CURRENT RESEARCH IN MOTIVATION

EDITED BY

Ralph Norman Haber
University of Rochester

HOLT, RINEHART AND WINSTON, INC.
New York   Chicago   San Francisco   Toronto   London

TO *Ruth and Sabrina*

PREFACE

IN THE PAST DECADE the concept of motivation has undergone vast changes as a result of the increased research and concentration on theory. So thick and fast, in fact, have developments come that older theoretical positions have been swamped with both newer and inconsistent data to explain and newer theoretical "heresies" with which to compete. While some of the older theories have held up well, others have fallen into disrepute, so that the organization of this field of study is fast losing its monolithic character. A few psychologists have even been heard to say publicly that the concept of motivation is no longer needed. While such statements cause me, as one who has spent much of his professional life teaching and investigating motivational processes, to cringe, they also have kept me continually examining anew the specific properties of the concept of motivation and the way it functions in general psychological theory. And my examination reinforces my belief in the importance of research in motivation. In this compendium of current studies I include a number of viewpoints stressing the value that motivational concepts have for psychology.

There is a need for such a collection of research papers and theories of motivation as I present, not only because these rapid developments in the field have been somewhat unorganized, but also because the field of motivational research has become so large that we may be approaching the point at which it can no longer be encompassed under a single rubric. This may, in fact, be the last time that a book can even pretend to include under one cover the range of topics that most psychologists would call motivational. I know that there are many psychologists who would not include in a course in motivation the scope of material I present in this book. Some emphasize the research and theory derived from animal studies; others specialize exclusively in studies of human motivation. It is my hope that my book will be large enough to satisfy the needs of instructors with these different viewpoints even if they wish to deal exclusively with their own areas. It is possible, also, that I have excluded topics that some instructors will consider part of the subject of motivation, though I expect this to be a less likely occurrence than that of finding those who feel I have stretched the term motivation to cover unrelated research concepts.

The compilation of these seventy-six papers was made possible by the generous cooperation of each of the authors and their publishers, for which I am most appreciative. I would like to acknowledge the help of Ruth Mallory and Martha Breen, each of whom greatly facilitated many of the details of preparation.

Finally, my deep appreciation goes to my wife, Ruth, who has shared with me most of the more arduous chores of editing.

R.N.H.

Rochester, New York
November 1965

CONTENTS

CURRENT RESEARCH IN MOTIVATION

INTRODUCTION

WHILE THERE HAVE BEEN MANY FORMAL ATTEMPTS to define the psychological concept of motivation, these have not met with much success. Indeed, though the study of motivation implies the study of the "whys" of behavior, these "whys" mean so many different things to different people that little consensus has ever been achieved. The breadth of this collection of readings is meant to portray the immense range of topics properly considered under the rubric of motivation, even though it would be rare to find any one person who would consider all of of these topics simultaneously to be motivational in content. I hope that one of the results of having this collection of papers available will be to show the linkage of many different areas, all having as a unifying theme some concern with the "whys" of behavior.

Explication of the "whys" of behavior has usually taken one of two forms: emphasizing the mobilization or release of energy, or elaborating a specification of the directionality of behavior. In other terms, these approaches are known, respectively, as *drive* or *incentive* theories of motivation. The former has traditionally placed greater weight on the conditions that release biological energy within the individual, energy that provides the motive power behind the behavior we call motivated. The latter theory has tended to ignore or minimize changes in energy, and has instead focused on the incentives that attract or repel an individual. In this sense, motivation is not the study of undirected energy, but of the pulling or repelling valances of goal events—the direction that behavior takes. In recent years, these two approaches in the definition of motivation and in the construction of motivational theories have somewhat tended to coalesce, although the two concepts are still separable in nearly every individual theory of motivation. Much of the content of the papers in this collection is concerned with this distinction and some of its implications.

The selection of papers was not based on historical trends. Older studies have been included only when their relevance to current research and theory is still explicit and stimulating. Therefore, for the student first approaching this field, this book will not convey many of the rather dramatic changes that have occurred in research and theory on motivational problems over the past decade or two. Most of these changes have paralleled similar ones in other fields of psychology, but perhaps they have occurred nowhere more dramatically than in the study of motivation.

One of the most important changes has been a shift from a primarily biological orientation, using concepts of special relevance to animal motivation, to a greater concern with those characteristics of motivated behavior unique to human beings.

While strong concern with human motivation has always existed, the predisposition was to use the concepts derived from research conducted exclusively with animals to explain human motivation. The change has come with the realization that since human motivation contains many characteristics that are not found in animals, it cannot be studied through extrapolation from animal research. Furthermore, many of the generalizations being made from concepts derived from research on animals are themselves being questioned today. Current research is beginning to catch up with much of the older thinking about mental content, particularly about fantasy behavior. Needless to say, fantasy in animals will never play a large role in theorizing about animal motivation and, therefore, the extension of concepts from animal research has not placed much emphasis on such processes in humans. As the section of the book on fantasy behavior will illustrate, fantastic processes can not only be used as an index of human motivation; they serve as an antecedent condition for motivational processes as well. It is these latter processes that cannot be discovered by extrapolation.

A second change over the last few years has been the shift in stress from drive variables to incentive variables. This has paralleled the reduction in a biological orientation, but has also come as a result of extensive questioning of the usefulness of the drive concept as the basic building block of motivational theory. Part of this shift has taken the form of placing more emphasis on incentives in the formal theories of motivation. But independent of theoretical changes much more research is being done on incentive variables directly, and such research ignores or controls drive parameters. Thus, incentives, which twenty-five years ago were relatively neglected in research, are now drawing a major share of attention.

One of the more important factors that has hastened the decline of drive interpretations of motivated behavior has been the increase of interest in studying exploration and curiosity and general activation or arousal processes. Since drive interpretations led to an examination of the internal environment of the organism, little attention was paid to the fact that human beings, like lower animals, spend large amounts of time engaged in the seemingly frivolous activity of being curious. Attempts to include this kind of behavior in a drive framework by creating a curiosity drive were neither particularly logical nor empirically successful. Curiosity and exploration and related processes have therefore come to occupy a larger and larger role in motivational theorizing, one quite independent of internal drive mechanisms. These phenomena have, as we shall see, themselves come to be the basic building blocks for some of the new cognitive theories of motivation.

Somewhat independent of the above changes is a shift from comprehensive formal theories of motivation to particularistic empirical approaches. The days of global theories seem to be fading, at least for the present. In their places are detailed investigations for special processes or concepts within areas of motivation, with only secondary interest in tying these together into a general theory. Research is limited in scope, hypotheses are concerned with a smaller range of data, and an appreciation of the multiplicity of factors underlying motivated behavior comes only from surveying the entire field, not from viewing any one theory.

Related to this change, which primarily reflects the breakup of the Hullian Behavior Theory as an encompassing theory for motivation (as well as for learning), a shift is occurring away from direct stimulus-response interpretations of motivational phenomena to cognitive interpretations. The most important characteristic of this change is the analysis of motivated behavior, not in terms of specific antecedent experiences, but in terms of the more generalized nature of previous experience. For example, recent interest has focused on some important qualitative differences between early as compared to later experience, with the finding that the specific nature of that early experience is not as important as the time at which it occurred. Thus, one is not fearful as an adult because of the specific fears he learned as a child, but rather because of the kind of experiences he had in handling and responding to fearful situations.

Finally, an important shift has brought the topics of unconscious motivation and defensiveness under more experimental control for their analysis and investigation. Motivational psychology seems to be moving away from very subjective interpretations of these processes, and is becoming willing to be more explicit about them. This has, of course, built up the experimental literature on these processes, and has provided greater support both for the older theoretical treatments, such as Freud's, and, in rather specific ways, for alternative formulations.

None of these changes have resulted as yet in the elimination of any of the traditional topics of motivation, but they have added a number of new ones, which are reflected in the Table of Contents. The editor had an immense latitude in what he selected for his collection, and for the reasons just discussed the selection task is doubly difficult when the topic is motivational processes. Seventy-six papers have been selected for inclusion. Of the thousands appropriate for a book of this title, nearly three hundred were seriously considered. Many important experimental and theoretical articles had therefore to be omitted to meet the demands of space. It might be difficult to justify in each instance why a particular paper was or was not included, though the brief introduction to each chapter provides a discussion of the range of the content of the chapter and the particular emphasis of each paper. This should provide some help in better appreciating the selection process.

The book is rather arbitrarily divided into nine chapters. The titles chosen for those chapters are descriptive and usually broad enough to include quite a breadth of material within them. The alternative of having many narrowly defined chapters was not used, primarily because this would tend toward one-article chapters in many instances. There are no speciality chapters, such as "The effects of motivation on . . . ," which might include perception, affiliation, social behavior, and the like. Some relevant material has been included on these topics, but formal chapters, while very important, have been dropped for reasons of space. Because of the arbitrariness of the chapter titles, and also of their ordering, it should be possible to use this book in sequences other than that chosen by the editor. For example, concentration primarily on human motivation, drawn from clinical and personality theories, can probably emphasize little of the first third of the book, though there is still a great amount of material there that is relevant. Likewise, a concern primarily with animal research on motivation will favor few selections from the last two or three chapters, while concentrating most heavily on the first two-thirds of the book. Even the entire range of material as broad as this collection can be covered in different sequences.

It is my hope that this book provides a collection of work that is representative of the field of motivation in the middle 1960s. This should be a picture of rapid growth and change, with more concern with careful empirical mapping of specific motivational processes than with building or supporting all-encompassing theories of motivation. Traditional views are giving way to bolder attempts to try out new ideas, many of which will undoubtedly be discarded. This is, however, a sign of the vitality that marks this area of research.

Chapter 1

INSTINCTIVE BEHAVIOR

A chapter on instinctive behavior is not usually found in a course on motivation, though it has great relevance to research on motivation. Innate interpretations are often attributed to motivational patterns of behavior particularly in the form: "He did such-and-such because it is just human nature." While such attempted explanations rarely contribute much understanding, it is possible that many motivational patterns of behavior may in fact occur fully organized without benefit of practice or imitation. It is therefore of great theoretical significance to examine instinctive behavior in relation to motivation.

One reason the topic is often left out is the disrepute it enjoys. A long controversy has plagued the concept, centering particularly on its proneness to circularity. Recently, however, a new tradition of animal behavioral research (ethology) has developed, sparked primarily by Konrad Lorenz and Niko Tinbergen and their students. This work has avoided the logical pitfalls of the concept, and in its place has raised questions of the interaction of learned and innate factors in motivational behavior much more clearly.

An instinct is defined as a pattern of behavior, usually complex in structure (to distinguish it from a reflex), which is found universally among the members of a species, occurs without the need for prior learning or experiences, is relatively invariant in form, and is reliably elicited or released by a particular and usually very simple stimulus. Ethological research has specialized primarily in looking for specific patterns of behavior that seem to occur in similar form each time and are found throughout the species in question. Then the attempt is made to determine both whether learning had shaped the pattern in any way and what is the nature of the releasing stimulus. Both of these tasks are very difficult, as attested to by the exhaustive work needed when even a simple instinct is being investigated. But both are crucial in this search for knowledge about instinctive behavior. Very elaborate experiments and controls over natural environments are needed even to begin to answer whether a particular pattern of behavior will occur without prior experience. Lehrman's research, discussed below, is a dramatic example of the difficulty and care that is needed to achieve clear answers. Search for the specific properties of the releasing stimulus represent some of the most detailed perceptual experiments in the literature, since systematic isolation of relevant parameters of the stimulus is required until the crucial aspect releasing the behavior is found.

There is nothing circular about this definiton of instinctive behavior, and theoretically it has the appearance of defining a reasonable class of behaviors. The controversy now is over the facts—can the patterns of behavior that fit this definition be isolated.

Beach, in an older paper, reviews both the logical and empirical concerns with the innate versus learned dichotomy. Lehrman presents one of the most incisive critiques of the ethologists' position on instinctive behavior. He argues, in part from his own data on mating behavior, that hormonal control of "instinctive" behavior requires relevant experiences of the particular organism before it develops full autonomous control over these patterns. This paper of Lehrman's will undoubtedly shape the direction of much of American research and theory on instinctive behavior for many years.

While ethologists have presented a number of specific mechanisms controlling instinctive behavior, two of these have caught the fancy of motivation-oriented psychologists. They have provided the basis for extended experimental programs and have been offered as foundations for other motivational processes. The more important of these is the concept of *imprinting*, first discussed by Lorenz in 1935. It refers to very rapid and relatively permanent learning that occurs during very early critical periods of an organism's life. Hess has perhaps contributed the most systematic research on imprinting, and the paper included here presents a wide range of the experimental data. Thompson and O'Kieffe show how early imprinting can serve to reduce the effects of stress. Several other studies are included in Chapters 4 and 6 that make use of imprinting-like concepts. The other motivation-relevant concept is *displacement,* which concerns primarily the behavioral outcome when two incompatible actions are both called for. Zeigler's very recent paper on the implications of this analysis for motivational theory is an excellent discussion of the problems of predicting conflict-like behavior. Psychologists have done relatively little work on what happens after a conflict occurs (see Chapter 7), but ethologists have focused closely on this. Displacement behavior is the term used to denote responses that are related to neither of the conflicted behavior systems, but rather seem to be innocuous responses that help reduce the tensions of the conflict without actually having to perform either of the conflicted actions.

This is a very narrow sampling of the three primary areas of overlap between instinctive behavior and motivation—early experience, imprinting, and displacement. But it does highlight the relevance of these concepts to motivational behavior. Ethologists have focused on animal behavior almost exclusively, though without ruling out the application of the concepts of instinctive behavior to human beings. While the general assumption is made that instinctive processes become less important as one moves up the phylogenetic scale and as their place is taken by learned behavior, there is no reason to believe that human beings do not possess some instinctive patterns of behavior. It should be expected, however, that such patterns, if they exist, may not be fully or permanently under the control of instinctive processes, but rather would be susceptible to the influences of acquired experiences. Much more work is obviously needed on the generality of instinctive behavior to human beings.

Psychological Review, 1955, vol. 62, pp. 401–410

The Descent of Instinct

Frank A. Beach

"The delusion is extraordinary by which we thus exalt language above nature:—making language the expositor of nature, instead of making nature the expositor of language" (Alexander Brian Johnson, *A Treatise on Language*).

The basic ideas underlying a concept of instinct probably are older than recorded history. At any rate they are clearly set forth in the Greek literature of 2,500 years ago. They have been controversial ideas and they remain so today. Nevertheless, the instinct concept has survived in almost complete absence of empirical validation. One aim of the present article is to analyze the reasons for the remarkable vitality of a concept which has stood without objective test for at least two millennia. A second objective is to evaluate the concept as it relates to a science of behavior.

Origins in Philosophy and Theology

The concept of instinct evolved in relation to the broad problems of human destiny, of Man's place in nature, and his position in this world and the next. From the beginning, instinct has been defined and discussed in terms of its relation to reason and, less directly, to the human soul.

During the fourth century B.C. the Greek philosopher Heraclitus declared that there had been two types of creation. Men and gods were the products of rational creation, whereas irrational brutes comprised a separate category of living creatures. Heraclitus added the observation that only gods and men possess souls. The close relation between rational powers and possession of a soul has been reaffirmed time and again during the ensuing 2,500 years. Heraclitus did not advance the concept of instinct but he laid the groundwork for its development.

Stoic philosophers of the first century A.D. held that men and gods belong to one natural community, since they are rational beings. All animals were specifically excluded since they are not creatures of reason and even their most complex behavior takes place "without reflection," to use the words of Seneca. This stoical taxonomy was both flattering and convenient since, according to the tenets of this school, members of the natural community were forbidden to harm or enslave other members.

It is significant that neither Heraclitus nor the Stoics based their conclusions upon objective evidence. Their premises concerning the psychology of animals were not derived from empirical observation; they were demanded by assumption of the philosophical position that animals lack a rational soul.

Aristotle, who was more of an observer than a philosopher, was of a different mind. In *Historia Animalium* Man is placed at the top of Scala Natura (directly above the Indian elephant), and is accorded superior intellectual powers, but none qualitatively distinct from those of other species.

In the thirteenth century Albertus Magnus composed *De Animalibus,* based chiefly upon the writings of Aristotle but modifying the Aristotelian position where necessary to conform to Scholastic theology. Albertus removed Man from the natural scale, holding that he is unique in possessing the gift of reason and an immortal soul. Animals, lacking reason, "are directed by their natural instinct and therefore cannot act freely."

St. Thomas Aquinas, student of Albertus, supported his teacher's distinction between men and animals. Animals possess only the sensitive soul described by Aristotle. The human embryo is similarly endowed, but the rational soul is divinely implanted in the fetus at some time before birth.[1] The behavior of man therefore depends upon reason, whereas all animals are governed by instinct. Like the Stoic philosophers, the Scholastics were unconcerned with factual evidence. Their emphasis upon instinctive control of

[1] It is not irrelevant to point out that weighty disputation concerning the exact age at which the soul enters the fetus retarded the advancement of embryological knowledge during its seventeenth century beginnings.

animal behavior was dictated by a need of the theological system, and in this frame of reference instinct was a useful concept.

Roughly four centuries after the time of St. Thomas Aquinas, René Descartes and his followers aggressively restated the existence of a man-brute dichotomy. The bare facts of the Cartesian position are common knowledge, but for the purpose of the present argument it is important to ask why Descartes felt so strongly about the matter—felt compelled to hold up man as the Reasoner, at the same time insisting that all other living creatures are only flesh-and-blood machines. The explanation stands out in the following quotation:

"After the error of atheism, there is nothing that leads weak minds further astray from the paths of virtue than the idea that the minds of other animals resemble our own, and that therefore we have no greater right to future life than have gnats and ants" (René Descartes, *Passions of the Soul*).

From Albertus to Descartes the argument runs clear. The theological system posits a life after death. Hence the postulation of the soul. But mere possession of a soul is not enough. Each man must earn the right of his soul's salvation. This in turn depends upon reason, which man exercises in differentiating good from evil, behavior which is sinful from that which is not. An afterlife is man's unique prerogative; no animals share it. They have no souls and therefore no need to reason. But how are the complex and adaptive reactions of subhuman creatures to be explained if not by reason, foresight, volition? They are comfortably disposed of as products of instincts with which the Creator has endowed all dumb brutes.

That the thirteenth-century point of

view persists today is shown by the following quotation:

> In animals there are only instincts, but not in man. As St. Thomas points out, there cannot be any deliberation in a subrational being (even though we may get the impression that there is). . . . Instincts in animals seem to operate according to the pattern of physical forces, where the stronger always prevails; for animals are utterly devoid of the freedom which characterizes man. . . . That is why when one studies human behavior one must rise above the purely animal pattern and concentrate upon those two faculties, intellect and will, which separate man from animal (Msgr. Fulton J. Sheen, *Peace of Soul*).

To summarize what has been said thus far, it appears that the descent of the instinct concept can be traced from early philosophies which set man apart from the rest of the living world and sought for him some divine affinity. This was achieved by claiming for man alone the power of reason. By a process of elimination the behavior of animals was ascribed to their natural instincts. During the Middle Ages this dichotomous classification became a part of Church doctrine, with the result that possession of reason and of a soul were inextricably linked to the hope of eternal life. Prescientific concepts of instinct were not deduced from the facts of nature; they were necessitated by the demands of philosophical systems based upon supernatural conceptions of nature.

Early Scientific Usage

When biology emerged as a scientific discipline, there was a general tendency to adopt the prescientific point of view regarding instinct. Some exceptions occurred. For example, Erasmus Darwin's *Zoonomia* expressed the theory that all behavior is a product of experience, but this point of view was subsequently disavowed by the grandson of its sponsor. Charles Darwin made the concept of instinct one cornerstone of his theory of evolution by means of natural selection.

To bridge the gap of the Cartesian man-brute dichotomy, and thus to establish the evolution of mind as well as structure, Darwin and his disciples amassed two types of evidence. One type purported to prove the existence of human instincts; the other pertained to rational behavior in subhuman species. The idea of discontinuity in mental evolution was vigorously attacked, but the dichotomy between instinct and reason was never challenged.

The nineteenth-century literature on evolution shows plainly that the concept of instinctive behavior was accepted because it filled a need in the theoretical system, and not because its validity had been established by empirical test.

Contemporary psychologists such as Herbert Spencer were influenced by the evolutionary movement, and the idea of an instinctive basis for human psychology became popular. William James, in Volume II of his *Principles*, insisted that man has more instincts than any other mammal. McDougall's widely read *Social Psychology* listed human instincts of flight, repulsion, parental feeling, reproduction, self-abasement, etc. Woodworth, Thorndike, and other leaders agreed that much of human behavior is best understood as an expression of instinctive drives or needs.

One of the difficulties with such thinking is that it often leads to the nominal fallacy—the tendency to confuse naming with explaining. Some psychological writers were guilty of employing the instinct concept as an explanatory device, and the eventual result was a vigorous revolt against the use of instinct in any psychological theory.

The Anti-instinct Revolt

Dunlap's 1919 article, "Are there any instincts?" (1919–1920), was one opening gun in the battle, but the extreme protests came from the most radical Behaviorists as represented by Z. Y. Kuo, who wrote on the subject, "A psychology without heredity" (1924). For a while the word "instinct" was anathema, but the revolt was abortive, and there were three principal reasons for its failure.

First, Kuo denied instinct but admitted the existence of unlearned "units of reaction." By this phrase he meant simple reflexes, but in using it he set up a dichotomy of learned and unlearned behavior which was fatal to his basic thesis. It merely shifted the debate to arguments as to the degree of complexity permissible in an unlearned response, or the proportion of a complex pattern that was instinctive. The second error consisted essentially of a return to the position taken by Erasmus Darwin at the close of the eighteenth century. Having averred that the only unlearned reactions consist of a few simple reflexes, the opponents of the instinct doctrine invoked learning to explain all other behavior. This forced them into untenable positions such as that of maintaining that pecking behavior of the newly-hatched chick is a product of head movements made by the embryo in the shell, or that the neonatal infant's grasp reflex depends upon prenatal exercise of this response. The

third loophole in the anti-instinct argument derived from a dualistic concept of the hereditary process. Admitting that genes can affect morphological characters, and simultaneously denying that heredity influences behavior, opponents of instinct were hoist by their own petard. If the physical machinery for behavior develops under genetic control, then the behavior it mediates can scarcely be regarded as independent of inheritance.

It is important to note that this war over instinct was fought more with words and inferential reasoning than with behavioral evidence. It is true that a few individuals actually observed the behavior of newborn children or of animals, but most of the battles of the campaign were fought from the armchair in the study rather than from the laboratory.

Current Thought in Psychology

Although there are militant opponents of the instinct doctrine among present-day psychologists, it is undoubtedly correct to say that the concept of instincts as complex, unlearned patterns of behavior is generally accepted in clinical, social, and experimental psychology. Among experimentalists, Lashley suggested that instinctive behavior is unlearned and differs from reflexes in that instincts depend on "the pattern or organization of the stimulus," whereas reflexes are elicited by stimulation of localized groups of sensory endings (1938).

Carmichael (1947) expressed agreement with G. H. Parker's statement that human beings are "about ninetenths inborn, and one-tenth acquired." Morgan (1947) studied food-hoarding behavior in rats, and concluded, "since it comes out spontaneously without training, it is plainly instinctive." The following quotation reveals that some modern psychologists not only embrace the concept of instinctive behavior, but consider it a useful explanatory device.

"Of the theories of hoarding which have been advanced, the most reasonable one in terms of recent data is that the behavior is instinctive . . ." (Waddell, 1951).

At least three serious criticisms can be leveled against current treatment of the problem of instinctive behavior. The first is that psychologists in general actually know very little about most of the behavior patterns which they confidently classify as instinctive. In his paper, "The experimental analysis of instinctive activities," Lashley mentions the following 15 examples:

1. Eating of Hydra by the Planarian, Microstoma.

2. Nest-building, cleaning of young and retrieving by the primiparous rat.

3. Restless running about of the mother rat deprived of her litter.

4. Homing of pigeons.

5. Web-weaving of spiders.

6. Migratory behavior of fishes.

7. Nest-building of birds, including several species.

8. Mating behavior of the female rat in estrus.

9. Dancing reactions of the honeybee returning to the hive laden with nectar.

10. Visual reactions of rats reared in darkness.

11. Responses of the sooty tern to her nest and young.

12. Reactions of the seagull to artificial and normal eggs.

13. Sexual behavior of the male rat.

14. Mating responses in insects.

15. Mating responses in domestic hens.

It is a safe guess that most American psychologists have never observed any of these patterns of behavior. At a conservative estimate, less than half of the reactions listed have been subjected to even preliminary study by psychologically trained investigators. The significance of this criticism lies partly in the fact that those psychologists who *have* worked in the area of "instinctive" behavior tend to be more critical of the instinct concept than are those who lack first-hand knowledge of the behavioral evidence.

Relevant to the criticism of unfamiliarity is the fact that the degree of assurance with which instincts are attributed to a given species is inversely related to the extent to which that species has been studied, particularly from the developmental point of view. Before the development of complex behavior in human infants had been carefully analyzed, it was, as we have seen, a common practice to describe many human instincts. Longitudinal studies of behavior have reduced the "unlearned" components to three or four simple responses not much more complex than reflexes (Dennis, 1941).

The second criticism is that despite prevailing ignorance about the behavior which is called instinctive, there is strong pressure toward premature categorization of the as yet unanalyzed patterns of reaction. The history of biological taxonomy shows that the reliability of any classificatory system is a function of the validity of identification of individual specimens or even populations. Unless the systematist is thoroughly familiar with the characteristics of a given species, he cannot determine its proper relation to other groups.

Similarly, until psychologists have carefully analyzed the salient characteristics of a given pattern of behavior, they cannot meaningfully classify or compare it with other patterns.

The third criticism of current treatment of instinctive behavior has to do with the classificatory scheme which is in use. When all criteria which supposedly differentiate instinctive from acquired responses are critically evaluated, the only one which seems universally applicable is that instincts are unlearned (Munn, 1938). This forces psychology to deal with a two-class system, and such systems are particularly unmanageable when one class is defined solely in negative terms, that is, in terms of the absence of certain characteristics that define the other class. It is logically indefensible to categorize any behavior as unlearned unless the characteristics of learned behavior have been thoroughly explored and are well known. Even the most optimistic "learning psychologist" would not claim that we have reached this point yet. At present, to prove that behavior is unlearned is equivalent to proving the null hypothesis.

Perhaps a more serious weakness in the present psychological handling of instinct lies in the assumption that a two-class system is adequate for the classification of complex behavior. The implication that all behavior must be determined by learning or by heredity, neither of which is more than partially understood, is entirely unjustified. The final form of any response is affected by a multiplicity of variables, only two of which are genetical and experiential factors. It is to the identification and analysis of all of these factors that psychology should address itself. When this task is properly conceived and executed there will be no need nor reason for ambiguous concepts of instinctive behavior.

Genes and Behavior

Experimental investigation of relationships between genetical constitution and behavior was exemplified by the pioneering studies of Yerkes (1913), Tryon (1929), and Heron (1935). Interest in this area has recently increased, and a large number of investigations have been summarized by Hall (1951) who anticipates a new interdisciplinary science of psychogenetics.

As Hall points out, the psychologist interested in examining gene-behavior relations has several approaches to choose from. He can compare the behavior of different inbred strains of animals currently available in the genetics laboratory. He can cross two strains and study the behavior of the hybrids. Selective breeding for particular behavioral traits is a well-established technique. The behavioral effects of induced mutations have as yet received very little attention but should be investigated.

It is known that selective breeding can alter the level of general activity (Rundquist, 1933), maze behavior (Heron, 1935), emotionality (Hall, 1938), and aggressiveness (Keeler & King, 1942) in the laboratory rat. Inbred strains of mice differ from one another in temperature preference (Herter, 1938), aggressiveness (Scott, 1942), and strength of "exploratory drive" (Thompson, 1953).

Various breeds of dogs exhibit pronounced differences in behavioral characteristics. Some are highly emotional, unstable and restless; whereas others are phlegmatic and relatively inactive (Fuller & Scott, 1954). Special breeds have been created by selective mating to meet certain practical requirements. For example, some hunting dogs such as the foxhound are "open trailers." While following a fresh trail they vocalize in a characteristic fashion. Other dogs are "mute trailers." The F_1 hybrids of a cross between these types are always open trailers although the voice is often that of the mute trailing parent (Whitney, 1929).

Inbreeding of domestic chickens for high egg production has produced behavioral deficiencies of various kinds. Although hens of some lines are excellent layers, they have almost totally lost the normal tendency to brood the eggs once they have been laid (Hurst, 1925). The maternal behavior of sows of different inbred lines of swine is strikingly different. Females of one line are so aggressively protective of their young that they cannot be approached during the lactation period. Sows of a second genetical line possess such weak maternal interest that they frequently kill their litters by stepping or lying on the young (Hodgson, 1935).

Study of the effects of controlled breeding cast doubt upon the validity of any classificatory system which describes one type of behavior as genetically determined and another as experientially determined. For example, by manipulating the genotype it is possible to alter certain types of learning ability. As far as present evidence can show, the influence of genes on learning is as important as any genetical effect upon other behavior patterns commonly considered instinctive. There is no reason to assume that so-called instinctive reactions are more dependent upon heredity than noninstinctive responses; hence genetical determination is not a differentiating criterion.

The Meaning of Genetical Determination

Behavior which is known to vary with the genotype is often incorrectly defined as "genetically determined" behavior. Although we can show a correlation between certain genes and particular behavior patterns, this is of course no proof of a causal relationship. Many other genes and nongenic factors are always involved in such correlations. This point is nicely illustrated by a series of experiments on audiogenic seizures in mice.

Susceptibility to fatal seizures is high in some inbred strains and low in others (Hall, 1947). When a high-incidence and low-incidence strain are crossed, the susceptibility of the F_1 generation is intermediate between those of the parental strains. So far the evidence strongly supports the conclusion that seizure incidence is genetically determined. However, the incidence of seizures can be altered without changing the genetic constitution.

This is accomplished by modifying the prenatal environment. Fertilized eggs recovered from the tubes or uterus of a female of one strain and introduced into the uterus of a female of a different strain will sometimes implant normally and produce viable young. This has been done using seizure-susceptible females as donors and seizure-resistant females as hosts. Under such conditions the genetical characteristics of the young are unaltered, but their susceptibility to fatal seizures is lower than that of their own genetic strain and higher than that of the "foster" mothers in whose uteri they developed (Ginsberg & Hovda, 1947).

Studies of this sort emphasize the important but often neglected fact that postnatal behavior is affected by factors acting upon the organism before birth. As Sontag has pointed out, this is true of human beings as well as lower species.

Fetal environment may play a part in determining characteristics of the physiological behavior of any newborn infant. We are too often inclined to neglect this source of modification of physiological potential. Too frequently we think of the individual as beginning life only at birth. Yet because it is during the period of intrauterine life that most of the cells of the vital organs are actually formed, it is during this period that "environmental" factors such as nutrition, oxygen, mother's hormones, etc. are most important in modifying their characteristics (1950, p. 482).

Another fundamental principle illustrated by the results of transplanting fertilized ova is that the uniformity of behavior which characterizes highly inbred strains of animals cannot be ascribed solely to homozygosity, but depends as well upon *minimal variability of the prenatal environment.* More broadly conceived, this principle implies that behavioral similarities and differences observable at birth are in part a product of intrauterine effects.

If forced to relinquish the criterion of genetical control, proponents of the instinct doctrine fall back upon the criterion of the unlearned nature of instinctive acts. Now learning is a process occurring through time, and can only be studied by longitudinal analysis. If instinctive acts are unlearned, their developmental history must differ in some significant fashion from that of a learned response.

The Ontogeny of Behavior

No bit of behavior can ever be fully understood until its ontogenesis has been described. Had psychologists always recognized this fact, much of the fruitless debate about unlearned behavior could have been avoided.

Perhaps the most widely cited psychological experiment on development and instinctive behavior is that of Carmichael, who studied the swimming behavior of larval amphibians (1927). He reared embryos in a solution which paralyzed the striped muscles but permitted normal growth. Animals that were thus prevented from practicing the swimming response were nevertheless capable of normal swimming when placed in pure water. These findings are often offered as proof of the claim that swimming is instinctive. However, to demonstrate that practice is not essential for the appearance of a response is only the beginning of the analysis. This point is clearly illustrated by certain observations of insect behavior.

Gravid female moths, *Hyponomenta padella,* lay their eggs on the leaves of the hackberry plant and die shortly thereafter. The eggs hatch, the larvae eat the leaves and eventually become mature. Females of this new generation in turn select hackberry leaves on which to deposit their eggs. Another race of moths prefers apple leaves as an oviposition site. The difference between the two races has been perpetuated, generation after generation, for many centuries. It would appear to be the example par excellence of a genetically controlled behavior trait. But such an explanation is insufficient.

When eggs of the apple-preferring type are transferred to hackberry leaves, the larvae thrive on the new diet. Thirty per cent of the females developing from these larvae show a preference for hackberry leaves when it comes time for them to deposit their eggs (Keeler & King, 1942).

The evidence is of course incomplete. Why only 30 per cent of the insects show a reversal of preference is not clear. It would be illuminating if the same experimental treatment could be repeated on several successive generations. Nevertheless it appears likely that the adult moth's choice of an oviposition site is influenced by the chemical composition of the food consumed during the larval period (Emerson, 1943). If this interpretation is correct, the data illustrate the fact that a complex behavior pattern may be "unlearned" and still depend upon the individual's previous history.

Comparable examples can be found in the behavior of vertebrates. Stereotyped patterns of behavior appear with great regularity in successive generations under conditions in which practice plays no obvious role. Nonetheless such "species-specific" responses may be dependent upon previous experience of the organism.

The maternal behavior of primiparous female rats reared in isolation is indistinguishable from that of multiparous individuals. Animals with no maternal experience build nests before the first litter is born, clean the young, eat the placenta, and retrieve scattered young to the nest (Beach, 1937). However, pregnant rats that have been reared in cages containing nothing that can be picked up and transported do not build nests when material is made available. They simply heap their young in a pile in a corner of the cage. Other females that have been reared under conditions preventing them from licking and grooming their own bodies fail to clean their young at the time of parturition (Riess, 1950).

There are undoubtedly many adaptive responses which appear *de novo* at the biologically appropriate time in the absence of preceding practice, but the possibility remains that component parts of a complex pattern have in fact been perfected in different contexts. Whether or not this is the case can only be determined by exhaustive analysis of the ontogeny of the behavior under examination. Nonetheless, to define behavior as "unlearned" in the absence of such analysis is meaningless and misleading.

Summary: The concept of instinctive behavior seems to have originated in antiquity in connection with attempts to define a clear-cut difference between man and all other animals. Human behavior was said to be governed by reasoning, and the behavior of animals to depend upon instinct. In his possession of the unique power of reason, man was elevated above all other creatures, and, incidentally, his use of them for his own purposes was thus morally justified.

Christian theologians adopted this point of view and averred that man was given the power of reason so that he could earn his own salvation. Similar privileges could not logically be accorded to lower animals. Therefore they were denied reason and their behavior was explained as a product of divinely implanted instincts. In both sacred and secular philosophies the concept of instinct served a practical purpose, although in no instance was there any attempt to validate it by examination of the empirical evidence.

The concept gained a central position in scientific thinking as a result of the Darwinian movement. Proponents of the evolutionary theory accepted uncritically the assumption that all behavior must be governed by instinct or by reasoning. Their aim was to demonstrate that animals can reason and that men possess instincts. The same dichotomy has persisted in experimental psychology. Attempts to eliminate the instinct concept were unsuccessful because those who made the attempt accepted the idea that all behavior is either acquired or inherited.

No such classification can ever be satisfactory. It rests upon exclusively negative definitions of one side of the dichotomy. It obscures the basic problems involved. It reflects an unnaturally narrow and naive conception of factors shaping behavior.

To remedy the present confused situation it is necessary first to refrain from premature classification of those kinds of behavior that are currently defined as unlearned. Until they have been systematically analyzed it will remain impossible to decide whether these numerous response patterns belong in one or a dozen different categories.

The analysis that is needed involves two types of approach. One rests upon determination of the relationships existing between genes and behavior. The other consists of studying the development of various behavior patterns in the individual, and determining the number and kinds of factors that normally control the final form of the response.

When these methods have been applied to the various types of behavior which today are called "instinctive," the concept of instinct will disappear, to be replaced by scientifically valid and useful explanations.

E. L. Bliss (Ed.), *Roots of Behavior*. New York: Paul B. Hoeber, Inc., 1962, pp. 142–156

Interaction of Hormonal and Experiential Influences on Development of Behavior[*][1]

Daniel S. Lehrman

Beach (1947), in his now-classic review of sexual behavior in mammals, pointed out that the mating patterns of various animals were influenced, in their development and expression, both by the effects of gonadal hormones and by the effects of individual experience. Further, different species and the two sexes within the same species might differ with respect to the relative degree of dependence of their sexual behavior upon the presence of various hormones and upon various situational and experiential factors.

Recent research makes it increasingly clear that the animal's individual experience plays a role in the development of many behavior patterns which are demonstrably hormone-induced and, conversely, that the effects of hormones play a role in many behavior patterns which are dependent upon the animal's previous experience (Lehrman, 1956b; Schneirla, 1956). It is the purpose of this chapter to review and discuss a number of instances of such interactive relationships between the effects of hormones and of individual experience.

* Copyright © 1962 by Hoeber Medical Division of Harper & Row, Publ., New York.
1 Work from the author's laboratory, reported in this paper, has been supported by Grant No. M2771 from the National Institute of Mental Health, U.S. Public Health Service, for which grateful acknowledgment is made.

Hormone-Experience Interactions

SEXUAL BEHAVIOR
IN THE GUINEA PIG

W. C. Young and his collaborators (Young, 1957) have carried out a many-sided analysis of the origin of individual differences in the sexual behavior of the guinea pig. Both male (Young and Grunt, 1951) and female (Goy and Young, 1957) guinea pigs show considerable individual variability in various quantitative measures of sex behavior, and these differences are persistent, so that they reflect stable differences among individuals, rather than fortuitous variations in the behavior of individuals. That these individual differences may be based in part upon genetic factors is indicated by the fact that consistent differences in the pattern and in the intensity of sexual behavior can be noted between animals of different inbred strains, and between inbred and heterogeneous strains, both in the male (Valenstein, Riss, and Young, 1954) and in the female (Goy and Young, 1957).

Grunt and Young (1952, 1953), investigating the nature of these genetic differences, divided groups of male guinea pigs into those showing high, medium, and low "sex drive," as measured by a score reflecting several different aspects of the sexual behavior pattern. When these animals were castrated, their sexual behavior scores all fell to the same minimal level. Some 16 weeks after castration, replacement therapy was instituted consisting of daily injections of testosterone propionate. This treatment resulted in the reinstatement of sex behavior. Further, when they were all injected with the same amount of male sex hormones, the animals tended to show the same relative amount of sex behavior as they had previously shown under the influence of endogenous androgen. A fourfold increase in the level of administered androgen, beyond that required for reinstatement of the pattern, had no further effect upon the sex behavior scores, and did not alter the relative standing of the different groups. Similar results have been obtained with females (Goy and Young, 1957). This indicates that the differences in the sex behavior of the various strains of guinea pigs are the result, not of differences in the amount of circulating sex hormones, but rather of differences in the responsiveness to sex hormones of the tissues mediating sex behavior.

The experiments cited so far make it clear that the sex hormones play an important role in establishing and maintaining sexual behavior in the guinea pig, and that this role varies, depending upon differences in the genetic constitution of the animals. A further group of experiments demonstrates the contribution of individual experience to the effectiveness of the hormonal induction of sex behavior, and the interaction of this contribution with that of genetic differences.

Valenstein, Riss, and Young (1955) reared different groups of male guinea pigs, of several different strains, under conditions of social isolation or of association with other animals of the same age. All animals were weaned from their mothers when they were 25 days old. The "isolated" males were raised in isolation after weaning, while the "social" males were kept with 3–5 females of the same age, until the age of 73 days. The animals were tested for sexual behavior, starting at 77 days of age.

In males of two inbred strains, the

"social" animals showed significantly higher scores on a variety of measures of sexual behavior than did the isolated animals. In the group of genetically heterogeneous animals, no such differences appeared. The authors suggested that this might be because the genetically heterogeneous males grow much more rapidly than do those of either of the two inbred strains, and thus might reach, within 25 days, a stage of development at which they could acquire the experience which contributes to the differences between isolated and social animals. They therefore repeated the experiment with genetically heterogeneous males, weaning them at 10 days of age instead of 25. Under these conditions, the social males had significantly higher scores than did the isolated ones.

It is thus apparent that experience during early life (i.e., before sexual maturity) contributes, in this species, to the development of the normal pattern of sexual behavior. In a further experiment, Valenstein, Riss, and Young (1955) found that caging with other males was just as effective as caging with females for the development of the normal sexual pattern. Since both intact males and estrous females may initiate mounting behavior, while spayed females do not, Valenstein and Goy (1957) next reared "social" animals by caging them with *spayed* females. This procedure resulted in a markedly lower level of sexual behavior than did rearing with either intact males or intact females. The experience involved in these experiments occurs before sexual maturity and is effective even in animals castrated at birth, indicating that the activity of the gonads is not necessary for the occurrence or effectiveness of the experience (Riss *et al.*,

1955). Essentially similar results, in all respects, are found when these experiments are repeated on females (Goy and Young, 1957).

These experiments, which only partially reflect the tenacity with which this group of investigators has explored this problem, demonstrate clearly that hormonal, genetic, and experiential influences all play substantial measurable roles in the development and expression of sexual behavior in this species. A final experiment by Valenstein and Young (1955) provides a direct demonstration of the interaction between the effects of both experience and hormones. This experiment is illustrated in Figure 1. Two groups of male guinea pigs were weaned from their mothers at the age of 25 days. Each animal of the "social" group was then caged with five females of the same size until the age of 73 days, and the "isolated" males were kept in isolation until the same age. From the age of 73 days, all the animals were kept under the same (isolated) conditions. They were given weekly tests of sexual behavior from 11 to 17 weeks of age, the results of which can be seen in the left-hand field of Figure 1. The social animals had, clearly and consistently, higher sexual behavior scores than the isolated ones. At the age of 17 weeks, some of the animals of each group were castrated, while the rest were left intact. The animals were then kept in isolation until they were 27 weeks old, without further sexual experience, except that the castrated animals were tested starting at 25 weeks, to make sure that their sexual behavior had regressed to the level characteristic of castrated animals. It will be seen that the sexual behavior of both the isolated-reared and the social-reared

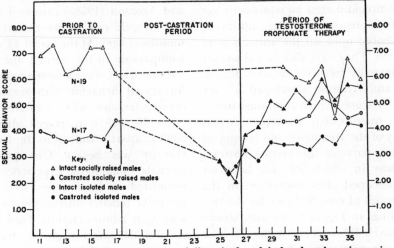

Fig. 1. Sexual behavior scores of socially raised and isolated male guinea pigs before castration (left), after castration (center), and during androgen replacement therapy (right). (From Valenstein and Young, 1955.)

animals had, by eight weeks after castration, regressed to the same minimal level. Starting at 27 weeks of age, all the castrated animals received replacement therapy consisting of daily injections of testosterone propionate, the dosage level being the same for the isolated-reared as for the social-reared animals. During the period of hormone therapy, the castrates and the noncastrated controls were given weekly tests for sexual behavior. The results of these tests are shown on the right-hand field of Figure 1, where it will be seen that, under the same hormone dosage, the sexual behavior of the social-reared castrates rose to a higher level than did that of the isolated-reared castrates, the level of sexual behavior eventually reached by each group approximating that maintained by the uncastrated animals which had been reared in the same manner.

SEXUAL BEHAVIOR IN CATS

Using a somewhat different technique, Rosenblatt and Aronson (1958a,

1958b) have investigated the relationship between the effects of both sexual experience and hormones upon sexual behavior in male domestic cats. These investigators allowed different groups of cats to have different amounts of sexual experience, then castrated them and studied the decline in sexual behavior after castration as a function of the amount of sexual experience before castration.

Two groups of animals were used: a group of maximally experienced animals which were allowed many opportunities to associate with sexually receptive females, so that each animal achieved from 32 to 81 copulations; and a group of minimally experienced males which were allowed no opportunity to copulate with females, some of the males merely being tested with females to determine the age at which sexual behavior matures, but being allowed no more than a single preliminary mounting of a female. After the maximally experienced animals had achieved the requisite amount of experience, and after an equivalent age had been reached in the minimally experienced ones, all the animals were castrated. They were then tested weekly with sexually receptive females. Rosenblatt and Aronson developed a "sex behavior score" which combined into a single quantitative measure various aspects of the frequency and latency of different parts of the mating pattern. The way in which this sex behavior score declined after castration, in the two groups of cats, is shown by the two light lines in Figure 2 (we may ignore the heavier lines for the moment). The upper curve (triangles) shows the change in sexual behavior score after castration, week by week, for the maximally experienced males, while the lower curve (circles) shows similar measurements for the minimally experienced males. It will be seen that sexual behavior in the experienced animals declined slowly and that 15 weeks after castration it was still at a higher level than that shown by the inexperienced animals.

Male cats castrated before puberty do not develop sex behavior (Rosenblatt and Aronson, 1958a) and the persistence of sex behavior in experienced animals after castration contrasts with the failure of inexperienced animals to develop sex behavior after (postpuberal) castration. This indicates that, while the presence of male hormone is essential for the development of the behavior, the sexual experience acquired under the influence of this hormone leads to changes in the animal which persist after the hormone is withdrawn, and which make possible the maintenance of sex behavior in its absence.

In a further experiment, Rosenblatt

and Aronson (1958a) castrated a number of male cats before puberty (at 4 months of age). At the age of 11 months (comparable to the normal age of sexual maturity), these animals were tested for sexual behavior with sexually receptive females, with negative results. After 10 such tests, staged about two weeks apart, androgen replacement therapy was begun. One group of animals (maximally experienced) was permitted to have access to sexually receptive females during the period of androgen administration. Four of the six animals of this group developed normal sexual behavior, achieving between 30 and 134 copulations. The animals of the second group were not permitted access to receptive females during the period of androgen therapy. Hormone treatment was then discontinued, for both groups of animals, and all animals were then subjected to weekly tests for sex behavior. The results of these tests are shown by the heavy lines in Figure 2. It will be seen that the occurrence of sex behavior in prepuberally castrated animals, injected with androgen after the age of normal

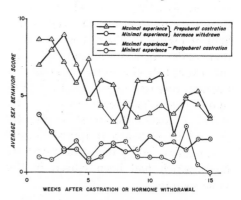

Fig. 2. Average sex behavior scores for 15 weeks following hormone withdrawal by castration or by cessation of androgen treatment, in male cats with and without sexual experience. (From Rosenblatt and Aronson, 1958a.)

puberty, is similar to that of intact animals, and that sexual experience acquired under the influence of this injected hormone has the same effect in organizing sexual behavior so that it can persist after the hormone is withdrawn as does sexual behavior occurring under the influence of endogenous hormone in intact, normal animals.

The effects of the hormone on the animal during prepuberal and early pubertal periods—and, indeed, during postpuberal periods before the actual occurrence of sexual experience—appear from these experiments not to be important as influences on the development of sexual behavior. On the other hand, regressive long-term changes following castration appear to make the expression of sexual behavior much more difficult, since long-term observations (lasting several years) after castration show that sexual behavior even in maximally experienced animals declines to a low level. When such animals are later injected with sex hormone for a period of several months, and then the hormone is withdrawn, subsequent weekly tests show that the sex behavior has risen to a level comparable to that shown just after the original castration, and that it declines at about the rate shown after the original castration by maximally experienced animals, *whether or not any additional sexual experience was allowed during the second period of hormone administration* (unpublished observations by Cooper, referred to by Rosenblatt and Aronson, 1958a). This indicates that the experience of sexual behavior, which can become organized and can develop only under the influence of male sex hormone, leads to long-persisting changes in organization, the effects of which are, in later life, interactive with the concurrent effects of sex hormones.

PARENTAL BEHAVIOR IN RING DOVES

Male and female ring doves (*Streptopelia risoria*) both share in the care of the eggs and young. The young are at first fed on "crop-milk," a substance produced by the walls of the parents' crops and regurgitated by them to the young (Craig, 1909). The dove's crop produces crop-milk under the influence of prolactin secreted by the bird's pituitary gland (Riddle, 1937). The pituitary, in turn, is stimulated to produce this hormone by stimuli arising from participation in the act of incubating the eggs (Patel, 1936). I have studied the effect of prolactin upon this parental regurgitation-feeding behavior, and the interaction between the effect of prolactin and that of previous parental experience (Lehrman, 1955).

Ring doves were injected with prolactin in sufficient quantity to cause complete development of the crop, and suppression of sexual behavior (Bates, Riddle, and Lahr, 1937). At the end of the seven-day injection period, the doves were placed singly in cages each containing a hungry young dove, 7 days of age. Equal numbers of male adults and female adults were used as experimental animals. Half of the subjects had had previous breeding experience consisting of the successful completion of two breeding cycles during which young were reared; the other half, of the same age as the experienced birds, had been kept in isolation since just before sexual maturity and had thus never had breeding experience. Control birds, both experienced and inexperienced, were tested without previous prolactin treatment.

No untreated birds, whether experienced or inexperienced, made any attempt to feed the young. Among the birds injected with prolactin, there was a striking difference between the behavior of the birds with, and those without, breeding experience. None of the inexperienced birds fed the young during a 24-hour test period. Among the experienced birds, 10 (out of 12) fed the squabs by regurgitating crop-milk to them, the average latency until the first regurgitation being about 60 minutes after the birds were introduced into the cage.

Although the inexperienced birds failed to feed the young in response to prolactin injection, their behavior was nevertheless quite different from that of inexperienced birds which had not been injected with prolactin. They showed no sexual behavior, were quieter, and exhibited various signs of tension, such as repeated swallowing, pecking at food without eating, etc. Under the prolactin treatment, the crops of the inexperienced birds developed just as much as did those of the experienced birds.

This experiment showed that, although prolactin induces various physiological changes in doves regardless of their previous experience, these changes lead to the performance of parental feeding behavior only in animals which have had previous breeding experience. A further experiment throws some light upon the mechanism of this relationship between the effects of prolactin and of the animal's earlier experience. Two groups of experienced doves were injected with prolactin, in the same manner as just described. One day before they were due to be tested with

young doves, the birds were injected intradermally with a long-acting local anesthetic. Half of the birds were anesthetized by small injections distributed through the skin over the crop and into the wall of the crop. The other half of the birds were injected with the same amount of the local anesthetic distributed in small injections in the skin of the back (a control for possible systemic effects). Local anesthesia of the crop prevented the appearance of regurgitation-feeding responses, *or of parental approaches to the young,* in 8 of the 12 birds so treated; the same anesthetic injected into the back failed to inhibit parental feeding responses in 10 of the 12 birds.

Since local anesthesia of the crop prevents the appearance of parental feeding responses after prolactin injection, it seems likely that afferent inflow from the crop, engorged by the effects of prolactin, is at least a part of the basis for the ability of prolactin to induce parental regurgitation behavior.

Riddle and Burns (1931) found that regurgitation responses of ring doves, originally occurring as a response to the forcible introduction of a drug tablet into the crop, readily became conditioned (after 3–13 trials) to the sound of the experimenter opening the door of the cage. The regurgitation response is thus apparently quite easily conditioned, and this may be a part of the basis for the difference in behavior between experienced and inexperienced birds injected with prolactin. Regurgitation responses originally elicited by tactual stimulation by the young, upon which the parents are sitting, may become conditioned to visual and auditory stimuli from the young; the parents may thus *approach* the young when their crops are engorged only after such conditioning, while before conditioning they respond only to tactual contact with the young which they are brooding. This view is supported by observations of experienced and inexperienced birds feeding newly hatched young for the first time.

Mrs. R. Wortis and I, in an unpublished experiment, have obtained somewhat similar data in relation to the elicitation of incubation behavior by progesterone. This hormone, injected into experienced ring doves, reliably induces the birds to sit on eggs (Riddle and Lahr, 1944; Lehrman, 1958a). We have subjected 10 pairs of birds with previous breeding experience and 10 pairs, of the same age, without breeding experience to a seven-day course of progesterone injections. At the end of the hormone treatment, the birds were introduced, in pairs, into standard breeding cages supplied with a nest and eggs. Doves that have not been injected with progesterone, placed in a similar situation, do not sit on the eggs until after several days, during which they first build a nest (Lehrman, 1958b, 1959).

A striking difference was observed in

TABLE 1

LATENCY OF INCUBATION RESPONSE OF PAIRS OF PROGESTERONE-INJECTED RING DOVES WITH AND WITHOUT PREVIOUS INCUBATION EXPERIENCE[*]

	Experienced		Inexperienced	
	Median	Range	Median	Range
Time to first standing on nest	<1 min.	<1 min.–3 min.	60.5 min.	<1 min.–>2 hr.
Time until incubation is established	21.5 min.	6 min.–3 hr.	24.5 hr.	82 min.–no response

[*] Measured from time birds are introduced into a cage containing nest and eggs.

the response of the experienced and of the inexperienced birds to the progesterone injection. These differences are summarized in Table 1. The experienced birds obviously approach and sit on the eggs more quickly and more often than do inexperienced birds subjected to the same hormone injection.

Discussion

HORMONE-EXPERIENCE INTERACTIONS

The groups of experiments described above do not by any means exhaust the possible types of interactions between hormonal and experiential effects. A number of other types could be cited. So-called "social-dominance" hierarchies, which depend upon relations among animals which recognize each other individually (Guhl and Ortman, 1953) can often be altered by the administration of sex hormones. For example, exogenous androgens have been reported to cause an increase in the "social status" of ring doves (Bennett, 1940), domestic hens (Allee, Collias, and Lutherman, 1939; Allee and Foreman, 1955), and chimpanzees (Clark and Birch, 1945), while estrogenic hormones tend to lower the standing of the animal, both in domestic hens (Allee and Collias, 1940) and male chimpanzees (Clark and Birch, 1946).

Experience of stress stimulation in infancy affects the development of the pituitary-adrenal relationship in rats, which in turn influences the animals' reactions when adult (Levine, 1960; Levine, Alpert, and Lewis, 1957). Other examples could be given.

It is obviously not possible to account for all of the effects described here by assuming a single type of interaction between the effects of experience and of hormones. Experiential influences upon behavioral responses to sex hormones in guinea pigs, as analyzed by Young and his co-workers, depend at least partly upon the animals' experience before they are sexually mature, while the experiential effects demonstrated in cats by Rosenblatt and Aronson clearly depend upon postpuberal sexual experience. In most of the work we have done on ring doves so far, it is apparent that animals with similar histories before sexual maturity may respond to exogenous hormones quite differently, depending upon differences in their reproductive experience when mature. The data on the effects of sex hormones upon social rank demonstrate still another possibility: here a continuing relationship, dependent upon the animals' experience with each other, is altered by the intrusion of the effects of sex hormones into the existing situation.

The implication of these studies is therefore not that any particular kind of relationship consistently or necessarily obtains between the effects of hormones and those of experience, but rather that a full understanding of the organization and causation of behavior patterns, even in those cases in which we have a good deal of knowledge of the physiological mechanisms, can only be achieved by analysis of the ontogeny.

In all the cases considered, and in many others, analysis of the ontogenetic processes contributing to the development of the behavior enormously expands and deepens our understanding of the nature of the behavioral organization, and this is true regardless of what conclusions are eventually reached, in any particular case, about the extent to which experiential factors do or do not play a role in the ontogeny.

SPECIES DIFFERENCES
AND PHYLOGENETIC PROBLEMS

The differences between guinea pigs and cats, just cited, imply that the relationships between experiential and hormonal determinants of behavior vary from species to species, and there is abundant evidence that such interspecific variability is no less striking with respect to the phenomena which we are discussing than with respect to any other biological processes. For example, socially reared rats and individually reared rats do not differ in their sexual behavior, in sharp contrast to the situation in guinea pigs (Beach, 1942, 1958).

Beach (1947) suggested, for mammals, that there is a regular phylogenetic progression in the physiological mechanisms underlying sexual behavior, with lower mammals being more dependent on the immediate presence of the relevant hormones, and relatively independent of influences from the cerebral cortex, while in higher mammals the increasing development of the cerebral cortex is associated with increasing modifiability of sexual behavior and increasing independence of such behavior from immediate control by gonadal hormones.

Beach's summary of the data available in 1947 demonstrated the existence of such trends among mammals. More recent discussions, however, suggest certain modifications of the details of these generalizations. For example, Rosenblatt and Aronson (1958a) point out that *prepuberally* castrated rats, hamsters, and guinea pigs may actually show somewhat more sexual behavior when tested as adults than do similarly treated cats or chimpanzees. In contrast, when experienced animals are castrated postpuberally, sexual behavior persists much longer in cats and primates than in the rodents. Formulations of the relative "importance" of hormonal and of cerebral influences must therefore depend, to some extent, upon the extent to which experience has contributed to the development of the behavior pattern in question.

L. R. Aronson (1959) points out that data from fishes, amphibians, reptiles, and birds, while they support the general picture of vertebrate sexual behavior as being related to gonadal activity, do not suggest that such behavior is more dependent upon gonadal hormones in these forms (which lack a cerebral cortex) than in mammals. Further, Aronson points out that different aspects of the mechanisms underlying sexual behavior, such as distance perception of the female, tactual sensitivity to the female, erection capacity, etc., may be differentially affected by hormones (Soulairac, 1952), and that individuals and species may differ from each other with respect to (1) the relative dominance of the various components in the sex behavior pattern and (2) the degree to which the various aspects of the pattern are affected by castration and by gonad hormone replacement therapy. It follows from this that, although phylo-genetic trends from lower to higher vertebrates are by no means obvious when we use generalized notions of "sex drive" or "sexual arousal" for our definition of sexual activity, detailed analysis of the part-processes involved in sexual behavior, and of their integration, will provide much better insight into evolutionary trends than we now have.

SOME REMARKS ON TERMINOLOGY

I have avoided the use of the term "learning," preferring the less restrictive expression "experiential influences." As Schneirla (1956, 1957) has pointed out, the concept of "experience" may be taken to connote *"all stimulative influences upon the organism through its life history."* Such stimulative influences begin to work before birth and include a wide variety of *kinds* of effect, from pervasive developmental influences of the chemical environment to the most specific kinds of learning as we know it in adult animals (Hebb, 1953b). The term "learning" inevitably brings to mind the principal parameters of the type of experiment ordinarily associated with "learning theory": performance improves as a regular function of practice on successive trials; performance tends to deteriorate as a regular function of periods of nonpractice; there are regular relationships between the rate of improvement of performance and such variables as the distribution of practice, various aspects of "reward," etc. "Learning" in this restricted sense undoubtedly does occur in connection with, and participates in the development of, various types of "species-specific" (Beach, 1960) or "instinctive" (Schneirla, 1956) behavior. However, it must be remembered that the concepts of "learning" which are derived from traditional learning experiments may be misleading when applied to the kinds of behavior which we are discussing here, for several reasons.

"Learning" and "Experiential Influences"

First, learning theory is almost entirely derived from experiments on adult mammals. Many of the experiential effects relevant to the development of the types of behavior considered in this paper occur at early developmental stages and have effects which are much more widely generalized among many aspects of the animal's behavior than is the case with the learning of specific responses, or specific associations, by adult animals. Carmichael (1936) has suggested that the effects of stimulation in very early developmental stages may be in part to alter growth patterns, including those of the nervous system, so that the effects of "maturation" in such cases may not be conceptually distinguishable from those of "learning" (Kuo, 1932). Hebb (1949) has similarly pointed out that distinctions between the effects of learning and of growth processes do not have the same significance in adult stages as in the more labile earlier stages of development. Indeed, different groups of laboratory rats reared under different living conditions may, when adult, perform quite differently in "standard" learning situations (Christie, 1951, 1952).

In general, while the concept of "experiential influences" certainly includes those ordinarily associated with the term "learning," it also includes so many other kinds of processes that it seems preferable, when trying to define

the basic problems of the ontogenetic relationships out of which behavioral organizations emerge, to use the more inclusive term, reserving finer distinctions, when useful, for those specific cases in which the actual mechanisms have been analyzed.

Motivation and "Experience"

There is a second reason for caution in the application of the paradigms of learning theory to the analysis of the ontogeny of species-specific behavior: such behavior often develops in association with physiological conditions which form the basis for strong motive states, and which limit the range of stimulation to which the animal can be effectively sensitive. For example, Aronson (1959) suggests that sex hormones cause cutaneous changes, changes in olfactory thresholds, and changes in the composition and strength of various muscles, and that these effects must be regarded as possibly relevant to the ways in which the hormones change sexual behavior. Similarly, the changes in bodily tensions associated with parturition appear to influence the behavior of the parturient mammalian mother toward her young (Schneirla, 1956), and the tension of milk in the mammary glands later plays a role in her nursing behavior (Cross, 1952). These effects imply changes in sensitivity, no doubt compounded by central effects of the hormones, which may add additional effects on sensitivity to various types of stimulation (Morgan, 1959). This suggests that in the study of the ontogeny of species-specific behavior, the analysis of the participation of experiential influences requires much closer attention to the effects of physiological and motivational conditions upon the effectiveness of "experience" than has traditionally been characteristic of learning experiments.

LOCUS OF EXPERIENTIAL EFFECTS IN BEHAVIOR SEQUENCES

The traditional test of the presence of "learning"—that performance should improve on successive repetitions of the behavior—is not always helpful in analyzing the participation of experiential influences in the development of hormone-induced instinctive behavior patterns.[2] For example, although experienced ring doves feed their young somewhat sooner after the eggs hatch than do inexperienced ones of the same age (Lehrman, 1955), these differences are quantitatively not large; and the fact remains that ring doves, like most other animals, can carry out the normal behavior patterns associated with the reproductive cycle on the first occasion when such a cycle occurs.

How can we reconcile the fact that animals can perform various behavior patterns adequately during the first reproductive cycle with the fact that, in many cases, experienced and inexperienced animals differ so strikingly in their behavioral response to injected hormones?

At least a partial solution to this problem may be found in the fact that experience during the early stages of a reproductive cycle may have important effects, not on behavior during the same stages of the next cycle, but upon be-

havior during subsequent stages of the same cycle. The attachment of the ring dove to its nest, which develops during the time when the nest is being built, may serve both to localize the laying of eggs in the nest and to ensure that, after the eggs are laid, the birds are bound to come into contact with the eggs in such a way as to lead to the stimulation of incubation behavior. Similarly, the fact that the birds are sitting on the eggs when they hatch makes possible the development of relationships between parents and young, even though the birds show no tendency to approach the young until after such relationships have been established. In this case, the experience that the birds have during early parts of the cycle has the effect of moulding a pattern of behavior toward the nest (and eggs) which, when it persists into the changed physiological condition of the next stage, contributes to the probability that the behavior appropriate to this next stage will occur. This is clearly an effect of experience, although it does not necessarily result in the behavior being more efficient during the second reproductive cycle than during the first, since the experience with the nest during the first cycle may help ensure adequate reactions to the eggs during that same cycle. However, we may take birds who are *not* now tied to the nest (e.g., reproductively inactive birds), and inject them with hormones which duplicate in them the physiological conditions characteristic of one of the later stages, such as the incubation period. We can then see a striking difference between the behavior of birds with previous breeding experience and that of birds without such experience. The latter, even though they are now in such a physiological condition that they would sit on eggs

2 Although various investigators have reported that maternal behavior is more efficient in multiparous than in primiparous mammals (Hediger, 1950; Ross *et al.*, 1956; Seitz, 1958), it is by no means clear whether this is the result of learning or of growth changes, since controls for age are usually absent in these reports (Dieterlen, 1959; Lehrman, 1961).

if they were (because of their experience during the immediately preceding stage) spending most of their time on the nests, do not, in a high percentage of the cases, approach the eggs. On the other hand, the birds with previous experience, subjected to the same hormone treatment, are induced to approach the eggs. What the previous breeding experience appears to have done is to make it possible for the birds to react in ways which they have previously found satisfying within the same physiological (i.e., motivational) condition. Because birds which *normally,* in the course of an ordinary breeding cycle, come into such physiological condition are at the time closely attached to the nest, they will inevitably come into contact with the eggs, which induce incubation behavior enabling them to learn to approach the eggs later on the basis of distance perception of them.

Thus we are able to account for the apparently contradictory facts that the birds sit adequately on their eggs during their *first* breeding experience, and that they will not sit on eggs offered by the experimenter, after hormone injection, unless they have had previous breeding experience.

Similarly, the behavior of the parturient mother cat toward her young, which consists of alternate vigorous licking (an extension of self-licking) and quiet lying in proximity to the neonates, facilitates the onset of suckling. This interaction between mother and young, based in part upon the physiological condition of the mother at parturition, has as a consequence the development of the somewhat different relationships which can be seen later.

This is clearly seen in sheep and goats, in which removal of the neonate from the mother for a short period after birth, or interference with the parturient mother's licking of the neonate, may seriously disturb the development of mother-young relationships (Blauvelt, 1955); Collias, 1956). The effects of short periods of separation (one-half hour to one hour) at birth may still be apparent two or three months later, in the form of weakened bonds between mother and young (Hersher, Moore, and Richmond, 1958).

The experience of the mother early during the parturient and postparturient periods, based in part upon her hormone-induced physiological condition, clearly contributes to the behavior which develops later, although this does not at all necessarily mean that the normal behavior of a primiparous mother and that of a multiparous one will be different (Schneirla, 1956). A further consideration is the fact that experience which takes place later in the reproductive cycle cannot be expected to be transferred intact into the earlier stages of the next reproductive cycles when the animal is in a quite different physiological condition.

Conclusion: It will be seen from these remarks, as well as from all of the descriptions of hormone-experience interactions described earlier in this paper, that analysis of the contribution of experiential influences to the development of hormone-induced behavior requires a formulation much broader and more subtle than would be suggested by simple questions implying (1) that "learning" is demonstrated only when the behavior improves on successive repetitions of the reproductive cycle or (2) that "learning" requires previous opportunity to observe another animal performing the activity.

Science, July 17, 1959, vol. 130, pp. 130–141

Imprinting[*][1]

Eckhard H. Hess

Students of behavior generally agree that the early experiences of animals (including man) have a profound effect on their adult behavior. Some psychologists go so far as to state that the effect of early experience upon adult behavior is inversely correlated with age. This may be an oversimplification, but in general it appears to hold true. Thus, the problem of the investigator is not so much to find out *whether* early experience determines adult behavior as to discover *how* it determines adult behavior.

Three statements are usually made about the effects of early experience. The first is that early habits are very persistent and may prevent the formation of new ones. This, of course, refers not only to the experimental study of animals but also to the rearing of children. The second statement is that early perceptions deeply affect all future learning. This concept leads to the difficult question whether basic perceptions —the way we have of seeing the world about us—are inherited or acquired.

The third statement is simply that early social contacts determine the character of adult social behavior. This is the phenomenon of imprinting.

At the turn of the century, Craig (1908), experimenting with wild pigeons, found that in order to cross two different species it was first necessary to rear the young of one species under the adults of the other. Upon reaching maturity the birds so reared preferred mates of the same species as their foster parents. Other interspecies sexual fixations have been observed in birds and fishes.

Heinroth (1910; Heinroth & Heinroth, 1924) and his wife successfully reared by hand the young of almost every species of European birds. They found that many of the social responses of these birds were transferred to their human caretaker. Lorenz (1935) extended these experiments, dealing especially with greylag geese.

Lorenz was the first to call this phenomenon "imprinting," although earlier workers had observed this effect. He was also the first to point out that it appeared to occur at a critical period early in the life of an animal. He postulated that the first object to elicit a social response later released not only that response but also related responses such as sexual behavior. Imprinting, then, was related not only to the problem of behavior but also to the general

[*] Reprinted from *Science* by permission.
[1] The work described in this article was supported in part by Grant No. M–776 of the National Institutes of Health, Public Health Service, Department of Health, Education and Welfare, Bethesda, Md.; by the Wallace C. and Clara A. Abbott Memorial Fund, of the University of Chicago, Chicago, Ill.; and by the Wallace Laboratories, New Brunswick, N.J.

biological problem of evolution and speciation.

Although imprinting has been studied mainly in birds, it also has been observed to occur in other animals. Instances of imprinting have been reported in insects (Thorpe, 1944), in fish (Baerends & Baerends-van Roon, 1950), and in some mammals. Those mammals in which the phenomenon has been found—sheep (Grabowski, 1941, deer (Darling, 1938), and buffalo (Hediger, 1938)—are all animals in which the young are mobile almost immediately after birth. Controlled experimental work with mammals, however, has just begun.

The first systematic investigations of imprinting were published in 1951. Simultaneously in this country and in Europe, the work of Ramsay (1951) and Fabricius (1951) gave the first indication of some of the important variables of the process. Ramsay worked with several species of ducks and a variety of breeds of chickens. He noticed the importance of the auditory component in the imprinting experiment and the effect of changes in coloring on parental recognition as well as on recognition of the parents by the young. His findings also showed that color is an essential element in recognition, while size or form seemed to be of less importance. Most of Ramsay's experiments dealt with exchange of parents and young and did not involve the use of models or decoys as imprinting objects, although he also imprinted some waterfowl on such objects as a football or a green box.

Fabricius carried on experiments with several species of ducklings and was able to determine approximately the critical age at which imprinting was most successful in several species of ducks. In some laboratory experiments he found it impossible to do imprinting in ducklings with a silent decoy—something which my coworkers and I were easily able to do a few years later in our Maryland laboratory. After the appearance of this pioneer work by Ramsay and by Fabricius, no relevant papers appeared until 1954. At that time Ramsay and Hess (1954) published a paper on a laboratory approach to the study of imprinting. The basic technique was modified slightly the following year and then was continued in the form described below. Papers in 1956 by Margaret Nice (1953) and by Hinde, Thorpe, and Vince (1956) include most of the pertinent materials published up to 1956 since Lorenz's classic statement of the problem.

Since 1956, however, there has been an increasing number of papers on imprinting in a variety of journals. However, most investigators report experiments which are primarily designed to look for ways in which imprinting can be likened to associative learning and are not primarily carried out to investigate the phenomenon itself. Later we shall return to a consideration of these experiments; for the present we shall concern ourselves mainly with the program carried out since 1951 at McDonogh and at Lake Farm Laboratory, Maryland, and at our laboratories at the University of Chicago.

Experimental Studies

Our laboratory in Maryland had access to a small duck pond in which we kept relatively wild mallards. The birds laid their eggs in nesting boxes, so the eggs could be collected regularly. After storage for a few days, the eggs were incubated in a dark, forced-air

ys before
ısferred to
... .tions were
taken to place the newly hatched bird
into a small cardboard box (5 by 4 by
4 inches) in such a way that it could
see very little in the dim light used to
carry out the procedure.

Each bird was given a number,
which was recorded on the box itself
as well as in our permanent records.
The box containing the bird was then
placed in a still-air incubator, used as
a brooder, and kept there until the
bird was to be imprinted. After the
young bird had undergone the imprinting procedure, it was automatically
returned to the box, and the box was
then transferred to a fourth incubator,
also used as a brooder, and kept there
until the bird was to be tested. Only
after testing was completed was the
duckling placed in daylight and given
food and water.

The apparatus we constructed to be
used in the imprinting procedure consisted of a circular runway about 5 feet
in diameter. This runway was 12 inches
wide and 12½ feet in circumference at
the center. Boundaries were formed by
walls of Plexiglas 12 inches high. A mallard duck decoy, suspended from an elevated arm radiating from the center of
the apparatus, was fitted internally with
a loud-speaker and a heating element.
It was held about 2 inches above the
center of the runway. The arms sus-
pending the decoy could be rotated by
either of two variable-speed motors.
The speed of rotating and intermittent
movement could be regulated from the
control panel located behind a one-way
screen about 5 feet from the apparatus.
The number of rotations of both the
decoy and the animal were recorded
automatically. Tape recorders with con-

tinuous tapes provided the sound that
was played through the speaker inside
the decoy. A trap door in the runway,
operated from the control panel, returned the duckling to its box.

IMPRINTING PROCEDURE

The young mallard, at a certain number of hours after hátching, was taken
in its box from the incubator and
placed in the runway of the apparatus
(Fig. 1). The decoy at this time was situated about 1 foot away. By means of a
cord, pulley, and clip arrangement, the
observer released the bird and removed
the box. As the bird was released, the
sound was turned on in the decoy
model, and after a short interval the
decoy began to move about the circular
runway. The sound we used in the imprinting of the mallard ducklings was
an arbitrarily chosen human rendition
of *"gock,* gock, gock, gock, gock." The
decoy emitted this call continually during the imprinting process. The duckling was allowed to remain in the apparatus for a specified amount of time
while making a certain number of turns
in the runway. At the end of the imprinting period, which was usually less
than 1 hour, the duckling was automatically returned to its box and placed
in an incubator until it was tested for
imprinting strength at a later hour.

TESTING FOR IMPRINTING

Each duckling to be tested was mechanically released from its box halfway
between two duck models placed 4 feet
apart. One of these was the male mallard model upon which it had been
imprinted; the other was a female
model which differed from the male
only in its coloration. One minute was

Fig. 1. The apparatus used in the study of imprinting consists primarily of a circular runway around which a decoy duck can be moved. In this drawing a duckling follows the decoy. The controls of the apparatus are in the foreground.

allowed for the duckling to make a decisive response to the silent models. At the end of this time, regardless of the nature of the duckling's response, sound was turned on simultaneously for each of the models. The male model made the "gock" call upon which the duckling had been imprinted, while the female model gave the call of a real mallard female calling her young.

Four test conditions followed each other in immediate succession in the testing procedure. They were: (i) both models stationary and silent; (ii) both models stationary and calling; (iii) the male stationary and the female calling; (iv) the male stationary and silent and the female moving and calling. We estimated these four tests to be in order of increasing difficulty. The time of response and the character of the call

note (pleasure tones or distress notes) were recorded. Scores in percentage of positive responses were then recorded for each animal. If the duckling gave a positive response to the imprinting object (the male decoy) in all four tests, imprinting was regarded as complete, or 100 percent.

Determination of the "Critical-Period"

To determine the age at which an imprinting experience was most effective we imprinted our ducklings at various ages after hatching. In this series of experiments the imprinting experience was standard. It consisted in having the duckling follow the model 150 to 200 feet around the runway during a period of 10 minutes. Figure 2 shows the scores made by ducklings in the different age

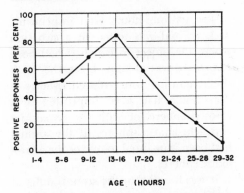

Fig. 2. The critical age at which ducklings are most effectively imprinted is depicted by this curve, which shows the average test score of ducklings imprinted at each age group.

groups. It appears that some imprinting occurs immediately after hatching, but a maximum score is consistently made only by those ducklings imprinted in the 13- to 16-hour-old group. This result is indicated in Fig. 3, which shows the percentage of animals in each age group that made perfect imprinting scores.

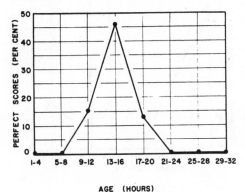

Fig. 3. Another way of showing the critical age is by plotting the percentage of animals in each age group that made scores of 100 percent in testing.

SOCIAL FACILITATION IN IMPRINTING

In order to find whether imprinting would occur in those ducklings which were past the critical age for imprinting—that is, over 24 hours of age—we attempted to imprint these older ducklings in the presence of another duckling which had received an intensive imprinting experience. Ducklings ranging in age from 24 to 52 hours were given 100 feet of following experience during a period of 30 minutes. The average score for the ducklings was 50 percent; this shows that some imprinting can occur as a result of social facilitation. Two conclusions can be drawn. (i) Social facilitation will extend the critical age for imprinting. (ii) The strength of imprinting in these older ducklings is significantly less than that when the animal is imprinted alone at the critical age under the same time and distance conditions; under the latter circumstances the average score made is between 80 and 90 percent. A further indication of this dissipation of imprintability with increasing age is obtained when we average the scores for those animals which were between 24 and 32 hours old. The average score for these animals was 60 percent, while the score made by older animals ranging in age from 36 to 52 hours was 43 percent. One last item points to the difference; even when the time and distance were increased during imprinting of the older ducklings there were no perfect scores. With such a large amount of distance to travel during the imprinting period, approximately 40 percent of the animals would be expected to make perfect scores if they were imprinted during the critical period.

Field Tests of Imprinting

In this same exploratory vein we have also carried out some studies under more normal environmental conditions. To do this we took animals imprinted in our apparatus and placed them in the duck-pond area, where they could either stay near a model placed at the water's edge or follow the model as it was moved along the surface of the duck pond, or go to real mallards which had just hatched their ducklings. Imprinted ducklings did not follow the live mallard females who had young of an age similar to that of the experimental animals. In fact, they avoided her and moved even closer to the decoy. Naive mallards, about a day old, from our incubator, immediately joined such live females and paid no attention to the decoys. These records, which we captured on motion-picture film, offer proof that what we do in the laboratory is quite relevant to the normal behavior of the animals and is not a laboratory artifact.

Color and Form Preferences in Imprinting Objects

An examination of the importance of the form and color of an imprinting object is relevant to any inquiry concerning factors contributing to the strength of imprinting (Schaefer & Hess, 1959).

Eight spheres approximately 7 inches in diameter in the colors red, orange, yellow, green, and blue, and in achromatic shades of near-black, near-white, and neutral grey were presented to 95 young Vantress broiler chicks as imprinting objects. The imprinting procedure was essentially the same as that described above in the duckling experiments. All the animals were exposed to one of the spheres during the critical period. Each imprinting experience lasted for a total of 17 minutes, during which time the imprinting object moved a distance of 40 feet.

Twenty-four hours after imprinting, each animal was tested in a situation where the object to which it had been imprinted was presented, together with the remaining four colored spheres if the animal had been imprinted to a colored sphere, or with the remaining two achromatic spheres, if the animal had been imprinted to one of the achromatic spheres.

It was found that the stimuli differed significantly in the degree to which they elicited the following-reaction. The stimuli, ranked in their effectiveness for eliciting following during imprinting, from the highest to the lowest, are: blue, red, green, orange, grey, black, yellow, white. These colors, in the same order, were increasingly less effective in terms of the scores made during the testing period. We concluded from this that the coloring of a stimulus is more important than its reflectance (Fig. 4).

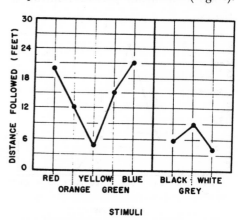

Fig. 4. Mean distance, in feet, traveled in the course of following response, by eight groups of animals, to eight different stimuli differing in color or reflectance.

In order to determine also form preferences in imprinting objects, we took the same spheres we used in determining color preferences and added superstructures of the same coloring, so that

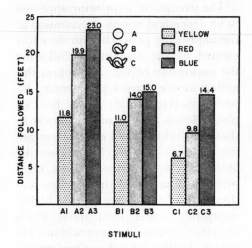

Fig. 5. Effectiveness of models in eliciting the following-reaction, expressed as a function of stimulus complexity and color.

the spheres had heads, wings, and tails (Fig. 5).

The addition of superstructures had a definite effect on the ease with which the following-reaction could be elicited: the plain ball was found to be the most efficient; the ball with wing and tail-like superstructures, less so; and the ball to which wings, tail, and head had been added, least efficient. We even presented a stuffed brown Leghorn rooster to the chicks, and it was found to be the least efficient model of all in eliciting the following response.

Auditory Imprinting in the Egg

Some investigators of imprinting have felt that vocalization of the incubating parent might cause imprinting to that vocalization even before the young fowl hatched. This seemed a likely hypothesis, so we carried out the following experiment. About 30 mallard eggs were incubated in an incubator with a built-in loud-speaker. For 48 hours before hatching these mallards were exposed

to a constantly played taped recording of a female mallard calling her young. Eggs were removed just before hatching and placed in a different incubator. Later, when tested, these young made no significantly greater choice of this source of sound than of the "gock" call used in our normal imprinting procedure. [A preliminary experiment was reported earlier (Ramsey & Hess, 1954).] Auditory imprinting, while the mallard is still in the egg, is therefore considered to be unlikely.

Law of Effort

We decided to vary independently the factors of time of exposure and the actual distance traveled by the duckling during the imprinting period. Since previous results had indicated that a 10-minute exposure period was sufficient to produce testable results, we decided to run a series of animals, varying the distance traveled but keeping the time constant at 10 minutes. We therefore used one circumference of the runway (12½ feet) as a unit and ran groups of animals for zero, one, two, four, and eight turns. This resulted in imprinting experiences in which the ducklings moved about 1 foot, 12½ feet, 25 feet, 50 feet, and 100 feet, respectively. All ducklings were imprinted when they were between 12 and 17 hours of age, in order to keep the variable of critical period constant. The results showed that increasing the distance over which the duckling had to follow the imprinting object increased the strength of imprinting. A leveling-off of this effect appears to occur after a distance of about 50 feet. These results are shown in Fig. 6.

In order to determine the effect of length of exposure time on imprinting

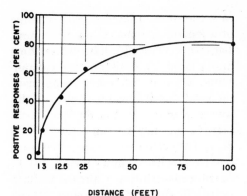

DISTANCE (FEET)

Fig. 6. Strength of imprinting as a function of distance traveled by ducklings, with exposure time held constant.

strength, we chose a distance that could be traversed by ducklings in periods of time as short as 2, 10, and 30 minutes. The scores made by animals imprinted for 2, 10, and 30 minutes, respectively, while traveling a distance of 12½ feet were essentially identical. Moreover, there is no significant difference between the findings for ducklings allowed to follow for a distance of 100 feet during a 10-minute period and those allowed 30 minutes to cover the same distance. These results are shown in Fig. 7.

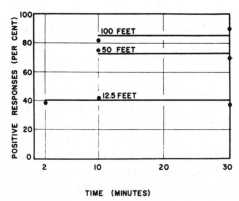

TIME (MINUTES)

Fig. 7. Strength of imprinting as a function of duration and exposure in minutes. Time had little effect on the test scores of the ducklings when the distance traveled was held constant.

The strength of imprinting appeared to be dependent not on the duration of the imprinting period but on the effort exerted by the duckling in following the imprinting object. To confirm this notion we tried two supplementary experiments (Hess, 1958). In the first, we placed 4-inch hurdles in the runway so that the ducklings not only had to follow the model but also had to clear the obstacles. As we suspected, the birds which had to climb the hurdles, and thus expend more effort, made higher imprinting scores than those which traveled the same distance without obstacles. In the second experiment we allowed the duckling to follow the decoy up an inclined plane, with similar results. After further experiments we came to the conclusion that we could write a formula for imprinting: the strength of imprinting equals the logarithm of the effort expended by the animal to get to the imprinting object during the imprinting period, or $I_s = \log E$.

Previous accounts in the literature on imprinting have made the following of a moving object a necessary condition of imprinting. Our results, as formulated in the law of effort, indicate that the amount of walking done by the animal during the imprinting period is of primary significance. The following experiment was therefore carried out. Two identical decoys were spaced 3 feet apart. A light over each decoy could be turned on and off so that only the model giving the "gock" call was illuminated in the darkened experimental apparatus, and the illumination was made to coincide with the call. When the duckling reached the lighted and calling model, the light and sound were turned off in that model and turned on in the other, which was 3 feet away. In this manner we could shuttle the animal back and forth and have it cover a distance similar to that used in the normal imprinting situation, where it walks behind a moving object.

Animals were run at four shuttles and 16 shuttles. The results show scores similar to those obtained previously for the 12½-foot and 50-foot distances (see Fig. 6). They indicate, again, that imprinting strength is a function of the distance walked by the duckling, regardless of whether or not the more complex perception of *following* a moving object is involved.

Fear Behavior and Locomotory Ability

In the light of the "critical period" results, the question arises as to what developmental changes might be taking place that would account for the limits of the critical period.

During the very early hours of their lives, animals show no fear. We conducted an experiment with 137 White Rock chicks of different ages (Hess, in press) and found that there is no fear up to 13 to 16 hours after hatching. Afterwards, the proportion of animals from age group to age group begins gradually to increase up to the age of 33 to 36 hours, when all animals show fear. Fear responses will prevent an animal from engaging in the kind of social behavior necessary for imprinting to take place, since a fearful animal will avoid rather than follow a potential imprinting object.

On the other hand, fear behavior cannot account for the limitation of imprinting before the peak of maximum effectiveness. Since the strength of imprinting is dependent on locomotor ac-

tivity, we postulated that the ability to move about might thus be an important factor. The ability to move about is a growth function and would limit the onset of the critical period. Hence, we tested 60 Vantress broiler chicks of White Rock stock of different ages to determine the development of increasing locomotor ability.

The two curves we obtained from these two experimental studies—one for increasing locomotor ability and one for increasing incidence of fear behavior with increasing age—were found to be in substantial agreement with the limits of the critical period. In fact, in plotting these two curves together, we obtained a hypothetical "critical period" for imprinting which strongly resembled the empirical one obtained for that breed.

It seems likely that all animals showing the phenomenon of imprinting will have a critical period which ends with the onset of fear. Thus, we can predict in a series of animals, knowing only the time of onset of fear, the end of imprintability for that species. Even in the human being one could thus theoretically place the end of maximum imprinting at about 5½ months, since observers have placed the onset of fear at about that time (Bridges, 1932; Spitz & Wolf, 1946a).

Innate Behavior Patterns and Imprinting

Most commonly the following-reaction to a certain model has been taken as a means of observing the progress of imprinting during the first exposure to the imprinting object and also as an indicator of the effectiveness of this exposure. However, the following-reaction is always accompanied by other innate behaviors which may also be observed and recorded. For the present purpose, the emission of "distress notes" or "contentment tones," maintenance of silence, and fixation of an object were checked for individual animals for a 2-minute period at the beginning of an imprinting session (Hess & Schaefer, 1959).

To differentiate between the "distress notes" and the "contentment tones" of chickens is comparatively easy, even for the layman who has never become familiar with them. "Distress notes" are a series of high-intensity, medium-pitch tones of approximately ¼-second duration in bursts of five to ten. Little pitch modulation occurs in this kind of call. "Contentment tones," on the other hand, are a series of high-pitch, low-intensity notes emitted in bursts of three to eight and with considerable pitch modulation during emission. The duration of the individual tones is much shorter, ¹⁄₁₂ of a second or less. During distress notes the animal usually holds its head high; during contentment tones it holds its head beak down. The designations *distress notes* and *contentment tones* are merely labels and should not necessarily be taken literally.

The subjects were 124 Vantress broiler chicks which had never experienced light until the time of the experiment. The experimental situation was much like the first 2 minutes of an imprinting experiment.

We found that the behavior of the animals changed markedly with age. The younger the animals were, the more pronounced was their striving to move under the cover of the nearby model. Figure 8 reflects the way in which this behavior diminished with age. Figure 9 shows that the proportion

of animals fixating, or orienting toward, the model also diminished with increasing age. Although it was considerably more difficult for the younger animals to cover even the short distance between their original location and the model because of their poor locomotor ability, the time it took these younger animals to reach the model was much shorter than the time it took the older animals. However, the mode of locomotion for these younger animals was not walking but, rather, a kind of tumbling; they used both feet and wings as supports, and this left them exhausted after reaching the model a few inches away.

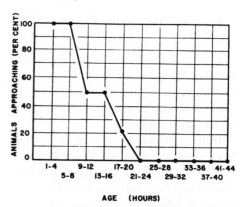

Fig. 8. Percentage of 124 chicks that approached the stimulus objects at different ages.

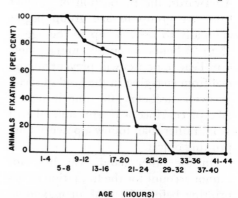

Fig. 9. Percentage of 124 chicks that fixated the stimulus object at different ages.

These results concerning behavior patterns during imprinting offer still further corroborating evidence for the location of the critical period as empirically determined. The emission of distress notes by animals older than 17 hours, even in the presence of an object that offers warmth and shelter, may be taken as an indication that a new phase of the animals' perception of their environment has set in. This behavior obstructs imprinting under the conditions of our laboratory arrangement. The high incidence of animals emitting contentment tones in the presence of the model is gradually replaced by an increasing number of animals emitting distress notes. No similar displacement occurs in animals remaining silent. The emission of contentment tones decreased as the animals became older, and the emission of distress notes increased at the same time.

The most important interpretation of these findings is that elicitation of following-behavior by various means after the critical period may not touch upon imprinting phenomena at all. Conventional training methods may be employed to overcome the fear response which the animals show after 17 hours, and it is not impossible to induce them, for example, to follow human beings. However, during the critical period, habituation or learning proper need not be considered as far as lowering of fear behavior is concerned, since at that time there is little or no fear present in the animals.

Drug Studies

The rapid drop in imprinting, then, appears to be coupled with the developing emotional response of fear—a response that makes imprinting impossible. To examine this aspect of imprinting, reduction of the emotional response by means of a tranquilizing drug (Hess, 1957) seemed a logical step. Meprobamate was chosen because of evidence that it would reduce emotionality without markedly influencing motility or coordination. Preliminary experiments with dosages of meprobamate showed clearly that the emotionality of the ducklings was markedly reduced. In fact, the ducklings showed no fear of strange objects or persons, even though they were at an age where marked fear is normally a certainty.

To obtain the maximal information from this experiment, we then decided to test animals under the following four conditions: (i) drug at 12 hours of age, imprinting at 24 hours of age when the effect of the drug had worn off; (ii) drug at 12 hours of age, imprinting at 14 to 16 hours of age, test when the drug effect had worn off; (iii) imprinting at 16 hours, test under drug later; and (iv) drug at 24 hours, imprinting at 26 hours, test when the drug effect had worn off.

In general, the procedure for imprinting and testing was the same as that which has been described. Control animals were given distilled water, and chlorpromazine and Nembutal were used to obtain additional information. The results are shown in Table 1.

It is obvious that, while meprobamate reduces fear or emotional behavior, it also makes imprinting almost impossible. It does not, however, interfere with the effects of imprinting. This is clear from the results of test (iii). Chlorpromazine allows a high degree of imprinting under all conditions, whereas Nembutal reduces imprinta-

TABLE 1

PERCENTAGE OF POSITIVE RESPONSES MADE BY DUCKLINGS UNDER DIFFERENT
CONDITIONS OF TESTING AND DRUG ADMINISTRATION

Conditions	Control H_2O	Memprobamate (25 mg/kg)	Nembutal (5 mg/kg)	Chlorpromazine (15 mg/kg)
Drug at 12 hr., imprinting at 24 hr.	14	54	31	57
Drug at 12 hr., imprinting at 14–16 hr.	62	8	28	63
Imprinting without drug at 16 hr., test under drug	61	65	61	58
Drug at 24 hr., imprinting at 26 hr.	19	17	16	59

bility at all points except under the conditions of test (iii).

From the data, it appears that we might interpret the action of the drugs as follows. If we assume that meprobamate and chlorpromazine reduce metabolism, then we could expect the high imprinting scores found at 24 hours of age [test (i)], because metabolism had been slowed and we had thus stretched out the imprinting or sensitive period. This did not occur when we used Nembutal or distilled water. The second point deals with the reduction of emotionality. In test (iv) we had little evidence of emotionality in the meprobamate and the chlorpromazine groups. Emotionality did occur in the control and in the Nembutal group. Thus far, the only way we can interpret this former result is to consider the law of effort. Here we had found that the strength of imprinting was a function of effort or of distance traveled. It may be that, since meprobamate is a muscle relaxant, these effects of meprobamate cut into the muscular tension or other afferent consequences and thus nullify the effectiveness of the imprinting experience. Since, under the same circumstances, we attain perfectly good im-

printing in all cases with chlorpromazine, this notion becomes even more tenable.[2]

Cerebral Lesions

In addition to drug effects we also studied the results of cerebral lesions on the imprinting behavior of chicks. This was done partly because we had noticed a loss of the fear response in some chicks that had undergone operations—chicks which were old enough to have this response fully developed.

Chicks with a type 1 lesion showed good imprinting at the age of 3 days. This is considerably better than the finding for the control chicks, which only occasionally show this behavior so late in their first few days. Even with this lesion, chicks at 5 and at 7 days showed no imprinting.

Chicks with type 2 lesion showed no imprinting, although some that had been prepared earlier gave no evidence of fear responses to strange objects.

Completely decerebrate animals were run only at 2 days of age, and they followed well, but the tests were inconclu-

[2] Further studies are in progress following up this hypothesis.

sive insofar as imprinting strength was concerned. Diagrams of the various lesions are shown in Fig. 10.

Although the number of animals used in this study is still small, this seems to be a fruitful avenue of approach. Control animals that have had sham operations act essentially like normal chicks. Other experiments involving electrical stimulation are being undertaken, since such stimulation may reinforce imprinting behavior.

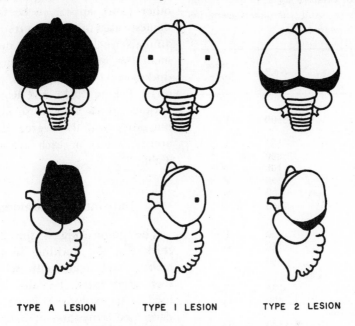

TYPE A LESION   TYPE I LESION   TYPE 2 LESION

Fig. 10. Three types of lesions in the chick brain, used to study the effect of extirpation on imprintability.

Genetic Studies

We have also considered the genetic side of imprinting. We kept ducklings which were highly imprintable and bred them separately from ducklings which showed very little imprinting response. We thus had two groups of offspring, those produced by "imprinters" and those produced by "non-imprinters." There was a clear and significant difference in the imprinting behavior of the two groups, even in the first generation. The offspring of imprintable parents were easily imprinted; those of less imprintable parents were difficult to imprint. The "imprinter" ducklings had imprinting test scores more than three times better than those of the "non-imprinter" ducklings. Similar results were also obtained in a study of bantam chicks. We are also following up those animals which have had experimental imprinting experiences to determine what influence, if any, these experiences have on their behavior as adults. So far the results are inconclusive, but they do suggest that experimental imprinting of mallards affects their behavior as adults, particularly with respect to courtship patterns.

Birds of various species show differing degrees of imprintability. Domestic

TABLE 2

NUMBER AND IMPRINTABILITY OF
DIFFERENT EXPERIMENTAL ANIMALS

*Most of the animals were imprinted in run-
way and mallard decoy situations. Some of
the Vantress broilers were imprinted on
colored spheres, and the sheep were imprinted on human beings.*

Animal	No.*	Imprinta-bility†
Ducks		
Wild mallard	3500	E+
Domesticated mallard	150	E
Peking	200	G
Rouen	100	F
Wood	50	P
Black	50	G
Total	4050	
Geese		
Canada	30	E+
Pilgrim	50	G
Total	80	
Chickens		
Jungle fowl	100	G
Cochin bantam	300	G
New Hampshire Red	100	G
Rhode Island Red	100	G
Barred Rock	200	G
Vantress broiler	500	G+
White Rock	100	F
Leghorn	200	P
Total	1600	
Other Fowl		
Pheasant	100	P
Eastern bobwhite quail	50	G
California valley quail	20	E
Turkey	30	F
Total	200	
Mammals		
Sheep	2	G
Guinea pig	12	G
Total	14	
Total	5944	

* Estimated for fowl, actual for mammals.
† E, excellent; G, good; F, fair; P, poor.

fowl do show imprinting responses, but
the results are not as clear as for wild
birds. We have had good success in
imprinting some breeds of chicks, and
the best imprinters among them are the
Vantress broilers. Leghorns, on the
other hand, appear to be too highly
domesticated to give clear results. Other
animals we have used in our experimentation are two kinds of geese, black
ducks, wood ducks, turkeys, pheasants,
quail. Peking ducks, and Rouens. The
various breeds we have so far used in
our work and the degree of imprintability found in each are shown in
Table 2.

Imprinting in Mammals

The guinea pig is similar to the
chick and the duckling in that it is
mobile and reasonably self-sufficient
soon after birth. For this reason we
used it in exploratory work. We first
developed a method of obtaining the
young from the mother with minimal
parental contact. This was done by
Caesarean section. However, further
work showed that it was sufficient to
obtain the young within an hour after
they were born, and for the moment we
are doing this. Guinea pigs imprint on
human beings and follow them about
as do the fowl with which we have been
working. The maximum effectiveness
of the imprinting experience seems to
be over by the second day. So far, in
using our imprinting apparatus with
our usual duck decoy we have obtained
best results sometime before the end of
the first day of age. Work is being continued so that we can have a more
standardized procedure before beginning a major program in this area.

Imprinting and Learning

The supposed irreversibility of imprinting has been particularly singled out by some investigators to show that imprinting is nothing but "simple learning"—whatever that is. We do have some isolated instances which point to a long-range effect, but systematic work is just now beginning in our laboratories. Canada goslings, imprinted on human beings for a period of a week or two, will from that time on respond to their former caretaker with the typical "greeting ceremony," as well as accept food out of his hand. This occurs in spite of the fact that they normally associate entirely with the Canada geese on our duck pond. A more striking case is that of a jungle fowl cock which was imprinted by me and kept away from his own species for the first month. This animal, even after 5 years—much of that time in association wth his own species—courts human beings with typical behavior, but not females of his own species. This certainly is a far-reaching effect and is similar to the findings of Räber (1948), who reported on a male turkey whose behavior toward human beings was similar. An increased amount of homo- sexual courtship in mallards has been observed with some of our laboratory imprinted animals, which, while not a statistically valuable finding, perhaps points also to long-range, irreversible effects.

Imprinting is currently receiving much attention, and papers on the subject are being published at an impressive rate. Unfortunately, most experimenters appear to be certain that imprinting is identical with simple association learning and design their experiments as studies in association learning. In many instances the animals are too old when used in the experiments to fall within the critical age for imprinting, with the result that only association learning can occur. Papers falling into this category are those of Jaynes (1956, 1957, 1958), Moltz & Rosenbaum, 1958b) and James (in press).

Our own experiments on the relation between association learning with food as a reward and imprinting during the critical period show four distinct differences.

In the first place, learning a visual discrimination problem is quicker and more stable when practice trials are spaced by interspersing time periods between trials than when practice trials are massed by omitting such intervening time periods. With imprinting, however, massed practice is more effective than spaced practice, as shown by our law of effort. Secondly, *recency* in experience is maximally effective in learning a discrimination; in imprinting, *primacy* of experience is the maximally effective factor. The second difference is illustrated by the following experiment. Two groups of 11 ducklings each were imprinted on two different imprinting objects. Group 1 was first imprinted on a male mallard model and then on a female model. Group 2, on the other hand, was first imprinted on a female model and subsequently on a male model. Fourteen of the 22 ducklings, when tested with both models present, preferred the model to which they first had been imprinted, showing primacy. Only five preferred the model to which they had been imprinted last, showing recency, and three showed no preference at all.

In addition, it has been found that the administration of punishment or painful stimulation increases the effectiveness of the imprinting experience, whereas such aversive stimulation results in avoidance of the associated stimulus in the case of visual discrimination learning.

Finally, chicks and ducklings under the influence of meprobamate are able to learn a color discrimination problem just as well as, or better than, they normally do, whereas the administration of this drug reduces imprintability to almost zero.

Imprinting, then, is an obviously interesting phenomenon, and the proper way to approach it is to make no assumptions. To find out its characteristics to explore its occurrence in different organisms, and to follow its effects would seem a worthwhile program of study.

What can we say in conclusion about the general nature of imprinting? Our best guess to date is that it is a rigid form of learning, differing in several ways from the usual association learning which comes into play immediately after the peak of imprintability. In other words, imprinting in our experiments results in the animal learning the rough, generalized characteristics of the imprinting object. Its detailed appreciation of the *specific*-object comes as a result of normal conditioning—a process which in the case of these animals takes a much longer time and is possible days after the critical period for imprinting has passed. It is an exciting new field and is certainly worthy of study.

Science, March 16, 1962, vol. 135, pp. 918–919.

Imprinting: Its Effect on the Response to Stress in Chicks[*][1]

William R. Thompson and M. W. O'Kieffe

Several writers have suggested a close relation between emotion and imprinting. Thus, maturation of fear may determine the critical period during which imprinting occurs (Hess, 1959b). Conversely, imprinting may have as a main function the reduction of fear in the young animal (Moltz, Rosenbaum, & Halikas, 1959; Harlow, 1959). Gray (1958) has reviewed evidence at the human level and suggests that, here also, lack of attachment to a parent or parent-surrogate has deleterious effects on emotional development.

The experiments reported here were aimed at providing further evidence on the relation between imprinting and emotion. Specifically, our aim was to examine both the effects of the imprinting experience and the presence of a surrogate mother on the responsiveness

* Reprinted from *Science* by permission. Copyright © 1962 by the AAAS.
[1] The research reported here was supported by a grant-in-aid from the National Science Foundation.

of chicks to stress. First an extreme and then a mild stress were used.

In the first experiment, 28 Vantress chicks from a local hatchery were used. To eliminate visual contact with each other or with the environment, the chicks were transferred to the lab in closed boxes at 3 hours of age. In the lab, they were kept in individual cages (9 by 8 by 5½ inches) covered with fine mesh nylon screening that allowed light and heat to enter but presumably prevented any effective perception of the environment outside the cages. Lighting was supplied by two 200-watt ceiling bulbs; cage temperature was maintained at approximately 88°F. The chicks were weighed individually at 3, 9, 12, and 16 hours. So they would have no visual contact with the environment, the chicks were placed in metal cans during weighing.

Experimental procedure was divided into two parts, imprinting and stress. Imprinting was as follows. Fourteen of the chicks, randomly assigned to the experimental group, were imprinted to surrogate mothers made of wadded linen wrapped in white cheesecloth and shaped so as to resemble an adult chicken. First, a surrogate was placed in the cage of each experimental chick from 4 hours of age until the introduction of stress at 60 hours. Second, each chick was given a 10-minute imprinting session with a moving surrogate at 8, 12, 16, and 20 hours of age. This was carried out in an unpainted wooden alley, 6 by 2 feet, with walls 3 feet high. Each chick was transferred to the alley in darkness. The room lights were then turned on, and the chick was allowed to follow a surrogate suspended in the alley and moved in front of the chick by the experimenter from behind a screen. Control chicks were kept in their home cages during this whole training session.

Stress involved total food and water deprivation at 60 hours of age. At this time, surrogates were removed from seven of the experimental cages and placed with seven control subjects. This procedure yielded four groups: imprinted with surrogate (IS), imprinted without surrogate (INS), nonimprinted with surrogate (NIS), and nonimprinted without surrogate (NINS). All chicks were weighed again at 60 and 94 hours, and at death.

In analyzing the data, two main variables were of interest in comparing the resistance of the four groups to stress: survival time and weight loss.

No significant differences between groups were found either in respect to survival time or weight loss. A significant negative correlation was found between age at death and percent weight loss ($r = 0.62$, $p < .01$), indicating, paradoxically, that chicks which showed the largest weight loss by 94 hours (all were still alive at this time) tended to live longer.

In view of these negative results, we designed a new experiment using a milder stress condition and a more sensitive index of responsiveness to stress.

In the second experiment, the subjects were a new group of 28 Vantress chicks, approximately 3 hours old at the time of pickup. Mode of transfer to the laboratory, housing conditions, and surrogates were as in the first experiment. However, a circular imprinting apparatus, like that of Hess (1959b), was used. This was made of white cardboard painted with irregular black lines. The outside circumference of the alley was 13 feet, the inside was 6 feet. The surrogate was suspended in the alley and moved manually by the experimenter from behind a screen. A view of the alley farthest from the experimenter was supplied by an appropriately located mirror.

Imprinting procedure was similar to that used previously. The 14 experimental chicks lived with a surrogate in their home cages and, in addition, were given three 10-minute imprinting sessions in the circular alley at 9, 12, and 15 hours of age. Each chick was removed from its cage to the alley in darkness and allowed to follow the moving surrogate. Mean following distances for all experimental chicks for the sessions at 9, 12, and 15 hours were, respectively, 164.5, 333.1, and 339.7 feet. Control chicks lived in their home cages during this time.

Stress was introduced at 28 hours of age. Each chick was carried in a metal can, in darkness, to a test box (2 by 2 by 1 foot) containing a doorbell. Half the experimentals and half the controls had a surrogate with them during stress sessions, thus giving four groups (IS, INS, NIS, NINS) as in the first experiment. Stress consisted of a 3-minute session during which the doorbell was rung for 10-second periods interspersed with 10-second periods of silence. After this 3-minute session, chicks were left in the test box for 5 minutes without the bell ringing. Two measures of the response to stress were used: activity-level and vocalization. Since the first of these yielded such low scores from all chicks, it is omitted in presentation of results. Vocalization was scored by a hand-counter in terms of number of "distress" peeps per minute during both the 3-minute sound trial and the subsequent 5-minute trial.

Mean peeps per minute in the two trials are shown in Table 1. A mixed

TABLE 1

MEAN DISTRESS CALLS PER MINUTE ELICITED IN IMPRINTED AND NONIMPRINTED CHICKS DURING AND FOLLOWING SOUND STRESS

See text for explanation of abbreviations.

Group	Distress calls per minute (mean)	
	During stress	After stress
IS	32.6	37.9
INS	28.7	31.1
NIS	47.1	89.6
NINS	21.3	41.9

model variance analysis indicated two significant effects: between stress and nonstress condition ($F = 20.26$, $p < .001$) and the interaction between imprinted-nonimprinted and stress-nonstress ($F = 12.48$, $p < .01$). All chicks tended to vocalize more following stress than during stress; this difference was larger for nonimprinted than for imprinted chicks.

Thus, we may conclude that although imprinting does not appear to affect responsiveness to severe stress, it does influence responsiveness to a mild stress inasmuch as imprinted chicks showed a reduced amount of "distress" vocalization following auditory stimulation.

Summary: Young chicks imprinted to surrogate mothers were compared with nonimprinted controls on two tests designed to measure resistance to stress. Half of each group was run with and without a surrogate present during the stress. One test involving survival time under starvation showed no effects. However, in the other test, imprinted chicks showed fewer distress calls in response to auditory stimulation than nonimprinted controls.

Psychological Bulletin, 1964, vol. 61, pp. 362–376

Displacement Activity and Motivational Theory:

A CASE STUDY IN THE HISTORY OF ETHOLOGY[1]

H. Philip Zeigler

The existence of species-specific behaviors raises three distinct sets of problems for the student of animal behavior (Lashley, 1938). The first concerns the nature of the response patterns which constitute the behaviors and the stimulus situations eliciting these response patterns. Take, for example, the instinctive behavior of nest building by birds. Construction of the nest involves the utilization by the bird of certain relatively stereotyped motor sequences, elicited by certain external stimuli. Thus nest building in the domesticated canary (Hinde, 1958) involves primarily three groups of distinct motor sequences: gathering, carrying, and building. All of these behaviors are obviously elicited by specific stimuli: gathering, by the presence of grass and/or feathers; carrying, by stimuli in the bill; building, by features of both the material and the nest site. Such sensorimotor sequences are character-

istic of all species-specific behaviors and the problems they raise are primarily those of the morphology and developmental history of such stimulus-response relationships.

It was to the latter problem that the early American behaviorists addressed themselves primarily, and current research on the effects of early experience upon adult behavior (Beach & Jaynes, 1954) is a direct descendant of the types of investigations carried out by Kuo (1932), Cruze (1935), and Carmichael (1936). These studies have had as their point of reference the perennial problem of the relative contributions of innate and acquired factors to the behavioral repertoire of organisms. Accordingly, they have been aimed at elucidating the developmental history of certain of the behavior patterns which are to be found in the repertoire of adult animals. In so doing, they have contributed notably to the solution of the first of the three groups of problems raised by species-specific behavior and clarified the conceptual difficulties involved in the artificial dichotomy between the innate and the acquired (Hebb, 1953a; Schneirla, 1956).

However, even when the developmental history of a given sensorimotor sequence has been sufficiently clarified, certain diverse characteristics of species-

[1] This paper is based, in part, upon discussions with various members of the Department of Zoology, Subdepartment of Animal Behavior, Cambridge University, during the author's tenure as a Postdoctoral Research Fellow, United States Public Health Service, 1958–60. Preparation of the manuscript was supported by Grant M–5214, National Institute of Mental Health, United States Public Health Service. For their detailed comments and criticisms of the manuscript, the author is indebted to R. A. Hinde and Hugh Rowell.

specific behavior confront us with a second group of problems. Consider once again the example of nest building. Even though the sensorimotor mechanisms involved in this behavior are presumably available throughout most of the bird's adult life, nest building takes place only at certain periods in the bird's life cycle. During these periods the bird is differentially responsive to stimuli which may have been consistently present in its environment, for example, grass and feathers, but which up to this time have been ignored. Such periodic or seasonal variations in the responsiveness of sensorimotor mechanisms are characteristic of many species-specific behaviors. Witness seasonal migrations in birds and fish, or the variations in sexual receptivity of female rats during the estrus cycle. Moreover, in addition to such relatively long-term variations, short-term variations in responsiveness are also common; that is, a constant stimulus presented at intervals to an animal does not elicit a constant response. The most obvious examples are to be found in connection with feeding and mating behavior. The animal that has eaten is no longer responsive to food, and sexual responsiveness in the male is considerably reduced following copulation. Similarly, feathers and grass may be available continuously, but nest building occurs in discrete bouts which alternate with other activities. The occurrence of nest building appears to reduce temporarily the responsiveness of the sensorimotor mechanisms involved in the behavior.

The third set of problems raised by species-specific behavior is best illustrated by the random exploratory behavior of a hungry animal, or the activity of an animal engaged in nest-site selection. Such animals appear to be reacting to the deprivation of some stimuli, and for this reason Lashley characterized such behaviors as reactions to a deficit. Thus when an animal builds a nest it is clearly reacting to specific stimuli, but nest-site selection and the fact that the nest is built to a definite form suggests, in addition, reactions to a deficit. Similarly, at a certain stage of nest building, the canary stops gathering grass and begins to collect feathers which are used for the soft, inner lining of the nest. There are no obvious external stimuli which are adequate to account for the onset of nest building, the changeover from grass to feathers, or the termination of the nest with the achievement of a definite species-specific form.

The problems raised by variations in responsiveness and reactions to a deficit, because they relate to the arousal, direction, and termination of behavior patterns rather than to their developmental history, are often grouped under the rubric of motivational problems. Ethological theories of motivation represented an attempt to deal systematically with such problems.

Drive Theory, Energy Models, and Motivation

In endeavoring to deal with the motivational aspects of behavior—learned or species-specific—many theorists have found it necessary to postulate the existence of either single- or multiple-drive processes. In either case, the drive is viewed as activating specific behavior patterns: different degrees of activation resulting in increases or decreases in the probability of occurrence of their correlated behavior patterns.

Implicit in many of these theories is

the concept of motivational energy, which is often treated as analogous to and comparable with physical, chemical, or electrical energy. While most contemporary theories of motivation have been variants of drive theory, for certain theorists, for example, Hull, Hebb, Spence, etc., the energy analogy is merely implicit and is represented by a general-drive variable whose function it is to energize behavior. For other theorists, for example, Freud, McDougall, Lorenz, and Tinbergen the centrality of the energy concept is indicated by the use of such terms as libido, psycho-physical energy, reaction-specific energy, motivational impulses, etc. These latter theorists, moreover, have made the energy analogy still more explicit by embodying it in electrical, mechanical, or hydraulic models. In these energy models of motivation (Hinde, 1960), variations in the quantity, quality, or distribution of such energy are used to account for those observed variations in the behavior of animals customarily grouped under the rubric of motivational changes.

Lorenz's theory, for example, was an attempt to account for the short-term variations in responsiveness typical of species-specific behavior. His observations that sensorimotor sequences become progressively more difficult to elicit with repeated presentations of the sign stimulus led him to suggest that these variations in responsiveness reflected variations in the level of accumulated action-specific energy in some hypothetical reservoir within the animal (Lorenz, 1950).

While such concepts might account for the motivational aspects of rather limited behavior patterns (consummatory behaviors), they were patently inadequate to deal with either long-term or with periodic variations in responsiveness or with the problems raised by appetitive behaviors—those behaviors which Lashley had characterized as reactions to a deficit. It was to deal with such behaviors that Tinbergen (1951) developed his hierarchical model of motivation. This model retained Lorenz's concept of action-specific energy but extended the concept considerably. Instead of postulating motivational energy whose action specificity was restricted to a particular, limited response pattern, he viewed motivational energy as being general to all the activities of a major instinct. He thus replaced action-specific energy with what might be termed drive-specific energy. Thus the same type of motivational energy could activate all the diverse sensorimotor mechanisms grouped by Tinbergen under the rubric of the reproductive instinct— mating, nest building, aggression, maternal behavior, etc. Each of these subinstincts, however, was also activated by motivational energy specific to it, which was accumulated in its own specific reservoir or center.

The difficulties inherent in the use of such energy models have been perceptively discussed by Lehrman (1953), Kennedy (1954), and Hinde (1959, 1960). Although none of these authors considers displacement activity in detail, it is clear from their comments that the concept of displacement activity has been among the problematic aspects of ethological theories of motivation. It is equally clear from Hinde's (1960) recent paper that the vicissitudes which this concept has undergone indicated the necessity for a revision of such theories. It is for this reason that the present paper is subtitled "A Case Study in the History of Ethology."

Displacement Activity

One of the most obvious characteristics of animal behavior is its directedness. Any individual pattern of behavior normally occurs as part of a sequence of functionally related behavior patterns. It appears to serve the same ends as do the behavior patterns which precede and follow it, and to share with them a common history of environmental stimulation. The grooming of birds, for example, normally occurs after bathing, when it serves to clean and resettle the feathers. It is thus associated with a recent history of certain types of environmental stimulation, for example, water or dirt on the feathers, and we should expect it to occur only in its proper place in the functional sequence and only in the presence of such stimulation. Should grooming occur in the absence of such stimulation and in the midst of a sequence of behaviors (e.g., fighting, mating, etc.) which does not include bathing, we should be justified in considering such grooming behavior anomalous, since it appears out of its usual behavioral context.

It is thus a matter of some surprise and considerable interest to find that out-of-context activities are observed quite frequently in the behavior of animals. Thus, for example, postures and movements normally associated with feeding, grooming, nest building, or sleeping in birds are often observed to occur out of context during aggressive or sexual encounters with other birds (Andrew, 1956a; Baggerman, Baerends, Helkens & Mook, 1956; Hinde, 1952; Lorenz, 1941; Makkink, 1931, 1936; Moynihan, 1953; Tinbergen, 1940). Similar observations have been recorded for fish (Tinbergen & van Iersel, 1947) and invertebrates (Bastock & Manning, 1955, Crane, 1957; Gordon, 1955). At the mammalian level, out-of-context behavior has been observed in rats (Bolles, 1960), cats (Armstrong, 1950), dogs (Schmidt, 1956), and wolves (Schenkel, 1947). Finally, both Lorenz (1950) and Tinbergen (1951) have suggested that such characteristic human behaviors as head scratching and tie straightening in emotional situations may be viewed as out-of-context activities (for an earlier review, see Armstrong, 1950a).

The possible theoretical significance of out-of-context activities was first noted, independently, by Kortlandt (1940) and Tinbergen (1940) who pointed out certain peculiarities in the behavior patterns themselves or in the conditions under which they occurred. First, such behaviors appeared to be most frequent in situations of either conflict or thwarting. A conflict situation may be characterized by the simultaneous activation of two or more incompatible behavior patterns. Such situations occur frequently during sexual (attack, escape, copulate) or aggressive encounters (attack, escape). The various behavior patterns elicited by the situation are incompatible and the animal generally alternates among them. Thwarting situations arise when a specific response pattern is activated but the animal is prevented from performing, completing, or continuing the response. A male stickleback, for example, cannot perform coition until the female follows him to the nest, and in the presence of incompletely aroused females will often display out-of-context nest-ventilation movements.

The out-of-context behaviors observed in conflict and thwarting situations were described as being different in kind and degree from the same behaviors in their normal context. To describe these differences, Tinbergen (1940) used such terms as irrelevant, frantic, and incomplete. The term irrelevant implied that the stimuli which normally elicit the behavior in an appropriate context were absent. Thus out-of-context feeding responses can take place in the absence of food. The terms incomplete and frantic referred to the fact that out-of-context activities are often broken off in the middle, seem hurried, and are eccentric, or imperfectly oriented. For example, bill wiping, a form of grooming in the zebra finch, is normally performed with the bird's body and head parallel to the branch or twig on which it is perched. It thus makes contact with the branch when the head is lowered and the bill wiped. By contrast, out-of-context bill wiping often takes place with the bird's body at right angles to the branch so that the bill wipes in mid-air (Morris, 1954).

Finally, it was noted that out-of-context activities occur most frequently when the two antagonistic response tendencies are in equilibrium, that is, when they are of (presumably) equal strength. For example, out-of-context nest digging in the stickleback was found to occur most frequently during aggressive encounters at the boundaries between two adjacent territories—a place where attack and escape behaviors would be elicited in equal degree. The incidence of such behavior could be greatly increased by crowding a large number of males into a small tank, thus increasing the number of immediately adjacent territories (Tinbergen & van Iersel, 1947).

The situations described above all share a common characteristic. In every case, a specific response tendency has been activated but its overt manifestation has somehow been blocked; either by the presence of an antagonistic response tendency, or by the absence of an appropriate stimulus situation.

On the basis of such observations, Tinbergen (1940) and Kortlandt (1940) postulated a motivational mechanism derived from and compatible with the type of drive theory current in ethology at the time. They suggested that, in the conflict situation, the motor patterns belonging to one of the drives (e.g., escape) are incompatible with the motor patterns belonging to the other (e.g., attack) drive. In the thwarting situation, they suggested, a given drive cannot express itself fully because the required releasing stimulus is not present. In either case, the result—in terms of an energy model—is a build-up of motivational energy which cannot discharge itself through the appropriate motor channels because these channels are blocked or otherwise unavailable. Tinbergen (1951) therefore suggested that such energy finds an outlet by discharging through the center of another instinct (p. 117). Since the center through which it discharges may have no functional relation to the center which is blocked, the resultant behavior will necessarily be out of context and occur in the midst of behavior sequences to which it is irrelevant. Out-of-context behaviors were thus viewed as resulting from a sparking over (Übersprung) of motivational energies from the motor system of one instinct to that of another, and were termed by Tinbergen Übersprungbewegungen (Tinbergen, 1940). The English equivalent, displacement activities, was suggested by Armstrong (1947). Grooming, which is observed to occur in the midst of an aggressive encounter would be called displacement grooming, since it has not been elicited by the normal stimuli for grooming nor activated by a grooming drive. Rather it is viewed as being motivated by energy from fleeing and/or fighting centers which has sparked over into the grooming center. As Kortlandt (1940) put it, the displacement activity is an expression not of its own drive (autochthonous motivation) but of a strange or different drive (allochthonous motivation).

The phenomenon of displacement activity had certain immediate implications for ethological drive theory. In Lorenz's original formulation of the theory, each fixed action pattern (sensorimotor sequence) in the animal's repertoire was presumably activated from a reservoir of motivational energy specific to that pattern. The phenomenon of displacement activity suggested that surplus energy, overflowing from a given reservoir, could activate behavior patterns not normally fed from that reservoir. Similarly, Tinbergen had originally viewed motivational impulses as being drive-specific; since they could activate only one hierarchical system of centers (e.g., that of the reproductive instinct). The discovery that motivational energy could spark over from one such hierarchical system to another, for example, from reproduction to body care, implied the existence of general as well as specific motivational energy. The theory which finally emerged (Tinbergen, 1951) combined both possibilities and provided for both general drive and multiple- or specific-drive processes. In this respect it was similar both to Freudian theory (Colby, 1955) and to much contemporary psychological theorizing.

Moreover, both Tinbergen (1951) and Lorenz (1957) suggested that the primary function of displacement activity is a cathartic one. It was viewed as permitting the resolution of conflicts between two antagonistic drives by acting as an outlet through which surplus motivational energy could blow off. Several writers (Armstrong, 1950; Bastock, Morris, & Moynihan, 1953) pointed to the obvious similarity between displacement activity in animals and a variety of neurotic and emotional behaviors in man, and in animals suffering from experimental neurosis—regression, object displacement, neurotic passivity, etc. Such similarities were of particular interest for psychoanalytic instinct theories (Barnett, 1955; Rapaport, 1960*b*). Furthermore, both Lorenz (1957) and Tinbergen (1951) pointed to the presence of displacement activities in man as "suggesting an instinctive organization in man basically similar to that found in animals [Tinbergen, 1951, p. 210]."

Finally, there occurred one of these processes of circular reasoning only too common in the early stages of theory development. On the one hand, the neatness and ease with which the ethological energy model accounted for the phenomenon of displacement activity was taken as an indication not only of the utility of the model, but of its validity. Conversely, the very plausibility of the model lent credence to a surplus-energy interpretation of displacement activity and militated against an explanation in more analytic terms. For this reason the surplus-energy interpretation presented by Tinbergen and Kortlandt in 1940 was to go essentially unchallenged for more than a decade.

The Causal Analysis of Displacement Activity

The publication, in the early fifties, of comprehensive statements of ethological theory (Lorenz, 1950; Tinbergen, 1951) elicited a barrage of criticisms from both psychologists (Lehrman, 1953) and ethologists (Hinde, 1959; Kennedy, 1954). These criticisms were instrumental in stimulating more detailed investigations of the factors underlying displacement activity. The results of these investigations cast serious doubt upon the motivational uniqueness of displacement activity.

It became apparent, for example, that under certain circumstances displacement activities need not be incomplete or imperfectly oriented but might be indistinguishable in form or orientation from the same behaviors in context. Thus displacement grooming in the zebra finch (Morris, 1954) might include the whole sequence of grooming movements—preening, stretching, shaking, scratching—used by the bird in normal grooming, while displacement feeding in this species could range from incomplete pecking at the floor to actual feeding in which the bird swallowed food. For additional examples see Armstrong (1950) and Andrew (1956b).

A second distinguishing characteristic of displacement activity had been its supposed irrelevance. Two assumptions appear to underlie the use of this term. First, the behavior was assumed to be independent of any other ongoing activity of the animal. However, it has been shown that the occurrence of one displacement activity rather than another in a given situation appears to be related to the animal's posture (Lorenz,

1957; Tinbergen, 1952). Secondly, it was assumed that the stimuli which normally elicit the activity were absent. This assumption too proved to have been unjustified, since a large body of evidence indicated that the nature of the displacement activity shown depended upon or was strongly influenced by the external stimulus situation. For example, displacement feeding in the turkey (Räber, 1948) might take the form of either eating or drinking depending upon the relative availability of food and water. Displacement feeding in the great tit (Hinde, 1952) might take the form either of turning over leaves, or pecking at the ground, depending upon whether the bird were perched in a tree or on the ground. Similarly, in the courtship of the zebra finch (Morris, 1954) the bird might show displacement feeding, if food were available; if a female were available (during a fight with another male) displacement mounting might take place, that is, mounting without either preliminary courtship or succeeding copulation. If neither of these alternatives were available, the bird might engage in displacement grooming or displacement sleeping.

Finally, Morris (1956) and Andrew (1956b) pointed out that conflict situations in birds and mammals are accompanied by a wide variety of autonomic responses including respiratory, circulatory, and thermoregulatory changes. These, in turn, would provide a host of stimuli arising from the feathers, blood vessels, and skin which might be expected to elicit a variety of grooming activities.

With the gradual accumulation of such observations it was becoming apparent that displacement activity is not irrelevant but is clearly causally related to the ongoing activities of the animal and/or the nature of the external stimulus situation. Nevertheless, a careful analysis of the motor patterns utilized as displacement activities indicates that there is some sense in which these patterns are unique.

Of all the motor patterns available in the animal's repertoire, only a limited number are ever observed to occur as displacement activities. The reader may have already noted that displacement grooming, feeding, and sleeping have been referred to most frequently. It is difficult to characterize such patterns except to note that they are common or readily available ones for the species in question (Lorenz, 1957). Grooming, for example, is one of the commonest behavior patterns of birds and mammals. Indeed, Bolles (1960) has reported that male rats in their home cages spend 40% of their waking hours in grooming behaviors. Similarly, oral activity, both in and out of feeding situations, is common in birds and mammals. As for relatively less-common activities (e.g., nest building, mounting, incubation), these are found to occur as displacement activities only when their threshold for occurrence has been temporarily lowered—either by internal (seasonal) changes or by the presence of external stimuli (e.g., a mate, a nest, or eggs). In short, the motor patterns exhibited most frequently as displacement activities in conflict or thwarting situations are precisely those which, *ceteris paribus,* are likely to occur with the greatest frequency even under normal circumstances.

This generalization has been shown to hold not only for complex behavior patterns such as feeding or grooming, but for the individual responses which constitute these complex behaviors. Grooming in birds, for example, may consist of the following set of responses: head shaking, preening, feather settling, bill wiping, and scratching. By studying the temporal organization of these responses, several investigators (Andrew, 1956a; Morris, 1954; van Iersel & Bol, 1958) have shown that there is a regular sequence of such responses, with one type of response regularly following a given response and preceding another. During normal grooming in the bunting, for example, bill wiping and feather settling are seen first, followed by preening and finally by scratching. Other things being equal, some types of grooming responses are more likely to occur during normal grooming than are others. It is precisely these low threshold grooming responses which are observed to occur most frequently as displacement activities.

The sole remaining characteristics of displacement activity which require explanation are the occurrence of the behaviors out of their normal contexts and in the midst of situations involving conflicting or thwarted response tendencies. Why, in addition, does displacement activity in conflict situations occur most frequently when the antagonistic response tendencies appear to be of equal strength? These characteristics constituted the crux of the problem of displacement activity and as the evidence began to accumulate several alternatives to the original surplus energy hypothesis began to emerge.

In a study of normal and displacement grooming in birds, Andrew (1956a) observed that not only was grooming one of the commonest activities in the birds' repertoire, it was also one of the most easily delayed, suppressed, or interrupted activities. If a bathing bird were frightened, for example, it would flee in the midst of bathing without responding to its wet plumage by a burst of grooming activity. Andrew further observed that when grooming did occur, it was most likely to take place at a time when the animal was changing over from one activity to another—an observation since confirmed and extended to the rat by Bolles (1960). Thus it might occur before and after bursts of locomotion, or after a sexual display but before nest-building activity.

On the basis of his observations, Andrew (1956a) presented a hypothesis which accounted for the occurrence of grooming as a displacement activity during conflict situations. He suggested that the peripheral stimuli which elicit grooming are continually present but that grooming is easily suppressed by other activities. In conflict situations, when a response tendency such as escape, which normally takes precedence over grooming, is blocked by an equally strong competing response tendency such as attack, grooming may occur in response to the usual peripheral stimuli. There are then two types of causal factors underlying displacement grooming—direct factors and indirect factors. Direct factors would include the presence of the peripheral stimuli normally eliciting the behavior, while the indirect factor was the extent to which other activities, incompatible with grooming are present.

Bindra (1959) independently suggested that displacement activity might be explained by reference to three variables: arousal level, habit strength, and sensory cues. He postulated that animals in conflict or thwarting situations are characterized by increased levels of arousal, and that in this condition the activities which are most likely to occur are those "which are prepotent in the animal's repertoire." The specific activity which occurs will be determined by the nature of the peripheral stimuli present.

A third hypothesis (the disinhibition hypothesis) was suggested by van Iersel and Bol (1958) and Sevenster (1960, 1961). It assumed that excitatory factors are constantly present in some degree for all behavior patterns, but that inhibitory relationships exist among various behavior patterns such that the activation of one such pattern suppresses the occurrence of others. In conflict situations, the antagonistic response tendencies tend to inhibit each other thus decreasing the inhibition each alone exerts on other activities. The degree of disinhibition, together with the extent to which internal factors and external factors (peripheral stimuli) are present for other activities determines which of these activities will be shown as a displacement activity.

All three of these hypotheses represent a considerable advance on the original "surplus" hypothesis. They all discard the untenable distinction between autochthonous and allochthonous motivation; they recognize the role of the stimulus situation and they describe the occurrence of displacement activity in terms of the probability of occurrence of other behavior patterns. However, the Bindra (1959) hypothesis involves the postulation of an intervening variable of arousal level; a concept whose formal properties have frequently been analogized to those of a general-drive concept (Hebb, 1955; Hinde, 1959). Similarly, both versions of the disinhibition hypothesis are phrased in terms of drives and centers.

Moreover, inhibition and disinhibition are simply more elaborate descriptive terms and their use in this context is tantamount to a restatement of the observation that grooming occurs more frequently in one situation than in another.

The problem of displacement activity has been considerably clarified by a recent experimental investigation of normal and displacement grooming in the chaffinch (Rowell, 1961). Rowell achieved a considerable degree of control of the relevant variables, of which the most important are the existence of a conflict situation and the presence of the peripheral stimuli eliciting grooming. Such stimulation was produced either by spraying the birds with a fine water spray, or by using a sticky birdseed which produced grooming responses restricted to the bill (bill wiping). Two kinds of approach-avoidance conflict situations were used, both of which could be varied in intensity.

By varying the amount and/or type of peripheral stimulation, Rowell was able to affect both the composition (body grooming versus bill wiping) and frequency of grooming responses in both normal and conflict situations. He concluded that the pattern and intensity of peripheral stimulation are the direct causal factors underlying grooming in all situations, thus confirming the first part of Andrew's (1956a) hypothesis.

He further demonstrated that the frequency of grooming varies inversely with the frequency of other activities such as locomotion and that grooming is possible only in the pauses between other activities. Furthermore, grooming does not occur in all such pauses, but only in those above a certain minimum length (which is always longer than the duration of the actual motor patterns involved in grooming). Finally, the different types of grooming responses take different lengths of time; the most common being of short duration and thus least susceptible to interruption by other activities. Not only the occurrence but also the composition of grooming is influenced by the length of time available. This confirms another portion of the Andrew (1956a) hypothesis which suggested that the presence or absence of behaviors incompatible with grooming constitutes an indirect causal factor underlying grooming.

One further factor remains to be considered. Displacement activity is most frequent when the conflicting response tendencies are equally balanced, that is, when the animal is in a state of motivational equilibrium with respect to these tendencies. In this situation, grooming may be expected to occur in response to the usual peripheral stimuli. The existence of such an equilibrium state is not directly observable but was inferred by Rowell from variations in the bird's behavior. Rowell reasoned that if, in an approach-avoidance situation, the animal pauses in its locomotion and then reverses its direction a state of equilibrium might be presumed to have been reached, since the approach tendency has changed into an avoidance tendency (or vice versa). If, as Andrew (1956a) had hypothesized, the presence of an equilibrium state is a major factor permitting grooming, grooming should be most frequent in those pauses involving changes of direction. This prediction was confirmed in Rowell's study and, independently, in a study by Tugendhat (1960a) of approach-avoidance conflicts in sticklebacks. It therefore appears that the equilibrium state is a permissive factor, and that variations in grooming behavior in such a situation are due simply to variations in the intensity and type of peripheral stimulation.

We are now in a position to account for all the observed characteristics of displacement grooming and to extend our explanation to other types of displacement activity. Behaviors observed to occur as displacement activities are those whose threshold for elicitation is low at the time. The most common displacement activities (feeding, grooming) are maintenance activities with very low thresholds. Other behaviors, for example, sexual and maternal behaviors, will occur as displacement activities when their thresholds have been reduced by the presence of hormones or of external stimuli such as nests, eggs, or other birds. The occurrence of displacement activity in conflict situations is due to the fact that such situations provide for the existence of equilibrium states which are characterized by the temporary absence of competing responses and the presence of pauses whose duration is long enough for the displacement activity to occur. Since different responses require different minimal lengths of time to occur, those which require long times are most likely to be interrupted by other activities. Thus the appearance of incompleteness or of frantic behavior is undoubtedly due to the fact that the duration of the equilibrium is generally too short to permit the complete occurrence of the entire behavior pattern. Finally, in thwarting situations the stimuli which would elicit normal, higher threshold responses are absent and other behaviors prepotent to some extent at the time may occur in response to their normal stimuli.

Such a causal analysis of displacement activity is a far cry from its original conceptualization as a mechanism which provided cathartic relief in neurotic conflicts by discharging surplus motivational energy.

Implications for Motivational Theory

The original attractiveness of ethological energy models of motivation was due, in part, to the ease with which they appeared to account for certain diverse motivational phenomena. The experimental analysis of instinctive behavior has now progressed to the point where alternative explanations of these phenomena are possible. Short-term variations in responsiveness, for example, may frequently be due not to the exhaustion of reaction-specific energy but to stimulus-specific habituation processes, or various types of sensory feedback (Bol, 1959; Hinde, 1959; Lehrman, 1956a). Reactions to a deficit may frequently be accounted for in terms of interactions between species-specific sensorimotor sequences and species-typical environments (Lehrman, 1956b; Van der Kloot & Williams, 1953a, 1953b) though in certain cases the past experience of the animal is also a crucial variable. Finally, it is now possible to account for displacement activity without recourse to energy models of motivation.

Such models, whether Freud's, McDougall's, Lorenz's, or Tinbergen's, have been inextricably linked with drive constructs, so that in discarding the energy aspects of the models we raise the possibility of discarding the drive constructs as well. However, it may be advantageous at the outset to distinguish between specific- and general-drive constructs and deal with them separately.

The term specific drive often reflects a confusion between functional and causal approaches to the analysis of behavior. On the one hand, such concepts are used as functional labels to categorize and describe groups of behavior patterns which appear to share a common function. The diverse activities involved in nest building, since they eventuate in a completed nest, are lumped together under the rubric of a nest-building drive or under the broader rubric of a maternal drive. However, since the activities involved in nest building appear to fluctuate together in time it is often assumed that they must share a common causal mechanism. Hence the concept of a specific drive is often invoked causally as an explanation for the spontaneous occurrence, temporal organization, and goal directedness of the behavior. It would obviously be advantageous to discard such constructs and replace them with explanations of the type exemplified by the causal analysis of displacement activity. Fortunately, such analyses are rapidly becoming available for almost every aspect of species-specific behavior including sexual behavior in mammals (Beach, 1956), incubation behavior in birds (Baerends, 1959), maternal behavior in birds and mammals (Lehrman, 1961), nest building in birds (Hinde, unpublished[2]) and cocoon spinning in silkworms (Van der Kloot & Williams, 1953a, 1953b), hunger in mammals (Miller, 1957b; Teitelbaum, 1962) and in the blowfly (Dethier & Bodenstein, 1958), exploratory behavior and play (Berlyne, 1960; Welker, 1961). The existence of such causal

[2] Conference on Sex and Behavior held in 1961–62 in Berkeley, California.

analyses has rendered the construct of specific drive superfluous.

Perhaps the most ubiquitous of the constructs invoked by motivational theorists is that of a general drive which functions solely to energize behavior. Although such a concept does not form an explicit part of either Lorenz's or Tinbergen's theory, it was implicit in the original formulation of the surplus hypothesis of displacement activity. For psychological theorists the concept of a general drive has occupied a central place in learning theory since Hull, even though the behavioral evidence customarily cited in its support has been frequently considered of dubious validity or doubtful relevance (Bolles, 1958; Estes, 1958b). The recent emergence of the concept of arousal within motivational theory represents an extension of the general-drive concept to problems other than those involved in learning—most notably to those of emotional behavior.

The term arousal was originally used in conjunction with physiological studies of a so-called arousal or activating system located in the brain stem. With the publication of papers by Duffy (1957), Lindsley (1951), Hebb (1955), and Malmo (1957), the implications of these physiological findings were explored by psychologists and the concept of arousal gained widespread currency (Berlyne, 1960; Bindra, 1959). As currently employed the term is indistinguishable in its functional properties from the concept of an energizing general drive. Some theorists have even identified general drive with the activity of the so-called nonspecific activating system of the brain stem (Hebb, 1958; Lindsley, 1957).

Such terms as arousal level and nonspecific activating system share an important feature with other drive constructs in that they have all the earmarks of what may be termed a blanket variable. They are invoked to account for a variety of diverse effects whose only common characteristic may be the fact that they all fluctuate together to some extent. Moreover, a concept of motivational energy is implicit in the arousal construct so that it is marred by the same conceptual difficulties inherent in general drive constructs. These conceptual difficulties, and certain recent developments in psychology and physiology suggest the need for a re-examination of the arousal concept.

The validity of the physiological evidence upon which the concept rests is currently being called into question. A recent group of studies (Adametz, 1959; Chow & Randall, 1960; Doty, Beck, & Kooi, 1959; Kreindler, Unger, & Volanskii, 1959) indicates that the integrity of the midbrain reticular formation is not an indispensable precondition for the existence of either physiological or behavioral arousal or for the occurrence of emotional behavior or learning. Studies by Sprague, Chambers, and Stellar (1961) suggest that affective responses to sensory stimuli may be mediated by structures other than the nonspecific reticular system. Detailed analyses of brain-stem organization indicate that the so-called activation effects of reticular stimulation are not the result of a unitary arousal system but are mediated by the effects of such stimulation upon a variety of diverse physiological mechanisms (Dell, 1958; Fuster, 1961). On the basis of a comprehensive review of the anatomy and physiology of the brain-stem reticular formation, Rossi and Zanchetti (1957) concluded that this structure was un-

likely to act indiscriminately as a sheer energizer.

Bindra (1959), noting that the various indices of arousal do not correlate very satisfactorily, has suggested that it may be premature to assume that these indices are representative of some unitary arousal process. Despite this caveat, explanations of emotional behavior in arousal terms continued to multiply. Indeed, it was because conflict and thwarting situations are customarily viewed as emotional situations that the concept of arousal played a central role in Bindra's hypothesis of displacement activity. As we have seen, such a concept has proved superfluous for the explanation of displacement activity and recent studies by Schachter and his associates suggest that an arousal construct may be equally superfluous for the understanding of other types of emotional behaviors as well (Schachter & Singer, 1962).

Finally, it has been suggested that given the fact that the central nervous system is continuously active it may not be theoretically necessary to postulate an energizing factor (Hinde, 1960). Several theorists have found it possible to discard general-drive constructs entirely and present alternative approaches to the motivational problems raised by learned and species-specific behaviors. The essential feature of all these approaches is the consideration that the occurrence of a specific response in a given situation is the outcome of its successful competition with other responses which themselves have a certain probability of occurrence in that situation (Bindra, 1961; Estes, 1958; Hinde, 1959). The similarity of this formulation to those proposed by Andrew and Rowell is obvious.

One final implication of the causal

analysis of displacement activity is worth considering. It will be recalled that the ethological investigators concentrated their attention not only upon the specific response under investigation (e.g., displacement grooming responses) but also upon the general behavioral context within which these responses occur. Now typically, as Bindra (1961) has pointed out, psychologists restrict their attention to the defined responses under investigation (e.g., running, bar pressing, key pecking) and ignore the matrix of general activity components (e.g., sniffing, grooming, walking, sitting) within which the defined response takes place. Bindra has convincingly demonstrated that a detailed consideration of such background behavior may shed considerable light upon the conditions underlying the emergence of the specific responses themselves. Accordingly,

it is to be hoped that in the future such a microanalysis of behavior will become a more widely-accepted technique in the study of both species-specific behavior and learning.

Summary: Behaviors occurring out of their characteristic motivational context and in the midst of conflict and thwarting situations have been called "displacement activities." Such behaviors were originally explained by reference to energy models of motivation. It is now known that the nature and intensity of such activities are primarily a function of 3 sets of variables: type and intensity of peripheral stimulation, the existence of behaviors incompatible with the activity in question, and the existence and duration of states of motivational equilibrium with respect to such incompatible behaviors. The implications of these findings for motivational theory are discussed and it is suggested that drive and energy concepts no longer serve any useful function in the study of species-specific behavior.

Chapter 2

PRIMARY AND SECONDARY DRIVES

Twenty years ago, and perhaps even ten, this chapter would have been the most important in any book on motivation. Primary drives were the major building block of Hullian motivation theory—the unlearned sources of energy that accounted for all of the energy underlying motivated behavior. Thus, it was an extremely parsimonious system.

As the next few chapters will show, this parsimony has not proved completely sufficient. The fertility of the concept has, however, accounted for an unprecedented amount of research utilizing it as a framework, and without doubt it is this volume of work that has helped to point the way to improvements in motivational theory.

The concept of drive is a highly technical precisely defined term. A primary drive is a general energizer, whose reduction is reinforcing. It is primary because both of these properties occur without learning. From this definition, a drive can be claimed to be influencing behavior only if it meets tests from two experimental situations. For a variable to be a general energizer, it must be shown to energize (increase in strength) all reaction tendencies present at the moment. If it energizes some but not others, then it is not a drive but rather some selective motivational mechanism, such as an incentive variable. For a variable to be reinforcing, its reduction must increase the probability of responses contingent upon its reduction, and, conversely, its increase (usually called punishment) must reduce the probability of contingent responses. If these tests are all met, then the variable may be called a drive. If the tests are satisfied without prior learning, it is a primary drive; otherwise it is a secondary drive.

Surprisingly few variables have met these tests. Some evidence exists that primary drives include four appetitional variables—deprivation of food (hunger), water (thirst), sex (sex), and anticipated reinforcement (frustration)—and one aversive drive—pain. Only two secondary drives have been demonstrated—the secondary drive of learned fear based on the primary drive of pain, and the secondary drive of learned frustration based on the primary drive of frustration. Wagner's paper on frustration in Chapter 3 provides the most clear-cut description of experiments designed to evaluate a variable for drive status. This paper can serve as a model for research within a drive conceptualization.

These definitions of drive just reviewed are arbitrary ones, originally offered by Hull and slightly refined by Brown, Spence, and some others.

They are simple, easily specified, and easily manipulated. Of course, many other definitions of motivational concepts could be offered, and many are explicit or implicit throughout this book. None however, come close to the parsimony and usefulness of this definition, and for that reason the definition has proved to be the most fruitful in directing and influencing research on motivation. It also provides most of the focus of discussion and argument. Most, though not all, of the work presented in this and the next chapter was derived from this definition, and these studies or discussions show different aspects of the usefulness of the drive concept so defined. In subsequent chapters, however, other studies will be presented that raise serious theoretical or empirical difficulties with this definition. Alternative definitions will be offered by some writers. Others will pointedly ignore the problems of formal definition for the moment, presenting their work as empirical studies of the relationship between classes of motivational variables, whether defined as drives or not.

Neal Miller's paper reviews some of the research carried out in his laboratory at Yale University over the past decade on sources of drive variables, and how they effect behavior. His work represents one of the most comprehensive attempts to study motivational interactions in animal studies, and this selection is merely one aspect of this program of research.

Dethier's work has been a masterful series of studies on hunger mechanisms in insects. While advancing knowledge of comparative psychology of motivation, it is even more important in isolating the mechanisms that control eating and satiation. This kind of work is now being done with higher organisms, much of it stimulated by his leads, and nearly all substantiating the pattern of findings he uncovered.

Sheffield has presented a number of studies that raise serious problems with the drive-reduction part of this definition of drive. In his two papers printed here for the first time, he brings some of this evidence together, along with a reformulation of the drive concept. While his work has been cited for over ten years as evidence against the classical concept of drive reduction, as presented above, these papers present for the first time a concise exposition of his revised interpretation of drive.

Judson Brown has long been identified with the classical drive theory, and included in this first of his papers is a defense of the drive-reduction aspect of drive theory, especially as an attempt to answer attacks on the drive concept from those who feel that the experiences of pleasure contradict the concept of drive. While his defense is not entirely satisfactory, it helps make the issues very explicit, which, as mentioned before, is one of the most import attributes of a precise theory.

Epstein and Levitt, and Kessen *et al.* present individual experiments that utilize aspects of the drive notion, to examine its effects on selected behavior patterns. Kessen's paper is particularly instructive because of the importance of careful specification of the measures employed in measuring drive. In fact, these results have been interpreted as some negative evidence of the generalized nature of primary drives.

Four papers are included on the secondary drive of fear. The two by Brown are classical studies, reprinted here because they are models of research in this area, and for their still valid implications. Walters reports a continuation of a series of studies with puzzling results for drive theory, or any other theory for that matter, for he finds that the effects of learned fear apparently persist in the face of extinction procedures and new learning. This is consistent with other evidence that learned fear is a very pervasive and powerful motivational influence on behavior.

American Psychologist, 1961, vol. 16, pp. 739–754.

Analytical Studies of Drive and Reward[1]

Neal E. Miller

I want to present some recent research which my students and I have been pursuing. These studies are interrelated, but they reflect a variety of my own interests as well as those of different students who have contributed greatly to them. Therefore, they cover quite a range, beginning with some purely behavioral studies, and ending with a combination of behavioral and physiological techniques.

In order to put these studies into proper context, I shall from time to time briefly summarize certain earlier work from my laboratory. For the ben-

1 Address of the President to the sixty-ninth Annual Convention of the American Psychological Association, New York City, September 3, 1961.

Work on the studies cited in this paper was supported by Grants MY647 and MY2949 from the National Institute of Mental Health of the National Institutes of Health; United States Department of Health, Education, and Welfare; Bethesda, Maryland. The work of Angus A. Campbell and Donald Novin was supported by Grant G5818 from the National Science Foundation, Washington, D.C.

efit of those who have not had extensive experience with research, I shall mention a few of the difficulties and failures, as well as those successes which ordinarily are all that is published and hence give a false impression of the actual process of groping forward into the unknown. But, even so, I shall not begin to do justice to the arduous exploration, only some of which has led forward.

While I realize all to well the difficulties of trying to prove the null hypothesis, I believe there should be more mention of negative results in publications, not only to give a truer picture of scientific research, but also to prevent later investigators, one after another, from proceeding in the same way into the same quagmires.

At the purely empirical level, drives and rewards obviously are important in the performance of learned behavior, be it individual or social, normal or abnormal. Thus all behavior theorists from Thorndike (1898) on have used the empirical law of effect in some form or other. Many advances have been made, and many more can be made, by staying at this level and applying the empirical law of effect to behavior in the laboratory and in the home, in the classroom, factory, and clinic. As you may know, I have made some such applications (Dollard & Miller, 1950; Miller, 1957b, 1959; Miller & Dollard, 1941). My present purpose, however, is to try to analyze some of the fundamental mechanisms involved in drive and reward.

Effect of Drive on Reward and Learning

Everyone agrees that the level of drive can affect performance, but there has been a long, vigorous controversy over whether it also affects learning. As you know, Tolman (1932) initiated this controversy which has been carried on by other expectancy theorists (Hilgard, 1956). He contended that animals exposed to a learning situation without any motivation learn "what leads to what," but do not display this "latent learning" until they are motivated to perform. One of the difficulties in resolving this controversy has been that in the complete absence of any motivation it is hard to get animals to expose themselves to the mazes and other types of learning situations commonly used. A completely unmotivated rat would be expected to sit completely still. But for the learning theorist there is not much future in watching rats sitting still. How can we surmount this difficulty?

As a means of exposing unmotivated rats to water, I asked one of my students, Donald Jensen, to try to develop

Fig. 1. The oral fistula used to elicit and record conditioned tongue licks.

a fistula into the mouth. With considerable ingenuity, he developed the polyethylene fistula illustrated in Figure 1. This enters in the back of the rat's neck (where it is hardest for him to bite or scratch it out), passes under the skin, is anchored by a blob of dental cement, plunges down through the snout, and emerges into a little metal tip on the top of the palate. With further perspicacity, Jensen suggested that this fistula might be used to elicit and record conditioned tongue licks. The tongue completes an electrical circuit with the little metal tip. This technique was further developed with the help of another student, Richard C. DeBold, who performed with me the following experiment on the effects of thirst on conditioned tongue licks.

During the first, or learning, phase of the experiment, 64 male albino rats were given a total of 150 trials during which a flickering light was a signal for an injection of water into the mouth. Every fifth trial was an unpaired test trial. All rats were on a schedule of 22-hour water deprivation. Four experimental groups were run with different strengths of thirst achieved by the following treatments immediately before each day's training: (a) *strong thirst* with no drinking before training; (b) *moderate thirst*, allowed to drink before training 70% of amount usually consumed; (c) *satiated* by drinking ad lib. One hour before training; (d) *supersatiated* by preceding procedure plus injection via the mouth fistula of an additional 70% of daily water consumption, most of which the rat allowed to drool out of his mouth. We wanted to be absolutely sure that this last group was completely satiated. And it really was.

As a control for spontaneous level of licking and for pseudoconditioning, four similar control groups were run with exposure to the same number of lights and injections which never were paired with each other. Figure 2 shows the results for these control rats. There is a low level of spontaneous licking which does not change throughout the training and is not markedly or consistently related to the level of thirst.

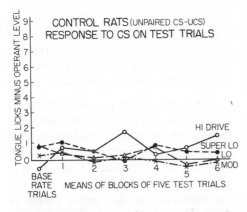

Fig. 2. **The four control groups for pseudo-conditioning show a low level of spontaneous licking which is not consistently related to number of training trials of level of thirst.**

Figure 3 shows that, during test trials, the performance of the satiated (LO) and supersatiated animals was approximately the same as that of the pseudoconditioning controls. The moderately thirsty animals showed definitely better conditioning, and the highly thirsty ones obviously were the best of all. There seems to be a clear relationship between drive and learning. How-

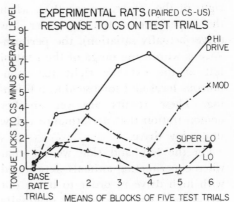

Fig. 3. **Performance during conditioning as a function of level of drive.**

ever, it is possible that the two non-thirsty groups actually were learning that the light led to the water, but were not performing because they were not motivated.

In order to test for such latent learning, half of the rats in each group were given five trials of exposure to the light alone (without water) when they were motivated by 22 hours of thirst. The other half were tested following normal satiation. The results are presented in Figure 4. Between the dotted lines just

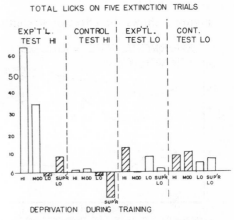

Fig. 4. **Performance during testing under high drive (22-hour water deprivation) or low drive (normal satiation), as a function of deprivation during training.**

right of the center, we see that, when the experimental test is under low drive (actually satiation), the performance is within the range of the control test at the extreme right for spontaneous level and for pseudoconditioning. These results are yet another demonstration that performance is low under low drive.

On the left-hand side we see that when experimental animals were tested with high drive in order to bring out any latent learning, those originally conditioned with high drive gave many conditioned licks; those originally conditioned with moderate drive gave approximately half as many conditioned licks; and those conditioned with low or superlow drives were within the range of spontaneous licks, as indicated by the control groups. Thus, when the effects of drive on learning are separated from those on performance by tests designed to bring out any latent learning, a clear-cut relationship between strength of drive and learning remains. This result is contrary to the prediction from Tolman's (1932) expectancy theory. It emphasizes the importance of drive.

Figure 5 shows the effect of strength

of drive on the unconditioned licks to the water during the training trials. It can be seen that the water elicited more licks in the thirstier rats. Contiguity theorists, following the Guthrie (1952) tradition, could use this relationship between the drive and the unconditioned response as a basis for explaining the superior learning of the more highly motivated group, without having to assume any relationship between the strength of thirst and the *rewarding* effects of water. Thus, while the results went against the expectancy theory, they did not differentiate between reinforcement based on contiguity alone and reinforcement based on contiguity plus reward. How can we differentiate between these two possibilities?

UNSUCCESSFUL ATTEMPTS TO
CONDITION RESPONSES ELICITED
BY ELECTRICAL STIMULATION
OF MOTOR CORTEX OF RAT

If one could elicit a response without motivation and reward, one might test between the contiguity and the reward theories of reinforcement. A considerable number of years ago, Roger Loucks (1935) apparently did this by implanting electrodes in the motor cortex of dogs. He paired a cue for over 600 trials with leg lifting elicited by stimulation of the motor cortex in three dogs without producing any conditioning. But by adding a food reward, he produced conditioning in two other dogs. This result seemed to show that contiguity alone was not sufficient for learning, while contiguity plus reward was.

I wanted to repeat this highly significant experiment and, in addition, to try a latent learning design to see whether, after pairing the cue with the

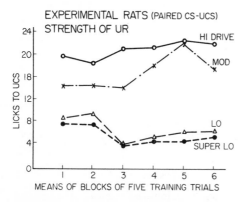

Fig. 5. Unconditioned licks during conditioning as a function of training trials and strength of drive.

motor response elicited by stimulating the cortex without reward, subsequent trials of pairing the motor response with reward (but without the cue), would cause the response to appear on final test trials with the cue but without motor stimulation or reward.

After considerable work, one of my students, Derek Hendry, found a place where leg movements could be elicited by stimulating the cortex of the rat, and also designed an apparatus for restraining the rat and recording the leg movements. But a large amount of additional effort yielded confusing and negative results.

Finally, we decided to see whether thirsty rats restrained in this way would learn the leg withdrawal as an instrumental response to get water without any central stimulation, much as they will learn to press a bar. They did not. Apparently rats react badly to restraint and are poor at learning discreet, leg retraction responses. We had achieved no results from almost a year of work on this project. Perhaps some radical, or even minor, change would make the procedure work, but it was time for Hendry to concentrate on a PhD thesis, so he prudently changed to a safer problem.

Meanwhile, I found that Giurgea (Doty & Giurgea, 1961) had been able to establish conditioning in an animal by pairing electrical stimulation of a sensory area with electrical stimulation of the motor cortex, provided the trials were very widely distributed. But did the motor stimulation which he used serve as a reward, either like the Olds and Milner (1954) stimulation in subcortical structures, or by relieving boredom? The latter hypothesis would explain the need for the wide distribution of trials since the novelty effect of

a stimulus is known to be subject to rapid habituation by massed trials and, as would be expected from this fact, Arlo Myers and I (1954) have found that widely distributed trials favor learning rewarded by weak exploration. Furthermore, Bower and I (1960) have found that strong reinforcement is required the more resistance a response must overcome. Thus, if massed trials generate more reactive inhibition, they should require more reward. Such considerations suggest that Giurgea might get conditioning, even with less widely distributed trials, provided he added a reward.

I have just speculated that stimulating the motor cortex might have a mild rewarding effect. One could test for such a reward by determining whether the cortical stimulation will help to maintain some other response, such as bar pressing originally learned for food. If the cortical stimulation is rewarding, it should help to prevent the extinction of such a response (Miller, 1961a).

On the other hand, it is possible that the elicitation of an arousal response, rather than reward, is the basic requirement for effective learning. It is also possible that contiguity alone is sufficient, or that where an additional resistance must be overcome, a central excitatory state must also be conditioned by contiguity to serve as a booster.

CAN RESPONSES IN THE SENSORY CORTEX BE STRENGTHENED BY REWARD?

At the moment I am shifting my efforts on this problem somewhat. I still am attempting to secure evidence on the effectiveness of contiguity alone compared with contiguity plus reward.

But at the same time, I am exploring the possibility of objectively studying certain phenomena which may be relevant to imagery, hallucinations, and mediating responses. Various investigators have electrophysiologically recorded so-called sensory conditioning. For example, if a tone is a cue for a distinctive rhythm of flashes of light, the evoked potential to the flashes originally recorded from the visual cortex can sometimes be recorded to the tone alone. But such conditioning characteristically is variable and does not persist for a large number of trials. We are trying to see whether it can be strengthened by adding a reward after the flashes. Will anticipatory evoked potentials from the visual cortex be learned if they are rewarded by giving food to a hungry animal? Can the flashes then be omitted and the distinctive rhythm of cortical potentials be made instrumental to securing reward? If so, will the activity producing these potentials have all of the functional properties of a cue producing response, such as a visual image (Miller, 1961a)? I had hoped to have answers for you, but as often happens, the solution to various technical problems has required more time than I anticipated. It is also possible that this will be one of the trails that, instead of leading to a break through the barrier mountains, leads into a box canyon.

WHAT DETERMINES
THE EFFECTIVE POINT
OF REINFORCEMENT
IN A TEMPORAL SEQUENCE?

To summarize our position so far, we have succeeded in securing a clear-cut demonstration of the effects of drive on learning, but have failed to solve a

second problem and to complete a related third one. Let us now turn to a fourth problem. At what point in a temporal sequence does reward occur?

Experiments by Thorndike (1933) purported to demonstrate a bi-directional gradient of reinforcement affecting acts occurring both before and after the reward. Probable sources of artifact in his data were discovered and his interpretation was seriously questioned (Jenkins & Sheffield, 1946). Looking for a simpler, more direct, test, one of my students, Mohammed Nagaty (1951) trained hungry rats some years ago to press a bar as soon as it was inserted. Next he habituated them to receive a pellet immediately before, as well as immediately after, pressing the bar. Then he found that rats with only the pellet *after* pressing omitted, extinguished at the same rate as those with the pellet omitted *both* before and after pressing the bar. These results, and various controls, showed that the pellet before pressing the bar was not an effective reward. But under these conditions some of the food probably still was being chewed and swallowed, the taste lingered in the mouth, and food certainly was entering the stomach and being digested *after* the bar was pressed. In short, part of the chain of events of food ingestion and digestion followed pressing the bar. Why did these later events in the chain have no rewarding effect?

In a recent attempt to answer this question, David Egger and I (1962) advanced the hypothesis that reward occurs primarily at the point at which new information is delivered. Normally, delivery of food to the cup, and certainly food in the mouth, invariably means that it can be chewed, tasted, swallowed, will reach the stomach, and be digested. Therefore, feedback from these subsequent links in the sequence conveys no new information; it is completely redundant. According to our hypothesis, in Nagaty's experiment all of the new information, and hence the reward, came when the food was delivered.

In order to test this hypothesis, we worked on the learning of secondary reinforcement. We chose the learning of secondary reinforcement instead of the learning of a movement, since it is easier to control the interval between a cue and reward than it is the timing of a movement made by an animal. Our specific hypothesis was that the secondary reinforcement value of a cue is a function of its information value.

Figure 6 summarizes the experimental situation. Look at the diagram next to the bottom labeled "redundant." The first single pellet always predicts the delivery, 2 seconds later, of the trio of pellets. This is analogous

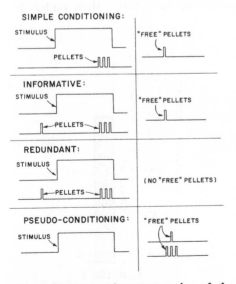

Fig. 6. Diagrammatic representation of the conditions in the first experiment on secondary reinforcement as a function of the information value of the CS.

to delivery of food predicting the taste, chewing, swallowing, and entry of food into the stomach. Thus, although the intervening stimulus is followed by additional pellets, it is redundant.

In the top diagram of simple conditioning, which represents the usual situation for learning secondary reinforcement, the stimulus is not redundant because there is no other way of predicting the trio of pellets.

But is there any other way of rendering the stimulus informative, while still having it always preceded by a pellet in order to control for any possible inhibitory aftereffect of the first bit of reward? Suppose we present unpredictably between trials a number of single free pellets, as is indicated in the diagram next to the top, labeled "informative." Then the stimulus is no longer redundant: it is a more reliable predictor of the trio of pellets than is the single pellet. From our hypothesis, we predict that with such a group the stimulus should become a stronger secondary reinforcer than it will in the redundant group given exactly the same treatment in all other respects, but without the additional presentation of some free pellets not followed by the trio of pellets.

Finally, the bottom diagram represents a control for pseudoconditioning in which presentations of the stimulus and the pellets never were paired.

In order to achieve the most sensitive test for secondary reinforcement, we first trained rats to press a bar for pellets, then extinguished them by disconnecting the pellet feeder mechanism, and finally gave them test trials during which every third press delivered the stimulus, but no pellets. Thus the measure of secondary reinforcement was relearning after extinction and is shown by the amount of bar pressing for the stimulus in excess of that shown by the pseudoconditioning, control group.

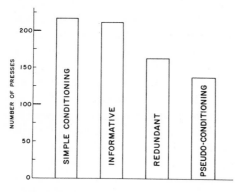

Fig. 7. **Food administered immediately before a CS does not interfere with the acquisition of secondary reinforcement, provided the stimulus is an informative predictor of additional food, but does produce a substantial reduction if it makes the CS redundant.**

Figure 7 presents the results. You can see that the informative group did as well as the group with the conventional simple conditioning procedure. The pellet of food a half-second before the stimulus had no obvious inhibitory aftereffect. Furthermore, as demanded by our hypothesis, the informative group performed significantly better than the redundant one.

Figure 8 summarizes the design of a similar experiment on the same problem. Since Stimulus 1 always precedes Stimulus 2, the latter is redundant and should acquire less secondary reinforcement value, even though it always precedes food. But there is a way to make S_2 informative. Present S_1 unpredictably a number of times without either S_2 of food. Then S_2 is a more reliable predictor of food than S_1 and is no longer redundant. From our hypothesis we predict that with a group given such training S_2 will be a stronger reinforcer

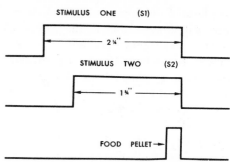

Fig. 8. **Design of stimulus sequence used in second experiment on secondary reinforcement as a function of the information value of the CS.**

than it will in a group given exactly the same number of identical pairings of S_1 plus S_2 with food, but without the additional presentations of S_1 alone.

Figure 9 presents the results of such an experiment (Egger & Miller, 1962). The ordinate is the number of bar presses, followed by S_2 as a secondary reinforcer for relearning after experimental extinction. You can see that there were more bar presses for S_2 under the informative than under the

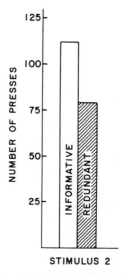

Fig. 9. **Results of a second experiment showing that a cue is a stronger secondary reinforcer when it is informative.**

redundant conditions. The results of this second experiment also are in line with the information hypothesis.[2]

But it is quite possible to interpret these results at a different level of analysis, using the drive-reduction hypothesis, which I have found it extremely fruitful to investigate, although I am not at all certain that it is true. According to the strong form of the drive-reduction hypothesis, the secondary reinforcer must produce a reduction in that part of the drive which can be modified by learning. Figure 10 presents a diagram of the theoretical analysis. On the left-hand side of this diagram you can see that, if most of the learnable drive already has been reduced by S_1, little drive-reduction remains to be conditioned to S_2. On the other hand, if S_1 often fails to predict food, much of the conditioned drive-reduction to it should be extinguished. Hence, as is illustrated on the right-hand side of the diagram, more of the drive-reduction should occur to, and be conditioned to, S_2.

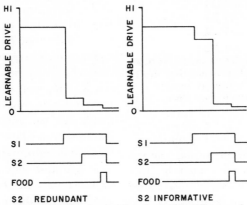

Fig. 10. Diagram showing how the difference in acquisition under the redundant and informative conditions might be explained by the drive-reduction hypothesis of reinforcement.

As you can see from the diagram, this type of an analysis demands that, if the secondary reinforcing value of our hitherto neglected stimulus, S_1, is tested, it should be greater under the conditions on the left-hand side when it is the reliable predictor (making S_2 redundant) than under those on the right-hand side when it is an unreliable predictor (making S_2 informative). Figure 11 shows that this is indeed the case.

2 Since the measure was the ability of the cue to substitute for food in inducing recovery from experimental extinction, only the difference between the informative and redundant condition is relevant; the performance under the redundant condition may have represented disinhibition or spontaneous recovery.

Although the preceding experiment is in line with the deduction made by applying the drive-reduction hypothesis, it would be much more satisfying if we could test the hypothesis in this and in other situations by some more direct, independent measure of the moment-to-moment level of the drive. The need for such a measure in this and in many other experiments is one of the things that has motivated me to explore physiological techniques. My original hope was that, if the neural centers controlling hunger and satiation could be located, it might be possible to use direct recordings from such centers as a meas-

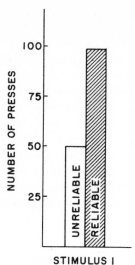

STIMULUS 1

Fig. 11. Confirmation of the prediction based on the theoretical analysis summarized in Figure 10. (Stimulus 1 is a stronger secondary reinforcer when it is a reliable than when it is an unreliable predictor.)

ure of drive. While I am less optimistic about this than when I started, the experimental program initiated by this hope has produced many interesting results.

EXPERIMENTS ON SENSORY FEEDBACK FROM THE MOUTH AND STOMACH

Before investigating the brain, however, I worked on some more peripheral mechanisms: the sensory feedback from the mouth and the stomach which I had speculated might be sources of reinforcement in puzzling over the results of Nagaty's experiment. Please fasten your seat belts while I summarize this old work quickly, in order to give the background for some new experiments.

If drive-reduction is the basis of reward, it is obvious that it must occur promptly after the food is received, or else it will be too late to reinforce the responses leading to food. Therefore,

the reduction in hunger must occur long before digestion and absorption have restored the cellular deficit. In order to study the effect on hunger of feedback from various links in the chain between the eating and absorption of food, Martin Kohn and I spent the better part of a year trying to develop a simple fistula through which food could be injected directly into the stomach of the rat. After trying many different techniques, we ended up with a great respect for the rat's incredible ability to extrude various foreign devices from his body even though these were held in by flanges which seemed to make such extrusion impossible. Fortunately, we eventually heard that Evelyn K. Anderson of the National Institutes of Health had developed a stomach fistula for the rat. Now that various workers in our laboratory have made a few minor improvements of their own, this technique, which originally gave us so much trouble, can be taught to a good undergraduate student in a couple of days. Our experience in this particular case is representative of what often occurs in the development of new techniques. They are extremely difficult before certain problems are solved and quite easy afterwards.

Experiments by Kohn (1951), Berkun, Marion Kessen, and myself (1952) showed that food injected directly into the stomach produced a prompt reduction in hunger, and taken normally by mouth produced an even greater reduction. Similarly, Woodrow, Sampliner and I (Miller, Sampliner, & Woodrow, 1957) found that water injected directly into the stomach produced a prompt reduction in thirst, but water taken normally by mouth produced an even greater reduction. With each of these drives the same results were secured by two different techniques for measuring drive: volume of food or water consumed, and rate of working for food or water by pressing a bar on a variable-interval schedule. Thus we were confident of the results which showed that the drive was regulated by immediate feedback from both the stomach and the mouth (Miller, 1957a). These prompt effects avoided the delay that would have been embarrassing to the drive-reduction hypothesis.

Meanwhile, Sheffield and Roby (1950) had shown that a nonnutritive but sweet substance, namely saccharine, could act as a reward for hungry animals even though all of it was excreted, so that it served no nutritional need. This finding has been used as an argument against the strong form of the drive-reduction hypothesis. But Edward Murray, Warren W. Roberts, and I showed that saccharine taken by mouth reduces the amount of food consumed immediately thereafter, which suggests that it temporarily reduces hunger as would be demanded by the drive-reduction hypothesis, and supplies additional evidence for an oral feedback controlling hunger (Miller, 1957a).

Recently, a student of mine, Derek Hendry, has observed that thirsty rats will lick at a cooling stream of air, and then has found that they will learn to press a bar to turn on the air briefly. Since the air increased evaporation, and hence the water deficit, he thought that this was evidence against the drive-reduction hypothesis. However, when at my suggestion he made the test for the effect of licking air on thirst, he found that a period of licking air not only reduced the immediately subsequent consumption of water, but also caused thirsty rats to reduce their rate of working for water by pressing a bar on a

variable-interval schedule. Thus it appears that the feedback from the mouth produced by licking a jet of air may temporarily somewhat reduce thirst (Hendry & Rasche, 1961).

But to return to our original story, if food injected directly into the stomach produces a prompt reduction in hunger, it should serve as a reward. And indeed Marion Kessen and I (Miller & Kessen, 1952) found that rats would learn to turn to the side of the T maze in which they received milk via fistula directly into the stomach rather than isotonic saline.

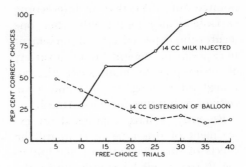

Fig. 12. One group of hungry rats learns to choose the side of a T maze where their stomachs are distended by milk injected directly via fistula; another group learns to avoid the side where their stomachs are distended by injection of liquid into a balloon. (From Miller, 1957a.)

Soon after that, we found that inflating a balloon in the rat's stomach would reduce the rate of bar pressing for food (Miller, 1955). We concluded that stomach distension probably reduced hunger. In that case, stomach distension should serve as a reward. But when we made the test, as Figure 12 shows, we found that the animals learned to avoid the side where their stomachs were distended by the balloon, in contrast to learning to go to the side where the stomach was distended by milk. This was nice in that the behavioral test showed up a qualitative difference, which otherwise might not have been suspected. But it complicated the theoretical picture (Miller, 1957a).

DESIGN TO TEST INTERVENING VARIABLE

Now for some time I had been advocating and also practicing the use of a variety of behavioral tests to cross-check each conclusion in order to avoid being mislead by side-effects which might be specific to a given type of test (Miller & Barry, 1960). Indeed, I insistently pointed out (1959) that an intervening variable is meaningful only when one secures the expected type of agreement in experiments designed to use a variety of techniques to manipulate the assumed intervening variable and a variety of techniques for measuring it.

Recently, I have completed an experiment of this type to compare the effects of three methods of manipulating thirst—water by mouth, by fistula, and in a stomach balloon—on three different measures of thirst: the volume drunk immediately afterwards, the amount of quinine in the water required to stop drinking, and the rate of working at pressing a bar rewarded by water on a variable-interval schedule.

Figure 13 presents the results of this experiment. Let us look at the two diagrams to the left and in the center showing results for measuring thirst by the volume of water drunk and by the amount of quinine required to stop drinking. In the open bars you can see that prefeeding increasing amounts of water—0, 5, 10 or 15 milliliters—produced progressive decrements in the scores on both tests. These decrements serve as a basis for calibrating the other effects.

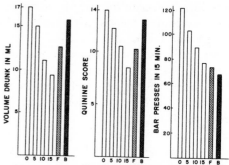

Fig. 13. Comparison of three different measures of the effect on thirst of three different types of pretreatment: Water drunk normally by mouth (0, 5, 10, or 15 milliliters); 15 milliliters of water injected via stomach fistula (F); 15 milliliters of water injected into stomach balloon (B). (The patterns of results measured by volume consumed or by quinine score are highly similar; the results measured by rate of bar pressing are different.)

Looking at the bar with single cross-hatching and labeled F, you can see that using the fistula to inject 15 milliliters of water directly into the stomach produced an effect roughly comparable to that of drinking 10 milliliters normally by mouth. Allowing for sampling errors, the effects are roughly comparable in both the left and middle diagrams. Now looking at the double cross-hatched bars labeled D, you can see that injecting into the balloon 15 milliliters of water to distend the stomach produced less effect than drinking 5 cubic centimeters normally by mouth. The effect is highly similar in both the left and middle diagrams. The general picture of agreement in these two diagrams is what might be expected if the different experimental operations—water via mouth, fistula, and in the balloon—all were manipulating a single intervening variable, namely, thirst, which was being measured by both of the tests: volume of water drunk, and amount of quinine required to stop drinking.

Now, shifting to the right-hand figure for results of the test which used rate of bar pressing as a measure, you can see that the effect of prefeeding various amounts of water was much like that in the preceding tests. The effect of injecting water by fistula was somewhat off. But the effect of inflating the balloon was grossly different. Instead of being almost negligible, *less* than drinking 5 cubic centimeters of water by mouth, it was *greater* than that of drinking 15 cubic centimeters of water by mouth.

From this result we draw two conclusions: First, in my previous work by relying on bar pressing as the sole test, I probably had been trapped into greatly overestimating the reduction in drive, if any, produced by inflation of a balloon in the stomach. Second, when the bar pressing test is also included, the overall results cannot be explained by the assumption of a single intervening variable, since the results of all three tests are not perfectly correlated, as they would have to be if they were all pure measures of the same unitary thing, namely, strength of thirst. Perhaps the bar pressing test is especially susceptible to distraction, pain, and nausea, possibly produced by inflating the balloon in the stomach. If so, this pain or nausea would be a second intervening variable.

In any event, the need for this particular type of experimental design is obvious. As I have pointed out before (Miller, 1957b), we have great confidence in the electron as an intervening variable, because electrons produced by a great variety of experimental operations: rubbing a cat's fur against amber, heating a metal in a vacuum, putting zinc and carbon in acid, or cutting a magnetic field with a wire, all have exactly the same charge when measured by a variety of techniques—repelling like charges on a droplet of oil, depositing silver in an electroplating bath, or creating magnetic lines of force when they move. It is this kind of agreement which gives us confidence.

In the behavioral sciences we need to make much more use of such cross-checking of hypotheses. With sufficient ingenuity, it is possible, not only in simple situations of the kind I have been describing, but also in dealing with many other problems. For example, in the area of personality development, certain clinical observations on children can be checked against controlled experiments on animals and also against anthropological observations on the effects of different conditions of child rearing in other cultures.

Brain Electrolytes and Thirst

To recapitulate briefly, I have described evidence that drive is important for learning. I have shown that the point in a temporal sequence, at which maximum reward effect is concentrated, can be described in terms of information theory and possibly explained in terms of the drive-reduction hypothesis of reinforcement. I have shown that the drives of both hunger and thirst are promptly reduced by feedback from both the mouth and the stomach. Now let me carry on the main story a bit further.

For some time, it has been believed that there are osmoreceptors in the brain which could be an additional mechanism involved in controlling thirst. A few years ago, Andersson (1953), in Stockholm, added convincing evidence by showing that minute injections in the region of the third ventricle of a satiated goat's brain, would elicit drinking if the solution injected (2% NaCl) had slightly more effective osmotic pressure than is normal for body fluids. My students and I confirmed this in the cat, and in addition showed that minute injections of pure water, which has less osmotic pressure than the body fluids, would have the opposite effect of reducing thirst. For both the increase and the reduction, we got the same results with two different measures: volume of water consumed and rate of performing a learned response to get water on a variable-interval schedule (Miller, 1961b). Thus we see that, in addition to being controlled by feedbacks from the mouth and stomach, thirst is controlled by receptors in the brain which respond to the state of the body fluid around them.

Still more recently a student of mine, Donald Novin (1962), has devised an ingenious technique for recording electrolyte concentration in the body fluids of normal rats free to move around in a small chamber. This is significant to

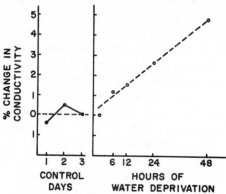

Fig. 14. Electrolyte concentration, as measured by conductivity, increases with hours of water deprivation. (From Novin, 1962).

our story because electrolyte concentration in the body is almost entirely due to the concentration of NaCl which in turn determines the effective osmotic pressure to which the "osmoreceptors" in the brain presumably respond.

Two platinum-black electrodes are chronically implanted in the rat's brain so that they can be connected to flexible leads. Since the electrolyte concentra-

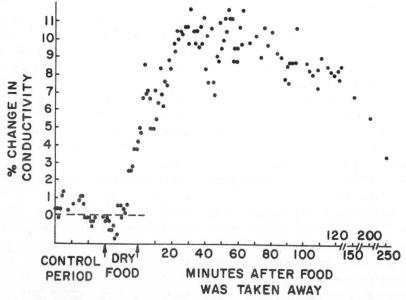

Fig. 15. Feeding dry food to a hungry rat increases electrolyte concentration, as measured by conductivity, which then decreases during the subsequent interval without access to water. (From Novin, 1962)

tion of various body fluids presumably is the same, the placement in the brain is for convenience, rather than having crucial significance. With suitable bridge circuits, the resistance between these two electrodes is used to measure electrolyte concentration. Let us see some of the results which he has secured in our laboratory.

Figure 14 shows the results of water deprivation. As the animal becomes dehydrated, we expect the concentration of electrolytes (primarily salt) in his blood to increase, so that the conductivity should increase. We can see that this is exactly what occurred.

If a hungry animal is fed dry food, it makes him thirsty. Figure 15 shows that this procedure also increases the electrolyte concentration as measured by conductivity. But looking at the right-hand side of the figure, we see a peculiar thing. Several hours after eating dry food, and without any opportunity to drink, the conductivity begins going

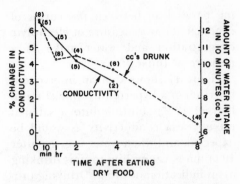

Fig. 16. After thirst is induced by feeding dry food to hungry rats, longer rest intervals without water produce a great reduction in thirst as measured either by conductivity or by volume of water drunk. (Separate tests are given at the end of each interval.) (From Novin, 1962)

down. According to this, the animal should be less thirsty even though it is longer since his last drink. Figure 16 shows the results of separate tests for thirst, administered at different times after dry food without water. You can see that the rats do indeed drink less after the longer times. There is a strik-

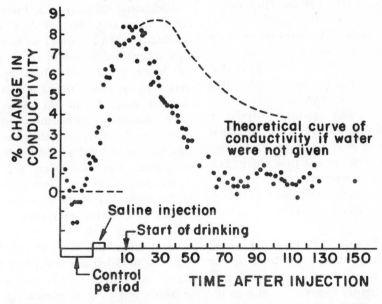

Fig. 17. An intravenous injection of hypertonic saline (1 milliliter of 12 percent) into a satiated rat increases thirst as measured by conductivity, so that when water is introduced, the rat starts drinking which restores conductivity to the baseline level for satiation. (From Novin, 1962)

ing parallelism between the curves of conductivity as a measure of electrolyte concentration and water-intake as a measure of thirst.

Figure 17 shows that an intervenous injection of a hypertonic saline (1 milliliter of 12%) solution into a satiated rat increases conductivity as would be expected, and when water is given after 10 minutes, causes him to start drinking as an indication of thirst. Drinking produces a drop in conductivity, which begins to occur rapidly enough so that it could be one of the factors involved in the eventual stopping of drinking.

The dotted theoretical curve of conductivity if water were not given is based on results of another experiment; the drop in it is produced by the excretion of salt by the kidneys. You should note for future reference that the empirical curve of conductivity comes back approximately to the same baseline level it had before the hypertonic saline was injected.

Looking at one type of experimental manipulation at a time, we have seen good qualitative agreement between the two measures: electrical conductivity and the volume of water drunk. If electrolyte concentration is the only intervening variable involved, we must expect a perfect positive correlation between these measures when the effects of different manipulations are compared. In order to test this, Novin performed an experiment, comparing the effects of normal deprivation and of intervenous injection of saline upon both measures.

Figure 18 shows the results. Looking to the left of the dotted line, we see that the water deprivation used produced a slightly *lower* level of conductivity than did the saline injection. But on the right-hand side of the dotted line, we see that the water deprivation

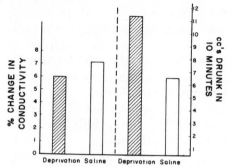

Fig. 18. An injection of hypertonic saline which produces a greater increase in conductivity than does a period of water deprivation, elicits less drinking than does the deprivation. Therefore, the change in effective osmotic pressure, measured by conductivity, cannot be the sole factor involved in thirst. (From Novin, 1962)

induced considerably *more* drinking than did the saline injection. This is not a perfect positive correlation; in fact, it is a negative one. Thus the results show that electrolyte concentration, which produces effective osmotic pressure, cannot be the sole factor involved.

Additional evidence of a discrepancy comes from the effect of drinking on conductivity. In Figure 17 we have seen that, after an injection of saline, drinking brings conductivity back approximately to the base-line of the preceding satiated state. Figure 19 shows that, after normal deprivation, drinking brings conductivity far below the satiation baseline level depicted by the solid horizontal line out from the little square on the ordinate. This is the kind of result that would be expected if the animal is drinking to restore a water deficit, rather than to bring electrolyte concentration back to a given level. Perhaps the so-called osmoreceptors are reacting not solely to effective osmotic pressure, but to total amount of dehydration. Perhaps there are some other receptors that react to the volume of body fluid. At least we know that elec-

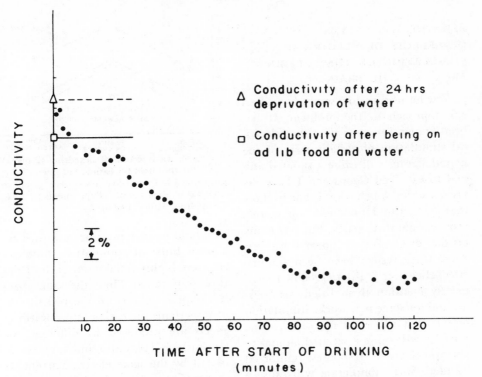

Fig. 19. Ad lib. drinking following water deprivation reduces conductivity far below the normal predeprivation base level. (Represented by the little solid line out from the hollow square. Contrast this with the effect of drinking induced by the hypertonic injection, as presented in Figure 17. (From Novin, 1962)

trolyte concentration cannot be the whole story.

Again we see the advantage of testing an intervening variable with a design comparing the effects of at least two different experimental manipulations upon at least two different measures.

UNSUCCESSFUL TESTS ON PARABIOTIC RATS

There has been a good deal of speculation that, in addition to the osmoreceptors, the brain contains receptors which respond to a hunger hormone, or the state of nutrients in the blood. In an attempt to locate some such humoral factor, Angus A. Campbell worked with me on parabiotic rats, or in other words, surgically created Siamese twins.

But an extensive amount of labor failed to secure any evidence for a hunger hormone, or indeed for the transfer of appreciable amounts of nutrients across the parabiotic barrier. Since then I have learned that Teitelbaum also has secured somewhat similar negative results with such rats.[3] Perhaps we need some other type of preparation to study this problem.

[3] Our observation was that having a well-fed partner did not appreciably increase the starvation time of the unfed one or increase the food consumption of the fed one. In a personal communication, P. Teitelbaum has told us that, in a similar experiment, the food intake of the fed member of the pair did not increase during the first several days, although it perhaps may have increased approximately 24 hours before the unfed member died of starvation.

BEHAVIORAL ANALYSIS
OF EFFECTS OF ELECTRICAL
STIMULATION OF THE "FEEDING
AREA" OF THE BRAIN

Now let us turn to a somewhat different approach to the problem. It has been known for some time that electrical stimulation of certain areas of the hypothalamus will cause a satiated animal to eat. Ted Coons and I have devised a series of behavioral tests to show that such stimulation does not merely arouse a gnawing reflex, but has many of the properties of normal hunger. Since these results have been summarized elsewhere (Miller, 1960b), I shall merely mention them briefly as background for some new work. Stimulation of this area will elicit not only eating, but also will cause a satiated animal to perform learned responses reinforced by food. Such stimulation will cause a satiated rat to bite food, but not to lap up pure water. However, the rat will lap up sugar water or milk. Therefore the response is not defined primarily by the motor movements, but rather by a sensory feedback, namely, the taste of food. As would be expected from the drive-reduction hypothesis of reinforcement, turning *off* such stimulation will act as a reward to produce the learning of a T maze. But paradoxically, turning *on* such stimulation also will serve as a reward. This result is contrary to the prediction from the drive-reduction hypothesis of reinforcement.

In Figure 20 the center points of the solid lines show that the appetite reducing drug, dexedrine, *increases* the threshold (in microamperes) for eliciting eating. But as the center points of the dotted lines show, the same injection of the same drug *reduces* the

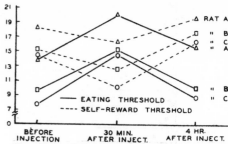

Fig. 20. An injection of dexedrine (2 mg/k) raises the threshold for eating, but lowers it for self-reward. (Twenty-five tests were given to each rat at each point.) (Experiments by E. E. Coons from Miller, 1960b)

threshold for bar pressing rewarded by a brief burst of stimulation. Both results are highly reliable for each of the three rats tested. Since the same drug has opposite effects on the two thresholds, perhaps the eating and rewarding effects are produced by different systems which are indiscriminately stimulated by the same electric current. If so, predictions from the drive-reduction hypothesis must be held in abeyance.

A CHEMICAL CODE IN THE BRAIN?

Another one of my students, Peter Grossman (1961), recently has devised a double cannula technique for stimulating the same "feeding area" of the rat's brain with minute amounts of crystalline substances. He has found that minute amounts of the adrenergic substances, adrenalin or noradrenalin, will cause satiated rats to eat and also to perform a learned response rewarded by food. By contrast, stimulation of the same area via the same cannula, by minute amounts of the cholinergic substances, acetylcholine or carbachol, will cause satiated rats to drink and also to perform learned responses rewarded by water.

Various control tests with other substances rule out pH, vasoconstriction or vasodilation, and osmotic pressure as the primary sources of these effects. More convincing still is the fact that an intraperitoneal injection of ethoxybutamoxane, which is an adrenergic blocking agent, practically eliminates the eating elicited by inserting the adrenergic noradrenalin into the brain, while leaving the drinking elicited by the cholinergic carbachol, practically unaffected. Similarly, an intraperitoneal injection of the cholinergic blocking agent, atropine sulfate, leaves the eating to centrally administered noradrenalin relatively unaffected, while practically eliminating the drinking to carbachol. These effects of the blocking agents are an elegant control to show that the drugs elicit eating and drinking via their adrenergic and cholinergic effects, respectively.

In rats with a cannula into this area of the hypothalamus, we apparently have a good method of investigating new compounds suspected to have central, adrenergic, or cholinergic effects, or to function as central blocking agents.

But are the effects we have just described involved in normal hunger and thirst? That they probably are is indicated by the fact that administering the appropriate blocking agent, either peripherally by intraperitoneal injection or centrally via the cannula into the brain, produced the appropriate differential effects on rats made hungry or thirsty by deprivation of food or water. The effects of the blocking agents on normal hunger and thirst are somewhat less complete than those on eating and drinking elicited centrally, but they are unmistakable. The adrenergic blocking agent produces a reliably greater decrement in food con-

sumption than does the cholinergic one; the cholinergic blocking agent produces a reliably greater decrement in water consumption than does the adrenergic one. Thus adrenergic and cholinergic effects seem to be involved in normal hunger and thirst, respectively. In short, this evidence, along with that of other more purely physiological studies, suggests a chemical code in the brain.

BASIS OF ANTAGONISM BETWEEN HUNGER AND THIRST

The effects we have just described give us an opportunity to answer a theoretically interesting question. It is known that water deprived animals stop eating dry food. Is this because the drive of thirst is centrally incompatible with the drive of hunger, or because bodily dehydration interferes with peripheral aspects of the hunger mechanism—for example, a dry mouth making it difficult to eat dry food?

Similarly, food deprived animals drink less water. Is this because the mechanism of the hunger drive is antagonistic to thirst or merely because animals not eating dry food do not require as much water?

In an attempt to answer these questions, Grossman secured the results shown in Figure 21. In the upper graph, you can see that direct stimulation of the hypothalamus by norepinephrine increased the food intake of normally hungry rats exposed only to food, while stimulation by carbachol markedly decreased it. Similarly, the lower graph shows that carbachol increased the drinking of normally thirsty rats exposed only to water, while norepinephrine decreased it. These results strongly suggest that there is

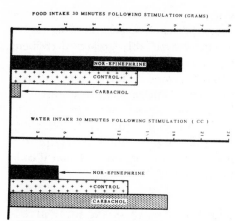

FOOD INTAKE 30 MINUTES FOLLOWING STIMULATION (GRAMS)

NOR-EPINEPHRINE

CONTROL

CARBACHOL

WATER INTAKE 30 MINUTES FOLLOWING STIMULATION (CC)

NOR-EPINEPHRINE

CONTROL

CARBACHOL

Fig. 21. When introduced into the "feeding area" of the lateral hypothalamus, minute amounts of adrenergic norepinephrine potentiate food intake induced by 24-hour deprivation, while cholinergic stimulation by carbachol interferes with food consumption. The same substances via the same cannula have opposite effects in similar tests for water consumption. (From Grossman, 1961)

some central way, analogous to reciprocal innervation, in which the drive mechanisms of hunger and thirst tend to inhibit each other.

These discoveries are being followed up in our laboratory. We have investigated the effects of injecting minute quantities of blood serum from hungry and satiated animals directly into the brain. Our preliminary results are negative. We are investigating the effects of other hormones and drugs, both in the feeding area and in the ventromedial nucleus, which is believed to be a satiation area. We are studying the effects of a bacterial toxin which seems to interfere with drinking (Dubos, 1961), and also, we find, with eating. We

are testing the effects of adrenergic and cholinergic blocking agents on direct electrical stimulation of the brain. We are confronted with many more interesting problems than there possibly is time to investigate.

A New Conception of the Brain

The work that I have just described on drive and reward as well as on the work on other topics by our Past President, Donald O. Hebb (1958), and by other laboratories in a number of nations, is opening up a new conception of the brain.[4] We no longer view the brain as merely an enormously complicated telephone switchboard which is passive unless excited from without. The brain is an active organ which exerts considerable control over its own sensory input. The brain is a device for sorting, processing, and analyzing information. The brain contains sense organs which respond to states of the internal environment, such as osmotic pressure, temperature, and many others. The brain is a gland which secretes chemical messengers, and it also responds to such messengers, as well as to various types of feedback, both central and peripheral. A combination of behavioral and physiological techniques is increasing our understanding of these processes and their significance for psychology.

[4] For an illuminating overview see Magoun (1958); for a comprehensive series of authoritative summaries, Field, Magoun, and Hall (1960).

Science, March 13, 1964, vol. 143, pp. 1138–1145

Microscopic Brains[*]

V. G. Dethier

The study of animal behavior is unique among the sciences because it begins historically and methodologically with human behavior, prescinds from human experience, and projects this experience into other animals. It is thus more disposed to subjectivity and introspection than the other sciences and constantly labors under the burden of containing these biases within the bounds of their historical context. The study of man himself is further complicated by the fact that the investigator is trying essentially to understand himself, and others through himself, and in so doing is employing a brain to understand a brain.

Students of behavior tend to seek in other animals that which they believe exists in themselves. They look for motivation, drive, emotion, perception, consciousness, ideation, mood, sensation, and learning. Common sense assures us that it would be absurd to deny the existence of these phenomena. Those to whom an appeal to common sense borders on scientific heresy need only peruse the *Handbook of Physiology* and dwell upon the chapter headings: "Drive and motivation," "Emotional behavior," "Attention, consciousness, sleep, and wakefulness," "Perception," "Thinking, imagery, and memory." These are real phenomena.

Faced with defining them, however, we bog down in a morass of ignorance, confusion, anthropomorphism, and verbal gymnastics to escape anthropomorphism.

Given this background, how can one ever study these states outside the context of human behavior? Certainly the most obvious and tangible approach is a search for physiological correlates. When a dog which is teased by a stranger bares its fangs, raises its hackles, snarls, and lunges, we say that it is enraged. Whether it is or not we shall probably never know, any more than we can ever know when a fellow human is enraged. On the other hand, we can ask meaningful and testable physiological questions about the dog's behavior in this situation, which so closely mimics our own emotion in comparable situations. We can investigate the conditions under which hair is erected, adrenalin is secreted, teeth are bared. It may even be possible to gain some insight into possible affective components of this behavior through employment of the self-stimulation techniques discovered by Olds and Milner, 1954; Olds, 1962.

Viewed in this light, it is clear that higher animals, mammals especially, exhibit a rich repertoire of behavior comprehended under the terms motivational, emotional, and so on which seems to be absent to varying degrees in the so-called lower animals. The farther removed an animal is from ourselves, the less sympathetic we are in ascribing to it those components of behavior that we know in ourselves. There is some fuzzy point of transition in the phylogenetic scale where our empathizing acquires an unsavory aura. Yet there is little justification for this schism. If we subscribe to the idea of a lineal evolution of behavior, there is no reason for failing to search for adumbrations of higher behavior in invertebrates. If, on the other hand, we believe in a behavioral dichotomy, in the idea that the invertebrates differ qualitatively from the vertebrates, it behooves us to put the belief to test.

In the latter part of the 19th century and the first quarter of the present one, students of behavior, especially of insect behavior, identified themselves so thoroughly with their subjects that their observations led to uncritical anecdotal interpretations (see Hingston, 1928). The reaction that followed is epitomized in the words of Schneirla (1953a): "Anthropomorphism is a doubtful practice for scientists interested in understanding the real nature of behavior." Yet without a disciplined anthropomorphism inquiry into behavior is hobbled. Anthropomorphism has an heuristic value at this stage of inquiry and should be exploited with more courage.

Consider for example the insects, whose patterns of behavior are so complex and humanly mimetic that they have been held up for emulation since Solomon's time. It is considered unforgivable for scientists to speak of the rage, aggression, awareness, sensation, drive, and wakefulness of insects. Only the poet is permitted to speak the phrase "mad as a hornet." Insects are said to be stimulus-bound and instinctively fixed—little machines in a deep sleep—which implies, of course, that higher animals are not. This juxtaposition raises some profoundly interesting questions: Do insects indeed lack higher categories of behavior or is it that being anatomically different from us they do not show, for example, emotion because their eyes are pupilless and immobile, because they do not cry, sweat, or sulk? Or is it that experimentalists do not ask these questions of insects, and hence by default have assigned them a behaviorally inferior role? Or is it that, truly lacking this behavior, insects show a deficit because their nervous system is handicapped by having fewer cells in its minute mass? Or is there perhaps a qualitative (recognizing, of course, that a sufficient number of quantitative differences constitute a qualitative one) difference between the mammalian and the insect nervous systems? And if the answers to the last two questions be in the affirmative, how does the conclusion affect our concepts of the evolution of animal behavior and of behavior in general?

The proper approach to this problem is one for pondering. Neurological analyses of behavior have proceeded for a long time on the assumption that unit analysis will yield the answers. There is a growing feeling in some quarters, however, that the key to understanding lies in other parameters of neuronal systems, a view espoused particularly by Bullock (1958). Physiologists studying behavior believe in any case that the ultimate solutions lie in a clearer understanding of sensory and synaptic events and nerve impulse transmission (for example, Roeder, 1962; Wiersma, 1962). A number of psychologists, on the other hand, believe that the complexity of events controlling behavior is too great to be analyzed in these terms and that large-scale psychological concepts must be used in conjunction with the smaller-scale neurological ones (Hebb, 1958). Guttman (1963) in a provocative essay on "Laws of behavior and facts of perception" proposes a methodological dualism for studying perception (sensation, sensory integration, and perception) on the one hand and what the animal "does" on the other. Gregory (1961) maintains that behavior should be analyzed as the output of a machine. The sentiments of the psychologists emphasize the reality of the questions I posed earlier, while the attitude of the cyberneticists, who would treat animals as machines, suggests that the questions might best be answered by experiments with simple organisms.

Motivation

Let us approach these problems by selecting what appears on the surface to be one of the more simple concepts and one most amenable to analysis—namely, the concept of motivation. And let us search for evidence of motivated behavior in the fly, as much for insight into the methods of analysis and for testing the applicability of the concept of motivation to *all* animals as for arriving at a definitive answer to the question of its existence in insects.

But first, what is motivation? This may be a brash question indeed. Most people, however, seem to have an intuitive idea what motivation is, although they either hesitate to commit themselves verbally or find the idea too elusive to state. Let us attempt to formulate a statement. Motivation is a specific state of endogenous activity in the brain which, under the modifying influence of internal conditions and sensory input, leads to behavior resulting in sensory feedback or change in internal milieu, which then causes a change (reduction, inhibition, or another) in the initial endogenous activity. The essence of motivation is endogenous activity, in the brain, correlated with a particular kind of behavior. The level of motivation can be inferred by the amount of work (frequency, speed, quantity, general activity, and so on) an animal will perform in order to carry out the specific behavior or by the intensity of adverse stimulation (for example, shock) that an animal will tolerate to the same end. This measure (drive) is not an infallible assessment of motivation because many other patterns of behavior exhibit orderly changes in activity associated with deprivation. The most unequivocal measure may be operant conditioning, as Teitlebaum has suggested (Teitlebaum, in press), because the operant is essentially a voluntary act, not dependent upon specific afferent input, that an animal can use to obtain reinforcement. Since the animal exerts control over the occurrence of its response, the behavior is distinct from reflexes and from complex fixed motor patterns. Demonstration of an endogenous center by electrical recording therefrom or by eliciting patterned behavior by local brain stimulation is not alone convincing evidence for motivation. Nor is the occurrence of vacuum activity—that is, spontaneous response during deprivation in the absence of specific stimulation. On the other hand, if the behavior in question cannot be manipulated operantly, this of itself is no indication of lack of motivation because the animal may be a "nonlearner." One might argue that if learning is a criterion for motivation and an animal cannot learn, then it cannot be motivated. Here, however, learning is proposed as a criterion for detecting motivation and not as a *sine qua non* for its existence. Conceivably an animal could be capable of exerting voluntary control over its behavior without exhibiting a demonstrable capacity for learning. One need not look far beyond our own species for examples.

Objections to this definition of motivation may be raised on the grounds that it is too restrictive and that it places a well-recognized category of behavior into a hypothetical and experimentally inaccessible area of the nervous system. On the other hand, the usual operational descriptions of motivated behavior may be so broad and undiscriminating as to construe all behavior as motivated. If, for example, motivated behavior is described simply as goal-directed behavior with a drive component (change in activity), then the phototactic behavior of a moth could conceivably be construed as motivated, the light being the goal, compulsive flight representing the drive component, and the moth coming to rest in the vicinity of the light representing drive reduction. Similarly, the chemotactic responses of male moths to the sex attractants of the female would also come under the category of motivated behavior because the female would be the goal, flight would be the drive component, and the cessation of flight and failure to fly again after contact with the female would represent drive reduction. Even more broad is the designation of all random, unoriented, restless behavior, the appetitive behavior of Lorenz, as the outward manifestation of a mounting internal drive. It would seem that definitions so broad as to encompass within their bounds at one and the same time tactic behavior and such acknowledged motivated behavior as feeding by the rat invite an informational loss and raise the danger of obscuring meaningful differences of a fundamental nature. It is hoped that the point of being able to distinguish in a given behavioral situation between the kind of mechanism that fits the restricted definition given initially and alternate kinds of mechanisms will become clear in the following examples.

Hunger in the Fly

Let us commence by selecting and analyzing in detail one of the more intensively studied kinds of behavior—namely, feeding behavior, or in the context of our questions, hunger and satiation. In ourselves, hunger is a state defined by absence of food and feeding. A number of sensations—fullness or hunger pangs, as the case may be, euphoria, distress, and others—are associated with hunger; that is, hunger has an affective component. It leads to highly motivated behavior. It has a drive component; hungry men and animals will learn to work hard for food and will tolerate high levels of aversive stimuli. Does this picture accurately represent the state of affairs in insects or are there fundamental differences? Is the insect merely a push-button machine whose behavior is satisfactorily explained in stimulus-response terms or is there more to the picture? Is it useful to investigate hunger and satiation instead of restricting inquiry to the regulation of feeding?

The normal pattern of feeding in the

blowfly is as follows (Dethier, 1955; Dethier, Evans, & Rhoades, 1956). The fly moves about actively and randomly, flying or walking. If odorous food is available, the fly orients to it by means of information received through olfactory receptors on the antennae and palpi (Dethier, 1952). Upon encountering the food the fly steps in it, thus stimulating taste receptors on the tarsi. These receptors trigger extension of the retractable proboscis, bringing marginal labellar taste hairs into contact with the solution. As these hairs are stimulated the labellar lobes are spread, bringing another set of taste receptors, the interpseudotracheal papillae, in touch with the solution. Sucking commences, food is swallowed, and at the conclusion of a meal some regurgitation occurs.

Feeding is thus under the control of four sets of sense organs: antennal and palpal olfactory organs, tarsal taste receptors, marginal labellar taste hairs, and interpseudotracheal taste papillae. Each locus contains receptors mediating acceptance and receptors mediating rejection. Feeding is monitored at each level and can be terminated if rejection receptors are stimulated or if acceptance receptors become adapted.

For any given state of the fly there are two stimulus variables influencing feeding activity: kind of sugar and concentration. These affect threshold of acceptance, speed of sucking, and duration of sucking. It is important to note that the order of effectiveness of sugars bears no relation to metabolic value. (Hassett, & Dethier, 1951). Thresholds, therefore, reflect stimulating effectiveness. All acceptable sugars can have the same effect behaviorally (for example, they may cause meals of equal volume to be taken) if concentrations are matched, as seen in preference tests. For any given sugar, the speed and duration of sucking depend solely on concentration unless an impeding factor such as viscosity begins to operate. The rate of sensory adaptation also varies as a function of concentration. It is through this mechanism that the duration of sucking is controlled.

The short-term pattern of feeding is determined by these factors and by postingestion factors. Feeding is largely driven by sensory input. As food is sucked into the esophagus by the pharyngeal pump, peristalsis originating in the esophagus drives the food first directly into the mid-gut, then into the crop, a blind diverticulum which serves as a storage reservoir. After intake is terminated (by sensory adaptation), antiperistalsis in the crop duct periodically returns slugs of food to the esophagus, whence peristalsis now drives it into the mid-gut, the crop valve having closed, the mid-gut valve being open. From the mid-gut food is absorbed into the blood, whence it is mobilized in the glycogen of the muscles and the fat body. There are thus four energy storage depots: crop, blood, glycogen, and fat body.

Thus a "meal" for the fly may be described as follows. Volumetric intake is under the control of the sensory input. When sensory adaptation occurs, feeding stops but may resume intermittently over the next few minutes as disadaptation and adaptation fluctuate. Soon, however, the meal terminates. Now the fly cannot be induced to feed further. At this juncture postingestion factors inhibit feeding, and the duration and time course of their operation depend upon the concentration and volume of sugar ingested. During this refractory period a number of physiological changes have been measured: rate of crop emptying, change in gut contents and motility, change in blood-sugar level, and changes in threshold (Evans & Dethier, 1957). The rate at which the crop empties by transferring solution to the mid-gut is at first rapid, then decreases slowly. At the same time the level of sugar in the blood increases shortly after feeding, then falls rapidly as the crop becomes empty. Coincident with these events the acceptance threshold, that is, the concentration of sugar required to reinitiate feeding, falls. In a series of operations involving ligaturing full and empty crops and mid-gut, loading the mid-gut by enema, injecting sugar into the blood, and making parabiotic twins of fed and hungry flies, Bodenstein and I (Dethier & Bodenstein, 1958) showed that the acceptance threshold remained unchanged. Transection of the recurrent nerve, however, that section of the stomatogastric nervous system supplying the alimentary canal, caused flies to become hyperphagic. In other words, the mechanism for shutting off ingestion no longer functioned normally. Bodenstein and I postulated that the recurrent nerve carries back to the brain inhibitory impulses which originate in receptors in the esophagus stimulated by the periodic regurgitation from the crop as it transfers fluid to the mid-gut. We suggested that the inhibitory feedback nullifies input from the oral taste organs, this being reflected as a rise in acceptance threshold. Reexamining the question, Evans and Barton Browne (1960) concluded that the mechanism did not involve a rise in sugar threshold but did involve a change in responsiveness to water (in which all sugar was

presented). In any case, events monitored in the esophageal region normally inhibit further intake.

Locomotor Activity

There is still another behavioral event correlated with deprivation, general bodily activity. When a fly is allowed to spend its entire life in a minute actograph under normal lighting conditions but without food, it exhibits a pronounced circadial activity rhythm. This rhythm persists in total darkness and can be reversed. In constant light, however, it is more or less completely damped. Under these conditions an emerging fly is quiescent, except for occasional short bursts of activity during the first 72 hours of life. At 72 hours activity begins in earnest, increases to a maximum at 84 to 96 hours, then begins to wane, foreshadowing death. If the fly is fed during its period of activity, movement drops to zero. The time required to attain once again the initial rate depends on the concentration and volume of ingested sugar.

Thus there are two overt behavioral manifestations of deprivation, increased activity and lowered acceptance threshold. It is possible to explain all of the feeding behavior of the fly in terms of these two variables. The lifetime feeding behavior of a fly and the behavior of a fly in a two-choice situation will illustrate this point. At the time of emergence from the pupal state the fly has completed all growth and cell division (gonads excepted) and can live out its full life span (about 60 days) on a diet of pure carbohydrate. Immediately upon emergence it takes very little 0.1-molar sucrose (a concentration insuring maximum longevity) but rapidly increases its consumption to a maximum by the 2nd or 3rd day. From then on intake is fairly constant except for minor fluctuations due to differences in activity. There may be a gradual decline with age; there is a precipitous decline before death.

With a more concentrated sugar—for example 1.0 molar sucrose—the overall pattern is similar but the volume intake is markedly increased during the first four days, and thereafter is considerably less than it is for 0.1-molar sugar. When the fly is presented alternately with "high" and "low" sugar at 48-hour periods, the volume of "low" sugar taken is always less than the volume of "high." Thus it might be said that the fly regulates its caloric intake. Since 0.1-molar sugar provided maximum longevity and since the volume of 1.0-molar, even though reduced, provided an excess of sugar, it would seem that the regulation is not absolute. The change in intake can be explained fully in terms of changes in activity and the dependence of rate of sucking, rate of adaptation and disadaptation, and rate of crop emptying upon the concentration of sugar encountered (Dethier & Rhoades, 1954). In a two-choice situation the fly always imbibes a greater volume of the more stimulating of the two solutions, whether it be a higher concentration of the same sugar or an intrinsically more stimulating one. In this situation a fly always takes a highly stimulating non-nutritive sugar in preference to a poorly stimulating nutritive one.

Thus the feeding behavior of the fly in choice situations and in deprivation and satiation can be adequately explained in stimulus-response terms. Is this the whole story? We now return to our primary questions. Clearly there are differences between a fed and an unfed fly, but is the unfed fly "hungry" and do we gain by asking if it is hungry? Is feeding behavior motivated behavior?

Measures of Motivation in the Fly

At the simplest level of inquiry one searches for a drive component. Is there a positive correlation between the general bodily activity of the fly and its state of deprivation? Clearly the answer is yes. As Green has shown (in press; Browne & Evans, 1960), however, the fly does not move faster; it merely moves more often. Will a hungry fly suck faster or eat longer than a satiated fly? Clearly, for a given concentration, the answer is yes. But this, at least hypothetically, is explainable in terms of interaction between a standard sensory input and a variable inhibitory feedback via the recurrent nerve. Will the fly work harder to obtain food? Here the answer is in doubt. A number of laboratories, our own included, have attempted over the last decade to induce a fly to press a bar for food or to run a maze. So far these attempts have met with consistent failure. Bar-pressing devices that flies can operate have been built, but the animals have never cooperated—possibly because the situation is too foreign to their natural history. Attempts have also been made to detect an increase in flying effort as measured by frequency of wing-beat when a deprived fly is exposed to the odor of food (Schoettle, 1963). In this case the fly was *Drosophila* and the food, bananas. A deprived fly did not fly any more vigorously than a satiated fly. In this connection it is of interest that hungry flies are more "persistent" in their efforts to come to food (as are hungry mosquitoes) and can be discouraged only with great effort, but this behavior is explainable on the basis of increased general activity with deprivation.

No attempts have yet been made to measure the amount of electric shock a fly will tolerate in order to obtain food, and this measure might be informative. Measurements have been made of the amount of adversely stimulating adulterants a fly will tolerate in its food as it gets hungrier, but the data cannot be interpreted as usefully as we would like. At first glance it appears that a hungry fly does indeed tolerate more salt than a fed fly, but this finding is deceptive. Feeding represents a favorable balance between acceptable and unacceptable sensory input. For example, if a small amount of salt is added to sugar, imbibition continues unabated; if more salt is added, sucking stops. Now if the sugar concentration is increased, intake resumes even though the high concentration of salt remains. In other words, the sensory input from sugar receptors must exceed the input from salt receptors if feeding is to result. It has been pointed out, however, that the sugar threshold drops with deprivation. That is to say, fewer sugar impulses are required to trigger the event, so when a deprived fly tolerates more salt in a standard sugar solution it means simply that the lower threshold to sugar is, in effect, an increase in sugar concentration; so the net result is a sugar-salt balance in the central nervous system still in favor of the sugar. It would be highly instructive to reapply the test of salt tolerance by adjusting the sugar concentration with each stage of deprivation to a threshold criterion. A few experiments of this sort were conducted by Has-

linger (1935) with a related fly, *Calliphora erythrocephala*. The rejection threshold for hydrochloric acid during starvation was measured by presenting the acid in a fructose solution, the concentration of which was varied so as to be just 3 times the threshold for fructose on each day of the test. Under these conditions no change in the rejection threshold for acid was observed. Similar results were obtained with unacceptable sugar alcohols, salts, and quinine. In other words, the insect did not tolerate more adversity. On the other hand, the efficacy of skin repellents against mosquitoes is an example of an adverse stimulus whose effectiveness clearly varies with the state of deprivation of the insect.

Endogenous Activity

Increased general activity correlated with deprivation can be analyzed through additional steps. The analysis introduces the concept of endogenous activity in the central nervous system. As Roeder (1955; 1962) has pointed out, reflex physiology with its assumption of neurological silence in the absence of overt stimulation has failed to provide a basis for explaining behavior even in insects. Endogenous activity in receptor and central neurons is widespread among invertebrates, having been first detected by Adrian in caterpillars (1930). Its characteristics and neuronal bases have been discussed most recently by Kennedy (1962), Van der Kloot (1962), and Bullock (1962). In general, insects have spontaneously active motor centers in the subesophageal ganglion through which stimuli act to excite thoracic locomotor centers. In the supraesophageal ganglion there are centers which inhibit the activity centers (Roeder, 1953). Recently Huber (1960) has shown by local brain lesions and point stimulation in the cricket that there are two centers in the brain concerned with locomotion, one in the corpora pedunculata which inhibits the subesophageal ganglion and one in the corpus centrale which excites the subesophageal ganglion. The subesophageal ganglion regulates the degree of excitation of the thoracic ganglion. Thus the head determines the onset and duration of locomotion and, in conjunction with head sensory input, the direction. The thoracic ganglion together with proprioceptive input from the legs actually promotes locomotion.

Ethologists have long contended that appetitive behavior (drive) derives from an endogenous activity reasonably supposed to be a manifestation of endogenous nerve activity. As Roeder (1955) has pointed out, it is not easy to devise experiments that will demonstrate a connection between appetitive behavior and endogenous neural activity. He and his co-workers (Roeder, Tozian, & Weiant, 1960) demonstrated that copulatory movements by the praying mantis are endogenous in origin and that both copulatory movements and endogenous activity of motor neurons supplying the abdominal appendages are under the inhibitory control of the subesophageal ganglion. Spontaneous activity in abdominal ganglia increases markedly when the ganglia are completely isolated from the rest of the nervous system (Roeder, Tozian, & Weiant, 1960; Weiant, 1958).

No such neat correlation has been demonstrated with the fly; it is more than likely, however, that a correlation exists. Unpublished experiments from our laboratory show that the fly is like other insects in that removal of the subesophageal ganglion results in akinesis. This finding suggests the presence of an excitatory locomotor center. The animal can still walk briefly in a coordinated fashion if strongly stimulated; hence the thoracic center by itself can pattern walking. Removal of the supraesophageal ganglion promotes continuous locomotion. It has been shown, furthermore, that the following factors do not affect locomotor activity: increase in weight after a meal, metabolic state (that is, nutritional state), blood sugar concentration, blood potassium level (Evans & Browne, 1960), age, stretch receptors in the abdomen or the crop or posterior portions of its duct, limitations on oxygen reaching the thorax and legs from the abdominal air sacs, or constant stimulation of oral receptors during regurgitation (Green, in press). Green (in press) has suggested that spontaneous locomotor activity in the fly is affected by a hormonal factor derived from the neurosecretory cells of the brain or the corpus cardiacum, or both.

Role of Hormones

Evidence to the effect that there are indeed hormonal changes associated with changes in general activity and with feeding has been obtained with other species of insects. Harker (1956) has reported, for example, that endocrine secretions from the subesophageal ganglion, and probably the corpora allata also, may be involved in circadian activity rhythms. In locusts starvation increases spontaneous locomotor activity (Edney, 1937), speed of movement, and time spent in marching (Ellis, 1951). When a locust has fed, the titer of potassium ions in the blood increases. It decreases with deprivation. For any given motor nerve output a starved locust (low potassium) responds with greater muscular activity than a satiated (high potassium) locust (Hoyle, 1954; 1955; Ellis & Hoyle, 1954). A satiated hopper will still march, but the sensory input required to initiate locomotion must be greater. Hormonal changes are also involved. Ecdysone, the hormone of the prothoracic gland, is involved in processes which lead to differential effects on activity of the central nervous system and motor nervous system. It increases electrical activity in the cord and decreases it in metathoracic motor nerves (Haskell & Moorhouse, 1963). Haskell and Moorhouse have postulated that the utilization of information by the centers depends on the influence of hormonal balance on integrative and other centers. That there are causal relations among feeding, hormone balance, and spontaneous activity in the central nervous system is almost certain. As early as 1934 Wigglesworth (1934) showed that after the bug *Rhodnius* has had a blood meal, the swelling of the abdomen sends messages via the ventral nerve cord to the brain whereupon the medial neurosecretory cells secrete a hormone which is eventually released by the corpora cardiaca to trigger a moult. Later Van der Kloot (1960) found that impulses would be recorded from the nervus cardiacium I when the abdomen was stretched, but only then. Feeding by a cockroach causes neurosecretory cells in the protocerebrum to become active (Clark & Langley, 1962) and the corpora cardiaca to release a pharmacologically

active substance into the blood (Davey, 1962a). The release of hormones at feeding is triggered by receptors in the labrum (Davey, 1962b). The secreted material causes an increase (13 to 21 percent) in heart rate over its initial value (Davey, 1962b). A hyperglycemic factor has been found in the corpus cardiacum (Steele, 1961). The corpora cardiaca also release active materials when animals are exposed to stress (for example, electrical stimulation, surgery, handling) (Hodgson & Geldiay, 1959). Extracts of corpus allatum depress spontaneous activity in the isolated nerve cord (Ozbas & Hodgson, 1958), while extracts from the corpora cardiaca inhibit impulses from the inhibitory center in the subesophageal ganglion and impulses impinging on efferent nerve cells in cercal and metathoracic ganglia (Milburn & Roeder, 1962; Milburn, Weiant, & Roeder, 1960).

All of these data, though fragmentary and derived from a number of species, support the general picture of a behavioral activity arising from spontaneous activity in the central nervous system and modified at feeding through the mediation of substances released into the blood by the endocrine system in such a manner that the modulating influence of sensory input on endogenous activity is altered.

This picture, however, does not differentiate fixed pattern behavior from the motivational behavior of our definition. It merely says that there are fixed patterns of behavior whose expression depends on endogenous neural activity modified by the internal environment and thus indirectly or directly by sensory input from the outside.

Fixed Patterns in the Brain

Extensive neurophysiological analyses have begun to reveal something of the neural mechanisms concerned in the execution of these patterns. The classical techniques of gross ablation (reviewed by Ten Cate, 1931) have been replaced by the more precise techniques of local lesions and local stimulation (Huber, 1955; 1959; 1960; 1962a, b, & c; Oberholzer & Huber, 1957; Vowles, 1954; 1958; 1961; Voskresenskaja, 1957; Voskresenskaja & Svidersky, 1961; Drescher, 1960; Maynard, 1956; 1962). According to Huber (1962b) these analyses reveal, in the cricket, two categories of behavior: (i) movement patterns in which the interplay of effectors can be modulated by different input from the periphery (for example, walking, copulation, egg-laying); (ii) movement patterns which are almost irrevocably set by the central nervous system (for example, grooming, singing, flying). Local stimulation of the brain elicits from specific points ordered and coordinated patterns. At any point, however, there are changes in latency, threshold, and activation (from activation to inhibition). In some cases (for example, acoustic behavior) where action depends on momentary endogenous states there are changes in threshold related to these. In other cases (for example, copulation and oviposition) only the first local stimulation is effective because a certain constellation of stimuli from the periphery is required. The behavior pattern evoked may be very complex and its various phases may come into action sequentially, depending on the order of their respective thresholds. For example, local stimulation in the cricket may produce

the following actions, in this order: increase in respiration, antennal and head movements, walking, jumping.

These analyses have shown, furthermore, that such a seemingly simple action as walking is in reality part of complex behavioral situations. As Huber (1960) has shown, one category of behavioral situation of which walking is an element is flight, hole inspection, and attack. Walking is also an element of food searching, burrow construction, courting, and postmating behavior. Brain stimulation in some animals caused locomotion coupled with orienting movements of the antennae and palpi, and feeding when food was encountered. A change in threshold with satiation was noted. Huber believes that the searching movements, together with the taking of food, support the hypothesis that activation of an eating drive has occurred.

A demonstration of "little motors" which can be stimulated electrically hardly confirms the idea of motivation. I am inclined to agree with Teitlebaum that there must be an element of arbitrariness in motivation to distinguish it from complex fixed motor patterns and that this can best be sought by seeking a behavior that builds up in the absence of stimulation, with some state of deprivation, has a drive component, is goal-directed and satiates, can then be correlated with endogenous activity in the central nervous system, and can be operantly conditioned. The endogenous element separates it from reflex systems; the element of operant manipulation separates it from fixed motor patterns.

The failure to be able to manipulate a fly operantly is indeed a stumbling block to applying the crucial test to its feeding behavior. In the absence of this test the behavior can be explained adequately in terms of stimulus-response combined with fixed patterns. The fly can still be a little machine—true, not a push-button one, but nonetheless a rigidly programmed one and to this extent different from the mammal.

At this point, until some success attends efforts to demonstrate operant conditioning, the analysis should probably be transferred to an insect whose learning ability is indisputable. The honey bee is an admirable example of a learner. Unfortunately there is not the wealth of physiological information that exists for the fly and the cockroach. One fact is important, however: the honey bee can be trained to come to a feeding place at a specific time for food (Beling, 1929). This finding suggests that bees are motivated in that they have "voluntary" control over a fixed pattern. The bee cannot be made to go for food at an hour (for example, 9 P.M.) when she does not normally fly, but she can be made to suppress her flying activity during the normal hours of flying except at the appointed hour and then to show appetitive behavior in advance of specific stimulation. She can be trained to go to different places (as many as five) at different times and will continue to do so without reinforcement for as long as 6 days. This behavior meets our specifications for motivated behavior.

If a motivated behavior can be shown in a learner such as the honey bee, it is not unreasonable to suspect that it is also characteristic of species with similar brains even though these species may not be capable of operant conditioning. All these things considered, therefore, it does not seem improbable that insects are capable of motivated

behavior even in the restricted context of our definition. This being the case, motivated behavior is not confined to the higher vertebrates and, at least insofar as this aspect of higher behavior is concerned, one need not propose a dichotomy of function. Furthermore, since the insect brain is obviously smaller and less complex, perhaps we must revise our estimates of the minimum requirements for certain kinds of behavior, because it follows that at least the potential for some kinds of learning and for motivation does not have a prerequisite of large mass, cell numbers, and complexity.

The Insect Brain

The foregoing conclusion drives us to look at the small insect brain from a new perspective and with less stultifying preconceptions. The brain of a blowfly weighs about 0.84 milligram (wet weight). Its maximum linear dimension is 1583 microns. It probably contains not more than 100,000 cells. The smallest brains of equal complexity in any insect with equally rich behavior are the brain of the culicoid midge or no-see-um and the brain of the African ant *Oligomyrmex*. The former is 200 microns in its greatest dimensions; the latter, 150 microns. In each case the brain consists of a central feltwork of nerve processes, the neuropile, interspersed with fiber tracts, the whole overlain cortically with the cell bodies. This neural mass is encased in a sheath of non-neural connective tissue cells or glial elements. The most striking organizational feature of the insect brain is the sharp separation of cell body regions and synaptic fields. In contrast to the vertebrate brain, where cell bodies may lie in intimate association with dendrite fields, most of the cell bodies of the insect brain lie far removed at the periphery.

At the next level of structural organization the brain consists of three divisions; protocerebrum, deutocerebrum, and tritocerebrum. In the protocerebrum there are three systems of association neurons: the paired corpora pedunculata (mushroom bodies), the corpus centrale, and the horse-shoe-shaped pons. The fibers of these systems do not leave the brain. Instead they form synaptic connections with afferent and efferent fibers from all parts. The protocerebrum also receives the afferent tracts from the eyes. Antennal tracts enter the deutocerebrum. The tritocerebrum connects with the visceral system.

The greatest mass of the brain (33 to 80 percent) is made up of the paired optic lobes (Hamström, 1928). Next in order of size (2 to 40 percent) are the mushroom bodies, between which lies the small central body. There are also small paired antennal centers (1.3 to 18 percent).

The greatest sensory input to the head in terms of the number of receptor units comes from the eyes and antennae. The optic lobes are concerned with accepting input from the visual cells and, through chiasmata, ganglion cells, and elaborate synaptic systems, integrating this information. The antennal centers are much less complicated, as befits a system that does not have to deal with the same number of variables as affect the visual system. Most of the sensory input from taste is collected by the subesophageal ganglion. Most auditory, tactile, and proprioceptive input is collected by the segmental ganglia elsewhere in the body.

The corpora pedunculata and corpus centrale are clearly the great integrative centers of the brain. The former, as the elegant work of Huber and Vowles has demonstrated, contain inhibitory systems for general activity, take part in controlling walking direction, serve as the integration sites for complex instinctive behavior, and are essential for learning.

A number of people who have studied the insect nervous system, most recently Vowles (1961), have put forward the hypothesis that the insect nervous system differs from the vertebrate at all functional levels. Because the cell bodies are small and lie at the periphery rather than surrounded by dendrites, and because the receptive areas of dendrites are smaller, it is argued that there are inherent limitations on integration. It might be concluded, according to this view, that the insects have evolved different types of nervous mechanisms. The alleged deficiencies of the neuron cannot be compensated for by increasing the number of cells. Indeed, in any case, size limits severely the availability of cell number. Not only is the number in the brain limited, the number available to the sense organs and motor systems is also limited. Vowles has suggested that as a result the perceptual world may be less rich and that the motor patterns are combinations of a few simple stereotyped movements limited by the absence of motor centers in the brain.

Systems analyses have tended in large measure to emphasize the simplicity and machine-like quality of the insect nervous system. Mittelstaedt's (1962) meticulous analysis of prey-capture by mantids can best be expressed in his own words. "The control pattern of the entire system, at the present state of analysis, thus appears to be a chain which includes a loop within which is a second loop. If set into operation by the mechanism which provides prey recognition, the optic loop first turns the head toward the prey and the proprioceptive loop adjusts the neck muscles' activity to the load until the position 'ordered' by the optic loop is reached, so that, at final steady-state, that 'order' is accurately proportional to the deviation of the head from the body axis, and thus also to the deviation of the prey from the body axis. The 'order' is then used to determine the deviation of the strike from the body axis, which—to produce a hit— should itself be accurately proportional to the deviation of the prey from the body axis. The proportionality factor, the 'calibration' of the system, has been, on the average, correctly set during phylogeny (through survival of the best calibrated!) and apparently cannot be altered during an animal's individual life."

Other analyses of systems which serve the dynamic equilibrium of insects, as, for example, the optomotor reaction (Hassenstein, 1951; 1958; 1959; Hassenstein & Reichardt, 1959) and the haltere flight control system of flies (Faust, 1952; Pringle, 1948; Schneider, 1953) have also contributed greatly to our knowledge of the mechanics of control systems. All systems analyses, however, have tended to show how reflex-oriented the animal is on the one hand (for example, prey-predator relationships and optomotor reactions) and how rigidly patterned it is on the other (for example, copulation by the mantis, and singing and locomotion by the cricket). But a systems analysis commences with the premise that the object of investigation is a machine; hence

the analysis is biased to demonstrate how the insect acts like a machine. In the words of Bullock (1962): "We form the concept of a nervous system especially dominated in lower forms where learning is not so conspicuous, by ready-made combinations of springs, levers, and catches, cocked and easily triggered or self-firing to cause a complex movement, perhaps steered or shaped by sensory input."

Higher Categories of Behavior

It is perfectly true that much of the behavior of an insect is reflex and instinctive. Yet the extent to which this picture represents an accurate profile of its comprehensive behavior is weakened by the very failure to search for the higher components of behavior. The one analysis which we have attempted to make in detail—namely, the analysis of motivated behavior— has shown, even when biased against success by particularly rigorous criteria, that such behavior very probably exists. Were we to investigate "mood" we might find that insects do not differ qualitatively from vertebrates. If by "mood" we mean a situation in which responses to stimuli are different at different times as a result of retention in the central nervous system of some result of previous stimulation, or metabolic change related to feeding or egg development, then there are numerous examples of behavior which at least superficially meet the criteria and are amenable to neurological analysis. If we inquire into perception instead of arguing seriously, as some do, that insects are stimulated and do not perceive, then we can test the hypothesis that their perceptual world is impoverished compared with our own. Hassenstein's analysis of perception of movement by the weevil which shows that the animal does not react to movement of "objects" or "contours" in a shaped optical environment is a step in this direction.

The problem of pain is another Pandora's box into which one may peek cautiously. It is well known that insects respond stoically to heroic surgery. On the other hand, an entire industry has been built upon the knowledge that insects avoid repellents. Students of learning utilized the knowledge that cockroaches avoid shock. It is also known that insects submitted to trauma of various kinds (for example, insecticides, shock, hyperactivity, immobilization, excessive handling) secrete into the blood various pharmacologically active materials (Hodgson & Geldiay, 1959; Beament, 1958; Davey, 1963). The fact that free nerve endings similar to the pain endings of vertebrates have not been discovered is not altogether relevant.

Pursuing the survey to its logical conclusion, we come finally to the problem of consciousness. Seeking for some physiological handhold on this problem, students of vertebrate behavior have struggled with interpreting the electroencephalogram. Electrical activity in the insect brain is, not surprisingly, generally different from that in the vertebrate brain. Whereas the latter is dominated by rhythmic slow waves and rarely shows mixed action potentials, the former exhibits spikes conspicuously and slow waves less predominately (Bullock, 1945). Slow rhythmic potentials do occur, however, in those portions of the brain having structured neuropile (for example, the optic ganglia) (Maynard, 1962). No attempt has been made to correlate changes in electrical activity of the brain with behavior such as sleep, anesthesia, and so on. The nearest approach is Schoonhoven's study (1963) which reveals that the brains of certain moths are not electrically silent during diapause, that period of growth cessation during which the insect is behaviorally inactive.

All of these fragmentary bits of information are provocative in suggesting that there is more to the behavior of insects than systems analyses and unit neurological analyses reveal. We might do well to accept in principle the dualistic methodology espoused by Guttman (1963), namely, to use, in addition to behavioristic and physiological analyses, concepts about psychological events which come to us through common sense, intuition, introspection, sensation, and perception. The idea of an extreme dichotomy that sets insects so far apart from vertebrates as to be qualitatively different is founded as much on a fear of anthropomorphism, however well disciplined, as on a paucity of data.

Perhaps these insects are little machines in a deep sleep, but looking at their rigidly armored bodies, their staring eyes, and their mute performances, one cannot help at times wondering if there is anyone inside.

A Drive-Induction Theory of Reinforcement[1]

Fred D. Sheffield

My title, as you have probably guessed, is worded to contrast the position I intend to discuss with the drive-reduction position of Hull (1943), Miller and Dollard (1941), Kendler (1951), and other members of what has come to be known as the "S–R reinforcement" group. I mentioned this title to one of the graduate students at Yale and he objected to the use of drive "induction." He argued that "induction" is the opposite of "deduction," not the opposite of "reduction." His logician's sense of "induction" is, however, listed as only the fifth meaning of the word in Webster's Collegiate Dictionary. In its more general meaning, "induction" is the noun form of "induce," which means to lead on, to bring about, or to cause. The first meaning of induction is *initiation* and the position I am going to advocate implies that animals learn responses that *initiate or arouse motivation*. This is an opposing position to that of the drive-reductionist group, which alleges that animals learn responses that bring about a decrease in motivation. In my version of the law of effect, rewards are factors that increase excitement, although I shall attempt to deduce my law of effect from contiguity.

I should preface all further remarks by saying that I anticipate and hope for objections and criticisms. I am a former student of the late Clark L. Hull, and one of the things Professor Hull used to drum into his students was that the advance of science is commonly impeded by people who are afraid to propose a novel position for fear of seeming stupid. I should also say that another one of Hull's precepts was that science proceeds toward the truth by a series of successive approximations; I think I have a new approximation to offer and I won't be offended if you help prove it is only approximate.

In preparing this paper I had a choice between whether to discuss the difficulties facing the drive-reduction theory and then present my proposed solution, or whether to discuss the proposed solution alone. I decided that the most important thing was to make the proposed solution understood, so I will concentrate on it.

Let me begin by way of an overall statement about my so-called "drive-*in*duction theory." In this theory the *incentive* aspect of rewards accounts for their effectiveness. The incentive aspect should be contrasted with the *relaxing* aspect that is so important to the drive-reduction position. If one dangles a carrot in front of a rabbit, it does not relax the rabbit; on the contrary it arouses him to action. This action will be simply reaching out his head to start nibbling if there is no obstacle, but if

[1] Paper read at Psychology Colloquium, Brown University, November, 1954; mimeographed copy prepared the same year for Professor N. E. Miller's graduate learning course at Yale University.

the carrot is on the wrong side of a wire screen, the action may involve considerable struggling. Once the rabbit starts eating he may begin to relax if he is very hungry, but the carrot reward was tension-*inducing* when first shown—it raised the general level of excitement for as long as it took him to get a bite. This tension-arousing, activity-motivating feature of all rewards I consider crucial to the instrumental learning process. My attempt will be to evolve a theory in which the motivation aroused by the reward gets channeled into the instrumental act, and relaxing aftereffects will be treated as basically irrelevant to the learning process per se.

Now for the details of the theory. A key concept is that of the *"consummatory response."* As ordinarily used in psychology, "consummatory response" refers to the response that consummates the drive or motive—that is, the response that removes the drive. Usually a single response does not do this and we use "consummatory response" to label the kind of behavior that will consummate the drive if the behavior is continued long enough—as eating when hungry. Consummatory behavior is circularly maintained—the response-produced stimuli elicit the response until the drive state is changed. There are often ambiguities in the concept that have to be settled for each particular case. In the sex drive, for example, we might want to call copulating the consummatory response when technically orgasm is the consummatory response. In the present formulation the important thing about consummatory behavior is that *it brings striving to an end;* it removes the internal or external stimuli for excitement and brings about the stimulation that the animal "does nothing to avoid, often doing such as to

maintain" in Thorndike's (1911) definition of a reward.

A second key concept is that of *frustration*. This is a somewhat ambiguous word in psychology and perhaps needs a special definition in the present context. I will use it to mean a circumstance in which the animal is in a drive state and in which the consummatory response is stimulated but is prevented from occurring for one reason or another. One can frustrate a hungry newborn baby by rubbing its lips with a nipple, always keeping the nipple out of the baby's mouth. The sucking response is reflexly stimulated but can be prevented from occurring by dodging the baby's reflexes. When the infant is more experienced, one can frustrate it when it is hungry simply by holding it in the nursing position. The cues have become conditioned to the sucking response and the baby is just as frustrated by conditioned arousal of the consummatory response as it is by stimulating its reflexes with an innately adequate stimulus.

This factor of *frustration through conditioned arousal* of the consummatory response involves an obvious deduction from classical conditioning, but the implied proposition has been so little used that it has an air of novelty to it. The proposition is that conditioned arousal of a consummatory response is inherently frustrating. Innate stimuli for a consummatory response are usually not frustrating for long because they come from "the real thing," that is, they come from a stimulus object that permits consummation. But after conditioning the neutral cues that accompany the consummatory response, when presented by themselves, stimulate the performance of the response under circumstances in which it cannot be executed completely. A carrot visually dangled in front of a rabbit is frustrating if and only if he has had past experience with eating carrots. All aspects of a maze are frustrating to the rat after a few trials except those cues that are part of the stimulus pattern invariably present during eating—and these are frustrating if food is omitted.

A third key concept is that of general *excitement* or excited emotion. We can relate this to muscular tonicity and to vigor of response. We can perhaps also relate it to activity of the autonomic nervous system. I am thinking of nothing more complicated than the autonomic-skeletal state of the organism present when we describe the individual as excited.

I am going to make some assumptions about this general state of excitement that are not part of the proven facts of psychology, although they may seem reasonable enough. One important assumption is that *a frustrating situation causes an increase in excited emotion,* that is, if a consummatory response is stimulated but not allowed to occur completely, the general level of excitement will be increased. I do not intend this general increase in excited emotion to imply a gradual thing; rather it is thought to be immediate— just like the case of the hungry infant who immediately starts to cry if the nipple is arbitrarily withdrawn with all the cues of nursing still present, or the hungry rat who struggles to hang onto the food dish that one starts to withdraw.

This frustration-excitement hypothesis will bother some because they think also of the frustration-depression hypothesis—the discouraging effect of frustration. They are thinking, however, about the "responding-in-vain"

aspect of prolonged frustration. Prolonged frustration and failure in the clinical sense may produce depression, but I would say this occurs only after a state of frustration no longer exists. The state of frustration is that in which the consummatory response is still being aroused but not satisfied, and I think it reasonable to assume that this is innately tension-inducing. I will mention later some supporting experimental evidence.

If we make this assumption, we can deduce an interesting proposition about what happens inside the organism in the course of repeated trials over a response sequence that terminates in the consummatory response for the drive present. What we can deduce is that the response-produced cues of the correct sequence will become a stimulus sequence of increasing excitement as the instrumental response sequence proceeds toward the final response. This follows simultaneously from (a) the fact that only those cues provided by correct performance of the instrumental response can become stably conditioned to the consummatory response in an instrumental learning situation and (b) the fact that earlier cues in the sequence are conditioned by progressively higher-order conditioning.

In bar-pressing, for example, the rat presses the bar and gets fed, which is perfect timing for conditioning the response-produced cues of bar-pressing to the consummatory response. If he makes the false response of touching the bar without pressing and dives into the food tray for food, the tray is empty and the false cue pattern is extinguished. Only the cues from the correct response get stably conditioned to the consummatory response. Note also that these correct response-produced cues are not to be thought of as simply proprioceptive. If, for example, one moves his head, he gets a sweeping visual change that is just as response-produced as the proprioceptive return from his neck muscles. In the present context, "response-produced" refers to all of the cues—proprioceptive, tactile, visual, auditory, and so forth—that are specific to the correct response and that are caused to impinge on the sensorium *because of the performance of the correct response*. It is an obvious deduction that the conditioned arousal of the consummatory response can stably work its way back along the cues from the *correct response* sequence and no other, and since the arousal occurs under circumstances in which the consummatory response cannot yet be performed we also deduce the accompanying presence of excitement through frustration.

The "working backward" of the conditioned consummatory response along the true path of a maze or any series of responses that makes up an instrumental sequence is a special form of higher order conditioning. If we think of a correct temporal sequence, R_1S_1, R_2S_2, R_3S_3, $R_CS_C \rightarrow R_CS_C$, in which R_C is the circularly maintained consummatory response, it is clear that R_C will become conditioned first to S_3; then, when well attached to S_3, it will occur in a favorable temporal location for conditioning to S_2. When R_C has moved back to S_2, it will be in a favorable temporal relation for optimum conditioning to S_1. If the animal makes a wrong response, R_C will not be reinforced because it will not lead to the next correct thing to do—only those things that move toward the goal or to the next correct phase are reinforced, in the Pavlovian sense of the term rein-

forcement. In any particular learning situation there will also be constant factors (such as the texture of the walls and floor of a maze) that will also be conditioned to the consummatory response and that will generalize immediately to the beginning of the sequence. Figure 1 shows the picture for a series of trials.

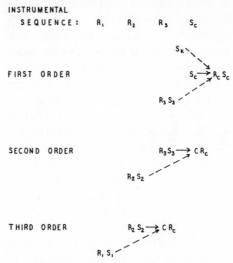

Fig. 1. Schematic diagram of the higher-order conditioning process in an instrumental sequence. Solid lines refer to previously established connections, the one between S_C and R_C being the innate consummatory reponse. Each response is assumed to have a unique response-produced stimulus, that for R_C being the consummatory stimulus, which circularly maintains R_C. CR_C refers to a conditioned component of R_C and S_k refers to constant stimuli unique to the situation but not different in different parts of the sequence.

These diagrams are of course of the over-simplified-paradigm variety, since the responses in a sequence are not discrete and since conditioning cannot be broken down into single successive steps. The general meaning is clear, however, and it can be seen that the conditioning of R_C to the later responses in the sequence proceeds more rapidly because it is always several trials ahead of the earlier parts of the sequence. The *ultimate weakened performance of higher order conditioning, as studied by Pavlov, is not expected,* however, since the terminal stimulus in the sequence is always reinforced. Pavlov never studied the conditioning of a *sequence* of stimuli invariably terminating in reinforcement; rather, he either stopped reinforcement of the first-order stimulus or reinforced it separately. As set up here, the conditioned response should merely move forward—in a progressively less firmly established form in the earlier stages of training but later at almost full strength throughout. An implication of this derivation is that frustration-excitement, due to this conditioned arousal of the consummatory response, will also work its way backward and be specific to cues of the true path or correct instrumental sequence.

A second important assumption is that excitement gets channeled into whatever skeletal response happens to be under way at the time the increase in excitement occurs. This is the major hypothesis in the drive-induction theory being proposed. As stated, it sounds rather obvious—if the excitement does not interfere with the ongoing behavior, or if it is not elicited by a stimulus for incompatible behavior, there is no place for it to show up except in an increased vigor of executing the behavior already under way. The important implication in the present context is a little less obvious, however—namely that after the first learning trial, the performance of the correct response provides response-produced cues for excitement; and this excitement necessarily feeds back into the performance.

Consider the rat as the choice point

in a T-maze on the second trial. He engages in what Tolman (1932) called "vicarious trial and error," making incipient starts in each direction. But the response-produced cues from starts in the correct direction are more strongly conditioned to the consummatory response, resulting in an increase in excitement that carries through from the start to actual entrance of the path. Or consider the rat in the Skinner box after the first reinforcement. He still has all the exploratory tendencies he had on the first trial but there is now a difference: A class of movements approximating the correct one in their response-produced cues are now more likely to be carried through if hesitantly started. Any one that, in its incipience, arouses the consummatory response through the conditioning mechanism will not be abandoned but rather will be somewhat aggressively executed.

In considering this mechanism you will recognize that the consummatory response will also be conditioned to various general and specific cues in the situation other than those strictly emanating from the instrumental response. If the rat was looking at the bar when he pressed it, the sight of the bar will arouse the consummatory response; this will feed into further looking at the bar, which will facilitate his performing the previous response by restricting his orientation to relevant cues. Such subsidiary conditioning has the effect of making the animal more active and exploratory in the right places. *The most general statement of the overall mechanism is that the animal is forced to follow courses of action that maximize conditioned arousal of the consummatory response.* This is so because, of the variety of acts possible at the outset, the ones that progressively acquire the power of arousing the excitement engendered by the unsatisfied consummatory response are going to get a booster feedback that makes them prepotent even before they become habitual and stereotyped. At the molar level of the law of effect the animal learns the responses that arouse the conditioned consummatory response; these, like all rewards that strengthen responses, are secondary rewards.

You may feel that in my thinking on this I am coming very close to an expectancy interpretation. You may argue that I might as well say the animal learns the response that maximizes his expectation of getting food. I don't mind this accusation so long as it does not carry with it the connotation that I am close to a *cognitive* interpretation. Expectancies at the human level are verbalized antedating responses and their prototype at the infant or animal level is always a conditioned response component that has moved forward in a regularly experienced stimulus-response sequence. To apply the concept of *cognition* at the animal level, however, is to suggest the rat can perceive the cause-and-effect relationship between his responses and the arrival of reward. I would argue that the nearest he comes to this is to get more excited when he has a tendency to do the things that have been successful on previous trials. The human also has this mechanism for correct responding but he has, as well, the ability to verbalize means-end relationships and to pick rationally the one that maximizes his expectation of reward. Contrary to being a cognitive interpretation, the proposed mechanism is one that blindly forces the animal to choose the behav-

ior route that is circularly energized by its previous association with the consummatory response. Professor Hull always sought a mechanism of reinforcement that would explain the adaptive nature of learning; the proposed mechanism is precisely as adaptive as the consummatory response itself.

Instrumental learning perceived in some such way as in the present proposal has many advantages in handling the facts of conditioning and reward learning. They would make too long a list to cover here and I shall therefore mention only two:

1. The proposed mechanism requires the use of only a contiguity principle of learning. Everything is deduced from (a) contiguity, (b) the exciting effects of frustrating a consummatory response, and (c) the channeling of excited emotion into the ongoing act. Each of these has a simple believability. Since the key conditioning involved in the treatment of reward learning is the conditioning of the consummatory response, this explanation helps make sense out of the fact that all of the principles of classical conditioning and reward learning are interchangeable if we substitute reward for unconditioned stimulus or vice versa.

2. It simplifies acquired drive and acquired reward by reducing them to the same thing, namely, cue patterns that elicit the consummatory response by way of conditioning. These patterns function as the reward does when it is presented and has not quite been used yet, that is, they arouse the consummatory response. The complete drive-reduction interpretation of acquired drives and rewards is very unwieldy and often, if not invariably, has to have the same stimulus serve as both an acquired drive and an acquired reward.

Moreover, the operations for establishing an acquired drive are usually identical with those for establishing an acquired reward. The difficulties inherent in the drive-reduction approach to secondary reward were appreciated by Hull (1943), as in the following quotations from *Principles of Behavior:*

Secondary reinforcement differs from primary reinforcement in that the former seems to be associated . . . with stimulation whereas the latter seems to be associated with the cessation of stimulation. . . . (p. 97)

So far as our present knowledge of habit structure goes, the habit structures mediated by the two types of reinforcement are qualitatively identical. This consideration alone constitutes a very considerable presumption in favor of the view that both forms are at bottom, i.e., physiologically, the same. (pp. 99–100)

I would underscore this statement by saying that regardless of what is thought of the present proposal, the smart theorist will look to *acquired* reward to get his ideas about how the reinforcement process works. My own position is that all reinforcement in the law-of-effect sense is based on acquired motivation—the strengthening of the instrumental act is a direct effect of the incentive value of the *reward at a distance*—which is of necessity an acquired affair. We are all born with consummatory responses. Once practiced, they become connected to cues, giving us incentives.

You will probably be interested in what kind of research a drive-induction orientation leads to. Since I do not want to give the impression of being an arm-chair theorist in any case, I shall refer to some figures from recent investigations. The first experiments carried out with this theoretical orientation I call the "moth-and-the-flame" experiments after the hypothetical model of a moth in a T-maze who learns to fly to the side with a lighted candle even though this increases stimulation and threatens survival. I reported these at a Brown Colloquium several years ago under the title "Studies in Sex and Saccharine."

The sex experiment I have reported elsewhere under the frivolous title "Coitus Reservatus in Rattus Norvegicus," and in print as "Reward value of copulation without ejaculation" (Sheffield, Wulff, and Backer, 1951). As these titles imply, the sex studies demonstrated that male rats will learn a response that leads to copulation without any drive reduction through ejaculation. This was without any experience with ejaculation either prior to or during the experiment, so acquired reward based on primary drive reduction was ruled out. An incidental finding was that copulation attempts with another male were also reinforcing for instrumental learning. This result was complicated by the fact that in prior sex tests the animals had previously copulated—without ejaculating—with a female. This introduced acquired reward as a possibility, but note that such acquired reward was not based on any primary reward in the form of ejaculation.

The early saccharine studies (Sheffield and Roby, 1950), demonstrated in several ways that hungry animals would learn a response rewarded by a solution of water sweetened with saccharine despite the fact that this neither reduced the drive nor satisfied the need. We could not rule out acquired reward by controlling previous experience with such sweet tastes as rats' mothers' milk but we ran animals over a time period sufficiently extended so that any acquired reward value should have been extinguished.

A more recent set of experiments with Roby and Campbell (Sheffield, Roby, and Campbell, 1954) using sweet solutions was published in the October 1954 *Journal of Comparative and Physiological Psychology* and I might mention its most salient findings. The purpose of the study was to find out —*assuming* that saccharine was innately reinforcing—whether nourishment added anything to instrumental learning. We compared a saccharine solution and a dextrose solution that had previously been roughly equated for strength of consummatory response as measured by drinking rate with very hungry animals. We also wanted the organism to have a chance to "discover," so to speak, that dextrose was a primary reward. That is, we wanted to maximize the acquired reward value of the taste of dextrose. For this purpose some animals were given prior experience with an opportunity to drink large quantities of dextrose when hungry. In all we used eight groups of rats in a runway habit, including a pure water control, two different concentrations of dextrose, and a group that received dextrose further sweetened with saccharine.

The important finding was that regardless of the factors influencing the strength of the consummatory response, the latter was the best final index of how well the animals would learn. Saccharine and dextrose concentrations which evoke equal drinking rates are equivalent as rewards. Adding saccharine to dextrose makes it a much better reward. Prior experience with drinking

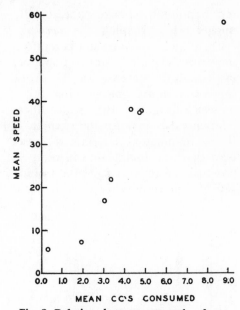

Fig. 2. Relation between strength of consummatory response and instrumental running response with reward solutions varying in sweetness, nourishment, and prior experience in the goal box. Speed scores are 100 x inverse of time to traverse a 4-ft. runway to get 4 min. access to the reward solution. Reading from left to right the reward groups are: water, no experience; 2% dextrose, no experience; 2% dextrose, dextrose experience; 2% dextrose, water experience; 2.6% dextrose, water experience; 2.6% dextrose, dextrose experience; 0.13% saccharin, no experience; 2% dextrose and 0.13% saccharin, no experience. (From Sheffield, Roby, & Campbell, 1954.)

dextrose gives it a temporary advantage on drinking rate that is lost in the course of training. The results are shown in Figure 2.

Another recent experiment with sweets that is not yet in print varied the strength of the consummatory response by varying the hunger of the animals. Thus we have shown that you can vary the consummatory response by changing the concentration of the sweet while keeping the *hunger constant* and get a corresponding change in reinforcing value; the present question is whether you can vary the consummatory response by changing the animals' hunger while keeping the *sweetness constant* and get a variation in reinforcing value. The same runway habit was used, and the reward was a sucrose concentration of 5 gms. per liter. It can be seen in Figure 3 that a nice linear relation exists between the strength of the consummatory response as measured by the drinking rate in the goal box and the reinforcing value as indicated by the runway speed.

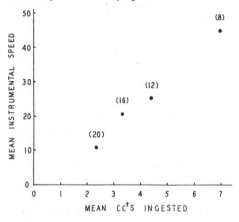

Fig. 3. Plot showing relation between consummatory and instrumental strength when the consummatory response strength was varied by independently varying daily food intake, as indicated at each point (in parenthesis) in terms of daily gram dry weight of Purina mash. The reward was a 4-min. opportunity to drink a 5% sucrose solution; the instrumental response was running down a 4 ft. runway to get access to the reward; speed scores are inverse of time multiplied by 100. Data based on last 12 of 24 training trials.

The upshot of these sweet experiments is that the vigor of the consummatory response is an excellent index of reward value regardless of its drive-reducing properties. This finding is demanded by the drive-induction theory and is crucial in contrasting it with the drive-reduction theory.

The other kinds of relevant recent experiments have been aimed at the frustration-excitement portion of the drive-induction theory. In a previous experiment (Sheffield and Campbell, 1954) it was found that a stimulus that regularly preceded daily feeding became a cue for increased excitement as measured by movements in an activity cage. This was an experimental check on the implication that conditioned arousal of the consummatory response would result in increased excitement. The experiment is probably familiar to most of you, but I will review it briefly. Rats lived in individual activity cages inside a soundproofed cabinet inside a soundproofed room. They were kept on a deprivation diet and fed only once a day by the sudden, automatic dropping of a single lump of wet mash into their activity cages. For experimental animals this feeding was preceded for five minutes by a conditioned stimulus consisting of a gross change in the auditory and visual field; for control animals the same feeding regime was followed and the conditioned stimulus was presented at the same time, but the food dropping came at random times before and after the conditioned stimulus so that no conditioning of the consummatory response would occur. Our control animals should therefore show adaptation to the conditioned stimulus pattern. But according to the frustration-excitement hypothesis—combined with the deduction of conditioned arousal of the consummatory response—the experimental animals should show a progressive increase in the amount of activity in response to the conditioned stimulus as days of training continue.

This increase in activity was very clear. As shown in Figure 4, the control animals show a decline and the experimental animals show a marked rise. The phenomenon will not be an unfa-

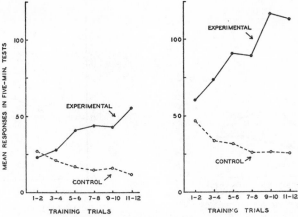

Fig. 4. Acquisition of consummatory excitement when a 5-min. environmental change regularly precedes daily feeding (experimental) compared with adaptation to the change when it is not correlated with feeding (control). The index of excitement is skeletal activity as reflected in movements of a stabilimeter cage. The environmental change (CS) in the left figure was cessation of exhaust-fan noise plus shift from dark to light; the CS in the right figure was cessation of exhaust fan plus shift from light to dark. (From Sheffield & Campbell, 1954.)

miliar one to those who have handled rats on a starvation diet and a daily feeding regime. When one comes around to feed them each day they quickly come to show great excitement to the cues provided by the caretaker just before he gives them their food. I suspect, however, that too many caretakers have regarded this as merely the activity of a high drive and did not realize they were the stimulus. The effect of hunger alone on activity is relatively slight—if at all existent—as demonstrated in an earlier study with Campbell (Campbell and Sheffield, 1953).

As part of the analysis in this experiment, we broke down activity during the five-minute conditioned stimulus into responses during successive minutes. The result was that coupled with the acquisition of activity was the formation of a gradient in which activity —and presumably excitement—was greatest just before the dropping of the food. This is comparable to the gradient of the moving forward of the conditioned consummatory response. The results are shown in Figure 5.

The subsequent experiments I want to mention were done with Sue Rosner and were aimed at finding out whether this actually was a gradient of arousal of the consummatory response or whether it merely reflected temporal summation due to the prolonged presence of a frustrating cue for the consummatory response. In these experiments the question raised was what happens if you present the CS without dropping the food after training. The CS, which in this case was a tone, lasted only five seconds during training, thus corresponding to the last five seconds before food dropped in the earlier study. During tests interposed after five, ten, and fifteen days of training, the CS was not followed by food and activity

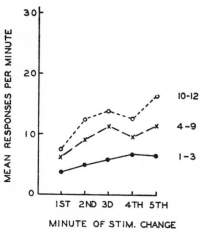 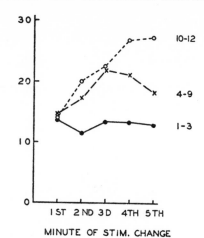

Fig. 5. Minute-by-minute random activity in a stabilimeter cage during a 5-min. CS regularly preceding daily feeding, broken down by stage of training. The breakdown is for the experimental groups shown in Fig. 4, and stage of training is indicated in terms of days (trials) of training. As in Fig. 4, results on the left are for a CS pattern of cessation of noise plus onset of light and results on the right are for a CS pattern of cessation of noise plus offset of light. (From Sheffield & Campbell, 1954.)

was recorded for five minutes. The activity obtained in the test on the sixteenth day is averaged for six subjects in Figure 6. It can be seen that there is a terrific response to tone, but as soon as the cue ends the excitement dissipates. The behavior is not that of a cognitive animal upset because the food did not arrive; activity subsides when the feeding cue disappears.

As a final test on the seventeenth day, the tone was presented and left on for five minutes instead of five seconds, no food being dropped. The activity with this test is shown in Figure 7. It can be seen that again there is an immediate and terrific response to the CS during the first five seconds of tone. There is no evidence for temporal summation, however; we get a distinct drop in which generalization decrement prevails as the usually five-second tone continues for longer periods. The second five seconds of tone is plotted in the figure and is significantly lower than the first. The results fortify an

interpretation of immediate excitement to the CS for the consummatory response and a high degree of specificity of conditioned cues involved. Thus the generalization decrement is large even

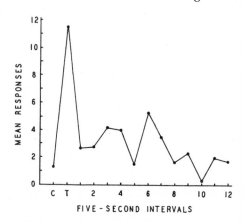

Fig. 6. The course of excited activity when a familiar 5-sec. food signal is presented but not followed by food. The ordinate shows mean stabilimeter activity responses of 6 rats, per 5-sec. interval of time. On the abscissa, C is a control rate based on the 60 secs. preceding the tone CS, T reflects the 5-sec. of tone, and the succeeding 12 points are 5-sec. intervals following cessation of tone CS.

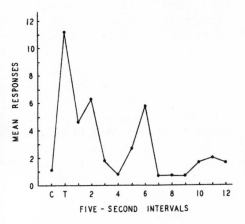

Fig. 7. The course of excited activity when a familiar 5-sec. food signal is not followed by food and is continued for 60 sec. beyond the usual time for presenting food. The ordinate and abscissa have the same meaning as in Fig. 6.

with the variation of the rather subtle factors involved in temporal duration of the cues.

These results are especially encouraging because they show (a) an immediate burst of excitement when the consummatory response is mobilized by a conditioned cue and (b) a high degree of discriminability of cues capable of arousing the response. These are both fairly crucial to the reinforcement mechanism proposed.

Addendum[2]

In all of the foregoing, the reinforcement mechanism has been discussed in terms of such "positive" reinforcements as food, sweet tastes, sex, and so forth. A critical question is whether funda-

[2] Not presented at the Brown Colloquium. The ideas included here were held back to answer the "$64 question" expected from the Brown audience. For some reason, the question was not asked. The question *was* asked by Professor Miller, and the Addendum was added when he requested a copy of the Brown talk to use in his learning course.

mentally the same mechanism is involved in the case of "negative" reinforcements such as shock, in which the response that terminates the stimulation, rather than the response that produces it, is acquired.

In response to this question, it may be said at the outset that my thinking has been oriented toward the positive-incentive problems without much thought to the negative-incentive case. My presumption is that the kind of excitement produced by mobilizing the consummatory response before consummation can occur is in some ways a different kind of excitement from that produced by pain, fear, and other noxious stimulations. Thus there is nothing comparable to the "freezing" of fear in the excitements produced by anticipatory consummatory behavior. A comparison of the two instrumental learning situations is therefore complicated to the extent that different kinds of "emotions" are involved. My basic assumption is, however, that "excitement" has a "g-factor" that is channeled into ongoing behavior regardless of whether the source is frustration of a consummatory response or stimulation of pain receptors.

As far as the mechanics of reinforcement are concerned, the chief difference between rewards and punishments in the present conception is that whereas rewards are stimuli that elicit behavior that in turn increases the reward stimulation, punishments are stimuli that directly produce excitement and elicit behavior that decreases punishing stimulation. The behaviors alluded to are in nearly all natural examples handled by innate reflexes. If a specific reward has no specific maintaining reflex, it innately elicits "holding still"; if a specific punishment has no specific avoiding reflex, it innately elicits restless motion. If a learned cue for a reward-maintaining response is presented and the maintaining response is interfered with, excitement is produced that channels into whatever the animal is doing that brings on the cue. The consequences of this have already been outlined. If a punishment is presented, there is some innate excitement immediately elicited along with any avoiding reflexes. This is different from a reward, which produces excitement only when its maintaining response is blocked. Moreover, in an instrumental learning situation the ongoing response when this excitement is directly aroused is at the onset of punishment a response that produces punishment, but this is normally superceded by a response that terminates punishment *while the excitement is still present*. The excitement will move forward to the first response, that is, the response that brought on the punishment; and if this alone described the mechanics of the situation, the response that produces punishment would be strengthened in the same manner as the response that is instrumental in producing reward. But the terminal response in the sequence—the one that is present when punishment ends—is going to move forward along with the excitement. To the extent, therefore, that this terminal response is incompatible with the response that produced punishment in the first place, it will supersede the latter response. That is, the correct response has the immediate excitement of pain channeled into it and it is located on a stable cue-response sequence along which it can move forward. It therefore becomes either the immediate response to the noxious stimulus or an anticipa-

tory response if there are cues that can trigger it off in advance.

When a one-year-old child sees its first candle it will reach out to touch the candle and react to the heat by a swift reflex withdrawal. This will not ordinarily stop the child from reaching again (the reaching part may even be strengthened) but is very likely to stop the touching part because the avoidant response is quickly conditioned and moves forward slightly enough in time that the cues of almost touching the flame evoke withdrawal.

No comparable incompatible response can stably move forward in the case of rewards. Anticipatory responses that do not lead to food, for example, would lose their ability to produce feedback excitement because they would not be reinforced as cues for the consummatory response. The consummatory act itself cannot move forward because it requires the reward stimulus for its execution. Responses that delay the consummatory act do not receive much feedback because they spoil the temporal relations that make for good conditioning of response-produced cues to the arousal of the consummatory response. Avoidant responses, on the other hand, can be executed in the absence of the punishment; there are no features of the learning situation that interfere with the moving forward of the terminal response, an inherent tendency of conditioned responses. An avoidant response will move forward to the point just ahead of punishment; at this point the maximum anticipatory excitement of incipient incorrect responses is channeled into the incompatible correct response. Avoidant responses can move still further forward but in so doing they lose the good temporal relation for conditioning and tend to weaken. This leads to some extinguished excitement to incipient errors. What the individual tends never to lose, therefore, is an excited correct response when he *almost* makes a mistake; otherwise he may develop a stable relaxed anticipatory response that is executed regularly but too far in advance of punishment to be carried out with much excitement.

Any punishment situation that could be rigged to prevent the moving forward of an incompatible terminal response would be expected to produce the paradoxical strengthening of the response that leads to punishment. Examples of what appears to be a compulsive approach to a punishing stimulus are not unknown. According to the present interpretation these arise when only the *excitement* moves forward to

the act that brings on the punishment. This would make a punishing situation comparable to a rewarding situation.

Between rewards and punishments are a number of stimulating situations that lead to undifferentiated excitement. These appear to be reinforcing, at least in younger people. Children readily learn responses that lead to loud noises and excessive activity, and even mildly noxious excitements like roller coasters and horror movies strengthen instrumental behavior. Experiences that come under the heading of "thrills" do not fit drive-reduction interpretations in any easy fashion. These appear to be examples in which general excitement moves forward but either involves no specific behavior that terminates the excitement or no terminal response incompatible with the response that brings on the excitement.

New Evidence on the Drive-Induction Theory of Reinforcement[1]

Fred D. Sheffield

Readers of the preceding paper are familiar with the drive-induction theory of reinforcement and the *old* evidence that supports it. In this paper I would like to expand my discussion of the hypothesis and present some of the al-

[1] This paper was originally read as an address given at the Stanford Psychology Colloquium, November 1960. As presented, it contained a detailed description of the reinforcement mechanism and supporting evidence, most of which has been deleted because it essentially repeated parts of the Brown Colloquium paper. What remains is primarily directed to the drive-induction hypothesis per se.

ready published evidence that supports it, the factors that modify or extend it, and some newly published evidence that helps clarify the issues involved.

Partly because of a bias for keeping theory abreast of research, I have been reluctant to publish a general theory of reinforcement. The nearest I have come so far to a published statement of my position was in a 1954 experimental article with Roby and Campbell, entitled "Drive Reduction versus Consummatory Behavior as Determinants of Reinforcement" (Sheffield, Roby, &

Campbell, 1954). This article reported a set of experiments which helped demonstrate that the amount of nourishment appears to be an irrelevant variable in determining the reward value of sweet substances. The main reason there is a statement of theory in the article is that the editors urged me to add something to the original manuscript to explain what I thought the alternative was to the drive-reduction position that the experiments failed to support. The statement gives the flavor of the theory as conceived at that time.

. . . in the case of instrumental learning with positive rewards the reward stimulus is at the outset of training an "unconditioned" stimulus for the consummatory response in the sense that it will regularly elicit the response when presented. It would be expected that this terminal consummatory response would become conditioned to immediate neutral cues, especially those which just precede the onset of the reward stimulus. On successive experiences after the first these cues will arouse the consummatory response *ahead* of the reward. Moreover, this arousal of the incomplete consummatory response will work its way from the goal backward over the instrumental sequence since only the cues in this sequence invariably precede reward. Thus performing the correct responses— and only the correct ones—becomes a cue-producing situation that arouses the incomplete consummatory response.

This inference can be made the basis for an explanatory mechanism if one assumes (a) that incomplete arousal of the consummatory response produces excitement if the animal is in the appropriate drive state and (b) such excitement is channeled into whatever [skeletal] response is being performed at the moment. The first of these assumptions is easy to accept—thus animals on a hunger regime, for example, are practically beside themselves with excitement when exposed to the cues that just precede the arrival of their daily ration in their living cages. If the second assumption corresponds with facts, correct responses would become prepotent over others because they alone would be performed with the added boost of excitement from anticipatory arousal of the consummatory response. And with several incipient response tendencies at a behavioral choice point, the one that arouses the consummatory response would be the most likely to carry through to completion. With training the correct sequence gets the advantage of more rehearsal and more vigorous performance than incorrect sequences.

This alternative to the "drive reduction" mechanism might be called the "drive induction" theory of rewards since it depends on arousal rather than reduction of excitement and treats rewards as incentives rather than satisfiers (Sheffield, Roby & Campbell, 1954, pp. 353–354).

Note that this is a theory about drive as well as a theory about reinforcement in instrumental learning. The basic assumption of the preceding passage is that "incomplete arousal of the consummatory response produces excitement if the animal is in the appropriate drive state." This is the drive-induction hypothesis and can be stated more explicitly as follows: *"If an animal is in a given drive state, and stimuli for the appropriate consummatory response are presented under circumstances in which the consummatory response cannot occur, the animal will innately respond with general excitement."*

To make this more meaningful let me use a concrete example. If a mother rat has recently produced a litter, she will—in her temporary hormonal condition—innately respond in such a way as to keep her entire brood next to her. This is accomplished simply by retrieving any that move away from the group. She executes the retrieving response more or less automatically and calmly when she notices a stray. But if a small wire-mesh cage is placed over the stray, so that the mother can see it and smell it but not retrieve it, the mother becomes quite agitated and displays what most observers would call excited emotion.

I have called this excitement from consummatory stimulation without consummation "drive induction." My reason for giving it this name was, as already noted, partly that it is the opposite of drive *re*duction and helped contrast my reinforcement position with the drive-reduction position. Another reason was that if one defines "drive" as the source of energetic activity (which was Woodworth's (1918) intent when he invented the concept), the source of the energetic activity, in cases in which the drive-induction hypothesis applies, is not the internal state per se but rather is the excitement induced by externally stimulating the consummatory response. The hormonal state of the post-parturitional female rat does not directly stimulate excitement; excitement is induced by the unconsummated external stimulation to retrieve. Similarly, the blood state that goes with hunger does not directly stimulate excitement; this is induced by unconsummated stimulation to eat. If you feel that "excitement-induction" would be a better name for the theory than "drive-induction," I would tend to agree, but am also tempted to make a further suggestion that we might profitably drop the word "drive" from psychological terminology.

Accepting, however, the conventional usage of the term "drive," I make a distinction between two kinds of drives and should hasten to point out that the drive-induction hypothesis is not intended to apply to all things that have been called "drives" by S–R psychologists. It applies to those internal states (such as hunger, sex, probably thirst, and so on) for which there is a clear-cut consummatory stimulus and a clear-cut innate consummatory response that, if properly executed, leads either to removal of the consummatory stimulus or to a change in the internal state—a change that renders the stimulus no longer effective. I do not apply it to the case of pain drive or to any of the sources of excitement and activity that come under the heading of a *strong external or internal stimulus* that by sheer strength of afferent input goads the animal into excited activity. My distinction in drives is thus between (1) *strong-stimulus* drives, which have tended to serve as the model for S–R psychologists and drive-*re*duction theorists, and (2) *excitability* or lowered-threshold drives, which do not exhibit excitement except in the presence of incomplete consummatory stimulation. The drive-induction hypothesis applies only to the latter kind—the "excitability" drives.

A concrete example of what I consider to be an excitability drive is hunger. The traditional treatment of hunger is that it is an excited state produced by strong stimulation from stomach contractions—that is, hunger pangs. I learned to discredit this conception some twenty-odd years ago when as a teaching assistant I was in charge of a drives-and-motives demonstration using laboratory rats. My observation then was that very hungry rats, like satiated rats, spend much of their time apparently sleeping. But they could be distinguished from satiated rats in three ways: they did more eating when given an opportunity, they showed a heightened startle-reaction to a sudden stimulus, and they showed a much greater restlessness when I came into the vivarium to give them their daily feeding. From these observations I came to the conclusion that hunger was not a stimulus, but rather *a state of increased reactivity that specifically lowers the threshold for the consummatory response, also lowers the threshold for general skeletal excitement, and maximizes excitement when food cues are provided in advance of eating.*[2]

It goes without saying that the first of these observations, lowered threshold for eating, is typical of hunger. The other two observations I later put to test in some experiments with Byron Campbell (Campbell & Sheffield, 1953; Sheffield & Campbell, 1954). These constitute some *old* evidence of the drive-induction theory and some of you may already be familiar with them although they perhaps will have a new meaning in the present context. In these experiments the animals temporarily lived in circular, individual, stabilimeter cages which recorded movements of the animal on a twenty-four-hour-a-day basis. The cages were in a soundproofed cabinet kept in a soundproofed room.

2 The usage of "lowered threshold" in this context has led to some misunderstandings. It does not refer to the simple sensory thresholds of psychophysics. In its strictest meaning, a "threshold" is an arbitrary point on the abscissa of the function relating response amplitude to stimulus intensity. As here used, a "lowered threshold" means that the entire function is raised, such that a more vigorous response is obtained if the adequate stimulus is held constant at any value on the abscissa (stimulus intensity). "Excitability" is perhaps the better concept, and the import here is that, in the higher drive state, the consummatory response is more readily and more vigorously elicited by the consummatory stimulus, the converse being true in the lower drive state. The mechanics are very likely different from the case of sensory thresholds, where "internal state" changes are likely to be in the receptors (e.g., dark adaptation in the retina). Excitability drive changes, as internal states, appear more likely to involve changes at the central level, or perhaps on the response side of the causal sequence between stimulus and response.

The purpose of the first experiment (Campbell and Sheffield, 1953) was to find out how much restless activity a rat shows in response to sheer starvation over a seventy-two-hour period and how his reactivity to a sudden external stimulus changed during this period. Rats lived in the cages for a control period of four days on an ad-lib diet. Then food was taken away and they were starved for three days. On each day activity was recorded not only over the twenty-four hours but also separately for ten minutes *before* and ten minutes *during* a marked change in the auditory and visual environment.

The results are shown in Figure 1, in which it is apparent that there is very little shift in absolute activity level as a function of increased hunger drive. It is also apparent that activity is always greater in the presence of the external stimulus although this diminishes during the ad-lib period. It is finally apparent that during starvation the downward trend of adaptation to the external stimulus is reversed and general reactivity instead shows a definite

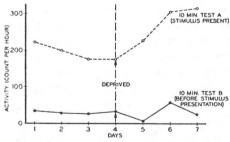

Fig. 1. The effect of food deprivation on the activity response to an environmental change. The solid line reflects 10-min. records before an environmental change, the dotted line reflects the subsequent 10 min., the change being cessation of exhaust-fan noise and onset of light. Feeding was ad lib until day 4, when all food was removed. Ten min. activity means (6 animals) are converted to hourly rates. (From Campbell & Sheffield, 1953)

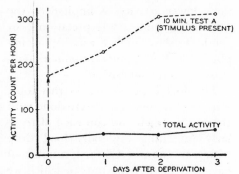

Fig. 2. A comparison of the effects of deprivation on activity versus the joint effect of deprivation and an environmental change. The solid line reflects mean hourly activity rate during a constant environment, based on 24-hour records; the dotted line reproduces the corresponding part of the dotted curve in Fig. 1. (From Campbell & Sheffield, 1953.)

rise with greater hunger. The fluctuations in the lower curve can be attributed to the instability of ten-minute tests; if the twenty-four-hour activity is used, the result is smoother, as shown in Figure 2. You will recall that the purpose of the experiment (Sheffield and Campbell, 1954) was to find out what happens to activity in response to this kind of constant environmental change. In this experiment the animals lived in soundproofed stabilimeter cages and were fed by a remote control device that dropped food into the cages without warning for one group and dropped food for the other group always at the end of a five-minute period of a fixed environmental change. Both groups were exposed to the external stimulus but for the former group the stimulus was uncorrelated with feeding while for the latter group it always just preceded feeding.

The results were that the activity response of the control group to the five-minute stimulus drops over successive days of exposure, whereas the activity response of the experimental group

shows a marked rise with successive days of training[3] I interpret the results as the conditioning of the consummatory response to the cues that always precede eating. As conditioning continues, the consummatory response is stimulated by the external cues, but cannot take place until the food arrives. The ensuing excitement shown in the form of restless activity I consider to be an innate response to consummatory stimulation in the absence of consummation.

These are, of course, experiments on *drive* and *drive induction* and do not involve any instrumental learning. Their relevance to the question of where the excitement comes from in the case of excitability drives is independent of their relevance to the reinforcement mechanism. The nature of the induced excitement is nevertheless crucial to the theory as a whole, and is the concern of the new evidence and unsettled issues referred to at the outset of this paper. The issues tend to be interrelated, and tend to focus on the questions of (a) what are the mechanics of the excitement produced by stimulating the consummatory response when it cannot occur and (b) what aspects of a consummatory response are conditioned when a stimulus regularly precedes execution of the complete consummatory response.

My original conception of the source of excitement was in terms of an emotional response to *frustration* as defined by presenting a consummatory stimulus but *preventing* the consummatory response. I had a frustration-excitement

[3] See fig. 4 of the Brown Colloquium paper, acquisition of consummatory excitement when a 5-min. environmental change regularly precedes daily feeding compared with adaptation to the change when it is not correlated with feeding.

hypothesis as a more general form of the frustration-aggression hypothesis. I thought in terms of interfering with a well-motivated response that is all set to go—even to the point of incipient contractions of the skeletal muscles involved. My idea was that if this state of affairs persisted for long enough it produced, innately, an emotional response comparable to the anger response Watson (1924) found when he confined the movements of a neonate.

This way of conceiving things led me to some expectations that turned out to be contrary to fact. One such expectation was that if a signal of a given duration regularly precedes food when hungry, maximal frustration should be produced if the food failed to come at the usual time. The experimental background of this expectation came from an incidental finding in the experiment mentioned in the preceding paper in which increased skeletal excitement was demonstrated when a five-minute signal regularly preceded the daily feeding.

The incidental finding that led me to expect maximal frustration was that there is a rising gradient of excited activity up to the fifth minute—the time when the dropping of food was most imminent.[4] There are two ways to interpret this gradient: one is that the consummatory response is being aroused more completely because the temporal cues are getting more like those that just precede feeding; the other is that temporal summation of frustration is making the animal more and more impatient. The experimental question was: What would happen if we didn't drop the food? Would the next minute

show lower activity, as implied by the similarity-of-cues interpretation or would it show higher activity, as implied by the temporal-summation-of-frustration hypothesis?

The first experiments on this topic were exploratory. They were done with Byron Campbell and consisted of regularly preceding the daily food drop with a five-minute CS for a number of days and then giving tests in which we either ended the CS without dropping the food or else continued the CS beyond the five-minute interval—again with no food. *We didn't get any sort of overshoot response when the usual food failed to arrive.* Skeletal excitement increased up to about the time of the usual feeding, but the animals calmed down after this point regardless of whether the CS terminated or whether it persisted beyond the usual time. This result was replicated in a more careful experiment, in which my colleague was Sue Rosner, and in which we used a five-second rather than a five-minute CS and in which the same stabilimeter apparatus was used as in the experiments with Campbell. Since the purpose was to get a very precise momentary analysis of excited activity, we recorded the reactions, not on magnetic counters as in the studies with Campbell but rather on an Esterline Angus polygraph running at a fairly fast speed so as to plot the instant-by-instant movements of the rats.

After training, the rats uniformly showed a burst of activity during the five-second CS, but this did not persist after the CS was terminated on test trials in which the CS was not followed by food. A summary of this fact is shown in Figure 3 which plots stabilimeter activity before, during, and after the five-second tone. The before meas-

[4] See fig. 5 in the Brown Colloquium paper, minute-by-minute random activity in a stabilimeter cage during a 5-min. CS regularly preceding daily feeding, broken down by stage of training.

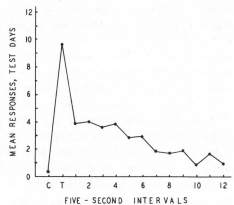

Fig. 3. The course of excited activity when a familiar 5-sec. food signal is presented but not followed by food. The ordinate shows mean rate (6 rats) per 5-second interval. The rate at C is based on a 60-sec. control period prior to the tone CS; T refers to the 5 sec. of tone; the succeeding 12 points are 5 sec. intervals after offset of the tone CS. The data shown are averages over 3 test trials, one each after 5, 10, and 15 days of training at one trial per day.

ure, labeled C for "control," is based on a five-minute observation period but is expressed, as at the rest of the points, in terms of responses per five-second interval totaled for six rats. The figure averages the three test trials in which food was not dropped. It is clearly apparent that activity is at a low ebb in these hungry rats before the CS for eating, is very high during the CS for eating, and falls off rapidly as soon as the CS for eating disappears. This verifies the similarity-of-cues hypothesis and means at the very least that if frustration has an effect on excited skeletal activity it is immediate and momentary and disappears almost as soon as the stimulus for the consummatory response disappears. Essentially the same result was found for a final test trial in which the tone persisted for one minute after the usual time of tone cessation and food dropping. I interpret the results as evidence *against* the idea that

consummatory excitement is anything like an anger response to frustration and as evidence *in favor* of the idea that consummatory excitement requires the immediate presence of the conditioned consummatory stimulus rather than being a somewhat delayed response to interference with the consummatory response.

Perhaps the most significant thing about these results is that they indicate that the excitement of conditioned consummatory stimulation is a highly immediate and precise thing. I didn't realize this until I saw the results, but I would be hard put to explain instrumental learning in terms of drive induction if the second assumption—the feedback assumption that excitement channels into the response of the moment—involved a kind of excitement that required a delay—and persisted after the cues for the consummatory response had subsided. What my mechanism depends on is an instantaneous excitement that starts fast and ends fast as a function of the cues of the moment. The experiment with Sue Rosner tends to confirm this. It fails to confirm some other current ideas, such as those of Amsel (1958), that involve an excited state *subsequent* to and produced by the failure of an expected reinforcement—at least in the case of rats.

There was another important finding in the Sue Rosner data which was not apparent in the original analysis of the data but which I had put on my agenda as a reanalysis after running into some puzzling findings in experiments with salivary conditioning in dogs. Actually I didn't have a chance to do the reanalysis until quite recently. In order to keep things in context rather than in historical order I will describe the

Rosner finding now and tell you about the puzzling dog result later. The moral is, of course, that one should never throw away old data; one never knows for sure that they won't take on new significance.

The purpose of the new analysis was to determine whether the excited activity moved forward to the beginning of the five-second tone or whether it concentrated on the end of tone where food was most imminent. The response on the first training trial is shown in the upper half of Figure 4. It shows a

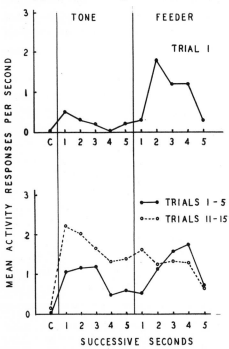

Fig. 4. Shift in location of excited activity during training with a 5-sec. tone CS that regularly precedes daily feeding. The top half shows the first day's result prior to any correlation of CS and food but after 5 days of experience with tone and food drop at noncorresponding times of day. The bottom half divides performance during training into early (days 1–5) and late (days 11–15) and reveals that the peak of activity shifts to the first second of tone. Point C on the abscissa refers to rate during a 5-min. control period prior to onset of tone.

small reaction to tone and a much larger reaction when food is dropped. I should point out that this first training trial was prefaced by five days of adaptation to the tone and experience with the dropping of food at a different time from the sounding of tone. I should also point out that the food-drop mechanism took a second or two from the time the button was pushed until the time the food fell into the food cup, which explains the delay in the peak of reaction to the sound, sight, and smell of the food when it suddenly dropped, as one entire wet-mash bolus. Finally I should point out that the peak of activity shown, a little after food appeared, is not the activity of eating. When the animal settles down to eat, the stabilimeter cage is essentially motionless; I am obliged to interpret as the peak of activity the initial excitement caused by the sound, sight, and smell of food arrival, all of which are conditioned stimuli coming within the drive-induction interpretation. The control point is based on a five-minute observation period before tone and food. The present figure is restricted in that it shows only the five seconds of tone and the first five seconds after tone. It does not show the subsidence to nearly zero activity that follows almost immediately after the low point achieved at the fifth second after the cessation of tone and the initiation of the food-drop mechanism.

The top half of Figure 4 is only a baseline for the relevant finding shown in the lower half. Here we see the trend of events as a result of training with the five-second food signal. If you look at the mean result for the first five training trials you see that what was a little hump of activity to the tone on the first trial has enlarged in size, although it is still smaller than the hump that goes with the presentation of food before eating begins. Now if you look at the result for the last five training trials, you see that the hump to tone is larger than that to food and that the highest point is during the first second of the tone CS. Consummatory excitement has moved forward (that is, occurs earlier) along what I here consider to be a generalization gradient of similarity of the beginning and end of tone. From the standpoint of the drive-induction mechanism of reinforcement the result is excellent because the ultimate excitement is so instantaneous to the food cue.

Now let me describe the laboratory "defeat" that led me to the reanalysis of the Rosner data. This "defeat" has actually more salience for the question of what is the nature of the conditioned consummatory response than for that of what are the mechanics of excitement due to conditioned arousal of the consummatory response, although it is relevant to both topics. The experiments had to do with old-fashioned salivary conditioning, using dogs, which is a rare type of research in this country. I shall not explain here how I became involved in this research but can assure you that it was in the interests of the reinforcement issue. The circumstances on which I am drawing can be summarized as follows: a five-second tone is sounded; this sound overlaps with that of a food delivery motor, and this in turn moves a circular belt to a position in which a ¾-inch ball of liverwurst drops into a wooden salad bowl in front of a semi-restrained dog. The dog's salivary response is recorded continuously and always shows a burst of saliva to liverwurst in the mouth. In a very few trials with this proce-

dure, the dog will start to salivate to the tone in advance of the liverwurst. Early in training you can measure conditioned salivation on every trial, even though you reinforce on every trial; the conditioned salivation is anticipatory and can be measured before the unconditioned response to food. If you continue this sort of training long enough, however, the *anticipatory* salivation may disappear permanently. *Conditioned salivation is still present* and can be readily demonstrated by leaving out the food, but it is no longer anticipatory. Rather it tends to come at about the same time that food comes— or about the time the dog would have salivated if food had come. Dogs differ in how clever they are about this, but apparently there is a general tendency —perhaps easy to understand—for the dog to discriminate the beginning of tone (which is never accompanied by food) from the end of tone and the sound of the delivery device (which is always accompanied by food).

This analysis not only conforms to the behavior of the dog but also fits discrimination theory. Furthermore it fits a more careful rereading of Pavlov's (1927) own experience, in which the anticipatory CR tended eventually to emerge only at the end of the CS and tended to "disappear" unless the experimenter kept lengthening the CS. In my experience, if you want to continue to get an anticipatory conditioned salivary response, you may have to engage in a battle of wits with the dog. Anything that makes it hard for the dog to tell when food will arrive fosters anticipatory conditioned salivation. You can lengthen and vary the duration of the CS; you can use partial reinforcement; you can space the trials and use a highly variable inter-trial interval;

but if there is some final way of the dog's sensing when the food is certain to arrive, his salivary response tends ultimately to wait for that certainty.

This outcome surprised me, although, as already noted, I eventually realized that it fits discrimination theory. A more important surprise, however, was the fact that the skeletal and instrumental behavior of the dogs did not follow the same history as the salivary behavior. Regardless of what the salivary response did, the dogs tended to orient to the food bowl and got set to eat when the CS started. This behavioral response to tone appeared before the first salivary response, persisted as an anticipatory response through training, and was more resistant to extinction than was conditioned salivation. It would appear that the digestive system requires more concrete evidence—or more precise timing—than the skeletal system.

It was these results that originally gave me the idea of reexamining Sue Rosner's data. If there is something special about skeletal excitement that makes it move forward and stay forward, one should find the same outcome in the rat data. The Rosner rat data are in this sense consistent with the dog data.

All of these results are relevant, as I see things, to the question of what aspect of the consummatory response is conditionable and what aspect moves forward to produce consummatory excitement. This is not only a problem for me but is also a problem for all of the incentive-oriented S–R theorists (e.g., Seward, 1950, 1956; Spence, 1956) who have extended a Hullian approach. Such theorists have placed more and more emphasis on "little rg," which in my terms is the "conditioned consum-

matory response." My preference in labeling stems from my respect for Sherrington (1906), who invented the consummatory response concept, and my disrespect for a teleological concept such as "goal" in mechanistic theories; but I think that regardless of label we will all have to give up the idea that what moves forward is some overt or peripheral portion of the consummatory response. I am already thinking, instead, of a central-nervous-system phenomenon which may show up in various ways at the behavioral level. The behaviorists who emphasize "little rg" have tended to identify it with such overt components as salivation and chewing movements. I can't speak for rats in this respect, but I can say that, for dogs, even a tricky experimenter may have trouble maintaining anticipatory salivation, and I can say *categorically* that I have never seen dogs make an anticipatory chewing movement when the unconditioned stimulus is food.

My attitudes on this issue are further influenced by some fairly recent evidence that tends to force reconsideration of what I once thought was a foolproof index of the consummatory excitement that would be expected in response to a conditioned stimulus for the consummatory response. My "foolproof" index was the vigor of the consummatory response itself when the consummatory object was presented. I have carried out a variety of experiments, using sex, sweets, variations in drive, and so forth, in which it always turned out that there was an almost linear relation between strength of consummatory behavior and strength of instrumental behavior.

Some of the evidence that gives me pause comes from a fairly recent Yale thesis by Doris Kraeling (1961). Kraeling used a straight runway and varied both concentration of sucrose and amount of time allowed to drink the solution, using three different concentrations and three different durations of drinking time in the goal box. She was doing a sophisticated study of the amount-of-reward factor and one of the purposes was to contrast consummatory stimulation with caloric intake by independently varying concentration of sucrose and amount ingested. From this standpoint a major finding was that a small amount of a higher concentration of sucrose uniformly produces faster running than much larger amounts that contained more calories but were of a weaker concentration. The strength of the instrumental response depended on the sucrose concentration, not on the calories ingested.

At the moment, however, I am interested in an important incidental finding of the study, namely that with practice—and Kraeling provided many trials—the *running response* curves separated and stayed separated for the three different sucrose concentrations that she used; the *consummatory response* curves, however, while starting well separated, came closer and closer together with practice. The relevant results are shown in Figure 5, which shows the ultimate separation in running speed, and Figure 6, which shows the ultimate "togetherness" of consummatory responding. Here we seem to have a case in which instrumental vigor is better identified with the strength of consummatory *stimulation,* ultimate vigor of consummatory responding being in the right rank order but remaining very much the same in absolute value regardless of the strength of stimulation.

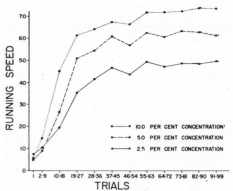

Fig. 5. Relation between instrumental speed of running and concentration of rewarding sucrose solution. The main finding shown in the figure is that after prolonged training the performance curves are still widely separated for 10%, 5%, and 2.5% concentrations. (From Kraeling, 1961.)

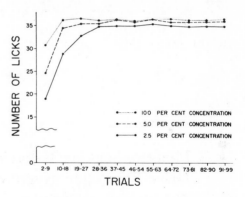

Fig. 6. Relation between consummatory vigor and concentration of rewarding sucrose solution. The main finding shown in the figure is that whereas consummatory vigor is well separated for the three sucrose concentrations in early trials, the differences become very slight (although statistically significant) after about 30 trials; when compared with Fig. 5, the results indicate that consummatory stimulation is a more important determiner than overt consummatory response vigor. (From Kraeling, 1961.)

One can of course discount the results by saying that with liquid food obtained from a drinking tube the vigor of the consummatory response is limited by the innate tongue-lapping rate of the rat, which is well known to be about seven laps per second whenever he laps. But one must also consider the possibility that strength of *consummatory activation,* at the level of the CNS, can continue to increase—in response to stronger stimulation—beyond the physiological limit of the vigor of the overt consummatory response. This might lead to the interesting situation in which one can tell more about the vigor of the internal central consummatory activation by looking at the vigor of the instrumental behavior than by looking at the vigor of the consummatory behavior.

To me this further suggests that I may have to start using constructs at the level of the central nervous system, a state of affairs that doesn't bother me in the least, because, as a natural scientist rather than a behaviorist, I

have always thought that psychology was predestined to have a permanent link with the CNS. What I have had in mind along these lines is the idea that the excitability-drive state sensitizes the activation mechanism for the appropriate consummatory response and that this mechanism channels impulses exclusively into the consummatory response when the innate consummatory stimulus is presented. When the mechanism is activated by a conditioned stimulus, however, and there is no controlling feedback from the innate consummatory stimulus, the activation spills all over the skeletal system; this spillover increases all skeletal tonicity and feeds into whatever skeletal responses are being executed at the moment.

Psychological Review, 1955, vol. 62, pp. 169–179

Pleasure-Seeking Behavior and the Drive-Reduction Hypothesis[1]

Judson S. Brown

During recent years, it has become increasingly apparent that notoriety, if not fame and fortune, can be achieved by repeatedly and vociferously attacking the drive-reduction hypothesis of reinforcement. Just why this hypothesis should have been singled out for special attention is not entirely clear. Perhaps it is indeed strikingly inferior

[1] Presidential address delivered at the twenty-sixth annual meeting of the Midwestern Psychological Association in Columbus, Ohio, 1954. The author is indebted to Drs. I. E. Farber and Kenneth W. Spence for their constructive criticisms of the manuscript.

to other conceptions. Perhaps it is one of the few whose formulation is specific enough to make attacks feasible. Or perhaps the onslaughts are manifestations of reaction formation by those whose drives have been reduced through the writing of other polemics. In any event, it must be admitted that these crusades have had a salutary influence. The defenders of the faith have been forced to think more clearly, to avoid circularities of definition, and to perform relevant supporting experiments.

Since these criticisms appear rather

frequently in the pages of our psychological journals and books, there is always the danger that such half-truths as they may contain will mislead the casual reader, and that any residual virtues of the drive-reduction assumption will be needlessly obscured or even forgotten. The purpose of this paper, therefore, is to re-examine some of these contentions and to re-emphasize some relatively neglected facts and theoretically plausible mechanisms that bear importantly on the issue. No attempt will be made, however, to defend the notion that drive reduction is, in addition to stimulus-response contiguity, a necessary mechanism for all learning. The concern of this discussion is not with the drive-reduction hypothesis of learning per se. Instead, attention is focussed on the problem of whether behavior commonly described as "pleasure seeking" or "stimulation seeking" constitutes a genuine exception to the drive-reduction interpretation, and whether, without undue strain, such behavior can be coordinated with that conception.

Surveys of the history of the drive-reduction view (Postman, 1947; Waters, 1934) show that the arguments of its opponents have been not only vigorous, but well diversified. Some writers, placing their trust in the principle of parsimony, have insisted that stimulus-response contiguity alone is sufficient to account for the growth of associative bonds, additional factors of decreased drive or tension being unnecessary. Others have held that the effects attending a consummatory response cannot act backward in time to affect the strength of a connection, or perhaps that "pleasant" consequences alone can produce learning, or even that learning can take place in the absence of both

motivation and motivation reduction.

The criticism most frequently raised of late, and the one we shall be concerned with here, has been phrased in a variety of different ways. In all of them, however, a central role has been assigned to the observation that *a response may be learned or maintained even though marked increases in stimulation occur while it is in progress or even after its termination.*

In one of the variations on this theme, emphasis is placed on the fact that organisms sometimes exhibit behavior that takes them from an initial state of relative quiescence into one marked by heightened activity and strong stimulation (McClelland, 1951). The individual who deserts the quiet comfort of his easy chair for a lurching, noisy ride on a roller coaster is regarded as epitomizing this behavior. He is described as seeking strong stimulation. Since the increased stimulation follows closely upon the response of getting into the roller coaster, and since that increase is sometimes equated with a rise in drive, a problem is said to be raised for the drive-reduction view. In essence, this is the problem of an organism's exhibiting behavior resulting in so-called pleasurable or positive stimulation. It is the problem of why, if the drive-reduction view is correct, men and animals ever behave so as to obtain more stimulation rather than less.

The same basic criticism is sometimes expressed as a dissatisfaction with the explanatory use by drive-reduction theorists of the concept of secondary reinforcement. Hilgard (1948), for example, points out that the phenomenon of secondary reinforcement is normally marked by an increase rather than a decrease in stimulation. If stimulus reduction is identified with drive reduction, then a rise in stimulation implies an increase in drive. As a consequence, appeals to secondary reinforcement to explain learning are said to lead to a weakening of the generality of the drive-reduction interpretation.

Still a third formulation of this objection arises from the finding that monkeys, when confined in an opaque-walled box, can learn manual responses for which no reward is given other than that of being allowed to look out of a window of the box (Butler, 1953). According to one interpretation of this result (Harlow, 1953b), the stimulation provided by the laboratory room beyond the box provides, or arouses, a drive. Consequently, if responses are actually learned when followed by such a drive increase, their acquisition cannot be ascribed to drive reduction. In short, if a response is followed by an increase in stimulation, irrespective of what happens then or later, and regardless of previous experiences with such stimulation, the drive-reduction concept is declared helpless to account for the learning of that response.

A fourth and final variation of this anti-drive-reduction motif rests on the supposed fact that organisms persist for unreasonably long periods in "behavior which is clearly punishing, or, at least more punishing than rewarding" (Postman, 1947), p. 546). The hypothetical author who is described as writing for a lifetime even though the completion of each opus is punished by an editor's rejection slip, and the masochist, are popular examples cited to support this notion. Though the cataloguing of such reactions as "more punishing than rewarding," is obviously unreliable, since hidden rewards may be operating, and "unreasonable persistence" is also difficult to assess, the belief in the existence of such persistent maladaptive behavior is apparently widespread.

To recapitulate, the drive-reduction assumption has been declared deficient for the following reasons: (*a*) Organisms seek out and approach situations or perform actions involving an increase rather than a decrease in stimulation. (*b*) The drive-reduction theorist is inconsistent if he tries to explain the learning of some responses by invoking the principle of secondary reinforcement with its attendant stimulation increments. (*c*) On the assumption that visual stimulation is drive arousing in monkeys, the acquisition of responses "rewarded" by such stimulation is evidence against the drive-reduction concept. (*d*) Organisms are supposed to persist unreasonably in behavior regarded by observers as more punishing than rewarding. In all of these criticisms, stress is laid on the fact that *when increases in stimulation occur after a response has been initiated or after it ceases, the tendency to perform that response is not always weakened, and may even become stronger.* This failure of increased stimulation to function as a kind of "negative reinforcer" is proposed as a major stumbling block for the drive-reduction interpretation.

As an initial step in attempting to answer these criticisms, it may be noted that the proponents of the above views, in order to stimulate thought and present the best possible case for their position, have often emphasized rather bizarre and extreme examples. But the problem raised by these examples is not confined to the bizarre and the abnormal. The phenomena are typical of the simplest and most conventional kinds of behavior. One need not turn to the masochist for pertinent data;

they abound in nearly all reactions. Though this point seems to have escaped notice, *almost every overt response, and many a covert one, is accompanied by an increase in stimulation.* In most instances, the level of stimulation provided by proprioceptive feedback and by fluctuating external cues must be higher during the response than either before or after. When a rat is first placed in a maze, it may not move at all for a while. When it does move, however, its reactions are likely to provide an increase in the level of both internal and external stimulation. But if stimulation is, in general, more intense at a later phase of the response than at the moment of its initiation, a problem arises as to whether this constitutes a rise in drive and hence an embarrassment for the drive reductionist. Clearly, this is the same problem that lies at the core of the criticisms that have been mentioned, and just as clearly, it too requires a carefully considered analysis.

Granting, then, that a great many responses, though probably not all, are attended by heightened stimulation, by what stratagems can these stimulus increments be coordinated with the suppositions of the drive-reduction view? One alternative might be to assume that *the sensory consequences of most responses are practically never intense enough to provide increments to the drive level.* But this assumption seems unsatisfactory for the following reasons: (*a*) it implies that when stimuli really are strong, a drive results, an implication that reintroduces the problem to be solved. (*b*) It tacitly assumes that when stimuli do produce a drive the response should be abandoned or at least not learned. (*c*) It raises the further problem of how to specify the precise level of intensity at which stimuli become or induce drives.

A second avenue of escape from this dilemma has been opened by one of Miller and Dollard's proposals (1941). They suggest that *heightened stimulation following a response is not incompatible with the drive-reduction position because such stimulation may lower the total stimulation to a level below that prevailing initially.* To use their example, an individual lost in a forest at night does get more stimulation when he sees a light in a cabin window. But seeing the light may actually decrease the totality of stimulation by eliminating internal excitations arising from anxiety or apprehension. Although this solution has substantial merit, the range of cases to which it applies appears to be relatively limited. Moreover, since the rise in stimulation is closer to the response than the decline, a problem remains as to why the decline should override the "punishing" effect of the more immediate rise.

A third possibility, the one to be defended here, is simply that *an increase in stimulation, even when relatively intense, need not always be categorized as an increase in drive.* That is, it is sometimes profitable to treat strong stimuli as drives in our formulations for predicting behavior, and sometimes not. The adoption of this view makes necessary the abandonment of the position that each and every stimulus necessarily has drive properties simply because it is physically intense. It means that the definition of a drive must include more than measurements of, or inferences about, the sheer physical strength of a stimulus. It means that a given stimulus may have drive value for some individuals, but not for others; or for one individual at one time, but not at another. This is apparently essentially the same point that Skinner (1938) makes when he asserts that a drive is not a stimulus.

With respect to the problem under consideration, this suggestion, that strong stimuli need not always engender drive, has numerous implications. Generally speaking, it makes imperative a careful re-examination of all instances in which strong stimulation is supposed to present a paradox for the drive-reduction view. Specifically, it leads to the conclusion that whenever the jostling and noise of the roller coaster can be disqualified as drive increments, the occurrence of the behavior does not constitute an anomalous example. The masochist who beats himself with a hammer may not be providing sensory excitation whose role as a behavior determinant is covariant with drive. In all these instances, the increase in physical stimulation is present, but the presumed increase in drive, along with its paradoxical implications, vanishes.

Merely to assert, however, that strong stimuli do not always function as drives does not contribute much to the resolution of our difficulties. We need to know when, and under what conditions, stimuli will or will not have drive-like effects. We need to list specific factors other than stimulus intensity which must be taken into account if a maximally useful definition of stimulus-induced drive is to be achieved. Whether the resulting definition is, in fact, useful, will depend on whether certain agreed-upon behavioral consequences are found to accompany or to follow the presentation or removal of the stimulus. Consequences such as the intensification of behavior or the occurrence of learning might serve adequately in this capacity, though no firm decision need be made here.

In attempting to specify these additional factors, let us first consider those which lead to the conclusion that a given stimulus, though strong, will *not* operate as a drive.

One factor capable of altering the drive properties of a stimulus is the amount and kind of previous experience that the organism has had with that stimulus. Thus *a physically intense stimulus tends not to produce a drive if an organism has been exposed on successive occasions to gradually increasing values of that stimulus and if each presentation has been followed by some kind of drive reduction.* Some of the most convincing evidence to support this contention comes from the conditioning studies of Pavlov. He found that stimuli such as strong electric shocks, wounding of the skin severe enough to draw blood, and cauterization of the skin lost their noxious aspects if, when used as conditioned stimuli for an alimentary response, their intensity was gradually increased. The process of neutralization was apparently quite complete, since according to Pavlov's report ". . . not even the tiniest and most subtle objective phenomenon usually exhibited by animals under the influence of strong injurious stimuli can be observed in these dogs. No appreciable changes in the pulse or in the respiration occur in these animals . . ." (1927, p. 30). Incidentally, the fact that the dogs in these experiments were fed for a few seconds after each stimulation appears to be especially significant. Prior to the conditioning training, each of the stimuli apparently had drive value. Marked alterations in respiration and pulse, as well as violent motor reactions directed toward removal of the stimuli or escape from them, were observed. That a complete tolerance was developed for these strong stimuli may be taken as evidence for their loss of drive-arousing capacity. According to Liddell (1944), the major findings in these studies have been amply corroborated in studies at the Cornell Behavior Farm.

Further striking evidence to support the view that stimuli normally describable as painful or drive arousing can lose these attributes and become neutral or even "pleasant" if presented at progressively increasing strengths and followed by primary rewards is to be found in Masserman's studies of "experimental masochism." In these experiments, cats were trained to press a switch to obtain food. Air blasts of gradually increasing intensity were then administered each time the switch was depressed. Under these conditions, the air blast can be raised to an intensity that ". . . would be tolerated by no 'normal' cat and yet, because it is now part of the signal-complex leading to feeding, the experimental animal not only is not disturbed by it but, even in the absence of the food reward itself, frequently works the switch to experience the air blast as a subsidiary goal" (1946, p. 57). That results of this kind are not restricted to animal subjects is apparent from Slutskaya's study (1928) in which infants who were pricked with a needle and then fed came to exhibit anticipatory eating responses to the sight of the needle.

In addition to these experimental data, there are abundant anecdotal illustrations, which, though less well documented, also tend to support this contention. Straight whiskey, when first ingested, typically elicits rather violent defense reactions. Because of this, the novice drinker usually begins with sweet liqueurs, "pink ladies," and wines, and slowly works his way through a series of beverages characterized by the gradual disappearance of cola and ginger-ale additives. Finally, only plain water or even nothing need be mixed with the raw product. To the hardened drinker, straight whiskey does *not* taste bad—not bad at all! (It is thus that a product euphemistically labeled "neutral spirits" becomes indeed psychologically neutral.) That the ingestion of alcoholic beverages is often followed by the reduction of one or more drives is common knowledge. It seems needless, therefore, to speculate here as to which drive, when reduced, provides the principal support for this process of neutralization.

Closely parallel steps seem to be involved in acquiring a taste for highly peppered sauces and in learning to eat the kinds of cheeses that Henning would certainly have located at the putrid corner of his olfactory prism. In each instance samples of the commodity, diluted to the point of toleration, are presented initially and are followed by gradually strengthened versions until a terminal level, limited apparently only by the manufacturer's ingenuity, has been reached.

This process of "demotivating" a strong stimulus seems to have much in common with the phenomenon of *negative adaptation,* especially as it has been described by Guthrie (1935). Though he would doubtless not regard the drive-reduction aspect as necessary, he might agree that the task of adapting the horse to the feel of saddle and rider by gradually increasing the weight on its back would be facilitated by the frequent administration of lumps of sugar and crisp Washington apples.

Under some conditions, it might be predicted that the intense propriocep-tive stimulation and muscular strain due to prolonged work should have drive-like effects. But if an organism gets appropriately reinforced training, it can acquire a tolerance for the stim-ulative effects of repetitive muscular effort that is little short of astounding. Rats and pigeons can be trained to make hundreds of responses for a single bite of food if the percentage of reinforcement is high initially, and if the reduction in frequency of reinforce-ment with further trials is sufficiently gradual. In such instances, apparently, the stimulation accruing from a multi-tude of successive reactions does not function as a drive, since behavior such as resting, though followed by the cessation of such stimulation, is not strengthened.

Having noted that, in certain learn-ing situations, strong stimuli tend to lose their drive-arousing functions, we may now inquire as to what mech-anisms may be involved in this process.

One such mechanism appears to be the transformation of a drive-arousing stimulus into a cue for specific re-sponses appropriate to the situation. In effect, *a stimulus loses its power to act as a drive as it acquires strong as-sociative connections to well-integrated, directed bits of behavior.* For the al-bino rat, a bright light has demon-strable drive properties. Responses in-strumental in escaping from the light, or in turning it off, are readily ac-quired. But if the light is located near food, and if, through appropriate training, it becomes associated with reactions of approaching and eating,

its original drive characteristics will be diminished.

This general notion, that the drive function of a powerful stimulus de-clines as it acquires new, behavior-directing properties is supported by several lines of evidence. Hebb, for example, makes essentially this point when he asserts that ". . . potentially painful stimulation is not disruptive (that is, not pain) when it forms part of a stimulation that has well-organized central effects" (1949, p. 199). In studies of widely distributed periodic reinforcement, stimuli arising from muscular tension and fatigue tend, early in learning, to prevent further responding. But after learning is well advanced, they function as cues for additional reactions. The drive aspects of the strong olfactory and gustatory stimuli arising from whiskey disappear as those cues become associated closely with elbow-bending and swallowing responses. The increase in pleasant affect found by Peters (1938) to ac-company the making of positive re-sponses to initially unpleasant stimuli may be a comparable phenomenon, and there are a number of parallels between his judgmental theory of feel-ing and the position taken here.

An unpublished experiment by Mil-ler and Davis[2] illustrates nicely both the manner in which a strong stimulus can acquire associative properties and the importance of making the increases in its intensity gradual if the process of demotivation is to be successful. In their study, rats were first trained to traverse a 2-meter alley for food. Mo-mentary shocks were then administered

[2] Miller, N. E., & Davis, M. The influence of the positions of reward and punishment in the response sequence. Personal communica-tion, 1953.

at a distinctively marked section in the middle of the alley. When shock intensity was strengthened gradually on successive trials, the animals continued to dash rapidly down to the end containing food. But when shock was increased suddenly, the phenomenon of continued running did not appear. Seemingly, when the shock was increased in small steps, it acquired a tendency to elicit running rather than stopping. By becoming associated with the approaching response it relinquished its power to act as a drive. On the basis of this evidence, then, it would appear that drive-arousing stimuli tend to become neutralized as they become converted to cues having strong associations with well-integrated, ongoing responses.

A second mechanism of importance in effecting the neutralization of strong stimuli during learning involves the acquisition by such stimuli of secondary reinforcing power. The presumption here is *that stimuli lose their driving potentialities, in part at least, as they acquire the capacity to reinforce antedating responses.* The loud buzz produced by the food-delivery magazine in a Skinner box may at first be drive arousing and disturbing to the naive rat. But after being repeatedly paired with food it gains the capacity to reinforce completely new acts and its manifest driving aspect is reduced.

Keller and Schoenfeld (1950) stress this mechanism in their analysis of human aversions. As has been done here, they note that originally unpleasant stimuli may lose this character and become acceptable, or even sought after, as a consequence of training. This modification of the properties of the stimulus they attribute not to the outweighing of the aversion by a conflicting drive, but to the aversive stimulus' becoming a secondary reinforcement. They apply this interpretation to masochism, as well as to laboratory studies in which electric shocks administered during reinforced bar-pressing trials acquire the capacity to produce a rapid acceleration in response rate during extinction.

Precisely what happens when a stimulus becomes transformed from a drive arouser to a secondary reinforcer is not clear. One interpretation, which is consistent with the drive-reduction view, would stress the kind of response that becomes associated with the stimulus when it acquires its reinforcing power. If that response is capable of interfering with, or reducing the drive condition of the moment, the net effect of the secondary cue will be an actual diminution in drive. Insofar as this holds true, it means that any inherent drive-arousing power of a secondarily reinforcing stimulus diminishes as it achieves the strength to elicit a drive-reducing reaction. An interpretation of this sort has been proposed for the special case of acquired drives by Miller and Dollard (1941). For them, cues can act as learned rewards or secondary reinforcers when they acquire a tendency to inhibit or relax a response that is functioning as a drive. This possibility, that some kind of drive-reduction process underlies the phenomenon of secondary reinforcement, has also been expressed by Mowrer (1951), Osgood (1953), and Farber (1954).

Evidence to support this view comes from diverse sources. Spragg (1940), for example, has shown that the intense drive resulting from the withholding of drugs in addicted monkeys can be temporarily reduced by a hypodermic injection of saline solution. The sight and feel of the needle seem to elicit responses of relaxing that are incompatible with whatever states or reactions characterize the condition of abstinence. Wolff and Goodell (1943) have found that the administration of a placebo falsely described as aspirin can produce an actual increase in a subject's threshold for pain. And Gantt (1948) has observed that anxiety symptoms in neurotic dogs are completely inhibited by sexual stimulation even prior to orgasm.

It thus appears that learning plays a significant part in the "demotivation" of strong stimuli by leading to the formation of close associations between those stimuli and ongoing activities and by building up the capacity of those stimuli to serve as reinforcers.

In addition to the role played by learning, there are at least two innate processes capable of accomplishing the same result, at least temporarily. One of these is the familiar mechanism of *sensory adaptation*. Instances of this are common in the visual and olfactory modalities, but more striking ones are to be found in research on cutaneous pain. Stone and Jenkins (1940), for instance, in a detailed review of such studies, report frequent confirmations of the phenomenon of adaptation to pain. In experiments employing needle algometers, complete pain adaptation was found in approximately 80 to 100 per cent of the instances in which it was studied.

The second innate mechanism may be described, for want of a better label, as *competitive stimulation*. This refers to the fact that the effective strength of pain-arousing stimuli can be weakened by the simultaneous presentation of other stimuli. Hardy and his collabo-

rators (Hardy, Wolff, & Goodell, 1940) state that the pain threshold for one region of the body can be raised as much as 35 per cent by intense stimulation of some other region, a finding confirmed by Parsons and Goetzl (1945). Hebb (1949) also remarks that stimuli normally capable of provoking pain, and hence presumably drive, may fail to do so when combined with other sources of stimulation. Just how widespread the action of this mechanism may be is uncertain, but it is a common observation that pain can often be reduced by tensing the muscles or by gritting the teeth.

These then are some of the qualifying factors which, when incorporated into a definition of stimulus-induced drive, lead to the decision that certain stimuli, even when physically intense, will not have drive-like effects on behavior. Referring back to the arguments of the anti-drive-reductionists, it should now be apparent that many of the supposed paradoxical effects of increased stimulation disappear in the light of these suggestions. A secondary reinforcer does involve an increase in stimulation, but not necessarily an increase in drive, and it may, in fact, evoke responses which actually reduce drive. The laboratory world, as seen from a window in a box, represents heightened stimulation for a monkey though not inevitably heightened drive. The masochist stimulates himself in a manner that could be painful and drive arousing for others, but not for him.

The solution we have proposed to the problems raised by the anti–drive-reductionists may appear to have achieved its goal at some sacrifice of objectivity. To assert that the drive-arousing potential of a stimulus is not necessarily correlated with its physical intensity is to maintain, of course, that certain characteristics of the organism must be listed among the elements of a definition of stimulus-produced drive. It means that a particular stimulus will not be drive arousing if an organism has had specific kinds of learning experiences with it, if his sensory receptors are in such and such a state of adaptation, or if he is being simultaneously titillated by certain other strong stimuli. This requirement, that the specification of stimulus-aroused drive include additional information about the state of the organism and its history, does to be sure, add complexity to the drive problem, but it presents no insurmountable obstacles. Drive states resulting from operations of deprivation are subject to the same kinds of restrictive specifications. A 24-hour period of food privation means one thing if the subject is old and obese, and something different if the subject is young and slender; it means one thing if the subject has been on an ad libitum diet for weeks, and something else if he has recently undergone a prolonged deprivation schedule. Drive level, defined either in terms of deprivation time or stimulation conditions, can be maximally useful only if additional data about an organism's previous experience, momentary states, and responses are taken into consideration.

In the preceding discussion, some of the conditions under which stimuli would *not* be expected to have drive-like effects have been examined in detail. Before concluding, it seems appropriate to consider briefly some instances in which stimuli *would* be expected to exhibit motivating effects. These are cases in which all the requirements of the definition, as amended by state-ments about previous experience, sensory adaptation, and so on, have been satisfied. But to grant that intense stimuli can qualify as contributors to drive level is to raise the original problem with which this discussion began. An admission has been made that responses followed by intense stimulation may be learned or perpetuated, at least when the stimuli are deleted from the category of drives. But can it be admitted that responses may be learned or maintained when their onset is followed by stimuli that cannot be stricken from the class of drives?

Either an affirmative or negative answer can be given to this question, depending on the nature and strength of responses evoked by the stimulus and on the relation between the time of drive increase and the time of occurrence of the response. The discussion of this matter can be conveniently organized with respect to these temporal relations.

Consider first the case where *the stimulus-produced increment to drive does not appear until after a response has terminated.* Here it is obvious that the drive, though genuine, cannot act to energize or intensify the completed reaction. Indeed, if the interval between the response and the stimulus is relatively long, the increment in drive should have no effect upon either the vigor of the behavior or upon the probability of its recurrence. As is well known, long-delayed punishments are quite ineffective as deterrents to the performance of undesirable responses. Moreover, if the onset of the drive is delayed, its reduction must also be postponed, and the effectiveness of any reinforcing power possessed by that reduction will be reduced. It seems unlikely, therefore, that a response will either be learned or unlearned if it is followed after an appreciable time by both an increase and a decrease in drive. The possibility remains, of course, that learning may occur under the special conditions suggested by Miller and Dollard, where the decrease is substantially greater than the increase, and where the temporal interval between response and stimulation reduction is minimal. It is also possible that when the time interval is short, the drive increment may lead to the abandonment of the response. Such a "punishing" effect might be observed when the cues for the completed response are still present and when the drive-arousing stimulus evokes reactions which are incompatible with the completed one.

Finally, let us examine the situation in which *the stimulus-initiated increment to drive is produced while a response is in progress.* Since the response is actually occurring, the tendency to perform it must be greater than that for any other act. If drive is assumed to intensify whatever response is dominant at the moment, it follows that the ongoing reaction, as long as it is dominant, will be facilitated rather than disrupted.

Evidence to support this contention is found in studies by Muenzinger (1934) and Drew (1938), who report that electric shock administered after the choice point facilitates learning, and in Ullman's (1951) experiment in which the rate of food consumption increased if rats were shocked while eating. Similarly, Miller (1948b) found that a momentary shock delivered to rats on the stem of an elevated T maze increased their speed of running and decreased their errors. His rats had been trained to run to food when hungry but were

thoroughly satiated at the time shock was administered.

It thus appears that *a step-up in drive occurring during a response can exert a dynamogenic influence on that response, providing the eliciting cues are exercising a high degree of control over the behavior.* Moreover, this magnifying effect should appear on the very first occasion when the drive is heightened, i.e., before the drive-initiating stimulus has had any opportunity to accumulate either associative connections with the ongoing action or any secondary reinforcing attributes. Any stimulus capable of arousing a drive, however, may also be rich in its own potentialities for eliciting specific movements. If so, its presentation may upset the initial dominance relations among the reaction tendencies, and the response in progress may suffer interference. The anti–drive-reductionists seem to feel that a negative effect of this kind should be predicted by their opponents' theory on every occasion when increased drive occurs during a response.

A drive reductionist can admit, therefore, that genuine drive increments can occur after the initiation of a response and that the response may, nevertheless, persist or even become stronger. And he can admit this without having to abandon his special hypothesis as to the mechanism of reinforcement. He merely asserts that the ongoing behavior should be intensified except when it is overridden by competitive reactions. Though he assumes that a reduction in drive is reinforcing, he need not also assume that an increase in drive, in and of itself, produces an obverse negative effect.

In summary, we have been concerned

in this discussion with some recent criticisms of the drive-reduction hypothesis of reinforcement. Though these criticisms differ in their manifest content, all are grounded in the observation that when a rise in stimulus intensity takes place during a response, or shortly thereafter, the probability that the response will recur does not always become less, and may even grow greater. If an increase in stimulation is alone sufficient to define heightened drive, then this observation constitutes an apparently crucial exception to the drive-reduction view, because the response is first followed by increased drive and only later by its decline. The fact that organisms often behave so as to obtain more stimulation rather than less, or to obtain so-called "pleasant" stimulation, constitutes, in essence, an identical apparent exception to the drive-reduction view.

In seeking to solve this problem, it has been denied that the drive state, if any, resulting from or induced by stimulation can be usefully defined solely in terms of the sheer physical intensity of the stimulus. The definition must be broadened to include such additional factors as amount and kind of previous experience with a stimulus, level of sensory adaptation, and degree and kind of simultaneous stimulation. When this is done, many of the supposed exceptions to the drive-reduction hypothesis are eliminated, since they can no longer be correctly described as involving increases in drive.

But even when all conditions of the modified definition have been met, some stimuli still qualify as drive arousers. The effects of these upon behavior can be coordinated with the drive-reduction view by contending that if they occur at appropriate times they will facilitate rather than disrupt behavior. Instances in which disruption does take place can be attributed to the elicitation of interfering responses by the drive-producing stimuli, and not to any negative motivational attributes inherent in them.

Journal of Abnormal and Social Psychology, 1962, vol. 64, pp. 130–135

The Influence of Hunger on the Learning and Recall of Food Related Words[1]

Seymour Epstein and Herbert Levitt

Despite a number of studies on the steering or directive effects of primary drives[2] on perception, association, and imagination (see, for example, Clark, 1952; Epstein & Smith, 1957; McClelland & Atkinson, 1948; Murray, 1959; Wispé, 1954), not a single such study

[1] This paper was presented, in part, at the American Psychological Association convention in 1958. The study was supported by Grant M–1293 from the National Institute of Mental Health, United States Public Health Service, as part of a project on the measurement of drive and conflict. At the time both authors were at the University of Massachusetts.

[2] Drive throughout this paper is defined as a state of activation with directive properties. For those who prefer to define drive as a state of activation only, the word "motive" could be substituted wherever the word drive appears.

has been reported on learning in humans. As for retention, there are a few studies with humans on the directive influence of acquired drives (Rapaport, 1950a), but none on primary drives.

The present study was undertaken to provide answers to the following questions: Does hunger at time of learning facilitate the learning and retention of words referring to food? Does hunger at time of recall facilitate the recall of words referring to food? Is there an interaction of hunger at time of learning and at time of recall upon recall of words referring to food? Are directive effects of hunger on learning and retention fairly general or do they vary as a function of specific characteristics of the stimulus?

A problem in working with the hunger drive in the laboratory is that if relatively high states of drive are to be obtained it is necessary to require abstinence from eating, which produces set effects that have been demonstrated to exert an influence as great as, or greater than, drive effects (Clarke & Epstein, 1957; Postman & Crutchfield, 1952; Taylor, 1956). Fortunately, several studies working within the normal food cycle have demonstrated directive effects of drive as a function of 4–6 hours of deprivation (Epstein & Smith, 1956; Lazarus, Yousem, & Arenberg, 1953; Postman & Crutchfield, 1952; Sanford, 1936, 1937).

Method

Subjects

Sixty subjects, paid at the rate of $1.00 per hour, were enlisted from four fraternities at the University of Massachusetts. Subjects were randomly assigned to four equal groups according to a 2 × 2 factorial design of hunger at time of learning and hunger at time of memory. Fifteen subjects

were hungry at learning but not hungry at recall, 15 were hungry at both learning and recall, 15 were not hungry at learning but were at recall, and 15 were neither hungry at learning nor recall. Hungry subjects were obtained by testing at 5:00 P.M., before the evening meal, and control subjects by testing at 6:30 P.M., after the evening meal. The group that was not hungry at learning and hungry at recall had a 23-hour memory interval, whereas the group that was hungry at learning and not hungry at recall had a 25-hour memory interval. Although the difference of 2 hours might be expected to influence total recall, there was no reason to believe it would influence selective recall, and, as it turned out, total recall was unaffected.

Procedure

For the learning session, a paired-associates list containing food words and control words was presented in four different random orders by a modification of a group method described by Saltz and Myers (1955). Standard instructions for learning paired associates were given, and subjects were required to raise their hands after reaching the criterion of one trial without error for the entire list. In order to reduce temptation to misrepresent, an appeal to honesty was made, and subjects were told they would have to remain for the entire session no matter when they were finished. Moreover, as each trial was represented by a separate page, cheating would have required turning pages, which could have been detected by the experimenter. In order to prevent overlearning for the more rapid learners, subjects were required to work on an anagrams task following completion of the learning task. From all observations it was evident that the instructions were adhered to. On the day following learning, three measures of memory were obtained. First the subject wrote down all the single words he recalled from the previous day, treating stimulus and response words independently. Next, the subject was given a test of recognition in which correct and incorrect words were included. Finally, a measure of relearning was obtained. The last two measures were discarded when it was found that scores were uniformly so high that there was not sufficient variance left to investigate.

Paired-associates list

The words to be learned consisted of 12 paired associates subdivided according to food relatedness and associative strength. High associative (HA) pairs consisted of a stimulus member paired with the word most often given to it in a preliminary word association test administered to 100 subjects from a comparable population. Low associative strength (LA) pairs consisted of a stimulus member paired with a word which it had never elicited as a response. There were four paired associates in which both members were food words—FRUIT-APPLE (HA), CHEESE-CRACKER (HA), WAFFLE-STEAK (LA), and CAKE-HAM (LA); four pairs in which both members were control words—CARPET-RUG (HA), LAMP-LIGHT (HA), ROOM-SOFA (LA), BED-WINDOW (LA); and four pairs in which one of the members was a food word and the other a control word, with order counterbalanced—EGG-STAIR (LA), STEW-CEILING (LA), HOUSE-BUT-TER (LA), and SCREEN-POTATO (LA). The control words were related to home objects in order to partly control for the uniform concept formed by the food words. The pairs that contained words from both concepts, henceforth referred to as the "mixed" category, were necessarily of low associative strength, resulting in an overall design that was not balanced, but from which balanced designs could be extracted.

Results

Learning

Scores consisted of the first trial at which two successive correct anticipations occurred. The data were first treated by an analysis of variance in a three-dimensional design of hunger at time of learning, food relevance of paired associates, and associative strength of paired associates, each represented at two levels. The four paired associates involving mixed concepts were not included in this analysis as

they did not occur at the level of high associative strength. In Table 1 it can be seen that hunger is significant as a main effect (.05 level). The hungry group learned words across classifications in fewer trials than the control group. However, there is no support for differential learning of pairs of food words and pairs of control words as a function of hunger (see sources of variance F × H and A × F × H). The remaining sources of variance, which are of only incidental interest, show that pairs of high associative strength were learned more rapidly than pairs of low associative strength (.01 level), and pairs of food words were learned more rapidly than pairs of control words (.01 level). There are significant differences (.01 level) between individual words

TABLE 1

ANALYSIS OF VARIANCE OF TRIALS TO CRITERION AS A FUNCTION OF HUNGER, ASSOCIATIVE STRENGTH, AND FOOD RELEVANCE

Source of variance	df	MS	F
Total between	59		
Hunger (H)	1	36.85	4.50*
Individual subjects (Ss)	58	8.19[a]	
Total within	420		
Associative strength (A)	1	531.30	116.77**
A × H	1	16.50	3.63
A × Ss	58	4.55[a]	
Food relevance (F)	1	107.35	41.61**
F × H	1	.61	—
F × Ss	58	2.58[a]	
A × F	1	55.36	21.13**
A × F × H	1	2.84	1.08
A × F × Ss	58	2.62[a]	
Words within categories (W)	4	23.14	8.67**
W × H	4	4.93	1.85
W × Ss	232	2.67[a]	
Total	479		

[a] Error term for the mean squares listed above it up to the next error term.
* Significant at .05 level.
** Significant at .01 level.

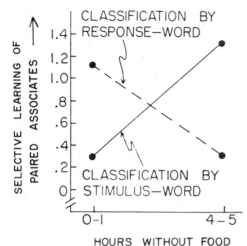

SELECTIVE LEARNING OF PAIRED ASSOCIATES →

CLASSIFICATION BY RESPONSE—WORD

CLASSIFICATION BY STIMULUS—WORD

HOURS WITHOUT FOOD

Fig. 1. Selective learning of food related paired associates as a function of whether the food word is a stimulus or response member. (Scores consist of mean trials to criterion for nonfood paired associates minus food paired associates, with food relevance determined independently for stimulus and response members. A high score indicates that food relevant paired associates were learned relatively rapidly.)

cept that the classification by stimulus and response membership replaced the classification by low and high associative strength. It was found that the hungry group learned paired associates relatively more rapidly than the control group when the stimulus member was a food word and less rapidly when the response member was a food word. This can be seen in Figure 1 where mean trials to criterion for control words minus food words is plotted as a function of time without food. (By subtracting food words from control words, rather than the other way around, all values were kept positive, and a high score made to indicate relatively rapid learning of paired associates containing food words.) The mean differences for the hungry and control groups are, re-

within categories, and there is a significant interaction (.01 level) between associative strength and food relevance, with a greater disparity between the learning of pairs of food and control words of low associative strength than between the learning of food and control words of high associative strength.

In a second analysis of the learning data, the mixed pairs, which had not been previously included, were substituted for the pairs of high associative strength, thereby producing an orthogonal arrangement according to whether a word was a stimulus member or a response member and a food word or a control word. Thus, the following combinations of words were represented in the paired associates: food-food, food-control, control-food, and control-control. The analysis of variance was identical to the preceding analysis ex-

TABLE 2

ANALYSIS OF VARIANCE OF TRIALS TO CRITERION AS A FUNCTION OF HUNGER AND FOOD RELEVANCE OF STIMULUS AND RESPONSE MEMBERS

Source of variance	df	MS	F
Total between	59		
Hunger (H)	1	76.40	2.56
Individual subjects (Ss)	58	29.81	
Total within	420		
Stimulus relevance (S$_r$)	1	76.40	12.67**
H × S$_r$	1	32.68	5.41*
Ss × S$_r$	58	6.03ᵃ	1.29
Response relevance (R$_r$)	1	57.86	14.57**
H × R$_r$	1	18.48	4.65*
Ss × R$_r$	58	3.97ᵃ	
S$_r$ × R$_r$	1	129.64	21.72**
H × S$_r$ × R$_r$	1	1.40	—
Ss × S$_r$ × R$_r$	58	5.97ᵃ	1.28
Individual words (W)	4	39.41	33.83
H × W	4	23.73	5.09**
Ss × W	232	4.66ᵃ	
Total	479		

ᵃ Error term for the mean squares listed above it up to the next error term.
* Significant at .05 level.
** Significant at .01 level.

spectively, 0.29 and 1.37 for classification by stimulus word and 1.12 and 0.31 for classification by response word. The analysis of variance indicates that both effects are significant at the .05 level (see Table 2, sources of variance $H \times S_r$ and $H \times R_r$). However the significant interaction of hunger and words within categories (see source of variance $H \times W$) indicates that the findings may be a result of the particular words selected, and that verification with a different set of paired associates is required.

Recall. Recall was analyzed by an analysis of variance for the variables of hunger at learning, hunger at recall, food relevance of the word recalled, and associative strength, with the mixed category treated as an additional level of associative strength. Scores were the number of words recalled within each of the six classifications formed by the two levels of food relevance and the three levels of associative strength. There were 14 entries rather than 16 for each condition, as 2 subjects failed to appear for the recall session.

In Table 3 it can be seen that there is a significant interaction (.01 level) for the variables of hunger at learning, hunger at recall, and food relevance of the word recalled. In Figure 2 it is apparent that the reason for the interaction is that an increase in recall of food words as a function of hunger at recall occurs only when the groups not hungry at learning are compared. If only subjects not hungry at learning are considered, the mean number of food words minus control words recalled is −1.79 for the condition of not hungry at recall, and 0.93 for the condition of hungry at recall. In contrast, when the same comparison is made for subjects who learned when hungry, the relative

TABLE 3

ANALYSIS OF VARIANCE OF NUMBER OF WORDS RECALLED AS A FUNCTION OF HUNGER AT TIME OF LEARNING, HUNGER AT TIME OF RECALL, ASSOCIATIVE STRENGTH, AND FOOD RELEVANCE

Source of variance	df	MS	F
Total between	55		
Hunger at learning (H_l)	1	.76	—
Hunger at recall (H_r)	1	.10	—
$H_l \times H_r$	1	1.45	1.02
Individual subjects (Ss)	52	1.41ª	
Total within	280		
Associative strength (A)	2	16.75	12.50**
$A \times H_l$	2	.08	—
$A \times H_r$	2	.25	—
$A \times H_l \times H_r$	2	3.18	2.37
$A \times Ss$	104	1.34ª	
Food relevance (F)	1	.29	
$F \times H_l$	1	.30	—
$F \times H_r$	1	2.35	2.67
$F \times H_l \times H_r$	1	8.03	9.12**
$F \times Ss$	52	.88ª	
$A \times F$	2	11.76	8.98**
$A \times F \times H_l$	2	4.15	3.17*
$A \times F \times H_r$	2	2.36	1.80
$A \times F \times H_l \times H_r$	2	.95	—
$A \times F \times Ss$	104	1.31ª	
Total	335		

ª Error term for the mean squares listed above it up to the next error term.
* Significant at .05 level.
** Significant at .01 level.

recall of food words varies little as a function of hunger at recall, with mean differences, respectively, of 0.43 and −0.29 for the not hungry and hungry conditions. It is of interest that neither hunger at learning nor at recall approaches significance for total words recalled. Apparently, hunger decreases recall of control words to about the same extent that it increases recall of food words.

There is a significant interaction for the variables of hunger at learning, food relevance, and associative strength

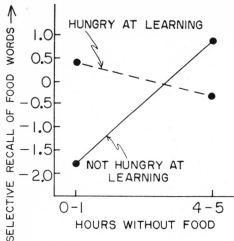

Fig. 2. Selective recall of food words as a function of hunger state during recall. (Scores consist of number of food words minus nonfood words recalled.)

(.05 level). In Figure 3 it can be seen that the relationship is a direct one for hunger at time of learning and relative recall of food words for the food words which had previously been presented in high associative strength pairs, and an inverse one for the food words pre-

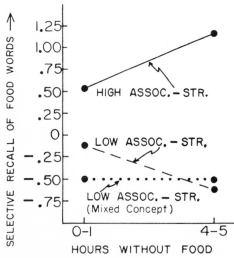

Fig. 3. Selective recall of food words as a function of hunger at learning and associative strength of the paired associates presented in the learning session. (Scores consist of number of food words minus nonfood words recalled.)

sented in low associative strength pairs. No relationship between relative recall of food words and hunger at recall is indicated for food words of low associative strength presented in mixed concepts.

Discussion

It would seem reasonable to expect that hunger at time of learning would facilitate the learning of food words, that hunger at time of recall would facilitate the recall of food words, and hunger at both times would result in the greatest degree of selective recall. Brown (1953), in a highly relevant discussion of the influence of hunger upon perception states that,

it would not be surprising if the hungry Ss, who possess both the internal cues and the visual cues, should do better than the nonhungry Ss, who possess only the visual cues. On the present view, the hungry group might also be superior to the nonhungry group on nonfood pictures, though their superiority should be less than in the case of the food pictures. Facilitation of performance on nonfood pictures would be attributed to the energizing effects of drive *per se*, not to the presence of hunger stimuli (p. 9).

Assuming that the same principles apply to learning as to perception, the finding of a general facilitating effect of hunger upon learning supports the position illustrated by Brown on the significance of the activating role of drive. However, the results on selective learning and recall appear to be far more complex than would be the case if drive produced cues simply combined with stimulus produced cues to facilitate drive related responses. Several studies on the influence of hunger upon perception and imagination have suggested that associated with every drive state there is a drive oriented autistic process and a reality oriented inhibitory process (Epstein, 1961; Epstein & Smith, 1956; Levine, Chein, & Murphy, 1942; McClelland & Atkinson, 1948; Sanford, 1937; Wispé, 1954). It is possible that the finding of facilitation in learning when the stimulus member is a food word was an example of the autistic process, and that the retardation in learning when the response member was a food word of the inhibitory process. If this is so, it would suggest that drives tend to induce sensitization in perception by inducing set effects or by some other means, and to induce defensiveness in overt response.

In regard to recall, it was found that the directive effect of hunger upon recall depended upon the hunger condition at learning. Only when learning took place in the nonhungry condition was selective recall as a function of hunger at recall demonstrated. This would suggest that drive-produced cues can interfere with as well as facilitate recall of drive related material.

The finding that hunger increased recall of food words without influencing total recall suggests that the directive effects of a drive may function as an attention or set producing phenomenon, i.e., by focusing attention in one direction, attention in other areas is diminished. In this respect, drive-produced set effects differ from other set effects only to the extent that the cues are internal and therefore less likely to be correctly labeled.

The effect of hunger on selective learning was more equivocal than its effect on selective recall. This is not surprising, as recall involves a greater separation from the stimulus than does learning. An increase in memory interval can be viewed in the same manner as an increase in ambiguity, i.e., both factors by reducing the degree to which the response is determined by the stimulus, increase the degree to which motivational and incidental factors play a role.

The finding that hunger during learning resulted in an increase in selective recall of food words of high associative strength but a decrease in recall of food words of low associative strength can be understood by considering the particular combinations of words investigated. High associative strength pairs consisted of combinations, such as CHEESE-CRACKER, which are commonly experienced together during reduction of hunger, while the same does not apply to the low associative strength combinations, such as WAFFLE-STEAK. It is likely that a drive arouses only those associations that have previously been associated with it or with its reduction, rather than all stimuli related to the drive in the individual's cognitive framework.

An obvious limitation in the present study is the very mild state of drive investigated. Coupled with the empirical nature of the study and the unanticipated findings, the need for verifications is apparent. However, it would seem that the "new look" is as appropriate for learning as it is for perception. Apart from theoretical considerations, the directive influence of drives on learning is of considerable practical significance and deserves more experimental attention than it has received.

Summary: The study was undertaken to investigate the influence of hunger on the learning and recall of words related to food. Thirty subjects learned a list of paired associates consisting of all possible combinations of food and nonfood words, immediately before the evening meal.

Thirty other subjects learned the same paired associates immediately after the evening meal. Half of each group was tested for recall the next day before the evening meal, and half after the evening meal. The recall task consisted of writing all the single words that could be remembered from the learning session of the previous day.

The major findings and conclusions were as follows:

1. The group hungry at learning learned more rapidly than the control group.

2. The group hungry at learning demonstrated relative facilitation in the learning of paired associates when the stimulus word was a food word, and relative retardation when the response word was a food word. This was interpreted as indicating that drives tend to induce selective facilitation in perception but inhibition in response for drive related material.

3. There was an interaction of hunger condition at learning and at recall upon selective recall of food words. Only when comparison was between the groups who were not hungry during learning was hunger during recall found to be directly associated with selective recall of food words. It was concluded that drive produced cues interfere with as well as facilitate recall of drive related material.

4. Increased recall of food words as a function of hunger occurred at the expense of a decrease in recall of control words. It was suggested that drive creates a selective set for drive related materials and consequent inattention to other material.

5. The group hungry at learning exhibited greater selective recall of food words presented in high associative strength pairs and less selective recall of food words presented in low associative strength pairs than the group not hungry during learning. It was concluded that drive tends to activate associations of stimuli that have been present during arousal or reduction of the drive, rather than of all stimuli related to the drive in the individual's cognitive framework.

Science, June 10, 1960, vol. 131, pp. 1735–1736.

William Kessen, Gregory A. Kimble, and Beverly M. Hillmann

Effects of Deprivation and Scheduling on Water Intake in the White Rat[*][1]

Miller (1957) has recently pointed out that different measures of what is held to be a unitary process—for example, the drive state of thirst—on occasion show rather wide variation one from another. The present report advances evidence that such variation occurs not only when different classes of behavior are observed as operational measures of the same drive, but also under circumstances where a single indicator varies with changes in laboratory routines.

In the first study, five albino rats of the Wistar strain were kept in individual cages in a darkened room over a period of several months. For the first 5 weeks of the study, the animals were permitted access to water for 1 hour a day (23-hour deprivation schedule); at the end of this period a series of depri-

[*] Reprinted from *Science* by permission. Copyright © 1960 by the AAAS.
[1] The research reported here was carried out in the psychology laboratories of Brown University, under the direction of Gregory A. Kimble.

vation tests was begun which extended over a period of 8 weeks (schedule condition). Two observations of drinking during a test period of 1 hour were made after deprivation of 4, 21, 22, 25, 26, and 30 hours, and one observation was made after 0 and one after 47 hours of deprivation. During this time, food was freely available to the animals, and, on days when a test was not scheduled, the animals drank at the usual 23-hour deprivation interval.

When these observations were completed, the animals were returned to free access to water as well as to food for 3 weeks, after which drinking tests were run at the same deprivation intervals used in the schedule condition. In this case, however, the animals were deprived of water *only* during the test interval (free access condition).

The results of the study are shown in Fig. 1. For animals on a free access base line, there is a relatively regular relation between deprivation interval and amount drunk. Intake in this condition shows a statistically significant increase between 0 and 4 hours of deprivation ($p < .05$), and between 4 hours

of deprivation and all other intervals ($p < .01$), but there is no significant variation among deprivation intervals of 21, 23, 25, 26, and 30 hours. On the other hand, the amount drunk from a schedule base line shows a striking inflection near the deprivation interval associated with scheduled drinking. This inflection is sharp enough to produce statistically significant differences in intake between 21- and 22-hour deprivation, between 22- and 25-hour deprivation, and between 25- and 30-hour deprivation (all differences at $p < .01$). It is interesting, too, to note that, although a significant increase in intake occurs between 0- and 4-hour deprivation in the schedule condition, there is a nonsignificant *drop* in intake between 4- and 21-hour deprivation.

Scheduling of drinking on a once-a-day cycle seems to have the effect of reducing differences in intake between some relatively short period of deprivation (in this case, 4 hours) and longer periods up to the deprivation interval associated with scheduled drinking, and then of producing a sharp rise in intake at deprivation intervals longer than the

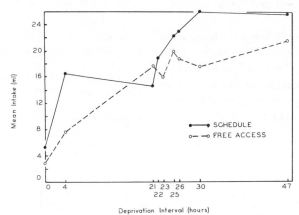

Fig. 1. Amount of water drunk during a test period of 1 hour following water deprivation of varying intervals for animals with free access to water and for animals with access to water limited to 1 hour a day.

one normally associated with scheduled drinking.

A second study was run in order to make a closer examination of intake at the lower end of the deprivation range. Ten albino Wistars were studied, five with free access to water at all times other than test intervals and five under 23-hour scheduled deprivation. Tests of water intake were run at 0, 1, 2½, 4, 5, 6, and 12 hours of water deprivation. In this study, the results of which are shown in Fig. 2, intake over the first 10 minutes of the test hour was analyzed because it had been shown that intake during the shorter period adequately represented intake over the entire hour.

It should be noted in Fig. 2 that, as the first study suggested, the rise of intake with deprivation appears to be sharper in the scheduled group than in the free access group. For example, intake for the schedule group was significantly different ($p < .01$) between the lower deprivation intervals (1- and 2½-hour) and the higher intervals (6- and 12-hour). The rise of intake in the free access group, although regular, did not reach conventional levels of statistical significance.

These studies confirm the observation of earlier workers (Horenstein, 1951; Koch & Daniels, 1945; Saltzman & Koch, 1949) that a sharp rise in consummatory behavior takes place between 0 and 4 to 6 hours of deprivation, but they also

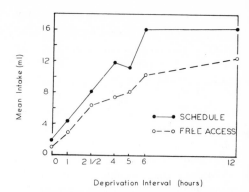

Deprivation Interval (hours)

Fig. 2. Amount of water drunk during a test period of 10 minutes following water deprivation of varying intervals for animals with free access to water and for animals with access to water limited to 1 hour a day.

suggest that part of this effect may be ascribable to the influence of caretaking schedules. Animals which have been "trained" to drink every 24 hours will show distortions of intake when compared with animals tested from a base line of free access to water. These distortions suggest caution in the use of hours of deprivation as a simple index of "thirst" and lend support to Miller's conclusions (1957; see also Mandler, 1957) about the complexity of drive measures in general.

Summary: Two studies are presented to demonstrate that the consummatory behavior of drinking in the rat is under the control of duration of water deprivation and that intake after deprivation is related to variation in the scheduling of the animals' opportunities for drinking.

Journal of Experimental Psychology, 1949, vol. 39, pp. 747–759

The Role of Fear in the Motivation and Acquisition of Responses[1]

Judson S. Brown and Alfred Jacobs

An important concept in a number of current theories of behavior is that the emotion of fear is (usually) a learned, anticipatory response to painful stimulation and that its significance as a behavior-determinant lies primarily in its motivational properties. The assumption that fear is a learned response stems from the fact that it can be elicited by (conditioned) stimuli which in the past have been closely associated with, or have been followed by, noxious (unconditioned) stimuli. The additional assumption that fear is (or produces) a drive, rests on the assertion that it exhibits certain of the major functional properties commonly attributed to primary drives such as hunger. Specifically, (1) the presence of fear is said to energize or motivate behavior, and (2) a reduction in fear is said to act as a reinforcement for the acquisition of new responses. Since the fear reaction is learned, the resulting drive is termed secondary or acquired to distinguish it from primary drives whose antecedent conditions are un-

like those typically observed in learning situations.

This conception, which is essentially a translation of certain Freudian (1936) ideas into stimulus-response terms, was first proposed by Mowrer (1939). Subsequently, he and others have applied the notion to the interpretation of a variety of behaviors and have carried out a number of experiments tending to support the hypothesis (Farber, 1948; May, 1948; Miller & Dollard, 1941; Mowrer, 1940; Mowrer & Lamoreaux, 1946a), which apparently provides the most convincing confirmatory evidence, forms the point of departure for the present investigation.

The procedure employed by Miller may be summarized briefly as follows. The apparatus consisted of an oblong box, divided by a sliding door into two compartments, one white with a grid floor, the other black with a smooth floor. During preliminary training trials, rats were allowed to escape a shock in the white compartment by running into the black, the door being open. On subsequent learning trials, the animals were placed in the white side with the door closed, but with no shock on the grid. If an animal made the 'correct' response of turning a small wheel (located over the door) within 100 sec., the door dropped and

[1] The second of the two experiments reported herein has been previously described in a paper presented by the second author at the 1948 meeting of the Midwestern Psychological Association. The authors are indebted to Dr. I. E. Farber for a careful reading of the manuscript and for numerous stimulating suggestions made during the course of the experiments.

the rat could escape into the black compartment. If the response was not made within the allotted time, the animal was lifted out of the box to await its next trial. The results obtained on the learning trials indicated clearly that if the wheel-turning response occurred a few times early in the series it was then rapidly learned, apparently being reinforced by the reduction in fear accompanying escape into the black compartment. Thirteen out of 25 animals showed clear-cut evidence of learning the new response. On subsequent trials, when the wheel-turning response was made 'incorrect' for these 13 rats, it extinguished rapidly, and a new 'correct' response of pressing a bar to open the door was readily learned. Since no shock was administered on any of the learning trials, the results were interpreted as indicating that the fear aroused by the stimuli from the white compartment provided a drive which led to random activity and hence to the initial correct responses, and that the reduction in fear accompanying escape from the white box operated to reinforce the wheel-turning and bar-pressing responses.

Although Miller's interpretation of his results in terms of fear and its reduction appears quite plausible, there are other interpretations that merit consideration. One alternative is to assume that frustration, not fear, is the important drive in the situation and hence that frustration-reduction is the significant reinforcing event. According to this hypothesis, the interrupting or blocking of any strong, on-going response produces a state of frustration or anger which functions as a drive. In Miller's experiment, the response which was blocked was that of running from the white box into the black, a response

which had been powerfully reinforced by shock-reduction during the training trials. On the learning trials, when this response was prevented from occurring by the closed door, the hypothetical frustration drive might well have been aroused. This drive, like that of fear, could lead to the appearance of varied activity and, eventually, to the correct response of turning the wheel. Since the opening of the door would permit the resumption of the running response, there would follow an almost immediate reduction in frustration. As a consequence, the tendency to perform the wheel-turning response would be strengthened by this decrease in drive.

The two experiments reported herein were designed to control for this possible frustration factor by eliminating the locomotor response from the initial training situation. The general procedure employed in both studies involved a number of training trials during which rats were placed in an oblong box and given paired presentations of a neutral (conditioned) stimulus and an electric shock. On subsequent learning trials, the conditioned stimulus was presented without shock and an opportunity was provided for the animals to execute a new response of crossing from one side of the box to the other by jumping over a barrier. If the barrier-crossing response occurred, the conditioned stimulus was immediately terminated. Learning was estimated from the latencies of the barrier-crossing responses. In the case of both experiments it was assumed that: (1) the pairing of the neutral stimulus and the shock would result in the development of a conditioned fear response; (3) the presence of fear would lead to varied responses, including that of crossing the barrier; and (3) the barrier-jumping reaction would be reinforced by the cessation of the conditioned stimulus and the consequent reduction in fear. It was also assumed that, since no specific escape response was reinforced by shock-reduction during training, the possibility of arousing frustration during the subsequent learning trials would be negligible. The two experiments differed with respect to certain details such as number of training trials, nature of the conditioned stimulus, and so on. These variations led to certain differences in the results which are believed to be of importance for interpretations of fear-motivated behavior.

Experiment 1

Apparatus

The apparatus consisted of an oblong box 14 in. long, 5 in. wide, and 5 in. deep (inside dimensions), painted flat black and provided with a grid floor. The grid was constructed of $\frac{3}{32}$-in. brass rods, spaced at intervals of $\frac{7}{16}$ in. The lid of the box was constructed by tacking celluloid to a light wooden frame hinged to the upper edge of the box. A removable barrier extended two in. above the grid floor when in position.

The shocking current was obtained from a 75,000-ohm potentiometer wired as a voltage divider across the 500-volt secondary of a conventional radio power transformer. The voltage was applied to the grid through a fixed resistor of 0.3 megohm. The shock-voltage values given below represent readings from a 2000-ohm-per-volt a.c. voltmeter connected across the output leads of the potentiometer at all times.

The conditioned stimulus was the sound produced by a high-frequency buzzer (Speedex Type) operating on six volts a.c. The latencies of the barrier-crossing responses were measured with a stop-watch from the onset of the conditioned stimulus until an animal had crossed completely over the barrier.

The room was in almost complete darkness save for the illumination provided by a 10-watt lamp suspended about 18 in. directly above the center of the box.

Subjects

Two groups of 10 rats, each consisting of eight hooded females and two albino males approximately 100 days old, were used as Ss. Within each sex the animals were assigned to the two groups at random.

Training Procedure

The procedure followed during training was designed to produce a conditioned fear response in the animals of the experimental group, but not in those of the control group. Each animal of the fear group was placed in the apparatus (with barrier absent) and given 40 paired presentations of buzzer and shock, 10 per day for four succeessive days. The buzzer was sounded for either 2, 3, or 4 sec. before the shock and continued to sound with the shock for either 3, 4, or 5 sec. Individual trials were spaced at intervals of either 4, 5, or 6 min. The durations of buzzer, buzzer with shock, and inter-trial interval were selected at random from the above ranges and the same sequence was administered to all animals. At the conclusion of each day's training, each animal was left in the apparatus for 10 min. before being returned to its home cage. The shocks were 160 volts for the females and 180–200 volts for the larger males. Food and water were present at all times in the home cages. The animals in the control group were trained in exactly the same manner as were those in the experimental group, except that *no shocks were given the controls at any time.*

Testing Procedure

The two-in. barrier was introduced into the center of the box and each animal was given 40 learning trials, 10 on each of four successive days. On each learning trial, an animal was placed in the box and the buzzer was sounded *but no shock was presented.* When the rat jumped the hurdle, the buzzer was immediately turned off. On the first day, successive trials were given at five-min. intervals. If a response had not occurred by the end of a continuous three-min. sounding of the buzzer, the buzzer was turned off and two min. were allowed to pass before the next trial. On Days 2, 3, and 4, the trials were run at four-min. intervals, the buzzer being turned off when the response was completed, or after an interval of two min. if no response occurred. The initial trial of the first day was given five min. after an animal was placed in the box; on the other days the interval preceding the first trial was three min. As in the case of the training procedure, the animals were returned to their cages 10 min. after the last trial of a day. The control and experimental animals were treated in an identical manner throughout the learning session.

Results

The outcome of the procedure followed in Experiment 1 is summarized in Table 1 where the mean log latencies (plus a constant of 1.0) for successive blocks of five learning trials have been listed for both the experimental and the control groups. These values have also been plotted in Fig. 1. The individual response latencies (in sec.) were transformed into logarithms in order to normalize the data for statistical treatment. The constant was added so that the values obtained here could be plotted to the same scale as those in the second experiment where a constant was added to avoid negative logarithms.

An examination of these statistics shows that the experimental animals exhibited a progressive decrease in the latency of the barrier-crossing response with successive non-shock trials. All but one of the experimental animals learned the new response with a fair degree of

promptness. The one that did not learn made only one barrier-crossing response during the 40 test trials. The scores for this animal have not been included in the treatment of the data. That the decrease in latency shown by the group as a whole can scarcely be attributed to chance is indicated by the highly significant value of *t* obtained from a comparison of the means of the first and the last five trials of this group. This *t*-value is the first shown in Table 2. By comparison, the control animals (not shocked during training) showed no progressive decrease in latency during

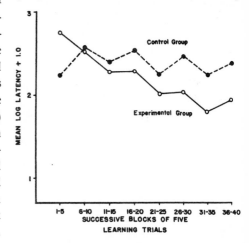

Fig. 1. Latencies of barrier-crossing responses made by the experimental and control animals on successive blocks of five learning trials. The experimental animals were presumably fearful and show evidence of improved performance with fear-reduction as the reinforcement for the new response. The non-fearful controls show no improvement. These curves were plotted from the values listed in Table 1.

TABLE 1

MEAN LOG LATENCIES (PLUS 1.0) FOR SUCCESSIVE BLOCKS OF FIVE LEARNING TRIALS

	Trials							
	1–5	*6–10*	*11–15*	*16–20*	*21–25*	*26–30*	*31–35*	*36–40*
Control Group	2.23	2.64	2.40	2.52	2.26	2.47	2.30	2.40
Exper. Group	2.75	2.54	2.28	2.29	2.01	2.04	1.81	1.95

TABLE 2

A Summary of Tests of Significance Computed Between Various Means for Both Experimental and Control Animals

Trials or Groups Compared	t	d.f.	P
1. Trials 1–5 vs. 36–40 (Exper.)	5.70	8	<.01
2. Trials 1–5 vs. 36–40 (Cont.)	2.00	9	<.10, >.05
3. Exper. vs. Cont.: Trials 1–5	4.40	17	<.01
4. Exper. vs. Cont.: Trials 36–40	2.97	17	<.01
5. Exper. vs. Cont.: Mean of all trials	1.55	17	<.20, >.10

the course of the learning trials. In fact, their mean reaction latency on trials 36–40 was longer than that on trials 1–5, although the difference is not significant, as may be seen from the second entry in Table 2.

It is important to note, however, that although the fear-group animals showed clear evidence of learning the new response and were significantly faster than the controls on the last five trials (fourth entry, Table 2), they were significantly slower than the controls on the first five trials (third entry in Table 2). As a result of this reversal in the relative proficiencies of the two groups, a statistical comparison of the *over-all means* of the two groups does not lead to the rejection of the null hypothesis (last value in Table 2).

One feature of the data that is of interest is the cyclic fluctuations in latency exhibited by both the control and experimental animals (Fig. 1). In the case of the controls, the mean latencies were longer on the last five trials of each day than on the first five. This suggests that exploratory tendencies were undergoing extinction during the course of each day's trials. Consistent with this interpretation is the fact that the controls also had shorter latencies on the first five trials of each of the last three days than on the last five trials of each preceding day. Conceivably, this reflects the spontaneous recovery of the

extinguished exploratory tendencies.

The cyclic fluctuations shown by the experimental animals were limited to the last three days of testing (trials 11–40) and were less marked than those of the controls. These might also be attributed to the extinction and spontaneous recovery of exploratory behavior on the assumption that the exploratory tendencies were superimposed upon the gradually developing tendency to cross the barrier in response to the buzzer. It is quite possible, however, that processes of extinction and spontaneous recovery were actually taking place in the case of either the jumping response or the fear response, or both.

Discussion

The major objective of the present study was to determine whether the rewarding and energizing functions commonly attributed to fear, but also ascribable in special cases to a drive resulting from the frustration of a locomotor response, would be exhibited under conditions unfavorable to the development of frustration. Since, in this experiment, clear evidence of learning was obtained under such conditions, it may be concluded that the *rewarding function* of fear-reduction receives additional experimental support, and that frustration, at least of the hypothesized variety, is apparently not an essential element.

It has been shown that the cessation of a normally neutral stimulus, after that stimulus has been repeatedly presented with a noxious one, acquires the property of strengthening new stimulus-response connections. In accounting for this empirical fact, it may be assumed that the pairing of the two stimuli results in the neutral one's becoming a conditioned stimulus which evokes a fear reaction. This reaction, which may be a fractional anticipatory component of the unconditioned response to the noxious stimulus, is presumed, perhaps by virtue of the stimulation it provides (Miller & Dollard, 1941), to add an increment to the general drive level of the animal. As a consequence, any new reaction occurring in close temporal proximity to the cessation of the fear response and the consequent drive reduction will be reinforced.

With respect to the *energizing function* of fear, it must be concluded that the present experiment yields no direct evidence that fear leads inevitably to an increase in random or exploratory movements. If such were the case, one would anticipate that the *initial* barrier-crossing responses of the fearful (experimental) animals would have been quicker than those of the controls, since on the first few trials, before any appreciable learning had occurred, the response latencies should reflect rather directly the tendency to make random movements. This expectation is not confirmed by the data. On the first trial, for example, the fearful animals were much slower than the controls, the mean log latencies for the two groups being 2.71 and 1.88 sec., respectively. And even at the end of the first five trials when the mean latency for

the controls had risen to 2.23 sec. (five trials combined) the fearful group was still significantly inferior to the controls.

From qualitative observations of the behavior of our animals it seems probable that the initial response latencies of the experimental rats were long because these animals were more prone to 'freeze' or crouch than were the nonfearful ones. In some instances, the fearful rats were fairly active when first placed into the apparatus but would immediately become immobile when the buzzer was sounded. It seems likely, therefore, that under the conditions of this study, fear was quite often accompanied by a reduction in random activity instead of by an increase in activity. Confirmatory evidence for these observations is provided by Miller (1948), who reports marked crouching on the part of some of his animals, and by Arnold (1945), who states categorically (though on the basis of only two or three studies) that fear is always accompanied by a reduction in somatic activity.

Although these findings appear to be inconsistent with the hypothesis that fear exhibits the energizing function of a drive, the hypothesis may be retained, provided one abandons the rather limited assumption that drives, when functioning as energizers, always lead to more vigorous overt or random action.[2]

2 It should be noted that although both Mowrer and Miller have, in general, restricted their treatments of the energizing function of fear to its role as a motivator of so-called random or trial-and-error behavior, neither of them has apparently held the view that random activity is the only variety of response that will be exhibited when the drive of fear is present. Such a view, however, of the energizing action of drives is rather commonly expressed in introductory treatments of motivation (see, e.g., Shaffer, 1936, p. 89).

Thus, it may be supposed, as Hull (1943) does, that the generalized drive state (D), to which all of the specific drives or needs contribute, combines in a multiplicative manner with the habit values of both learned and innate responses ($_sH_R$'s and $_sU_R$'s). Other things equal, the response which occurs is that having the strongest habit, irrespective of the specific drives which are the major contributors to the strength of D. If crouching is exhibited instead of random activity, then the strength of the crouching habit must be greater than that for random action, and the stronger the drive, the more intense the crouching will be. According to this conception, then, *the presence of fear may act as an energizer (by virtue of its contribution to D) and yet lead in certain instances to an increase in immobility.*

The question remains, of course, as to why the habit of crouching should be strong for fearful animals but not for non-fearful ones, or for ones highly motivated by hunger, thirst, etc. One answer, suggested by Miller (1948), is that crouching occupies a dominant position in the hierarchy of innate responses to the stimuli accompanying (or arising from) fear. Hungry animals do not crouch because hunger-produced stimuli are different from fear-produced stimuli and are not innately associated with responses of immobility.

It is also possible that crouching is *learned* during the shock trials, and that it becomes conditioned to the fear stimuli, as well as to stimuli provided by the shock and the apparatus. Crouching or freezing would certainly be reinforced if they occurred at the time the shock was turned off or if they led in some way to either a complete or partial reduction of shock.[3] Although no systematic observations were made of such behavior, the impression is strong that the initial reactions of the animals to shock were almost always ones of rather violent action. Immobility reactions never became dominant until after a number of shock trials had been administered. Similar observations of the learning of immobile reactions to escape shock have been made by Mowrer (1940). We would conclude tentatively, therefore, that responses of crouching or standing still may well have been acquired during the course of the training trials in our experiment, and that in all probability these responses were conditioned to both external and internal stimuli by the reinforcing effect of reductions in shock intensity.[4]

[3] A reduction in shock intensity would result if an animal's position led to an increase in contact area and a decrease in current density through the tissues of its feet. Or, complete elimination of shock could be effected by an animal's standing on its hind feet and touching only one side of the shock circuit. When such postures were adopted in this experiment, it was noted that marked increases could be produced in the shock voltage without disturbing the animals. This constitutes objective evidence that the animals were not feeling the shock at those times. On a few occasions it was even necessary to move an animal forcibly into a new position in the apparatus so that further shock trials could be given.

[4] It seems highly probable that, if crouching can be learned as a reaction to fear, animals could also be trained to be exceptionally active in the presence of fear by suitably reinforcing such activity. Confirmatory evidence for this possibility has been obtained in a previous experiment by one of the present authors (Brown, 1948). In that experiment, rats that had been given strong shocks at the end of a short straight alley, and who were therefore presumably quite fearful, exhibited vigorous avoidance responses when placed back into the alley even when no shock was present. In Miller's experiment discussed above, the initial training procedure was also such as to

Although in this experiment the evidence for learning appears to be relatively unambiguous, since the fearful animals were significantly superior to the controls when compared on the last five trials, it is possible that some of the drop in the curve of Fig. 1 for the fear group could have been due to factors other than learning. In particular, the initial fall of the curve, at least to the point where it crosses the control-group curve, might indicate merely that the freezing responses were becoming extinguished and that the level of general activity was increasing. An increase in activity level would be quite likely to lead to shorter response latencies. Thus it was felt that the interpretation of at least the first segment of the curve was difficult and that further experimentation was needed.

Experiment 2

Purpose

The second experiment was conducted to determine whether by modifying the procedure of the first, the degree of freezing exhibited by the fearful rats could be substantially reduced while maintaining fear at a sufficiently high level to enable it to serve in a reinforcing capacity. The changes in procedure were designed to reduce the opportunities for the animals to learn to crouch, and to make conditions more favorable for the learning of the new response. Specifically, the procedure of the second experiment when compared with that of the first

reinforce the tendency of his animals to be active when fearful. Such a tendency might be strengthened (by fear reduction) in the case of those animals that learned to escape, and extinguished in the case of those that failed to learn, thus permitting the crouching response to become dominant in the latter group.

involved (1) a reduction in the number of shock trials, (2) a change from steady shock to pulsating shock, (3) a change in the conditioned stimulus, (4) a modification of the learning procedure, making it unnecessary for the animals to shuttle back and forth in the apparatus, and (5) the introduction of an irrelevant (hunger) drive.

Apparatus

The same basic apparatus described above was used. The box was modified to permit the introduction of a guillotine-type door which extended down through the top at the center and rested directly on the upper edge of the two-in. partition. This served to divide the box into two compartments of equal size and appearance.

Because of noticeable fluctuations in both the frequency and intensity of the buzzer used in Experiment I and because of its somewhat raucous sound, a new conditioned stimulus was introduced. This consisted of a light and tone presented together, both being interrupted 100 times per min. by a commutator on a small synchronous motor. The light was provided by an inside-frosted 10-watt lamp suspended 12 in. above the exact center of the box. The tone, generated by a resistance-capacitance oscillator and fed directly into a five-in. permanent magnet speaker, had a frequency of 2000 cycles and an intensity, measured at the top of the box, of about 70 db. above a reference level of 10^{-16} watts/cm.^{2} This compound stimulus of pulsating light and tone was employed in order to achieve distinctiveness without at the same time increasing intensity to the painful or slightly noxious level. The shock was the same as in Experiment I, except that the circuit was interrupted at the same rate as were the light and tone. This modification was introduced because exploratory work revealed that with intermittent shock there was apparently less chance that the animals would adopt a crouching position which would effectively reduce the shock intensity.

The latency of each response on the learning trials was measured by means of a Standard Electric Timer. The timer was started automatically when the guillotine door was lifted (to allow the animal to cross the barrier) and stopped when the door was lowered following a response.

Subjects

The experimental and control groups each consisted of eight naive albino rats between 60 and 120 days of age. Five of the animals in each group were females, three were males. Within each sex, animals were assigned at random to the two groups.

Training Procedure

The purpose of the training trials, as in Experiment I, was to develop in the experimental animals a conditioned fear response to the tone-light stimulus. These animals received a total of 22 training trials (as contrasted with 40 in Experiment I); 10 trials were given on each of two successive days and two on the third day. The trials were alternated, half of them being administered in one compartment and half in the other. Each trial consisted of a nine-sec. presentation of the conditioned stimulus, with the interrupted shock presented during the last six sec. of the period. Normally, the shock was set at 150 volts, but occasionally it was raised to 180 if an animal showed no signs of receiving the shock. Successive training trials were run at intervals of three min. One min. after a trial, the animal was moved to the opposite compartment where the next trial followed in two min. After the last trials of the first two days, the animals remained in the box for two min. before being returned to their home cages. Two min. after the second trial of the third day, the animals were removed to a carrying cage, where they remained for five min. before being returned to the apparatus for the learning trials.

All animals were run under a 22-hour hunger drive. They were fed in separate feeding cages one hour after the completion of each day's trials. The purpose of the hunger drive was to raise the general activity level of the animals and hence to increase the probability that the desired response of crossing the barrier would occur promptly on the initial learning trials.

The procedure employed in the training of the control animals was identical with that described above for the experimentals, except that the controls were never shocked.

Testing Procedure

On each test (learning) trial an animal was placed in one of the compartments, whereupon the door was lifted and the light-tone stimulus was presented *without shock*. As soon as the response of crossing the hurdle occurred, the light and tone were shut off and the door was lowered. After the lapse of two min., the animal was returned to the first compartment for the next trial. In the event that the barrier-crossing response did not occur within one min., the light-tone stimulus was terminated and the door was lowered, the animals being left in the compartment for an additional min. At the end of this period, they were lifted out of, and immediately replaced in, the same compartment and a new trial was begun. The test trials for both groups were identical, all animals receiving 40 trials, 10 on each of four successive days. The test trials for half of the animals in each group consisted in going *from* the compartment in which they had received their last training trial; the other half went *into* the compartment where the last training trial had been given.

Results and Discussion

The major findings of the second experiment are summarized in Table 3,

TABLE 3

MEAN LOG LATENCIES (PLUS 1.0) FOR SUCCESSIVE BLOCKS OF FIVE LEARNING TRIALS

	Trials							
	1–5	6–10	11–15	16–20	21–25	26–30	31–35	36–40
Control Group	2.09	2.26	2.14	2.35	2.10	2.39	2.19	2.50
Exper. Group	2.02	1.50	1.23	0.94	1.08	1.19	1.10	1.25

TABLE 4

Tests of the Significance of Differences Between Various Means
Obtained from the Experimental and Control Groups

Trials or Groups Compared	t	d.f.	P
1. Trials 1–5 vs. 36–40 (Exper.)	4.48	7	<.01
2. Trials 1–5 vs. 36–40 (Cont.)	6.03	7	<.01
3. Exper. vs. Cont.: Trials 1–5	0.45	14	<.70, >.60
4. Exper. vs. Cont.: Trials 36–40	6.61	14	<.01
5. Exper. vs. Cont.: Mean of all trials	9.06	14	<.01

where the mean log latencies (plus 1.0) for successive blocks of five trials are given. These values are plotted in Fig. 2 to the same scale as that of Fig. 1. The results of tests of significance applied to the data are given in Table 4.

From the curves of Fig. 2, it is apparent that, in broad outline at least, the results of the second experiment parallel and confirm those of the first. All of the eight experimental animals learned the new response, and a comparison of the group means for the first and last blocks of five trials shows that the decrease in latency was highly

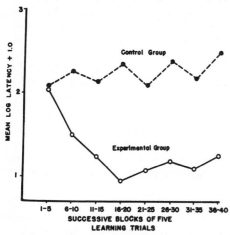

Fig. 2. A graphic presentation of the values listed in Table 3. The resulting curves are comparable to those in Figure 1, and reveal the marked superiority of the fearful experimental animals over the non-fearful controls in the learning of the barrier-crossing response in the second experiment.

significant. The control animals, by contrast, not only showed no improvement in performance, but instead showed a significant decrement. The general thesis concerning the reinforcing effect of fear-reduction thus receives additional experimental support.[5]

When one compares the curves for the two control groups in the first and second experiments, it is seen that they are roughly alike in absolute height and both show similar cyclic fluctuations in latencies with successive blocks of trials. The two curves differ in that the one for the second control group starts at a lower point and ends at a higher point than that for the first group. The fact that the second group

[5] Since the control-group animals were never shocked, there is a possibility that the experimental animals learned to jump the barrier simply to escape from a compartment in which they had been shocked. The response might have been reinforced if, for some obscure reason, the cues of the escaped-into compartment aroused less anxiety than those of the escaped-from compartment. Subsequent to the preparation of this article, an additional control group of eight animals was run to test this possibility. These new animals were trained under precisely the same conditions as were the members of the experimental group in Experiment 2. On the subsequent learning trials, however, both the light-tone stimulus and the shock were omitted. The performance of these animals was quite similar to that of the controls in Experiment 2, no learning being exhibited. The mean log latencies (plus one) for successive blocks of five trials were 2.26, 2.22, 2.24, 2.56, 2.45, 2.52, 2.44, and 2.60.

shows a significant increase in latency may be the result of differences between the two conditioned stimuli. The somewhat raucous buzzer in Experiment 1 could well have been annoying to the animals, and its cessation following a response might have functioned, therefore, as a reinforcing event. Such reinforcement would tend to counteract increases in response latency resulting from the weakening of exploratory tendencies.

A comparison of the two experimental groups reveals that the second showed a marked superiority (shorter latencies) over the first at all stages of learning. Furthermore, the second group differed much more widely from its comparable control group than did the first. Evidently the altered procedures of the second experiment led to more efficient learning. It is impossible, however, to determine from the data just which procedural modifications were primarily responsible for this increase in efficiency.

One feature of interest regarding the curves for the experimental groups is that the animals in the second experiment reached their maximum level of proficiency by the 20th trial and from then on exhibited a fairly progressive decline in performance. This was not the case in the first experiment. Although a statistical comparison of trials 16–20 with trials 36–40 for the second experimental group yielded a nonsignificant t of 1.7, six of the eight animals had longer mean latencies on the later block of trials than on the earlier one. It is possible, therefore, that the barrier-crossing response was becoming extinguished in spite of the reinforcement provided by fear reduction. Such a decrement in performance could occur as the result of the accumulation of fatigue or work inhibition,

even if the level of fear and the reinforcement it provided remained unchanged. But this seems somewhat unlikely, in view of the fact that the response was not especially effortful and the trials were spaced at intervals of a little over two minutes. On the other hand, the decrement in performance could be attributed to a partial extinction of the fear response with a consequent loss in its capacity to provide both an increment to the drive and adequate reinforcement for the jumping response. But if the fear did extinguish, the question immediately arises as to why the reinforcing property attributed to fear-reduction could apparently strengthen the jumping response but not the fear response itself. To our knowledge, there is as yet no completely satisfactory answer to this question; and any attempt to consider the problems which it raises concerning the acquisition and extinction of fear would take us far beyond the intended scope of the present paper.

One of the important outcomes of the second experiment is the manner in which the data bear, though somewhat obliquely, it is admitted, upon the problem of crouching discussed previously. In this regard, it should be noted that the mean scores on the first five-trial block for the experimental and control groups are almost identical, there being no statistical basis for the rejection of the null hypothesis. In the first experiment, however, the experimental group was significantly *inferior* to its comparable control group on the first five trials. Now, if the assumption is made that long response latencies on early trials are indicative of crouching (which was not, of course, measured directly) it follows that the animals in the second experiment crouched less (relative to their own controls) than did those in the first experiment. At first thought it might seem that such a reduction in crouching could be attributed to the fact that the animals in the second study were hungry whereas those in the first were not; but this hypothesis may be rejected on the grounds that both the controls and the experimentals in the second study were tested under the same conditions of food deprivation. More reasonably, it could be argued that the degree of immobility in the second experiment diminished either because the fearful animals were less fearful (they received fewer shocks) or because the experimental conditions (pulsating shock, etc.) were less favorable for the learning of the freezing responses. In any event, it seems fairly certain that the experimental animals in the second study *were fearful,* since they readily acquired the new response when it was followed by the cessation of the fear-arousing conditioned stimulus, and *in spite of the presence of this fear they did not crouch more on the early trials than did their non-fearful controls.* Accordingly, we would surmise that fear is not always accompanied by crouching and that the procedural changes of the second experiment probably acted to diminish crouching by reducing the opportunities for its acquisition.

Finally, it should be pointed out that the lack of a significant difference between the performance of the experimental and control groups on the first five-trial block can be interpreted as indicating not only that fear is not always accompanied by crouching, but also that it does not always lead to an increase in general activity level. As in the case of the first experiment, it can be assumed that the *energizing function* of the acquired drive of fear is to intensify whatever responses are dominant, with both innate and acquired habits or predispositions being the determiners of response dominance. As a consequence, almost any degree of overt activity, ranging from vigorous action to rigid immobility, could be exhibited by fearful animals if the appropriate habits were present.

Summary: 1. Two experiments have been described in which an investigation was made of the assumption that fear functions as a drive to motivate or energize behavior and that fear-reduction serves as a reinforcing event in the learning of new responses. In both studies, the methods employed in establishing the fear reaction and in measuring its reinforcing properties were designed to minimize the possibility of arousing some other emotional state such as frustration or conflict to which the results might be attributed instead of to fear. The two experiments differed with respect to certain details of procedure, the results of which are believed to be of importance in the interpretation of fear-motivated behavior.

2. The general procedure of both studies involved a number of training trials during which rats were placed in an oblong box and given paired presentations of a conditioned stimulus and an electric shock. Control animals received the conditioned stimulus but not the shock. On subsequent learning trials the conditioned stimulus was presented alone to all animals and an opportunity was provided for them to perform a new response of crossing from one side of the box to the other by jumping over a central barrier. When the new response was made, the conditioned stimulus was immediately terminated.

3. The assumptions underlying this procedure were: (a) that the paired presentation of the conditioned stimulus and shock, even though no specific escape response was systematically reinforced, would lead to the development of a conditioned fear reaction elicitable by the conditioned stimulus alone; (b) that the conditioned fear would motivate the behavior of crossing the barrier;

and (c) that the reduction in fear, occasioned by the cessation of the conditioned stimulus following the new response, would act to strengthen the tendency to perform that response.

4. Since in both experiments the fearful animals learned the new response, whereas their comparable controls did not, the conclusion is drawn that fear-reduction functions much like other drive-reductions to reinforce new responses. The data do not indicate, however, that fear, in spite of its apparent drive properties, is necessarily accompanied by an increase in overt activity. Instead, it appears that fear acts to intensify whatever response is dominant at the moment, whether it be a response of crouching or one of a more active variety. Although the determination of response dominance may be a function in part of innate factors, significant changes in the characteristics of the dominant response to fear can apparently occur as the result of learning.

Journal of Experimental Psychology, 1951, vol. 41, pp. 317–328

Conditioned Fear as Revealed by Magnitude of Startle Response to an Auditory Stimulus[1]

Judson S. Brown, Harry I. Kalish, and I. E. Farber

During recent years considerable emphasis has been placed upon the importance of fear or anxiety as a determinant of behavior. According to one interpretation (Miller, 1948; Miller & Dollard, 1941), fear is a conditioned, anticipatory response to impending painful stimulation. This response, it is further assumed, functions as a secondary motivational system and should exhibit, therefore, certain of the major properties commonly ascribed to primary drive states..In particular, (1) fear should act to intensify other response tendencies during the period of its evocation, and (2) it should, if reduced in strength following a response, function as a reinforcing event leading to the strengthening of that response.

1 This study was supported in part by a research grant from the United States Public Health Service covering Research Project MH–2C, entitled *Anxiety and Frustration in Human and Animal Behavior.*

In experimental studies designed to explore this conception, the resulting conclusions have been based almost entirely upon demonstrations of the reinforcing properties of fear reduction (Brown & Jacobs, 1949; Farber, 1948; May, 1948; Miller, 1948a; Mowrer, 1940). Typically, the procedures have been of the following general sort. A period of training is first introduced during which a neutral stimulus (or stimuli) is paired with a noxious one (usually electric shock). The noxious stimulus is presumed to act as a UCS eliciting a pain reaction, and the neutral one is assumed to become the CS. Following the initial training trials, the animal is presented with the CS alone. On the basis of the foregoing assumptions, any response that occurs during the presentation of the CS should be strengthened if it is followed closely by the elimination or diminution of the conditioned (fear-arousing) stimulus. The presence of fear under these conditions is demonstrated by the fact that new responses are learned, and by the fact that old responses (those occurring during the conditioning trials) may show extreme persistence (Farber, 1948) despite the absence of primary reinforcement.

Although the successful clarification of a number of problems has resulted from the use of this fear-reduction method, it suffers from several practical disadvantages. For instance, it is impossible by means of this procedure to determine the latency with which the fear response is aroused following the onset of the CS, or to determine the course of its development during the time the CS is acting. Furthermore, the testing trials, during which the UCS is omitted, may constitute extinction trials insofar as fear is concerned. If the response to be learned is low in initial relative strength, the fear may extinguish before the reaction has occurred frequently enough to become learned. And finally, if the conditions of the testing situation differ markedly from those obtaining during the conditioning trials, the animals may learn rather quickly to differentiate between the conditioning and test trials, i.e., fear may not be elicited in the test situation. This could occur either because the cues present during testing are inadequate to arouse fear or because they elicit responses that inhibit fear.

In view of these limitations of the fear-reduction method, it has appeared desirable to explore other procedures. The present paper reports one such method that appears to hold considerable promise for future investigations in the area of fear in particular and in the field of conditioning in general.

This method is based upon the presumed intensifying or motivating properties of fear rather than upon its reinforcing properties.

On the assumption that fear has drive properties, it follows within the framework of Hull's theory (1943) that stimulus-response tendencies should be enhanced by its presence. It is immaterial whether such tendencies are the result of previous learning or whether they are innate. In theory, if the response being measured is highest in the animal's repertoire (including responses that may accompany fear), that response will occur more frequently and will have a greater amplitude and shorter latency when fear is present than when it is not. Furthermore, the stronger the fear, the more marked should be its effect upon these measurable features of the response.[2]

In the present study, the response selected for measurement was the startle reaction of rats to an explosive auditory stimulus. One of the original bases for choosing the startle response was the frequently heard clinical observation that anxious patients exhibit exaggerated startle reactions to sudden loud sounds. It does not follow from this

[2] It should be noted that these statements are not inconsistent with the observation that an increase in drive does not lead to the indiscriminate strengthening of *every* response. One must consider the nature of the responses that are elicited by the stimuli associated with the drive itself. For instance, Estes and Skinner (1941) have shown that the presence of fear may inhibit bar-pressing, and Miller, Brown, and Lipofsky (cited in Miller, 1944) have shown that under proper conditions, increasing fear strengthens overt avoidance but not approach, whereas increasing hunger strengthens approach but not avoidance. It is only when the drive stimuli do not themselves elicit competing response tendencies that an increase in drive will lead to an intensification of the overt responses ordinarily elicited in a given situation.

alone, of course, that rats will necessarily behave like clinical patients; but if fear has motivational properties in patients as well as in rats, the theory would predict that both would show magnified startle responses when anxious.

In general, the present method involved the use of a stabilimeter-like apparatus capable of recording the magnitude of a rat's jump to a loud sound. In order to demonstrate the utility of the technique, rats were given a series of trials designed to condition the fear reaction, with interspersed test trials to measure the startle response. The training trials were followed by three series of extinction trials. As will be shown below, the startle response was found to increase as a function of the number of fear-conditioning trials, to undergo progressive diminution (extinction) when the UCS was omitted, and to exhibit spontaneous recovery from extinction after an interval of 24 hr.

Apparatus

The apparatus used in recording the startle reactions of the rats was a modified version of a rat stabilimeter previously employed by one of the present authors (Brown, 1939). The basic sensing element was a postage scale (Hanson, Model 1509, 5-lb. capacity) from which the platform, the calibrated dial with its protective glass, and the pointer had been removed. A new platform, 2.75 in. wide and 7.5 in. long, made of .25-in. plywood, was attached to the scale. A grid, constructed of brass welding rods (.094-in. diameter) spaced at .437-in. intervals in bakelite supporting strips, was secured to the platform. A space of .5 in. was provided under the grid to reduce the possibility of its being shorted by feces or urine.

Surmounting the grid was a detachable, bottomless confinement box (2.37 in. wide, 7.37 in. long, 5.5 in. high, inside dimen-

sions). The top and front side were formed of thin Plexiglass, and the two ends and the other side were of thin plywood. The box, the mounting platform with its supporting rod, and the grid weighed a total of 487 gm. When a rat was placed on the grid and the confinement box fastened down around it, any loud sharp sound would produce a startle reaction that would cause the platform to be momentarily depressed below its normal position. These downward movements of the platform were transmitted by means of a thread to an ink-writing muscle lever whose deflections were recorded on a 5-in. tape moving at .53 in. per sec. Prolonged oscillations of the system were prevented by a damping device consisting of a plunger in an oil-filled cylinder. Following an abrupt, extreme displacement, the system would come to rest in two or three cycles. Downward movements of the platform were amplified approximately 16 times, on the average, by the muscle lever which measured 4.53 in. from pivot point to writing tip. The maximum angular deviation of the lever permissible with the 5-in. polygraph was about 31°, which yielded a deflection on the record of 2.36 in. No attempt was made in reading the records to correct for the arc distortion of the stylus or for the nonlinearity introduced at the point where the recording thread was coupled to the stylus. Dynamic tests of over-all reactions of the system to suddenly imposed forces were made by dropping a 50-gm. bag of steel shot from various distances upon the top of the confinement box. On these tests, the platform was loaded with 310 gm. (the mean weight of all rats used in the experiment). These measurements revealed that the relation between the deflection of the recording pen and the fall of the 50-gm. weight was roughly linear within a height-of-fall range of 15 to 200 mm., corresponding to a pen-deflection range of 17 to 50 mm. Above and below these limits, the departures from linearity were rather marked.

The presentation of the CS and UCS was controlled automatically by a group of decade-type, electronic interval-timers (Hunter & Brown, 1949). The CS consisted of the simultaneous activation of a buzzer (Edwards, Model 1872, operated on 6 v. a.c., situated about 2.5 ft. from the confinement box) and a light (60-w. frosted lamp, 6 in. in front of the transparent side of the confinement box). The UCS for the fear reaction was a 60-cycle shock of either 70 or 80 v. (see footnote 3) applied to the grid through a series resistance of 330,000 ohms. The startle stimulus was produced by a toy pistol (Super Nu-Matic Paper Buster Gun) held about 2 ft. from the confinement box. The sound resulting from the "firing" of this gun, which reached the rat primarily through a number of holes drilled in the top of the box, was sufficiently loud and sharp to produce a marked startle reaction, yet not so loud as to require the use of a sound-shielded room. Although the gun was fired manually rather than automatically, the timing error thus introduced was quite small (estimated maximum deviation ±.25 sec.). The E was well practiced and timed his reactions by means of a clock hand making one complete revolution in 10 sec. The exact time at which the startle stimulus occurred was registered on the record by an electromagnetic signal marker. This marker was connected to the output of an amplifier which was activated in turn by a microphone placed near the toy pistol.

Procedure and Subjects

In broad outline, the experimental procedure described below was designed to develop a conditioned fear reaction in an experimental group of animals and to make it possible to determine whether the presence and magnitude of this anxiety state could be inferred from changes in the strength of a startle reaction *which was itself never conditioned during the experiment.*

Initial Tests

Since there appeared to be some possibility that magnitude of startle might be significantly related to body weight, each S was given an initial series of five presentations of the startle stimulus alone on the day preceding the actual emotional conditioning. The product-moment correlation between mean amplitude of startle on these initial tests and body weight was found to be .20 ($N = 30$) for a weight range of 232 to 368 gm. It was concluded, therefore, that body weight, as a significant variable, could

be largely ignored. The variability of the unconditioned reactions to the sound was rather large, however, and it was decided to match the members of the experimental and control groups on the basis of these initial tests of reaction amplitude.

Conditioning and testing procedure

On each of the four days following the initial test day Ss of the experimental group were given a series of 10 trials, seven of which were conditioning trials. On all conditioning trials, the light-buzzer CS was presented for 5 sec., with the UCS (shock) being presented for the last 2 sec. of this period.[3] This procedure was based on the assumption that the pairing of the light-buzzer combination and shock (even though no overt response was systematically reinforced) would lend to the arousal of an anticipating fear reaction which would reach its greatest intensity at about the time the shock was normally applied. The other three trials (trials 4, 7, and 10) were tests on which the CS was presented as usual but with the startle stimulus introduced 3 sec. after the onset of the CS *in place of the shock.* The heights of all jumps to these startle stimuli were recorded. These test trials were, of course, the critical trials introduced to determine the possible facilitative effect of fear upon startle. Successive trials on any one day were administered at intervals ranging from 20 to 40 sec., the average intertrial interval being about 30 sec.

The control Ss were given the same number of trials, at the same rate, as were the experimental Ss. For the controls, however, the CS and UCS were never presented simultaneously. On alternate trials, the UCS (duration, 2 sec.) either preceded the CS by 3 sec. or followed the CS by 3 sec. By this procedure, the control Ss received exactly the same number of presentations of the

[3] The strength of shock given each S was either 70 or 80 v., depending upon its degree of sensitivity. Rough determination of the reactivity level of all Ss were made on the initial test day following the five startle trials. The assignment of shock voltages was based upon visual inspections of the average amplitude of activity tracings provided by the recording system when shock was applied. The number of Ss receiving the 80-v. shock was the same in both groups.

light-buzzer and the same number of shocks as did the experimentals. This served to control for possible changes in magnitude of startle attributable to pseudo-conditioning. The controls, like the experimentals, were given three startle tests on the fourth, seventh and tenth presentations of the CS for any one day. The gun was fired 3 sec. after the onset of the light-buzzer stimulus in order to duplicate exactly the tests given the experimental animals.

Extinction trials

On the day following the completion of the conditioning trials, all Ss were first given two paired (or unpaired, in the case of the controls) presentations of light-buzzer and shock, followed immediately by 12 nonreinforced presentations of the light and buzzer. On each of these extinction trials, the startle stimulus was presented at the usual time, i.e., 3 sec. after the onset of light and buzzer. Startle responses were recorded on each trial. The mean intertrial interval was again about 30 sec. Two additional series of extinction trials were given on the next two days in exactly the same manner, with the single exception that no more shocks were given the members of either group.

Subjects

Thirty hooded, male rats, divided into two equal groups, were used. Their ages ranged from 90 to 120 days, and all had been previously used in a bar-pressing experiment which did not involve shock.

Results

Acquisition

The results obtained from measurements of startle-response amplitude on each of the four conditioning days and on the preceding "matching" day are presented in Table 1. The *S's* scores for the four conditioning days were means of the startle responses elicited on the three test trials of each days. The values listed in the "Matching Pretest" column were computed for the experimental and control groups after match-

TABLE 1

Magnitude of Startle Responses on a Pretest Day Used for Matching Groups and on Four Succeeding Days During Which Experimental *Ss* Were Conditioned

Group	Measure in mm.	Matching Pretest	Successive Conditioning Days			
			1	2	3	4
Experimental	M	12.3	20.7	23.9	25.5	25.1
	Mdn	9.6	19.7	23.3	24.3	25.0
	SD	9.9	14.8	14.0	14.0	13.5
Control	M	11.8	13.7	15.6	15.0	11.9
	Mdn	9.2	11.7	8.3	11.7	10.3
	SD	10.4	9.9	13.2	13.7	10.0

ing on the basis of the initial day's tests. These values were included in the table to indicate the approximate magnitude of the startle response prior to the conditioning of the emotional reaction.[4]

From an inspection of the tabulated values and of the graphic plot of the medians in Fig. 1, it will be seen that the experimental *Ss* showed a marked increase in magnitude of startle re-

[4] This measure of "zero conditioning" is not, it is recognized, entirely adequate since it was obtained from reactions to sound alone. A more appropriate measure would have been magnitude of startle response to sound *plus* light and buzzer. Thus it is possible that the presence of the light and buzzer might have some inherent dynamogenic effect upon startle and that our zero point is therefore spuriously low. We would reject this possibility, however, on the grounds that the control group's scores for successive days (especially the medians) do not deviate markedly from those of the matching day in spite of the additional facilitative effect that could have been produced by the residual emotional effects of shock at the time the sound was given. In any event, it is obvious that the experimental and control groups were highly similar in terms of their startle responses prior to training, and it is doubtful that the addition of the light and buzzer would have had a *differential effect* upon their reactions.

sponse as a result of the anxiety-conditioning trials. By contrast, the responses of the control Ss appeared to show no such systematic change in magnitude, the mean for the last day of training being almost identical with that obtained on the initial test day. The *net* over-all increase in mean response magnitude between the pretest day (Day 0) and Day 4 shown by the experimental group as compared with the controls is highly significant ($t = 3.3$, $df = 14$, $p = < .01$). The tentative conclusion may be drawn, therefore, that the paired presentation of the CS and the shock led to the development of a conditioned fear state that functioned to facilitate the Ss' startle reactions to the sound.

In addition to the gross finding that magnitude of startle was intensified by fear, it is also apparent that the process of intensification was, within limits, a progressive one. The curve of median values, plotted in Fig. 1, resembles rather closely more conventional negatively accelerated curves of conditioning. It is also evident, however, that the growth of fear is an extremely rapid process when compared with the speed of acquisition of a skeletal response in a classical conditioning situation. From our data, it would appear that the reaction was quite strongly conditioned by the end of the first day. This observation regarding the rapidity of emotional conditioning is further supported by the finding that on the initial startle trial of Day 1, given after only three paired presentations of light-buzzer and shock, the experimental group showed a mean startle response of 21.7 mm., whereas the comparable mean for the controls was only 8.5 mm. It is conceivable, therefore, that if a large number of Ss were run so as to stabilize plots of reactions on individual test trials, the curve reflecting the acquisition of fear in this situation would exhibit an even more precipitous rise than that suggested by Fig. 1.

Qualitative observations of the behavior of the Ss during the conditioning series revealed that their reactions to the CS resembled somewhat those reported by Upton (1929) for guinea pigs and by Wever (1930) for cats. In the case of the experimental rats, it was noted that quite early in the conditioning series the onset of the CS was often followed by a marked reduction in general activity level accompanied by rapid, shallow breathing reminiscent of the "flutter phenomenon." The controls, on the other hand, were more prone to exhibit this behavior during the interval *following* the cessation of the CS. For them, it appeared as if the termination rather than the onset of

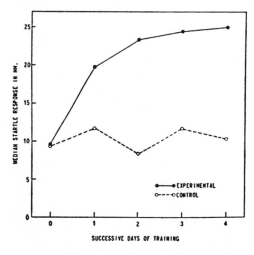

Fig. 1. Curves showing the differential facilitative effect of fear conditioning upon magnitude of startle response to an explosive sound. The training procedure was designed to induce a state of fear in the experimental animals but not in the controls. The values plotted at the zero point on the abscissa were obtained from measurements of startle on the day prior to the initiation of training.

TABLE 2

MAGNITUDES OF STARTLE RESPONSES FOR SUCCESSIVE BLOCKS OF THREE TRIALS
DURING EACH OF THREE DAYS OF EXTINCTION TRIALS

Group	Meas-ure	Successive Blocks of Three Extinction Trials Each											
		Day 1				Day 2				Day 3			
		1	2	3	4	5	6	7	8	9	10	11	12
Experi-mental	M	25.0	18.4	11.5	12.4	17.7	15.0	12.3	11.6	13.0	16.1	11.7	11.8
	Mdn	19.3	16.7	10.3	7.0	16.3	9.0	8.0	5.0	7.7	11.3	7.3	11.3
	SD	16.9	11.9	8.9	10.1	14.0	13.8	13.0	13.1	10.6	16.2	11.3	12.2
Control	M	12.7	11.7	7.9	10.7	8.6	5.6	7.0	6.6	9.2	7.3	7.3	6.5
	Mdn	11.7	8.0	8.7	7.0	7.3	3.3	6.7	6.3	5.0	8.3	6.3	4.3
	SD	10.2	10.0	6.0	9.3	5.4	5.6	4.6	6.1	8.8	5.3	5.7	5.6

the CS had become the critical environmental change arousing fear. This observation is supported in part by additional data included in the Discussion.

Extinction

On the assumption that the data obtained during the acquisition trials reflected the growth of a conditioned fear reaction, it appeared reasonable to expect that with the omission of shock, the reaction would show such additional phenomena of classical conditioning as extinction and spontaneous recovery. In order to examine this possibility,

three days of extinction trials were introduced following the acquisition series. The descriptive statistics obtained from the extinction-trial data are presented in Table 2. These values were computed from distributions of individual scores, each of which was a mean of three successive extinction trials. A plot of the median values from the table is provided in Fig. 2 to facilitate visual inspection.

It will be seen from the first day's data that the vigor of the startle reaction exhibited by the experimental *Ss* underwent a progressive decline as

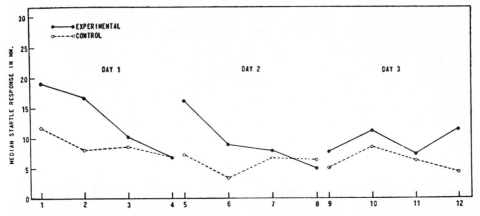

Fig. 2. Magnitude of startle responses exhibited by the experimental (fearful) and control (non-fearful) groups on three successive days during which the previously conditioned, fear-arousing stimulus was repeatedly presented without being followed by the unconditioned stimulus of electric shock.

a function of the number of non-reinforced trials. The control *Ss* also showed a slight decrement in response strength which could have been due to adaptation, or to the extinction of a small amount of anxiety, or to both. Negative adaptation could also, of course, have been a factor contributing to the fall in the experimental-group curve. The difference between the means for the experimental group on the first and fourth blocks of trials was highly significant ($t = 3.13$, $df = 14$, $p = <.01$). Since the controls also showed a slight drop, the *net* decrease for the experimental group relative to the controls was of course reduced, and was found to be significant at about the $.10 > p > .05$ level of confidence. It seems reasonable to infer from this evidence, then, that the fear which was presumably responsible for the intensification of the startle response, declined in strength as the result of the operation of omitting the shock.

From the experimental-group data of the second extinction day it is evident that the 24-hr. interval separating the fourth and fifth blocks of trials led to the spontaneous recovery of the startle response and hence, by inference, to the recovery of the extinguished fear response. The means for the control *Ss*, by contrast, showed a decrement rather than an increase, with the medians showing no appreciable change. A statistical evaluation of the net mean change from Blocks 4 to 5 for the experimental versus the control *Ss* yielded a *t* of 2.00, with a *p* between .05 and .06. This suggestive evidence for the difference effects of the passage of time upon the responses of the two groups is in accord with the notion that fear, as reflected by startle responses, is a conditionable state or response having functional properties in common with other conditionable reactions.

With further nonreinforced trials on the second day, the indicator reaction for the experimental group again declined in much the same manner as on Day 1. Spontaneous recovery, though in reduced amount as would be expected from other conditioning data, was again shown by the experimental group at the start of Day 3. This finding tends to support the conclusion that the spontaneous recovery of the second day was a genuine phenomenon, but it should be noted that the means (though not the medians) for the control group were also greater at the start of Day 3 than at the end of Day 2. No clear indication of the occurrence of further progressive extinction was provided by the third day's data.

Discussion

The results of the present experiment have provided additional support for the supposition that the paired presentation of a neutral and a noxious stimulus results in the acquisition, by the neutral stimulus, of the capacity to elicit an emotional response of fear or anxiety.[5] That this conditioned fear state appears to possess motivating or energizing properties akin to those of primary drives is suggested by the finding that at the time fear was presumably aroused, the innate startle responses of rats to a loud sound were considerably intensified. Moreover, since the degree of intensification of startle varied con-

[5] This statement involves no implicit hypotheses as to the basic conditions for this acquisition. It in no way implies, for example, that the mere contiguity of the two stimuli is regarded as sufficient for the learning of the emotional reaction.

comitantly with operations known to affect strength of conditioning, and since the startle reaction was itself never directly conditioned, it may be assumed that the effect of these operations was to change the degree of fear. Thus it can be inferred that fear was increasing progressively with number of conditioning trials, that it was being extinguished, and that it had spontaneously recovered, from the observation that these classical conditioned-response properties were exhibited by the nonconditioned startle reaction.

Although the startle response has been termed *nonconditioned* throughout this study, the fact that this reaction *can* be conditioned (Hunter, 1937; Landis & Hunt, 1939) makes it necessary to consider the possibility that the obtained results could be attributed to learned modifications of the startle tendency instead of to the energizing property of fear. In the present experiment, the jump response was elicited on 12 occasions (three times on each of four training days) in the presence of the CS, and it would be on these trials, therefore, that direct conditioning of startle might have taken place. Thus it might be supposed that the response was conditioned through the action of sheer contiguity of stimulus and response or because of the reinforcement provided by the offset of the sound stimulus. Although this is a logical possibility, it does not provide an acceptable explanation of the differences between the experimental and control groups. Inasmuch as both groups were given precisely the same number and kind of test trials, they had exactly the same opportunity for the startle to become conditioned in the suggested manner.

An alternative and more plausible

hypothesis is that the tendency to jump to the shot in the presence of the light and buzzer was increased because of the *reinforcing effect of fear reduction* attending the cessation of the CS, rather than the energizing effect of the anxiety elicited by the CS. The fact that the responses of the controls showed no significant increase is perfectly compatible with this proposal since, for them, the CS should have led to little or no anxiety as compared with the experimentals. Although this hypothesis differs from the major one of the present paper, it leads to precisely the same conclusions with respect to the growth and decay of fear.

Evidence can be cited, however, which favors the conclusion that the major determinant of the increase in startle was the dynamogenic rather than the reinforcing action of fear. Thus it may be recalled that the average jump of the experimental *Ss* to the *first* presentation of the startle stimulus, introduced after three conditioning trials, was 21.7 mm., almost twice as large as the mean response of the same *Ss* on the matching trials of the previous day. Since the startle stimulus had not, prior to this first test, been followed by fear reduction, it appears unlikely that this marked increase in strength could have been due to a learned modification of the startle tendency. We conclude, therefore, that although the possible role of fear reduction cannot, and should not, be completely dismissed, a more defensible hypothesis is that the observed effects were primarily due to the energizing function of fear.

A still further interpretation of the present findings might rest upon the possibility that the experimental *Ss*, but not the controls, were learning to adopt a specific posture in response to the CS. If this were the case, it is conceivable that the enhancement of the startle to the shot could be explained in terms of the sheer "mechanical advantage" provided by the learned postural adjustment. Successive changes in the posture, and hence in its capacity to facilitate jumping, would be presumed to have taken place during the training and extinction trials. Since no precise records were made of the animals' postural or gross muscular adjustments to the light and buzzer, it is possible that such adjustments could have occurred.

With respect to this hypothesis, it may be noted initially that fear has been defined simply as a conditioned anticipatory response to impending painful stimulation. This response, or response pattern, may be assumed to produce intense stimulation, and thereby, a state or process having certain of the properties of primary drives. In this formulation no attempt has been made to specify whether the anticipatory responses need be central or peripheral, skeletal or visceral. Nor have any assumptions been made as to whether the physical mechanisms underlying the intensifying function of fear are hormonal, neural, or mechanical. The basic hypothesis that fear acts as an energizer would not, therefore, be invalidated by the observation that postural adjustments were present or by the finding that these adjustments were facilitative in a purely mechanical fashion.

It should be observed, however, that perhaps not *all* responses elicited by the cues associated with a noxious stimulus should be considered as fear reactions. Some of these anticipatory responses may produce little stimula-

tion and therefore have little or no drive value, and it is conceivable that some conditioned postural adjustments are of this sort. It is important to note that if the intensification of startle is due solely to the mechanical advantage inhering in such postures then the range of responses susceptible to enhancement as a result of this reaction is probably severely restricted. Response patterns having motivational properties are usually assumed to have the capacity of intensifying a rather wide variety of reactions. It is doubtful that there would be much utility in ascribing drive characteristics to a response if its intensifying action were limited to a single other reaction. Whether the anticipatory responses in the present situation have such restricted effects is, of course, a question that must be answered by further investigation.

It may be recalled that one of the rather casual observations of the present study was that the going-off of the CS rather than its onset appeared to be the critical fear-arousing event for the *Ss* of the control group. Quantitative data supporting this supposition were obtained from eight *Ss* following the completion of the main experiment. In this exploratory study, four rats from each of the original experimental and control groups were given ten reconditioning trials on each of two successive days. The procedure was identical with that of the principal study except for the startle test trials. On these trials, the startle stimulus was presented 3 sec. *after the termination* of the CS instead of 3 sec. after its onset, as had previously been the case. On the assumption that fear should have been greatest at about the time the shock was normally received, it follows that 3 sec. after the termination of the CS, the controls, that were shocked on alternate trials at that time, should have had a higher degree of fear than the experimentals. That this was apparently the case is indicated by the fact that the mean response of the controls on the six test trials of the two days was 13.9 mm., as compared to a mean of 6.9 mm. for the experimental *Ss*.

Although this reversal in the relative response strengths of the two groups is reasonably striking, the finding must be regarded as quite tentative. It may be remarked, incidentally, that the ease with which it was possible to make this additional observation would appear to constitute one of the major advantages of the present method. To have attempted to demonstrate the fear-arousing properties of the cessation of a stimulus by methods involving reinforcement through fear reduction would have been far more laborious.

Finally, it should be pointed out that the present experiment is to a certain degree similar to the "sensitization" study of Prosser and Hunter (1936). They observed that a weak auditory stimulus originally incapable of eliciting a startle response of the gastrocnemius muscle of the rat would acquire the capacity to do so after it had been paired with shock. Their conclusion that excitability is increased by shock and therefore facilitates startle is consistent with our findings that startle is intensified by fear. In their experiment, however, no obvious additional stimulus capable of arousing a conditioned fear state preceded the weak sound. Hence, it seems likely that their observed sensitization was due to the effects of *residual* excitement from preceding shocks rather than to a *con-ditioned* excitement as in the present experiment.

Summary: 1. Previous experimental demonstrations of the motivational aspects of fear or anxiety as a determinant of behavior have been based primarily upon the reinforcing property of fear reduction. Although this approach has been quite successful, a number of practical disadvantages can be discerned in the method. The present paper describes an alternative method of studying fear, which rests upon assumptions concerning the energizing rather than the reinforcing properties of fear.

2. Rats were placed in a stabilimeter-like device and given a series of training trials, each of which consisted in the presentation of a neutral stimulus and a shock. For an experimental group, the two stimuli were paired in a manner designed to produce a conditioned pain response (fear or anxiety) to the neutral stimulus; for a control group, the temporal intervals between the stimuli were such as to reduce or prevent the formation of fear. Under neither procedure was any overt response systematically reinforced. Following the conditioning series, extinction trials (CS presented alone) were given on each of three successive days. To test for the presence of fear, a loud, sharp sound was substituted at the time shock was customarily applied (to the experimental *Ss*) and the magnitude of the startle response was recorded. On the assumption that the startle reaction would be a function of the strength of the conditioned fear state, it was predicted that vigor of startle would vary concomitantly with operations designed to produce acquisition, extinction, and spontaneous recovery of fear.

3. The results for the training series showed a significant increase in the average startle response of the experimental *Ss* relative to the controls (whose reactions changed but little during these trials). Data from the series of extinction trials revealed that the startle response in the experimental group declined progressively during the nonreinforced trials of the first day, recovered spontaneously during the interval separating the first and second days, de-

clined again on the second day, and tended to show recovery again between the second and third days.

4. It is concluded that the results of the experiment provide further support for the assumption that the pairing of a neutral and a noxious stimulus leads to the develop-

ment of a conditioned fear reaction having motivational concomitants. It is further held that the momentary strength of this reaction can be inferred from the extent to which some other reaction, in itself never directly conditioned to the fear cues, is intensified at the time of fear arousal.

American Journal of Psychology, 1964, vol. 77, pp. 75–83.

The Latency of the Conditioned Fear-Response

R. A. Champion

The concept of emotional activity figures prominently in both abnormal psychology and in the theory of behavior, and appears to provide a promising avenue by which the experimental psychologist might contribute to the understanding of clinical problems. The possibility of a link of this kind may be increased by the clearer specification of and distinction between two types of emotional activity, in the form of anxiety or emotionality, on the one hand, and the hypothetical fear-response, on the other hand. Both of these types of emotional activity are said to be derivable from painful or noxious stimulation, but the former may best be regarded as a persisting state of the organism, while the latter is thought of as a specific response.

Spence, for example, has offered a theory of emotionally-based drive which is studied through the manipulation of airpuffs administered between conditioning trials or the selection of high and low scorers on a self-inventory test of manifest anxiety (1958), but it seems that he is dealing with an hypothetical 'state' variable, even though he describes it as an emotional response and

uses the designation r_e. Miller, on the other hand, represents a group of workers who have given rather more attention to the specific, discrete response of fear, originating as a component or concomitant of pain, but learnable in the sense that it is capable of being elicited by some neutral stimulus consistently presented with the painful stimulus (1951b). While the distinction between emotionality and fear in these terms may be important, the two processes should still be conceived of as having common properties and as being in no way opposed. Motivational properties are attributed to fear, and the fear-response may be thought of as occurring with such frequency as to equal emotionality in persistence. The distinction must be made, however, for it is only the fear-response which has been shown to be learnable and therefore directly dependent upon environmental cues rather than merely building up with successive noxious stimulations (Brown, Kalish, & Farber, 1951).

Detailed consideration of the processes involved in the acquisition and extinction of the hypothetical fear-response (Champion, 1961), a necessary prelude to any clinical application, leads to the latency of the response as a crucial feature, and the following experiment was designed to yield further information about this property of fear. The relevance of this information is readily illustrated in the rationale of Mowrer's recent elaboration of his 'two-factor' theory of behavior (1960b). Mowrer argues that the conditioned occurrence of not only fear but also the cessation of fear (hope) acts to govern overt, instrumental behavior. There is reason to suppose, however, that the fear-response is mediated in part at least by the action of the relatively slow autonomic nervous system, so that its latency may well be longer than that of the responses which Mowrer assumes it to govern.

The most fruitful procedure for determining the latency of the conditioned fear-response appears to be the probe-stimulus (*PS*) technique devised by Brown and his associates (Brown, Kalish & Farber, 1951). By this means Spence and Runquist produced evidence that fear has a latency greater than 0.5 sec. and possibly of the order of 4.5 sec. (1958); Ross interpreted data gathered in a similar way to mean that the latency of the response is longer than 0.5 sec. and may exceed 2 sec. (1961). A common feature of these two experiments, however, was the use of a reflex (eyeblink) as the index of conditioned fear, whereas the theorizing of Mowrer, for example, is more concerned with the effects of fear on instrumental responses. It was thought, therefore, that the available evidence should be confirmed under these more general conditions. Unfortunately, any move to study the wider effects of fear leads to a further problem in the

ambiguity of the expected direction of the effect. Those who have used the PS technique hitherto have assumed that, having motivational properties, fear activates any concomitant response which clearly dominates all other competing responses. Mowrer, on the other hand, works with the assumption that one main effect of fear is to inhibit other responses (1960b) and Mowrer and Aiken, for example, have used decrement in feeding rate in rats as an index of the strength of fear (1954). In addition to Mowrer's distinction between active and passive avoidance learning (1960b), the apparent incompatibility of the opposing effects of fear might be resolved with the idea that weak to mild fear has a dynamogenic effect on a dominant contemporary response, whereas the stimulus-properties of strong fear arouse responses which interfere with and dominate all other contemporary responses. It is also possible that, although fear activates the dominant contemporary response, this is not the one that *E* is studying, so that the test-response is weakened by a more direct form of competition. In the absence of prior knowledge about the strength of fear in absolute terms, and of the exact dynamics of the test-situation, it as not clear at the outset of the present study whether the index of fear would be provided by the enhancement of or interference with the test-response.

The fear-response was conditioned in this experiment by consistently presenting a tone (*CS*) in conjunction with shock (*UCS*). Late in training the shock was replaced on some trials by a probe-stimulus (*PS*) in the form of a light to which *S* had been instructed to give a key-pressing response, and the theoretical effect of fear was measured in the reaction-time (RT, or latency) of this test-response to the light-signal. To locate the peak of strength of fear as a CR, the PS was inserted at varying time-intervals after the CS. A particular methodological problem concerned the advisability of using a control-group of S^s to whom the CS and UCS would not be presented in conjunction, as a check on the conditioning of fear. In the other experiments cited, UCS–CS trials were run for this purpose (backward conditioning), but recent evidence of true backward conditioning of the long-latency GSR suggests that such a control may be reduced in effectiveness if the fear-response also proves to have a relatively long latency (Champion & Jones, 1961). It was decided, therefore, that no such control would be exercised, in the expectation of no disadvantage if previous findings were confirmed.

Method

Subjects

The Ss were 45 volunteers from a course in introductory psychology. The results for one S were discarded after the completion of the experiment when a check showed that he had already served in a similar experiment.

Apparatus

The CS was a 2000-cps, sine-wave tone of 60 db. spl and 8 sec. duration delivered to S through headphones, and the UCS was a 90-cps, 0.5-sec., spike-wave shock of 2.27 ma. (as measured with a 15,000-ohm resistor in place of S) with a peak-to-peak voltage of 34 v. The UCS was administered through thimble-type electrodes of German silver, $\frac{1}{2}$ in. in length, attached to the index and middle fingers of the right hand. The interval between the onset of CS and UCS was held constant at 0.5 sec. The PS was a 0.5-sec. flash of a 6-v. DC lamp placed near S's right hand, and S was required

to respond to the PS with the right hand by pressing a telegraph key on which was mounted a 4×2-in. wooden platform as a hand-rest. An electronic chronoscope was started with the onset of the PS and stopped by pressure on the key so as to measure the RT.

Procedure

S was placed in a sound-reduced room separate from that containing E and the main apparatus, and all measures were taken in one session of about 45-min. duration. The session began with 5 practice trials of the key-pressing response to the PS and one presentation of the UCS alone. Then followed 6 presentations of the CS–PS sequence as a fore-test; the CS preceded by the PS by each of the 6 intervals to be used later in locating the fear response, viz. 0.5, 1.5, 2.5, 3.5, 4.5, and 5.5 sec. These intervals were used in a different predetermined random order for each S, with the restriction that no interval occurred on any ordinal trial on more than 10 or less than 6 occasions over the group of Ss as a whole. It should be noted that the CS of 8 sec. overlapped the PS by at least 2 sec.

The second stage in the procedure consisted of 9 CS–UCS trials to obtain a conditioned fear-response; to prevent 'surprise' reactions on S's part in later tests, one CS–PS trial was inserted after the second and fifth CS–UCS trials, the CS–PS interval being varied among Ss. The main measures were taken in the third stage of the procedure which took the form of an after-test. Training trials (CS–UCS) were continued, but were interspersed with CS–PS trials as tests of the strength of fear. Further 6 CS–PS trials were used, at each of the intervals listed above and in a predetermined random order subject to the same restriction as in the fore-test, with the further proviso that no S receive the same random order in the after-test as in the fore-test. Test trials (CS–PS) were run after training Trials 9, 10, or 11, 12 or 13, 14 or 15, 16 or 17, and 18 or 19. The exact points at which CS–PS trials were inserted were predetermined at random within these limits with the restriction that such trials be not separated by 1, 2, or 3 CS–

UCS trials more than twice in the sequence for any one S. Throughout the session as a whole trials were separated by 45, 50, or 55 sec. in prearranged random order. The CS–PS trials were preceded by a verbal 'ready' signal given by E over an intercom approximately 4 sec. before the onset of the CS, but no warning signal of any kind was given on CS–UCS trials.

Results

In keeping with the theoretical considerations outlined above, the effect of the conditioning procedure on the test-response showed some inconsistency. Of the 264 CS–PS trials run in the after test there was a decrement in performance relative to the fore-test measure in 62 cases, but these were scattered over Ss and CS–PS intervals. For this reason, and because of the presence of some extreme scores in the data, the measures on the fore- and after-tests were first analyzed separately and by means of nonparametric tests.

The fore- and after-test data are represented in Fig. 1. It will be recalled that the CS–PS trials consisted of a 'ready' signal, followed 4 sec. later by the onset of the CS, followed in turn by the PS at intervals varying from 0.5 sec. to 5.5 sec. in 1.0-sec. steps. The RT of the key-pressing response to the PS in the fore-test did not vary with the CS–PS interval to a significant degree; a Friedman analysis of variance gave a X^2 value of 0.09 ($p > 0.99$ for $5df$). In the after-test, however, following a number of CS–UCS trials, significant differences emerged ($X^2 = 12.13$, $p < 0.05$ for 5 df). Comparing the results on the various CS–PS intervals in the after-test by means of rank tests, there were significant differences between 0.5 and 2.5 sec. ($Z = 2.58$, $p < 0.01$), 0.5 and 4.5 sec. ($Z = 2.64$,

$p < 0.01$), and 2.5 and 5.5 sec. ($Z = 2.57$, $p < 0.05$). One other comparison, that between 4.5 and 5.5 sec., approached significance ($Z = 1.86$, $p = 0.06$). Assuming that the main effect of fear in this experiment was to reduce the RT of the test-response, the latency of the fear-response appears to be greater than 0.5 sec. but less than 5.5 sec.

A feature of the results of the after-test was the performance of the test-response with a CS–PS interval of 3.5 sec., which deviated from the trend of the data as a whole. This result could emerge if the conditioned fear-response was at its peak about 3.5 sec. after the onset of the CS, and if the stimulus-properties of this relatively strong fear-response were to elicit a number of other responses which competed with the test-response so as to induce its performance. To test this possibility, further analyses were made of the data of those Ss who showed some consistency in their reaction to the conditioning of fear. When the data of the

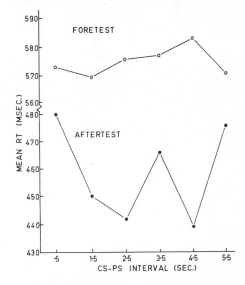

Fig. 1. Performance as a function of CS-PS interval on the fore- and after-tests.

fore- and after-test for each S at each CS–PS interval were represented in the form of a decrease or increase in the RT (gain or loss in performance, respectively) as a result of conditioning, there proved to be 14 Ss whose RT decreased at all 6 CS–PS intervals ('gainers') and 9 Ss whose RT increased at 3 or 4 intervals. ('losers'). No S showed an increase in RT at as many as 5 or 6 intervals. If it be allowed that the test-response of key-pressing was activated by fear in the group of Ss showing gains in performance, then their peak performance should have occurred at about 3.5 sec., if such is the latency of the conditioned fear-response. If the other group of Ss showed a high frequency of loss in performance because the test-response of key-pressing was not dominant and was interfered with (or inhibited) by some other response, then their poorest performance should have occurred at about 3.5 sec. by the same token. The obtained results of these two groups of selected Ss are depicted in Fig. 2; their

form is in keeping both with the general theoretical expectations about the dynamics of the fear-response and with the hypothesis that the fear-response has a latency of the order of 3.5 sec. The data were combined for statistical tests ($N = 23$), allowing for the difference in the expected direction of the effect with 'gainers' and 'losers.' Applications of rank-tests showed significant differences between change in performance at CS–PS intervals of 0.5 and 3.5 sec. ($T = 64.5$, $p < 0.05$), and 3.5 and 5.5 sec. ($T = 59.5$, $p < 0.05$). As a final check, the same test was applied to all other Ss who showed two gains or two losses at the two CS–PS intervals in question; for 0.5 sec. vs. 3.5 sec. ($N = 8$) there was a significant difference of the form predicted ($T = 5$, $p < 0.05$ for a one-tailed test), but there was no significant difference under these conditions between change in performance at 3.5 sec. and 5.5 sec.

Discussion

The general conclusion to be drawn from the data of this experiment is that the conditioned fear-response has a latency of the order of 3.5 sec., being greater than 0.5 sec. but less than 5.5 sec. This conclusion is compatible with the data of Spence and Runquist, and the significant difference in performance on the after-test between the CS–PS intervals of 0.5 and 4.5 sec. in the present study confirms their main result (Spence & Runquist, 1958). The finding of Ross that the latency of the response was greater than 0.5 sec. is also confirmed (1961). This latter E varied the CS–UCS interval from group to group during training and concluded that little if any conditioning of fear occurred with a 0.5-sec. interval, although he noted that Spence

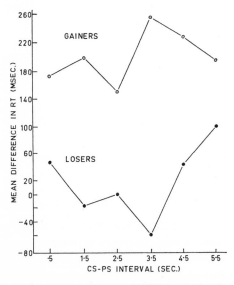

Fig. 2. Mean difference in RT for Ss showing gains and losses at various CS-PS intervals (N for 'Gainers' = 14; for 'Losers' = 9)

and Runquist used this interval. The evidence presented by Ross in support of the conclusion that the latency of conditioned fear may be longer than 2 sec. was obtained only with CS–UCS intervals of 2 and 5 sec. These observations suggest that the optimal CS–UCS interval for the conditioning of fear remains to be established, but they do not necessarily affect the conclusion that, once generated, the conditioned fear-response has a latency greater than 0.5 sec.

It may be supposed that the inferior performance at the 0.5 and 5.5-sec. CS–PS intervals in this experiment is an artifact due to the technique of testing each S at each interval. It will be appreciated that the CS (tone) acted as a form of 'ready' signal for the reaction to light as the probe-stimulus, and in the terminology of the RT experiments this meant irregular variation in the duration of the foreperiod. Under conditions of this type, Woodrow found that well-practiced Ss tended to give their shortest average RT with warning intervals of intermediate length in any given series of intervals, instead of with an interval of 2 sec. as when the duration of the foreperiod was held constant (1914); thus the 2.5, 3.5, and 4.5-sec. intervals of this experiment may have been favored. At least two considerations, however, seem to rule out this possibility. First, the group of Ss showing a high frequency of decrement in performance from fore- to after-test ('losers' in Fig. 2) gave exactly the opposite result, performing best at the extreme rather than the intermediate values. Secondly, examination of results in the fore-test, before any conditioning, showed that although performance at each interval improved somewhat as the given interval was used further toward the end of the

series of six trials, this improvement did not vary in any meaningful way from interval to interval, and it is unlikely that the intermediate intervals gained more than other intervals in the remaining eight CS–PS trials, including the trials of the after-test.

Another methodological point concerns the ambiguity in the predicted effect of conditioned fear, ranging from activation to inhibition of the test-response. It was inferred that the inversion at 3.5 sec. in the main data of the after-test (Fig. 1) was due to the interfering effects of fear, and the interests of consistency might demand that fear also be assumed to occur strongly at 0.5 and 5.5 sec. Conversely, complete concentration on the activating effect of fear could lead to the conclusion that the response is strongest at 2.5 and 4.5 sec. In the present instance it is thought that the ambiguity has been resolved by preference to the performance of the groups of 'gainers' and 'losers', and to previous findings. The solution to the problem in general terms, however, appears to be more appropriately found in prior experimental control so as to insure either the clear dominance of, or interference with, the test-response. In retrospect, for example, clearer results might have been obtained in this study if the Ss had practiced the key-pressing response to a greater extent before fear-conditioning.

Two features of the present data appear to be of general theoretical significance. First, the findings suggest that when one and the same stimulus elicits both the fear-response and an overt, instrumental response, the latter will occur before the former. This being so, fear cannot unfailingly prevent a given response from occurring, although it may have a modifying or inhibiting effect once the response has begun. Secondly, the data provide further evidence that fear may modify a contemporary response through activation as well as inhibition. The possibility of some consistency in an individual's reaction to fear, as exemplified in the groups of 'gainers' and 'losers,' may relate back to emotionality as a 'state' variable. It is most likely that the occurrence of an increment or a decrement in performance as a result of fear-conditioning depends on the dynamics of the experimental situation at the moment the *PS* is administered, in terms of the present experiment, as well as on *S*'s past experience in similar situations. In addition to these factors, however, there may be some inherent property of the organism which contributes to the nature of the reaction to fear. It might be fruitful to conduct an experiment of the present type on groups of high-anxious and low-anxious *S*s, perhaps with the expectation that the former group would present responses to fear which would in turn in-

terfere with all but the very simplest (reflex) test-response to a *PS*. The same procedure could be used to test the effects of anxiety-inducing and anxiety-reducing drugs on the conditioning of fear in humans.

Summary: A fear response to a tone was conditioned in a group of 44 *S*s by consistently pairing the tone with shock. Late in training the shock was replaced on some trials by a light in response to which *S* had been instructed to press a key as quickly as possible, and the tone was presented 0.5, 1.5, 2.5, 3.5, 4.5, and 5.5 sec. before the light. By comparison with similar tests of *RT* before fear-conditioning, this use of the probe-stimulus technique produced data which suggested that the fear-response has a latency greater than 0.5 sec. and possibly of the order of 3.5 sec. This conclusion was confirmed by an examination of the results of those of *S*s who showed some consistency in their reaction to fear-conditioning by way of gains or losses in performance. Some theoretical implications of these findings were discussed, with particular reference to Mowrer's theory of behavior and to the distinction between anxiety and fear.

Canadian Journal of Psychology, 1963, vol. 17, pp. 412–418.

Frequency and Intensity of Pre-Shock Experiences as Determinants of Fearfulness in an Approach-Avoidance Conflict[1]

Gary C. Walters

Kurtz and Walters (1962) have recently reported that rats subjected to brief experiences of intense electric

[1] This paper is based upon a dissertation directed by K. H. Kurtz, submitted in partial fulfillment of the requirements for the Ph.D. degree at the University of Buffalo.

shock displayed a greater sensitivity to punishment in a subsequent conflict test than animals receiving no pre-shock experiences. Further, pre-shock has been shown to have an enduring effect upon the organism in that such experiences result in exaggerated fear reactions even after a period of one year has elapsed between pre-shock and subsequent testing (Walters & Rogers, 1963). These results have been interpreted as supporting the hypothesis that prior experiences of aversive stimulation sensitize an organism, predisposing it to react with "increased fearfulness" during subsequent encounters with aversive stimuli. However, a number of other investigators have reported habituation of unconditioned responses to electric shock when a long series of shocks was administered (Kellogg, 1941; Kimble, 1955; MacDonald, 1946; Seward & Seward, 1934). These reports suggest that prolonged exposure to moderate intensity shock may result in habituated or decreased fear reactions. If this is the case, one might expect animals subjected to such experiences to react with decreased rather than increased fearfulness during subsequent encounters with aversive stimuli.

Accordingly, the present study deals with the effects of variations in the number and severity of pre-shock experiences on later fearfulness. As in the Kurtz and Walters study, fearfulness was assessed using an approach-avoidance test.

Method

Subjects

The Ss were 96 male albino rats obtained from Holtzman Animal Farms and were approximately 54 days old at the start of the experiment. The Ss were housed in individual cages throughout the experiment.

Apparatus

Shock compartment. The Ss received their initial shock experiences in a compartment with floor dimensions of 2 by 6 in. The floor was composed of two unpainted metal strips, each ¾ in. in width, separated by ½ in. The side walls, also made of unpainted metal, were 7 in. high. The ceiling and ends were made of white opaque plastic. Both the floor plates and side walls served as electrodes; E could reverse the polarity of both the floor and side wall electrodes if S appeared to be escaping shock by supporting itself on surfaces of like polarity. The details of the construction of this apparatus are given elsewhere (Kurtz & Walters, 1962). The shock circuit was designed to deliver a current of either 0.60 or 1.25 ma., depending upon the group to which S was assigned. Approximately 235 v., 60 cycle ac, through a 200,000-ohm resistance in series with S was used to deliver the 1.25 ma. current; 110 v., was applied through this same circuit to deliver the 0.60 ma. current.

Runway. The floor and side walls of the alley used for approach-avoidance testing were made of wood painted a glossy gray; the top was enclosed by wire mesh. The alley was 48 in. long (excluding the start box and goal box), and 4 in. high. To aid in determining the distance traversed by the rat, the floor was marked into 1-in. segments numbered from 1 to 48. The starting box was a 7-in. extension of the alley, separated from the rest of the runway by an opaque guillotine door. The goal box was 10½ in. long, 4 in. wide, and 4 in. high. A second guillotine door prevented S from leaving the goal box after entering it. The floor of the goal box consisted of two metal plates running the length of the box and separated by a half-inch gap. The plates were each 1¾ in. wide and constituted shock electrodes. Metal side walls also served as electrodes in the event that Ss touched them with their paws while shock was being delivered. Food reinforcements—a wet mash of Purina Lab Chow and milk—was presented in a small food cup mounted on the far side of the goal-box wall. Further details of the construction of the apparatus are presented elsewhere (Kurtz & Walters, 1962).

Procedure

The 96 Ss were shocked, trained, and tested in "squads" of 12 animals each. Ss were assigned to a given squad at random, with the restriction that at least one S from each of the four treatment conditions be included in each squad.

Original treatment. The 96 Ss were randomly divided among four treatment groups, three shocked and one non-shocked. Ss in the shocked groups were assigned to one of the following three shock conditions: Prolonged Intense Group (PIG)—200 shocks of 1.25 ma. intensity; Brief Intense Group (BIG)—10 shocks of 1.25 ma. intensity; Prolonged Moderate Group (PMG)—200 shocks of 0.60 ma. intensity.

At 54 days of age Ss in the three shocked groups were placed individually into the treatment apparatus, where they received a series of shocks, each of 5-sec. duration, delivered without warning on the average of one shock per minute. The total time spent in the shock box was 3 hr. and 20 min. The Ss in the BIG received their 10 shocks concurrently with the last 10 shocks delivered to Ss in the PIG. Ss in the Non-shocked Group (NSG) were confined in the apparatus for the same amount of time but were not shocked.

Runway training. Beginning on the eighth day of a 23-hr. feeding regimen, all Ss were trained to run from the start box to the goal box of the runway to obtain food. Ten training trials were given each day for four consecutive days. Each trial was run as follows: S was placed in the start box and after a 5- to 10-sec. delay the guillotine door was raised. After entering the goal box S was allowed to eat a bite of food, after which it was returned to the start box for the next trial.

Approach-avoidance testing. The day after concluding approach training each group was randomly divided into two subgroups, one receiving shocks of 1.25 ma., the other receiving shocks of 0.60 ma. in the goal box immediately after beginning to eat. All shocks at the goal were ½ sec. in duration, each S receiving only one shock on any given trial. Five test trials were given, two on the first day of testing and three on the second. Trials were staggered so that one trial was completed by all Ss before the next trial was begun. The time between trials varied between 1 and 6 min. The following measures were recorded on each test trial: (1) time taken to

leave the start box; (2) time taken to reach the goal box and begin eating (exclusive of start box time); and (3) distance run before the first reversal of direction (measured by position of front paws). If S did not enter the goal within 5 min. after the start box door was lifted, it was removed from the runway and given a total time score of 300 sec.

Results

Goal-Approach Training

The performance of each S on a given day was summarized by the median time score achieved on the 10 training trials of that day. The median of these individual scores (median of the medians) was used to summarize the performance of each group on each day of training. A Kruskal-Wallis one-way analysis of variance (Siegel, 1956) did not indicate a significant variation among the four groups ($H = 4.70$, p > .20). By the final day of training, the distributions of running times were virtually indistinguishable, the group medians varying between 2.5 and 2.8 sec. The differences among the four groups did not approach statistical significance ($H = 3.31, p > .30$).

Approach-Avoidance Testing

The performance of the four subgroups receiving moderate shock at the goal is summarized in Figures 1A, 1B, and 1C; Figures 1D, 1E, and 1F show the results of the four subgroups receiving intense shocks.

To obtain an over-all evaluation of the differences among subgroups, summary scores were obtained of each subject's performance by taking the median of the five daily scores for that subject. In turn, the median of the individual medians was used to summarize the 12 individual scores in each subgroup, as

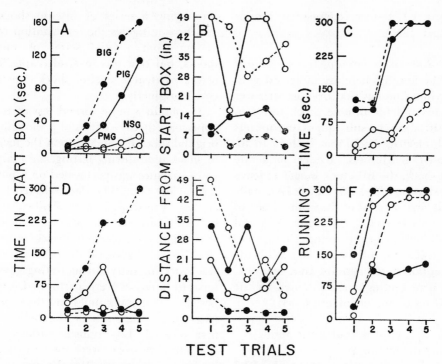

Fig. 1. Alleyway performance during approach-avoidance conflict testing. A, B, and C represent the performance of the groups receiving moderate test shock; D, E, and F the performance of the groups receiving intense test shock.

TABLE 1

GROUP MEDIANS OF SUMMARY SCORES OF TEST PERFORMANCE

	Intensity of test shock					
	Intense	Moderate	Intense	Moderate	Intense	Moderate
Shock experience prior to testing	time in start box (sec.)		running time (sec.)		point of first reversal (in. from start box)	
Brief intense	214.5	53.0	300.0	300.0	2.0	8.0
Prolonged intense	17.0	30.0	137.0	266.0	17.5	12.0
Prolonged moderation	40.0	12.0	300.0	71.5	12.5	44.0
Non-shocked	24.0	5.0	251.0	75.5	27.5	39.5

reflected in Table 1. Tests of significance reported below are based upon the individual subject's summary scores.

A Kruskal-Wallis one-way analysis of variance (Siegel, 1956) indicated that the four groups represented in each figure differed significantly ($p > .01$).

A natural baseline for assessing the test results is the NSG performance. A second point of reference is provided by the BIG, since earlier studies have found evidence that this treatment leads to increased fearfulness (Kurtz & Pearl, 1960; Kurtz & Walters, 1962). Except where otherwise indicated, tests of significance were made using the Mann-

Whitney U test for independent groups (Siegel, 1956).

The Effect of a Series of Intense Shocks

The findings here are in accord with previous findings that brief experiences of unavoidable intense shock result in sensitization to subsequent encounters with electric shock, that is, lead to increased fearfulness. Under moderate test shock, the BIG took longer to leave the start box ($p < .05$, Figure 1A), made their first reversal of direction closer to the start box ($p < .05$, Figure 1B), and exhibited longer running times than the NSG ($p < .05$, Figure 1C). With the exception of the running time measure, the same findings were obtained for the BIG tested under intense shock.

The Effects of a Prolonged Series of Intense Shocks

Under moderate test shock the BIG and the PIG did not differ appreciably on any measure of their test performance (see Figures 1A, 1B, and 1C). Like the BIG, the PIG differed from the NSG on each performance measure ($p < .05$). These results indicate that a prolonged series of intense shocks has much the same effect as a brief series of intense shocks when subsequent test shock is moderate.

Under conditions of high test shock, on the other hand, the effects of intense shocks in the original treatment situation depended upon whether the original series of shocks was brief or prolonged. Although the BIG clearly showed sensitization under high test shock, the PIG hardly differed in performance from the NSG. In fact, this group differed significantly from the BIG on each of the three measures ($p < .05$, see Figures 1D, 1E, and 1F). This pattern of results suggests that

prolonging a series of intense shocks somehow mitigates the sensitization resulting from a brief series of such shocks, but that this reversal is specific to the particular level of shock experienced originally.

To obtain a more formal test of the hypothesis that the effects of prolonging original shock depended upon the level of shock used during testing, an analysis of variance was performed on a portion of the data. The data selected for analysis constituted a two-by-two design in which one factor was level of the original prolonged shock series (PMG *versus* PIG) and the other factor was shock intensity during testing. Two separate analyses were performed, one based upon starting times and the other based upon measures of the point of first reversal. Log transformations of the summary scores were used in these analyses. The scores for the running time measure did not meet the assumption of normality necessary for an analysis of variance. Neither main effect was significant when tested against the within-groups error term. However, the interaction between level of test shock and level of original treatment shock was significant at the .01 level, confirming the inference that the effects of prolonging shock depend upon the level of test shock.

Prolonged Series of Moderate Shocks

No statistical differences were found between the performance of the PMG and the NSG tested under moderate shock (see Figures 1A, 1B, and 1C). The PMG did differ from the BIG on each of the three performance measures ($p < .05$). Under intense test shock there was a tendency toward sensitization in the PMG, although the only measure on which this group differed significantly from the NSG was the point of first reversal ($p < .05$, see Figure 1E). This finding is similar to the pattern of results found when the PIG was tested under a moderate shock level. In both instances a test shock intensity different from that used during original treatment resulted in some degree of sensitization.

Discussion

The results confirm previous findings (Kurtz & Pearl, 1960; Kurtz & Walters, 1962; Pearl, 1961) and offer further support for the hypothesis that brief experiences of intense fear predispose an organism to react with exaggerated fear during subsequent encounters with aversive stimulation. In addition, these earlier findings were extended by showing that sensitization also results from a prolonged series of moderate intensity shocks when subjects receiving this type of treatment were tested under an intense shock level. Prolonging the experiences of shock resulted in a reversal of the sensitizing effects observed following experiences of brief shock, provided the same level of shock was used during both original treatment and testing.

It seems unlikely that the transfer of fear from treatment to test situation can be accounted for solely in terms of simple stimulus generalization of fear. A stimulus generalization hypothesis would predict that subjects subjected to a prolonged shock series would have acquired a stronger association of fear with cues in the treatment apparatus and thus have exhibited greater transfer than the brief shock groups. This was clearly not the case since greater transfer was obtained under brief treatment shock. Further, Kurtz and Pearl (1960)

have shown that transfer results even after the extinction of fear responses associated with cues in the treatment compartment.

If the operations which produce fear lead to a permanent increase in the drive level of the organism it would be expected that treated animals would have shown faster learning during runway training since the fear and hunger drives would be combined. Since, in the present study, no differences were found during training, it seems clear that original shock experiences do not result in a permanent increase in the general drive level of the organism. Rather, there are certain residual effects of original shock experiences which function to increase drive level in later encounters with shock. This implies that such residual effects do not lead to a chronically raised level of fear, but to increased reactivity of the organism in a fear-arousing situation. Therefore, in a test situation where the fear drive is used to motivate the to-be-learned response (for example, avoidance conditioning), increased fear drive should result in faster learning of the treated animals. Results consistent with this interpretation have been reported by Baron, Brookshire, and Littman (1957) and Kurtz and Pearl (1960). However, in the present study, where we are dealing with the punishment of a previously learned behaviour, it would be expected that increased fear drive would result in greater disruption of the learned behaviour.

The reversal of the sensitizing effect of pre-shock under certain conditions cannot be considered as a true "adaptation" phenomenon since, strictly speaking, this would imply that the pre-shocked animals were *less* disrupted during testing than the non-shocked control animals: this was not the case. It must be pointed out, however, that some investigators have reported findings which were interpreted as demonstrating that pre-shock experiences do serve to "adapt" the organism to later fear experiences (Baron, *et al.,* 1957; Baron & Antonitis, 1961; Kamin, 1961). These seemingly discrepant findings are in line with Selye's (1952) more general conception of the dual nature of exposure to stress upon later reactivity under stress. Selye has shown that under some circumstances prior exposure to stress serves to make the organism more resistant to subsequent stress while under others the organism is rendered more susceptible to the debilitating effects of stress. In terms of the behavioural effects of pre-shock experiences it seems obvious that we will have to determine the conditions under which each of these phenomena occur.

Chapter 3

PUNISHMENT, FRUSTRATION, AND STRESS

Punishment has been a difficult topic in motivational theory, as Solomon's review and discussion so amply point out. Its effects cannot be predicted on the basis of the way rewards influence behavior, since the relationships are much more complex. A reward gives information about what is correct—hence it can facilitate the selection and reinforcement of the correct response. Punishment indicates what is not correct, but gives little additional information about what is correct. In addition, punishment is usually an aversive primary drive (pain) which nearly always is accompanied by a secondary drive of fear. Hence, in addition to its effects on the punished behavior, a new drive is present, one that may energize many other behaviors. Thirdly, individuals learn specific techniques and mechanisms for handling punishment, such as fleeing, fighting back, identifying with the aggressor, withdrawing, and the like, and these will be elicited by punishment, quite independent of the effects of the punishment on the punished behavior. Finally, a fourth effect of punishment has recently been investigated. If aversive stimulation is prolonged in application, the organism is said to be in a state of stress. In addition to the learned and unlearned motivational patterns of behavior that may result, profound biological adaptive reactions occur as a consequence of this continual stress. These adaptations initially allow the fullest mobilization of resources to meet the stressor, but if it is prolonged sufficiently, the resultant internal and external behaviors may be very maladaptive.

The interaction of these four factors have required elaborate conceptualizations of punishment. Some of these are discussed by Solomon and by Martin. Brown *et al.* present evidence on some seemingly paradoxical effects of punishment, which are a direct result of the third factor mentioned above. This kind of paper, along with a number of recent similar results from other experiments, lends support for many of the human clinical behavior patterns that seem to be paradoxical effects of punishment—especially that of masochism.

The study by Lefkowitz *et al.* also concerns these interactions, specifically the second and third factors. Their study investigates the responses of children as a function of the kind and amount of punishment administered to them during normal socialization. The body of research on this problem is growing, and while some of the data are contradictory, the pattern of results reported here is representative.

While only one paper is included on frustration, quite an extensive literature has recently developed on some new and powerful conceptualizations of this topic. Amsel's work has been the most pioneering, by showing the continuity of the concept of frustration to that of the primary aversive drive of pain. He has postulated an implicit internal response that occurs whenever an individual is frustrated (a condition that follows the non-occurrence of an expected reinforcement). This response is very much like the internal emotional response produced by pain. Using this analogy, a number of predictions regarding frustrative behavior can be made, quite similar to those regarding behavior following pain. (See Brown, Martin, and Morrow's and Martin's papers in Chapter 2.) Wagner summarizes the work of Amsel and others on the success of these formulations, and then reports a number of his own studies extending this research.

Material on stress reactions is not usually included in motivational theories, though it is difficult to see why not. The effects are certainly motivational in outcome, and the mechanisms parallel many of those discussed in the regulation of drive behavior (Chapter 2) and in central nervous system arousal (see Chapter 4). Brady's paper is perhaps the most explicit example of maladjustive behavior resulting from prolonged attention. Notice that the stressor here is not being shocked—the yoked controls did not ulcerate. Rather it is the continual vigil to be on guard against danger—thus the "executive syndrome." Ader and Conklin, and Denenberg and Whimbey present one type of experiment showing how stress effects can be relatively permanent, and can even be transmitted to offspring. There is very extensive support for this finding. Finally, Deevey develops the argument that the stress reaction emanating from overcrowding in asocial mammals accounts for the rhythmical population cycles found in these mammals. While population cycles are a far cry from motivation, the mechanism accounting for them are most explicitly motivational in character.

American Psychologist, 1964, vol. 19, pp. 239–253.

Punishment[1]

Richard L. Solomon

First, an introduction: I will attempt to achieve three goals today. (*a*) I will summarize some *empirical generaliza-*

1 This is a slightly revised text of the author's Presidential Address to the Eastern Psychological Association, New York City, April 1963. The research associated with this address was supported by Grant No. M-402 from the United States Public Health Service.

tions and problems concerning the effects of punishment on behavior; (*b*) I will give some demonstrations of the *advantages of a two-process learning theory* for suggesting new procedures to be tried out in punishment experiments; and (*c*) finally, I shall take this opportunity today to *decry some unscientific legends* about punishment, and to do a little pontificating—a privilege that I might be denied in a journal such as the *Psychological Review,* which I edit!

Now, for a working definition of punishment: The definition of a punishment is not operationally simple, but some of its attributes are clear. A punishment is a noxious stimulus, one which will support, by its termination or omission, the growth of new escape or avoidance responses. It is one which the subject will reject, if given a choice between the punishment and no stimulus at all. Whether the data on the behavioral effects of such noxious stimuli will substantiate our common-sense view of what constitutes an effective punishment, depends on a wide variety of conditions that I shall survey. Needless to say, most of these experimental conditions have been studied with infrahuman subjects rather than with human subjects.

Sample Experiments

Let us first consider two sample experiments. Imagine a traditional alley runway, 6 feet long, with its delineated goal box and start box, and an electrifiable grid floor. In our first experiment, a rat is shocked in the start box and alley, but there is no shock in the goal box. We can quickly train the rat to run down the alley, if the shock commences as the start-box gate is raised and persists until the rat enters the goal box. This is *escape* training. If, however, we give the rat 5 seconds to reach the goal box after the start-box gate is raised, and only then do we apply the shock, the rat will usually learn to run quickly enough to avoid the shock entirely. This procedure is called *avoidance* training, and the resultant behavior

change is called *active* avoidance learning. Note that the response required, either to terminate the shock or to remove the rat from the presence of the dangerous start box and alley, is well specified, while the behavior leading to the onset of these noxious stimulus conditions is left vague. It could be any item of behavior coming *before* the opening of the gate, and it would depend on what the rat happened to be doing when the experimenter raised the gate.

In our second sample experiment, we train a hungry rat to run to the goal box in order to obtain food. After performance appears to be asymptotic, we introduce a shock, both in the alley and goal box, and eliminate the food. The rat quickly stops running and spends its time in the start box. This procedure is called the *punishment procedure,* and the resultant learning-to-stay-in-the-start-box is called *passive* avoidance learning. Note that, while the behavior *producing* the punishment is well specified, the particular behavior *terminating* the punishment is left vague. It could be composed of any behavior that keeps the rat in the start box and out of the alley.

In the first experiment, we were teaching the rat *what to do,* while in the second experiment we were teaching him exactly *what not to do;* yet in each case, the criterion of learning was correlated with the rat's receiving *no* shocks, in contrast to its previous experience of receiving several shocks in the same experimental setting. One cannot think adequately about punishment without considering what is known about the outcomes of both procedures. Yet most reviews of the aversive control of behavior emphasize active avoidance learning and ignore passive avoidance learning. I shall, in this paper, emphasize the similarities, rather than the differences between active and passive avoidance learning. I shall point out that there is a rich store of knowledge of active avoidance learning which, when applied to the punishment procedure, increases our understanding of some of the puzzling and sometimes chaotic results obtained in punishment experiments.

But first, I would like to review some of the empirical generalities which appear to describe the outcomes of experiments on *punishment* and passive avoidance learning. For this purpose, I divide the evidence into 5 classes: (*a*) the effects of punishment on behavior previously established by *rewards* or positive reinforcement, (*b*) the effects of punishment on *consummatory* responses, (*c*) the effects of punishment on complex, sequential patterns of *innate* responses, (*d*) the effects of punishment on discrete reflexes, (*e*) the effects of punishment on responses previously established by punishment—or, if you will, the effects of punishment on active escape and avoidance responses. The effectiveness of punishment will be seen to differ greatly across these five classes of experiments. For convenience, I mean by *effectiveness* the degree to which a punishment procedure produces *suppression* of, or facilitates the *extinction* of, existing response patterns.

Now, let us look at punishment for *instrumental responses or habits previously established by reward or positive reinforcers.* First, the outcomes of punishment procedures applied to previously rewarded habits are strongly related to the *intensity of the punishing* agent. Sometimes intensity is independently defined and measured, as in the case of electric shock. Sometimes we

have qualitative evaluations, as in the case of Maier's (1949) rat bumping his nose on a locked door, or Masserman's (Masserman & Pechtel, 1953) spider monkey being presented with a toy snake, or Skinner's (1938) rat receiving a slap on the paw from a lever, or my dog receiving a swat from a rolled-up newspaper. As the intensity of shock applied to rats, cats, and dogs is increased from about .1 milliampere to 4 milliamperes, these orderly results can be obtained: (*a*) *detection* and *arousal,* wherein the punisher can be used as a cue, discriminative stimulus, response intensifier, or even as a secondary reinforcer; (*b*) *temporary suppression,* wherein punishment results in suppression of the punished response, followed by complete recovery, such that the subject later appears unaltered from his prepunished state; (*c*) *partial suppression,* wherein the subject always displays some lasting suppression of the punished response, without total recovery; and (*d*) finally, there is *complete suppression,* with no observable recovery. Any of these outcomes can be produced, other things being equal, by merely varying the intensity of the noxious stimulus used (Azrin & Holz, 1961), when we punish responses previously established by reward or positive reinforcement. No wonder different experimenters report incomparable outcomes. Azrin (1959) has produced a response-rate *increase* while operants are punished. Storms, Boroczi, and Broen (1962) have produced long-lasting suppression of operants in rats.[2] Were pun-

2 Since the delivery of this address, several articles have appeared concerning the punishment intensity problem. See especially Karsh (1963), Appel (1963), and Walters and Rogers (1963). All these studies support the conclusion that shock intensity is a crucial variable, and high intensities produce lasting suppression effects.

ishment intensities different? Were punishment durations different? (Storms, Boroczi, & Broen, 1963, have shown albino rats to be more resistant to punishment than are hooded rats, and this is another source of discrepancy between experiments.)

But other variables are possibly as important as punishment intensity, and their operation can make it unnecessary to use *intense* punishers in order to produce the effective suppression of a response previously established by positive reinforcement. Here are some selected examples:

1. *Proximity* in time and space to the punished response determines to some extent the effectiveness of a punishment. There is a response-suppression gradient. This has been demonstrated in the runway (Brown, 1948; Karsh, 1962), in the lever box (Azrin, 1956), and in the shuttle box (Kamin, 1959). This phenomenon has been labeled the gradient of temporal delay of punishment.

2. The conceptualized *strength* of a response, as measured by its resistance to extinction after omission of positive reinforcement, predicts the effect of a punishment contingent upon the response. Strong responses, so defined, are more resistant to the suppressive effects of punishment. Thus, for example, the overtraining of a response, which often decreases ordinary resistance to experimental extinction, also increases the effectiveness of punishment (Karsh, 1962; Miller, 1960a) as a response suppressor.

3. *Adaptation* to punishment can occur, and this *decreases* its effectiveness. New, intense punishers are better than old, intense punishers (Miller, 1960). Punishment intensity, if slowly increased, tends not to be as effective as

in the case where it is introduced initially at its high-intensity value.

4. In general, resistance to extinction is decreased whenever a previously reinforced response is punished. However, if the subject is habituated to receiving shock together with positive reinforcement during reward training, the relationship can be reversed, and punishment during extinction can actually increase resistance to extinction (Holz & Azrin, 1961). Evidently, punishment, so employed, can functionally operate as a *secondary reinforcer,* or as a cue for reward, or as an arouser.

5. Punishments become extremely effective when the response-suppression period is tactically used as an aid to the reinforcement of new responses that are topographically *incompatible* with the punished one. When new instrumental acts are established which lead to the old goal (a new *means* to an old *end*), a punishment of very low intensity can have very long-lasting suppression effects. Whiting and Mowrer (1943) demonstrated this clearly. They first rewarded one route to food, then punished it. When the subjects ceased taking the punished route, they provided a new rewarded route. The old route was not traversed again. This reliable suppression effect also seems to be true of temporal, discriminative restraints on behavior. The suppression of urination in dogs, under the control of *indoor stimuli,* is extremely effective in housebreaking the dog, as long as urination is allowed to go unpunished under the control of *outdoor stimuli.* There is a valuable lesson here in the effective use of punishments in producing *impulse control.* A *rewarded alternative,* under discriminative control, makes passive avoidance training a potent behavioral influence. It can produce a highly re-

liable dog or child. In some preliminary observations of puppy training, we have noted that puppies raised in the lab, if punished by the swat of a newspaper for eating horsemeat, and rewarded for eating pellets, will starve themselves to death when only given the opportunity to eat the taboo horsemeat. They eagerly eat the pellets when they are available.

It is at this point that we should look at the experiments wherein punishment appears to have only a temporary suppression effect. Most of these experiments offered the subject *no* rewarded alternative to the punished response in attaining his goal. In many such experiments, it was a case of take a chance or go hungry. Hunger-drive strength, under such no-alternative conditions, together with punishment intensity, are the crucial variables in predicting recovery from the suppression effects of punishment. Here, an interesting, yet hard-to-understand phenomenon frequently occurs, akin to Freudian "reaction formation." If a subject has been punished for touching some manipulandum which yields food, he may stay nearer to the manipulandum under low hunger drive and move farther away from it under high hunger drive, even though the probability of finally touching the manipulandum increases as hunger drive increases. This phenomenon is complex and needs to be studied in some detail. Our knowledge of it now is fragmentary. It was observed by Hunt and Schlosberg (1950) when the water supply of rats was electrified, and we have seen it occur in approach-avoidance conflict experiments in our laboratory, but we do not know the precise conditions for its occurrence.

Finally, I should point out that the attributes of effective punishments vary *across species* and *across stages in maturational development* within species. A toy snake can frighten monkeys. It does not faze a rat. A loud noise terrified Watson's little Albert. To us it is merely a Chinese gong.

I have sketchily reviewed some effects of punishment on *instrumental* acts established by *positive reinforcers*. We have seen that any result one might desire, from response enhancement and little or no suppression, to relatively complete suppression, can be obtained with our current knowledge of appropriate experimental conditions. Now let us look at the effects of punishment on *consummatory acts*. Here, the data are, to me, surprising. One would think that consummatory acts, often being of biological significance for the survival of the individual and the species, would be highly resistant to suppression by punishment. The *contrary* appears to be so. Male sexual behavior may be seriously suppressed by weak punishment (Beach, Conovitz, Steinberg, & Goldstein, 1956; Gantt, 1944). Eating in dogs and cats can be permanently suppressed by a moderate shock delivered through the feet or through the food dish itself (Lichtenstein, 1950; Masserman, 1943). Such suppression effects can lead to fatal self-starvation. A toy snake presented to a spider monkey while he is eating can result in self-starvation (Masserman & Pechtel, 1953).

The interference with consummatory responses by punishment needs a great deal of investigation. Punishment seems to be especially effective in breaking up this class of responses, and one can ask *why,* with some profit. Perhaps the intimate temporal connection between drive, incentive, and punishment results in drive or incentive becoming conditioned-stimulus (CS) patterns for aversive emotional reactions when consummatory acts are punished. Perhaps this interferes with vegetative activity: i.e., does it "kill the appetite" in a hungry subject? But, one may ask why the same punisher might not appear to be as effective when made contingent on an *instrumental* act as contrasted with a consummatory act. Perhaps the nature of operants is such that they are separated in time and space and response topography from consummatory behavior and positive incentive stimuli, so that appetitive reactions are not clearly present during punishments for operants. We do not know enough yet about such matters, and speculation about it is still fun.

Perhaps the most interesting parametric variation one can study, in experiments on the effects of punishment on consummatory acts, is the *temporal order* of rewards and punishments. If we hold hunger drive constant, shock-punishment intensity constant, and food-reward amounts constant, a huge differential effect can be obtained when we reverse the order of reward and punishment. If we train a cat to approach a food cup, its behavior in the experimental setting will become quite stereotyped. Then, if we introduce shock to the cat's feet while it is eating, the cat will vocalize, retreat, and show fear reactions. It will be slow to recover its eating behavior in this situation. Indeed, as Masserman (1943) has shown, such a procedure is likely, if repeated a few times, to lead to self-starvation. Lichtenstein (1950) showed the same phenomenon in dogs. Contrast this outcome with that found when the temporal order of food and shock is *reversed*. We now use shock as a discriminative stimulus to signalize the availability of food. When the cat is performing well, the shock

may produce eating with a latency of less than 5 seconds. The subject's appetite does not seem to be disturbed. One cannot imagine a more dramatic difference than that induced by reversing the temporal order of reward and punishment (Holz & Azrin, 1962; Masserman, 1943).

Thus, the effects of punishment are partly determined by those events that directly precede it and those that directly follow it. A punishment is not just a punishment. It is an event in a temporal and spatial flow of stimulation and behavior, and its effects will be produced by its temporal and spatial point of insertion in that flow.

I have hastily surveyed some of the effects of punishment when it has been made contingent either on rewarded *operants* and instrumental acts or on *consummatory* acts. A third class of behaviors, closely related to consummatory acts, but yet a little different, are *instinctive act sequences:* the kinds of complex, innately governed behaviors which the ethologists study, such as nest building in birds. There has been little adequate experimentation, to my knowledge, on the effects of punishment on such innate behavior sequences. There are, however, some hints of interesting things to come. For example, sometimes frightening events will produce what the ethologists call displacement reactions—the expression of an inappropriate behavior pattern of an innate sort. We need to experiment with such phenomena in a systematic fashion. The best example I could find of this phenomenon is the imprinting of birds on moving objects, using the locomotor following response as an index. Moltz, Rosenblum, and Halikas (1959) in one experiment, and Kovach and Hess (1963), see also Hess (1959a,

1959b) in another, have shown that the punishment of such imprinted behavior sometimes depresses its occurrence. However, if birds are punished prior to the presentation of an imprinted object, often the following response will be energized. It is hard to understand what this finding means, except that punishment can either arouse or inhibit such behavior, depending on the manner of presentation of punishment. The suggestion is that imprinting is partially a function of fear or distress. The effectiveness of punishment also is found to be related to the critical period for imprinting (Kovach & Hess, 1963).

However, the systematic study of known punishment parameters as they affect a wide variety of complex sequences of innate behaviors is yet to be carried out. It would appear to be a worthwhile enterprise, for it is the type of work which would enable us to make a new attack on the effects of experience on innate behavior patterns. Ultimately the outcomes of such experiments *could* affect psychoanalytic conceptions of the effects of trauma on impulses of an innate sort.[3]

A fourth class of behavior upon which punishment can be made contingent, is the simple, discrete reflex. For example, what might happen if a conditioned or an unconditioned knee

[3] Since the delivery of this address, an article has appeared on this specific problem. See Adler and Hogan (1963). The authors showed that the gill-extension response of *Betta plendens* could be conditioned to a previously neutral stimulus by a Pavlovian technique, and it could also be suppressed by electric-shock punishment. This is an important finding, because there are very few known cases where the same response can be both conditioned and trained. Here, the gill-extension response is typically elicited by a rival fish, and is usually interpreted to be aggressive or hostile in nature.

jerk were punished? We are completely lacking in information on this point. Can subjects be trained to inhibit reflexes under aversive motivation? Or does such motivation sensitize and enhance reflexes? Some simple experiments are appropriate, but I was unable to find them in the published work I read.

A fifth class of behavior, upon which punishment can be made contingent, is behavior *previously established by punishment procedures:* in other words, the effect of passive avoidance training on existing, active avoidance learned responses. This use of punishment produces an unexpected outcome. In general, if the same noxious stimulus is used to punish a response as was used to establish it in the first place, the response becomes strengthened during initial applications of punishment. After several such events, however, the response may weaken, but not always. The similarity of the noxious stimulus used for active avoidance training to that used for punishment of the established avoidance response can be of great importance. For example, Carlsmith (1961) has shown that one can increase resistance to extinction by using the same noxious stimuli for both purposes and yet decrease resistance to extinction by using equally noxious, but discriminatively different, punishments. He trained some rats to run in order to avoid shock, then punished them during extinction by blowing a loud horn. He trained other rats to run in order to avoid the loud horn, then during extinction he punished them by shocking them for running. In two control groups, the punisher stimulus and training stimulus were the same. The groups which were trained and then punished by different noxious stimuli extinguished more rapidly during punishment than did the groups in which the active avoidance training unconditioned stimulus (US) was the same as the passive avoidance training US. Thus, punishment for responses established originally by punishment may be ineffective in eliminating the avoidance responses they are supposed to eliminate. Indeed, the punishment may strengthen the responses. We need to know more about this puzzling phenomenon. It is interesting to me that in Japan, Imada (1959) has been systematically exploring shock intensity as it affects this phenomenon.

Our quick survey of the effects of punishment on five classes of responses revealed a wide variety of discrepant phenomena. Thus, to predict in even the grossest way the action of punishment on a response, one has to know *how* that particular response was originally inserted in the subject's response repertoire. Is the response an instrumental one which was strengthened by reward? Is it instead a consummatory response? Is it an innate sequential response pattern? Is it a discrete reflex? Was it originally established by means of punishment? *Where,* temporally, in a behavior sequence, was the punishment used? How *intense* was it? These are but a few of the relevant, critical questions, the answers to which are necessary in order for us to make reasonable predictions about the effects of punishment. Thus, to conclude, as some psychologists have, that the punishment procedure is typically either effective or ineffective, typically either a temporary suppressor or a permanent one, is to oversimplify irresponsibly a complex area of scientific knowledge, one still containing a myriad of in-

triguing problems for experimental attack.

Yet, the complexities involved in ascertaining the effects of punishment on behavior *need not* be a bar to useful speculation ultimately leading to experimentation of a fruitful sort. The complexities should, however, dictate a great deal of caution in making dogmatic statements about whether punishment is effective or ineffective as a behavioral influence, or whether it is good or bad. I do *not* wish to do that. I would like now to speculate about the data-oriented theories, rather than support or derogate the dogmas and the social philosophies dealing with punishment. I will get to the dogmas later.

Theory

Here is a theoretical approach that, for me, has high pragmatic value in stimulating new lines of experimentation. Many psychologists today consider the punishment procedure to be a special case of avoidance training, and the resultant learning processes to be theoretically identical in nature. Woodworth and Schlosberg (1954) distinguish the two training procedures, *"punishment for action"* from *"punishment for inaction,"* but assume that the same theoretical motive, a "positive incentive value of safety" can explain the learning produced by both procedures. Dinsmoor (1955) argues that the facts related to both procedures are well explained by simple stimulus-response (S-R) principles of avoidance learning. He says:

If we punish the subject for making a given response or sequence of responses—that is, apply aversive stimulation, like shock—the cues or discriminative stimuli for this response will correspond to the warning signals that are typically used in more direct studies of avoidance training. By his own response to these stimuli, the subject himself produces the punishing stimulus and pairs or correlates it with these signals. As a result, they too become aversive. In the meantime, any variations in the subject's behavior that interfere or conflict with the chain of reactions leading to the punishment delay the occurrence of the final response and the receipt of the stimulation that follows it. These variations in behavior disrupt the discriminative stimulus pattern for the continuation of the punishment chain, changing the current stimulation from an aversive to a nonaversive compound; they are conditioned, differentiated, and maintained by the reinforcing effects of the change in stimulation [p. 96].

The foci of the Dinsmoor analysis are the processes whereby: (*a*) discriminative stimuli become aversive, and (*b*) instrumental acts are reinforced. He stays at the quasi-descriptive level. He uses a peripheralistic, S-R analysis, in which response-produced proprioceptive stimuli and exteroceptive stimuli serve to hold behavior chains together. He rejects, as unnecessary, concepts such as fear or anxiety, in explaining the effectiveness of punishment.

Mowrer (1960) also argues that the facts related to the two training procedures are explained by a common set of principles, but Mowrer's principles are somewhat different than those of either Woodworth and Schlosberg, or Dinsmoor, cited above. Mowrer says:

In both instances, there is fear conditioning; and in both instances a way of behaving is found which eliminates or controls the fear. The only important distinction, it seems is that the stimuli to which the fear gets connected are different. In so-called punishment, these stimuli are produced by (correlated with) the behavior, or response, which we wish to block;

whereas, in so-called avoidance learning, the fear-arousing stimuli are not response-produced—they are, so to say, extrinsic rather than intrinsic, independent rather than response-dependent. But in both cases there is avoidance and in both cases there is its antithesis, punishment; hence the impropriety of referring to the one as "punishment" and to the other as "avoidance learning." Obviously precision and clarity of understanding are better served by the alternative terms here suggested, namely, passive avoidance learning and active avoidance learning, respectively. . . . But, as we have seen, the two phenomena involve exactly the same basic principles of fear conditioning and of the reinforcement of whatever action (or inaction) eliminates the fear [pp. 31–32].

I like the simple beauty of each of the three unifying positions; what holds for punishment and its action on behavior should hold also for escape and avoidance training, and vice versa. Generalizations about one process should tell us something about the other. New experimental relationships discovered in the one experimental setting should tell us how to predict a new empirical event in the other experimental setting. A brief discussion of a few selected examples can illustrate this possibility.

Applications of Theory

I use a case in point stemming from work done in our own laboratory. It gives us new hints about some hidden sources of effectiveness of punishment. Remember, for the sake of argument, that we are assuming many important similarities to exist between active and passive avoidance-learning processes. Therefore, we can look at active avoidance learning as a theoretical device to suggest to us new, unstudied variables pertaining to the effectiveness of punishment.

Turner and I have recently published an extensive monograph (1962) on human traumatic avoidance learning. Our experiments showed that when a very reflexive, short-latency, skeletal response, such as a toe twitch, was used as an escape and avoidance response, grave difficulties in active avoidance learning were experienced by the subject. Experimental variations which tended to render the escape responses more emitted, more deliberate, more voluntary, more operant, or less reflexive, tended also to render the avoidance responses easier to learn. Thus, when a subject was required to move a knob in a slot in order to avoid shock, learning was rapid, in contrast to the many failures to learn with a toe-flexion avoidance response.

There are descriptions of this phenomenon already available in several published experiments on active avoidance learning, but their implications have not previously been noted. When Schlosberg (1934) used for the avoidance response a highly reflexive, short-latency, paw-flexion response in the rat, he found active avoidance learning to be unreliable, unstable, and quick to extinguish. Whenever the rats made active avoidance flexions, a decrement in response strength ensued. When the rats were shocked on several escape trials, the avoidance response tended to reappear for a few trials. Thus, learning to avoid was a tortuous, cyclical process, never exceeding 30% success. Contrast these results with the active avoidance training of nonreflexive, long-latency operants, such as rats running in Hunter's (1935) circular maze. Hunter found that the occurrence of avoidance responses tended to

produce more avoidance responses. Omission of shock seemed to reinforce the avoidance running response. Omission of shock seemed to extinguish the avoidance paw flexion. Clearly the operant-respondent distinction has predictive value in active avoidance learning.

The same trend can be detected in experiments using dogs as subjects. For example, Brogden (1949), using the forepaw-flexion response, found that meeting a twenty/twenty criterion of avoidance learning was quite difficult. He found that 30 dogs took approximately 200–600 trials to reach the avoidance criterion. The response used was, in our language, highly reflexive— it was totally elicited by the shock on escape trials with a very short latency, approximately .3 second. Compare, if you will, the learning of active avoidance by dogs in the shuttle box with that found in the forelimb-flexion experiment. In the shuttle box, a large number of dogs were able to embark on their criterion trials after 5–15 active avoidance-training trials. Early escape response latencies were long. Resistance to extinction is, across these two types of avoidance responses, inversely related to trials needed for a subject to achieve criterion. Conditions leading to quick acquisition are, in this case, those conducive to slow extinction. Our conclusion, then, is that high-probability, short-latency, *respondents* are not as good as medium-probability, long-latency operants when they are required experimentally to function as active avoidance responses. This generalization seems to hold for rats, dogs, and college students.

How can we make the inferential leap from such findings in active avoidance training to possible variations in punishment experiments? It is relatively simple to generalize across the two kinds of experiments in the case of CS-US interval, US intensity, and CS duration. But the inferential steps are not as obvious in the case of the operant-respondent distinction. So I will trace out the logic in some detail. If one of the major effects of punishment is to motivate or elicit new behaviors, and reinforce them through removal of punishment, and thus, as Dinsmoor describes, establish avoidance responses incompatible with a punished response, how does the operant-respondent distinction logically enter? Here, Mowrer's two-process avoidance-learning theory can suggest a possible answer. Suppose, for example, that a hungry rat has been trained to lever press for food and is performing at a stable rate. Now we make a short-duration, high-intensity pulse of shock contingent upon the bar press. The pulse elicits a startle pattern that produces a release of the lever in .2 second, and the shock is gone. The rat freezes for a few seconds, breathing heavily, and he urinates and defecates. It is our supposition that a conditioned emotional reaction (CER) is thereby established, with its major stimulus control coming from the sight of the bar, the touch of the bar, and proprioceptive stimuli aroused by the lever-press movements themselves. This is, as Dinsmoor describes it, the development of acquired aversiveness of stimuli; or, as Mowrer describes it, the acquisition of conditioned fear reactions. Therefore, Pavlovian conditioning variables should be the important ones in the development of this process. The reappearance of lever pressing in this punished rat would thus depend on the extinction of the CER and skeletal freezing. If no further shocks are administered, then the CER should extinguish according to the laws of Pavlovian extinction, and reappearance of the lever press should not take long, even if the shock-intensity level were high enough to have been able to produce active avoidance learning in another apparatus.

Two-process avoidance theory tells us that something very important for successful and durable response suppression was missing in the punishment procedure we just described. What was lacking in this punishment procedure was a good operant to allow us to reinforce a reliable avoidance response. Because the reaction to shock was a respondent, was highly *reflexive,* and was quick to occur, I am led to argue that the termination of shock will *not* reinforce it, nor will it lead to stable avoidance responses. This conclusion follows directly from our experiments on human avoidance learning. If the termination of shock is made contingent on the occurrence of an operant, especially an operant topographically incompatible with the lever press, an active avoidance learning process should then ensue. So I will now propose that we shock the rat until he huddles in a corner of the box. The rat will have learned to *do* something arbitrary whenever the controlling CSs reappear. Thus, the rat in the latter procedure, if he is to press the lever again, must undergo *two* extinction processes. The CER, established by the pairing of CS patterns and shock, must become weaker. Second, the learned huddling response must extinguish. This combination of requirements should make the effect of punishment more lasting, if my inferences are correct. Two problems must be solved by the subject, not one. The experiments needed to test these speculations are, it would appear, easy to design, and there is no reason why one should not be able to gather the requisite information in the near future. I feel that there is much to be gained in carrying on theoretical games like this, with the major assumptions being (a) that active and passive avoidance learning are similar processes, ones in which the same variables have analogous effects, and (b) that two processes, the conditioning of fear reactions, and the reinforcement of operants incompatible with the punished response, may operate in punishment experiments.

There is another gain in playing theoretical games of this sort. One can use them to question the usual significance imputed to past findings. Take, for example, the extensive studies of Neal Miller (1959) and his students, and Brown (1948) and his students, on gradients of approach and avoidance in conflict situations. Our foregoing analysis of the role of the operant-respondent distinction puts to question one of their central assumptions—that the avoidance gradient is unconditionally steeper than is the approach gradient in approach-avoidance conflicts. In such experiments, the subject is typically trained while hungry to run down a short alley to obtain food. After the running is reliable, the subject is shocked, usually near the goal, in such a way that entering the goal box is discouraged temporarily. The subsequent behavior of the typical subject consists of remaining in the start box, making abortive approaches to the food box, showing hesitancy, oscillation, and various displacement activities, like grooming. Eventually, if shock is eliminated by the experimenter, the subject resumes running to

food. The avoidance tendency is therefore thought to have extinguished sufficiently so that the magnitude of the conceptualized approach gradient exceeds that of the avoidance gradient at the goal box. The steepness of the avoidance gradient as a function of distance from the goal box is inferred from the behavior of the subject *prior* to the extinction of the avoidance tendencies. If the subject stays as far away from the goal box as possible, the avoidance gradient may be inferred to be either displaced upward, or if the subject slowly creeps up on the goal box from trial to trial, it may be inferred to be less steep than the approach gradient. Which alternative is more plausible? Miller and his collaborators very cleverly have shown that the latter alternative is a better interpretation.

The differential-steepness assumption appears to be substantiated by several studies by Miller and his collaborators (Miller & Murray, 1952; Murray & Berkun, 1955). They studied the displacement of conflicted approach responses along both spatial and color dimensions, and clearly showed that the approach responses generalized more readily than did the avoidance responses. Rats whose running in an alley had been completely suppressed by shock punishment showed recovery of running in a similar alley. Thus the inference made was that the avoidance gradient is steeper than is the approach gradient; avoidance tendencies weaken more rapidly with changes in the external environmental setting than do approach tendencies. On the basis of the analysis I made of the action of punishment, both as a US for the establishment of a Pavlovian CER and as a potent event for the reinforcement of instrumental escape and avoidance responses, it seems to me very likely that the approach-avoidance conflict experiments have been carried out in such a way as to produce inevitably the steeper avoidance gradients. In other words, these experiments from my particular viewpoint have been inadvertently biased, and they were not appropriate for testing hypotheses about the gradient slopes.

My argument is as follows: Typically, the subject in an approach-avoidance experiment is trained to perform a specific sequence of responses under reward incentive and appetitive drive conditions. He runs to food when hungry. In contrast, when the shock is introduced into the runway, it is usually placed near the goal, and no specific, long sequence of instrumental responses is required of the subject before the shock is terminated. Thus, the initial strengths of the approach and avoidance instrumental responses (which are in conflict) are not equated by analogous or symmetrical procedures. Miller has thoroughly and carefully discussed this, and has suggested that the avoidance gradient would not have as steep a slope if the shock were encountered by the rat early in the runway in the case where the whole runway is electrified. While this comment is probably correct, it does not go far enough, and I would like to elaborate on it. I would argue that if one wants to study the relative steepnesses of approach and avoidance responses in an unbiased way, the competing instrumental responses should be established is a *symmetrical* fashion. After learning to run down an alley to food, the subject should be shocked near the goal box or in it, and the shock should not be terminated until the subject has escaped all the way into the start box.

Then one can argue that two conflicting instrumental responses have been established. First, the subject runs one way for food; now he runs the same distance in the opposite direction in order to escape shock. When he stays in the start box, he avoids shock entirely. Then the generalization or displacement of the approach and avoidance responses can be fairly studied.

I am arguing that we need *instrumental*-response balancing, as well as *Pavlovian*-conditioning balancing, in such conflict experiments, if the slopes of gradients are to be determined for a test of the differential-steepness assumption. Two-process avoidance-learning theory requires such a symmetrical test. In previous experiments, an aversive CER and its respondent motor pattern, not a well-reinforced avoidance response, has been pitted against a well-reinforced instrumental-approach response. Since the instrumental behavior of the subject is being used subsequently to test for the slope of the gradients, the usual asymmetrical procedure is, I think, not appropriate. My guess is that, if the symmetrical procedure I described is actually used, the slopes of the two gradients will be essentially the same, and the recovery of the subject from the effects of punishment will be seen to be nearly all-or-none. That is, the avoidance gradient, as extinction of the CER proceeds in time, will drop below the approach gradient, and this will hold all along the runway if the slopes of the two gradients are indeed the same. Using the test of displacement, subjects should stay in the starting area of a similar alley on initial tests and when they finally move forward they should go all the way to the goal box.

The outcomes of such experiments

would be a matter of great interest to me, for, as you will read in a moment, I feel that the suppressive power of punishment over instrumental acts has been understated. The approach-avoidance conflict experiment is *but one* example among many wherein the outcome *may have been* inadvertently biased in the direction of showing reward-training influences to be superior, in some particular way, to punishment-training procedures. Now let us look more closely at this matter of bias.

Legends

Skinner, in 1938, described the effect of a short-duration slap on the paw on the extinction of lever pressing in the rat. Temporary suppression of lever-pressing rate was obtained. When the rate increased, it exceeded the usual extinction performance. The total number of responses before extinction occurred was not affected by the punishment for lever pressing. Estes (1944) obtained similar results, and attributed the temporary suppression to the establishment of a CER (anxiety) which dissipated rapidly. Tolman, Hall, and Bretnall (1932) had shown earlier that punishment could enhance maze learning by serving as a cue for correct, rewarded behavior. Skinner made these observations (on the seemingly ineffective nature of punishment as a response weakener) the basis for his advocacy of a positive reinforcement regime in his utopia, *Walden Two*. In *Walden Two*, Skinner (1948), speaking through the words of Frazier, wrote: "We are now discovering at an untold cost in human suffering—that in the long run punishment doesn't reduce the probability that an act will occur [p. 260]." No

punishments would be used there, because they would produce poor behavioral control, he claimed.

During the decade following the publication of *Walden Two*, Skinner (1953) maintained his position concerning the effects of punishment on instrumental responses: Response suppression is but temporary, and the side effects, such as fear and neurotic and psychotic disturbances, are not worth the temporary advantages of the use of punishment. He said:

In the long run, punishment, unlike reinforcement works to the disadvantage of both the punished organism and the punishing agency [p. 183].
The fact that punishment does not permanently reduce a tendency to respond is in agreement with Freud's discovery of the surviving activity of what he called repressed wishes [p. 184].
Punishment, as we have seen, does not create a negative probability that a response will be made but rather a positive probability that incompatible behavior will occur [p. 222].

It must be said, in Skinner's defense, that in 1953 he devoted about 12 pages to the topic of punishment in his introductory textbook. Other texts had devoted but a few words to this topic.

In Bugelski's (1956) words about the early work on punishment: "The purport of the experiments mentioned above appears to be to demonstrate that punishment is ineffective in eliminating behavior. This conclusion appears to win favor with various sentimentalists [p: 275]." Skinner (1961) summarized his position most recently in this way:

Ultimate advantages seem to be particularly easy to overlook in the control of behavior, where a quick though slight advantage may have undue weight. Thus, although we boast that the birch rod has been abandoned, most school children are still under aversive control—not because punishment is more effective in the long run, but because it yields immediate results. It is easier for the teacher to control the student by threatening punishment than by using positive reinforcement with its *deferred, though more powerful,* effects [p. 36.08, italics mine].

Skinner's conclusions were drawn over a span of time when, just as is the case *now,* there was no conclusive evidence about the supposedly more powerful and long-lasting effects of positive reinforcement. I admire the humanitarian and kindly dispositions contained in such writings. But the scientific basis for the conclusions therein was shabby, because, even in 1938, there were conflicting data which demonstrated the great effectiveness of punishment in controlling instrumental behavior. For example, the widely cited experiments of Warden and Aylesworth (1927) showed that discrimination learning in the rat was more rapid and more stable when incorrect responses were punished with shock than when reward alone for the correct response was used. Later on, avoidance-training experiments in the 1940s and 1950s added impressive data on the long-lasting behavioral control exerted by noxious stimuli (Solomon & Brush, 1956). In spite of this empirical development, many writers of books in the field of learning now devote but a few lines to the problem of punishment, perhaps a reflection of the undesirability of trying to bring satisfying order out of seeming chaos. In this category are the recent books of Spence, Hull, and Kimble. An exception is Bugelski (1956) who devotes several pages to the complexities of this topic.

Most contemporary *introductory psychology* texts devote but a paragraph or two to punishment as a scientific problem. Conspicuously, George Miller's new book, *Psychology, the Science of Mental Life,* has no discussion of punishment in it.

The most exhaustive textbook treatment today is that of Deese (1958), and it is a thoughtful and objective evaluation, a singular event in this area of our science. The most exhaustive journal article is that by Church (1963), who has thoroughly summarized our knowledge of punishment. I am indebted to Church for letting me borrow freely from his fine essay in prepublication form. Without this assistance, the organization of this paper would have been much more difficult, indeed.

Perhaps one reason for the usual textbook relegation of the topic of punishment to the fringe of experimental psychology is the wide-spread belief that punishment is unimportant because *it does not really weaken habits;* that it pragmatically is a *poor controller* of behavior; that it is extremely *cruel* and unnecessary; and that it is a technique leading to *neurosis* and worse. This legend, and it is a legend without sufficient empirical basis, probably arose with Thorndike (1931). Punishment, in the time of Thorndike, used to be called punishment, not passive avoidance training. The term referred to the use of noxious stimuli for the avowed purpose of discouraging some selected kind of behavior. Thorndike (1931) came to the conclusion that punishment did not really accomplish its major purpose, the destruction or extinction of habits. In his book, *Human Learning,* he said:

Annoyers do not act on learning in general by weakening whatever connection they follow. If they do anything in learning, they do it indirectly, by informing the learner that such and such a response in such and such a situation brings distress, or by making the learner feel fear of a certain object, or by making him jump back from a certain place, or by some other definite and specific change which they produce in him [p. 46].

This argument is similar to that of Guthrie (1935), and of Wendt (1936), in explaining the extinction of instrumental acts and conditioned reflexes. They maintained that extinction was not the weakening of a habit, but the replacement of a habit by a new one, even though the new one might only be sitting still and doing very little.

When Thorndike claimed that the effects of punishment were indirect, he was emphasizing the power of punishment to evoke behavior other than that which produced the punishment; in much the same manner, Guthrie emphasized the extinction procedure as one arousing competing responses. The competing-response theory of extinction today cannot yet be empirically chosen over other theories such as Pavlovian and Hullian inhibition theory, or the frustration theories of Amsel or Spence. The Thorndikian position on punishment is limited in the same way. It is difficult to designate the empirical criteria which would enable us to know, on those occasions when punishment for a response results in a weakening of performance of that response, whether a habit was indeed weakened or not. How can one tell whether competing responses have displaced the punished response, or whether the punished habit is itself weakened by punishment? Thorndike could not tell, and neither could Guthrie. Yet a legend

was perpetuated. Perhaps the acceptance of the legend had something to do with the lack of concerted research on punishment from 1930–1955. For example, psychologists were not then particularly adventuresome in their search for experimentally effective punishments.

Or, in addition to the legend, perhaps a bit of softheartedness is partly responsible for limiting our inventiveness. (The Inquisitors, the Barbarians, and the Puritans could have given us some good hints! They did not have electric shock, but they had a variety of interesting ideas, which, regrettably, they often put to practice.) We clearly need to study new kinds of punishments in the laboratory. For most psychologists, a punishment in the laboratory means electric shock. A few enterprising experimenters have used air blasts, the presentation of an innate fear releaser, or a signal for the coming omission of reinforcement, as punishments. But we still do not know enough about using these stimuli in a controlled fashion to produce either behavior suppression, or a CER effect, or the facilitation of extinction. Many aversive states have gone unstudied. For example, conditioned nausea and vomiting is easy to produce, but it has not been used in the role of punishment. Even the brain stimulators, though they have since 1954 tickled brain areas that will instigate active escape learning, have not used this knowledge to study systematically the punishing effects of such stimulation on existing responses.

While the more humanitarian ones of us were bent on the discovery of new positive reinforcers, there was no such concerted effort on the part of the more brutal ones of us. Thus, for reasons that now completely escape me, some of us in the past were thrilled by the discovery that, under some limited conditions, either a light onset or a light termination could raise lever-pressing rate significantly, though trivially, above operant level. If one is looking for agents to help in the task of getting strong predictive power, and strong control of behavior, such discoveries seem not too exciting. Yet, in contrast, discoveries *already have* been made of the powerful aversive control of behavior. Clearly, we have been afraid of their implications. Humanitarian guilt and normal kindness are undoubtedly involved, as they should be. But I believe that one reason for our fear has been the widespread implication of the *neurotic syndrome* as a *necessary* outcome of all severe punishment procedures. A second reason has been the general acceptance of the behavioral phenomena of rigidity, inflexibility, or narrowed cognitive map, as *necessary* outcomes of experiments in which noxious stimuli have been used. I shall question *both* of these conclusions.

If one should feel that the Skinnerian generalizations about the inadequate effects of punishment on instrumental responses are tinged with a laudable, though thoroughly incorrect and unscientific, sentimentalism and softness, then, in contrast, one can find more than a lurid tinge in discussions of the effects of punishment on the *emotional* balance of the individual. When punishments are asserted to be ineffective controllers of instrumental behavior, they are, in contrast, often asserted to be devastating controllers of emotional reactions, leading to neurotic and psychotic symptoms, and to general pessimism, depressiveness, constric-

tion of thinking, horrible psychosomatic diseases, and even death! This is somewhat of a paradox, I think. The convincing part of such generalizations is only their face validity. There *are* experiments, many of them carefully done, in which these neurotic outcomes were clearly observed. Gantt's (1944) work on neurotic dogs, Masserman's (1943) work on neurotic cats and monkeys, Brady's (1958) recent work on ulcerous monkeys, Maier's (1949) work on fixated rats, show some of the devastating consequences of the utilization of punishment to control behavior. The side effects are frightening, indeed, and should *not* be ignored! But there *must be* some rules, some principles, governing the appearance of such side effects, for they *do not* appear in all experiments involving the use of strong punishment or the elicitation of terror. In Yates' (1962) new book, *Frustration and Conflict,* we find a thorough discussion of punishment as a creator of conflict. Major attention is paid to the instrumental-response outcomes of conflict due to punishment. Phenomena such as rigidity, fixation, regression, aggression, displacement, and primitivization are discussed. Yates accepts the definition of neurosis developed by Maier and by Mowrer: self-defeating behavior oriented toward no goal, yet compulsive in quality. The behavioral phenomena that reveal neuroses are said to be fixations, regressions, aggressions, or resignations. But we are not told the necessary or sufficient experimental conditions under which these dramatic phenomena emerge.

Anyone who has tried to train a rat in a T maze, using food reward for a correct response, and shock to the feet for an incorrect response, knows that there *is* a period of emotionality during early training, but that, thereafter, the rat, when the percentage of correct responses is high, looks like a hungry, well-motivated, happy rat, eager to get from his cage to the experimenter's hand, and thence to the start box. Evidently, merely going through conflict is not a condition for neurosis. The rat is reliable, unswerving in his choices. Is he neurotic? Should this be called subservient resignation? Or a happy adjustment to an inevitable event? Is the behavior constricted? Is it a fixation, an evidence of behavioral rigidity? The criteria for answering such questions are vague today. Even if we should suggest some specific tests for rigidity, they lack face validity. For example, we might examine *discrimination reversal* as a test for *rigidity*. Do subjects who have received reward for the correct response, and punishment for the incorrect response, find it harder to reverse when the contingencies are reversed, as compared with subjects trained with reward alone? Or, we might try a *transfer test,* introducing our subject to a new maze, or to a new jumping stand. Would the previously punished subject generalize more readily than one not so punished? And if he did, would he then be *less discriminating* and thus neurotic? Or, would the previously punished subject generalize poorly and hesitantly, thus being *too discriminating,* and thus neurotic, too? What are the criteria for behavioral *malfunction* as a consequence of the use of punishment? When instrumental responses are used as the indicator, we are, alas, left in doubt!

The most convincing demonstrations of neurotic disturbances stemming from the use of punishment are seen in Masserman's (Masserman & Pechtel, 1953) work with monkeys. But here the criterion for neurosis is *not* based on instrumental responding. Instead, it is based on emotionality expressed in consummatory acts and innate impulses. Masserman's monkeys were frightened by a toy snake while they were eating. Feeding inhibition, shifts in food preferences, odd sexual behavior, tics, long periods of crying, were observed. Here, the criteria have a face validity that is hard to reject. Clearly, punishment was a dangerous and disruptive behavioral influence in Masserman's experiments. Such findings are consonant with the Freudian position postulating the pervasive influences of traumatic experiences, permeating all phases of the affective existence of the individual, and persisting for long time periods.

To harmonize all of the considerations I have raised concerning the conditions leading to neurosis due to punishment is a formidable task. My guess at the moment is that neurotic disturbances arise often in those cases where *consummatory* behavior or *instinctive* behavior is punished, and punished under *nondiscriminatory* control. But this is merely a guess, and in order for it to be adequately tested, Masserman's interesting procedures would have to be repeated, using discriminative stimuli to signalize when it is safe and not safe for the monkey. Such experiments should be carried out if we are to explore adequately the possible effects of punishment on emotionality. Another possibility is that the number of rewarded behavior alternatives in an otherwise punishing situation will determine the emotional aftereffects of punishments. We have seen that Whiting and Mowrer (1943) gave their rats a rewarding alternative, and the resulting behavior was highly reliable. Their rats remained easy to handle and eager to enter the experimental situation. One guess is that increasing the number of behavioral alternatives leading to a consummatory response will, in a situation where only one behavior alternative is being punished, result in reliable behavior and the absence of neurotic emotional manifestations. However, I suspect that matters cannot be that simple. If our animal subject is punished for Response A, and the punishment quickly elicits Response B, and then Response B is quickly rewarded, we have the stimulus contingencies for the establishment of a masochistic habit. Reward follows punishment quickly. Perhaps the subject would then persist in performing the punished Response A? Such questions need to be worked out empirically, and the important parameters must be identified. We are certainly in no position today to specify the necessary or sufficient conditions for experimental neurosis

I have in this talk, decried the stultifying effects of legends concerning punishment. To some extent, my tone was reflective of bias, and so I overstated some conclusions. Perhaps now it would be prudent to soften my claims.[4] I must admit that all is not lost! Recently, I have noted a definite increase in good

parametric studies of punishment on several kinds of behavior. For example, the pages of the *Journal of the Experimental Analysis of Behavior* have, in the last 5 years, become liberally sprinkled with reports of punishment experiments. This is a heartening development, and though it comes 20 years delayed, it is welcome.

Summary: I have covered a great deal of ground here, perhaps too much for the creation of a clear picture. The major points I have made are as follows: *First, the effectiveness of punishment as a controller of instrumental behavior varies with a wide variety of known parameters.* Some of these are: (*a*) intensity of the punishment stimulus, (*b*) whether the response being punished is an instrumental one or a consummatory one, (*c*) whether the response is instinctive or reflexive, (*d*) whether it was established originally by reward or by punishment, (*e*) whether or not the punishment is closely associated in time with the punished response, (*f*) the temporal arrangements of reward and punishment, (*g*) the strength of the response to be punished, (*h*) the familiarity of the subject with the punishment being used, (*i*) whether or not a reward alternative is offered during the behavior-suppression period induced by punishment, (*j*) whether a distinctive, incompatible avoidance response is strengthened by omission of punishment, (*k*) the age of the subject, and (*l*) the strain and species of the subject.

Second, I have tried to show the theoretical virtues of considering active and passive avoidance learning to be similar processes, and have shown the utility of a two-process learning theory. I have described some examples of the application of findings in active avoidance-learning experiments to the creation of new punishment experiments and to the reanalysis of approach-avoidance conflict experiments.

Third, I have questioned persisting legends concerning both the ineffectiveness of punishment as an agent for behavioral change as well as the inevitability of the

---

[4] Presidential addresses sometimes produce statements that may be plausible at the moment, but on second thought may seem inappropriate. In contrast to my complaints about inadequate research on punishment and the nature of active and passive avoidance learning are Hebb's (1960) recent remarks in his APA Presidential Address. He said: "The choice is whether to prosecute the attack, or to go on with the endless and trivial elaboration of the same set of basic experiments (on pain avoidance for example); trivial because they have added nothing to knowledge for some time though the early work was of great value [p. 740]."

neurotic outcome as a legacy of all punishment procedures.

Finally, I have indicated where new experimentation might be especially interesting or useful in furthering our understanding of the effects of punishment.

If there is one idea I would have you
retain, it is this: Our laboratory knowledge
of the effects of punishment on instrumental and emotional behavior is still
rudimentary—much too rudimentary to
make an intelligent choice among conflicting ideas about it. The polarized doctrines
are probably inadequate and in error. The
popularized Skinnerian position concern-

ing the inadequacy of punishment in suppressing *instrumental* behavior is, if correct
at all, only conditionally correct. The
Freudian position, pointing to pain or
trauma as an agent for the pervasive and
long-lasting distortion of *affective* behavior
is equally questionable, and only conditionally correct.

Happily, there is now growing attention
being paid to the effects of punishment on
behavior, and this new development will
undoubtedly accelerate, because the complexity of our current knowledge, and the
perplexity it engenders, are, I think, exciting and challenging.

Psychological Bulletin, 1963, vol. 60, pp. 441–451

Reward and Punishment Associated with the Same Goal Response:

A FACTOR IN THE LEARNING OF MOTIVES[1]

Barclay Martin

It is common to postulate the existence of acquired or learned motives to
account for those persisting patterns of
purposeful human behavior that are associated with no obvious primary reinforcement. Some of this purposeful behavior is no doubt rewarded by primary
reinforcements about which we are presently more or less ignorant, or is rewarded so intermittently that the primary reinforcement escapes notice.
When there is no primary reinforcement present and behavior persists, we
are dealing, of course, with the phenomenon of resistance to extinction.

[1] The author wishes to thank Leonard Ross
for his helpful comments on this paper. Support during the preparation of the paper was
provided in part by the Research Committee
of the Graduate School from special funds
voted by the State Legislature.

Our current knowledge about antecedent learning conditions that affect resistance to extinction of responses, although still incomplete, provides us
with several empirical principles that
are probably powerful enough to account for much of the purposeful yet
innately nonrewarding behavior that
we observe in ourselves and others. The
resistance to extinction of responses
learned under partial, or varied reinforcement or varied stimulus conditions
are examples of such principles. Another, and even more striking example,
is the almost nonextinguishability of
avoidance responses learned after a few
severe traumatic experiences (Solomon
& Wynne, 1954).

In this paper attention will be directed to a type of antecedent condition that has not received much experimentation, but which may contribute strongly to resistance to extinction; namely, the condition where reward and punishment are associated with the same goal response during learning. Naturally, one boundary condition that must be imposed is that the punishment has to be introduced in such a way that the goal response is not completely inhibited during acquisition. Somewhat paradoxically it is expected that punishment of the goal response in this way will lead to greater persistence at making this goal response during extinction than if reward only had been experienced. The remainder of the paper will be devoted to reviewing research relevant to this proposition, and then outlining a theoretical formulation to account for this predicted phenomenon.

Relevant Research

Sears, Whiting, Nowlis, and Sears (1953) and Sears, Maccoby, and Levin (1957) report findings consistent with this expectation in regard to dependency behavior in children. In both studies there is evidence that the more dependency responses, such as clinging to and resisting separation from mother, are punished the greater is the strength of these dependency responses. No matter how carefully performed, correlational studies of this kind provide only indirect evidence for the basic proposition since there is no experimental control over the antecedent conditions. Perhaps, for example, excessively dependent children cause their parents to be more punishing of dependency responses rather than vice versa. There have also been studies, including the

two referred to above, which find that aggressive tendencies increase as punishment for aggression increases. Since aggression is a common response to punishment in general, maybe innately so to some extent, the issue is considerably complicated in this case and, accordingly, studies involving aggression as the goal response will not be reviewed.

It may have occurred to the reader that associating reward and punishment with the same goal response is identical to the procedure employed by several investigators in an attempt to produce experimental neuroses (cf. Maier, 1949; Masserman, 1943). In most such studies, however, the punishment was introduced in such a way as to completely inhibit or otherwise disorganize the behavior; or the animal had no freedom to approach or withdraw in the situation. Masserman (1943), however, does report "counterphobic" behavior in three cats which had received punishing air blasts in association with feeding. One cat, for example, at the feeding signal would run to the food box, insert his head beneath the lid, and then, instead of feeding, would remain immobile staring at the experimenter for prolonged periods. Maier (1949) was consistently able to produce responses in rats that were extremely resistant to extinction by confronting them with an insoluble discrimination problem in the Lashley jumping box apparatus. However, as several investigators have pointed out, for example, Eglash (1954), the punishing air blast necessary to make the rat jump could continue to serve as a powerful motivator of a stereotyped avoidance response. At any rate, the presence of the initial air blast makes the situation too complicated to analyze in terms of reward and punishment associated with the same goal response.

There have been some studies, not necessarily oriented towards producing experimental neurosis, in which less disorganizing punishments have been associated with goal responses. Fisher (1955) using puppies as subjects experimentally manipulated rewards and punishments associated with approaching an experimenter, a response roughly analogous to dependency or adult seeking behavior in children. He split litters of puppies into four groups of six puppies each at 18 days of age and provided different social experiences for these groups until the puppies were 15 weeks old. The two groups relevant to the present question were referred to as the Indulged group and the Punished-Indulged group. The puppies in the former group experienced 100% reward whenever they approached the experimenter during half-hour sessions conducted five times per week throughout the training period. Reward consisted of being petted and fondled by the experimenter. The puppies in the Punished-Indulged group experienced the five per week reward sessions just the same as the Indulged group but in addition also experienced five half-hour sessions per week in which they were punished every time they approached the experimenter. Punishment consisted of being switched or handled roughly, and during six sessions of being electrically shocked. A "dependency" test was conducted during the fourth, fifth, twelfth, and thirteenth weeks of training and on the third and fifth days after completion of training. This test consisted of having a human sit quietly in the corner of a room while an observer recorded the amount of time the puppy spent near the human through a one-way mirror. Differences between the two groups were not significant at the fourth and fifth weeks; however, by the twelfth and thirteenth weeks and even more so on the third and fifth days after termination of the experimental training periods, the Punished-Indulged group spent significantly *more* time near the human than did the Indulged group. These differences were due to relative increases in time for the Punished-Indulged group. The Indulged group continued to spend about the same amount of time near the experimenter. An important observational note is that two of the six puppies in the Punished-Indulged group spent no time whatsoever near the human on the twelfth- and thirteenth-week tests, and in spite of this the group as a whole spent over twice as much time near the human than did the Indulged group in which there were no zero time scores. These two puppies, however, during the posttraining tests did approach the human and spent more time near him than their litter mates in the Indulged group. The behavior of these two puppies points to the existence of strong avoidance tendencies along with the approach tendencies in these Punished-Indulged puppies. The fact that the Punished-Indulged puppies scored significantly higher on a standardized timidity test also underscores the presence of fearfulness around humans.

These results suggest that punishment has added in some way to the persistence of the goal response beyond the effects of 100% reward; however, this experiment was not conducted for the purpose of testing this theoretical proposition and there are several factors present that could account for the results on a different basis. One possibility is that the obtained result may reflect nothing more than the partial reinforcement effect, that is, reward was received on a 50% partial reinforcement basis and if punishment had no effect at all or even a mildly inhibitory one, conceivably the partial reinforcement effect could account for the obtained difference with the 100% reward group. Also, the Punished-Indulged group received twice as many total sessions as the Indulged group, and furthermore, the use of switching, rough handling, and shock as punishments introduces the complication of varied reinforcement. In order to test for an effect of punishment above and beyond that due to partial reinforcement, it would have been necessary to have had a control group that received 50% reward and 50% nonreward to have kept the total number of training sessions constant, and to have employed only one type of punishment in the experimental group.

Although this paper is primarily concerned with extinction effects, a number of studies have found punishment to produce a facilitating effect during the acquisition phase of learning. Such an effect in acquisition may or may not involve the same mechanisms as a similar effect in extinction, but is closely enough associated with the present problem to warrant inclusion in this review. In a series of studies using rats as subjects Muenzinger has demonstrated convincingly that shock plus eventual food reward associated with the correct response in a visual discrimination problem in a T maze produces more rapid learning than just reward by itself (Muenzinger, 1934; Muenzinger, Bernstone, & Richards, 1938; Muenzinger & Powloski, 1951). It is important to give the shock *after* the choice point since giving it before the

choice point retards learning (Muenzinger & Wood, 1935); also pretraining to approach shock in order to get food produced a facilitating effect in a subsequent discrimination problem where shock was associated with the correct choice (Muenzinger & Baxter, 1957; Muenzinger, Brown, Crow, & Powloski, 1952). Muenzinger suggested that these results might be accounted for on the basis of the emphasis or alerting effect of shock.

Freeburne and Taylor (1952) report more rapid discrimination learning when rats were shocked for both right and wrong responses than in a no-shock control group. Prince (1956) failed to confirm the findings, although he did find the usual shock-right facilitating effect, and in addition found that the shock-right effect was greater the more trials the rats were allowed to get food reward for making the correct response before shock was introduced. Wischner (1947) failed to obtain the shock-right effect in a noncorrection situation, and Fairlee (1937) found that learning was markedly retarded if shock was given at the "moment of choice" in a T maze.

Although most of the above rat studies indicate that shock associated with the correct response can facilitate learning, none bears conclusively on the question of the effect of punishment on the goal response, since in all cases the onset of shock occurred during or immediately after the rat left the choice point in the maze, and the rat made the goal response after shock termination. Thus, the running-toward-the-goalbox response can be conceived as being reinforced by shock termination upon completion of the total response as well as by whatever food rewards may be provided.

Drew (1938) did administer shock directly through the food in the goal box in a discrimination learning problem when the rat made the correct response. He found in comparison to a no-shock group that learning was facilitated to about the same extent as in shock-right or shock-wrong conditions where shock was given immediately after the choice point. In a different situation altogether Holz and Azrin (1962) trained two pigeons to peck a plastic disc for food reward under a fixed-interval reinforcement schedule. A moderately intense electric shock given with every response produced no permanent change in responding. When this same punishment was given only during the first part of each interval, response rate decreased in this part of the interval. However, when this punishment was given only during the last part of the interval, the punished responses actually increased slightly, while the unpunished responses decreased. The results of both Drew, and Holz and Azrin suggest that punishment may have a facilitating effect even when it occurs in close spatial or temporal proximity to the goal response. Holz and Azrin suggest that the results of their study can be accounted for on the basis of the "discriminative properties" of punishment. That is, punishment by virtue of past association with reward now serves as a cue tending to elicit the rewarded response.

There are only a few studies that have investigated extinction effects after rewarding and punishing the same response. Farber (1948) shocked rats at a choice point in a **T** maze while the rats were learning a position response and found much greater resistance to extinction in these rats than was the case for nonshocked controls. Farber suggested

that during extinction the fear conditioned to the earlier parts of the maze could be reduced by going to the always "safe" goal box. Again, this explanation does not necessarily include the situation where the goal response itself is punished.

Logan (1960) reports extinction data in a study that is very relevant to the present issue. Rats learned to run down a straight runway for food reward, and in some cases were given a 150 millisecond shock of progressively increasing intensity in the goal box when they were an inch or two in front of the food cups. Groups were run under a variety of conditions, but those most appropriate for comparison here are as follows: one group received 100% reward and no shock; a second group received 100% reward and 50% shock; and a third received 50% reward and 50% shock with reward and shock never occurring in the same trial. Although the extinction curve of the third group is presented in a different graph from the others and no statistical analyses are provided for these comparisons, the results appear to clearly confirm the present thesis. The 50% reward-50% shock group showed the least tendency to extinguish, whereas the 100% reward group showed the greatest rate of extinction. In fact, the 50% reward-50% shock group showed no tendency to extinguish whatsoever over the 48 extinction trials.

Unfortunately Logan does not provide extinction data on a 50% reward, 50% nonreward group, which would allow one to see if shock produced an effect beyond that expected by partial reinforcement. Actually, such a comparison might not be a clear-cut test of the facilitating effects of punishment. Many theories have been proposed to account for the partial reinforcement effect. To the extent that the "generalization decrement" or the ease with which animals can discriminate between the conditions of acquisition and extinction is an important determinant of the partial reinforcement effect, this factor would work against the facilitating effect of punishment. Thus, the half shock, half reward group should extinguish more readily than a half reward, half nonreward group, since the change to extinction should be easier to discriminate in the former. If in spite of this factor working against it, punishment were to prolong extinction beyond that found for a partial reinforcement condition it would be dramatic evidence for the issue at hand. As mentioned, however, results on a regular partial reinforcement group were not included.

The fact that the 100% reward, 50% shock group showed greater resistance to extinction than the 100% reward group clearly supports the idea that punishment, shock in this case, produces an effect that cannot be accounted for in terms of partial reward reinforcement since reward occurred on all acquisition trials in both groups. Logan (1960) briefly comments that the facilitating effect of shock

suggests that shock acts directly to increase the persistence of the approach tendency and does not maintain extinction performance simply through a lessening of the avoidance tendency [p. 221].

There is evidence that the presence of an electrically charged grid before the safe area increases resistance to extinction of learned escape responses to this goal area beyond that obtained when no shock at all is given during

extinction (Gwinn, 1949; Moyer, 1957; Solomon, Kamin, & Wynne, 1953; Whiteis, 1956). Contradictory findings by Moyer (1955) and Seward and Raskin (1960) most likely indicate that the phenomenon is obtained only within certain boundary conditions. Although these studies again point to the possible facilitating effect of punishment received *before* the final goal is achieved, the presence of shock during "extinction" and the fact that the reward consisted of escape from shock make these studies somewhat tangential to the present analysis.

Ullman (1951, 1952) reports interesting results in which "compulsive eating symptoms" are produced in rats. After several free eating sessions in a compartment, shock was introduced during the first 5 seconds of each minute for eight 20-minute sessions, during which food was available and the rats were hungry. Finally the rats were put in the compartment while food satiated but given the same shock sequences for four 20-minute sessions. The rats ate more while the shock was on than off, and the relative preference for eating during shock increased when they were food satiated. These results suggest that eating, even when not hungry, reduced the aversiveness of the shock; and that furthermore the shock stimuli perhaps came to serve as both cue and energizer for making the eating response when no primary hunger motivation was present.

Punishment has been given to human subjects under shock-right and shock-wrong conditions in simple maze learning situations, and learning was found to be superior for shock-right with low shock intensity, but superior for shock-wrong with high shock intensity (Feldman, 1961). Freeburne and Schneider (1955) found that shock-right, shock-wrong, and shock for both right and wrong responses facilitated learning compared to a no-shock condition. They also found that continuing shock during extinction produced greater persistence at making the correct responses than when shock was discontinued. A comparison of extinction results between a group that received shock for right responses during acquisition and a group that received no shock for right responses during acquisition, where neither group received any reinforcement during extinction, was not reported. Such a comparison would be more relevant to the issue at hand. In general, there is some question as to how relevant studies of college students doing simple learning tasks in psychological laboratories can be to the basic question being raised, considering the complexity of the motivational patterns operating in a college student that would affect his interpretation of the situation and his persistence at the task during extinction.

Some Theoretical Considerations

The idea that inconsistent administration of rewards and punishments by parents will result in psychological "fixations" in children is not a new one in the literature (cf. Fenichel, 1945, p. 66). And assuming that the empirical phenomenon is a real one, there will, of course, be no dearth of explanations for it. The question becomes one of what kind of formulation is most likely to clarify the mechanisms involved and at the same time suggest fruitful lines of empirical research. Before turning to my own preference for a theoretical formulation, reference will be made to other writers' theories that are pertinent to this issue.

Whiting (Sears et al., 1953) has suggested that conflict is necessary to provide drive strength for secondary motivational systems, for example:

only those actions which are followed by both reward and punishment become part of a secondary motivational system [and] the conflict between these two incompatible expectancies provides the drive strength for instigating the originally reinforced action [p. 180].

According to Whiting, conflict per se would seem to be the source of facilitative drive. In another publication Whiting and Child (1953), in attempting to account for displaced aggression, introduce the notion that acquired fear resulting from previous punishment adds to the general drive level present and thereby increases the strength of the displaced response beyond that expected from ordinary stimulus generalization.

Although Miller (1944, 1959) has both theorized and experimented extensively with respect to conflict behavior, he has not dealt to any great extent with the condition in which the punishment is applied in such a way that the animal never stops making the complete approach response; nor has he considered the effect of such antecedent training on extinction. Miller (1959) does, however, suggest in passing the possibility that punishment may have a facilitating effect upon the approach response.

It is entirely possible that administering at the goal shocks that are too weak to stop the animal from approaching and eating will be found to have the dynamogenic effect of increasing speed of running or strength of pull instead of reducing them as would be expected from algebraic summation [p. 225].

Festinger's (1961) theory of cognitive dissonance would seem to predict the phenomenon at issue here, although Festinger's theory so far has been applied primarily to the partial reinforcement situation or situations in which subjects had to exert effort or submit to boredom rather than experience clearcut punishments. Nevertheless, it would seem to follow from the general line of thinking involved in dissonance theory that if a subject has experienced punishment as well as reward associated with a goal response, he would be inclined to reduce dissonance by telling himself that this was a wonderful goal response indeed, and well worth persisting for.

Continuing in the cognitive vein, Tolman's (1948) conception of narrowed cognitive fields produced by high motivation or stress would seem to predict perseveration in extinction after reward and punishment. That is, because he is not attending to other possibilities the animal would continue making the same response much longer than if his cognitive field had not been constricted by stress. Easterbrook (1959) brings what amounts to this same theoretical position up-to-date in an excellent integration of research that can be accounted for by the notion of cue utilization, essentially the same notion as Tolman's cognitive field.

My own preference in theoretically analyzing the situation in which reward and punishment are associated with the same goal response is to employ some of the constructs used in current S-R behavior theory. The following represents logical deductions of a relatively nonquantitative sort from these constructs with regard to this particular situation rather than the introduction of any basically new constructs.

This analysis involves in part an extension of the formulations developed by Amsel (1958) to account for the effects of nonrewarded trials when given in association with rewarded trials. Following Amsel it is suggested that r_g-s_g be considered the general term to apply to all anticipatory responses and their stimulus properties, that become conditioned to stimuli that precede the goal response. Let r_r-s_r, then, represent a subdivision of r_g-s_g which includes all anticipatory reward responses and their associated stimulus properties, and let r_p-s_p represent anticipatory punishment responses and their stimulus properties.[2] In this formulation r_r-s_r refers to more than the merely observable fractions of a consummatory response such as chop licking or salivating, and is meant to include any central nervous system or other reaction conditioned to stimuli that precede a rewarded goal response. Such r_r-s_r have activating or energizing properties and may also participate in the secondary reinforcement process in the sense that any change in the stimulus situation producing an increase in r_r-s_r would be reinforcing. Spence (1960), however, would apparently restrict the function of r_r-s_r to an energizing one and not include a secondary reinforcing property.

The r_p-s_p subdivision of r_g-s_g is conceived to be similar to but perhaps somewhat more inclusive than the construct of acquired fear. Thus, r_p-s_p consists of all reactions, observable or otherwise, that become conditioned to

---

2 This terminology might be confusing in that Spence and his associates have habitually limited the use of r_g-s_g to anticipatory reward reactions. However, it seems to the writer that Amsel's suggestion was a good one, and that the interest of overall clarity is best served by defining r_g-s_g as the generic term. Thus, r_r-s_r is similar to the more restricted meaning that r_g-s_g has been given in the past.

stimuli that precede an aversive or punishing experience.

And similar to $r_r\text{-}s_r$, $r_p\text{-}s_p$ have energizing properties, and in addition have the capacity to play a role in the process of secondary negative reinforcement, that is, any change in the stimulus situation producing a decrease in $r_p\text{-}s_p$ would be reinforcing. Thus, in simplified summary, when they occur separately the presence of $r_r\text{-}s_r$ will cause the animal to attempt to increase these $r_r\text{-}s_r$ in number and strength. The complicating feature in this analysis becomes apparent when we consider the possibility that $r_r\text{-}s_r$ may come to serve as conditioned stimuli to evoke $r_p\text{-}s_p$, and at the same time $r_p\text{-}s_p$ may come to serve as conditioned stimuli to elicit $r_r\text{-}s_r$.

The constructs of $r_r\text{-}s_r$ and $r_p\text{-}s_p$ are similar, respectively, to anticipatory positive affect change and anticipatory negative affect change suggested by McClelland, Atkinson, Clark, and Lowell (1953). And accordingly, deductions from the McClelland et al. theory of motivation should lead to similar expectations with regard to the effect of rewarding and punishing the same goal response. Also, the constructs of hope and fear proposed by Mowrer (1960) in the revision of his two-factor learning theory are no doubt similar, respectively, to $r_r\text{-}s_r$ and $r_p\text{-}s_p$.

Amsel (1958) employed the term $r_f\text{-}s_f$, to refer in similar fashion to the conditioned fraction of the frustration state induced by nonreward. One might think of punishment in terms of a dimension of severity starting at nonreward frustration; in which case $r_p\text{-}s_p$ become simply stronger $r_f\text{-}s_f$. However, the term punishment as used in this paper is reserved for situations in which the animal is subjected to clearly noxious stimulation. It is possible, though, that the inevitable frustration or conflict accompanying a punished response adds to the nature and strength of $r_p\text{-}s_p$.

There are three primary considerations that would lead to the expectation of greater resistance to extinction with punishment than without it. The first reason is that more activation or drive should be present than if only reward had been given in acquisition. The sources of this additional activation can be somewhat arbitrarily separated as follows: (a) anticipatory punishment, $r_p\text{-}s_p$, elicited by external or internal stimuli preceding the goal response that would have been present if there had been no reward or reward motivation, such as thirst or hunger; and (b) $r_p\text{-}s_p$ elicited by drive stimuli associated with reward motivation and stimuli associated with anticipatory reward, $r_r\text{-}s_r$. The a and b division simply serves to point up two important sources of cues to which $r_p\text{-}s_p$ has been conditioned and with respect to which extinction of $r_p\text{-}s_p$ must occur. The drive or energizing properties of $r_p\text{-}s_p$ should facilitate the dominant approach tendency during extinction, perhaps by a multiplicative relationship with the strength of the approach habit. That increased activation or arousal does facilitate a dominant response tendency in a given situation, at least within certain limits, hardly needs documentation.

The second consideration is that during the learning process the anticipatory punishment responses, $r_p\text{-}s_p$, have been part of the stimulus situation in which the approach response has been reinforced and made dominant over avoidance responses, and thus eventually $r_p\text{-}s_p$ serve as additional cues tending to elicit approach responses. This is essentially the mechanism that Amsel (1958) employed to account for the partial reinforcement effect: namely, that the stimulus properties of the anticipatory frustration reaction, r_f-s_f, come to serve as cues eliciting the approach response. Likewise, Holz and Azrin (1962) employ the same idea in proposing that the discriminative properties of punishment come to elicit the goal response.

It is even possible that r_p-s_p come to elicit additional amounts of r_r-s_r and that accordingly there is more anticipatory reward or secondary reinforcement experienced at a distance from the goal than would have been the case without punishment. In general, either overt approach responses or anticipatory reward responses associated with the stimulus properties of r_p-s_p should prolong extinction. The control over the dominant response by the stimulus properties of r_p-s_p may, in part, correspond to Tolman's notion of stress induced narrowing of the cognitive field.

The third reason that punishment should prolong extinction is that there is good evidence that anticipatory punishment, r_p-s_p, is more resistant to extinction than acquired reward, r_r-s_r. Solomon and Wynne (1954) summarized the research bearing on this assumption and were so impressed by the resistance to extinction of acquired fear, especially when the initial reinforcement was quite severe or traumatic, that they postulated a partially irreversible effect, that is, that acquired fear *never* completely extinguishes. Thus, if some aspect of r_p-s_p does extinguish relatively slowly, its effect both in terms of augmenting the general level of activation present and as a stimulus

associated with the approach response should persist for a relatively long time.

There are, of course, factors working against the thesis proposed in this paper. Two such factors would seem to be of primary significance. First, some avoidance tendency in all likelihood does develop with respect to a goal response that has been punished, and such an avoidance tendency might be quite resistant to extinction. Second, the conditions of acquisition and extinction should be more readily discriminated when punishment as well as reward is discontinued. This would be especially true if the comparison group involved partial reward reinforcement.

It should be emphasized again that the hypothesized increased resistance to extinction effect of punishment is expected to occur only within certain boundary conditions, the most important of which involves the strength of avoidance relative to approach tendencies produced in acquisition. Factors such as the intensity and frequency of punishment, the gradualness with which it is introduced, and the amount of reward-only training given before punishment is introduced are undoubtedly important in creating the circumstances under which the expected effect will occur.

Summary: Research is reviewed which provides support for the thesis that, within certain boundary conditions, the association of punishment with a goal response during learning adds to the persistence of the response during extinction beyond the effects of reward-only during learning. Some theoretical considerations are offered to account for this phenomenon which make use of the constructs of anticipatory punishment responses, r_p-S_p, and anticipatory reward responses, r_r-S_r.

Journal of Comparative and Physiological Psychology, 1964, vol. 57, pp. 127–133

Self-Punitive Behavior in the Rat:

FACILITATIVE EFFECTS OF PUNISHMENT ON RESISTANCE TO EXTINCTION[1]

Judson S. Brown, R. C. Martin, and Mitchell W. Morrow

Broadly conceived, the experiments reported below bear on the question of why organisms sometimes behave so as to expose themselves repeatedly to aversive stimuli even when less punishing alternatives might be chosen. That such behavior does occur is attested to by Masserman's (1946) studies of experimental masochism, by demonstrations of the facilitative effects of punishment upon resistance to extinction (Gwinn, 1949; Solomon, Kamin, & Wynne, 1953; Whiteis, 1956) and by such experiments as those of Pavlov (1927) and of Miller (1960) in which aversive stimuli appear to lose their negative properties.

Nevertheless, some investigators (e.g., Imada, 1959; Moyer, 1955, 1957; Seward & Raskin, 1960) have not obtained confirmatory results in similar situations and the reasons for the discrepancies remain to be identified. Further experimentation is needed, therefore, to determine whether punishment indeed increases resistance to extinction and especially to provide more adequate information concerning variables necessary for the development and maintenance of seemingly maladaptive, self-punitive behavior.

Experiment 1

Method

Subjects. Fifty-four male hooded rats of the Long-Evans strain served as Ss. These were purchased from a commercial supplier and were 90–110 days old when first introduced into the experimental apparatus.

Apparatus. The main components of the equipment were a start box and a straight runway, both of which had grid floors and glass lids, plus a goal box that was fitted with a wooden floor and a Masonite lid. The start box (18 in. long × 5 in. wide × 11.5 in. high, inside) was divided into an upper and a lower compartment by a trap-door-like floor hinged along one edge 7 in. above the grid floor. A door at the end of the start box provided the means whereby Ss could be introduced into the upper compartment, and a 4.5 × 5 in. barrier at the alley end of that compartment prevented Ss from prematurely escaping into the alley. When the trap-door floor was automatically released S fell to the grid floor below where it was then free to run through the alley to the goal box.

The runway (6 ft. long × 3.5 in. wide × 11.5 in. high, inside) was uniform throughout save for narrow wooden strips across the top at the 2- and 4-ft. positions. These

[1] These studies were carried out in the Department of Psychology at the University of Florida and were supported by Grants M-4952 and MH-06900 from the National Institutes of Health. The authors are indebted to Robert D. Fitzgerald for a critical reading of the manuscript.

strips served to support cadmium sulphide photocells which pointed downward and were energized by infrared light sources below the grid floor. Additional vertically oriented light beams and photocells were situated at the juncture of the start box and alley and at the entrance to the goal box. By means of these devices and associated electronic equipment, measurements (to the nearest $\frac{1}{100}$ sec.) could be made of starting time (the interval between the release of the floor flap and the occlusion of the first light beam), the time consumed in traversing each of three 2-ft. alley segments, and total time (starting time plus the sum of the three segment times).

The goal box (18 in. long × 10 in. wide × 11.5 in. high, inside) was painted black, in contrast to the start box and runway which were light gray. A guillotine door at the entrance to the goal box prevented Ss from attempting to retrace once the goal box had been entered completely.

The grid floors were fashioned of $\frac{3}{32}$-in. stainless steel rods set into plastic side rails at .5-in. intervals. The six 1-ft. grid sections comprising the runway floor and the 18-in. section under the start box could be selectively energized by 60-cycle current from a variable-voltage autotransformer fed through a series resistor of 10,000 ohms. The open circuit voltage across all grid sections was monitored by means of a vacuum tube ac voltmeter. The shock intensities specified below were the open circuit voltages read from this meter.

A 60-w. lamp, suspended about 8 in. above the center of the start box served as a CS. A motor-driven circuit breaker in series with the lamp provided two .25-sec. "on" and two .25-sec. "off" periods per second.

Procedure. The general procedure involved shock-escape training for all Ss followed by "extinction" trials during which shock was interposed between the start and goal boxes for two groups of Ss but not for a third.

In detail, when Ss were received from the supplier they were given unrestricted access to food and water for 2–3 days and were then placed on a regular feeding schedule calling for 14–16 gm. of Purina laboratory chow per day for 7 days. During this period water was constantly available

and all Ss were handled for a few minutes each day. The food deprivation regimen was instituted in the hope that variability might be reduced and fear increased, since the results of one study (Meryman, 1952) had indicated that hungry rats were more fearful than nonhungry ones. All experimental trials were administered when Ss were approximately 22 hr. hungry.

The next 4-day period was devoted to preliminary habituation training, each S being permitted to explore all sections of the apparatus for 10 min. per day. On the first of these days, each S was carried directly from its home cage to the maze; on the second day, a short waiting period in a carrying cage preceded the 10-min. familiarization period; and on the third and fourth days, the experience of being dropped from the upper compartment of the start box to the grid floor beneath was added to the sequence.

Shock-escape training was administered at the rate of 10 trials per day for the next 4 days. Trials 1 and 2 were run with the 6-ft. alley removed and the start box connected directly to the goal box. The shock was set at 50 v. for all 10 trials of the first day. Three trials were then given with a temporary 2-ft. long alley inserted between the start and goal boxes, followed by three trials in traversing a temporary 4-ft. alley. On Trials 9 and 10 of the first acquisition day Ss were required to traverse the entire 6-ft. runway to escape shock. The shock voltage was raised to 60, 70, and 75 v. on Days 2, 3, and 4, respectively, to offset possible adaptation effects.

On every trial S was put into the starting compartment through the end door, after which the guillotine door at the entrance to the goal box was immediately raised. This latter event, accompanied by some uncontrolled and unspecifiable auditory cues, initiated the following automatically timed sequence of events: (*a*) after a 3-sec. delay the blinking light began to flash, followed 3 sec. later by (*b*) the whirring sound of the trap-door release motor, and finally, in about 2 more sec. by the release and fall of the floor itself. After S was started in this manner, the light continued to blink until the infrared beam at the entrance to the goal box was intercepted. This latter event automatically cut off the blinking light and stopped the third-segment and total-time clocks. The *S* was permitted to remain in the dark goal box with the guillotine door closed for about 20 sec. before being removed to an individual chamber in the carrying cage to await the next trial. The *S*s were run in squads of six, two members of the squad being randomly assigned to each of three groups. The daily food ration was allotted to each *S* approximately 15 min. after it had been returned to its home cage.

Extinction trials were begun on the fifth day following the initiation of escape training. At this time the six members of each squad were randomly assigned in equal numbers to three groups differing with respect to whether shock was present in the runway during extinction and with respect to its spatial location and extent. One group, the *short-shock group,* encountered shock only in the final 2-ft. segment of the alley. The second group, designated the *long-shock group,* was shocked throughout the entire 6-ft. runway, but not in the start box. The third group, termed the *no-shock group,* was never shocked during extinction, and no *S*, of course, was ever shocked in the goal box. On all these trials shock intensity was fixed at 60 v.

Extinction trials were continued under these conditions for 6 days (provided *S*s continued to run) at the rate of 10 trials per day with approximately the same intertrial interval (i.e., 5–7 min.) as that employed during acquisition. If *S* failed to reach and enter the goal box within a criterional time of 60 sec., extinction trials were discontinued and arbitrary time scores of 60 sec. were entered in the protocols for that *S*. Exploratory studies had shown that a single failure to leave the start box within 1 min. was highly predictive of complete extinction in this situation.

Results

While starting and running times were recorded throughout the escape training phase, these data, because of their lack of direct relevance to the purposes of this study, have not been included in this report. It is worth

noting, however, that the training procedures described above led to remarkably fast escape learning. Typically, asymptotic performance level was reached in 5–10 trials with the full length runway. Moreover, none of the *S*s had to be discarded for failing to learn or for acquiring successful shock-escape responses other than running.

The extinction data plotted in Figure 1 may be taken as representative of the major results of Experiment 1. This figure shows the speed with which the entire 6-ft. alley was traversed by each of the three groups on each of the 6 extinction days. Each point represents a mean of 18 reciprocals which has been multiplied by 6 to yield ft/sec, each of the reciprocals, in turn, being based on an individual *S*'s median running time for 10 daily trials. It is clear from this figure and from statistical analyses of these data that extinction took place in all groups; and, although the shocked *S*s ran somewhat faster than the nonshocked *S*s, the main "groups" effect was not significant

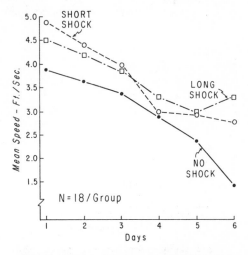

Fig. 1. Showing the mean speeds with which short-shock, long-shock, and no-shock groups traversed the 6-ft. straight runway during each of the 6 extinction days in Experiment 1.

$(F < 1.0)$. Thus these data provide no support for the expectation that punishment prolongs the extinction process. This conclusion is further buttressed by the observation that the groups did not differ markedly with respect to the number of Ss that had met the extinction criterion by the end of the sixth day. At that time, five of the no-shock, six of the long-shock, and seven of the short-shock Ss had quit running.

By and large, the data obtained from measurements of starting speed and of running speed in the individual 2-ft. segments of the alley were consistent with the above conclusions. However, one effect approaching statistical significance was that of groups in the case of last-segment running speeds ($F = 3.08$, $df = 2/51$, $p > .05$).

Running speeds in the three alley sections averaged over 6 days are shown in Figure 2. From this it is evident that the no-shock group tended to slow down as the goal box was neared, the long-shock group ran at a relatively constant speed, and the short-shock Ss

accelerated as the goal was approached. An analysis of variance of these data yielded the only highly significant finding of the study, namely, the interaction of groups by alley segments ($F = 12.2$, $df = 2/51$, $p < .001$).

In summary, Experiment 1 provided no substantial evidence indicating that punishment prolonged extinction. But neither did the study show that extinction was accelerated by shock, as might be expected on the basis of traditional conceptions of punishment as a behavior deterrent. This latter finding encouraged the authors in the belief that even relatively minor changes in experimental conditions might result in the prolongation of extinction by shock. The second experiment reported below confirmed this expectation.

Experiment 2

An examination of the conditions prevalent during Experiment 1 and an analysis of the behavior exhibited by Ss tested therein suggested the need for the changes introduced in Experiment 2. For one thing, shock intensity may have been high enough during extinction to evoke responses incompatible with running. Moreover, our acquisition data, supported by Martin's (1962) study of resistance to extinction as a function of number of escape training trials, suggested that the strength of the escape might actually be increased if escape trials were reduced from 40 to 20. It had also been observed during Experiment 1 that, generally speaking, running speeds were slowest at the start of each day, a warm-up-like increment appearing with additional trials. This indicated the desirability of changing the procedure so that the first no-shock trials of ex-

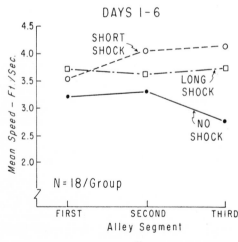

Fig. 2. Comparative running speeds exhibited by the three groups of Ss in each of the 2-ft. segments of the alley. (Each point represents a mean based upon all 60 extinction trials in Experiment 1.)

tinction would not coincide with the first trials of a day. Finally, it was felt that a more gradual transition from shock during acquisition to no-shock during extinction might diminish the contrast between the two procedures and thereby prolong extinction.

Method

Subjects. The Ss were 48 male hooded rats (Long-Evans strain) ranging in age from 100–140 days at the beginning of experimentation.

Apparatus. With the exception of one modification, the apparatus used in Experiment 2 was the same as that in Experiment 1. The sole change involved the substitution of an intermittently sounding buzzer for the blinking light. This modification was dictated by the observation that Ss in Experiment 1 seemed to become more excited by the whir of the trap-door release motor than by the onset of the blinking light. The buzzer, constructed of a dc relay energized by a 60-cycle source, was mounted on the side of the start box and produced not only a clearly audible sound but also tactually detectible (by Es) vibrations of the start box and of its grid floor. The sound level in the start box, as measured by a General Radio sound level meter ("C"-scale weighting) was about 53 db. above a reference level of 0.0002 dynes/cm^2 without the buzzer turned on. It increased to 67 db. when the buzzer was added and to 70 db. when the floor-release motor began to whir. With respect to duration of on-off periods, relation to floor-drop time, etc., the parameters of the buzzer variable were identical with those of the blinking light in the first experiment.

Procedure. The pre-experimental handling, feeding, and habituation procedures were the same as those followed in Experiment 1. The number of escape-training trials was reduced from 40 to 20, though the rate (10 trials per day) was not altered. The shock voltages were modified in several ways. During the escape trials of Day 1, 45 v. was applied to all grid sections. This was raised to 50 v. during the second day's training session. The shock used for the short-shock Ss in the third segment and

for the long-shock Ss in the alley was 50 v. for the first trial of the first extinction day and 45 v. for all subsequent trials. The no-shock Ss received 50, 45, 40, 30, and 20 v. in the start box and in the alley during Trials 1–5, respectively, of the first extinction day and no shock anywhere thereafter. The same series of progressively declining voltages was applied to the start-box grid for the long-shock group and to the start-box grid and the grid of the adjacent 4-ft. alley segment for the short-shock group. On the sixth trial of the first extinction day, and on all subsequent extinction trials, the shock conditions for the short-shock and the long-shock groups were precisely like those holding throughout extinction in Experiment 1 save that the voltage in the electrified sections was maintained at 45 rather than at 60.

With respect to number of extinction trials, extinction criterion, intertrial intervals, etc., both experiments were identical. Starting times were not recorded, however, in Experiment 2, since this measure appeared to be the least stable in Experiment 1 and since a temporary shortage of timing devices made it mandatory to reduce the number of measures taken on each trial. Two Es were responsible for the training and testing of all Ss. Five replications (N = 6 per replication) were run by one E and three by the other.

Results

Summaries of the running-speed data derived from times recorded from the first and third 2-ft. segments of the runway are provided in Figures 3 and 4. From the curves in Figure 3 it is apparent that the long-shock group proved to be most resistant to extinction, followed sequentially by the short-shock and no-shock groups. Analysis of variance provided unequivocal support for the view that the differences, as revealed by Figure 3, were genuine, since the main treatment effect was highly significant ($F = 12.34$, $df = 2/45$, $p < .001$), as were the "days" effect ($F = 7.81$, $df = 5/225$, $p < .001$) and

FIRST SEGMENT

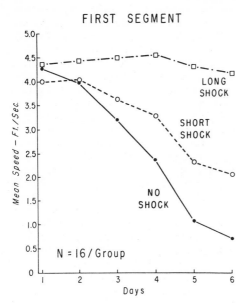

Fig. 3. These extinction curves exhibited by the three groups of Experiment 2 were derived from measurements of running speed in the first 2-ft. segment of the alley.

THIRD SEGMENT

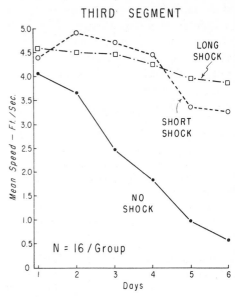

Fig. 4. The curves shown in this figure reveal the performance of the three groups in the last 2-ft. segment of the alley, which was adjacent to the goal box. The measures plotted here are the same as those in Figure 1, with which this figure may be compared.)

the interaction of days by treatments ($F = 10.62$, $df = 10/225$, $p < .001$). The conclusion that the groups differed in their tendency to resist extinction is further strengthened by the observation that of the 16 Ss in each group only 1 long-shock S had met the 60-sec. extinction criterion by the end of the sixth day whereas 6 of the short-shock and 11 of the no-shock Ss had ceased running by that time.

The trends apparent in Figure 3 are paralleled by data presented in Figure 4 and also by plots of middle-segment running times (not shown). Analyses of variance of second- and third-segment running speeds yielded, in each case, highly significant ($p < .001$) main effects of days, of treatments, and their interaction. A comparison of Figures 3 and 4 shows that while the long-shock Ss may have performed with slightly less vigor in the third (final) segment,

the short-shock Ss ran with augmented speed, and that both groups differed markedly from the no-shock group. The tendency for the short-shock Ss to accelerate as the goal-box was neared, which was also observed in Experiment 1, is revealed most clearly when the data are plotted as in Figure 5. The fact that the long-shock Ss ran faster in all segments and the short-shock Ss ran faster in the third segment than the no-shock Ss can be attributed in part, to the energizing effect of shock. But the finding that the short-shock Ss ran faster in the second than in the first segment cannot be ascribed to the energizing effects of shock and requires another interpretation.

Analysis of variance applied to the data in Figure 5 yielded a main effect ($F = 13.70$, $df = 2/45$, $p < .001$) and a segments by groups interaction that

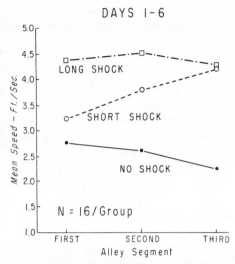

DAYS 1-6

N = 16/Group

Fig. 5. This figure, like Figure 2, shows that the three groups differed with respect to whether they tended to speed up or slow down in traversing the alley. (The goal-gradient-like acceleration shown by the short-shock Ss appears to be of special interest.)

were highly significant ($F = 12.50$, $df = 4/90$, $p < .001$). In none of the analyses were replications effects found to be significant sources of variance.

Discussion

The data of our two experiments, and especially those from Experiment 2, indicate that shock in the runway not only failed to accelerate extinction, as might be predicted from the supposition that shock should act to punish approach reactions, but instead, functioned to prolong extinction. The persisting behavior involved repeated approaches toward and toleration of stimuli, which, if defined in terms of Ss' original escape reactions would have to be labeled noxious. It seems justified, therefore, to describe such behavior as "masochisticlike".

Theoretical interpretations consistent with the results of our study prove to be surprisingly numerous. Mowrer's (1950) theory of this perseverative type of behavior, which he dubbed the "vicious circle" phenomenon, has considerable appeal. According to his view, the initial escape training should result in the conditioning of fear to the cues provided by the buzzer, the start box, and the alley. Then during extinction S runs because it is afraid, running produces shock which prevents (or retards) the process of fear extinction, and fear reduction perpetuates running. To this we may add the notions that shock reduction is itself a potent reinforcer for running and that shock onset may potentiate in-progress running responses.

Applied to our results, Mowrer's theory suggests that the no-shock Ss should quit running first, as they did, because their relatively long exposure to the runway cues in the absence of shock provided them with the most favorable conditions for fear to become extinguished and with no opportunity for fear to be further reinforced. The order in which the short-shock and long-shock groups extinguished would follow from the same principles.

Guthrie's (1935) concept of negative adaptation or habituation could also be applied to our data. According to this view, noxious stimuli lose their power to evoke escape reactions if they are repeatedly presented when responses that are incompatible with escape are dominant. Under such conditions, the aversive stimulus loses its negative properties to the degree that it becomes a conditioned cue for the incompatible reactions. In our studies the tactual cues provided by shock were part of the stimulus complex to which running became associated during the training series. Shock thus evoked approach reactions that interfered with responses of backing up or withdrawing; and during extinction the shocked Ss persisted in running because shock evoked and maintained forward-running behavior.

Our results are also consistent with interpretations stressing the similarity of acquisition to extinction conditions. Perhaps no-shock Ss extinguished most readily because they experienced the most marked change from acquisition to extinction, short-shock and long-shock Ss, respectively, being exposed to less drastic changes.

While the procedures used in our second study yielded unequivocal evidence that the aversive stimulus prolonged extinction, we are not yet able to pinpoint the crucial factor or factors. It would appear, however, that the to-be-punished response must be so well established that it will be evoked with a high degree of probability by the situational cues even when conditions are changed from acquisition to extinction plus punishment. Moreover, the intensity of the punishing stimulus should be moderate—this reduces the likelihood that competing responses will be elicited—and the shift from the acquisition to the extinction-plus-punishment phases should be gradual. Last of all, the motivational processes involved in the initiation of the response should perhaps be maintained or supported by the punishment to which the response leads. It may be worth noting that in the study by Seward and Raskin (1960) in which no evidence was found for increased resist-ance to extinction under punishment, few of the above requirements were met. The forward-going tendency was quite weak, the punishment was intense, and the transition from acquisition to extinction was abrupt.

A final point concerns the tendency of short-shock Ss in both experiments to speed up, even before they reached the shock in the final 2-ft. section of the alley. Speed-of-locomotion gradients have been frequently observed in studies involving the use of appetitive reinforcers but the authors are unaware of prior reports of such gradients in situations where Ss are approaching a punishing stimulus. If the phenomenon is genuine, it may prove useful to assume that a short-shock S is motivated in the middle segment by a fractional anticipatory shock-approach or shock-escape reaction that is logically comparable to the Hull-Spence $r_g - s_g$—K mechanism.

Summary: In 2 experiments rats were trained to escape from an electrified start box and runway into a safe goal box. During subsequent "extinction" trials the start box was made safe for all Ss, but some groups could not reach the safe goal box without enduring shock in part or all of the alley. Ss shocked in this way in the 1st study failed to stop running sooner than those given no shock, and in the 2nd study, shocked Ss resisted extinction significantly longer than nonpunished Ss. Fewer escape training trials, weaker shock, and more gradual transition from escape training to extinction characterized the 2nd study relative to the 1st. Various theories capable of explaining this masochistic-like behavior are examined.

Merrill-Palmer Quarterly, 1963, vol. 9, pp. 159–174

Punishment, Identification and Aggression[1]

Monroe M. Lefkowitz, Leopold O. Walder, and Leonard D. Eron

Punishment and the expression of aggressive behavior have been found in several studies to be positively associated (Sears, Whiting, Nowlis, and Sears, 1953; Sears, Maccoby, and Levin, 1957; Bandura and Walters, 1959; Miller and Swanson, 1960). Yet, the results of other studies show that punishment may have an inhibiting effect on the expression of aggressive behavior (Doob and Sears, 1939; Hollenberg and Sperry, 1951). Even within the same study, both directions of relationship obtain. For example, Sears, Maccoby, and Levin (1957) found that punishment may be shown to be an antecedent of aggressive behavior, when mild and infrequent, but when frequency and severity increase, punishment seems to produce aggression anxiety which inhibits the expression of aggression. Moreover, in a follow-up study of the same subjects six years later (Sears,

1 The data were obtained as part of a larger program of research dealing with the psychosocial development of aggressive behavior and supported by USPHS Grant M–1726. Support was also obtained from the Columbia County Tuberculosis and Health Association, Inc., and from the Hudson Lions Club. Grateful acknowledgment is extended to all of the school officials, parents, and children of Columbia County for their cooperation in this study. Appreciation is also rendered to Watson Scientific Computing Laboratory at Columbia University in New York City for the free use of their computing equipment.

1961), the data indicate that antisocial aggression is not significantly related at all to punishment—although the direction of the relationship was inverse. It should be noted, that in the later study the measure of aggression was independent of the rating of punishment, while in the earlier study both measures were obtained from the same respondent. The results of still another study illustrate that a positive relationship prevails between socialization anxiety and the choice of aggressive explanations as the cause of illness (Whiting and Child, 1953).

A third variable relating both to punishment and to aggression is the internalization of guilt, which in a broader context may be termed "identification." Several theories concerned with identification suggest that love-oriented disciplinary techniques—love conditionally granted or withheld depending upon obedience—foster developmental identification, whereas physical punishment engenders identification with the aggressor or defensive identification (Bronfenbrenner, 1960; Freud, 1937; Mowrer, 1950; Sanford, 1955). In the main, these theories tend to be supported empirically by studies concerned with child-rearing practices. Although some of the findings are not entirely unequivocal, Sears, Maccoby, and Levin

(1957) found that love-oriented discipline was more effective in child socialization and the development of conscience than was physical punishment. Moreover, the use of physical punishment by the parent as a disciplinary measure was related to aggressive behavior in the child. But, in a later study of the same subjects (Sears, 1961), no significant relationship was found between the use of withdrawal of love as a child-rearing practice and development of conscience in the child. Supporting data for the first finding derive from the work of Miller and Swanson (1960), who found that psychological punishment engendered greater guilt feelings than physical punishment. Furthermore, physical punishment seemed to produce more aggression in their subjects than psychological punishment. The results of two recent studies question the parsimony of those theories which hold that identification with the aggressor (Freud, 1937) or defensive identification (Mowrer, 1950) is the dynamic principle which best explains the imitative learning of aggression. In one of these studies (Bandura and Huston, 1961), it was found that observation of aggressive models in itself, regardless of the quality of the relationships between model and child, is enough to yield imitative aggression in children. Similarly, in the other study (Bandura, Ross, and Ross, 1961), ". . . subjects readily imitated aggressive models who were more or less neutral figures . . ." (p. 582).

The aim of the current research is to examine some of the relationships obtaining among punishment, identification, and aggression when the measure of aggression is derived independently of the punishment and identification measures and when punishment is ex-

amined by two analyses. One analysis of punishment would be as a dichotomy between its physical and non-physical aspects and would necessitate the combining of fathers and mothers into groups which say they use no physical punishment, as compared to those in which either parent admits to any use of physical punishment. The other analysis would deal with punishment as a scaled quantity ranging from zero to four physical punishments. Treating punishment as a continuous variable and then observing changes in aggression and identification at different points of the punishment continuum, should yield further information concerning the inhibiting or instigating effects of punishment on aggression. In addition, data pertaining to the effect of increasing punishment on confessing behavior (the measure of identification) may be obtained and the co-variation between confessing and aggression may be observed. Dichotomization of punishment into physical and non-physical categories would render data on the efficiency of these two kinds of disciplinary techniques as "conscience-building" phenomena.

Method

Subjects

The subject-population was comprised of all the third grade boys and girls in a semi-rural area of Columbia County, in the State of New York, as of 1959–1960. These children were approximately eight years of age. Data were also gathered from as many of the parents of these children as would consent to be interviewed. The pool of subjects involved consisted of 875 children, 555 fathers and 699 mothers.

Measuring Devices and Procedure

Punishment. All parents interviewed were asked to respond to 24 precoded questions dealing with punishment for specific acts. Of the 24, four were concerned solely with physical punishment:

1. If you heard (name) say mean things to another child, would you wash out his mouth with soap? (no, yes, cannot respond).

2. If (name) were rude to you, would you wash out his mouth with soap? (no, yes, cannot respond).

3. Would you spank (name) until he cries—if he were rude to you? (no, yes, cannot respond).

4. If (name) got very mad at you, would you slap him in the face? (no, yes, cannot respond).

The remaining 20 items were categorized under love withdrawal, restraint, isolation, shame, threat, and reasoning. Parental punitiveness was assumed to vary directly with the number of "yes" responses to the four physical punishment items. Due to the importance of the father in socialization of the child (Eron, Banta, Walder, and Laulicht, 1961), classification by number of physical punishment items chosen (where the number could range from zero to four) was performed separately for mothers and fathers.

Identification. As part of the interviewing procedure, all parents were asked questions designed to elicit information concerning their child's internalization of the socializing agents' interdictions. Confessing behavior, it was assumed, would tap this function. Consequently the following two items—modification of two questions in the Sears, Maccoby, and Levin study (1957)—were used:

1. When you ask (name) about something naughty he has done, how often does he deny it? Does he deny it: 1. all of the time? 2. most of the time? 3. some of the time? 4. almost never? 5. never?

2. When (name) has done something naughty and you haven't seen him do it, how often does he come and tell you about it without you having to ask him? 1. never? 2. almost never? 3. some of the time? 4. most of the time? 5. all of the time?

Aggression. This measure, a peer-rating sociometric technique, patterned after the "Guess Who" format, enabled aggression ratings to be obtained independently of the parents. Essentially, every child in a class rates every other child in that class on ten items dealing with aggression. This aggression index has been described in detail elsewhere. (Walder, *et al.,* 1961).

Social Status. A measure of social status —occupation—was employed in order to determine what relationship, if any, obtained between severity of punishment and social status. Kohn (1959) finds that both middle and working-class parents make use of physical punishment with about the same frequency. However, Bronfenbrenner reports (1958) that, ". . . working-class parents are consistently more likely to employ physical punishment, while middle-class families rely more on reasoning, isolation, appeals to guilt, and other methods involving the loss of love" (p. 424).

The measure in the present study was obtained from the parental interviews by determining the father's occupation and classifying the response according to the listing in the 1950 Census of Population, Classified Index of Occupations and Industries. In this classification, the ratings vary from zero, comprising professional, technical, and kindred workers, to nine, the category for laborers. Lower ratings correspond to higher social status job categories.

Results

Table 1 lists the range of physical punishment alternatives, shows the number of mothers or fathers choosing any one classification, and shows the number of boys and girls within each punishment alternative. Regarding sex differences, it was found that boys make significantly higher scores than girls on the peer-rating measure of aggression. In an analysis of directional tendencies, however, the findings for boys and for girls on punishment and aggression are consistent with the overall pattern with the exception of those groups in the highest physical punishment category. Since the N's in this category are small (Table 1), the reliability of this finding

TABLE 1

MEAN AGGRESSION AND CONFESSING SCORES CLASSIFIED ACCORDING TO
NUMBER OF PHYSICAL PUNISHMENT ITEMS ADMITTED BY PARENTS

Physical Punishment	Mothers				
	N	Aggression	Confessing	Boys	Girls
0	428	11.08	6.30	219	209
1	180	13.71	5.82	94	86
2	63	16.19	5.52	35	28
3 & 4	28	18.39	5.46	18	10
	Fathers				
0	353	9.79	5.96	167	186
1	138	14.96	5.19	80	58
2	45	15.16	5.78	28	17
3 & 4	19	14.89	5.16	11	8

is questionable. Consequently, no separate analysis for boys and girls was undertaken in this study.

Illustrated in Table 1 is the consistent increase in children's mean aggression scores as the number of physical punishment items chosen by mothers varies from zero out of four possibilities to three and four-out-of-four possibilities. (Categories three and four were combined because of the small N's when considered separately.) In order to determine whether or not these mean aggression scores were significantly different from each other, an analysis of variance for randomized groups was performed, the results of which are presented in Table 2. The obtained F ratios of 5.30 for mothers, and 7.26 for fathers are significant beyond the .01 level-of-confidence, indicating that in both cases the four aggression means are not all estimates of a common population mean.[2]

To answer the question of how these means differ, t tests comparing each mean with every other mean, were per-

formed.[3] These data, presented in Table 3 show that children's mean aggression scores differ significantly when mother reports using no physical punishment, as against their choices of one, two, three, and four physical punishment items. When mother reports using any degree of physical punishment, however, children's mean scores in these categories do not differ significantly from each other.

In the case of fathers, the increase in aggression is not as consistent as for mothers, in that the largest aggression mean coincides with the next to the largest number of physical punishment items. Although the F ratio is significant, indicating that the four means represent different populations, the t test analysis indicates that significant differences exist between mean aggression scores only when fathers admit to using no physical punishment as com-

[2] All probabilities are stated on the basis of two-tailed tests.

[3] Attempted first was an analysis according to Duncan's new multiple range test (Edwards, 1960) as extended for the case of unequal replications (Kramer, 1956). Because of the conservative nature of this test when applied to the case of unequal N's, significant differences between means were very likely masked.

TABLE 2

ANALYSIS OF VARIANCE OF AGGRESSION MEANS OF CHILDREN FOR FOUR
CATEGORIES OF PUNISHMENT AS REPORTED BY PARENTS

Source of Variation	Mothers				
	SS	df	MS	F	p
Between	2,955.60	3	985.20	5.30	< .01
Within	129,115.09	695	185.78		
Total	132,070.69	698			
	Fathers				
Between	3,492.23	3	1164.08	7.26	< .01
Within	88,389.59	551	160.42		
Total	91,881.82	554			

TABLE 3

THE *t* TESTS BETWEEN CHILDREN'S MEAN AGGRESSION SCORES FOR
FOUR CATEGORIES OF PUNISHMENT CHOSEN BY PARENTS

Physical Punishment Comparisons	Mothers		
	M	t	p
0–1	11.08		
	13.71	2.25	< .05
0–2	11.08		
	16.19	9.12	< .01
0–3 & 4	11.08		
	18.39	3.18	< .01
1–2	13.71		
	16.19	1.17	n.s.
1–3 & 4	13.71		
	18.39	1.56	n.s.
2–3 & 4	16.19		
	18.39	0.58	n.s.
	Fathers		
0–1	9.79		
	14.69	4.27	< .01
0–2	9.79		
	15.16	2.93	< .01
0–3 & 4	9.79		
	14.89	1.93	n.s.
1–2	14.96		
	15.16	—	—
1–3 & 4	14.96		
	14.89	—	—
2–3 & 4	15.16		
	14.89	—	—

pared to their choice of one and two of the four physical punishment items. There is no significant difference in aggression scores, however, between the use of no physical punishment and the choice of three or four physical punishments,

In observing the mean scores of the

items designed to measure children's confessing behavior as reported by mothers, Table 1 depicts a consistent decrease in these scores alongside the increase in both physical punishment items and aggression scores. An analysis of variance presented in Table 4, yields an F ratio equal to 7.61, significant beyond the .01 level-of-confidence, implying that these means are not estimates of a common population mean.

Insofar as children's confessing behavior as reported by fathers is concerned, a glance at Table 1 shows an inconsistent decrease in these scores paralleling the increase in aggression scores. However, an analysis of variance presented in Table 4 yielded an F ratio of 8.33 which is significant beyond the .01 level-of-confidence, indicating that the mean confessing scores did not arise from the same population.

When the relationship between confessing behavior and aggression is considered, inspection of the Pearson Product Moment correlations in Table 5 shows that these measures are negatively related for all classifications of punishment. Assuming the null hypothesis of zero correlation between aggression and confessing in the four punishment populations for both mothers and fathers, the results of t tests indicate that in certain punishment categories the null hypothesis is to be accepted and in others it is to be rejected. In the case of mothers, confessing behavior and aggression are inversely related and statistically significant at the .01 level in the zero physical punishment class and in the maximum physical punishment class; significance is at the .05 level-of-confidence in the second punishment category. For fathers, Table 5 shows that the negative relationship between confessing and aggression is significant at the .05 level-of-confidence only in the category of maximum punishment. Finally, it may be observed that with one exception, for the case of fathers, all of the correlations increase in absolute value as the degree of punishment increases.

In analyzing children's aggression and confessing scores as they relate to physical punishment, the question arose as to how non-physical relates to physical punishment. For each category of punishment, therefore, and for both parents, the mean number of punishment items other than physical was computed. Presented in Table 6, these

TABLE 4

ANALYSIS OF VARIANCE OF MEAN SCORES OF CHILDREN'S CONFESSING BEHAVIOR
AS REPORTED BY PARENTS FOR FOUR CATEGORIES OF PUNISHMENT

Source of Variation	Mothers				
	SS	df	MS	F	p
Between	62.63	3	20.84	7.61	< .01
Within	1,900.94	695	2.74		
Total	1,963.57	698			
	Fathers				
Between	65.98	3	21.99	8.33	< .01
Within	1,453.94	551	2.64		
Total	1,519.92	554			

TABLE 5

CORRELATION BETWEEN PEER-RATING MEASURE OF AGGRESSION AND
CHILDREN'S CONFESSING SCORES REPORTED BY PARENTS

Physical Punishment	Mothers			
	N	r	t	p
0	428	—.13	2.60	.01
1	180	—.15	2.05	.05
2	63	—.23	1.82	n.s.
3 & 4	28	—.50	2.93	.01
	Fathers			
0	353	—.07	1.26	n.s.
1	138	—.16	1.88	n.s.
2	45	—.14	.93	n.s.
3 & 4	19	—.52	2.49	.05

TABLE 6

AVERAGE NUMBER OF PUNISHMENT ITEMS OTHER THAN PHYSICAL CHOSEN BY
PARENTS IN THE DIFFERENT PHYSICAL PUNISHMENT CATEGORIES

Physical Punishment	Mothers	
	N	$\overline{X}$
0	428*	8.77
1	180	10.26
2	63	10.65
3 & 4	28	12.61
Total	699	
	Fathers	
0	353**	8.50
1	138	9.51
2	45	10.87
3 & 4	19	14.05
Total	555	

* Three chose none of the punishment alternatives.
** Four chose none of the punishment alternatives.

data show that the mean number of non-physical punishment items used by parents increases directly with their choice of physical punishment items. The analysis of variance of these means shown in Table 7 presents F ratios of 23.25 and 25.47 for mothers and fathers respectively. Significant beyond the .01 level-of-confidence, the analysis indicates that these mean scores did not arise from the same population.

An inadvertent finding was the comparatively large number of mothers and fathers who claimed that they used none of the physical punishment alternatives. Another, was that both mothers and fathers, although interviewed separately, on the whole agree so closely in their use of punishment. As shown in Table 8, 781 or 62 per cent of mothers and fathers, said they used no physical punishment and this number decreases

TABLE 7

ANALYSIS OF VARIANCE OF MEAN NUMBER OF PUNISHMENT ITEMS OTHER THAN PHYSICAL CHOSEN BY PARENTS IN THE FOUR CATEGORIES OF PUNISHMENT

Source of Variation	Mothers				
	SS	df	MS	F	P
Between	685.12	3	228.37	23.25	< .01
Within	6,797.29	695	9.78		
Total	7,482.41	698			
	Fathers				
Between	756.51	3	252.17	25.47	< .01
Within	5,456.89	551	9.90		
Total	6,213.40	554			

markedly as physical punishment increases. Reading across the table, it can be seen that the per cent of mothers and fathers choosing each class of punishment is almost identical.

To answer the question of whether degree of physical punishment is confounded with social status, the means of fathers' occupational ratings on the 1950 census listing of occupations were computed for each class of punishment and are presented in Table 9. The analyses of variance depicted in Table 10 resulted in F ratios of 1.16 for mothers and 1.64 for fathers. Since neither of these ratios is statistically significant, the null hypothesis that these means arose from a common population cannot be rejected. Therefore, it may be concluded that social status as measured by fathers' occupation is not a factor entering into the number of physical punishment items chosen by parents.

Heretofore, analyses have been performed separately for mothers and fathers. But, since mothers and fathers of the same family do not necessarily agree in their statements about punishment, analyses of the same variables were performed for families. Such analyses meet the condition, discussed earlier

in this report, of dichotomizing physical and non-physical punishment. Table 11 indicates that in 233, or 43 per cent of the families, *both* mother and father chose zero out of four physical punishments. Furthermore, there were 312 families, or 57 per cent in which either father or mother chose one or more physical punishments. Mean aggression scores as well as mean confessing scores differ significantly for both groups. Aggression and confessing scores are not significantly correlated in the case of zero physical punishment but are significantly correlated negatively when either father or mother admit to the use of one or more physical punishments. The t of 4.03, significant beyond the .01 level-of-confidence, indicates that the null hypothesis of zero correlation in the population may be rejected.

Because of the positive relationship between number of physical and non-physical punishment items chosen by parents, the bearing of solely physical punishment on aggression and confessing is unclear. Consequently, Pearson Product Moment correlation coefficients were computed between other-than-physical punishment scores, and scores

TABLE 8

PER CENT OF MOTHERS AND FATHERS CHOOSING EACH CLASS OF PUNISHMENT

Physical Punishment	Mothers	%	Fathers	%	Both	%
0	428	61	353	64	781	62
1	180	26	138	25	318	25
2	63	9	45	8	108	9
3 & 4	28	4	19	3	47	4
Total	699		555		1264	

TABLE 9

MEAN OF FATHERS' OCCUPATION FOR EACH
CATEGORY OF PUNISHMENT

Physical Punishment	Mothers	
	N	Mean Fathers Occupation
0	428	4.00
1	180	4.37
2	63	4.24
3 & 4	28	4.04
	Fathers	
0	353	3.88
1	138	4.29
2	45	3.76
3 & 4	19	4.68

TABLE 10

ANALYSIS OF VARIANCE OF OCCUPATION MEANS FOR
FOUR CATEGORIES OF PUNISHMENT

Source of Variation	Mothers				
	SS	df	MS	F	p
Between	18.69	3	6.23	1.16	n.s.
Within	3,742.45	695	5.38		
Total	3,761.14	698			
	Fathers				
Between	28.64	3	9.55	1.64	n.s.
Within	3,207.35	551	5.82		
Total	3,235.99	554			

on aggression, and scores on confessing. This analysis was done for 232 of the 233 families analyzed in Table 11 and the other-than-physical punishment score was the sum of non-physical punishment items chosen by mother and father. Other-than-physical punishment correlates .03 with children's aggression and —.01 with children's confessing. Neither of these coefficients is statistically significant.

Finally, analysis of Table 12 shows

TABLE 11

MEAN AGGRESSION AND CONFESSING SCORES AND THE CORRELATION
BETWEEN THEM GROUPED BY FAMILIES

Physical Punishment	Families	%	Aggres- sion	t	Confes- ing	t	r	t
0	233	43	8.57		12.61		−.10	n.s.
				5.03**		5.71**		
1+	312	57	14.07		11.31		−.22	4.03**

** Significant beyond the .01 level of confidence.

TABLE 12

MEAN NUMBER OF OTHER PUNISHMENTS AND MEAN SOCIAL
STATUS SCORES COMPUTED FOR FAMILIES

Physical Punishment	Families	Other Punishment	t	Social Status	t
			5.60**		1.52
0	233	17.44		3.82	
1+	312	19.85		4.14	

** Significant beyond the .01 level of confidence.

that those families choosing zero physical punishment also use significantly less other punishments than those families choosing one or more physical punishments. The t of 5.60 is significant beyond the .01 level-of-confidence. Again, mean scores on social status do not differ significantly between those groups.

Discussion

The almost consistent increase in children's mean aggression scores, paralleling the increase in physical punishment, suggests that punishment enhances rather than inhibits the expression of aggression. It appears that even when parents responded that they used all of the physical punishment choices available, aggression anxiety was not produced in their children. Generally, these findings support the results of other studies showing the more punishment the more aggression.

The increase in aggression with the increase in physical punishment seems to support the concept of imitation or role-modeling as illustrated by the studies of Bandura and Huston (1961) and Bandura, Ross, and Ross (1961). On the other hand, increases in the choice of physical punishment items by parents is associated with a decrease in the amount of confessing behavior of their children. In short, physical punishment seems *not* to foster the kind of identification which is measured by items dealing with the internalization of guilt. Rather, the children of those families choosing no physical punishments have significantly lower aggression scores than those whose families choose one or more of the physical punishments. Thus, punishment other than physical seems more effective in the development of conscience—or in socialization. These results follow in the same direction as those of Sears, Maccoby, and Levin (1957) and Miller and Swanson

(1960). Moreover, the data of the present study take into account the responses of both parents.

The negative correlations between aggression and confessing scores indicate that those children who have internalized the interdictions of the socializing agent are less aggressive than those who have not. Moreover, since the absolute value of these correlations increases with the increasing use of physical punishment the role of the latter as a socializing technique becomes manifest. Specifically, the more the use of physical punishment by the parents the less likely is the aggressive child to have incorporated those qualities which are assumed to comprise the construct termed "conscience." The results are not completely unequivocal: for mothers, the small but significant negative correlation within the category of zero physical punishment (Table 5) suggests that physical punishment may not always be a necessary aspect of the high-aggression, low-identification pattern.

Categorizing family units into physical and non-physical punishment groups (since parents do not always use the same form of punishment) leads to a more conclusive analysis of the aggression-identification relationship. Reference to Table 11 illustrates that when both father and mother choose none of the physical punishment alternatives, the correlation between aggression and confessing is not significant. On the other hand, when either father or mother admits to the use of one or more physical punishments, the correlation is low, but significant. Thus, it appears probable that physical punishment has an important effect on the relationship between aggression and confessing. To eliminate equivocation

concerning the relationship of physical punishment to aggression and confessing, it was attempted to show that punishment other than physical is unrelated to these child variables. Such lack of relationship was found to be the case as reported in the section on results. Therefore, within the context of this study, it seems reasonable to conclude that it is not punishment generally, but physical punishment specifically, which is related positively to aggression and negatively to identification.

It should be emphasized that in the separate analyses for mothers and fathers, several of the correlations under discussion are not statistically significant. Yet, it is instructive to note that both significance and the greatest magnitude of correlation occur in the maximum categories of physical punishment (Table 5). This observation seems to underscore, again, the importance of physical punishment in the foregoing correlations.

Considering that mothers and fathers were interviewed separately, the close agreement in the choice of punishment items as illustrated in Table 8 may be construed as a kind of reliability of this questionnaire technique, in obtaining information about child-rearing practices such as punishment. Also, these data dispute the notion that fathers employ harsher disciplinary techniques than mothers. That such a relatively high percentage of parents choose none of the physical punishment items is open to several interpretations: the use of physical punishment may be believed by the parent to be socially unacceptable to the interviewer; the range of physical punishments offered was too narrow; or, parents are considerably sophisticated and are aware of the implications of physical versus non-physical punishment as it relates to child behavior and personality. Which is the correct interpretation cannot be determined from the current analysis.

Finally, the finding that there was no difference in fathers' mean occupation scores among the different categories of physical punishment is consistent with Kohn's results (1959), but inconsistent with those of Bronfenbrenner (1958). Actually, Bronfenbrenner's finding that lower social status families are more inclined to use physical punishment than those families in the middle and upper social status categories seems to parallel a generally held notion about child-rearing practices within these classes. The current results in conjunction with Kohn's data—which show that working and middle-class parents use physical punishment approximately to the same extent—suggest that physical punishment may not be a class-bound phenomenon. From the present data, it seems reasonable to conclude that social status as measured by father's occupation is not a determinant in the amount of physical punishment chosen by parents. Actually, Bronfenbrenner (1958) suggests that a change may be occurring in the disciplinary techniques employed by the working-class and he hints at a reduction in "cultural lag." Evidence from the present study is consistent with his hypothesis that the working-class parent, as a result of greater income and education, is emulating the disciplinary techniques of the middle-class.

Summary: The study was concerned with an examination of some of the relationships among punishment, identification, and aggression. Data on punishment and identification were gathered from 699 mothers and 555 fathers through separate individual interviews. Children's aggression scores were obtained by a peer-rating technique independent of parental ratings. Generally, children's mean aggression scores were found to increase as the number of physical punishment items chosen by parents increased, whereas mean confessing scores, the measure of identification, decreased. Throughout the range of physical punishment, aggression and confessing were found to be negatively correlated but not statistically significant in all cases. Although physical and non-physical punishment were found not to be independent, the foregoing relationships concerning aggression, identification and punishment may be attributed to the physical component in punishment. This conclusion was reached by demonstrating that non-physical punishment is unrelated either to aggression or to identification. Finally, it was found that reported use of physical punishment was unrelated to social status. The results were discussed and, where possible, comparisons were made with the findings of other studies in this area.

Frustration and Punishment[1]

Allan R. Wagner

Although both the withholding of reward and the application of a noxious stimulus typically act to produce a subsequent decrement in the learned behaviors that they follow, few students of the learning process would fail to point out important differences in the manner of this effect. Thus, for example, while nonreinforcement may be treated as "weakening" a response tendency, punishment is more likely to be viewed as "suppressing" such a tendency. Although there has been good reason for such distinctions (for example, Estes, 1944), it may be that their emphasis has tended to obscure equally as important communalities that exist between the effects of punishment and nonreinforcement in some situations.

The present paper will describe a line of theory and research that, while not denying differences between nonreinforcement and punishment, makes explicit a variety of similarities between the two events in the context of instrumental reward learning.

Theoretical Background

The theoretical considerations that have led to the research to be described are perhaps most clearly detailed in the treatment of punishment presented by Miller (1959, 1960b, 1961a) and the

[1] Preparation of this paper, as well as the research reported, was supported in part by National Science Foundation Grants G–13080 and G–24015.

treatment of frustrative-nonreinforcement developed by Amsel (1958, 1962) and Spence (1960, Chap. 6). Reference, however, to recent reviews of nonreward by Amsel (1962) and of punishment by Church (1963) indicates that many of the separate features would be acceptable to a variety of theorists.

According to Miller, punishment, in addition to producing overt motor activity, also produces a primary emotional response. This emotional behavior may become conditioned to the stimuli that immediately precede it, and, following stimulus generalization, should be elicited by cues in a stimulus response chain that regularly antedates a noxious event. The conditioned emotional response, or *fear* as it is commonly called, is assumed not only to increase *S*s' drive level, but also, through its characteristic response produced stimuli, to tend to elicit overt unlearned or previously learned responses. These fear-mediated responses, when they are incompatible with a punished response, are held to be largely responsible for the decremental effects of punishment.

According to a highly similar analysis offered by Amsel and Spence, following some number of reinforcements necessary to build up anticipatory reward responses, nonreinforcement also will elicit a primary, aversive emotional response. This emotional response of *frustration* is assumed to be directly related in intensity to the magnitude of anticipatory reward. Just as fear will come to be elicited by cues that antedate punishment, a conditioned anticipatory form of the frustration response may be elicited by cues in an instrumental chain that precedes frustrative-nonreinforcement. Similarly, as the decremental effect of punishment may be ascribed largely to fear-mediated "avoidance" responses, the decremental effect of nonreinforcement is presumed to be due—at least in part—to learned or unlearned responses, elicited by anticipatory frustration, that are incompatible with the frustrated response.

It is clear that the studies of Miller, Amsel, and Spence have, to this degree, offered quite analogous treatments of punishment and frustrative-nonreward. If more than a conceptual similarity exists in the mechanisms involved, it should be possible to demonstrate that punishment and frustrative-nonreward interact similarly with a variety of experimental manipulations. The following experiments were designed to evaluate this possibility. In large part, the strategy has been to examine an effect that has been associated with noxious stimulation or punishment, asking whether the same, or a similar, effect will occur if frustrative-nonreward rather than noxious stimulation is employed as the "aversive" event.

Experimental Findings

DRUG-INDUCED RECOVERY
FROM INHIBITION

A well-known property of the response decrement, or "inhibition," produced by punishment is that it is particularly susceptible to the depressant action of certain drugs. Rats that have learned to traverse a runway for food reward, but that have been inhibited by punishing electric shocks, may be made to resume the running response if they are first injected with appropriate dosages of alcohol or sodium amytal (Miller, 1961). This occurs even though the same drugs will depress the running of Ss that have had only reward training. Apparently these drugs reduce punishment-produced avoidance tendencies more than they do food-rewarded approach tendencies. Miller has proposed that they have this differential effect as the result of a selective action upon the conditioned fear response.

A reasonable question is whether such drugs will likewise reduce inhibition produced by nonreinforcement in instrumental reward situations. That is, following the administration of one of these depressants, will there occur an increase in the performance of a response that has been decreased by nonreinforcement? To the extent that extinction is the result of competing responses mediated by anticipatory frustration, and to the extent that this emotional response is selectively reduced (as fear is assumed to be), such should indeed be expected.

The results of several studies are encouraging to this position. In an unpublished study, Wagner, Pendleton, and Perry trained rats in a differential, instrumental conditioning situation with black versus white runways. In a random half of the trials, Ss were run in an alley of one brightness and reinforced with 1.2 gm. of wet mash. In the other half of the trials they were run to the opposite brightness and nonreinforced. Running speeds at first increased in both alleys, but at the end of

70 total trials a consistent discrimination had developed, so that the speeds of running to the reinforced brightness were appreciably faster than the speeds to the nonreinforced brightness. At this point each S was tested on several days in both runways, following intraperitoneal injections of either 1200 mg/kg alcohol or an equal volume of physiological saline.

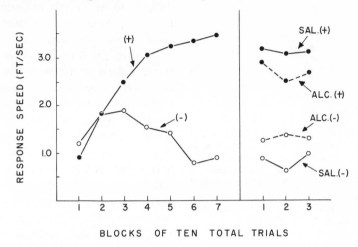

Fig. 1. Mean response speeds of 15 Ss to rewarded (+) and nonrewarded (−) discriminanda during original training, and during subsequent test trials following alcohol or saline control injections.

Figure 1 presents the pre-drug discrimination speeds and the results of the subsequent drug tests. As may be observed, during the test trials alcohol, as compared to the saline control, reduced the speed of approaching in the rewarded alley. Of primary interest, however, is the drug's effect on the response in the nonreinforced alley. Here it may be seen that the drug *increased* the speed of the response that had been inhibited by the preceding nonreinforced discrimination trials. This latter observation is consistent with the findings of Blough (1956) and Miller (1961). The former, using alcohol and sodium pentobarbital, and the latter, using sodium amytal, have both reported that the respective drugs decreased the inhibitory effects of a signal for nonreward.

While each of these drug effects is consistent with the prediction from frustration theory, it cannot be ruled out that they merely reflect an impairment in sensory acuity. Figure 1, indeed, presents exactly the expected picture if such were the case—a tendency when tested under the drug, toward convergence of the speeds to the positive and negative discriminanda. A more convincing test would appear to require a situation that is less dependent upon sensory discrimination.

A study by Barry, Wagner and Miller (1962) was designed to allow such a test. Rats were first trained, on a continuous reinforcement schedule, to run down a simple runway for 0.314 gm. food reward. This running response was then partially inhibited by two days of five nonreinforced trials each. Finally, on each of the next two days, before receiving additional nonreinforced "test"

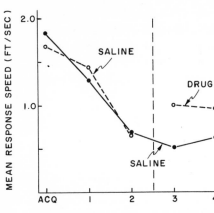

Fig. 2. Mean response speeds on last day of acquisition and subsequent extinction days for two groups of 8 Ss normally receiving saline prior to running. The dashed vertical line indicates point at which one group was shifted to alcohol or sodium amytal injections. (Barry, Wagner, & Miller, 1962)

trials, some Ss were injected with either 1200 mg/kg alcohol or 20 mg/kg sodium amytal, while others received equal-volume injections of physiological saline.

Figure 2 presents the final acquisition and subsequent extinction speeds for Ss that also received saline control injections during acquisition and during the initial extinction phase. Since alcohol and sodium amytal produced essentially identical effects, the results from Ss tested with both drugs have been combined. As may be seen in the figure, injections of the drugs increased the speed of the approach response, which had been inhibited by nonreinforced extinction trials. This result, which is highly significant, closely parallels the increase in speed produced by these drugs when shock has been used (Miller, 1961) to depress performance rather than experimental extinction, and is consistent with the dual assumptions made concerning the role of anticipatory frustra-

tion and the action of the drugs upon this response. Furthermore, since the simple acquisition and extinction procedures involved did not necessitate a sensory discrimination, it would appear difficult to deduce these findings from the assumption that the drugs merely reduced sensory acuity.

Another possibility, however, is that this finding is an indirect result of stimulus change. Considerable data indicate that an instrumental response that has been learned under appetitional rewards, but then inhibited by punishment in the same stimulus situation, will be more likely to occur if the stimulus situation is slightly or moderately changed. Miller and several of his students (e.g., Miller & Kraeling, 1952; Berkun, 1957), in a series of studies on "displacement," trained rats, for example, to run down a narrow, black runway for food reward. Electric shock punishments were then introduced at the goal until the Ss would refuse to approach it. The Ss were then tested in a slightly different runway, such as one that was wider and brighter. Under such modified stimulus conditions, the Ss showed a significant increase in their number of approaches to the goal. In interpreting this finding, as well as many other interesting conflict phenomena, Miller (1959) has proposed that the generalization gradient of fear-motivated avoidance responses is steeper than that of food-rewarded approach responses. Hence, when the stimulus situation is moderately changed, as by changing the width and brightness of the alley, fear-mediated avoidance responses suffer more of a generalization decrement than does the approach response.

If avoidance responses mediated by

anticipatory frustration also have a characteristically steep generalization gradient, the reduction in inhibition observed by Barry, Wagner, and Miller may have been an indirect result of the stimulus change from the sober to the drugged state, rather than a direct effect of the drug.

As a result of such reasoning, other *S*s, also receiving the drugs during acquisition and during the initial extinction trials, were run in the same experiment. Half of these *S*s then received test trials under drug and half were shifted to saline. If the previous findings were a result only of stimulus change, then a similar increase in extinction performance should have been observed in those *S*s shifted from drug to saline. In fact, no such increase occurred. Those *S*s that continued to be injected with one of the drugs during the test trials ran faster than those shifted to saline.

"DISPLACEMENT" OF INHIBITED RESPONSES

Although the above drug effects cannot thus be attributed simply to stimulus change, it would still be expected, if the proposed similarity between punishment and nonreinforcement is taken seriously, that some degree of stimulus change following a period of acquisition and extinction *would* lead to a recovery in performance. For example, Miller, *et al*'s demonstrations of displacement should also have been possible if frustrative-nonreinforcement had been used to inhibit running rather than punishment. The following study sought to test this possibility.

Rats were trained over 56 trials of continuous reinforcement, to run down a simple runway for 1.0 gm food re-

wards. The running response was extinguished over 24 nonreinforced trials. Half of the *S*s were trained and their responses then extinguished in a three-inch wide, black runway and half in a six-inch wide, white runway. On each of the last two days of extinction, each *S* was given a single, nonreinforced, test trial in its usual alley and an equivalent test trial in the opposite, that is, novel alley. If, following Miller's fear analysis, avoidance responses mediated by anticipatory frustration generalize less to the novel alley than do the approach response, *S*s should run faster in the novel alley than in that in which they had received both rewards and frustrative-nonreward.

Shifting to a novel situation may have other effects, however, in addition to producing generalization decrements in the respective approach and avoidance tendencies. To control for any systematic effects of novelty, such as an increase in fear or a decrease in stimulus satiation, additional *S*s were run in each alley merely by being placed in the start box and removed from the goal box. These *S*s never received food reward and hence also never received frustrative-nonreward. After an equal number of exposures to a given alley as was received by the experimental *S*s, these *S*s were also tested in the novel alley as well as in their original runway.

Figure 3 presents the running speeds over acquisition and extinction for experimental *S*s and over the exposure trials for control *S*s. As may be seen, by the end of extinction experimental *S*s were running somewhat slower than control *S*s. Figure 4 presents the results of the test trials for the two groups. There was a small, but consistent and

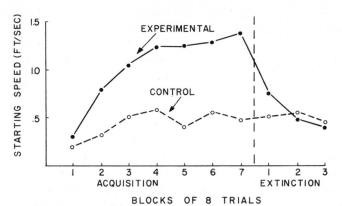

Fig. 3. Mean starting speeds for 16 Experimental Ss, which received food-rewarded acquisition and nonrewarded extinction trials, and 16 non-fed control Ss.

statistically reliable, increase in speeds for the experimental Ss when tested in the novel alley as compared to their usual alley. On the other hand, there was a reliable decrease in speeds for the control Ss. Although the absolute magnitude of the observed "displacement" effect was small, the qualitative features of the results were the same as those observed by Miller et al. when shock was used to depress performance.

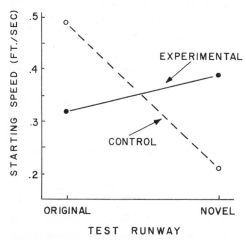

Fig. 4. Mean starting speeds for two groups whose prior performance was described in Figure 3, when tested in original, and moderately different, novel runway.

LEARNING RESISTANCE TO FEAR AND FRUSTRATION

It has been emphasized that the decremental effects of fear and anticipatory frustration are assumed to be dependent upon their mediating responses that are *incompatible* with the instrumental response. To the degree that Ss can be trained so that fear or anticipatory frustration will elicit responses that are *compatible* with the instrumental response, these emotional consequences of punishment and nonreinforcement should have less of a decremental effect. Miller (1960) has suggested that this type of training may take place when punishment intensity is built up gradually over trials at a reward goal, since rats given this treatment develop a resistance to the decremental effects of intense punishment. Such Ss presumably are rewarded during training for approaching in the presence of fear, so that increasingly strong fear can become a cue for approaching.

This is also one of the arguments invoked by Amsel (1958) to explain the common observation in instrumental reward situations, that Ss who are only inconsistently reinforced are more resistant to extinction than are continuously reinforced Ss. He has pointed out that the intensity of frustration elicited by nonreinforcement should increase gradually during acquisition as anticipatory reward increases. Partially reinforced Ss, have, then, presumably been reinforced during acquisition for continuing to approach in the presence of at first weak, but then increasingly intense anticipatory frustration cues. They are hence less likely to have avoidance responses elicited by these cues when they occur during extinction than are continuously reinforced Ss that have not had such training.

Brown and Wagner, in a recent study (1964), proposed that if there is a similarity between the emotional responses of fear and anticipatory frustration as has been suggested here, it would be reasonable to expect some degree of transfer of behaviors learned in the presence of one of these responses to occasions when the other response is aroused. Thus, it might be expected that Ss that have learned to approach in the presence of anticipatory frustration would also persist in approaching in the presence of fear. Likewise, Ss trained to approach in the presence of fear might be expected to continue to approach in the presence of anticipatory frustration.

To test this prediction, three groups of rats were trained in a straight runway. Group C received a simple continuous reinforcement schedule, with only a food reward on all trials. Group N received exposure to nonreinforcement during acquisition on a random 50 percent reinforcement schedule. Group P received exposure to punishment during acquisition, with electric shock on 50 percent of the trials, in addition to food reward on all trials. All groups received 114 acquisition trials, during which time the shock intensity gradually increased from 75 volts to 235 volts in Group P. Following training, each of the three groups was divided into two subgroups for testing. One group was tested with consistent nonreinforcement (extinction), the other with consistent food reward and 235-volt shock punishment. All shocks were given 1.0 seconds after S made contact with the reward pellet, and a variety of precautions were taken to ensure that punishment and nonreward were not confounded during either training or testing.

Test trial performance of the several groups may be seen in Figure 5. Exposure to either nonreinforcement or punishment during acquisition successfully produced resistance to the decremental effects of the event: the running speeds of Group P Ss tested with punishment and Group N Ss tested with nonreinforcement decreased only negligibly over the six-day test period. Of major interest, however, was the sizable and statistically reliable transfer of the effects of the two experimental training conditions: Group N Ss were less slowed by punishment and Group P Ss were less slowed by nonreinforcement than were the corresponding Group C Ss. These results would appear to provide reasonable encouragement to the view that there is some degree of communality in the emotional responses of fear and anticipatory frustration.

CONDITIONED FRUSTRATION AND FEAR

The above studies are among the sizable number (Amsel, 1958 and 1962;

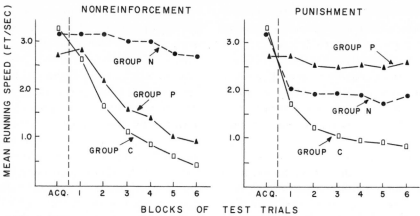

Fig. 5. Mean runway speeds on last day of acquisition and subsequent test trials for groups trained with nonreinforced (N), or punished (P) trials interspersed during acquisition, as compared with a continuously reinforced (C) group. Separate graphs are presented for the 15 Ss in each group tested with nonreinforcement and the 15 Ss tested with punishment. (Brown & Wagner, 1964)

Wagner, 1961 and 1963a) that attest to the usefulness of the assumption that anticipatory, aversive, emotional responses are an important product not only of punishment but also of frustrative-nonreinforcement. If such is the case, however, it should be amenable to more direct demonstration.

The aversive motivational properties of *fear* have been demonstrated by showing that the presence and the removal, respectively, of cues previously associated with painful stimulation, could produce energizing and reinforcing effects. Brown, Kalish, and Farber (1951) showed that the vigor of the unconditioned startle response to a sudden loud noise was increased by the presence of cues previously paired with electric shock. In addition, Miller (1948a) and Brown and Jacobs (1949) showed that escape from cues previously paired with shock provided an adequate reinforcement for the learning of a new response, such as lever pressing or hurdle crossing.

The following study (Wagner, 1963b) was designed to evaluate the proposal

that cues associated with frustrative-nonreward may come to elicit *anticipatory frustration* and hence also have aversive motivational properties. Since anticipatory frustration has been compared to fear in many aspects of detail, the techniques employed were closely patterned after those that had proved useful in the above mentioned investigations of fear. In separate test situations it was attempted to determine (a) whether the presence of cues previously paired with frustrative-nonreward would potentiate the unconditioned startle response, and (b) whether the cessation of such cues would serve as reinforcement for a simple hurdle-crossing response.

In the first experiment, two groups of rats received nonreinforcement randomly interspersed according to a 50% schedule among food-rewarded trials in a U-shaped runway. For Ss in the experimental group an interrupted light and white noise stimulus (CS) was presented on nonreinforced trials when an S broke a photocell beam located two feet before the empty food cup. The

Ss in the second group were run as controls. They were given the same experience with frustrative-nonreward in the runway as were the experimental Ss, that is, they were run on the same 50 percent reinforcement schedule. They also received the same exposure to the CS, but in a neutral cage, unassociated with feeding or frustrative-nonreward.

Over five consecutive days 116 runway trials were administered. These were sufficient to produce discriminative behavior in the runway speeds of the experimental Ss. That is, by the end of the 116 trials each of the experimental Ss would slow down or stop and turn around when the CS came on.

Following its last acquisition trial, each S was then given 20 spaced test trials in a stabilimeter device which recorded the amplitude of the S's startle response to a sudden, loud 1000-cycle tone. During the three seconds preceding each startle tone the CS was presented.

Figure 6 presents the mean startle response for the two groups over two consecutive blocks of ten trials. In the first ten-trial block there was a significantly greater startle in the experimental as compared to the control group. By the second block of ten trials there was a negligible difference in the opposite direction.

The obtained difference in startle amplitudes between experimental and control Ss over trials one through ten is in obvious agreement with the frustration-theory prediction. The more vigorous reaction of experimental Ss to the startle tone is consistent with the view that the CS produced a relative increase in emotionality for those Ss for which it had previously been paired with frustrative nonreward. Not predictable was the degree of persistence of this potentiation. Exposure of experimental Ss to the CS on test trials, without the primary event of frustrative-nonreward, represented extinction, and should have progressively diminished the effectiveness of the CS over the course of testing. That the potentiating effects of the CS for experimental Ss disappeared by the second block of test trials may indicate that the extinction of conditioned frustration is characteristically rapid, or perhaps that only a low level of conditioning had been attained by the start of testing.

In the second experiment, control and experimental Ss were trained in an identical fashion to those in the first experiment. They were tested, however, to determine whether the cessation of the CS would serve to reinforce a new response. The test apparatus consisted of an aluminum box with two identical compartments. The compartments were separated by a door which could be partially dropped through the floor, to provide a one-inch hurdle. An S was

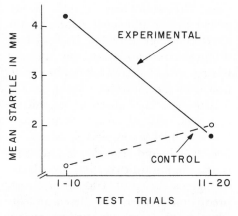

Fig. 6. Mean startle response of two groups of 9 Ss to an abrupt tone preceded by a CS. For Experimental Ss the CS was previously paired with frustrative-nonreinforcement. (Wagner, 1963b)

placed in one compartment with the door closed. Two minutes later the door was opened, presenting the CS and allowing S to cross to the opposite side. When S crossed the hurdle the CS terminated and the door was raised. Ninety seconds later the door was again opened, presenting the CS and allowing S to return to its original side which again terminated the CS. Sixteen successive trials were run in this shuttle fashion, on each of which response time was recorded.

Figure 7 presents the mean hurdle-crossing speeds over the first and last half of the test series for experimental and control Ss. As may be seen, the experimental group responded faster than the control group over both blocks of trials, but this difference was more pronounced in the last half than in the first half of the test series. The latter observation is crucial to the proposal that CS cessation was uniquely reinforcing for experimental Ss. The appearance of faster over-all speeds for experimental Ss could be attributed to the energizing effects of the CS pre-

viously demonstrated with the startle procedure. Differential reinforcement for hurdle-crossing, on the other hand, implies a divergence of the hurdle-crossing speeds of the two groups with additional hurdle-crossing trials. Statistical analyses revealed the obtained divergence to be reliable, as was the absolute difference between the two groups over the last block of trials.

It is apparent from Figure 7 that the reliable divergence in the trials of the two groups is largely a result of a decrease in control-group speeds. The small increase observed in experimental-group speeds during testing did not approach statistical reliability. That escape from the CS served to *maintain* the hurdle-crossing response for experimental Ss, in spite of the tendency observed in control Ss for speeds to decrease across trials, seems adequate to demonstrate its effectiveness as a reinforcer. At the same time, the failure to find an absolute increase in experimental S speeds indicates that the magnitude of this reinforcing effect cannot be considered large in comparison to other variables inherent in the test situation. This again may be due, as suggested by the transitory nature of the startle findings, to a low level of conditioned frustration at the start of testing, or to its relatively rapid extinction over the course of testing.

Although the absolute magnitude and persistence of the effects are small, the obtained differences between experimental and control Ss in both startle and hurdle-crossing are clearly in agreement with frustration-theory predictions. When considered in conjunction, the results from the two testing situations appear to place the concept of conditioned frustration on firmer ground. Likewise, the similarity

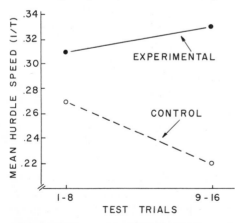

Fig. 7. **Mean speed of hurdle-crossing and CS-termination for two groups of 12 Ss. For Experimental Ss the CS was previously paired with frustrative-nonreinforcement. (Wagner, 1963b)**

of the present findings to those obtained in investigations of fear (Brown,
Kalish and Farber, 1951; Miller, 1948b;
Brown and Jacobs, 1949) provide further indication that nonreinforcement
in appetitional reward situations may
be difficult to distinguish in certain of
its behavioral effects from other "aversive" stimulation.

Summary: Regardless of one's theoretical disposition, it would appear difficult to
escape the conclusion that punishment and
nonreinforcement share a variety of effects
in instrumental reward learning. To the
degree that investigation continues to show
such similarities, the more it seems reasonable to attempt similar treatments of the
two events, such as the fear and anticipa-
tory-frustration theories that have been
described.

If the response decrement produced by
punishment is to be characterized as being
frequently unstable and impermanent, the
present data on depressant drugs and
stimulus change would suggest that part of
the response decrement produced by
frustrative-nonreward should be similarly
characterized.

If the practical use of punishment is to
be cautioned against, because of untoward

emotional effects that may become conditioned to the learning situation, the studies
on conditioned frustration would serve to
emphasize that simple nonreinforcement
may not be a panacea.

If the technique of gradually increasing
the noxious stimulation associated with a
behavior is to be considered as a method
for training "courage," the data on resistance to extinction would advise that a side
effect may be a decrease in sensitivity to
those occasions when the behavior is no
longer rewarded and appropriate.

This is still not to make the point that
nonreinforcement and punishment are
identical in their over-all effect. The two
events may serve as stimuli to elicit different immediate, overt responses. They undoubtedly lead to different incentive motivations, as in only one case does S learn
that reward no longer occurs. Furthermore,
the primary emotional response to nonreinforcement may not only differ in intensity from that which may be produced by
punishment, but, over a series of trials, is
presumably more transitory, since it is
assumed to decrease as anticipatory reward
decreases. The point is simply that there
are similarities that do exist, that may be
of theoretical and practical significance,
and that should not be ignored merely
because there are also important differences.

Science, October 18, 1963, vol. 142, pp. 411–412

Handling of Pregnant Rats: Effects on Emotionality of Their Offspring[*][1]

Robert Ader and Peter M. Conklin

By using conditioning techniques, it
has been shown that prenatal maternal
"anxiety" increases offspring emotional-

* Reprinted from *Science* by permission.
Copyright © 1963 by the AAAS.
1 Supported by grant MH 03655 from the
National Institute of Mental Health.

ity in the rat (Thompson, 1957; Ader &
Belfer, 1962; Doyle & Yule, 1959; Hockman, 1961). The effects which might
obtain from other types of behavioral
treatment of a pregnant animal are not
known. Various manipulations, notably

"handling," decrease emotionality in the rat when administered postnatally. The present study, then, was designed to determine the effects of prenatal handling, that is, handling of the pregnant animal, on emotionality of the offspring.

Data were obtained from a total of 138 offspring of primiparous Sprague-Dawley rats. These females were placed with males each evening and pregnancy was determined by vaginal smears taken the following morning. By random selection, half the pregnant animals remained unmanipulated and half were handled for 10 minutes three times daily (once each morning, afternoon, and evening) throughout the period of gestation. Pregnant animals were group-housed until approximately 1 week before delivery when they were individually placed into nesting cages. Handling consisted of picking up the animal and holding it loosely in one hand.

Litters were culled to seven or eight pups within 48 hours of birth and cross-fostering was also accomplished within this time. An equal number of litters remained with their natural mothers, were cross-fostered to mothers of that same group, or were cross-fostered to mothers of the opposing group. After this time the nesting cages in which the animals were housed were not cleaned and the pups were not manipulated in any way until weaning at 21 days. After weaning, animals were segregated by sex and treatment, and group-housed in standard laboratory cages. Food and water were available at all times.

Approximately half the animals were tested for emotionality at 45 days and 120 animals were tested at 100 days in an open-field situation. The field was 5 ft (1.5 m) in diameter and marked off into 7.5-inch (19-cm) squares and four concentric circles. Behaviors recorded were squares traversed and entries into the inner concentric circles (inversely related to emotionality), and defecation (directly related to emotionality). At 100 days all animals were also observed in an emergence-from-cage test in which the time required by animals to emerge from their open home cage (directly related to emotionality or "timidity") was recorded up to a maximum of 900 seconds.

Beginning at weaning a biweekly record of body weight was kept for 13 weeks. These data indicated no difference in the absolute weight or rate of growth between the prenatally handled and control animals.

Taken together, the emotionality data did not reveal any consistent tendency for animals fostered to handled mothers to differ from those fostered to control mothers. The data obtained from the open-field are given in Table 1. An analysis of variance applied to squares traversed revealed no differences as a function of group, sex, fostering, previous experience in the field, or

TABLE 1

OPEN-FIELD BEHAVIOR IN PRENATALLY HANDLED (H) AND CONTROL (C) OFFSPRING

Group	Squares traversed (mean No.)	Animals entering inner circles (%)	Animals defecating (%)
H ($N = 28$)	25.6	14.3	17.9
C ($N = 30$)	29.5	16.7	63.3
p	>.10	>.10	>.01
H ($N = 59$)	25.2	45.8	20.3
C ($N = 61$)	23.2	27.9	45.9
p	>.10	>.10	>.01

any interaction of these. Inspection of the data on the percentage of animals entering inner circles did not suggest the presence of any interactions within either the 45- or 100-day tests. Chi-square analyses indicated that a somewhat larger percentage of the combined offspring of handled mothers approached the center of the field at 100 days, but not on the earlier test.

Defecation in the open-field also showed no interaction effects. Within each subgroup of handled and control offspring at both 45 and 100 days, an equal or greater number of control offspring relative to handled offspring defecated. Chi-square analyses indicated that the number of prenatally handled animals defecating in the field was significantly lower than the number of control offspring on both tests ($\chi^2 = 10.54$; $\chi^2 = 7.71$).

The F test showed a significant Group $\times$ Fostering interaction on the

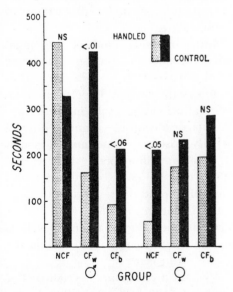

Fig. 1. Mean time required by prenatally handled and control offspring to emerge from their home cage. (NCF = non-cross-fostered; CF_w = cross-fostered within group; CF_b = cross-fostered between groups.)

emergence-from-cage test. Among males there was no difference between the non-cross-fostered handled ($N = 7$) and control ($N = 10$) groups, whereas both cross-fostered groups of prenatally handled animals ($N = 11$ and 20) emerged significantly sooner than controls ($N = 10$ and 12). Among females it was the cross-fostered groups ($N = 13$ and 11 for handled and 10 and 9 for control animals) which did not differ significantly, but the non-cross-fostered offspring of handled mothers ($N = 12$) emerged significantly sooner than controls ($N = 13$). These data are presented in Fig. 1.

In contrast to the greater offspring emotionality effected by prenatal maternal "anxiety," prenatally handled animals appear to be less emotional than controls. To the extent that high emotionality may be considered maladaptive, such results serve to contradict any orientation or expectation that only deleterious effects can result from prenatal manipulation.

It has been hypothesized by Thompson (1957) that the behavioral effects of prenatal maternal manipulations are brought about by the hormonal changes which occur in the mother in response to the anxiety-provoking stimulation. Presumably, these changes are transmitted to the fetus via the maternal-fetal blood exchange. If such are the mediating mechanisms, it would follow from the present data that the response of the pregnant (or for that matter, the nonpregnant) animal to handling is qualitatively and/or quantitatively different from the response to some if not all other forms of "stressful" stimulation of the kind commonly used in studies of environmental influences on behavior. Such a hypothesis has implications for the design of research on

the effects of "early" as well as prenatal experiences since it would appear
that one cannot necessarily generalize
from the effects of one type of manipulation to another. Unfortunately, little
is known at this time about the psychophysiological responses concomitant
with handling or other behavioral manipulations.

Summary: Pregnant rats were either
unmanipulated or were handled for 10
minutes three times daily throughout pregnancy. Offspring remained with their natural mothers or were cross-fostered within
and between experimental and control
groups. When tested at 45 and 100 days of
age, the offspring of handled mothers were
found to be generally less emotional than
the controls.

Scientific American, 1958, vol. 199, no. 4, pp. 95–103

Ulcers in "Executive" Monkeys*

Joseph V. Brady

Physicians and laymen alike have
long recognized that emotional stress
can produce bodily disease. Psychic
disturbances can induce certain skin
and respiratory disorders, can set off
attacks of allergic asthma and may even
play a part in some forms of heart
disease. Of all the body's systems, however, the gastrointestinal tract is perhaps the most vulnerable to emotional
stress. The worries, fears, conflicts and
anxieties of daily life can produce
gastrointestinal disorders ranging from
the "nervous stomach" which most of
us know at first hand, to the painful
and often disabling ulcers which are
the traditional occupational disease of
business executives.

Emotional stress appears to produce
ulcers by increasing the flow of the
stomach's acid juices. The connection
between emotional disturbance, stomach secretion and ulcers is well docu-

mented. A recent study of 2,000 Army
draftees, for example, found that those
who showed emotional disturbance and
excessive gastric secretion during their
initial physical examination developed
ulcers later on under the strains of
military life.

But not every kind of emotional
stress produces ulcers, and the same
kind of stress will do so in one person
and not in another. Experimental investigation of the problem is difficult.
Animals obviously cannot provide
wholly satisfactory experimental models
of human mind-body interactions.
They can, however, be studied under
controlled conditions, and it is through
animal experiments that we are finding
leads to the cause of ulcers as well as
to the effect of emotional stress on the
organism in general.

Various investigators have succeeded
in inducing ulcers in experimental animals by subjecting them to physical
stress. But the role of the emotional
processes in such experiments has been

uncertain. Experiments on dogs by George F. Mahl of Yale University Medical School indicate that a "fear producing" situation lasting many hours increases the animals' gastric secretions, but these animals do not develop ulcers. William L. Sawrey and John D. Weisz of the University of Colorado produced ulcers in rats by subjecting them to a conflict situation: keeping them in a box where they could obtain food and water only by standing on a grid which gave them a mild electric shock. But this experiment, as Sawrey and Weisz themselves pointed out, did not prove conclusively that emotional stress was the crucial factor in producing the ulcers.

Our studies of ulcers in monkeys at the Walter Reed Army Institute of Research developed somewhat fortuitously. For several years we had been investigating the emotional behavior of these animals. In some of our experiments we had been keeping monkeys in "restraining chairs" (in which they could move their heads and limbs but not their bodies) while we conditioned them in various ways. Since these procedures seemed to impose considerable emotional stress on the animals, we decided that we ought to know something about their physiological reactions. Preliminary investigation showed that stress brought about dramatic alterations in the hormone content of the animals' blood, but a more extensive study of 19 monkeys was brought to a halt when many of them died.

At first we considered this merely a stroke of bad luck, but the post-mortem findings showed that more than bad luck was involved. Many of the dead monkeys had developed ulcers as well as other extensive gastrointestinal damage. Such pathological conditions are normally rare in laboratory animals, and previous experiments with monkeys kept in restraining chairs up to six months convinced us that restraint alone did not produce the ulcers. Evidently the conditioning procedures were to blame.

One of the procedures which showed a high correlation with ulcers involved training the monkey to avoid an electric shock by pressing a lever. The animal received a brief shock on the feet at regular intervals, say, every 20 seconds. It could avoid the shock if it learned to press the lever at least once in every 20-second interval. It does not take a monkey very long to master this problem; within a short time it is pressing the lever far oftener than once in 20 seconds. Only occasionally does it slow down enough to receive a shock as a reminder.

One possibility, of course, was that the monkeys which had developed ulcers under this procedure had done so not because of the psychological stress involved but rather as a cumulative result of the shocks. To test this possibility we set up a controlled experiment, using two monkeys in "yoked chairs" in which both monkeys received shocks but only one monkey could prevent them. The experimental or "executive" monkey could prevent shocks to himself and his partner by pressing the lever; the control monkey's lever was a dummy. Thus both animals were subjected to the same physical stress (*i.e.*, both received the same number of shocks at the same time), but only the "executive" monkey was under the psychological stress of having to press the lever.

We placed the monkeys on a continuous schedule of alternate periods of shock-avoidance and rest, arbitrarily

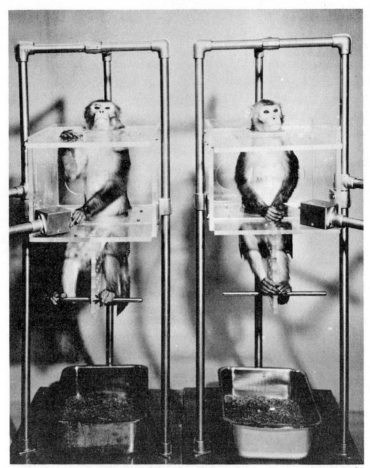

Fig. 1. Conditioning experiment involves training monkeys in "restraining chairs." Both animals receive brief electric shocks at regular intervals. The "executive" monkey (left) has learned to press the lever in its left hand, which prevents shocks to both animals. The control monkey (right) has lost interest in its lever, which is a dummy. Only executive monkeys developed ulcers.

choosing an interval of six hours for each period. As a cue for the executive monkey we provided a red light which was turned on during the avoidance periods and turned off during the "off" hours. The animal soon learned to press its lever at a rate averaging between 15 and 20 times a minute during the avoidance periods, and to stop pressing the level when the red light was turned off. These responses showed no change throughout the experiment.

The control monkey at first pressed the lever sporadically during both the avoidance and rest sessions, but lost interest in the lever within a few days.

After 23 days of a continuous six-hours-on, six-hours-off schedule the executive monkey died during one of the avoidance sessions. Our only advance warning had been the animal's failure to eat on the preceding day. It had lost no weight during the experiment, and it pressed the lever at an unflagging

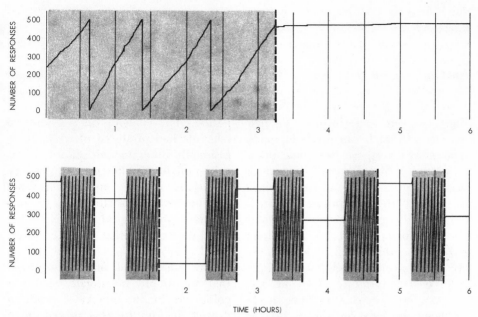

TIME (HOURS)

Fig. 2. Responses of monkeys were recorded automatically. Slope of the lines shows the rate of lever-pressing (vertical lines indicate resetting of stylus). Upper chart shows responses of an executive monkey during the last half of a six-hour avoidance session (gray area) and the first half of a six-hour rest period; shocks were programmed every 20 seconds. Monkeys kept on this schedule developed ulcers. Lower chart shows responses during a 30-minutes-on, 30-minutes-off schedule with shocks programmed every two seconds. Monkeys on this schedule failed to develop ulcers, despite more intense activity and presumably greater psychic stress.

rate through the first two hours of its last avoidance session. Then it suddenly collapsed and had to be sacrificed. An autopsy revealed a large perforation in the wall of the duodenum—the upper part of the small intestine near its junction with the stomach, and a common site of ulcers in man. Microscopic analysis revealed both acute and chronic inflammation around this lesion. The control monkey, sacrificed in good health a few hours later, showed no gastrointestinal abnormalities. A second experiment using precisely the same procedure produced much the same results. This time the executive monkey developed ulcers in both the stomach and the duodenum; the control animal was again unaffected.

In a series of follow-up experiments which is still in progress we have tried to isolate the physiological and psychological factors which produce the "laboratory ulcers." For example, one of our groups suggested that the "social" interaction between the two monkeys might be important. Certainly the most casual observation showed that considerable "communication" was going on between the two animals, who were seated within easy chattering distance of each other. We therefore studied several pairs of animals isolated from each other in soundproof "telephone booths." Unfortunately isolation failed to protect the executive monkeys, for they continued to develop ulcers.

More recently, however, we have found a factor or group of factors which does seem to be critical in producing ulcers. What we have learned seems to pivot on our chance selection of six hours as the interval for shock-avoidance and for rest in the conditioning procedure. We made this discovery when we sought to improve on the results of our experiments. Though laboratory animals can rarely be made to develop ulcers, we had come upon a procedure that seemed to produce ulcers "to order." The only uncertainty was the length of exposure required. This varied greatly among individual monkeys; some came down with ulcers in 18 days, others took as long as six weeks. If we could develop a technique guaranteed to produce ulcers in, say, 10 days, we could stop the shock-avoidance sessions on the eighth or ninth day, apply various therapeutic measures and study the monkey's response to them.

It seemed reasonable to assume that we might induce ulcers more rapidly and dependably by simply increasing the stress on the animals. We therefore put several monkeys on an 18-hours-on, six-hours-off schedule. After a few weeks one of the animals died, but of tuberculosis, not ulcers. The rest continued to press their levers week after week with no apparent ill effects. Finally, when it began to seem as if we might have to wait for the animals to die of old age, we sacrificed them— and found no gastrointestinal abnormalities whatever!

We put another group on an even more strenuous schedule: 30 minutes on and 30 minutes off, with the shocks programmed for every two seconds rather than every 20. Again one of the animals died, this time of a generalized virus infection unrelated to ulcers. The others, after weeks of frantic lever

pressing, showed no gastrointestinal changes.

We had to conclude that the crucial factor was not the degree or even the frequency of stress but was to be sought in the relationship between the length of the stress period and that of the rest period. The six-hours-on, six-hours-off schedule had produced ulcers (and occasionally other somatic disorders) despite individual differences in monkeys, variations in diet and maintenance routines and gross alterations in preliminary physiological tests. No other schedule we had tried produced ulcers at all.

This unexpected finding suggested that we should investigate what was going on in the monkeys' stomachs during the conditioning procedure. A standard technique for investigating gastric process in experimental animals makes use of an artificial opening, or fistula, in the animal's abdominal and stomach walls through which the contents of its stomach can be sampled. Such fistulas have played an important role in expanding our knowledge of the gastrointestinal system. In the early 19th century the famous U. S. Army surgeon William Beaumont made the first systematic study of the digestive process with the cooperation of a young Canadian who had a fistula due to an imperfectly healed gunshot wound. More than a century later Stewart G. Wolf, Jr., and Harold G. Wolff at the Cornell University Medical College, with the help of a man who had a similar injury, conducted a pioneer investigation of the relationship between emotional stress and ulcers. They found that situations which produced feelings of anxiety or aggression in their subject stepped up his gastric secretions and engorged his stomach wall with blood. Physiological changes of this sort, they believed, are the precursors of ulcers.

Edwin Polish of our department of neuroendocrinology has been studying the stomach acidity of some of our executive monkeys by means of artificial fistulas. His measurements, though far from complete, seem to provide one possible explanation of the results of our experiments.

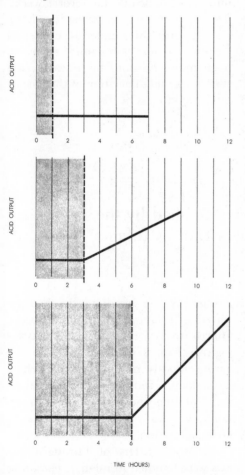

TIME (HOURS)

Fig. 3. Stomach acidity of executive monkeys, as shown in these highly simplified charts, did not increase during avoidance sessions (gray area) but rather during the subsequent rest periods. The greatest increase followed a six-hour session; no rise followed a one-hour session.

The stomach secretions of the executive monkeys do indeed become considerably more acid, but not (as one might expect) during the avoidance periods. When the animals are actually pressing the levers the acidity of their stomachs rises little. The significant increase in acidity begins at the end of the avoidance session and reaches a peak several hours later, while the animal is presumably resting. This finding suggests a close relationship between the formation of ulcers and the cyclic character of the six-hours-on, six-hours-off procedure. Emotional stress, it appears, must be intermittent—turning the animal's system on and off, so to speak—if it is to cause ulcers. Continuous emotional stress seems to permit a stable adjustment (at least for a while) under which ulcers do not develop. It is tempting to consider the analogy of the vacuum tube or light bulb which seems to last much longer under conditions of continuous current than when it is subjected to frequent heating and cooling.

Like most analogies, this one limps badly and has its limitations. For example, our experiments show that periodic stress does not always bring on ulcers, and Polish's findings are consistent with this. His measurements indicate that the greatest increase in acidity occurs after a six-hour avoidance session. After a three-hour session acidity rises, but less sharply; after a one-hour session it does not rise at all [see Fig. 3]. Periodic emotional stress apparently causes ulcers only if its period coincides with that of some natural rhythm of the gastrointestinal system.

Obviously our knowledge of the physiological and psychological processes which produce ulcers is far from complete. Our understanding of even the relatively well-controlled experiment I have described is just beginning to progress beyond the primitive level. We have yet to discover why emotional stress steps up the stomach's acidity later rather than immediately. We are still looking for a method of producing ulcers at will, in days rather than weeks. Eventually we hope to learn to detect an incipient ulcer before the animal collapses, by examining the subject's blood, urine and other secretions, thus making post-mortem examinations unnecessary.

There are many other questions about the effects of emotional stress which we have not yet begun to investigate. Really thorough examination of the experimental animals might well show other types of damage of which we are at present unaware. The two monkeys which died of causes unrelated to ulcers, for example, may have succumbed because their resistance had been lowered in some way by psychological stress. It would be surprising to find physical processes wholly unimpaired in monkeys who have been on a 30-minutes-on, 30-minutes-off schedule for several weeks. The opportunity to bring psychosomatic relationships under experimental scrutiny in the laboratory seems to open broad horizons for research into the causes and alleviation of this poorly understood class of ills.

Science, November 29, 1963, vol. 142, pp. 1192–1193.

Behavior of Adult Rats Is Modified by the Experiences Their Mothers Had as Infants[*][1]

Victor H. Denenberg and Arthur E. Whimbey

Handling rats in infancy has marked effects upon their subsequent behavioral and physiological processes (Denenberg, 1962; Denenberg & Karas, 1960; 1961; Levine, 1956; 1962; Morton, Denenberg, & Zarrow, 1963; Tapp & Markowitz, 1963). To date no one has investigated whether the handling of female rats in infancy affects their offspring. Modifications of the offspring's characteristics could occur during their fetal period, as a result of physiological changes induced in the

mother by the handling she had received in infancy, or they could occur after birth as a result of either physiological changes (which could, for example, modify milk supply or behavioral changes induced in the mother by the handling she had received in infancy. We now report results of such an investigation.

About 45 litters of Purdue-Wistar rats were handled in infancy. Handling consisted of removing a complete litter from the home cage (leaving the mother in the cage), placing the pups on shavings in a can for 3 minutes, and then returning the pups to their home

* Reprinted from *Science* by permission. Copyright © 1963 by the AAAS.
1 Research was supported in part by a grant from the National Science Foundation.

cage. This was done once a day from day 1 through day 20 of life. About 45 other litters were not disturbed during this time. Once these litters were born the shavings in their cages were never changed; food and water were supplied without opening the cages.

At 21 days the handled and non-handled litters were weaned, and the females were placed in specially designated cages. When mature, the females were bred to a random sample of colony males; the males were systematically moved from one cage to another and were exposed equally often to handled and nonhandled females.

When pregnant, the females were placed in stainless-steel maternity cages. The day after birth all litters were sexed, and those containing more than eight pups were reduced to four of each sex when possible, but never to less than two of one sex. No litter containing less than seven pups was used. The litters were then returned to their natural mothers. At this time (i) some litters were left with their natural mothers, (ii) other litters were fostered to mothers that had had the same experience (handled or not handled) in infancy as the natural mothers, and (iii) still other litters were fostered to mothers that in infancy had received the treatment opposite to that of the natural mothers. Fostering was done by moving the mothers from one cage to another, leaving the pups in the cage in which they had been born. In most instances fostering took place between litters born on the same day; in six cases the foster mother had given birth 1 day earlier than the natural mother, and in one case the foster mother had given birth 3 days earlier than the natural mother. Except for fostering, the litters were not disturbed. At 21

days the pups from 55 litters were weaned, weighed, sexed, earpunched, and placed in laboratory cages with littermates of the same sex.

Starting at 50 days of age, the animals were given 4 days of open-field testing. The field was 45 inches (115 cm) square, painted flat black, with walls 18 inches (46 cm) high. The floor was marked off in 9-inch (23-cm) squares by thin white lines. A rat was placed in one corner of the field, and its behavior was observed for 3 minutes. Total numbers of squares entered and boluses defecated were recorded. Two males and two females from each of 47 litters were tested in the open field. Testing was completed at 53 days, at which time the animals were again weighed.

The body weights at 21 days are summarized in Table 1. The weights of all animals within a litter were averaged to give one mean litter weight, thus yielding a Between Litter Error Mean Square based upon 49 degrees of freedom. To determine whether fostering had any effect, the two nonfostered groups (A and D) were compared with the two groups in which litters were fostered to mothers with the same infantile experiences as the natural mothers (groups B and E). No significant effects were found. Therefore, the fostering variable was ignored in assessing the prenatal and postnatal contributions of the mothers toward the body weight of the offspring. The analysis of these data found that the postnatal factor was significant ($F = 5.08$, $p < .05$). Young reared by mothers that had been handled in infancy (groups C, D, and E) weighed significantly more than pups reared by mothers that had not been handled in infancy (groups A, B, and F). The only

TABLE 1

MEAN BODY WEIGHT, IN GRAMS, AT 21 DAYS, MEAN NUMBER OF SQUARES ENTERED,
AND MEAN NUMBER OF BOLUSES DEFECATED DURING 4 DAYS OF OPEN-FIELD TESTING.
THE N PER MEAN IS GIVEN IN PARENTHESES.

Group	Experience of natural mother in infancy	Postnatal fostering of pups	21-days body wt.	Squares entered Male	Squares entered Female	Boluses Male	Boluses Female
A	Not handled	Not fostered	35.87 (69)	75.69 (16)	118.62 (16)	7.12 (16)	4.19 (16)
B	Not handled	Fostered to nonhandled mother	36.93 (62)	47.00 (16)	67.94 (16)	6.37 (16)	4.37 (16)
C	Not handled	Fostered to handled mother	41.29 (62)	90.56 (16)	97.75 (16)	12.31 (16)	5.56 (16)
D	Handled	Not fostered	40.81 (70)	53.06 (16)	58.69 (16)	10.87 (16)	7.81 (16)
E	Handled	Fostered to handled mother	38.87 (56)	50.64 (14)	70.93 (14)	10.50 (14)	12.21 (14)
F	Handled	Fostered to nonhandled mother	38.24 (101)	53.69 (16)	85.94 (16)	6.87 (16)	5.37 (16)

significant difference among the body weights in adulthood was between males and females.

The data for open-field behavior are summarized in Table 1. In the analysis of variance the scores of the 4 animals within each litter were combined to give one litter score, thus yielding a Between Litter Error Mean Square based upon 41 degrees of freedom. To evaluate the sex variable and all interactions with this variable, the male and female means were obtained separately for each litter, and the Between Litter × Sex Error Mean Square (df = 41) was used in the denominator of these F tests.

When the two nonfostered groups (A and D) were compared with the two groups in which fostering was done between mothers with the same experience in infancy (B and E), a significant interaction ($F = 4.58$, $p < .05$) was obtained between the presence or absence of fostering and the mother's experience in infancy; those young which were born of and reared by nonhandled mothers and which were not fostered (group A), were significantly more active than the other three groups. Therefore, the four fostered groups were used to evaluate the prenatal and postnatal contributions of the mothers toward the activity pattern of the offspring. A significant interaction ($F = 4.81$, $p < .05$) was found between the prenatal and postnatal mothers. Young born of mothers that had not been handled in infancy, and fostered to handled mothers (group C), were significantly more active than young from the other three groups (B, E, and F); the next most active group was the complement of this—rats born of handled mothers and reared by nonhandled mothers (group F). The sex variable was significant ($F = 6.87$, $p < .05$ but did not interact significantly with any of the maternal variables.

The test evaluating the fostering effect found that offspring born of and raised by mothers that had been handled in infancy (groups D and E) defecated significantly more ($F = 7.69$, $p < .01$) than offspring born of and raised by nonhandled control mothers (groups A and B); the procedure of fostering did not have any significant effect. The test separating the prenatal and the postnatal factors found that the postnatal mother was the significant contributor: young raised by mothers that had been handled in infancy (groups C, D, and E) defecated more ($F = 6.62$, $p < .05$) than young raised by mothers that had not been handled in infancy (A, B, and F). Again the sex factor was significant ($F = 9.15$, $p < .01$). Though sex did not interact significantly with any of the maternal variables, the Sex × Prenatal Mother interaction approached significance ($F = 3.49$, $p < .07$).

The results clearly establish that the experiences which the mother received while an infant were profound enough to modify her offsprings' body weight at weaning and open-field behavior in adulthood. These modifications were mediated through both the prenatal mother-fetus relationship and the postnatal mother-young interaction. The generality of this phenomenon has been confirmed by Grota (1963), who extrauterized fetuses (that is, removed the fetuses from the uterus but left them in the body cavity) of rat mothers which had been handled or not handled in infancy. Grota found that, for handled mothers, fetuses reared in the uterus had a higher survival rate between birth (by means of cesarean delivery) and weaning than those reared in the body cavity; extrauterization of fetuses in nonhandled mothers did not affect postnatal survival rate. In addition, Grota found that both the prenatal and postnatal mother contributed significantly to the weaning weights of pups delivered by cesarean section.

Summary: Some rat pups were handled for 20 days in infancy, while others were not. When the rats reached adulthood the females were bred. Some of the offspring were left with their natural mothers, others were fostered to mothers of the same background (handled/nonhandled) as that of their natural mothers, while still others were fostered to mothers with a different background from that of their natural mothers. The offspring were weaned and weighed at 21 days; at 50 days, activity and defecation scores were obtained in the open field. The weights at weaning and the defecation scores at 50 days were significantly influenced by the experience in infancy of the "postnatal" mother, whether she was the natural mother of a foster mother. The natural mother and the foster mother jointly affected the open-field activity of the offspring.

The Yale Review, December 1959, vol. 49, pp. 161–179.

The Hare and the Haruspex: A Cautionary Tale

Edward S. Deevey

Fifteen thousand years ago, when some of our more sensible ancestors had retired to paint pictures in caves in the south of France, the Scandinavian peninsula lay buried under a glacier. Even as recently as the seventh millennium B.C., when the arts and vices of civilization were already flourishing in the towns of Mesopotamia, the part of the earth's crust that is now Scandinavia was still depressed by the weight of half a mile of ice. Although the country has been rebounding at a great rate ever since, many Scandinavians remain depressed today. One reason may be that the Ice Age, as any Eskimo knows, is not yet over. The Scandinavian Airlines tourist who comes and goes like a swallow in the opalescent summer rarely glimpses the wintry or Pleistocene side of Nordic character, which accounts for its toughness, but which also results in some of the world's highest rates of alcoholism and suicide.

Perhaps because it was colonized so recently, the land the Norse called *Midgard* has always been treated as such—as middle ground, that is—by some of its inhabitants; as a good place to be *from,* on the way to some such place as *Asgard,* the abode of the gods. Rome, Byzantium, Normandy, and Britain were all chosen in their turn as earthly versions of Asgard. For a while, in the later Stone Age, the earliest emigrants could simply retrace their fathers' footsteps back to Europe, for the Danish Sounds were dry then, and dry land in the southern North Sea made Britain a peninsula before Scandinavia became one. By Roman and Viking times, given access to long ships, emigration continued to be almost as easy as it was fashionable. If one looks at a map of the land of the midnight sun (and remembers what happens when the sun goes down) it is easy to picture history as a series of glacial pulsations, or Gothic spurts, extruding adventurous Northmen toward successive seats of power, and milder winters. Nowadays, possibly because the northern winter is improving, the emigrants are less warlike than

they used to be, and Visigoths and Vikings have tended to give way to movie actresses and physicists. The last of the great landwasters, Gustavus Adolphus, died more than three hundred years ago. It was only a few years before his time—in 1579 to be exact—that the animal kingdom seems to have caught the idea and carried it on, for that is the first year in which the now-famous lemmings are known to have been on the march.

Biologists, of whom I am one, have been taking a lively interest in lemmings lately. These rat-sized hyperborean field mice were unknown in the ancient world, and even the sagas are strangely silent about them. They really began to draw attention only in Queen Victoria's time, and especially in England, when the notion somehow got about that Plato's Atlantis lay on the Dogger Bank, under the North Sea. The lemmings' efforts to emigrate from Norway were then explained as vain attempts to recover a lost homeland, now occupied by such thoroughly English creatures as the haddock and the sprat. The fact that Swedish lemmings march in the wrong direction, toward the Baltic, tends to undermine this theory, but science has not come up with a better explanation until very recently. Biologists always hesitate to impute human motives to animals, but they are beginning .to learn from psychologists, for whom attributing animal motives to humans is part of the day's work. What is now suspected is that the lemmings are driven by some of the same Scandinavian compulsions that drove the Goths. At home, according to this view, they become depressed and irritable during the long, dark winters under the snow. When home becomes intolerable, they emigrate, and their behavior is then described by the old Norse word, *berserk.*

A lemming migration is one of the great eruptions of nature, and its reverberations, like fallout, are of more than local concern. Biologists like to picture nature in the abstract as a sort of irregular lattice, or Mondrian construction, composed of feeding relations, whose seemingly random placement is ˝actually so tightly organized that every strut depends on all the others. The lemmings' place in this picture is that of a strut more easily fretted than most, because, like other vegetarians that nourish a variety of carnivores, they are more fed upon than feeding. As Caruso's vocal cords, suitably vibrated, could shatter glassware, the whole of animate creation sometimes seems to pulsate with the supply of lemmings. In normal years they live obscurely, if dangerously, in the mountains of Scandinavia, and on the Arctic tundra generally. Periodically, despite the efficient efforts of their enemies—which include such mainstays of the fur industry as the marten and the white fox—their reproductive prowess gets the upper hand, and the tundra fairly teems with them. At such times, about every four years somewhere in Norway, though any given district is afflicted less frequently, the balance of nature goes entirely awry, and the Mondrian composition seems to degenerate into parody. Sea birds give up fishing and flock far inland to gorge on lemmings, while the more local hawks and owls hatch and feed families that are several times larger than usual. Foxes, on the shores of the Arctic Ocean, have been known to hunt for lemmings fifty miles out on the pack ice. The reindeer, which ordinarily subsist on reindeer moss, acquire a taste for lemmings just as cattle use salt. Eventually, faced with such troubles (but not necessarily *because* of them—I'm coming to that), lemmings are seized with the classic, or rather Gothic, obsession, and millions of them desert the tundra for the lowlands.

The repercussions then begin in earnest. As the clumsy animals attempt to swim the lakes and rivers, the predatory circle widens to include the trout and salmon, which understandably lose interest in dry flies. The forested lowlands, already occupied by other kinds of rodents as well as by farmers and their dogs and cats, are not good lemming country—the winters are too warm, for one thing—but while the lemmings press on as though aware of this, they show no sign of losing their disastrous appetites. When the crops are gone, though seldom before, exorcism by a Latin formula is said to have some slight effect in abating the plague. Finally the vanguard may actually reach the sea, and having nowhere else to go, plunge in—sometimes meeting another army trying to come ashore from a nearby island. A steamer, coming up Trondheim Fjord in November 1868, took fifteen minutes to pass through a shoal of them, but they were swimming *across* the fjord, not down it to the sea. The landward part of their wake is a path of destruction, strewn with dead lemmings, and an epidemic focus of lemming fever— which is not something the lemmings *have,* but a kind of tularemia that people get from handling the carcasses. As the Norwegians take up this unenviable chore their thoughts rarely turn to Mondrian or any other artist;

the better-read among them may wonder, however, who buried the six hundred members of the Light Brigade.

American lemmings migrate too, but their outbreaks are observed less often, because no cities lie in their path. Knowledgeable bird-watchers are kept posted, nevertheless, by invasions of snowy owls, which leave the tundra when the lemming tide has passed its flood, and appear in such unlikely places as Charleston, the Azores, and Yugoslavia. Every four years or so, therefore, the lemmings affect the practice of taxidermy, and the economics of the glass-eye industry, as the handsome but unhappy birds fall trophy to amateur marksmen while vainly quartering the fields of France and New England. Closer to the center of the disturbance, the cities of western Norway see lemmings before they see owls, and they are not unknown as far away from the mountains as Stockholm, though spring fever is reported to be commoner than lemming fever along the Baltic beaches of Sweden. Oslo is ordinarily too far south, but was visited in 1862, in 1876, in 1890, and again in 1910. The 1862 migration, coinciding with the Battle of Antietam, may have been the greatest of the century, and one of its episodes was touching, if not prophetic. The Norwegian naturalist Robert Collett saw them, he said, "running up the high granite stairs in the vestibule of the University" (of Oslo). Evidently they were begging to be investigated by professors. The Norwegian savants were busy, however, and scorned the impertinent intrusion. In 1862 the discoverer of the death wish, Sigmund Freud, was a six-year-old boy in far-away Freiburg, and if he ever saw a lemming or shot a snowy owl his biographers have repressed it.

That the lemmings are neurotically sick animals, at least during migration, has not escaped the notice of close, or even of casual, observers. For one thing, they wander abroad in the daytime, as small mammals rarely do. For another, when crossed or cornered they show a most unmouselike degree of fight; as Collet said, "they viciously drive their sharp teeth into the foot, or the stick advanced toward them, and allow themselves to be lifted high up by their teeth." Descriptions of the last snarling stages of the march to the sea recall the South Ferry terminal at rush hour, or a hundred-car smashup on a California turnpike. In his authoritative and starkly titled book, *Voles, Mice, and Lemmings,* the English biologist Charles Elton summed up "this great cosmic oscillation" as "a rather tragic procession of refugees, with all the obsessed behaviour of the unwanted stranger in a populous land, going blindly on to various deaths." Offhand, however, neurosis does not seem to explain very much of this, any more than shellshock is a cause of war, and in trying to understand the upheaval the experts have tended to set the psychopathic symptoms to one side while looking for something more basic.

That something, presumably, would be some property of the lemmings' environment—food, predators, disease, or weather, or perhaps all working together—that periodically relaxes its hold on the mournful numbers. Find the cause of the overcrowding, so the thinking has run, and you will find why the lemmings leave home. But this thinking, though doubtless correct, has been slow to answer the question, because it tends to divert attention from the actors to the scenery. The oldest Norse references to lemmings confuse them with locusts, and the farmer whose fields are devastated can hardly be expected to count the pests' legs and divide by four. More detached students know that mammals do not drop from the sky, but in their own way they too have been misled by the locust analogy, supposing that lemmings swarm, as locusts do, because of something done *to* them by their surroundings. The discovery that the migrations are cyclical, made only a few years ago by Elton, strengthened the assumption that some environmental regularity, probably a weather cycle, must set the tune to which the lemmings, their predators, and their diseases respond in harmonics. Close listeners to nature's symphony soon reported, however, that it sounded atonal to them, more like Berg's opera *Wozzeck*, say, than like Beethoven's Sixth. Cycles of heavenly conjunctions were also looked into, but while the tides are pulled by the sun and moon, and the seasons are undeniably correlated with the zodiac, nothing in astrology reasonably corresponds to a four-year cycle.

If the lemmings' quadrennial fault lies, not in their stars, but in themselves, it is easy to see why the fact has been missed for so long. One reason, of course, is that most of their home life takes place under several feet of snow, in uncomfortable regions where even Scandinavians pass little time outdoors. The main trouble has been, though, as a quick review of thirty years' work will show, that the lemmings' path is thickly sown with false clues. Among these the snowy owls and white foxes rank as the reddest of herrings. The idea that the abundance of prey is controlled by the abundance of predators is a piece of folklore that is hard to uproot, because, like other superstitions, it is sometimes

true. The farmers and gamekeepers of Norway have acted on it with sublime confidence for more than a hundred years, backed by a state system of bounty payments, and hawks, foxes, and other predators are now much scarcer than they are in primeval Westchester County, for example. The result has been that while the grouse-shooting is no better than it used to be, the lemmings (and the field mice in the lowlands, where varmints are persecuted most actively) have continued to fluctuate with unabated vigor. A pile of fox brushes, augmented mainly every fourth year, remains as a monument to a mistaken theory, but their owners may take some gloomy pride in having furnished a splendid mass of statistics.

An even more seductive body of data exists in the account books of the Arctic fur trade, some of which go back to Revolutionary days. They give a remarkable picture of feast or famine, most kinds of skins being listed as thousands of times more plentiful in good years than in lean. Those that belonged to the smaller predators, such as the white fox and the ermine, rise and fall in numbers with the hauntingly familiar four-year rhythm, and the trappers' diaries (which make better reading than the bookkeepers' ledgers) show that their authors placed the blame squarely, or cyclically, on lemmings. Farther south there are periodic surges among such forest-dwellers as the marten and the red fox, whose fluctuating food supply is field mice. Lynx pelts, known to the trade under various euphemisms for "cat," show a still more beautiful cycle of ten years' length, which certainly matches the abundance of snowshoe hares, the lynxes' principal prey. The ten-year pulse of lynxes was extricated, after a brief but noisy academic scuffle, from the coils of the eleven-year sunspot cycle, and by the mid-'thirties the theory of mammal populations had settled down about like this: the prey begin to increase, and so do their slower-breeding predators; at peak abundance the predators nearly exterminate the prey, and then starve to death, so clearing the way for the prey to start the cycle over again.

The simple elegance of this idea made it enormously appealing, not least to mathematicians, who reduced it to equations and found it to have an astonishing amount of what they call *generality*. In physics, for instance, it is the "theory of coupled oscillations"; as "servomechanism theory" it underlies many triumphs of engineering, such as remote control by radar; in economics, it explains the tendency for the prices of linked products, such as corn and hogs, to chase each other in perpetually balanced imbalance. Regardless of the price of hogs, or furs, however, some killjoys soon declared that the formulae seemed not to apply to rodents. Some populations of snowshoe hares, for example, were found to oscillate on islands where lynxes, or predators of any sort, were scarcer than mathematicians. Besides, the equations require the coupled numbers of predator and prey to rise and fall smoothly, like tides, whereas the normal pattern of mammal cycles is one of gradual crescendo, followed abruptly by a crashing silence. A Russian biologist, G. F. Gause, was therefore led to redesign the theory in more sophisticated form. The predator, he said, need not be a fur-bearing animal; it can be an infectious disease. When the prey is scarce, the chance of infection is small, especially if the prey, or host, has survived an epidemic and is immune. As the hosts become more numerous, the infection spreads faster, or becomes more virulent, until the ensuing epidemic causes the crash.

In this new, agar-plated guise the theory was not only longer, lower, and more powerful; it was testable without recourse to the fur statistics, the study of which had come to resemble numerology. Made newly aware of lemming fever and tularemia, pathologists shed their white coats for parkas, and took their tubes and sterilizers into the field. The first reports were painfully disappointing: wild rodents, including lemmings, harbored no lack of interesting diseases, but the abundance of microbes had no connection with that of their hosts. Worse, the animals seemed to enjoy their ill health, even when their numbers were greatest, and when they died there was no sign of an epidemic. Not of infectious disease, anyway; but there was one malady, prevalent among snowshoe hares, that certainly was not infectious, but that just as certainly caused a lot of hares to drop dead, not only in live-traps, but also in the woods when no one was around. Long and occasionally sad experience with laboratory rabbits suggested a name, shock disease, for this benign but fatal ailment, the symptoms of which were reminiscent of apoplexy, or of insulin shock. The diagnosis, if that is what it was, amounted to saying that the hares were scared to death, not by lynxes (for the bodies hardly ever showed claw-marks), but, presumably, by each other. Having made this unhelpful pronouncement, most of the pathologists went home. The Second World War was on by that time, and for a while no one remembered what Collet had said about the lemmings: "Life quickly leaves them, and they die from the slightest injury . . . It is constantly stated by eyewitnesses, that they can die from their great excitement."

These Delphic remarks turned out to contain a real clue, which had been concealed in plain sight, like the purloined letter. An inquest on Minnesota snowshoe hares was completed in 1939, and its clinical language describes a grievous affliction. In the plainer words of a later writer,

This syndrome was characterized primarily by fatty degeneration and atrophy of the liver with a coincident striking decrease in liver glycogen and a hypoglycemia preceding death. Petechial or ecchymotic brain hemorrhages, and congestion and hemorrhage of the adrenals, thyroid, and kidneys were frequent findings in a smaller number of animals. The hares characteristically died in convulsive seizures with sudden onset, running movements, hind-leg extension, retraction of the head and neck, and sudden leaps with clonic seizures upon alighting. Other animals were typically lethargic or comatose.

For connoisseurs of hemorrhages this leaves no doubt that the hares were sick, but it does leave open the question of how they got that way. Well-trained in the school of Pasteur, or perhaps of Paul de Kruif, the investigators had been looking hard for germs, and were slow to take the hint of an atrophied liver, implying that shock might be a social disease, like alcoholism. As such, it could be contagious, like a hair-do, without being infectious. It might, in fact, be contracted in the same way that Chevrolets catch petechial tail fins from Cadillacs, through the virus of galloping, convulsive anxiety. A disorder of this sort, increasing in virulence with the means of mass communication, would be just the coupled oscillator needed to make Gause's theory work.

So theatrical an idea had never occurred to Gause, though, and before it could make much progress the shooting outside the windows had to stop. About ten years later, when the news burst on the world that hares are mad in March, it lacked some of the now-it-can-be-told immediacy of the Smyth Report on atomic energy, but it fitted neatly into the bulky dossier on shock disease that had been quietly accumulating in the meantime.

As a matter of fact, for most of those ten years shock disease was a military secret, as ghastly in some of its implications as the Manhattan Project. Armies are not supposed to react like frightened rabbits, but the simple truth, that civilians in uniform can suffer and die from shock disease, was horrifyingly evident in Korea. As was revealed after the war, hundreds of American captives, live-trapped while away from home and mother, had turned lethargic or comatose, or died in convulsive seizures with sudden onset. Their baffled buddies gave it the unsympathetic name of "give-up-itis."

Military interest in rodents was whipped up long before 1939, of course, but its basis, during more ingenious ages, was not the rodents' psyches. Rats have fought successfully, if impartially, in most of mankind's wars, but the Second World War was probably the first in which large numbers of rodents were deliberately kept on active duty while others were systematically slaughtered. To explain this curious even-handedness, and at the risk of considerable oversimplification, we may divide military rodents (including rabbits, which are not rodents, but lagomorphs, according to purists) into two platoons, or squadrons. First, there are wild, or Army-type rodents, which not only nibble at stores but carry various diseases; they are executed when captured. Then there are domestic, cabined, or Navy-type rodents; during the war these were mainly watched by Navy psychologists in an effort to understand the military mind. The story of the first kind was superbly told by the late Hans Zinsser in *Rats, Lice, and History,* a runaway best-seller in the years between World Wars. Conceivably as a result, there were no outbreaks of louse-borne typhus in the Second World War, but in the course of their vigil wildlife men continued to run into pathologists at Army messes around the world. The yarn of the Navy's rats has never been publicized, however (except, obliquely, in such studies of mass anxiety as William H. Whyte's *The Organization Man*).

The kind of nautical problem the psychologists had in mind was not the desertion of sinking ships, but the behavior of men under tension. The crowding of anxious but idle seamen in submarines, for instance, had had some fairly unmartial effects, which needed looking into. As subjects, when mariners were unavailable, the psychologists naturally used rats, which can be frustrated into states of high anxiety that simulate combat neurosis. So now, to recapitulate, there were *three* kinds of rodent experts in the Pacific theatre— zoologists, pathologists, and psychologists—and when they met, as they often did at the island bases, something was bound to happen. What emerged was a fresh view of rats, with which some of the lonelier islands were infested. These were no ordinary rats, but a special breed, like the Pitcairn Islanders, a sort of stranded landing-party. They were descendants of seagoing ancestors, marooned when the whalers had left; but, as the only wild mammals on the islands, they had reverted to Army type. It was soon noticed that when they entered messhalls and BOQ's they solved intellectual problems with great acumen, along with some anxiety-based bravado. Outdoors, on the other hand, their populations went up and down, and when abundant they terrorized the nesting seabirds or ran in droves through the copra plantations. Often, too, they simply dropped dead of shock. In short, they were rats, but whereas in confinement they behaved like psychologists, when at liberty they acted remarkably like lemmings.

If islanded feral rats contributed to the lemming problem, biologists could take wry pleasure in the fact, for most of the rats' contributions to insular existence—to the extinction of hundreds of kinds of interesting land birds, for instance—have been a lot less positive. Then, too, a back-to-nature movement led by psychologists promised to be an exhilarating experience, especially if it included an id-hunt through Polynesia. I have to admit, though, that it didn't work out quite that way, and my account of events in the Pacific theatre may be more plausible than accurate. The published facts are scanty, and my own duty as a Navy biologist was spent amid barnacles, not rodents, on the Eastern Sea Frontier. My first-hand knowledge of Pacific islands, in fact, is confined to Catalina, where rats are visible only on very clear days. What I *am* sure of is that startling things were learned in many countries, during the war years, about the capabilities of many kinds of animals besides rats. When these were added up it was not incredible that rodents might suffer the diseases of suburbia; some students would not have been surprised, by then, if bunnies were found to say "boo" to each other in Russian.

1. Bees, for example, were proved to be able to tell other bees, by means of a patterned dance like a polonaise, the direction and the distance from the hive at which food could be found, as well as the kind of flower to look for and the number of worker-bees needed to do the job. For compass directions they report the azimuth of the sun, but what they perceive is not the sun itself, but the arrangement of polarized light that the sun makes around the sky.

2. Navigating birds, on the other hand, take bearings on the sun directly, or on the stars, but when visual cues fail they fall back on an internal chronometer, conceivably their heart-beat, to reach their destination anyway.

3. Prairies dogs in their towns pass socially accepted facts, such as the invisible boundaries between their neighborhoods, from one generation to the next; they do it by imitating each other, not by instinct, and European chickadees do the same with their trick, invented about 1940, of following milkmen on their routes and beating housewives to the bottled cream.

4. Ravens and jackdaws can count up to six or seven, and show that they can form an abstract concept of number by responding, correctly, whether the number is cued by spots on cards, by bells or buzzers, or by different spoken commands.

5. A Swedish bird called the nutcracker remembers precisely where it buried its nuts in the fall, and digs them up, in late March, say, confidently and without errors through two feet of snow.

6. For its sexual display, an Australian species called the satin bowerbird not only constructs a bower, or bachelor apartment, decorating it with flowers and *objets d'art,* as do other members of its family, but makes paint out of charcoal or fruit-juice and paints the walls of its bower, using a pledget of chewed bark for a daub.

7. Bats avoid obstacles in total darkness, and probably catch flying insects too, by uttering short, loud screams and guiding themselves by the echoes; the pitch is much too high for human ears to hear, but some kinds of moths can hear the bats coming and take evasive action.

Made groggy by facts like these, most of them reported between 1946 and 1950, biologists began to feel like the White Queen, who "sometimes managed to believe as many as six impossible things before breakfast." Still, no one had yet spent a winter watching rodents under the snow, and the epicene behavior of bower-birds was not seen, then or since, as having any direct bearing on mammalian neurosis. If anything, the intellectual feats of birds and bees made it harder to understand how rodents could get into such sorry states; one might have credited them with more sense. Until new revelations from the Navy's rats laid bare their inmost conflicts, the point was arguable, at least, that anxiety is a sort of hothouse bloom, forced in psychologists' laboratories, and could not survive a northern winter.

As a footnote in a recent article makes clear, the United States Navy takes no definite stand on rodents. "The opinions or assertions contained herein," it says (referring to a report on crowded mice), "are the private ones of the writer, and are not to be construed as official or reflecting the views of the Navy Department or naval service at large." This disavowal is a little surprising, in that its author, John J. Christian, as head of the animal laboratories of the Naval Medical Research Institute at Bethesda, Maryland, can be considered the commander of the Navy's rodents. Ten years ago, though, when he wrote what may be thought of as the Smyth Report on population cycles, his opinions were temporarily freed from protocol. An endocrinologist and Navy lieutenant (j.g.), Christian had left the Fleet and gone back to studying mice at the Wyeth Institute, in Philadelphia. His luminous essay was published where anyone at large could read it, in the August, 1950 issue of the *Journal of Mammalogy*, under the title "The Adreno-Pituitary System and Population Cycles in Mammals." In it Christian said, in part:

We now have a working hypothesis for the die-off terminating a cycle. Exhaustion of the adreno-pituitary system resulting from increased stresses inherent in a high population, especially in winter, plus the late winter demands of the reproductive system, due to increased light or other factors, precipitates population-wide death with the symptoms of adrenal insufficiency and hypoglycemic convulsions.

Dedicated readers of the *Journal* remembered the snowshoe hares' congested adrenals, and did not need to be reminded that shock is a glandular disorder. They also knew their scientific Greek, and easily translated *hypoglycemia* as "lack of sugar in the blood"; but what they found new and fascinating was Christian's clinical evidence— much of it reported by a young Viennese internist named Hans Selye—tending to show that rodents might die, of all things, from a surfeit of sexuality. Most people had thought of rabbits as

adequately equipped for reproduction, but that is not the point, as Christian developed it: what does them in is not breeding, exactly, but concupiscence. Keyed up by the stresses of crowded existence—he instanced poor and insufficient food, increased exertion, and fighting—animals that have struggled through a tough winter are in no shape to stand the lust that rises like sap in the spring. Their endocrine glands, which make the clashing hormones, burn sugar like a schoolgirl making fudge, and the rodents, not being maple trees, have to borrow sugar from their livers. Cirrhosis lies that way, of course, but death from hypertension usually comes first.

In medical jargon, though the testy author of *Modern English Usage* would protest, the name for this state of endocrine strain is *stress*. As the physical embodiment of a mental state, anxiety, it is worth the respectful attention of all who believe, with mammalogists, that life can be sweet without necessarily caramelizing the liver. Despite its technicality, the subject is uncommonly rewarding. It is not only that seeing a lemming as a stressed animal goes far toward clearing up a famous mystery. And, although the how and why of psychosomatic ailments in wild rodents are undeniably important to tame men, the problems of gray flannel suits are not my main concern. The real attraction of stress, at least for a biologist, consists simply in the way it works: it turns out to contain a whole array of built-in servomechanisms. That is, the coupled oscillation of hosts and diseases, which Gause thought might underlie the fluctuating balance of nature, is mimicked inside the body, and may be said to be controlled, by mutual interaction between the glands. Biologists are impressed by abstract resemblances of this sort, which, after all, are their version of *generality*. In explaining stress by means of some fairly garish metaphors, therefore, I find it soothing to remember that what is called "imagery" in some circles is "model-making" in others.

As it happens, the master himself is no slouch at imagery. Selye's recent book, *The Stress of Life,* is notable, among other things, for its skillful use of the didactic, or Sunday-supplement, analogy. Without plagiarizing his exposition, though, it is possible to speak of vital needs as payable in sugar, for which the liver acts as a bank. Routine withdrawals are smoothly handled by hormones from the pancreas and from the adrenal medulla, which act as paying tellers; but the top-level decisions (such as whether to grow or to reproduce) are reserved for the bank's officers, the adrenal cortex and pituitary glands. Stress, in Selye's view, amounts to an administrative flap among the hormones, and shock results when the management overdraws the bank.

If the banking model is gently dissected, it reveals its first and most important servomechanism: a remarkably bureaucratic hookup between the adrenal cortex, acting as cashier's office, and the pituitary, as board of directors. Injury and infection are common forms of stress, and in directing controlled inflammation to combat them the cortex draws cashier's checks on the liver. If the stress persists a hormone called cortisone sends a worried message to the pituitary. Preoccupied with the big picture, the pituitary delegates a vice-presidential type, ACTH or adrenocorticotropic hormone, whose role is literally to buck up the adrenal cortex. As students of Parkinson would predict, the cortex, bucked, takes on more personnel, and expands its activities, including that of summoning more ACTH. The viciousness of the impending spiral ought to be obvious, and ordinarily it is; but while withdrawals continue the amount of sugar in circulation is deceptively constant (the work of another servomechanism), and there is no device, short of autopsy, for taking inventory at the bank. If the pituitary is conned by persisting stress into throwing more support to ACTH, the big deals begin to suffer retrenchment. A cutback of ovarian hormone, for instance, may allow the cortex to treat a well-started foetus as an inflammation to be healed over. Likewise, the glandular sources of virility and of maternity, though unequally prodigal of sugar, are equally likely to dry up. Leaving hypertension aside (because it involves another commodity, salt, which needn't be gone into just now), the fatal symptom can be hypoglycemia. A tiny extra stress, such as a loud noise (or, as Christian would have it, the sight of a lady rabbit), corresponds to an unannounced visit by the bank examiner: the adrenal medulla is startled into sending a jolt of adrenalin to the muscles, the blood is drained of sugar, and the brain is suddenly starved. This, incidentally, is why shock looks like hyperinsulinism. An overactive pancreas, like a panicky adrenal, resembles an untrustworthy teller with his hand in the till.

Haruspicy, or divination by inspection of the entrails of domestic animals, is supposed to have been extinct for two thousand years, and no one knows what the Etruscan soothsayers made of a ravaged liver. Selye would snort, no doubt, at being called a modern haruspex, but the omens of public dread are at least as visceral as those of any other calamity, and there are some sound Latin precedents—such as the geese whose gabbling saved Rome—for the view that emotion is communicable to and by animals. More recently, thoughtful veterinarians have begun to notice that neurotic pets tend to have neurotic owners, and a report from the Philadelphia zoo blames "social pressures," on the rise for the last two decades, for a tenfold increase of arteriosclerosis among the inmates. If Selye seems to be playing down anxiety—the word is not even listed in the index of his book —I can think of two possible reasons, both interesting if not entirely convincing. Anxiety is an ugly word, of course, and using it can easily generate more of it, just as calling a man an insomniac can keep him awake all night; Selye, as a good physician, may well have hesitated to stress it in a popular book about stress. More important, probably, is the fact that Selye, like any internist, begins and ends his work with bodily symptoms, and only grudgingly admits the existence of mind. A curious piece of shoptalk, which he quotes approvingly and in full from a San Francisco medical man (not a psychiatrist), suggests that some of his professional colleagues, like too many novelists, have read Freud without understanding him:

The dissociation of the ego and the id has many forms. I had an American housewife with dermatomyositis [an inflammation of skin and muscles] [the brackets are Selye's] who had been taught how to play the piano when she was little, and had continued for the entertainment of the children, but didn't get very far. When she started on large doses of ACTH she was suddenly able to play the most difficult works of Beethoven and Chopin—and the children of the neighbours would gather in the garden to hear her play. Here was a disso-

ciation of the ego and the id that was doing good. But she also became a little psychotic, and so her dosage of ACTH had to be lowered, and with every 10 units of ACTH one sonata disappeared. It all ended up with the same old music poorly performed.

The false note here, of course, is that business about "the dissociation of the ego and the id." Whatever the id may be, it is not considered innately musical, and *my* professional colleagues would count it a triumph to be able to teach it anything, even "Chopsticks." Still, we may take the anecdote as showing *some* kind of mental effect of stress; what the psychologist sees as rather more to the point is the obverse of this: moods and emotions cannot be injected hypodermically, but their cost is paid in sugar, and their action on the cortex is precisely that of ACTH. Christian finds, for instance, that crowding mice in cages enlarges their adrenals, but fortunately, in experiments of this sort, it is not always necessary to kill the animals to learn the answer. A microscopic sample of blood reveals a useful clue to endocrine tension: college students at exam time show a shortage of the same type of white cell that is also scarce in the blood of crowded mice. (The skittish blood cells are called *eosinophils;* I mention this because the word is sure to turn up in detective stories before long.) The fact that tranquillizing drugs do their work by blocking various hormones opens up another line of evidence, as well as a fertile field for quackery. But the surest sign that anxiety is stress—and its most lurid property—is its ability to visit itself on the unborn. The maker of this appalling discovery, William R. Thompson of Wesleyan University, tells us nothing of the sins of his rats' fathers, but his report shows all too clearly that the offspring of frustrated mothers, part of whose pregnancy was spent in problem boxes with no exit, carried the emotional disturbance throughout their own lives. Nestling birds can learn the parents' alarm call while still inside the egg (as the nearly-forgotten author of *Green Mansions* was among the first to notice), but the mammalian uterus is more soundproof, and the only reasonable explanation of Thompson's results is that the aroused maternal hormones perverted the silver cord, and made it a pipeline to a forbidden supply of sugar.

Circumspectly, now, so as to forestall any harumphs from the naval service at large, we may return to Christian's crowded mice. In outward demeanor the ordinary house mouse, *Mus musculus*, is the least military of rodents, but his dissembling is part of the commando tradition, and he would not have got where he is today without a lot of ruthless infighting. Nowadays house mice spend little time outdoors if they can help it, but in more rustic times they often scourged the countryside, like Marion's men, and the tenth-century Bishop of Bingen (who perished in the Mouse Tower) learned to his cost that country mice can be pushed too far. Recently, at some of our leading universities (Oslo, strange to say, has *still* not been heard from), mouse-watching has proved informative, if not exactly edifying, and I cull a few tidbits from the notes of some shocked colleagues:

The first thing to notice is that the old murine spirit of mass emigration is not yet dead, despite the effeteness of modern urban living. Not long ago an outbreak was observed—provoked, in fact—at the University of Wisconsin, where the scientists had set up a mouse tower, or substitute patch of tundra, in a junkroom in the basement of the zoology building, and set traps (not enough, as it turned out) in the neighboring offices and laboratories. Nothing happened for a while, except that the food—half a pound of it a day—kept disappearing. Then, in Browning's words, "the muttering grew to a grumbling; and the grumbling grew to a mighty rumbling"; and the experiment, though publishable, became unpopular; the room was simply overstuffed with mice, like a sofa in a neglected summer cottage.

Chastened, yet encouraged by this experience, the zoologists fell back on emigration-proof pens, where they could keep tab on the mice. Taking census whenever they cleaned the cages (which was pretty often, at someone's pointed insistence), they noticed that the numbers went up and down, but, as there were no seasons or predators and food was always abundant, the fluctuations made little sense at first. Gradually, though, when one of the observers, Charles Southwick, thought to count the tiffs as well as the mice, the shiny outlines of a servomechanism came into sight: as each wave of numbers crested and broke, the scuffles averaged more than one per mouse-hour, and hardly any young mice survived to the age of weaning. Putting the matter this way lays the blame, unchivalrously, on the mothers, and in fact, as the tension mounted, their nest-building became slovenly and some of them failed to nurse their litters, or even ate them (proper mouse food, remember, was always plentiful). But the males were equally responsible, though for different hormonal reasons. Like chickens with their peck-order, the buck mice were more concerned for status than for posterity, and the endocrine cost of supremacy was sexual impotence. In one of the pens two evenly-matched pretenders played mouse-in-the-manger with the females, and suppressed all reproduction until they died.

While the Wisconsin mice were either suffering from stress or practicing a peculiarly savage form of moral restraint, mice at other centers were also made unhappy, or at least infertile, by being given plenty of food, space, and sexual access. It came as no great surprise, then, when the adrenals of Christian's mice were found to swell, as he had predicted eight years before, in proportion to the numbers of their social companions. The really arresting experiment, which dilutes the inhumanity of some of the others, shows that rodents—rats, at any rate—*prefer* to be crowded and anxious. At the National Institutes of Health, in Bethesda, John C. Calhoun allowed litter-mates to grow up in one large pen, where every rat had an individual food hopper. From the start, when eating, they huddled like a farrow at a single hopper; later, though free to roam, eat, and nest in four intercommunicating pens, these rats and their descendants spent most of their time in one of the four, and as I write this they are still there, paying for their sociability in lowered fertility and shortened lives. For his part, my friend Calhoun coined a phrase that deserves to outlive his rats, and is still musing on *pathological togetherness*.

At this point in the argument, explaining the lemmings' periodic dementia should be anticlimatically easy. I seem to have overstated the case, in fact, for it seems less Gothic than *gothick*, like some of the more un-

necessary behavior described by the brothers Grimm. The cycle starts where population problems always do, with the lemmings' awesome power of procreation. Nubile at the age of thirty-five days, averaging seven or eight young at a cast, a female lemming may have worries, but barrenness is not one of them, and four litters is par for a summer's dalliance. Lemming life is more austere in winter, but not much. As long as food is plentiful under the snow, the winter sports of pullulation and fighting continue as at a disreputable ski resort. The wonder is—until we remember the owls and foxes above and the weasels *in* the runways—that it takes as long as four years for the numbers to become critical, like the mass of an atomic bomb. When the Thing goes off, then, it is the younger lemmings that emigrate, in search of a patch of tundra that is slightly more private than the beach at Coney Island; though less overtly anxious to begin with, presumably, their state of mind on reaching downtown Oslo is another matter entirely. The older, better-established residents, or those with stouter livers, stay home, and die of shock—having first passed on the family disease to the next generation. Before the epidemic of stress has run its course, it spreads to the predators, too (though *this* form of lemming fever is caught, ironically, from *not* eating lemmings). The snowy owl that died at Fayal, Azores, in 1928 may or may not have known that it had really reached Atlantis, but in being shot by an anxious man it provided a textbook, or postgraduate, example of a coupled oscillation.

If all this is true, and I think it is, the Norse clergymen who exorcised the lemmings in Latin were clearly on the right track, and what the Scandinavians need is a qualified haruspex. Before they hire one, though (I am not a candidate), or resort to spraying the tundra with tranquillizers (which would be expensive), there is one tiny reservation: there is not a scrap of *direct* evidence that the lemming suffers from stress. Come to think of it, no one has yet spent a winter watching lemmings under the snow. (Some Californian zoologists lived for several winters in Alaska, trying valiantly to do just that, but the runways are pretty small for Californians, and for most of the time there was trouble finding *any* lemmings). Except for some circumstantial lesions of the skin, which could be psychosomatic, like shingles (and which ruin the lemming's pelt), the case for contagious anxiety therefore rests on a passel of tormented rodents, but not as yet on *Lemmus lemmus.* That animal has baffled a lot of people, and I could be mistaken too. But if I am, or at least if the lemmings' adrenals are not periodically congested, I will eat a small population of them, suitably seasoned with Miltown. Fortunately, lemmings are reported to taste like squirrels, but better; in Lapland, in fact, with men who know rodents best, it's lemmings, two to one.

Chapter 4

AROUSAL AND ACTIVATION

This is a new chapter in motivation thinking—ten years ago because of lack of data it is unlikely that it could have been included. Even so, some of the thinking underlying the concepts of arousal and activation was already in the literature at that time—in fact, three of the four papers included here date from the 1950s. This is not because there are fewer recent studies, but because these are particularly clear.

The concepts of arousal and activation make possible large leaps ahead in understanding motivational processes. They have forced a recognition that central nervous system behavior has two components: a patterning that occurs at its higher centers, and a level of activity that occurs in the lower centers. A single sensory imput contributes to both of these—the patterning at the terminus of the sensory pathway, and arousal of the brain stem through which collaterals of that sensory pathway pass.

This discovery is not merely one of understanding pathways better. These two processes initiated by stimulation have very different though interacting functions, as Malmo spells out in some detail. The most important for motivational theory is the notion of an optimal level of arousal or activation—Malmo's U-shaped function. Many others have utilized this concept, particularly Berlyne and Hunt (see Chapter 5), for it provides a basis for arousal-seeking, as well as arousal-avoiding behaviors—both highly important and difficult motivational problems.

Hebb has perhaps contributed more to this area theoretically than any other psychologist, beginning with his attention to a careful separation of the level of arousal of the nervous system and the pattern of activity within it. This was most explicitly spelled out in his *Organization of Behavior* in 1949, and from slightly different points of view in a number of subsequent papers, including the one printed here. His work and thinking has perhaps altered the course of contemporary psychology more than any other single man. His work, taken in conjunction with several others (who are included in subsequent chapters) will lay the foundation for the next several decades.

Duffy's paper is a short historical account of the development of the concept of activation, which she facilitated by her own work. Malmo has drawn on some of Hebb's work, as well as much of his own, to present a general theoretical discussion of activation, as a dimension of behavior that underlies motivational as well as other processes. Finally, Fuster, working in Lindsley's laboratory at UCLA, provides a single experimental demonstration of the effects of reticular activity on more complex behavioral processes.

Psychological Review, 1955, vol. 62, pp. 243–254.

Drives and the C.N.S. (Conceptual Nervous System)[1]

D. O. Hebb

The problem of motivation of course lies close to the heart of the general problem of understanding behavior, yet it sometimes seems the least realistically treated topic in the literature. In great part, the difficulty concerns that c.n.s., or "conceptual nervous system," which Skinner disavowed and from whose influence he and others have tried to escape. But the conceptual nervous system of 1930 was evidently like the gin that was being drunk about the same time; it was homemade and none too good, as Skinner pointed out, but it was also habit-forming; and the effort to escape has not really been successful. Prohibition is long past. If we *must* drink we can now get better liquor; likewise, the conceptual nervous system of 1930 is out of date and— if we must neurologize—let us use the best brand of neurology we can find.

Though I personally favor both alcohol and neurologizing, in moderation,

the point here does not assume that either is a good thing. The point is that psychology is intoxicating itself with a worse brand than it need use. Many psychologists do not think in terms of neural anatomy; but merely adhering to certain classical frameworks shows the limiting effect of earlier neurologizing. Bergmann (1953) has recently said again that it is logically possible to escape the influence. This does not change the fact that, in practice, it has not been done.

Further, as I read Bergmann, I am not sure that he really thinks, deep down, that we should swear off neurologizing entirely, or at least that we should all do so. He has made a strong case for the functional similarity of intervening variable and hypothetical construct, implying that we are dealing more with differences of degree than of kind. The conclusion *I* draw is that both can properly appear in the same theory, using intervening variables to whatever extent is most profitable (as physics for example does), and conversely not being afraid to use some theoretical conception merely because it might become anatomically identifiable.

[1] Presidential address, Division 3, at American Psychological Association. New York, September, 1954. The paper incorporates ideas worked out in discussion with fellow students at McGill, especially Dalbir Bindra and Peter Milner, as well as with Leo Postman at California, and it is a pleasure to record my great indebtedness to them.

For many conceptions, at least, Mac-Corquodale and Meehl's (1948) distinction is relative, not absolute; and it must also be observed that physiological psychology makes free use of "dispositional concepts" as well as "existential" ones. Logically, this leaves room for some of us to make more use of explicitly physiological constructs than others, and still lets us stay in communication with one another. It also shows how one's views concerning motivation, for example, might be more influenced than one thinks by earlier physiological notions, since it means that an explicitly physiological conception might be restated in words that have—apparently—no physiological reference.

What I propose, therefore, is to look at motivation as it relates to the c.n.s.—or conceptual nervous system—of three different periods: as it was before 1930, as it was say 10 years ago, and as it is today. I hope to persuade you that some of our current troubles with motivation are due to the c.n.s of an earlier day, and ask that you look with an open mind at the implications of the current one. Today's physiology suggests new psychological ideas, and I would like to persuade you that they make psychological sense, no matter how they originated. They might even provide common ground—not necessarily agreement, but communication, something nearer to agreement—for people whose views at present may seem completely opposed. While writing this paper I found myself having to make a change in my own theoretical position, as you will see, and though you may not adopt the same position you may be willing to take another look at the evidence, and consider its theoretical import anew.

Before going on it is just as well to be explicit about the use of the terms motivation and drive. "Motivation" refers here in a rather general sense to the energizing of behavior, and especially to the sources of energy in a particular set of responses that keep them temporarily dominant over others and account for continuity and direction in behavior. "Drive" is regarded as a more specific conception about the way in which this occurs: a hypothesis of motivation, which makes the energy a function of a special process distinct from those S-R or cognitive functions that are energized. In some contexts, therefore, "motivation" and "drive" are interchangeable.

Motivation in the Classical (Pre-1930) C.N.S.

The main line of descent of psychological theory, as I have recently tried to show (Hebb, 1953), is through associationism and the stimulus-response formulations. Characteristically, stimulus-response theory has treated the animal as more or less inactive unless subjected to special conditions of arousal. These conditions are first, hunger, pain, and sexual excitement; and secondly, stimulation that has become associated with one of these more primitive motivations.

Such views did not originate entirely in the early ideas of nervous function, but certainly were strengthened by them. Early studies of the nerve fiber seemed to show that the cell is inert until something happens to it from outside; therefore, the same would be true of the collection of cells making up the nervous system. From this came the explicit theory of drives. The organism is thought of as like a machine, such as the automobile, in which the steering mechanism—that is, stimulus-response connections—is separate from the power source, or drive. There is, however, this difference: the organism may be endowed with three or more different power plants. Once you start listing separate ones, it is hard to avoid five: hunger, thirst, pain, maternal, and sex drives. By some theorists, these may each be given a low-level steering function also, and indirectly the steering function of drives is much increased by the law of effect. According to the law, habits—steering functions—are acquired only in conjunction with the operation of drives.

Now it is evident that an animal is often active and often learns when there is little or no drive activity of the kinds listed. This fact has been dealt with in two ways. One is to postulate additional drives—activity, exploratory, manipulatory, and so forth. The other is to postulate acquired or learned drives, which obtain their energy, so to speak, from association with primary drives.

It is important to see the difficulties to be met by this kind of formulation, though it should be said at once that I do not have any decisive refutation of it, and other approaches have their difficulties, too.

First, we may overlook the rather large number of forms of behavior in which motivation cannot be reduced to biological drive plus learning. Such behavior is most evident in higher species, and may be forgotten by those who work only with the rat or with restricted segments of the behavior of dog or cat. (I do not suggest that we put human motivation on a different plane from that of animals [Brown,

1953]; what I am saying is that certain peculiarities of motivation increase with phylogenesis, and though most evident in man can be clearly seen with other higher animals.) What is the drive that produces panic in the chimpanzee at the sight of a model of a human head; or fear in some animals, and vicious aggression in others, at the sight of the anesthetized body of a fellow chimpanzee? What about fear of snakes, or the young chimpanzee's terror at the sight of strangers? One can accept the idea that this is "anxiety," but the anxiety, if so, is not based on a prior association of the stimulus object with pain. With the young chimpanzee reared in the nursery of the Yerkes Laboratories, after separation from the mother at birth, one can be certain that the infant has never seen a snake before, and certainly no one has told him about snakes; and one can be sure that a particular infant has never had the opportunity to associate a strange face with pain. Stimulus generalization does not explain fear of strangers, for other stimuli in the same class, namely, the regular attendants, are eagerly welcomed by the infant.

Again, what drive shall we postulate to account for the manifold forms of anger in the chimpanzee that do not derive from frustration objectively defined (Hebb, Thompson, 1954)? How account for the petting behavior of young adolescent chimpanzees, which Nissen (1953) has shown is independent of primary sex activity? How deal with the behavior of the female who, bearing her first infant, is terrified at the sight of the baby as it drops from the birth canal, runs away, never sees it again after it has been taken to the nursery for rearing; and who yet, on the birth of a *second* infant, promptly picks it up and violently resists any effort to take it from her?

There is a great deal of behavior, in the higher animal especially, that is at the very best difficult to reduce to hunger, pain, sex, and maternal drives, plus learning. Even for the lower animal it has been clear for some time that we must add an exploratory drive (if we are to think in these terms at all), and presumably the motivational phenomena recently studied by Harlow and his colleagues (Harlow, 1953; Harlow, Harlow, Meyer, 1950; Butler, 1953) could also be comprised under such a drive by giving it a little broader specification. The curiosity drive of Berlyne (1950) and Thompson and Solomon (1954), for example, might be considered to cover both investigatory and manipulatory activities on the one hand, and exploratory, on the other. It would also comprehend the "problem-seeking" behavior recently studied by Mahut and Havelka at McGill (unpublished studies). They have shown that the rat which is offered a short, direct path to food, and a longer, variable and indirect pathway involving a search for food, will very frequently prefer the more difficult, but more "interesting" route.

But even with the addition of a curiosity-investigatory-manipulatory drive, and even apart from the primates, there is still behavior that presents difficulties. There are the reinforcing effects of incomplete copulation (Sheffield, Wulff, & Backer, 1951) and of saccharin intake (Sheffield & Roby, 1950; Carper & Polliard, 1953), which do not reduce to secondary reward. We must not multiply drives beyond reason, and at this point one asks whether there

is no alternative to the theory in this form. We come, then, to the conceptual nervous system of 1930 to 1950.

Motivation in the C.N.S. of 1930–1950

About 1930 it began to be evident that the nerve cell is not physiologically inert, does not have to be excited from outside in order to discharge (Hebb, 1949, p. 8). The nervous system is alive, and living things by their nature are active. With the demonstration of spontaneous activity in c.n.s. it seemed to me that the conception of a drive system or systems was supererogation.

For reasons I shall come to later, this now appears to me to have been an oversimplification; but in 1945 the only problem of motivation, I thought, was to account for the *direction* taken by behavior. From this point of view, hunger or pain might be peculiarly effective in guiding or channeling activity but not needed for its arousal. It was not surprising, from this point of view, to see human beings liking intellectual work, nor to find evidence that an animal might learn something without pressure of pain or hunger.

The energy of response is not in the stimulus. It comes from the food, water, and oxygen ingested by the animal and the violence of an epileptic convulsion, when brain cells for whatever reason decide to fire in synchrony, bears witness to what the nervous system can do when it likes. This is like a whole powder magazine exploding at once. Ordinary behavior can be thought of as produced by an organized series of much smaller explosions, and so a "self-motivating" c.n.s. might still be a very powerfully motivated one. To me, then, it was astonishing that a critic could refer to mine as a "motivation-less" psychology. What I had said in short was that any organized process in the brain is a motivated process, inevitably, inescapably; that the human brain is built to be active, and that as long as it is supplied with adequate nutrition will continue to be active. Brain activity is what determines behavior, and so the only behavioral problem becomes that of accounting for *in*activity.

It was in this conceptual frame that the behavioral picture seemed to negate the notion of drive, as a separate energizer of behavior. A pedagogical experiment reported earlier (Hebb, 1930 was very impressive in its indication that the human liking for work is not a rare phenomenon, but general. All of the 600-odd pupils in a city school, ranging from 6 to 15 years of age, were suddenly informed that they need do no work whatever unless they wanted to, that the punishment for being noisy and interrupting others' work was to be sent to the playground to play, and that the reward for being good was to be allowed to do more work. In these circumstances, *all* of the pupils discovered within a day or two that, within limits, they preferred work to no work (and incidentally learned more arithmetic and so forth than in previous years).

The phenomenon of work for its own sake is familiar enough to all of us, when the timing is controlled by the worker himself, when "work" is not defined as referring alone to activity imposed from without. Intellectual work may take the form of trying to understand what Robert Browning was trying to say (if anything), to discover what it is in Dali's paintings that can interest others, or to predict the out-

come of a paperback mystery. We systematically underestimate the human need of intellectual activity, in one form or another, when we overlook the intellectual component in art and in games. Similarly with riddles, puzzles, and the puzzle-like games of strategy such as bridge, chess, and *go;* the frequency with which man has devised such problems for his own solution is a most significant fact concerning human motivation.

It is, however, not necessarily a fact that supports my earlier view, outlined above. It is hard to get these broader aspects of human behavior under laboratory study, and when we do we may expect to have our ideas about them significantly modified. For my views on the problem, this is what has happened with the experiment of Bexton, Heron, and Scott (1954). Their work is a long step toward dealing with the realities of motivation in the well-fed, physically comfortable, adult human being, and its results raise a serious difficulty for my own theory. Their subjects were paid handsomely to do nothing, see nothing, hear or touch very little, for 24 hours a day. Primary needs were met, on the whole, very well. The subjects suffered no pain, and were fed on request. It is true that they could not copulate, but at the risk of impugning the virility of Canadian college students I point out that most of them would not have been copulating anyway and were quite used to such long stretches of three or four days without primary sexual satisfaction. The secondary reward, on the other hand, was high: $20 a day plus room and board is more than $7000 a year, far more than a student could earn by other means. The subjects then should be highly motivated to continue the experiment, cheerful and happy to be allowed to contribute to scientific knowledge so painlessly and profitably.

In fact, the subject was well motivated for perhaps four to eight hours, and then became increasingly unhappy. He developed a need for stimulation of almost any kind. In the first preliminary exploration, for example, he was allowed to listen to recorded material on request. Some subjects were given a talk for 6-year-old children on the dangers of alcohol. This might be requested by a grown-up male college student, 15 to 20 times in a 30-hour period. Others were offered, and asked for repeatedly, a recording of an old stock-market report. The subjects looked forward to being tested, but paradoxically tended to find the tests fatiguing when they did arrive. It is hardly necessary to say that the whole situation was rather hard to take, and one subject, in spite of not being in a special state of primary drive arousal in the experiment but in real need of money outside it, gave up the secondary reward of $20 a day to take up a job at hard labor paying $7 or $8 a day.

This experiment is not cited primarily as a difficulty for drive theory, although three months ago that is how I saw it. It *will* make difficulty for such theory if exploratory drive is not recognized; but we have already seen the necessity, on other grounds, of including a sort of exploratory-curiosity-manipulatory drive, which essentially comes down to a tendency to seek varied stimulation. This would on the whole handle very well the motivational phenomena observed by Heron's group.

Instead, I cite their experiment as making essential trouble for my own treatment of motivation (Hebb, 1949)

as based on the conceptual nervous system of 1930 to 1945. If the thought process is internally organized and motivated, why should it break down in conditions of perceptual isolation, unless emotional disturbance intervenes? But it did break down when no serious emotional change was observed, with problem-solving and intelligence-test performance significantly impaired. Why should the subjects themselves report (a) after four or five hours in isolation that they could not follow a connected train of thought, and (b) that their motivation for study or the like was seriously disturbed for 24 hours or more after coming out of isolation? The subjects were reasonably well adjusted, happy, and able to think coherently for the first four or five hours of the experiment; why, according to my theory, should this not continue, and why should the organization of behavior not be promptly restored with restoration of a normal environment?

You will forgive me perhaps if I do not dilate further on my own theoretical difficulties, paralleling those of others, but turn not to the conceptual nervous system of 1954 to ask what psychological values we may extract from it for the theory of motivation. I shall not attempt any clear answer for the difficulties we have considered—the data do not seem yet to justify clear answers—but certain conceptions can be formulated in sufficiently definite form to be a background for new research, and the physiological data contain suggestions that may allow me to retain what was of value in my earlier proposals while bringing them closer to ideas such as Harlow's (1953) on one hand and to reinforcement theory on the other.

Motivation and C.N.S. in 1954

For psychological purposes there are two major changes in recent ideas of nervous function. One concerns the single cell, the other an "arousal" system in the brain stem. The first I shall pass over briefly; it is very significant, but does not bear quite as directly upon our present problem. Its essence is that there are two kinds of activity in the nerve cell: the spike potential, or actual firing, and the dendritic potential, which has very different properties. There is now clear evidence (Clare & Bishop, 1955) that the dendrite has a "slow-burning" activity which is not all-or-none, tends not to be transmitted, and lasts 15 to 30 milliseconds instead of the spike's one millisecond. It facilitates spike activity (Li, Choh-Luh & Jasper, 1953), but often occurs independently and may make up the greater part of the EEG record. It is still true that the brain is always active, but the activity is not always the transmitted kind that conduces to behavior. Finally, there is decisive evidence of primary inhibition in nerve function (Lloyd, 1941; Eccles, 1953) and of a true fatigue that may last for a matter of minutes instead of milliseconds (Brink, 1951; Burns, 1955). These facts will have a great effect on the hypotheses of physiological psychology, and sooner or later on psychology in general.

Our more direct concern is with a development to which attention has already been drawn by Lindsley (1951): the nonspecific or diffuse projection system of the brain stem, which was shown by Moruzzi and Magoun (1949) to be an *arousal* system whose activity in effect makes organized cortical activity possible. Lindsley showed the

relevance to the problem of emotion and motivation; what I shall attempt is to extend his treatment, giving more weight to cortical components in arousal. The point of view has also an evident relationship to Duffy's (1941).

The arousal system can be thought of as representing a second major pathway by which all sensory excitations reach the cortex, as shown in the upper part of Fig. 1; but there is also feedback from the cortex and I shall urge that the *psychological* evidence further emphasizes the importance of this "downstream" effect.

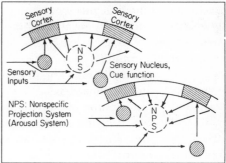

Fig. 1.

In the classical conception of sensory function, input to the cortex was via the great projection systems only: from sensory nerve to sensory tract, thence to the corresponding sensory nucleus of the thalamus and thence directly to one of the sensory projection areas of the cortex. These are still the direct sensory routes, the quick efficient transmitters of information. The second pathway is slow and inefficient; the excitation, as it were, trickles through a tangled thicket of fibers and synapses, there is a mixing up of messages, and the scrambled messages are delivered indiscriminately to wide cortical areas. In short, they are messages no longer. They serve, instead, to tone up the cortex, with a background supporting action that is completely necessary if the messages proper are to have their effect. Without the arousal system, the sensory impulses by the direct route reach the sensory cortex, but go no farther; the rest of the cortex is unaffected, and thus learned stimulus-response relations are lost. The waking center, which has long been known, is one part of this larger system; any extensive damage to it leaves a permanently inert, comatose animal.

Remember that in all this I am talking conceptual nervous system: making a working simplification, and abstracting for psychological purposes; and all these statements may need qualification, especially since research in this area is moving rapidly. There is reason to think, for example, that the arousal system may not be homogeneous, but may consist of a number of subsystems with distinctive functions (Olszewski, 1954). Olds and Milner's (1954) study, reporting "reward" by direct intracranial stimulation, is not easy to fit into the notion of a single, homogeneous system. Sharpless' (1954) results also raise doubt on this point, and it may reasonably be anticipated that arousal will eventually be found to vary qualitatively as well as quantitatively. But in general terms, psychologically, we can now distinguish two quite different effects of a sensory event. One is the *cue function,* guiding behavior; the other, less obvious but no less important, is the *arousal* or *vigilance function.* Without a foundation of arousal, the cue function cannot exist.

And now I propose to you that, whatever you wish to call it, arousal in this sense is synonymous with a general drive state, and the conception of drive therefore assumes anatomical and physiological identity. Let me remind

you of what we discussed earlier: the drive is an energizer, but not a guide; an engine but not a steering gear. These are precisely the specifications of activity in the arousal system. Also, learning is dependent on drive, according to drive theory, and this too is applicable in general terms—no arousal, no learning; and efficient learning is possible only in the waking, alert, responsive animal, in which the level of arousal is high.

Thus I find myself obliged to reverse my earlier views and accept the drive conception, not merely on physiological grounds but also on the grounds of some of our current psychological studies. The conception is somewhat modified, but the modifications may not be entirely unacceptable to others.

Consider the relation of the effectiveness of cue function, actual or potential, to the level of arousal (Fig. 2). Physiologically, we may assume that cortical synaptic function is facilitated by the diffuse bombardment of the arousal system. When this bombardment is at a low level an increase will tend to strengthen or maintain the concurrent cortical activity; when arousal or drive is at a low level, that is, a response that produces increased stimulation and greater arousal will tend to be repeated. This is represented by the rising curve at the left. But when

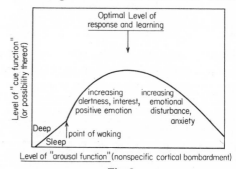

Fig. 2.

arousal is at a high level, as at the right, the greater bombardment may interfere with the delicate adjustments involved in cue function, perhaps by facilitating irrelevant responses (a high D arouses conflicting $_sH_R$'s?). Thus there will be an optimal level of arousal for effective behavior, as Schlosberg (1954) has suggested. Set aside such physiologizing completely, and we have a significant behavioral conception left, namely, that the same stimulation in mild degree may attract (by prolonging the pattern of response that leads to this stimulation) and in strong degree repel (by disrupting the pattern and facilitating conflicting or alternative responses).

The significance of this relation is in a phenomenon of the greatest importance for understanding motivation in higher animals. This is the *positive attraction of risk taking,* or mild fear, *and of problem solving,* or mild frustration, which was referred to earlier. Whiting and Mowrer (1943) and Berlyne (1950) have noted a relation between fear and curiosity—that is, a tendency to seek stimulation from fear-provoking objects, though at a safe distance. Woodworth (1921) and Valentine (1930) reported this in children, and Woodworth and Marquis (1947) have recently emphasized again its importance in adults. There is no doubt that it exists. There is no doubt, either, that problem-solving situations have some attraction for the rat, more for Harlow's (1953) monkeys, and far more for man. When you stop to think of it, it is nothing short of extraordinary what trouble people will go to in order to get into more trouble at the bridge table, or on the golf course; and the fascination of the murder story, or thriller, and the newspaper accounts of

real-life adventure or tragedy, is no less extraordinary. This taste for excitement *must* not be forgotten when we are dealing with human motivation. It appears that, up to a certain point, threat and puzzle have positive motivating value, beyond that point negative value.

I know this leaves problems. It is not *any* mild threat, *any* form of problem, that is rewarding; we still have to work out the rules for this formulation. Also, I do not mean that there are not secondary rewards of social prestige for risk taking and problem solving—or even primary reward when such behavior is part of lovemaking. But the animal data show that it is not always a matter of extrinsic reward; risk and puzzle can be attractive in themselves, especially for higher animals such as man. If we can accept this, it will no longer be necessary to work out tortuous and improbable ways to explain why human beings work for money, why school children should learn without pain, why a human being in isolation should dislike doing nothing.

One other point before leaving Fig. 2: the low level of the curve to the right. You may be skeptical about such an extreme loss of adaptation, or disturbance of cue function and S-R relations, with high levels of arousal. Emotion is persistently regarded as energizing and organizing (which it certainly is at the lower end of the scale, up to the optimal level). But the "paralysis of terror" and related states do occur. As Brown and Jacobs (1949, p. 753) have noted, "the presence of fear may act as an energizer . . . and yet lead in certain instances to an increase in immobility." Twice in the past eight months, while this address was being prepared, the Montreal newpapers reported the behavior of a human being who, suddenly finding himself in extreme danger but with time to escape, simply made no move whatever. One of the two was killed; the other was not, but only because a truck driver chose to wreck his truck and another car instead. Again, it is reported by Marshall (1947), in a book that every student of human motivation should read carefully, that in the emotional pressure of battle no more than 15 to 25 per cent of men under attack even fire their rifles, let alone use them efficiently.

Tyhurst's (1951) very significant study of behavior in emergency and disaster situations further documents the point. The adult who is told that his apartment house is on fire, or who is threatened by a flash flood, may or may not respond intelligently. In various situations, 12 to 25 per cent did so; an equal number show "states of confusion, paralyzing anxiety, inability to move out of bed, 'hysterical' crying or screaming, and so on." Three-quarters or more show a clear impairment of intelligent behavior, often with aimless and irrelevant movements, rather than (as one might expect) panic reactions. There seems no doubt: the curve at the right must come down to a low level.

Now back to our main problem: If we tentatively identify a general state of drive with degree of arousal, where does this leave hunger, pain, and sex drives? These may still be anatomically separable, as Stellar (1954) has argued, but we might consider instead the possibility that there is just one general drive state that can be aroused in different ways. Stellar's argument does not seem fully convincing. There are certainly regions in the hypothalamus that

control eating, for example; but is this a *motivating* mechanism? The very essence of such a conception is that the mechanism in question should energize *other* mechanisms, and Miller, Bailey, and Stevenson (1950) have shown that the opposite is true.

But this issue should not be pressed too far, with our present knowledge. I have tried to avoid dogmatism in this presentation in the hope that we might try, for once, to see what we have in common in our views on motivation. One virtue of identifying arousal with drive is that it relates differing views (as well as bringing into the focus of attention data that may otherwise be neglected). The important thing is a clear distinction between cue function and arousal function, and the fact that at low levels an increase of drive intensity may be rewarding, whereas at high levels it is a decrease that rewards. Given this point of view and our assumptions about arousal mechanisms, we see that what Harlow has emphasized is the exteroceptively aroused, but still low-level, drive, with cue function of course directly provided for. In the concept of anxiety, Spence and Brown emphasize the higher-level drive state, especially where there is no guiding cue function that would enable the animal to escape threat. The feedback from cortical functioning makes intelligible Mowrer's (1952) equating anxiety aroused by threat of pain, and anxiety aroused in some way by cognitive processes related to ideas of the self. Solomon and Wynne's (1950) results with sympathectomy are also relevant, since we must not neglect the arousal effects of interoceptor activity; and so is clinical anxiety due to metabolic and nutritional disorders, as well as that due to some conflict of cognitive processes.

Obviously these are not explanations that are being discussed, but possible lines of future research; and there is one problem in particular that I would urge should not be forgotten. This is the cortical feedback to the arousal system, in physiological terms: or in psychological terms, the *immediate drive value of cognitive processes,* without intermediary. This is psychologically demonstrable, and *has* been demonstrated repeatedly.

Anyone who is going to talk about acquired drives, or secondary motivation, should first read an old paper by Valentine (1930). He showed that with a young child you can easily condition fear of a caterpillar or a furry animal, but cannot condition fear of opera glasses, or a bottle; in other words, the fear of some objects, that seems to be learned, was there, latent all the time. Miller (1951) has noted this possibility but he does not seem to have regarded it very seriously, though he cited a confirmatory experiment by Bregman; for in the same passage he suggests that my own results with chimpanzee fears of certain objects, including strange people, may be dealt with by generalization. But this simply will not do, as Riesen and I noted (Hebb and Riesen, 1943). If you try to work this out, for the infant who is terrified on *first* contact with a stranger, an infant who has never shown such terror before, and who has always responded with eager affection to the only human beings he has made contact with up to this moment, you will find that this is a purely verbal solution.

Furthermore, as Valentine observed, you cannot postulate that the cause of such fear is simply the strange event,

the thing that has never occurred before. For the chimpanzee reared in darkness, the first sight of a human being is of course a strange event, by definition; but fear of strangers does not occur until later, until the chimpanzee has had an opportunity to learn to recognize a few persons. The fear is not "innate" but depends on some sort of cognitive or cortical conflict of learned responses. This is clearest when the baby chimpanzee, who knows and welcomes attendant *A* and attendant *B,* is terrified when he sees *A* wearing *B*'s coat. The role of learning is inescapable in such a case.

The cognitive and learning element may be forgotten in other motivations, too. Even in the food drive, some sort of learning is fundamentally important: Ghent (1951) has shown this, Sheffield and Campbell (1954) seem in agreement, and so does the work of Miller and his associates (Berkun, Kessen, Miller, 1952; Miller, Kessen, 1952; Miller, 1953) on the greater reinforcement value of food by mouth, compared to food by stomach tube. Beach (1939) has shown the cortical-and-learning element in sex behavior. Melzack (1954) has demonstrated recently that even pain responses involve learning. In Harlow's (1953) results, of course, and Montgomery's (1953), the cognitive element is obvious.

These cortical or cognitive components in motivation are clearest when we compare the behavior of higher and lower species. Application of a *genuine* comparative method is essential, in the field of motivation as well as of intellectual functions (Hebb & Thompson, 1954). Most disagreements between us have related to so-called "higher" motivations. But the evidence I have discussed today need not be handled in such a way as to maintain the illusion of a complete separation between our various approaches to the problem. It *is* an illusion, I am convinced; we still have many points of disagreement as to relative emphasis, and as to which of several alternative lines to explore first, but this does not imply fundamental and final opposition. As theorists, we have been steadily coming together in respect of ideational (or representative, or mediating, or cognitive) processes; I believe that the same thing can happen, and is happening, in the field of motivation.

The Nature and Development of the Concept of Activation[1]

Elizabeth Duffy

The concept of "activation" or "arousal" did not develop within the past decade, or even within the past score of years. Nor did it arise in the first instance from the work of electroencephalographers. It grew rather from the work of a relatively small group of physiological psychologists who believed it worthwhile to investigate the functioning of parts of the body other than the nervous system. Electroencephalography added great impetus to the development of the concept, supplied the term that has now been adopted for it, and made converts of many who were unwilling to accept the concept before there was evidence of what type of anchorage it might have in the nervous system.

In the early stage of its development, the concept of activation was referred to as the degree of excitation or energy mobilization of the organisms (Duffy, 1934, 1941b, 1949, 1951). Its theoretical development depended upon the ex-

perimental findings of investigators who were studying such functions as tension of the muscles, the electrical resistance of the skin, cardiovascular activity, body temperature, and similar phenomena. Most of these investigators studied the functioning of the various systems independently of each other and in relation to some specific condition of the organism, such as "emotion" or sleep, though some recorded groups of measures under these conditions. Relationships between the physiological responses and the particular condition of the organism were generally reported.

Some investigators, however, were impressed with the organismic character of the excitation of the individual. Charles Féré (1900), had been concerned with what he called "dynamogenesis," or the energizing effect of increased muscular tension upon a wide variety of responses. Walter B. Cannon (1929), in his study of the physiological changes occurring during the excited "emotions," conceived of a general increase in energy as one of the results. The writer (Duffy, 1934) suggested

[1] With slight alterations, a symposium paper presented at the American Psychological Association meeting in September, 1963.

abandoning the term "emotion" which had never been defined in any precise fashion, and directing attention to the degree of excitation of the organism, which, it was suggested, might affect both sensory and motor processes, and indeed every aspect of behavior. In Duffy (1941a), she proposed a continuum of "energy level," or "level of reactivity," as one of three basic concepts which, taken together (and with appropriate subheads), could replace the traditional, overlapping, and ill-defined terms that constituted the descriptive categories of psychology. In an address in 1950, published the following year (Duffy, 1951), she developed more fully the concept of "energy mobilization" as a continuum of organismic excitation, varying with the stimulus situation and with internal factors, and producing important changes in behavior of many kinds. The electroencephalogram, skin-resistance, and muscle-tension were among the physiological phenomena shown to change in a continuum with changes in the stimulus situation, the task demands, and the general organic condition of the individual. Now, however, in accordance with an earlier conclusion (Duffy, 1949), only "energy mobilization" and "direction" were considered basic descriptive categories, since the previously included "response to relationships" was regarded as an aspect of the maintenance of direction in behavior.

During this span of years, Darrow (1936) pointed to "the preparatory and facilitative" functions of changes in electrical skin-resistance and blood-pressure and G. L. Freeman (1938) discussed the "postural substrate" as an energizer of overt phasic responses and developed more fully a number of hypotheses in connection with the energetics of behavior (Freeman, 1948).

Widespread interest in the concept of activation arose with the discovery of the activating function of the reticular system and related brain structures. In 1951, Donald B. Lindsley published his "activation theory of emotion," which referred to the activation pattern of the electroencephalogram. He did not at that time conceive of a continuum of activation, but discussed rather the EEG changes occurring in "emotion" and those occurring during sleep, with no attention devoted to intermediate conditions. Later, he began thinking tentatively in terms of a continuum. Schlosberg, Hebb, Malmo, Berlyne, Bindra, and others focused attention upon this concept and have made use of it in interesting fashion. In the meantime, the writer had prepared a manuscript for a book on the subject, kindly read by Malmo and others at McGill in 1955, summarized in part in an article (Duffy, 1957), but delayed in publication for five years (Duffy, 1962).

What, then, is the concept and what need does it fill? The writer will reply from her own point of view since there are differences of opinion not yet capable of resolution.

In her thinking, a concept of this sort became a necessity to account for the fact that an individual—that is, an organism taken as a whole—is sometimes excited, sometimes relaxed, and sometimes in a variety of intermediate conditions. While the various systems of the organism are not equally activated at a given moment, it seems apparent that it is the organism as a whole that is showing the higher or lower degree of excitation, and not just a particular system within the organism such as the skeletal muscles.

Objections to a concept of general activation have been raised in some quarters, though there has been wide acceptance of it in others. Those who have objected have done so usually on one or another of the following bases, which will be discussed briefly:

1. They mistakenly conclude that the concept of general activation refers to something nonphysiological, over and above the totality of the activation of the various parts of the organism. It should be emphasized that the concept does not refer to psychic energy, so-called, or to any mysterious addition to the excitation of the tissues of the organism. Indeed, activation may be defined in terms of such excitation as measured by the various indices mentioned above.

2. They correctly state that it is not clear how this general activation should be measured—and the writer, herself, is committed to definition in terms of measurement. At present, we can point to a number of still imperfect techniques of measurement, any one of which, taken separately from a *group* of subjects and correlated with factors of stimulation and of response, will reveal significant relationships. Though the general line of approach seems to be reasonably clear, we do not as yet know how our measures may best be combined, which single measures are most significant, or even, in many cases, the best techniques for securing the single measures. Yet R. C. Davis, Lundervold, and Miller (1957) found what they called a "general response pattern" to certain stimuli, described as consisting of increased muscle-tension, increased sweat-gland activity, increased heart-rate, and increased respiration-rate and amplitude. They noted that this pattern was, on a small scale, that which accompanies exercise and which is also supposed to be present in "emergency reaction." The response variables were said to behave with reasonable consistency from subject to subject under their experimental conditions. Activity of the brain was not recorded but, if it had been, there seems every reason to believe that central and peripheral measures of excitation would have shown covariation.

3. Objectors to the concept of general activation often point to the rather low intercorrelations of physiological measures obtained by a number of investigators, thus suggesting less integrated functioning of the organism than the data of either physiology or everyday observation would make plausible.

Yet the low intercorrelations exist. The writer has suggested that they may be accounted for by such factors as the following:

(a) There is a difference in the latency of various physiological responses, so that one function may be at its peak while another is just beginning to be activated.

(b) It seems clear, from the investigations of J. I. Lacey and his collaborators (J. I. Lacey and B. C. Lacey, 1958a), that in nearly half of the population at least, excitation may, in consistent fashion, be shown most markedly in one system by one individual and in another system by another individual. This fact, of course, makes measurement of general activation more difficult, but it scarcely negates the conception of an activated *individual* rather than merely an activated system within the individual.

It is of interest that the Laceys themselves, while denying general activation as a concept, speak of "autonomic reactivity" after measuring cardiac activity and the electrical activity of the skin which, in their investigations, showed little correlation (J. I. Lacey and B. C. Lacey, 1958b).

(c) Homeostatic mechanisms in some instances, as for example heart-rate and blood-pressure, may show antagonistic actions between the systems after a certain degree of activation has been reached.

(d) More than in most areas of psychology, errors of measurement are likely to occur, because of lack of precise information as to what should be measured and in what way, and because of lack of adequate attention to the numerous controls that are necessary.

(e) Finally, it appears that response is specifically adjusted to the stimulus situation, within the ability of the individual to make an adjustment. While the individual as a whole may be more activated or less activated at a given time, the locus of the maximum activation may vary with the requirements of the situation as perceived by the individual. For example, in what is loosely called "fear" the individual wants less of the stimulus, and he may either retreat as rapidly as possible or he may cower in a given spot, being in both cases more highly activated than usual but showing, perhaps, a somewhat different pattern of activation in his various systems. In this sense, a concept of activation might be considered to be both general and specific.

Perhaps it is in order here to point out that while intercorrelations of physiological measures are generally low, *intra*correlations, or correlations of measures within the same individual, appear to be considerably higher. And the latter are, after all, what a concept of general activation requires.

Definitions of activation have sometimes been classified as either "central" or "peripheral." Those called "central" define activation in terms of neural action in certain centers, while those that have been called "peripheral" define activation in terms of measures of excitation in any part of the organism, including changes recorded from brain centers. It would seem that the definitions described as peripheral differ from those described as central chiefly by placing more emphasis upon operational definitions, and thus they are less involved in actual or potential disputes in regard to the relationship between the central and the peripheral functions. The *measures* of activation employed by those adhering to the one type of definition do not appear to differ from those employed by those adhering to the other type of definition.

For some purposes, activation produced by certain types of stimulus conditions, such, for example, as those referred to as motives, may be of more interest to the investigator than those produced by other conditions, as, for example, exercise. Under these circumstances, the investigator must attempt to hold constant any factors affecting activation (such as movement) whose influence he does not wish to have reflected in his measures. The situation is basically no different from that encountered in the design of other types of experiment. Yet the wide variety of factors that can produce changes in activation with resultant changes of a similar kind in behavior, is in itself of interest.

The concept of activation, as the writer has employed it, refers not to the energy that is potentially available to the organism, but to that actually released through activity in the tissues. The concept is, of course, amenable to modification as new data become available.

The degree of activation, as shown by the writer in various publications (Duffy, 1962) appears to affect both sensory sensitivity and motor response, and is involved in those consistencies of behavior that we call personality characteristics. Its determinants are both physiological and psychological. The concept appears to hold great promise both for particular explanations and for unifying a wide range of phenomena that are of concern to the psychologist. It is gratifying to note the extent to which it has been, and is now being, employed for these purposes.

Psychological Review, 1959, vol. 66, pp. 367–386.

Activation: A Neuropsychological Dimension[1]

Robert B. Malmo

There have been three main lines of approach to the problem of activation: (*a*) through electroencephalography and neurophysiology, (*b*) through physiological studies of "behavioral energetics," and (*c*) through the learning theorists' search for a satisfactory measure of drive. Before attempting a formal definition of activation, I shall briefly describe these three different approaches to the concept.

NEUROPHYSIOLOGICAL APPROACH: LINDSLEY'S ACTIVATION THEORY[2]

The neurophysiological approach to activation had its origin in electroen-

[1] Support for some of the research reported herein has come from the following sources: National Institute of Mental Health, National Institutes of Health, United States Public Health Service: Grant Number M–1475; Medical Research and Development Division, Office of the Surgeon General, Department of the United States Army: Contract Number DA–49–007–MD–626; Defence Research Board, Department of National Defence, Canada: Grant Number 9425–04; and National Research Council of Canada: Grant Number A. P. 29.

Grateful acknowledgment is made to A. Amsel, R. C. Davis, S. M. Feldman, P. Milner, M. M. Schnore, R. G. Stennett, D. J. Ehrlich and L. R. Pinneo for constructive criticism of the manuscript.

The main parts of this paper were presented in a Symposium entitled, "Experimental Foundations of Clinical Psychology," under the chairmanship of Arthur J. Bachrach, at the University of Virginia, April 1–2, 1959. To Ian P. Stevenson, who was the discussant of my paper on that Symposium, I owe a debt of gratitude for his very helpful comments.

cephalography (EEG). Early workers in the EEG field soon discovered that there were distinctive wave patterns characterizing the main levels of psychological functioning in the progression from deep sleep to highly alerted states of activity (Jasper, 1941). In deep sleep large low-frequency waves predominate. In light sleep and drowsy states the frequencies are not as low as in deep sleep, but there are more low-frequency waves than in the wakeful states. In relaxed wakefulness there is a predominance of waves in the alpha (8–12 c.p.s.) range that gives way to beta frequencies (approximately 18–30 c.p.s.) when the *S* is moderately alert. Under highly alerting and exciting conditions beta waves predominate. In ad-

[2] I am using neuropsychology in a rather broad sense, meaning to include the work often referred to by the term "psychophysiology." This usage implies that the chief problems being studied are psychological ones, and it also stresses the importance of neurophysiological techniques. It is true that, strictly speaking, many of the physiological techniques in use are not neurophysiological ones; yet our main interest lies in the central neural control of the physiological functions under study rather than in the peripheral events themselves.

Later on in the paper I shall attempt a formal definition of activation. For the first section of the paper, I believe that it will be sufficient to say that in using the term "activation" I am referring to the intensive dimension of behavior. "Arousal" is often used interchangeably with activation; and level of drive is a very similar concept. For instance, a drowsy *S* is low, an alert *S* is high in activation.

dition to the increased frequency of the waves under these conditions of heightened alertness there is also a change from a regular synchronized appearance of the tracing to an irregular desynchronized tracing, usually of reduced amplitude.

For Lindsley's theory, desynchronization (called "activation pattern") became the single most important EEG phenomenon. My use of the term "desynchronization" is purely descriptive. Desynchronization or "flattening" in the EEG tracing was consistently found associated with increased alertness in a large variety of experiments with animal and human Ss. The consistency and generality of this phenomenon suggested the existence of mechanisms in the brain mediating behavioral functions having to do with levels of alertness, although at the time that the original observations were made it was not at all clear what these neural mechanisms were.

With the discovery of the ascending reticular activating system (ARAS), however, there was rapid and very significant advance in theory and experimentation. Some of the most important general findings have been as follows: (a) Lesions in the ARAS abolished "activation" of the EEG and produced a behavioral picture of letehargy and somnolence (Lindsley, 1957). (b) The "activation pattern" in the EEG was reproduced by electrical stimulation of the ARAS. Furthermore, in the monkey, Fuster (1958) recently found that concurrent ARAS stimulation of moderate intensity improved accuracy and speed of visual discrimination reaction. He also found that higher intensities had the opposite effect, producing diminution of correct responses and increase of reaction times. Interpretation of these latter findings is complicated by the fact that they were obtained with stimulation intensities higher than the threshold for the elicitation of observable motor effects such as generalized muscular jerks. It is not stated whether intensity of stimulation was systematically studied. In any event, these observations of deleterious effect from high intensity stimulation are of considerable interest because they are what might be expected according to the activation theory.

The activation theory as first stated by Lindsley (1951)—although introduced in the handbook chapter on emotion—was, from the outset, conceived by him to be broader than an explanatory concept for emotional behavior. The theory was elaborated by Hebb (1955) in an attempt to solve the problem of drives. With the continuous flow of new experimental data on the ARAS (Lindsley, 1957), this area of neuropsychological investigation appears to be heading toward an important breakthrough. I shall attempt to state very briefly the main points of the current theory, drawing upon the ideas of several authors. According to this theory, the continuum extending from deep sleep at the low activation end to "excited states"[3] at the high activation end is very largely a function of cortical bombardment by the ARAS, such that the greater the cortical bombardment the higher the activation. Further, the relation between activation and behavioral efficiency (cue func-

[3] The expression "excited states" is frequently used to refer to the upper end of the activation continuum. In using this term I do not wish to imply increased overt activity. In fact, overt activity may be reduced to a very low level at the high end of the continuum, when—for example—a person is immobilized by terror.

tion or level of performance) is described by an inverted **U** curve. That is, from low activation up to a point that is optimal for a given function, level of performance rises monotonically with increasing activation level, but beyond this optimal point the relation becomes nonmonotonic: further increase in activation beyond this point produces a fall in performance level, this fall being directly related to the amount of the increase in level of activation.

Principles of neural action that could account for the reversal in the effects of nonspecific neural bombardment of the cortex by the ARAS have long been known (Lorente de Nó, 1939, p. 428). Circulation of neural impulses in a closed chain of neurons (or "cell assembly" to use Hebb's [1949] term) may be facilitated by impulses arriving outside the chain (e.g. from the ARAS). According to Lorente de Nó's schema, such extraneous impulses have the effect of stimulating certain neurons subliminally thus making it possible for an impulse from within the chain to finish the job, that is make it fire at the appropriate time in the sequence, when alone, without the prior hit, it would have failed to fire it.

Again, according to the same account by Lorente de Nó (1939, p. 428), the deleterious effects of overstimulation from impulses outside the chain can be explained. A neuron in the chain may fail to respond to stimulation if owing to repeated activity it acquires a high threshold, and this failure to transmit the circulating impulses would mean cessation of activity in a cell assembly. I proposed this kind of explanation previously (1958) to account for the downturn in the inverted **U** curve as an alternative to Hebb's suggestion that

"the greater bombardment may intermonotonic. Therefore, finding the nonmonotonic relation in such simple responses as bar pressing and salivation raises strong doubts that the habit interference explanation can account for fere with the delicate adjustments involved in cue function, perhaps by facilitating irrelevant responses (a high D arouses conflicting $_sH_R$'s?)" (Hebb, 1955, p. 250).

It seems reasonable to suppose that as diffuse bombardment from the ARAS greatly exceeds an amount that is optimal for some simple psychological function being mediated by a particular cell assembly, the operation of that cell assembly will be impaired, and that the performance being mediated by it will suffer accordingly. This line of reasoning suggests that the inverted **U** relation should be found in quite simple psychological functions. Present evidence appears to support this suggestion. A recent (unpublished) experiment by Bélanger and Feldman, that I shall describe later in this paper, indicates that in rats the inverted **U** relation is found with simple bar pressing performance, and an experiment by Finch (1938) suggests that even such a simple response as the unconditioned salivary response yields the inverted **U** curve when plotted against activation level.

It may be noted that according to a response competition hypothesis, the inverted **U** relation should appear most prominently in complex functions where opportunities for habit interference are greater than they are in the case of simple functions. According to the response competition hypothesis, in the limiting case where response is so simple that habit interference is negligible, the relation between response strength and activation level should be the seemingly pervasive phenomenon of the inverted **U** curve.

PRINCIPLE OF ACTIVATION GROWING OUT OF WORK ON BEHAVIORAL INTENSITY

Even before the EEG work on desynchronization, the behavioral evidence had suggested the existence of some brain mechanism like the ARAS. The writings of Duffy (1951, 1957), Freeman (1948), and others of the "energetics" group have long stressed the importance of an intensity dimension in behavior.

In an attempt to obtain a measure of this intensity variable, Duffy relied mainly on records of muscular tension (1932) while Freeman's favorite indicator was palmar conductance (1948). These workers concluded from their experiments that there was a lawful relationship between a state of the organism, called "arousal," "energy mobilization," "activation," or simply "intensity" and level of performance. Moreover, they suggested that the relationship might be described by an inverted **U** curve (Duffy, 1957). This suggestion has proved heuristic as indicated by the current experimental attack on the inverted **U** hypothesis (Stennett, 1957a; Bindra, 1959; Cofer, 1959; Kendler, 1959).

The inverted **U** shaped curve has been shown to hold in numerous learning and performance situations where the amount of induced muscle tension was varied systematically (Courts, 1942). It is tempting to conclude that tension induction is simply one of the many ways to increase activation level, but as Courts' (1942) discussion suggests this conclusion would be premature. It is possible that squeezing on a dynamometer, a typical means of inducing tension in these experiments, may produce generalized activation effects as some data from Freeman indicate (1948, p. 71). But Freeman's data are insufficient to establish this point, and there are alternative explanations for the relationship between the performance data and induced tension (Courts, 1942). By repeating the induced-tension experiments with simultaneous recordings of EEG and other physiological functions it would be possible to determine how general the effects of inducing tension actually are. Such direct tests of the activation hypothesis are very much needed.

DRIVE AND ACTIVATION

A third approach to the activation principle was made by learning theorists, especially those of the Hull school. I have argued elsewhere (Malmo, 1958) that general drive (D), without the steering component, became identical in principle with activation or arousal. Set aside for the moment the attractive possibility of using ARAS as a neural model for mediation of D, and consider only the methodological advantages of physiological measures in the quantification of D. It seems that none of the other attempts to measure D have been really satisfactory, and that physiological indicants where applied have been surprisingly effective. Learning theorists up to the present time have made only very occasional use of physiological measures. For instance, in arguing that a previously painful stimulus had lost its drive properties, Brown (1955) cited the absence of physiological reaction when the stimulus was applied. More recently, Spence (1958) has reported some success with physiological measures in his studies of "emotionally-based" drive.

In keeping with traditional views concerning the place of physiological measures in psychology, on those few occasions that they were employed at all they were applied to aversive or emotionally based drive. According to the activation principle, however, it should be possible to use physiological measures to gauge appetitionally based as well as aversively based drive. This means, for instance, that in a water deprivation experiment there should be close correspondence between number of hours of deprivation and physiological level. That is, heart rate, for example, should be higher in an animal performing in a Skinner box after 36 hours of deprivation than after 24, higher still after 48 hours of deprivation and so on. In my Nebraska Symposium paper I stated that, as far as I was aware, this kind of experiment had not been reported (Malmo, 1958, p. 236).

Bélanger and Feldman in Montreal have recently completed such an experiment, and, as can be seen by inspecting Fig. 1, the results were as predicted by the activation hypothesis. Heart rate in rats showed progressive change corresponding with increasing hours of water deprivation. Although there were only seven rats in the group, this change in heart rate was highly significant. Deprivations were carried out serially on the same group of animals, commencing at 12 hours and proceeding to 24, 48 hours and so on with sufficient hydration (four to seven days) between deprivation periods to prevent any cumulative effects from affecting the experiments. Heart rate was picked up by means of wire electrodes inserted

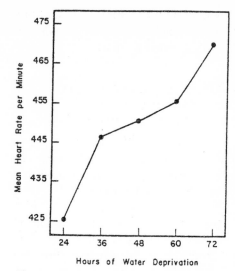

Fig. 1. Data from Bélanger and Feldman showing relation between water deprivation and heart rate in rats $(N = 7)$. See text for explanation.

in the skin of the animals and was amplified and registered graphically by means of a Sanborn electrocardiograph. Particular care was taken to record heart rate under nearly the same conditions of stimulation each time, that is, when the animal was pressing on the lever in the Skinner box or during drinking from the dispenser immediately after pressing. Under these conditions it was not possible to obtain sufficient heart-rate data at the 12-hour deprivation interval. Testing the animal under constant stimulating conditions is a very important methodological consideration. Some exploratory observations indicated that heart-rate measurements taken in a restraining compartment did not agree with those taken under the carefully controlled stimulus conditions provided by the Skinner box. I shall return to this finding later on because, aside from its methodological importance, I believe that it has considerable theoretical significance as well.

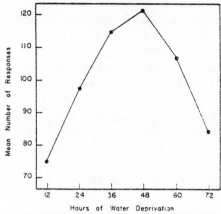

Fig. 2. Data from Bélanger and Feldman showing relation between water deprivation and Skinner box performance in rats ($N = 7$). See text for explanation.

Figure 2 presents the behavioral data which are again in remarkably good agreement with prediction from the activation hypothesis. Up to the 48-hour deprivation interval there is an increasing monotonic relationship between number of bar presses and hours of deprivation which is strictly in accordance with Hullian theory. The accompanying rise in heart rate suggests that for this part of the curve, hours of deprivation and the physiological indicant are roughly equivalent as measures of drive. But after the 48-hour point on the curves, the combined heart rate and behavioral data support predictions previously made from activation theory (Malmo, 1958) and suggest that the Hullian position requires revision. This kind of downward turn in the response curve has usually been attributed to a physical weakening of the animal due to the deprivation of food or water. In the absence of physiological data such an assumption appeared reasonable in many cases, although it did not account for response decrement in certain experiments where physical weakening seemed to be ruled out (Finan, 1940; Freeman, 1940; Fuster, 1958; Kaplan, 1952; Stennett, 1957a). Attack on this problem with physiological methods should soon provide a definitive answer concerning the main determinants of this response decrement. The present experiment represents an important first step in a program of animal studies that should go a long way towards solving this problem. It is not claimed that this one experiment demolishes the inanition hypothesis, but it does seem that the results are opposed to it. Heart rate in the Minnesota starvation experiments was found lowered in the weakened individuals (Malmo, 1958, p. 252) whereas heart rate in the present experiment was markedly increased during the period when number of responses was declining. Moreover, Bélanger was careful to record the weights of the animals all through the experiments, and he observed only very slight changes in weight, even at the 72-hour deprivation interval. Again, it should be stressed that all through the experiment the animals received four to seven days of hydration between conditions. Furthermore, it is interesting to note that the animals continued to press the bar at fairly regular intervals in the high deprivation conditions (with response decrement). That is, their behavior did not appear as though they had "given up." The acts of pressing continued to occur regularly, only they were separated by longer temporal intervals than under more optimal conditions of deprivation.

The increasing monotonic curve for heart rate did not seem to be simply due to the physical conditions of exertion associated with the act of bar pressing. It is true that up to the peak of the performance curve increasing heart rate was accompanied by increasing frequency of bar pressing, but past this point, heart rate continued to show rise despite the decline in exertion due to bar pressing. One might conjecture that exercise may have had greater effect on heart rate under extreme deprivation, but this would be counterbalanced—to some extent, at least—by the reduced number of presses.

To control for possible serial effects in this experiment there were two checks. First, he obtained similar findings from a second group of rats in which the order of deprivation conditions was reversed, commencing with the 72-hour deprivation condition, and finishing with the 12-hour condition. Second, the group of rats that had the ascending order of deprivation intervals were tested one week after the end of the experiment under the 60-hour deprivation condition. Mean number of responses was 96.7 and mean heart rate was 458.9 beats per minute, thus providing good agreement with the results that were obtained in the main experiment.

Finally, it is possible to speculate along various lines about how the heart rate data could be accounted for without involving the concept of activation. Obviously, further experimentation is needed, but it is encouraging nonetheless that the first animal experimentation specifically designed to explore the relation between appetitional drive and activation turned out according to prediction.

Characteristics of Activation

The three approaches described in the previous section appear to lead to the same fundamental concept of activation. It will, of course, be difficult to state a precise definition of activation that will satisfy everyone. Neurophysiologically oriented workers will maintain a healthy scepticism concerning the so-called "peripheral" indicants of activation. The "energetics" group while welcoming the extended use of what is essentially their own methodology will in company with some learning theorists look askance at theoretical models that verge on neurologizing. Despite differences in point of view, however, it seems worthwhile to attempt to deal with certain major characteristics of activation on which we may expect a large measure of agreement.

ACTIVATION LEVEL A PRODUCT OF MULTIPLE FACTORS

When a man is deprived of sleep for some 60 hours his activation level appears higher than it was before he had suffered sleep loss. Physiological indicants reveal an upward shift in activation level that is gradual and progressive throughout the vigil (Malmo, 1958). Having once demonstrated these physiological changes it is tempting to dispense with physiological recording in further work, assuming that 60 hours of deprivation will invariably produce a heightened state of activation. Such an assumption, however, cannot be made. An example will make clear why this assumption is untenable. A sleep-deprived S requires constant stimulation to prevent him from going to sleep. It is a general finding in such studies that despite the best intentions of the S to remain awake he will "catnap" if left alone. When he is working at a task trying to keep his efficiency from falling, the effect of major sleep loss is to produce a large increase in activation level. The important point to see here, however, is that the higher activation level is a combined product of the stimuli and their demands on him plus the condition of sleep loss. Without such stimulation, the *S* would surely fall asleep and we know from our studies of sleep that physiological levels drop very rapidly as one drifts into sleep. It is obvious, therefore, that in the absence of the task, physiological indicants at 60 hours' deprivation would show lower, not higher, activation in comparison with the rested condition.

That the "drive state" is in large part determined by environmental stimulating factors is indicated also by the observations of Bélanger and Feldman in their water deprivation experiments. Incidental observations suggested that, in addition to being more variable, heart rates recorded from the animal in a restraining compartment seemed to be consistently lower than those that were recorded when the animal was pressing the lever or drinking. In the restraining compartment the animal could view the lever through glass so that apparently mere sight of the lever was insufficient stimulation to produce the full effect upon heart rate that was produced by the acts of pressing on the lever and drinking. It thus appeared that, with deprivation time approximately the same, activation level differed appreciably depending upon the conditions of external stimulation. These observations were merely incidental ones in this experiment, and they should be repeated; but they encourage the point of view that activation level is in large part a function of environmental stimulating conditions. The experiments of Campbell

and Sheffield (1953) seem to point in the same direction. In the absence of sufficient environmental stimulation, food deprived rats are no more active than satiated ones, but with stimulation they are much more active than the satiated controls.

Returning to the example of the water deprived rat in the Skinner box, the two major factors determining the level of activation in that situation are (*a*) the internal conditions produced by deprivation and (*b*) the environmental stimulating conditions. To restate a point previously made, level of activation does not seem to be simply determined by the condition of deprivation alone. This would mean that depriving an animal of water per se could not produce some direct effect on motor mechanisms such as a simple discharge into the cardiac accelerating mechanism, leading to increased heart rate. Instead of some direct effect of this kind leading immediately over to some observable effector action, deprivation appears to have a sensitizing effect that is undetectable (or latent). According to this view, when appropriate stimulation does occur, the previously latent effect of deprivation will show itself in the heart rate: within limits, the longer the period of deprivation the higher the heart rate. Furthermore, according to activation theory, the same central mechanism that increases heart rate also acts to increase bombardment of the cerebral cortex. As previously stated, this central mechanism is presumed to be the ARAS.[4]

What could be the means of sensitiz-

[4] It is very likely that the descending reticular activating system is involved here too, but, at the present stage of knowledge in this field, it does not seem wise to introduce further complications into the neuropsychological model.

ing cells in the ARAS by a condition such as deprivation of water or food? If some hormone like epinephrine were released by deprivation, it is conceivable that this hormone could act to sensitize the ARAS cells in degree proportional to the amount of time that the animal had been deprived. As a matter of fact, hormonal sensitization of neural mechanisms is a currently active area of research (Saffran, Schally, & Benfey, 1955; Dell, 1958).

There are some real difficulties in defending the position that the ARAS is a unitary intensity-mediating mechanism, because the ARAS does not appear to be a homogeneous anatomical system. Indeed, as Olszewski (1954) has shown, these central brain stem structures appear very complex and highly differentiated. This unreassuring fact must not be forgotten, but neither should it be accepted as precluding the unitary function. As Lashley points out in the discussion of Olszewski's paper, structural differences are not reliable indices of function when unsupported by other evidence.

As a matter of fact, there is some important functional evidence which encourages the unitary view despite the structural complexity of the ARAS. Dell (1958) has found that: "Epinephrine does not activate selectively mammillothalamocingular systems, . . . but instead activates the ascending reticular system *en masse,* thus leading to a generalized cortical arousal" (p. 370). Control experiments showed that the activation effect was due to a direct action of the epinephrine at the reticular level and not to an effect on the cerebral cortex. Similar results have been obtained by Rothballer (1956).

Another kind of difficulty for the quantitative view would be posed by showing that patterned discharge from

the ARAS to the cortex (not merely total quantity of discharge) was the crucial factor in supporting some behavioral action. Don't the effector patterns of standing, walking, and righting pose just such a difficulty? The relation of midbrain mechanisms to posture seems to be clearly one in which patterns of discharge from the midbrain are important. But the decorticate mammal (guinea pig, rabbit, cat, dog) in which the cortex of both hemispheres has been removed shows approximately normal postural and progressional activities (Dusser de Barenne, 1934, p. 229). Since the activation concept under review deals with bombardment of the cerebral cortex, it appears that these noncortically mediated response patterns fall outside of phenomena under present consideration.

I should add, finally, that my admittedly speculative suggestion concerning hormonal sensitization is by no means essential to the main point which is that the behavioral evidence clearly shows the effects of deprivation to be latent (i.e. unobservable) under certain conditions. Moreover, this stress placed on the latent effects of deprivation is not mere hairsplitting. In addition to being required for an explanation of the Montreal experiments, this concept of latent deprivation effects appears to account in large measure for the findings of Campbell and Sheffield (1953), and more generally for the failure of random activity to adequately serve as a measure of drive or activation (Malmo, 1958).

ACTIVATION
AND THE S—R FRAMEWORK

As the product of interaction between internal (perhaps hormonal) conditions and external stimulating ones, activation cannot be very reasonably classified as either stimulus or response. This means that the physiological measurements that are used to gauge level of activation do not fit very well into the S–R formula. It is perhaps useful to think of these physiological conditions as part of O in the S-O-R formula (Woodworth & Schlosberg, 1954, p. 2).

The momentary physiological reaction to a discrete stimulus like the sudden rise in palmar conductance accompanying pin-prick is not of primary concern to us in our study of activation. This kind of S–R reaction, important as it undoubtedly is for investigating other problems, is of little relevance for the study of activation, compared with the longer lasting changes. As Schlosberg has put it to me in personal communication, in employing skin conductance to gauge level of activation, one observes the "tides" and not the "ripples." I do not mean to disparage studies that use physiological reactions as R terms in the strict S–R sense. It is just that in this paper I am concerned with physiological functions only insofar as they are related to activation.

It may be queried whether we are dealing with a needless and hair-splitting distinction by saying that activation is not a response. However, the kind of difference I have in mind appears quite distinct and useful to keep in mind, though it should not be stressed unduly. Basically, it is the same distinction which Woodworth and Schlosberg (1954) make when they draw particular attention to the difference between slow and rapid changes in skin conductance. As examples of rapid changes in skin conductance, there are the "GSRs" as R terms in conditioned responses, and in free association tests. Examples of slow skin-conductance

changes, on the other hand, are the gradual downward drifts that occur over hours during sleep (see Fig. 4), the slow downward changes in skin conductance in Ss as they become gradually habituated to an experimental situation (Davis, 1934; Duffy & Lacey, 1946), and (going up the activation scale) the progressive upward changes in conductance during a vigil (Malmo, 1958).

I would not deny that there are stimuli and responses going on in the physiological systems, but at the present time I see no way of identifying and handling them. It should be added, however, that this does not give one license to completely disregard the antecedents of physiological changes. For instance, if the hand of a sleeping S becomes hot by being covered with heavy bedclothing the local thermal sweating induced thereby will bring about a sudden rise in palmar conductance which has nothing to do with activation. Or sleep may be induced by certain drugs which have a specific stimulating effect on respiration, such that respiration rate will not fall during sleep as it usually does (see Fig. 5 for curve obtained under nondrug conditions). Furthermore, artifacts due to movement and postural shifts may prevent muscle potentials from serving as reliable indicants of activation level.

LIMITATIONS
OF THE ACTIVATION CONCEPT

I am not attempting to solve the problem of selection, i.e., the problem of finding the neurophysiological mechanisms that determine which cues in the animal's environment are prepotent in the sense of winning out over other cues in triggering off a pattern of effector action. This point seems clear enough, especially when it is stressed that activation has no steering function; and yet there is still the risk that some critics may misunderstand and state as one shortcoming of this theory that it does not adequately handle the problem of selection. The theory may be open to criticism on the grounds that it is limited, but it should not be criticized for failing to do something which it was not intended to do.

It will be noted that in general an attempt is made to raise theoretical questions that stand a good chance of being answered by available experimental techniques. Schematically, the experimental paradigm is as follows:

Activation
    level: Low Moderate High
Expected perform-
    ance level: Low Optimal Low

It is important to stress that the measure denoted by "moderate activation level" has meaning only in relative (not in absolute) terms. That is, the level is "moderate" because it is higher than that of the low activation condition, and lower than the level of the high activation condition. Comparisons are invariably of the within-individual, within-task kind, which means that the level of activation which is found to be optimal for one task is not directly compared with the level of activation which is found to be optimal for a different task. Thus, at the present stage of theorizing, no attempt is made to deal with the question of whether tasks which differ in complexity, for example, also differ with respect to the precise level of activation which is optimal for each one. However, I have dealt elsewhere (Malmo, 1958) with the related question of response competi-

tion, suggesting an alternative to the response competition explanation for decrement in performance with increased activation (or D).

Again, the theoretical formulations may be criticized for being too narrow. But it must be kept in mind that their narrowness is due to the close nexus between theory and experiment in this program. These formulations may also be criticized for an unjustifiable assumption in the postulation of a communal drive mechanism. One may well ask where the evidence is that proves the existence of a state of general drive. In dealing ith this kind of question, it is essential to refer back to the outline of the experimental paradigm. The experimental induction of the three discriminable activation levels referred to in the outline depends upon the controlled variation of certain conditions in the S's environment. The fact that by varying conditions as dissimilar as appetitional deprivations and verbal incentives it is possible to produce similar shifts in physiological indicants provides a sound basis for introducing the operationally defined concept of activation level that cuts across traditional demarcation lines of specific drives. All this, of course, does not constitute final proof for a communal drive mechanism. Certainly further data are required before it is even safe to conclude equivalence of drive conditions in the alteration of physiological levels, to say nothing of proving the existence of a communal drive mechanism.

Interrelations Between Physiological Indicants of Activation

Criticism directed against physiological measures as indicants of activation usually involve one or both of the following points. The first objection is that intercorrelations between physiological measures are so low that it is unreasonable to consider their use for gauging a single dimension of behavior. A second objection is that activation properly refers to events in the brain and that the correspondence between these central events and what may be observed in such peripheral functions as heart rate, respiration, muscle tension and the like is not close enough to permit valid inferences from the peripheral events to the central ones. In the following section, I shall attempt to answer these criticisms.

INTRA- AND INTERINDIVIDUAL
CORRELATIONS AMONG
PHYSIOLOGICAL INDICANTS
OF ACTIVATION

In an unpublished paper, Schnore and I have discussed certain misconceptions that have confused some critics of physiological methods. The most serious misunderstanding concerns correlations among physiological measures. It is true that *inter*individual correlations are low, but this fact is actually irrelevant insofar as using these measures to gauge activation is concerned. The important question is whether significant *intra*individual correlations are found in a sufficiently high proportion of individuals, and the answer appears to be yes (Schnore, 1959).

What the low *inter*individual correlations mean, of course, is that an individual in any given situation may have a heart rate that is high relative to the mean heart rate for the group, and at the same time have a respiration rate or a blood pressure that is low

relative to the group mean. These findings are in line with the principle of physiological specificity that is now supported by several lines of evidence.[5] Physiological specificity is a separate problem that is in no way crucial for the activation hypothesis. An illustration will make this clear. Take a rather extreme example of an individual with very *high* heart rate (say 95 when the mean for his group under specified conditions is 75) and very *low* palmar conductance (50 micromhos when the group mean is 100). In an experiment with varied incentive, in going from a low incentive to a high incentive condition this S will likely show an increase in heart rate from 95 to say 110 and an increase in palmar conductance from 50 to say 60 micromhos. The main point is that even though the S's heart rate is already high compared with the mean for his group, it goes still higher (concordantly with palmar conductance) when the stimulating situation increases the level of activation. This is the kind of intraindividual correlation between physiological measures[6] that is required for gauging the dimension of activation and, to repeat,

[5] The general principle of physiological specificity states that under significantly different conditions of stimulation individuals exhibit idiosyncratic but highly stereotyped patterns of autonomic and somatic activation. I use the term *physiological specificity* as a generic reference to autonomic-response stereotypy (Lacey & Lacey, 1958) to symptom specificity (Malmo & Shagass, 1949), and to stereotypy of somatic and autonomic activation patterns (Schnore, 1959).

[6] It is not claimed, however, that all physiological measures are equally useful for the purpose of gauging activation level. On the contrary, as Schnore's experiments have suggested, some measures appear superior to others, and eventually we may be able to select the most discriminating ones and thus improve our measurement (Schnore, 1959).

the evidence strongly indicates that the intraindividual correlations are sufficiently high for this purpose.

Relations Between Central and Peripheral Indicants of Activation

As previously noted, the pioneer EEG workers observed definite changes in EEG pattern accompanying major shifts in the conscious state of the *S*. Moreover, they recognized a continuum of increasing activation usually referred to as the sleep-waking-excitement continuum, just as other workers like Freeman (1948) and Duffy (1957) employing peripheral measures of palmar sweating and muscular tension recognized it. Among the early workers in this field, Darrow (1947) studied EEG and other measures simultaneously, but only very recently have techniques been made available that can provide the kind of quantitative EEG measurements required for critical comparisons along the activation continuum. That is, from simple inspection of the raw EEG tracing it is possible to see gross differences between sleeping and waking, or between a drowsy, relaxed state and one of extreme alertness. But for experiments on activation it is necessary to have an instrument that will reveal measurable differences for "points" lying closer to each other on the activation continuum. For example, it is essential to have a measure that will discriminate reliably between a moderately alert and a highly alert state. For such discriminations the method of inspection will not do, and a device for objective quantification of the wave forms is required.

Because of its complexity the EEG tracing has been difficult to quantify, and although gross differences in activation level could be detected by simple inspection of the tracing, this method was too crude for more detailed work. However, with the advent of EEG frequency analysers, quantification of the EEG looked promising because these analysers were designed to provide quantified EEG data for each of many different narrow frequency bands. Unfortunately, these instruments have not proved useful because of insufficient stability. In our laboratory we have been trying band-pass filters to provide stable quantification of various selected frequency bands in which we are primarily interested (Ross & Davis, 1958). Results thus far appear highly encouraging.

DATA INDICATING RELATIONSHIPS BETWEEN EEG AND OTHER PHYSIOLOGICAL FUNCTIONS

In a recent sleep deprivation experiment, we found that palmar conductance and respiration showed progressive rise during the vigil, indicating increasing activation with deprivation of sleep. In the same experiment we recorded EEG and, by means of a band-pass filter, obtained a quantified write-out of frequencies from 8–12 per second, in the alpha range. It will be recalled that the classical picture of activation is reduction in the amount of alpha activity. Therefore, what we might expect to find in this experiment is progressive decrease in the amount of alpha activity. As a matter of fact, this is exactly what was found (Malmo, 1958, p. 237).

As Stennett (1957b) has shown, however, the relationship between EEG alpha activity and other physiological variables is sometimes curvilinear.

In the sleep deprivation experiments physiological measurements were taken under highly activating conditions and at this high end of the continuum further increase in activation seems invariably to decrease the amount of alpha activity. But at the lower end of the continuum with the S in a drowsy state, increased activation has the opposite effect on alpha activity. An alerting stimulus, instead of producing a flattening of the EEG tracing, will actually produce an augmentation of the alpha activity. This has sometimes been referred to as a "paradoxical" reaction, although it seems paradoxical only when it is assumed that the relation between activation level and alpha amplitude is a decreasing montonic one throughout the entire activation continuum. But Stennett (1957b) has shown that the relationship is not monotonic. From his data he plotted a curve which has the shape of an inverted U. From this curve it would be predicted that with a drowsy S, stimulation should *increase* alpha amplitude. From the same inverted U curve it would also be predicted that an S whose activation level was sufficiently high (past the peak of the curve) before stimulation would show a *decrease* in alpha amplitude. Actually, some unpublished experiments on startle by Bartoshuk fit these predictions very well.

Recent data indicate the usefulness of a 2–4 c.p.s. band-pass filter in experiments on sleep. The data in the figures that follow represent mean values from three men who slept all night in our laboratory after serving as Ss in our sleep deprivation experiments.

Bipolar sponge electrodes, soaked in electrode jelly and attached to the S by Lastonet bands, were used for the parietal EEG placement (two thirds of the distance from nasion to inion, and 3 cm. from the midline on each side). The primary tracing was recorded by an Edin Electroencephalograph, and the two secondary tracings were integrations of the EEG potentials that were passed through band-pass filters for selective amplification of signals in the 2–4 and 8–12 c.p.s. frequency bands. Measurements on the secondary tracings were carried out with special rulers, and these measurements were converted to microvolt values by reference to calibration standards.

Method of recording and measuring palmar conductance was similar to that described by Stennett (1957a).

Electrocardiograms were picked up from electrodes placed on contralateral limbs, and heart rates were determined from measurements of electrocardio-tachometric tracings. Respiration rates were obtained by means of a Phipps and Bird pneumograph.

All three Ss slept well throughout the night (approximately from 10 P.M. to 9 A.M. after some 60 hours without sleep). Physiological recordings were carried out continuously during the whole period of sleep in each case, and except for occasional attention to electrodes (e.g. application of electrode jelly and saline to electrodes) the Ss were undisturbed.

Four pairs of cellulose sponge electrodes were attached to the four limbs (to the pronator teres muscles of the arms and the peroneal muscles of the legs) for the purpose of recording muscle potentials. Primary muscle-potential tracings were recorded on the chart of a custom built Edin electromyograph (EGM). Electronic integrators (employing the condensor charge–discharge principle, like those

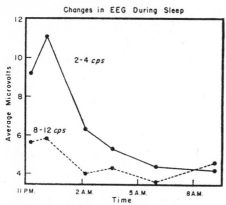

Fig. 3. Mean EEG values from three healthy young male Ss during a night's sleep. Subjects had been sleep-deprived. Band-pass filters were used in connection with electronic integrators to provide quantitative data in the two different frequency bands.

used for the secondary EEG tracings), attached in parallel across the galvanometers of this EMG unit, integrated the muscle potentials over successive 4-second periods.

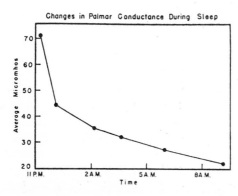

Fig. 4. Mean palmar conductance values from the same Ss, at the same times during sleep as in Figure 3.

These muscle-potential tracings were used to record movements and periods of restlessness during sleep. Five-minute periods free from muscle-potential activity and preceded by at least 5 minutes of movement-free trac-

ings were chosen for measurement in order to provide the values plotted in Fig. 3-5. The actual lines plotted on the baseline represent the medians for the three Ss. In each instance the three times were close to one another.

In Fig. 3 observe that following a brief rise early in sleep the upper curve for 2–4 c.p.s. falls continuously during the entire period of sleep. This curve is consistent with published accounts of changes in EEG during sleep noted by inspection of the raw tracings (Lindsley, 1957, p. 68). Early in sleep there is an increase in slow waves around 2–4 cycles per second, but as sleep continues these waves are replaced by even slower ones. As far as I am aware, the data in Fig. 3 represent the first use of a 2–4 band-pass filter to quantify the EEG. The curve for 8–12 c.p.s. EEG also shows some fall, and the voltage is low in accordance with the well-known disappearance of alpha waves from the raw tracings during sleep.

Figures 4 and 5 show data for palmar conductance, heart rate, and respiration, that were recorded at the same time as the EEG data. From the second plotted point on, there is rather close resemblance between these curves and the one for 2–4 c.p.s. EEG. It seems likely that a band-pass filter for fast frequencies in the beta range might yield a continuously falling curve commencing with drowsiness and continuing through the onset and early stages of sleep. There are serious technical difficulties in quantifying the next step of frequencies above the alpha band, but we are hopeful that a band-pass filter that has recently been constructed in our laboratory will overcome these difficulties.

DIRECT ALTERATION OF *ARAS* ACTIVITY BY MEANS OF ELECTRICAL STIMULATION AND RELATED ANIMAL EXPERIMENTATION

The most relevant experiment on direct stimulation of the ARAS is, as far as I know, the one by Fuster (1958) that was mentioned earlier. By stimulating in the same part of the ARAS that produces the EEG picture of activation, Fuster was able to produce improved discrimination performance in the monkey. Presumably, this effect was achieved by causing a larger number of impulses from the ARAS to bombard the cortex. The assumption would be that before the onset of electrical stimulation the cortex was not receiving sufficient bombardment for optimal performance (Hebb, 1955) and that ARAS stimulation brought total bombardment in the cortex closer to the optimal value. The situation may not be as simple as this, but the success of the Fuster experiment encourages further experimentation along these same lines. Finding that level of performance can be altered by electrical stimulation of the ARAS opens up the

exciting possibility that if amount of neural activity in the ARAS can be measured, we might find a direct correlation between a central measure of activation and level of performance. For instance, the Bélanger and Feldman experiment described earlier might be repeated with the addition of recordings from the ARAS. The aim of such an experiment would be to determine whether the continuous rise in the heart rate curve with increasing deprivation times could be matched by a similar rise in amplitude of deflections from recording in the ARAS with implanted electrodes. Recent neurophysiological experiments appear encouraging with respect to the feasibility of such an approach (Li & Jasper, 1953, pp. 124–125; Magoun, 1958, p. 68).

Effects of Increased Activation on Localized Skeletal-Muscle Tension in Psychiatric Patients

The implication of activation theory for various clinical phenomena might very well be the topic of a separate paper. Certainly there is not space to deal at length with the topic here. I have chosen, therefore, to present a few recent observations, chiefly in order to suggest how level of activation may be studied in relation to a clinical phenomenon.

The graph in Fig. 6 illustrates what appears to be a general finding in patients complaining of tensional discomfort in a localized muscular site. The data for the curves plotted in the figure were obtained from a psychiatric patient, a 42-year old woman who complained of muscular discomfort localized in the left thigh. In the session when these data were taken electromyograms (EMGs) were recorded from

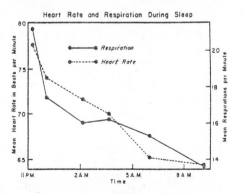

Fig. 5. Mean values for heart rate and respiration from the same Ss at the same times during sleep as in Figures 3 and 4.

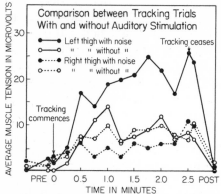

Fig. 6. Mean muscle tension from left thigh and right thigh from patient with complaint of tensional discomfort in the left thigh. Note that when patient was performing the tracking task under distraction (loud noise), tension rose in the left thigh but not in the right. See text for explanation.

various muscles over the body; those from the left and right thighs are shown in the figure. The patient was engaged in pursuit tracking using an apparatus similar to the one employed by Surwillo (1955, 1956). Figure 6 shows that when a loud distracting noise, of the kind described by Schnore (1959), was presented during tracking, the tension in the left thigh was very much higher than that of the right thigh. When tracking was carried out under free conditions this tensional difference between thighs was not observed.

Interpretation of these data seems quite straightforward. When level of activation was increased by presenting a loud distracting noise the effect was shown entirely in one muscle group, the left thigh, which was the symptom area in this patient. Simultaneous recordings of tension from other parts of the body showed that the tension was specific to the left thigh and was not merely increased on the whole left side of the body.

The specificity of the left thigh in indicating the higher activation is quite clear. Observe that tension in the thigh muscles on the opposite side of the body actually fell slightly under the activating condition.

The same procedure was carried out with a second patient, a young girl of 28, who complained of a distressing feeling of tightness in the neck on the right side. Results were similar to the ones obtained in the previous case, with activation again showing its effect specifically in the symptom area. When the loud distracting noise was turned on during tracking, tension in this area showed marked increase whereas tension in the muscles on the left side of the neck showed no rise whatever.

Very similar results were obtained from two additional patients whose areas of tensional discomfort were localized in still different parts of the body. One woman with complaint of tension on the left side of her neck served as a useful control for the patient previously described with tension localized in the opposite side of the neck. No tracking experiment was carried out with this patient. Apparently the sight of the EMG recording room for the first time was itself sufficient to increase the amplitude of muscle potentials from the symptom area so that they become appreciably higher than those on the opposite side of her neck. The other woman (fourth patient in this series) complained of tensional discomfort that appeared to originate in the left shoulder. EMGs were recorded from the left and right shoulders of this patient while she lay in bed listening to the playback of a recorded interview. During the first part of the playback, tension was about the same on the two sides of the body. But when the topic concerning her dead sister commenced to come over the speaker, tension in the left shoulder became much greater than that in the right.

As far as could be determined, the EMG data from all these patients were consistent in suggesting that for skeletal-muscle tension in patients with well-developed tensional symptoms, increasing the activation level up to a certain point has the effect of raising muscle tension in one localized muscle group, the one in which the patient complained of tensional discomfort. It was not necessary for the patient to actually feel the discomfort during the experimental session for this differential result to appear. I have been using the term "symptom area" to refer to the muscle group where the discomfort was localized when present.

Interesting findings that appear to parallel those from the patients were obtained from three young male nonpatient Ss in our recent investigation of sleep deprivation. As previously mentioned, evidence from EEG, palmar conductance, and respiration indicated that activation during tracking increased progressively with hours of sleep deprivation. In addition to these other physiological tracings, EMGs from various areas over the body were also recorded. One muscle area, a different one for each S, showed significant rise in tension over the vigil. It was the neck muscles in one S, the forehead in another, and the biceps muscle of the right arm in the third. In each case the one muscle showed statistically significant rise in tension, and in none of the Ss was there significant tensional rise in any other muscle. In fact, there was regularly progressive and very significant fall in the tension of the left forearm in all three Ss. As far as I know, none of the men actually complained of tensional discomfort in the areas showing rise in tension during the vigil.

Where high level activation is long continued as in a vigil or in certain psychoneurotic patients, it appears that skeletal tension may become localized to a single muscle group. The discomfort associated with this tension in some patients can become extremely severe. It should be noted that in one-session experiments, where rise in activation was for relatively short intervals of time, tensional rise occurred in more than one muscle group (Surwillo, 1956; Stennett, 1957a).

Methodologically, these results are important because they reveal a difference between EMGs and some other physiological measures with respect to gauging activation. Unlike heart rate or respiration rate that invariably yields one measure no matter how it is recorded, there are as many measures of muscle tension as there are muscles that can be recorded from. It appears that when sufficient care is taken, EMGs may be very valuable in helping to gauge activation, but that considerable caution is required in the interpretation of results, and especially in the interpretation of negative results.

From the clinical point of view it seems an interesting speculation that the patient's localized muscle tension may itself actually increase the general activation level. (I do not mean the level of muscle tension all over the body.) Two main assumptions are involved in this suggestion. The first one is that the area of localized muscle tension in the patient acts like tension that is induced, for example, by having an S squeeze on a dynamometer. From the generalized effects of tension induction on learning and performance it is clear that the effects of increased muscle tension are quite general ones. Though crucial physiological data are missing in these experiments, as previously mentioned, one very likely explanation of these results is that the local increase in muscle tension somehow produces an increase in the general level of activation, with rise in heart rate and blood pressure, with fall in level of EEG alpha, and so on. This is the second assumption. The results of two recent experiments are in line with this assumption. Meyer and Noble (1958) found that induced tension interacted with "anxiety" in verbal-maze learning ("anxiety" measured by means of the MAS [Taylor, 1953]), while Kuethe and Eriksen (1957) in a study of stereotypy likewise reported a significant interaction between these two variables when "anxiety" was experimentally produced by means of electric shocks. The MAS appears to select individuals who are significantly above the mean in activation, and from the results of Schnore (1959) and Feldman (1958) it seems safe to conclude that anticipation of shock also leads to increased levels of physiological activity. In short, generalizing from the induced tension experiments, it seems reasonable to suppose that a patient's muscular tension in a small focal area might have the general effect of increasing activation. If such is the case symptomatic treatment might have significant general as well as specific effects. Although based on only one patient, Yates' (1958) results from symptomatic treatment of tics seems encouraging with respect to the feasibility of research in this general area.

Summary: The neuropsychological dimension of activation may be briefly described as follows. The continuum extending from sleep at the low activation end to "excited" states at the high activation end is a function of the amount of cortical bombardment by the ARAS, such that the greater the cortical bombardment the higher the activation. The shape of the curve relating level of performance to level of activation is that of an inverted U: from low activation up to a point that is optimal for a given performance or function, level of performance rises monotonically with increasing activation level; but past this opitmal point the relation becomes nonmonotonic: further increase in activation beyond this point produces fall in performance level, this fall being directly related to the amount of the increase in level of activation.

Long before the discovery of the ARAS the behavioral evidence of Duffy, Freeman, and others of the "energetics" group had suggested the existence of some such brain mechanism. Moreover, learning theorists of the Hull school have in their concept of the general drive state come very close to the activation principle. Up to the present time they have employed physiological measures only sparingly and have restricted their use to the aversive aspects of drive. But with evidence that such measures may also be applied to nonaversive (appetitional) drive, it seems likely that the present rather unsatisfactory measures of drive may eventually be replaced by physiological indicants.

Activation has a number of main characteristics that may be listed as follows: (*a*) Activation has no steering function in behavior. (*b*) It is considerably broader than emotion. (*c*) Activation is not a state that can be inferred from knowledge of antecedent conditions alone, because it is the product of an interaction between internal conditions such as hunger or thirst, and external cues. (*d*) Activation does not fit very well into the S-R formula. It is a phenomenon of slow changes, of drifts in level with a time order of minutes (even hours) not of seconds or fractions thereof. (*e*) Activation is a quantifiable dimension and the evidence indicates that physiological measures show a sufficiently high intra-individual concordance for quantifying this dimension.

It is suggested that activation is mediated chiefly through the ARAS which seems, in the main, to be an intensity system. Neurophysiological findings strongly suggest that it may be possible to achieve more precise measurement of activation through a direct recording of discharge by the ARAS into the cerebral cortex. Research on this problem is urgently needed.

The concept of activation appears to have wide application to phenomena in the field of clinical psychology. As one illustration, in this paper, activation was applied to clinical phenomena of tensional symptoms.

Science, 1958, vol. 127, p. 150

Effects of Stimulation of Brain Stem on Tachistoscopic Perception[1]

Joaquin M. Fuster

This report concerns part of a study conducted on rhesus monkeys to investigate the effects of electrical stimulation of different sites in the brain on tachistoscopic perception.

For this investigation the animals were first trained to discriminate between stereometric objects presented in pairs, by placing food reward under one of the objects of each pair. After this preliminary training without restriction of exposure duration, each animal was subjected to several series of trials at different exposures; the number of correct responses was noted, and the reaction time was automatically measured. The testing apparatus was a modification of that used by Harlow, which for our purposes was transformed into a tachistoscope (Fig. 1). Its main feature was an argon-mercury bulb which was used to flash briefly a light of controllable duration and constant intensity upon the objects. The pairs of white objects (for

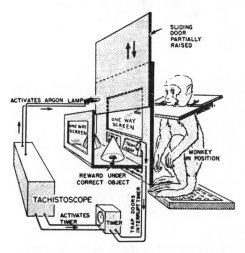

Fig. 1. Testing apparatus for visual discrimination. The monkey is shown in one of the plastic collars (schematically represented) by which the animals were permanently held to protect the electrode mount from their hands and to restrict them partially for performing the experimental task.

1 This work was aided by grants from the following sources: Carnegie Corporation of New York; Office of Naval Research contract NR–144–102, Nonr 233(32); U.S. Public Health Service, grant B–611; Ford Foundation. I am especially indebted, also, to Robert B. Livingston, H. W. Magoun, Donald B. Lindsley, and K. F. Killam for their help and advice throughout the course of this investigation.

example, a cone and a 12-sided pyramid of similar proportions) were placed in a dark field in front of the animal. A brief acoustic signal preceded by 2 seconds the illumination of the objects; this signal was in no case concomitant with the visual stimulus. Selection of the correct member of each pair was always followed by a food reward. The position of the correct member was changed randomly from trial to trial.

Electrodes were implanted in the animals' brains so that the effects of electrical stimulation could be studied. To date, six animals have been used in the investigation. The electrode placements were histologically verified. As a rule, currents were always used that did not cause any apparent effect on the normal behavior of the awake animal, regardless of the placement of the electrodes. A biphasic square wave current, of 300 cy/sec. and intensities between 100 and 300 μa, was used as a norm. Each animal was used as its own control. In the experimental series, the electrical stimulation was applied during each trial period, starting 2 seconds in advance of the flash and persisting until the animal had made its choice.

Stimulation of the core of the brain stem at the level of the mesencephalon consistently increased the animals' efficiency at discrimination, as indicated by significantly higher percentages of correct responses and shorter reaction times as compared with the controls (Fig. 2). Stimulation through the same electrodes with intensities higher than the threshold for the elicitation of observable motor effects, such as generalized muscular jerks (startle reaction), eye movements, pupillary oscillations, vocalization, and so forth, had a deleterious effect on the performance of the animals, as indicated by the diminution

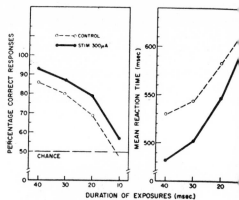

Fig. 2. Effects of stimulation of the brain stem on tachistoscopic discrimination. Each plotted point is based on 100 trials.

of correct responses at all exposure durations and prolongation of reaction time. These effects were consistent and reproducible from animal to animal.

The same areas which upon mild stimulation facilitated tachistoscopic discrimination have previously been shown to evoke electroencephalographic and behavioral arousal in the sleeping or relaxed animal (Moruzzi & Magoun, 1949; Segundo, Arana, & French, 1955). These areas are in the rostral part of the brain stem activating system, which is mostly composed of the reticular formation of the midbrain tegmentum. Evoked potentials of long latency to sensory stimuli are also picked up in these areas (French, Verzeano, & Magoun, 1953). This was verified in the present investigation, by using the same electrodes for recording.

Both perceptual and motor processes involved in tachistoscopic discrimination appear to be facilitated by stimulation of the reticular activating system. It is difficult to determine whether the effects on reaction time are a direct consequence of the facilitatory effect on perception or independent of it. However, it seems likely that the reticular facilitation is primarily upon "central integrative time," rather than upon peripheral transmission time.

These findings give support to the hypothesis that the reticular activating system, whose primary role has been demonstrated to be that of central mediator for the achievement and maintenance of wakefulness by means of activation of the cortex, extends its function to the alert state as a further manifestation of the same physiological role, subserving basic attentive behavior. Its different degrees of excitation underlie the gradation of this function from deep sleep to extreme alertness. Excitation of this brain stem system induces general activity of the cortex (arousal), presumably facilitating its receptivity to the sensory impulses ascending over the classic sensory paths. The facilitation of tachistoscopic discrimination by electrical stimulation of the same system may be considered as an example of such an effect on visual perception.

Chapter 5

EXPLORATORY BEHAVIOR

This, too, is a new chapter in the study of motivation, and its appearance has represented a major revolution in thinking about motivated behavior. Because it is new, it means slightly different things to different psychologists, a fact that accounts for the somewhat greater heterogeneity of the papers. Running through each paper, however, is the notion that higher organisms are motivated by novelty, that they are curious, and that they explore in the absence of motivation supplied by primary and secondary drives. Furthermore, and most importantly, if they are deprived of the opportunity to perform these activities, especially in early life, irreparable effects occur that cannot be explained simply in terms of the missing activities.

The eleven papers in this section include a number of different aspects of exploratory behavior. Their selection represented one of the most difficult editorial tasks because of the great variety of conceptualizations and as yet little agreed-upon coherence. Each of the papers, however, represents an important contribution or illustrates a different example of the motivational relevance of exploratory behavior.

Berlyne's work is placed first partly because of the range of variables covered in the study, but mainly because of his contributions to this field. Perhaps more than anyone else he has added empirical data to a theoretical framework. This paper is an excellent example of his work.

The next two papers are also empirical experiments designed to specific aspects of this topic. Wendt *et al.* show that deprivation of visual experience serves as a motivator to monkeys to seek and continue visual exploration. Sackett *et al.* show in a similar vein that after visual deprivation even hungry rats prefer a visually complex environment to food rewards. Following their paper are two letters, one by Hillix suggesting an interpretation more consistent with drive theory, and an answer by Sackett defending his interpretation. This pair of letters are most effective in making the distinction between these interpretations clear, and in showing how different exploratory behavior is from that predicted by a drive interpretation.

The theoretical paper by McClelland and Clark is an attempt to spell out a model of what antecedent conditions lead to positive and negative affect—pleasure and pain. It is also a proposal to reintroduce these affective concepts back into motivational psychology by providing operational definitions that are not circular. The proposal to make affective processes dependent upon a discrepancy between expectancy (previous experience) and current stimulation was adapted from Hebb and is similar to related proposals offered by Berlyne, Hunt, Malmo, and others. These terms, and the concepts behind them had been nearly outlawed from experimental psychology since the days of Watson, partly because of the subjectivism they inspire, and partly because of the difficulties in defining them either operationally or logically. McClelland and Clark have provided such a definition, and have permitted the opening of a freer theoretical environment for motivational theories. Their particular definition may turn out to require modification; to date, too few experiments have been performed to determine this, although the paper by Haber represents with some success a direct test of the theory.

Gilmore has written an historical-theoretical review of the research on play behavior. While play clearly falls under this general topic, it has been poorly integrated and even more inadequately understood. Gilmore discusses some of the reasons for this and presents the two major theoretical attempts to explain the motivational antecedents and effects of play behavior. Even these two models, of Freud and Piaget, have not been able to lead to much experimental research; Gilmore points out the reasons for this along with the results of an extensive experiment of his own.

The last three papers represent perhaps the newest and most far-reaching extension of this topic. In a number of recent articles, including this one, Hunt has presented and reviewed the evidence of the variation in stimulation, the opportunities to respond to such variation, and its effects on development of normal motivational patterns in infancy and childhood. The important part of this developmental process is its generality—apparently the particular characteristics of the stimuli being explored are unimportant. The importance lies rather with the development of strategies for interacting with the environment, strategies that underlie intelligence, curiosity, internalization of many motivational processes—in fact nearly everything that distinguishes an alert, active, creative individual from one who is none of these things. It is perhaps with this paper that motivational theory comes farthest from a simple drive theory of motivation. It does not deny that drives exist, but it diminishes their importance with respect to nearly all patterns of motivated behavior. The continued elaboration and support for work in this direction should bring the most profound changes in the next decade, and this paper will be one of the guideposts.

Two slightly older papers have also been providing seminal influences. Bowlby, primarily studying children who were isolated from parents and placed in emotion- and novelty-sterile environments in wartime Britain, found different patterns of disturbance depending upon the time at which the separation occurred. Separation prior to six months seemed to have few permanent effects, and those that occurred were easily overcome when the separation ended. Those, however, occurring between six months and two-to-three years were nearly irreversible in their effects, in that return to normal daily family life could not correct the emotional and intellectual defects. While these results were studied without benefit of experimental controls and thus are undoubtedly the result of a number of factors acting together, the extent of the result adds further support to the importance of activities at these ages. The final paper, by Harlow and Zimmermann, studies the same kinds of problems in infant primates, in which much more experimental control is possible. This work clearly shows the relative importance of support and comfort as maternal activities, as compared to feeding functions in the well-being and development of infants.

Electroencephalography and Clinical Neurophysiology, 1965, vol. 18, pp. 156–161.

Effect of Stimulus Complexity and Incongruity on Duration of EEG Desynchronization[1]

D. E. Berlyne and P. McDonnell

Introduction

A substantial body of experimentation has shown exploratory responses to occur as part of a comprehensive "orientation reaction," which includes all the indices of heightened arousal (Robinson and Gantt, 1947; Sokolov, 1958; Berlyne, 1960). The most important determinants of the strength and direction of exploratory behavior are the "collative" stimulus properties (e.g. novelty, surprisingness, complexity, incongruity, ambiguity), so called because they derive from collation or comparison of stimulus elements experienced at different times or in different por-

tions of a stimulus field (Berlyne, 1960). Investigation of the influence of collative variables on the orientation reaction is therefore called for in order to round out the picture. Since, as more and more writers are recognizing, the newer concept of "arousal" has much in common with the older concept of "drive," verification that collative variables affect arousal processes would have far-reaching implications for motivation theory (Berlyne, 1960, 1963a, in press).

Previous experiments have shown that the magnitude of the galvanic skin response (GSR) increases with degree of inter-response *conflict* (suspected of underlying all the collative variables), with *surprisingness* and with *novelty* (Berlyne, 1961; Berlyne *et al.*, 1963). The independent variables of the experiment to be reported were those

[1] This investigation was supported by Public Health Research Grant MH-06324 from the National Institute of Mental Health. The data were collected by P. McDonnell for a thesis submitted in accordance with the requirements for the M.A. Degree of the University of Toronto.

LOW-COMPLEXITY CATEGORIES

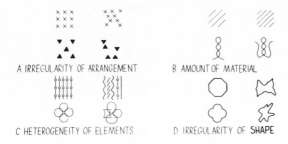

HIGH-COMPLEXITY CATEGORIES

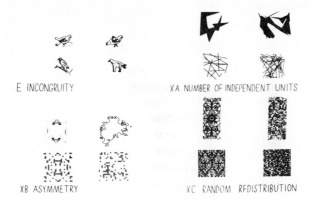

Fig. 1. The stimulus material.

represented by the patterns displayed in Fig. 1. These are all variables that might be covered by terms such as *complexity* and *incongruity* in everyday parlance. They have been shown to have significant and, on the whole, similar effects on the duration of exploratory inspection and on the direction of exploratory choice (Berlyne, 1957, 1958, 1963b; Berlyne and Lawrence, 1964; Berlyne and Lewis, 1963), on ratings of "pleasingness" and "interestingness" (Berlyne, 1963b; Berlyne

and Lawrence, 1964), and on paired-associate verbal learning (Berlyne *et al.*, in preparation).

These complexity and incongruity variables were found to have no effect on the GSR when the patterns received 0.2 sec exposures (Berlyne and Lawrence, 1964). With 3-second exposures, the incidence of the GSR was greater for more complex or irregular patterns but only when subjects were extrinsically motivated (that is, instructed to attend carefully for the sake of a later recognition test). Furthermore, the effect, though statistically significant, was not commensurate with the pronounced effects that these same variables have been found repeatedly to exert on exploration and other forms of behavior. It was therefore decided to examine the influence of these variables on the EEG component of the orientation reaction (that is, alpha blocking) in the hope that this might provide a more direct and sensitive measure of heightened arousal in the form of visual attentiveness. The hypothesis to be tested was that more complex or incongruous stimulus patterns would evoke longer-lasting desynchronization.

Method and Material

Apparatus

A Grass Model 5 polygraph was used to record EEG on two channels with 5P1 preamplifiers. A third channel marked time in seconds and registered the beginning and end of each stimulus pattern. A tracing was taken from each side of the head by means of one silver-disc electrode attached to an adjustable head-band and placed over the upper occipital area and one electrode attached to the ear-lobe with a plastic clip.

The subject sat in an easy-chair, facing a screen, in a dimly lit 7 x 12 foot compartment within a shielded chamber. The experimenter and the polygraph were stationed in an adjoining compartment within the shielding. A Kodak Carousel automatic projector was placed outside the shielding and projected slides through a nipple. It was controlled by Hunter timers and set to show slides for 3 seconds each with intervals of 15 seconds.

Subjects

In all, 107 male students from first, second, and third year nonspecializing psychology classes were tested. Of these, 19 were discarded for the following reasons: 11 because alpha waves occupied less than 25 percent of the tracing in the absence of

stimulation, 1 because of persistent alpha waves, 5 because of apparatus failures, 2 because they disclosed that they had seen the patterns previously. This left 88 subjects whose tracings were analyzed.

Design

The stimulus material consisted of negative slides (white on black) of the 32 patterns in Fig. 1. The patterns were divided into two subsets, A and B, of 16, each containing the more complex (more irregular, more incongruous) member (the right-hand one in Fig. 1) of one pair and the less complex member of the other pair in each of the 8 categories. Subsets A and B were then each arranged in a sequence that was randomized except that each successive group of four contained first the two patterns from one category and then the two from another category. The more and less complex items were thus evenly distributed through the sequence. Of the 88 subjects, 22 received subset A in the original sequence, 22 subset B in the original sequence, 22 subset A in the original sequence reversed, and 22 subset B in the original sequence reversed.

Each of these groups of 22 subjects was further divided into an *extrinsically motivated* and a *non-extrinsically motivated* subgroup of 11 subjects each. The extrinsically motivated subjects were instructed to look at the patterns carefully because they were later to undergo a "visual-discrimination test" in which they would be required to pick out the patterns that were about to be shown among others. The non-extrinsically motivated subjects were told that they were simply to look at the patterns. It was stressed that this was not a learning task and that no questions would be asked about the patterns at any time. The experimental patterns were each shown twice in succession to study possible habituation with repetition.

Procedure

After the subject had been seated and the electrodes had been placed, the experimenter spent about 15 min talking to him and endeavoring to put him at his ease. The experimenter then left the compartment to calibrate the polygraph and obtain a sample of the subject's resting EEG response with eyes closed, after which the instructions appropriate to the subject's subgroup were given.

A tray of 10 practice slides was then projected. There followed four trays each containing first 2 practice slides and then 4 patterns, shown twice consecutively, belonging to the experimental sequence. The practice slides bore patterns of the same general nature as the experimental patterns. They were used in order to habituate orientation reactions to the sounds made by the projector and to allow time for alpha waves to appear.

Between succeeding trays, the door of the experimental compartment was opened, and the subject was informed that there would be another tray. Between the third and fourth trays, the light was turned on for 30 seconds and the subject was told that there would be a brief delay. These measures were taken in the hope of staving off habituation and drowsiness.

Scoring

In general, the scoring criteria were those adopted by Wilson and Wilson (1959) in their study of desynchronization in response to repeated flashes of light. The tracing from the side of the head that showed the greater alpha amplitude or the greater frequency changes in response to stimulation was selected for analysis, but the other tracing was used in case of ambiguity. The scoring was done by an experimenter who did not know at the time which response corresponded to which stimulus pattern. Desynchronization was deemed to have occurred when either alpha waves decreased in amplitude by at least 50 percent or the dominant frequency exceeded 13 c/seconds.

The time between the disappearance of alpha activity or the onset of stimulation, whichever occurred later, and the first return of at least 3 alpha waves after stimulation ended was taken as the duration of desynchronization. If no alpha waves appeared between the appearance of one stimulus pattern and the appearance of the next, that trial was assigned a score of 17.6 seconds. This was the time elapsing between the appearance of one pattern on the screen and the onset of the sound from the projector that heralded the appearance of the next pattern. Fig. 2 shows samples of different forms of tracing that were obtained and how duration was measured in each case.

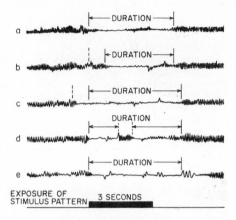

Fig. 2. Samples of different forms of EEG response, showing how duration of desynchronization was measured in each case.

Results

As in other experiments using the same stimulus material, the results for the 8 categories of patterns, representing distinct though related variables, were analyzed both separately and collectively.

Table 1 shows the mean durations of desynchronization for less and more complex patterns. The mean was greater for the more complex patterns over all categories and in every category except Category D. According to analyses of variance (see the last two columns in Table 1), the difference was significant at the .001 level for all categories together, at the .01 level for Category B, and at the .05 level for Categories A, E, and XC.

The means for extrinsically and nonextrinsically motivated subjects were 6.0 and 6.1 seconds respectively. Those for the first and second presentations of patterns were 6.0 and 6.1 seconds

TABLE 1

MEAN DURATION OF EEG DESYNCHRONIZATION
(IN SECONDS)

	Category	Less Complex	More Complex	F(1,258 df)	P
A	Irregularity of Arrangement	5.8	6.5	6.08	<.05
B	Amount of Material	5.7	6.6	10.17	<.01
C	Heterogeneity of Elements	6.0	6.4	—	NS
D	Irregularity of Shape	6.3	6.0	—	NS
E	Incongruity	5.4	6.5	6.28	<.05
XA	Number of Independent Units	5.7	6.1	—	NS
XB	Asymmetry	6.0	6.3	—	NS
XC	Random Redistribution	5.6	6.2	4.98	<.05
	All Categories	5.8	8.3	24.95	<.001

respectively. Neither these differences nor any of the interactions reached significance.

There was, on the other hand, a significant tendency for desynchronization to become briefer as the session continued. The ranking correlation coefficient (Kendall's *tau*) between how early an exposure came in the sequence and how long a period of desynchronization it evoked was −.48, and $p < .001$.

Discussion

The hypothesis that more complex or incongruous stimulus patterns evoke longer-lasting desynchronization has thus received confirmation. On the basis of this and previous experiments, we can put forward with fair confidence the view that the collative stimulus properties influence arousal processes. In this experiment, the effect occurred even when there was no extrinsic motivation and subjects were given no special reason to attend to, or be aroused by, the stimulus patterns. No extrinsic reward or punishment hinged on absorption of the information contained in them, and no motor activity, other than eye movements, depended

on them. So the findings are consonant with the conclusion, suggested by a variety of other phenomena, that such characteristics of the external environment as novelty, surprisingness and complexity can induce heightened drive independently of visceral needs and nociceptive events. An essential link in the extensions of motivation theory that have been proposed to take account of exploratory and other behavior governed by collative variables (Berylne, 1960, 1963a, 1964) has been corroborated.

The exact significance of the relation between duration of desynchronization and stimulus complexity remains, of course, to be worked out. Since more complex or incongruous stimulus patterns can be said, granted certain assumptions, to have a higher information content, it might be conjectured that desynchronization continues until the bulk of the information with which a pattern is charged has been assimilated and uncertainty has fallen to a threshold value. This conjecture would explain why alpha activity takes longer to reemerge after a pattern bearing more information has been encountered. It is, however, hard to reconcile with the fact that the second presentation of a pattern evoked, on the average, as protracted a spell of desynchronization as the first presentation although much of the information must surely have been absorbed by the time the first presentation ended. All we can suppose at present is that the duration of desynchronization somehow measures the extent to which the impact of a stimulus pattern activates the arousal system.

It is rather surprising that desynchronization was not more prolonged after the first presentation of a pattern than after the second presentation and that it was not lengthened by extrinsic motivation. In an earlier experiment sampling the effects of the same stimulus patterns on the GSR (Berlyne *et al.*, 1963), there was a marked drop in GSR incidence from the first to the second and third presentation, and extrinsic motivation raised GSR incidence significantly. The fact that our patterns were much more intricate and more heavily laden with information than the flashes and tones that are usually used in EEG work may have had something to do with these negative findings. After many more presentations of one pattern, habituation would surely have appeared. Russian writers, especially Sokolov (1958), have regularly reported that "signal stimuli," that is, stimuli whose information content must be processed in order to guide a motor response, evoke more pronounced and extinction-resistant orientation reactions than others. On the other hand, Wilson and Wilson (1959) found that whether or not subjects had to perform a motor response to their light flashes (squeezing a rubber bulb) made no difference to the duration of desynchronization.

Numerous experiments have shown that indices of the orientation reaction will wane as an identical stimulus is repeated, reviving when a change is introduced. Our finding that the duration of desynchronization decreased as exposures of patterns succeeded one another, even though one pattern was replaced by another after every two exposures, shows that the response to novelty as such will habituate if novel stimuli continue to appear. This extends what Berlyne *et al.* (1963) found with the same visual patterns and the GSR and what Kratin (1959) found with sounds changing in pitch and the EEG.

Summary

1. Human subjects were exposed to a sequence of visual patterns, each shown twice consecutively. Exposures lasted 3 seconds and were separated by intervals of 15 seconds. The patterns belonged to 8 categories, representing various complexity and incongruity variables.

2. More complex or incongruous patterns evoked, on the average, longer desynchronization than less complex or incongruous patterns (6.3 seconds as compared with 5.8 seconds). The difference was found to be statistically significant when the data for all 8 categories were examined together and when the data for 4 of the categories (representing irregularity of arrangement, amount of material, incongruity and random redistribution) were examined separately.

3. No significant difference appeared between first and second presentations of the same patterns between subjects who were extrinsically motivated (told to attend carefully for the sake of a later recognition test) and not extrinsically motivated, and none of the interactions was significant. There was, however, a significant tendency for desynchronization to grow shorter as the session continued.

4. The findings are discussed in relation to theoretical and experimental work on motivational aspects of exploratory behavior and related phenomena.

Science, January 25, 1963, vol. 139, pp. 336–338

Self-Maintained Visual Stimulation in Monkeys After Long-Term Visual Deprivation[*][1]

Richard H. Wendt, David F. Lindsley, W. Ross Adey, and Stephen S. Fox

It was established in an earlier study (Fox, 1962) that the amount of visual stimulation a monkey will give itself is a function of the duration of deprivation from light just prior to the test period. At the same time it was suggested that the response rate is also a function of the long-term level of visual input from the environment. In the study reported here, monkeys with very different histories of exposure to visual stimulation were compared with respect to their rates of self-maintained visual stimulation after deprivation from light of fixed duration immediately prior to the test.

Within the first month of life two monkeys [one a *Macaca mulatta,* one a *Macaca irus* (a cynomolgus)] were taken from their mothers and maintained separately in totally dark air-conditioned boxes that were partially sound-proof and large enough to allow adequate exercise (see Lindsley, Wendt, Fugett, Lindsley, & Adey, 1962). These boxes were located in a light-tight

room; bottle feeding, handling, and feeding with solid foods were carried out in total darkness or with the animal's face effectively masked. To prevent retinal degeneration and blindness (Riesen, 1958) the monkeys were exposed to diffuse unpatterned light for 1 hour daily, as follows. Each animal was removed from the living quarters in total darkness and seated in a restraining chair. Its neck was placed in a horizontal pillory which restrained the head comfortably and prevented the admission of light from below. Two domes of frosted Lucite, placed one inside the other, were positioned over the head of the animal so as to admit only unpatterned light from an incandescent light source housed in a chamber which covered the top of the chair. After this daily 1-hour exposure to light the monkeys were returned to the dark living quarters. The control animals were two monkeys (one a *Macaca mulatta,* the other a *Macaca irus*), of the same age as the experimental animals, that had been raised normally.

After 16 months under these conditions a phase of daily test sessions was initiated in which the rate of self-maintained visual stimulation was measured for both groups. Each animal was placed in a restraining chair and

* Reprinted from *Science* by permission. Copyright © 1963 by the AAAS.
1 We thank Richard Fugett for his part in caring for the animals. This study was conducted at the University of California, Los Angeles. It was supported by the U.S. Public Health Service (grant B-1883) and by the U.S. Air Force Office of Scientific Research [contract AF 49 (638)-686].

allowed to press a lever with its hands. Each lever press produced light for 1 second inside the chamber above the translucent domes. The duration of the light was independent of the duration of the initiating lever press, and independent of lever presses made while the light was on. Two measures were recorded: (i) the total number of responses (lever presses) and (ii) the total number of illuminations. In this way it was possible to determine the total duration of light produced by the animal and to obtain some general index of the monkey's motivational state as measured by the total number of responses. The test session for each experimental animal was terminated when the monkey had produced light of total duration of 1 hour. The regimen established during the first 16 months of life was thereby maintained. In order that the control animals and the experimental animals should experience equivalent periods of visual deprivation in each 24-hour period immediately prior to the test session, the control animals were caged in totally dark living quarters, when they were not in the test apparatus, during the phase of test sessions. The test session for the control animals was arbitrarily fixed at 2 hours. Thus, both the experimental and the control animals were maintained in darkness for at least 22 hours each day during the phase of test sessions. All the animals were tested daily, with the exception of occasional missed days distributed randomly throughout the 19 weeks of the study.

Within the first week of test sessions the animals that had been raised in darkness showed rates of response strikingly higher than even the highest rates for the control animals of this or the earlier study (Fox, 1962). In the second week of test sessions the average response rate for the two experimental animals had risen to 3400 and 2350 responses per hour, respectively, as compared with averages of 100 per hour for the two controls. The dark-reared animals maintained this high rate of response consistently in test sessions extending over a period of nearly 5 months; there was no indication of a decline in response rate during this period. By contrast, response rates for the control animals were never higher than about 500 responses per hour, even after these animals had been maintained in continuous darkness, except during the test sessions, for 9 weeks.[2] Comparable differences between results for the experimental and the control animals were also seen when the total number of illuminations per hour was taken as a measure of response.

One might raise the question, Was the response rate in fact maintained by the visual stimulation which followed each lever press or was it maintained by kinesthetic or auditory stimulation produced by the act of manipulating the lever? To answer this question, different experimental conditions were established: from week 7 to week 10 the daily test session for the experimental animals consisted of a continu-

[2] A third experimental animal (*M. mulatta*), which was subjected to visual deprivation for a shorter period, showed a similar but less marked elevation of response rates. Testing of this animal was begun after 15 weeks of visual deprivation, when the monkey was 4 months old. Its rate of responding for light (1500 to 2000 responses per hour for weeks 2 to 8 of testing) was significantly higher than that of its normal control of the same age, yet lower than the response rates of the other two experimental animals. It is not known whether the intermediate response rate of this experimental animal is related to the shorter period of visual deprivation or due simply to factors of motor development.

ous session divided into three periods. The initial period was a 1-hour extinction period during which the monkeys had access to the lever as usual but a lever press did not turn on the light. During the second period the animals were allowed to press the lever freely and each lever press produced light, as in the test sessions for weeks 1 to 6. After the animals had pressed the lever enough times to produce a total of 30 minutes of light, the light was automatically turned on and remained on continuously for a period of 30 minutes —the third and final period of the test session. On this regimen each experimental animal continued to receive daily a total of 1 hour of light.

Under these conditions the experimental animals quickly became quite sophisticated, and extinction of lever pressing was rapid during the initial, dark period of each test session, the rate for each experimental animal being about 200 responses per hour. Response rates were equally low when the light was continuous, during the final period of the test session. By contrast, the experimental animals responded at rates of between 2000 and 3000 responses per hour during the second period of the test session. Thus, the experimental animals responded at very low rates when lever pressing did not produce light, or when the light was already present, but at very high rates when lever pressing produced light.

From weeks 10 to 19 the experimental animals were placed on a schedule of 6-hour daily test sessions, in order that the effect of long test sessions on the response rates might be studied. It was found that response rates declined only about 15 percent from hour 1 to hour 6 of the test sessions for the

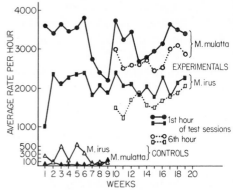

Fig. 1. Average rates of lever pressing for unpatterned light for experimental monkeys and for normal control monkeys during 19 weeks of test sessions. The points joined by solid lines represent the average number of lever presses produced by the animal during the first hour of its test sessions for the week indicated. The points joined by dotted lines for the experimental animals (weeks 10 to 19) represent the average number of lever presses produced by the animal during hour 6 of its test sessions for the week indicated. Data presented for the experimental animals for weeks 7 to 9 are rates for the second period only of the test sessions; rates during the initial, extinction period were excluded from the calculation.

Macaca mulatta and less for the *M. irus* (see Fig. 1). Furthermore, there was no evidence of a decline in response rates during this 10-week period, average rates of response having been approximately as high on week 19 as on week 10. The observation that the light-deprived animals pressed the lever for light at rates of 2000 to 3000 presses per hour for 6 continuous hours daily over a period of 10 weeks afforded a striking demonstration of the insatiable character of the behavior.

It should be emphasized that the experimental animals did not differ in spontaneous behavior, except in their high rates for response light, or in physical development from the normal controls. Since the experimental design prevented assessment of factors such as isolation from other animals and reduced auditory stimulus, we cannot be certain that light deprivation was the essential factor in producing the high rates of self-maintained visual stimulation, although this seems highly likely. It does appear that an animal's previous visual experience is an important determinant of his later need for visual stimulation, but it is not yet known whether visual deprivation occurring early in an animal's life and deprivation occurring late in its life are equally effective in producing the behavior described.

Although studies of normal animals have revealed regulation by the animal of visual input (Fox, 1962; Lockhard, 1962), the relationship of the phenomenon described here to the many findings on sensory restriction reported in the literature is not clear. The persistent electrophysiological changes reported by

Fourment and her co-workers (Fourment & Scherrer, 1961; Fourment & Cramer, 1961) for rabbits exposed to long-term super- or subnormal illumination may be relevant, indicating underlying neural mechanisms.

We conclude that the effects of short-term experimental sensory deprivation cannot be isolated from the total sensory history of the animal. The basic question of the origin of the apparently insatiable responding for light, at extremely high rates, will remain unanswered until extensive developmental studies are undertaken.

Summary: Newborn monkeys reared in darkness for 16 months, except for daily 1-hour periods of exposure to unpatterned light, were allowed to press a lever to obtain unpatterned light. The animals showed apparently insatiable responding, at rates that were extremely high as compared with rates for normally reared control animals.

Science, May 27, 1963, vol. 141, pp. 518–520.

Food versus Perceptual Complexity as Rewards for Rats Previously Subjected to Sensory Deprivation[*][1]

Gene P. Sackett, Patricia Keith-Lee, and Robert Treat

Theory and research in the study of motivation assume that a hungry animal will learn those responses that produce food and cease making responses that do not produce food. Drive theories, especially, assume that operations such as deprivation of food or water

[*] Reprinted from *Science* by permission. Copyright © 1963 by the AAAS.
[1] A paper based on this study was read by one of us (G.P.S.) at the Midwestern Psychological Association meeting, Chicago, 1963.

are sufficient conditions for producing motivation, and that the presence of food or water after a particular response is a sufficient condition for learning that response, provided enough learning trials have been given. This report questions the assumption that food reward is a *uniformly* sufficient condition for reinforcing behavior in hungry animals (see for example Hull, 1943; Brown, 1961; Mowrer, 1961). Specifically, it is asked if hungry animals, reared in an environment where they were deprived of varied visual stimulation during behavioral development, will prefer to eat food, or prefer to have commerce with visually complex stimuli.

Thirty-six hooded rats were weaned and placed in cages made out of 1-qt metal fruit cans, one rat per can, on the evening of the day on which their eyes opened. The median age of eye-opening was 15 days. These animals remained in the cans for the next 45 days. Half of the cans were painted white. A 6-volt light bulb, bolted to the inside of the can top, provided 24-hour illumination for each white can. The open end of the can was placed on hardware cloth, which served as the bottom of the cage. The animals could not see out of the side or top of the cage, and could see brown paper, only, through the hardware cloth. The other cans were painted black, and were placed in a different, completely dark room. The dark-reared animals received light (.01 mlam) for 15 minutes on each day. The experimental animals, subjected to sensory deprivation, thus consisted of (i) 18 animals, half male and half female, reared in a constantly lighted, white cage, and (ii) 18 animals, half male and half female, reared in a constantly dark, black cage. Control animals, ten males and ten females, were also weaned on the day that their eyes opened, and were immediately placed, three rats per cage, in the normal colony environment.

After the 45th day of sensory deprivation, the deprived rats were placed in colony cages under the identical conditions of the normally reared animals. At the time of this experiment, the rats were 125 to 140 days old. There-

fore, the deprived animals had been living under normal visual stimulating conditions for 65 to 80 days. The subjects had not been deprived of food or water, or subjected to any procedures involving electric shock or other noxious stimuli.

The apparatus was a wooden T-maze with a 6- by 12-inch start-box, a 6- by 12-inch straight alley from start box to the end of the choice-point area, and 6- by 24-inch detachable goal arms. The floor and walls of the start-box and straight alley were unpainted masonite. One of the goal arms was half black and half white. One wall was white, the other black. Half of the floor area, that adjacent to the black wall, was black, while the floor adjacent to the white wall was white. This goal arm is referred to as the *simple*-stimulus goal. The floor and walls of the second goal arm contained a black-and-white checkerboard pattern. There were approximately equal numbers of black and white 1-inch squares in the pattern. This goal arm is referred to as the *complex*-stimulus goal.

For half of the experimental animals and half of the control group, food was placed in the simple-stimulus goal. For the other half of the subjects in each rearing condition, food was placed in the complex-stimulus goal. Thus, half of the rats received food in the half-black, half-white goal if they chose that arm on a trial, while the remaining half received food in the checkerboard-patterned goal.

Twenty-five massed trials were given to each subject on one day. The goal arm containing food was on the right or left side of the maze on any trial as determined by a random schedule.

Two days before the start of experimental trials the animals were deprived of food, but not of water. After 24 hours of food deprivation, the animals were adapted to the maze start-box and choice-point area, and were allowed to eat 15 of the food pellets (45 mg) used as reinforcement, which were scattered about the maze floor at the choice point. The rat could neither see into, nor enter, either goal arm. This adaptation period lasted for 10 minutes. Experimental trials began 24 hours after adaptation. The subject received no food between the adaptation and test periods.

Immediately before the start of the first experimental trial, the subject was placed in the goal arm which would contain food on his test trials. Two pellets were placed in a small cup at the back of the goal arm. The subject was allowed 1 minute to eat the pellets and to explore the goal area. Trial No. 1 commenced 45 seconds after the end of this pretrial feeding period.

On each experimental trial the animal was allowed a maximum of 5 minutes to leave the start-box and enter one of the goal arms. A choice-response was defined as entering the goal far enough so that the experimenter could close the goal-box door, touching no more than the rat's tail. After a choice, the animal was left in the goal arm for 30 seconds. The time between trials was 45 seconds.

The difference in number of correct responses, defined as choice of the goal containing food, between males and females was not significant. The difference between animals reared in the constantly lighted, white cans, and in the constantly dark, black cans, was also not significant. The interactions of sex, and white versus black rearing cages, with the goal-stimulus complexity variable were also not significant

(all $P > .25$). Therefore, the data are pooled for males and females, and for both black and white rearing cages.

The mean number of correct responses on the 25 trials made by subjects in each rearing and goal-stimulus condition are as follows: (i) sensory deprivation, food in checkerboard goal, 16.6; (ii) sensory deprivation, food in half-black, half-white goal, 12.1; (iii) normal rearing, checkerboard goal, 15.3; and (iv) normal rearing, half-black, half-white goal, 15.5. Analysis of variance indicates that goal stimulus and the goal stimulus × rearing condition interaction are statistically significant (both $P < .01$). Thus the mean of 15.9 correct responses for all subjects that could obtain food at the checkerboard goal is significantly higher than the mean of 13.8 for the subjects that could obtain food at the simple-stimulus goal. The interaction of rearing condition and goal stimulus is produced because the mean number of responses to food by animals reared in sensory deprivation and tested with food in the simple-stimulus goal is significantly lower than the means for the other three groups.

A second breakdown of the data is shown in Fig. 1. This figure presents the mean percentage of correct responses on each trial for each of the four groups, averaged in blocks of five trials. The striking finding illustrated here is that little or no learning to go to food occurred in the group reared in sensory deprivation that received food in the simple-stimulus goal. In fact, the first four points for this group are either at or below the 50-percent performance level expected on the basis of chance. To further illustrate the nature of this finding, on 21 out of the 25 trials a majority of the subjects in this group chose the checkerboard goal

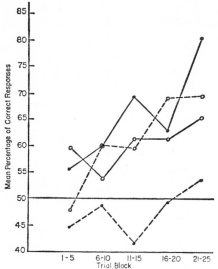

Fig. 1. Percent of subjects in each group going to the goal arm containing food on each trial, averaged over blocks of five trials. Solid line, filled circles: rats subjected to sensory deprivation, food offered at patterned goal; dashed line, filled circles: rats subjected to sensory deprivation, food offered at half-black, half-white goal; solid line, open circles: normal rats, food offered at patterned goal; dashed line, open circles: normal rats, food offered at half-black, half-white goal.

rather than the half-black, half-white goal containing food $(P < .01)$. All curves for the other groups show the typical increasing function characteristic of learning data. It is also instructive to note that on the first block of trials even the normally reared animals tested with food on the simple-stimulus side exhibit a tendency to choose the more complex, checkerboard stimulus.

These results reveal one major empirical fact. Under the conditions of this experiment, food is not a uniformly reinforcing substance serving to increase the probability of responses associated with it. If the rat has been reared in visual sensory deprivation, even though he has not been subjected to sensory deprivation during his adult life, he does not prefer a response alternative

leading to food. Instead, he tends to choose a response alternative leading to a more perceptually complex, stimulating situation. Further, these data hint, although they do not show as clearly, that, for an animal subjected to sensory deprivation, the probability of going to food is higher than that for a normally reared animal if food is found in a complex visual-stimulus situation.

One problem concerning effects of sensory deprivation might be raised to question these results. The procedure used may have detrimentally affected the vision of the visually deprived animals. This problem is answered indirectly by the fact that the animals subjected to sensory deprivation and receiving food in the checkerboard goal *did* discriminate between the two goal stimuli. Thus, although retinal damage may have occurred, it was not sufficient to eliminate the subjects' ability to make a pattern discrimination.

If they can be replicated, results such as were found in this study must motivate a change in some of the current thinking concerning the necessary and sufficient conditions for choice behavior and for reinforcement. In the light of these data, the so-called "primary" biological needs, as such, do not appear to be the uniformly sufficient, let alone the necessary, conditions for motivation that have been assumed in the past. And, substances satisfying these "primary" biological needs do not appear to be the generally sufficient conditions thought to reinforce behavior and lead to learning.

The findings of this study are consistent with a number of investigations and formulations, such as the work of Harlow (1953a), Harlow & McClearn (1954), Harlow, Blazek & McClearn (1956), Dember (1956), Levin & Forgays

(1960). Their reports, concerned with the so-called curiosity, exploratory, and/or manipulatory motives, illustrate the importance of temporal changes in stimulation, and the complexity of environmental stimulation as determinants of the activation and persistence of approach responses. The present study expands on this earlier work, indicating that (i) need for perceptual experience, like need for food, may involve biological processes just as basic as the classical "primary" biological needs; and (ii) the effects of early perceptual deprivation on later behavior may persist, in the form of an extremely strong motive to respond to complex stimulation, throughout the life of the organism.

Summary: Rats raised in darkness or in a constantly lighted white cage go to food in a T-maze if the food is located in a checkerboard goal. They do not go to food if the food is located in a visually less complex, half-black, half-white goal. Normally raised rats go to food regardless of the visual complexity of the goal.

Science, November 22, 1963, vol. 142, pp. 1021–1022

Sensory Deprivation of Rats

A LETTER TO THE EDITORS OF *Science*

W. A. Hillix*

In a recent report (Sackett, Keith-Lee, & Treat, 1963) the authors say that "If the rat has been reared in visual sensory deprivation, even though he has not been subjected to sensory deprivation during his adult life, he does not prefer a response alternative leading to food. Instead, he tends to choose a response alternative leading to a more perceptually complex, stimulating situation."

The observation that is supposed to justify this statement is that rats reared in either uniformly white or uniformly black quart cans later fail to show typical learning to go to food placed in a half-white, half-black alley; they learn more quickly to go to food in an alley painted in a checkerboard pattern. The authors claim that "perceptual complexity" accounts for the difference.

I would claim that prolonged association of the simple stimuli with noxious conditions can more parsimoniously account for the difference. Eight years ago, Goodson and Brownstein (1955) showed that rats would avoid stimuli which had previously been associated with electric shock. It does not surprise me to find that they will also avoid stimuli which have been associated with 45 days of close confinement. Had I been confined for a third of my life as these rats had, I would go rather hungry before entering a situation which was reminiscent of that confinement. The authors could hardly have designed a "simple" arm for their maze

(half black, half white) better calculated to elicit any existing avoidance
responses from rats reared under both
of their "sensory deprivation" conditions.

The data themselves lend credence to
the logical possibility that creating a
secondarily motivating stimulus, rather
than perceptual deprivation, is the
critical step. As the authors themselves
point out, a majority of the sensory-
deprived subjects avoid the half-black,
half-white arm of the maze on 21 of the
25 massed learning trials. The authors'
Fig. 1, however, gives some indication
that the degree of avoidance lessens,
and hence that food *is* acting as a reinforcer. The tendency to go to the complex stimulus (away from the noxious
stimulus?) is certainly not increasing, as
it should if commerce with the complex
stimulus is truly preferred to food.

The figure, then, presents evidence
which is exactly contrary to the authors'
statement that "Under the conditions
of this experiment, food is not a uniformly reinforcing substance serving to

increase the probability of responses
associated with it." It is true that the
probability of response to the food side
in the critical group is not greater than
.5, but I doubt if many drive theorists
would make the blanket assertion that
it should be, given some imbalance in
the original probabilities of response,
and given some arbitrary limit on the
number of trials.

In summary, the authors have interpreted their results as supporting their
preconceptions despite the lack of the
controls necessary to justify the interpretation. I am not an exponent of a
"drive theory," but if I were, I would
not be concerned in the slightest with
the results reported. Rather, I would
suggest that the experiment be repeated
with appropriate controls, including a
group of animals which are restricted
45 days in the presence of a complex
stimulus. I would predict that such
animals would appear to be seeking
commerce with *simple* stimuli, if these
simple stimuli were less like the stimuli
associated with restriction.

Science, November 22, 1963, vol. 142, p. 1022.

Sensory Deprivation in Rats: A Reply to Hillix

A LETTER TO THE EDITORS OF *Science*

Gene Sackett*

This reply to the criticism by Hillix
might aptly be titled "To approach or
to avoid: that is the question." A control group composed of animals reared

in isolation in a visually complex environment certainly would have provided a valuable addition to our study.
Unfortunately, such a group was not
available at the time. However, data
will soon be made available concerning
rats reared under the same isolation

conditions as in our report, but in a black-white checkerboard environment. When run in a three stimulus, free-choice, situation involving no food deprivation or food rewards, these animals prefer a *checkerboard* visual stimulus similar to that present during restricted rearing, rather than the "simple stimuli . . . less like the stimuli associated with restriction" referred to by Hillix in his prediction. Also, a study by Musselman (1962, 1963) involving normally reared rats run without food deprivation or reward is pertinent. When adapted to a checkerboard stimulus and subsequently tested in a free-choice situation, these rats prefer the original complex stimulus to more "simple" stimuli (black, white, or black and white stripes). In this study, as in ours, animals adapted to more simple stimuli choose a more complex stimulus on the subsequent free-choice test trial.

Hillix's argument seems to stem from the anthropomorphic assumption that relative environmental confinement is a noxious stimulus for the hooded rat, perhaps even as noxious as electric shock. Some evidence on this point does not support his contention. Total confinement by binding or other means certainly has produced noxious physiological effects on rats. However, data by Welker (1959) show that rats prefer a small, dark, confined area to a larger, well-lighted area in a novel exploratory situation. Data by Berlyne (1955) reveal that close confinement (in a much smaller area than that employed in our experiment) immediately prior to testing had no effect on either the subsequent amount of exploration or on the particular stimulus objects explored, even though some of these objects were present during confinement. If confinement serves to produce "secondarily motivating stimuli," then certainly the negative effects of such stimuli should have operated in Berlyne's study. In fact, I do not know of any valid experimental basis for assuming that relative confinement produces negative motivational effects in the rat, especially effects comparable to those of electric shock. Further, and most important, it should be noted that in our study the degree of confinement in relation to the size of the quite young animals was not exceptional, particularly when compared with the degree of confinement present in "normal" laboratory rearing cages housing four or five rats. In fact, our purpose for concluding the confinement period at 45 days was to keep the average amount of cage space per rat approximately equal for both restricted and normally reared control subjects.

Although these comments do not resolve the criticism of our interpretation, it does not appear to us that Hillix's alternative conceptualization "can more parsimoniously" account for our data. Admittedly, the results might be interpreted by several alternative explanations. At issue seems to be the basic orientation of the behavioral scientist toward his subject matter. Hillix's explanation appears oriented toward the fairly common viewpoint that behavior proceeds as a function of avoiding stimuli and their consequences. Our explanation, like that of Montgomery (1953a, 1955) in explaining exploratory behavior, Dember (1956) in explaining spontaneous alternation, and Fiske and Maddi (1961) in attempting a general theory of the effects of sensory stimulation, is oriented toward explaining at least certain behaviors as a function of approaching stimuli and their consequences. I hope that rather than leading to further argument, our study and the many others pointing in a similar direction will lead instead to sound research aimed at resolving such conflicts in theoretical orientation toward the study of what might be called sensory motivation.

David C. McClelland, John W. Atkinson, Russell A. Clark, and Edgar L. Lowell, *The Achievement Motive,* New York: Appleton-Century-Crofts, Inc., 1953, from Chapter 2, pp. 42–66.

Discrepancy Hypothesis*[1]

David C. McClelland and Russell A. Clark

Antecedent Conditions for Affective Arousal

Let us now focus our attention on the all-important problem of identifying the antecedent conditions which produce affective arousal. For if we know them, we are in a position, according to the theory, of knowing how to create a motive by pairing cues with those conditions, according to the principles discussed in the next main section on *the acquisition of motives* (see Chapter 7). Considering the antecedent conditions for affective arousal inevitably gets us into some ancient controversies over what causes pleasure and pain (McDougall, 1927; Beebe-Center, 1932; Dallenbach, 1939; Hebb, 1949). There is not the space here to review these controversies or to attempt to resolve them. Instead, we can only indicate what appears to us to be a promising approach to a general theory. This approach can only be outlined roughly here in the form of a series of propositions which seem promising to us but which will require experimentation and more detailed exposition in further publications.

AFFECTIVE AROUSAL IS
THE INNATE CONSEQUENCE
OF CERTAIN SENSORY
OR PERCEPTUAL EVENTS

It is probable (though not necessary) that the basic mechanism which gives rise to *sensory* pleasantness (e.g., sweetness) and unpleasantness (e.g., bitterness) is similar to that which gives rise to pleasantness-unpleasantness at a more complex perceptual level (pleasant music vs. dissonant music). In this connection we use the term *sensory* to refer roughly to simple variations in stimulus dimensions (e.g., stimulus intensity), whereas *perceptual* refers primarily to more complex variations in stimulus events.

* Reprinted by permission of Appleton-Century- Crofts.
[1] D.C.McC. and R.A.C. are largely responsible for this section, which was written after the main body of the text had been completed.

POSITIVE AFFECT IS THE RESULT
OF SMALLER DISCREPANCIES OF A
SENSORY OR PERCEPTUAL EVENT
FROM THE ADAPTATION LEVEL
OF THE ORGANISM; NEGATIVE
AFFECT IS THE RESULT OF
LARGER DISCREPANCIES

The salt curve in Figure 1 illustrates this postulated relationship from the hedonic reactions to increasing salt concentrations in the mouth. Fifty years ago it was a commonplace assumption that increasing sensory intensity in *any* modality produced a pleasantness-unpleasantness curve like this (Beebe-Center, 1932, p. 166). The new feature of such a curve for us is that, like Hebb, we would plot it not against increasing intensity as such but against size of discrepancy between the stimulus (perception) and the adaptation level of the organism (expectation). Such a modification has several advantages which we

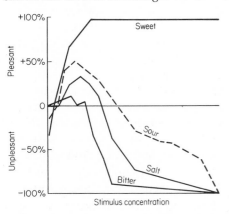

Fig. 1. Preponderance of "pleasant" or "unpleasant" judgments in relation to the concentration of a liquid solution. The ordinate gives per cent "pleasant" minus per cent "unpleasant." The abscissa is proportional to the concentration, the full length of the baseline standing for 40 per cent cane sugar, for 10 per cent salt, and for .004 per cent quinine sulphate (all by weight). Data of R. Engel, from Woodworth and Schlosberg, 1954, p. 661.

will enumerate, but among them is the fact that it brings the "discrepancy hypothesis" as to the source of affect within the realm of quantitative testing according to Helson's formulae (1948) for determining adaptation level and discrepancies from it. In the discussion which follows we have obviously leaned heavily on Helson's formulations of the concept of adaptation level.

NATURAL ADAPTATION LEVELS
FOR VARIOUS SENSORY
RECEPTORS DIFFER

Such a hypothesis is apparently essential to a discrepancy hypothesis because of the known fact that some receptors give rise most readily or "naturally" to pleasantness and others to unpleasantness. In Figure 1 the two curves for sweet and bitter sensations illustrate this point. Thus sugar appears to give rise to pleasurable sensations across the entire range of stimulus intensity. In terms of the discrepancy hypothesis, this suggests that a discrepancy from the natural adaptation level (AL) large enough to produce unpleasantness is not possible. The bitter curve, on the other hand, is quite different: here nearly all intensities of stimulus concentration tested give rise to negative affect. The fact that the absolute threshold for sugar is considerably above what it is for bitter (Praffman, 1951) suggests the following interpretation. The threshold for sweet is relatively high and the range of stimulation to which it is sensitive sufficiently narrow so that large discrepancies from AL which probably lies near the threshold are impossible. With bitter the threshold is so low that small fractions of the maximum concentration used in Figure 1 still represent fairly large discrepancies from an *AL* near the threshold. At this stage of our knowledge easy generalizations must be avoided, but it seems obvious even now that ultimately the natural *AL* for a receptor will turn out to be somewhere near its threshold (modified perhaps by the normal stimulation impinging on it) and that the size of the discrepancies which will yield positive and negative affect will be a joint rational function of the three constants in receptor functioning—the lower threshold, the upper threshold, and the Weber fraction.

What is clearly needed is a survey of all sensory qualities in terms of the discrepancy hypothesis as to what produces positive and negative affect. Such a survey cannot be attempted here both because of space limitations and because of the obvious complexity of some of the problems to be solved. Take pitch, for example. At first glance, it would look as if a few moments at the piano would easily disprove the discrepancy hypothesis. If two notes of small discrepancy in pitch, such as C and C-sharp, are played together in the middle pitch range, the effect is normally unpleasant; whereas if two notes farther apart in pitch, such as C and E, are played together, the effect is pleasant. Isn't this just the reverse of what our hypothesis would predict? It is, unless one considers the fact that two notes fairly close together produce a larger number of audible beats per second than two notes farther apart. It has long been recognized (Woodworth, 1938, p. 515) that unpleasantness is a function of these beats which represent discrepancies from an evenly pitched sound. Thus if size of discrepancy is measured in terms of "frequency of beats," it appears that the two tones close together are *more discrepant* than

those farther apart and should therefore be more unpleasant. But this is only the beginning of what could be a thorough exploration of the esthetics of music according to this principle. Variables which appear to influence the pleasantness of combinations of tones, for example, include the absolute pitch of the two tones, the pattern of overtones, simultaneity vs. succession in sounding the two tones, and the like.

Or to take one more example—that of color. If our *AL* theory is correct, one would have to predict that dark-skinned peoples of the world would have different color *AL*'s from looking at each other than would light-skinned people. Consequently, the discrepancy in wavelength terms from the *AL*'s which should yield maximum pleasure in countries like India and the United States ought to be different. In these terms one might explain the fact that in India red is the most preferred color and white is the color of mourning, whereas in the United States blue-green is most preferred and black is the color of mourning (Garth, *et al.*, 1938). It is at least suggestive that nearly complementary skin color bases should produce complementary pleasant and unpleasant colors, but the most important point to note here is that our theory would argue for a *natural* basis for color preferences based on dominant or recurrent experiences rather than for a purely accidental basis subsequently reinforced by culture, as current thinking would appear to emphasize. Obviously such natural preferences can be changed by the culture or by the individual through particular experiences (e.g., there are plenty of American children who prefer red), but the point is that U.S. and Indian populations as groups should show different color preferences according to the principle that moderate discrepancy from different skin color AL bases will yield pleasure in colors of different wavelength composition.

These two examples should be sufficient to illustrate the deductive fertility of the discrepancy hypothesis and also the need for the kind of careful analysis of different sensory qualities which is beyond the scope of this introductory treatment.

A DISCREPANCY BETWEEN ADAPTATION LEVEL AND A SENSATION OR EVENT MUST PERSIST FOR A FINITE LENGTH OF TIME BEFORE IT GIVES RISE TO AN HEDONIC RESPONSE

There are several reasons for making this assumption. In the first place, Beebe-Center and others have noted that certain types of sensations—e.g., taste, smell, pain—give rise to affective responses more readily than others— e.g., sight, hearing. A possible explanation for this fact would be "receptor lag" or "AL lag." That is, for the first group of sensations AL may change rather slowly, so that the discrepancy caused by a new stimulus will last long enough to give an hedonic report. In taste and smell, for instance, there appear to be purely "mechanical" reasons for the relative slowness with which previous concentrations of stimulator substances are changed by new substances. Thus a change might occur at one point in the receptor surface while the rest of the surface was still responding to earlier chemicals. In vision and hearing, on the other hand, the AL appears to respond rapidly to new sensations so that only major shifts in intensity will cause a discrepancy from

AL to persist long enough to give rise to an hedonic response.

A second reason for the discrepancy-persistence hypothesis is that the hedonic j.n.d. seems to be larger than the sensory j.n.d. That is, in all modalities the discrepancies required to produce a just noticeable difference in hedonic tone seem to be larger than those required to produce a report of a difference in sensation. Unfortunately, adequate data on this point are apparently not available at present, although the problem is one that may be attacked easily experimentally. What is needed is a repetition of some of the standard psychophysics experiments in which hedonic judgments are called for under exactly the same conditions as judgments of *heavier, brighter, longer,* and so on. Usually these two types of judgments have been made separately. It would not be surprising if the hedonic j.n.d. turned out to be some function of the Weber fraction for each modality. The meaning of all this in terms of the present hypothesis is simply that a larger than just noticeable sensory difference is required to maintain a discrepancy over AL long enough to give rise to a just noticeable hedonic effect.

A third reason for the discrepancy-persistence hypothesis is simply to avoid making the whole of behavior affectively toned. After all, every sensory event might be considered, at least in some marginal sense, a discrepancy from some "expectation" and should therefore lead to some kind of affective arousal, were it not for some principle requiring a minimum degree of stability in the expectation or AL so that a discrepancy from it *could* persist. In short, the simple occurrence of an event is not sufficient to set up an AL such that any further modified occurrence of that same event will produce a discrepancy sufficient to cause affect. Rather the *AL* must be built up to a certain minimum level of stability through successive experiences, as in memory or psychophysical experiments, before discrepancies from it will produce affect. A case in point is provided by Hebb's young chimpanzee which did not fear a detached chimpanzee head until it had formed through experience a stable expectation of what a chimpanzee should look like (Hebb, 1949).

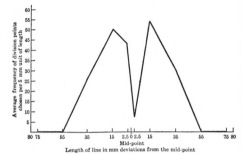

Fig. 2. **Unequal division points of a straight line chosen as most pleasing. From Angier, 1903.**

DISCREPANCIES FROM ADAPTATION LEVEL WILL GIVE RISE TO A POSITIVE-NEGATIVE AFFECT FUNCTION IN EITHER DIRECTION ALONG A CONTINUUM

In many instances, events can differ from expectation only uni-directionally. Thus after the shape of the human figure has been learned, discrepancies can occur only in the direction of being less like the expected shape. But with many dimensions, particularly intensity, discrepancies are bi-directional and may have somewhat different affective consequences depending on their direction. For example, does a decrease of so many j.n.d.'s from an *AL* have the same hedonic tone as an increase of the same number of j.n.d.'s?

The simplest assumption is that the hedonic effect is the same regardless of the direction of the discrepancy. But the evidence for the assumption is not very convincing. It consists for the most part of some early experiments in esthetics such as the one summarized in Figure 2. Angier (1903) simply asked his subjects to divide a 160 mm line unequally at the most pleasing place on either side of the midpoint. The results in Figure 2 were obtained by

averaging the frequencies of choices per 5 mm unit between 5–25 mm, 25–45 mm, 45–65 mm, 65–75 mm discrepancies, and plotting them with the actual frequencies for the 5 mm discrepancies on each side of the midpoint. Since Angier did not permit his subjects to choose the midpoint and since he forced them to make half of their judgments on either side of the midpoint, the data do not really test our hypothesis crucially. He should rather have let a large number of subjects choose any division points at all along the line. Still, Angier's introspective data from his subjects led him to conclude that "most of the subjects, however, found a slight remove from the center disagreeable" (1903, p. 550). Furthermore it is clear that his subjects did not like to divide the line near its extremities on either side. In short, there is evidence for the typical hedonic curve for discrepancies *in both directions* from the center which must be assumed to represent some kind of an *AL* based on symmetry, balance, and so forth. A similar bimodal preference curve for rectangles of different width-length ratios is reported by Thorndike (see Woodworth, 1938, p. 386), if the exactly balanced ratio of .50 is taken as the *AL*.

When an attempt is made to discover

the same principle in the operation of sensory modalities, however, the situation becomes complex. Consider Alpert's data in Figure 3 as an example. The lower curve, which again is the typical hedonic function for discrepancies from *AL*, was obtained in the following way. Subjects inserted one eye in a translucent "Ganzfeld" about the size of an egg cup. Around the outside of the cup, red lights were placed so as to produce inside it a diffuse red light covering the entire visual field and presumably stimulating largely only one set of receptors—the cones. In the center of the cup a small spot subtending about 18 degrees of visual arc was distinguishable from the rest of the field by a hazy dark line, produced by the fact that the spot was separately illuminated from behind. First the subject adjusted the illumination of the reddish spot until it matched the reddish "Ganzfeld" in all respects as closely as possible. Then the experimenter set a Variac which also controlled lamp volt-

age for the spot in such a way that if he switched off the "constant" lamp just adjusted by the subject and switched on the "variable" lamp for about two seconds, the subject got a glimpse of the spot as more or less intense than the surrounding "Ganzfeld." The subject made a judgment of pleasantness-unpleasantness on a scale of +3 to −3 *after* the "variable" lamp had been switched off and the "constant" lamp back on. Each subject made four judgments at each of the lamp voltage settings shown on the abscissa of Figure 3. The "spots" of different intensity were presented in random order four separate times. The procedure was duplicated for different illuminations of the "Ganzfeld" (i.e., for different adaptation levels). There were 10 subjects and the two curves in Figure 3 represent the average judgments of all of them under two adaptation level settings—one in which the "Ganzfeld" illumination was low (< .5 foot candles) and the other in which it was high (about 3 foot candles according to G.E. photometer). Each subject's judgments under all conditions were converted to a common scale of standard scores with a mean of 50 and an *SD* of 10. Thus the fact that the dotted line in Figure 3 is above 50 throughout most of its course means that most of the subjects' judgments in this condition were above their individual hedonic means *for the whole series of judgments* (including a series with a moderate *AL* not reproduced here).

Three conclusions can be drawn from Figure 3: (1) When the *AL* is low, and the receptors are close to the "resting" state, increases in stimulation produce first positive affect and then negative affect as postulated above. See solid line in Figure 3. (2) When the *AL*

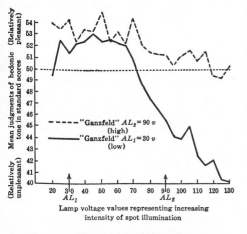

Fig. 3. Hedonic tone judgments for discrepancies in spot illumination above and below low (AL₁) and high (AL₂) "Ganzfeld" illuminations. Red light, 10 subjects making 4 judgments at each lamp voltage value. Data from Alpert, 1953.

is high, well above the resting state, all increases in stimulation tend to produce negative affect and all decreases tend to produce positive affect. See dotted line in Figure 3. (3) There is no marked evidence in these curves either (a) for large decreases in stimulation leading to negative affect or (b) for stimulation around the AL producing a neutral hedonic response. Neither (a) nor (b) should be considered as conclusive negative evidence, however. With respect to (a), common experience suggests that eating ice cream after drinking coffee is more painful than under normal conditions. On the surface, it would appear that this is because the low temperature of the ice cream represents a much larger discrepancy downwards from the heightened AL of the mouth or teeth produced by drinking coffee. But the problem is complicated by the fact that the heat and cold receptors may be different and related in an unknown way. That is, ice cream may not be a decrease in stimulation for warm receptors but an *increase* in stimulation for cold receptors. The virtue of using red illumination in the present experiment is that it presumably limits the effects of stimulation largely to one set of receptors—the cones. In short, the question of whether decreases in stimulation ever produce negative affect and of whether the hedonic curve is therefore alike on both sides of AL must be left open at the present time.

With respect to (b) there is a slight (though probably insignificant) dip in the lower hedonic curve for values of the spot which are close to those of the "Ganzfeld" AL. It can be argued that the reason the dip is not more striking is that at least two other AL's are operating in this situation. The first is the natural or physiological AL of the re-

ceptor which here and in other similar figures seems to lie somewhere around the threshold of the receptor. The illumination of the "Ganzfeld" was apparently close enough to this value for the lower curve in Figure 3 not to produce a major modification in its shape. The second AL is that produced by the *series* of spot stimuli of varying intensity. This can be calculated by Helson's formula (1947) to be equivalent to a lamp voltage value of around 63 volts, which is considerably *above* the "Ganzfeld" AL value and which may interact with it in some way to obscure further the dip in hedonic tone for values approximating AL. Generally speaking, the principle appears to hold for the lower curve if the AL is taken to be the physiological AL, and for the upper curve if the AL is taken to be the "Ganzfeld" value. Although both of these assumptions seem reasonable, once again the question must be considered open as to whether values approximating the AL always tend to take on a neutral hedonic tone, at least until we have more accurate ways of figuring out how AL's are shifted by exposure to various experiences.

INCREASES AND DECREASES IN STIMULUS INTENSITY CAN BE RELATED TO MOTIVATION ONLY IF ADAPTATION LEVEL AND LEARNING ARE TAKEN INTO ACCOUNT

Our view of motivation differs from Miller and Dollard's (1941) in two important ways. First, the effects of changes in stimulus intensity must always be referred to AL, and second, such changes produce affect immediately and motives only through learning. More specifically, an increase in stimulus intensity (a "drive" for Miller and Dollard) provides the basis for a motive only if it represents a large enough discrepancy from *AL* to produce positive or negative affect. It elicits a motive only if it or the situation producing it has been associated with such affect in the past. A decrease in stimulus intensity (a "reward" for Miller and Dollard) either provides the basis for an approach motive if it produces positive affect or removes the cues which have been redintegrating negative affect and thus eliminates an avoidance motive. Thus "drive" and "reward" in Miller and Dollard's sense are seen to be special cases of a more general theory.

Let us leave aside for the moment the question of whether motives or drives are always learned and look more closely at the question of the relation of stimulus intensity to *AL*. For us, it is not intensity per se which is important but discrepancy from *AL*. It follows that many strong stimuli will be unpleasant, but not all. It depends on over-all *AL*. Thus if a person is in dim illumination (bottom curve in Figure 3), a light with a lamp voltage value of 90 will produce marked negative affect; but if the illumination is already that bright, the same light will produce a rather indifferent response (upper curve in Figure 3). It is for this reason apparently that biting one's lips or otherwise hurting one's self helps relieve pain.

CHANGES IN ADAPTATION LEVEL,
WITH ATTENDANT HEDONIC
CHANGES, MAY BE PRODUCED
BY SOMATIC CONDITIONS

This is an obvious point and a few illustrations will serve to demonstrate its importance. The somatic conditions may be either chemical (hormonal) or neurological in nature. Pfaffman and Bare (1950) have demonstrated that the preferences for lower salt concentrations shown by adrenalectomized rats cannot be explained by a lowering of the *sensory* threshold of the nerves responding to salt. An explanation in our terms would simply be that the central *AL* has been lowered by chemical changes in the bloodstream so that lower salt concentrations on the tongue will produce a pleasurable discrepancy from it. That is, Pfaffman and Bare found that the lower concentrations had always produced action potentials in the gustatory nerve, although they did not produce preference behavior in the normal rat. The reason for this in our terms is that they were sufficiently near the normal *AL* not to evoke preference behavior. Figure 4, which is plotted from Harriman's data (1952), shows in detail what happens to salt preferences in adrenalectomized rats when salt has been removed from their diet. The solid curve shows the amount of salty water of different concentrations consumed by normal rats on a normal diet (including about 1 per cent salt) when they could choose between it and distilled water. The dotted curve

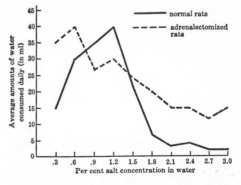

Fig. 4. Data plotted from Harriman (1952) showing average amounts of salty water of different concentrations consumed by normal (solid line) and adrenalectomized rats (dotted line) on a salt-free diet.

shows the same results for the adrenalectomized animals on a salt-free diet.

The solid curve shows substantially the same relationship obtained for humans as presented in Figure 1 and it can be explained by the same assumptions—namely, that the AL for salt is somewhere below .3 per cent salt but above the absolute threshold for discrimination of salty from non-salty water which is at least as low as .01 per cent concentration of salt (Pfaffman and Bare, 1950). The AL empirically is that concentration which a rat will not consistently approach or avoid as compared with distilled water. The dotted curve suggests that for the operated animals the AL has now moved to lower concentrations, so that a .3 per cent solution represents a "pleasurable" discrepancy whereas before it was relatively "neutral." The fact that formerly preferred concentrations (.9 per cent and 1.2 per cent) are now *less* preferred also supports the idea that the AL has been lowered, since these now represent larger (and therefore less pleasant) discrepancies from it. But how about the tail end of the dotted curve? Should not the adrenalectomized animals find the high salt concentrations even less pleasant than the normals, if their AL has been lowered? According to the discrepancy hypothesis they should, but these data are not conclusive evidence that they do not. That is, the operated animals may find the strong concentrations even more unpleasant than the normals do, but drink more of them in short "swallows" because the "after-taste" remains pleasant longer. In other words, if the salt solutions dissipate according to a negative decay function, there may be an appreciable time period after exposure to a strong concentration when the stimulus is pleas-

ant, if the AL is low as in operated animals. Thus the operated animals may drink for the pleasant after-taste of strong concentrations; the normal animals may not because the dissipating solution reaches the higher AL sooner. At least the possibility is worth exploring.

In this fashion, changes in positive and negative affect resulting from the same stimulation on different occasions can be accounted for by chemical effects on AL. Such a hypothesis should be especially valuable in accounting for changes in the pleasurableness of sexual sensations accompanying certain hormonal cycles in lower animals (cf. Ford and Beach, 1951). Similarly Head's observations on the effects of thalamic lesions show that neurological damage can affect AL. Take this case, for example: "In one case a tube containing water at 38° C applied to the normal palm was said to be warm, but the patient cried out with pleasure when it was placed on the affected hand. His face broke into smiles and he said, 'Oh! that's exquisite,' or 'That's real pleasant'" (quoted in Beebe-Center, 1932, p. 391). Or another: "When a pin was lightly dragged from right to left across the face or trunk of one of the patients suffering from a lesion affecting the left side, she exhibited intense discomfort as soon as it had passed the middle line. Not only did she call out that it hurt more, but her face became contorted with pain. Yet careful examination with algesimeters showed that on the affected side her sensitivity to such stimulation was, if anything, slightly lowered" (Beebe-Center, 1932, p. 390). It is difficult to think about such findings in any other terms but some neurological effects on a central AL

such that identical stimulations would produce different effects.

An interesting consequence of this proposition is that it suggests a reason why the sources of positive and negative affect may be different for different physiques. Thus if the AL for kinaesthetic sensations from large well-developed muscles is higher, it would be easy to understand why more activity would be required to get pleasurable discrepancies from the AL than for a weaker physique with lower kinaesthetic AL. In fact, one should argue that the amount of activity which produces pleasure for the mesomorphic physique (and consequently approach motives) might well produce too large a discrepancy, negative affect, and avoidance motives for the ectomorph. It might not be too far-fetched to attempt to account for the dominant sources of pleasure in each of Sheldon's somatotypes (1940) in terms of different AL's set up in different sensory modalities by different types of physiques. The argument would run something like this: The endomorph appears to get most of his pleasure from his gut because the AL for gut sensations is relatively high for such physiques and it takes gut sensations of greater intensity (or variety) to produce the discrepancies necessary for pleasure; the mesomorph appears to get most of his pleasure from his muscles because the AL for kinaesthetic sensations is relatively high and more variations in kinaesthetic sensations are required to give pleasure; the ectomorph appears to get more of his pleasure from minimal sensory stimulation because the AL for skin sensations is so low that moderate deviations from it give pleasure, and so forth. Such hypotheses are obviously incomplete and highly tentative, but they can certainly be tested experimentally and made more precise by isolating such physique types and determining their hedonic thresholds for various sensory qualities.

Finally, this proposition provides a basis for explaining Freud's libidinal development hypothesis, which has proven so fruitful clinically but so difficult to understand in terms of traditional "objective" theories of motivation. The explanation runs briefly as follows: "Erogenous zones" are skin areas where AL's are so low that relatively light tactual stimulation gives rise to sufficient discrepancies from AL to yield pleasure. If Freud is correct, it should be possible to demonstrate objectively that a constant tactual stimulus will give rise to pleasure responses in infants more readily in certain areas than in others. For the mouth, this seems well established, if the sucking response is taken as indicative of pleasure (i.e., because it is an approach response). For the anal and genital regions the facts are less well established. Freud's second hypothesis is that the erogenous sensitivity of these regions shifts as the child matures. In our terms, this simply means that changes in somatic conditions, produced here by maturation, modify AL's so that, as in the case of Head's patient, the same stimulus has a different hedonic effect. For example, the innate AL to mouth stimulation may increase with age so that touching the lips in the same way no longer yields pleasure and, at the same time, the anal region may become especially sensitive to tactual stimulation, and so on. The rise and fall in sensitivity of these various skin areas can certainly be measured behaviorally and understood in terms of physiologically produced changes in AL.

CHANGES IN ADAPTATION LEVEL,
WITH ATTENDANT HEDONIC
CHANGES, MAY BE PRODUCED
BY EXPERIENCE

This proposition opens up a whole new area that needs careful experimental exploration. We know some things but not nearly enough about how this happens. Thus Helson (1948) has demonstrated how an anchor or a series of stimuli can modify an *AL* in various modalities. His formulae even make assumptions as to the relative weights of background and figural stimulations in determining an *AL* produced by a series of stimuli. Furthermore, we know that hedonic judgments show the same type of central tendency, contrast, and assimilation effects that led Helson to formulate his notion of *AL* (Beebe-Center, 1932). This is as it should be, because as *AL*'s shift in the "physical dimensions of consciousness" there should be corresponding shifts in hedonic reactions if they are a function of the size of discrepancies between new stimuli and the sensory *AL*. But the most clear-cut evidence we know of which demonstrates that the hedonic curve is shifted as a function of shifts in sensory *AL* is that which has already been presented in Figure 3 and discussed above. (See also Beebe-Center, 1932, p. 238.)

In the absence of more such data at a more complex level, we must work with qualitative observations to some extent. Take Hebb's treatment of the "fear of the strange" as a point of departure. "About the age of four months the chimpanzee reared in the nursery, with daily care from three or four persons only and seeing few others, begins to show an emotional disturbance at

the approach of a stranger (Hebb and Riesen, 1943). The disturbance increases in degree in the following months. . . . Chimpanzees reared in darkness, and brought into the light at an age when the response (to a strange face) would be at its strongest, show not the slightest disturbance at the sight of either friend or stranger. *But* some time later, after a certain amount of visual learning has gone on, the disturbance begins to appear exactly as in other animals" (Hebb, 1949, pp. 244–245). He also reports that "a model of a human or chimpanzee head detached from the body" produces marked affective arousal in half-grown or adult chimpanzees but not in younger chimpanzees. From all this he concludes that "the emotional disturbance is neither learned nor innate: a certain learning must have preceded, but given that learning the disturbance is complete on the first appearance of certain stimulus combinations" (Hebb, 1949, p. 245). This is the crux of the matter as far as our theory of the conditions necessary for affective arousal (either positive or negative) is concerned. An *AL* must be built up in certain areas of experience (though it appears to be innately given for sense modalities) and then increasing descrepancies from that *AL* give rise first to positive and then to negative affect, as in Figure 1. *The AL may be acquired, the affective reactions to discrepancies from it are not;* they appear maximally the first time the discrepancy occurs and with less intensity thereafter because the new experience automatically interacts with the *AL*, changes it, and thereby reduces the discrepancy. Hence there is ultimate boredom or adaptation to pain or pleasure (satiation) as we shall see in a moment.

EVENTS CAN DIFFER FROM EXPECTATIONS ON A VARIETY OF DIMENSIONS

The example we have chosen from Hebb to illustrate the preceding point is important because, unlike the sensory AL's which we have been discussing, it deals with changes in *patterns* of stimulation rather than with changes in *intensity* levels. Thus we have to expand the AL concept to include expectations about shapes (e.g., faces) or any other events that the organism has had occasion through past experience to build up expectations about. This expansion, while absolutely necessary for a complete theory, raises certain practical problems in defining the size of a discrepancy between expectation and perception—a variable which we must be able to determine quite precisely if we are going to be able to predict whether a given discrepancy will give rise to positive or negative affect.

Basically, the problem is one of isolating dimensions along which two events can differ and then attempting to define degrees of difference objectively. Thus the events can differ in intensity, extensity, clarity, quality, certainty, and so on, and traditional psychophysics gives us plenty of cues as to how degrees of difference along these dimensions can be determined. So far we have talked largely about intensity differences, but differences in quality (or similarity) can be treated the same way. Thus one would predict on the basis of the discrepancy hypothesis that an artificial language consisting of highly probable syllabic combinations would be more amusing than one consisting of highly improbable syllabic combinations, or that nonsense syllables that sounded like English (NOQ) would be more amusing than ones that didn't (VOQ). And so forth. The research along these lines that needs to be done appears almost limitless.

Most events, of course, can differ from expectation in a variety of ways. Suppose a rat runs down an alley, turns left, proceeds three or four steps further, finds and eats a food pellet of a certain size and consistency. If this series of events occurs with sufficient frequency, we argue that the rat has built up a chain of associations of high probability or certain "expectations" as to what will happen. But these expectations, redintegrated partially when the rat is placed in the maze, may fail to be exactly confirmed in a variety of ways. An obstacle may delay him so that it takes him longer to get to the food. We may substitute mash for a food pellet, or a large pellet for a small one. He may eat the food where it is or pick it up and carry it somewhere else to eat it. And so forth. According to the discrepancy hypothesis, certain predictions about this process can be made. So long as the animal is uncertain in his expectations (i.e., is still learning the habit), there will be a tendency to limit the variability of responses so as to increase the probability of expectations until events represent only moderate and hence pleasurable deviations from them. But once the habit is overlearned the animal will tend to introduce variations once more —now to *increase* uncertainty to a "pleasurable" level. In short, exactly confirming certain expectations produces boredom and a tendency to discontinue the act unless enough minor variations are permitted to produce positive affect. The evidence for this hypothesis from animal learning is considerable. Thus the tendency toward variability in routine behavior has been found by many learning psychologists and is perhaps best illustrated by Heathers' (1940) report that rats alternate the paths they choose to get food when either is equally good. They are apparently operating according to the same general principle when they prefer a path to food with a barrier in it to an unobstructed path to food (Festinger, 1943), or prefer seeds which are difficult to crack open to seeds which are not so difficult (Yoshioka, 1930). Other similar examples of "inefficient" preferences have been collected by Maltzman (1952). In these and other such cases, the rat may prefer what looks like an inefficient response because it involves minor variations from expectation along such dimensions as time delay, spatial location, size of expected object, nature of expected object, and so forth—variations which according to the discrepancy hypothesis should yield pleasure. Research on this problem has to be done with care because as soon as the modification is major (for example, when the time delay becomes too long), then, of course, negative affect results and the preference of the animal is reversed. To complicate the matter even more, one should know how certain, or overlearned, the expectations are before predicting the effects of variations from them. If the expectations are of low probability, then confirmation should produce negative affect as in "fear of the strange." If they are of moderate probability, precise confirmation should produce pleasure (as in reading a detective story or playing solitaire). If the expectations are of high probability,

then precise confirmation produces boredom or indifference (as in reading over again the detective story one has just finished, to use Hebb's example). The hedonic effects of the interaction of degrees of certainty of an expectation on the one hand, and degrees of deviation of an event from that expectation on the other, have yet to be worked out experimentally, but there is no reason why they could not be, using either animal or human subjects.

FRUSTRATION IS A SOURCE OF NEGATIVE AFFECT

A special note is in order as to where the notion of frustration or conflict as a drive (Whiting, 1950; Brown and Farber, 1951) fits into this scheme. Frustration in their terms results essentially from competition of response tendencies in such a way that F (frustration) is increased by reducing the difference in strength between the two opposed tendencies and also by increasing the absolute strength of both of them. Such statements are completely in line with our assumptions, with some exceptions to be noted in a minute. That is, we too would argue that the more nearly equal in strength two response tendencies are, the more they would give rise to negative affect (F); because such competition means that if either response is made, the expectation based on the other is not confirmed; or that if neither is made, both are unconfirmed. Similarly, the effects of nonconfirmation should be greater, the greater the strength of the response tendency. There are two differences between our scheme and theirs, however: (1) We would argue that when the size of the discrepancy between the stronger and weaker response tendencies is large, there should be a stage when the competition of the weaker response tendency should give rise not to frustration but to pleasure, if the stronger tendency is confirmed. This would require a modification in their formula for computing F such that for a certain range of discrepancies between the two tendencies it would yield negative F values (signifying pleasure). (2) They treat F as if it were a drive, whereas in our terms F in itself is simply negative affect and does not become a motive until anticipations of it or by it are elicited.

THE ACHIEVEMENT MOTIVE DEVELOPS OUT OF GROWING EXPECTATIONS

So far our scheme has been stated in fairly abstract form. A concrete example involving the development of the achievement motive may help explain its application in practice. Suppose a child is given a new toy car for Christmas to play with. Initially, unless he has had other toy cars, his expectations (or AL's) as to what it will do are non-existent, and he can derive little or no positive or negative affect from manipulating it until such expectations are developed. Gradually, if he plays with it (as he will be encouraged to by his parents in our culture), he will develop certain expectations of varying probabilities which will be confirmed or not confirmed. Unless the nonconfirmations are too many (which may happen if the toy is too complex), he should be able to build up reasonably certain expectations as to what it will do *and confirm them*. In short, he gets pleasure from playing with the car. But what happens then? Why doesn't he continue playing with it the rest of his life? The fact is,

of course, that his expectations become certainties, confirmation becomes 100 per cent, and we say that he loses interest or gets bored with the car; he should get bored or satiated, according to the theory, since the discrepancies from certainty are no longer sufficient to yield pleasure. However, pleasure can be reintroduced into the situation, as any parent knows, by buying a somewhat more complex car, by making the old car do somewhat different things, or perhaps by letting the old car alone for six months until the expectations about it have changed (e.g., decreased in probability). So, if a child is to continue to get pleasure from achievement situations like manipulating toy cars, he must continually work with more and more complex objects or situations permitting mastery, since, if he works long enough at any particular level of mastery, his expectations and their confirmation will become certain and he will get bored. The situation is analogous to the experiments by Washburn, Child, and Abel (cf. Beebe-Center, 1932, p. 238) which show that pleasure decreases on successive repetitions of simple popular music, whereas it increases on successive repetitions of severely classical music. In the first instance, expectations or AL's are readily formed and confirmed to the point of boredom, whereas they take much longer to form with classical music—so long in fact that some people never expose themselves to such music often enough to get pleasure from having them confirmed. Thus pleasure from anything—be it mastery, music, or modern art—depends on a moderate degree of novelty, which has to become ever greater as expectations catch up with it. But note that there are limits on this developmental process: not every child will develop a very high level achievement motive or esthetic appreciation motive. In the first place, there limits placed by native intelligence: the possibilities of a toy car or a comic book may never be exhausted as far as a moron is concerned because they never become certain enough for him to be bored over trying them out. Thus one would expect some kind of a correlation between the mastery level involved in n Achievement for a given person and his intelligence.

In the second place, there are limits placed on the development of n Achievement by the negative affect which results from too large discrepancies between expectations and events. Thus Johnny may develop expectations as to what a model airplane or a solved arithmetic problem looks like, but he may be unable to confirm these expectations at all, or only very partially. The result is negative affect, and cues associated with these activities may be expected to evoke avoidance motives. To develop an achievement approach motive, parents or circumstances must contrive to provide opportunities for mastery which, because they are just beyond the child's present knowledge, will provide continuing pleasure. If the opportunities are too limited, boredom should result and the child should develop no interest in achievement (and have a low n Achievement score when he grows up). If the opportunities are well beyond his capacities, negative affect should result, and he may develop an avoidance motive as far as achievement is concerned. Since a fairly narrow range of circumstances will conspire to yield a high achievement approach motive, it would not be surprising to discover that individuals or

groups of individuals in different cultures differ widely in the amount of achievement motivation they develop.

IN HUMAN ADULTS ADAPTATION LEVELS ARE NUMEROUS AND COMPLEX SO THAT A SINGLE EVENT MAY HAVE SEVERAL HEDONIC CONSEQUENCES

Take flunking out of school, for example. One might argue that if the student half expected it, he should feel pleasure since his expectation is confirmed. Although it is true that he may get some fleeting satisfaction from having predicted correctly, this is more than outweighed by the nonconfirmation of other expectations built up over his whole life history such as doing a good job, being a professional man, etc. So far we have been dealing largely with low level expectations and AL's taken one at a time for the sake of simplicity, but obviously in real life situations, after the person has matured, the calculus of pleasure and pain becomes exceedingly complex. Consider, for example, the traditional argument used against hedonic theories of motivation to the effect that adults at any rate frequently do things, out of a sense of duty or what not, which are distinctly unpleasant. What about the martyr, for example? Can he be seeking pleasure or avoiding pain? The answer is "yes," in the larger sense in which positive and negative affect are defined here. If a man builds up a conception of the Universe—an expectation of the way in which moral or spiritual laws govern it and his place in it—which is sufficiently firm and well defined, it may well be that the anticipated nonconfirmation of such an expectation through transgression of those laws would produce sufficient negative affect so that a man would choose the lesser negative affect of burning at the stake. One of the virtues of our view of motivation is precisely that it permits the development of new, high level motives as experience changes the person's expectations or adaptation levels. Whereas the rat or the child may be primarily governed by variations from sensory or simple perceptual expectations, the adult will be ruled by discrepancies in higher level cognitive structures (beliefs) which may lead to action in direct opposition to simple sensory pleasures and pains.

Journal of Experimental Psychology, 1958, vol. 56, pp. 370–375.

Discrepancy from Adaptation Level as a Source of Affect[1]

Ralph Norman Haber

This study is an attempt to specify the antecedent conditions which produce affective arousal. Little theorizing or research has been done in this area even though the concepts of "affect" and "affective arousal" are being included in contemporary theories of motivation (Atkinson, 1954; McClelland, Atkinson, Clark, & Lowell, 1953; Olds, 1955; Young, 1955). Whenever such a concept is employed, the theorist is pressed to find an antecedent definition of it, since in most cases a consequent defined concept of affect leads to circularity. McClelland, Atkinson, Clark, and Lowell (1953) have developed a theory based, in part, on Hebb's (1949)

1 This research was performed at Wesleyan University while the author was on a Behavioral Science Fellowship from the Ford Foundation, and also with the assistance of a Grant-in-Aid from the Ford Foundation to David C. McClelland. The author gratefully acknowledges this double debt to the Ford Foundation and especially to Dr. McClelland. Portions of this paper were read at the 1958 APA convention.

neurological model of the origin of affect and Helson's (1947) notion of adaptation level. According to McClelland's discrepancy hypothesis as to the origins of affect, "Positive affect is the result of smaller discrepancies of a sensory or perceptual event from the adaptation level of the organism; negative affect is the result of larger discrepancies" (1953, p. 43). The discrepancy hypothesis predicts that affects as a function of discrepancy from the adaptation level (AL) should be a symmetrical "butterfly" curve, as shown in Fig. 1. Affect is now stated to be a function, not of increasing physical intensity per se, but of the size of the discrepancy between the adaptation level (expectation or adaptation) of the organism, and the stimulus (perception).

The concept of adaptation level was developed by Helson. He regarded the AL as being experientially determined: "The effects of stimulation form a (central) spatio-temporal configuration in

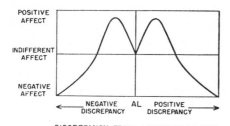

DISCREPANCY FROM ADAPTATION LEVEL

Fig. 1. Affect as a function of discrepancies above and below the AL (hypothetical).

which order prevails." Within this pattern, "there is assumed a stimulus that represents the pooled effects of all the stimuli, and to which S is attuned or adapted" (Helson, 1947, p. 2).

Hebb's (1949) neurological model of the origins of affect holds, briefly, that when nerve impulses reach the cortex, they set up cell assemblies; patterns of excitation in specific nerve nets that follow designated paths and orders of firing. After the assemblies have been established, according to Hebb, further excitation may have several effects. If the incoming impulses are in the same pattern as the established assembly, the assembly short-circuits, i.e, the excitation of any one element in the assembly will fire the whole pattern. This corresponds to boredom—to complete and exact fulfillment of all "expectations." If, however, these impulses are sufficiently different from the assembly to alter it slightly or to add new patterns to it, the conscious experience is pleasure or positive affect. The final possibility is excitation so different as to completely disrupt the assembly, resulting in displeasure or pain.

The present experiment is designed to test the discrepancy hypothesis as an explanation of variation in affect experienced in the "temperature sense." The adaptation level is that temperature of water to which S's hands are adapted, and discrepancies are different temperatures of water in which S's hands are put. The S is asked to judge his affective reaction to the temperature changes by comparing simultaneously two discrepancies from the same AL, one for each hand.

Adaptation occurs immediately to temperatures identical with the normal skin temperatures of S, and in a matter of seconds to temperatures slightly above or below normal skin temperature, where a slight time lag is required for the skin temperature to shift to this new value. When the adapting temperature is increased sufficiently above or below skin temperature so that adaptation is impossible, then no AL can be established because the adapting temperature will feel warm or cool itself. Discrepancies beyond this point should no longer produce the relationship postulated in Fig. 1. The exact nature of the reaction to them cannot be predicted in advance, except that for very high temperatures it should be unpleasant to practically all further increases in temperature and for very low temperatures it should be unpleasant for all further decreases in temperature.

Method

Apparatus

The comparison stimuli were ten 10-qt. buckets of water arranged in a horseshoe, with an eleventh bucket as the standard stimulus, designated the AL bucket. The S sat in the center of the horseshoe, which was small enough to allow him to put both hands in all possible combinations of buckets. Heat was provided by 11 600-w. heating units, each with a variable resistor, and each connected to a variable transformer, having a maximum output of 7.5 amp. and 135 v. Water temperatures could be held constant over time by making heat input equal heat loss from the body of water. Adjustment and control of temperatures was possible to a degree finer than necessary for the discriminations made in this experiment. The size of the buckets was sufficient to prevent any shifts in temperatures resulting from immersion of the hand of S for short periods of time. All temperatures are stated in degrees Centigrade.

Procedure

The Ss were eight paid male Wesleyan University undergraduates. They were tested in individual sessions, each varying from 1 to 2 hr. In each session there were 80 to 135 judgments. As S entered the horseshoe for each session, the skin temperature of his hand was recorded by a chemical thermometer on the palm. Then he was told which bucket was the standard or AL bucket and was told to place both hands in it to the wrists. A light mark on the wrist was used to assure uniformity of immersion. The S was instructed to report when the water in the AL bucket felt neutral (i.e., no temperature sensation) to both hands. This was to obtain initial adaptation. Then S was instructed to place each hand simultaneously in a different comparison bucket, the correct ones being designated each time by E. The S then had to remove one of his two hands, the one that felt less pleasant. His report was required within 3 sec. after immersion, and no indifferent report was allowed. Then both hands were returned to the AL bucket and the process was repeated. It was emphasized by E that there was no "gimmick" or game to outguess, but that each choice was to be made on the basis of the pleasantness or unpleasantness of the individual comparison.

The temperature of the AL bucket was designated as 0° discrepant from the AL. Then all the comparison buckets were also designated as a specific discrepancy from the AL. Hence, if the temperature of the AL bucket was 33° and the two comparison buckets were 34° and 36°, then S had to make a hedonic choice between a discrepancy of +1° and +3°. If the AL was 34° and the two comparison buckets were the same as above, then the choice involved a

0° versus a +2° discrepancy. Table 1 shows the frequency of presentation of each comparison.

TABLE 1

FREQUENCY OF PRESENTATION OF EACH COMPARISON IN EACH SESSION

	0°	1°	2°	3°	7°
1°	15				
2°	15*	15*			
3°	15	15	15*		
7°	5	5	5*	5	
15°	5	5	5*	5	5

* In some sessions, a 2° discrepancy was not used. Its exclusion leaves a logarithmic scale of discrepancies.

The Weber fraction for temperature sensation yields a j.n.d. of less than .1° in either direction (Geldard, 1953) when the water is at skin temperature. This j.n.d. increases rapidly so that it is over 2.9° when the temperature is 48°. In view of this, the discrepancies chosen for the study are far enough apart to be easily discriminated.

In the climate of central Connecticut in spring, the average skin temperature is about 33°. However, extra buckets were maintained in the horseshoe to insure proper discrepancies in terms of the skin temperature of each S as he began the session. This was necessary when S's skin temperature differed by more than a degree from 33°.

Three separate functions of the relationship between affect and discrepancy from AL were studied. (a) Five Ss were used to establish the function when the AL was set at or near skin temperature and the comparison buckets *increased* by discrepancies of 0°, 1°, 3°, 7°, and 15°. Each S served in two sessions with these settings. (b) The same five Ss were used to establish the function when the AL was set at or near skin temperature and the comparison buckets *decreased* by discrepancies of 0°, 1°, 3°, 7°, and 15°. Each S served in two sessions with these settings. (c) Three Ss were used to study the effects on the butterfly function when the AL was *increased* above skin temperature. Each of these Ss completed two sessions for each setting of the AL: 33°, 34°,

35°, 36°, 38°, and 40°, or 12 sessions for each S. In every one, the comparison buckets increased by discrepancies of 0°, 1°, 2°, 3°, 7°, and 15° from the AL. (There were no equivalent sessions for systematic decreases in the AL.) Note that for these three Ss, when the AL was set near their skin temperature (one of the 6 AL's used), the same function was being tested as the five Ss used in Part a. Hence, data relevant to the AL set near skin temperature will be presented for eight Ss.

The data were paired-comparison judgments, which were transformed into a continuous scale of preferences on the basis of the number of times a discrepancy was preferred in relation to the number of times it was offered. Hence, if a particular discrepancy was offered 55 times, and in these it was preferred 40 times, it had a value of 73%. If some other discrepancy was offered 55 times and preferred 31 times, it had a value of 56%. The significance of the difference between any two values was tested by a χ^2 technique. For example, to test the difference between the 0 and the 1 discrepancies for a given S, a 2×2 χ^2 table was used, with marginals labeled: discrepancy, 1 and 2; and preference; preferred to all others; not preferred to all others. The judgments of preference between the 0° and 1° were split, half being included for the 0° and half for the 1°. This avoided double counting and inflated N's.

All tests of significance were applied to one S at a time, and used data of only one session. For each S in each session, two χ^2 tests were computed, testing the highest preferred discrepancy against the two adjacent discrepancies. Hence, if the 1° discrepancy was preferred the most, it was compared to discrepancies of 0° and 3°.

The presentation order of the stimuli was randomly varied from session to session and from S to S, as was the position of the stimuli in the horseshoe. The buckets were so arranged that there were at least two buckets for each discrepancy stimulus, one on either side of the standard bucket. This prevented Ss from learning place cues as quickly, and allowed the same comparisons to be tested using different pairs of buckets. Consistent hand preferences were looked for by interspersing choices between equal stimuli. No S had to be eliminated on this

account. The S never had to make judgments between stimuli where one was above and the other below the AL. Stimuli above the AL were always in a different session from stimuli below the AL. This was done to avoid any difficulties arising out of the possibilities of two distinct receptor systems being in operation, one for cold and another for hot.

TABLE 2

AFFECT AS A FUNCTION OF THE
DISCREPANCY OF TEMPERATURES
ABOVE AND BELOW THE
ADAPTATION LEVEL

(Cell entries are the percentages of times each discrepancy was chosen in relation to the number of times it was offered as a choice with all other discrepancies.)

S	Discrepancy					
	0°	1°	2°	3°	7°	15°
Above the Adaptation Level						
S_1	64	96		46	6	0
S_2	49	100		57	6	0
S_3	68	98		40	6	0
S_4	38	69		94	6	0
S_5	34	70		94	12	0
S_6	60	94	74	13	4	0
S_7	40	85	72	30	4	0
S_8	14	44	74	98	4	0
Below the Adaptation Level						
S_1	62	94		48	8	0
S_2	62	100		44	6	0
S_3	68	100		38	6	0
S_4	66	98		42	6	0
S_5	72	94		40	6	0

Results

When the AL was set at or near the skin temperature for each S and the comparison buckets increased by a logarithmic scale (discrepancies of 0°, 1°, 3°, 7°, and 15° with the inclusion of a discrepancy of 2° for three Ss), affect first increased and then decreased. This was found with all eight Ss. For five Ss, the

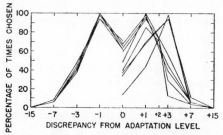

Fig. 2. Affect as a function of discrepancies of temperatures above and below the AL. Data taken from Table 2.

maximum pleasure point (MPP) was a $+1°$ discrepancy. For each of these Ss, $+1°$ was significantly $(P < .01)$ preferred to either $0°$ or the next highest discrepancy. Three Ss preferred a $+3°$

TABLE 3

AFFECT AS A FUNCTION OF DISCREPANCY OF TEMPERATURES ABOVE THE ADAPTATION LEVEL, WHEN ADAPTATION LEVEL WAS INCREASED FROM 33° TO 40°

(*Cell entries are the percentages of times each discrepancy was chosen in relation to the number of times it was offered as a choice with all other discrepancies.*)

S	AL	Discrepancy					
		$0°$	$1°$	$2°$	$3°$	$7°$	$15°$
S_6	33°	60	94*	74	13	4	0
	34°	74	91*	47	13	4	0
	35°	73	88*	48	13	4	0
	36°	97*	73	43	13	4	0
	38°	97*	72	43	13	4	0
	40°	100*	71	42	13	4	0
S_7	33°	40	85*	72	30	4	0
	34°	63	92*	61	21	4	0
	35°	59	99*	56	13	4	0
	36°	84	86*	43	13	4	0
	38°	98*	72	44	13	4	0
	40°	100*	71	42	13	4	0
S_8	33°	14	44	74	98*	4	0
	34°	15	55	70	86*	4	0
	35°	21	46	75	85*	4	0
	36°	56	67	75*	27	4	0
	38°	60	71*	61	35	4	0
	40°	100*	71	42	13	4	0

* Indicates the most preferred discrepancy.

discrepancy as the MPP. Analogous χ^2's reached at least the same significance levels. For each S in every session, there was only one maximum for the function, with a decrease on both sides of the maximum point.

When discrepancies less than the AL were tested, all five Ss preferred an MPP of $-1°$ discrepancy below the AL. All 20 χ^2 tests were significant $(P < .01)$. Hence, for the five Ss tested for both wings of the "butterfly," affect was symmetrically related to the discrepancies in each direction from the AL (see Table 2 and Fig. 2).

In studying the effect of increasing the value of the AL with all three Ss, the AL could be increased from 33° to 35° without changing Ss' preferred discrepancy (MPP); $+3°$ in one case, and $+1°$ in the other two. As the AL increased further, the difference between the MPP and the AL decreased until, for one S, the MPP for an AL of 36° was also 36°; i.e., a zero discrepancy was preferred. For the second S, the MPP was equal to a zero discrepancy at an AL of 38°. The third S did not reach

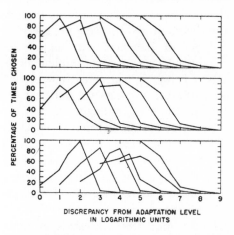

Fig. 3. Affect as a function of discrepancy of temperatures above the AL, when the AL is increased from 33° to 40°. Data taken from Table 3.

an MPP of zero discrepancy until the AL had reached 40°. Above these points, the affect curve decreased in a linear fashion as discrepancy from AL increased further. With these three Ss, it was impossible to establish complete adaptation above 38°. This was defined as not being able to report the neutral sensation in the AL bucket. Above this value, all Ss reported a feeling of warmth.

Discussion

These results supply ample support for the discrepancy hypothesis as to the sources of affect in the temperature sense. For an AL set at or near skin temperature, affect increased and then decreased as a regular function of discrepancies from the AL when the discrepancies were both above the AL and below it. AL's were also established above normal skin temperatures in three Ss up to 38°. Geldard (1953, p. 220) reports that a temperature of 38° takes 4–5 min. to adapt, while in this experiment, Ss rarely took that much time to report adaptation. Since Ss knew the session would last only as long as the time required to make the specified number of judgments, in some cases they may have reported complete adaptation before it had actually occurred, to speed up a somewhat boring task. If this happened, it might explain the leveling out of the "butterfly" effect. It is interesting to speculate as to whether the butterfly would have remained intact if adaptation had been complete at higher temperatures. Following Hebb's theory, this should be expected, because once a cell assembly is established, a slight discrepancy from it should be pleasurable. But if the assembly is not fully organized (i.e.,

adaptation is incomplete), then the discrepancy is measured from whatever assemblies are organized. This implies that if adaptation to 40° is not complete, 41° is not a discrepancy of +1° but really +3° or +4°, depending upon the maximal temperature to which S is adapted. Accepting this reasoning, affect is produced according to the discrepancy hypothesis whenever adaptation is complete, and that in the temperature sense, there is a considerable range over which adaptable AL's can be established.

This experiment involved the actual adaptation of the sense organs, not the central tendency of a series of sensations over time as in many of Helson's examples. The discrepancy hypothesis is applicable to this latter case, where the cell assembly would be the pattern of central nervous system activity resulting from repeated stimulation of a sensory nerve. Alpert (1953) demonstrated the establishment of an adaptation level defined as the summation of previous auditory stimulation. He chose a pattern of very unfamiliar beats, making up a unique rhythm, as a single stimulus, and presented it many times. He argued that, at first, it would be so discrepant from previous AL's for rhythm that it should be unpleasant. As it was repeated, the previous AL's would be modified to include this new pattern. In this way, the discrepancy should decrease and the stimulus would become more pleasant. Eventually, the AL should become identical with the new pattern and the affect would be indifferent. Alpert verified these predictions.

The discrepancy hypothesis is not the only possible explanation of affect. Any of the various forms of a tension reduction theory (e.g., Miller & Dollard, 1941) might be extended to explain affect by assuming that central nervous excitation is minimal when the end-organs are adapted, and that any change from adaptation will produce an increase in stimulation. If increases in stimulation set up a drive state which S tries to reduce (which would appear to be a behavioral definition of negative affect), then a zero discrepancy from the AL should be preferred over all larger discrepancies, according to this theory. This prediction is clearly not borne out by these data, where small discrepancies from AL are decidedly preferred to zero discrepancies. This implies that increases in stimulation can be pleasurable, i.e., sought in themselves and not simply as a means to anxiety reduction, a fact that some tension-reductionists (e.g., Farber, 1953, p. 5; Myers & Miller, 1954) are just coming to recognize. Olds' data (1955) on the reinforcing effects of *increases* in septal stimulation also support this view. These data seem

more in line with a two-factor theory of motivation: that individuals may approach "pleasurable" objects in addition to avoiding "unpleasurable" ones. The discrepancy hypothesis is an attempt to give an independent definition to what is pleasant or unpleasant, independent of the resulting approach or avoidance behavior.

Summary: The Ss adapted both hands to water at or near skin temperature, and then placed each in water of different temperatures, behaviorally making an affective response as to the more pleasant temperature by withdrawing immediately the less comfortable hand. The results showed that small discrepancies from the adaptation level of the hands were more preferred than either larger discrepancies or zero discrepancies. Adaptation levels were then established above normal skin temperature in three Ss. The affective function shifted from a "butterfly" to a monotonically decreasing curve when the adaptation level was increased sufficiently. The discussion pointed out some of the implications of these data for motivational theories.

Play: A Special Behavior

J. Barnard Gilmore

Certainly everyone knows what play is not, even if everyone can't agree on just what play is. Play seems to represent that definitionally impossible "wastebasket" category of behavior, the unmotivated act. Consider these traditional definitions of play (they are actually miniature theories of play) as drawn from Mitchell and Mason (1934):

Spencer: Activity performed for the immediate gratification derived, without regard for ulterior benefits; Lazarus: Play is ac-

tivity which is in itself free, aimless, amusing or diverting; Seashore: Free self expression for the pleasure of expression; Dewey: Activities not consciously performed for the sake of any result beyond themselves; Stern: Play is voluntary, self-sufficient activity; Patrick: Those human activities which are free and spontaneous and which are pursued for their own sake alone, interest in them is self-sustaining, and they are not continued under any internal or external compulsion; Allin: Play refers to those activities which are accompanied by a state of comparative pleasure, exhilaration, power, and the feeling of self-initiative;

Curti: Highly motivated activity which, as free from conflicts is usually though not always, pleasurable (pp. 86–87).

It is clear that the person who wishes to understand play behavior has set himself a difficult task if he uses either his intuitive sense of the term or the above comments as a beginning point of reference, since the definition of play will determine both the theorizing about and the research done with play. To be scientifically workable, any definition must be precise; but "play" is an abstract and global sort of behavior, one that eludes precision. In the past, play has been a thing to be inferred, not the sort of behavior that elicits clear agreement with respect to its presence or absence.

It will be the purpose of this paper to explore the possible causes and effects of play in children, as suggested both by theorists of play and by research on play behavior. Play will be defined arbitrarily by the following behavioral example: a young child takes a piece of cloth and, as if the cloth were human, makes it "go to sleep." While behaviors as divergent as the dancing-like movements of apes and the sober assembly of model airplanes by adolescents have been considered to be play, we will knowingly restrict ourselves to this narrow (and not necessarily "pure") case. Perhaps in thinking about this one small play episode, concepts and distinctions will emerge that could lead to a clearer and more extensive definition of play.

Theories dealing with the causes and the effects of play fall into two general categories. First are those theories concerned only with the antecedents of play and with the inferred purposes of play; these theories regard the specific content of play behaviors as irrelevant. These theories will be termed *classical theories* of play since they spring from the psychological *zeitgeist* prior to World War I. A second general category of play theories, more recent in origin, views the specific form that play takes as being crucial for specifying the causes and effects of play. The play theories of Piaget and of psychoanalysis represent this type of theory.

The Classical Theories of Play

One of the oldest theoretical statements concerning the significance of play is attributed both to Schiller (1873) and to Spencer (1873), although it appears likely that its germ was to be found in educational literature long before their time. Briefly stated, this theory holds that play is the result of a surplus of energy, a surplus that exists because the young are freed from the business of self-preservation through the actions of their parents. The energy surplus finds its release in the aimless exuberant activities that we term play. This theory is usually referred to as the *surplus energy theory* of play. It postulates, first, a quantity of energy available to the organism and, second, a tendency to expend this energy, even though it is not necessary for the maintenance of a life balance, through goalless activity (play). In the terms of the surplus energy theory, then, the play behavior represented by the young child's making a cloth toy "go to sleep" would be seen as essentially unpredictable and meaningless behavior, pushed into being by the automatic production of unneeded energies. The going-to-sleep-play could just as well have been any other sort of play-like behavior with no consequences for the surplus energy theory of play. The surplus energy theory of play is an appealing one, and it has been put forward in a variety of forms, most notably by Tolman (1932), Tinklepaugh (1942), and Alexander (1958).

A second classical theory of play sees this activity not as the product of a surplus of energy, but rather as the product of a deficit of energy. Play is here seen as a method by which spent energy can be replenished. This theory, the *relaxation theory* of play is associated primarily with Lazarus (1883) and with Patrick (1916). Essentially, play is seen by these men as a mode of dissipating the inhibition built up from fatigue due to tasks that are relatively new to the organism. Thus, play is found most often in childhood. Play not only replenishes energy for the as-yet-unfamiliar cognitive activities of the child, but, because it also reflects "deep-rooted race habits" (by which is meant phylogenically acquired behaviors that are *not* therefore new to the organism), play is the one activity that shows very little build-up of inhibition over time. This theory of play would view the "making-the-toy-sleep" episode as a simple restful activity reflecting perhaps an inherited ability to show simple symbolization, an activity caused by the fact that the child was psychically too fatigued to do anything else.

A great many of the general theorists who have considered the meaning of play have seen it as a form of instinctive behavior. The number of theorists who have seen play in this light approaches two dozen, as cited by Britt and Janus (1941) and by Beach (1945). Perhaps the most eloquent of these theorists is Karl Groos (1898, 1908a) whose theory has come to be known as the *preexercise theory* of play. Play for

Groos is seen as the product of emerging instincts, something that fixes these instincts and exercises them in preparation for their maturation time. The episode of play we have taken for our working definition would be explained by the preexercise theory as possibly the first stirrings of a parental instinct.

At about the time Karl Groos' preexercise theory was becoming known, G. Stanley Hall (1906) put forward his *recapitulation theory*, which saw play not as an activity that developed future instinctual skills, but rather one that served to rid the organism of primitive and unnecessary instinctual skills carried over by heredity. Hall was the first to conceive of stages of play; he postulated that each child passes through a series of play stages corresponding to, and recapitulating, the cultural stages in the development of races. Wundt (1913) was another well-known proponent of the recapitulation theory of play. The recapitulation theory would seem to place the episode of "making-the-cloth-toy-sleep" in the category of a vestigal primitive behavior, perhaps magicoreligious in original intent.

Another theory-like approach to play came from the work of Appleton (1910). She studied play in primitive cultures and in children, and she concluded that play is a response to a generalized drive for growth in the organism; it is not instinctual preexercise as conceived by Groos. Appleton saw as the basis for play a hunger in the organism for growth to a stage at which the instinct can operate. Thus, play serves to facilitate the mastery of skills necessary to the function of adult instincts. The child plays because he wants this mastery and he "knows" that play is the method by which he may achieve it. There are other theories of play, mostly in the educational literature, which are akin to this one in their stress of a self-actualizing basis for play, but they will not be traced here. Theories of play such as Appleton's we will term *growth theories.*

Similar to the growth theories are the ego-expanding theories of play put forward first by K. Lange (1901), and later by Claparède (1911, 1934). "Ego" here means the reality-meeting and reality-mapping aspects of cognitive life. Thus, Lange sees play as being nature's way of completing the ego and Claparède sees play as an expressive exercising of the ego and the rest of the personality, an exercising that strengthens developing cognitive skills and aids the emergence of additional cognitive skills.

These, then, are the purely classical theories of play. They are classical insofar as all of them view the specific content of play behaviors as being more or less incidental to the causes of play generally. Surprisingly, there are essentially no research data relevant to these theories of play, so that if one wishes to evaluate their worth he must rely on observations and personal impressions (see Hurlock, 1934). This is not to imply that the classical theories of play are untestable. On the contrary. A direct consequence of the surplus energy theory of play, for instance, is that children should play more when rested than when they are fatigued. Speaking generally, this seems to be the case, yet the limits of this "truth" need empirical testing. A direct consequence of the relaxation theory of play would be that any person should do better on a new task following a period of play than after having done some different new task. Perhaps there is more reason to question this hypothesis than was the

case with the hypothesis drawn from the surplus energy theory of play.

The preexercise theory of play is only as impressive as the concept of human instincts. If one grants the existence of a parental instinct, then it should be possible to design an experiment that denies the opportunity for parent-role play and evaluates the influence of this restriction on later parental behavior. The recapitulation theory predicts that children's play should mirror the development of cultures, so that we should never see a child play at a "higher" function before he first plays at a "lower" one. Of those we have called classical theories of play, only the growth theories and the ego-expanding theories of play admit of no ready, testable derivatives. From the standpoint of the person who wishes to understand the causes and the effects of play, the classical theories have only two major drawbacks. First, they do not undertake to explain the wide individual differences found in human play behavior, and second, they have produced no important research data to support their various positions.

The newer theories of play differ from the classical play theories primarily in that they invoke explanations of play behavior based on dynamic factors of individual personality, and they are geared to explaining individual shifts in play behavior. These newer theories of play will be called the *infantile dynamics theories* of play, after Piaget. The most elaborated of the infantile dynamics theories are those of Piaget and psychoanalysis; but two early theories belonging in this category are those of Lewin (1933) and Buytendijk (1934).

For Lewin, play occurs because the cognitive life-space of the child is still unstructured, resulting in a failure to discriminate between the real and the unreal. It is easy then, for the child to pass into the region of playful unreality where things are changeable and arbitrary. Lewin does not elucidate this thesis further, except to state that in childhood a force or tendency arises to leave the region of reality, especially when this region is dominated by an "overstrong pressure."

Like Lewin, Buytendijk holds that a child plays because he is a child, because his cognitive "dynamics" do not allow any other way of behaving. The four main characteristics of the child's dynamics that determine this fact for Buytendijk are: a lack of motor and mental coherence or coordination, an inability to delay or detour, a need to achieve sympathetic understanding (what he has called a "pathic" attitude) as opposed to objective knowledge, and an ambivalence toward all objects, especially strange ones. Thus, play is an expression of the child's uncoordinated approach to the environment; it allows a pathic understanding of the environment and achieves immediate ends. But play is also ambivalent and reflects only a temporarily prepotent approach tendency to objects. Play for Buytendijk is rhythmic, reflecting the relaxation phase of a tension-relaxation cycle. Finally, Buytendijk's infantile dynamics theory asserts that children (as well as animals) "play" only with images, which constitute the actual expression of the child's pathic understanding. Within the framework of the infantile dynamics theory, play is the child's way of thinking. In these last theories of play the explanation of our definitional example of play would be that it represents a straightforward working outcome of the "forces" identified in the

theories. Thus, the play of "making-the-cloth-sleep" is the symbolic way children come to comprehend the act of going to sleep, when they try to think about such a thing. Piaget's theory would offer a generally similar explanation for such play behavior.

Piaget's Theory of Play

Piaget's theory of play goes a good deal beyond that of Buytendijk. While Piaget sees play as the inevitable result of the child's cognitive structure, he has formulated the problem more precisely. "Play is but a part of the whole infantile dynamics, and although we agree that it derives from them, the question to be answered is in what conditions it does so, and why it does not always do so" (1945, p. 160).[1]

Speaking generally, Piaget sees play as the product of a stage of thinking, through which the child must pass in developing from an original egocentric and phenomenalistic viewpoint to an adult's objective and rationalistic outlook. More specifically, in situations in which the person has any basis for behaving, every human encounter with the environment has two discriminable aspects that are central to Piaget's general theory of behavior. On the one hand, a person recognizes, categorizes, and utilizes events in terms of previous

[1] Piaget's entire discussion of his theory of play is contained in his book *Play, Dreams and Imitation* in Childhood. This book is quite difficult to read or to interpret without prior grounding in Piaget's more general theory of behavior, as put forward in his many other works. Since these other works are not directly relevant to Piaget's theory of play, however, only the 1945 work has been cited in this paper. For the interested reader, an excellent introduction to Piaget has been written by J. H. Flavell and published by Van Nostrand: *The Developmental Psychology of Jean Piaget* (1962).

habits, conventions, and preferences. He bends reality to fit what he "knows." On the other hand, a person notes unique aspects of a new encounter and takes account of these in an effort to change, modify, or in some way adjust himself to better fit the new reality. These two aspects of behavior are always fused and always present. One aspect can *predominate* over the other, however, and distinguishing them at the theoretical level is crucial for Piaget's theory of behavior and play. Piaget implies that these two aspects of behavior spring from different sources, appear at different times, and develop at different rates. It is this fact of cognitive dynamics that is said to lead us to see so much play in children.

Play, for Piaget, is all behavior in which the aspect of adjustment to fit reality, (that is, the aspect of mental accommodation to things as they really are) is deemphasized. Play occurs insofar as behavior is purely one of "taking in," of bending reality to fit one's existing forms of thought. Since this is an aspect of all behavior, every behavior has at least some play-like aspects. One can't speak of play versus non-play in the Piagetian schema of things; behaviors are only less or more playful insofar as they do or do not make some attempt to cope with reality.

Piaget has distinguished three broad categories of play. Early in a child's life any newly mastered motor ability will be performed over and over in different contexts. All objects that the infant encounters are bent to fit this new behavior pattern regardless of their suitability. No new learning takes place during such behavior, and there is every evidence of pleasure from the child. This is an example of what Piaget has distinguished as practice

play. The definitional play example of making the rag "go to sleep," which was taken as the model for this paper, is an example of what Piaget has distinguished as symbolic play. The rag is treated as if it were alive, and it is played with so as to symbolize what is salient for the child in the concept of going to sleep. Piaget distinguishes a third major category of play that he has termed "games with rules." This type of play develops latest in children, and is exactly what its title suggests.

Piaget has said that play is seen insofar as thoughts and objects are bent to fit existing concepts or thought patterns while some obvious and logical aspects of things are ignored, or deemphasized. This is precisely what occurs in dreaming, and Piaget sees a close link between the play of children and the dreaming process. Just why we revert to a play-like mode of thought in sleep is not a matter that Piaget's theory has undertaken to explain. Instead, *the process is accepted as a given,* and Piaget is content to describe and label the important aspects of this process.

In the same way, Piaget has described how the traditional play of childhood comes about. As a newborn, a human has only the most rudimentary reflex abilities to recognize and incorporate his experiences, or to make allowances for any unique aspects of his experiences. (And these, remember, are the two functions with which Piaget's theory always deals.) Piaget postulates, however, a tendency in all living organisms to make repeated contact with any slightly novel event; and in the newborn, this tendency "forces" new awareness, new habits, new expectations, and new distinctions regarding the environment as a whole. There is, then, an increase in the modes of response to the environment, and the two functions with which Piaget deals become more discriminable, each from the other. The infant gradually becomes able to act by habit and to ignore the now reduced number of unique components to a given experience. Thus, as the infant becomes able to behave in a play-like fashion, that is, without regard to any but the familiar and habitual aspects of the situation, this very potential for play begins to be immediately realized. The play potential is realized for the same sorts of reasons that a coin tossed many times will realize its potential for showing some "heads." It is the nature of the child that his cognitive structure will lead to play.

Why then does play drop out as the child grows up? Piaget suggests there are two answers. First, as we have noted, adults can and do show some play-like behavior, as for instance in dream life. But they also do so, to varying degrees, in many other areas. Doodling is an example of one of the *most* play-like adult behaviors. Thus, one answer is that play doesn't drop out, it remains in certain new areas of adult experience and in "unconscious" behaviors. A second answer as to why play drops out seems to be that as the child has more experiences, he can more easily respond to things as they are, rather than to things only insofar as he has known them. Put another way, the child acquires new possibilities for inventing improved, more rational, modes of handling encounters with the unfamiliar environment. With the development of this ability, then, the tendency to resort to actions that are only partially appropriate to a situation (play behavior) is reduced. Eventually,

with adult mastery of the environment, the person has a greatly reduced "need" to resort to bending reality to fit his state of the moment.

To summarize Piaget's position so far, play is the behavior seen whenever there is a preponderance of that aspect of all behavior that involves taking in, molding, and using things, all in terms of one's current inclination and habit, without deference to any aspects of so behaving that might not "fit" in some sense. Play *can* occur only insofar as behaviors are sophisticated enough to show differentiation between (a) the taking-in aspect of behavior that bends reality to fit the self and (b) the self-modifying aspects of behavior that bend the self to fit reality. Play *can* occur only insofar as there are many different modes of thought and action into which reality may be bent. Thus it is that the newborn shows no play, and that until middle childhood more and more play is seen. Finally, play *will not* occur insofar as more adaptive responses become familiar and can be easily invented when needed. Thus it is that play is reduced in prominence in late childhood.

Piaget's theory calls for a sharp distinction between the causes of play and its effects. It is to the latter that we next turn. There are two important by-products of play behavior according to the Piagetian formulation. The first such by-product is joy, pleasure, or some closely related affective state. This is clearest in the earliest "practice play" behavior of children. The infant of eight months will repeat a movement that shakes a rattle over and over again, while showing the most obvious signs of delight. For Piaget, play brings with it "the functional pleasure of use." At older ages the pleasure seen in play is primarily one of efficacy (see White, 1959); that is, it is the less visible pleasure of self-assertion. Yet as the child grows older and his play becomes more symbolic, the pleasure attendant on play becomes less obvious. Even so, pleasure is one of Piaget's implicit criteria of play behavior, and the absence of pleasure from what might otherwise be considered play behavior suggests that a reality-based attempt to learn may be prominent in such behavior.

The second by-product of play, within the framework of Piaget's theory, is an adaptive one. Play is seen as functioning in such a way that it prevents new abilities, both physical and mental, from being lost due to disuse. Play fixes and retains the new abilities since it is just such abilities that are likely to be getting the most attention when "reality" is getting very little. Thus, on the basis of Piaget's theory, if play behavior were to be prevented somehow—a difficult thing since the sources of play are presumed to be internal—then many fewer abilities and concepts would remain available to the child. (As it stands however, Piaget's theory would not preclude the possibility of reforming all abilities that were once available.) It can be seen that an understanding of play behavior may well have important implications for the education of all young children.

On the basis of his theory of play and his more general theory of cognitive development, Piaget has developed a system for categorizing various types of play behavior. We shall not explore this system here, except to note that Piaget has set aside two categories to identify play that, in addition to the typical by-products already noted, serves to reduce an unpleasantness for the child. The first such category of play

has been termed *compensatory combinations,* and it refers to behavior that "improves" reality by distorting it to fit more agreeable and desired thoughts. For example, Piaget's daughter pretended to be carrying her newborn cousin after being told that she must not touch the baby. The second such category of play Piaget has termed *liquidating combinations,* and it refers to behavior that has been freed from a need to allow for the presence of strong affect that, originally, came connected with the play-provoking situation. For example, having been frightened by the sight of a dead duck, Piaget's daughter later played at imitating the motionless bird and made her dolls "see" a dead duck without fear. In setting aside these two special categories of play, Piaget has recognized a possible source of play that is taken as the core for what we shall term the *cathartic theory* of play, of which the *psychoanalytic theory* of play is the most recent and most lucid variant.

The Cathartic and Psychoanalytic Theories of Play

The cathartic theory of play has roots that extend as far back as the writings of Aristotle (see Mitchell & Mason, 1934). Briefly, the cathartic theory sees play as reflecting the child's attempt to master situations that at first were too much for him. Carr (1902) was among the earliest to put forward this theory of play. Groos (1908b) extended his preexercise theory of play somewhat to include a cathartic aspect. Reaney (1916), Robinson (1920), and Curti (1930), all have elaborated variations on the cathartic theory of play.

The psychoanalytic theory of play is

a special case of the more general cathartic theory. The psychoanalytic play theory was first introduced by Freud (1908, 1920, 1926) incidental to considerations of phantasy and repetition behaviors. Freud thought of play as being closely related to phantasy behavior, in fact he defined play as phantasy woven around real objects (toys), as contrasted with pure phantasy, which is daydreaming. Play, for Freud, shares many of the unconscious determinants that shape dream life, and in this respect Freud's theory of play is similar to that of Piaget.

Freud distinguished two classes of wishes, either of which he considered to be a necessary source of play. First, there are the wishes a child has to be big, grownup, or in the shoes of someone more fortunate. Thus, in accordance with an inherited tendency to seek immediate pleasure, even if this pleasure must be in part hallucinated, the child phantasies some situation he would like to see exist. Second, the child can be driven into play by his wishes to take the active role in all painful encounters that have been passively suffered. Play arising from this source does so in accordance with an inherited tendency to repeat, over and over, any experience that has been too much for the child. Thus, Erikson has observed:

[Individual child play] often proves to be the infantile way of thinking over difficult experiences and of *restoring a sense of mastery,* comparable to the way in which we repeat, in ruminations and in endless talk, in daydreams and in dreams during sleep, experiences which have been too much for us (1959, p. 85).

In the psychoanalytic theory of play "a sense of mastery" is the most typically cited *effect* of play. It is important to note, however, that this mastery feeling is necessarily restricted to play that serves to reverse a previous painful experience. Play that is purely wish fulfillment will have as its effect the feeling of "pleasure" that is presumed to be inherent in all reductions of psychic tension according to psychoanalytic theory. Play that springs from wishes can have the effect not only of a circumvention of reality, but, as Waelder (1933) has pointed out, play can also circumvent the action of the superego. In play one can presumably achieve the physically or the morally impossible.

More recently there have been some important refinements of, and additions to, the more general psychoanalytic theory of play described so far. Anna Freud (1936) has pointed out that one effect of imitative play, in those cases where the imitated object is feared, is a lessening and binding of the fear either of the object or of what the object may represent for the child. Thus, play may serve not only to lower anxiety around a given context through promotion of active coping devices, but it may serve a *defensive* purpose as well by denying any grounds for anxiety. The exact formula under which imitative play may accomplish any defensive ends has not been suggested. One could speculate, however, that it does so under the magic formula: "Since the object and I are so alike, it will fear me just as I fear it; it will also love me just as I love me, and it will not surprise me by anything it may do, for I would be likely to do similar things myself."

Erikson (1937, 1940, 1950, 1951, 1959) is well known for his recent contributions to a psychoanalytic theory of play.

While agreeing with Freud regarding the major sources of play, Erikson has emphasized the coping effects of play. He has said: "I propose the theory that the child's play is the infantile form of the human ability to deal with experience by creating model situations and to master reality by experiment and planning" (1950, p. 195). Perhaps more important has been Erikson's contribution of the concept of play disruption. Not only does anxiety lead to play of a relevant nature, suggests Erikson, but play can get out of hand, as it were, thus mobilizing the very anxiety with which it is trying to deal. The result is an abrupt stop in play behavior. Says Erikson: "The human animal not only plays most and longest, it also remains ready to become deadly serious in the most irrational contexts" (1940, p. 562). In addition to Erikson, a number of psychoanalytic theorists have put forward their own elaborations of the theory of play introduced by Freud. Among the most notable are Klein (1929), Peller (1954), and Alexander (1958).

With this background on the cathartic theories of play, consider how they would account for the making-the-rag-go-to-sleep play of our working example: There is a certain degree of psychic pain caused the young child when he is told to go to sleep, for the child wishes both to comply and to remain awake. Further, the child does not want to feel he must submit to adult demands. Thus, the sleep play of our example occurs as a cathartic, wish-impelled response to this lingering psychic pain. It is regrettable that the precise manner in which psychic conflict produces play behavior is not spelled out in any of the cathartic theories. While the implication that

play occurs as a response instrumental to the reduction of psychic pain is always strong, the cathartic theories of play have never quite made the full distinction that pain reduction as an *effect* of play does not demonstrate that pain is necessarily a *cause* of play behavior.

On Evaluating the Infantile Dynamics Theories of Play

The psychoanalytic theory of play and Piaget's theory of play are well developed and explicit, but, curiously enough, these theories, too, have led to little, if any, research. Both theories are based on close and careful observation, yet neither has led to an experimental assessment. A search of the play literature reveals that the two great areas in which play has been studied are those of (a) cataloguing the leisure activity of children according to their location along many different dimensions, and (b) observing the doll "play" of different children for components of various behaviors, especially aggression.

A comprehensive summary of all but the recent studies of play preferences can be found in Britt and Janus (1941). This research is of tangential relevance to the theories under consideration, however, and much of it suffers from a variety of limiting problems in design. More relevant is the research with doll play, a literature that has been summarized by Levin and Wardwell (1962). Doll play assessment derives from psychoanalytic theory; it proceeds on the assumption of the validity of psychoanalytic hypotheses. Thus, while doll play research has provided certain observational data that generally can be interpreted as supporting the psychoanalytic theory of play, such research is not free from its own assumptions and is not directed specifically toward testing the psychoanalytic theory of play. There is nothing unscientific about the study of play or about the testing of play theories, yet to date only the author (Gilmore, 1964) seems to have a relevant test of the infantile dynamics play theories of Piaget and psychoanalysis.

On the basis of Piaget's general theory of play, especially on the basis of his comments regarding the role of novelty in predisposing play and regarding pleasure as an accompaniment (albeit a presumed effect) of play, Gilmore hypothesized that children would prefer to play with toys that were somewhat novel for them, as opposed to simple toys. It was further hypothesized that anxious children would prefer to play with novel toys over simple toys less than would nonanxious children, but would prefer to play with toys relevant to the source of their anxiety (as opposed to irrelevant toys) more than would nonanxious children. children. Three studies were conducted to check these hypotheses.

The first study, observational in design, employed children hospitalized for tonsillectomy as "anxious" subjects. Matched control subjects, ranging in age from five years through eight years, were seen in their school. All subjects were presented with toys representing dimensions of (a) novelty (or complexity) and (b) relevance and irrelevance to hospitalization. The primary measure of play was the time each subject spent touching the toys. The results of this study strongly supported the hypothesis that anxious children prefer anxiety-relevant toys more than do nonanxious children. All children preferred novel toys, however, and there was

no evidence to support the hypothesis that nonanxious children would prefer novel toys more than would anxious children. This first study admitted of two important possibilities, however. Children who came for tonsillectomy may still have been different than their matched control counterparts, thus determining their preference for hospital-relevant toys. And it may have been the *interest* of the hospital routine that led to hospital play, without the children's obvious anxiety having been in any way causal. A second, experimental study was done to control these possibilities.

In the second study, then, children were randomly assigned to an anxious or nonanxious condition. Subjects volunteered to join a club and expected some sort of initiation, possibly painful, involving the eyes or the ears. Anxious subjects were further divided, on a random basis, into two groups, those expecting auditory and those expecting visual pain. The remaining group, of nonanxious subjects, was told there would be no painful initiation. Play materials were presented twice to every subject, before and after "the initiation." The toys represented both (a) novel or simple and (b) auditory- or visual-relevant dimensions. Thus, toys which were anxiety-relevant for half the anxious subjects were the anxiety-irrelevant toys for the remaining half of the anxious subjects, and vice versa. Time spent with the toys again served as the measure of play. The "initiation" assessed the fear level of each subject, and results from this measure gave excellent evidence that the anxiety manipulations were effective as intended.

In this experimental, second study, results for the auditory fear group gave further support to the hypothesis that anxious children prefer anxiety-relevant toys over anxiety-irrelevant toys. It was suggested that a ceiling effect may have prevented similar results from appearing in the visual fear group since even when not anxious, all subjects preferred the visual toys. Again, no evidence was found to support the hypothesis that anxious children will prefer novel toys less than will nonanxious children. Novel toys were heavily preferred to simple toys by all subjects.

A third study was done to check on the stability of the auditory fear data in view of the absence of similar findings in the visual fear condition. In this third study, an auditory fear group and a nonanxious control group were created exactly as in the previous study. Further, a new, nonanxious "auditory control" group was set up in which subjects expected an enjoyable auditory "initiation." This new group served to control completely for any possibility that the *salience* of the forthcoming auditory experience might be producing the auditory-toy play instead of the anxiety generated by the expectation. As in the second study, results showed that the anxiety manipulations worked as intended. Further, both the standard control subjects and the new auditory control subjects showed play preferences mirroring those of the previous control group. Thus, the salience of the expected auditory initiation does not seem to account for the findings of these studies. However, the new auditory fear subjects showed a significant *avoidance* of anxiety-relevant toys when they were anxious.

The findings of this third study were just opposite to the findings of the previous study, and they did not support the hypothesis derived from the

psychoanalytic theory of play. There was no noticeable difference between the schools or subjects in these last two studies on the basis of which to explain the dramatic shift in observed play under conditions of anxiety. There was, however, a suggestion that the anxious subjects in this third study were more afraid than were the previous anxious subjects. Recalling Erikson's description of play disruption when anxiety becomes too great, it might be postulated that unusually anxious subjects in this third study found the anxiety-relevant toys too frightening to play with.

Two conclusions seem warranted from these three studies viewed as a whole. First, toy novelty or simplicity does not interact appreciably with a child's anxious state to produce changes in toy preferences. All children seem to prefer novel (or complex) toys over "simple" toys. Thus, the data from these studies fit the Piagetian theory of play without, at the same time, providing great support for it. Secondly, one can conclude that the presence of anxiety changes a child's preferences for toys relevant to his anxiety, but this change can be an increased or decreased preference, depending upon as yet unspecified additional factors. Thus, the psychoanalytic theory of play received some tentative support from the data of these studies, especially if that play theory is expanded to include play-avoiding behavior under conditions of heightened anxiety.

The studies just described constitute only the beginning of what will certainly have to be a great many experiments probing the causes and effects of play. Play is a special behavior, one that will be difficult to explore for many initially unsuspected reasons. The ery ambiguity of the term "play," the uncertainty as to just how different behaviors may be to still qualify as "play," will constantly work to divide and confuse all who do not first consider and communicate their personal definitions of the term. And if research on theories of play is to be carried out, a satisfactory dependent measure of play will have to be devised. Gilmore (1964) used as his play criterion the touching of toys, but this measure has obvious limits. These are only the first of the problems that research in play will meet.

If research on play is scarce and difficult to do, it cannot also be said that theories of play are either scarce or untestable. A great deal of theoretical attention has been paid to play behavior. A great many hypotheses stand ready to be investigated on the basis of the theories of play. The question remains: Why will a young child take a piece of cloth and "make it go to sleep?"

The Epigenesis of Intrinsic Motivation and Early Cognitive Learning[1]

J. McV. Hunt

Even as late as 15 years ago, a symposium on the stimulation of early cognitive learning would have been almost impossible. It would have been taken by most people as a sign that both participants and members of the audience were too soft-headed to be considered seriously. Even as late as 15 years ago, there was simply no point in talking about such a matter, for no possibility of altering cognitive capacity, or intelligence, was conceived to exist. To be sure, there was, before World War II, some evidence that suggested, even strongly, that cognitive capacities might be modified by early experience; but such evidence as existed was "too loose" to convince anyone who embraced the assumptions that intelligence is fixed and that development is predetermined (see Hunt, 1961). These two assumptions—and I believed and taught them just as did most of us—were considered to be among the marks of a "sound" and "hard-headed" psychologist. Had we psychologists absorbed the implications of Johannsen's (1903) distinction between the genotype and the phenotype and his notion that the phenotype is always a product of continuous, on-going, organism–environment interaction, we should never have held these two assumptions with such certainty; but of the two fathers of the science of genetics we knew only Mendel. Since World War II, however, the various investigations of the effects of infantile ·experience has piled up sufficient evi-

[1] This paper was originally prepared for the symposium on the Stimulation of Early Cognitive Learning, chaired by J. R. Braun and presented at the Annual Meeting of the American Psychological Association, Philadelphia, Pennsylvania, 30 August 1963. It was written with the support of Public Health Service Grant MH K6–18,567.

dence to nearly destroy the credibility of these two dominant assumptions of our post-Darwinian tradition.

The change in conceptions started with the work of Sigmund Freud, but it has recently taken some abrupt new turns. Freud's (1905) theory of psychosexual development attributed great importance to the effects of early infantile experience and especially to the preverbal fates of instinctive modes of pleasure-getting. The earliest studies of the effects of infantile experience assumed these effects to be on the emotional rather than on the intellectual aspects of personality (Hunt, 1941). Yet the studies of the effects of the richness of environmental variations encountered during infancy on adult maze-learning ability in rats (Hebb, 1947) and in dogs (Thompson & Heron, 1954) have proved to be most regularly reproducible. These studies stemmed from the neuropsychological theorizing of Donald Hebb (1949) and his distinction between "early learning," in which "cell-assemblies" are developed, and "later learning," in which these assemblies are connected in various kinds of "phase sequences." The studies showed that those rats encountering the larger number of environmental variations during infancy received higher scores on the Hebb-Williams (1946) maze-test of animal intelligence than did those encountering fewer variations (see Forgays & Forgays, 1952; Forgus, 1954; Hymovitch, 1952).

In Hebb's (1947) original study of this kind, the number of variations in environment ranged from the many supplied by pet-reared rats in a human home to the few supplied by cage-rearing in the laboratory. A similar approach was employed by Thompson & Heron (1954), and dogs pet-reared from

weaning until eight months of age proved to be markedly superior in performance on the Hebb-Williams test at 18 months of age (after ten months with their cage-reared litter-mates in a dog pasture) to those litter-mates individually cage-reared from weaning to eight months. In fact, the pet-reared dogs appeared to differ more from their cage-reared litter-mates than did the pet-reared rats from their litter-mates. From this I am inclined to infer that the degree of the adult effect of such infantile experience increases as one goes up the vertebrate scale. I tend to attribute this apparent increase in the effect of infantile experience to the increasing proportion of the brain that is without direct connections with receptor input and/or motor output (see Pribram, 1960). I refer here, of course, to the notion of the A/S ratio first put forth by Hebb (1949).

This notion, that the degree of effect of the richness of variations in environment encountered during infancy on adult cognitive capacities increases with the size of the A/S ratio, suggests that the results of these animal studies should probably generalize to the human species. Incontrovertible evidence concerning this suggestion is hard to come by. Nevertheless, a combination of observations strongly supports the suggestion that such early experience has marked effects on the rate of human development and perhaps also has effects on the level of adult intellectual ability.

First, the evidence concerning effects of early experience upon the rate of human intellectual development is fairly compelling. It has long been noted that children being reared in orphanages show retardation in both their functional development and their motivational apathy. These observations were long discounted because of the notion that only those genotypically inferior remain in orphanages, but the well-known studies of René Spitz (1945, 1946) helped to rule out this attribution of the retardation to a selection of genotypes. Unfortunately, Spitz's observations could be discounted on other grounds (see Pinneau, 1955). More recently, however, Wayne Dennis (1960), whose prejudices would appear from his previous writings to favor the traditional assumptions of "fixed intelligence" and "predetermined development," has found two orphanages in Teheran where retardation is even more extreme than that reported by Spitz. Of those infants in their second year, 60 percent were still unable to sit up alone; of those in their fourth year, 85 percent were still unable to walk alone. Moreover, while children typically creep on all fours rather than scoot, as did the children in a third orphanage in Teheran (one for demonstration purposes), those in these two typically chose scooting. By way of explanation, Spitz emphasized the emotional factors associated with lack of mothering (a one-to-one interpersonal relationship) as the basis for the greater retardation observed at "foundling home" than at "nursery." Dennis, on the other hand, has attributed the extreme retardation in sitting and walking to lack of learning opportunities, or more specifically, to the "paucity of handling, including failure of attendants to place children in the sitting position and the prone position" (1960, p. 58). These may well be important factors, but I suspect that yet another factor is of sufficient importance to deserve specific investigative attention—namely, a paucity of variation in auditory and visual inputs, or, perhaps I should say a paucity of meaningful variation in these inputs. On the visual side, these Teheran infants (i.e., those in the orphanages in which 90 percent of the children are recorded as having been under one month of age at the time of admission) had plenty of light, but they continually faced homogeneous off-whiteness interrupted only by passing attendants who seldom stopped to be perceived. On the auditory side, while the noise level of the surrounding city was high and cries of other children were numerous, seldom did clear variations in sound come with such redundancy as to become recognizable and very seldom did such sound variations herald any specific changes in visual input. Thus, opportunities for the development of specific variations in either type of input and opportunities for auditory-visual coordinations were lacking. Moreover, since no toys were provided, the children had little opportunity to develop intentional behavior calculated to make interesting spectacles last. Dennis has reported the most extreme case of mass retardation of which I know. Although signs of malnutrition were present, Dennis was inclined not to consider it a major factor because of the vigor he observed in such automatisms as head shaking and rocking back and forth, and because he could see no way in which malnutrition could call forth scooting rather than creeping. Moreover, the role of heredity was minimized by the facts that the children in the demonstration orphanage, where retardation was much less marked, came from the one admitting neonates, and that they were probably chosen from those most retarded at the time of transfer.

Second, the evidence concerning the

permanence of such effects is highly suggestive if less compelling than that concerning rate of development. Whether or not such retardation as that observed in Teheran inevitably leaves a permanent deficit cannot be stated with certainty. You will recall that Dennis observed that once these children in the orphanage learned to walk, they appeared to walk and run as well as other children do. But do not most intellectual and social functions demand a much more broadly integrated and more finely differentiated set of autonomous central processes than do such motor functions as walking and running? Certainly this is suggested by the fact that the dogs pet-reared by Thompson and Heron (1954) are much superior to those cage-reared in solving various problems in the Hebb-Williams mazes even after a period of ten months of running free in the dog pasture. Moreover, permanence of the effects of infantile experience is also strongly suggested by the results of Goldfarb's (see 1955) studies, in which adolescents, orphanage-reared for approximately their first three years, showed lower IQs, less rich fantasies, less tendency to take and hold onto a task, and more social problems than did adolescents (matched with those orphanage-reared for educational and socioeducational status of their mothers) who were reared in foster homes for those first three years. And again, permanence of intellectual deficit is also suggested by the finding in Israel that children of Jewish immigrants from the Orient persist in their scholastic inferiority to children of Jewish immigrants from Western countries, and by the observations that children from the slums in America persist in scholastic inferiority

to children from middle-class parents, even though the slum children may be advanced at least in motor development at ages from one to two years. In spite of these strong suggestions, it would be exceedingly interesting to have direct evidence from test performances at adolescence of these orphanage-reared Iranians for comparison with the test performances of family-reared Iranians or of adolescents reared in the demonstration orphanage. It is also important to determine whether the intellectual deficit from defective early experience is irreversible, or persists because of the way in which human children are usually treated once they achieve certain ages. If the latter alternative is the case, it should be possible to devise corrective experiences to overcome the deficit. This would be re-studying the issues that concerned Itard and Seguin. Getting the evidence necessary to decide such issues is exceedingly difficult.

Early Cognitive Learning and the Development of Intrinsic Motivation

Combining such bits of evidence as I have indicated with the geneticist's conception of genotype-environment interaction and with the biologist's notion of organism-environment interaction now makes it quite sensible to attempt to stimulate early cognitive learning. This evidence, however, hardly indicates how to go about it. Perhaps the most fruitful source of suggestions about how to proceed comes from an examination of the relationship between the development of intrinsic motivation and early cognitive learning.

CHANGES IN TRADITIONAL ASSUMPTIONS OF MOTIVATION

One of the leading traditional assumptions about motivation, namely, that painful stimulation during infancy leads inevitably (through something like Pavlovian conditioning) to increased proclivity to anxiousness and to reduced capacity for adaptation or learning, has been called into serious question by evidence from studies of the effects of painful infantile experience. Various investigators have found that rats submitted to painful electric shock, like those handled and petted, defecate and urinate less in an unfamiliar situation than do those left unmolested in the maternal nest (see Denenberg, 1959, 1962; Denenberg & Karas, 1960; Denenberg, Morton, Kline, & Grota, 1962; Levine, 1956, 1957, 1958, 1959). If proneness to defecate or urinate in an unfamiliar situation is an index to anxiousness, these findings appear to deny the notion that anxiousness is an inevitable consequence of painful stimulation and to suggest that painful stimulation may be a special case of the principle that variation in inputs helps to immunize an animal to fear of the strange. Moreover, investigators have found that encounters with electric shock before weaning may increase the adult ability of rats to learn, at least when this ability is indexed by means of the number of trials required to establish an avoidance response to painful stimulation (see Brookshire, 1958; Brookshire, Littman, & Stewart, 1961; Denenberg, 1959; Denenberg & Bell, 1960; Denenberg & Karas, 1960; Levine, 1956, 1958; Levine, Chevalier, & Korchin, 1956). Encounters with painful electric shock in infancy appear to

share with petting and handling the same kind of effects upon avoidance conditioning just as they share similar effects upon later defecation and urination in an unfamiliar situation. At least, this appears to be true for rats, but it may not be true for mice (see Lindzey, Lykken, & Winston, 1960).

Perhaps this surprising similarity in the effects of painful stimulation and in the effects of petting and handling is an artifact of comparing the effects of each of these kinds of encounters with the effects of leaving the infant rat unmolested in the maternal nest. In such comparisons, painful shock, petting, and handling all constitute variations in receptor inputs or in environmental encounters. It has been argued that these various kinds of input are equivalent in their effects on still unweaned rat pups and that it is only stimulation per se that counts in early infancy (Levine, 1959). This, however, can hardly be so, for Salama & Hunt (1964) have found that rats shocked daily during their second ten days of life show substantially less "fixation" effect of shock at the choice-point in a T-maze than do their litter-mates that were petted or handled. The petted and handled rats in this experiment showed "fixation" effects that did not differ significantly from those of litter-mates left unmolested in the maternal nest. The findings of this experiment show that some of the effects of shock in early infancy differ markedly from those of petting and handling, but the fact that shock in infancy reduces rather than increases the "fixation" effects of shock at the choice-point in the maze is again highly dissonant with the assumption that painful stimulation must inevitably increase proclivity to anxiousness. Long ago, the Spartans based their child-rearing on the principle that infants should be exposed to pain and cold to toughen them against future encounters with such exigencies. The evidence may indicate that they were not entirely wrong. On the other hand, the status of this issue is hardly such as to warrant any abrupt change in our tradition of protective tenderness toward our young.

Another change in our conception of motivation derives from recognition that there is a motivating system inherent in an organism's informational interaction with the environment. Although it is quite clear that painful stimulation, homeostatic needs, and sex all constitute genuine motivating systems, a very large share of an organism's interaction with the environment is informational in character. It occurs through the distance receptors, the eyes and the ears, and, to a much lesser degree, through touch. Elsewhere I have documented the basis for the notion that a motivating system inheres within this informational interaction (Hunt, 1963a). For instance, the Russian investigators have found both an emotional aspect and an attentional aspect to even an infant mammal's response to change in visual or auditory input. This is what they call the "orienting response." The emotional aspect of this "orienting response" can be registered by such expressive indicators as vascular changes (plethysmograph), changes in blood pressure (sphygmomanometer), changes in heart rate (cardiotachometer), changes in palmar sweating (electrical conductance of the skin), changes in muscular tension (electromyograph), and changes in brain potentials (electroencephalogram). For these changes, see Razran (1961). The attentional aspect can be

seen in the cessation of ongoing activities and the efforts to turn to the source of input. The fact that this "orienting response" is present at birth, or as soon as the ears are cleared and the eyes are open, indicates that it is a fundamental, ready-made mechanism. The fact that this response has both emotional and attentional aspects indicates, at least to me, that it is motivational, and the fact that the "orienting response" occurs to changes of ongoing input through the eyes and ears indicates that its motivational power is intrinsic within the organism's informational interaction with the environment.

STAGE ONE IN THE EPIGENESIS OF INTRINSIC MOTIVATION: THE "ORIENTING RESPONSE"

Indications of the motivational importance of this "orienting response" and of encounters with variations in inputs derive from the marked retardation observed in children whose auditory and visual inputs have been severely restricted. Here the extreme retardation observed by Dennis (1960) in the Teheran orphanages has the dramatic import, if I am correct, that the major factor in its causation lies in homogeneity of reception input. Furthermore, in light of our traditional behavioristic belief that the observable motor response is all-important in development, it is worth noting that the marked retardation that I am attributing to homogeneity of input does not occur with inhibition of motor function during the first year. Again, this latter observation is by Dennis, or by Dennis & Dennis (1940). You will recall that the distribution of ages for the onset of walking in Hopi children cradled for their first year did not differ rom the distribution of ages for onset f walking in Hopi children reared in n unrestrained fashion. While the motions of the legs and arms of the radled infants were restrained during most of their waking hours, the fact hat these cradled infants were often arried about, once they were 40 days ld, means that they probably encountered an enriched variety of redundant hanges in auditory and visual input. uch a comparison suggests that it may e changes in perceptual input rather han opportunity for motor response hat is most important in the motivation of psychological development during the earliest months (see also Fiske : Maddi, 1961).

irst Suggestion for Stimulating Early Cognitive Learning

This brings me to my first concrete uggestion for stimulating cognitive development during the earliest months, nd the process can begin at the child's irth. I suggest that the circumstances e so arranged that the infant will encounter a high variety of redundant hanges of auditory, visual, and tactual nputs.

But this suggestion needs elaboration. While changes in ongoing stimuation are probably of basic motivaional importance, it may not be mere hange in itself that is sufficient to oster cognitive development; redundance of the input changes and of inermodal sequences of input changes re probably necessary. Piaget's (1936) bservations of his own infants suggest hat, during approximately the first alf-year, one of the major accomplishments of interaction with the environment consists in the coordination of vhat are at birth largely independent ensorimotor systems. According to Piaget, these systems include sucking, listening, looking, grasping, vocalizing, and wriggling. Without use, any one of these systems will wane. As is well known to any farm boy who has pail-fed a calf, the sucking wanes after ten days or two weeks of pail-feeding and the calf can be trusted completely among fresh cows with full udders. Moreover, the work of Alexander Wolf (1943) and of Gauron & Becker (1959) on the effects of depriving infant rats of audition and vision on the readiness of these systems to respond in adulthood, coupled with the work of Brattgård (1952) and of Riesen (1947, 1958, 1961) showing that the visual system fails to develop properly when rabbits and chimpanzees are reared in darkness, indicates that this principle holds for listening and looking as well as sucking. Parenthetically, I should add that the role of organism-environment interaction in early development appears also to be tied biochemically with later capacity to synthesize RNA, as the work of Brattgård (1952), Hydén (1959), and others (see Riesen, 1961) appears to indicate. Perhaps the earliest of such interactions serve chiefly to sustain and to strengthen and develop the individual ready-made sensorimotor organizations or, as Piaget terms them, the "reflexive schemata." Very shortly, under typical circumstances, however, the sounds that evoke listening come to evoke looking, and the things seen come to evoke grasping and reaching, and the things grasped come to evoke sucking, etc. Such changes indicate progress in the coordination of the originally separate systems. During this phase, which is the second stage in Piaget's (1936) system, the progressive organization of schemata consists chiefly in such coordination, and it appears to consist in sequential organization, of which Pavlov's *conditioning* and Guthrie's *contiguity learning* are special cases.

If one tries to imagine how one can introduce redundant changes in visual and auditory inputs in order to provide for the sequential coordination of listening with looking, of looking with reaching, etc., one finds it no easy matter without actually having on hand human beings whose approaches and withdrawals supply the auditory-input changes that are regularly followed by visual-input changes. I have found myself wondering if the emphasis on mothering may not have a somewhat justified explanation in that it is the human infant's informational interaction with this coming and going of the mother that provides the perceptual basis for this coordination of relatively independent schemata.

STAGE TWO IN THE EPIGENESIS
OF INTRINSIC MOTIVATION

But the nature of this intrinsic motivational process changes with experience. Any attempt to stimulate early cognitive learning must, I believe, take this change in form, or epigenesis, into account if it is to be at all successful. Moreover, if this epigenesis is taken into account, the circumstances encountered by the infant should not only motivate a rapid rate of cognitive development but should contribute substantially to the satisfaction the infant gets from life. As observers of infant development have long noted, the human infant appears to learn spontaneously, that is, in the absence of the traditional extrinsic motivators, and to get superb enjoyment from the process (see Baldwin, 1895; Bühler, 1918, 1928;

Hendrick, 1943; Mittlemann, 1954). This is a new notion to most of us, but it is also old. For instance, it was implicit in the "self-activity" of Froebel (1887) and in the "intrinsic interest" of Dewey (1900). Moreover, Maria Montessori (1909), to whose work I shall return shortly, built her system of education for young children on the notion that children have a spontaneous interest in learning.

In what appears to be the first major transition in the structure of intrinsic motivation, the infant, while continuing to respond to changes in ongoing stimulation, comes to react toward the cessation of inputs which have been encountered repeatedly in a fashion designed to continue them or to bring them back into perceptual ken. Piaget (1936) called this a "reversal transformation." He considered it to be the beginnings of intention. Each of you who has ever dandled an infant on your knee is familiar with at least one example: when you stop your motion, the infant starts a motion of his own that resembles yours, and when you start again, the infant stops. The prevalence of infants' actions that are instigated by an absence of repeatedly encountered changes in input suggests, at least to me, that the repeated encounters with a given pattern of change in receptor input lead to recognition that provides one basis, and I believe it an important one, for cathexis, emotional attachment, and positive reinforcement (see Hunt, 1963b). My colleague Morton Weir prefers to refer to what attracts the infant as "predictability." Perhaps this is the better term. I have, however, preferred "recognition" because I suspect that what is happening is that the repeated encounters with a pattern of change in ongoing input serve to build into the storage of the posterior intrinsic system of the cerebrum a coded schema that can be matched to an input from the repeatedly encountered pattern of change. As the pattern is becoming recognizable, or when it is newly recognized, I suspect it provides a joyful basis of cathexis and positive reinforcement. I believe, at least tentatively, that it is this recognition that is one of the most consistent evokers of the infant's smile. Such an interpretation gains some support from the fact that maternal separation and encounters with unfamiliar persons bring little emotional disturbance, anxiety, or grief until the second half of the first year of life (Freud & Burlingham, 1944). In fact, these observations of emotional disturbance are important indicators that the cathexis or maternal attachment has been formed. It is this emotional disturbance that supports the observation that an infant acts to retain or to obtain a pattern of familiar input that attests his cathexis of that pattern. Moreover, it should be noted that emotional distress accompanies maternal deprivation only after the age at which objects have begun to acquire permanence for the child. Presumably this permanence of objects is based on the development, in the course of repeated encounters with a pattern of change in input, of a set of semiautonomous central processes that can represent the pattern deriving from an encounter with an object.

Parenthetically, may I suggest also that the following-response within what is called "imprinting" may well be a special case of this more general principle that emotional attachment grows out of the recognition coming from repeatedly encountering an object, place, or person; the fact that the following-response occurs after a shorter period of perceptual contact with an object in a species such as the grey-leg goose, or in the sheep or deer, than is required in species such as the chimpanzee or man suggests that the number of encounters, or duration of perceptual contact, required may well be a matter of the portion of the brain without direct connections with receptors or motor units, or what Hebb (1949) has termed the A/S ratio.

Out of such observations comes the empirical principle, which I have imbibed from Piaget (1936), that "the more an infant has seen and heard, the more he wants to see and hear." The avidity of an infant's interest in the world may be seen to be in large part a function of the variety of situations he has encountered repeatedly. Moreover, it would appear to be precisely the absence of such avid interest that constitutes the regularly observed apathy of orphanage-reared children who have encountered only a very limited variety of situations. It may well be that this seeking of inputs that have been made familiar by repeated encounters is what motivates the behavior Dennis & Dennis (1941) have termed "autogenous." Outstanding examples of such behavior are the hand-watching and the repetitive vocalizations called "babbling." It is, apparently, seeking to see the hands that motivates the motions to keep them within view, thereby providing the beginnings of eye-hand coordination. It is, apparently, seeking to hear voice sounds that motivates spontaneous vocalizing and keeps it going, thereby providing the infant with a beginning of ear-vocal coordination.

Second Suggestion for the Stimulation of Early Cognitive Learning

This brings me to my second suggestion for fostering early cognitive learning. It comes in connection with the development of intrinsically motivated intentions or plans, as the terms *intention* and *plan* are utilized by Miller, Galanter, & Pribram (1960). In fact, it is in connection with this development of intrinsically motivated intentions or plans that one basis for this change in the conception of motivation may be seen. Psychologists and psychoanalysts have conceived of actions, habits, defenses, and even of every thought system, as an attempt to reduce or eliminate stimulation or excitation within the nervous system arising out of painful stimulation, homeostatic need, or sex. To anyone who has observed and pondered the struggle of a young infant to reach and grasp some object he sees, it is extremely difficult to find such an extrinsic motivational basis for his reaching and grasping. What is suggested by Piaget's observations is that in the course of repeated encounters with an object, there comes a point at which seeing that object becomes an occasion for grasping it. In this coordination between looking and grasping, it would appear that grasping the object becomes a goal even though it is quite unrelated to pain, to homeostatic need, or to sex. Once an infant has the grasping goal of an object he has seen repeatedly, his various other motor schemata of striking, pushing, and even locomotion become also means to achieve this goal. Anyone who ponders this phenomenon in the light of the traditional theory of extrinsic motives will ask, "but why grasp the object?" And, "why grasp one object rather than another?" My tentative answer to these questions is that the object has become attractive with the new-found recognition that comes with repeated visual or auditory encounters. While reading Piaget's (1936, 1937) observations, one gets the impression that a smile very frequently precedes the effort to grasp, as if the infant were saying, "I know what you are, I'll take hold of you." Of course, nothing is so explicit; he has no language; he is merely manifesting a kind of primordial plan or intention. It is my hypothesis that this primordial intention is instigated by recognitive perception. If this hypothesis is true, then once an infant is ready to grasp things and to manipulate them, it is important that he have perceptual access to things he can grasp. It is important that there be a variety of such things that he has encountered earlier. The more varied the objects that are available, the more interest the infant will have in his world and the more sources of attractive novelty he will have later on.

As already indicted, it is probably also important that the infant have an opportunity to interact with human beings as well as with inanimate objects. Perhaps one of the chief functions of early interaction with human beings is to make the vocalized phones of the parental language and the gestures of communication familiar, for one of the most common forms of action designed to hold onto newly recognized inputs is imitation.[2] Such imitation is important for socialization and for intellectual development because the roots of human culture reside in the sounds of language and the various gestures of com-

---

[2] This conception of imitation differs radically from that given by Miller & Dollard (1941), but it does not deny that their conception may be true under certain circumstances.

munication. An infant imitates first those phones and gestures that are highly familiar to him. In fact, one of the most feasible ways to start an interactive relationship with a young infant is to make one of the sounds that he is making regularly or to perform one of his characteristic gestures. The very fact that the sounds or gestures are the infant's helps to insure his recognition of them. Seeing them in another person commonly brings delighted interest and, not infrequently, imitative effort to recover them when the adult has stopped. The infant's jouncing in the dandling relationship is a special case of such imitative effort. Again we have a kind of encounter hard to arrange without involving human beings. This paucity of encounters that can be arranged without human beings supports the idea that the stories of feral men, including Romulus and Remus, are probably myths.

STAGE THREE IN THE EPIGENESIS OF INTRINSIC MOTIVATION

The second major transformation in intrinsic motivation appears to occur when repeatedly encountered objects, places, and events become "old stuff." The infant then becomes interested in *novelty*. The breakdown of the meaning of a given input with repeated perceptual encounters and the monotony that comes with repeated participation in given events are phenomena that psychologists have long observed (see Titchener, 1926, p. 425). Hebb (1949, p. 224), moreover, has observed that a major source of pleasure resides in encountering something new within the framework of the familiar. The sequence—of "orienting response" to stimulus change, recognition with re-

peated encounters, and interest in the variations within the familiar—may well be one in the interaction of an organism with each completely new class of environmental phenomena. What look like stages in the development of the first year may possibly be derived from the fact that an infant tends to be repeatedly encountering a fairly extended variety of situations at a fairly consistent rate. In any event, in his observations of his own children, Piaget (1936) noted that this interest in novelty appears toward the end of the first year.

There are those who dislike the very notion of such an epigenesis in the structure of motivation. There are those who seek single explanatory principles. Some have tried to explain this series of transformations in terms either of a process in which the new is continually becoming familiar or of a process whereby the earlier interest in the familiar exists because recognizability itself is novel at this phase. We may someday get a biochemical understanding of this phenomenon, but such attempts to find a unitary psychological principle of explanation are probably doomed to failure. Numerous studies indicate very clearly that organisms first respond to change in ongoing inputs. It is less certain that they next prefer the familiar, but the evidence is abundant that they later prefer objects and situations that are relatively less familiar than others available (see Dember, Earl, & Paradise, 1957; Hebb & Mahut, 1955; Montgomery, 1952, 1953a.) There is one instance in which a study shows that the lowly rat will endure even the pain of electric shock to get from his familiar nest-cage to an unfamiliar situation where there are novel objects to manipulate (Nissen, 1930).

Studies also exist, moreover, in which organisms withdrew in fear from "familiar objects in an unfamiliar guise." These were objects that could never have been associated with painful stimulation in their previous experience because the animals had been reared under known conditions at the Yerkes Primate Laboratory. Festinger (1957) has, also, found people withdrawing from information dissonant with their strong held beliefs, plans, or commitments.

It is no easy matter to characterize properly what is essential in that glibly called "novelty." I believe, however, that we can say that novelty resides within the organism's informational interaction with its environment. I have termed this essence "incongruity" (Hunt, 1963a); Berlyne (1960) has written of the "collative variables" underlying "arousal potential"; Festinger (1957) has talked of "dissonance"; Hebb (1949) has written of the stage of development in cortical organization; and Munsinger & Kessen (1964), are using the term "uncertainty." Whatever this essence is called, too much of it gives rise to withdrawal and gestures commonly connoting fear. Too little appears to be associated with boredom. That novelty that is attractive appears to be an optimum of discrepancy in this relationship between the informational input of the moment and the information already stored in the cerebrum from previous encounters with similar situations.

Once interest in novelty appears, it is an important source of motivation. Perhaps it is the chief source of motivation for cognitive learning. Interest in novelty appears to motivate the improvement of locomotor skills, for the novel objects "needing" examination or

manipulation are typically out of reach. It appears to motivate imitation of unfamiliar verbal phones and unfamiliar gestures and even of fairly complex actions. Imitated vocalizing of unfamiliar phones and vocal patterns appears to be exceedingly important in the acquisition of language. The notion that all infants vocalize all the phones of all languages (Allport, 1924) has long been hard to believe. The social side of language acquisition appears to be more than the mere reinforcing with approval or notice of those vocal patterns characteristic of the parents' language. If the interest in novelty provides an intrinsic motivational basis for (imitatively) vocalizing phones that have never been a part of the infant's vocal repertoire, then we have a believable explanation for the fact that most of the first pseudo-words are approximations of adult vocalizations that have occurred repeatedly in connection with novel and exciting events. Repetition of encounters with a given class of events may be presumed gradually to establish central processes representative of that class of event, that is, *images*, if you will. Imitation of the novel phones verbalized by adults in association with the class of events may provide the infant with a vocalization that can serve him as a sign of his image. Later, reinforcement, partially based on approval-disapproval and partially based on growing cognitive differentiation, may lead gradually to images and phonemic combinations that are sufficiently like those of the people taking care of an infant to permit communication.

Once language is acquired, the human child comes into basically the same existential situation in which all of us find ourselves. He then has two major sources of informational input: first, the original one of perceiving objects and events and, second, the new one of learning about them through the language of others. One of his major intellectual tasks is to make what he learns about the "real world" through the communications of others jibe with what he learns about it directly through his own receptors. This is a creative task of no mean proportion, and it is not unlike the task with which mature men of science are continuously concerned. This is one of George Kelly's (1955) major points.

The considerations already outlined in connection with my suggestions concerning repeated encounters with a given class of stimulus change and "recognition" show again the basis for the principle that "the more a child has seen and heard, the more he wants to see and hear" and do. If an infant has encountered a wide variety of changes in circumstances during his earliest days, and if he has encountered them repeatedly enough to become attached to them through recognition, and if he has had ample opportunity to act upon them and to manipulate them, he will become, I believe, ready to be intrigued by novel variations in an ample range of objects, situations, and personal models.

The fact that too much novelty or incongruity can be frightening and too little can be boring, however, creates a problem for those who would stimulate cognitive development. They must provide for encounters with materials, objects, and models that have the proper degree of that incongruity (Hunt, 1963a). This is one aspect of what I have termed the "problem of the match" (Hunt, 1961b, pp. 267ff.).

Third Suggestion for the Stimulation of Early Cognitive Learning

Consideration of the problem of the match brings me to my third concrete suggestion for stimulating cognitive learning in the very young. I must confess that I have borrowed this suggestion from Montessori (1909; see also Fisher, 1912). The first portion of this suggestion is that careful observation be made of what it is in the way of objects, situations, and models for imitation that interests the infant. Once it is clear what objects and models are of interest, then I suggest providing each infant with an ample variety of them and with an opportunity to choose spontaneously the ones that intrigue him at a given time. This latter suggestion assumes, of course, that the infant is already comfortable, that he feels safe, and that he is satisfied so far as homeostatic needs are concerned. I really feel that we do not have to worry too much about gratifying the sex appetite of a child under three years of age.

When I wrote *Intelligence and Experience* (1961b), this problem of providing a proper match between the materials with which a child is confronted by teachers and what he already has in his storage loomed large because of our tremendous ignorance of the intricacies involved. This ignorance is a major challenge for investigation; in the meantime, however, as Jan Smedslund pointed out to me in a conversation in Boulder last summer, Montessori long ago provided a practical solution. She based her system of education on intrinsic motivation, but she called it "spontaneous learning." She provided young children with a wide variety of materials, graded in difficulty and roughly calculated to be the range of materials that would provide a proper match for children of ages three to six if they were given opportunity for choice. She also gave each of the children in her school an opportunity to occupy himself or herself with those materials of his or her own individual choice. To do this, she broke the lock-step in the educational process. A Montessori school was socially so structured that the children were obviously expected to occupy themselves with the materials provided. Moreover, by having together within a single room children ranging in age from three to six years, she provided a graded series of models for the younger children and an opportunity for some of the older children to learn by teaching the younger ones how to do various things. You will be interested to know that a substantial proportion of the slum children in Montessori's school began reading and writing before they were five years old. In the Casa di Bambini, which Montessori founded in 1907 in the basement of a slum apartment-house in Rome, the teacher was the apartment-house superintendent's 16-year-old daughter who had been trained by Montessori. You will also be interested to know that the old nursery school bugaboo that children have very brief spans of attention did not hold. Dorothy Canfield Fisher (1912)—the novelist who spent the winter of 1910–1911 at the original Casa di Bambini—has written that it was common to see a three-year-old continuously occupied with such a mundane task as buttoning and unbuttoning for two or more hours at a stretch.

Montessori's contributions to the education of the very young were discussed with excitement in America until the time of World War I. Thereafter the discussion ended almost completely. I suspect that this occurred because Montessori's theoretical views were so dissonant with what became about then the dominant views of American psychologists and American educators. Her theory that cognitive capacity could be modified by proper education was dissonant with the dominant and widely-prevailing notions of "fixed intelligence" and "predetermined development." These notions were implicit in the doctrine of a constant IQ. Her notion of spontaneous learning was sharply dissonant with the doctrine that all behavior is extrinsically motivated by painful stimulation, or homeostatic need, or sex. Moreover, the importance she attributed to sensory training was dissonant with what became the prevailing presumption that it is the observable motor response that counts. We need to reexamine her contributions in the light of the theoretical picture that has been emerging since World War II. I am grateful to Jan Smedslund for calling her contributions to my attention.

My discourse has skipped roughly half of the second year and all of the third year of life, because interest in novelty typically makes its earliest appearance toward the end of the first year or early in the second. (Montessori's schools took children only at three years of age or older.) I suspect that the basic principle involved in stimulating cognitive learning is fairly constant once the interest in novelty appears. On the other hand, I would not be surprised if it were precisely during this period between 18 months and three years of age that lower-class families typically most hamper the kind of cognitive learning that is later required for successful performance in school and in our increasingly techno-logical culture. Let me explain briefly.

During the first year, the life of an infant in a family crowded together in one room—as Oscar Lewis (1961) has described such living in his *Children of Sanchez* and as I have observed it in the slums of New York—probably provides a fairly rich variety of input. On the other hand, once an infant begins to use his new-found locomotor and lin-guistic skills, his circumstances in a lower-class setting probably become anything but conducive to appropriate cognitive learning. Using his new loco-motor skills gets him in the way of problem-beset adults and, all too likely, may bring punishment which can be avoided only by staying out of their way. This in turn deprives the infant of the opportunity to hear and imitate the verbal phones that provides the basis for spoken language. If a slum child should be lucky enough to ac-quire the "learning set" that things have names and to begin his repetitive questioning about "what's that?", he is not only unlikely to get answers but also likely to get his ears cuffed for ask-ing such silly questions. Moreover, in the slum setting of lower-class family life, the models that an infant has to imitate are all too often likely to result in the acquisition of sensorimotor or-ganizations and attitudes that interfere with rather than facilitate the kinds of cognitive learning that enable a child to succeed in school and in a techno-logical culture such as ours. How long such interference with development can last without resulting in a permanent reduction in cognitive potential re-mains an unsolved problem. It is likely, however, that day-care centers and nursery schools prepared to face such children with situations, materials, and models that are not too incongruous with the schemata and attitudes that they have already acquired, can coun-teract much of the detrimental effect of lower-class life. Such pre-school ex-perience during the second and third, and possibly even during the fourth, years of life can perhaps serve well as an antidote to this kind of cultural deprivation (see Hunt, 1964).

Summary: I have limited my discussion to the implications, for the stimulation of early cognitive learning, of the epigenesis of intrinsic motivation that I believe I can see taking place during preverbal develop-ment. I have identified three stages of in-trinsic motivation that are separated by two major "reversal transformations." In the first of these, repeated encounters with pat-terns of change in perceptual input lead to recognition that I now believe to be a source of pleasure and a basis for cathexis or for affectional attachment. The second consists in a transition from an interest in the familiar to an interest in the novel. During the first few months, when the child is responsive chiefly to changes in the char-acter and intensity of ongoing stimulation, I suspect it is most important to provide for repeated encounters with as wide a variety as possible of changes in receptor input. It may also be important to provide for sequential arrangements of these inputs that will provide a basis for a coordination of all combinations of the ready-made re-flexive sensorimotor systems. As the infant becomes attached to objects, people, and situations by way of the hypothetical joys of new-found recognition, it is probably most important to provide opportunities for him to utilize his own repertoire of in-tentional activities to retain or elicit or manipulate the objects, people, and situa-tions, again in as wide a variety as is feasi-ble. Once interest in novelty appears, I suspect it is most important to give the child access to a variety of graded materials for manipulation and coping and to a variety of graded models for imitation.

With what little we now know of what I call the "problem of the match," I suspect it is important to follow Montessori's principle of trusting to a considerable degree in the spontaneous interest of the individual infant instead of attempting to regiment his learning process in any lock-step method of preschool education.

Maternal Care and Mental Health. Geneva: World Health Organization, 1952. Chapter 1, pp. 11–14; Chapter 4, pp. 46–51; Chapter 5, pp. 52–58.

Maternal Care and Mental Health

J. Bowlby

Some Origins of Mental Ill-Health

Among the most significant developments in psychiatry during the past quarter of a century has been the steady growth of evidence that the quality of the parental care which a child receives in his earliest years is of vital importance for his future mental health. Such evidence came first from the psycho-analytic treatment of adults and then from that of children. It has been greatly amplified during the past decade by information gathered by psychologists and psychiatrists working in child guidance and child care—two fields affording unrivalled opportunities for first-hand observation both of the developing child and of his milieu.

Largely as a result of this new knowledge, there is today a high level of agreement among child-guidance workers in Europe and America on certain central concepts. Their approach to cases, their investigations, their diagnostic criteria, and their therapeutic aims are the same. Above all, the theory of etiology on which their work is founded is the same.

The basic principles of this theory of the origins of mental health and mental illness will be discussed more fully later. For the moment it is sufficient to say that what is believed to be essential for mental health is that the infant and young child should experience a warm, intimate, and continuous relationship with his mother (or permanent mother-substitute) in which both find satisfaction and enjoyment. Given this relationship, the emotions of anxiety and guilt, which in excess characterize mental ill-health, will develop in a moderate and organized way. When this happens, the child's characteristic and contradictory demands, on the one hand for unlimited love from his parents and on the other for revenge upon them when he feels that they do not love him enough, will likewise remain of moderate strength and become amenable to the control of his gradually developing personality. In this complex, rich, and rewarding relationship with the mother in the early years, varied in countless ways by relations with the father and with siblings, that child psychiatrists and many others now believe to underlie the development of character and of mental health.

A state of affairs in which the child does not have this relationship is termed 'maternal deprivation'. This is a general term covering a number of different situations. Thus, a child is deprived even though living at home if his mother (or permanent mother-substitute) is unable to give him the loving care small children need. Again, a child is deprived if for any reason he is removed from his mother's care. This deprivation will be relatively mild if he is then looked after by someone whom he has already learned to know and trust, but may be considerable if the foster-mother, even though loving, is a stranger. All these arrangements, however, give the child some satisfaction and are therefore examples of partial deprivation. They stand in contrast to the almost complete deprivation which is still not uncommon in institutions, residential nurseries, and hospitals, where the child often has no one person who cares for him in a personal way and with whom he may feel secure.

The ill-effects of deprivation vary with its degree. Partial deprivation brings in its train acute anxiety, excessive need for love, powerful feelings of revenge, and, arising from these last, guilt and depression. These emotions and drives are too great for the immature means of control and organization available to the young child (immature physiologically as well as psychologically). The consequent disturbance of psychic organization then leads to a variety of responses, often repetitive and cumulative, the end products of which are symptoms of neurosis and instability of character. Complete deprivation, with which we shall be dealing principally in this report, has even more far-reaching effects on character development and may entirely cripple the capacity to make relationships.

The evidence on which these views are based is largely clinical in origin. Immensely valuable though this evidence is, it is unfortunately neither systematic nor statistically controlled, and so has frequently met with scepticism from those not engaged in child psychiatry.

Investigators with a statistical bent have worked with the concept of the 'broken home' and a number of studies have demonstrated a relation between maladjustment and this situation. As an example an extensive study undertaken by Menut (1943) may be quoted. He compared 839 children suffering from behaviour disorders with nearly 70,000 controls from the schools of Paris, and found that of the problem children 66% came from broken homes while of the controls only 12% did so. In a subsequent more detailed study of 100 of the problem children from broken homes he assessed the broken home itself as being a main causative factor in 84.

But though these studies have been of value in amplifying and confirming clinical evidence of the far-reaching importance of the child's early experience in his home, the concept of the broken home is scientifically unsatisfactory and should be abandoned. It includes too many heterogeneous conditions having very different psychological effects.

In place of the concept of the broken home we need to put the concept of the disturbed parent-child relationship which is frequently, but not necessarily, associated with it. If the child's developing relationships with his mother and his father are used as the focal point, data of far greater precision emerge, and much that is obscure in the origins of mental illness begins to become clear. An illustration of the fruitfulness of this standpoint is a recent study by Stott (1950), who has published the full case-histories of 102 persistent offenders aged between 15 and 18 years who were in an English Approved School. In this comparatively large series he has demonstrated clearly how anxieties arising from unsatisfactory relationships in early childhood predispose the children to respond in an antisocial way to later stresses. Most of the early anxiety situations noted by Stott are particular aspects of maternal deprivation.

Naturally, parent-child relationships have many dimensions and there are many other ways besides deprivation, arising from separation or outright rejection, in which they may become pathogenic. The commonest are (*a*) an unconsciously rejecting attitude underlying a loving one, (*b*) an excessive demand for love and reassurance on the part of a parent, and (*c*) a parent obtaining unconscious and vicarious satisfaction from the child's behaviour, despite conscious condemnation of it. These themes, however, do not concern this report; nor does it treat in detail the child's relation to his father. The reason for this is that almost all the evidence concerns the child's relation to his mother, which is without doubt in ordinary circumstances by far his most important relationship during these years. It is she who feeds and cleans him, keeps him warm, and comforts him. It is to his mother that he turns when in distress. In the young child's eyes father plays second fiddle and his value increases only as the child's vulnerability to deprivation decreases. Nevertheless, as the illegitimate child knows, fathers have their uses even in infancy. Not only do they provide for their wives to enable them to devote themselves unrestrictedly to the

care of the infant and toddler, but, by providing love and companionship they support her emotionally and help her maintain that harmonious contented mood in the aura of which the infant thrives. In what follows, therefore, while continual reference will be made to the mother-child relation little will be said of the father-child relation; his value as the economic and emotional support of the mother will be assumed.

Theories which place the origins of mental disturbances in these intimate domestic events are, of course, in strong contrast to the theories which stem from the German school of psychiatry. These stress constitutional and inherited factors, at times to a point reminiscent of Calvinistic predestination. Suffice it to say that evidence for these extreme views does not exist and that the relative weights of nature and nurture remain still to be determined. In this connexion, it is useful to remember that recent work in embryology has produced a steady accumulation of evidence that pathological changes in the embryo's environment may cause faults of growth and development exactly resembling those that in the past have been ascribed to pure genetic causes (Corner, 1944). This is a finding of great importance, which, as will be seen, is exactly paralleled in psychology. It is to be emphasized, however, that such findings in no way contradict theories postulating the adverse influence of hereditary factors, except in so far as these are held in the extreme form that hereditary factors alone account for all differences in human behaviour. Indeed, all those subscribing to the views set out in this report believe that in the final analysis hereditary factors will be shown also to play a part and that the greatest scientific progress will be made when the interaction of the two can be studied.

A second far-reaching biological principle also stems from embryology, namely, the discovery that the harmful effects on the embryo of trauma, intoxication, infection, and other potentially damaging processes vary not only with the nature of the offending agent and the structure and function of the tissue mainly attacked but also with the maturity of that tissue. In the psychological field this principle is illustrated in the now classic work of Hunt (1941), who demonstrated experimentally that the starvation of rats on the 24th day of life left traces on behaviour clearly discernible in adult life, while a similar experience at 36 days had no such effect.

Finally, it may be noted that in the physiological sphere it has been observed that the evil effects on an organ are especially far-reaching when noxious influences operate during its earliest phases of development, as for instance in the case of rubella where maximal damage is caused between the sixth and tenth weeks of foetal life. The identity of the biological principle at work here and that invoked by psychiatrists who impute far-reaching effects to certain emotional experiences occurring in the earliest phases of mental functioning, as early as the first six months of life, will be apparent. It may be said, therefore, that these theories, so far from being inherently improbable, are strictly in accord with accepted biological principle.

Interim Conclusions

The evidence has been reviewed at some length because much of it is still little known and the issue of whether deprivation causes psychiatric disturbance is still discussed as though it were an open question. It is submitted that the evidence is now such that it leaves no room for doubt regarding the general proposition—that the prolonged deprivation of the young child of maternal care may have grave and far-reaching effects on his character and so on the whole of his future life. Although it is a proposition exactly similar in form to those regarding the evil after-effects of rubella in foetal life or deprivation of vitamin D in infancy, there is a curious resistance to accepting it. Indeed, there are still psychiatrists in all countries who challenge these conclusions, though it is to be remarked that few of them have had training in child psychiatry or experience of work in a child-guidance clinic. Their clinical work is confined to the examination of older patients of an age when it is difficult or impossible to obtain light on what really happened in their early years. Moreover, so embittered and distorted is the information patients commonly give about their childhood experiences that many psychiatrists and even psycho-analysts have regarded their stories as no more than fantasies and have wholly discounted the really adverse effects of an unhappy childhood. It is, of course, true that there are still far too few systematic studies and statistical comparisons in which proper control groups have been used. Relatively few studies taken by themselves are more than suggestive. But when all the evidence is fitted together it is seen to be remarkably consistent and this, taken with the considered opinions of experienced child-guidance workers in many different countries, leaves no doubt that the main proposition is true. Reluctance to accept it is, perhaps, because to do so would involve far-reaching changes in conceptions of human nature and in methods of caring for young children.

However that may be, although the main proposition may be regarded as established, knowledge of details remains deplorably small. It is as though it had been established that an absence of vitamin D caused rickets and that calcium was in some way involved, but as yet no quantitative measures were available and there was complete ignorance of the many interrelated associated factors. That deprivation can have bad consequences is known, but how much deprivation children of different ages can withstand has yet to be determined. The evidence may now be summarized and such conclusions drawn as are permissible.

In the first place, there is abundant evidence that deprivation can have adverse effects on the development of children (*a*) during the period of separation, (*b*) during the period immediately after restoration to maternal care, and (*c*) permanently. The fact that some children seem to escape is of no consequence. The same is true of the consumption of tubercular-infected milk or exposure to the virue of infantile paralysis. In both these cases a sufficient proportion of children is so severely damaged that no one would dream of intentionally exposing a child to such hazards. Deprivation of maternal care in early childhood falls into the same category of dangers.

Most of the evidence in respect of long-term effects refers to the grave disturbances following severe deprivation; it is easiest to work from these established connexions to those which are less well understood. The evidence

suggests that three somewhat different experiences can each produce the affectionless and psychopathic character:

(*a*) lack of *any* opportunity for forming an attachment to a mother-figure during the first three years (Powdermaker, Bender, Lowrey, Goldfarb);

(*b*) deprivation for a limited period—at least three months and probably more than six—during the first three or four years (Bowlby, Spitz & Wolf);

(*c*) changes from one mother-figure to another during the same period (Levy and others).

Though the gross results of these different experiences appear the same it seems probable, both for theoretical and empirical reasons, that close study will reveal differences. For instance, it may well be that the discrepancy as regards stealing between the children studied by Bowlby (1944, 1946) and by Goldfarb (1943) would be explained in this way. All of Goldfarb's cases had been institutionalized from soon after birth until they were three years old. None of Bowlby's had—they were all products of deprivation for a limited period, or of frequent changes. It may well be that their stealing was an attempt to secure love and gratification and so reinstate the love relationship which they had lost, whereas Goldfarb's cases, never having experienced anything of the kind, had nothing to reinstate. Certainly it would appear that the more complete the deprivation in the early years the more isolated and asocial the child, whereas the more that deprivation is interspersed with satisfaction, the more ambivalent and antisocial he becomes. Lowrey (1940) may well be right in his belief that "children placed in institutions for short periods after the age of 2 do not develop this isolated type of personality or show the same behavior patterns"; research at present in progress at the Tavistock Clinic tends to confirm this. Nevertheless, Carey-Trefzer (1949) and Bowlby have each recorded a sufficient number of cases where the development of extremely antisocial characters, unable to make stable relations with anyone though not complete isolates, appeared to follow changes from one mother-figure to another during the fourth year, to make it clear that very evil results may follow even at this age. Naturally, the effects on personality development at any given age will depend on the exact nature of the experience to which the child is submitted, information about which is all too frequently missing from records. Indeed, one of the great shortcomings of present evidence is a lack of detail and precision on this point. It has already been remarked that implicit in Goldfarb's writings is the assumption that all infants and toddlers in institutions have similar experiences. Not only is it clear that they do not, but the more one studies all the data on the subject, the more he becomes convinced that the outcome is to a high degree dependent on the exact nature of the psychological experience. If further research is to be fruitful, it must pay minute attention not only to ages and periods of deprivation, but also to the quality of the child's relation to his mother before deprivation, his experiences with mother-substitutes, if any, during separation, and the reception he gets from his mother or foster-mother when at last he becomes settled again.

Though all workers on the subject are now agreed that the first year of life is of vital importance, there is at present some debate regarding the age at which deprivation has the most evil consequences. Bowlby, after reviewing his cases, noted that the separations which appeared pathogenic had all occurred after the age of six months and in a majority after that of 12 months, from which he was inclined to conclude that separations and deprivations in the first six months of life were less important for the child's welfare than later ones. This has also been the view of Anna Freud (Burlingham & Freud, 1943). It has, however, been called in question explicitly by Spitz & Wolf (verbal communication), and implicitly by Klein (1948a), whose data are of a very different kind, having been derived retrospectively from the psycho-analytic treatment of children and adults. Goldfarb also has attached especial importance to the first half-year, although his data do not really warrant the conclusion he draws from them. Nevertheless, this study of Goldfarb's (1945), in which he examines the social adjustment of adolescents in relation to the age at which they were admitted to the institution, points unmistakably to the special vulnerability of the child during the first year in comparison to later ones. Bender's references (1946, 1947) to children in whom the deprivation was limited to the first year and who none the less showed the classical retardation and personality distortion provide further evidence regarding the first year as a whole, though they do not contribute to the debate regarding the baby's vulnerability during the first half of it in particular.

For the present, therefore, it may be recorded that deprivation occurring in the second half of the first year of life is agreed by all students of the subject to be of great significance and that many believe this to be true also of deprivation occurring in the first half, especially from three to six months. The balance of opinion, indeed, is that considerable damage to mental health can be done by deprivation in these months, a view which is unquestionably supported by the direct observations, already described, of the immediately adverse effects of deprivation on babies of this age.

There is, however, a further point—the time limit within which the provision of mothering can make good some at least of the damage done by deprivation in these early months. The comparative success of many babies adopted between six and nine months who have spent their first half-year in conditions of deprivation makes it virtually certain that, for many babies at least, provided they receive good mothering in time, the effects of early damage can be greatly reduced. What Goldfarb's work demonstrates without any doubt is that such mothering is almost useless if delayed until after the age of $2\frac{1}{2}$ years. In actual fact this upper age limit for most babies is probably before 12 months. But the probable existence of a safety limit should not give rise to complacency: the fact that it may be possible to make good some of the damage done by deprivation in the early months is no excuse for permitting it to be inflicted in the first place.

So much for the fully fledged forms of psychopathic character and the experiences which produce them, a sequence of events now widely recognized by child psychiatrists. Ever since Levy's first paper, however, psychiatrists concerned with this problem have pointed to the existence of less gross conditions to which less severe deprivation could give rise and which are far and away more frequent. Not only are there the many partial and covert forms of psychopathic personality, including Fitzgerald's hysterics (1948), but many conditions of anxiety and depression almost certainly stem from deprivation experiences or have been exacerbated by them.

Such examples, Levy writes, are seen in those adults whose social life represents a series of relationships with older people every one of whom is a substitute mother. They may be single or in combination, the point being simply that the patient must, throughout life, be in contact with a person from whom the same demands are made that were thwarted in the original experience with the mother. The life pattern then becomes dependent on maintaining such relationships. When one of them is broken there is a period of depression, or a feeling that 'something is terrifically lacking', until another relationship is made. Another type of reaction is seen in the form chiefly of excessive demands made on the person who is selected to satisfy the privations of early life . . . The problem is always the same—excessive demands for food, for money, for privileges.

Not infrequently people with these troubles deny their existence by an excessive show of cheerfulness and activity—the hypomanic reaction. This is an attempt to convince themselves that God's in his heaven, all's right with the world, a state of affairs of which they are far from sure. Naturally the hypomanic method meets with some success but, based as it is on a denial, is in constant danger of cracking and leaving its owner in a state of despair. Moreover, even while it succeeds, the press of activity and intolerance of frustration are very trying to others, while, as Bowlby (1944, 1946) and Stott (1950) have shown, it not infrequently leads to delinquency.

Though such cases are sadly numerous, they are mercifully more accessible to psycho-analytic therapy than the severe forms. On the immense therapeutic task set by the fully fledged psychopaths all are agreed. Levy described them in 1937 as having a poor prognosis, a view endorsed by every worker since. Because of their almost complete inability to make relationships, the psychotherapist is robbed of his principal therapeutic tool: he should, of course, be skilled in the management of patients who hate him; he has yet to learn methods of affecting for the better patients who have no feelings for him at all. The findings of Powdermaker et al. (1937) in this regard are especially clear. Working over a period of some six years in a small home for delinquent girls between the ages of 12 and 16, therapy was given to 80 of them. Half were successes and half failures. Response to therapy was related neither to intelligence nor to heredity. Its relationship to the girls' early family experiences, however, was striking.

The failure in treatment of all those who had suffered rejection or had never had a libidinal tie recalls Goldfarb's remark (1947) that he has never seen "even one example of significantly favorable response to treatment by traditional methods of child psychiatry". Bender (1947) goes so far as to say that "once the defect is created it cannot be corrected", and recommends that methods of care should make no attempt to be therapeutic or corrective but "should be protective and should aim to foster a dependent relationship". Others are more hopeful and believe that if the child is permitted to regress to completely infantile modes of behaviour there is a chance of his developing afresh along better lines. The work of Jonsson at the Children's Village at Skå near Stockholm is an example of a European experiment along these lines. Here the children are encouraged to become highly dependent on their house-mothers and are permitted to regress to such infantile behaviour as taking their food from a baby's feeding-bottle. This, and similar experiments in the USA, are conceived on sensible lines, though there is debate regarding the optimal degree of control which should be exercised over the children. It will be many years before the success of these methods can be judged.

The evidence available suggests that nothing but prolonged residence with an adult, with insight into the problem,

TABLE 1

RELATION OF THERAPEUTIC RESPONSE OF DELINQUENT GIRLS
TO THEIR EARLY FAMILY EXPERIENCES (POWDERMAKER *et al.*)

Early family experience	Effect of therapy	
	success	failure
No rejection and some constructive family tie present	25	0
Rejection by some member of the family but some constructive tie present also	12	10
Neurotic and ambivalent relationships	3	13
Complete rejection or no libidinal tie	0	17
Totals	40	40

Note: P is less than .01.

skill in handling it, and unlimited time to devote to her charge, is likely to be of much avail. This is not only very expensive but could never be made available to more than a tiny fraction of cases. Far more practicable, and in the long run far cheaper, is to arrange methods of care for infants and toddlers which will prevent these conditions developing.

Theoretical Problems

The theoretical problems regarding personality development and its dependence on a continuous relationship with a nurturant figure during the critical period of ego and super-ego development in the early years are of the greatest interest. It would not be appropriate in this report to do more than touch on them, however, since they are very complex and by no means clearly understood. On the other hand, progress in understanding the practical issues involved is to a high degree dependent on progress in theoretical insight.

The development of the personality is a process whereby we become less and less at the mercy of our immediate environment and of its impact upon us, and more and more able to pursue our own goals, often over long periods of time, and to select and create our own environment. Such a process implies, among other things, a capacity to abstract common properties, to think in symbolic terms, and to plan ahead—all attributes of what Goldstein & Scheerer (1941) have termed the abstract attitude. Only when this abstract attitude is developed has the individual the capacity to control his wish of the moment in the interests of his own more fundamental long-term needs.

One expects the child of three, or even five, to run into the road to seek his ball—at those ages he is still largely at the mercy of the immediate situation. As he grows older, however, he is expected to take more things into account and to think ahead. By 10 or 11 he is capable of pursuing goals some months distant in time. At 16 or 18 the more developed boy or girl is able to perform prodigious feats of abstraction in time and space. Using psycho-analytic terms, this is the process whereby the individual frees himself from slavery to his instincts and the reign of the pleasure principle, and develops mental processes more adapted to the demands of reality.

The psychic machinery which we develop within ourselves to harmonize our different and often conflicting needs and to seek their satisfaction in a world realistically apprehended is our ego. Its functions are many and include appraisal of our long- and short-term needs, their arrangement in an order of priority, the inhibition of some and the acceptance of others, so that action may be purposeful and integrated instead of haphazard and self-frustrating. Because one of our foremost long-term needs is to remain on friendly and cooperative terms with others, we must keep their requirements firmly in the front of our minds; and so important is this for us that we differentiate, within our ego, machinery specially designed for the purpose—our conscience or super-ego. It is evident that both ego and super-ego are absolutely dependent for their functioning on our ability to maintain the abstract attitude and it is not surprising that during infancy and early childhood these functions are either not operating at all or are doing so most imperfectly. During this phase of life, the child is therefore dependent on his mother performing them for him. She orients him in space and time, provides his environment, permits the satisfaction of some impulses, restricts others. She is his ego and his super-ego. Gradually he learns these arts himself and, as he does so, the skilled parent transfers the roles to him. This is a slow, subtle, and continuous process, beginning when he first learns to walk and feed himself and not ending completely until maturity is reached.

Ego and super-ego development are thus inextricably bound up with the child's primary human relationships; only when these are continuous and satisfactory can his ego and super-ego develop. In dealing here with the embryology of the human mind one is struck by a similarity with the embryological development of the human body, during the course of which undifferentiated tissues respond to the influence of chemical organizers. If growth is to proceed smoothly, the tissues must be exposed to the influence of the appropriate organizer at certain critical periods. In the same way, if mental development is to proceed smoothly, it would appear to be necessary for the undifferentiated psyche to be exposed during certain critical periods to the influence of the psychic organizer, the mother. For this reason, in considering the disorders to which ego and super-ego are liable, it is imperative to have regard to the phases of development of the child's capacity for human relationships. These are many and, naturally, merge into one another. In broad outline the following are the most important:

(*a*) The phase during which the infant is in course of establishing a relation with a clearly identified person—his mother; this is normally achieved by five or six months of age.

(*b*) The phase during which he needs her as an ever-present companion; this usually continues until about his third birthday.

(*c*) The phase during which he is becoming able to maintain a relationship with her in absentia. During the fourth and fifth years such a relationship can only be maintained in favourable circumstances and for a few days or weeks at a time; after seven or eight the relationship can be maintained, though not without strain, for periods of a year or more.

The process whereby he simultaneously develops his own ego and super-ego and the capacity to maintain relationships in absentia is variously described as a process of identification, internalization, or introjection, since the functions of ego and super-ego are incorporated within the self in the pattern set by the parents.

The ages by which these phases are completed no doubt vary greatly from child to child in the same way that physical maturation varies. For instance, the capacity to walk matures at any time between 9 and 24 months, and it may well be that psychic maturation is equally variable. If this is so, it will be wise to be concerned in research with developmental rather than chronological age, since it seems fairly certain that the kind and degree of psychological disorder following deprivation is dependent on the phase of development the child is in at the time. In postulating this, well-established embryological principles are again followed. As Corner (1944) states:

abnormalities are produced by attacking, at just the right time, a region in which profound growth activity is under way . . . Possible abnormalities will tend to fall into classes and types corresponding to the most critical stages and regions in development. Injuries inflicted early will in general produce widespread disturbance of growth . . . late injuries will tend on the other hand to produce local defects.

Furthermore, he notes that

a given undifferentiated tissue can respond to an organizer only during a limited period. It must have reached a certain stage of differentiation before it can respond; and later its character becomes fixed, so that it can yield only a more limited type of response.

The period during which the child's undifferentiated psyche can respond to the influence of the maternal 'organizer' is similarly limited. Thus the evidence is fairly clear that if the first phase of development—that of establishing a relation with a clearly differentiated person—is not satisfactorily completed during the first 12 months or so, there is the greatest difficulty in making it good: the character of the psychic tissues has become fixed. (The limit for many children may well be a good deal earlier). Similarly, there appears to be a limit by which the second and third phases must be completed if further development is to proceed.

Now it is these vital growth processes which are impaired by the experience of deprivation. Clinically, it is observed that the egos and super-egos of severely deprived children are not developed— their behaviour is impulsive and uncontrolled, and they are unable to pursue long-term goals because they are the victims of the momentary whim. For them, all wishes are born equal and equally to be acted upon. Their

capacity for inhibition is absent or impaired, and without this a limited, precise, and consequently efficient mode of response cannot develop. They are ineffective personalities, unable to learn from experience and consequently their own worst enemies.

The theoretical problem is to understand how deprivation produces this result. The two main approaches to its solution are Goldfarb's discoveries (1943) regarding the impairment of abstract thinking in these patients, and the clinical findings regarding their inability to identify or introject. Each approach carries us some distance, but the day has yet to come when they lead to a unified body of theory.

Goldfarb's findings in regard to the serious and specific impairment of the capacity for abstract thinking, which was present in every one of his cases, might be held to explain the failure of ego and super-ego development, since, as already remarked, this capacity is of the essence of their functioning. But even if this is so there remains the puzzle as to why deprivation should impair the capacity for abstract thinking. One possibility is that this capacity not only underlies ego functioning, but can develop only if ego functioning itself develops favourably. This will need investigation.

The failure of ego development in deprived children is perhaps more easily understood when it is considered that it is the mother who in the child's earliest years fulfils the function of his ego and super-ego. The institution children studied by Goldfarb and by Bender had never had this experience, and so had never had the opportunity of completing the first phase of development—that of establishing a relationship with a clearly identified mother-figure. All they had had was a succession of ad hoc agents each helping them in some limited way, but none providing continuity in time, which is of the essence of ego functioning. It may well be that these grossly deprived infants, never having been the continuous objects of care of a single human being, had never had the opportunity to learn the processes of abstraction and of the organization of behaviour in time and space. Certainly their grave psychical deformities are clear examples of the principle that injuries inflicted early produce widespread disturbance of growth.

In the institutional setting moreover there is less opportunity for the child who has learned the processes of abstraction and mental organization to exercise them. In the family, the young child is, within limits, encouraged to express himself both socially and in play. A child of 18 months or 2 years has already become a character in the family. It is known that he enjoys certain things and dislikes others, and the family has learned to respect his wishes. Furthermore, he is getting to know how to get his parents or his brothers and sisters to do what he wants. In this way he is learning to change his social environment to a shape more congenial to him. The same occurs in his play, where in a symbolic way he is creating and recreating new worlds for himself. Here are the exercise grounds for ego and super-ego. In any institutional setting much of this is lost; in the less good it may all be lost. The child is not encouraged to individual activity because it is a nuisance; it is easier if he stays put and does what he is told. Even if he strives to change his environment he fails. Toys are lacking: often the children sit inert or rock themselves

for hours together. Above all, the brief intimate games which mother and baby invent to amuse themselves as an accompaniment to getting up and washing, dressing, feeding, bathing, and returning to sleep—they are all missing. In these conditions, the child has no opportunity of learning and practising functions which are as basic to living as walking and talking.

The case of the child who has a good relation with his mother for a year or two and then suffers deprivation may be rather different. He has passed through the first phase of social development, that of establishing a relationship, and the trauma affects the second phase in which, though ego and super-ego development is proceeding apace, the child's awareness of his relative lack of skill in these matters is reflected in his limpet-like attachment to his mother, to whom he constantly looks for help. Only if she is with him or near at hand can he manage his environment and manage himself. If he is suddenly removed from her, to hospital or institution, he is faced with tasks which he feels to be impossible. In a traumatic situation of this kind it is usual for such skill as has already been learned to be lost. There is usually a regression to primitive functioning and increased difficulty in learning afresh. This well-known principle of the theory of learning may account for the regression to and fixation of those children at primitive modes of thinking and behaviour, and their seeming inability to progress to more mature methods.

A further principle of the theory of learning is that an individual cannot learn a skill unless he has a friendly feeling towards his teacher, and is ready to identify himself with her and to incorporate her (or some part of her) into himself. Now this positive attitude towards his mother is either lacking in the deprived child or, if present, is mixed with keen resentment. How early in a child's life deprivation causes a specifically hostile attitude is debatable, but it is certainly evident for all to see in the second year. No observation is more common than that of the child separated for a few weeks or months during the second, third, and fourth years failing to recognize his mother on reunion. It seems probable that this is sometimes a true failure to recognize, based on a regression in the capacity to abstract and identify. At others, it is certain that it is a refusal to recognize, since the children, instead of treating their parents as though they were strangers, are deliberate in their avoidance of them. The parents have become hated people. This hostility is variously expressed. It may take the form of tempers and violence; in older children it may be expressed verbally. All who have treated such children are familiar with the violence of their fantasies against their parents whom they feel have deserted them. Such an attitude is not only incompatible with their desire for love and security, and results in acute conflict, anxiety, and depression, but is clearly inimical to their future social learning. So far from idolizing their parents and wishing to become like them, one side of them hates them and wishes to avoid having anything to do with them. This is the dynamic of aggressively delinquent behaviour and may also be the dynamic of suicide, which is the result of the same conflict fought out between different systems within the self.

In other cases the child has suffered so much pain through making relationships and having them interrupted that he is reluctant ever again to give his heart to anyone for fear of its being broken. And not only his own heart: he is afraid, too, to break the heart of new persons whom he might love because he might also vent his anger on them. Older children are sometimes aware of this and will remark to a therapist: "We had better not become too familiar, for I am afraid I shall get hostile with you then" (quoted by Tibout, 1948). It is feelings such as these which underlie the withdrawal response. To withdraw from human contact is to avoid further frustration and to avoid the intense depression which human beings experience as a result of hating the person whom they most dearly love and need. Withdrawal is thus felt to be the better of two bad alternatives. Unfortunately, it proves to be a blind alley for no further development is then possible; progress in human relations necessitates the individual taking the other road, in which he learns to tolerate his ambivalent feelings and to bear the anxiety and depression which go with them. But experience shows that once a person has taken refuge in the relative painlessness of withdrawal he is reluctant to change course and to risk the turmoil of feeling and misery which attempting relationships brings with it. As a result his capacity to make affectionate relationships and to identify with loved people becomes inhibited and any treatment offered is resisted. Thenceforward he becomes a lone wolf, pursuing his ends irrespective of others. But his desire for love, repressed though it is, persists, resulting in behaviour such as promiscuity and the stealing of other people's posssessions. Feelings of revenge also smoulder on, leading to other antisocial acts, sometimes of a very violent character.

Deprivation after the age of three or four, namely in the third phase, does not have the same destructive effect on ego and super-ego development and on the ability for abstract thinking. It still results, however, in excessive desires for affection and excessive impulses for revenge, which cause acute internal conflict and unhappiness and very unfavourable social attitudes.

In both the second and third phases the child's restricted sense of time and his tendency to misapprehend a situation add greatly to his difficulties. It is exceedingly difficult for grown-ups to remember that the young child's grasp of time is meagre. The child of three can recall the events of a few days ago and anticipate those of a day or two hence. Notions such as last week or last month, next week or next month are incomprehensible. Even for a child of five or six, weeks are immensely long and months almost timeless. This very restricted time-span has to be understood if the despair which the young child feels at being left alone in a strange place is to be fully realized. Though to his mother it may seem not only a finite but relatively brief time, to him it is eternity. It is this inability to imagine a time of deliverance which, together with the sense of his helplessness, accounts for the overwhelming nature of his anxiety and despair. Perhaps the nearest to it the grown-up can conceive is to imagine being committed to prison on an indeterminate sentence.

This analogy is apt, since the notion of punishment is itself not far from many a child's mind as the explanation of events. All clinicians have come across children who have seriously believed that their being sent away from home was to punish them for being naughty, a misconstruction which is often made even more terrifying and distressing by being unexpressed. At other times children imagine that it has been their fault that the home has been broken up. Commonly there is bewilderment and perplexity regarding the course of events, which leads the child to be unable to accept and respond to his new environment and the new people caring for him. Naturally a child who has suffered gross privation in early infancy, or who for other reasons cannot make relationships, will not be affected in these ways, but will greet each change with the genial indifference apparent in Levy's case already quoted. But for the child who has had the opportunity to make relationships it is not so easy to change loyalties. Indeed, very many of the problems which arise as a result of moving an older child to a foster-home are caused by the failure to recognize the deep attachment which a child has for his parents, even if they are exceedingly bad and have given him little affection. Unless these perplexities are cleared up and these loyalties respected, the child will remain anchored in an unsatisfactory past, endlessly trying to find his mother and refusing to adapt to the new situation and make the best of it. This results in a dissatisfied restless character unable to make either himself or anyone else happy.

By and large, then, the theoretical framework of developmental phases of ego functioning and of capacity to make object relationships, and of the periods within the life cycle by which they must be completed, seems to fit the clinical evidence. No doubt as understanding increases the three main phases described here will be subdivided into many subphases, and one will learn to discern the particular psychic forces which are brought into play by deprivation in each of them.

In this brief sketch no attempt has been made to go into detail nor to compare and discuss the views of the many psycho-analysts and psychologists who have contributed to our understanding. Those familiar with the literature will know where the writer's debts lie.

Science, August 21, 1959, vol. 136, pp. 421–431.

√ Affectional Responses in the Infant Monkey[*][1]

Harry F. Harlow and Robert R. Zimmermann

Investigators from diverse behavioral fields have long recognized the strong attachment of the neonatal and infantile animal to its mother. Although this affectional behavior has been commonly observed, there is, outside the field of ethology, scant experimental evidence permitting identification of the factors critical to the formation of this bond. Lorenz (1937) and others have stressed the importance of innate visual and auditory mechanisms which, through the process of imprinting, give rise to persisting following responses in the infant bird and fish. Imprinting behavior has been demonstrated successfully in a variety of avian species under controlled laboratory conditions, and this phenomenon has been investigated systematically in order to identify those variables which contribute to its development and maintenance [see, for example, Hinde, Thorpe, and Vince (1956), Fabricius (1951), Hess (in press),

Jaynes (in press), and Moltz and Rosenblum (1958b)]. These studies represent the largest body of existent experimental evidence measuring the tie between infant and mother. At the mammalian level there is little or no systematic experimental evidence of this nature.

Observations on monkeys by Carpenter (1934), Nolte (1955), and Zuckermann (1933) and on chimpanzees by Köhler (1925) and by Yerkes and Tomilin (1935) show that monkey and chimpanzee infants develop strong ties to their mothers and that these affectional attachments may persist for years. It is, of course, common knowledge that human infants form strong and persistent ties to their mothers.

Although students from diverse scientific fields recognize this abiding attachment, there is considerable disagreement about the nature of its development and its fundamental underlying mechanisms. A common theory among psychologists, sociologists, and anthropologists is that of learning based on drive reduction. This theory proposes that the infant's attachment to the mother results from the association

* Reprinted from *Science* by permission.
[1] Support for the research presented in this article was provided through funds received from the graduate school of the University of Wisconsin; from grant M–772, National Institutes of Health; and from a Ford Foundation grant.

of the mother's face and form with the alleviation of certain primary drive states, particularly hunger and thirst. Thus, through learning, affection becomes a self-supporting, derived drive (Dollard & Miller, 1950, p. 133; Mussen & Conger, 1956, pp. 137, 138). Psychoanalysts, on the other hand, have stressed the importance of various innate needs, such as a need to suck and orally possess the breast (Hinde, Thorpe, & Vince, 1956), or needs relating to contact, movement, temperature (Ribble, 1943; Winnicott, 1948), and clinging to the mother (Bowlby, 1958).

The paucity of experimental evidence concerning the development of affectional responses has led these theorists to derive their basic hypotheses from deductions and intuitions based on observation and analysis of adult verbal reports. As a result, the available observational evidence is often forced into a preconceived theoretical framework. An exception to the above generalization is seen in the recent attempt by Bowlby (1958) to analyze and integrate the available observational and experimental evidence derived from both human and subhuman infants. Bowlby has concluded that a theory of component instinctual responses, species specific, can best account for the infant's tie to the mother. He suggests that the species-specific responses for human beings (some of these responses are not strictly limited to human beings) include contact, clinging, sucking, crying, smiling, and following. He further emphasizes that these responses are manifested independently of primary drive reduction in human and subhuman infants.

The absence of experimental data which would allow a critical evaluation of any theory of affectional develop-

ment can be attributed to several causes. The use of human infants as subjects has serious limitations, since it is not feasible to employ all the experimental controls which would permit a completely adequate analysis of the proposed variables. In addition, the limited response repertoire of the human neonate severely restricts the number of discrete or precise response categories that can be measured until a considerable age has been attained. Thus, critical variables go unmeasured and become lost or confounded among the complex physiological, psychological, and cultural factors which influence the developing human infant.

Moreover, the use of common laboratory animals also has serious limitations, for most of these animals have behavioral repertoires very different from those of the human being, and in many species these systems mature so rapidly that it is difficult to measure and assess their orderly development. On the other hand, subhuman primates, including the macaque monkey, are born at a state of maturity which makes it possible to begin precise measurements within the first few days of life. Furthermore, their postnatal maturational rate is slow enough to permit precise assessment of affectional variables and development.

Over a 3-year period prior to the beginning of the research program reported here, some 60 infant macaque monkeys were separated from their mothers 6 to 12 hours after birth and raised at the primate laboratory of the University of Wisconsin. The success of the procedures developed to care for these neonates was demonstrated by the low mortality and by a gain in weight which was approximately 25 percent greater than that of infants raised by their own mothers. All credit for the success of this program belongs to van Wagenen (1950), who had described the essential procedures in detail.

These first 3 years were spent in devising measures to assess the multiple capabilities of the neonatal and infantile monkey. The studies which resulted have revealed that the development of perception, learning, manipulation, exploration, frustration, and timidity in the macaque monkey follows a course and sequence which is very similar to that in the human infant. The basic differences between the two species appear to be the advanced postnatal maturational status and the subsequent more rapid growth of the infant macaque. Probably the most important similarities between the two, in relation to the problem of affectional development, are characteristic responses that have been associated with, and are considered basic to, affection; these include nursing, clinging, and visual and auditory exploration.

In the course of raising these infants we observed that they all showed a strong attachment to the cheesecloth blankets which were used to cover the wire floors of their cages. Removal of these cloth blankets resulted in violent emotional behavior. These responses were not short-lived, indeed, the emotional disturbance lasted several days, as was indicated by the infant's refusal to work on the standard learning tests that were being conducted at the time. Similar observations had already been made by Foley (1934) and by van Wagenen (1950), who stressed the importance of adequate contact responses to the very survival of the neonatal macaque. Such observations suggested to us that contact was a true affectional

variable and that it should be possible to trace and measure the development and importance of these responses. Indeed there seemed to be every reason to believe that one could manipulate all variables which have been considered critical to the development of the infant's attachment to a mother, or mother surrogate.

To attain control over maternal variables, we took the calculated risk of constructing and using inanimate mother surrogates rather than real mothers. The cloth mother that we used was a cylinder of wood covered with a sheath of terry cloth,[2] and the wire mother was a hardware-cloth cylinder. Initially, sponge rubber was placed underneath the terry cloth sheath of the cloth mother surrogate, and a light bulb behind each mother surrogate provided radiant heat. For reasons of sanitation and safety these two factors were eliminated in construction of the standard mothers, with no observable effect on the behavior of the infants. The two mothers were attached at a 45-degree angle to aluminum bases and were given different faces to assure uniqueness in the various test situations (Fig. 1). Bottle holders were installed in the upper middle part of the bodies to permit nursing. The mother was designed on the basis of previous experience with infant monkeys, which suggested that nursing in an upright or inclined position with something for the infant to clasp facilitated successful nursing and resulted in healthier infants (see van Wagenen, 1950). Thus, both mothers provided the basic known requirements for adequate nursing, but the cloth mother provided

[2] We no longer make the cloth mother out of a block of wood. The cloth mother's body is simply that of the wire mother, covered by a terry-cloth sheath.

Fig. 1. Wire and cloth mother surrogates.

an additional variable of contact comfort. That both of these surrogate mothers provided adequate nursing support is shown by the fact that the total ingestion of formula and the weight gain was normal for all infants fed on the surrogate mothers. The only consistent difference between the groups lay in the softer stools of the infants fed on the wire mother.

Development of Affectional Responses

The initial experiments on the development of affectional responses have already been reported (Harlow, 1958; Harlow & Zimmermann, 1958) but will be briefly reviewed here, since subsequent experiments were derived from them. In the initial experiments, designed to evaluate the role of nursing on the development of affection, a cloth mother and a wire mother were placed in different cubicles attached to the infant's living cage. Eight newborn monkeys were placed in individual cages with the surrogates; for four infant monkeys the cloth mother lactated and the wire mother did not, and for the other four this condition was reversed.

The infants lived with their mother surrogates for a minimum of 165 days, and during this time they were tested in a variety of situations designed to measure the development of affectional responsiveness. Differential affectional responsiveness was initially measured in terms of mean hours per day spent on the cloth and on the wire mothers under two conditions of feeding, as shown in Fig. 2. Infants fed on the cloth mother and on the wire mother have highly similar scores after a short adaptation period (Fig. 3), and over a 165-day period both groups show a distinct preference for the cloth mother. The persistence of the differential responsiveness to the mothers for both groups of infants is evident, and the over-all dif-

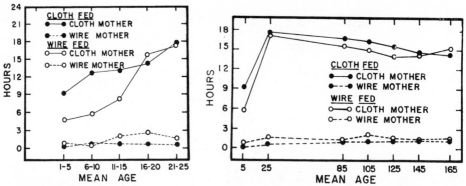

Time spent on cloth and wire mother surrogates. Fig. 2 (left). Short term. Fig. 3 (right). Long term.

ferences between the groups fall short of statistical significance.

These data make it obvious that contact comfort is a variable of critical importance in the development of affectional responsiveness to the surrogate mother, and that nursing appears to play a negligible role. With increasing age and opportunity to learn, an infant fed from a lactating wire mother does not become more responsive to her, as would be predicted from a derived-drive theory, but instead becomes increasingly more responsive to its nonlactating cloth mother. These findings are at complete variance with a drive-reduction theory of affectional development.

The amount of time spent on the mother does not necessarily indicate an affectional attachment. It could merely reflect the fact that the cloth mother is a more comfortable sleeping platform or a more adequate source of warmth for the infant. However, three of the four infants nursed by the cloth mother and one of the four nursed by the wire mother left a gauze-covered heating pad that was on the floor of their cages during the first 14 days of life to spend up to 18 hours a day on the cloth mother. This suggests that differential heating or warmth is not a critical variable

within the controlled temperature range of the laboratory.

Other tests demonstrate that the cloth mother is more than a convenient nest; indeed, they show that a bond develops between infant and cloth-mother surrogate that is almost unbelievably similar to the bond established between human mother and child. One highly definitive test measured the selective maternal responsiveness of the monkey infants under conditions of distress or fear.

Various fear-producing stimuli, such as the moving toy bear illustrated in Fig. 4, were presented to the infants in their home cages. The data on differential responses under both feeding conditions are given in Fig. 5. It is apparent that the cloth mother was highly preferred to the wire mother, and it is a fact that these differences were unrelated to feeding conditions—that is, nursing on the cloth or on the wire mother. Above and beyond these objective data are observations on the form of the infants' responses in this situation. In spite of their abject terror, the infant monkeys, after reaching the cloth mother and rubbing their bodies about hers, rapidly come to lose their fear of the frightening stimuli. Indeed, within a minute or two most of the babies were

Fig. 4. Typical fear stimulus.

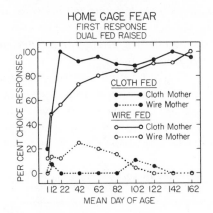

HOME CAGE FEAR
FIRST RESPONSE
DUAL FED RAISED

CLOTH FED
●——● Cloth Mother
●······● Wire Mother
WIRE FED
○——○ Cloth Mother
○······○ Wire Mother

PER CENT CHOICE RESPONSES

MEAN DAY OF AGE

Fig. 5. Differential responsiveness in fear tests.

visually exploring the very thing which so shortly before had seemed an object of evil. The bravest of the babies would actually leave the mother and approach the fearful monsters, under, of course, the protective gaze of their mothers.

These data are highly similar, in terms of differential responsiveness, to the time scores previously mentioned and indicate the overwhelming impor-

tance of contact comfort. The results are so striking as to suggest that the primary function of nursing may be that of insuring frequent and intimate contact between mother and infant, thus facilitating the localization of the source of contact comfort. This interpretation finds some support in the test discussed above. In both situations the infants nursed by the cloth mother developed consistent responsiveness to the soft mother earlier in testing than did the infants nursed by the wire mother, and during this transient period the latter group was slightly more responsive to the wire mother than the former group. However, these early differences shortly disappeared.

Additional data have been obtained from two groups of four monkeys each which were raised with a single mother placed in a cubicle attached to the living-cage. Four of the infants were presented with a lactating wire mother and the other four were presented with a nonlactating cloth mother. The latter group was hand-fed from small nursing bottles for the first 30 days of life and then weaned to a cup. The development of responsiveness to the mothers was studied for 165 days; after this the individual mothers were removed from the cages and testing was continued to determine the strength and persistence of the affectional responses.

Figure 6 presents the mean time per day spent on the respective mothers over the 165-day test period, and Fig. 7 shows the percentage of responses to the mothers when a fear-producing stimulus was introduced into the home cage. These tests indicate that both groups of infants developed responsiveness to their mother surrogates. However, these measures did not reveal the differences in behavior that were displayed in the

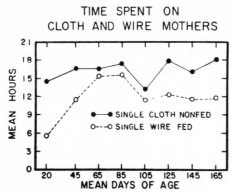

Fig. 6. Time spent on single mother surrogates.

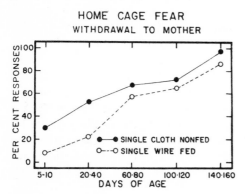

Fig. 7. Responsiveness to single surrogate mothers in fear tests.

reactions to the mothers when the fear stimuli were presented. The infants raised on the cloth mother would rush to the mother and cling tightly to her. Following this initial response these infants would relax and either begin to manipulate the mother or turn to gaze at the feared object without the slightest sign of apprehension. The infants raised on the wire mother, on the other hand, rushed away from the feared object toward their mother but did not cling to or embrace her. Instead, they would either clutch themselves and rock and vocalize for the remainder of the test or rub against the side of the cubicle. Contact with the cubicle or the

mother did not reduce the emotionality produced by the introduction of the fear stimulus. These differences are revealed in emotionality scores, for behavior such as vocalization, crouching, rocking, and sucking, recorded during the test. Figure 8 shows the mean emotionality index for test sessions for the two experimental groups, the dual-mother groups, and a comparable control group raised under standard laboratory conditions. As can be seen, the infants raised with the single wire mother have the highest emotionality scores of all the groups, and the infants raised with the single cloth mother or with a cloth and wire mother have the lowest scores. It appears that the responses made by infants raised only with a wire mother were more in the nature of simple flight responses to the fear stimulus and that the presence of the mother surrogate had little effect in alleviating the fear.

During our initial experiments with the dual-mother conditions, responsiveness to the lactating wire mother in the fear tests decreased with age and opportunity to learn, while responsiveness to

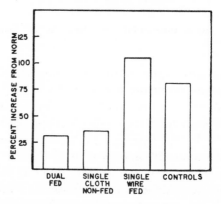

Fig. 8. Change in emotionality index in fear tests.

the nonlactating cloth mother increased. However, there was some indication of a slight increase in frequency of response to the wire mother for the first 30 to 60 days (see Fig. 5). These data suggest the possible hypothesis that nursing facilitated the contact of infant and mother during the early developmental periods.

The interpretation of all fear testing is complicated by the fact that all or most "fear" stimuli evoke many positive exploratory responses early in life and do not consistently evoke flight responses until the monkey is 40 to 50 days of age. Similar delayed maturation of visually induced fear responses has been reported for birds (Fabricius, 1951), chimpanzees (Hebb, 1949, pp. 241 ff.), and human infants (Jersild & Holmes, 1935, p. 356).

Because of apparent interactions between fearful and affectional developmental variables, a test was designed to trace the development of approach and avoidance responses in these infants. This test, described as the straight-alley test, was conducted in a wooden alley 8 feet long and 2 feet wide. One end of the alley contained a movable tray upon which appropriate stimuli were placed. The other end of the alley contained a box for hiding. Each test began with the monkey in a start box 1 foot in front of the hiding box; thus, the animal could maintain his original position, approach the stimulus tray as it moved toward him, or flee into the hiding box. The infants were presented with five stimuli in the course of five successive days. The stimuli included a standard cloth mother, a standard wire mother, a yellow cloth monster with the head removed, a blank tray, and a large black fear stimulus, shown in Fig. 9. The infants were tested at 5, 10, and

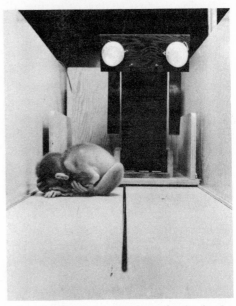

Fig. 9. Response to the fear stimulus in the straight-alley tests.

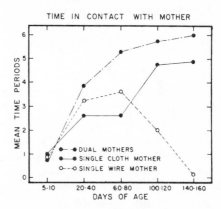

TIME IN CONTACT WITH MOTHER

MEAN TIME PERIODS

DAYS OF AGE

● —● DUAL MOTHERS
●——● SINGLE CLOTH MOTHER
○--○ SINGLE WIRE MOTHER

Fig. 10. Responsiveness to mother surrogates in the straight-alley tests.

20 days of age, respectively, and then at 20-day intervals up to 160 days. Figure 10 shows the mean number of 15-second time periods spent in contact with the appropriate mother during the 90-second tests for the two single-mother groups, and the responses to the cloth mother by four infants from the dual-mother group.

During the first 80 days of testing, all the groups showed an increase in response to the respective mother surrogates. The infants fed on the single wire mother, however, reached peak responsiveness at this age and then showed a consistent decline, followed by an actual avoidance of the wire mother. During test sessions 140 to 160, only one contact was made with the wire mother, and three of the four infants ran into the hiding box almost immediately and remained there for the entire test session. On the other hand, all of the infants raised with a cloth mother, whether or not they were nursed by her, showed a progressive increase in time spent in contact with their cloth mothers until approaches and contacts during the test sessions approached maximum scores.

The development of the response of flight from the wire mother by the group fed on the single wire mother is, of course, completely contrary to a derived-drive theory of affectional development. A comparison of this group with the group raised with a cloth mother gives some support to the hypothesis that feeding or nursing facilitates the early development of responses to the mother but that without the factor of contact comfort, these positive responses are not maintained.

The differential responsiveness to the cloth mother of infants raised with both mothers, the reduced emotionality of both the groups raised with cloth mothers in the home-cage fear tests, and the development of approach responses in the straight-alley test indicate that the cloth mother provides a haven of safety and security for the frightened infant. The affectional response patterns found in the infant monkey are unlike tropistic or even complex reflex responses; they resemble instead the diverse and pervasive patterns of response to his mother exhibited by the human child in the complexity of situations involving child-mother relationships.

The role of the mother as a source of safety and security has been demonstrated experimentally for human infants by Arsenian (1943). She placed children 11 to 30 months of age in a strange room containing toys and other play objects. Half of the children were accompanied into the room by a mother or a substitute mother (a familiar nursery attendant), while the other half entered the situation alone. The children in the first group (mother present) were much less emotional and participated much more fully in the play activity than those in the second group (mother absent). With repeated testing, the security score, a composite score of emotionality and play behavior, improved for the children who entered alone, but it still fell far below that for the children who were accompanied by their mothers. In subsequent tests, the children from the mother-present group were placed in the test room alone, and there was a drastic drop in the security scores. Contrariwise, the introduction of the mother raised the security scores of children in the other group.

We have performed a similar series of open-field experiments, comparing monkeys raised on mother surrogates with control monkeys raised in a wire cage containing a cheesecloth blanket from days 1 to 14 and no cloth blanket subsequently. The infants were introduced into the strange environment of the open field, which was a room measuring 6 by 6 by 6 feet, containing multiple stimuli known to elicit curiosity-manipulatory responses in baby monkeys. The infants raised with single mother surrogates were placed in this situation twice a week for 8 weeks, no mother surrogate being present during one of the weekly sessions and the appropriate mother surrogate (the kind which the experimental infant had always known) being present during the other sessions. Four infants raised with dual mother surrogates and four control infants were subjected to similar experimental sequences, the cloth mother being present on half of the occasions. The remaining four "dual-mother" infants were given repetitive tests to obtain information on the development of responsiveness to each of the dual mothers in this situation. A cloth blanket was always available as one of the stimuli throughout the sessions. It should be emphasized that the blanket could readily compete with the cloth mother as a contact stimulus, for it was standard laboratory procedure to wrap the infants in soft cloth whenever they were removed from their cages for testing,

weighing, and other required laboratory activities.

As soon as they were placed in the test room, the infants raised with cloth mothers rushed to their mother surrogate when she was present and clutched her tenaciously, a response so strong that it can only be adequately depicted by motion pictures. Then, as had been observed in the fear tests in the home cage, they rapidly relaxed, showed no sign of apprehension, and began to demonstrate unequivocal positive responses of manipulating and climbing on the mother. After several sessions, the infants began to use the mother surrogate as a base of operations, leaving her to explore and handle a stimulus and then returning to her before going to a new plaything. Some of the infants even brought the stimuli to the mother, as shown in Fig. 11. The behavior of these infants changed radically in the absence of the mother. Emotional indices such as vocalization, crouching, rocking, and sucking in-

Fig. 11. Subsequent response to cloth mother and stimulus in the open-field test.

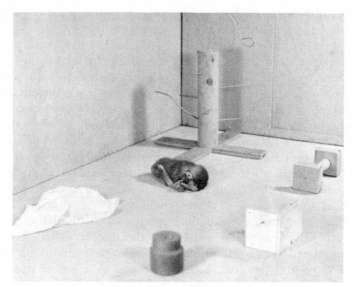

Fig. 12. Response in the open-field test in the absence of the mother surrogate.

creased sharply. Typical response patterns were either freezing in a crouched position, as illustrated in Fig. 12, or running around the room on the hind and clutching themselves with their arms. Though no quantitative evidence is available, contact and manipulation of objects was frantic and of short duration, as opposed to the playful type of manipulation observed when the mother was present.

In the presence of the mother, the behavior of the infants raised with single wire mothers was both quantitatively and qualitatively different from that of the infants raised with cloth mothers. Not only did these infants spend little or no time contacting their mother surrogates but the presence of the mother did not reduce their emotionality. These differences are evident in the mean number of time periods spent in contact with the respective mothers, as shown in Fig. 13, and the composite emotional index for the two stimulus conditions depicted in Fig. 14.

Although the infants raised with dual mothers spent considerably more time in contact with the cloth mother than did the infants raised with single cloth mothers, their emotional reactions to the presence and absence of the mother were highly similar, the composite emotional index being reduced by almost

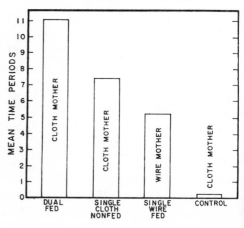

Fig. 13. Responsiveness to mother surrogates in the open-field test.

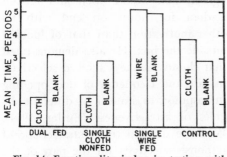

Fig. 14. Emotionality index in testing with and without the mother surrogates.

half when the mother was in the test situation. The infants raised with wire mothers were highly emotional under both conditions and actually showed a slight, though nonsignificant, increase in emotionality when the mother was present. Although some of the infants reared by a wire mother did contact her, their behavior was similar to that observed in the home-cage fear tests. They did not clutch and cling to their mother as did the infants with cloth mothers; instead, they sat on her lap and clutched themselves, or held their heads and bodies in their arms and engaged in convulsive jerking and rocking movements similar to the autistic behavior of deprived and institutionalized human children. The lack of exploratory and manipulatory behavior on the part of the infants reared with wire mothers, both in the presence and absence of the wire mother, was similar to that observed in the mother-absent condition for the infants raised with the cloth mothers, and such contacts with objects as was made was of short duration and of an erratic and frantic nature. None of the infants raised with single wire mothers displayed the persistent and aggressive play behavior

that was typical of many of the infants that were raised with cloth mothers.

The four control infants, raised without a mother surrogate, had approximately the same emotionality scores when the mother was absent that the other infants had in the same condition, but the control subjects' emotionality scores were significantly higher in the presence of the mother surrogate than in her absence. This result is not surprising, since recent evidence indicates that the cloth mother with the highly ornamental face is an effective fear stimulus for monkeys that have not been raised with her.

Further illustration of differential responsiveness to the two mother surrogates is found in the results of a series of developmental tests in the open-field situation, given to the remaining four "dual-mother" infants. These infants were placed in the test room with the cloth mother, the wire mother, and no mother present on successive occasions at various age levels. Figure 15 shows the mean number of time periods spent in contact with the respective mothers

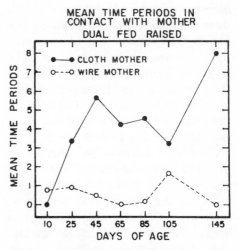

Fig. 15. Differential responsiveness in the open-field test.

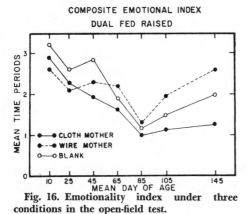

Fig. 16. Emotionality index under three conditions in the open-field test.

for two trials at each age level, and Fig. 16 reveals the composite emotion scores for the three stimulus conditions during these same tests. The differential responsiveness to the cloth and wire mothers, as measured by contact time, is evident by 20 days of age, and this systematic difference continues throughout 140 days of age. Only small differences in emotionality under the various conditions are evident during the first 85 days of age, although the presence of the cloth mother does result in slightly lower scores from the 45th day onward. However, at 105 and 145 days of age there is a considerable difference for the three conditions, the emotionality scores for the wire-mother and blank conditions showing a sharp increase. The heightened emotionality found under the wire-mother condition was mainly contributed by the two infants fed on the wire mother. The behavior of these two infants in the presence of the wire mother was similar to the behavior of the animals raised with a single wire mother. On the few occasions when contact with the wire mother was made, the infants did not attempt to cling to her; instead they would sit on her lap, clasp their heads and bodies, and rock back and forth.

In 1953 Butler demonstrated that mature monkeys enclosed in a dimly lighted box would open and reopen a door for hours on end with no other motivation than that of looking outside the box. He also demonstrated that rhesus monkeys showed selectivity in rate and frequency of door-opening in response to stimuli of different degrees of attractiveness (Butler, 1954). We have utilized this characteristic of response selectivity on the part of the monkey to measure the strength of affectional responsiveness of the babies raised with mother surrogates in an infant version of the Butler box. The test sequence involves four repetitions of a test battery in which the four stimuli of cloth mother, wire mother, infant monkey, and empty box are presented for a 30-minute period on successive days. The first four subjects raised with the dual mother surrogates and the eight infants raised with single mother surrogates were given a test sequence at 40 to 50 days of age, depending upon the availability of the apparatus. The data obtained from the three experimental groups and a comparable control group are presented in Fig. 17. Both groups of infants raised with cloth mothers

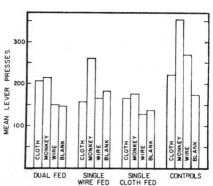

Fig. 17. Differential responses to visual exploration.

showed approximately equal respon-siveness to the cloth mother and to another infant monkey, and no greater responsiveness to the wire mother than to an empty box. Again, the results are independent of the kind of mother that lactated, cloth or wire. The infants raised with only a wire mother and those in the control group were more highly responsive to the monkey than to either of the mother surrogates. Fur-thermore, the former group showed a higher frequency of response to the empty box than to the wire mother.

In summary, the experimental analy-sis of the development of the infant monkey's attachment to an inanimate mother surrogate demonstrates the over-whelming importance of the variable of soft body contact that characterized the cloth mother, and this held true for the appearance, development, and mainte-nance of the infant-surrogate-mother tie. The results also indicate that, with-out the factor of contact comfort, only a weak attachment, if any, is formed. Finally, probably the most surprising finding is that nursing or feeding played either no role or a subordinate role in the development of affection as meas-ured by contact time, responsiveness to fear, responsiveness to strangeness, and motivation to seek and see. No evidence was found indicating that nursing medi-ated the development of any of these responses, although there is evidence in-dicating that feeding probably facili-tated the early appearance and increased the early strength of affectional respon-siveness. Certainly feeding, in contrast to contact comfort, is neither a neces-sary nor a sufficient condition for affec-tional development.

One of the outstanding characteris-tics of the infant's attachment to its mother is the persistence of the rela-tionship over a period of years, even though the frequency of contact be-tween infant and mother is reduced with increasing age. In order to test the persistence of the responsiveness of our "mother-surrogate" infants, the first four infant monkeys raised with dual mothers and all of the monkeys raised with single mothers were separated from their surrogates at 165 to 170 days of age. They were tested for affectional retention during the following 9 days, then at 30-day intervals during the fol-lowing year. The results are of necessity incomplete, inasmuch as the entire mother-surrogate program was initiated less than 2 years ago, but enough evi-dence is available to indicate that the attachment formed to the cloth mother during the first 6 months of life is en-during and not easily forgotten.

Affectional retention as measured by the modified Butler box for the first 15 months of testing for four of the infants raised with two mothers is given in Fig. 18. Although there is considerable vari-ability in the total response frequency from session to session, there is a con-sistent difference in the number of re-sponses to the cloth mother as con-trasted with responses to either the wire

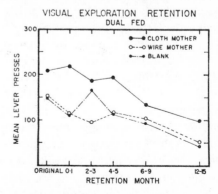

Fig. 18. Retention of differential visual-ex-ploration responses.

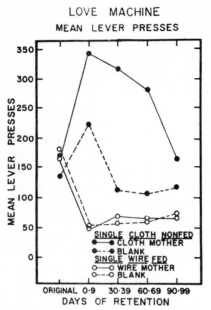

LOVE MACHINE
MEAN LEVER PRESSES

Fig. 19. Retention of differential visual-exploration responses by single-surrogate infants.

highly significant reduction in general level of responding. Although incomplete, the data from further retention testing indicate that the difference between these two groups persists for at least 5 months.

Affectional retention was also tested in the open field during the first 9 days after separation and then at 30-day intervals. Each test condition was run twice in each retention period. In the initial retention tests the behavior of the infants that had lived with cloth mothers differed slightly from that observed during the period preceding separation. These infants tended to spend more time in contact with the mother and less time exploring and manipulating the objects in the room. The behavior of the infants raised with single wire mothers, on the other hand, changed radically during the first retention sessions, and responses to the mother surrogate dropped almost to zero. Objective evidence for these differences are given in Fig. 20, which reveals the mean number of time periods spent in contact with the respective mothers. During the first retention test session, the infants raised with a single wire mother showed almost no responses to the mother surrogate they had always known. Since the infants raised with both mothers were already approaching the maximum score in this measure, there was little room for improvement. The infants raised with a single nonlactating cloth mother, however, showed a consistent and significant increase in this measure during the first 90 days of retention. Evidence for the persistence of this responsiveness is given by the fact that after 15 months' separation from their mothers, the infants that had lived with cloth mothers spent an average of 8.75 out of 12 possible time periods in

mother or the empty box, and there is no consistent difference between responses to the wire mother and to the empty box. The effects of contact comfort versus feeding are dramatically demonstrated in this test by the monkeys raised with either single cloth or wire mothers. Figure 19 shows the frequency of response to the appropriate mother surrogate and to the blank box during the preseparation period and the first 90 days of retention testing. Removal of the mother resulted in a doubling of the frequency of response to the cloth mother and more than tripled the difference between the responses to the cloth mother and those to the empty box for the infants that had lived with a single nonlactating cloth mother surrogate. The infants raised with a single lactating wire mother, on the other hand, not only failed to show any consistent preference for the wire mother but also showed a

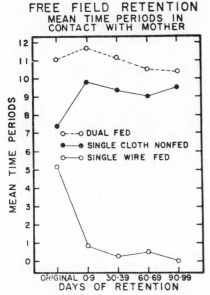

FREE FIELD RETENTION
MEAN TIME PERIODS IN
CONTACT WITH MOTHER

o—o DUAL FED
•—• SINGLE CLOTH NONFED
o—o SINGLE WIRE FED

Fig. 20. Retention of responsiveness to mother surrogates in the open-field tests.

contact with the cloth mother during the test. The incomplete data for retention testing of the infants raised with only a lactating wire mother or a nonlactating cloth mother indicates that there is little or no change in the initial differences found between these two groups in this test over a period of 5 months. In the absence of the mother, the behavior of the infants raised with cloth mothers was similar in the initial retention tests to that during the pre-separation tests, but with repeated testing they tended to show gradual adaptation to the open-field situation and, consequently, a reduction in their emotionality scores. Even with this over-all reduction in emotionality, these infants had consistently lower emotionality scores when the mother was present.

At the time of initiating the retention tests, an additional condition was introduced into the open-field test: the surrogate mother was placed in the center of the room and covered with a clear Plexiglas box. The animals raised with cloth mothers were initially disturbed and frustrated when their efforts to secure and contact the mother were blocked by the box. However, after several violent crashes into the plastic, the animals adapted to the situation and soon used the box as a place of orientation for exploratory and play behavior. In fact, several infants were much more active under these conditions than they were when the mother was available for direct contact. A comparison of the composite emotionality index of the babies raised with a single cloth or wire mother under the three conditions of no mother, surrogate mother, and surrogate-mother-box is presented in Fig. 21. The infants raised with a single cloth mother were consistently less emotional when they could contact the mother but also showed the effects of her visual presence, as their emotionality scores in the plastic box condition were definitely lower than their scores when the mother was absent. It appears that the infants gained considerable emotional security from the presence of the mother even though contact was denied.

In contrast, the animals raised with only lactating wire mothers did not show any significant or consistent trends during these retention sessions other than a general over-all reduction of emotionality, which may be attributed to a general adaptation, the result of repeated testing.

Affectional retention has also been measured in the straight-alley test mentioned earlier. During the preseparation tests it was found that the infants that had only wire mothers developed a general avoidance response to all of the stimuli in this test when they were

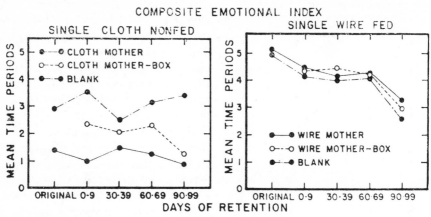

Fig. 21. Emotionality index under three conditions in the open-field retention tests.

about 100 days of age and made few, if any, responses to the wire mother during the final test sessions. In contrast, all the infants raised with a cloth mother responded positively to her. Maternal separation did not significantly change the behavior of any of the groups. The babies raised with just wire mothers continued to flee into the hiding booth in the presence of the wire mother, while all of the infants raised with cloth mothers continued to respond positively to the cloth mother at approximately the same level as in the preseparation tests. The mean number of time periods spent in contact with the appropriate mother surrogates for the first 3 months of retention testing are given in Fig. 22. There is little, if any, waning of responsiveness to the cloth mother during these 3 months. There appeared to be some loss of responsiveness to the mother in this situation after 5 to 6 months of separation, but the test was discontinued at that time as the infants had outgrown the apparatus.

The retention data from these multiple tests demonstrate clearly the importance of body contact for the future

maintenance of affectional responses. Whereas several of the measures in the preseparation period suggested that the infants raised with only a wire mother might have developed a weak attachment to her, all responsiveness disappeared in the first few days after the mother was withdrawn from the living-cage. Infants that had had the opportunity of living with a cloth mother showed the opposite effect and either became more responsive to the cloth mother or continued to respond to her at the same level.

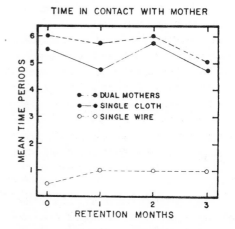

Fig. 22. Retention of responsiveness to mother surrogates in the straight-alley test.

These data indicate that once an affectional bond is formed it is maintained for a very considerable length of time with little reinforcement of the contact-comfort variable. The limited data available for infants that have been separated from their mother surrogates for a year suggest that these affectional responses show resistance to extinction similar to the resistance previously demonstrated for learned fears and learned pain. Such data are in keeping with common observation of human behavior.

It is true, however, that the infants raised with cloth mothers exhibit some absolute decrease in responsiveness with every one of the major test situations. Such results would be obtained even if there were no true decrease in the strength of the affectional bond, because of familiarization and adaptation resulting from repeated testing. Therefore, at the end of 1 year of retention testing, new tests were introduced into the experimental program.

Our first new test was a modification of the open-field situation, in which basic principles of the home-cage fear test were incorporated. This particular choice was made partly because the latter test had to be discontinued when the mother surrogates were removed from the home cages.

For the new experiment a Masonite floor marked off in 6- by 12-inch rectangles was placed in the open-field chamber. Both mother surrogates were placed in the test room opposite a plastic start-box. Three fear stimuli, selected to produce differing degrees of emotionality, were placed in the center of the room directly in front of the start-box in successive test sessions. Eight trials were run under each stimulus condition, and in half of the trials the most direct path to the cloth mother was blocked by a large Plexiglas screen, illustrated in Fig. 23. Thus, in these trials the infants were forced to approach and bypass the fear stimulus or the wire mother, or both, in order to

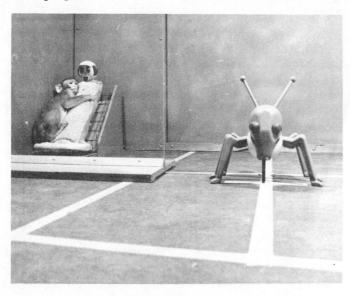

Fig. 23. Typical response to cloth mother in the modified open-field test.

reach the cloth mother. Following these 24 trials with the mothers present, one trial of each condition with both mothers absent was run, and this in turn was followed by two trials run under the most emotion-provoking condition: with a mechanical toy present and the direct path to the mother blocked.

We now have complete data for the first four infants raised with both a cloth and a wire mother. Even with this scanty information, the results are obvious. As would be predicted from our other measures, the emotionality scores for the three stimuli were significantly different and these same scores were increased greatly when the direct path to the mother was blocked. A highly significant preference was shown for the cloth mother under both conditions (direct and blocked path), although the presence of the block did increase the number of first responses to the wire mother from 3 to 10 percent. In all cases this was a transient response and the infants subsequently ran on to the cloth mother and clung tightly to her.

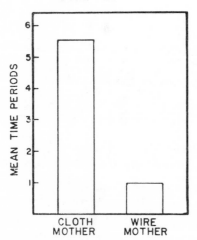

TIME IN CONTACT WITH MOTHERS
DUAL FED

MEAN TIME PERIODS

CLOTH MOTHER   WIRE MOTHER

Fig. 24. Differential responsiveness in the modified open-field test.

Objective evidence for this overwhelming preference is indicated in Fig. 24, which shows the mean number of time periods spent in contact with the two mothers. After a number of trials, the infants would go first to the cloth mother and then, and only then, would go out to explore, manipulate, and even attack and destroy the fear stimuli. It was as if they believed that their mother would protect them, even at the cost of her life—little enough to ask in view of her condition.

The removal of the mother surrogates from the situation produced the predictable effect of doubling the emotionality index. In the absence of the mothers, the infants would often run to the Plexiglas partition which formerly had blocked their path to the mother, or they would crouch in the corner behind the block where the mother normally would have been. The return of the mothers in the final two trials of the test in which the most emotion-evoking situation was presented resulted in behavior near the normal level, as measured by the emotionality index and contacts with the cloth mother.

Our second test of this series was designed to replace the straight-alley test described above and provide more quantifiable data on responsiveness to fear stimuli. The test was conducted in an alley 8 feet long and 2 feet wide. At one end of the alley and directly behind the monkeys' restraining chamber was a small stimulus chamber which contained a fear object. Each trial was initiated by raising an opaque sliding door which exposed the fear stimulus. Beginning at a point 18 inches from the restraining chamber, the alley was divided lengthwise by a partition; this provided the infant with the choice of entering one of two alleys.

The effects of all mother combinations were measured; these combinations included no mothers, two cloth mothers, two wire mothers, and a cloth and a wire mother. All mother conditions were counterbalanced by two distance conditions—distances of 24 and 78 inches, respectively, from the restraining chamber. This made it possible, for example, to provide the infant with the alternative of running to the cloth mother which was in close proximity to the fear stimulus or to the wire mother (or no mother) at a greater distance from the fear stimulus. Thus, it was possible to distinguish between running to the mother surrogate as an object of security, and generalized flight in response to a fear stimulus.

Again, the data available at this time are from the first four infants raised with cloth and wire mothers. Nevertheless, the evidence is quite conclusive. A highly significant preference is shown for the cloth mother as compared to the wire mother or to no mother, and this preference appears to be independent of the proximity of the mother to the fear stimulus. In the condition in which two cloth mothers are present, one 24 inches from the fear stimulus and the other 78 inches from it, there was a preference for the nearest mother, but the differences were not statistically significant. In two conditions in which no cloth mother was present and the infant had to choose between a wire mother and no mother, or between two empty chambers, the emotionality scores were almost twice those under the cloth-mother-present condition.

No differences were found in either of these tests that were related to previous conditions of feeding—that is, to whether the monkey had nursed on the cloth or on the wire monkey.

The results of these two new tests, introduced after a full year's separation of mother surrogate and infant, are comparable to the results obtained during the preseparation period and the early retention testing. Preferential responses still favored the cloth as compared to the wire mother by as much as 85 to 90 percent, and the emotionality scores showed the typical 2:1 differential ratio with respect to mother-absent and mother-present conditions.

The researches presented here on the analysis of two affectional variables through the use of objective and observational techniques suggest a broad new field for the study of emotional development of infant animals. The analogous situations and results found in observations and study of human infants and subprimates demonstrate the apparent face validity of our tests. The reliability of our observational techniques is indicated, for example, by the correlation coefficients computed for the composite emotional index in the open-field test. Four product-moment correlation coefficients, computed from four samples of 100 observations by five different pairs of independent observers over a period of more than a year, ranged from .87 to .89.

Additional Variables

Although the overwhelming importance of the contact variable has been clearly demonstrated in these experiments, there is reason to believe that other factors may contribute to the development of the affectional response pattern. We are currently conducting a series of new experiments to test some of these postulated variables.

For example, Bowlby (1958) has suggested that one of the basic affectional variables in the primate order is not just contact but *clinging* contact. To test this hypothesis, four infant monkeys are being raised with the standard cloth mother and a flat inclined plane, tightly covered with the same type of cloth. Thus, both objects contain the variable of contact with the soft cloth, but the shape of the mother tends to maximize the clinging variable, while the broad flat shape of the plane tends to minimize it. The preliminary results for differences in responsiveness to the cloth mother and responsiveness to the inclined plane under conditions that produce stress or fear or visual exploration suggest that clinging as well as contact is an affectional variable of considerable importance.

Experiments now in progress on the role of rocking motion in the development of attachment indicate that this may be a variable of measurable importance. One group of infants is being raised on rocking and stationary mothers and a second group, on rocking and stationary inclined planes. Both groups of infants show a small but consistent preference for the rocking object, as measured in average hours spent on the two objects.

Preliminary results for these three groups in the open-field test give additional evidence concerning the variable of clinging comfort. These data revealed that the infants raised with the standard cloth mother were more responsive to their mothers than the infants raised with inclined planes were to the planes.

The discovery of three variables of measurable importance to the formation and retention of affection is not surprising, and it is reasonable to assume that others will be demonstrated. The data so far obtained experimentally are in excellent concordance with the affectional variables named by Bowlby (1958). We are now planning a series of studies to assess the effects of consistency and inconsistence with respect to the mother surrogates in relation to the clinical concept of rejection. The effects of early, intermediate, and late maternal deprivation and the generalization of the infant-surrogate attachment in social development are also being investigated. Indeed, the strength and stability of the monkeys' affectional responses to a mother surrogate are such that it should be practical to determine the neurological and biochemical variables that underlie love.

Chapter 6

REWARDS AND INCENTIVES ✓

While the natural location of a chapter on rewards should be contiguous with both the drive and punishment chapters, a number of recent changes in motivational theory have made this material very much less dependent upon a drive model. Many theorists and researchers are not using a drive model at all, but are placing their emphasis on the characteristics of the reward process itself, regardless of the drive conditions of the organism.

The drive model is just as explicit about the definition of rewards as it is about those of drives. A reward is any stimulus event that increases the probability that associated responses will occur. This is a completely empirical definition and does not require any statement about why certain stimuli (such as food) have this property. Some rewards are primary, in that they will result in these changes in probability without prior experience with the reward. Other rewards are secondary, in that they have to be paired with primary rewards (such as a bell with food) before they will increase the probability of associated responses.

The first three papers are most closely allied with drive model conceptions, particularly as elaborated by Spence. Spence has added to the basic Hullian behavior theory the importance of incentives as an independent variable in the prediction of behavior. The particular formulation he has chosen, both theoretically and as a result of many studies, however, retains drive as a multiplicative factor, thus requiring drive to be greater than zero before a response will occur, regardless of the strength of incentives. Much of the evidence of the previous chapter is in disagreement with this requirement.

These three papers, while using language derived from Spence's theory, each present results that raise different problems with this mode of handling incentive motivation. Kraeling's work represents the results of one of the most careful separations of the particular parameters of incentives—nutritive value, consummatory response, and affective value. While Spence would expect that the incentive value would be primarily due to the strength of the consummatory response, Kraeling finds instead that the affective value, varied by the concentration of the taste solutions, is the primary determinant of incentive value. Davis and Keehn's data are also consistent with Kraeling's findings, and they suggest other relationships between consummatory response and incentive value. Trapold explores another line of derivation from Spence's work, in which he examines the effects of an incentive, learned in one context, upon un-learned responses tested in another context.

In an independent line of work, Kessen has been examining the reward value of sucking in the human newborn. The classical explanation is that sucking has acquired incentive value because of its association with food —a primary reward. Kessen's results seem to imply the opposite—that sucking may be an innate reinforcer, whose power to quiet an infant is independent of prior association with food and hunger reduction. Per-haps food is a secondary reward, based on its pairing with sucking?

The next group of four papers is drawn from quite a different ap-proach, centering primarily around the work of David McClelland. McClelland does not focus on drive states at all; he is most concerned with the association of certain rewards, defined in terms of the affective states they produce, with specific patterns of behavior in childhood. One of the most difficult problems for any theory of motivation to handle is to explain the incredible strength of learned motivational processes. Drive-based theories have tended to base them entirely on fear—the only major secondary drive. The first paper by McClelland is designed to show that great strength of early learning is really to be expected, particularly the learning of motives. Thus, this is not a problem at all, given his analysis. Argyle and Robinson's work on achievement motivation, fol-lowing the extensive research begun primarily by McClelland and Atkin-son, also stresses previous affective learning.

The next two papers, by McClelland, Atkinson, Clark, and Lowell, and by Feather, working in Atkinson's laboratory at Michigan, present general motivational theories based on incentive rather than on drive mechanisms. These models, though not widely appreciated, represent about the only formal alternatives to a drive-type model of motivated behavior, such as that proposed by Hull, Spence, and Mowrer, or implied in Freud, among others.

The McClelland *et al.* model was derived as a parallel to the discrep-ancy hypothesis presented in the previous chapter, though they can be considered independently. Feather, however, has attempted to avoid some of the problems attendant on the identification of affect states. He explicitly compares ways in which this model would handle several motivational phenomena in comparison to similar treatment by Mowrer. The paper presented here is valuable for its explicit statements and comparisons of two major motivational positions.

The last three papers in this chapter represent another and quite different approach to the nature of incentives and rewards—that of dissonance theory, as developed by Leon Festinger and some of his stu-dents. Festinger argues that adherence to the secondary-reward model of Hull, for example, overlooks the problems that occur when rewards are felt to be insufficient. He suggests that when a person finds himself in such a situation he often has to psychologically reevaluate the reward upwards, so that he now sees its value as commensurate with the effort he is investing in order to attain it. Thus, one of the determinants of rewards is quite independent of an individual's previous history of rewards—in fact a paucity of prior reward may increase the incentive value of a stimulus. Festinger's paper reviews several experiments supporting this line of reasoning. The other two papers present individual experiments related to this work. Carlsmith and Aronson show that correctly anticipating a bad outcome is preferred to having an unexpected good outcome occur—that is, the agreement with expectancy is more important than the incentive value of the outcome per se. Lewis presents further evidence of the relationship of effort to reward value and discusses the data he obtained in relation to several alternative theoretical treatments.

This chapter on incentive motivation presents three rather different approaches—two rather recent and one based on nearly forty years of work. All three of these positions are different from the basic building blocks of drives, though the first position is an outgrowth of the drive model, in the sense that drives and incentives are seen as working together. Selection pressures have severely restricted the choice of papers to be included in this chapter. Several other somewhat independent lines of work that have had to be ignored for the purposes of this book are also prominent in the literature on incentives. Nearly all of the work, however, both that which is included and that which had to be left out, is fairly recent and, while each of these approaches has accounted for an impressive amount of data and research, it is not yet possible to determine which of these will prove to be the most valuable.

Journal of Comparative and Physiological Psychology, 1961, vol. 54, pp. 560–565

Analysis of Amount of Reward as a Variable in Learning[1]

Doris Kraeling

Several studies (e.g., Crespi, 1942; Grindley, 1929; Zeaman, 1949) have demonstrated a positive relationship

between amount of food reward and instrumental response strength. Quantity of food was varied either by the use of single food pellets of different weights or by the use of different numbers of food pellets of equal weights. When quantity of food is varied by these methods, three separate factors are commonly confounded: intensity of

[1] This paper is based on a dissertation submitted to the Faculty of the Graduate School of Yale University in partial fulfillment of the requirements for the PhD degree. The author wishes to express her appreciation to F. D. Sheffield for his guidance, and to W. Kessen and F. A. Logan, the other members of the thesis advisory committee. The author is also indebted to D. R. Williams for constructing the apparatus.

taste stimulation, duration of ingestion time, and amount of nutrient. It is important to assess the relative contribution of these factors to the relation between amount of reward and response strength.

An alternative method of studying the amount of reward, which permits separation of the above three factors, is by the use of liquid reward. The effectiveness of sweet liquids as rewards for instrumental learning has been shown in a number of studies over the past ten years (e.g., Dufort & Kimble, 1956; Guttman, 1953, 1954; Sheffield & Roby, 1950; Sheffield, Roby, & Campbell, 1954; Young & Shuford, 1954).

The present experiment was designed to investigate the effects upon response strength of concentration of sucrose solution, time of exposure to the sucrose solution, and amount of caloric intake from the obtained volume of sucrose solution.

Method

Design

Concentration of sucrose solution and time of exposure to the sucrose solution were varied factorially to form a three-by-three matrix. The three concentrations of sucrose solution used were 2.5%, 5.0%, and 10.0%; the three times of exposure to the sucrose solution were 5 sec., 25 sec., and 125 sec. By simultaneously manipulating concentration and time of exposure, the design also involved variation in amount of caloric intake.

The Ss were run in two replications of 36 animals each. To balance for order of handling, a replication was run in four successive sets of 9 animals each. The animals within a set were randomly assigned to the nine cells of the design.

Subjects

The Ss were 72 male albino rats of the Sprague-Dawley strain from the Blue Spruce Farms, Altamount, New York. They were approximately 100 days old at the beginning of the experiment.

Apparatus

The apparatus consisted of an alley and a device to record each tongue lap an animal made while drinking from a tube at the end of the alley.

The alley contained a 6-in.-long by 6-in.-wide by 9-in.-high start box, a 4-ft.-long by 4-in.-wide by 9-in.-high runway, and a 12-in.-long by 6-in.-wide by 9-in.-high goal box. The start box and the goal box had hinged floors and guillotine doors to prevent retracing. The interior of the alley was painted black, with the exception of an aluminum plate covering the last 8 in. of the floor of the goal box. There was a circular aperture 1 in. in diameter centered 2½ in. above the floor at the end of the goal box. The tip of a drinking tube came just up to the aperture so that the animal could contact the fluid in the tube only with its tongue.

Three Standard Electric timers recorded the following three durations of time: the time from the opening of the start-box door to the time the animal left the start box; the time from leaving the start box to entering the goal box; the time from entering the goal box to taking the first lick from the drinking tube.

Three drinking tubes, with tube openings approximately 3.9 mm. in diameter, were used for the three concentrations of sucrose solution and were rotated from day to day among them. Each drinking tube was fitted into a 10-cc. graduated cylinder which could be attached to a hinged panel used to hold the tube in the aperture of the goal box during the exposure period and to automatically withdraw the tube at the end of the period.

The device to record tongue laps was similar to that used by Stellar and Hill (1952). An electronic relay fired with each lick that the animal made while drinking from the tube. One lead from the circuit was attached to the metal plate on the floor of the goal box; the other lead was in the fluid contained in the graduated cylinder. The electronic relay operated a bank of seven counters and a cumulative recorder. Licks were registered on separate counters for each 5-sec. interval of the first 25 sec. of the exposure period and on one counter for the remaining 100 sec. The seventh counter registered the total number of licks, and so provided a check on the accuracy of the individual counters.

Procedure

Upon receipt from the breeding laboratories, the animals were placed in the colony room on ad libitum feeding with Purina checkers for several days. The animals were then housed in individual cages in the experimental room and were adapted to a feeding schedule in which they received 12 gm. (dry weight) of Purina mash for 24 days and 11 gm. (dry weight) of mash and 1 gm. of sugar for the remaining 3 days before the start of training. Commercially available ABDEC vitamins were added to the daily diet. Water was continuously available to the animals from trays in their living cages.

During training, the animals were given one trial per day for 99 days. On each trial, the animal was placed in the start box and allowed to go down the runway to obtain the appropriate concentration of sucrose solution from the drinking tube for the appropriate period of time. Immediately after this period of time had elapsed and the drinking tube had been automatically withdrawn, the animal was picked out of the goal box. If the animal did not leave the start box within 300 sec., it was placed in the runway; if it did not leave the runway within 300 sec., it was placed in the goal box. One hour after each animal had been run, it was fed 11 gm. of mash and enough sugar to make up the difference between 1 gm. and the amount it had obtained from the sucrose solution in the goal box.

Sucrose solutions were made of commercial sugar and distilled water every nine days. The three concentrations contained 2.5 gm. of sugar, 5.0 gm. of sugar, and 10.0 gm. of sugar for each 100 cc. of water. In terms of percentage by weight, the concentrations of sucrose solution used were 2.4, 4.8, and 9.1. An electrolytic test of each concentration of sucrose solution, made daily over one nine-day period, showed that the strength of the solution was not changed during the course of nine days.

Results

In the analysis of the data, trials were treated in successive blocks of nine, the animal's score in each block being its median for those particular nine trials. The only exception to this procedure was the exclusion of the first trial from the first block. When successive blocks were grouped over different portions of training, the score of an animal was the mean of these median scores.

Instrumental behavior was analyzed in terms of "running speed" defined as

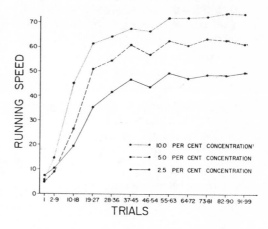

Fig. 1. Strength of instrumental response, broken down by concentration of sucrose solution.

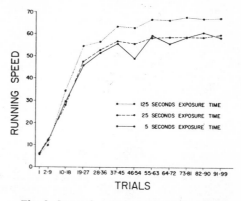

Fig. 2. Strength of instrumental response, broken down by time of exposure to the sucrose solution.

100 divided by the time taken from leaving the start box to entering the goal box.

Curves of running speed over all blocks of trials are presented for the three concentrations of sucrose solution in Figure 1 and for the three times of exposure to the sucrose solution in Figure 2. Analyses of variance were performed on mean running speeds for the first three blocks of trials and mean running speeds for the last three blocks of trials. Concentration of sucrose solution had a significant effect upon running speed for the trials early in training ($F = 13.73$; $df = 2, 54$; $p < .01$) and for the trials late in training ($F = 12.12$; $df = 2, 54$; $p < .01$). Time of exposure to the sucrose solution did not have a significant effect either for the early training trials ($F = 0.74$; $df = 2, 54$) or for the late training trials ($F = 1.99$; $df = 2, 54$). As is apparent in Figure 2, despite the non-significance of the effect of time of exposure, the 125-sec. group did have a consistently higher running speed throughout training than the 25-sec. and 5-sec. groups.

To assess the effect of amount of caloric intake upon instrumental behavior, empirically determined mean total caloric intake and mean running speed for the nine-group breakdown by concentration and time of exposure are presented in Table 1. It is apparent that there was a relatively poor relationship between total caloric intake and running speed. Running speed was more closely related to concentration of sucrose solution. In each instance in which the running speed of a group having a higher concentration value could be compared with that of a group having a higher total caloric intake value due to a longer time of exposure to a lower concentration, the running speed of the former group was greater. For example, with regard to the data based upon the last three blocks of trials, the group that received the 5.0% concentration for a 5-sec. period of time ingested a mean of 0.07 calories and ran at a mean speed of 59.7, while the group that received the 2.5% concentration for a 25-sec. period of time ingested more calories, 0.12, but ran at a lower speed, 44.9. This pattern held consistently for all such diagonal comparisons of the table, both for the

TABLE 1

BREAKDOWN OF MEAN RUNNING SPEED AND MEAN
CALORIC INTAKE (IN PARENTHESES)

Time of Exposure (sec.)	First Three Blocks of Trials			Last Three Blocks of Trials		
	Sucrose Concentration (%)			Sucrose Concentration (%)		
	2.5	5.0	10.0	2.5	5.0	10.0
5	21.7 (0.02)	29.4 (0.05)	35.8 (0.11)	44.4 (0.03)	59.7 (0.07)	70.9 (0.14)
25	20.8 (0.08)	27.0 (0.21)	39.9 (0.46)	44.9 (0.12)	61.5 (0.28)	70.3 (0.57)
125	23.4 (0.38)	29.9 (1.07)	45.2 (2.25)	57.0 (0.57)	66.1 (1.28)	78.5 (2.61)

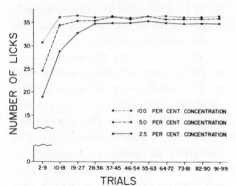

Fig. 3. Strength of consummatory response during the first 5 sec., broken down by concentration of sucrose solution.

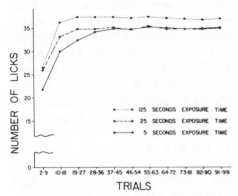

Fig. 4. Strength of consummatory response during the first 5 sec., broken down by time of exposure to the sucrose solution.

first three blocks of trials and for the last three blocks of trials.

An index of consummatory behavior was available for analysis, the number of individual tongue laps involved in the ingestion of the sucrose solution during successive intervals of time.

Curves of number of licks during the first 5 secs. are presented for the three concentrations of sucrose solution in Figure 3 and for the three times of exposure to the sucrose solution in Figure 4. Analyses of variance were performed on mean number of licks during the first 5 sec. for the first three blocks of trials and on mean number of

licks during the first 5 sec. for the last three blocks of trials. Concentration of sucrose solution had a significant effect upon the number of licks for the trials early in training ($F = 15.78$; $df = 2, 54$; $p < .01$) and for the trials late in training ($F = 3.56$; $df = 2, 54$; $p < .05$). The effect of time of exposure to the sucrose solution was also significant for the early training trials ($F = 7.76$; $df = 2, 54$; $p < .01$) and for the late training trials ($F = 8.01$; $df = 2, 54$; $p < .01$). As is apparent in Figure 4, the significant effect of time of exposure was largely attributable to the difference between the 125-sec. group and the other two groups.

The similarity in Figures 1 and 3 and in Figures 2 and 4 suggested a close relation between instrumental behavior and consummatory behavior. However, the analyses of variance revealed that while the factor of concentration of sucrose solution continued to account for the major proportion of the variance in instrumental behavior throughout training, it became relatively less important in accounting for the variance in consummatory behavior in the later training trials. With regard to running speed, the factor of concentration accounted for 47% of the variance for the first three blocks of trials and 54% of the variance for the last three blocks of trials. With regard to number of licks during the first 5 sec., the corresponding values were 38% and 21%. To obtain an estimate of the extent of the relation between instrumental behavior and consummatory behavior, Pearson r correlation coefficients were computed for the 18-group breakdown by concentration, time of exposure, and replication. The r between mean running speed and mean number of licks during the first 5 sec. for the first three

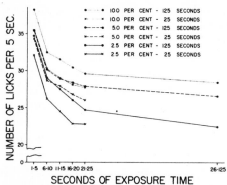

Fig. 5. Strength of consummatory response as a function of interval of time of exposure, broken down by concentration of sucrose solution and time of exposure to the sucrose solution. (These data are based upon trials late in training.)

blocks of trials was +.77 ($p < .01$), that for the last three blocks of trials +.50 ($p < .05$).

A further result was that number of licks during a given interval of time declined with continued exposure to the sucrose solution. For animals exposed to the sucrose solution for 25 sec. there was a progressive drop in number of licks during the five successive 5-sec. intervals. For animals allowed to drink for 125 sec. a similar drop existed during the first 25 sec. and continued during the remaining 100 sec., as estimated by the number of licks during that 100-sec. interval divided by 20. Relevant data, based upon the last three blocks of trials, are shown in Figure 5. Analyses of variance performed on mean number of licks during the first 25 sec. yielded a pattern of results similar to that obtained for number of licks during the first 5 sec.

Discussion

Within the range of values used in this study, intensity of taste stimulation is the critical aspect of reward in rela-

tion to instrumental response strength. Concentration of sucrose solution was a major determinant of running speed; time of exposure to the sucrose solution and amount of caloric intake were not. The implication of earlier studies of amount of reward (e.g., Crespi, 1942; Zeaman, 1949) has been that the amount of nutrient ingested is critical. The main effect of amount of reward in these studies, however, was found with small amounts of food, in which case the smallest amounts would not provide a full mouthful of food and intensity of taste stimulation would have been operative in affecting instrumental response strength. Crespi found significant differences between the running speeds of animals receiving .02, .08, and .32 gm. of food but failed to find dependable differences for animals receiving .32, 1.28, and 5.12 gm. of food. Zeaman, in applying the sign test to the latencies of the final six trials of his groups receiving .05, .20, .40, .80, 1.60, and 2.40 gm. of food, failed to find dependable differences in the upper values.

Concentration of sucrose solution was also an important determinant of the strength of the consummatory response. It was more important early in training than later in training. Early in training, consummatory behavior is competing with exploratory behavior in the goal box. At this stage, the number of licks during a given interval of time depends to a considerable extent on how much of that time the animal spends at the drinking tube rather than on how rapidly the animal licks while at the tube. Under these conditions, differences in taste stimulation would be expected to have a relatively pronounced effect on the prepotency of the consummatory response in relation to other behavior. Later in training when the animal spends most of its time at the tube regardless of the concentration of the sucrose solution in the tube, the different intensities of taste stimulation would be expected to produce less markedly differential rates of licking.

Duration of ingestion time had a significant effect upon consummatory response strength throughout training. The result cannot be interpreted as due to variation in the amount of practice at the consummatory response with consequent variation in habit strength (Spence, 1956). If such were true, the effect would be expected to be apparent at the early phase of training but not at the end of training, when practice should be sufficient to bring the groups differing in time of exposure to the sucrose solution to the same asymptote of habit strength.

In general, a relatively good relationship existed between instrumental response strength and the strength of the consummatory response. This confirms a similar relationship reported in a study by Sheffield, Roby, and Campbell (1954). The relation may be interpreted in terms of Seward's tertiary-motivation hypothesis (Seward, 1950), Sheffield's drive-induction hypothesis (Sheffield et al., 1954), or Spence's incentive-motivation hypothesis (Spence, 1956). According to each of these positions, variation in the properties of the consummatory response would be expected, through classical conditioning of parts of the consummatory response to cues accompanying the instrumental response, to have differential effects on instrumental response strength.

However, it should be noted that the strength of the instrumental response was largely determined by concentration of sucrose solution throughout training, whereas concentration became less important in determining the strength of the consummatory response as training proceeded. Instrumental behavior was affected by concentration of sucrose solution in ways which could not be predicted merely from the observed strength of the consummatory response. Therefore, a simple view that the strength of the consummatory response is critical in reward in relation to instrumental behavior is not consistent with the results. An alternative view is that the intensity of taste stimulation is a critical factor and that the relationship between instrumental response strength and consummatory response strength arises because under certain conditions consummatory response strength is a good index of consummatory stimulation.

Summary: The purpose of the study was to investigate the effect upon instrumental response strength of three factors commonly confounded in investigations of amount of food reward: intensity of taste stimulation, duration of ingestion time, and amount of nutrient.

A sweet liquid, a sucrose solution, was used as the reward for the instrumental response of running in a straight alley. Intensity of taste stimulation was varied by varying the concentration of the sucrose solution, and duration of ingestion time was varied by varying the time of exposure to the sucrose solution. The amount of caloric intake was, therefore, a joint function of concentration and time of exposure. Measures were taken of running time in the alley and of number of individual tongue laps involved in the ingestion of the sucrose solution.

The main findings were: (*a*) concentration of sucrose solution was a major determinant of the strength of the instrumental response throughout training; (*b*) time of exposure to the sucrose solution did not have a significant effect upon the strength of the instrumental response; (*c*) total amount of caloric intake was poorly related to the strength of the instrumental response, as compared with concentration of sucrose solution; (*d*) concentration of sucrose solution was an important determinant of the strength of the consummatory response, this effect being greater early in training than late in training; (*e*) time of exposure to the sucrose solution was an important determinant of the strength of the consummatory response.

The data are interpreted as indicating that intensity of taste stimulation is a critical aspect of reward in relation to instrumental response strength. Whereas there is, generally, a good relationship between instrumental response strength and the strength of the consummatory response, intensity of consummatory stimulation affects instrumental behavior in ways which cannot be predicted merely from the observed strength of the consummatory response.

Science, July 31, 1959, vol. 130, pp. 269–270

Magnitude of Reinforcement and Consummatory Behavior[*][1]

John D. Davis and J. D. Keehn

In place of Hull's (1943) original associative interpretation, Spence (1956) has recently argued for a motivational theory of the effects on behavior of different reward magnitudes. Spence bases part of his argument upon empirical data collected in his own and other laboratories. But greater attention is given to indirect evidence derived from a theoretical analysis of runway behavior. According to this theory, part of an animal's consummatory behavior in a goal box becomes conditioned to stimuli in that goal box, and ultimately, through generalization, anticipatory goal responses (r_g) are elicited by stimuli in the runway. When s_g represents feedback stimulation from the response r_g, the mechanism r_g-s_g is said to maintain running in the alley. In particular, this r_g-s_g mechanism is assumed to possess motivational properties "that vary with the magnitude or vigor with which it occurs" (Spence, 1956; p. 135).

Whether or not this assumption is necessary is not certain (see Estes, 1958), but it is inadequate as stated, owing to the ambiguity of the term *vigor*. The vigor of a response might, for instance, refer to the magnitude, or strength, of the response—that is, the amount of effort that goes into a single occurrence of that response; it might refer to the rate at which that response occurs (when it does occur); or it might refer to the persistence of that response in competition with other responses. Thus, *vigor* might refer to the intension, tempo, or perseveration of a response, or to any combination of these and other response dimensions (Gilbert, 1958). Only the first and second of these dimensions appear to have been considered by Spence—that is, he questions whether different magnitudes of reward produce different r_g's in terms of strength or intension (Estes, 1958, p. 137) or whether

[*] Reprinted from *Science* by permission.

[1] This study was supported in part by a grant from the Rockefeller Foundation to the arts and sciences division of the American University of Beirut. The data were collected at the University of Illinois.

the effect is on the tempo of a single r_g (Spence, 1956, p. 147), and, with some reservations, he concludes that the second alternative is correct—on the basis of experiments reported by Guttman (1954) and by Sheffield, Roby, and Campbell (1954). However, neither of these studies is pertinent, because although they show that different reward conditions lead to different operant and consumption rates, there is no indication whether these were due to the tempo, perseveration, or latency of the consummatory behavior. That is, the consummatory response may have occurred more slowly (when it did occur) with smaller rewards rather than larger ones; it may have occurred at the same tempo but less often in the sense that more, or longer, pauses intervened between sequences of consummatory responses; or it may have begun at different latencies after the reinforcing solutions became available.

Despite Spence's contention to the contrary (1956, p. 144), it is possible to measure consummatory behavior directly in a Skinner-box situation. This method, first employed by Kappauf and later by Stellar and Hill (1952), has been utilized by one of us to record the drinking behavior of white rats when presented with various concentrations of sucrose, saccharin, and sodium chloride in distilled water solutions.

The apparatus was a 15- by 6- by 6-in. compartment wired so that a small current (less than 1 μa) flowed each time the animal's tongue made contact with the fluid under test. This current was amplified sufficiently to operate a relay which activated a Gerbrands-type cumulative recorder. Each lick of the fluid from a drinking tube with a 3-mm opening, which protruded into the cage, advanced the pen one step across the recording paper, with the result that a curve directly reflecting the rate of consumption of the fluid in the tube was automatically produced. The apparatus was installed in a large darkened and sound-shielded room. None of the noises of the apparatus were audible to the human ear from inside the room.

Each one of four rats of the Sprague-Dawley strain was tested with all of the solutions used in the experiment. The animals were first adapted for 10 days to a 23½-hour drinking rhythm, with access to tap water for ½ hour out of each 24 hours. The sodium chloride tests were then run for ½-hour sessions, with 2-day intervals between the test sessions. For the 2 days following each test day the animals were given only tap water to drink, so as to equalize as far as possible the degree of water deficit prior to the tests. If, for example, on a test day a large quantity of the proffered fluid was consumed, the tap-water intake on the following day was reduced. It has been observed, however, that by the third day following a large intake the amount of tap water consumed is about the same as that normally consumed by a rat that has been deprived of water for 23½ hours. The concentrations of the sodium chloride solutions employed were 0.50, 0.86, 2.0, and 3.0 percent, respectively. All the solutions used were percentage (weight/volume) preparations in distilled water. At the end of the sodium chloride tests the same procedure was followed with saccharin and sucrose solutions, in that order. After the licking rates for these solutions for water-deprived rats had been determined, the saccharin series was repeated when the animals had been sated with food and water.

The results in all cases were clear-

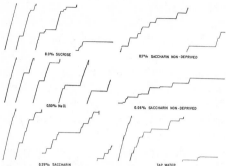

Fig. 1. Cumulative curves of the response of one animal given access to the six fluids indicated. Unless otherwise indicated the animal had been deprived of water for 23½ hours prior to the test. Each full excursion of the pen represents 1000 licks, and each graph represents 30 minutes of drinking. Thus, for example, when the deprived animal was offered 0.50 percent NaCl, it made approximately 4500 tongue laps in a 30-minute period.

cut; the local rate of drinking an acceptable solution was constant for each animal. If an animal drank all, it drank at a constant rate, regardless of its state of deprivation and the concentration of the solution under test. Figure 1 presents typical examples of all the records collected and shows some of the licking curves for one of the animals given access to tap water, 0.50-percent sodium chloride, 0.25-percent saccharin, and 8.0-percent sucrose, respectively, when water-deprived and to 0.6-percent and 0.10-percent saccharin when satiated. The curves that were produced by the other three animals are identical with respect to the major characteristic performance.

Although Gilbert (1958) reports individual differences in tempo of bar pressing, no such differences in licking rates were observed in these studies. The local rates of responding remained between five and six licks per second for all animals under all conditions. Variations in the total amount of intake were a function solely of the

duration of the pauses and the lengths of the sustained drinking periods. That is, differences in quantities of liquid consumed per unit of time represent not, as Spence (1956) appears to believe, differences in the tempo of the consummatory response but differences in the perseveration of that response.

It seems clear, then, that the tempo, although not necessarily the intension (Gilbert, 1958), of the consummatory response must be ruled out as a determiner of instrumental performance with different reinforcing stimuli. If some characteristic of the consummatory act itself is to be used to account for these differences, perseveration seems the most likely, in our current state of knowledge (Steller & Hill, 1952). Although the local rate of licking is a constant, independent of individual subject differences and the chemical composition of the fluids investigated in this study, other dimensions of the licking operant are not. Latency, perseveration, and duration of the operant may all vary with differing test fluids, as Gilbert (1958) has demonstrated with another operant. An investigation of the dimensions of the consummatory operant would appear to be necessary before an adequate explanation of the effect of the quantity or quality of a reinforcing substance on instrumental behavior can be given. Clearly the amount of reward substance consumed per unit of time is too coarse a measure. It does not describe how the substance is consumed. It tells nothing about the temporal distribution of pauses, about the duration of sustained periods of drinking, or about the rate of drinking when it occurs.

Summary: The rates at which white rats licked saline, sucrose, and saccharin solutions, respectively, were measured by cumulative recording of tongue contacts with the solution in question. The local rate of licking was constant for all solutions, but differences in the distribution of sustained periods of licking were related to the type and concentration of the fluid consumed.

Journal of Comparative and Physiological Psychology, 1962, vol. 55, pp. 1034–1039

The Effect of Incentive Motivation on an Unrelated Reflex Response[1]

Milton A. Trapold

According to current behavior theory of the Hull-Spence variety (cf., Spence, 1956), at least one of the effects of the reward given at the end of an instrumental response chain is that it provides for a learned source of motivation, *incentive motivation*. Thus, when a rat receives reward at the end of a straight runway, there is an increment in (or maintenance of) a learned process which on subsequent trials will motivate or energize the response of locomoting down the runway.

At a more explicit theoretical level, incentive motivation has been identified with the anticipatory goal response $(r_g - s_g)$ mechanism (Spence, 1951, 1956). These conditioned anticipatory goal responses are assumed to have a motivational capacity which is positively related to the magnitude of reward, and the conditioning of $r_g - s_g$ is assumed to be the mechanism underlying the learning of incentive motivation.

While the $r_g - s_g$ conception of reward effects has been of considerable usefulness in the theoretical integration of a number of phenomena of learning, there are several questions regarding this mechanism that remain unanswered. One of the most important of these is the exact sense in which $r_g - s_g$ is to be considered motivating. For example, in recent years a number of writers (Brown, 1961; Farber, 1955; Spence, 1956) have re-emphasized with regard to the more traditional forms of motivation (e.g., food or water deprivation, conditioned fear, anxiety, etc.) the *general drive* conception of motivation first made explicit by Hull (1943). According to this view, motivational variables are considered general response energizers in the sense that all motivational variables multiply all response tendencies, and thus any motivational variable will enhance the speed, amplitude, or vigor of any response elicited in its presence.

Empirically, this conception of the operation of motivational variables has received a great deal of support in a variety of testing situations and with

[1] This investigation was completed in partial fulfillment of the requirements for the PhD degree for the Department of Psychology, State University of Iowa. Sincere appreciation is expressed to K. W. Spence, under whose supervision this work was done. This research was conducted during the writer's tenure as a National Science Foundation Cooperative Fellow.

a variety of motivating operations (cf., Brown, 1961; Spence, 1956), and one can now ask whether incentive motivation—the state of affairs consequent upon presenting an organism with a stimulus which has consistently been paired with a primary reinforcer—is to be considered motivational in this same response-general sense. This is tantamount to asking whether *any* response elicited in the presense of an r_g-evoking stimulus will be facilitated, and whether this facilitation is a function of the magnitude of reward.

Experiments showing a positive relation between instrumental-response performance and magnitude of reward imply that when both the incentive and the instrumental response are conditioned to the same stimuli and based upon the same reward, the instrumental response will be facilitated by the simultaneous presence of incentive motivation. Another group of experiments (Estes, 1943, 1948; Walker, 1942) has shown that the instrumental response will also be facilitated when the incentive and instrumental response are based upon the same reward, but are conditioned, at least in part, to different stimuli.

While these experiments provide some evidence for a motivational function of stimuli which have been paired with reward, nonmotivational interpretations of the data are also available. The ideal situation for the demonstration of the response-general energizing or motivating properties of incentive would be one in which the reference response is completely independent, as far as the history of the S is concerned, of both the reward substance upon which the incentive is based and the stimuli to which the incentive is conditioned. This would insure that any facilitation would not be due to the introduction into the effective stimulus complex of additional stimuli (either the incentive-evoking stimulus itself, or stimulus components of responses it may evoke) to which the reference response is conditioned.

One technique by which these conditions may be met is the "probe stimulus" technique introduced by Brown, Kalish, and Farber (1951). This technique, which has proven quite useful in the study of the general facilitating properties of both hunger and conditioned fear (Armus, 1960; Brown et al., 1951; Fogel, 1961; Meryman, 1952, 1953; Ross, 1960; Spence & Runquist, 1958), is based upon the reasoning that if a variable has general motivating or energizing properties, it should exert these on a reflex response as well as on a learned response. Thus, to demonstrate the general energizing properties of fear, Brown et al. paired a CS with shock and then showed that the amplitude of the reflex startle response of the rat to a sharp auditory stimulus was greatly enhanced when the startle response was evoked in the presence of this CS.

The present experiment attacks the question of whether incentive motivation functions as a general response energizer using a variation of the probe stimulus technique with the startle reflex of rats as the reference response.

Method

Subjects

The Ss were 60 male hooded rats aged 150 to 165 days at the beginning of the experiment.

Apparatus

The main apparatus was a stabilimeter similar to that described by Brown, Kalish, and Farber (1951). This consisted of an aluminum confinement box 2.5 in. wide, 5.75 in. high, and 7.0 in. long, with a wire-mesh floor and top and mounted such that changes in the applied force on the floor of the confinement box caused it to move slightly against the restraint of a spring, the amount of movement being approximately proportional to changes in the applied force. These movements of the stabilimeter, which served as a measure of the startle response, were recorded on moving paper by means of a mechanical connection with the recording pen. This pen, constructed as a first class lever, also amplified the stabilimeter movements by approximately 16:1. An adjustment in this recording system allowed the pen to be centered individually for each S.

The reward employed for the conditioning of $r_g - s_g$ was a solution of sucrose (table sugar) in tap water. This liquid reward was chosen because of the relative ease with which it can be delivered automatically in any desired amount and because it has been shown to be a very effective reinforcer in instrumental learning studies (Collier & Myers, 1961; Goodrich, 1960; Guttman, 1953). The system for delivering the sucrose consisted of an open bottle of the solution mounted 30 in. above the floor of the confinement box and a small brass fountain inserted through the end wall of the confinement box. The bottle was connected to the fountain by latex tubing, and a solenoid valve between the bottle and fountain permitted any quanity of sucrose to be delivered automatically.

The CS employed throughout was a single 150-w. frosted light bulb suspended 12 in. above the top of the confinement box plus the low humming noise provided by the motor and gear train of the paper drive on the recording equipment. The duration of the CS, the amount of sucrose, and the point at which the sucrose was delivered were controlled by a bank of silent decade-type timers.

The startle stimulus was produced by manually firing a single cap in a commercial cap pistol at a distance of approximately 2 ft. from the confinement box.

Procedure

For 2 weeks prior to the beginning of the experiment, all Ss were habituated to a feeding regimen of 1-hr. access to Purina lab pellets daily. During this period, Ss were also handled and given experience in the carrying cages that would later be used to transport them to the experimental room.

During all subsequent phases of the experiment, each S was run at approximately the same time each day. The Ss were transported in squads from the main colony room to the experimental room in a portable carrying cage, but to avoid giving Ss any experience with the startle stimulus other than that received when they were actually in the stabilimeter, this carrying cage was left in the adjoining hallway and Ss were taken into the experimental room one at a time to receive their daily treatment. To the human ear, the startle stimulus fired in its normal position inside the experimental room produced only a faint click in the hallway.

All Ss received their daily ration of 1-hr. free access to food in the home cage approximately 15 min. after the last S had been given its day's treatment.

Adaptation to the startle stimulus. In this phase of the experiment, all Ss were treated exactly alike. On each of 3 days, each S was removed from the carrying cage and taken into the experimental room where it was placed in the confinement box of the stabilimeter and given a series of five presentations of the startle stimulus according to a predetermined schedule of variable intertrial intervals with a mean of 45 sec. To avoid giving Ss any experience with the hum produced by the chart drive of the recording equipment (which would later become part of the CS), the amplitude of the startle response was recorded on these adaptation trials by manually drawing the paper under the recording pen.

Conditioning. At the conclusion of the adaptation trials, Ss were randomly assigned to one of three groups, two experimental groups and a control group. For the experimental groups, the daily treatment consisted of 10 conditioning trials and two test trials. On conditioning trials the CS was presented for 5 sec., and at the end of the third second, 0.5 ml. of the appropriate concentration of sucrose was delivered to the fountain. For one experimental group (Group E-24) the sucrose concentration was 24% (by weight), and for the other experimental group (Group E-6) it was 6%. The test trials were of two types; on one test trial of each day (CS-test) the CS and sucrose were presented as on a regular conditioning trial, but in addition the startle stimulus was presented 2.75 sec. after the onset of the CS (i.e., just before the sucrose). On the other trial (No CS-test) the startle stimulus was presented alone. On these No CS-tests, the amplitude of the startle response was recorded by manually drawing the chart paper under the recording pen.

The control group was treated exactly like the experimental groups except that they never received sucrose. That is, each day the control Ss received 10 trials on which the CS appeared for 5 sec. and two test trials, one of which involved the CS and the startle stimulus and the other of which involved the startle stimulus alone.

For all groups, both conditioning trials and test trials were presented according to a prearranged schedule of variable intertrial intervals with a mean of 45 sec. A random half of the Ss in each group received the CS-test trial following the fourth conditioning trial of a day and the No CS-test trial after the ninth conditioning trial, while the other half of each group received the test trials in the reverse order.

Conditioning was continued with this daily procedure for a total of 10 days, giving a total of 100 conditioning trials and 10 each of the two kinds of test trials.

Extinction. Extinction involved only one change in procedure from conditioning; all sucrose was deleted from both conditioning and CS-test trials for the experimental groups. Extinction was continued for 4 days, with the same procedure as used in conditioning, i.e., 10 extinction trials and two test trials per day.

Response Measures

In all phases of the experiment, the response measure was the amplitude of the pen deflection caused by the startle response. This was measured to the nearest millimeter with no attempt to correct for arc-distortion.

On all trials except test trials, a record was also kept of what will hereafter be referred to as *instrumental responses.* An instrumental response was defined as any instance during the initial 3 sec. of the CS of S's nose entering the depression in the fountain into which the sucrose was delivered. These responses were scored in an all-or-none manner, and each trial was scored either as having shown or not having shown such a response.

Results

Startle Amplitude

A summary of the results obtained with the startle-amplitude measure is presented in Table 1. The data from conditioning and extinction were analyzed separately by mixed analyses of variance; both analyses included

TABLE 1

MEAN STARTLE AMPLITUDES FOR BLOCKS OF TWO CS- AND NO CS-TEST TRIALS
FOR ALL GROUPS IN BOTH ACQUISITION AND EXTINCTION

Group	Test	Trial Blocks						
		Acquisition					Extinction	
		1	*2*	*3*	*4*	*5*	*1*	*2*
E-24	CS	10.6	10.6	9.4	8.3	12.0	9.0	8.6
	No CS	9.4	9.6	7.8	8.6	7.2	7.5	12.8
E-6	CS	11.8	8.2	8.6	9.6	10.3	10.5	11.4
	No CS	9.4	11.5	7.3	11.8	8.6	10.6	9.5
C	CS	15.6	11.0	10.0	9.8	10.8	6.8	7.4
	No CS	10.8	10.2	8.4	10.0	9.0	8.6	9.6

groups, trials, and the counterbalanced factors of type of test trial and order of testing. In the acquisition analysis the criterional measure was the mean startle amplitude on the two tests of a given type in a block of 20 conditioning trials, with two such trial blocks (Trials 1–20 and 81–100) comprising the trial variable in the analysis. In the extinction analysis the criterional measure was the startle amplitude on the single test of a given kind in a block of 10 extinction trials, with two such trial blocks (Trials 1–10 and 31–40) being included.

The acquisition analysis showed only the effect of type of test trial to be significant beyond the .05 level ($F = 9.52$, $df = 1/54$). However, the fact that neither the type of test × trials nor the type of test × groups interaction even approached significance indicates that this effect of type of test trial was independent of the CS's having been paired with sucrose for two of the groups.

The extinction analysis also yielded only one variance source significant beyond the .05 level, namely, the interaction between order of testing and trials ($F = 4.68$, $df = 1/54$). On the first block of extinction trials Ss receiving the CS-test first gave the larger mean startle amplitude (10.5 mm. vs. 7.4 mm.), while on the last block of extinction trials this relationship reversed (13.2 mm. vs. 7.4 mm.). However, the interaction effects which comprised the error term against which this order × trials interaction was evaluated displayed significant heterogeneity of variance across the six subgroups of the experiment when tested by Bartlett's test ($\chi^2 = 12.08$, $df = 5$). This increases by an unspecifiable amount the probability of falsely rejecting the hypothesis of no interaction, and when taken in conjunction

with the fact that this was the only significant effect in the entire analysis, and that there was no a priori reason to expect such an effect, it seems reasonable to retain the hypothesis of no interaction in the face of this significant F ratio.

Instrumental Responses

Figure 1 presents the data from the instrumental response measure in terms of the mean percentage of responses in blocks of 10 trials. It can be seen that both experimental groups showed definite acquisition and subsequent extinction of this response while the control group maintained a constant low operant level throughout both periods.

In view of the obvious differences between the experimental and control groups, the analyses of these data were restricted to the experimental groups. The acquisition and extinction data were analyzed separately by mixed analyses of variance with main factors of groups, trials, and order (referring to the order of CS- and No CS-test). For both analyses the criterional measure was the number of responses in a block

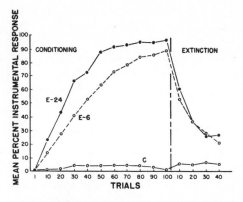

Fig. 1. Mean percentage of instrumental approach responses by blocks of 10 acquisition and extinction trials. (The abscissa point marked 1 gives the percentage on the first trial.)

of 10 trials; the acquisition analysis included three such trial blocks (Trials 1–10, 41–50, and 91–100) and the extinction analysis included two (Trials 1–10, and 31–40).

The acquisition analysis revealed the effects of groups, trials, and trial × groups all to be significant at the .05 level or better ($F = 18.38, 388.80, 5.20$; $df = 1/36, 1/36, 2/72$, respectively). In the extinction analysis, only the trials variable reached the .05 level of significance ($F = 138.6, df = 1/36$).

Discussion

The results from the conditioning period of this experiment show clearly that the minimal instrumental response involved in obtaining the reward from the fountain was facilitated by the presence of a stimulus that had been paired with a reward, and that the degree of this facilitation was positively related to the magnitude of reward. The results obtained with the startle response measure, on the other hand, showed no such facilitation. No differences were obtained among the CS-test performances of the various groups, and although CS-test trials gave generally larger startle responses than the No CS-test trials, this effect was approximately constant for all groups and was not related to trials in any systematic manner. Hence, it seems reasonable to conclude that the startle response was unaffected by being evoked in the presence of a stimulus that had been consistently paired with reward.

The extinction data revealed essentially the same picture. The rapid drop in the instrumental response measure in extinction represents, at least in part, the extinction of $r_g - s_g$ and the consequent decrease in energization of the in-

strumental response, whereas the startle amplitude measure showed no significant effects other than the questionable order × trials interaction.

This overall pattern of results, then, leads to the conclusion that while the instrumental response involved in obtaining the reward was facilitated by the incentive stimulus, the startle response, which was in no way instrumental, was not facilitated. Following the reasoning presented in the introduction, these results would be taken as indicating that incentive motivation does not function as a general response energizer, but somehow exerts its facilitative effect only on some subset of behavior which at the very least includes the response instrumental to obtaining the reward in a particular situation.

The generality of this conclusion, of course, cannot be determined from the present experiment. Similar experiments employing different reference responses, different reward substances, and different conditioning situations will be necessary to determine the limits of the classes of responses facilitated or not facilitated by incentive motivation.

Summary: This study attempted to determine if incentive motivation—the state of affairs consequent upon presenting an organism with a stimulus that has regularly been paired with food ($r_g - s_g$)—functions like drive as a general energizer of all responses evoked in its presence. The problem was attacked using the "probe stimulus" technique in which the amplitude of a reflex response is employed as an index of the general energizing properties of a variable.

The experiment employed three groups of 20 rats; the apparatus was a small stabilimeter, the movements of which were recorded graphically, and provided a measure of the startle response.

All Ss were first habituated to a 24-hr. feeding cycle and given a series of adaptation trials to the startle stimulus (report from firing a cap pistol). Two (experimental) groups then received 10 trials daily for 10 days on which a CS was paired with 0.5 ml. of a sucrose solution. For one group the solution contained 6% sucrose and for the other, 24%. On these trials, the control group was presented with the CS only. All Ss also received two test trials each day. On one test trial the startle response was elicited in the presence of the CS; on the other test trial it was elicited in the absence of the CS. A subsequent ·4-day extinction series followed the same procedure except for the omission of sucrose for all Ss. In addition to ·the startle response measures, a record was also kept of instrumental approach responses to the food cup during the CS period of all nontest trials.

The results of this experiment were completely opposed to a general energizing conception of incentive motivation. Both experimental groups showed acquisition and extinction of the instrumental approach responses, with the 24% group showing the faster acquisition but with no differences in rate of extinction. The startle amplitude data, on the other hand, showed no differences attributable to the pairing of the CS with sucrose. Thus, it was tentatively concluded that while incentive motivation serves to facilitate some subset of behavior which at least includes the class of responses instrumental to obtaining the reward, it does not indiscriminately facilitate any and all responses evoked in its presence.

Journal of Comparative and Physiological Psychology, 1963, vol. 56, pp. 69–72

The Effect of Nonnutritive Sucking on Movement in the Human Newborn[1]

William Kessen and Anne-Marie Leutzendorff

The sucking behavior of the young human infant has been closely studied for a variety of reasons—as an indicator of individual variation (Balint, 1948; Kessen, Williams, & Williams, 1961), as related to tensional states (Wolff, 1959), as a response undergoing changes with practice (Davis, Sears, Miller, & Brodbeck, 1948), as a modifying influence on autonomic responses (Lipton, Richmond, Weinberger, & Hersher, 1958), as a discriminating response for psychophysical studies (Bronshtein, Antonova, Kamenetskaya, Luppova, & Sytova, 1958), and, in most careful descriptive

detail, as part of a complex behavior system involving respiration and swallowing (Peiper, 1956). Attention has also been devoted to the place of the sucking response in theories of behavior. The central role of sucking in psychoanalytic theory has often been rehearsed (see, for a recent explication, Lustman, 1956) and this "alimentary reflex" is at the foundation of recent Russian treatments of early learning (Kasatkin, 1952). Bowlby (1958) has discussed sucking as critical in the formation of the "child's tie to his mother" and Piaget goes so far as to state that "psychology begins with the use of this [sucking] mechanism" (Piaget, 1952, p. 39).

[1] The research reported here was supported in part by Research Grant M–1787, from the National Institute of Mental Health, United States Public Health Service.

By far the larger part of research on sucking, whether related to theory (e.g., Davis et al., 1948) or not, has been concentrated on the local topographical features of the response with relatively little attention being given to concomitant or consequent changes in other responses of the infant. Recently, Kessen and Mandler (1961) have proposed that the sucking response acts as an inhibitor of distress, quieting the infant even if the sucking is not followed by food ingestion. An elemental implication of this position is that nonnutritive sucking, that is, sucking without consequent ingestion of food, should show clear-cut effects on responses of the infant that are reasonably held to indicate distress. The present study was designed to demonstrate the effect of the sucking response on several measures of newborn responding—chiefly general movement.

Method

Subjects

The Ss were 15 male and 15 female human newborn infants, 24 to 60 hr. old when first observed. Nine of the males were circumcised during the course of the study. The Ss were observed four times during the lying-in period: in the morning and the afternoon of the first day on which they were observed (called *Day 1* later in this report) and in the morning and the afternoon of the following day (*Day 2*). Median age of Ss at the first observation was 52 hr.

Apparatus

The Ss were placed supine on a mattress fitted to an equipment cart adapted for photographic observation. An overhead girder, approximately 3 ft. above S, supported a fixed motion camera (Bell & Howell, 16-mm., Model DL-70). Pens of an Esterline-Angus operations recorder were operated by six telegraph keys arranged in two banks of three keys, one bank on each side of the observation cart (see Kessen, Hendry, & Leutzendorff, 1961 for an illustration of the apparatus).

Procedure

Approximately 1 hr. after their mid-morning feeding and again approximately 2 hr. after their early afternoon feeding, Ss were brought from their nursery to the observation room, a normally unoccupied nursery on the same floor of the hospital.[2] All Ss were awake at the beginning of each observation; if a baby was crying loudly, he was held or rocked until he stopped crying. Ss were dressed in diaper and hospital shirt throughout the observations. Two preliminary 5-min. observations were made of each S. In one of these, hand-mouth contacting and hand-face contacting were observed and recorded; in the other, mouthing and crying were recorded. Data collected during these observations (which took place before the photographic series described below) will not be presented in this report. After the second 5-min. observation, E changed the infant's diapers; this served to insure that the photographic series was started dry and that all Ss were roused by roughly equivalent handling.

The photographic series consisted of two runs of film. The first was 30 sec. in duration, during which time the infant was not stimulated (Baseline). The camera was rewound and, approximately 60 sec. after the end of the first run, the second run of film, 75 sec. in duration, was made. This run recorded the behavior of S during 15 sec. without stimulation (Prestimulation), 30 sec. of stimulation (Stimulation), and 30 sec. after stimulation (Poststimulation). For 20 Ss, additional recordings were made on the operations recorder of mouthing and crying throughout the photographic series.

Stimulation was of two kinds. To observe the effects of nonnutritive sucking, E put an ordinary hospital bottle-nipple stuffed with cotton over his index finger and inserted the nipple into the infant's mouth (this procedure is called *Nipple* hereafter). As a rough control for tactile contact and to insure that response to sucking was not

2 The writers are deeply indebted to M. J E. Senn and to the staff of Grace-New Haven Community Hospital for their generous cooperation.

merely undifferentiated response to any stimulation, each S was also stimulated by E's stroking of S's forehead with a hospital diaper at an interval of from 1 to 2 sec. (*Forehead*). During each of the four observation periods, either the Nipple or the Forehead procedure was applied during the Stimulation period. Ss were assigned to one of two balanced orders for the four observations, either Nipple-Forehead-Forehead-Nipple or the converse. Thus, each S was observed under Nipple stimulation and under Forehead stimulation on each of 2 days.

Immediately after the photographic series, Ss were returned to their nursery.

Response Measures

When S was observed to be moving his lips in a way characteristic of sucking—i.e., mouthing—whether or not his mouth was then being simulated, one of the telegraph keys operating a pen of the operations recorder was depressed. The resulting record was divided into 1-sec. intervals; if mouthing occurred at any time during an interval, that interval was given a score of one. Thus, mouthing scores in an observation period of 15 sec. could range from zero to 15. Similarly, whenever S was observed to cry—only audible exhalations were scored—a second telegraph key was depressed. The resulting record of crying was scored just as mouthing was. Both mouthing and crying measures have been shown to produce high interobserver reliability (Kessen et al., 1961).

The measure of primary interest in the present study was general movement. The method of measuring movement and its rationale have been described in detail elsewhere (Kessen, Hendry, & Leutzendorff, 1961). Briefly summarized, the method assesses the mean displacement of the infant's hands and feet over periods of 5 sec. A film-frame from the beginning of an observation is back-projected onto a glass surface and the positions of the infant's hands and feet are marked on tracing paper overlying the glass surface. Then, a film-frame taken 5 sec. after the first is projected and the new positions of hands and feet are marked. This procedure is repeated to the end of a film run. The mean linear displacement of the four limbs between examined frames constitutes the index of movement used. The film record was calibrated to provide a measure of displacement in cm. per limb per 5-sec. interval. The measure can be obtained with high interobserver reliability and has been shown to vary systematically between Ss and across days of the lying-in period (Kessen et al., 1961). In the present study, the film runs were measured with the start of stimulation and the end of stimulation as zero points, that is, the points from which 5-sec. intervals were determined.

Results and Discussion

The effect of Nipple and Forehead stimulation on newborn movement is shown in Figure 1. The Movement Index shown on the ordinate is a measure in cm. of mean limb displacement per 5-sec. interval. The abscissa is marked off in temporal intervals of 5 sec. Thus, the first open circle in the lower graph indicates that in the first 5 sec. of the Baseline period, the mean limb displacement of the 30 Ss was just over 3 cm. During Baseline and Prestimulation periods, there is no difference in the movement measure for the two conditions. Immediately after the beginning of stimulation, however, there is a precipitous drop in mean movement under Nipple stimulation, and this reduction is maintained throughout the period of stimulation. As soon as stimulation ends, the infants' movements increase until, 25 sec. after the end of stimulation, movement has returned almost exactly to its Baseline level for both stimulation conditions. An analysis of variance of movement over the last three periods of stimulation showed a highly significant difference between Nipple and Forehead stimulation ($F = 33.76$, $df = 1/87$) and no statistically significant variation

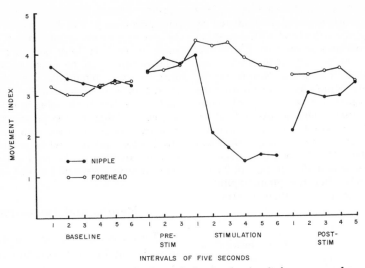

Fig. 1. The effect of nipple and forehead stimulation on newborn human movement.

ascribable to sex, day of observation, their interactions, or their interactions with the stimulation conditions. Moreover, Forehead stimulation does not reliably change the movement index from Prestimulation levels. The suddenness of the drop in movement index under Nipple stimulation was assessed in an analysis of data from the Nipple Stimulation period alone. The overall drop across the six Stimulation intervals is significant ($F = 14.82$, $df = 5/308$), with almost all of the variance accounted for by the drop from the first interval to the second ($F = 69.73$, $df = 1/308$). In short, inserting a stuffed nipple into the mouth of a newborn infant results in a sudden and reliable drop in movement.[3]

The effects of Nipple and Forehead stimulation on two other responses of the infants are shown in Figure 2. In general, changes in mouthing and

crying with stimulation parallel those in movement. Comparing the change from Baseline to Stimulation period of Nipple and Forehead stimulation, analysis of variance showed a significant relative increase in mouthing ($F = 47.61$, $df = 1/19$) and a significant relative decrease in crying ($F = 17.51$, $df = 1/19$). As was the case with movement, there is almost a complete return to Baseline levels of responding within 30 sec. of the end of stimulation.

The effects of nonnutritive sucking on newborn movement can be clearly described from these results, but interpretation of the facts is less obvious. Because all infants who were observed had been fed a number of times prior to observation, it is possible to maintain that the changes in behavior consequent on oral insertion of a stuffed nipple are the result of secondary reinforcement learned from the association of nipple and sucking with food. Although such an interpretation puts inordinate demands on the notion of secondary reinforcement—i.e., that high values of secondary reinforcement can

[3] The failure to find changes in movement consequent on brief "spontaneous" hand-mouth contacts by the child (Williams & Kessen, 1961) may most reasonably be ascribed to the very short duration of most such contacts.

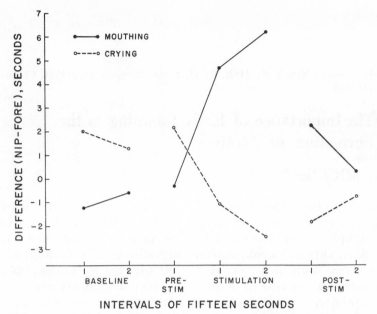

Fig. 2. The effect of nipple and forehead stimulation on newborn crying and mouthing. (See text for description of the conditions of observation.)

be acquired in 10–20 feedings—the question should be answered by observation of infants who have not yet been fed. A second question posed by the observations reported here concerns the nature of the event controlling changes in movement. It is plausible to believe that the intensity or frequency of the sucking response is relevant to the degree of diminution in movement—that is, that the infant who sucks throughout nipple stimulation will show a greater reduction in movement than the less industrious sucker. However, there was not enough variation in duration of mouthing during nipple stimulation among Ss in the present study to draw even tentative conclusions on this issue. Finally, it remains to be seen whether the effect described here is related to the potentially reinforcing properties of sucking. The change in newborn movement consequent on nonnutritive sucking clearly does not,

in the circumstances of the present study, persist long past the termination of stimulation. The effect of contingent nonnutritive sucking on the probability of a selected response must be studied in order to determine further functional properties of this "inhibitor of distress."

Summary: 30 newborn human infants were observed on 4 occasions during the lying-in period to determine the behavioral consequences of nonnutritive sucking. On 2 of these occasions a bottle-nipple placed over E's finger was inserted in S's mouth for 30 sec.; on the other 2 occasions E stroked S's forehead lightly with a cloth for 30 sec. Determinations were made of S's movement and, for 20 Ss, of mouthing and crying. Within 5 sec. of nipple insertion S's movement dropped to a significantly lower level; within 25 sec. after the removal of the nipple S's movement had returned to baseline levels. Nipple insertion produced a significantly higher level of mouthing and a significantly lower level of crying. No significant effects of the forehead stimulation were found.

Personality, New York: Holt, Rinehart and Winston, Inc., 1951, Chapter 12, pp. 441–458.

√The Importance of Early Learning in the Formation of Motives[*]

David C. McClelland

Let us begin where most theories of motivation have begun in recent years: with two simple assumptions—namely, that the important psychogenic motives are learned (not instinctual), and that they are somehow acquired by association with primary biological pleasure and pain. For the moment let us put aside the pleasure-pain problem and ask what it is that makes this particular kind of learning so persistent and powerful. Psychologists have studied the learning process in the laboratory in great detail. They have set up nonsense syllable pairs for human beings to associate, distinctive goal boxes for rats to associate with food pellets, and token rewards for chimpanzees to associate with oranges or bananas. In all of these learning situations, what the organism acquires is rather rapidly forgotten. Certainly it shows none of the persistence which we must assume characterizes human motivation. Yet the stubborn fact remains that psychologists believe motives are learned in the same way as other responses are learned. What is the solution to this apparent paradox?

[*] Reprinted by permission of the author and Holt, Rinehart and Winston, Inc. Copyright 1951 by David C. McClelland. The excerpt, which appears as part of chap. 12 in *Personality*, pp. 441–458, has been given the above title for this volume.

So far, the only clue we have mentioned is that avoidance learning is harder to extinguish than other kinds of learning—a clue which, as we have just seen, has led to the elaboration of a theory of secondary motivation which is based on the notion of anxiety reduction and which we have found inadequate on other grounds. But suppose we take a closer look at avoidance learning. Why is it relatively harder for the rat to unlearn an avoidance response? Naïvely we could say that he keeps running to avoid a nonexistent shock simply because he doesn't know it has been turned off. His learned response *prevents* him from finding out that conditions have changed. But can't this situation be generalized? Are there not many situations in which the rat or the human being would have difficulty in discovering that conditions are now changed from what they were before—conditions that do not necessarily involve avoidance learning? In general we might predict that the more disorderly and confused the original conditions of acquisition were, the harder it would be to set up conditions which were sufficiently different from them for the organism to perceive the difference and unlearn a response no longer appropriate.

Let us follow this clue a little further: very few laboratory experiments are sufficiently "messy" and disorderly to make the discrimination between learning and extinction difficult for the animal. In their zeal for experimental control, psychologists may have over-reached themselves. They have usually provided *one* cue that is always relevant, *one* response which is always appropriate to the reward, and *one* particular set of time relations between the events in the cue-response-reward sequence. The reasons for such careful control are excellent. If psychologists are to be able to determine the relations among their analytic units (cue-response-reward) they must control some while they systematically vary others. But it is just this control which may be creating the difficulties for explaining the persistence of certain types of "real life" learning. For the fact of the matter is that in life there is seldom any such regularity in the conditions of learning as we introduce normally into laboratory experiments. Stimulus, response, and reward do not occur in any regular sequence. Sometimes a response is rewarded, sometimes not; sometimes it is punished. Sometimes a reward is so delayed that it is difficult or impossible for the organism to determine what response was instrumental in producing it. In fact, learning in natural life situations often takes place under such irregular, changing, and inconsistent conditions that an experimenter who is absorbed in his consistent cue-reward sequences might wonder how anything is *ever* learned under such conditions. But things *are* learned under such conditions and when they are, they should be very hard to unlearn because the learning is so general in the first place, so compounded of different cues, responses,

rewards, and punishments, that it will be hard for the person ever to discover that conditions have changed, that some general expectation he has formed is no longer being confirmed.

Fortunately the mature organism has developed its symbolic and anticipatory capacities to the point where such irregularities in external conditions are usually not so important. Language is a great help to human beings. Thus Johnny has no difficulty in learning that he is being punished for having filched some cookies three hours earlier rather than for riding his tricycle, which is what he is doing when his father discovers his theft. A rat might have trouble figuring out what the punishment was for. But Johnny's father simply tells Johnny that he is punished because he stole the cookies, and, if Johnny understands language, the act of stealing cookies will be symbolically redintegrated and directly associated with the punishment that follows. So it is with many situations. Our symbolic capacities free us from too great a dependence on external regularities and enable us to produce the same kind of regularities internally as the experimenter produces by control of external conditions.

But not always. Sometimes associative connections must be formed under such irregular conditions that they should be very difficult to regularize symbolically. This should be particularly true of early childhood before symbolic control has developed to any very great extent. Following our clue has now led us back to the position taken [earlier] that early childhood ought to be the time when the opportunity to form strong, generalized, and persistent associations is greatest. As we discovered, there are many reasons based on learning theory why early childhood experiences should have the great importance assigned to them by the psychoanalysts. Many of these same reasons would lead us to expect that these experiences may form the basis we have been seeking for the formation of the strong secondary motives that obviously persist for long periods in a person's life. In the first place, if we accept the principle of mass action or the greater over-all responsiveness of the infant to stimulation, it would be logical to assume that many more of the infant's associations would have an affective component. Since pleasure and pain (or affective arousal) are easier to produce in an organism which has not yet developed its discriminatory or symbolic capacities, it should follow that many more situations in infancy would get associated with affective states than would be true later on.

In the second place, the connection for the infant between a situation or response and the state of affective arousal must be very vague and general at best, before symbolic control has been achieved. Whatever else can be said about the behavior of parents, it must be much more irregular than the behavior of an animal experimenter trying to get a rat to acquire a strong secondary drive. There are inevitably delays, inconsistencies, and indeterminacies in the association of situations and responses to primary pleasure and pain. For example, if Johnny gets praised occasionally for doing a variety of things like building blocks, throwing a ball, saying a new word, etc., a general connection is set up between "doing something" and pleasure. Johnny is probably not quite sure what the "something" is that leads to pleasure because the reward occurs in a hit-or-miss fashion and because he can't tell the difference

very well between one response and the next, but a very general connection is made. Because it is so general, the connection will also be hard to extinguish. Perhaps he isn't rewarded for throwing the ball on several different occasions. But in the first place, he may not perceive this (the lack of reward may be associated with some other act out of the many he is performing) and in the second, even if he did perceive it, that would be no reason to give up, since he was also not rewarded during the acquisition of the association. Furthermore, there are many other acts in the hierarchy associated with this type of reward which have not been extinguished.

For an older child, on the other hand, the specific connection between a particular response and reward would be much more easily formed and also more easily extinguished since a new (nonrewarded) situation could be more easily distinguished from the old, particularly after the use of language had developed to the point where the parents could explain the situation was different. In short, early childhood would seem to be the ideal time to form strong, affective associations which are so general that they will be hard to extinguish. So we now have a hypothesis as to how persistent secondary motives are acquired and why childhood is so important in their formation. Our next problem is to attempt to state more precisely what conditions lead to the development of (a) strong and (b) general associations of an affective nature. Actually there will be some overlap in our treatment of these two attributes of motivational associations for the simple reason that resistance to extinction is commonly used to measure *both* strength of an association and its generality. Nevertheless, each attribute has also some different measuring operations: strength may also be measured by amplitude, frequency of occurrence in competition with other responses, and latency; generality may be inferred from the irregularity of the conditions of learning. Hence the two attributes will be treated separately in the following discussion, although they are inseparable in some cases.

Conditions Influencing Primarily the Strength of Affective Associations

PRIMACY

[Earlier] we discussed briefly why early associations should have some advantage over later ones just because they occurred first and would not therefore be assimilated into a preexisting apperceptive mass. But we did not specifically discuss the problem of strength. As a matter of fact, there are a number of animal experiments which show that early associations are stronger. Hunt's initial study of feeding frustration in young rats (1941) is a case in point. He found that if rats were irregularly deprived of food .n infancy they tended to hoard more as adults, when deprived of food again, than did rats whose initial feeding frustration occurred after the organism had matured. Why should this be so? An explanation apparently requires the notions that deprivation cues get associated with anxiety or affective arousal, that hoarding is an instrumental response which reduces this anxiety, and that *the affective arousal is more intense in infancy than later.* Consequently, when the cues are reinstated in adulthood they arouse a greater anxiety in the rats deprived in infancy, which in turn motivates more

instrumental hoarding behavior. Similar results have been obtained by Wolf (1943), who has reported the relatively greater permanent effect of early over late sensory deprivation in rats. Animals whose eyes or ears had been temporarily sealed off during the nursing period consistently performed less well in a competitive situation in adulthood which required the use of these sense modalities, despite the fact that tests of the sensitivity of sight or hearing under noncompetitive situations showed no impairment. Rats which had been deprived later in life did not show the same inadequacy in the face of adult frustration. While the results of this experiment cannot be interpreted with any great certainty, they can be understood in terms of a hypothesis which states that the early-deprived rats had formed a strong association between frustration and dependence responses involved in nursing which was reinstated when frustration occurred in later life. Again the evidence is that the early association has a stronger or more permanent effect.

Unfortunately it is difficult to perform comparable experiments on human infants and to observe their effect in later life. Most reports at the human level have dealt with motor and intellectual rather than motivational phenomena. Thus Dennis has reported (1938) that marked deprivation of social stimulation in young human infants had little effect on their motor development. In a very well-known study McGraw compared the development of a pair of identical twins, Johnny and Jimmy, after treating Johnny to very unusual, accelerative training techniques. She found that the untaught twin caught up very quickly with his brother and the two showed no marked differences later in motor coordination and intellectual capacity. Nevertheless, she did find (1935, 1939) that the special training had had rather marked effects on such personality variables as self-confidence and initiative. Jimmy remained much more cautious than his accelerated brother. This suggests that generalized learning in infancy involves primarily affective pleasure-pain associations which will influence the motivational or emotional aspects of personality in later life more than the purely intellectual or motor aspects.

INVOLVEMENT OF THE
AUTONOMIC NERVOUS SYSTEM

We have been arguing that affective arousal (pleasure and pain) is somehow at the root of motivational associations. Affective arousal is normally accompanied by some kind of discharge over the autonomic nervous system which is characteristically conceived as both *intense* and *diffuse*. From this we may infer that one of the reasons why affective learning is stronger or harder to extinguish is that it is more intense, more diffuse, perhaps more "primitive" than associations involving more highly differentiated cortical control. Mowrer (1947) has been so impressed by the differences between learning which involves the autonomic as compared with the central nervous system that he has been led to the conclusion that different kinds of learning are mediated by the two systems. He argues that learning proceeds according to the contiguity principle in the autonomic system and according to the law of effect in the central nervous system. The evidence which he accumulates for two kinds of learning is considerable but it does not lead necessarily to his conclusion that

the distinction between the two depends on whether the autonomic or the central nervous system is involved. On anatomical grounds one simply cannot make as sharp a distinction between the two nervous systems as Mowrer's theory requires. Nevertheless, autonomic discharge *can* be taken as a sign of the fact that a central state of considerable intensity and diffuseness has been aroused and one can reason from this that associations involving the autonomic effector system will be stronger and harder to extinguish than those which do not lead to such a discharge. The exact reason why this is so is not known but a suggestion can be made: perhaps affective states are less under cortical control and are therefore less easily aroused symbolically in their full intensity. If this were so, one could argue that they will be harder to extinguish, just as it is hard to extinguish any response which cannot readily be evoked symbolically. One of the benefits of psychotherapy may be that affective states are sufficiently reinstated to become associated with symbolic cues, which can then be attached to new responses which will take the place of the old, maladaptive, affective ones.

Whatever the reason for the apparently greater intensity of affective states associated with autonomic discharge, it again seems likely that they are more apt to be aroused in early childhood (cf Jersild, 1942). Prior to the development of cortical control, nearly any stimulus will involve some autonomic discharge. As the child matures, the affective component apparently gets less and less and more and more specifically attached to certain cues or responses. This suggests that motives may become progressively harder to form with age although clearly a traumatic incident at any age should be sufficient to form the kind of strong affective association that is required. The only difficulty is that even here the association is apt to be much more specific (e.g., a phobia) than the generalized hedonic associations required for "true" motivation. Aside from their greater susceptibility to autonomic involvement, children are also more apt to be subjected to the kinds of experiences which lead directly to affective arousal. They are less able to protect themselves against relatively intense pains such as being stuck by a pin, severe colic, falling out of bed, etc. They are subjected to a great deal more direct reward and punishment by parents, etc. It is in these terms that we can best understand McGraw's finding that generalized associations involving affective arousal from early reward and punishment for roller-skating, climbing boxes, etc., had more permanent effects than the rather specific instrumental associations involved in acquiring such particular motor skills.

TIME DISCRIMINATION
AND INTENSITY

The psychoanalysts have not been slow to recognize the greater affective intensity of early childhood experiences, but as might be expected they tend to attribute them to other, more subjective factors. Chief among these has been the suggestion that the intensity of pleasure and pain is greater because the infant has not as yet learned to discriminate time, to anticipate in particular that certain experiences will come to an end. Affective states for the infant should have in consequence a certain "timeless" quality which is difficult for adults to comprehend and which psychoanalysts have tried to get

them to comprehend by stepping up the vividness of the language they use to describe the infant's phenomenal world. Perhaps Flugel (1945) presents the most common-sense description of the infant's inferred states of mind, based on much stronger statements made by child analysts like Susan Isaacs and Melanie Klein. "The very young child, with no more than a minimal appreciation of time, is unable to bear tension; he does not possess the knowledge, so consoling to older human beings, that loss, frustration, pain, and discomfort are usually but temporary and will be followed by relief. Consequently a very small change in a situation (e.g., a less comfortable posture or pressure of his clothes, a less easy grasp of a nipple or a less ready flow of milk) will convert a pleasant satisfying stimulus into an unpleasant dissatisfying one." (1945, p. 109.) "In moments of satisfaction everything is well, and the breast—and later the mother—is an entirely good object, the prototype perhaps of the fairy godmother or genie who fulllls all wishes completely and instantaneously. At moments of dissatisfaction the child feels that all is lost, that he is overwhelmed by distress, and that the object or parent is entirely bad, hostile, and frustrating." (1945, p. 117.) While many experimentalists (Orlansky, 1949) would doubtless object to the anthropocentric language used by Flugel and the psychoanalysts in an attempt to explain the child's world of experience, yet they could certainly agree that the absence of time discrimination would give an "all-or-nothing" characteristic to pleasure or pain experiences which would probably serve to make them more intense than for older organisms that can anticipate the cessation of either pleasure or pain. This lack of discrimination alone would go a long way toward explaining why it is that associations formed between events and pleasure and pain in early childhood should have a persistence and affective intensity that would be hard to equal in the laboratory.

THE PARADOXICAL EFFECTS OF FREQUENCY OF REWARD

Nearly all learning theorists assume that the frequency of occurrence of an association has something to do with increasing its strength, even though they may disagree as to whether frequency causes or merely carries the influences which produce an increase in strength. They also commonly assume that persistence or resistance to extinction is a measure of the strength of an association. Yet there have always been some facts that do not fit both of these assumptions. Sometimes, the more frequently a response has been reinforced the *easier* it is to extinguish. How can an operation both strengthen and weaken a response at the same time? Pavlov (1927) found that conditioned salivary responses which had been greatly overlearned could sometimes be extinguished on a single trial. Under these circumstances, how could trials to extinguish be a measure of the strength of a connection? Obviously, one or the other of the original assumptions must be in error. The question has come up again and again in learning theory in the controversy over whether a partially learned discrimination can be reversed without loss of learning time (cf. Hilgard & Marquis, 1940). The so-called "continuity" theorists have accepted both of the two assumptions just stated and argued that the more frequently one response to a discrimination situa-

tion has been reinforced, the longer it will take to extinguish that response and shift to the opposite one. The noncontinuity theorists have argued that this does not seem to be necessarily so.

Without going into the intricacies of this particular argument we can note that frequency of reward has two effects which should influence the extinction process differently. In the first place, frequency probably permits the association to be strengthened as the continuity theorists argue. However, in the second place, the more frequent the reward has been, the easier it is for the organism to perceive that there has been a change in conditions when the reward is withdrawn in the extinction condition. The stronger the original association, the more distinctive and specific it is and the greater the contrast with the new situation in which the animal no longer receives reward under the same conditions. Consequently the animal should find it easier to discriminate the new (extinction) situation from the old (acquisition) situation. Really the animal is faced with a *problem in successive discrimination* which will be easier in direct relation to the distinctiveness of the difference between conditions of learning and extinction. The greater the frequency of reward during acquisition, the more distinctively different a series of non-rewarded trials and the easier extinction should be. If original learning is pushed far enough, as in the case of Pavlov's overlearning experiments, a single nonreinforced trial may be sufficient to distinguish the new situation from the old and to produce the appropriate response of not responding. To summarize, the more frequently an association is reinforced, the stronger it will become, but also the more specific and in consequence the more easily extinguished. Evidence for these two conflicting effects of the frequency of reward has been discovered by Gwinn (1950) working with the fear response in rats. He found that when he increased the frequency of strong shocks which mature rats received in a compartment, the rats ran out of the compartment faster on the first few extinction trials, which is consistent with the first assumption that frequency of an association increases its strength. But he also found, paradoxically, that the same rats *extinguished more quickly,* which is consistent with the second assumption that these rats were able to distinguish the non-shock situation in extinction from the shock situation in training more easily than the rats who had only been shocked a few times during training.

The bearing of this point on the formation of motives in human beings is interesting, although somewhat conjectural at this stage. Learning psychologists who have attempted to apply their principles to child rearing have up to now usually argued that the way to strengthen a desirable habit or attitude is to reward it consistently. Thus it might be suggested that if Johnny's father wants Johnny to strive for achievement, he ought to reward Johnny for any little efforts toward achievement that he makes. In the light of our present analysis this might strengthen the specific response of achieving for daddy's approval, but if Johnny ever found himself in a situation where approval was not forthcoming, we might expect that the response would also extinguish rather rapidly. It is on just such a basis that we could distinguish between a *habit* of achieving in response to specific situations to get a specific reward and an achievement *motive* which is based on a generalized association between *various* responses and *possible* achievement rewards.

Again, age at which stress is placed on achievement (or other forms of adjustment) seems important. A parent may be extremely consistent in stressing achievement (from his viewpoint) but may begin his consistent disciplining at too early an age for the child to discover and symbolize the consistency. If so, he will tend to develop what we have just called an achievement motive rather than an achievement habit. Thus Friedman (1950), in studying the extent to which children in various cultures were required to do things for themselves, found that early stress on independence training was significantly related to the amount of achievement motivation expressed in the mythology of the cultures concerned. Later stress, however, was not as closely related to mythological nAchievement, which suggests that children in such cultures did not develop the strong *generalized* affective associations needed for high imaginative nAchievement but developed instead achievement "habits" which, as in the hypothetical case of Johnny, would be more specifically tied by language to particular situations and rewards.

Conditions Affecting Primarily the Generality of Affective Associations

Frequency of reward is a good transition from conditions increasing strength to those increasing generality of associations since, as we have seen, it serves simultaneously to increase strength and decrease generality, particularly if continued long enough. What are some of the other conditions influencing generality of associations, particularly as they may be present in childhood, when motives are presumably learned? Linton has considered the problem in a general way as follows:

> The more specific a response the easier it is to extinguish it. The reason for this is fairly obvious. Laboratory experiments have shown that habits are extinguished either when they fail to achieve the desired ends or when they expose the individual to too much punishment. Owing to environmental or other changes, a response which is linked with a single situation or with a very small number of situations, can easily become subject to the conditions which will lead to extinction. More generalized responses on the other hand are likely to be rewarded in connection with some situations even when they are unrewarded or punished in connection with others. It is a common experience that while specific patterns of overt behavior are fairly easy to extinguish, value-attitude systems are extremely hard to extinguish. Such systems tend to survive even when their overt expressions have been inhibited in many situations and to reassert themselves with almost undiminished vigor when new situations involving the particular value factor arise. (1945, p. 115.)

If the word *motive* is substituted for the phrase "value-attitude system" in this quotation, it summarizes in a general way one of the main reasons why motives are so persistent.

Furthermore, Linton goes on to link the formation of generalized value-attitudes to early childhood. They "seem to be easy to establish in childhood but exceedingly difficult to establish in adult life" possibly because of "some inability on the part of the small child to differentiate between related situations" (1945, p. 116). In short, he has stated our general thesis that affective associations laid down in childhood are often so exceedingly general because of the child's undeveloped powers of discrimination that they persist because it is difficult to produce the conditions that would make it possible to extinguish them. This argument assumes that associations do not decay simply through disuse, which seems a safe assumption in view of the fairly overwhelming evidence that it is what happens *in time* rather than time itself that causes forgetting (cf. McGooch, 1942). What more specifically are some of the conditions that promote generality of initial learning?

LACK OF SYMBOLIC CONTROL

We have already discussed above the great advantages that human beings have in being able to free themselves from environmental sequences by symbolic manipulation. The use of symbols, especially language, favors specificity of learning largely because it enables the child to make the discrimination much more easily between when it is appropriate to make a response and when it is not. He can group together what would otherwise be a large number of complex experiences, often separated by varying time intervals, under a single heading and say, for instance, "Oh, mummy loves me if I try hard." The younger child does not have this advantage: all he can learn is that there is a vague class of activities which is followed by something pleasant (e.g., "mummy's love"). Since he cannot define the boundaries of the class very well or decide whether a given act belongs to it or not, he may, if pressure for achievement is put on him at this age, learn to "be kept on his toes by a nameless, shapeless, unlocated hope of enormous achievement," as Bateson so nicely phrases it. Language also makes it easier to decide when effort is *not* called for. If the child has named the class of activities which require effort (e.g., schoolwork), he can the more readily distinguish activities that do not require effort (e.g., household chores). But if the independence training is itself so general that no such specific learning is possible, or if it occurs so early in life that adequate symbolization is impossible, then we have the conditions for the formation of an extremely general achievement association which will be very hard to extinguish.

GENERALIZED THREATS AND PROMISES

We have also already mentioned the fact that avoidance learning may be hard to extinguish because it leads to a response which does not permit the person to discover that the situation is changed. Technically this is somewhat different from general learning, but it delays extinction in the same way. Furthermore, it suggests a type of learning situation which may prevent unlearning because the responses are instrumental to goals which are so high, vague, or indeterminate that *it is impossible for the person to evaluate how well he is doing.* At one extreme, a child may be punished regularly for stealing candy. He knows he will be spanked if he takes it and may learn to inhibit this response. Later on he may try taking it again and if he goes unspanked will soon extinguish the inhibitory response. At the other extreme, a child may be told if he steals candy that "something bad" will happen to him, his conscience will hurt him, God will disapprove, etc. This too will in time inhibit his response but now if he breaks through this inhibition at any

time he has no way of knowing accurately whether he is being punished or not. "Something bad" may not happen immediately, but it may later; sins may be stored up in heaven, etc. In short, prohibitions established on the basis of vague threats are much harder to unlearn than those established by direct punishment, just as Mackinnon discovered (cf. Murray, 1938). The same argument holds for vague promises of reward. The vaguer and more general they are, the harder it will be for the child to discover whether the achievement behavior (for instance) he is showing does or does not lead to the promised gratifications.

IRREGULARITY OF ORIGINAL LEARNING CONDITIONS

For a number of years learning theorists have known that random reinforcement during learning will delay extinction over what it is for 100 per cent reinforcement (cf. Humphreys, 1939). Many studies summarized by Jenkins and Stanley (1950) have shown that this phenomenon is very general and occurs whether reinforcement is periodic (e.g., every second minute), aperiodic (e.g., randomly distributed around two minutes), or in fixed ratio (e.g., for every third response). An explanation of the delay in extinction can readily be made in terms of our analysis of the influence of frequency of reinforcement on the distinctiveness of acquisition as compared to extinction conditions. Whenever reinforcement occurs with less than 100 per cent regularity, acquisition conditions become more similar to extinction conditions and it gets harder for the animal to discriminate between the two and learn to stop responding. Stated in its most general form, our proposition is that *any method of increasing the similarity between acquisition and extinction will delay extinction.*

But randomizing reinforcement is only one way of making the discrimination between learning and extinction difficult. Many other kinds of irregularities may be introduced. Even in these experiments the correct *response* is never varied (as it often would be in life situations), nor are the relevant *cues.* In other words, in a typical experiment bar-pressing remains the response which produces the food, although it may not bring food on a particular occasion. McClelland and McGown (1950) performed an experiment in which the reinforcement factor was held constant at 100 per cent but the relevant cues and responses to receiving food were varied. They trained two groups of white rats to associate a goal box with food, one in the standard specific way and the other in an irregular, "general" way. The goal box consisted of a circular alley. In the specific alley-trained group a barrier was inserted in the alley and food reward on the training days was *always* placed just in front of this barrier. Consequently the rats in this group learned to enter the circular alley, turn left, and run a certain fixed distance to find a food pellet. They learned to associate a particular left-turning response, a particular location in the alley, and a particular time delay with food reward.

The group of rats which received generalized reinforcement training were treated quite differently. They too were always fed in the circular alley but there was no barrier in it and the reinforcement was given in such a way as to prevent the animal from associating any particular response, or portion of the alley, or time delay with food reward. This was done by leaving the food rewards in different sections of the circular alley and by sometimes feeding the animal only when he *stopped* in a certain section of the alley. In other words, the occurrence of the food reward in the goal alley was so irregular with respect to time and place and so inconsistent with respect to the response reinforced that the rats must have formed only a very general association between the circular alley and food reward. After both groups of rats had received 100 per cent reinforcement in the goal alley on three successive days in this fashion, the crucial test was made of determining which group would continue to run into the alley longer when the food reward was withdrawn. Both groups showed evidence of·the fact that the goal alley, by being associated with food, had attained some secondary reinforcing power. That is, both groups ran into the goal alley more often and faster on the test day than did control groups which had not received reinforcement in it. The group which had been rewarded for a specific response during training extinguished rather rapidly as in all other experiments of this sort. But the general group behaved quite differently. In the first place, the rats in this group ran into the goal alley significantly faster than the specific animals did, showing that the generalized training had developed a more powerful secondary reward. In the second place, they showed little evidence of extinction in the twenty-five extinction trials given them. On the contrary, they showed slight evidence of a tendency to run faster at the time when the "specific" animals had definitely begun to extinguish.

So far then as this experiment goes, it confirms the hypothesis that generalized learning is stronger (speed-of-running measure) and will persist longer than specific learning. It tests the hypothesis, however, only in an over-all fashion. Actually three factors associated with reward were controlled in the specific group and varied in the general group —namely, the response, the time delay, and the place where the food was. Each of these should be studied separately to discover whether it is the variation in the responses rewarded or the place rewarded or the delay of reward which accounts for the persistence of the secondary reinforcing power of the goal alley. Needless to say, all these factors are varied under the normal conditions in which the child is learning something. Prior to the development of language there must be a good many associations which can best be described as "something good" following "something" else at some time or other.

A peculiarly important form of irregularity in learning not so far mentioned is that in which both reward and punishment (or pleasure and pain) get mixed up in the same association. Suppose the rats in McClelland and McGown's experiment had also been shocked occasionally just as they were eating the food. What would have happened then? Would this have delayed extinction still more? As a matter of fact there is some evidence on this point: Drew (1938) found that electrifying the food a rat was eating greatly increased the rate of consumption. What is being built up here is an association which involves elements both of pleasure and pain—an association which appears to be "stronger" and should be harder to extinguish by non-reward if Farber's previously reported similar experiment (1948) may be taken as indicative of what would happen.

Such associations have very great importance in psychoanalytic theory and in understanding the problems of neurosis. In these areas the term *ambivalence* is commonly applied to them. How such mixed, ambivalent associations are supposed to be acquired in early childhood is again clearly described by Flugel (1945). After pointing out that a very small change in the situation may "convert a pleasant satisfying stimulus into an unpleasant dissatisfying one," he states "Thus the child can both love and hate the same objects in rapid succession or alternation and his love and hate alike tend to work on the all-or-nothing principle— there are not the qualifications and quantitative variations that are found in later life." (1945, p. 109.) The breast which does not supply the milk may be regarded as "bad" or frustrating one moment and as "good" the next, when milk flows and satisfies hunger. Thus many objects must in the beginning be associated *with both pleasure and pain* in ways that the infant is incapable of separating. As both Lewin (1935) and Miller (1944) have pointed out, ambivalence or an approach-avoidance conflict is one of the most serious and insoluble types of conflict. As such it may create a secondary disturbance or tension which becomes an important and persistent new motive with tension reduction as its goal. But note in particular that associations which contain pain and punishment to begin with should be exceedingly difficult to extinguish by additional punishment or non-reward later on. Theorists have wondered why a child's love for his mother may persist despite all sorts of discouragements, punishment, evidence of dislike and rejection, etc. One of the reasons may well be that the child acquired his original regard for his mother under conditions which contained a good deal of punishment to begin with. So the "new" punishing situations are not sufficiently different from the "old" learning conditions to make the unlearning of the old response likely or even possible. Ambivalent associations should be harder to unlearn than non-ambivalent ones, if this reasoning is correct.

UNREPRODUCIBILITY OF THE CONDITIONS OF LEARNING

A related but somewhat different reason why early learning may be so general that it is hard to extinguish arises from the fact that many of the discriminations a child subsequently makes have not been made at the time the learning in question took place. Chief among these is the distinction between self and not-self, between inner and outer sensations. In Flugel's words, "There is no adequate distinction between sensations and their accompanying feelings and impulses, nor—more important still—between these feelings and impulses and the associated outer objects." (1945, p. 110.) In short, things happen in the child's life—pleasurable things and painful things—and the child has no clear notion as to whether the pain comes from within (proprioceptive sensations) or without (sensations from the eye or other distance receptors). Thus the pleasure from sucking may become associated *both* with internal hunger sensations and with external visual ones (the breast). We could expect then a kind of generalized

association between eating pleasure and a set of cues not yet discriminated into inner and outer sources which we might label *proto-perceptive*. Later on, however, the child discriminates quite clearly between what happens inside him and what happens in the outside world. Now suppose we had the job of extinguishing an association involving proto-perceptive cues after the inner and outer discrimination had been clearly established. Would it not be difficult? How could we go about re-establishing the cue situation which was present when the association was learned? What we would be most likely to do is to reproduce the external part of the cue compound (e.g., the mother) and expect that new associations learned to this aspect of the compound would replace the old ones. But such a procedure would probably not be very efficient, although some retroactive inhibition through partial similarity in the cue situations should occur. In short, it may be hard to unlearn some early affective associations because they were learned *under cue conditions which cannot be reinstated and attached to new responses.* This point need not only apply to inability to distinguish inner from outer stimuli, of course; it should hold for any peculiar cue conditions of infancy that are hard to reinstate. In fact, the same argument was presented in a more general way [earlier when] we pointed out that as children grow larger it becomes difficult to reinstate exactly what they perceived when they were small and looking at the underneath surfaces of the world. And if cue patterns cannot be reproduced with a fair degree of accuracy, it will be difficult to unlearn the associations involving them.

For all these reasons and for others

which are closely related, affective associations formed in early childhood are apt to be strong and very resistant to unlearning or forgetting. From the theoretical viewpoint there is no reason why such associations could not be formed *at any time in life* but more of the conditions we have laid down are apt to occur in childhood, particularly at the preverbal level. Thus we have made a beginning at least toward solving one of the two major difficulties associated with contemporary theories of motivation—namely, the difficulty of explaining their extraordinary persistence and strength in the light of our knowledge of the transitoriness of most laboratory learning.

British Journal of Social and Clinical Psychology, 1962, vol. 1, pp. 107–120.

Two Origins of Achievement Motivation[1] 441 ✓

Michael Argyle and Peter Robinson

Introduction

A great deal of research has been carried out in connection with the achievement motive. This seems to have two basic aspects, 'motive to achieve'—an approach motive, and 'motive to avoid failure'—an avoidance motive. Most of the research has been conducted with a measure (nAch) which seems to be primarily an index of 'motive to achieve'. This research suggests that the achievement motive is a drive which can be aroused experimentally, varies between people and is acquired (McClelland *et al.*, 1953; Atkinson, 1958). It is generally assumed that the two aspects of this drive are acquired through processes of reward and punishment.

THE EFFECTS OF REWARD AND PUNISHMENT ON nACH

Winterbottom (1953) studied 29 eight- to ten-year-old boys and their mothers. Achievement motivation was measured by the content analysis of imaginative stories, and mothers were interviewed concerning their socialization techniques. The use of verbal and material rewards for fulfilling demands for achievement was unrelated to nAch scores, but physical rewards (kissing and hugging) were so related ($p < 0.05$). None of the three types of punishment considered bore any relation to nAch. Crandell, Preston & Rabson (1960) studied 30 three- to five-year-olds and their mothers. Achievement motivation was assessed not by the projective method but by ratings of achievement efforts at school; material rewards for

1 This research was supported by the M.R.C. who gave a grant for research assistance.

We are grateful to Adrienne Dunn, Helen Ross, Dr. Richard Lynn, Ken Hignett and David Moseley for assistance in the administration of tests, and to the Teachers and children of the City of Oxford High School, Didcot Girls Grammar School, Wallingford Grammar School, Banbury Grammar School, Bromsgrove County High School, Witney Secondary Modern School and Headington Secondary School.

achievement were rated in the home. A correlation of 0.42 ($p < 0.01$) was found between the two variables. This study differs from the others reported in that achievement motivation was measured from ratings, and in that the subjects were so young. Child, Storm & Veroff (1958) carried out a cross-cultural study of 52 societies. Achievement motivation was assessed from a content analysis of 12 randomly chosen folktales from each society, treating the stories as TAT protocols. Various aspects of socialization were rated on 7-point scales by judges using the available ethnographic materials. It was found that a combination of reward for achievement and punishment for absence of achievement-oriented behaviour correlated 0.34 with nAch ($p < 0.06$). However if societies using rigid or compulsive child-rearing are considered separately, this correlation rises to 0.57 ($n = 9$), and nAch is also correlated with punishment for presence of achievement ($r = 0.68$, $p < 0.05$), and conflictful handling of achievement ($r = 0.44$). However, for the 10 societies which do not use rigid methods of socialization, these correlations are insignificant or negative. Similarly, punishment for absence of achievement is very effective in societies low in general indulgence ($r = 0.80$, $p < 0.01$), but not in societies high in indulgence ($r = 0.08$). This important study suggests that reward, and particularly punishment, can produce nAch only in a rigid and non-indulgent setting. Achievement motivation was found to be higher in societies where training was non-rigid ($r = 0.56$) and indulgent ($r = 0.29$), so the question arises, what are the origins in these other societies?

There is, however, some evidence that success at specific tasks does result in greater efforts being made to perform the tasks. Keister (1938) found that nursery school-children came to show more persistence at tasks as a result of success and praise for performance at progressively more difficult tasks. P.S. Sears (1940) found that the level of aspiration increases as a function of success in previous tasks.

It has been found by Robinson (1961) and others that nAch is correlated with I.Q. at about 0.40. This is consistent with the idea that academic success leads to greater achievement motivation. Robinson also found that British school-children who had been selected for grammar school at 11+ had a higher nAch than children of the same I.Q. who were not selected. This confirmed his hypothesis that success would increase nAch.

To summarize, emotional rewards for achievement, punishment for non-achievement in a rigid non-indulgent setting, and experience of success at tasks, may all contribute to the development of nAch.

THE INFLUENCE OF EXHORTATION ON nACH

It was thought at one time that training for independence and self-reliance produced achievement motivation. McClelland & Friedman (1952) in a cross-cultural study of 8 American Indian societies found that nAch as measured from folk-tales was correlated with earliness and severity of independence training; however, Child, Storm & Veroff (1958) found no such relation with self-reliance training in their study of 52 societies, nor in a re-analysis of the McClelland & Friedman data. Rosen & d'Andrade (1959) point out that encouragement of independence in general must be distinguished from encouragement of independent achievement in particular.

Winterbottom (1953) found that the mothers of boys higher on *n*Ach had made demands for independence and mastery at an earlier age: only the achievement-related demands showed a significant difference. Rosen and d'Andrade (1959) studied 40 nine- to eleven-year-old boys and their parents by setting up experimental tasks in the home and observing parental reactions. Boys high in *n*Ach had parents who set high standards for them and expected them to do well; their mothers, but not their fathers, showed a type of interaction corresponding to a combination of warmth and rejection. Kagan & Moss (1959) found that maternal concern with achievement was significantly higher for high *n*Ach girls; they found no such relation for boys. Wolf (1938) found that persistence at tasks in children was correlated with a high level of demands by adults which were reasonable in the light of the child's ability.

Whereas it has usually been supposed that *n*Ach is acquired by rewards and punishments which occur *after* the achievement-behaviour (or lack of it) has taken place, we now have evidence that exhortations and setting of standards *before* the behaviour may also be effective. We shall postulate that when there are appropriate relations between parent and child—warmth and dependency probably—then these exhortations will become "introjected", i.e. applied by the child to himself and experienced as an "ought". It is quite likely that this process can ultimately be reduced to more familiar principles of learning: for instance the child may

have been rewarded for carrying out parental exhortations on previous occasions and thus acquired a learning set to obey all such demands.

It is proposed to test this hypothesis in the current investigation. It is predicted that *n*Ach will be correlated with (i) the strength of parental demands for achievement, and (ii) the reported strength of super-ego demands for achievement.

IDENTIFICATION WITH ACHIEVEMENT-ORIENTED PARENTS AS A SOURCE OF *n*ACH

It is postulated that children often identify with their parents, and that when their parents are hard-working and successful they will wish to be like their parents and thus acquire a high *n*Ach. This is a second type of learning which is not easily reducible to familiar learning processes. Again it is possible that identification and imitation is rewarded by parents, e.g. mother may praise a boy for being like his father, and thus create a learning set to imitate. Alternatively it could be due to a desire to acquire status in fantasy, or to clarify the self-concept.

Two predictions follow:—*n*Ach should correlate with (i) the reported achievement orientation of the parents, and (ii) identification with parents.

Method

Subjects

Five hundred and one subjects were used in all, 236 girls and 265 boys, the results being computed separately for groups varying between 39 and 106 in size. Most of the subjects were grammar school children aged between thirteen and seventeen; there were also two groups of students.

Design and procedure

Data were collected in the classroom, in the absence of the regular teacher, and were completed within a single period in most cases. The design was correlational; for each homogeneous sample correlations were computed between the relevant variables.

Measurement of Variables—projective measure of achievement motivation (n*Ach*)

The McClelland–Atkinson method of measurement was used. Three of the following four pictures were used—boy at desk, operation scene, men with machine, man at drawing board (Atkinson 1958, p. 488, pictures 8, 7, 2, 28). These were reproduced on cardboard, size 2 ft. $\times$ 1 ft. 6 in. and shown for 15 seconds each. The four questions were written on the blackboard as a guide to the stories (1. What is happening? Who are these people? 2. What has led up to this situation? 3. What is being thought or wanted? By whom? 4. What will happen next?). Subjects were given 4 minutes to write each story, with the exception of the 59 grammar school boys, who were given 12 minutes and who produced rather more achievement imagery. The initial instructions were as follows, and were designed to produce a relaxed condition:

'You are going to see a series of pictures, and your task is to write a story that is suggested to you by each picture. Try to imagine what is going on in each picture. Then tell what the situation is, what led up to the situation, what the people are thinking and feeling, and what they will do. The questions on the board are to guide you.

'In other words, write as complete a story as you can—a story with plot and characters.

'You will have four minutes for each story. Write your first impressions and work rapidly. I will keep time.

'There are no right or wrong stories or kinds of stories, so you may feel free to write whatever story is suggested to you when you look at a picture. Spelling, punctuation, and grammar are not important. What is important is to write out as fully and as quickly as possible the story that comes to your mind as you imagine what is

going on in each picture. Are there any questions?'

The reliability of scoring obtained was not as high as that reported by some previous investigators, and was in the area of 0.50. Subsequently we used the scores of the scorer (Robinson) who agreed most closely with the practice manual provided by Atkinson (1958). Test-retest reliability over an interval of two years was obtained for one group, and yielded a reliability of 0.44 ($n = 59$). However, examination of the stories produced by different administrators suggests that the contents are extremely sensitive to minor variations of the testing situation and relations with the tester.

Separate scores were obtained for the hope of success (nAch+) and the fear of failure (nAch−), as distinguished by Clark, Teevan & Ricciuti (1956).

Measurement—the questionnaire measure of achievement motivation (Q-ach)

Previous investigations by Robinson (1961) had led to the construction of a questionnaire. This consisted of two sets of questions corresponding to a hope of success factor and a fear of failure factor. Scores on the two sub-tests correlated with scores on nAch+ and nAch− respectively. The scale will be referred to as Q-ach, while the projective measure will be called nAch.

Measurement—uses of the semantic differential and Q-sort

In order to measure *strength of parental achievement tendencies, strength of parental achievement demands,* etc., the semantic differential was used (cf. Osgood *et al.*, 1957). Since the original semantic differential does not contain any scales dealing with achievement, a number of such scales were inserted. Out of the six scales introduced, only three were significantly intercorrelated, and these were retained. They are: hard-working—easy going, top-of-the class—bottom-of-the-class and clever—stupid. Average ratings on the 7-point scales were used to obtain scores on these variables.

Several sets of semantic scales were completed by each subject, including (a) THE

KIND OF PERSON MY FATHER IS, (*b*) THE KIND OF PERSON MY FATHER THINKS I OUGHT TO BE. It was found that when there was an 'ought' or similar instruction, subjects tended to use the categories showing maximum achievement, so that there was little variation between subjects. To meet this difficulty a miniature Q-sort was constructed, in which 2 out of 10 attributes to be ranked refer to achievement. The reciprocal of the average rank of these two attributes is taken as the achievement score.

Measurement—Identification

Three methods of measurement were employed:

1. The similarity of scoring THE KIND OF PERSON I WOULD MOST LIKE TO BE and MY FATHER (etc.) on the Semantic Differential and Q-sort. In the case of the Q-sort, the similarity was measured by the rank-order correlation between the two sets of rankings. For the semantic differential, various measures ·of semantic distance were compared and finally the easiest to compute was used—the mean difference of scale ratings—since this correlated highly with more complex measures.

This measure of identification was used since it is closest to our conceptualization of this variable. There might be some advantage in using an independent measure of the attributes of the other person; on the other hand this measure shows how far a subject wants to be like his perception of the other.

2. An alternative measure used was similar to the first, but based only on the scoring of the achievement scales on the modified semantic differential. It seemed possible that a subject could identify with some attributes of another person, but not with all of them.

3. Finally, a direct measure was used, consisting of a number of items such as 'I would like to do the sort of work that my father does', 'My father is the best person to go to for advice', with a 5-point scale of agreement.

Measurement—guilt and self-aggression

In connection with certain unexpected results obtained, which are presented in this paper, it is necessary to describe the relevant measuring instruments. Guilt was measured by means of a scale developed in another study and purified by means of factor analysis. Self-aggression was measured by means of a modified version of one of the aggression scales devised by Sears (1961). The new version has higher correlations between the items than the original one had: the average correlation between items and the total score is now 0.50. Use was also made of a set of inter-correlated intropunitive jokes being compiled by the first author. Subjects indicate how funny they find the jokes: the scores are averaged and are taken as a measure of self-aggression.

Results

Introductory note on selection of data to be used

Although 501 subjects were tested altogether, not all of the tests were given to all the subjects. Several samples of subjects were discarded because the projection test for *n*Ach did not produce enough achievement related imagery (the reasons for this were discussed above). Other groups of subjects were discarded because the semantic measure of parental demands did not have enough variance (this was replaced by a Q-sort measure as described above).

Relations between the different measures of achievement motivation

Total *n*Ach scores correlated with total Q-ach scores at 0.22 ($p < 0.01$). The subscores for *n*Ach+ and Q-ach+ had a small correlation of about 0.10, while *n*Ach− and Q-ach− correlated at 0.17 ($p < 0.05$). The approach and avoidance scores for each measure had correlations that were either zero or slightly negative. There is little evidence here that the projective and questionnaire measures were measuring the same variable. Further evidence on this

TABLE 1

Correlations Between Achievement Motivation and the Reported Strength
of Parental Demands for Motivation

		nAch+	nAch−	Q-ach+	Q-ach−
Father's	(boys)	0.23 (n = 59)	0.25	−0.18 (n = 44)	0.17
	(girls)	0.07 (n = 39)	0.31*	0.10 (n = 79)	−0.09
Mother's	(boys)	0.23 (n = 59)	0.25	−0.16 (n = 44)	0.10
	(girls)	−0.01 (n = 39)	0.07	−0.09 (n = 79)	0.13

In Tables 1–5 * indicates $p < .05$, ** $p < .01$, *** $p < .001$, italics $p < .10$, using a one-tailed
test where applicable.

question will be obtained from the correlations of each measure with other variables.

*Achievement motivation in relation to
the introjection of parental demands*

The most direct evidence on this hypothesis consists of the correlations between achievement motivation and reported parental demands for achievement. The relevant correlations are given in Table 1.

Although only one correlation is significant at the 5 per cent level, several more are significant at the 10 per cent level, and nearly all the nAch correlations are positive. There is no confirmation of a relation between parental demands and Q-ach, however. The nAch correlations are higher if the upper half of subjects on parental identification are considered separately, in the case of mother-son relations.

Since parental demands are assumed to operate via their introjection, it would be expected that super-ego demands for achievement would correlate with achievement motivation. Unfortunately SE (ach) as measured on the

semantic differential has a very small variance—most subjects ascribe maximum achievement demands to the super-ego. A better test of this hypothesis is provided by the samples for whom a Q-sort measure was used. The only such sample available consisted of 40 female students. The findings are shown in Table 2.

*Achievement motivation and parental
achievement*

The correlations between achievement motivation and reported parental achievement orientation are given in Table 3. The latter variable consists of average ratings on the inter-correlated semantic scales of hard-working (v. easy-going), top-of-the-class (v. bottom-of-the-class) and clever (v. stupid).

It can be seen that most of the correlations are in the expected direction, two of them being significant. The strongest relations are between Q-ach+ and father's achievement for boys, and nAch+ and mother's achievement for girls. However, the correlations are in general higher for father than for

TABLE 2

Correlations Between Achievement Motivation and SE(ach)

	nAch+	nAch−	Q-ach+	Q-ach−
SE(ach)	0.03 (n = 40)	0.30 (p < 0.025)	0.13 (n = 84)	−0.21 (p < 0.025)

mother. Thus the weakest relation is the mother-son one.

Relations between achievement motivation and identification with parents

The correlations between achievement motivation and several measures of identification are given in Table 4.

The correlations increase with the directness of the measures of identification used. In addition the correlations are in general higher for Q·ach than for nAch, if the results ·for the same populations are compared (not shown in this table).

Combined influence of parental achievement and identification with parents on achievement motivation

There are two possible ways of studying the joint influence of these two variables. One way is simply to calculate multiple correlations for particular samples, the other to find the correlation of achievement motivation with variable A when only those high on variable B are considered.

The multiple correlations can be inferred from Tables 3 and 4; since all of the correlations are positive, the multiple correlations are in general higher than those shown here, and correspondingly significant at a higher level.

Various analyses have been made by dividing samples at the mid-point on one variable to find the correlation of the upper half on a second variable. This was carried out for the most reliable sample for which nAch was measured—the 59 High School boys. The correlation of total nAch and mother's achievement orientation rose from 0.10 to 0.22 if the upper half on maternal identification is considered; the same does not apply to father. The mother-son correlation is the weakest, but is apparently strengthened when only those

TABLE 3

CORRELATIONS BETWEEN ACHIEVEMENT MOTIVATION
AND REPORTED PARENTAL ACHIEVEMENT TENDENCIES

	nAch+	nAch−	Q-ach+	Q-ach−
Father (boys)	0.13 (n = 59)	0.10	0.31* (n = 112)	0.07
Father (girls)	0.20 (n = 39)	0.04	0.16 (n = 130)	0.12
Mother (boys)	−0.03 (n = 59)	0.14	−0.03 (n = 112)	0.11
Mother (girls)	0.32* (n = 39)	0.22	0.06 (n = 130)	−0.05

TABLE 4

CORRELATIONS BETWEEN ACHIEVEMENT MOTIVATION AND IDENTIFICATION

		nAch+	nAch−	Q-ach+		Q-ach−
Father (boys)	EI/F (Sem. Diff.)	0.05 (n = 59)	−0.03	0.05	(n = 112)	0.13
	EI/F(ach)	0.17	0.20			
	Ident. (Quest.)			0.37***	(n = 86)	0.22*
Father (girls)	EI/F	0.10 (n = 39)	0.19	0.01	(n = 130)	0.07
	Ident.			0.24*	(n = 102)	0.31**
Mother (boys)	EI/M	−0.03 (n = 59)	0.06	0.18*	(n = 112)	0.12
	EI/M(ach)	0.19	0.26*			
	Ident.			0.36***	(n = 86)	0.52***
Mother (girls)	EI/M	0.02 (n = 39)	0.15	0.05	(n = 130)	0.10
	Ident.			0.20*	(n = 102)	0.42***

high in maternal identification are considered. This provides an explanation of the weak mother-son relation—this is the lowest of the four identifications.

Achievement motivation in relation to guilt and self-aggression

An unexpected pattern of findings was obtained with measures of guilt and self-aggression, which were administered to the subjects for quite different purposes. Table 5 shows the correlations in question.

by studying the relation between them and by examining their relations with other variables measured. The relations between the two measures are positive, but low. Between $nAch+$ and Q-ach+, $r = 0.10$ $(n = 200)$; between $nAch-$ and Q-ach-, $r = 0.17$ $(p < 0.05)$. Turning to the correlations with other variables, we find that the predictions about identification are best confirmed for Q-ach, as compared with $nAch$. On the other hand, the introjection predictions are best confirmed for $nAch-$. This

TABLE 5

Correlations Between Achievement Motivation, Guilt and Self-aggression

	$nAch+$	$nAch-$	Q-ach+		Q-ach-
Guilt (boys)	0.29* $(n = 59)$	−0.11	0.11	$(n = 198)$	0.25
(girls)	0.27 $(n = 39)$	−0.28	0.17	$(n = 197)$	0.19*
Self-aggression (boys)			0.40***	$(n = 86)$	0.35**
(girls)			0.42***	$(n = 106)$	0.49***
Intropunitive jokes (boys)			0.11	$(n = 42)$	0.18

Discussion

Validity of measures of achievement motivation

The projective measure of $nAch$ has previously been shown to be valid in the sense that scores can be increased by experimental arousal of the drive (McClelland *et al.*, 1949). On the other hand, studies of the association between $nAch$ and external measures, e.g. of performance at tasks or academic achievement with I.Q. held constant, have not consistently confirmed the validity of this measure. Another questionnaire measure—the achievement scales of the California Personality Inventory (Gough 1957)—was found to be a successful predictor of over-achievement in school and college, with I.Q. held constant.

Further light on the validity of these two kinds of measure can be provided

suggests that there may be different elements within achievement motivation, which have different socialization origins and ways of functioning.

The Introjection Hypothesis

The hypothesis is generally confirmed by the positive correlations with reported parental demands (Table 1), especially with $nAch$, though these are not at a high level of significance. The hypothesis is also supported by the correlation of 0.30 between $nAch-$ and super-ego demands. As mentioned above, the best results here in terms of satisfactory measures obtained, were found from students and it is possible that younger subjects would give better correlations. It is understandable that $nAch-$ should be acquired by means of this mechanism. Super-ego demands are commonly of a negative character, so it would follow that an avoidance drive would result. These demands are generally unconscious, and this explains why the drive should appear in nAch but not in Q-ach.

We also find that this mechanism is dependent on sufficient identification with or closeness to the parents: the correlations are higher if only those subjects who identify most with their parents are considered.

The Identification Hypothesis

Reported parental achievement has a generally positive relation with achievement motivation; this is particularly true of the same-sex parent, and in the case of boys and fathers, for Q-ach+. The results for parental identification are better for the most direct measures of identification, but the results are consistently positive for all measures and for most parent-child combinations. While the mother-son relation is weakest on the parental achievement relation, this is strengthened if only those high in maternal identification are considered. This confirms the idea that parental achievement is only effective if there is sufficient identification with the parent.

Achievement and self-aggression

The correlation consistently found with guilt and self-aggression was not predicted, so it remains to consider the explanation of this finding.

(a) Self-aggression may produce self-rejection and low self-evaluation, and lead to enhanced achievement efforts. If this were so, there should be a negative correlation between nAch and self-estimates of achievement. This however is not found. Similarly we should expect more self/ego-ideal conflict to go with high nAch. Such a relation was found by Martire (1956) for subjects

producing high nAch stories under both the aroused and relaxed conditions; we used only the relaxed condition and found no consistent relation here.

(b) If nAch− is due to punishment for failure, and if guilt feelings are also due to punishment, it would be expected that nAch− and guilt would be correlated. However, as Table 5 shows, it is nAch+ which has the higher correlation with guilt: this could conceivably be due to punishment for the *absence* of achievement producing both nAch+ and guilt.

(c) Guilt and self-aggression could be in part the result of low actual achievement in combination with a high nAch. We have seen that guilt is correlated with nAch; is it also correlated with low self-estimates of achievement? Our results show that it is consistently correlated in this way, in one sample reading −0.36 ($p < 0.01$). It looks as if this is the most likely of the three explanations offered.

Problems about the direction of causation

Our results all take the form of correlations between pairs of measures, where both measures were taken from the same subjects. Several distinct problems of interpretation arise. In the first place, the correlation may arise out of a shared 'response set', e.g. acquiescent subjects may tend to agree more strongly with all the items. This could not affect the projection test results, and it is difficult to see how the Q-ach scores could be affected by the same response set as the Semantic Differentials. Secondly there may be contamination between measures, i.e. one measure may affect the results on another, e.g. through a desire to appear consistent or via the arousal of some drive state. The projection test was always given first in order to avoid any inter-test influences on this very sensitive measure. However it is possible that people who really have a high *n*Ach tend to ascribe high achievement tendencies or demands to their parents as a further projective manifestation of the drive. McClelland *et al.* (1953, p. 276 f.) found that the correlations between parental attitudes and *n*Ach were the same when the former were estimated by the children or by a psychiatrist; however, no reports on achievement were included here.

A third possibility is that the correlations found are due to a different causal process from that hypothesized. For instance, children with high *n*Ach are thereby likely to have more successful parents. While this is obviously unlikely, it is possible that *n*Ach leads to greater parental identification when parents are themselves successful.

Conclusion

Five hundred grammar school children and others were given projective and questionnaire measures of achievement motivation as well as semantic differential or Q-sort tests to assess their relations with parents. Achievement motivation, especially as measured by projective test, was correlated with reported strength of parental achievement demands; the fear of failure component also correlated with reported super-ego demands for achievement.

Achievement motivation, especially as measured by questionnaire, was found to be correlated with the reported achievement tendencies of the same-sexed parent, and with identification with parents. Both processes were dependent on their being sufficient identification with parents.

Achievement motivation correlated with measures of guilt and self-aggression; since the latter also correlated with low self-ratings of achievement it was suggested that the guilt is produced by high motivation and low achievement in this sphere.

Summary: A review of previous investigations shows that achievement motivation can be produced by rewards and punishment in childhood only under special conditions not usually encountered. It is postulated that two other types of learning may also occur (*a*) the introjection of parental exhortation and standards, (*b*) identification with achievement-oriented parents and others. These hypotheses were tested in a correlational study of five hundred grammar school and other children. Achievement motivation was measured both by the content analysis of imaginative stories and by a questionnaire; relations with parents were obtained from a modified version of the semantic differential. Both hypotheses were confirmed, though both processes were found to work only when there was sufficient identification with parents. An additional finding was that achievement motivation was found to be correlated with various measures of self-aggression and guilt.

The Achievement Motive. New York: Appleton-Century-Crofts, Inc., 1953, Chapter 2, pp. 27–42, 67–75

The Affective Arousal Model of Motivation* ✓

David C. McClelland, John W. Atkinson, Russell A. Clark, and Edgar L. Lowell

Our reservations with respect to contemporary motivation theory have led us to attempt to rough out proposals for an alternative theory which may now or ultimately meet some of these objections and handle the data at least as well as the other models discussed. We are well aware of the incompleteness, as of this writing, of our theoretical thinking, but we will attempt to state our views as precisely and forcefully as we can in the hope that we can stimulate more serious discussion and experimental testing of motivational theory. At several points we will be obliged to present alternative hypotheses, since we do not as yet have the data to decide between them. But we agree with Hull and others that the only way to make progress in a field is "to stick one's neck out" and to state implicit theoretical assumptions as explicitly as possible.

Our definition of a motive is this: *A motive is the redintegration by a cue of a change in an affective situation.* The word *redintegration* in this definition is meant to imply previous learning. In our system, all motives are learned. The basic idea is simply this: Certain stimuli or situations involving discrepancies between expectation

(adaptation level) and perception are sources of primary, unlearned affect, either positive or negative in nature. Cues which are paired with these affective states, changes in these affective states, and the conditions producing them become capable of redintegrating a state (A') derived from the original affective situation (A), but not identical with it. To give a simple example, this means that if a buzzer is associated with eating saccharine the buzzer will in time attain the power to evoke a motive or redintegrate a state involving positive affective change. Likewise, the buzzer if associated with shock will achieve the power to redintegrate a negative affective state. These redintegrated states, which might be called respectively *appetite* and *anxiety,* are based on the primary affective situation but are not identical with it.

The term *change in affect* is used in two separate senses. It refers on the one hand to the fact that *at the time of arousal* of a motive, the effective state which is redintegrated must be different from the one already experienced by the organism, and on the other hand to the *possibility* that *at the time of acquisition* of a motive, the affective state with which the cue gets associated must be undergoing a change. We are agreed that a "change in affect" at the

* Reprinted by permission of Appleton-Century-Crofts.

time of arousal in the first sense must occur, but we see two possibilities on the acquisition side of the picture— one, that the association is with a *static* affective state; the other, that it is with a *changing* affective state. To elaborate this point further, the first alternative states simply that any cue associated with a situation producing affect will acquire the power to evoke a "model" of that situation (A') which will serve as a motive. The second alternative requires that the cue be associated with a *changing* state—of going from "shock" to "no shock" or from neutrality to pleasure, and so forth. The difference between the two possibilities is illustrated in the following diagram:

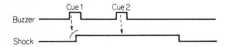

According to the first hypothesis, both cue 1 and cue 2 should be capable of evoking an avoidance motive, since they have both been paired with the affective state arising from shock. According to the second, alternative hypothesis, cue 2 should have weak or nonexistent motivating power since it has not been associated with a *change* in affect. It should be possible to determine which of these alternatives is correct by experimentation along these lines. Finally, it should be repeated that both hypotheses assume that the redintegrated affect *at the time of arousal* must represent a change over the present affective state of the organism.

In the discussion so far there has been some ambiguity as to just what is redintegrated—the affective state or change, the conditions which produced it, or both. Actually, the ambiguity

reflects some uncertainty as to which alternative is correct and also some difficulty in expressing simply exactly what happens. By far the most likely possibility is that both the situation *and* the affect it produces are redintegrated. Thus the redintegrated "situation" defines the goal in the usual sense (e.g., sugar in the mouth), and the redintegrated "affect" (e.g., reaction to the sugar in the mouth) determines whether the goal is motivating or not. For the sake of simplicity, phrases like redintegrated "affective state" or "affective change" are used throughout this chapter to refer both to the affective reaction itself and the situation which produced it.

Two main questions connected with the concept of redintegrated affective state still remain to be answered. Why, first of all, should we have decided to base motives on affect? Secondly, how are we to determine the existence of affective arousal? It will be difficult to do complete justice to these questions, but a word on each may help indicate the progress of our thinking.

Why Affect as a Basis for Motives?

We have decided to base motives on affective arousal, following Young's lead (1949) for several reasons. In the first place, it seems apparent that the motive concept will be useful only if it has some kind of a limited base. That is, if all associations are motivating, then there seems no particular reason to introduce the concept of motivation to apply to a particular subclass of association. Thus the associations involved in forming motives must be in some way different from other types of associations. And we have chosen affective states as the basis for motives rather than biological needs or strong stimuli because of the limitations of those concepts already discussed. A more positive reason for choosing affective states as primary is that they are "obviously" important in controlling behavior, at least at the common-sense level. The hedonic or pleasure-pain view of motivation is certainly one of the oldest in psychological thinking and can be traced at least to Plato's *Protagoras*. Furthermore, in order to get motives in the laboratory we commonly pair cues with affective states resulting from shock, saccharine in the mouth, food deprivation, and the like. Operationally we manipulate states which we know subjectively will produce pleasure and pain when we work with motives.

Another reason for choosing affect as the basis for motives rather than tissue needs, etc., is the overwhelming evidence for the importance of selective sensitivity in guiding and directing behavior in lower animals. Tinbergen (1951) has collected dozens of cases which illustrate how special stimuli are required to release a particular "consummatory" response particularly in submammalian species. Young (1949) has repeatedly called attention to the different palatability of various foods for the white rat. Weiner and Stellar (1951) have demonstrated unlearned salt preferences in the rat. And so forth. The list could easily be extended. The usual reaction by theorists to these facts is to assume that they are not characteristic of the human animal, which is obviously much more dependent on learning than on innate reactions to particular "releasing" stimuli. The difference is nicely highlighted by Ford and Beach (1951), who show how human sexual behavior is much less dependent than the behavior of lower animals on particular external signs and internal hormonal conditions.

But all of this seems no reason to assume a sharp discontinuity between man and other animals with respect to the factors controlling behavior. Rather we have been struck by the possibility that man's behavior may also be guided by selective sensitivity to particular kinds of situations. The difference may be one of degree rather than kind. With man the "releasing" situations may be much less specific than the dot on a gull's beak which releases pecking behavior of a gull chick, but they may exist just the same (see Chapter 5). And the consummatory reactions elicited by such situations may also be much less specific and rigid than the pecking, fighting, courting responses shown in lower animals; in fact, the interesting possibility pursued here is that in man these specific overt reactions to "releasing" stimuli are attenuated and occur instead as diffuse reactions of the autonomic nervous system signifying what we usually call "affect." Thus our motivational system for man has been constructed to parallel the analysis of instinctive behavior in lower animals made by Tinbergen (1951) and others. Certain types of situations (see Chapter 6) innately release reactions which are diffuse and covert in man rather than specific and overt, but which are consummatory in the same sense in that they ultimately exhaust themselves. These diffuse reactions are what we mean by affect, and they can be observed either through verbal reports and autonomic reactions, or inferred from approach and avoidance behavior, as we shall see in the next section. Man's advantage over lower animals lies precisely in the wider range of situations which will produce affect and in the lack of overt specificity of the affective reaction. Thus he can build a wide variety of motives on a much broader base, but to our mind it is essentially the same base as that which is responsible for guiding and directing the behavior of lower animals.

Behavioral Effects of Affective Arousal

But how do we propose to define pleasure and pain or affective arousal? We certainly do not intend to fall into the trap of arguing that pleasurable sensations are those that lead to survival, and painful ones those that ultimately lead to maladaptation and death. This answer lands us back in the same difficulties that face the biological need theory of motivation. Let us first attempt to define affect by anchoring it on the behavioral side. It might seem more logical to consider first the antecedent conditions of affect (see Chapter 6) rather than its behavioral consequences, but the behavioral approach is more familiar because it is the one that has been customarily employed in attempts to measure affect or pleasure and pain (cf. Lindsley, 1951). Thus, at a certain gross level, one can distinguish affective states from other states by the effects of autonomic activity—changes in respiration rate, in electrical skin resistance, in blood pressure, and the like. Thus one might initially state as a generalization that an affective state is present whenever the *PGR* shows a significant deflection, and that anyone who wants to establish a motive can simply pair cues with such deflections or the conditions which produced them. Autonomic accompaniments of emotions

may not be perfect indexes of their presence, but they are sufficiently good to provide a very practical basis for deciding in a large number of cases that affective arousal has occurred.

Since autonomic measures apparently cannot be used at the present time to distinguish sensitively between positive and negative affective states, we will need to attack this problem in some other way. There are several possibilities. Among humans, expressive movements can readily be interpreted as indicating pleasant or unpleasant feeling states, particularly facial expressions (Schlosberg, 1952). Impromptu vocalizing seems also to be a good indicator of mood. Probably the most sensitive and frequently used index to hedonic tone is verbal behavior. If the person says "I dislike it," "I'm unhappy," or "it hurts," we take it as a sign of negative affect. If he says "I feel good," or "I like it," we take it as a sign of positive affect. One difficulty with these expressive signs is that they are not infallible. They can all be "faked," or changed by learning.

And what about animals? They can't talk, it would be difficult to try to interpret the facial expression of a rat or an elephant, and no one has made a careful study of animal vocalization patterns in response to pleasure and pain. In the case of some animals, certain innate response patterns are readily interpreted as signifying positive or negative affect—e.g., purring or spitting in the cat; licking, tail-wagging, or growling in the dog, and so on. More attention should be given to the study of the expressive signs of affect, but until it is, we must be satisfied with stopgap measures. Probably the most useful of these with adult animals is simple preference or approach behavior in contrast to avoidance behavior.

Sometimes there are reflex responses that are clearly approach or avoidance in nature—e.g., sucking, grasping, swallowing, spitting, vomiting, blinking—and in some instances they may provide direct evidence of positive or negative affective arousal. That is, eye-blinking in response to a puff of air, if accompanied by an autonomic response, would give evidence that affect was present and that this affect was negative in nature. Cues paired with the air puff would in time come to elicit an avoidance motive (as indicated by the presence of an avoidance *response*—the conditional or anticipatory eye-blink). But since reflexes are few in number and sometimes hard to classify as approach or avoidance (e.g., the knee jerk), better evidence for the existence of affective arousal is to be found in *learned* approach and avoidance behavior (locomotor, manual, verbal). There is an apparent circularity here, because what we are saying is that we can tell whether affective arousal occurred only after the organism has learned an approach or avoidance response in the service of a motive. Are we not first making a motive dependent on affective arousal and then saying we can find out whether affective arousal occurred if a motive has been formed which leads to approach or avoidance behavior? The answer is "Yes, we are," but the argument is not completely circular (cf. Meehl, 1950). Thus in one experiment we can determine that salty water leads to learned approach or preference behavior in the rat and we can then *infer* from this that it produes positive affective arousal. This inference (that salty water "tastes good" to the rat) can then be used as the basis for new learning experiments, theorizing,

and so on. In this way we can gradually build up classes of objects, situations, response categories, or sensations which must produce affective arousal and then try to generalize as to what they have in common, as we have in Chapter 6. In brief, the notion here is to use autonomic responses to indicate the presence of affect and approach and avoidance (either learned or reflex) to distinguish positive from negative affect.

There is one misconception which may arise in connection with this definition that it is well to anticipate, however. The terms *approach* and *avoidance* must not be understood simply as "going towards" or "away from" a stimulus in a spatial sense. Thus "rage," when it goes over into attack, is an "avoidance" response, even though it involves "going towards" something. *Avoidance* must be defined in terms of its objective—to discontinue, remove, or escape from a certain type of stimulation and not in terms of its overt characteristics. Attack has, as its objective, removal of the source of stimulation in the same sense that withdrawal does. *Approach* must also be defined functionally—i.e., it is any activity, the objective of which is to continue, maintain, or pursue a certain kind of stimulation. Because of the ambiguity involved in using these terms, it might be better to substitute others like *stimulus enhancement* or *stimulus reduction,* but approach and avoidance have the advantage of common usage and if it is understood that they are used in a functional sense, difficulties should not arise in using them as the primary means of defining positive and negative affect on the response side. It is perhaps worth noting that Dearborn (1889) and Corwin (1921) came to the same decision long ago after recording involuntary "pursuit" (extension) and "withdrawal" (flexion) movements to pleasant and unpleasant stimuli, respectively.

DISTINGUISHING THE EFFECTS OF AFFECT AND MOTIVE

Analytically speaking, there are three events involved in the development of a motive, any of which may have observable and distinguishable behavioral effects. In order of occurrence, they are:

A. The situation producing affect

B. Redintegration of (A)

C. Response learned to (B)

We have discussed the problem of measuring the behavioral effects of A in the previous section. How can the effects of A and B be distinguished, if at all? The simplest assumption would seem to be the one that Hull made years ago (1931), to the effect that a cue paired with a goal response will evoke a fractional anticipatory portion of it. The notion behind this is that the redintegrated response is like the original but fractional in nature, that is, consisting of a portion of the total goal response which is perhaps less in intensity or duration. The difficulty with this idea has been discussed at some length by Mowrer (1950). In general, the objection is similar to the one made against the substitution hypothesis in conditioning experiments. That is, formerly it was commonly assumed that in conditioning the conditioned stimulus simply substituted for the unconditioned stimulus in evoking the unconditioned response. But, as Hilgard and Marquis (1940) point out, the conditioned response is in fact often quite different from the unconditioned response. It is not necessarily a miniature replica or fractional portion of the original unconditioned response. For example, there is evidence that the normal response in rats to the primary affective state produced by shock is squealing, defecating, and intense variable behavior, whereas the normal response to anticipation of shock (e.g., to fear) is different, probably crouching (Arnold, 1945). The evidence that crouching is the normal response to fear is not conclusive, as Brown and Jacobs (1949) point out, because it can be eliminated by certain experimental procedures; but the probability is still fairly great that the response to fear differs in important ways from the response to shock. Therefore it would seem unwise at this state of our knowledge to assume that the fear response is just a partial copy of the shock response. At the phenomenological level, it seems that shock produces two distinguishable response elements—pain, which is the immediate reaction to shock, and fear, which is the anticipatory redintegration of the pain response. These two responses are clearly different. That is, if one's teeth are hurt by drilling in the dentist's chair, the sight of the chair may evoke a subjective feeling we label fear, but it does not evoke a "fractional" pain in the teeth.

When we consider the third event in the sequence of motive formation—namely, the responses learned to the redintegrated affect—the picture becomes even more complex. Our position is that the genotypic responses to redintegrated positive or negative affect are "functional" aproach or avoidance. Thus from avoidance we can infer that negative affect has occurred if we lack a direct independent response definition of negative affect. But at the phenotypical level, the responses learned to redintegrated negative or positive affect may be very varied. A rat can be trained to run at as well as away from a shock (Gwinn, 1949). Rage and fear are genotypically avoidance responses, but phenotypically the former involves approach and the latter withdrawal. Similarly, love and contempt or scorn are genotypically similar in that they both involve attempts to maintain a source of stimulation, but phenotypically love involves "going towards" an object and scorn involves "keeping your distance" from the scorned object. A classification of emotions on a pleasant-unpleasant dimension and on an attentive-rejective one succeeds in ordering satisfactorily nearly all the facial expressions of emotion, according to Schlosberg (1952), a fact which tends to confirm our position that one must distinguish basically between positive and negative affect on the one hand and learned reactions to it, however classified, on the other. If the learned reactions are classified as to whether they phenotypically involve "going towards" or "away from" something, as they were approximately on Schlosberg's attentive-rejective dimension, then one gets a fourfold table in which Love, Contempt, Rage, and Fear represent the four major types of emotional reactions.

But obviously such classifications of phenotypic reactions can vary tremendously. The important points to keep in mind theoretically are (1) that they are surface modes of reaction with two basic objectives—to approach or maintain pleasure and to avoid or reduce pain, and (2) that they are acquired and hence take time to develop and show characteristic individual differences.

MEASURING MOTIVES THROUGH THEIR EFFECTS

The fact that the learned reactions to motives may vary so much suggests that it may be difficult to identify motives through their effects. The first problem is to decide at what point the stream of behavior indicates the presence of a motive. It may be helpful to begin the analysis with a simple case in which the behavior produced by affect can be distinguished from that which reflects the subsequent redintegration of affect. Consider the startle reaction (Landis and Hunt, 1939). A pistol shot produces varied autonomic and reflex effects which are signs of affective arousal. The fact that this arousal is negative can be inferred after the long latency "voluntary" avoidance responses appear which are signs of an avoidance motive cued off by the shot or its "startle" effects because of the former association of such cues with negative affect. A necessary inference from this is that the first time startle is elicited (as perhaps in the Moro reflex in infants), it should not produce the longer latency co-ordinated avoidance behavior which Landis and Hunt observed in adults.

This suggests that one of the important ways in which motivated behavior may be identified is in terms of the *coordination* of responses or in terms of some kind of a response *sequence,* which terminates when the organism arrives somewhere with respect to a source of affect. The terms *approach* and *avoidance* imply a sequence of responses which has a *goal*—e.g., arriving at or away from a situation producing affect. The general definition is "goal-oriented free choice with habit and situational factors controlled." Under this we have placed approach and avoidance behavior, the only criterion one can use with animals, and the choice of certain "classes of goal-oriented thoughts" for inclusion in fantasy, the criterion we have used in measuring achievement motivation. These criteria are similar in implying choice responses with respect to a goal. We mean by the term *goal* here the same thing we meant earlier when we were distinguishing between genotypic and phenotypic approach and avoidance, between the functional significance of an act (e.g., avoiding a stimulus) and the modality of the act itself (which may involve attacking the stimulus). The goal is the functional significance of the act. Let us be more specific. Any response an animal makes involves choice in a sense. Any succession of responses also involves co-ordination in the sense of alternation of effector pathways, and so on. But only when the succession becomes a sequence which results in approach to or avoidance of a situation can we argue that there is evidence for the existence of a motive.

In dealing with verbal responses in a story the problem is simpler. Many thoughts (e.g., "the boy is happy") indicate the presence of affect, but only those thoughts chosen for inclusion which imply affect in connection with a particular situation are evidence for the existence of a motive (e.g., "the boy wants to do a good job"). In this example, "wanting to do a good job" defines an end situation which would produce positive affect (see below), and the fact that the subject chooses to include such a statement is taken as evidence that he is motivated for achievement. That is, he has made a "goal-oriented" choice by making a statement about an achievement situation ("good

job") which would inferentially produce positive affect (the boy "wants" it). Thus with such a measure of motivation we do not need the evidence of a co-ordinated though perhaps variable sequence of responses with a certain end, since the end ("good job") is directly stated, and it is this end state, with its accompanying affect rather than mere co-ordination, which seems to be the necessary criterion for deciding that behavior is showing evidence of the existence of motivation.

In short, in verbal behavior the "redintegrated affective situation" may be reflected directly and need not be inferred from a sequence of responses signifying approach and avoidance.

But why in the definition do we insist on "free" choice with certain factors controlled? The argument runs like this. Since general locomotor approach and avoidance are learned so early and so well in the life history of the organism, they can be utilized in normal animals to test the strength of a motivational association, provided the testing situation is a "free" one—provided the rats' "habits" are normal and provided the situation is a normal one for the rat. That is, it would be fair to test for the existence and strength of a rat's hunger motive by measuring the number of times he runs toward food as compared with other objects when placed on an open table top, provided his past experience has been normal." But obviously if his past experience has not been normal—if he has lived in a vertical cage with no chance to walk in a horizontal dimension, if he has never had the opportunity to connect the sight of food with certain affective states (taste, reduction in hunger pangs), if he has been taught to run only when mildly hungry and to sit when very hungry—

then the situation will not give a "fair" measure of his hunger motive. The number of times he ends up in the vicinity of the food could still be recorded in such cases, but it might be a measure of things other than hunger. It would measure hunger according to our argument if, and only if, it made use of a highly overlearned response (i.e., a "normal" habit) in a situation which did not clearly evoke incompatible responses (i.e., a "normal" situation).

In a sense, this is fairly similar to the state of affairs when a human being is telling a story in response to a picture. That is, for most subjects putting thoughts into words or verbalizing is a highly overlearned response. Furthermore, in the fantasy situation no particular set of responses is supposed to be perceived as especially appropriate. Fantasy is a "free" response situation, provided the picture is not too structured. It might not be for a certain class of persons, for professional writers, for example, because they may have learned a particular set of responses to use in such a situation, just as the rats who have been trained to sit still when hungry have learned a particular set of responses which prevent us from measuring their motivation in the usual way. But except for professional authors, individuals should have no particular set of verbal response tendencies which seem appropriate because of past experience with such situations. In contrast, if we ask a subject if he would like to get a good grade in a course, the fact that he answers "yes" is of no particular significance for diagnosing his achievement motivation, because we can assume that he will have learned that this is an appropriate response to such a question. Here the social reality or the modal cultural pattern determines his response. It is just for this reason that we prefer pictures which are not so structured as to elicit one particular response by common social agreement. We want the restraints on the free choice of responses by the subject reduced to a certain necessary minimum.

Furthermore, the fantasy situation is "free" because the testing conditions do not place any external constraints on the responses which are possible. Thus the subject can write about anything— about killing someone, committing suicide, touring the South Seas on a pogo stick, having an illegitimate child, and so forth. Anything is symbolically possible. Thus the choice of response patterns is not limited by what can be done under the conditions in which the motive strength is to be tested. Here our measure of human motivation has a great advantage over measures of animal motivation, but in both cases the problem is the same: to minimize or know the situational and habit determinants of behavior. This position fits into the general theoretical framework described elsewhere by McClelland (1951) in which he argues that behavior is determined by situational (perceptual) factors, by habit (memory) factors, and by motivational factors. It follows that if one wants a particular response to reflect motivation primarily, the strength of the other two determinants must either be known, minimized, or randomized. In the elementary state of our present knowledge, the best procedure would appear to be to use highly overlearned responses in "free" situations. There is, therefore, some theoretical justification for our empirical finding that motives can be measured effectively in imagination

The Acquisition of Motives

Now that we have considered the possible antecedent conditions for affective arousal (see McClelland & Clark, 1953, as reprinted in Chapter 5), what about the parallel problem of the antecedent conditions for motive formation? By our definition of a motive, the solution to this problem is straightforward. A motive is formed by pairing cues with affective arousal or with the conditions, just discussed, that produce affective arousal. These cues may be unconnected with affective arousal or they may be response-produced cues resulting from affective arousal. That is, the following sequence of events may occur:

cies between expectations and perceptions. A motive is the learned result of pairing cues with affect or the conditions which produce affect.

THE ACQUISITION OF MOTIVES OF DIFFERENT STRENGTH

Since motives are learned, the conditions for their acquisition that we must consider are largely those which are traditionally called the "laws of learning." That is, the strength of a motivational association should be a function of the same factors, such as contiguity, which have been assumed to govern the strength of any association. But what exactly is meant by the term *strength*

Large discrepancy⟶ Negative⟶ Autonomic⟶ Distinctive--→ Avoidance
from AL   affect   response   cues   motive

The first three links in this chain are unlearned (as indicated by solid arrows), but the last link is a learned association (as indicated by a broken arrow) based on previous pairings of such autonomic cues with negative affect. Thus the cues for setting off a motivational association may lie in the behavioral effects of the affect itself. Take Hebb's half-grown chimpanzees, for example. The sight of a detached plaster head produces negative affect that leads to diffuse autonomic responses which have been associated with negative affect in the past and which consequently evoke fear (the redintegrated portion of negative affect). Fear in turn elicits coordinated avoidance responses which continue until the situation which touched off the sequence changes—e.g., until the head is out of sight or if that is impossible, until the animal "adapts" to it.

But the main point is that affect is the innate result of certain discrepan-

of a motive? At least three meanings can be distinguished. Strength may refer to the likelihood or *probability* that a motive will be aroused by a particular cue; it may refer to the *intensity* of the motive once aroused; or it may refer to the pervasiveness or *extensity* of the motive, by which is meant the variety of circumstaces under which it will appear. Table 1 has been prepared to summarize very briefly the different variables which we believe will influence these three aspects of motive strength and also the response variables by which these aspects of motive strength may be most conveniently measured. The sequence across the table from antecedent variable to hypothetical construct to response variable is not exact or exclusive. Thus "rate of affective change" almost certainly influences motive intensity as well as motive dependability.

Most of the variables in the table are fairly self-explanatory and are drawn

TABLE 1

MOTIVE STRENGTH AS A HYPOTHETICAL CONSTRUCT CONCEIVED AS VARYING
IN THREE DIMENSIONS, EACH OF WHICH IS DETERMINED PRIMARILY
BY CERTAIN ANTECEDENT VARIABLES AND MEASURED PRIMARILY
BY CERTAIN RESPONSE VARIABLES

Antecedent variables *influencing*	*Dimensions of MOTIVE STRENGTH*	*as reflected in the most relevant* response variables
Frequency of association of cue with affective change contiguity between cue and affective change Rate of affective change	Motive *Dependability*	Probability that a choice response will occur per unit time
Amplitude of affective change	Motive *Intensity*	Intensity of the choice response (Response amplitude, number of *R*'s per unit time, latency or speed of *R*)
Variety of cues connected with affective change	Motive *Extensity*	Variety of cues eliciting *R* or resistance of choice response to extinction

with one or two exceptions from prevailing theories of the factors which influence learning. Probably the simplest way to explain how they are all supposed to operate is to choose an hypothetical example which will illustrate each of them in turn. Let us take a frog as our experimental animal and place him in a water-filled container which is equipped with a platform onto which he can jump if he wants to. Let us further suppose that pouring hot water on a frog will evoke a negative affective change. Leaving aside for a moment the problem of how the frog acquired the instrumental response necessary for avoidance, we can further assume that the goal-oriented choice response we will be interested in observing here is whether or not he jumps out of the water onto the platform. As a conditioned stimulus we may use anything to which he is sensitive, say a light touch on the head. Now we begin

the conditioning procedure and pair the touch on the head with a "shot" of hot water. The first two antecedent variables in the table are the familiar conditioning variables, which state simply that the more frequently the cue (touch) is paired with the affective change (produced by hot water) and the more contiguous the association, the greater the probability that the motive will be aroused, as can be demonstrated by the greater frequency of the avoidance response of jumping onto the platform for a given number of taps on the head. The third variable, *rate of affective change,* is, on the other hand, a relatively unfamiliar one, although it has been used by Gwinn (1949) to explain certain effects of punishment in rats. What it states is that if the temperature in the water is changed slowly so that the affective change is spread out over time, it will produce a less dependable affective association. Or to turn this statement around, the more rapid the affective change, the more effective it is in producing a motivational association. There is little evidence that we know of which supports the importance of this variable directly, although it has seemed to us to follow logically from some of our other assumptions. That is, a slow change in water temperature would presumably raise the adaptation level so that the temperature increase from beginning to end would provide less discrepancy from AL at any given moment, and hence less negative affect, than would the same increase over a shorter period of time. By this interpretation, rate of change reduces to a special case of amplitude of the affective change, the next variable to be considered. That is, the more rapid the change, the greater the affect; and the greater the affect, the stronger the motive. Rate of change may also exert an influence indirectly through its effect on contiguity. Often the initial change in affect (as produced by an increase in temperature) provides cues that get associated by contiguity with further changes in affect (discomfort from the heat), but if the connection has been noncontiguous, as in slow changes in temperature, it will provide a more imperfect means of eliciting anticipatory negative affect.

The *amplitude of affective change* in our frog experiment could be controlled not only by rate of change but more simply by varying the temperature of the hot water. The assumption is that up to a certain point the hotter the water, the more vigorous would be the response to the conditioned stimulus (touch). The vigor of the response could be measured by the number of responses made per unit time (if he were blocked from escaping),

by the latency of the avoidance response, by its speed, or by the strength of pull against a thread attached to some kind of recording instrument.

Our fifth variable, the variety of cues connected with affective change, also represents something of a new emphasis. The reason for its inclusion becomes quite apparent in the light of some recent studies by V. F. Sheffield (1949) and by McClelland and McGown (1953). These authors were interested in explaining why it was that extinction takes longer after partial reinforcement during learning. Both researches come to the conclusion that the reason for the delay in extinction is that some of the cues present during extinction were also present during acquisition in the partially reinforced group, namely, those cues resulting from non-reinforcement. This can be interpreted further as follows. It means in effect that the greater the similarity between the cues in the extinction and the acquisition conditions, the longer the extinction will take because the animal will find it harder to distinguish between extinction and acquisition conditions. In the ordinary learning experiment, where the animal has received 100 per cent reinforcement or reward, he is commonly extinguished under conditions of zero reinforcement. This constitutes such a major change in stimulating conditions that he can discriminate the difference without too much difficulty and learn that a different response is appropriate under such markedly changed conditions. But the perceptual difference between 50 per cent reinforcement in learning and zero reinforcement in extinction is not so large, and the animal should therefore take longer to make the discrimination and learn not to respond in extinction. To generalize this example a little, we can state that *the greater the variety of cues to which a response is attached, the harder it will be to extinguish it completely,* because the more difficult it will be to reinstate all the original cues and extinguish the response to them. Therefore, the more varied or irregular the conditions of acquisition, the more generalized the association will be and the harder it will be to extinguish it by any specific non-reinforcement. In our hypothetical frog experiment there are a number of ways in which the cue conditions during acquisition could be varied. We could use different conditioned stimuli (light and sound as well as touch); we could *vary* the time between the conditioned stimulus and unconditioned stimulus (hot water); we could sometimes fail to introduce the hot water after the conditioned stimulus (partial reinforcement), and so on. A rough measure of the generalized nature or extensity of the affective association is *the number of trials* it takes the animal to give up making the avoidance response completely when any particular conditioned stimulus is presented repeatedly without the unconditioned stimulus. That is, the more general the association, the harder it should be for the animal to discriminate the new situation (extinction) from the old (acquisition). So he should take more trials to extinguish. In passing it should be noted that, since "trials to extinction" measures primarily, though not exclusively, the *extensity* aspect of motive strength, it may not give exactly the same results as measures of other aspects of motive strength, such as strength of pull, latency, speed, and so forth.

Another, perhaps more direct, test of extensity of an association would be to explore the limits of the generalization gradients from some particular conditioned stimulus. Thus, one could certainly predict that the generalization gradients would be much wider for animals trained under a variety of conditions than those trained very regularly with a particular stimulus of a particular intensity, and so on.

These three aspects of motive strength are of great importance at the human level. We expect to find with further research that there are some subjects whose achievement motive is aroused by a great variety of cues. Other subjects may have achievement motives which are aroused only by very specific situations (e.g., playing cards, winning at football, making feminine conquests). People will also vary in the intensity as well as the extensity of their motives. Some will have an intense desire to succeed at cards, others only a mild desire in this area but an intense desire to get good grades in a course. It should be possible to plot for each individual a graph which would show the intensity of his achievement motive or achievement *interest,* in each of several different areas. Our present measure of n Achievement represents a kind of averaging out of these two variables so as to obtain one index for each person. Motive dependability is in a sense the primary aspect of strength, since a motive must be first aroused before its intensity and extensity can be measured. The best measure here seems to be the regularity with which a given cue, if repeated over and over again, will give rise to the achievement motive. Thus we might find some subjects who wanted to win at cards all the time; others only part of the time and some not at all. On the face of it, there seems no reason to assume that this variable is perfectly correlated with intensity. It is at least logically possible that a subject who is only occasionally aroused might, if aroused, show a very strong achievement motive. Conversely, a person who is always aroused by a particular situation might be aroused at a relatively low level of intensity. To sum up, we expect to be able to measure independently at the human level the three aspects of motive strength theoretically distinguished here—e.g., dependability, intensity, and extensity. Motives also differ in kind as well as in strength of course (see below), so that the complete description of a motive will have four dimensions—quality (goal or scoring definition), extensity, intensity, and dependability.

Types of Affective Change and Types of Motives

As previously indicated, it is possible to distinguish two aspects of motives based on whether the choice response made involves approach or avoidance. These two types of behavior seem sufficiently different to warrant speaking of two different aspects of motivation. For one thing, Miller (1944), Clark (1952), and others have commonly assumed that approach and avoidance gradients differ markedly in slope. For another, we have found fairly convincing evidence in our own data for two aspects of the achievement motive, one of which seems characterized by defensiveness and a fear of failure, the other by increased instrumental striving and hope of success. Finally, if we consider the way in which motives are supposed to be learned, some should be acquired under circumstances in which pleasure results from successful achievement, whereas others should be acquired under circumstances in which negative affect results from failure.

In addition to these two basic aspects of motivation, there is at least the logical possibility of two other types which would result from other kinds of affective change. Thus the two types we have already mentioned might be thought of as resulting primarily from first, an increase in pleasure (an approach motive) and, second, from an increase in pain (an avoidance motive). But, at least theoretically, cues may also be associated with a decrease in pain or with a decrease in pleasure. One would expect the former to lead to approach behavior and the latter to avoidance behavior of a sort. At the present writing, however, there is very little evidence for the existence of either of these aspects of motivation, despite the current popularity of the notion that stimulus reduction is particularly important in motivation theory. Thus in a preliminary experiment Lee (1951) has shown that a cue paired with *onset* of shock will lead to intense avoidance behavior when presented in a new situation, whereas a cue associated with *offset* of shock will not lead to approach behavior, as it should, but to a somewhat less intense avoidance behavior. It may be that reduction in shock gains its apparent "rewarding" effect because it removes cues arousing an avoidance motive and not because it is in itself a positive goal. In common-sense language, a rat may learn to run off a charged grid not because the "safety box" attracts him (approach motive) but because the grid cues off an avoidance or fear motive which is no longer cued off in the safety box so that he stops running when he gets there. On the whole, however, further exploration of motives based on *decreases* in affective states is definitely called for.

Psychological Review, 1963, vol. 70, pp. 500–515

Mowrer's Revised Two-Factor Theory and the Motive-Expectancy-Value Model[1]

N. T. Feather

In two recent volumes Mowrer (1960a, 1960b) has presented a major revision of his original two-factor theory. The main aim of the present paper is to show how certain basic concepts in this revised two-factor theory, viz., *fear, hope, relief,* and *disappointment,* can be reinterpreted in terms of a model which involves the concepts of motive, expectation, and incentive value (Feather, 1959a). It will be argued that this model provides an alternative conceptualization to Mowrer's theory with differential testable implications.

In his original two-factor theory Mowrer (1947) distinguished between *solution* or instrumental learning and *sign* learning or conditioning. Solution learning applied to the learning of instrumental habits, and sign learning to the learning of fears. Mowrer assumed that the habits formed in solution learning were strengthened by reward, that this type of learning was mediated by the action of the central nervous system, and that it involved the skeletal musculature. In contrast, the learning of fears (or sign learning) was assumed to proceed by a principle of contiguity, to be mediated by the action of the autonomic nervous system, and to involve the glands and smooth muscles.

[1] I am indebted to R. P. McDonald for his helpful comments and suggestions about this paper.

This latter type of learning permitted an interpretation of the effects of punishment on behavior, not in terms of a weakening of habits (cf., early Thorndike) but rather as involving the conditioning of fear. Adjustments of the organism were then assumed to be in the direction of fear reduction. Mowrer argued that, in *passive* avoidance learning, the fear which was conditioned to *response-correlated* stimuli resulted in conflict and, if intense enough, in response inhibition. In *active* avoidance learning the organism was assumed to reduce fear elicited by *external* stimulation by active avoidance of the situation.

Revised two-factor theory (Mowrer, 1960a, 1960b) is in a sense, more unified than the original two-factor theory in that it no longer involves a distinction between sign learning and solution learning. In this new theory *all* learning is sign learning, and solution learning is a derivative thereof. Mowrer still refers to his theory as two-factored, however, because he assumes that there are two types of reinforcement, viz., incremental or drive induction (the type of reinforcement involved in punishment) and decremental or drive reduction (the type of reinforcement involved in reward). The focus of the revised theory is on the learning of *emotions.* Mowrer's interest in the conditioning of emotions is now broadened, and conditioned hopes and fears become the basic concepts in discussing the effects of rewards and punishments on behavior. The emotions of relief and disappointment also play important roles in the revised theory.

The distinctions made by Mowrer between his concepts of fear, hope, relief, and disappointment are perhaps best represented in terms of a conditioning situation which involves a signal or conditioned stimulus (CS) and a shock or unconditioned stimulus (UCS). Shock onset is assumed to elicit pain and the emotional response of fear. After frequent pairings in which the CS overlaps the onset of shock, the signal is converted into a "danger signal" and the subject is able to react with fear before shock onset, i.e., fear becomes anticipatory. The emotional response called "relief" occurs when the danger signal is terminated and there is no shock onset. Relief corresponds to reduction in the conditioned fear, and is referred to by Mowrer as secondary reinforcement Type 1. It is apparent that both fear and relief are closely associated with the stage of conditioning involving shock *onset*. In contrast, both hope and disappointment are more closely associated with the stage of conditioning in-

volving shock *offset*. Shock offset is accompanied by a subsiding of the emotional upset, or fear reduction. With frequent pairings in which the CS overlaps shock offset, the signal is converted into a "safety signal" and the subject is able to react with reduction in fear before the offset of the shock, i.e., fear reduction becomes anticipatory. Mowrer calls this anticipatory response "hope," and maintains that hope is the basis of secondary reinforcement Type 2. Disappointment corresponds to a recrudescence of fear (or helplessness) when the safety signal is terminated and there is no shock offset. In summary, fear is elicited when the danger signal is on, and relief occurs when the danger signal is removed. Hope is elicited when the safety signal is on, and disappointment occurs when the safety signal is removed. In the conditioning paradigm considered, fear and relief, and hope and disappointment, relate to different stages in the temporal sequence of events, viz., shock onset and shock offset, respectively.· These similarities and differences in the four emotions, in relation to the conditioning paradigm, are presented in Table 1.

It is apparent from Table 1 that secondary decremental reinforcement, or reduction in learned fear, is common to

TABLE 1

MOWRER'S CONCEPTS OF FEAR, HOPE, RELIEF, AND DISAPPOINTMENT IN RELATION TO A CONDITIONING PARADIGM

	Danger signal prior to shock onset	Safety signal prior to shock offset
Onset of signal	*Fear* Increase in learned fear Secondary punishment, Type 1 Anticipatory	*Hope* Decrease in learned fear Secondary reinforcement, Type 2 Anticipatory
Offset of signal	*Relief* Decrease in learned fear Secondary reinforcement, Type 1 Not anticipatory	*Disappointment* Increase in learned fear Secondary punishment, Type 2 Not anticipatory

the emotions of relief and hope. In contrast, secondary incremental reinforcement, or increase in learned fear, is common to the emotions of fear and disappointment. Mowrer's revised two-factor theory is, therefore, *basically fear-centered*. Each of the four emotions involves a change in the strength of fear. In the case of fear and hope this change is anticipatory whereas for relief and disappointment the change is not anticipatory. The analysis also indicates that while fear and relief may occur in the absence of the primary, noxious event, i.e., shock, both hope and disappointment imply the presence of the primary noxious event. Finally, we should note that Mowrer extends the above form of analysis to situations involving the appetitional drives of hunger and thirst, where hunger fear and thirst fear are assumed to be important variables.

As in the original two-factor theory, fear is assumed to mediate passive avoidance learning when conditioned to response-correlated stimuli and active avoidance learning when conditioned to independent, external stimuli. Hope, or anticipated fear reduction, is now regarded as the basis of habit. Mowrer argues that when hope is conditioned to response-correlated stimuli it "feeds back" to facilitate the response. When hope is conditioned to independent, external stimuli, it is assumed to mediate approach behavior. Revised two-factor theory therefore accounts for the effects of rewards and punishments on behavior not in terms of a strengthening or weakening of associations, but rather as involving the facilitating and inhibiting effects on responses of conditioned hope and conditioned fear. As stated by Estes (1962), ". . . the overt behavior is appropriately modified by the type of emotion it leads to, the organism tending to continue behaviors that give rise to hope and desist from those that give rise to fear [p. 118]."

Mowrer (1960b, p. 320) considers that revised two-factor theory has perhaps its "closest approximation" in Tolman's conception of learning (Tolman, 1932) which emphasizes the acquisition of sign-gestalts or expectations. In fact, Mowrer (1960b) at times appears to identify hopes and fears with expectations. Thus he states, "In two-factor theory, 'expectations' are of two major varieties: hopes and fears, representing, respectively, anticipations of good and bad events (significates) to come [pp. 325–326]." But it is important to note that Mowrer's "expectations" are rather different from Tolman's. Tolman's concept of an expectation is identified as an hypothesis about the implications of action in a situation, as a *cognitive* anticipation of "what leads to what" if a particular course of action is taken. The cognitive or representational aspect of meaning (as distinct from the evaluative aspect) is discussed by Mowrer (1960a) in his second volume. There he introduces the concept of *image* which is defined as a conditioned sensation and which is used as the important basis for the cognitive and mnemonic aspects of learning. Mowrer's discussion suggests that he would identify a cognitive expectation, in Tolman's sense, as an image. It is apparent, however, that he is unhappy with the concept of a purely cognitive expectation since he believes that it leaves unanswered the important question of the relationship of actual behavior to cognition. Thus he repeatedly cites Guthrie's (1952) criticism of Tolman's learning theory, viz., "In his concern with what goes on in the rat's mind, Tolman has neglected to predict what the rat will do. So far as the theory is concerned the rat is left buried in thought . . . [p. 143]."

Mowrer's solution to this problem is to consider expectations as having both dynamic (emotional) and cognitive (imaginal) aspects. Such a conceptualization, he claims, avoids the difficulty inherent in Tolman's analysis, which may have arisen from a false antithesis between intellect and emotion. For Mowrer (1960a) this antithesis is unjustified for, in thinking, affective, and cognitive components are assumed to be interwoven. His argument is perhaps clearest in his discussion of vicarious trial and error behavior,

we must be careful not to *leave* the rat at the choice point *"lost* in thought." We must somehow get him "going" again, and eventually to his goal. If, in thought, we are merely dealing with expectancies in the sense of "pure cognitions," there is an acute problem here. But if, instead, we view these expectancies more dynamically (as hopes and fears), then we have a basis for expecting thought to be closely related to, and to eventuate in, overt motion [p. 216].

It may be possible, however, to retain the concept of a purely cognitive expectation and to incorporate it into a theoretical model which avoids the criticism by Guthrie that the organism is left "lost in thought." In one of his last papers Tolman (1955) attempted to do just this by specifying concepts of need, expectation, and valence which were assumed to interact to determine performance. Tolman's model is one of a class involving concepts akin to motive, expectation, and incentive value. Other such models have been developed by Lewin, Dembo, Festinger, and Sears (1944) in the analysis of level of aspiration behavior, by Rotter (1954) in his

social learning theory, by subjectively expected utility (SEU) theorists in the analysis of decision making (Edwards, 1954), and by Atkinson (1957) in discussion of achievement motivation.[2] The similarities and differences between these models have been summarized in a recent paper (Feather, 1959a). The existence of this class of models suggests the possibility of an alternative approach to the conceptualization of fear, hope, relief, and disappointment, and it is to such an alternative that we now turn.

An Alternative Conceptualization

We will now present as an alternative to Mowrer's interpretation of fear, hope, relief, and disappointment, a theory which employs the concepts of *fear motivation* and *hope motivation*. These two concepts are not identified as the emotional responses of fear and hope, respectively. Rather they are to be considered as theoretical concepts which may be developed within a class of models involving the concepts of motive, expectation, and incentive value (Feather, 1959a). However, we would expect measures of fear motivation and hope motivation to correlate positively with measures of the emotional responses of fear and hope, respectively.

The particular motive-expectancy-value model presented in this paper is based on Atkinson's (1957) theory of achievement motivation, and a version of it, applied to the achievement con-

[2] The level of aspiration model, the social learning model, and the SEU decision model do not explicitly include a concept of motive but Atkinson (1958, p. 305) argues that concepts such as valence, reinforcement value, and utility can be conceived as the multiplicative combination of motive and incentive value.

text, has been used by the writer in the analysis of persistence (Feather, 1961, 1962). *Motive* is conceived as a relatively stable personality disposition which may, in some cases, have an innate basis (cf., Eysenck's, 1957, concept of a predisposition to emotionality), but which is more likely the product of early learning, possibly according to principles formulated by McClelland (1951, pp. 441–475). More specifically, motives are conceived as dispositions within the person to approach certain classes of objects or events and to avoid certain other classes of objects or events. The objects or events which are approached are called positive incentives or rewards; the objects or events which are avoided are called negative incentives or punishments. Expectations and incentive values are assumed to be more closely related to aspects of a situation. An *expectation* is conceived as a cognition about the consequences of behavior in a situation, a sign-significate relationship which captures the idea of "what leads to what." Its strength may be indexed in terms of a subjective probability about the occurrence of the consequence, given the act (Rotter, 1954; Atkinson, 1957). This concept of expectation has been formalized as an S_1-R_1-S_2 representation by MacCorquodale and Meehl (1953) and recent studies have investigated some of the factors which influence its strength (cf., Feather, 1963b). The *value* of an incentive is assumed to be related to qualitative and quantitative aspects of a reward or punishment (e.g., amount of food, palatability of food, intensity and/or duration of shock). In most situations incentive values are probably independent of expectations. In an achievement situation, however, where performance is evaluated against standards of excellence, incentive values of success and failure are related to subjective probability of success (Feather, 1959b).

The above concepts are in no way teleological. Each refers to a present condition, and measures of the strength of motives, expectations, and incentive values can be, and have been, developed. Atkinson and Litwin (1960), for example, have examined the construct validity of the Test of Insight (French, 1958) and the Test Anxiety Scale (Mandler & Sarason, 1952) as measures of the strength of the motives to achieve success and to avoid failure respectively. Two recent volumes edited by Lindzey (1958) and by Atkinson (1958) have considered problems in the assessment of human motives. A variety of papers concerned with the measurement of subjective probability are now available, some of which present direct methods of measurement (e.g., Adams & Adams, 1961; Feather, 1963; Galanter, 1962), while others employ more indirect approaches (e.g., Becker, 1962; Edwards, 1962). Finally, there is an increasing literature, particularly from decision theory, on the measurement of incentive values or utilities (e.g., Becker, 1962; Edwards, 1954; Galanter, 1962).

Motives, expectations, and incentive values are assumed to combine (perhaps multiplicatively) to determine *motivation* either to approach a positive incentive or to avoid a negative incentive. For example, in Atkinson's (1957) theory of achievement motivation, the motivation to achieve success is taken as the multiplicative combination of motive to achieve success, subjective probability (or expectation) or success, and positive incentive value of success, and the motivation to avoid failure is taken as the multiplicative combination of motive to avoid failure, subjective probability (or expectation) of failure, and negative incentive value of failure.

In the motive-expectancy-value model we identify *hope motivation* as motivation to approach a positive incentive or reward. Hope motivation is therefore not equated with expectation of a reward nor is it considered in terms of fear reduction. Rather, expectation of reward is taken as a necessary but not a sufficient condition of hope motivation. Hope motivation, in the sense of motivation to approach a reward, is also assumed to depend upon the strength of the relevant motive and the magnitude of the positive incentive value. In the case of a hungry child, for example, who has learned to obtain cookies from a jar on the pantry shelf, strength of hope motivation (and its emotional correlate of hope) would depend on the strength of the child's motive to approach food (a relatively stable personality disposition related to early learning), the degree to which he expects to find the cookies in the jar (an expectation based on past experience and influenced by the present situation), and the positive incentive value of the food (related to the number and quality of the cookies).

In a corresponding way, *fear motivation* is identified as motivation to avoid a negative incentive or punishment. In the conditioning paradigm considered previously, we would argue that the amount of fear motivation (and its emotional correlate of fear), which is elicited with onset of the danger signal, will depend on the degree to which the punishment is expected. But, we would further maintain that the amount of aroused fear motivation is also a function of the intensity of the shock and its duration (aspects of the punishment which should affect its negative incen-

tive value), and of a relatively stable disposition (or motive) to avoid the punishment.

Provided expectations and incentive values are *independent,* confirmation of an expectation of reward should lead to an increase in the strength of the expectation and, hence, to an increase in hope motivation. For example, if the hungry child found cookies in the jar, his expectation would be confirmed and strengthened. When he is again hungry and decides to get the cookies, hope motivation would be stronger due to the increased strength of the expectation of reward. In a corresponding way, provided expectations and incentive values are independent, confirmation of an expectation of punishment should determine an increase in fear motivation. The repeated occurrence of shock following the danger signal would lead to an increase in the strength of the expectation of punishment and, hence, to a higher level of fear motivation when the danger signal is presented.

Increases in hope and fear motivation may also occur when expectations are "overconfirmed" in the sense that there is an unexpected increase in the quality or amount of the reward or punishment. Here the increase in motivation appears to be determined mainly by the increase in incentive value although, since expectations which are overconfirmed are presumably also strengthened, increases in motivation may also be determined by the strengthened expectations. One aspect of Crespi's (1942) classic investigation indicates the improvement in performance which follows a sudden increase in the amount of reward. His interpretation of this effect (Crespi, 1944), in terms of an increase in "emotional drive" or "eagerness," is analogous to the increase in hope motivation which, in the present model, is assumed to follow overconfirmation of a reward.

Relief and disappointment may also be conceptualized in terms of the motive-expectancy-value model. *Motivational relief* is assumed to occur when nonconfirmation of an expectation of punishment determines a decrease in fear motivation (i.e., a decrease in motivation to avoid the punishment). Thus, for example, when shock does not follow the danger signal, the expectation of punishment is not confirmed and fear motivation would decrease. Motivational relief is identified as this decrease in fear motivation, and we would expect measures of motivational relief to correlate positively with measures of relief conceived as an emotional response.

Correspondingly, *motivational disappointment* is assumed to occur when nonconfirmation of an expectation of reward determines a decrease in hope motivation (i.e., a decrease in motivations to approach the reward). Thus, for example, if the hungry child finds that there are no cookies in the jar, his expectation of reward is not confirmed and hope motivation would decrease. Motivational disappointment is identified as this decrease in hope motivation, and we would expect measures of motivational disappointment to correlate positively with measures of disappointment conceived as an emotional response.

Provided expectations and incentive values are independent, repeated nonconfirmation of an expectation of punishment should determine continued motivational relief and a progressive decrease in fear motivation. Similarly, provided expectations and incentive values are independent, repeated non-

confirmation of an expectation of reward should determine continued motivational disappointment and a progressive decrease in hope motivation.

Both motivational relief and motivational disappointment are therefore assumed to follow *nonconfirmation* of expectations and to involve reduction in fear motivation and hope motivation, respectively. An expectation of reward or punishment is not confirmed when the expected reward or punishment does not eventuate, i.e., there is *no* reward or punishment. Motivational relief and motivational disappointment would also occur under conditions where *partial* confirmation of an expectation leads to a decrease in motivation, that is, where the expected reward or punishment does occur but in reduced amount or quality. An expectation of reward would be only partially confirmed if the amount of the expected reward were suddenly reduced (cf., Crespi's experiment, 1942), or if there was a sudden reduction in the quality of the expected reward (cf., Tinklepaugh's experiment, 1928). Partial confirmation of an expectation of reward would determine a decrease in hope motivation, i.e., motivational disappointment. Similarly, if an expectation of punishment were only partially confirmed, due to an unexpected decrease in the intensity of punishment, there would be a decrease in fear motivation, i.e., motivational relief.

In summary, motivational relief and motivational disappointment are defined in terms of reduction in fear motivation and hope motivation, respectively, where this reduction is determined by nonconfirmation or partial confirmation of the corresponding expectation. In contrast, provided incentive values and expectations are inde-

TABLE 2

FEAR MOTIVATION, HOPE MOTIVATION, MOTIVATIONAL RELIEF, AND MOTIVATIONAL DISAPPOINTMENT IN RELATION TO CONFIRMATION AND NONCONFIRMATION OF EXPECTATIONS WHEN INCENTIVE VALUES AND EXPECTATIONS ARE INDEPENDENT

	Expectation of punishment	Expectation of reward
Confirmed or overconfirmed	Increase in fear motivation	Increase in hope motivation
Not confirmed or partially confirmed	Motivational relief	Motivational disappointment

Note.—Strength of motivation is assumed to be positively related to strength of motive, level of expectation, and magnitude of incentive value.

pendent, the development of increments in fear motivation and hope motivation would follow confirmation or overconfirmation of expectations. The similarities and differences in hope motivation, fear motivation, motivational disappointment, and motivational relief are summarized in Table 2 for the more usual case where incentive values and expectations are assumed to be independent.

It is apparent from Table 2 that fear motivation and motivational relief form a pair, and that hope motivation and motivational disappointment form a pair. It is important to note that, unlike Mowrer's approach, these four concepts are not defined as different aspects of the fear response. Hope motivation is not anticipated fear reduction, nor is motivational disappointment considered to be a recrudescence of the emotion of fear. Instead the four concepts are explicated within the framework of a motive-expectancy-value model.

The preceding discussion has been concerned with the more common case of the motive-expectancy-value model, where incentive values and expectations are assumed to be independent. It is reasonable to assume, for example, that the positive incentive value of food is not related in any systematic way to the expectation of food, or that the negative incentive value of shock is not systematically related to the expectation of shock. But there are situations where we would expect incentive values and expectations to be *related* (cf., Feather, 1959a). One such situation is the achievement situation where a person's performance at a task can be evaluated against standards of excellence. Here we would expect the positive incentive value of success to be greater for success at a difficult task (low expectation of success) than for success at an easy task (high expectation of success). Correspondingly, we would expect the negative incentive value of failure at a task to be greater for failure at an easy task (low expectation of failure) than for failure at a difficult task (high expectation of failure). These dependencies between incentive values and expectations are assumed in the theory of achievement motivation (Atkinson, 1957; Feather, 1962). It is interesting to consider the concepts of hope motivation, fear motivation, motivational disappointment, and motivational relief with respect to this particular motive-expectancy-value model.

In the theory of achievement motivation "hope for success" motivation is taken as the multiplicative combination of motive to achieve success (M_s), expectation of success (P_s), and positive incentive value of success (I_s). Similarly, "fear of failure" motivation is taken as the multiplicative combination of motive to avoid failure (M_{af}), expectation of failure (P_f), and negative incentive value of failure (I_f). In the model, the positive incentive value of success is taken as the complement of the subjective probability of success (i.e., $I_s = 1 - P_s$), and the negative incentive value of failure is taken as minus the complement of the subjective probability of failure—i.e., $I_f = -(1 - P_f)$. Hence the theory makes the quite explicit assumption that incentive values and expectations are related. It follows from these assumptions that hope for success motivation is curvilinearly related to subjective probability of success (P_s), increasing to a maximum value as P_s increases to .50, and thereafter decreasing in value as P_s further increases. Similarly, fear of failure motivation is curvilinearly related to subjective probability of failure (P_f), increasing to a maximum value as P_f increases to .50, and thereafter decreasing in value as P_f further increases. These curvilinear relationships are indicated in Table 3 for different motive strengths.

Table 3 implies that, insofar as the theory of achievement motivation is concerned, the occurrence of motivational relief or motivational disappointment will depend upon the *strength* of the corresponding expectation. Motivational relief would occur when nonconfirmation of a *weak* expectation of failure determines a decrease in fear of failure motivation. Let us assume, for example, that a person with a weak expectation of failure (e.g., $P_f = .30$) succeeds at a task (i.e., the expectation is not confirmed). This success should determine a decrease in his expectation of failure at the task for future attempts (e.g., P_f may decrease from .30 to .20). Table 3 shows that such a decrease in a weak expectation of failure (from $P_f = $

.30 to $P_f = .20$) would determine a decrease in fear of failure motivation i.e., motivational relief, and that this decrease would be greater for a stronger motive to avoid failure.

Correspondingly, motivational disappointment would occur when nonconfirmation of a weak expectation of success determines a decrease in hope for success motivation. Let us assume, for example, that a person with a weak expectation of success (e.g., $P_s = .30$) fails at a task (i.e., the expectation is not confirmed). This failure should determine a decrease in his expectation of success at the task for future attempts (e.g., P_s may decrease from .30 to .20). Table 3 shows that such a decrease in a weak expectation of success (from $P_s = .30$ to $P_s = .20$) would determine a decrease in hope for success motivation, i.e., motivational disappointment, and that this decrease would be greater for a stronger motive to achieve success. In other words, motivational relief would follow success at a task considered to be easy, and motivational disappointment would follow failure at a task considered to be difficult.

But what would happen if a *strong* expectation of failure $(P_f > .50)$ or a strong expectation of success $(P_s > .50)$ were not confirmed? The theory of achievement motivation implies that this condition would not determine motivational relief or motivational disappointment but, rather, *increments* in fear of failure and hope for success motivation, respectively. For example, if a person with a strong expectation of failure (e.g., $P_f = .70$) were to succeed at a task, this success would determine a decrease in his expectation of failure at the task for future attempts (e.g., P_f may decrease from .70 to .60). Table 3 shows that such a decrease in a strong

TABLE 3

RELATIONSHIPS OF HOPE FOR SUCCESS MOTIVATION AND FEAR OF FAILURE
MOTIVATION TO EXPECTATIONS OF SUCCESS AND FAILURE

Expectation of success (P_s)	Incentive value of success (I_s)	Hope for success motivation when		Expectation of failure (P_f)	Incentive value of failure (I_f)	Fear of failure motivation when	
		$M_s = 1$	$M_s = 2$			$M_{af} = 1$	$M_{af} = 2$
.9	.1	.09	.18	.1	$-.9$	$-.09$	$-.18$
.8	.2	.16	.32	.2	$-.8$	$-.16$	$-.32$
.7	.3	.21	.42	.3	$-.7$	$-.21$	$-.42$
.6	.4	.24	.48	.4	$-.6$	$-.24$	$-.48$
.5	.5	.25	.50	.5	$-.5$	$-.25$	$-.50$
.4	.6	.24	.48	.6	$-.4$	$-.24$	$-.48$
.3	.7	.21	.42	.7	$-.3$	$-.21$	$-.42$
.2	.8	.16	.32	.8	$-.2$	$-.16$	$-.32$
.1	.9	.09	.18	.9	$-.1$	$-.09$	$-.18$

Note.—M_s = Strength of motive to achieve success; M_{af} = Strength of motive to avoid failure; $I_s = 1 - P_s$; $I_f = -(1 - P_f)$; Hope of success motivation = $(M_s \times P_s \times I_s)$; Fear of failure motivation = $(M_{af} \times P_f \times I_f)$.

expectation of failure (from $P_f = .70$ to $P_f = .60$) would determine an increase in fear of failure motivation and that this increase would be greater for a stronger motive to avoid failure. Similarly, hope for success motivation would increase following nonconfirmation of a strong expectation of success, the increase being greater for a stronger motive to achieve success. In other words, an increase in fear of failure motivation would follow success at a task considered to be difficult, and an increase in hope for success motivation would follow failure at a task considered to be easy.

Hence, in the theory of achievement motivation, which assumes dependencies between incentive values and expectations, nonconfirmation of an expectation does not necessarily determine motivational relief or motivational disappointment. The definition of these two concepts involves not only nonconfirmation of an expectation but also a decrease in the corresponding motivation. These two requirements are met

in the theory of achievement motivation only when weak expectations are not confirmed. By the same token, in the theory of achievement motivation, *confirmation* of an expectation does not necessarily determine increases in hope for success or fear of failure motivation. Assuming that confirmation of an expectation would increase its strength, increases in hope for success or fear of failure motivation would occur only if a weak expectation (i.e., P_s or $P_f < .50$) were confirmed. Confirmation of a strong expectation of success ($P_s > .50$) or a strong expectation of failure ($P_f > .50$) would determine decreases in hope for success and fear of failure motivation, respectively. The general rule is that, whenever confirmation or nonconfirmation of an expectation of success or failure shifts the strength of the expectation *towards* the intermediate value (i.e., $P_s = P_f = .50$), then the corresponding motivation increases. But, whenever confirmation or nonconfirmation of an expectation of success or failure shifts the strength of the expectation *away from* the intermediate value, then the corresponding motivation decreases.

The relationships of fear of failure motivation, hope for success motivation, motivational relief, and motivational disappointment to confirmation and nonconfirmation of expectations, in the theory of achievement motivation, are summarized in Table 4.

Table 4 is obviously more complex than Table 2. This greater complexity is an outcome of the dependencies between incentive values and expectations assumed in the theory of achievement motivation which, together with the assumption of multiplicative combination of variables, determine curvilinear relationships between strength of motivation and level of expectation. In the more general case of the motive-expectancy-value model, strength of motivation is assumed to be positively related to strength of motive, level of expectation, and magnitude of incentive value. The variables are assumed to be independent and, hence, the relationships of fear motivation, hope motivation, motivational relief, and motivational disappointment to confirmation, and

nonconfirmation of expectations (as summarized in Table 2) are of a simpler order.

Some Experimental Evidence

An examination of Table 3 indicates that the motivational disappointment which would occur when a relatively weak expectation of success ($P_s < .50$) is reduced in strength to a very weak expectation of success (e.g., $P_s = .10$) by nonconfirmation, would be greater when the weak expectation is high in value (e.g., $P_s = .40$) rather than low in value (e.g., $P_s = .20$), and would be greater for a strong motive to achieve success (e.g., $M_s = 2$) than for a weak motive to achieve success ($M_s = 1$). More specifically, we can advance the following two hypotheses:

Hypothesis 1 states that, providing expectations of success are relatively weak, for a given strength of the motive to achieve success, motivational disappointment accompanying reduction of a weak expectation of success to a low value should be positively related to the initial expectation of success.

Hypothesis 2 states that, providing

TABLE 4

Fear of Failure Motivation, Hope for Success Motivation, Motivational Relief, and Motivational Disappointment in Relation to Confirmation and Nonconfirmation of Expectations when Incentive Values and Expectations are Related

	Strong expectation of failure ($P_f > .50$)	Weak expectation of failure ($P_f < .50$)	Strong expectation of success ($P_s > .50$)	Weak expectation of success ($P_s < .50$)
Confirmed	Decrease in fear of failure motivation	Increase in fear of failure motivation	Decrease in hope for success motivation	Increase in hope for success motivation
Not confirmed	Increase in fear of failure motivation	Motivational relief	Increase in hope for success motivation	Motivational disappointment

expectations of success are relatively weak, for a given initial expectation of success, motivational disappointment accompanying reduction of a weak expectation of success to a low value should be positively related to the strength of the motive to achieve success.

Hypotheses 1 and 2 together involve a more general prediction to cover the case where both strength of motive and initial expectation of success vary among subjects. This prediction is as follows:

Hypothesis 3 states that, providing expectations of success are relatively weak, motivational disappointment accompanying reduction of a weak expectation of success to a low value should tend to be positively related to strength of initial hope for success motivation.

The predictions in Hypotheses 1 and 2 both involve this principle since initial hope for success motivation would be stronger for higher initial expectations of success (cf., Hypothesis 1), and for stronger motives to achieve success (cf., Hypothesis 2). But Hypotheses 1 and 2 refer to more controlled situations where either the strength of motive to achieve success or the initial expectation of success is held constant. Hypothesis 3 is concerned with the more general situation where both strength of motive to achieve success and initial expectation of success vary among subjects.

Although the above hypotheses have not been explicitly tested, some relevant evidence has recently been obtained by the writer in an investigation of persistence (Feather, 1963). Sixty male subjects worked individually at an insoluble, unicursal puzzle with the opportunity of turning to an alternative puzzle of the same type whenever they desired. The insoluble puzzle was presented to subjects as very difficult. Each subject was, in fact, told that only 5% of university students were able to solve it. The alternative puzzle, which was soluble, was presented to the subjects as intermediate or average in difficulty, and each subject was told that 50% of university students were able to solve it. This information about the difficulty levels of the two puzzles was given to each subject before he began to work at the first puzzle. As a check on the effectiveness of the fictitious group norm procedure, each subject was required to estimate his chances of success for each puzzle using a rating scale numbered from 0 to 100 in steps to 10. This probability estimate, obtained before the subject commenced the puzzle, is assumed to indicate the strength of his initial expectation of success (P_s).

For each puzzle the task was to trace over all the lines of a diagram without lifting the pencil from the diagram and without tracing over any line twice. Copies of the insoluble first puzzle (Item 1), printed on cards, were placed in a stack in front of the subject. Similarly, copies of the soluble second puzzle (Item 2), printed on cards, were placed to one side of the subject, but he could not see the content of Item 2 before he began to work at it. Each subject was allowed to work at an item for as many trials as he chose, taking up to 40 seconds for each trial. He could quit Item 1 whenever he desired and turn to Item 2. The measure of persistence was the number of trials taken by the subject at Item 1 before turning to Item 2.

Following the test of persistence, each subject completed a postperformance questionnaire. Among other questions, the subject was asked how concerned he felt about succeeding at Item 1 (i.e., how much he desired to succeed), how disappointed he felt at failing at Item 1, how anxious or worried he felt about his performance at Item 1, and how annoyed he felt about his lack of progress at Item 1. These questions were presented in Likert form and required answers on a five-category scale which was scored from one to five in the direction of increasing strength of the feeling. To check on changes in expectation of success with repeated failure at Item 1, each subject was also asked what he estimated his chances of success to be after he had completed about half the number of trials he took at Item 1, and also just before he finished working at this item. These "middle" and "final" probability estimates were obtained using the same rating scale as was employed to obtain "initial" probability estimates prior to performance at Item 1.

Need Achievement scores based on stories written to six pictures under neutral conditions according to the standard procedure (McClelland, Atkinson, Clark, & Lowell, 1953) provided measures of the strength of motive to achieve success (M_s). Mandler-Sarason Test Anxiety scores provided measures of the strength of motive to avoid failure (M_{af}). Both the projective test of n Achievement and the Test Anxiety Scale were administered to the subjects some weeks prior to the test of persistence.

The experimental situation described above fulfills the conditions for the occurrence of motivational disappointment according to the theory of achievement motivation. Item 1 was presented to the subjects as very difficult and,

hence, initial expectations of success should tend to be relatively weak. Furthermore, each trial taken by the subject at Item 1 resulted in failure since the puzzle was insoluble. Hence the weak initial expectation of success was not confirmed by success and, by assumption, this weak expectation should tend to decrease in strength with repeated failures,[3] and determine decreases in hope for success motivation.

Table 5 presents intercorrelations between subjects' ratings of their concern about succeeding at Item 1, their disappointment about failure at Item 1, their anxiety about failure at Item 1, their annoyance about failure at Item 1, and their chances of success prior to performance at Item 1 (initial probability estimates).

Table 5 shows that ratings of achievement concern correlate $r = .52$ ($p < .00,1$, $df = 58$) with ratings of disappointment. If we assume that these ratings can be taken as measures of hope motivation and motivational disappointment, respectively, this result is consistent with the predicted positive relationship stated in Hypothesis 3. Table 5 also shows that ratings of disappointment correlate $r = .28$ ($p < .05$, $df = 58$) with estimates of probability of success obtained prior to performance at Item 1. Assuming that these ratings can be taken as measures of motivational disappointment and initial expectation of success respectively, this result is consistent with the predicted positive relationship stated in Hypothesis 1. Ratings of disappointment are also

[3] Analysis of probability estimates reveals a tendency for an increase from the initial estimate to the middle estimate, followed by a decrease to the final estimate. This puzzling trend may be a function of the very low norm (5%) reported to the subjects.

TABLE 5

INTERCORRELATIONS OF RATINGS OF ACHIEVEMENT CONCERN,
DISAPPOINTMENT ABOUT FAILURE, ANXIETY
ABOUT FAILURE, ANNOYANCE ABOUT FAILURE,
AND INITIAL PROBABILITY ESTIMATES

	Disappointment about failure	Anxiety about failure	Annoyance about failure	Initial probability estimate
Concern about achievement	.52***	.22	.29*	.14
Disappointment about failure		.47***	.35**	.28*
Anxiety about failure			.58***	—.03
Annoyance about failure				.08

* $p < .05$.
** $p < .01$.
*** $p < .001$.

positively correlated with n Achievement scores $(r = .18)$ but this correlation is not statistically significant. If we assume that these measures can be taken as indicating degree of motivational disappointment and strength of motive to achieve success, respectively, this lack of a significant positive relationship fails to support Hypothesis 2.

These data are therefore consistent with the predictions stated in Hypotheses 1 and 3. It is important to note, however, that the above experiment was not specifically designed as a test of the three hypotheses concerning motivational disappointment, and offers only suggestive evidence. The data contained in Table 5 are rather incidental to the main aim of the investigation which was to investigate differences in persistence.[4] However, more rigidly con-

[4] Results indicate that persistence at Item 1 is positively related to initial estimates of probability of success (P_s) for the subjects classified as high in n Achievement and low in Test Anxiety, but there is no relationship between persistence and initial estimates of P_s for the subjects classified as low in n Achievement and high in Test Anxiety. This result accords with the prediction based on the motive-expectancy-value model.

trolled investigations of the above hypotheses should be possible. One might, for example, attempt to control the number of failures the subjects undergo at the task rather than to allow this to vary, as in the present investigation, and one might also systematically vary initial expectations of success at the insoluble task. One might also try to devise alternative methods of measuring motivational disappointment and hope for success motivation additional to the rather simple rating measures used in the above study. In future research, it should also be possible to investigate predictions about motivational relief, in an achievement context, which parallel those stated in the above hypotheses. For example, according to the theory of achievement motivation, we would predict that, providing expectations of failure are relatively weak, for a given strength of the motive to avoid failure, motivational relief accompanying reduction of a weak expectation of failure to a low value should be positively related to the initial expectation of failure. Such predictions could be investigated in an achievement situation where a subject experiences repeated success at an easy task.

Future research could also study the relationship of motivational disappointment to hope motivation, and motivational relief to fear motivation in situations other than the achievement situation. As we have indicated, the achievement situation is rather exceptional in that the conceptualization of achievement-related motivation involves the assumption of dependencies between incentive values and expectations. The analysis for the more usual case, where incentive values and expectations are assumed to be independent, would be simpler. We would predict that, for this more usual case, motivational disappointment accompanying reduction of an expectation of reward to a low value should tend to be positively related to the strength of initial hope motivation. Similarly, motivational relief accompanying reduction of an expectation of punishment to a low value should tend to be positively related to strength of initial fear motivation. Unlike the hypotheses presented for the achievement situation, neither of these two predictions is qualified by an assumption about the strength of the initial expectation of reward or punishment.

But what of the relationships between hope motivation and fear motivation, or between motivational relief and motivational disappointment? It seems to the writer that Mowrer's revised two-factor theory would lead to the prediction of positive interrelationships between measures of the four emotions of fear, hope, relief, and disappointment on the basis of intensity of fear.[5] When fear is strong, relief (or fear reduction) should be strong, hope (or anticipated fear reduction) should be strong, and disappointment (or fear induction) should be strong. The strength of hope, relief, and disappointment should tend to decline as fear becomes less intense. However, an analysis based on the motive-expectancy-value model need not lead to this prediction. In the first place there is no necessary assumption in the motive-expectancy-value model that reward is equivalent to fear reduction. In fact, the model is more hedonistic in its orientation. Secondly, even though it may be possible to devise reward and punishment situations which determine relatively constant expectations and incentive values among the subjects, hope motivation and fear motivation would still be influenced by the particular motives which are aroused. These motives are not necessarily positively correlated. In fact, in the theory of achievement motivation (Atkinson, 1957), it is assumed that the motive to achieve success (M_s) and the motive to avoid failure (M_{af}) are *independent* dispositions of the personality. Several studies (Atkinson, 1958; Feather, 1963), in which strength of M_s is inferred from analysis of TAT protocols and strength of M_{af} is inferred from scores on the Test Anxiety Questionnaire (Mandler & Sarason, 1952), provide evidence which is consistent with this

5 The generally positive intercorrelations in Table 5 are not inconsistent with this prediction. An important exception is the absence of a significant positive correlation between ratings of anxiety about failure and achievement concern. Furthermore, ratings of disappointment are the only measures to show a significant positive correlation with initial estimates of probability of success. These latter results are consistent with the derivation from the theory of achievement motivation.

assumption. Thus, given expectations and incentive values which are relatively uniform in strength among the subjects, prediction of the relationship between measures of hope motivation and measures of fear motivation would depend on assumptions about the relationship of the underlying motives. In the present conceptualization these motives are taken as relatively stable personality dispositions and need not be positively correlated. Nor are they considered to involve changes in the level of fear.

The writer believes that the concepts of fear motivation, hope motivation, motivational relief, and motivational disappointment, which have been developed in this paper, provide an alternative to Mowrer's conceptualization permitting differential, testable predictions.

Summary: This paper presents alternatives to Mowrer's concepts of fear, hope, relief, and disappointment. The 4 concepts which are presented are not defined as increments or decrements in the fear response (as in Mowrer) but are developed within the framework of a motive-expectancy-value model. Fear motivation is defined as motivation to avoid a negative incentive or punishment, hope motivation as motivation to approach a positive incentive or reward, motivational relief as reduction in fear motivation following nonconfirmation or partial confirmation of an expectation of punishment, and motivational disappointment as reduction in hope motivation following nonconfirmation or partial confirmation of an expectation of reward. This alternative conceptualization makes a clear distinction between cognitive expectations and hope and fear motivation in that an expectation is assumed to be a necessary but not a sufficient condition of motivation. Some research implications are considered.

American Psychologist, 1961, vol. 16, pp. 1–11.

The Psychological Effects of Insufficient Rewards

Leon Festinger

Some fields of Psychology have for many years been dominated by ideas concerning the importance of rewards in the establishment and maintenance of behavior patterns. So dominant has this notion become that some of our most ingenious theoretical thinking has been devoted to imagining the existence of rewards in order to explain behavior in situations where, plausibly, no rewards exist. It has been observed, for example, that under some circumstances an organism will persist in voluntarily engaging in behavior which is frustrating or painful. To account for such behavior it has, on occasion, been seriously proposed that the cessation of the frustration or pain is rewarding and thus reinforces the tendency to engage in the behavior.

I want to maintain that this type of explanation is not only unnecessary but also misleading. I certainly do *not* wish to say that rewards are unimportant, but I propose to show that the absence of reward or the existence of inadequate reward produces certain specific consequences which can account for a variety of phenomena which are difficult to deal with if we use our usual conceptions of the role of reward.

Before I proceed, I would like to say that most of the thinking and most of the experimental work which I will present are the result of collaboration between Douglas H. Lawrence and myself. Indeed, whatever you find interesting in what I say you may safely attribute primarily to him.

I will start my discussion in a rather roundabout manner with some remarks which concern themselves primarily with some aspects of the thinking processes of human beings. Human thinking is sometimes a strange mixture of "plausible" and "magical" processes. Let us examine more closely what I mean by this. For example, imagine that a person knows that some event is going to occur, and that the person can do something to prepare himself to cope more adequately with the impending event. Under such circumstances it is very reasonable (perhaps you might even want to use the word "rational") for the person to do whatever is necessary in preparation for the coming event. Human thinking, however, also works in reverse. Consider a person who goes to a lot of trouble to prepare himself for a future event which might possibly occur. Such a person will subsequently tend to persuade himself that the event is rather likely to occur. There is nothing very plausible or rational about this kind of mental process—rather, it has almost a magical quality about it. Let me illustrate this briefly by describing an experiment recently conducted by Ruby Yaryan (Yaryan & Festinger, 1960).

Under the pretext of investigating the manner in which students study for examinations, she asked subjects to study a list of arbitrary definitions of symbols in preparation for a possible test. Two conditions were experimentally created for the subjects. Half of the subjects were told that, if they actually took the test, this list of definitions of the symbols would be in their possession during the test, and so, all that was necessary in preparation was to familiarize themselves with the list. This was, essentially, an "easy preparation" condition. That is, not much effort was required of the subjects in advance preparation for the test.

The other half of the subjects were told that, if they actually took the test, they would *not* have the list of definitions with them and so it was necessary for them to memorize the symbols and their definitions in preparation for the test. It is clear that this constitutes a much more "effortful preparation" condition. Considerable effort was required of these subjects in advance preparation for the possible test.

It was carefully explained to each subject that not everyone would actually have to take the test. Specifically, they were told that only half of the people in the experiment *would* take the test. It was also carefully explained that the selection of who would, and who would not, have to take the test had already been made in consultation with their teachers (the subjects were all high school girls). Nothing that happened during the experiment would affect whether or not they took the test —this had already been decided in advance for each of them.

After they finished studying the list of definitions, they were asked a number of questions to preserve the fiction that the experiment was concerned with study habits. Each subject was also asked to indicate how likely she thought it was that she, personally, would have to actually take the test. The results show, quite clearly, that subjects in the effortful preparation condition, on the average, thought it was more likely that they would have to take the test than did subjects in the easy preparation condition. In other words, those who were experimentally induced to engage in a lot of preparatory effort, persuaded themselves that the thing they were preparing for would actually occur.

The relevance of this experiment to the problem of the effects of inadequate rewards will become clearer in the following example which illustrates the same psychological process. Consider some person who is strongly attracted to some goal. It is quite reasonable for this person to be willing to expend more effort, or to endure more pain, in order to reach the goal than he would be if he were less attracted. Once more, however, one finds the same process of reasoning in reverse. That is, if a person exerts a great deal of effort, or endures pain, in order to reach some ordinary objective, there is a strong tendency for him to persuade himself that the objective is especially valuable or especially desirable. An experiment conducted by Elliot Aronson and Judson Mills (1959) shows the effect quite nicely.

The subjects in the experiment by Aronson and Mills were college girls who volunteered to join small discussion groups. Each subject, when she appeared for the discussion group, was told that, instead of being put into a new group, she was being considered for inclusion in an ongoing group which had recently lost one of its members. However, the subject was told, because of the group's concern that the

replacement be someone who would be able to discuss things freely and openly, the experimenter had agreed to test the replacement before admitting her to the group. Some subjects were then given a very brief and not painful test while others were given a rather extended and embarrassing test. The experimenter then, of course, told each subject that she had done well and was admitted to the group. Thus, there were some subjects who had attained membership in the group easily and some subjects who had endured a painful experience in order to be admitted to the group.

The experimenter then explained to the subject that the discussion was carried on by means of an intercommunication system, each girl being in a separate room. She was brought into her room which contained a microphone and earphones. The experimenter told her that the others had already started and perhaps it would be best for her not to participate in the discussion this time but just to listen. Next meeting, of course, she would participate fully. Speaking into the microphone the experimenter then went through the illusion of introducing her to the three other girls in the group. He then "disconnected" the microphone and gave the subject the earphones to wear. The subject then listened for about 25 minutes to a tape recording of a rather dull and halting discussion. All subjects, of course, heard exactly the same tape recording thinking they were listening to the actual live group discussion.

When the discussion was finished, the experimenter explained to the subject that, after each meeting, each of the girls filled out a "post-meeting reaction form." She was then given a questionnaire to complete which asked a variety of questions concerning how interesting she had found the discussion to be, how much she liked the other members of the group, and other similar questions. The results show, as anticipated, that those subjetcs who had gone through a painful procedure in order to be admitted to the group thought the discussion was more interesting and liked the other group members better than did those who had gained admission to the group easily. In other words, we see the same process operating here as we noted in the previous experiment. If someone is somehow induced to endure embarrassment in order to achieve something, she then persuades herself that what she has achieved is valuable.

In both of the examples which I have discussed (and one could present many more examples of similar nature) a situation has been produced where the organism has two pieces of information (or cognitions) which do not fit together. In the first example, these two pieces of information were: (*a*) I have worked hard in preparation for an event. (*b*) The event is not too likely to occur. In the second example, the two cognitions which did not fit together were: (*a*) I have endured pain to attain an objective. (*b*) The objective is not very attractive. This kind of "nonfitting" relationship between two pieces of information may be termed a dissonant relation (Festinger, 1957). The reason, of course, that dissonance exists between these cognitions is that, psychologically, the obverse of one follows from the other. Psychologically, if an objective *is* very attractive, it follows that one would be willing to endure pain to attain it; or if the objective is *not* attractive, it follows that one does *not* endure pain to attain it. This specification of why a given relation between cognitions is dissonant also provides the clues to predicting specifically how the organism will react to the existence of the dissonance. Assuming that the organism will attempt to reduce the dissonance between the cognitions, there are obviously two major classes of ways in which this can be done. He can attempt to persuade himself that the pain which he endured was not really painful or he can attempt to persuade himself that the objective *is* very attractive.

I will not spend any more time than this in general theoretical discussion of the theory of dissonance and the reduction of dissonance. I hope that this small amount of general theoretical discussion will be enough to give context to the specific analysis of the psychological effects of insufficient rewards.

Let us consider in more detail what is suggested by the example of the experiment by Aronson and Mills and by the theory of cognitive dissonance. In that experiment the dissonance which was created was reduced by enhancing the value of the goal. This suggests that organisms may come to like and value things for which they have worked very hard or for which they have suffered. Looking at it from another aspect, one might say that they may come to value activities for which they have been inadequately rewarded. At first glance this may seem to contradict a widely accepted notion in Psychology, namely, that organisms learn to like things for which they *have* been rewarded. In a sense it is contradictory, but not in the sense that it denies the operation of this widely assumed process. It does, however, state that another process also operates which is rather of an opposite character.

Let us analyze the situation with which we are concerned somewhat more carefully and more precisely. We are concerned with the dissonance between two possible cognitions. One of these is a cognition the organism has concerning his behavior, namely, I have voluntarily done something which, all other things being equal, I would avoid doing. The other is a cognition about the environment or about the result of his action, namely, the reward that has been obtained is inadequate. As we mentioned before, this dissonance can be reduced if the organism can persuade himself that he really likes the behavior in which he engaged or if he enhances for himself the value of what he has obtained as a result of his actions.

There is, of course, another way to reduce the dissonance, namely, for the organism to change his behavior. That is, having done something which resulted in an inadequate reward the organism can refuse to perform the action again. This means of reducing the dissonance is undoubtedly the one most frequently employed by organisms. If the organism obtains information which is dissonant with his behavior, he usually modifies his behavior so that it fits better what he knows concerning his environment. Here, however, I am going to consider only situations in which this means of reducing dissonance is not available to the organism. That is, I will consider only situations in which the organism is somehow tricked or seduced into continuing to engage in the activity in spite of the dissonance which is introduced. Under these circumstances we would expect one of the two previously mentioned dissonance reduction mechanisms to be used.

If one thinks for a while about the possible behavioral consequences of such a psychological process as we have described, an explanation suggests itself for the well-known finding that resistance to extinction is greater after partial reward than after complete reward.

Before I explain this more adequately I would like to digress for a moment. Since much of the research on the effects of partial reward has been done on rats, and since the experiments that Lawrence and I have done are also on rats, the question will inevitably arise as to whether or not I really think that rats have cognitions and that rats reduce dissonance the way humans do.

First for the matter of cognitions in rats: All that is meant by cognition is knowledge or information. It seems to me that one can assume that an organism has cognitions or information if one can observe some behavioral difference under different stimulus conditions. If the organism changes his behavior when the environment changes, then obviously he uses information about the environment and, equally obviously, can be said to have cognitions.

Now for the question of whether or not rats reduce dissonance as humans do: Although Lawrence keeps telling me that rats are smarter than humans, I suspect that the rat is a rather stupid organism and does not reduce dissonance nearly as effectively as the human being does. I suspect that the mechanisms available to the rat for dissonance reduction are very limited and that the amount of dissonance which gets effectively reduced is relatively small. Still, I suspect that they *do* reduce dissonance. At any rate, if we find that the theory of dissonance can make valid predictions for rat behavior, this will be evidence that they do, indeed, reduce dissonance.

Now to return to the matter of the increased resistance to extinction following partial reward. Let us examine what occurs, psychologically, during a series of trials on which the behavior of an organism is only occasionally rewarded. Imagine a hungry animal who dashes frantically down some runway and into some so-called "goal box" only to find that there is nothing there. The cognition that he has obtained nothing is dissonant with the cognition that he has expended effort to reach the goal box. If this state of affairs were continually repeated, as we all know, the animal would reduce the dissonance by refusing to go to the goal box, that is, he would change his behavior. But, in a partial reward situation, the animal is tricked into continuing to run to the goal box because an appreciable number of times that he goes there he does find food. But, on each nonrewarded trial dissonance is introduced when the animal finds the goal box empty. The assumed process of dissonance reduction would lead us to expect that, gradually, the animal develops some extra preference either for the activity or for the goal box itself. A comparable animal that was rewarded every time he ran to the goal box would not develop any such extra preference.

Consider the situation, then, when extinction trials begin. In addition to realizing that food is no longer present, the partially rewarded animal also has to overcome his extra preference before he stops going to the goal box. We would thus expect "extinction" to take longer for a partially rewarded animal than for an animal that was always rewarded. The magnitude of the difference should be far greater than just the slight effect which would exist if the 100% animal discovers more rapidly that the situation has changed.

If this explanation is correct, then the greater resistance to extinction following partial reward is a direct consequence of the process of dissonance reduction. This, of course, immediately suggests an extension of this line of reasoning to situations other than those involving partial reward. *Any* procedure which introduces dissonance during the training trials should similarly be expected to increase resistance to extinction since the same kind of dissonance reduction process should operate.

Let us, however, try to be precise about what kinds of procedures would introduce dissonance for an organism during training trials in an experiment. It is, fortunately, possible to define this operationally in a precise manner. Let us imagine that we test an organism in a single choice situation. In the case of a rat, for example, this might be simply an apparatus where, from the starting point the animal can turn either right or left. Let us further imagine that the organism we are testing is quite hungry and that, whichever alternative he chooses, he obtains food. We can, then, vary one at a time a variety of factors to discover what the organism will ordinarily avoid doing. One would, of course, find many such factors which would lead the organism not to choose the alternative with which that factor is associated. Dissonance will be created for the organism if he is somehow tricked into consistently engaging in an activity involving such a factor.

This may sound very involved so let me try to say it again, this time, a bit less abstractly. Imagine that we test rats in a simple left-right choice apparatus and, no matter whether the animal goes left or right, he obtains food. But, imagine that, if he goes left, the animal must swim through water to get to the food but, if he goes right, there is simply a short run down an alley to the food. Let us further imagine that, under such circumstances, the animal will consistently choose to go to the right, that is, he will avoid swimming through water. Armed with this knowledge concerning the behavior of the rat we can then assert the following: if one puts a rat in a situation where we somehow trick the rat into consistently swimming through water, dissonance will have been created.

Remembering what we have already said about the ways in which dissonance can be reduced in this kind of situation (provided that we are successful in tricking the organism into continuing to engage in the activity) we would then arrive at the following statement: any condition which the animal will avoid in the above mentioned test situation will increase resistance to extinction in a nonchoice situation.

Let us look at some of the data which exist which are relevant to this statement. We know that if a hungry rat is put in a situation where he has a choice between a goal box where he is rewarded 100% of the time and a goal box where he is rewarded only part of the time, he will fairly consistently go to the place where he is rewarded 100% of the time. And, of course, we also know that where no choice is involved, partial reward increases resistance to extinction. But there are other variables or conditions which should increase resistance to extinction in a similar manner if our theoretical analysis is correct.

Consider the question of delay of

reinforcement. Once more, thinking of our hypothetical test situation, we can be reasonably certain that a rat, if faced with a choice where one alternative led to immediate reward while the other alternative involved an appreciable delay before the rat was allowed to continue to the goal box to obtain food, the rat would rather consistently choose the alternative that led to immediate reward. We should then expect that, in a nonchoice situation, delay of reward should lead to greater resistance to extinction. Existing data show that this is indeed correct. Appreciable delay of reward does lead to greater resistance to extinction. I will briefly review some of the data which exist on delay of reward to give you some idea of the effect which is obtained.

The usual experiment has been done on extinction following delay of reinforcement compares one condition in which the rats encounter no enforced delay between starting down a runway and obtaining food in the goal box with other conditions in which, on some trials, the rats are detained in a delay chamber before being allowed to proceed to the food. The usual period of delay which has been used has been about 30 seconds. Crum, Brown, and Bitterman (1951) and Scott and Wike (1956) both find that a group of rats delayed on half the trials shows much greater resistance to extinction than a group which was never delayed. In another experiment, Wike and McNamara (1957) ran three groups which differed in the percentage (and of course, number) of trials on which they were delayed. They find that the larger the percentage or number of trials on which the animal experiences delay, the greater is the resistance to extinction. The same kind of result is obtained by

Fehrer (1956) who compared rats who were delayed for 20 seconds on *every* trial with ones who were never delayed. She also finds that delay results in increased resistance to extinction.

Before we proceed to other matters, I would like to briefly raise a question concerning one kind of explanation that has frequently, in one form or another, been offered to account for increased resistance to extinction after partial reward. The basis of this kind of explanation, whether it be in terms of expectancy, or conditioning of cues, or any of a number of other varieties, rests in pointing out that there is more similarity between acquisition and extinction for partial reward conditions than for 100% reward conditions. I would like to point out that this type of explanation is clearly not very useful in explaining the increased resistance to extinction after delay of reward. From the point of view of the explanation I am here proposing, however, partial reward and delay of reward clearly involve the same psychological processes.

Let us go on now to examine the matter of work and effort. I am sure it is fairly obvious to all of you now what I want to say about work and effort. If we return to a consideration of our hypothetical test situation we know that, given a choice between an effortless path to food and a path requiring expenditure of effort, the hungry animal will choose the effortless path rather regularly. Hence, in accordance with our analysis concerning dissonance and dissonance reduction, we would expect the requirement of greater effort during acquisition to lead to increased resistance to extinction.

It is surprising that, in spite of the relative consistency of results among the studies which exist in the literature, the effect of effort during acquisition on resistance to extinction has not been generally noted. People have rather tended to note the finding that the greater the effort required during extinction, the faster does extinction occur. But the data are also clear with respect to the effect of effort during acquisition. They show quite clearly that, holding effort during extinction constant, the more effort required during acquisition, the more resistance there is to extinction. The data from one of the more adequately controlled experiments will suffice to illustrate the effect.

Aiken (1957) reports an experiment in which the animal was required to press a panel in order to gain access to food. Some rats were required to exert little effort while others were required to exert considerable effort during training. Half of the animals in each condition were extinguished with the low effort requirement and half with the high effort requirement. Holding effort during extinction constant, the results show clearly that the average number of trials to a criterion of extinction was considerably greater for the high effort acquisition condition than for the low effort acquisition condition. Other experiments in the literature also show this same effect if one examines the data carefully. It should once more be pointed out that any explanation of this effect which depends upon a notion of similarity between acquisition and extinction conditions is clearly inadequate.

One could list many other specific conditions which, analyzed in the same way, would be expected to increase resistance to extinction. I have chosen the three preceding ones to discuss because reasonably good data concerning them exist in the literature. Now, however, I would like to return to a more thorough consideration of the partial reward situation.

I have stated that, on nonrewarded trials in a partial reward situation, dissonance is introduced into the animal's cognition when he realizes that there is no food available. The amount of dissonance can, of course, vary in magnitude. It is important for us to consider the operational variables which will affect the total magnitude of dissonance which is introduced in this manner. This total magnitude of dissonance, of course, will determine how much dissonance reduction occurs through the development of extra preferences (always assuming that the animal does not change his behavior) and hence will determine the resistance to extinction.

In the past, it has generally been assumed that the major operational variable affecting resistance to extinction is the ratio of reward. That is, the smaller the proportion of rewarded trials, the greater the resistance to extinction. However, one might reason that since dissonance is created for the animal on every nonrewarded trial, it seems plausible to suppose that the major operational variable which will affect the resistance to extinction is, rather, the sheer total number of nonrewarded trials which the animal has experienced rather than the ratio of nonreward. From the data in published experiments it is impossible to assess whether or not this is correct since these two variables are completely confounded in the literature. Experiments on partial reward have always held constant either the number of rewarded trials or else the total number of trials that the animal experiences. It is clear,

of course, that when either of these quantities is held constant, the number of nonrewarded trials is perfectly correlated with the ratio of nonreward and so the effects cannot be separated.

It is possible, perhaps, to get some hunch about this, however, from examining the results of experiments which have used rather few training trials. If we are correct, these experiments should show very weak effects of partial reward on resistance to extinction. Sheffield (1949), for example, using a total of 30 trials (only 15 nonrewarded trials) found very small differences between extinction after partial and complete reward. Wilson, Weiss, and Amsel (1955) and also Lewis (1956), replicating the Sheffield experiment almost exactly, also find such small differences that it requires an analysis of covariance to make them appear significant. However, Weinstock (1954), using a similar apparatus, but employing 75 training trials, finds huge and unmistakable differences.

It is unnecessary to belabor the matter by quoting many studies here since it is all a matter of hunch and impression. In general, when one goes through the literature one gets the impression that the experiments which show small effects after partial reward have tended to employ rather few trials. But comparison of this kind between different experiments done by different experimenters is a very shabby business at best since the variation from experimenter to experimenter can be quite large for unknown reasons. The question seemed important enough, however, so that Lawrence and I thought it worthwhile to do a study which could answer the question. The study was carried out through the kind efforts of John Theios. I would like to describe it to you briefly.

The general design of the study is very simple and does not differ in any essential way from the usual study which has been done on the effects of partial reward. The major difference was that we were primarily concerned with seeing the effects of the absolute number of nonrewarded trials and with being able to separate these effects from the effects of ratio of reward. We employed four different conditions of "number of unrewarded trials." Some groups experienced 0 unrewarded trials; some groups of animals experienced a total of 16 unrewarded trials in the apparatus; still other groups experienced a moderate number of unrewarded trials, namely, 27; and finally some groups were run who experienced very many unrewarded trials, namely, 72.

Within these conditions, by varying the total number of trials, different conditions of ratio of reward were set up. Some animals were run with 33% reward, others with 50% reward, and still others with 67% reward. Of course, it was not possible to vary the ratio of reward for animals in the condition of 0 unrewarded trials but the animals were run for varying numbers of trials anyhow. Table 1 shows the total design. The numbers in the cells indicate the total number of

trials after preliminary training which the animals in that condition ran. During preliminary training, of course, all groups were rewarded 100% of the time. There were between 11 and 16 animals in each condition. It will be noted that we did not run a condition of 67% reward and 27 unrewarded trials. The reason for this is simple. We ran out of patience and decided this condition was not essential.

It will also be noted that three groups of 0 unrewarded trials were run so that the total number of trials brackets the entire range for the other groups.

Figure 1 shows the results of the experiment. Along the horizontal axis of the figure are indicated the various values of number of unrewarded trials which we employed and along the ordinate are the average number of trials to reach a criterion of extinction. Each circle on the figure represents the results for one of our experimental conditions. The empty circles represent the data for those with the fewest total number of trials. Thus, except for the 0 unrewarded trials conditions, these empty circles represent the data for the 33% reward conditions. Similarly, the dark circles represent the longest number of total trials and hence, for the

TABLE 1

TOTAL NUMBER OF TRIALS AFTER PRELIMINARY TRAINING IN PARTIAL REWARD EXPERIMENT

Reward Schedule	Number of Unrewarded Trials			
	0	16	27	72
33%		24	43	108
50%		31	54	144
67%		48		216
100%	0			
	54			
	216			

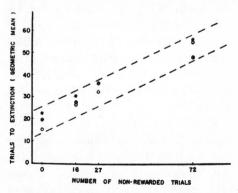

Fig. 1. Number of trials to extinction after partial reward.

partial reward groups, represent the 67% reward conditions.

It is clear from an examination of the figure that, holding constant the number of unrewarded trials, there were only slight differences among the different conditions of ratio of reward. On the other hand, the variable of total number of unrewarded trials has a large and significant effect. It would, indeed, seem that in these data the only variable affecting resistance to extinction after partial reward is the number of unrewarded trials. The results of the experiment are hence quite consistent with the interpretations which we have made from the theory of dissonance.

These data are, of course, encouraging but certainly not conclusive. It would be nice to be able to have more direct evidence that nonreward tends to result in the development of extra preferences. From the point of view of obtaining such more direct evidence concerning the validity of our theoretical interpretation, the partial reward situation is not very adequate. For one thing, our theoretical analysis states that quite different processes occur, psychologically, on rewarded and on unrewarded trials. In a partial reward situation, however, the animal experiences both kinds of trials and, hence, an attempt to separate the effects of the two kinds of trials is bound to be indirect. And, of course, the possibility always exists that the increased resistance to extinction may depend upon some more or less complicated interaction between rewarded and unrewarded trials.

It would then be desirable to be able to compare pure conditions of reward and nonreward. That is, we could test the theory more adequately if we could compare the resistance to extinction of two groups of animals, one of which had always been rewarded in a given place, and the other of which had *never* been rewarded in that same place. This, of course, presents technical problems of how one manages to induce an animal to consistently go to a place where he never gets rewarded. This problem, however, can be solved by employing a variation of what is, essentially, a delay of reward experiment. With the very able assistance and hard work of Edward Uyeno we proceeded to do a series of such experiments in an attempt to get more direct validation of our theoretical derivations. I would like to describe some of these experiments for you.

The apparatus we used was a runway with two boxes in addition to the starting box. The two boxes were, of course, quite easily distinguishable. We will refer to one of them as the end-box and to the other as the mid-box. From the starting place, the animal was to run through a section of alley to the mid-box and then through another section of alley to the end-box. One group of rats was fed on every trial in the mid-box and also fed on every trial in the end-box. We will refer to this group as the 100% reward condition. Another group of rats was never fed in the mid-box but, instead, was delayed there for the same amount of time that it took the other to eat its food. These animals then continued to the end-box where they were also fed on every trial. We will refer to this group as the 0% reward condition. The designations of 100% and 0% reward refer, of course, to the reward in the mid-box. Both groups were rewarded on every trial in the end-box and this, of course, is what induced the animals in the 0% reward condition to run consistently to a place where they were never rewarded.

The procedure which was employed in extinction was also somewhat different from the usual procedure in a delay of reward experiment. Because we were interested in comparing the two groups of animals in their willingness to go to the mid-box where one group had always, and the other group had never, been fed, we ran extinction trials only from the starting position to the mid-box. During extinction, of course, no food was present for either condition and after a short period of time in the mid-box the animals were returned to their home cage. Thus, from this experiment we have a better comparison of the effects of reward and of nonreward. Figure 2 shows the average running times for the two groups during extinction.

The figure shows the data for the first 30 extinction trials averaged in groups of 3 trials each. It is clear from the figure that there is a very marked difference between the two groups of animals. Those who were always fed in the mid-box start off running quite fast (reflecting their speed of running dur-

ing acquisition) but slow down very rapidly. Those animals that were never fed in the mid-box start off more slowly (again reflecting their speed of running acquisition) but they do not show as rapid a rate of extinction. Indeed, between the fourth and fifth blocks of trials the two curves cross over and thereafter the animals run considerably faster to a place where they have never been rewarded than they do to a place where they have always been rewarded.

One may certainly conclude from these data that increased resistance to extinction results from nonreward and that an explanation of the partial reward effect in terms of some interaction between reward and nonreward is not very tenable. Actually, in the experiment I have just described we ran a third group of animals which was rewarded 50% of the time in the mid-box and the results for these animals during extinction fall nicely midway between the two curves in Figure 2. The resistance to extinction of those who were never fed in the mid-box is greater than that of either of the other two groups of animals.

At the risk of being terribly repetitious, I would like to remind you at this point of the explanation I am offering for these data. Briefly, dissonance is introduced as a result of the insufficient reward or absence of reward. As long as the organism is prevented from changing his behavior, the dissonance tends to be reduced by developing some extra preference about something in the situation. The existence of this extra preference leads to the stronger inclination to continue running during extinction trials.

If this explanation is correct, however, one should be able to observe the effects of this extra preference even in a

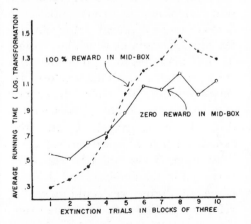

Fig. 2. Running time during extinction in single mid-box experiment.

situation where all the motivation for food was removed. Indeed, it would seem that this would be a better test of this theoretical explanation. We consequently repeated the experiment I have just described to you with one modification. Three days were allowed to elapse between the end of acquisition and the beginning of extinction. During these 3 days food was always present in the cages so that by the time the extinction trials started the animals were quite well fed and not hungry. Food remained always available in their cages during the extinction period. In addition, during the 3 intervening days, each animal was placed for periods of time in the end-box without food being available there. In other words, there was an attempt to communicate to the animal that food was no longer available in the apparatus and anyhow the animals were not very motivated for food.

Extinction trials were, of course, run just from the starting box to the mid-box. Three trials were run each day and Figure 3 shows the results for the first 10 days of extinction. It is clear from an examination of the figure that the

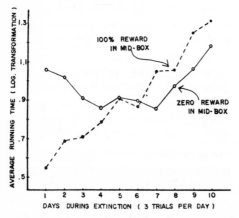

Fig. 3. Running time while satiated during extinction in single mid-box experiment.

results are very similar to the previous results and are, in a sense, even stronger. Those animals who were always fed in the mid-box start off relatively fast and as extinction trials progress the curve shows steady and rather rapid increase in running time. In short, one obtains a familiar kind of extinction curve for these animals.

The group that was never fed in the mid-box, however, shows a very different pattern of behavior. They start off much more slowly than the other group but, for the first 4 days of extinction, they actually run faster than at the beginning. By the seventh day the two curves have crossed and thereafter the 0% reward group runs faster than the 100% reward group. It is also interesting to note that, for the 0% reward group, through the eighth day, one can see no evidence of any extinction having occurred at all. If one is inclined to do so, one can certainly see in these data some evidence that an extra preference of rather weak strength exists for the animals that were never rewarded in the mid-box.

We were sufficiently encouraged by these results so that we proceeded to perform what I, at least, regarded as a rather ambitious experiment. Before I describe the experiment, let me briefly explain the reasoning which lay behind it. It is plausible to suppose that the extra preference which the organism develops in order to reduce dissonance may be focused on any of a variety of things. Let me explain this by using the experiment I have just described as an illustration. Those animals who were never fed in the mid-box, and thus experienced dissonance, could have developed a liking for the activity of running down the alley to the mid-box, they could have developed a preference for some aspect of the mid-box itself, or they could have developed a preference for any of the things they did or encountered subsequent to leaving the mid-box. Experimentally, of course, there was no control over this.

It occurred to us, in thinking about this, that if the dissonance were reduced, at least to some extent, by developing a preference for something about the *place* where the dissonance was introduced, then it would be possible to show the same effects in a very well controlled experiment. In other words, if the dissonance introduced by absence of reward were reduced, at least in part, by developing some liking for the place where they were not rewarded, then one could compare two groups of animals, both of which experienced the identical amount of dissonance, but who would be expected to develop preferences for different places.

To do this we used the same basic technique as in the previous two experiments I have described but with an important modification. Instead of one mid-box, two mid-boxes were used. From the starting box the animals went to Mid-box A, from there to Mid-box B, and from there to the end-box where all animals received food on every trial. Two groups of animals were run in this experiment. Group A was delayed in Mid-box A for a period of time and then was allowed to run directly through Mid-box B to the end-box. Group B was allowed to run directly through Mid-box A but was delayed for a period of time in Mid-box B before being allowed to go to the end-box. In other words, both groups of animals had identical experience. The only difference between the groups lay in the particular box in which they were delayed. (All three boxes were, of course,

quite distinctive.) For the extinction trials the animals were satiated as in the preceding experiment. For the extinction trials the animals were run only from Box A to Box B. That is, during extinction the animals were placed directly into Box A, the door was then opened, and when they ran to Box B were removed to their home cage.

Thus, Group A during extinction was running away from the place where they had been delayed, while Group B was running to the place where they had been delayed. If some extra preference had developed for the place where they had been delayed, we would expect Group B to show more resistance to extinction than Group A. In short, during extinction, Group B should behave like the 0% reward groups in the previous experiments. Group A, however, should behave during extinction more like the 100% reward animals in the preceding experiments.

Figure 4 shows the data for these two groups of animals for the first 10 days of extinction, three trials having been run on each day. The two curves in the figure must, by now, look very familiar

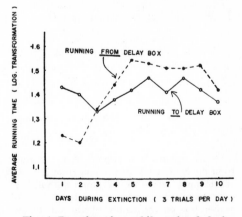

Fig. 4. Running time while satiated during extinction in double mid-box experiment.

to you. The same result is obtained as in the two previous experiments. The initial difference between the two groups again reflects their previous running speed in that section of the apparatus. During acquisition, Group B ran more hesitantly in the section between the two mid-boxes than did Group A. This difference, of course, still exists at the start of the extinction trials. Thereafter, however, Group A, which was running away from its delay box, rapidly increases its running time. Group B, which was running to its delay box, does not increase its time at all and shows no evidence of any extinction during 30 trials. By the fourth day of extinction, the two curves have crossed and thereafter Group B consistently runs faster than Group A.

If one looks carefully at all the data, I think one finds reasonable evidence

that insufficient reward does lead to the development of extra preference. This extra preference, at least in the white rat, seems to be of a rather mild nature, but the magnitude of the effect is quite sufficient to account for the increased resistance to extinction after partial reward or after delay of reward.

Let us then briefly examine the implications of these findings and of the theory of dissonance for our traditional conception of how reward functions. It seems clear that the inclination to engage in behavior after extrinsic rewards are removed is not so much a function of past rewards themselves. Rather, and paradoxically, such persistence in behavior is increased by a history of non-rewards or inadequate rewards. I sometimes like to summarize all this by saying that rats and people come to love things for which they have suffered.

Journal of Abnormal and Social Psychology, 1963, vol. 66, pp. 151–156

Some Hedonic Consequences of the Confirmation and Disconfirmation of Expectancies[1]

J. Merrill Carlsmith and Elliot Aronson

Recent investigations have suggested that theories of cognitive consistency can be adapted to account for individual differences in self-concept (Aronson & Carlsmith, 1962; Deutsch & Solomon, 1959). For example, Aronson and Carl-

[1] This research was supported by a grant from the National Science Foundation (NSF-G-16838) administered by the junior author. The experiment was conducted while the senior author was on the tenure of an NSF fellowship. The authors are indebted to W. G. Cochran for advice on the analysis of the data.

smith, using the theory of cognitive dissonance (Festinger, 1957) as a point of departure, suggested that dissonance occurs most often when an individual's behavior is at variance with his self-concept—i.e., at variance with his expectancy concerning his own behavior. The authors reasoned that, theoretically, behavior which is inconsistent with a self-relevant expectancy should arouse dissonance; dissonance would be aroused whether the self-concept involved is positive or negative. For example, the self-concept "I am not generous" would be dissonant with the cognition "I gave $1,000 to charity." To test this hypothesis, Aronson and Carlsmith conducted a laboratory experiment which demonstrated that subjects who expected to perform poorly on a particular task, but performed well, expressed greater dissonance (discomfort) than subjects who expected to perform poorly and *did* perform poorly.

In the above experiment, Aronson and Carlsmith dealt with a specific and limited kind of expectancy—an expectancy which involved a self-conception regarding one's ability on a particular task. The present experiment is an attempt to generalize this prediction to make it applicable to any expectancy. That is, rather than limiting the prediction to situations involving a person's disconfirmed expectancy about his own behavior, it is now suggested that dissonance is aroused whenever any event occurs which disconfirms any strong expectancy. Thus, the following prediction can be made: If a person firmly expects a certain event and it does not occur, he will experience dissonance. His cognition that he expects the event to occur is dissonant with his cognition that the event did not occur.

Festinger has described dissonance as a state of "psychological discomfort." Previous experiments testing derivations from his theory have inferred the existence of dissonance from observable manifestations of attempts to reduce it. The present experiment was designed to measure the existence of dissonance on a more directly hedonic level. If dissonance arises from the disconfirmation of an expectancy, then a disconfirmed expectancy should result in a hedonically negative state. If one assumes that this negative hedonic tone generalizes to objects in the environment, one can make the following prediction: If a person expects a particular event (X) and instead, a different event (Y) occurs, he will experience dissonance. Consequently, he would judge Y to be less pleasant than if he had had no previous expectancy.

Procedure

In general, the procedure involved: leading the subject to expect that a solution the subject was about to taste would be bitter (or sweet), experimentally varying the strength of his expectancy, experimentally confirming or disconfirming this expectancy, and measuring the subject's perception of the taste of the solution.

The subjects were 52 college students who were paid volunteers. When the subject arrived, the experimenter said that he was a graduate student who was working for two psychologists simultaneously, and that these psychologists were interested in totally different problems. In order to conserve time and money, the experimenter continued, they had decided to attack these two problems in the same experimental session. Thus, the experiment would actually consist of two unrelated experiments which could be done at the same time.

The experimenter explained that the problem one of the psychologists was interested in was people's sensitivity to interpersonal cues—cues emanating from another person which might indicate something about how that person was feeling or what he was thinking.

> For example, suppose that every time I was about to fly into a rage, I performed some idiosyncratic movement, say scratching my head. If you were interested in knowing whether I was about to fly into a rage (so you could escape), you might learn this correlation and thus be able to predict my behavior.

The experimenter explained that the ability to notice such cues was an extremely important part of one's sensitivity to the feeling of others—that all people had such mannerisms, and that people who could learn to identify them quickly were able to predict feelings and thoughts of others and were thus considered perceptive, sensitive, insightful. The experimenter explained that he was interested in studying this process in a highly controlled laboratory situation. He then proceeded to describe the task.

On the table in front of the subject were 24 small paper cups, each containing about 2 cubic centimeters of solution. One half of the cups contained a sweet solution, the other half a bitter solution. The experimenter explained that he would present the subject with a solution which the subject was to taste. Before the subject tasted the solution, the experimenter would present a signal which would indicate whether the solution would taste bitter or sweet. On the basis of this signal the subject was to make a prediction before tasting the solution. The experimenter said that the signals would be mannerisms of his—scratching his head, stroking his nose, etc.

Some of the signals will mean that the next solution will be sweet; some will mean that the next solution will be bitter; some will be completely irrelevant. Your job is to learn what the signals mean and to predict the flavor of the next solution you taste.

One of the variables of interest in the experiment, the experimenter explained, was the effect of motivation on this ability, i.e., whether obtaining a reward for being correct would increase a person's efficiency. In order to test this, two groups were to be studied. One group, which the subject would be a member of, was an experimental group. For this group, there would be monetary payoffs for correct predictions. The subject would win $.50 for every correct guess, and would lose $1.00 for each incorrect guess. The experimenter lent the subject $5.00 with which to play the game, and explained that if the subject ended the experiment with less than $5.00, no money would change hands. There were 18 trials; thus, the subject could win up to $9.00, but

could not lose. Most subjects won between $1.00 and $2.00.

The experimenter continued,

As I mentioned before, I am actually working for two psychologists and I am trying to get data for two separate experiments simultaneously. The other psychologist, Dr. _____, is interested in the perception of taste. Specifically, he is interested in developing a psychophysical scale of taste. The problem is the following: Suppose I gave you two sweet solutions, and one contained twice as much saccharin as the other. Physically, such a solution would be twice as sweet, but psychologically it probably wouldn't be; i.e., it probably wouldn't taste twice as sweet to you. It might taste just a little sweeter, it might taste ten times as sweet. This is what we are trying to find out. We would like a scale, a set of numbers to apply to these solutions, so that if we call one solution "10" and one "20," we can be sure that the latter will taste twice as sweet as the former, regardless of what the physical concentrations actually are.

The experimenter then explained that the subject was to rate each solution he tasted by the method of magnitude estimation. The experimenter told the subject that he would first give him a standard solution which would be called "10." There would be one standard for the sweet, one for the bitter. The test solutions were to be compared with the standards and were to be assigned numbers which were proportional to how sweet or bitter they tasted.

Thus, if it tastes twice as sweet as the standard, you would call it "20," if it tastes half as sweet, call it "5."

The experimenter emphasized that any number could be used. Two scales were to be determined—one for sweet, one for bitter. The experimenter explained that the two scales were completely independent; on each scale a higher number would represent more concentration, i.e., more sweet or more bitter.

The experimenter reviewed briefly the whole sequence which was: the experimenter gave the signal, the subject guessed sweet or bitter, the experimenter gave him the cup, the experimenter told him whether he was correct or not just as the subject tasted the solution, the subject estimated the sweetness or bitterness of the solution.

The experimenter first presented two standards of each solution. One other standard of each solution was given after the ninth trial. The experimenter waited for one minute after each trial in order to allow any aftereffects of the taste to dissipate.[2] Fresh water was available at all times if the subject wished to rinse his mouth. In actuality, all of the sweet solutions and all of the bitter solutions contained precisely the same physical concentration. The sweet solution was a saccharin solution of 2 grams per liter. The bitter was a quinine sulfate solution of .080 grams per liter.

The signals actually used were extremely simple. They consisted of the experimenter's moving his hand to his ear, forehead, and chin as a signal for bitter; nose, forehead, and chin as a signal for sweet. Most subjects learned these signals in three to five trials.

After it was clear that the subject had learned the signals, the experimenter gave the signal for one solution while presenting the subject with the other solution, which caused the subject to be wrong on that trial. The experimenter then resumed the correct signals, and waited until the subject had been correct for four or five trials, at which point the experimenter again gave a misleading signal.

The assumption in this procedure is that the saccharin solution will taste pleasant, and the quinine solution will taste unpleasant. Further, it is assumed that a sweeter solution will taste more pleasant, and a more bitter solution more unpleasant. Evidence in support of these assumptions is reviewed by Pfaffman (1958). In this experiment, this assumption was clearly satisfied for most subjects. For example, many of the subjects spontaneously remarked how unpleasant the quinine sulfate solution tasted, and one subject could not complete the experiment because she feared it would make her sick. However,

there were a few subjects who found the bitter solution to be rather pleasant. Also, there were some subjects who found the saccharin solution unpleasant. In order to be certain that we used only subjects for whom the sweet and bitter solutions were, respectively, pleasant and unpleasant, all subjects were asked the following questions at the conclusion of the experiment:

Would you say the standard sweet solution was pleasant or unpleasant?
Was a sweeter solution more pleasant?
Would you say the standard bitter solution was pleasant or unpleasant?
Was it more unpleasant as it got more bitter?

It will be remembered that all of the solutions were of the same strength; the subjects, however, showed considerable variability in their ratings. Thus, the phrase "a sweeter solution" did have meaning for the subject.

For the analysis of the data on sweet solutions, only those subjects were used who found the solution to be more pleasant as it became sweeter. Similarly, only the data of subjects who found the bitter solution to be more unpleasant as it became more bitter were used in the analysis of bitter solutions. Because of this precaution, the data of 10 of the 52 subjects were eliminated in the analysis of sweet solutions;[3] the data of 3 of the 52 subjects were eliminated in the analysis of the bitter solution.[4]

At the close of the experiment, the experimenter told the subject the true purpose of the experiment and discussed the need for deception.

---

[2] Evidence is presented by Nielson (1958) to show that aftereffects of quinine dissipate in about 50 seconds.

[3] The surprisingly large number of subjects who found the sweet solutions to be unpleasant may be partially explained by the fact that six of them were among the last seven subjects who participated in the experiment. When the experimenter tasted to check this phenomenon, he found that the solution had become stale and indeed was slightly unpleasant.

[4] Five additional subjects were discarded from the analysis: one because he guessed the purpose of the experiment; one because the quinine made her feel sick and she could not complete the experiment; three because they failed to learn the signals.

Results

The hypothesis under consideration is the following: If a person expects a particular event (X) and instead, a different event (Y) occurs, he will experience dissonance. Consequently, he will judge Y to be less pleasant than if he had had no previous expectancy. In terms of the present operations, if a person expects a solution to be sweet, but finds that it is bitter, he will judge the solution to be less pleasant (more bitter). Similarly, if he expects a solution to be bitter, but finds that it is sweet, he will again judge the solution which disconfirms his expectancy to be less pleasant (less sweet).

Before discussing the results, several things should be noted. When the subject is incorrect, there are clearly several factors operating: He loses money ($1.00), he is wrong, and an expectancy is disconfirmed. These can be separated in the analysis. There are some trials on which the subject is incorrect, but has no clear expectancy about what the solution will be. That is, on early trials, before he has learned the signal system, or on trials following a disconfirmation when he feels he does not understand the signal system, the subject does not have a firm expectancy. But when he has predicted correctly for several successive trials, he expects very strongly that the next solution will be what the signal has led him to predict. For this reason, in the analysis we look for trials on which the subject was correct (Correct), trials on which he was incorrect but had no strong expectancy (Incorrect), and trials on which he was incorrect and strongly expected to be correct (Disconfirmation). It was decided to define Disconfirmation by in-

cluding those trials on which all of the following occurred: the subject was incorrect, the experimenter gave an incorrect signal, the subject had been correct on the previous two trials of that flavor. These criteria are probably conservative, in the sense that an independent measure of strength of expectancy might identify some trials as Disconfirmation which we have classified as Incorrect.

Figure 1 shows the mean ratings of sweetness and bitterness for each trial for the Incorrect and Disconfirmation conditions. Because of large differences between subjects in both means and variances, each subject's ratings were transformed to standard scores with a mean of 10 and a variance of 1. Since no subjects had expectancies disconfirmed on the first five trials, the results for these trials are not included.

In examining the theoretical ideas outlined earlier, the following comparisons are of interest. The difference between being correct and being incorrect with an expectancy should be largest, since it contains the effect due to being wrong, the effect due to losing money, and the effect due to having an expectancy disconfirmed. The difference between being correct and being incorrect with no expectancy gives an estimate of the effects of being wrong and losing money. But the crucial comparison is between being incorrect with an expectancy (Disconfirmation) and being incorrect without an expectancy (Incorrect). This provides a control for effects of being wrong and losing money, and should reflect only the effect of having one's expectancies disconfirmed.

Because it was impossible to control completely the trial on which a subject

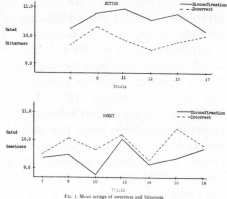

Fig. 1. Mean ratings of sweetness and bitterness.

was correct or incorrect, the effects due to treatments are partially confounded with the effects due to trials. To eliminate this confounding, and get unbiased estimates of treatment effects, an analysis of variance was performed. Although the unequal number of cases in the cells precluded use of the standard formulas for the analysis of variance, it was possible to use a standard analysis of variance model. A least squares solution was obtained, giving unbiased estimates of all treatment effects, and yielding all F and t tests. The analysis of variance is shown in Table 1. It is ap-

TABLE 1

ANALYSIS OF VARIANCE

Source	df	SS	MS	F
Sweet				
Trials	6	32.99	5.50	7.33*
Treatments	2	15.09	7.54	10.06*
Error	250	186.90	.75	
Total	258	234.98		
Bitter				
Trials	5	5.28	1.06	1.29
Treatments	2	11.95	5.98	7.29*
Error	256	210.62	.82	
Total	263	227.85		

* $p = .001$.

TABLE 2

UNBIASED ESTIMATES OF THE EFFECTS OF TREATMENTS ON THE PERCEPTION OF TASTE

Taste	Correct	In-correct	Discon-firma-tion	t
Sweet	10.09ᵃ	9.89	9.47	C × I: 1.32 C × D: 4.58**** I × D: 2.54**
Bitter	10.15ᵇ	9.86	10.57	C × I: 1.86* C × D: 2.89*** I × D: 3.77****

ᵃ Higher scores mean more sweet.
ᵇ Higher scores mean more bitter.
* $p < .10$.
** $p < .02$.
*** $p < .01$.
**** $p < .001$.

parent that the treatment effects are highly significant for both sweet and bitter ($p < .001$ in both cases).

As may be seen in Figure 1, or from the overall means in Table 2, the results for the sweet solutions are completely in line with the hypothesis. The subject perceived the solution as most sweet on trials when he correctly predicted that it would be sweet. On trials when he was incorrect, but had no expectancy, the solution was perceived as less sweet; the least pleasant of all were the cases in which a sweet solution disconfirmed an expectancy.

The bitter solutions were perceived as most bitter on trials when the subject was incorrect with a firm expectancy. The means for the other two groups are in the opposite direction from what one might have predicted from a simple-minded interpretation of association theory; thus, the solution was perceived as more bitter on trials when the subject was correct than on trials when he was incorrect but had no expectancy. This difference is not significant, however ($t = 1.86$, $p < .10$); nor is the comparable difference for the sweet solutions ($t = 1.32$).

The conclusion suggested by these results is that there is no clear effect on the perception of taste due to the subject's being incorrect *if he had no expectancy*. However, when the subject is incorrect, and a firm expectancy is disconfirmed, there is a clear and strong effect on the taste of the solutions which disconfirms the expectancy. Bitter solutions which disconfirm expectancies are perceived as more unpleasant (more bitter); sweet solutions which disconfirm expectancies are perceived as less pleasant (less sweet).

It should be noted that our results for bitter and sweet move, as predicted, in opposite directions. For the bitter solution, a disconfirmed expectancy resulted in a rating of more bitter (higher rating); for the sweet solution a disconfirmed expectancy resulted in a rating of less sweet (lower rating). Consequently, an alternative explanation involving the possible assimilation of the rating toward the expected taste could account for the results involving the sweet solution but would predict the opposite for the bitter solution. Likewise, an alternative explanation involving the possible exaggeration of the strength due to surprise (contrast effect) could account for the results involving the bitter solution, but would predict the opposite for the sweet solution. There would seem to be no reason to predict contrast in one flavor and assimilation in the other. It appears that the only unitary explanation for the results is one that takes into account the affectual direction of the two continua, thus predicting opposite results for bitter and sweet.

Our theory leads to the prediction that the stronger the expectancy, the greater the negative affect following its disconfirmation. Such a prediction is apparently contrary to affectual theories which suggest that positive affect follows a departure from an expected result (e.g., McClelland, 1953; White, 1959). For example, McClelland's discrepancy hypothesis holds that stimuli widely discrepant from a person's adaptation level produce negative affect; stimuli mildly discrepant from a person's adaptation level produce positive affect; stimuli which coincide with a person's adaptation level produce boredom. Here, level of adaptation can be considered to be identical with an expectancy which has been formed by repeated invariant events. This hypothesis was confirmed in an experiment by Haber (1958) who found that subjects who had adapted to a given temperature preferred a slight change in temperature to either no change or to a large change. It would be of interest to determine the condition under which a disconfirmed expectancy is pleasant or unpleasant. For example, in the present experiment the expectancy was ego involving—i.e., the subject felt that he was *right* when he made his prediction. This was not the case in Haber's experiment. Moreover, in the present experiment, disconfirmation and confirmation had important consequences for the future; i.e., a disconfirmed expectancy meant that the subject would have to reformulate his ideas if he wanted to be correct on the next trials. In addition, it is clear that certain kinds of situations are inherently more boring than others. In the case of a very boring situation, a disconfirmed expectancy might be a welcome relief from boredom. It is clear that there are many variables which must be taken into account before a precise statement can be made concerning the relationship between affect and the disconfirmation of an expectancy. What this study has demonstrated is that under certain conditions (not boring, future relevant, and ego involving) the disconfirmation of a strong expectancy leads to negative affect.

Summary: In a test of the hypothesis that events which disconfirm expectancies will be perceived as unpleasant, Ss tasted a random sequence of sweet and bitter solutions. On the basis of certain sgnals given by the E, they developed expectancies or hypotheses about whether the next solution would be bitter or sweet. On trials when the Ss' expectancies were disconfirmed due to incorrect signals, the solutions were judged to taste more unpleasant. Thus, a bitter solution was rated more bitter; a sweet solution was rated less sweet. The results were interpreted in terms of Festinger's theory of cognitive dissonance.

Journal of Comparative and Physiological Psychology, 1964, vol. 57, pp. 367–372

Some Nondecremental Effects of Effort[1]

Michael Lewis

The relationship between effort and performance is neither simple nor straightforward. Hull (1943, 1952) believed that any increment in the amount of effort required of an organism to complete a response leads to a corresponding decrement in the tendency of the organism to perform that response. Experimental demonstrations of this phenomenon have acquired a singular importance in providing the empirical basis for the Hullian concepts of conditioned and reactive inhibition. Thus formulated, these concepts of inhibition have been assigned a significant role in the interpretation of such seemingly diverse behavioral phenomena as experimental extinction, discrimination,

and spontaneous recovery. Other investigators (Aiken, 1957; Applezweig, 1951; Maatsch, Adelman & Denny, 1954) have shown, however, that animals will produce an effortful response in an extinction series for as long as an equivalent group of animals will continue making a considerably less effortful response, provided that each group was extinguished at the same effort level that had been used in acquisition. Thus, although the animals in the high-effort group expended more energy per response unit, they demonstrated as much resistance to extinction as did animals in the low-effort group. The results of Wright's (1937) and Child's (1946) work have demonstrated that, contrary to the so-called "law of least effort," under certain conditions, children confronted with two or more alternatives will choose the most effortful pathway to reach a goal. In addition, Olds' (1953), Aronson's (1961), and Lewis' (1964) results suggest that the more effort an

[1] The experiments, conducted at the University of Pennsylvania, were supported by the National Institute of Mental Health Grants No. MF-11,965 and M-1260 and by a National Institute of Mental Health Grant No. M-4202 to R. L. Solomon. This paper was read at the Eastern Psychological Association Convention in New York, April 1963.

individual expends to acquire an object, the greater is his preference for that object. Each of these areas of investigation raises serious questions for an interpretation of effort that specifies only its decremental effect.

Three experiments were designed to test the hypothesis that the value of an object is functionally related to the amount of effort required to obtain that object. The value of the object, in this case Rice Krispies (RK), was defined in two ways: (a) the effect on an animal's running speed in a straight-alley maze; and (b) the reward value measured in two ways: the *rate* of eating and the *amount* eaten under near satiation.

Experiment 1

Method

Subjects. Twenty female albino rats 90–110 days of age were assigned randomly to two groups: a high-effort group (HE) and a low-effort group (LE). The two groups were equal with respect to mean body weight. One LE S died during the course of the experiment.

Apparatus. The equipment consisted of a training box, a straight-alley maze, and a feeding box. The training box was 3¼ × 36 × 10 in., with a wire-mesh floor and ceiling. The box was painted black. A pulley was attached to one end of the box. Either an 80-gm. or 5-gm. weight was suspended from the pulley by a nylon thread. The thread could be fastened to S's harness by a removable metal clip. The straight-alley maze was 3 × 37 × 4 in. The floor and sides of the maze were gray, and it was covered with a transparent plastic ceiling. Two guillotine-type doors separated the maze into three compartments: a start, a running area, and a goal area. Photoelectric cells operating two electronic clocks provided a measure of the time elapsed from the raising of the start door until S entered the goal area. The feeding compartment was 4 × 9 × 3 in. Except for a transparent plastic ceiling, it was constructed entirely of wood and was painted gray.

Procedure. In the pretraining phase Ss were tamed and acquainted with the apparatus. After 4–5 days of taming, each S was fitted with a rubberband harness which was placed over its forelegs and chest. After a short period of adaptation to the harness, Ss were placed on a 23-hr. deprivation—1-hr. feeding schedule, with water continuously available.

Once each day during the pretraining, Ss were placed in the end of the training box where the pulley was located, and Purina lab chow was placed at the other end of the box (the goal area). No weights were attached to Ss during this period. The entire pretraining period lasted 10 days. On the first day of the training stage, weighted thread was attached to Ss when they were placed in the training box, and Rice Krispies (RK) were substituted for Purina lab chow. The high-effort group of Ss (HE) pulled the thread weighted with 80 gm.: the low-effort group (LE) pulled the thread weighted with 5 gm. Twenty RK pellets were placed in the goal area. After 2 min., Ss were removed from the training box and were fed Purina lab chow in their home cages. This procedure was followed for 9 successive days, one trial per day. In the test phase, begun on the tenth day following the initiation of training, Ss were placed in the straight-alley maze with no weight attached. Each S had five successive trials in the maze. Each of the four trials was terminated when S had consumed the two RK pellets in the goal area, or as soon as 1 min. had elapsed, whichever occurred first. On Trial 5 S was given a maximum of 2 min. to consume 20 RK pellets. After S ate the RK pellets, or after 2 min. had elapsed, S was removed from the maze and placed in the home cage. On the second day of the test stage, Ss were again placed in the training box and were given an additional training trial under the effort conditions. Thus, during the test phase, training days were alternated with test days, until a total of 8 test days and 7 training days had been completed.

On the eighth test day, Ss were returned to their home cages and were allowed free access to food and water for 24 hr. At the end of that time Ss were deprived of food for 3 hr. and were then placed in a feeding compartment for 30 min. Each compartment contained 10 gm. of RK pellets.

Measures. Measures obtained on each S were (a) time to reach goal area in the test maze, (b) rate of eating in the test maze, and (c) number of RK pellets consumed under near satiation conditions. The first measure simply was the time to reach the goal area. The second measure was the amount of time S required to consume 20 RK pellets on the fifth trial of the test days. The third measure was the weight of the RK pellets consumed in the feeding compartment after 24 hr. of ad-lib. food and water. The pellets were weighed before and after the 30-min. feeding, and the difference between the weights provided this score.

Results

Figure 1 presents the results obtained from an analysis of the time taken to reach the goal area in the test maze. The Mann-Whitney U test (Siegel, 1956) applied to individual S's median running speed across all trials failed to reach significance. An analysis of each day's running scores by the Mann-Whitney U test, revealed that the HE group ran significantly faster than the LE group on Days 4 and 7 ($U = 22, 24$; $p < .05$, respectively). Similarly, the HE Ss ate faster than did the LE Ss, but these differences fell short of statistical significance ($CR = 1.50, df = 17$).

The last measure, based on the number of RK pellets consumed under near satiation conditions, did significantly differentiate the groups. The HE Ss consumed significantly more RK pellets than did the LE Ss ($U = 7, p < .002$).

Discussion

The experimental procedure did influence differentially the two effort groups. While the results are modest, they all point to an effort effect. To test the reliability of these findings and to

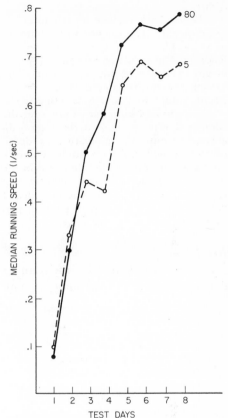

Fig. 1. Median running speed of each effort group over the 8 test days (5 trials per test day).

determine whether the obtained difference varied as a function of the amount of weight placed on Ss, the entire experiment was repeated.

Experiment 2[2]

Although the second study was in most essential respects a replication of the first, it seemed advisable to include two intermediate weight groups, consisting of Ss that pulled 30-gm. and 55-gm. weights in the training trials.

[2] The data of Experiment 2 were collected by Jerry Keller.

Method

Subjects. Forty female albino rats, 90–110 days old, were assigned to four groups of 10 Ss. These Ss were obtained from the Rockford Farm Colony. Several Ss (7) died during the course of this experiment. Elimination of these Ss reduced the 30-gm. and 80-gm. groups to 7 and 6 Ss, respectively.

Apparatus and procedure. Except for the additional weights used in the intermediate-effort groups, the apparatus was identical to that used in the first study. The procedure was the same as that followed in the previous experiment except that the test phase of the experiment was extended 4 days, allowing 10 rather than 8 sets of performance trials in the test maze.

Results

Presented in Figure 2 are the running data obtained in the test maze. A com-

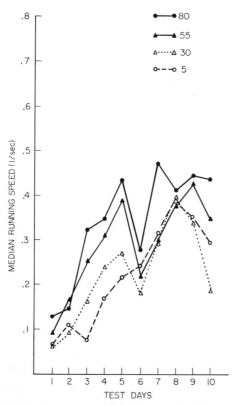

Fig. 2. Median running speed of each effort group over the 10 test days (5 trials per test day).

parison of Ss' median running speeds across all trials revealed the superior performance of the 80-gm. group as compared to the 5-gm. and 30-gm. groups ($U = 14$, $p < .05$; $U = 8$, $p < .01$, respectively). No other comparisons were significant. The data indicate a fairly consistent monotonic relationship between effort and running speed for the first 5 days.[3] The analysis by day for the difference between 80-gm. and 5-gm. groups revealed that the 80-gm. group showed superior performance on Days 3, 4, 5, and 7 ($U = 3$, $p < .001$; $U = 16$, $p < .06$; $U = 9$. $p < .01$; $U = 18$, $p < .09$, respectively). It should be noted that the heavily weighted group diverges from the lightly weighted group at the third, fourth, and fifth days. This pattern is quite similar to that observed in the first experiment.

The eating rate results are shown in Table 1. Comparisons among the individual groups indicate only one significant difference, namely, the 80-gm. group ate the pellets significantly faster than did the 5-gm. group ($U = 10$, $p < .02$).

Also shown in Table 1 are the amounts of RK consumed following 22-hr. free feeding. While the 80-gm. group ate more RK than the 5-gm.

TABLE 1

EATING BEHAVIOR OF THE Ss BY WEIGHT PULLED DURING TRAINING

Group	Amount eaten (gm. in ½ hr.)		Rate of eating (No. of RK in 10 sec.)
	Mdn.	M	Mdn.
80 gm.	5.0	4.2	2.44
55 gm.	3.0	3.3	2.39
30 gm.	2.5	3.0	1.36
5 gm.	1.0	2.2	1.60

[3] The E usually assigned to run Ss was ill and another E took his place on Days 6 and 7.

TABLE 2

BEHAVIOR MEASURES OF Ss DURING
TRAINING PERIOD

Group	Mdn. RK consumed[a]	Mdn. time (in sec.) spent in goal area[b]	Mdn. time (in sec.) to reach Goal[c]
80 gm.	15.9	98.2	7.8
55 gm.	16.5	83.8	4.7
30 gm.	11.2	85.6	6.5
5 gm.	13.4	75.8	6.8

[a] Kruskal-Wallis $H = 10.7$; $.01 < p < .02$.
[b] Kruskal-Wallis $H = 12.5$; $p < .01$.
[c] Kruskal-Wallis $H = 9.33$; $.02 < p < .05$.

group, the only significant difference between the groups is that the 80-gm. group ate more RK than the 30-gm. group ($U = 8$, $p < .03$). It should be noted, however, that the means and medians show a monotonic inverse relationship to the amount of weight applied to Ss in the training series. The probability that this predicted ordering would occur by chance is $p = .04$.

Table 2 presents the results obtained from an analysis of Ss' behavior in the training box. The 80-gm. group ate significantly more RK and remained in the goal area a significantly greater period of the time than did the 5-gm. group ($U = 11$, $p < .05$; $U = 4$, $p < .02$). For the most part, these findings indicate that the heavier weighted Ss tended to require less time to reach the goal area, consume more RK pellets, and remain in the goal area longer than did the lighter weighted Ss.

Discussion

The second experiment provided additional evidence for the nondecremental effect of effort. Because of the differential and high mortality rate among Ss in this experiment, as well as their general irritability, the results might be explained by differential health and strength: those 80-gm. Ss who survived may have been healthier and stronger than Ss in the 5-gm. condition. This position would also have to argue that the death of the 5-gm. S in Experiment 1 left that group with healthier and stronger Ss. On the basis of a health rather than an effort argument, the 5-gm. group should have performed better than the 80-gm. in the first experiment. This was not the case. Nor can this argument account for the superior behavior of the 55-gm. group in which no animals died. Nevertheless, in order to establish firmly that the observed effect was produced by effort, a third experiment was performed.

Experiment 3[4]

Method

Subjects. A high-effort (80 gm.) group and a low-effort (5 gm.) group, each containing 15 Ss, were used.

Apparatus and procedure. These were exactly the same as in Experiment 1.

Results

Figure 3 presents the running speed data. The 80-gm. group once again performed better than the 5-gm. group in the straight-alley runway. The over-all test of significance, individual Ss' median running speed across trials, was just short of significance ($U = 84$, $p < .10$). While an analysis by day revealed no significant differences, the fourth and fifth days showed the greatest differences between the two groups. This superior performance and consummatory behavior was consistent with the results of both Experiments 1 and 2.

Both the eating rate measure and the

4 The data of Experiment 3 were collected by Faith Lubin.

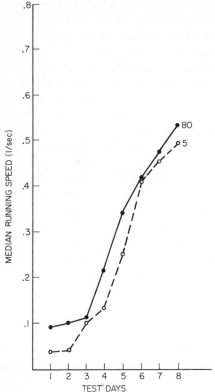

Fig. 3. Median running speed of each effort group over the 8 test days (5 trials per test day).

straight-alley maze, faster eating rate, and greater amount of food consumed. Differences in the performance data were not great but the consistent superiority of Ss trained under high effort, especially on the first 5 days, appears to indicate more than a superficial similarity between experimental results. Consummatory behavior proved to indicate more strongly the differential effect of the training conditions. The results of all three experiments indicate a limited effort effect, and it must be concluded, therefore, that for the rat, the effort variable has a weak influence on the shift in the value of a stimulus-event. Festinger (1961) in discussing the effect of effort also has suggested that "this extra preference, at least in the white rat, seems to be of a rather mild nature . . . [p. 11]."

Several theoretical positions can account for the presented findings. Festinger's cognitive dissonance theory (1957, 1961) has led him to conclude that when an organism obtains an "insufficient reward" following an expenditure of energy, he will either discontinue his effortful activity, or attribute additional value to the activity or to other aspects of the goal situation. This development of an "extra preference" for the activity or situation is seen as the consequence of the dissonance-reducing activity of the organism.

A second model of behavior could argue that high effort interferes with a goal-directed response, and therefore results in frustration (Brown & Farber, 1951; Hull, 1952; Sears, Maccoby, & Levin, 1957). Such an interpretation would maintain that the effort itself did not directly affect the value of the external reinforcer, but rather that affected drive level and the consequent reinforcement value of drive reduction.

amount consumed measure provided evidence to indicate that the 80-gm. group ate faster and ate more than the 5-gm. group. These differences were, however, short of significance ($U = 86$, $p < .15$; $U = 93$, $p < .20$, respectively).

Discussion

The results of all three experiments provide support for the hypothesis that effort can affect the value of a goal object as a reinforcer during the initial effort experience. Specifically, the data support the hypothesis that Ss expending the greatest effort in the training series develop the strongest preference for the food, and that this preference is reflected in faster performance in the

The same kind of interpretative problem exists where frustration is defined as withdrawal or delay of expected reward (Amsel, 1958).

A third interpretation could emphasize the fact that proprioceptive stimuli associated with high effort are more intense or perceptually articulate (have greater S_D value), and that their discriminative properties enhance their derived (secondary) value for any given amount of original external reinforcement. After training with differential effort, in any subsequent test of the value of a reinforcer in which a response at all similar to the training response is used, the apparent value of the external reinforcer might seem greater for a group trained under high effort. This effort effect, however, could be attributed to the greater secondary reinforcement value in the cue properties of the "new" response because of its similarity to the original training response. Thus, in the test maze, the response of moving forward to the goal area could have generalized more strongly for the high-effort group than for the low-effort group, and could thereby account for the former group's greater running speed. While this explanation can account for the running data, it cannot explain the differences found between the effort groups by the consummatory measure.

Finally, a fourth interpretation might emphasize the attentional factor. The technique of fastening a weight to S's harness not only produces more effortful responding, but also seems to reduce activity not directed toward obtaining the goal (e.g., jumping about, exploratory behavior, examination of the harness) among the high-effort, rather than the low-effort Ss. These observations suggest that the latter group of Ss acquired responses which were inconsistent with the behavior of moving forward to the goal area and eating the RK. Further, it would be reasonable to expect that competing responses acquired in the training box would be generalized to the test maze, with the consequence that the low-effort group would be at a disadvantage until the competing responses were extinguished in this setting. If these suppositions are valid, one would expect the presence of competing responses adversely to affect the performance and consummatory behavior of the low-effort group in the training box as well as in the test maze. Examination of the data in Experiment 2 supports this interpretation. The groups that pulled the heavier weight tended to perform and eat faster than groups that pulled the lighter weight in both the training box and test maze.

Summary: 3 experiments, designed to test the hypothesis that the reward value of an object is functionally related to the amount of effort required to obtain that object, were carried out in which several groups of rats were trained to pull 5–80 gm. weights in order to obtain a minimal amount of a relatively unique food reward. The weight that S pulled was constant from trial to trial. 3 independent measures of value were used: performance in a straight-alley maze; rate of eating; amount eaten under near satiation. Results of all 3 experiments were consistent, and while attaining limited statistical significance, tended to occur for all measures in the predicted direction.

Chapter 7

CONFLICT

The study of conflict has been one of the most extensively investigated areas of motivated behavior. The reason seems quite clear—several very explicit models, especially those of Neal Miller and Kurt Lewin, were available. These models were easily tested and easily generated new predictions about conflict behavior. Lewin's was not presented in quite as flexible a form, and was gradually absorbed by Miller's conflict-gradients model, which has dominated the field for over twenty years.

The papers in this section were all chosen to illustrate various aspects of conflict behavior and the different ways it is studied. Not all of the results are in perfect agreement, but this area is perhaps clearer than any other in the psychology of motivation. The basic tenets of Miller's model seem well established. The research issues now center on the extension of the assumptions in the model and the nature of some of the processes, especially the interaction among the approach and avoidance gradients.

While Worell's paper is the only one included that bears directly on the motivational patterns that arise during conflict, this aspect is present at one level or another in each of these papers. In this sense, in addition to having to solve the conflict itself, an individual also has to face the arousal of new motives that reflect his previous feelings about being in conflict. As with punishment, which arouses new means of handling the punishment independent of the effects on the punished behavior, conflict has similar properties and effects. In this sense, merely knowing the relevant gradients and distance is not sufficient to predict all of the possible behavior patterns during conflict.

American Psychologist, 1961, vol. 16, pp. 12–24

Some Recent Studies of Conflict Behavior and Drugs[1]

Neal E. Miller

Clinical studies of mental disease indicate the extreme importance of fear and conflict, two factors which usually are closely interrelated. Studies of men in combat show clearly that practically all of the common symptoms of neuroses, and even psychoses, can be produced by intense fear and conflict. Similarly, experimental studies on animals show that fear and conflict can produce behavioral disturbances, and even psychosomatic symptoms such as stomach acidity, ulcers, cardiac symptoms, and increased susceptibility to infection. Even in normal life, fear and conflict contribute significantly to human physical and mental fatigue.

My earlier work on conflict behavior (Miller, 1944, 1959) was closely integrated by theory. I started with principles which had been abstracted from results of experiments in the simplified conditioning situation, and made a few additional assumptions. First, very simple deductions from these principles were tested in very simple experimental situations. Then, step by step, attempts were made to apply the joint action of a number of principles to more complex situations with additional experimental checks at each successive stage

of development. The studies I am talking about here are related to the same theory; but they also attempt to investigate new variables which ultimately should be incorporated into the theory, after we have enough data to formulate reasonably probable principles. Since I am investigating a variety of such variables, the studies are somewhat heterogeneous.

In both the former work and these studies, I have benefited greatly by interaction with my students. The work I report here is that of the entire group in my laboratory. It continues to be a great pleasure to work with such wonderful groups of students and collaborators.[2]

Effects of Sodium Amytal on Conflict

First, I shall describe some studies of effects of drugs on fear and conflict done in collaboration with Herbert

[1] Work on this paper and on studies cited in it was supported by Grants M 647 and MY 2949 from the National Institute of Mental Health, United States Public Health Service.

[2] In addition to those mentioned in the text, I want to acknowledge the help on various experiments of K. Gustav Ogren and Charles W. Alkire, who helped in the construction of the apparatus; Arlo K. Myers, Gordon H. Bower, who helped in a supervisory capacity; and the following who helped with the running of experimental animals: Nariyuki Agarie, Edward E. Etheridge, Elizabeth S. Jackson, Libby Michel, Phyllis Miller, Roberta Pritzker, Gerald Schwartz, Gail E. Tidd, Russell Tousley, Sylvia A. Wagner, and Hanna B. Weston.

Barry, III. One of our purposes is to study how performance in a number of experimental situations which presumably measure fear is changed by various drugs which presumably affect fear. We want to see whether fear behaves as a single unitary variable, or whether certain drugs have more effect on the crouching freezing pattern, while others have more effect on startle and avoidance responses, or whether the results are still more complex (Miller & Barry, 1960).

In the course of this work, we have devised a number of techniques for getting repeated measures of conflict behavior, so that each animal can be used as his own control, and so that a variety of drugs can be tested with the same group of animals.

Another of our purposes (which is the basis of the work to be exemplified here) is to make analytical studies of the behavioral effects of certain drugs which are definitely known to have interesting effects on human behavior. I shall illustrate our work by presenting some results of an analytical series of experimental studies still in progress on one of the drugs with interesting clinical effects, amobarbital sodium, commonly called sodium amytal. I believe that in a modest and incomplete way the studies of this drug illustrate a type of work which is needed on a variety of selected drugs, each of which has well-established, but different, psychological effects on the human subject.

A decade ago, John Dollard and I (1950) advanced the hypothesis that the therapeutic effects of this drug, which are especially notable in combat neuroses, are produced by reducing the avoidance component of an approach-avoidance conflict more than the approach one. In fairly extensive exploratory work on rats, Baily and I (1952) were unable to demonstrate such an effect, but we did readily get the fear-reducing effect in an experiment on cats. In the current experiment on rats under the supervision of Barry, this drug has produced unusually consistent effects in ameliorating approach-avoidance conflict. The unexplained discrepancy with the early exploratory results on rats is puzzling and indicates the danger of generalizing too widely from observations of drug effects in a single experimental situation.

Figure 1 shows the effects of an intraperitoneal injection of 20 mg/kg of amobarbital sodium, commonly called sodium amytal, on a variety of experimental tests of fear and conflict in the albino rat. Let me briefly describe the tests.

In the *telescope alley* test, on the first trial, the rats run 1 foot to the reward, where they never receive electric shock. (Therefore this trial is labeled "0" on the ordinate which indicates threat of shock.) On each successive trial, the rats are required to run an additional foot and occasionally receive the shocks at the goal which, when they occur, are stronger the longer the distance to the goal. Incidentally, the shocks in all of our experiments are given through a series resistance of approximately 200,000 ohms, which accounts for the high voltages. The current is 60 cycle ac.

In this test the cues for danger are primarily proprioceptive and visual. The response, which is running, involves considerable movement and is rewarded every trial.

In the *automated conflict* test, the rats press a bar for a reward on a variable interval schedule. The first 2 minutes are safe, but after that, an increasingly loud tone signals unpredict-

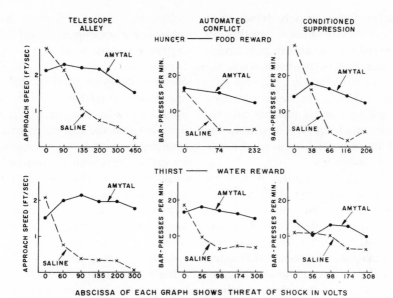

ABSCISSA OF EACH GRAPH SHOWS THREAT OF SHOCK IN VOLTS
SODIUM AMYTAL 20 mg/kg 20 minutes before test

Fig. 1. Effects of an intraperitoneal injection of 20 mg/kg of amobarbital sodium (sodium amytal) administered to Sprague-Dawley albino rats 20 minutes before testing in six experiments on fear and conflict by different techniques described in the text.

able shocks on the bar which, when they occur, are increasingly strong the louder the tone. For the last 2 minutes, the tone and shock are turned off. The cues for danger are primarily auditory, the test chamber severely limits movement, and the response of standing on the hind legs and pressing a bar is rewarded on a variable interval schedule.

The *conditioned suppression* test is similar except that the shock is delivered via the grid floor and is inescapable, so that we are measuring conflict with "freezing," rather than with active withdrawal from the bar. Except for the minor innovation of the gradually increasing tone correlated with increasingly strong shocks, this last test is identical, of course, with the conditioned emotional response (CER) which has been developed out of Estes and Skinner's (1941) classic paper and

has been extensively used by Hunt (1956), Brady (1956), and others.

On the test trials shown in Figure 1, no electric shocks were given, so we are dealing with the effects of fear, rather than of pain plus fear. In order to control for any effects specific to the approach drive, animals in the experiments represented in the top row were motivated by hunger and rewarded by food, while those in the bottom row were motivated by thirst and rewarded by water.

It can be seen that the results under all of these various conditions were highly similar. Looking at the beginning of each curve, which represents performance with little or no fear, it can be seen that, in general, the amytal reduced performance below the placebo level. This part of the test acts as a control to show that the effects of the amytal were not simply to produce an increase in the approach drive, or to act as a general stimulant. As the rats encountered cues to which increasingly strong fear had been conditioned, the performance following placebo was markedly reduced. But the performance under sodium amytal was not affected nearly as much by the fear-inducing cues. Thus, amytal improved the performance under fear.

The fact that so similar results appear in tests involving different cues, different responses, and different drives, makes it unlikely that the effects are specific to the peculiarities of a certain testing situation. The remarkable agreement in the results of the six different experiments makes it clear that sodium amytal definitely reduced the relative strength of fear in our different conflict situations.

Having experimentally demonstrated a striking effect on rats consonant with clinical observations on people, the next step is to determine how this effect is produced. More precise knowledge of the detailed behavioral effects of this drug is needed in order to know under what circumstances a fear-reducing effect can be expected to occur. It is also needed as a basis for relating behavioral effects to results secured with powerful new neurophysiological and biochemical techniques for studying the action of drugs on different parts of the brain.

PRIMACY OF HABIT VERSUS
DIRECT ACTION ON FEAR

In all of the preceding experiments, the amytal improved performance by reducing the relative strength of the fear-motivated habit. How was this effect achieved: directly by a selective action on the brain mechanisms involved in fear, or indirectly by other means? For example, in all of these experiments, as well as in all other experiments that I know of on the effects of drugs on conflict, the habit of approach was established first, and the habit of avoidance second. Perhaps the drug reduced the fear-motivated avoidance not because it has a selective effect on certain fear centers, but rather because it has a selective effect on the more recently established habit.

Perhaps there is something special about the first habit to be established in any situation that makes it more resistant to drug effects—and also to other interventions. In their trail blazing papers on primary inhibition, Szwejkowska (1959) and Konorski and Szwejkowska (1952) have shown that whether a cue is first presented in an excitatory or inhibitory role makes a great deal of difference in the ease of subsequent excitatory or inhibitory conditioning, even after several reversals of the role. Perhaps primacy is more important than we have realized. How can we test for its effects in our experiments on drugs?

In the simplest of a series of experiments on this problem, we trained an animal first to go right in a T maze and then to go to the left. After the second habit was fairly well established, we tested with injections of drug or saline. The sodium amytal produced an increase in errors which would be consistent with the primary hypothesis. Since the errors did not reliably exceed the 50% that would be expected by chance, we were unable to discriminate a differential resistance of the first-established habit to the drug from a mere increase in random behavior.

In another experiment, we tried establishing the fear of the tone in a

Skinner box first before we trained the animal to press a bar to secure food there. In the hope of attaching the fear specifically to the tone, and avoiding too much fear of the whole situation, we started out with weak shocks first and gradually increased them after the animal had a chance to learn the discrimination. This procedure apparently was reasonably successful, because it was not extraordinarily difficult subsequently to train the animals to eat and then to press the bar during silent periods in the Skinner box. Then we tested for the effects of sodium amytal. If this drug primarily affects fear, results should be similar to our previous ones, but if it primarily affects the most recent habit, our results should be completely reversed.

Figure 2 shows the results. You can see that the results were similar to our previous ones; the sodium amytal had the greater effect on fear, even though it was the first-established habit. In this experiment we may have had some residual fear of the general testing situation. Such fear would account for the low initial rate of bar pressing and for the fact that the amytal had some beneficial effect on performance even

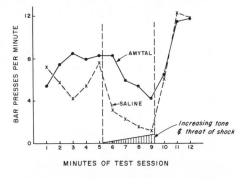

Fig. 2. In the conditioned suppression test, sodium amytal affects the habit motivated by fear rather than the habit established most recently. (The rats had learned to fear the tone before they learned to press the bar.)

before the fear-evoking tone was sounded.

In another experiment on the same topic, we used a technique analogous to our telescope alley. We used a shuttle alley 8 feet long with a light bulb at either end. Five seconds after the light at one end started flashing, an electric shock was delivered through the sections of the grid floor. This shock was strongest at the lighted end and progressively weaker in farther sections, with the one at the opposite end having no shock. In this way, we trained the rats to shuttle from one end of the alley to the other, always staying away from the flashing light. After they had learned this, we gave the hungry rats trials of being started at alternate ends of the darkened alley, and finding food pellets in tiny cups in the center of each 1-foot section. Then they were given trials with the light flickering at the far end from the start. On these trials shocks occurred on the grid at unpredictable times, being stronger, as before, nearer to the flashing light. The rat was taken out after he had been in the alley 2 minutes, or had taken the pellet in the section nearest the flashing light.

Following this training, the animals were given the drug and placebo tests. During these test trials, no shock was actually given. The results are presented in Figure 3. It can be seen that under amytal, the animals approached farther toward the flashing light into sections with a higher threat of shock than they did after a placebo. Since the habit of approaching was established after the fear of the sections near the flashing light, we would expect exactly the *opposite* results if the main effect of the amytal had been to weaken most the most recently established habit.

The results of these two different

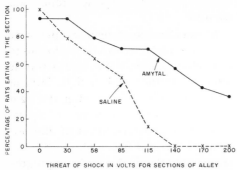

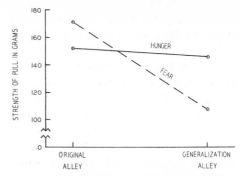

Fig. 3. In the shuttle alley, sodium amytal reduces the strength of the originally learned habit of avoiding electric shock associated with a flashing light more than it does that of the subsequently learned habit of advancing to eat pellets of food found in cups spaced at 1-foot intervals.

Fig. 4. The gradient of stimulus generalization of avoidance motivated by fear contrasted with that of approach motivated by hunger. (The strength of pull of each rat was measured twice in the same alley in which he was originally trained and twice in a different alley, with the sequence of testing balanced.) (From Murray & Miller, 1952)

experiments indicate that the amytal did not produce its fear-reducing effects merely by weakening the more recently established habit.

STIMULUS CHANGE VERSUS DIRECT ACTION ON FEAR MECHANISM

As background for the next experiment, I shall remind you of some older results which extend the notion that the gradient of avoidance is steeper than that of approach from the original gradients in space, to gradients of stimulus generalization. Edward Murray and I (1952) trained one group of hungry rats, which wore harnesses attached to a string, to run down a wide white alley to secure food at the goal. We trained another similar group to run down the same alley to avoid electric shock by reaching an island of safety at the goal. Two more groups were similarly trained in a narrow black alley. Then half of each group was tested in the *same* alley in which they had been trained, and the other half was tested in the *other* alley for stimulus generalization. The rats were

temporarily restrained halfway down the alley while their strength of pull was measured. You can see by Figure 4 that the gradient of stimulus generalization of avoidance was steeper and crossed that of approach. This means that a change in the stimulus situation weakens tendencies to avoid more than those to approach.

Doris Kraeling and (Miller & Kraeling, 1952) tested th application of this principle to a conflict situation by training one group of hungry rats to run down the wide white alley, and another group to run down the narrow black alley to get food. Then, both groups were given increasingly strong shocks at the goal until the avoidance prevented them from reaching it. After this, one-third of each group was given test trials in the same alley, one-third in a somewhat different grey alley of intermediate width, and one-third in the opposite alley. As you can see from Figure 5, more of the rats reached the goal when tested in the different alleys than when tested in the same one. The

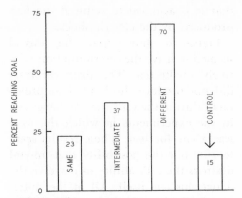

Fig. 5. Effects of stimulus generalization on an approach-avoidance conflict. **More rats reached the goal when tested in a different alley than when tested in the one in which the approach and avoidance tendencies were originally established.** (From Miller and Kraeling, 1952)

change in cues had altered the balance of conflict in favor of approaching.

But this is exactly the same kind of effect that was produced by the sodium amytal. Perhaps this drug does not have a direct effect specific to the fear mechanism, but only affects fear indirectly by changing the stimulus situation. How can we test for this?

To test for this possibility, we performed another experiment in which we gave half of the animals their avoidance training in the normal state, as is customarily done, but gave the other half their avoidance training under the influence of the drug. Then half of each of these two groups was tested following isotonic saline, and the other half following drug injection. This experiment was performed in the telescope alley.

The 2 × 2 design and results are summarized in Table 1. Adding up the rows shows the effect of having had the amytal during training. The effect is in the direction of fear-reduction, but is not reliable. Adding up the columns shows the effect of amytal during test-

TABLE 1

AVERAGE SPEED OF APPROACH IN THE LAST 6 INCHES OF THE TELESCOPE ALLEY DURING A SERIES OF TESTS FOR FEAR WITHOUT SHOCKS

Training	Testing		
	Amytal	Saline	Sum
Amytal	1.00	.82	1.82
Saline	1.14	.54	1.68
Sum	2.14	1.36	3.50

Notes.—Trials in which the rat failed to reach the goal are scored as zero speed. Speed of approach is in feet per second.

ing. The difference is larger and is statistically reliable. The superior performance during amytal shows that the drug has reduced fear even when any effects of stimulus change are completely balanced out. Finally, computing the interaction by comparing the two diagonals suggests that stimulus change did reduce fear somewhat in the groups that were changed, but the difference is not statistically reliable.

POSSIBLE EFFECTS OF AMYTAL ON DISCRIMINATION

Although the sodium amytal does not produce its apparently fear-reducing effect primarily by changing the stimulus situation, it is possible that it has another effect on cues. Perhaps it interferes in some way with the ability of the rat to discriminate the cues of danger. For example, it might make him less perceptive of presence or absence of the tone which signals presence or absence of the possibility of electric shocks in the Skinner box. In this case the behavior would be changed toward the average of that in the safe and dangerous conditions. Compared with the sober state, performance would be depressed then in the safe and improved in the dangerous conditions, which is exactly what we observed. The notion that this drug affects the subject's ability to discriminate is made plausible by the fact that one of its main effects is on the reticular activating system which is known to affect the perception of cues (Magoun, 1958). How can we check this possibility?

To test for this possibility, we trained a new group of rats in a different discrimination in the same apparatus. Instead of signaling shock, the same tone signaled that the bar no longer delivered food. After the rats had learned the discrimination which reduced their rate to approximately the same level as the shock did, we gave them tests with sodium amytal and other drugs.

If this different discrimination is not affected by the drug, it will show that the drug does not destroy the animal's ability to react discriminatively to the tone. If, on the other hand, we secure the same results as with fear, there will be two possibilities: (a) the drug may have disrupted the discrimination, or (b) the drug may have produced a direct reduction in the frustrational inhibition, presumably produced by the nonrewarded trials, in the same way

that it is assumed to reduced the fear produced by the electric shocks.

Figure 6 shows that the amytal seemed to leave the discrimination relatively unaffected. The drug certainly did not produce the kind of improvement during the tone that we have seen in the experiments in which the tone was a cue for fear. These results seem to rule out the possibility that amytal destroys the rat's ability to perceive the dangerous cue itself. All of the differences on this graph are highly reliable. Perhaps the greater depressing effect of the drug during the nontone intervals in this experiment is due to the fact that there was no general fear of the experimental situation for it to relieve.

On thinking over this experiment, however, another possibility occurred to us. You will note that the onset of the tone does not produce an immediate large decrease in the rate. The difference seems to build up during the 8-minute interval during which the loudness of the tone increases. Perhaps the nice dip in the curves of Figure 6 does not represent a discrimination at all, but merely the cumulative effects of the nonreinforced bar presses during the test period with tone.

In order to check on this possibility, we retrained the animals with the tone on at full intensity for 1-minute intervals, alternating with 1-minute silent intervals during which the customary schedule of reward was resumed. Since this schedule of reward was a 1-minute variable interval one, the reward would not be delivered during approximately half of the positive silent intervals. Therefore, one would not expect much extinction to occur during any given 1-minute nonrewarded negative interval with tone. Any difference between the tones and the silent periods would be

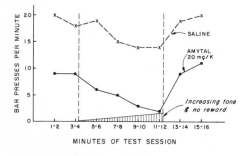

Fig. 6. Sodium amytal does not seem to reduce the decrement produced by a gradually increasing tone which has always been associated with nonreward in a Skinner box.

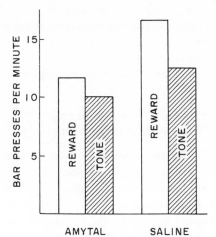

Fig. 7. **Results of a test in which a 1-minute tone is the cue for nonreward, while a 1-minute silent period is the cue for a variable interval schedule averaging one reward a minute. Under these most stringent conditions in the Skinner box, the drug appears to reduce but does not eliminate the discrimination.**

due primarily to the learned discrimination that reward never occurs during the tone, but sometimes occurs during the silent period.

After the animals had learned this discrimination, each one was tested in a balanced order for effects of injections of sodium amytal versus control solutions. The results are presented in Figure 7. It can be seen that the results are similar to those of Figure 6 and different from those in our previous experiments in which the same cue is used for fear instead of for nonreward. Although the sodium amytal seems to have reduced the discrimination, the difference between the rewarded silent period and the nonrewarded tone is still reliable. Furthermore, the difference between the experimental and the control groups is not reversed as it was when the response decrement was produced by fear instead of by nonreward.

We also ran a similar type of test in the alley situation. Instead of giving stronger shocks for trials with longer runs as we did in the telescope alley tests, we reduced the quantity of reward which was four pellets for the first trial of running the 1-foot length, two for the second trial of running the 2-foot length, one for the third trial, and zero for the fourth, fifth, and sixth trials. (Half of the animals had the opposite sequence of the large rewards for the long runs and the small ones for the short ones.) We called this the *frustration alley* test.

Figure 8 shows the results of this experiment. In this case you can see that the amytal speeded up running on the nonrewarded trials much as it did on the fear trials in Figure 1. Apparently, the amytal either counteracted the effects of frustration, or reduced the discriminability of the cues indicating that the trial was going to be nonrewarded.

This experiment and the immedi-

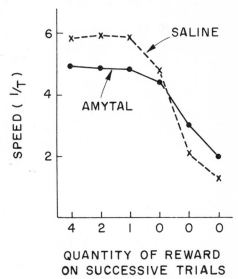

QUANTITY OF REWARD
ON SUCCESSIVE TRIALS

Fig. 8. **In the frustration alley, amytal produces results similar to those in previous tests with fear (depicted in Figure 1), and different from those in the Skinner box (as depicted in Figures 6 and 7).**

ately preceding two were designed to test the same thing, namely, the effects of amytal on the rat's ability to discriminate the cues used in preceding experiments on fear. The fact that the experiments in the Skinner box and in the alley yielded opposite results poses a dilemma. Are the effects related to possible differences in the degree to which the discriminations were learned, to the different cues used (distance versus tone), to the different types of responses required (running versus balancing on the hind legs and pressing a bar), to the different schedules of reinforcement (100% for the best distances in the alley and a 1-minute variable interval schedule, involving nonrewarded bar presses even without the tone in the Skinner box), or to yet other unsuspected differences between the two situations? We hope to perform soon more experiments to try to find out. In the meantime, we cannot be sure exactly what mixture of effects sodium amytal has.

The possibility that drugs may affect the subject's discriminative reaction to cues, makes it harder to interpret the results of complex experiments in which the same subjects are trained in a variety of different habits under the discriminative control of different stimuli, although such procedures also have their legitimate uses. We certainly shall want to proceed with our plan to test amytal (and the rest of our drugs) in simplified situations in which one group is trained only to approach motivated by hunger and another group is trained only to avoid motivated by fear, using the strength-of-pull technique (or possibly a strength-of-push technique) to measure the effects of the drug separately on each of these two tendencies acting singly.

We plan also to measure drug effects in a simple test of experimental extinction. Finally, dose-response studies are essential; they may help us better to analyze the effects of this drug.

TRANSFER OF FEAR-REDUCTION FROM DRUGGED TO SOBER STATE

If a drug produces a differential reduction in fear, by any one of a number of mechanisms, it may have some therapeutic usefulness as a chronic medication for people who need to have all of their fears reduced somewhat, or may help to tide a person over a transient situation which is producing too much general anxiety.

In many cases, however, it is necessary to reduce a specific unrealistic fear which is far too strong without producing an equivalent reduction in realistic fears, such as those of reckless driving. Since we cannot expect any drug to have such a discriminative action tailored to the needs of the culture at a given moment in history, the patient can only be helped by retraining, or, in other words, psychotherapy. Even here, a temporary use of the drug might theoretically be useful in order to help the person to become able to practice the responses he needs to learn. But as John Dollard and I (1950) pointed out, such new learning under the influence of the drug will not be useful unless it ultimately can be transferred to the normal nondrugged state. Perhaps drugs differ in this significant aspect of their effectiveness. How can we test for this?

In one of the few studies on this problem, Hunt (1956) recently found that experimental extinction of fear under chlorpromazine did not transfer effectively to the normal state. But human patients usually are not merely extinguished on their fears; they also are rewarded for performing the correct response in spite of fear. Thus the approach-avoidance conflict situation seemed to me more relevant than simple experimental extinction. It also seemed more likely to show a positive transfer effect because the reward would be expected to add counter-conditioning to the extinction of fear.

Hungry albino rats were trained to press a bar with food as a reward on a 100% schedule. Then the bar was electrified for unpredictable brief periods approximately half of the time. The strength of these shocks was increased until such a strong conflict was established that the rats would not press the bar.

After this conflict had been set up, the rats were given a retraining session in the apparatus with the shock turned off. During this session half of them had received a dose of amytal, and the other half a placebo injection. Figure 9 shows the results. You can see that during the extinction session, labeled "Drug Test," more of the amytal than the control animals resumed pressing

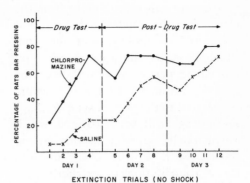

Fig. 10. While chlorpromazine (2 mg/kg intraperitoneally 45 minutes before the test) produces less initial improvement than does sodium amytal, more of the gain seems to persist during subsequent tests without drugs.

the bar. On another day, the rats were given post-drug tests to see whether the superiority during retraining with drug transferred to the normal nondrugged state. You can see that it did not. But the apparent inferiority of the drug group is not statistically reliable.

Figure 10 shows the results of a similar experiment with 2 mg/kg of chlorpromazine. Although the initial fear-reducing effects with this drug do not seem to be as striking as those with sodium amytal, there is less loss with transfer to the normal state. The superiority of the chlorpromazine group on the post-drug test approaches statistical reliability. We are performing dose-response studies essential to establish more definitely the apparent differene in transfer of the effects of these two drugs. If indeed there is less decrement in the transfer of training from the drugged to the normal state with chlorpromazine, this difference may be related to the fact that this drug has less extensive effects on the reticular formation than does sodium amytal.

Meanwhile, these experiments clearly show that it is unsafe to assume that

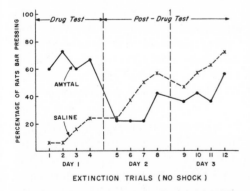

Fig. 9. The therapeutic effects of sodium amytal fail to transfer from the drugged to the nondrugged condition.

therapeutic transfer will occur from the drugged to the nondrugged state. It is also unsafe to assume that the drug which produces the greatest effect on immediate performance will have the greatest ultimate effect on learning transferred to the normal state. Perhaps some drugs will be discovered which are markedly superior in this crucial respect. Such a drug could make a major contribution to psychotherapy.

Need for Basic Studies to Establish a Science of Psychopharmacology

The work I have just described is a progress report rather than a completed program. By now it should be clear that an adequate study of even certain aspects of the behavioral effects of a single drug is a major project. Nevertheless, I believe it is necessary for us to take the time to be analytical and precise in determining the exact behavioral effects of a variety of drugs already known in a general way to have interesting clinical effects. Then we should advance to the further step of trying to find lawful relationships between these behavioral effects and the action of the drug on different parts of the brain as determined by techniques of neurophysiology, biochemistry, and biophysics. Out of such work may come a better understanding of how the brain functions to control behavior. Out of such work may emerge a basic science of psychopharmacology. As I have said before, the principles of such a basic science should eventually supply a rational basis for practical applications to mental health in the same way that organic chemistry provides a rational basis for the synthesis of new compounds.

Can Conflict Be Specific to a Drive or to an Anticipatory Goal Response?

In addition to the work on the effects of drugs, my students and I have been doing a number of other experiments on conflict behavior. One of these experiments stems from the attempt to apply learning theory to problems of neuroses and psychotherapy (Dollard & Miller, 1950). We have assumed that fear and avoidance can be specifically attached to the cues involved in certain drives, and to the thoughts aroused by specific drives. Cheng Fayu and I tested this assumption in a situation in which approach responses were punished if motivated by one drive, but not if motivated by a different one. The experiment was designed to determine the role of cues from the drive, and also from distinctive anticipatory goal responses to the drive.

Rats were trained to run down a short alley, jump over a low hurdle, land on a platform recording their response, and then pass under a curtain which hid the reward in the goal box. On some days they were run only when hungry and on others only when thirsty.

The foregoing part of the design was to determine the role of drive; the following part was to determine that of distinctive anticipatory goal responses. Half of each of these groups found dry food in the goal box on days when they were hungry and only water in the goal box on days when they were thirsty. For these animals, the distinctive goal responses of chewing or lapping would be expected to become anticipatory, and hence to provide distinctive cues in addition to those involved in the drive itself. According to our theory, antici-

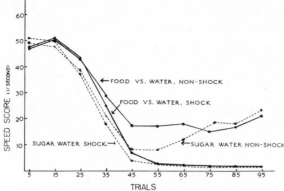

Fig. 11. In a conflict situation, the avoidance of exactly the same place can be made dependent upon the drive motivating approach. The discrimination is learned more quickly when the consummatory responses, and hence presumably the anticipatory goal responses, are made more distinctive.

patory goal responses should serve primitive cue-producing functions similar to the much more sophisticated responses of labeling involved in human speech and thought (Miller, 1935).

The other half of each of these groups found sugar water in the same identical drinking spout on both days, and hence performed exactly the same goal response to either hunger or thirst. These animals were satiated on pure sugar before runs on thirst days. They would not be expected to be helped by cues from distinctive anticipatory goal responses.

The results are presented in Figure 11. The dotted lines in the graph show that the animals which were running to drink sugar water from the spout eventually learned not to run on the days when they were motivated by the dangerous drive, but to run when they were motivated by the acceptable drive. It should be noted that this experiment is superior to most others which have demonstrated reasonably rapid learning of a good discrimination between drives, in that the learning to respond

to the cues from the drive is not confounded with learning to go to different places, or to get different goal objects which elicit different anticipatory goal responses.

The solid lines in the curve show the behavior of animals which were trained in the same way except that they received dry food when hungry and water when thirsty. It can be seen that these rats, which had the benefit of cues from distinctive anticipatory goal responses, learned the discrimination faster. The difference is highly reliable. This is exactly what would be predicted from the assumption that Dollard and I have made that distinctive cue-producing responses facilitate the learning and performance of discriminative behavior. According to us it is the loss of these cue-producing responses that makes behavior following repression less adaptive (Dollard & Miller, 1950).

Does Fear Become Consolidated with Time?

In lay and clinical experience there are two schools of thought which make different assumptions concerning the setting or forgetting of fear after a traumatic event. One school of thought recommends that a person suffering a fear-inducing accident when practicing an activity, such as flying an airplane or riding a horse, should go back to it immediately before the fear has a chance to become set. The opposite school of thought recommends an immediate rest to allow the fear to subside. Of course, these human examples may be complicated by the effects of verbal rehearsal during the intervening intervals. Nevertheless, the notion has been advanced by a number of different people that a basic physiological process of consolidation occurs shortly after a new learning experience (Coons & Miller, 1960; Hebb, 1949). Thus it seemed worthwhile to Edgar Coons, James Faust, and me to investigate this problem with animals.

In the first experiment, hungry rats received 30 trials at the rate of 5 a day running down an elevated strip to food. Then they were divided into two matched groups. On the first trial of the next day, upon touching the food, each rat received a traumatic electric shock at the goal and then was immediately removed to its home cage. Thirty seconds later the rats in the first group were returned to the runway for a test, while those in the second group were tested 24 hours later. The time required to touch food was recorded with a 5-minute maximum limit. It can be seen from the left-hand side of Figure 12 that the rats tested 24 hours later required twice as long to go back to touch the food than those tested 30 seconds afterwards. Since the difference is highly reliable, we may conclude that the relative strength of avoidance, and hence presumably of

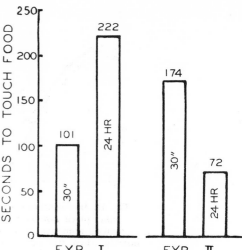

Fig. 12. Whether or not a 24-hour interval produces consolidation or forgetting of fear depends upon details of the experimental situation, which were designed to affect the degree to which the interval of time restored or altered the pattern of cues present when the traumatic shock was received.

fear, increased during the 24-hour interval immediately following the strong electric shock.

We have considered a number of hypotheses to explain these results. One is that the fear is consolidated during the interval. Another is that the excitement produced by the electric shock has a dynamogenic effect that increases the rat's tendency to run up to the goal immediately afterwards. Another is that under the particular conditions of this experiment, the stimulus conditions for the 30-second group differed more than did those for the 24-hour group from the ones immediately preceding the strong shock. Then it follows that the greater stimulus change for the 30-second group should produce a greater decrement in avoidance than in approach, so that this group would reach the goal sooner.

To describe this stimulus-change hypothesis in more detail, let us note that, when the animals received their shock, it was the first trial of the day, and they had not received any immediately preceding shock. For these animals tested 24 hours later, it was again the first trial of the day, and as before, they had not received any immediately preceding shock. But for the 30-second group the conditions were different in that it was the second trial of the day and they had just received an electric shock. Assuming that some sort of after-effects from the immediately preceding trial and/or shock persist, these would be expected to change the stimulus situation. These changes should produce a greater decrement in the avoidance motivated by fear than in the approach motivated by hunger. Therefore, these animals should show relatively less avoidance.

How can we test this hypothesis? Suppose we change the conditions so that the two factors—an immediately preceding trial and an immediately preceding shock—make the training and test conditions more similar for the 30-second group instead of for the 24-hour one. Then, we will expect the direction of the difference of the two groups to be reversed. The other two hypotheses would not predict such a reversal.

To test this prediction, we ran additional animals in another experiment exactly similar to the foregoing one, except that, instead of giving them their shock in the runaway on the first trial of the day, we gave it to them on the third trial. We also gave them a shock in a quite different apparatus 30 seconds before their shock trial in the alley. When these animals were being trained to avoid the goal by being shocked there, they had the stimulus after-effects of an immediately preceding trial and shock. But when tested

24 hours later, they were in a somewhat different stimulus context of no immediately preceding trials and no immediately preceding shock. Therefore, we would expect their avoidance to be relatively weaker on this test 24 hours later, so that the results would be completely opposite to those of the preceding experiment.

The right-hand side of Figure 12 shows the results of the second experiment. It can be seen that the results are opposite to those in the first experiment. The difference is highly reliable ($p < .01$). Instead of being consolidated with time, the relative strength of fear was reduced in the second experiment. The stimulus-change hypothesis was confirmed. Under the conditions of these experiments, differences in the stimulus traces were shown to be more important than any setting or forgetting of fear with time.

The results of these two experiments impress us with the importance of trying to analyze the exact stimulus conditions under which the fear was originally established and those under which it is tested.

Learning Resistance to Stress

The final experiments I shall describe have to do with learning resistance to pain and fear in an approach-avoidance conflict situation. Can resistance to stressful situations be learned? If such learning is possible, what are the laws determining its effectiveness and generality?

In one experiment on this topic, which is reported in more detail elsewhere (Miller, 1960), albino rats were trained to run down an alley for food. Their criterion task was to continue running in spite of 400-volt electric

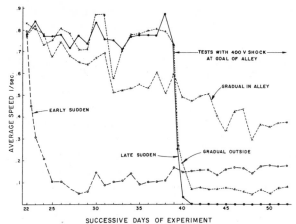

SUCCESSIVE DAYS OF EXPERIMENT

Fig. 13. Hungry rats may be trained to resist stress by continuing to run down an alley to a goal where they receive both food and electric shock. Under these conditions, previous overlearning of the habit of running to food decreases, rather than increases, resistance to stress. (From Miller, 1960)

shocks administered through a 250,000-ohm series resistance for .1 second immediately after they reached the goal. Some of these animals were introduced to the shock suddenly, others were given special training to resist the shock by receiving first mild shocks at the goal, followed by trials with shocks of gradually increasing strength.

The results are presented in Figure 13. You can see that the animals that had been habituated to gradually increasing shocks in the alley continued to run faster than those in the sudden groups which had not received the same type of training.

Was the superior performance of the gradually habituated group a general effect of mere exposure to the shocks, or, as our theoretical analysis demanded, was it an effect dependent upon specific rewarded training in the criterion situation? This was tested by giving another group the same gradual habituation to the same shocks administered at a different time of day in a distinctive box outside of the alley. You

can see that this group was not appreciably helped. Apparently, mere exposure to tough treatments will not necessarily improve resistance to stress in a different criterion situation.

As a control for the effect of additional training trials in the alley, we ran one group which was suddenly exposed to 400-volt shocks at the goal on the same trial that the gradual group received its first mild shocks, and we ran another group which was suddenly exposed to the 400-volt shocks at the same time that the gradual group reached the level of 400 volts. As you have already seen, the performance of both of these groups was poorer than that of the rats receiving the gradually increasing shocks at the goal of the alley. But looking at the curves for these two groups immediately after the sudden shocks were introduced, we can see a surprising fact. The speed of the group shocked late in training falls off much more rapidly than that of the one shocked early in training. This difference, which is reliable at the

.02 level of confidence, confirms earlier suggestive results in our laboratory by Eileen Karsh. It is directly contrary to the widely-held notion that overtraining will increase resistance to stress.

The results of the foregoing experiment suggest that it should be feasible and profitable to analyze further at both the animal and human level, the laws governing the learning of resistance to stresses, such as pain, fear, fatigue, frustration, noise, nausea, and extremes of temperature.

Two of my colleagues, David Williams and Herbert Barry, III, have already performed an interesting experiment providing behavioral evidence for the counterconditioning of fear. Rats were trained on a variable interval schedule of food reward. On exactly the same variable interval schedule, they were given a gradually increasing series of electric shocks for pressing the bar. For one group the food and shock schedules were in phase, so that every time they got a shock, a pellet of food was promptly delivered; for the other group, the schedules were out of phase, so that they received the same number and distribution of shocks, but at times when food was not delivered. You should note that for each bar press in both groups, the probability of food or shock was equally great and equally unpredictable. Nevertheless, the correlation of shock with food apparently rendered shock less disrupting to the rat, because the animals in the in-phase group continued pressing through considerably higher levels of shock than those in the out-of-phase group.

At present we are trying to secure objective measures of the counterconditioning of physiological responses to pain, a phenomenon suggested by

Pavlov (1927). If we succeed, we want to study this phenomenon in greater detail to determine how it is affected by factors such as strength of drive, amount and schedule of reward, and experimental extinction.

Summary: In the first part of this paper I have described a series of experiments analyzing how a drug with well-established clinical effects on human behavior may act to achieve some of these effects. Amobarbital sodium, commonly called sodium amytal, was the drug selected for his first series of experiments. As the first step, we established that we could produce in experiments on rats, effects which appear to parallel the fear-reducing effects of this drug in human conflict situations. These effects were repeated in experiments in three different types of apparatus with the approach motivated by two different drives.

In further experiments, we found that this fear-reducing effect was not primarily produced indirectly by drug induced changes in the stimulus situation. We also found that it was not primarily due to a greater effect of the drug on the more recently established habit of avoidance; similar effects were secured when avoidance was learned first.

One series of experiments suggested that the fear-reducing effects of the drug in the Skinner box were not due merely to interference with the rat's ability to discriminate the tone used as a cue for danger in that situation. But another experiment in the alley situation showed that the drug either did interfere with discrimination, or produced recovery from experimental extinction. Thus, although a number of indirect modes of action have been ruled out, we have not yet decisively narrowed down the drug's fear-reducing effects to a direct action on the fear mechanism.

Finally, we found that the beneficial effects of the sodium amytal on relearning in a conflict situation did not generalize from the drugged to the normal state. Chlorpromazine yielded more promising results on this crucial test. Dose-response studies are in progress to determine the generality of the difference between the drugs in this respect.

In another series of experiments we have seen that fear and conflict can be conditioned specifically to the cues of a given drive, so that whether or not a given response will elicit conflict can depend on the motivation for that response. When distinctive anticipatory goal responses are present, they improve the discrimination.

We have also seen that some conditions can produce an apparent consolidation of fear with the passing of time, while other conditions produce an apparent forgetting of fear. In these experiments, the crucial factor seems to be the extent to which the elapsed time changes or restores the cues present immediately before the traumatic electric shock.

Finally, we have seen that it is possible to increase the resistance to the stress of pain and fear by appropriate training. But one of the most obvious methods, overlearning, can reduce, rather than improve, the resistance of the habit to disruption by fear.

Psychological Review, 1961, vol. 68, pp. 354–358

Motivational Effects in Approach-Avoidance Conflict

R. A. Champion

It is to be expected that Miller's recent contribution to Project A (Miller, 1959) will reawaken interest in the formal analysis of conflict in S–R terms and prompt further experimentation in this area of theoretical and practical importance. Following his original treatment, which he set down in somewhat general terms (Miller, 1944), Miller has now presented a more formal and detailed consideration of conflict as an example of theory construction, but it is clear that his interest in the matter persists at the experimental as well as at the theoretical level. Miller's contributions have been closely paralleled by those of Hull (1938, 1952), similarly limited to behavior in space for the most part and treated by Miller as supplementary to rather than as competing with his own formulation. Before further work is undertaken in this context, however, some attention should be given to an apparent inconsistency in the S–R theory of conflict as proposed by Miller and Hull. The difficulty in question is most clearly exemplified in approach-avoidance conflict and the following discussion is therefore limited to this particular form of the general situation in which opposing tendencies to move in space are elicited simultaneously. The basic assumptions of both Hull and Miller are represented in Figure 1; the avoidance tendency is stronger than the approach tendency at the point of reinforcement (O) and the avoidance gradient has a steeper slope so as to produce intersection of the gradients (I) at a point of equilibrium on the distance dimension (d). The chief situation in which tests of these assumptions have been made is that of the rat in a straight alley; under these conditions Brown (1948) has confirmed that the gradients differ in slope and Miller (1944) has observed that rats released at the far end of the alley stop at an intermediate point on the way to the goal.

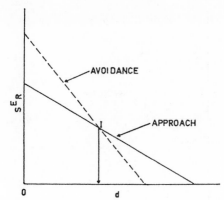

Fig. 1. The basic assumptions in the S-R theory of approach-avoidance conflict. (The gradients are represented as linear for the sake of simplicity.)

The inconsistency in this S–R treatment of conflict emerges when Hull and Miller turn to the effects of changes in the drive level of the organism in a state of approach-avoidance conflict. The factors involved here are best illustrated in the experiments of Miller (1944, 1959) designed to test these effects. Hungry rats were trained to run the length of an alley with food reward at its closed end so as to generate an approach gradient. They were then given a brief electric shock while eating in the goal box in order that an avoidance gradient might also be set up. The approach gradient, established with hunger drive and period of deprivation, was systematically varied in later test trials without shocks, half the rats being run with a strong hunger drive and half with a weak hunger drive. When placed at the far end of the alley the rats characteristically ran some way to the goal box and then stopped, but the more hungry rats ran nearer to the goal box than did the less hungry rats. Furthermore, it must be assumed that the avoidance training not only generated an avoidance gra-

dient but also introduced the acquired drive of fear. For reasons which remain to be clarified, rats given a weaker shock during this training also approached closer to the goal than did rats given a stronger shock.

Both Hull and Miller handle these results very simply by assuming that an increase in hunger raises the approach gradient whereas an increase in fear raises the avoidance gradient, bringing the point of intersection nearer to or further from the goal, respectively, as exemplified in Figure 2. The two theorists show some disagreement as to the exact nature of the gradient movement. In his earliest theorizing Hull (1938) stated that "an increase in drive such as hunger presumably increases both the height and the slope of the positive gradient" (p. 293) and this type of movement is demanded by his Postulate VIII (1952) which assumes a multiplicative relationship between generalized habit strength and drive strength in the production of excitatory potential. Miller has followed Hull in at least one

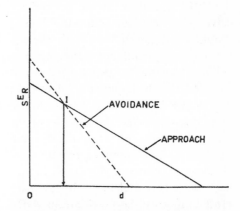

Fig. 2. The Hull-Miller interpretation of a reduction in the strength of fear in approach-avoidance conflict. (In comparison with Figure 1 the avoidance gradient has been lowered throughout its course so that the point of intersection, I, moves toward the goal, O, on the distance dimension, d.)

case (1948, pp. 170–171) but has more generally assumed that the gradient is raised or lowered by an equal amount throughout its course (e.g., Miller, 1959) as if the outcome was produced by the addition of drive strength and habit strength. The available experimental evidence (Brown, 1948) does not clearly indicate whether the effect is multiplicative or additive.

The significant inconsistency at which these comments are directed is shared by the two theorists, deriving from another of Hull's postulates and from experimental evidence obtained by Miller. In his *Principles of Behavior* (1943) Hull included a Postulate 7 which stated that "any effective habit strength $(_sH_R)$ is sensitized into reaction potentiality $(_sE_R)$ by all primary drives active within an organism at a given time" (p. 253). Thus it would seem improper for Hull to assume or deduce that an increase in the hunger drive affects only the approach gradient and that an increase in the fear drive affects only the avoidance gradient. If the 1943 postulate about generalized drive is to be taken literally then it should be deduced that both the approach and avoidance gradients, involving specific or generalized habit strength, should be equally affected by any change in drive strength regardless of its nature, so that the location of the point of intersection (I) on the distance dimension (d) should remain unchanged, as shown in Figure 3. It may have been this difficulty which caused Hull to modify the postulate in *A Behavior System* (1952) to read thus: "Postulate VD. At least some drive conditions tend partially to motivate into action habits which have been set up on the basis of different drive conditions"

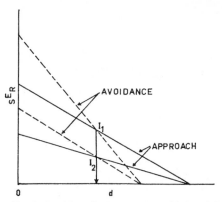

Fig. 3. A theoretical outcome which might be expected if Hull's 1943 postulate about generalized drive is applied. (With any decrease in drive strength the two gradients are lowered but the location of the point of intersection on the distance dimension is unchanged—I_1 and I_2.)

(p. 7). In that form, however, the postulate allows such a degree of ambiguity as to render it unworkable.

As well as quoting Hull's concept of generalized drive with approval, Miller (1948) has presented experimental evidence which clearly supports it. Thirsty rats were trained to run an alley with water reward; when the same animals were tested without water deprivation they ran faster when hungry than when not hungry. In another experiment hungry rats were trained in a T maze with food reward. When they were satiated with food it was found that they ran faster immediately after receiving a shock on a grid away from the maze or in the maze itself, and that this effect persisted after the shocks given in the maze had been omitted for some time. Miller interpreted all these effects in terms of drive generalization, arguing that the innervating effects of the strong stimuli present in thirst generalize to the stimuli of hunger, and from hunger to pain and fear. Thus Miller was also obliged to deduce that hunger would affect the avoidance tendencies in the conflict situation and that fear would affect the approach tendencies.

In the latest account of his theory of conflict, Miller (1959) appears to have arrived at a formulation which is comparable with that expressed in Hull's 1952 postulate. In his own Postulate D, Miller (1959) assumes that "the strength of tendencies to approach or avoid varies directly with the strength of the drive upon which they are based" (p. 205). At the same time, however, he allows "it is entirely possible that administering at the goal shocks that are too weak to stop the animal from approaching and eating will be found to have the dynamogenic effect of increasing speed of running or strength of pull" (p. 225). Perhaps Miller's (1959) present position is best summarized in these statements:

I would tentatively say that any specifiable conditions may be defined as increasing a drive when they specifically increase the performance of responses rewarded by the offset of these conditions, or by the goal objects that produce satiation. In using the word "specific," I do not mean to imply that the increase in drive cannot also increase the performance of other responses, but that it should produce a greater increase in the responses that have been specifically rewarded by the reduction in, or the goal objects of, that drive . . . (p. 240).

One aim of this discussion has been to show that deductions from the S–R theory of conflict are not as simple and straightforward as they may have earlier seemed (e.g., Miller, 1944, p. 437). Nevertheless the discussion has led to the "obvious" compromise between the concept of generalized drive on the one hand and differential movement of the gradients of approach and avoidance on the other hand; i.e., although both gradients are assumed to be affected by any change in drive strength, one gradient will move more than the other depending upon the nature of the drive which varies. It now remains to be shown how the differential gradient movement can take place, and the reason should be found in contemporary behavior theory in the interests of internal consistency. The most likely reason, and one which Miller almost makes explicit, is to be found in the directing role of the drive stimulus. As Hull (1952) has put it, "each drive condition generates a characteristic drive stimulus which is a monotonic increasing function of this state" (Postulate VC). Thus if, in the experimental situation of Miller (1944) cited above, the rats learn approach when hungry and avoidance when fearful, the stimuli of hunger will form part of the complex eliciting approach and the stimuli of fear will form part of the complex eliciting avoidance. The mere presence of the drive stimuli, however, does not necessarily provide for the required differential gradient movement with changes in type of motivation. On the contrary, a variety of effects may be predicted depending upon the strength of the two or more sources of drive present when the gradients are established. For example, if the rat learns to approach the goal under 12-hour food deprivation then it might be expected to approach *less* rapidly under 48-hour deprivation if only the change in drive stimulus were taken into account, because there would have been some alteration in the eliciting stimulus complex. The factor which, in theory, will actually produce the required differential gradient movement is the dynamism (V) of the drive stimulus. According to Hull's Postulate VIII (1952):

$$sE_R = D \times V \times K \times sH_R$$

so that in the conflict situation, neglecting incentive effects (K):

$$sE_R+ = D \times V_h \times sH_R+ \quad \text{(approach)}$$
$$sE_R- = D \times V_f \times sH_R- \quad \text{(avoidance)}$$

where V_h and V_f represent the dynamism of the drive stimuli for hunger and fear, respectively. Thus, in addition to the generalized effects of changes in D, a change in V_h will affect sE_R+ alone (approach) and a change in V_f will affect sE_R- alone (avoidance), and the differential gradient movement may be attributed to the selective dynamogenic effects of the drive stimuli.

Some further complications which might be taken into account are due to the particular technique which the experimenter uses in producing approach and avoidance tendencies simultaneously in the one organism. The point is best made by referring again to the experiment of Miller (1944) in which rats were trained to approach one end of an alley when hungry and were then shocked there while eating. In the "partial definitions" of his miniature system Miller (1959) states that "the animals running to food are being trained to approach under the motivation of hunger" and "animals running away from electric shock are being trained to avoid under the motivation of fear." As already implied, the exact predictions to

be made in the situation of Miller with changes in hunger on later test trials depend in part on the constant *strength* of the hunger drive at the time of approach training, because the strength of the hunger drive is being changed in the one animal. The avoidance training, on the other hand, presents a different type of complication if separate groups of rats are given shocks varying in strength from group to group. Since drive strength is here varied during acquisition it is likely that the height, slope, and even the shape of the avoidance gradient will also vary from group to group. Therefore, as far as changes in strength of fear are concerned there may be a more potent cause of differential gradient movement than drive-stimulus dynamism. The position may be further complicated by the fact that the animals are also hungry at the time the shocks are administered. In view of these complications there would seem to be ample scope at present for further experimentation in which other methods of approach and avoidance training are used.

Summary: Attention has been drawn to an apparent inconsistency in the S–R treatment of conflict as presented by Miller and Hull. Whereas both theorists refer to drive generalization as a feature of S–R theory, neither takes it into account when dealing with motivational changes in approach-avoidance conflict and both simply assume that hunger affects only the approach gradient while fear affects only the avoidance gradient. The internal consistency of the S–R theory is better preserved if the differential gradient movement is ascribed to the dynamogenic effects of the drive stimuli.

Journal of Abnormal and Social Psychology, 1962, vol. 64, pp. 438–445

Response to Conflict as Determined by Prior Exposure to Conflict[1]

Leonard Worell

Clinical descriptions frequently contain statements indicating that people who are faced with strong conflicts demonstrate inefficient behavior not only in relation to these strong conflicts but also in resolving comparatively mild conflicting situations. A "neurotic" individual, for example, who presumably reacts with strong conflicting tendencies only in certain areas, may be characterized as generally indecisive. Thereby, the implication is conveyed that the person's exposure to severe conflict has significantly contributed to his inefficient handling of weaker conflicts. In spite of these recurrent observations, the problem of the generalization of the effects of conflict has received scant experimental attention. With small exception research in the area of conflict has concentrated on (a) the behavioral consequences of variations in several characteristics of conflicting responses, such as their relative strength, approach avoidance, etc., and (b) the role of individual differences in conflict resolution (Andreas, 1958; Berlyne, 1960; Block & Peterson, 1955; Brown, 1942; Cartwright, 1941; Castaneda & Worell, 1961; Hovland & Sears, 1938; Kaufman & Miller, 1949; Scodel, Ratoosh, & Minas, 1959; Sears & Hovland, 1941;

Worell & Castaneda, 1961b; Worell & Hill, 1962. This paper continues Worell & Castaneda, 1961a) the investigation of a third area; that in which conflict serves as an antecedent to performance in other than the conflict situation. The general question under consideration is as follows: Does responding to conflict have an effect on the resolution of relatively weak conflict situations?

Our attention will be restricted to two separate but related facets of this general problem. First, we will describe two opposing theoretical formulations that deal with the effects on the individual of exposure to different degrees of conflict. These hypothetical consequences will then be used to anticipate the performance of subjects in a subsequent conflict situation. Second, we will consider the issue of the degree of conflict itself. In this connection, the importance for performance of the absolute and relative strength of conflicting tendencies will be examined.

The two theoretical approaches will be designated as the *competing response* and the *dynamogenic* hypotheses. These hypotheses may be, respectively, subsumed under the long-standing distinction made by psychologists between associative or learned and nonassociative approaches. According to the com-

[1] The present research was assisted by a grant from the Research Foundation of Oklahoma State University.

peting response view, it is assumed that responding to different levels of conflict leads to the learning of differing conflict-specific responses. For example, a person who is protractedly exposed to relatively strong conflict might be expected to learn such responses as withholding a decision or considering each alternative more carefully, etc. Then, in new but similar situations, the individual may be expected to invoke those behaviors which he has previously learned. Thus, with the competing response view, the effects of conflict are expected to have a limited generality—limited by the similarities between earlier and later conflict situations.

Sharply contrasted to the foregoing position is the dynamogenic view which proposes that conflict generates motivational consequences. The general suggestion that conflict may possess tension arousing or drive properties has been frequently made (Brown & Farber, 1951; Lewin, 1933; Miller, 1944; Miller & Stevenson, 1936). In addition, several studies designed to test this suggestion have agreed in finding heightened force of response as the degree of conflict is increased (Castaneda & Worell, 1961; Finger, 1941; Worell & Castaneda, 1961b). These results are consistent with the view that one consequence of conflict is an elevation of drive or motivation and that increasing degrees of conflict produce greater increments in drive. If conflict generates drive, then the effects of conflict on performance in a contiguously presented task would be expected to be evident irrespective of the similarity between the conflict and later performance situation. This is based on a view of drive as an indiscriminate energizer of performance (Hull, 1943).

Findings relevant to these alterna-

tives were recently obtained by Worell and Castaneda (1961a), where the generalization of the effects of conflict was examined in relation to learning. In two experiments, subjects were exposed to either high or low experimentally induced conflict prior to the presentation of each pair of two verbal paired-associates tasks. Different degrees of conflict were aroused by the simultaneous exposure of two lines of either equal or unequal length, while the paired associates lists contained words with either high or low amounts of intralist competition. The findings indicated that the conflict conditions did not significantly affect performance.

The foregoing findings are not compatible with expectations derived from the dynamogenic hypothesis. On the other hand, according to the competing response view, no necessary effects of conflict would be anticipated since the conflict and learning conditions were quite dissimilar. Consequently, in the present study, the degree of similarity between the conflict situation and the subsequent performance situation has been increased. Descriptively, subjects here are exposed to varying degrees of discrimination conflict and are then all placed into a weak discrimination conflict situation. Thus, the responses required in both the earlier and later conflict situations are the same, but the stimulus similarity changes to varying degrees for the subjects in the various conflict groups. In these situations, our interest is in a particular performance measure—namely, the time to initiate a decision or reaction evocation latency.

Given a weak conflict situation following differential conflict training, the following predictions would be made with the competing response and dynamogenic positions. From the standpoint of the competing response view, subjects who have been formerly trained under strong conflict should be slower in the weak conflict situation than those who had experienced less severe conflict training conditions. In this it is assumed that prior exposure to strong conflict has led to the learning of conflict-specific responses which are transferred to the new but similar situation. On the other hand, from the dynamogenic view, subjects who were formerly exposed to strong conflict should be faster than subjects exposed to weaker conflicts. This is based on two considerations: first, that increased conflict is associated with increased drive, and secondly, that increased drive, as determined by the Taylor Manifest Anxiety scale, has been found to produce faster speeds in the same relatively weak conflict situation as used here by Worell and Castaneda (1961b).

The second concern of this paper is with the problem of the degree or amount of conflict. Writings on conflict have frequently made reference to the importance of either or both the relative and absolute strengths of conflicting tendencies in defining amount of conflict. In general, studies designed to determine the effects of these two characteristics on temporal performance have varied the strengths of the conflicting tendencies by variations in either training procedures or stimulus intensity. The justification for using training procedures seems apparent; the logic for employing variations in the intensity of two or more simultaneously presented stimuli seems to be based on the repeated finding that increasing response strengths tend to be associated with increasing intensities of *single* stimuli.

The results of studies aimed at testing the assumption that the absolute strengths of competing tendencies are influential in determining the amount of conflict have been either negative or at best equivocal. For example, Berlyne (1957) exposed subjects to either two equally bright or two equally dim stimuli and found that the weaker intensities were associated with significantly *longer* response times. Castaneda and Worell (1961) found a similar, but insignificant, trend for increased speed of response to occur with increased intensities in an experiment which presented subjects with either two relatively bright or two relatively dim lights separated by equal log brightness differences. None of these results is in accord with expectations based on absolute strengths (Andreas, 1958; Bilodeau, 1950), since increased intensities should have produced longer response times. However, Andreas has obtained results agreeing with these expectations in his finding that response times were lengthened with increased amounts of training to the conflict stimuli.[2] In contrast, Bilodeau, also employing training procedures designed to increase the strengths of the competing tendencies, failed to find a significant decrease in movement time as the absolute strengths increased.

In contrast to the findings with absolute strengths, the results of studies directed toward the effects of the absolute *difference* in strength between or

[2] The studies performed by Andreas (1958) and Broadhurst (1957) used measures of temporal performance that were composites of reaction evocation time and what may be termed "movement" time. Since the meaning of a composite measure may be expected to vary considerably depending on what is involved in the movement performance, it is difficult to compare the results of studies using such a measure with those using reaction evocation latency.

the relative strengths of conflicting tendencies on temporal performance have been with few exceptions positive. Thus, studies by Bilodeau (1950), Brown (1942), Cartwright (1941), Castaneda and Worell (1961), Korman (1960), Worell and Castaneda (1961b), and Worell and Hill (1962) have agreed in finding that speed of response increases as the competing tendencies become more unlike in strength. However, no differences in temporal performance as a function of variations in relative strength have been obtained by both Andreas (1958) and Broadhurst (1957).[3]

Aside from empirical examinations of the problem of the amount of conflict, at least two theoretical formulations have been advanced which specifically incorporate either or both the relative and absolute strengths of conflicting tendencies in their approaches. First, in a detailed attempt to integrate a construct of frustration within a Hullian framework, Brown and Farber (1951) developed the position that frustration arose as a consequence of the magnitudes of *both* the absolute and relative strengths of competing tendencies. Moreover, their proposal suggests that somewhat greater importance should be given to the absolute strengths in producing frustration. In contrast, in a recent paper (Worell, 1961) where an attempt was made to account for the performance of differentially motivated subjects in learning and performance tasks involving competing response tendencies, a set of theoretical propositions based *solely* on the relative strengths of conflicting tendencies was discussed. In view of the rather general interest in the problem of the degree of conflict, the present study will examine the effects of the

3 See Footnote 2.

relative and absolute strengths of conflicting tendencies on both immediate performance and performance in a subsequently encountered conflict task.

Method

Design

All subjects were initially exposed to a low conflict condition in a brightness discrimination apparatus for a predetermined series of trials. In part, this procedure was used to assess whether the subjects in the subsequently separated groups demonstrated initially equivalent performances. Following exposure to low conflict, subjects were placed into either high, intermediate, or low conflict conditions for an additional fixed number of trials. The simultaneous presentation of either two equally dim or two equally bright lights constituted the high conflict condition. Intermediate conflict was determined by the exposure of a relatively bright and dim light, while low conflict consisted of the appearance of a very bright and very dim light. In all, five groups were given differential conflict training. Two groups were exposed to high conflict, two groups received intermediate conflict, and one group was given low conflict. Comparisons between the high, intermediate, and low conflict conditions provide information relevant to the effects of the relative strengths of conflicting tendencies, while comparisons between the two groups in each of the high and intermediate conditions are relevant to the role of the absolute strengths. To assess the effects of these conditions, all subjects were finally placed in the original low conflict situation.

Apparatus

The apparatus is the same as that described elsewhere (Worell & Hill, 1962). Briefly, it consisted of two windows set into a black panel, a start platform attached to the base of the panel with a visual ready signal directly above, and a push button on both the left and right edges of the start platform. A Standard Electric timer was activated with the illumination of the windows and was terminated when the subject removed his hand from the start platform. The lights in both windows were turned off by the subject pressing either push button. Reaction latency, or time from the illumination of the windows to removal of the hand from the start platform, was recorded to the nearest 1/100 second. These reaction time scores were converted to reciprocals (1/RT × 1000), so that all performances are presented in terms of speed of response.

The stimuli consisted of four different brightnesses, 2.8, 8.8, 90.9, and 291.4 foot candles, obtained by measurements at each window with a Macbeth illuminometer. The two brightest stimuli (90.9 and 291.4) and the two dimmest (2.8 and 8.8) were separated by differences of approximately .50 log units, while the two intermediate stimuli (8.8 and 90.9) were separated by an approximate 1.0 log unit difference.

Procedure

Each subject, participating individually, was instructed to push the button below either the "brighter" or "dimmer" light,

depending upon the condition to which he was assigned. The subject was informed that the experiment was concerned with the accuracy of visual discrimination. The instructions did not contain any implication that speed was considered important.

All subjects were given a total of 64 discrimination trials. The first 16 of these constituted familiarization trials with low conflict; the intermediate 24 trials presented the experimentally induced conflict conditions; and the final 24 trials presented low conflict to all subjects again. In those conditions where two unequally bright stimuli were administered, the position of the correct stimulus was randomized such that the same stimulus did not appear more than three consecutive times in the same location.

Subjects

The subjects were 70 volunteer females from introductory psychology who were

TABLE 1

Mean Speeds of Response

Group[a]	I[b]	Preconflict performance	Conflict training	Post-minus preconflict performance
I (291.4 and 291.4)	B	19.14	7.86	−3.98
	D	14.37	6.34	.43
II (2.8 and 2.8)	B	18.27	9.87	12.96
	D	15.72	8.11	8.67
III (291.4 and 8.8	B	15.02	18.71	29.27
	D	15.29	19.68	37.30
IV (90.9 and 2.8)	B	20.00	22.24	20.42
	D	16.68	18.74	13.43
V (291.4 and 2.8)	B	17.91	23.23	27.54
	D	16.07	20.96	23.16

[a] The numerical values given next to each numbered group reflect the intensity values of the conflict stimuli.

[b] The designation (B) and (D) represents the Bright and Dim instructional condition, respectively.

randomly assigned, 14 per group, to one of five groups. Within each group the brighter of the two stimuli was designated as the correct stimulus for half of the group and the dimmer for the remaining half.

Results

The mean speed scores ($1/RT \times 1000$) for all subgroups during the three major phases of the experiment are presented in Table 1. Figure 1 contains the data for the five major conflict groups with the bright-dim conditions combined over successive eight trial blocks. The data for the various groups were analyzed and will be discussed separately for the three major phases of the experiment.

Preconflict performance

In order to determine whether the subjects in the conflict groups demon-

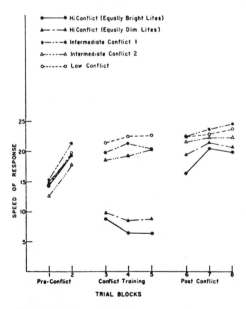

Fig. 1. Response speeds over trials for the five conflict groups during preconflict conditions. (Each trial block represents the average performance on eight trials. Intermediate Conflict 1 corresponds to Group III; Intermediate Conflict 2 to Group IV (see Table 1.)

strated comparable performances prior to exposure to conflict, a Lindquist (1953) Type III analysis of variance was performed on the preconflict training performances. The summary of this analysis appears in Table 2 and indicates that there were only two significant effects; that for the bright-dim instructional condition was significant at less than the .05 level, while the trials effect was significant well beyond the .001 level. Of particular interest is the absence of significant performance differences between the groups who were subsequently given the differential conflict treatments. The finding that speed increases with trials has been obtained many times before and indicates that performance becomes more rapid with practice. On the other hand, the finding of a significant difference between the bright-dim instructional conditions is of some interest. An examination of Table 1 indicates that there is a strong tendency for the subjects who were instructed to respond to the brighter stimulus to be faster. This result is in accord with a portion of the results obtained in a previous study (Castaneda & Worell, 1961). It would appear that through previous experience individuals may learn to respond to the "brighter" stimuli when relatively bright stimuli are present, and that forcing them to respond to dimmer stimuli may arouse interfering or incompatible tendencies. In other words, the instruction to respond to the dimmer stimulus seems to have increased the degree of conflict.

Conflict training

The mean speeds of performance for the five conflict groups are presented in the middle portion of Table 1. A second Lindquist (1953) Type III analysis

TABLE 2

Summaries of Analyses of Variance

Source	Preconflict performance			Conflict training			Postconflict performance		
	MS	df	F	MS	df	F	MS	df	F
Instructions (I)	13,353.64	1	4.73*	8,771.38	1	—	21.69	1	—
Conflict (C)	2,306.62	4	—	130,938.53	4	24.38***	7,620.97	4	3.98**
I × C	1,564.40	4	—	1,796.17	4	—	441.82	4	—
Error (b)	2,825.01	60		5,370.64	60		1,914.47	60	
Trials (T)	60,108.72	1	271.29***	38.32	2	—	4,812.09	2	21.91***
T × I	33.71	1	—	30.57	2	—	322.41	2	—
T × C	174.32	4	—	933.33	8	5.69***	46.35	8	—
T × I × C	292.94	4	—	157.96	8	—	431.09	8	—
Error (w)	221.57	60		164.15	120		219.58	120	

* $p = <.05$.
** $p = <.01$.
*** $p = <.001$.

was performed on the data during conflict training and is summarized in the middle portion of Table 2. This analysis provided two significant effects; the main effect of conflict was significant well beyond the .001 level as was the interaction of trials and the conflict conditions. An examination of the performances of the conflict groups during conflict training in Figure 1 indicates quite clearly the greater speeds of the low and intermediate conflict groups when compared with the two high conflict groups. In relation to the significant trials and conflict interaction, a further inspection of Figure 1 shows that while the low and intermediate conflict groups tended to increase in speed over trials, the high conflict groups tended to become slower. The foregoing results support the view that the conflict training conditions produced marked speed differences between the various groups.

A further analysis was made of the simple effects to determine whether the absolute strengths of competing tendencies provided significant differences in addition to those that are apparent for the relative strengths of these tendencies. It will be recalled that the two high conflict groups were exposed to either two equally bright or two equally dim stimuli. Since the difference in strength between the two stimuli was the same for either pair of stimuli, the major difference between the conditions is in terms of the absolute intensity of the stimuli. Likewise, one pair of intermediate conflict stimuli was made up of the 291.4 and 8.8 brightnesses, while the other pair consisted of the 90.9 and 2.8 brightnesses. In each case, there was about a 1.5 log unit difference between the stimuli. Assuming that within the present range of values, equal log differences represent subjectively equal differences, the major difference between the two intermediate conflict conditions also is in terms of the absolute intensity of the stimuli. Analyses revealed that the differences between the two high conflict groups and between the two intermediate conflict groups were not significant. Thus, there is no evidence for an effect of the absolute intensities on conflict performance.

Postconflict performance

The principal interest of this study was in the effects of prior exposure to different levels of conflict on performance in weak conflict situations. In order to determine these effects, an analysis was performed on the difference scores for each individual between preconflict performance (Trials 9–16) and postconflict performance (divided into successive eight trial blocks). The mean values for postconflict minus preconflict performance are presented in Table 1. The summary of an analysis of variance performed on these data may be seen in the third column of Table 2. This analysis provides two significant effects; the effect of trials was significant beyond the .001 level and the effects of conflict beyond the .01 level. Once again, the trials effect indicates that performances tend to become more rapid with practice (Figure 1). Of particular interest, however, is the significant conflict effect which suggests that previous exposure to various levels of conflict led to significant differences in the speed of resolving weak conflict situations. Reference to Table 1 and Figure 1 indicates that the two high conflict groups were slower than the two intermediate and lone low conflict groups. Moreover, the differences between these groups tend to persist over the entire 24 trials that (the weak conflict condition) were presented in Figure 1.

Discussion

The principal findings provide clear support for the view that the effects of conflict generalize to other related but less conflictful situations. It was found that individuals whose behavioral efficiency was impaired by exposure to relatively severe conflicts also demon-strated impaired ability to resolve subsequent weaker conflicting tendencies. When the present results are contrasted with those obtained in previous work (Worell & Castaneda, 1961a), there is a strong indication that generalization of the effects of conflict occurs along dimensions of similarity. Thus, in the former study where there was a minimal similarity between the conflict situation and the learning conditions, the generalization of conflict effects was only manifest when one took into consideration the nature of the individual's response to conflict. In the present study where there was a relatively high degree of similarity between the conflict situation and the subsequent performance task, a striking effect of conflict on later performance in a weaker conflict situation was found. From the standpoint of clinical approaches, these findings are in accord with what would be expected if one views personality as being a function of both the individual and the situation. Thus, the tendency to characterize an individual as generally indecisive may be adequate for a few persons, but that better prediction of behavior might be achieved by taking into account the specific nature of previously experienced conflicts and the present conflict situation.

The behavior of subjects in weak conflict following exposure to varying severities of conflict is consistent with expectations derived from the competing response formulation. It will be recalled that this hypothesis proposed that there would be a generalization of competing responses from the conflict training situation to the weak conflict situation, such that the behavior of subjects in weak conflict following performance under strong conflict would be significantly impaired. At the present time the exact nature of these hypothesized competing responses is unknown. Such responses, however, as hesitancy or holding back a response or learning to spend more time in looking from one alternative to the other appear to be likely possibilities. Although the identification of these responses would be of some value, the consistency of the obtained data with the general competing response position is of most immediate importance.

Although the findings support the competing response formulation, they do not eliminate the importance of the dynamogenic view, or at least a modified version of this view. For example, it might be maintained that the greatest amount of emotionality or drive was aroused in both high conflict groups, but that this heightened emotionality acted in concert with the competing response tendencies. Thus, the tension aroused by the conflict conditions might be seen as having increased the general level of drive and thereby augmented the strengths of the competing tendencies. Such a "feedback" view has been discussed by both Brown and Farber (1951) and Worell (1961). Although admittedly speculative, this reasoning does serve to highlight our lack of independent evidence about the degree of emotionality engendered in any of our groups. In any event, whatever the status of conflict produced drive may be under the present circumstaces, it seems apparent that a primary place must be made for some sort of associative (and in this case a competing response) formulation.

Apart from the competing response and dynamogenic views, an alternative explanation based on failure may be considered. It is possible that the various conflict training conditions were seen as differentially difficult by the subjects and that this varying difficulty produced differing levels of feelings of failure. In relation to this point, it should be noted that an attempt was made to minimize the possibility of failure occurring by having every response made by the subject to the conflict situation be a correct one. Thus, at all times the conflict situation was removed by the subject pressing the button under either simultaneously exposed light. Even if feelings of failure were not eliminated by this procedure, however, all that a precisely defined "failure" hypothesis would provide in terms of prediction would be a specification of the kinds of competing responses aroused as a function of conflict. In short, the general predictions made in this experiment would not differ from those made with the competing response formulation, since the "failure" hypothesis would be a special case of the competing response formulation.

In addition to these considerations, the findings relevant to the role of the absolute and relative strengths of conflicting tendencies deserve some attention. Our results suggest that the strength or degree of conflict varies with the *difference* in strength between competing tendencies. Hence, the more closely competing tendencies approximate one another in strength the greater the degree of conflict. On the other hand, we have found that the absolute strengths do not contribute significantly to performance. Here, subjects exposed to either high conflict condition or to ether intermediate conflict condition did not differ significantly in speed. As a result, within the present definition of absolute strength, strength of conflict appears to be principally, if not exclusively, based on the difference in strength between competing tendencies. Aside from the fact that other ways of manipulating absolute strength may provide different results, it is worth remembering that the present conflict conditions might be regarded as primarily involving conflict between two approach responses. Whether conflict situations which contain avoidance tendencies will provide similar results remains to be seen.

Summary: As a partial outgrowth of the frequent clinical observation that individuals who are faced with strong conflicts show inefficient handling of these conflicts and weaker conflicts as well, the problem of the generalization of the effects of conflict was investigated. The first question that was examined was whether prior exposure to conflict affected performance in a new but similar conflict situation. In order to anticipate performance in a conflict situation following differential conflict training, two alternative hypotheses, termed the competing response and dynamogenic, were considered. According to the competing response view, exposure to conflict was assumed to lead to the learning of certain conflict-specific responses and performance in a new but similar conflict situation was expected to be affected by the generalization of these responses from previous conflict experiences. According to the dynamogenic view, conflict was assumed to generate drive and performance in a subsequent conflict situation would be affected as a function of augmented drive levels. The second interest of this study was in the problem of the degree or strength of conflict. An attempt was made to determine the role of the absolute and relative strengths of conflicting tendencies in performance.

To test these considerations, five groups of subjects were exposed to three successive phases of an experimental procedure. Initially, all subjects were exposed to a weak conflict situation. Following this, the subjects in the various groups were given training in responding to one of five levels (severities) of conflict. Finally, all subjects were again exposed to the original weak conflict situation. The findings indicated (a) that prior exposure to strong conflict led to a significant impairment of speed performance in weak conflict, and (b) that the degree of conflict was dependent on the relative strengths of or the difference in strength between competing tendencies and not on the absolute strengths of these tendencies. The significance of these results for our hypotheses and personality predictions was discussed.

Science, 1960, vol. 132, pp. 1769–1770.

Simultaneous Generalization Gradients for Appetitive and Aversive Behavior

*Eliot Hearst**

When an organism is trained to make a response in the presence of a particular stimulus, this response will also normally occur in the presence of other stimuli that are physically similar to the original conditioning stimulus. The result of this phenomenon is often a "gradient of stimulus generalization" —an orderly decline in the probability of response, which takes place as the physical difference between the original stimulus and various test stimuli is increased. Stimulus generalization is a major explanatory concept in such areas as learning theory, psychotherapy, and abnormal psychology (see Mednick & Freedman, 1960).

The study reported here was designed to determine whether there is any difference between generalization gradients for reward-controlled and punishment-controlled behavior. The technique used to investigate this problem permitted a comparison of the two gradients for individual subjects and may be applicable to other problems in experimental psychology and psychopharmacology.

Five young male rhesus monkeys were the subjects. The experimental test chamber was a commercially produced model (Foringer) which provided an automatic mechanism for reward delivery, an electrifiable grid, implementation for two possible responses (pulling a chain which hung in the center of the chamber and pressing a lever mounted on one wall), and a 110 v a-c, 60-watt house light mounted above a circular screen of milk glass in the top of the chamber. During generalization testing the intensity of this house light was varied in discrete (though unequal) steps by means of a group of fixed resistors in series with the house light. The 11 possible test-light intensities were calibrated on several occasions with a General Electric foot-candle light intensity meter placed approximately 1 foot below the glass screen on which the house light was projected.

All the subjects were first trained to press the lever, which postponed shock for 10 seconds; by responding at least once every 10 seconds the subjects could avoid shock entirely (Sidman, 1953b).

During this training period, and all subsequent training periods prior to the generalization test, the house light was on continuously at its maximum intensity (28.1 ft-ca).

After the animals became proficient at avoiding shocks, the chain was introduced into the apparatus, and each pull of the chain was rewarded with a pellet of food. The avoidance schedule was still in effect, so that lever-pressing continued even during the learning of the chain-pulling response. Eventually all the subjects learned to press the lever to avoid punishment and to pull the chain to produce food reward on a 2-minute variable-interval schedule (Ferster & Skinner, 1957).

After ten additional sessions of exposure to the concurrent schedules of reward and avoidance in the presence of the brightest light intensity[1], a generalization test session was programmed. During this test, light of 11 different intensities was presented, 12 times at each intensity, in a mixed order. Each stimulus presentation lasted 30 seconds. No rewards or punishments were obtainable during this test. The test procedure was quite similar to that of Guttman and Kalish (1956).

For several experimental sessions after this generalization test the subjects were put on concurrent reward-avoidance schedules as before; they were

[1] Note that the animals were not given any discrimination training—that is, they were not exposed to any other house-light intensities during training in the experimental chamber. One subject, however, usually had to be left in the apparatus overnight, since his daily session began at 5 P.M.; at the conclusion of the session the house light went out, and the animal remained in complete darkness until the next morning. The generalization data for this subject did not differ in any obvious way from those for the other subjects.

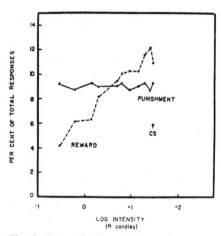

Fig. 1. Generalization gradients for reward-controlled and punishment-controlled behavior.

then given a second generalization test.[2]

Chain-pulls and lever-presses in response to each of the 11 light intensities were recorded. Generalization gradients, relating response strength (the ratio of total number of responses to each intensity to total number of responses to all intensities) to log intensity of the test light are shown in Fig. 1. These data are group means for the two generalization tests combined. Considered separately, the data for individual subjects are very similar to the group results.

Figure 1 displays a clear difference between avoidance and reward gradients. The reward gradient is much steeper; it was found that the subjects were all much more likely to respond to stimuli of a high intensity (close to that of the conditioned stimulus) than to stimuli of much lower intensity than the conditioned stimulus. In contrast, the avoidance gradient is almost completely flat; subjects were just as likely

to respond to the dimmest as to the brightest test light.[3]

Since the rate of avoidance responding was much higher than the rate of responding for food reward, the differences in shape of the generalization gradients might be attributable to differential response rates rather than to motivational or reinforcement factors (reward versus punishment). However, at least one similar study (Guttman & Kalish, 1956) has shown that lowered response rate leads to a flattening of generalization gradients, a finding which would imply the opposite effect from that obtained in the experiment discussed here.

The finding of virtually indiscriminate avoidance response, in contrast to the well-discriminated rewarded response, may have relevance to clinical descriptions of hypersensitivity and seeming irrationality under conditions of strong anxiety; an "anxious" patient may respond strongly to stimuli which are only remotely similar to an original anxiety-provoking stimulus. There are experimental data from studies of human beings which also show a greater than normal amount of stimulus generalization in subjects who are highly anxious (see, for example, S. A. Mednick, 1957; Hilgard, Jones & Kaplan, 1951) or even schizophrenic (Bender & Schilder, 1930; Garmezy, 1952b), or who are made anxious experimen-

---

[2] One subject contracted a digestive-tract infection and died before a second test was possible.

[3] After the conclusion of this experiment subjects were given discrimination training, so that they learned to press the lever and pull the chain only during light of one intensity (the brightest or dimmest, depending on the subject) and to cease responding when the light was of a different intensity (at the other end of the intensity continuum). Here, too, preliminary results showed avoidance gradients to be flatter than reward gradients. Both gradients were much steeper than before discrimination training, however.

tally (Bersh, Notterman & Schoenfeld, 1956).

Summary: In the presence of a bright light five monkeys were trained to press a lever to avoid shock and to pull a chain for food reward. When tested with a series of lights dimmer than the conditioning stimulus, the monkeys showed a sharp gradient of effect for the rewarded response, in contrast to a very flat gradient for the avoidance response.

Journal of Comparative and Physiological Psychology, 1963, vol. 56, pp. 1027–1031

Escape from a Stimulus Associated with Both Reward and Punishment

Eliot Hearst[1]

After association with reward or punishment a neutral stimulus usually develops positively or negatively reinforcing properties of its own. A response that terminates a conditioned positive stimulus should have a low probability of occurrence whereas a response that terminates a conditioned negative stimulus should have a high probability of occurrence (Azrin, Holz, & Hake, 1962; Dinsmoor, 1962; Kelleher & Gollub, 1962).

In this experiment we studied the effects of a stimulus that was associated with both reward and punishment. Rats were permitted to terminate the stimulus—and thus prevent rewards and punishments—by making a lever response. The stimulus may be described as "conflict-producing" since Ss had to risk punishment in order to obtain reward and had to forego reward in order to avoid punishment. The frequency of stimulus termination ("escape from the stimulus") served as a measure of the relative aversiveness of

the stimulus. Depending on the drive strengths involved and on the relative frequencies of reward and punishment, the stimulus could presumably exhibit a wide range of positively and negatively reinforcing effects.

Stimulus termination frequency was examined as a function of the intensity of punishment, the amount of food deprivation, and the presence or absence of food reward.

Method

Subjects

The Ss were five[2] male albino rats of Osborne-Mendel strain, numbered consecutively from MO-9 to MO-13. All were 99–100 days old at the beginning of training and had not been used in any prior work. Throughout the study Ss were maintained at 75% of their free-feeding weights by the use of condensed milk reinforcements during test periods and supplementary Purina rat pellets after sessions and on weekends.

---

[1] The expert technical assistance of Alice Torovsky and Minnie B. Koresko is gratefully acknowledged.

[2] Initially, two other rats were scheduled to be experimental Ss, but they never learned to press the lever, even though they were exposed to several different shock levels with and without accompanying food rewards.

Water was continuously available in the home cages of all Ss.

Apparatus

The experimental box was a commercially produced model (Foringer). A modified telegraph key served as the response lever. Whenever rewards were due, a motor-driven dipper delivered .1 ml. of condensed milk, presented for 3 sec., to a slot below and to the left of the lever. The milk solution was a mixture of equal volumes of sweetened condensed milk and tap water. A small stimulus light, mounted to the left of the dipper slot, went on while the dipper was available to S. Electric shocks of approximately .37-sec. duration were administered through a grid scrambler that randomly reversed the polarity of the voltage on the grid floor of the box. The floor, walls and lever were all connected into the shock circuit. When appropriate, a clicking noise was used as a stimulus. A system of timers, relays, counters, and cumulative recorders automatically programed shocks, food rewards, stimuli, etc., and recorded response data.

Procedure

All experimental sessions lasted 90 min. and occurred daily except for weekends.

The first experimental procedure involved reward only. In the presence of one stimulus condition (S^D)—a clicking noise for three Ss and a period of silence for two Ss—condensed milk rewards were delivered on a 1-min. variable interval schedule (VI 1). These rewards were response-independent, i.e., they were presented without regard to the behavior of Ss. A single lever press, however, produced a 5-min. time out from the "free" reinforcements. During this time out the other stimulus condition—a silent period for three Ss and a clicking noise for two Ss—was in effect and no rewards were possible. As soon as the 5-min. time out ended, S^D conditions were reinstated. If S never depressed the lever, S^D remained on for the entire session. Lever responses during time outs had no effect.

After Ss had been exposed to this procedure for 16 sessions, a free-shock contingency was added to the free-reward contingency during S^D. Shocks, .88 ma. in intensity, were delivered on a 4-min. variable interval schedule (VI 4) in S^D. Under this procedure Ss received both intermittent rewards (VI 1) and intermittent shocks (VI 4) during S^D. As before, a lever response terminated S^D for 5 min., and removed the possibility of rewards and shocks. The Ss remained on this concurrent reward-shock procedure for 17 sessions.

For the remainder of this phase of the experiment the frequency of S^D-escape behavior was studied as a function of (a) shock intensity, and (b) the presence or absence of concurrent food reward. Four shock intensities were tested (0.00, 0.22, 0.88, and 1.24 ma.), each with and without accompanying food reinforcement. Shocks were always programed on a VI 4 schedule and food rewards on a VI 1 schedule. Both VI tapes ran only during S^D.

Different Ss received the eight possible combinations of reward and shock intensity in a different mixed sequence. Each S was usually exposed to a particular combination for a standard stability period of 10 consecutive experimental sessions. Occasionally, several extra days had to be added to this 10-day standard because of an apparatus failure or obvious instability in an S's records. In all cases, only the last five sessions on a particular combination were used in calculating mean performance; each such 5-day mean will be called a "de-

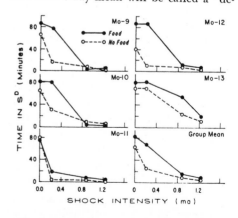

Fig. 1. Mean time spent in S^D as a function of shock intensity (maximum time = 90 min.). (The solid curves were obtained when both food and a given shock intensity were possible in S^D, the dashed curves when only shock was possible. Separate curves for the five individual Ss and for the group are shown.)

termination." At least two determinations were obtained for every S at each of the eight possible combinations of reward and shock intensity.

Variation of hunger drive

After this phase of the experiment had been completed, four of the five Ss were tested either hungry or satiated under several food-shock conditions. The details of these tests are described in the description of the results.

Results

Figure 1 compares mean time spent in S^D for the food and no-food conditions under the four different shock levels. The data points for each individual S are means of at least two determinations at each combination of reward condition and shock intensity.

When no food was possible in S^D, relatively little time was spent in S^D under shock intensities .22 ma. and higher. The amount of time S^D remained on was a decreasing function of shock intensity; Ss terminated S^D more quickly as shock levels were increased to higher values. Among the individual Ss, MO-11 appeared comparatively sensitive and MO-13 comparatively insensitive to the shocks.

The addition of the food contingency modified the functions of Figure 1 over their no-food values. More time was generally spent in S^D when food was available. Moreover, total S^D time declined less rapidly as a function of shock intensity than it did under the no-food condition.

When neither food nor shock was given in S^D ("no-food" curves for 0 ma. shock intensity), Ss usually left S^D on for most of the session. This finding indicated (a) that S^D was not inherently very aversive, and (b) that in this situation Ss do not often press for mere

stimulus change. It is clear, however, that Ss do terminate S^D occasionally under no-shock conditions, and that this is more likely to happen under no-food conditions than under food conditions.

An analysis of variance was applied to the group data summarized in Figure 1. Each S provided at least two determinations (in four cells there were three determinations) for each of the eight possible treatments. This test revealed significant differences among the four shock intensities ($F = 232.9$, $df = 3/44$, $p < .01$), the five Ss ($F = 18.8$, $df = 4/44$, $p < .01$), and the two food conditions ($F = 93.6$, $df = 1/44$, $p < .01$), as well as a significant interaction between shock intensity and food condition ($F = 7.84$, $df = 3/44$, $p < .01$). For each S the greatest increase in S^D-time brought about by the addition of food rewards occurred at a moderate shock level (.22 ma. or .88 ma.) rather than at a very strong shock or no shock at all.

Another aspect of behavior in this situation deserves brief mention. The rate of time-out lever pressing, which had no programed consequence, was found to increase significantly as the shock intensity increased ($p < .01$ from an analysis of variance of the group data). Increased time-out responding at high shock levels may simply be an example of response induction (Reynolds, 1961), or may have been anticipatory in nature, i.e., served to prepare S in some way for short latencies of response to S^D onset.

Variation of Hunger Drive

The prior phases of the experiment had focused on the aversive factors in the situation. Tests were next scheduled in which the degree of hunger was varied. First, Ss were placed on a schedule where food reward and shock of a mild intensity occurred on the same variable interval schedules as previously. Just as before, Ss were tested at 75% body weight and had not eaten since the end of the last experimental session, approximately 22½ hr. earlier. For Rats MO-9, 10, and 12 the "mild" shock was .22 ma.; for Rat MO-11 it was 0.16 ma. At these shock levels hungry Ss rarely terminated the stimulus (see Table 1).

TABLE 1

EFFECT OF FOOD DRIVE ON MEAN TIME (MINUTES) SPENT IN S^D "HUNGRY" VALUES WERE TAKEN FROM DAYS IMMEDIATELY PRECEDING SATIATION TESTS

	Food and mild shock		Food and no shock	
	Hungry	Satiated	Hungry	Satiated
MO-9	81.45	58.34	91.39	80.48
MO-10	72.27	33.75	81.52	72.07
MO-11	68.58	33.43	85.05	86.32
MO-12	91.32	12.43	78.33	66.35
Group M	78.41	34.49	84.07	76.31

Rat MO-13 began to exhibit great variability in baseline performance during this stage of the experiment. Its previous levels of response to mild shocks could not be recaptured; S usually terminated S^D much more frequently than before. Therefore, variation of hunger drive under a mild shock condition was not carried out with this S.

After Ss had stabilized on the "food-mild-shock" procedure under "hungry" conditions, they were given two tests when milk-satiated. These satiation tests occurred at least a week apart and were separated by several tests under the usual hunger conditions. To satiate Ss, we permitted them free access to a pan of condensed milk for 30 min. before experimental tests. Then we fed them additional milk with an eye dropper until several minutes had passed in which they refused to accept any more milk. The Ss took about 25–30 gm. of milk during this satiation period.

Table 1 shows that hungry Ss spent much more time than satiated Ss in the stimulus accompanied by food and mild shock. In none of the four individual Ss was there overlap between measurements taken while satiated and measurements taken under hungry conditions.

One control experiment was necessary to clarify interpretation of these differences between hungry and satiated Ss. It was possible that, under conditions of satiation, Ss might find a food-associated stimulus aversive, even if mild shocks were not given in the stimulus.

Therefore, Ss were placed on the food-no-shock condition for several weeks, until their behavior had stabilized. They were then given three satiation tests in the same way as described previously. Hungry Ss left S^D on for most of the session under this procedure, just as they had under the food-mild-shock condition. When Ss were satiated, however, mean S^D time declined only slightly (Table 1).

An analysis of variance (factorial design) for hunger condition (hungry vs. satiated), shock condition (mild vs. no shock), and Ss ($N = 4$) revealed differences between hunger conditions and between shock conditions to be significant at well beyond the .01 level. In addition, the Hunger Condition × Shock Condition interaction was significant beyond the .01 level. This latter result supports the conclusion that the effect of satiation is greater under the food-mild-shock condition than under the food-no-shock condition. Thus, it appears that the decline in S^D time brought about by satiation in the mild-shock condition is primarily related to the presence of shocks and cannot simply be attributed to a change in the incentive value of milk rewards for satiated Ss.

Discussion

The present technique has proven sensitive to variations in both appetitive and aversive factors. Rat Ss terminate a stimulus that is correlated with both reward and punishment less frequently than a stimulus that is correlated only with punishment. If the stimulus is correlated only with reward, Ss rarely terminate it. Satiated Ss terminate stimuli correlated with shocks of an intensity they accept when hungry.

The no-food curves of Figure 1 revealed that the frequency of termination of a shock-correlated stimulus is directly related to the intensity of the shocks. Studies of the relationship between shock intensity and measures of discriminated avoidance learning (e.g., Brush, 1957) have often displayed very minor differences among different shock levels. In the procedure of the present study individual Ss supplied data at several different shock levels. Our Ss could supply data at several shock levels because the effects of a given shock intensity were reversible; after just a few sessions at a new shock intensity, the performance of Ss usually shifted accordingly. Perhaps the effects of different shock intensities are more clearly seen when individual Ss have a chance to sample several shock values, in contrast to the "group-single value" experimental designs often used in the past.

Hearst and Sidman (1961) have reported data from experimental situations quite similar to the present one. In those experiments Ss were sometimes rewarded and sometimes punished for pressing a lever in the presence of S^D; they could, however, produce a time out from both reward and punishment by pressing a second lever. The Hearst-Sidman situation differs from the present one primarily in that rewards and punishments were response-correlated in the former case, whereas they were response-independent here. With response-correlated punishment there are three typical adjustments that S may make to the situation: (a) S may stop responding on the first lever, thereby preventing both reward and punishment; (b) S may press the second lever and produce time outs, thereby preventing both reward and punishment; and (c) S may persist in pressing the first lever, thereby continuing to produce both reward and punishment. Hearst and Sidman were particularly interested in alternative b—as were Egger and Miller (1960) in another study—since frequent production of time outs would lead to the significant conclusion that escape from a conflictful situation could in itself be positively reinforcing (see also a discussion of "conflict-induced drives" in Miller, 1959; Miller & Barry, 1960). Hearst and Sidman, however, obtained a variety of effects with the response-correlated procedure; no more than half the Ss showed a type b adjustment.

With the response-independent procedure, there are only two main adjustments to consider, and these are comparable to b and c above; (a) S may press the lever to produce time outs, thereby preventing both reward and punishment; or (b) S may allow S^D to remain on, thereby permitting rewards and punishments to continue. In the response-independent situation S can avoid shocks only in an "active" way, i.e., by pressing the lever in S^D, whereas in the response-correlated situation shocks can be avoided in both an "active" and a "passive" manner, i.e., either by the production of time outs or by a cessation of responding on the lever that produces the punishment. The type of stimulus termination examined in the response-independent situation does not, therefore, qualify as escape from conflict, or as an indicant of a conflict-induced drive, since lever presses in S^D not only remove S from a concurrently positive and negative stimulus, but also avoid shock. Therefore, the response-correlated procedures seem to provide a more relevant testing ground for the escape from conflict possibility, even though those procedures are more complicated and lead to a greater variety of effects than the one studied here.

Summary: Rats could terminate a stimulus associated with intermittent, response-independent rewards and shocks. Each S served as its own control and was tested on a variety of shock intensities. Stimulus termination rate was found to be directly related to shock intensity. Except at very high shock intensities Ss terminated the stimulus less frequently when both food and shock were possible than when only shock was possible. Variations in hunger drive also affected the frequency of stimulus termination. The present technique may prove useful as a relatively simple method for studying conflict behavior and secondary reinforcement.

Journal of Abnormal and Social Psychology, 1961, vol. 63, pp. 530–533

The Extinction of Fear as a Function of Distance Versus Dissimilarity from the Original Conflict Situation[1]

Thomas Elder, Charles D. Noblin, and Brendan A. Maher

Murray and Berkun (1955) have combined Miller's (1944, 1948) conflict and displacement models to form a three-dimensional scheme that generated predictions concerning the simultaneous operations of conflict and displacement. Conflict is derived from a set of assumptions relating response strength to the

[1] This study was supported by funds from Grants G 3852/6433 from the National Science Foundation to Brendan A. Maher.

It was read in abbreviated form at the annual meeting of the Southeastern Psychological Association, Atlanta, Georgia, 1960.

distance of the subject from the goal (Miller, 1944); displacement is based upon a similar set of assumptions concerning the difference in similarity between an original and other stimulus objects (Miller, 1944). Murray and Berkun diagrammatically represent this three-dimensional system by two horizontal axes at right angles to each other, representing distance and similarity scales, respectively. A third axis extends vertically from the point of intersection of the two horizontal axes and represents a scale of response strength. By placing two points on each of the three axes, two planes are obtained: one representing approach and one representing avoidance tendency, from which are derived specific predictions of behavior.

Applying the model to the behavior of rats, they deduced that subjects trained to approach-avoidance conflict in an original alley would, whenever possible, leave that alley to enter a different one and that the more dissimilar the new alley the nearer subjects would approach the goal. As a test of these deductions, they first trained rats to run an alley for food and on later trials established conflict by administering shock while the subjects were eating. These subjects were then placed at the starting end of the original alley and could either remain in this alley or could leave and enter new and different alleys adjacent and parallel to the original. Windows were spaced at equal intervals along the common walls of adjacent alleys to permit crossing from one to another. Tracings of the movements of the rats through the maze followed the pattern predicted; i.e., the subjects ran farther down the most dissimilar alley, and farther down the moderate alley than down the original. They also reported that goal responses occurred first in the most dissimilar alley, second in the intermediate, and finally in the original alley. Third, they observed that subjects entered the most dissimilar alley through windows farther down the intermediate alley than the windows used when crossing from the original to the intermediate alley. These results were interpreted as confirmation of deductions from, and support for, the three-dimensional model insofar as it predicts the locus of "dis-

placement" to be a function of the similarity between the original and the test situations.

A recent study (Maher, Elder, & Noblin, 1962) in which it was necessary to replicate the Murray and Berkun (1955) experiment has confirmed all but one of these findings. In this it was found that rats tend to enter more dissimilar alleys through the windows nearest the start end of the runways rather than windows spaced farther down the alleys. This finding was combined with the observation that Murray and Berkun always located the most dissimilar alley farthest away from the original, thus confounding distance and dissimilarity and making it impossible to decide if the subjects are entering new and different alleys as a response to distance cues or as a response to similarity cues.

If distance is the critical factor, then by deleting the principle of generalization from the three-dimensional formulation, and extending the assumptions about distance of the subject from the goal to include the distance of other alleys from the original, a simplified model evolves from which the same prediction (i.e., the "therapeutic effect") can be generated.

The purpose of the present study was to devise a situation in which the spatial distance of dissimilar alleys and the dissimilarity of distant alleys from the original could be systematically altered, thereby subjecting to empirical tests two alternate deductions: Subjects trained to approach-avoidance conflict should either enter and run farther down the most dissimilar alley as predicted by the three-dimensional model; or as the simpler formulation predicts, they should enter and run down the alley most distant from the original.

Method

Apparatus

The apparatus (see Figure 1) consisted of four alleys each of which was 48 inches long, 5 inches wide, 6 inches deep, white, grey, black, and white, respectively. The alleys and walls of the alleys contained four 2.5 inch square windows equally spaced along the walls of the alleys, each of separate construction so the parallel arrangement could be varied. A food cup 1.5 inches in diameter was attached to an end wall of each alley with the rim of the cup 3 inches from the floor. The floors of the alleys were covered with .25 inch hardware cloth. Hooks were placed on the outside of the end walls and a spring extended from the hooks on each end of the first alley to the hooks on the ends of the fourth alley to hold the four runways securely in parallel. A removable cover was constructed of .5 inch hardware cloth and placed on top of the four-alley combination.

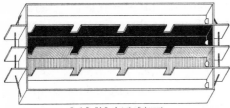

Fig. 1. Parallel alleys for testing displacement.

Fig. 1. Parallel alleys for testing displacement.

Subjects

The subjects were 24 male, albino rats of the Sprague-Dawley strain. These were randomly assigned to six groups of four and placed on a 24 hour food deprivation schedule 7 days prior to runway training. All subjects were fed 8 grams of Purina dog chow cubes daily, and a plentiful supply of water was available at all times.

Procedure

On the first day of training each of the 24 subjects received 25 successive reinforced approach trials in a white alley, hereafter designated as the original alley. A windowless wall was inserted between the original and adjacent alley to prevent the subject from entering other alleys during training trials. This procedure was repeated on the second day. On the third day subjects each received 10 warm-up trials, after which they received shock at the goal end of the original alley. The .75 milliampere shock was administered when the subject made a circuit between the metal food cup and the hardware-cloth floor. Shock trials were continued until the subject no longer ran beyond a point 18 inches from the start end of the runway.

Testing trials commenced immediately following the shock trials. The windowless wall between the original and the adjacent alley was removed and a wall with windows inserted in the maze.

Since the original alley was the same for all subjects, only the parallel position of the others was altered. This permitted six possible parallel arrangements of the four alleys, with one group of subjects assigned to each arrangement. Thus each group was tested under a different color/position combination.

A test trial consisted of placing the subject at the start of the original alley, the experimenter tracing its path through the maze. A trial terminated with the subject's making the goal response in any one of the runways or until a period of 2 minutes had elapsed. A goal response was defined by the subject's reaching up and placing its nose down into the food cup. Each subject received a maximum of 4 test trials on the first day and 10 test trials on each day thereafter until a criterion of two successive goal responses in the original alley had been reached.

Results

A mean distance score was computed for each subject by summing the number of eighth's of the distance traveled down the alley on each trial, and dividing by the total number of trials in which the subject entered that particular alley. Such scores were computed for each of the 24 subjects, the mean result for the entire sample being given

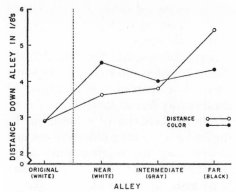

Fig. 2. Mean distances traveled down each alley.

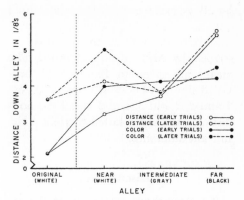

Fig. 3. Mean distance scores on early trials compared with later trials.

in Figure 2. The broken vertical line in the figure identifies scores obtained in the original from scores in the interchangeable alleys.

In order to test the effects of distance and/or color, a mixed analysis of variance on distance scores in the interchangeable alleys was used. As the summary in Table 1 shows, the distance variable produced the only significant effect. Variance due to groups (i.e., between-subjects, Distance × Color interaction) approached but did not reach

TABLE 1

SUMMARY OF ANALYSIS OF VARIANCE ON SUBJECTS' MEAN DISTANCE TRAVELED DOWN ALLEYS 2, 3, AND 4

Source	df	SS	MS	F
Between-subjects	11	145.04		
Groups (G)	2	47.61	23.80	2.20
Error (b)	9	97.43	10.82	
Within-subjects	60	419.23		
Distance (D)	2	96.23	48.11	9.56*
Color (C)	2	6.31	3.16	.63
Trial blocks (T)	1	2.51	2.51	.50
D × T	2	5.90	2.95	.59
C × T	2	11.74	5.87	1.17
G × T	2	9.78	4.89	.97
D × C$_{(w)}$ × T	2	2.84	1.42	.28
Error$_{(w)}$	47	236.31	5.03	
Total	71	564.27		

* $p < .01$.

the minimum significance level, and color appears to have had little or no effect. An unexpected result was that trials in the first half did not differ significantly from trials in the second half. Figure 3 shows that the only difference observed between early and later trials was in the original alley ($p < .001$ by a one-tailed sign test). The range of trials required to reach the criterion of two successive goal responses in the original alley was from 6 to 21 with a mean of 10.2.

To test Murray and Berkun's (1955) prediction that subjects should tend to use windows increasingly farther down toward the goal of increasingly dissimi-

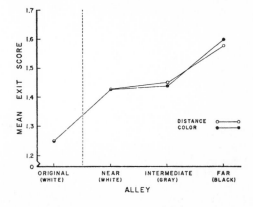

Fig. 4. Mean exit scores for each alley.

lar alleys, exit scores for the alleys along a distance as well as a similarity dimension were derived in the manner described by Murray and Berkun. The means are given in Figure 4. A one-tailed sign test between scores of Alleys 1 and 2, 2 and 3, and 3 and 4 for both distance and color failed to yield a significant difference.

Discussion

The hypothesis derived from the approach-avoidance-displacement model that subjects should run farther down more dissimilar alleys is rejected. The alternative hypothesis that rats trained to approach-avoidance conflict run farther down adjacent alleys as function of the spatial distance of the other alleys from the original is supported. However, the failure of the gradient to shift toward the goal ends of the neighboring alleys, and the dramatic forward shift of the point of intersecting approach-avoidance gradients in the original alley raises some doubt as to the nature of the therapeutic effect produced by experience in the other alleys. The tendency for subjects to leave the original alley and enter some alleys may, perhaps, be most parsimoniously viewed as *escape* behavior, rather than as a response to conflict generalized to other situations.

A possibility exists, however, that the dissimilar alleys did have a therapeutic effect, as a function not of *degree* of dissimilarity but of dissimilarity per se. While the behavior of subjects in the dissimilar-white alley differed from that observed in the original-white alley, thereby seeming to cast doubt on this hypothesis, these two alleys, similar in color, may have been dissimilar in some uncontrolled respect such as odor.

At this point, the conclusion drawn from this study is restricted to the inference that the three-dimensional model of Miller and others is open to question insofar as it utilizes a dissimilarity dimension to account for displacement.

Summary: The influence of distance was compared with that of dissimilarity in producing displacement behavior in an approach-avoidance conflict. Twenty-four white rats were used in a design that permitted separation of the effect of these two variables. Increasing reappearance of the approach response was significantly related to distance but not to dissimilarity. Tentative explanations are offered in terms of escape behavior, or of uncontrolled similarity cues such as odor. The Miller model of approach-avoidance-displacement is not supported by these data.

Science, September 30, 1960, vol. 132, pp. 896–897

Feeding in Conflict Situations and Following Thwarting[*][1]

Beatrice Tugendhat

Several studies have shown that the concept of drive as an energizer of all behavior that leads to the consummatory response is inadequate to describe the changes in a behavior pattern that accompany a high score in consummatory activities (Hinde, 1959). Further, Miller (1957) has reported two conditions that increase the amount of food intake while exerting differential effects on a number of other presumptive measures of strength of hunger. These findings are disturbing, as various investigators who have described the effects of frustration (see Marx, 1956) and conflict (Siegel & Brantley, 1951) as increasing drive strength have estimated the strength of drive by measuring a few, often a different few, of the many quantifiable aspects of a behavior pattern. The present report questions the description of such effects in terms of a unitary intervening variable.

Three-spined sticklebacks (*Gasterosteus aculeatus*, L.) were maintained in

aquaria divided by a partition into a food area and a living area. A portion of the partition was removed to permit 1 hour of access to the food at 1-, 2-, or 3-day intervals. For the thwarted feeding sessions the food was covered by a transparent plate for $\frac{1}{2}$ to 2 hours. After intervals ranging from 3 minutes to 4 hours, access to the food area with the plate removed was allowed. In conflict sessions, the fish received electric shock at varying intensities (42 volts, 84 ma; 66 volts, 112 ma; 108 volts, 210 ma) through a pair of electrodes immersed in the water. The first two entries into the food area or the 10th and 20th grasp at food were the occasions for administering shock.

Tubifex worms were scattered in the food area. Samples taken from the tanks indicated that there were over 30 times as many worms present as the fish would remove in the feeding session. To test whether a change in the behavior of the prey would make them less available to their predators, the feeding responses of the fish were imitated by poising over the prey and touching them with the end of a broad pencil at a rate corresponding to that of the feeding stickleback. There were no significant changes in the reaction of the prey to the repetition of this stimulation.

[*] Reprinted from *Science* by permission. Copyright © 1960 by the AAAS.
[1] The experiments on which this report is based were performed at the Oxford University Department of Zoology. Grateful acknowledgment is made to Dr. N. Tinbergen for his encouragement and helpful criticisms. The research was carried out while I was in receipt of a Miss Abbott's School Alumnae Fellowship, offered by Brown University, and of an intermediate and terminal predoctoral grant, awarded by the National Science Foundation.

TABLE 1

Feeding behavior: (*A*) following 1, 2, and 3 days deprivation (*N*=9); (*B*) in successive 15-minute periods of the feeding session, 2 days deprived (*N*=9); (*C*) in conflict sessions with high, medium, and low shock (*N*=12); (*D*) following thwarting (*N*=6). Significant differences: Italic type indicates that the difference between vertically adjacent pairs of numbers is statistically significant. In *A* and *C*, the pairs of asterisks indicate that the difference between the pairs of numbers not vertically adjacent are statistically significant. In *C*, bold-face type indicates that the differences between normal controls and all shock intensity tests considered together are statistically significant.

	Completed	Initiated	$\dfrac{Initiated}{Completed}$	Duration completed (0.10 min)	Total time feeding (min)
A. Days deprived					
1	*132*	612	*4.39*	3.8*	21.8
2	*196*	717	*3.52*	3.3	21.2
3	*252*	778	*2.87*	2.8*	21.7
B. Successive 15 min of feeding session					
1st	*63*	172	*2.75*	2.6	*4.3*
2nd	*54*	193	*3.46*	3.2	*5.7*
3rd	*43*	182	*3.98*	3.7	5.8
4th	*36*	169	*4.50*	4.0	5.6
C. Conflict: normal control; high, medium, low shock					
N	**196**	**756**	**3.83**	3.3	**22.8**
High	125*	551	3.27	2.8	13.7*
Md.	155	580	3.64	3.0	17.5
Low	197*	646.	3.36	2.9	19.4*
D. Thwarted and normal control; 1, 2, 3 days deprived					
1, N	155	*536*	*3.12*	4.0	21.3
1, T	180	*686*	*3.44*	4.0	25.8
2, N	191	*557*	*2.74*	4.0	22.2
2, T	209	*701*	*2.98*	3.7	25.2
3, N	223	577	*2.50*	3.5	*19.3*
3, T	*164*	671	*3.60*	3.9	*25.4*

Sticklebacks feeding on their ground-living prey swim near the floor of the tank and occasionally tilt their bodies to remain poised over the worms which are half-embedded in the sand. The eye movements during fixation on the prey are quite distinctive. Fixations may be followed by grasping the prey, scored as *completed feeding responses*. Each fixation, whether it led to the grasp or not, was scored as an *initiated feeding response*. Behavior such as attacks, returns to the living area, swimming up and down the walls of the food area, and so forth, has been grouped together as a bout of *nonfeeding behavior*. Such activities would appear in the absence of food and their frequency and duration could be changed by varying conditions other than deprivation. Then, *total time spent feeding* measures the predominance of feeding behavior in the 1-hour session, while the *ratio of initiations to completions* measures the predominance of one element in the feeding behavior pattern. In a bout of feeding, it is possible that few completions are performed because the *duration* of feeding responses is very long.

Behavior was recorded on a machine that moved a strip of paper at the rate of 5.6 cm/min (Trotter, 1959). The frequency, duration, and order of succession of responses could be obtained from the records.

Increased deprivation time results in a greater number of completed feeding responses, a shortened duration of feeding responses, and a decrease in the ratio of initiated to completed feeding responses (Table 1, *A, B*). But neither the number of initiations nor the total time spent feeding is reliably increased by deprivation.

These effects on feeding behavior are reversed in the course of the feeding session, as the fish become satiated: the frequency of completions decreases, response duration becomes longer, and there are more initiations per completion. The time spent feeding and the frequency of initiations increase at the beginning of the feeding session, remain at high values, and then fall off slightly at the end of the hour.

Hunger shows its effects on the predominance of completions over initiations, not on the predominance of feeding behavior over nonfeeding behavior.

In the conflict sessions (Table 1, *C*), the total time spent feeding is below normal values, and more markedly so for increasing shock intensities. But the ratio of initiations to completions is lower than normal, and the duration of feeding responses is below normal. These latter two effects are not changed by increasing shock intensities.

Nonfeeding behavior has become more predominant in the conflict sessions, but when feeding behavior is shown it is like that of very hungry fish.[2] As a result, over half the fish performed more completed feeding responses than normally under conditions of low shock, with some fish scoring as much as 40 percent over normal values.

As the feeding session progresses, the usual satiation changes occur and deviations from normal feeding scores are less marked. For example, the initiated to completed response ratio is below normal throughout the session, but reliably below normal only for the session as a whole or for the first 15 minutes of the session (Siegel & Brantley, 1951).

The effects of thwarting (Table 1, *D*) resemble those of conflict in that the fish may perform more or fewer completed feeding responses than normally. But now total time spent feeding and the frequency of initiations have increased, whereas the initiation to completion ratio is higher than normal.

It is noteworthy that the usual differences in feeding behavior for the three deprivation conditions have disappeared in the tests that follow thwarting.

The effects of thwarting and of conflict must be specified in terms of measures that indicate the predominance of the observed pattern of behavior over its alternatives and the predominance of high and low intensity forms of the behavior pattern. A model linking these two aspects of motivated behavior has been described (Tugendhat, 1960).

Summary: It is possible to quantify many different aspects of feeding behavior. In order to specify and differentiate the effects of deprivation levels, conflict, and thwarting, one cannot use only a single measure of this behavior pattern.

---

[2] The conflict study shows how cessation of feeding occurs. In the course of normal feeding sessions, only increases in time spent feeding were reliable. Though interruptions of feeding involving returns to the living area are few at the end of the session, these are of a reliably longer duration and extend further away from the food area. In the stickleback's normal environment this should increase the likelihood of exposure to stimuli that evoke behavior incompatible with feeding and thus end feeding activities.

Journal of Abnormal and Social Psychology, 1962, vol. 65, pp. 1–5

Maternal Permissiveness Toward Aggression and Subsequent TAT Aggression

Donald Weatherley

A number of theorists working within the framework of a Hullian-derived learning theory (e.g., Bandura & Walters, 1959; Sears, Maccoby, & Levin, 1957), have argued that the extent to which a parent is permissive toward a child's aggression is an important determinant of that child's subsequent aggressiveness. According to this approach, aggression is a learned response. An individual's readiness to aggress is assumed to depend in part on the extent to which aggressive behavior has been successful in removing frustrations in the past. Such success constitutes one way in which aggression is reinforced. When a parent is relatively permissive toward a child's aggression it may be expected that the child will more frequently exhibit aggressive behavior and thereby increase the likelihood that his aggressive behavior will be associated with reinforcement.

But it is not only through its influence upon aggressive tendencies per se that degree of maternal permissiveness can affect subsequent aggressive behavior. When a mother permits very little aggression by restraining, punishing, or redirecting the child's aggressive behavior when it occurs, she must communicate to the child disapproval of such behavior, however subtle this communication might be. Consequently, internal and external cues relevant to aggression may come to evoke anxiety responses in the child which function to inhibit the direct expression of aggression. The greater the mother's disapproval, the stronger should be the internal restraints against aggression which develop in the child.

The effects of parental attitudes toward aggression are presumed to extend into adulthood. In the study reported here, two groups of college girls, who differ in the extent to which their mothers reported a permissive attitude toward childhood aggression, were compared with respect to their aggressive responses in TAT productions, under conditions of high and low aggression arousal and high and low cue relevance for aggression. An extension of the Miller approach-avoidance model was involved in the derivation of the predictions which were made. This paradigm has been used by a number of investigators (e.g., Clark, 1955; Scott, 1956; Weatherley, 1961) who have found that the experimental arousal of socially disapproved motives can lead to a diminution of expression of those motives in thematic test protocols. This finding suggests that the cues relevant to the arousal of a motive may also arouse an anxiety response which acts to depress the expression of the motive to a level below that obtained under neutral conditions.

In the present study a formulation based on the Miller goal-gradient model led to the expectation that experimental arousal of aggression would have a differential effect upon the TAT aggression of subjects differing in the degree of maternal permissiveness for aggression they experienced as children.

Figure 1 depicts the model used. The net aggressive response strength for either group of subjects at any point along the horizontal axis is the difference between the height of the appropriate approach gradient and the matching avoidance gradient at that point. As can be seen, the subjects treated relatively permissively as children—High Maternal Permissiveness (MP) subjects—may be expected to express more TAT aggression at Point A than the subjects whose mothers treated them relatively nonpermissively in childhood—Low MP subjects. This is true also at Point B and at all points in between. Furthermore, as arousal and/or cue relevance is increased from A to B, the High MP subjects should show an increase in TAT aggression, while the Low MP subjects should show a decrease.

The placement of points along the hypothetical dimension of arousal and/or cue relevance in Figure 1 is, of course,

arbitrary; it is impossible to determine on an a priori basis what experimental operations and material will precisely correspond to Points A and B. In order to provide a broad sample of possible points along this dimension, two levels of aggression arousal and two levels of aggressive cue value of TAT cards were used.

Each subject told stories to TAT cards of high and low cue relevance for aggression under conditions of either high or low aggression arousal. Thus the variables of maternal permissiveness, degree of arousal, and cue value of TAT cards were ordered in a $2 \times 2 \times 2$ factorial design.

On the basis of the model depicted in Figure 1 two predictions were made: High MP subjects will express more TAT aggression in general than will Low MP subjects; High MP subjects will show a greater increase in TAT aggression as the cues and arousal conditions for aggression are increased than will Low MP subjects.

In addition to the TAT measure, subjects were asked to rate their subjective feelings during the experiment on several dimensions. No predictions were made concerning these measures; they were obtained to help evaluate the effectiveness of the aggression arousing situation and to supplement the information obtained from the TAT data.

Method

Procedure

The data reported in this paper were obtained from 100 female undergraduate students who volunteered to participate in the study. The data were collected in small group sessions. Half of the subjects served under High Arousal conditions: They were subjected to an aggression arousing situation immediately following which a TAT

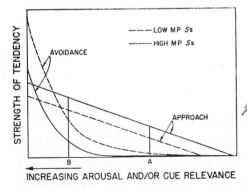

Fig. 1. Model depicting the aggressive approach and avoidance gradients of High and Low MP subjects.

measure of aggression and ratings of the subjects' subjective feelings were obtained.

Aggression arousal was accomplished by making highly insulting and depreciating comments to the subjects in the course of administering a brief paper-and-pencil task to them. The insulting was done by the author. A different experimenter obtained the TAT stories and ratings of subjective feelings, ostensibly as part of a study of "creativity." The situation was arranged in such a way that the subjects would not perceive a relationship between the aggression arousing situation and the subsequent measures.

The same procedure was followed for the other half of the subjects who served under Low Arousal conditions, with the exception that the paper-and-pencil task was administered in a friendly, non-provoking way.

TAT Measure

Four TAT cards were used: 8BM, 2, 18GF, and 6GF. These TAT pictures, in the order named, were successively projected on a screen for 20 seconds. The subjects were given 4 minutes to write a story about each one. The usual group TAT instructions were used (McClelland, Atkinson, Clark, & Lowell, 1953).

The TAT cards were chosen to represent two levels of aggressive cue relevance. Cards 8BM and 18GF were assumed to be relatively high in aggressive cues (i.e., the pictures are easily interpreted as suggesting some aggressive action); Cards 2 and 6GF were assumed to be relatively low in aggressive cue relevance.

Each TAT story was scored in terms of the total number of aggressive acts mentioned in it.

Subjective Feeling Ratings

Immediately after completing their TAT stories, but before they were given any information regarding the true purpose of the experiment, all subjects were asked to rate the degree to which they had experienced certain feelings at the time they were about to begin their first TAT story. They were asked to estimate the extent they had felt "tired," "happy," "tense," "bored," "angry." For each of these feelings a sub-

ject's answer consisted of a check mark placed on a line 7 centimeters long ranging from Not at all to Very much so. The score for each item was the distance of the check mark from the Not at all end of the scale in centimeter units.

Maternal Questionnaire

When the subjects were told of the real nature of the study at the end of the experimental sessions they were also asked to supply the names and addresses of their mothers. The mothers were subsequently contacted by mail and asked to complete a short, four-item questionnaire about their daughters. Two of these items are germane to the present report. They were designed to provide an index of the extent to which each subject's mother permitted the subject to aggress when the subject was a child. (Mothers were instructed to answer the questions in terms of how things were when the subject was less than 10 years old.) One item pertained to aggression toward parents, the other to aggression toward other children. Both were multiple-choice items containing four alternatives.[1]

[1] These two items were:

1. Sometimes children get into quarrels with friends or other neighborhood children. To what extent did you permit your daughter to quarrel with children (other than brothers and sisters) when she was growing up? a. An effort was usually made to stop such quarreling immediately whenever it was observed. b. Some quarreling was permitted if it didn't last too long, or become a heated argument. c. Quarreling was usually permitted to continue, unless someone was really being hurt in the verbal battle. d. Such quarreling was almost never interfered with. It was considered to be a matter for the children to work out for themselves.

2. Sometimes young children become angry at their parents and say angry things to them. How much of this sort of anger did you permit in your daughter when she was growing up? a. None whatsoever at any time. b. It was *occasionally* all right for her to become angry at her parents if there was good reason but she was never permitted to be rude in expressing her anger. c. She was *usually* allowed to express her anger toward her parents when she felt angry, but open "sassing" of her parents was prevented whenever possible to do so. d. She was given full opportunity to express her anger, even when it meant being rude to her parents on occasion.

A copy of the complete questionnaire used may be obtained from the author.

The responses to these items were combined by weighting each alternative in terms of the degree of permissiveness it indicated and adding the two scores. On the basis of a median split of these combined responses, each subject was categorized as having experienced as children either high maternal permissiveness (High MP subjects) or low material permissiveness (Low MP subjects) toward aggression.

The brevity of the maternal questionnaire apparently facilitated cooperation. Ninety-seven percent of the questionnaires sent out were completed and returned.

Results

TAT Aggression

The mean aggression scores obtained for each of the eight cells of the design are presented in Table 1. A triple classification analysis of variance was performed on these data. The only significant main effect found was that of cue relevance of cards, with the cards defined as high in cue relevance for aggression eliciting significantly more aggression ($p < .001$) than those low in cue relevance.

The first prediction was not confirmed. The overall mean number of aggressive acts produced by High MP subjects (5.02) was greater than that produced by Low MP subjects (4.43), but this difference was not statistically significant ($p < .10$).

On the basis of Prediction 2 it was expected that there would be a significant interaction between the variables of permissiveness and arousal and/or between permissiveness and TAT aggressive cue relevance. Neither of these double interactions approached statistical significance. However the analysis of variance did reveal a significant triple interaction ($p < .02$) among the variables of permissiveness, arousal, and TAT cue relevance.

As can be seen in Table 1, Low and High MP subjects did differ in their reaction to aggression arousal in the direction anticipated in Prediction 2 if only responses to the High Cue cards are considered. High MP subjects when

TABLE 1

MEAN NUMBER OF AGGRESSIVE ACTS
IN TAT STORIES

	High Arousal		Low Arousal	
	High MP subjects (N=23)	Low MP subjects (N=27)	High MP subjects (N=23)	Low MP subjects (N=27)
High aggressive cue cards	3.65_b	2.89_{bc}	2.74_c	2.85_{bc}
Low aggressive cue cards	1.87_a	1.89_a	1.78_a	1.22_a

Note.—Means with the same subscript are *not* significantly different from each other, by the Duncan (1955) multiple range test, at the .05 level.

TABLE 2

MEAN SUBJECTIVE FEELING RATINGS

Feeling rated	High MP subjects (N=46)	Low MP subjects (N=54)	Significance of differences
Tired	4.41	3.80	ns
Happy	4.76	4.04	$p < .02$
Tense	2.59	3.57	$p < .02$
Bored	2.76	2.84	ns
Angry	1.12^a	1.28	$p < .05$

[a] A square root transformation of ratings on the Angry dimension was performed after an inspection revealed unequal variances within cells.

aroused showed a significant increase ($p < .05$) in aggression on the High Cue cards as compared with High MP subjects under Low Arousal conditions.

Low MP subjects showed no such increase. In the case of responses to the TAT cards low in aggressive cues, however, aggression arousal had no differential effect upon High and Low MP subjects.

Feeling Ratings

Separate analyses of variance were performed on the data obtained from each of the five feelings rated. Only in the case of the self-ratings on the Happy dimension did the results under High Arousal 'conditions differ from those obtained under Low Arousal conditions. Subjects under High Arousal conditions rated themselves as significantly less happy than control subjects ($p < .01$). In no case was there a significant interaction between the variables of arousal and degree of maternal permissiveness on these measures. However, on several of the feelings rated, High and Low MP subjects did differ in their mean self-ratings, irrespective of whether they served under the High or Low Arousal conditions.

Table 2 contains mean self-rating scores for High and Low MP subjects on each of the feelings rated. As this table indicates, Low MP subjects rated themselves as significantly less happy ($p < .02$), more tense ($p < .02$), and more angry ($p < .05$) than did the High MP subjects.

Discussion

The model depicted in Figure 1 asserts that the net aggressive response strength of High and Low MP subjects should change differentially as arousal and/or cue conditions are increased. This principle was supported by the finding that insult produced an increase in the TAT aggression of High MP subjects, but not Low MP subjects. Moreover, this finding is consistent with the results of previous studies (Bandura & Walters 1959; Sears et al., 1957) which have indicated that maternal permissiveness toward aggression increases the likelihood of subsequent aggression.

Yet there is reason to doubt that the High MP subjects are necessarily more aggressive than the Low MP subjects under a variety of circumstances. Contrary to the expectation based on the model, they expressed no more TAT aggression in general than the Low MP subjects. Furthermore, the difference between High and Low MP subjects in reaction to insult occurred only on the TAT cards which had a strong "picture-pull" for aggression. This pattern of finding argues against a conception of the High MP subjects as individuals characterized by relatively strong, highly generalized readiness to aggress. Their heightened aggressiveness in the face of provocation and cues relevant to aggression can be viewed as an appropriate reaction to the stimulus situation. That the Low MP subjects showed no such increase in aggression, on the other hand, may be taken as an indication of inhibiting influences operating in these subjects. This interpretation proposes that High and Low MP subjects differ primarily in the extent to which they tend to inhibit the expression of aroused aggression rather than in the strength of their aggressive tendencies per se.

The subjects' ratings of their subjective feelings are noteworthy in this connection. The Low MP subjects, as compared with High MP subjects, rated themselves as feeling significantly more tense, more angry, and less happy. Their greater subjective tension and anger in the absence of even a comparable readiness to express overt aggression in the TAT situation supports the proposition that the Low MP subjects are more inclined to inhibit aggression than are High MP subjects.

Thus the data imply that relatively nonpermissive maternal attitudes toward childhood aggression are associated with the development of relatively strong internal restraints against expressing aggression. While the establishment of firm controls over aggressive tendencies may be regarded as a desirable goal, the self-ratings obtained in the present study also suggest that a more dysphoric subjective state may be another, less desirable correlate of nonpermissive maternal attitudes.

Summary: One hundred college girls told stories to two TAT cards high in aggressive cues and to two TAT cards low in cues for aggression. Half of the subjects told their stories after they had been subjected to an aggression arousing situation; the other half responded to the TAT cards without prior aggression arousal. The subjects were further categorized, on the basis of questionnaires completed by their mothers, as having experienced either relatively high maternal permissiveness (High MP subjects) or relatively low maternal permissiveness (Low MP subjects) toward aggression in childhood.

Two predictions were made: High MP subjects will express more TAT aggression in general than will Low MP subjects; High MP subjects will show a greater increase in TAT aggression as the cues and arousal conditions for aggression are increased than will Low MP subjects.

The data revealed that the High MP subjects did not express more TAT aggression in general than the Low MP subjects. High MP subjects did, however, show an increase in TAT aggression as arousal conditions were increased when responding to TAT cards high in aggressive cue relevance. No such increase occurred in the case of the Low MP subjects. Self-ratings made during the experiment indicated that the Low MP subjects felt significantly more angry, more tense, and less happy than the High MP subjects, irrespective of the degree of aggression arousal to which they were subjected.

Stop

Chapter 8

ANXIETY AND GUILT

This chapter and the next concern human motivational properties almost exclusively. It is true that these concepts, especially anxiety, have been used to refer to the behavior of animals, but most of those usages have been very loose and bear only a distant resemblance to the meanings here. For example, most of the research with animals operationally define anxiety in such a way as to make it indistinguishable from fear—a learned expectation of a noxious event. The clinical usage, however, strongly influenced by psychoanalytic theory, defines anxiety as a specific state of anticipation of discomfort or noxious feelings, not from some external source such as a shock or another person, but from the anticipation of becoming aware of one's impulses that are usually defended against. Thus, it is clear that the shuttle-box is not a place to study anxiety, though fear can be manipulated there with ease. Whether guilt and anxiety are not experienced by animals, or whether they cannot be investigated even if present, is not known at the moment, though, as in the following chapter, it may turn out that little fruitful knowledge will be acquired on these topics with animals as subjects. Research with animals has selectively borrowed parts of the meanings and ignored others, so that the oft-made objection that anxiety is not being studied in such experiments is usually a valid criticism.

The first two papers, by Sarnoff and his students, are excellent demonstrations of the presence and effects of anxiety, especially in that they pinpoint the differences between anxiety and fear. Byrne shows another facet of anxiety and its relationship to affiliation. Alpert and Haber discuss some of the problems in the prediction of achievement anxiety, especially in terms of some of the theortical concepts underlying the self-administered paper-and-pencil-scales used to assess achievement anxiety. Finally, in this section, Kessen and Mandler present a short but theoretically most important paper reviewing evidence regarding a causal relationship between anxiety and physical pain. They feel that this relationship—one that would be predicted by most learning theory interpretations of motivation—is not at all clear. Specifically, they present evidence that pain or pain-reduction are not necessary for anxiety to build up or to be controlled.

Three different papers have been selected on the study of guilt. This is a topic even more confusing in its experimental treatment than anxiety, and these three examples are not immune from problems. They do, however, give a sampling of the meanings of the concept of guilt and discuss its effects on behavior and how these can be investigated.

Journal of Abnormal and Social Psychology, 1961, vol. 62, pp. 356–363

Anxiety, Fear, and Social Affiliation

Irving Sarnoff and Philip G. Zimbardo[1]

In his recent monograph, Schachter (1959) reports that anticipated exposure to a painful external stimulus determines the degree to which persons wish to affiliate with each other: the greater the anticipated pain, the stronger the desire to await the onset of that pain in the company of others in the same predicament. In attempting to account theoretically for this finding, Schachter mentions such motivational forces as the subjects' needs for reassurance, distraction, escape, and information. However, among the various possible explanations, Schachter appears to favor one derived from Festinger's (1954) theory of social comparison processes. Adapting that theory to the phenomena under investigation, Schachter postulates that the arousal of any strong emotion evokes a need for comparison. Emotions are assumed to be quite unspecific states of affect. Hence, persons can only evaluate the quality, intensity, and appropriateness of their emotions

properly by comparing their own reactions with those of others. Moreover, novel emotion producing stimuli should induce a greater tendency to affiliate than familiar stimuli. By definition, a novel stimulus is one that is more difficult to fit into a person's established frame of reference for emotive states. Accordingly, the individual is more obliged to seek out others in order to define the emotional effects of novel stimuli.

The explication of Schachter's (1959) results in terms of the theory of social comparison processes is appealingly parsimonious. However, it requires the assumption that *all* emotive states have the same effect on affiliative behavior. Thus, Schachter, like many contemporary psychologists, does not deal with the possible conceptual distinctions between fear and anxiety. Yet, it seems to us that, by adopting an alternative assumption about the psychological properties of emotions, to be presented briefly below, it is possible to formulate predictions concerning affiliative responses that could not have been derived from the theory of social comparison processes. Indeed, by employing Freud's (1949a, 1949b) conceptual distinctions between fear and anxiety, we are led to predict a tendency toward

[1] The authors are indebted to the Yale Communication Research Project, directed by C. I. Hovland, for its material support of this study, and to C. I. Hovland for his encouragement and helpful suggestions. Our thanks are extended to Jacob Rabbie and Harold Gerard for their contributions to the study. We also wish to acknowledge the expert and enthusiastic participation of our research assistants, Ted Sheldon, Sally Whitcher, and Ira Grushow.

social isolation—rather than affiliation —as a consequence of certain conditions of emotional arousal.

The present experiment was, thus, undertaken with two objectives: to assess the empirical validity of conceptual differentiation between fear and anxiety, and to evaluate the extent to which the theory of social comparison processes may be applied to the relationship between all emotions and affiliative behavior. In order to implement these objectives, we have conducted an experimental investigation of the differential effects of fear and anxiety upon social affiliation.

FUNCTIONAL RELATIONSHIP BETWEEN EMOTIONS AND MOTIVES

The guiding assumption of our experiment holds that all emotions are consciously experienced epiphenomena of motives.[2] When our motives are aroused, we experience subjective reactions to which we learn, over time, to attach commonly agreed upon labels that signify the various emotions.

Motive, on the other hand, is defined as a tension producing stimulus that provokes behavior designed to reduce the tension. Each of our motives (innate or learned) requires the performance of a *different* response for the maximal reduction of its tension.

FEAR AND ANXIETY VIEWED AS MOTIVES

The motive of fear (which Freud called objective anxiety) is aroused whenever persons are confronted by an external object or event that is inher-

[2] The concept of motivation which we have chosen to employ has been elaborated elsewhere (Sarnoff, 1960a).

ently dangerous and likely to produce pain. Only one type of overt[3] response can maximally reduce our fear: separation from the threatening aspects of the feared object, accomplished by flight from the object, at one extreme, and conquest, at the other. In the case of fear, then, one's energies are mobilized toward dealing with the external stimulus; to eliminate, through some mode of escape or attack, the threat that is clearly and objectively present in the stimulus.

If we examine the consequences of anxiety (which Freud termed neurotic anxiety), we see no such correspondence between the internal disturbance of the person and an objectively harmful environmental stimulus. Instead, anxiety is typically aroused by stimuli which, objectively considered, are *innocuous*.[4] For example, in the case of the classical phobias, harmless objects possess a special motivational significance for certain people. These objects activate some motive other than fear, and this other motive, in turn, arouses the consciously perceived motive of anxiety. Hence, the emotional reaction of the anxious person is inappropriate to the

[3] Space limitations do not permit a consideration of the two types of covert (ego defensive) responses, denial and identification with the aggressor, which persons may employ in their efforts to cope with external threat. A full discussion of these ego defenses is presented by Sarnoff (1960a).

[4] In fact, since anxiety arousing stimuli are often related to unconscious libidinal motives, they may be regarded by most people as intrinsically pleasurable, rather than in any way painful. For example, owing to the manner in which their heterosexual motives have been socialized, some men may tend severely to repress their sexual cravings for women. Hence, when such men are shown photographs of voluptuous nudes, stimuli which might be quite evocative of pleasurable fantasies among most of their fellows, they are likely to experience anxiety (Sarnoff & Corwin, 1959).

inherent characteristics of the external stimulus.

Regardless of their content, the motives whose arousal evokes anxiety share a common property: they are all *repressed*. These repressed motives continue unconsciously to press for the reduction of their tensions; and anxiety signals the threat of possible expression of these repressed motives. Consequently, the person develops a number of additional ego defenses that function to safeguard the initial effects of repression. If the ego defenses do their work effectively, the motives are kept under repression, the inner danger passes and the individual's anxiety is reduced.

IMPLICATIONS OF THE MOTIVES OF ANXIETY AND FEAR FOR AFFILIATIVE BEHAVIOR

It follows from the foregoing discussion that, when their anxieties are aroused, people are more inclined to become preoccupied with the reassertion of inner self-control than with modes of dealing with the anxiety evoking external object. Because the anxious person tends to be aware of the element of *inappropriateness* in his feelings, he is loath to communicate his anxieties to others. To avoid being ridiculed or censured, he conceals anxiety aroused by stimuli which he guesses do not have a similar effect upon others, and which, he feels, ought not so to upset him. Thus, when anxiety is aroused, a person should tend to seek isolation from others. On the other hand, when fear is aroused and he is unable to flee from the threatening object, he welcomes the opportunity to affiliate. Since the usual responses to fear, flight and fight, are restricted in the experimental situation,

the subject seeks other fear reducing responses. Therefore, the probability of affiliation increases because it mediates fear reduction through the potentiality for catharsis and distraction as well as the emotional comparison offered by interpersonal contact.

We are led, therefore, to the hypothesis that the motives of fear and anxiety should influence social affiliation behavior differently: the greater the fear aroused, the more the subjects should choose to be together with others while they await actual contact with the fear arousing object. Conversely, the greater the anxiety elicited, the more the subjects should choose to be alone while they await contact with the anxiety arousing object.

Method

The experiment was presented to the subjects as a physiological investigation of the cutaneous sensitivity of various parts of the body. A 2×2 design was used in which two levels of fear and of anxiety were experimentally aroused. The dependent variable of social affiliation was measured by having the subjects state whether they preferred to spend an anticipated waiting period alone or in the company of others.

Subjects

The subjects were 72 unpaid, male undergraduate volunteers from six introductory psychology classes in Yale University. An additional 36 subjects were used to pretest the manipulations and measuring devices, and an additional 13 subjects were excluded from the analyses because they did not qualify as acceptable subjects, i.e., were friends, misunderstood the instructions, did not believe the rationale.

Procedure

Background information was collected by an accomplice alleged to be from the counseling program of the Student Health

Department. A questionnaire was designed
to obtain background information on the
subjects and also their preferred mode of
defense mechanism. The latter data were in
response to four Blacky cards. As in a recent experiment by Sarnoff (1960b), each
card was accompanied by three alternatives
that were to be rank ordered according to
the subjects' reaction to the theme of the
card (sibling rivalry, achievement, and two
of sucking). The alternatives reflected predominantly an acceptance of the motive,
projection of the motive upon others, or a
reaction formation against the motive.

About one month later, the experimenter
was introduced to the psychology classes as
a physiological psychologist studying physiological responses to sensory stimuli. The
subjects were subsequently recruited individually, and randomly assigned to the
four experimental treatments. The specious
purpose of the experiment and of the conditions of waiting were further established
by marking the experimental room "Sensory Physiology Laboratory" and two
nearby rooms "Waiting Room A" and
"Waiting Room T." Because of absentees,
the size of the groups tested varied from
three to five, and was usually composed of
four subjects. In order to avoid the development of superficial friendships during
the experiment, and eliminate the possibility that the subjects might react to cues
from each other or from the experimenter,
the subjects were isolated in adjacent cubicles, no communication was allowed, and
the tape-recorded instructions were presented through earphones.

The experimental conditions and instructions common to all subjects will be
presented first. After rolling up their
sleeves, removing their watches from their
wrists, and gum or cigarettes from their
mouths ("They interfere with the recording
electrodes"), the subjects were told:

Our experiment falls in the general
area of physiological psychology. As you
may know, one branch of physiological
psychology is concerned with the reactions of the sense organs to various kinds
of stimulation. Our present experiment
deals with the skin [or mouth] as an organ of sensation. We are interested in
studying individual differences in response to particular stimuli applied to it.

There has been a good deal of controversy about the relative sensitivity of
the fingertips [lips] as compared to the
palms [tongue], and upper surface of the
hand [palate]. Our experiment will help
to provide data upon which we may be
able ultimately to draw a detailed map
of the cutaneous sensitivity of the human
hand [mouth].

In order to measure your physiological
reactions, we are now going to attach
some instruments to your arm and finger
[corner of your mouth]. These instruments are electrodes which are connected
to a machine which records exactly the
strength of your response to each stimulus. . . . Electrode jelly will be applied
first to the area to insure that we get a
good electrical contact. (The electrodes
were then attached by a female laboratory assistant of middle age.)

In order to provide a reasonable basis for
asking the subjects to wait in other rooms
(and, thus, for making the choice of affiliation or isolation), the subjects were told
that it was necessary to assess their basal
rates of responding prior to the application
of the actual stimuli. They were led to believe that their individual sensitivities were
being recorded while they viewed a series
of slides of a typical subject who had participated in the experiment. They anticipated that a waiting period would come
after the slides, and then in the second—
and purportedly major—part of the experiment their direct reactions to the actual
stimuli would be measured. Accordingly,
they were told:

Now that your basal rates have been
recorded on our polygraph recorder, it
will take us about 10 minutes while we
tally the data and reset our measuring
instruments so that they will be geared
to your individual basal rates as you are
run one at a time through the rest of the
experiment. While we are doing these
things, we are going to ask you to wait in
other rooms which are available to us.
We will come to get you when it is your
turn to go through with the experiment.
Incidentally, we have found that some of
our subjects prefer to do their waiting
alone, while others prefer to wait together with other subjects. Therefore, we
are going to give you your choice of

waiting alone or with others. In either case, you will be ushered to a comfortable room furnished with adequate reading material.

After indicating their preference of waiting alone or together with others, the subjects also indicated the intensity of this preference on an "open-ended" scale in which 0 represented a very weak preference and 100 a very strong preference. On this relatively unstructured scale there was as much as 175 points of difference between subjects (from "75-alone" to "100-together").

Presentation of the slides during the experiment served two purposes in addition to the one previously mentioned. The content of the slides (appropriate to each experimental treatment) served to reinforce the subjects' differential expectations of the nature and severity of the stimulus situation. Furthermore, the subject seen in the slides became a focal point for measuring the effectiveness of the experimental manipulations. It was assumed that a direct attempt (by means of a scaled question) to appraise the level of the subjects' fear or anxiety would be likely to: sensitize them to the true purpose of the experiment; yield unreliable results since the subjects might neither be consciously aware of, nor able to verbalize, their anxiety reaction; and evoke resistance since some subjects might not want to admit to being anxious or fearful, calling their masculinity into question.

Therefore, it was necessary to use an indirect, disguised measure to evaluate whether the experimental inductions had actually aroused two levels of both fear and anxiety. Immediately after the slides had been shown (but before the affiliation choices had been made), the subjects were told:

As you may know, an individual shows his physiological reaction in a variety of behavioral forms. We are interested in seeing whether it is possible to estimate how ill-at-ease or upset individuals are at the prospect of receiving the stimulation in this experiment. Recalling the subject whom you just saw in the slides, how upset or ill-at-ease did he seem to you? Please assign a number anywhere from zero to 100 to indicate your feeling.

(Zero = unconcerned, at ease; 100 = extremely concerned and ill-at-ease.)

Since the subject in the slides was a posed model instructed to remain poker faced throughout, it was assumed that there was no objective difference in his expression. Thus, any systematic difference in ratings between groups should reflect a projection of the subjects' own motives upon this screen.

However, because the content of the slides was not identical for every group but rather "tailored" to each specific treatment, it was possible that the model may have actually looked more fearful in the slides shown to the subjects in the High Fear than in the Low Fear condition. As a control check on this possibility, four additional introductory psychology classes ($N = 108$) served as judges. They were told that the slides were of a typical subject in a recently completed experiment, and their task was to estimate how ill-at-ease and concerned he appeared (on the same scale used by the experimental subjects). Two of the classes saw only the face of the model (the rest of the slide was blacked out) and were told only that he was a subject in a physiological experiment in which stimuli were applied and responses measured. The other two classes saw the entire stimulus field of the slides and were given the same complete description that the experimental subjects received. Since each class of judges rated the slides for all four experimental treatments, the order of presentation was counterbalanced.

After the projective measure of motive arousal and the measure of affiliation, the electrodes were removed and a measure taken of the subjects' reasons for choosing to affiliate or be isolated. This was done with the rationale that a social psychologist had become interested in the fact that some of our subjects preferred to be together while others preferred to be alone, and he had asked us to get some information for him about the reasons underlying this preference.

The questionnaire, designed by Gerard and Rabbie (1960), contained both open-ended and structured questions asking for reasons for the affiliation choice. Finally, the subjects noted whether or not they wished to continue in the experiment. Only one subject (in the High Fear condition) refused to remain for the "stimulation" part of the experiment.

The true purpose, hypothesis, design, and reasons for the various deceptions (and, at a later time, the results) were explained fully to each subject.

High Fear

A high level of fear was induced by leading the subjects to anticipate a series of painful electrical shocks. Although they expected to endure each of the shocks for 2 minutes, the subjects were assured that the shocks would not cause damage or injury.

The female assistant (dressed in a white lab coat, as was the experimenter) then attached electrodes to each subject's arm and fingertip and strapped his arm onto a cotton-padded board. The leads from the electrodes appeared to go to a polygraph recorder, which also was seen in the series of slides of the typical subjects. Another slide showed an enormous electrical stimulator, and the implication was that it was behind a curtain in the experimental room. It was called to the subjects' attention that:

> The four dials shown in the upper right-hand corner of the stimulator enable us to regulate automatically the frequency, duration, delay, and intensity of the shock you will get.

The other slides portrayed the subject with earphones and electrodes attached (like the subjects themselves), "listening to the instructions", and then "about to receive his first painful shock," administered by the experimenter, who could be seen in the background manipulating the dials on the stimulator. A final situational factor that may have enhanced the effectiveness of the High Fear manipulation was that the experimental room housed electrical generators which made a continuous buzzing sound, a cue interpreted by the High Fear subjects as the electrical stimulator "warming up," but unnoticed or quickly adapted to by the other subjects. An unobtrusively posted sign reading "Danger/High Voltage," present only for the High Fear subjects, gave further credence to this notion.

Low Fear

In the Low Fear condition the word "shock" was never used, and all cues in the situation associated with shock, fear, or pain were removed; i.e., no white lab coats, arms not strapped to boards, etc. The expectations of these subjects were guided by instructions stating that our methodology was to apply a 10-second stimulus of very low intensity that would be just sufficient to elicit a measurable physiological response.

In the series of slides viewed by these subjects, the imposing electrical stimulator was replaced by a small innocuous looking apparatus (actually a voltmeter), and the experimenter was seen not in the active role as an agent of pain, but in the passive role of recording data from the polygraph recorder.

High Anxiety

Anxiety was manipulated by arousing a motive that was assumed to have been repressed by most of the subjects. In Freudian terminology, the motive might be called "oral libido," a desire to obtain pleasurable gratification by sucking on objects that is clearly related to infantile nursing experiences. The female breast is, of course, the prototype of such objects, but others include nipples, baby bottles, and pacifiers. Thus, to arouse this oral motive and, hence, the anxiety that should follow its arousal, subjects in the High Anxiety condition were led to believe that they would have to suck on a number of objects commonly associated with infantile oral behavior. They were told that their task would be to suck on these objects for 2 minutes while we recorded their physiological responses from the skin surfaces stimulated by the objects. In clear view in front of the subjects were the following items: numerous baby bottles, oversized nipples, pacifiers, breast shields (nipples women often wear over their breasts while nursing), and lollipops.

The same variety of stimulus objects was shown arrayed in front of the subject in the slides. He could be seen, tongue hanging out, lips puckered, about to suck his thumb (as one of the objects of stimulation) or one of the other objects. Subjects were told that the contact taped to the mouth recorded the direct reaction to the oral stimulation, while the arm contact recorded peripheral reactions.

Low Anxiety

The instructions to the Low Anxiety subjects did not mention "suck," nor any stimulation that they would receive from putting the objects in their mouths. Moreover, they were led to believe that they would keep each object in their mouths for only 10 seconds. The stimulus objects were not in immediate proximity to the subjects while their electrodes were being attached. The stimulus objects which they anticipated putting in their mouths were shown in the slides: whistles, balloons, "kazoos," and pipes. Since these objects do not require sucking (but rather, in general, blowing), the model's tongue was not seen as he prepared to use the stimuli in the slides.

EVIDENCE OF THE EFFECTIVENESS OF THE EXPERIMENTAL MANIPULATIONS

In using the subjects' estimates of the degree to which the model seen in the slides was upset by the prospect of receiving the stimulation in the experiment, it was assumed that the subjects would tend to project their induced level of fear and anxiety. Table 1, which presents the mean projection scores for each experimental treatment, offers evidence that this assumption was valid and the manipulations effective. The High Arousal subjects perceived the model to be significantly[5] more upset, concerned, and ill-at-ease than did the Low Arousal subjects.

Our theoretical distinction between fear and anxiety, and the way these concepts were operationally defined in this experiment, lead to the prediction that, assuming similarity of past experi-

[5] All p values reported throughout the paper are based on two-tailed tests of significance.

TABLE 1

MEAN PROJECTION SCORES FOR EACH EXPERIMENTAL TREATMENT

Motive	Level of Arousal		p value
	Low	High	
Fear	24	42	$< .01 (t = 3.05)$
Anxiety	14	31[a]	$< .01 (t = 2.95)$
	ns	ns	

Note.—The larger the score, the greater the degree of projection.

[a] Variance greater than in High Fear group, $p < .10$; SD for High Anxiety = 24, for High Fear = 16.

ence, persons facing the same clearly, objectively present threat should react in a relatively homogeneous fashion. This close correspondence between stimulus and response is not assumed to hold for anxiety. We have already noted that a stimulus that produces anxiety for some persons is not an anxiety producing cue for many others. Since the significance of the stimulus depends upon its symbolic and generally idiosyncratic associations, one would expect that a stimulus which elicited anxiety for persons with relevant predispositions (repressed motives) would have less effect on those who had more adequately resolved the conflict over the expression of the same motives. Thus, one way of determining whether our experimental manipulations produced two different motives, fear and anxiety (rather than only two levels of one motive), is to compare the variability in response between treatments.

The heterogeneity of response in the High Anxiety group is, as predicted, greater than in the High Fear and the Low Arousal conditions. The same difference in response variability between the High Anxiety group and all other groups is manifested as well in the dependent variable of social affiliation. The questionnaire data to be presented in a later section offer further support to the distinction between fear and anxiety.

Before presenting the major results, it is necessary to account for two possible sources of artifact in the just reported data on projection. They are: by chance sampling, the High Arousal groups could have contained more subjects who characteristically used projection as a mechanism of defense than the Low Arousal groups; and the subject seen in the High Fear and High Anxiety slides was objectively more upset and concerned than he was in the Low Fear and Low Anxiety slides. If either of these alternatives were true, then the projection measure would not be a reflection of differences due to the experimental arousals of levels of fear and anxiety.

The pretest data of the subjects' mode of defense preference on the Blacky Projection test show no initial significant difference between any of the groups in their tendency to use projection.

Among the groups of neutral judges who evaluated all the slides shown in the study, from 68%–98% reported perceiving either no difference in the degree to which the model appeared upset, or a difference opposite to that reported in Table 1. This result holds for both fear and anxiety, and regardless of the order of presentation or amount of the stimulus field seen (model's face only or entire slide). Thus, it appears that the projection measure can be used as an index of the efficacy of the experimental conditions and manipulations.

EFFECTS OF FEAR AND ANXIETY ON SOCIAL AFFILIATION

The results bearing upon the hypothesis of the study are presented in Table 2, where for each condition the mean intensity of desire to affiliate, as well as the number of subjects choosing to affiliate and to be alone, are presented. It is evident that there is a strong positive relationship between fear and the index of affiliative tendency, but a strong negative relationship between anxiety and affiliation, so that as fear increases affiliation also increases, while an increase in anxiety results in a decrease in affiliation. Thus, our prediction of an interaction between kind of motive and level of arousal is clearly supported by the data. While some 95% of the High Fear subjects chose the "together" alternative (with more than 0 intensity), only 46% of the High Anxiety subjects chose to wait together. The marked mean difference between these groups in intensity of choice (51.0–8.0) is significant well beyond the

TABLE 2

RELATIONSHIP OF MOTIVE TO SOCIAL AFFILIATION

	Mean Affiliation Strength[a]	Number of Subjects Choosing	
		Together	Alone or "0-Together"
Fear			
Low	34.0	12	3
High	51.0	19	1
Anxiety			
Low	27.0	11	4
High	8.0	10	12

Interaction: (Motive × Level) $p < .05$, $t = 2.30$, $df = 68$.

[a] The larger the score, the greater the affiliation tendency; isolation intensity score subtracted from affiliation intensity score.

.01 level ($t = 3.63$). The large mean difference in affiliative tendency between the High and Low Fear groups ($p < .07$, $t = 1.96$) represents a replication of Schachter's (1959, p. 18) results. While the mean difference between High and Low Anxiety was even larger than that between the Fear conditions, it only approached significance ($p = .16$, $t = 1.46$) due to the marked heterogeneity of variance of the High Anxiety group.

REASONS GIVEN FOR AFFILIATION CHOICE

The final measure taken was a questionnaire that explored the reasons the subjects gave for choosing to wait together with others or to wait alone. The 11 structured items on the questionnaire each presented a possible motive for affiliation; and each was accompanied by a 70-point scale on which the subject indicated how important he thought the motive was in determining his choice. The highly significant interaction between experimental treatment and questions ($p < .001$, $F = 3.74$, $df = 30.570$) on a repeated-measurement analysis of variance justified a search for those questions (motives for affiliation) that differentiated the groups.

Since there were too few subjects choosing the alone condition, the analysis is limited to those wanting to affiliate. The motives for affiliation that were most important for the High Fear subjects and most distinguished them from the Low Fear subjects were (the lower the mean, the greater the importance; 10 = extremely important):

1. I am not sure whether I am reacting in the same way as the others to the prospect of getting shocked and would like to compare my reactions to theirs. [Emotional comparison] High Fear $\bar{x} = 38$, Low Fear $\bar{x} = 54$, $p < .001$.

2. I feel worried about getting shocked and would like to know to what extent the others are worried too. [Extent of comparison] High Fear $\bar{x} = 40$, Low Fear $\bar{x} = 61$, $p < .001$.

3. I want to be distracted in order to take my mind off the prospect of getting shocked. [Distraction] High Fear $\bar{x} = 44$, Low Fear $\bar{x} = 59$, $p < .01$.

4. I am worried about the prospect of getting shocked and felt that talking with someone about it would get it off my chest. [Catharsis] High Fear x = 50, Low Fear $\bar{x} = 59$, $p < .05$.

The reasons for affiliation given spontaneously to a single open-ended question also reflect the importance of these same considerations. Among High Anxiety subjects choosing to be alone, the major reason given spontaneously and supported by the scaled questions is the desire "to be alone to think about personal affairs and school work."

Curiosity as to "what the others were like" was important, but equally so across all conditions. Of least importance among all subjects are the following motives for affiliation ("oral stimulation" substituted for "shock" for Anxiety groups):

"It would be clearer in my own mind as to how I feel about getting shocked if I could express my reactions to someone else." "I anticipated that the others would offer reassuring comments." "I want to be with others to reassure myself that I am not the only one who was singled out to be shocked." "I feel that perhaps together we could somehow figure out a way to avoid getting shocked."

There are several large differences between the High Fear and High Anxiety groups; with the former finding the following motives as significantly more important: emotional comparison, extent of comparison, distraction, catharsis, and the physical presence of others ($p < .05$ in each instance). Similarly, an internal analysis of the High Fear group reveals these same motives (especially catharsis and emotional comparison) to be more important for those subjects who chose to affiliate most strongly than for those below the group median in affiliation strength.

ORDINAL POSITION AND ITS
RELATION TO AFFILIATION

While the reasoning used in the planning of the present study did not include predictions of the effects of ordinal position upon affiliation, data relevant to this question was nevertheless obtained, to check on Schachter's (1959) finding that affiliation tendencies increased with emotional arousal only among first- and only-born children. This finding is duplicated in the present study. First-born children want to affiliate significantly more than later-borns under conditions of high fear, but not when the level of fear is low. While the mean affiliation intensity for the first-born High Fear subjects was 62, it was only 23 for the later-born High Fear subjects ($p = .05$, $t = 2.10$). This same general finding holds for the High Anxiety group, but again the within-group variability does not permit the large mean difference obtained (16 for first-borns and -3 for later-borns) to be statistically significant.

Discussion

Since our basic hypothesis has been supported, our results lend credence to the previously drawn conceptual distinction between fear and anxiety. In view of the fact that our anxiety arousing stimulus was specifically designed to tap only one kind of repressed motive, it of course remains an empirical question whether or not the evocation of other types of presumably repressed motives also leads to social isolation.

In order to predict the consequences of the arousal of a motive, therefore, it is necessary to know which responses are required to reduce its tension. The probability of the social comparison response is, thus, a function of: the kind of motive aroused, the intensity of the motive, the degree of novelty of the emotional experience, the response hierarchy associated with the specific motive, and certain attributes of those with whom the person is to affiliate.

We do not question the assumption that the need for some kind of cognitive-emotional clarity and structure is a basic human motive. However, we feel that the need for self-evaluation is not the *most* salient motive aroused in the experimental situations that Schachter (1959) and we employed. We do not view the cognitive need to structure a vague emotional state as the primary motive in these experiments; we see social comparison not as an end in itself but merely as one of the several responses that are *instrumental* in reducing the tension associated with the situationally more salient motives of fear and anxiety.

Strict application of the theory of emotional comparison processes to the present experimental situation should lead one to predict greater affiliation tendencies for the High Anxiety subjects than the High Fear subjects, since the Anxiety situation was more unusual than that of Fear, and the emotion aroused was probably more novel and vague. The opposite prediction, supported by the results, demands an approach, such as the one followed here, that specifies the probability of the response alternatives evoked by the dominant motives aroused.

As the emotional experience becomes very novel and unusual, the need for comparison of one's reactions with others should increase, and, hence, intensify affiliation tendencies. The induction of esoteric states of consciousness by "anxiety producing drugs" (being studied presently by Schachter) may be the kind of situation in which emotional comparison theory offers the best explanations and predictions. Under such circumstances, it may be possible to create emotional states that are epiphenomena of motives whose neurophysiological bases had never previously been set into motion. A more natural counterpart of this novel emotional experience occurs the first time a person experiences the emotions associated with the death of a loved one.

The predictive importance of knowing the specific responses appropriate to the motive aroused is clearly illustrated by the following examples. If a person's guilt is aroused, his response to feelings of guilt should be to seek out others only if they could be expected to punish him and, thus, to expiate his guilt, but not to affiliate with individuals perceived as unable to fill this role. Similarly, if repressed homosexual anxieties are aroused, isolation should generally be preferred to affiliation, as with oral anxiety in the present study. However, affiliation tendencies should increase if the subject is allowed to wait with females, but not if he can wait only in the company of males.

While our questionnaire data offer support for the importance of emotional comparison, they also point up the role of other motives such as need for catharsis and distraction. The marked difference in the importance of the reasons given for affiliation between the High Fear and High Anxiety groups is perhaps the most substantial evidence that the experimental manipulations have indeed led to the arousal of two quite different motives.

A final point of interest concerns the data about ordinal position. The finding that first-born children show greater affiliation tendencies than later-born children when either fear or anxiety are aroused supports Schachter's (1959) results. Theoretical and experimental attempts to uncover the dynamics underlying this "static" variable should prove interesting and fruitful.

Summary: This experiment tests the utility of the psychoanalytic distinction between fear and anxiety for making differential predictions about social affiliation. It also assesses the breadth of generalization of Schachter's (1959) empirical finding of a positive relation between emotional arousal and affiliation. Seventy-two subjects were randomly assigned to four experimental treatments in which low and high levels of fear and anxiety were manipulated. The success of these inductions was established by a projective device and questionnaire data. The dependent variable of social affiliation was measured by having the subjects choose to await the anticipated exposure to the stimulus situation either alone or together with others.

The results show that, while the desire to affiliate increases as fear increases (a replication of Schachter's, 1959, results), the opposite is true for anxiety; as anxiety increases the desire to affiliate decreases. Thus, as predicted, our findings lend empirical support to the theoretical distinction between fear and anxiety. At the same time, our results suggest that the theory of social comparison processes may not be adequate to account for the general relationship between emotions and affiliative tendencies.

Journal of Personality, 1959, vol. 27, pp. 374–385

Castration Anxiety and the Fear of Death[1]

Irving Sarnoff and Seth M. Corwin

Beginning with its formulation by Freud (1949a), the concept of castration anxiety has been widely invoked by psychoanalytically oriented therapists in their attempts to account for a variety of clinical phenomena (cf. Esman, 1954; Fodor, 1947; Kobler, 1948; Rothenberg & Brenner, 1955; Starcke, 1921). In recent years, several correlational studies have provided some empirical support for the concept of castration anxiety (Friedman, 1952; Schwartz, 1955; Schwartz, 1956). The present experiment was undertaken to contribute further data to aid in the scientific evaluation of the usefulness of the concept. Specifically, this experiment concerns the relationship between castration anxiety and the fear of death.

The Concept of Castration Anxiety

Freud first put forward the concept of castration anxiety in connection with his theory of the Oedipal conflict and the psychological processes employed in its resolution. Briefly, Freud postulated that the male child becomes motivated, at one stage in his psychosexual development, to possess his mother sexually. However, such a desire cannot be countenanced by the child's father. Indeed, the latter threatens to castrate

his son if he should persist in his illicit cravings. Presumably, this threat of castration may be made directly and literally, or it may be conveyed indirectly and symbolically. In any case, the threat is perceived by the child and it arouses his intense fear. To reduce this fear, the child must learn to behave in a way which will no longer provoke his father's jealous anger.

From the standpoint of the growing child, the effort to resolve the Oedipal conflict is an ongoing one whose outcome is not conclusively determined until after he has reached adolescence. In the course of this protracted effort, the child may draw upon a number of the mechanisms which are available in his repertoire of ego defense. According to psychoanalytic theory, however, the following three ego defenses are of principal importance in the child's struggle to attain mastery over the various facets of the Oedipal conflict: *identification, repression,* and *displacement.* Identification and repression are employed earlier than the mechanism of displacement. Nevertheless, after these ego defenses have been brought into play, they become part of the individual's habitual mode of coping with the Oedipal conflict.

When the conflict emerges during the phallic stage, the child, first of all, identifies with his threatening father. That is, the child adopts his father's sexual

[1] The authors wish to thank Professor Arthur R. Cohen for his helpful suggestions in regard to the preparation of this paper.

taboos and accepts the idea that it is wrong for a son to have sexual desires for his mother. Having internalized his father's prohibitions, the child then represses his sexual feelings for his mother. With this repression, the child ceases to be conscious of any sexual yearning for her.

The repression of sexual desire for the mother is followed by the latency period, a period of several years during which the child's sexual drive is relatively weak and quiescent. During this period, too, the child continues to cement his identification with his father. Hence, for a time, the child appears to be at peace with himself and the Oedipal conflict seems to have been mastered. Inevitably, however, the calm of the latency period is shattered by the onset of puberty. For the physiological changes of adolescence stir up imperative sexual tensions for which some outlet must be found, and sexual desires which had been dormant and unconscious throughout the latency period now tend to break through the barrier of repression which the child had built up against them.

In the throes of his reactivated sexuality, the adolescent may again be inclined to covet his mother. But any such inclination evokes the anticipation of castration which originally induced the child to renounce his mother as a sexual object. The adolescent is obliged to repress any newly awakened sexual desire for his mother, but must find some way of gratifying his urgent sexual cravings. Consequently, he is led to employ still another mechanism of ego defense, displacement. He diverts his sexual interest away from his mother and toward females whom he may consciously covet and pursue without arousing his castration anxiety. In ef-

fecting this displacement, the sexually mature male finally succeeds in establishing a lasting resolution of the Oedipal conflict.

Ideally, during the Oedipal period, the child is exposed only to that degree of castration threat which is sufficient to induce the repression of his sexual feelings for his mother alone. When the child attains adulthood, he should experience no anxiety when his heterosexual desires are aroused by any woman other than his mother, for he has learned to anticipate castration only when his mother is the object of his sexual desire. In actuality, however, children are exposed to varying degrees of castration threat; and if the amount of threat has been excessive, the individual may be led to repress his sexual feelings not only for his mother in particular, but also for women in general. In such cases the arousal of his repressed sexuality by *any* female may elicit the anxiety which has become associated with the incipient manifestation of a highly punishable motive. For a man who has suffered excessive threat of castration in childhood, therefore, sexual arousal, even by a female who is not his mother, is likely to evoke the anticipation of castration.

The Psychodynamic Relationship Between Castration Anxiety and the Fear of Death

Because men differ in respect to the degree of castration threat they have experienced in childhood, they may be expected to respond with differing degrees of castration anxiety to the same sexually arousing stimulus. Indeed, even in the absence of a particular external stimulus, men who, as children, were severely threatened with castration may be subject to chronic anxiety. This anxiety stems from the fact that their chronically repressed desires for sexual contact with women strive continually to break through into consciousness. Naturally, such individuals usually do not know that it is their own sexual motives which stimulate this anxiety, nor are they likely to be aware of the specific danger, castration, which they dread. Nevertheless, their underlying anxiety, as in the case of other strong unconscious affects, may be expected to color the content of their conscious thoughts, and they ought to become preoccupied with ideas which symbolically reflect the castration anxiety of which they are unaware. Hypochondria is an excellent clinical example of the way in which intense—but unconscious—castration anxiety may be indirectly expressed through a host of conscious fears concerning possible sources of infectious disease or bodily deterioration. Indeed, these hypochondriacal fears may, in some cases, actually focus on infections which could damage sexual organs. However, even in such instances, the individual is not likely to perceive the relationship between his conscious fear and the unconscious castration anxiety which it reflects. His concern tends to be outward rather than inward; and he spends his time and energy in attempts to escape infection.

Just as unconscious castration anxiety may be manifested in conscious fears of bodily injury, it may also manifest itself in a fear of the most extreme consequence of injury: death. Thus, it happens that individuals who are in the best of health and have never actually experienced any serious accident or illness may be obsessed by morbid and unremitting fears of dying or of being killed. These fears may become so acute that the individual is reluctant to go to sleep lest he should never awaken again.

Of course, the conscious fear of death may be developed for a variety of reasons, the most obvious of which concern the aftermath of traumatic events, such as military combat, which might have terminated the individuals' existence. Still it would appear, in view of the preceding theoretical account, that an individual who has suffered intense castration threats should have a greater habitual fear of death than an individual who has been less severely threatened. Individuals who have severe castration anxiety ought also to show more fear of death after the arousal of that anxiety than individuals whose castration anxiety is less intense. In arriving at these deductions, we have assumed that people with different degrees of castration anxiety have experienced differential degrees of castration threat for the expression of their sexual feelings. However, we shall not address ourselves directly to an investigation of these presumed developmental differences in this experiment. Instead, we shall focus exclusively on the impact of castration anxiety on the conscious fear of death, after that anxiety has been stirred by the perception of sexually arousing stimuli.

In line with this reasoning, the central hypothesis of this experiment may be stated as follows: *Individuals who have a high degree of castration anxiety will show a greater fear of death after being exposed to sexually arousing stimuli than individuals who have a low degree of castration anxiety.*

Method

General Design

The experiment followed a "before-after" design which provided for the arousal of two levels of sexual feeling among Ss possessing two degrees of castration anxiety. Castration anxiety was measured in pre-experimental sessions. Thus, the experiment studied the interaction of castration anxiety and sexual stimulation in determining the fear of death.

Subjects

Ss were 56 male undergraduates of Yale College. They were unpaid volunteers, recruited from among the general college population. Ss were run through the experiment one at a time in a dormitory room.

Rationale

This experiment was presented to the Ss as an investigation of some of the psychological factors which influence the appreciation of art. Ss were told that the investigators were interested in seeing how different individuals react to the same work of art, and how various attitudes and opinions are related to esthetic reactions. Ss were informed that they would first fill out a questionnaire which covered a number of opinions pertinent to our research objectives. After they had filled out this questionnaire, Ss were told that they would be shown several pictures about which they would be asked to write their esthetic reactions.

The Opinion Questionnaire

The first of the pre-experimental measures consisted of a 22-item Likert-type scale. Included among these 22 items was a seven-item Fear of Death scale and a five-item Morality scale, both of which are described below. The 10 remaining items in the questionnaire were interspersed among the items of these two scales. These 10 "filler" items pertained to various aspects of esthetic preference. They were included for two reasons: (a) to inhibit the emergence of a response set to the other items and

(b) to support the rationale of the experiment.

Ss indicated the extent of their agreement or disagreement with each item in the questionnaire. These responses were coded in terms of a six point scale ranging from $+3$ (Strongly Agree) to -3 (Strongly Disagree). Ss were not permitted to take a mid-point on the scale; they were obliged to indicate some degree of agreement or disagreement with each statement.

The Fear of Death Scale (FDS). Since all the items in the questionnaire were devised on an a priori basis, and since the FDS measure was the basic dependent variable of the study, it was felt advisable to attempt to weed out those FDS items which were grossly nondiscriminating. Accordingly, after the "before" measures were collected, an item analysis was performed on the seven-item FDS. Two items failed to discriminate between the high and low scorers. Thus, the hypothesis was tested by using a summated score of the five items which were retained.

The following are the five items which comprised the final version of the FDS:

1. I tend to worry about the death toll when I travel on highways.

2. I find it difficult to face up to the ultimate fact of death.

3. Many people become disturbed at the sight of a new grave, but it does not bother me. (reverse scores)

4. I find the preoccupation with death at funerals upsetting.

5. I am disturbed when I think of the shortness of life.

The Morality Scale (MS). The MS was included in the study in order to serve as an internal control for the plausible alternative hypothesis that a post-experimental increase in fear of death might be the result of an increase in guilt following contact with stimuli which violate one's moral values. Such a reaction following sexual arousal could induce an unconscious need for punishment in the guilty S and this need, in turn, might express itself in an increased fear of death. The MS consisted of five items dealing with attitudes toward sexual behavior. The MS items, constructed in the same a priori fashion as the FDS and contained in the same questionnaire as the FDS, were also subjected to an item analysis. Since the original MS items discriminated adequately between high and low scorers, they were all retained in the final version of the MS.

The following are the examples of items contained in the MS:

1. Although many of my friends feel differently, I feel that one should wait until he is married to have intercourse.

2. I am frequently disturbed by the complete lack of sexual control in the relationships of my friends and their dates.

The Measure of Castration Anxiety (CA)

After the administration of the scales described above, our measure of castration anxiety was obtained in the following way: Ss were presented with the so-called castration anxiety card of the Blacky Test (Blum, 1949). This card shows a cartoon depicting two dogs; one dog is standing blindfolded, and a large knife appears about to descend on his outstretched tail; the other dog is an onlooker to this event. Ss were asked to look at this card and then rank three summary statements which purported to summarize the situation which was depicted. Actually, each statement was composed, on an a priori basis, to express a different degree of anxiety, ranging from slight to intense. Thus, Ss attached a score of 3 to the statement they felt best reflected the emotions of the onlooking dog, a score of 2 to the statement they felt fit the situation least. The distribution of the scores turned out to be quite skewed: most Ss assigned a score of 3 to the low CA alternative, a score of 2 to the medium CA alternative, and a score of 1 to the high CA Alternative. The 36 Ss who showed this pattern of scores were placed in the Low CA group. The remaining 20 Ss were categorized in the High CA group. Below are the summaries used for the Blacky card. (L represents the Low castration anxiety statement, M, medium castration anxiety, and H, high castration anxiety.)

L. The Black Dog appears to be experiencing some tension as he watches the scene in front of him. However, the sight of the amputation has little emotional sig-

nificance for him, and he views the situation in a fairly detached manner.

M. The Black Dog is evidently quite frightened by what is going on in front of him. He is afraid that his tail might be next to be amputed. Nevertheless, he is able to bear up to the situation without becoming deeply upset or overwhelmed by anxiety.

H. The sight of the approaching amputation is a deeply upsetting experience for the Black Dog who is looking on. The possibility of losing his own tail and the thought of the pain involved overwhelm him with anxiety.

The Experimental Conditions

Approximately four weeks after they filled out the "before" measures, the Ss participated in the experiment. Since the experimental design called for variation in arousal of sexual stimulation, two experimental conditions were created: High and Low sexual arousal (HAS and LAS). The experimental manipulations were administered individually, with 29 Ss in the HAS condition and 27 Ss in the LAS condition.[2]

It was decided that the easiest and most manageable arousal of sexual feelings would be by means of photographs of women. To produce the HAS condition, a series of four pictures of nude women were presented one at a time. These pictures were artistically mounted as if they were prints or lithographs. E said that these pictures were designed to study individual differences in esthetic reactions to the same work of art. To heighten the impact of the arousal, Ss were given four minutes to write down their reaction to each picture. According to the rationale of the study, this writing was done in order to provide a record of the Ss' responses to the esthetic qualities of the picture.

In the LAS condition, the procedure was identical except for the fact that four pictures of fully clothed fashion models, taken

2 To insure a sufficient number of HCA Ss within the HAS and LAS conditions, half of the Ss were randomly selected from the HCA and LCA Ss and assigned to the HAS condition. The other half were assigned to the LAS condition. Two Ss who had been assigned to the LAS condition failed to appear for the experimental session.

from a magazine, were used instead of nudes.

After the experimental manipulations, Ss were required to fill out the following measures which are relevant to the data reported here: a rating scale designed to ascertain whether or not the HAS and LAS conditions succeeded in evoking different intensities of stimulation, the FDS scale, and the MS scale.

The postexperimental check on the sexually arousing quality of the manipulations indicated that the HAS pictures were clearly perceived as more sexually arousing than the LAS pictures. On a scale ranging from O (not at all arousing) to 100 (intensely arousing), the HAS Ss had an average score of 59, whereas the LAS Ss had an average score of 35. The difference between these means was well beyond the .001 level of significance. Thus, there can be little doubt concerning the difference in sexual stimulation of the two conditions of arousal.

It may also be relevant to note that, in postexperimental interviews, none of the Ss indicated that they had been suspicious about our stated research objective. Moreover, although some of the Ss in the HAS condition could not completely conceal their chagrin or embarrassment upon seeing the nudes, they did not doubt that we were interested in studying individual differences in reactions to the pictures.

Results and Discussion

The hypothesis tested in this experiment holds that HCA Ss will become more afraid of death after exposure to the HAS condition than LCA Ss. To test this hypothesis, the change in the Ss' level of fear of death was assessed by comparing their pre-experimental FDS scores with their postexperimental FDS scores. This comparison produced a "shift" score for each S, indicating by what amount and in which direction his "after" FDS score differed from his "before" FDS scores. A positive (+) shift score thus indicated that an S

exhibited more fear of death, while a negative (−) shift score was indicative of a decrease in fear of death.

A t test showed that there was no difference between the high and low arousal groups in their initial level of fear of death. However, a strong relationship was found between fear of death and castration anxiety. The phi coefficient is .612, a figure which is significant at the .01 level. This result is in accordance with the anticipations previously stated in the theoretical section. As a result of this relationship, however, the HCA Ss tended to have higher pre-experimental FDS scores than the LCA Ss. Consequently, it is clear that HCA Ss entered the experimental conditions with less possibility for upward movement in the FDS than the LCA Ss. Conversely, the LCA Ss had less possibility for downward movement. Therefore, it was deemed advisable to test the hypothesis both with and without attention to the Ss' initial level of fear of death.

Table 1 presents the results pertinent to the basic test of our hypothesis. Without controlling for initial position on the FDS, the predicted difference between HCA and LCA Ss in mean FDS shift scores under the HAS condition is significant at the .03 level, whereas no statistically reliable difference between the HCA and LCA Ss is obtained under the LAS condition. A test of the difference between the differences in mean FDS scores (the difference between HCA and LCA Ss under the HAS condition compared with the difference between HCA and LCA Ss under the LAS condition) yields a t of 4.35. This result, which is statistically significant at beyond the .001 level, appears clearly to indicate that the arousal of sexual feeling interacted

TABLE 1

ANALYSIS OF MEAN FDS SHIFT SCORES
(Differences Between HCA and LCA Ss Within High, Low, and Combined
Levels of Pre-experimental FDS Under HAS and LAS Conditions)

Strength of sexual arousal	Level of pre-experimental FDS	Strength of castration anxiety					
		HCA		LCA			
		N	Mean FDS shift	N	Mean FDS shift	Difference between means	p
HAS	High and low	11	+3.36	18	+ .45	+2.91	.03
LAS	High and low	9	−1.11	18	− .05	−1.06	n.s.
HAS	High	8	+1.88	6	+ .33	+1.55	n.s.
	Low	3	+7.33	12	+ .50	+6.83	.001
LAS	High	6	−2.00	7	−1.86	− .14	n.s.
	Low	3	+ .67	11	+1.10	− .43	n.s.

with level of castration anxiety in accord with our a priori predictions.

Mention ought, perhaps, to be made of the fact that both HCA and LCA Ss show a negative shift score, i.e., a decrease in the fear of death, under identical conditions. Thus when high and low levels of pre-experimental FDS are combined under the LAS condition, as in Table 1, HCA Ss get a mean negative shift score of −1.11 while the mean FDS shift score for LCA Ss is −.05. Similarly, it can be seen in Table 1 that, within the high level of pre-experimental FDS, but again under the LAS condition, HCA Ss obtained a mean FDS shift score of −2.00 as compared to −1.06 for LCA Ss. If we discount, as virtually negligible, the LCA shift score of −.05, the remaining three negative FDS shift scores seem best accounted for by the effects of statistical regression. Since the LAS condition arouses so little sexual feeling, it seems to permit the occurrence of the same sort of regression effects that are typically found among control groups: a

drop in mean retest score for initially high-scoring Ss and a rise in mean retest score for initially low-scoring Ss. This is exactly what appears to have happened with initially high and low scoring HCA and LCA Ss under the LAS conditions. Thus, both HCA and LCA Ss who are high in pre-experimental FDS show negative mean FDS shift scores. On the other hand, both HCA and LCA Ss who are low in pre-experimental FDS show positive shift scores under LAS conditions. Finally, HCA Ss who tend, as we have indicated, to have high pre-experimental FDS scores as a consequence of the positive correlation between FDS and CA, also decrease in FDS under the LAS condition when the high and low levels of pre-experimental FDS are combined.

In order to test the possibility that results might be accounted for by a guilt reaction to infringement of moral values concerning the sexual feelings aroused by the HAS, the mean FDS shift scores of the high and low MS Ss were compared under both HAS and

TABLE 2

DIFFERENCES BETWEEN HMS AND LMS Ss IN MEAN FDS SHIFT SCORES
UNDER HAS AND LAS CONDITIONS

| | Strength of morality | | | | |
| | HMS | | LMS | | |
Strength of sexual arousal	N	Mean FDS shift	N	Mean FDS shift	Difference between means	p
HAS	15	+2.13	14	+.93	+1.20	n.s.
LAS	13	−1.08	14	+.22	−1.30	n.s.

LAS conditions. The results of this analysis, presented in Table 2, indicate that, although there appears to be a slight tendency for Ss high in MS to show higher FDS shift scores than Ss low in MS, the difference is far from statistical significance. The possibility, then, that an infringement of moral values induced by the nudes caused an increase in fear of death is not supported.

It should be noted, finally, that our measure of the morality variable appears to be quite independent of the castration anxiety and fear of death measures. The product-moment correlation between pre-experimental FDS and pre-experimental MS was only −.034, while the correlation between CA and pre-experimental MS was also low and statistically insignificant (a phi coefficient of .105).

The results of the present experiment are interpreted as lending support to the validity of the Freudian concept of castration anxiety. Such an interpretation seems especially warranted since the plausible alternative explanation which we investigated failed to yield significant changes in the fear of death when Ss were categorized in terms of their moral scruples against sexual behavior. Since our pre-experimental measures of castration anxiety and morality were found to be quite independent of each other, we may conclude, with some confidence, that it was the arousal of castration anxiety rather than guilt feelings which produced the significant differences which we obtained.

Of course, nothing that was done here bears directly on the question of the etiology of castration anxiety. However, by demonstrating that sexually arousing stimuli exerted predicted and differential effects upon individuals with varying degrees of castration anxiety, we have provided circumstantial evidence which is consonant with Freud's emphasis on the significance of the sexual motive in the genesis of castration anxiety.

Summary: The aim of this experiment was to test an hypothesis concerning the psychodynamic relationship between castration anxiety and the fear of death. Specifically, the hypothesis predicted that persons who have a high degree of castration anxiety (HCA) would show a greater increase in fear of death after the arousal of their sexual feelings than persons who have a low degree of castration anxiety (LCA).

Fifty-six male undergraduates of Yale College were assigned to two experimental conditions in a "before-after" design which permitted the manipulation of two levels of sexual arousal. Before being exposed to one or the other of these manipulations, Ss filled out booklets containing a scale designed to measure the fear of death (FDS), a questionnaire concerning moral standard of sexual behavior (MS), and a measure of castration anxiety (CA).

High arousal of sexual feeling (HAS) was induced by showing the Ss four pictures of nude females. The condition of low arousal of sexual feeling (LAS) consisted of showing Ss four pictures of fashion models. Following the experimental manipulations, Ss again filled out the original FDS. In addition, Ss answered a questionnaire aimed at checking on the degree of sexual arousal which Ss perceived in the experimental manipulations.

The results clearly confirmed the hypothesis: HCA Ss showed a significantly greater increase in fear of death than LCA Ss after being exposed to the sexually arousing stimuli of the HAS condition. There were no significant differences in mean FDS shift scores between HCA and LCA Ss under the LAS condition. A postexperimental check of the difference in perceived arousal of sexual feelings revealed that Ss perceived the HAS condition as significantly more arousing than the LAS condition. A plausible alternative explanation of the obtained results was investigated and rejected. Thus, it was found that Ss who differed in the strength of their moral standards of sexual behavior did not differ significantly in their mean FDS scores after being exposed to the HAS condition.

Journal of Abnormal and Social Psychology, 1961, vol. 63, pp. 660–662

Anxiety and the Experimental Arousal of Affiliation Need[1]

Donn Byrne

The effect of experimentally aroused affiliative motivation on responses to projective tests has been investigated in order to develop a TAT scoring system for n Affiliation. Shipley and Veroff (1952) employed a sociometric procedure as the arousing condition. Their scoring system focused on imagery involving affiliation-deprivation. They cross-validated their scoring categories by comparing responses of freshmen accepted and rejected by college fraternities. Atkinson, Heyns, and Veroff

[1] This investigation was supported in part by research grants (EF-140, EF-143) from the University of Texas Research Institute. The author would like to express his appreciation to John Sheffield and Carole Calvert who served as research assistants and to Elaine Abbott who scored the affiliation need protocols.

(1954) attempted to broaden the definition of affiliation imagery by including any statement of concern over establishing, maintaining, or restoring a positive affective relationship with another person or persons. They also maximized the difference between the experimental and control groups used in the procedure for analyzing the responses. Again, a sociometric rating experience constituted the arousal condition. In both studies, and with somewhat different scoring systems, more affiliation responses occurred in the stories of the aroused subjects.

The experimental conditions that have defined affiliation arousal have been such that both positive and negative cues probably are present.

Affiliation need is conceptualized as an approach tendency, and the score as it is defined by the Mighigan group is largely oriented toward approach responses. However, imagery motivated primarily by fear of rejection may have been confounded with that motivated primarily by hope of affiliation because of the nature of the arousal conditions that have been used. If arousal conditions that involve ratings by others actually do evoke avoidance responses, such conditions should evoke feelings of anxiety as well as affiliation need.

A further consideration is whether affiliation arousal would be expected to evoke anxiety to the same extent in all subjects. When TAT protocols are obtained in a neutral situation and scored for n Affiliation, the resulting individual differences are assumed to indicate variations in characteristic motivational states. Persons who are found to have high need for affiliation should be most responsive to affiliation arousing cues in their environments. That is, external stimulus conditions and internal motivational state should interact. French and Chadwick (1956), using their own projective measure of affiliation need, found the greatest increase in n Affiliation in an arousal condition for subjects whose scores were highest in a neutral condition. Perhaps experimental manipulations designed to arouse affiliative motivation are only effective with those subjects for whom such environmental cues are initially salient. Therefore, if anxiety is evoked by affiliation arousal, one might reason that its intensity should be a function of an individual's characteristic level of n Affiliation.

These two considerations lead to the hypotheses that (a) anxiety is evoked by the experimental arousal of affiliation motives and (b) the amount of anxiety is a positive function of n Affiliation determined in a neutral situation.

Method

Procedure

As part of another study, 84 students (44 males, 40 females) enrolled in introductory psychology courses at the University of Texas were seen in groups of 5–10. They were seated in a small amphitheater equipped with a large one-way mirror. They were given a paper-and-pencil task requiring about 15 minutes time.

For the experimental group, the following instructions were given:

Before you begin, there is something else I would like to tell you about. You are actually taking part in two experiments at the same time.

One way to make judgments about people is to observe them carefully. The study of the expressive movements has taught psychologists a lot about the meaning of the many little unconscious gestures, facial expressions, body movements, etc. in which all of us engage in our everyday behavior. We have some evidence that such things have a lot to do with a person's popularity. So, during the rest of the session today, I and my two assistants will be watching each of you very closely.

This mirror here is actually a one-way screen. In the room next to this one, two research assistants are already taking notes on various aspects of your behavior. They are both graduate students in psychology. I'll show you where they are. (Lights in experimental room are turned off and those in the observation room turned on momentarily.)

Before the hour is over, we will have assigned a rating to each of you with respect to your general popularity, your attractiveness to the opposite sex, how likeable you seem, etc.

Following this, the experimenter left the subjects alone and noisily entered the observation room.

Anxiety ratings

Immediately following the paper-and-pencil tasks, the experimenter returned and administered a questionnaire dealing with reactions to the experiment. Two six-point self-rating scales dealt with their feelings of nervousness and uneasiness during the preceding 15 minutes and their estimates as to how nervous or uneasy most of the other students in the room probably felt. On each scale, the descriptive points were "completely calm," "relatively calm," "a little uneasy," "quite uneasy," "very uneasy," and "extremely uneasy."

The anxiety score consists of the combined responses to these two scales. The split-half reliability of this instrument was found to be .72, corrected by the Brown-Spearman formula.

Affiliation need

One week later, a different experimenter using a different experimental room administered four TAT slides according to Atkinson's (1958, pp. 836–837) instructions. The slides consisted of Pictures 28, 83, 102, and 103 in the list presented by Atkinson (1958, pp. 832–834). A research assistant used the Heyns, Veroff, and Atkinson (1958) manual to score the protocols.

A subsample of 29 protocols was scored independently by an experienced scorer at the University of Michigan. The correlation of .95 between the two sets of scores indicates high interjudge reliability. For the 84 subjects, the mean n Affiliation score was 2.67 with a standard deviation of 2.54. Subjects were divided approximately at the median into low ($N = 38$, scores of 0-2) and high ($N = 46$, scores of 3-10) groups.

Results

The means and standard deviations of the anxiety ratings are presented in Table 1. The interaction between experimental conditions and affiliation need in evoking anxiety was examined in a two-way analysis of variance. Disproportionality among the number of cases in the four cells was corrected

using the procedure outlined by Wert, Neidt, and Ahmann (1954). The results of this analysis are reported in Table 2.

Neither n Affiliation nor the experimental conditions were related to self-ratings of anxiety.[3] The interaction between the two independent variables, however, was statistically significant. The major source of the difference is between the High and Low n Affiliation groups in the experimental condition. Subjects high in affiliation need indicated significantly greater anxiety in response to affiliation arousing cues than subjects low in affiliation need ($t = 2.61$, $df = 34$, $p < .02$). Also, the difference between the experimental

TABLE 1

MEANS AND STANDARD DEVIATIONS
OF ANXIETY RATINGS

	Control group			Experimental group		
	N	M	SD	N	M	SD
High n Affiliation	27	3.81	1.16	19	4.42	.88
Low n Affiliation	21	4.00	1.23	17	3.59	.97

TABLE 2

SUMMARY OF ANALYSIS OF VARIANCE
OF ANXIETY RATINGS AS INFLUENCED
BY EXPERIMENTAL CONDITIONS
AND AFFILIATION NEED

Source	SS	df	MS	F	p
Experimental conditions	.4072[a]	1	.4072	.33	*ns*
Affiliation need	1.3438[a]	1	1.3438	1.09	*ns*
Interaction	5.2843[a]	1	5.2843	4.28	<.05
Within (error)	98.8233	80	1.2353		

[a] Adjusted.

[3] It was the failure of the arousal instructions to evoke anxiety that led to the present investigation.

and control conditions approaches significance for the subjects high in n Affiliation ($t = 1.90$, $df = 44$, p between .05 and .10).

Another way of examining the data is through a correlational approach. Anxiety ratings and n Affiliation scores correlated .45 ($p < .01$) in the experimental condition and $-.12$ (ns) in the control condition.

Discussion

The results suggest that manipulations designed to arouse affiliation need evoke anxiety, at least in persons whose fantasy productions give evidence of concern over establishing, maintaining, or restoring positive affective relationships. Arousal conditions that involve a high probability of success should be less likely to evoke such anxiety than arousal conditions that involve the strong possibility of failure. A separation of these positive and negative qualities in the arousal condition might lead to a more specific differentiation of hope of success and fear of failure with respect to affiliation imagery in thematic material. As Shipley and Veroff (1952) have suggested, the ability to specify whether individuals are motivated primarily by positive, negative, or mixed affiliative needs would seem to permit more accurate behavior predictions in affiliation relevant situations.

From another viewpoint, the findings suggest that the present n Affiliation scoring system identifies those individuals who are likely to be made anxious by a situation containing an affiliation threat. Presumably these same high n Affiliation subjects would respond with greater pleasure to the promise of an affiliative reward than would subjects low in n Affiliation. Other motivational scoring schemes might also be used in a similar way to predict those who would be made anxious by threat relevant experimental conditions or made pleased by reward relevant conditions.

A word should be added about the failure of the experimental condition to evoke more anxiety than the control condition. Remarks by various subjects suggested that the room in which the experiment was conducted was somewhat anxiety provoking in and of itself. If so, perhaps the instructions only served to define the source of anxiety cues. Without those instructions (in the control group), the array of individual hypotheses about the threat presented by the room was unrelated to n Affiliation. However, when other subjects (in the experimental group) were informed that they were being observed and rated, the source of concern became relatively specific. Those who feared, for example, the possibility of electric shock were now able to relax while those with strong affiliation motives perceived the cues as increasingly stressful.

Summary: The experimental conditions employed in studies of n Affiliation probably contain a mixture of positive and negative cues. If so, such arousal conditions should evoke anxiety as well as n Affiliation. The hypothesis was tested that anxiety is evoked by the experimental arousal of affiliation motives and that the amount of anxiety is a positive function of n Affiliation determined in a neutral situation.

In the experimental group, subjects were aware of being watched through a one-way mirror and rated for popularity, attractiveness, etc. while completing a paper-and-pencil task. The control group simply completed the paper-and-pencil task. All subjects then rated themselves and others in the group with respect to feelings of nervousness and uneasiness. At another testing session, TAT slides were shown, and the protocols were scored for n Affiliation.

Experimental conditions and affiliation need interacted to influence the anxiety self-ratings. In the experimental group, subjects high in n Affiliation rated themselves significantly more anxious than did those subjects low in n Affiliation; in the control group, affiliation need was unre- lated to anxiety ratings. Manipulations designed to arouse affiliation need thus appear to evoke anxiety in persons whose fantasy productions give evidence of concern over affiliation. Also, the present n Affiliation scoring system identifies those individuals who are made anxious by an affiliation threat.

Journal of Abnormal and Social Psychology, 1960, vol. 61, pp. 207–215

Anxiety in Academic Achievement Situations[1]

Richard Alpert and Ralph Norman Haber

As part of the effort to define and measure the variables of which test performance is a function, this study was designed to evaluate, both experimentally and theoretically, the paper-and-pencil instruments currently being used in American research for the measurement of individual differences in anxiety as it affects academic achievement performance. In addition, it includes a description of a new achievement-anxiety scale which has been devised to indicate not only the presence or absence of anxiety, but also whether the anxiety facilitates or debilitates test performance.

Three separate problems are considered: (*a*) the relationship between scales which are designed to measure general anxiety and scales specifically designed to measure test anxiety (spe- cific anxiety scales), and a comparison of the relative efficacy of the general and specific scales as predictors of academic achievement performance; (*b*) the relationship between the construct of anxiety and that of aptitude and the methodological problems involved in separating these two operationally; and (*c*) the direction of the effect of anxiety upon academic achievement performance.

Procedure and Subjects

Procedurally, this research involved the administration of a variety of anxiety scales to introductory psychology students and to freshmen at Stanford University. The scales used included the Taylor Manifest Anxiety Scale (MAS) (Taylor, 1953), the Welsh Anxiety Index (AI) (Welsh, 1952), the Freeman Anxiety Scale (AS) (Freeman, 1953); the Mandler-Sarason Test Anxiety Scale (TAS) (Mandler & Sarason, 1952), and the Achievement Anxiety Test (AAT), which has two scales discussed below. Analysis of the data involved intercorrelating these scales and studying their relationship to a measure of verbal aptitude, the Scholastic Aptitude Test (SAT) (College Entrance Examination Board, 1956), and to a set of academic performance indices, in-

[1] The support provided by the National Science Foundation (G-1787 and G-3045) is gratefully acknowledged. We also wish to thank R. R. Sears, Q. McNemar, and Jan Pierce for their help and support, and the Stanford University Office of the Registrar and Computing Center for their cooperation.

Part of this report appeared as a portion of a doctoral dissertation at Stanford University by the first author.

cluding college grade-point average and the final examination, mid-term examination, and course grades in the introductory psychology course. Only male Ss were included in the data analyses. For the students enrolled, the scales were either administered during the first class meeting of the quarter to the entire class (Fall 1955, Winter 1956, and Spring, 1956, with Ns of 93, 92, and 98, respectively), or as part of smaller group experiments which were required of all students (Spring, 1956, subsample, N = 40). Therefore, these data are representative of the population of the students from the introductory course in psychology, which is taken by 75% of the students in the university. For the freshmen, the scales were group administered as part of the freshman evaluation program.

The scores for the Scholastic Aptitude Test (administered to the students during their senior year in high school) and the grade-point averages were obtained from the Registrar of the university. The final examination, course, and midterm grades were obtained from class records. All of these data were collected without the Ss' awareness either that it had been collected or that data of this nature would be related in any way to their responses on the anxiety scales.

In view of the finding of Davids (1955a) that scores on anxiety scales are affected by the Ss' particular motivation for filling out anxiety questionnaires, it must be noted that Ss completed the present questionnaires with the understanding that the data were being collected as part of a large ongoing research program conducted by the Psychology Department and that their answers would be used for research purposes only. In some instances, Ss' affiliation motivation might have been aroused when, for example, the entire class was asked to fill out a questionnaire as a favor to the experimenter; at times when the questionnaire was administered in experimental session, the fulfillment of course requirements was the major motivation. In all situations, however, it was emphasized that the data would *not* be made available either to the university administration or to the faculty and that no selection of any kind would be based on the results of the questionnaire. There is no reason to believe that motivational differences in any way differentially affected the responses.

General versus Specific Anxiety Scales

The first concern in constructing a measuring instrument which will predict the effect of anxiety in academic performance is one of defining the population of experiences and behaviors which the item responses are to reveal. There are current in the literature two divergent positions regarding this matter. One position is exemplified by Taylor (1953) with her Manifest Anxiety Scale and the other by Mandler and Sarason (1952) with their Test Anxiety Scale.

Taylor's general anxiety scale is made up of items drawn from the MMPI and is concerned with a wide variety of situations other than test taking. Underlying the construction of the MAS is a theoretical assumption that there is a relatively constant "level of internal anxiety or emotionality," and also "that the intensity of this anxiety could be ascertained by a paper-and-pencil test consisting of items describing what have been called overt or manifest symptoms of this state" (Taylor, 1953, p. 285). If Taylor is correct in positing such a general anxiety state, then it should follow that a single measure of a set of manifest anxiety responses gathered from many situations would be an adequate predictor of the presence and effects of anxiety responses in *any* situation, whether it be eyelid conditioning (Spence & Taylor, 1951; Taylor, 1951), therapeutic sessions (Peck, 1951), serial learning (Taylor & Spence, 1952), or academic performance. At present, however, there is some evidence (Child, 1954; Mandler, 1954) of *intra*-individual differences in anxiety both in content and intensity from one situation to another. This evidence warrants further examination of the basic general-anxiety-state assumption underlying the construction of the Taylor MAS-type scale before applying such a scale as extensively as has been done in the past. Too often, conclusions have been drawn on the basis of correlations with the MAS regarding the presence or absence of anxiety or the effects attributable to anxiety without due consideration of the possible limitations of a general scale of this type as a sensitive indicator of anxiety in any limited, recurring type of situation.

Mandler and Sarason, who represent the alternative current position, maintain that the items composing the measuring instrument should be concerned with the specific situations in which it is to be used. These investigators, studying stress in academic achievement situations, devised the Test Anxiety Scale (TAS), ". . . a questionnaire which was specifically concerned with the Ss attitudes and experiences in a testing situation" (Mandler & Sarason, 1952, p. 166). Thus, the TAS provides a score indicating the recalled intensity of certain experiences and behaviors immediately antecedent to or concomitant with the taking of various types of examinations in the past. The implication of this type of scale is that the increased situational specificity of its item content will allow for a more sensitive measurement of anxiety and its effect in the academic achievement situation. It follows that for other situations other specific scales will be needed; and, only if these specific scales, each shown to be valid in its own situation, turn out to be highly intercorrelated may one posit a general anxiety state and thus justify a single measure of anxiety for all situations.

The relative merits of situational specificity versus generality of item content can be evaluated by two statistical techniques. The first is a comparison of the intercorrelations among a variety of general and specific scales administered to the same subjects. The Taylor MAS, the Welsh AI, and the Freeman AS are used as measures of general or manifest anxiety; the Mandler-Sarason TAS and the two scales of the AAT are used as measures of specific anxiety. High intercorrelations among all six scales would support the theoretical assumption of a single underlying state, and thus the appropriateness of a single general measure. On the other hand, low intercorrelations would support the use of scales which are specific to the situations in which they are to predict. Table 1 reports the intercorrelations of the measures of anxiety for an N of 40 (the only sample that received all six scales). Because in all instances inspection of the scatter diagrams revealed no departure from linearity, only product-moment correlation coefficients were computed.

As Table 1 indicates, the correlations among the general anxiety scales range from .32 to .39. The correlations between the general and specific scales range from .24 to .38. The correlations among the specific anxiety scales range from .40 to .64, all of which appear to be higher than any of the correlations involving the general scales. This observation is supported by significance tests of the differences between correlations, which indicate that in most instances the intercorrelations among the specific scales are significantly higher

TABLE 1

INTERCORRELATION AMONG SIX MEASURES OF ANXIETY

$(N = 40)$

Test	REL	AI	AS	TAS	AAT−	AAT+
General Anxiety Scales:						
MAS	.89	.39**[a]	.32*	.32*	.38*	−.33*
AI	.84		.34*	.28	.37*	−.25
AS	.73			.38*	.30	−.24
Specific Anxiety Scales:						
TAS	.82				.64**	−.40*
AAT−	.87					−.48**
AAT+	.83					

Note.—Reliability of the scales appear in Column 1.
[a] Based on the nonoverlapping items. When overlapping items are included, $r = .89$.
* Significant at .05 level.
** Significant at .01 level.

than the correlations involving the general scales either with each' other or with the specific scales. This seems to throw some doubt on the comparability and, therefore, substitutability of a general anxiety scale for a specific anxiety scale.

A factor analysis was also performed (Alpert, 1957) on this matrix of correlations, but although the above conclusions were supported by this analysis, such support is little more than suggestive because of the hazards of drawing conclusions from a factor analysis based on only 40 cases.

A second technique for determining the substitutability of the general for the situationally specific anxiety scales, far more rigorous than merely intercorrelating the scales, is to compare the two types of scales as predictors of various measures of academic performance. If the general scales predict as well as the specific scales, there is justification for the use of a single general measure for the detection of anxiety in all situations. If, on the other hand, the specific scales are able to account for

significantly more of the variance in the performance measures than are the general scales, then there is justification for the use of scales which are specific to the situation in which they are used.

Table 2 presents the correlations between the six anxiety scales and four measures of academic performance. These are average correlations, based on combined samples with total Ns ranging from 40 to 379. Thus, these relationships are based on all samples for which both the appropriate anxiety and performance scores were available. Before averaging was attempted, a check was made to be sure that neither the means and the standard deviations of all the samples nor the correlations to be averaged were significantly different. No differences were found in any of these comparisons.

The data summarized in Table 2 indicate that the specific anxiety scales are more often significantly correlated with academic performance measures than are the general anxiety scales. Accepting the 5% level of significance (two-tailed) as a criterion, only one of

TABLE 2

$(N = 40$ to $379)$

Test	Grade-Point Average	Course Exam Grade	Final Exam Grade	Midterm Exam Grade
		Psych 1	Psych 1	Psych 1
General Anxiety Scales:				
MAS	.01	−.08	−.02	−.19
AI	−.04	−.05	−.03	−.22*
AS	−.06	.14	.15	—
Specific Anxiety Scales:				
TAS	−.24*	−.21	−.16	−.32*
AAT−	−.25*	−.26*	−.28*	−.25*
AAT+	.37*	.23*	.26*	.21

* Significant at .05 level.

the 11 available correlations for the general scales reached significance, while 9 of the 12 correlations involving the specific scales reached significance.

The implications of the findings are reasonably clear. Specific anxiety scales and general anxiety scales measure, to a significant extent, something different. Furthermore, it appears that the variable which the specific scales measure, and which the general scales do not, is involved in academic performance to such an extent that the specific scales are better predictors of academic performance than are the general anxiety scales.

One may tentatively conclude, therefore, that further use of a general anxiety scale as an appropriate operation for the measurement of academic achievement anxiety is unwarranted. However, the next section, on the relationship of these various anxiety scales to aptitude must be considered before this can become a final conclusion.

The Relationship between Anxiety and Aptitude

In evaluating the efficacy of the various scales in the academic situation, one must take cognizance of the relationship between the anxiety measures and intellectual ability because interest is centered in a scale which predicts performance variance attributable to something other than aptitude. On this basis, it seems desirable for an anxiety scale to correlate highly with performance and only slightly with aptitude.

The equivocal results reported in the literature regarding the relationship between anxiety and aptitude become more clear if one takes into consideration the type of anxiety scale used, the heterogeneity of the population measured, and the nature of the aptitude measure (most importantly, whether it was timed and, therefore, under pressure, or untimed). (See Alpert, 1957, for a more extensive review of these variables.) Since the present study is concerned with a highly intellectually homogeneous college population and with an aptitude test given under pressure conditions, the literature involving comparable populations and test conditions is of most direct concern. It indicates that the general anxiety scales are not related to timed aptitude tests in homogeneous college populations (Davids & Eriksen, 1955; Schulz & Calvin, 1955), whereas specific anxiety scales are related to this kind of aptitude test (Sarason & Mandler, 1952). The data presented in Table 3 support these findings. Here the general anxiety scales are not significantly related to aptitude, but all the specific scales are significant beyond at least the 5% level.

There are four possible explanations for this difference:

1. The specific scales are in part a measure of intellectual ability. That is, for some reason, intelligence, *independent of actual anxiety level*, affects the individual's response to a specific anxiety measure. General scales are free of an intellectual ability component according to this argument.

2. A specific anxiety scale is an appropriate vehicle for rationalization or justification of poor academic performance. Because people of lower intelligence are more apt to have experienced the effects of the results of poor academic performance in the past, more of them would be inclined to use such rationalization than would people of higher intelligence, and the specific scales are more sensitive to rationalization attempts.

3. There are stress cues connected with the taking of timed college aptitude tests. These cues elicit anxiety responses which affect the aptitude test performance. The specific scales are sensitive to the presence of anxiety of the type reflected in the aptitude tests, but the general scales are not similarly sensitive.

4. The more intelligent the individual, the less anxiety he manifests in test situations because he has less objective reason to fear the experience. The specific scales, which are able to measure this interaction, are, therefore, a sensitive index of anxiety in a college population, whereas the general scales are not.

The last of these arguments is the only one which maintains that the obtained correlation is a measure of the relationship between the two constructs of anxiety and aptitude. The first three suggest that the correlation between the measures is an artifact which appears because of poor test construction or the conditions of measurement. While the present studies were not designed to evaluate these various explanations, they do provide suggestive evidence of their relative validity.

The first explanation holds that if an anxiety scale which is correlated with an aptitude measure is, because of some characteristic such as its format, simply

TABLE 3

CORRELATIONS BETWEEN SIX ANXIETY
SCALES AND A MEASURE·
OF VERBAL APTITUDE (SAT)

($N = 40$ to 379)

Test	Verbal Aptitude		
	N	r	P
General Anxiety Scales:			
MAS	198	+.10	ns
AI	153	+.13	ns
AS	40	−.24	ns
Specific Anxiety Scales:			
TAS	154	−.18	.05
AAT−	379	−.29	.001
AAT+	379	+.21	.001

a measure of aptitude itself, then one would expect that the aptitude and anxiety measures would account for the same variance in academic performance. If this were, in fact, the case, then a multiple correlation based on the best weighted combination of aptitude and anxiety would not be expected to account for significantly more of the variance in academic performance than would aptitude alone. Tables 4 and 5 present multiple correlations of aptitude and anxiety, predicting grade-

TABLE 4

MULTIPLE CORRELATIONS PREDICTING
GRADE-POINT AVERAGE (GPA) FROM
A COMBINATION OF VERBAL
APTITUDE AND ANXIETY

Test	N	R^a	r^b	r^c	p^d
AAT−	93	.46	−.45	.27	.001
AAT−	92	.29	−.08	.29	ns
AAT−	98	.53	−.40	.43	.001
TAS	40	.46	−.27	.41	ns
AAT+	93	.42	.36	.27	.01
AAT+	92	.43	.32	.29	.01
AAT+	98	.58	.50	.43	.001

[a] GPA · Apitude & Anxiety.
[b] GPA · Anxiety.
[c] GPA · Aptitude.
[d] For adding anxiety to aptitude.

TABLE 5

MULTIPLE CORRELATIONS PREDICTING FINAL
EXAMINATION GRADE FROM A
COMBINATION OF APTITUDE
AND ANXIETY

Test	N	R^a	r^b	r^c	p
AAT−	93	.49	−.48	.30	.001
AAT−	92	.42	−.02	.42	ns
AAT−	98	.35	−.34	.16	ns
TAS	40	.40	−.35	.25	.05
AAT+	93	.36	.25	.30	.05
AAT+	92	.47	.23	.42	.05
AAT+	98	.32	.28	.16	ns

[a] Final examination grade—Anxiety & Aptitude.
[b] Final examination grade—Anxiety.
[c] Final examination grade—Aptitude.

point average and final examination grade. Also, they indicate the significance of the addition of the anxiety measure in the predictions. The general anxiety scales are not included in the tables because they are not correlated with achievement performance and hence, could make no contribution to the prediction of such performance.

The debilitating scale of the AAT adds significantly, over and above aptitude, to the prediction of the grade-point average (GPA) in two out of three instances, and in one out of three for the final examination grade. The facilitating scale of the AAT adds significantly, over and above aptitude, to the prediction of GPA in the three instances reported, and in two out of the three instances for the final examination grade. The Mandler-Sarason TAS adds significantly to prediction of final examination grade, but not for GPA, in the only samples whose data are available. These findings refute the argument that the specific scales which are correlated with aptitude are simply measures of aptitude, because the results indicate that specific anxiety scales are able to account for variance in academic performance other than that accounted for by a measure of aptitude. This does not mean to say that these anxiety instruments are not, in part, measures of intellectual ability; it does say, however, that they are something more than that—and that therefore they are able to account for added variance in academic performance, and, as such, are valuable supplements to a measure of aptitude.

The second explanation holds that the significant correlation of specific anxiety scales with aptitude is really the result of a mediating process of rationalization and justification for poor performance. In order to evaluate this· argument, the entering freshman class was given a specific anxiety scale. Freshmen entering Stanford have, in the majority, a past history of similar academic success experiences in high school, and they have had no past experience with the college academic performance criteria which anxiety scales were to predict. The AAT was administered to the entire freshman class at Stanford during their orientation week in the Fall of 1955. After the end of their first year, a random sample of 96 was drawn and the AAT was correlated with their grade-point averages. Correlations of .42 with the facilitating scale and −.29 with the debilitating scale were obtained. Both correlations are significant beyond the 1% level. Comparing these correlations with those obtained for a sample of 70 upperclassmen for whom exactly comparable data were on hand, no significant differences were found.

This is a weak refutation of the second explanation, at least at the college level. But, of course, college students have had anxiety experiences regarding high school achievement, and thus, it is still possible that the freshmen could be rationalizing via the AAT for their high school grades. But the two scales were correlated with high school grade-point average .29 and −.21, respectively. These correlations are both significant at the 5% level, and they are not significantly different from .42 and −.29. Thus, it seems the data cannot provide a definite answer to the issue involved—nor, probably, can any correlational study of this nature.

Third, if a timed aptitude test arouses stress cues, which elicit anxiety responses which affect the aptitude test performance, then a correlation between an anxiety measure and an aptitude measure could be interpreted to mean that the anxiety scale measures the anxiety which is a component in the aptitude test situation and which is reflected in the aptitude test scores. If this were true, then it would follow that an *aptitude* measure would correlate more highly with an anxiety-provoking college examination than with one that aroused little anxiety. Because the final examinations require more involvement on the part of the student and count more toward his total grade, these tests should be more anxiety-provoking than the mid-term examination. From this reasoning, these two examinations were compared to provide the anxiety difference against which to test the aptitude measure. In no sample was there a significantly greater correlation between aptitude and final examination than between aptitude and midterm examination. These findings constitute a weak refutation of the third explanation.

A more definitive technique for evaluation of this explanation would be to administer the aptitude test to a group of students before and after they had been subjected to a course of psychotherapeutic treatment directed at the reduction of examination anxiety. If the increase in the mean aptitude score for the group receiving psychotherapy were significantly larger than any increase in the control group which had not received the psychotherapy, then we would have strong support for the third explanation of the relationship between aptitude and anxiety. This experiment would be similar to that by Pomeroy (1950), who demonstrated increases in finger-maze performance after only 10 min. of cathartic-type therapy. Until such time as appropriate data are available, however, one must hold in abeyance any final conclusions regarding the validity of this explanation.

In summary, regarding these three explanations, the first is refuted, doubt cast on the second, and the third neither refuted nor supported. Present evidence allows one to say only that either the third or the fourth explanation (that is, that the obtained correlation is a measure of the relationship between the two constructs—anxiety and aptitude) may be correct, or that both of them may be true. Had the first and second explanations been supported, they would support a preference for the use of a general anxiety scale because it is free of the contaminating influence of aptitude. The last two explanations support a preference for a specific anxiety scale because of its greater sensitivity. Since the evidence does indicate that these explanations are more probably correct, one has further support beyond that derived from the analysis of the interrelationships of the anxiety scales for the use of the specific rather than the general anxiety scales for prediction in academic performance situations.

Direction of Effect

A study of the anxiety literature leads to the question of how anxiety, when aroused in an examination, will affect performance; that is, whether it will facilitate it, debilitate it, or perhaps have no effect on it at all. On the basis of their earlier theoretical considerations, Sarason, Mandler, and Craighill (1952) state the following hypothesis:

When a stimulus situation contains elements which specifically arouse test or achievement anxiety, this increase in anxiety drive will lead to poorer performance in individuals who have test-irrelevant [incompatible or interfering] anxiety responses in their response repertory. For individuals *without such response tendencies,* [italics added] these stimulus elements will raise their general drive level and result in improved performance (p. 561).

The implication is that measurable anxiety responses, when present, are debilitating to performance, an implication which is reflected in the Mandler-Sarason TAS. All the items of the TAS are unidimensional, i.e., anxiety responses are either debilitating or not (e.g., "While taking a course examination, to what extent do you worry? Worry a lot . . . [to] . . . Worry not at all." [Item No. 35]). From the absence of negative responses for an *S,* that is, a low score on the test, they infer that when anxiety-provoking cues are present in the environment, "these stimulus elements will raise [his] general drive level and result in improved performance for that *S.*" (Sarason, Mandler, & Craighill, 1952, p. 561). This results in their confounding the two alternatives of a facilitating effect of anxiety and no effect of anxiety on academic performance and leads to their failure to allow for a third alternative, the possible existence of an individual whose anxiety responses in an anxiety-provoking situation do not affect test performance either by improving or by depressing the score. Such an individual would have to be described in their formulation as one whose negative or debilitating response effect is just counteracted by the increased task-performance drive.

There is another approach which does not require this unwarranted inference and according to which an anxiety scale would measure the presence and intensity of both kinds of anxiety responses, those which facilitate performance and those which interfere with it. If an individual scored low on both of these scale components, he would be considered to be unaffected (insofar as test performance was concerned) by anxiety-provoking cues. In other words, the facilitating effects of anxiety would then be measured independently and not inferred from the absence of negative responses. This independent measure would allow for the possibility of the absence of both types of response as well as for the presence of either one.

Theoretically, Mandler and Sarason would predict, on the basis of their ideas, that two such independent measures of anxiety would be highly negatively correlated. That is, if an individual had a great deal of facilitating anxiety, he would have little debilitating anxiety and vice versa. This is the assumption underlying their scale because it allows them to use. only the debilitating index and to infer facilitating anxiety from the absence of debilitation. This assumption may be unnecessary. In fact, these two constructs of debilitating and facilitating anxiety may be uncorrelated. Thus, an individual may possess a large amount of both anxieties, or of one but not the other, or of none of either. The nature of this correlation can be determined empirically following the construction of two such independent measures of anxiety, a scale measuring the facilitating effects of anxiety on achievement performance, and a separate scale measuring the debilitating effects of anxiety on achievement performance.

The Achievement Anxiety Test (AAT) was constructed to make this determination. It consists of two independent scales: a facilitating scale of nine items based on a prototype of the item—"Anxiety helps me to do better during examinations and tests"; and a debilitating scale of 10 items based on a prototype of the item—"Anxiety interferes with my performance during examinations and tests." Both scales have gone through numerous revisions based upon item analyses, correlations with various criteria, and theoretical reformulations. The test-retest reliabilities for a 10-week interval are .83 and .87, respectively. The test-retest reliability over an 8-month period is .75 for the facilitating scale and .76 for the debilitating scale. The two scales are administered in one questionnaire, the items randomly mixed (as presented below). The Ss answer each item on a five-point scale, indicating the degree to which the item applies to them. The AAT includes neutral buffer items in addition to the items listed. The numbers in the parentheses to the right are the actual item numbers on the AAT.

Facilitating Anxiety Scale

1. I work most effectively under pressure, as when the task is very important. Always —Never. (2)

2. While I may (or may not) be nervous before taking an exam, once I start, I seem to forget to be nervous. I always forget—I am always nervous during an exam. (9)

3. Nervousness while taking a test helps me do better. It never helps—It often helps. (11)

4. When I start a test, nothing is able to distract me. This is always true of me— This is not true of me. (12)

5. In courses in which the total grade is based mainly on *one* exam, I seem to do better than other people. Never—Almost always. (14)

6. I look forward to exams. Never—Always. (16)

7. Although "cramming" under pre-ex-

amination tension is not effective for most people, I find that if the need arises, I can learn material immediately before an exam, even under considerable pressure, and successfully retain it to use on the exam. I am always able to use the "crammed" material successfully—I am never able to use the "crammed" material successfully. (19)

8. I enjoy taking a difficult exam more than an easy one. Always—Never. (21)

9. The more important the exam or test, the better I seem to do. This is true of me —This is not true of me. (24)

Debilitating Anxiety Scale

1. Nervousness while taking an exam or test hinders me from doing well. Always—Never. (1)

2. In a course where I have been doing poorly, my fear of a bad grade cuts down my efficiency. Never—Always. (3)

3. When I am poorly prepared for an exam or test, I get upset, and do less well than even my restricted knowledge should allow. This never happens to me—This practically always happens to me. (5)

4. The more important the examination, the less well I seem to do. Always—Never. (6)

5. During exams or tests, I block on questions to which I know the answers, even though I might remember them as soon as the exam is over. This always happens to me—I never block on questions to which I know the answers. (10)

6. I find that my mind goes blank at the beginning of an exam, and it takes me a few minutes before I can function. I almost always blank out at first—I never blank out at first. (15)

7. I am so tired from worrying about an exam, that I find I almost don't care how well I do by the time I start the test. I never feel this way—I almost always feel this way. (17)

8. Time pressure on an exam causes me to do worse than the rest of the group under similar conditions. Time pressure always seems to make me do worse on an exam than others—Time pressure never seems to make me do worse on an exam than others. (18)

9. I find myself reading exam questions without understanding them, and I must go back over them so that they will make sense. Never—Almost always. (23)

10. When I don't do well on a difficult item at the beginning of an exam, it tends to upset me so that I block on even easy questions later on. This never happens to me—This almost always happens to me. (26)

Part of the refinement of the scales was accomplished through means of empirical techniques. After a large number of items had been constructed for each scale, the scales were used to predict several performance criteria, such as grade-point averages and final examination grades. These data were item-analyzed to give the correlation of each item with the criterion. Those items were retained which were highly correlated with the criteria but which were not correlated with each other. In this way, it was hoped to minimize the intercorrelation of the scales without affecting their validity coefficients. The final correlations between the facilitating and debilitating scales were $-.37$, $-.34$, $-.43$, and $-.48$, drawn from four different samples. For these four samples, the average means and standard deviations for the facilitating and debilitating scales of the AAT were as follows: for the AAT+, $M = 27.28$, $SD = 4.27$; for the AAT−, $M = 26.33$, $SD = 5.33$. The average correlation for the combined N (379) was $-.37$. All these correlations are significant beyond the 1% level. Hence, in spite of efforts to separate the two scales empirically, a low but significant correlation remains. The point seems made, however, that the correlation is neither perfect nor high as Mandler and Sarason imply and require as an assumption for the use of their scale.

In general, the two scales of the AAT correlated about equally, though oppo-

TABLE 6

MULTIPLE CORRELATIONS PREDICTING
GRADE-POINT AVERAGE (GPA)
FROM THE AAT

N	R[a]	r[b]	r[c]	r[d]	p[e]	p[f]
93	.50	.36	−.45	−.37	.001	.05
92	.32	.32	−.08	−.34	ns	.01
96	.54	.50	−.40	−.43	.05	.001

[a] GPA · AAT+ & AAT−.
[b] GPA · AAT+.
[c] GPA · AAT−.
[d] AAT− · AAT+.
[e] Significance of adding AAT−.
[f] Significance of adding AAT+.

site in sign, with the other variables discussed in this paper (see Tables 1, 2, and 3). The important question is whether, when predicting an academic performance score such as college grade-point average, there is any advantage in using both scales rather than using merely a conventional debilitating anxiety scale such as the AAT− alone or the Mandler and Sarason TAS. These two measures of debilitating anxiety (the AAT− and the TAS) correlate .64 with an N of 40, indicating considerable equivalence. Table 6 answers the question of whether a scale which measures the facilitating effect of anxiety justifies itself. In the last two columns to Table 6 it can be seen that for three separate samples, the multiple correlations, using both the plus and minus scales to predict grade-point average, are significantly better predictors than the minus or the plus scales alone.

It seems clear, therefore, that the incorporation of items designed to measure facilitating anxiety into a scale which already effectively measures debilitating anxiety can significantly increase the prediction of academic performance scores.

Summary: The results support the following conclusions:

1. Specific anxiety scales (scales having items specific to the academic test situation) and general anxiety scales are measuring, to a significant extent, something different from one another.

2. The specific anxiety scales are better predictors of academic performance than are the general anxiety scales.

3. The general anxiety scales are not significantly related to verbal aptitude, while the specific anxiety scales are all related to aptitude.

4. The specific anxiety scales, although more highly correlated with aptitude than the general anxiety scales, are, nevertheless, more often than the general anxiety scales, able to account for variance in academic performance other than that accounted for by a measure of aptitude.

5. An explanation of the relationship between anxiety scales and measure of aptitude, based on the use of an anxiety scale as a vehicle for rationalization or justification by students with poor past performance in academic situations, is not supported by these data.

6. On the basis of these data, no conclusion may be reached about explanations of the relationship between anxiety scales and measures of aptitude on the assumption that aptitude scores are, themselves, affected by anxiety. A possible experiment which may clarify this issue is suggested.

A scale for the measurement of "facilitating" anxiety was constructed, which added significantly to the prediction of grade-point average when it was combined with a measure of "debilitating" anxiety. The theoretical and practical significance of these findings was discussed.

Psychological Review, 1961, vol. 68, pp. 396–404

Anxiety, Pain, and the Inhibition of Distress[1]

William Kessen and George Mandler

Theories of anxiety have been developed from evidence as diverse as the avoidance behavior of animals and the symptomatic behavior of human neurotics; the language of these theories ranges from existentialism to learning theory. For all the differences in detail, however, there is a remarkable similarity in the approach of different theorists to the problem of anxiety.[2]

We will, in the present paper, examine the proposition that these theoretical communalities do not fully encompass available data about human and animal distress and then go on to present several theoretical propositions supplementary to current theories of anxiety.

[1] Parts of this paper were read at the 1960 meetings of the Western Psychological Association at San Jose, California; it was written during the authors' stay at the Center for Advanced Study in the Behavioral Sciences, Stanford, California, and was prepared in relation to USPHS Research Grants M-1787 and M-2442.

[2] "Anxiety" has come to be one of psychology's umbrella constructs; it covers so wide an area of research and speculation that no precise specification of its usages is possible. Nonetheless, as in the case of "learning" or "perception," "anxiety" is a useful summary expression for a set of different but related observations (see Mandler & Kessen, 1959, for a discussion of problems in the definition of theoretical terms). The theoretical differentiations which are proposed here are held to be relevant to the study of avoidance behavior, of physiological indicators of visceral disturbance, and of reported phenomenal distress.

Briefly and without extenuation, the following shared characteristics of contemporary theories of anxiety can be noted. First, there exists an archetypical event or class of events which evokes anxiety primitively or innately or congenitally. For Freud (1936), this original inciter was overstimulation; for Mowrer (1939), it is pain; for Miller (1951), the "innate fear reaction"; for Rank (1929), birth trauma; for Selye (1956), stress; for the existentialists, it is the very fact of being human and alive. The second communality in theories about anxiety is the postulation that, somehow, the response to the archetypical event is transferred to previously innocuous events, events either in the external environment or in the action of the organism. The typical assumption has been that this association takes place with contiguous occurrence of trauma and neutral event, although the students of human learning have been more detailed than this in discussing the conditioning of fear (see, for example, Dollard & Miller, 1950). Finally, it is assumed that the events terminating or reducing anxiety are closely related to the events which evoke it. Thus, the primitive danger of overstimulation is controlled by a reduction in level of stimulation; similarly, the "fear" of electric shock is reduced by moving away from events associated with shock, presumably in inverse analog to the model of hunger and thirst, where a deficit of some substance (deprivation) is repaired by its replacement (eating or drinking).

These common elements of present day conceptions of anxiety—the archetypical evoker, the mechanism for association to previously neutral events, and the parallelarity of the elicitation and the reduction of anxiety—have produced discernible biases in contemporary psychology. In theory, in research, and apparently in therapy, the problem of anxiety has come to be, on one hand, largely a problem of trauma —that is, what events set off the anxiety—and on the other hand, largely a problem of flight—that is, what responses will lead away from the inciting event. In what follows, we will examine the place of the "trauma" or "archetype" notion by examining in detail the best candidate for primary primitive evoker of anxiety—pain—and then we will go on to a consideration of a position that is alternative to, but not necessarily incompatible with, the common elements of anxiety theory sketched out here.[3]

Death of Pain

We will defend the position—coming to be widely held in American psychology—that a theory of anxiety based solely on pain as an archetypical precondition is untenable. The evidence at hand suggests two conclusions: first, that pain is not a necessary condition

[3] No attention will be given to the problem of individual differences in anxiety (Mandler & Sarason, 1952; Taylor, 1953); presumably they can be represented, at least theoretically, as parametric variations of the general theoretical formulations which we are considering in this paper.

for the development of anxiety and avoidance behavior; and second, that when pain is apparently a sufficient condition for the development of anxiety, there is at work a variety of factors rather than a single innate link.

There are three areas of evidence that support the conclusion that anxiety can occur even when pain does not occur. First, there are external events other than pain which arouse, without prior experience of association with pain, behavior which bears the marks of distress or anxiety. Of particular interest to our argument in the next section are the startle and distress responses of the newborn human infant to loud noise or to loss of support (Peiper, 1956; Watson, 1919). Among animals, escape, avoidance, and species-appropriate signs of distress to nonpainful events have been reported in abundance by ethologists; the mobbing of chaffinches at the appearance of an owl reported by Hinde (1954) is an example in point. Unless a severe twist is given to the behavioral interpretation of "anxiety," these cases, among others, stand against the Original Pain principle.

More striking as a demonstration of the separability of pain and anxiety is the behavior of human beings afflicted with congenital analgesia. This apparently inherited syndrome consists typically of a complete absence of pain sensitivity despite otherwise normal registration of the environment. A review of the 30-odd cases reported in the literature (Fanconi & Ferrazzini, 1957) shows the severely debilitating effects accompanying the absence of pain mechanisms. The patients are usually discovered to be mutilated during childhood; undiscovered fractures, scarred tongues and limbs, are among the injuries found. Despite the fact that these patients fail to develop specific adaptive avoidance behavior in the face of many injurious and noxious situations, anxiety toward other—nonpainful—events always seems to develop normally. The conclusion applied to one such case by West and Farber (1960) can be generalized to all observed cases of congenital analgesia: "anxiety plays a motivating role in determinating certain aspects of the patient's behavior." In brief, the development of anxiety and avoidance behavior is not halted by the absence of pain sensitivity, even though the avoidance of normally painful events is absent.

The foregoing two points have shown that distress will develop in the absence of pain. A third collection of evidence supports the assertion of the disjunction without conclusively demonstrating the absence of an association with pain, but the data, when seen all in a row, strongly indict an exclusive commitment to a pain-traumatic theory of anxiety. We refer here to the occurrence of anxiety or discomfort when highly practiced and well organized responses are interrupted. The early research of Lewin and his students and that of more recent workers (for example, Lewin, 1935; Marquis, 1943) suggest that the interruption of highly motivated, well-integrated behavior arouses emotional responses much like anxiety. To these data can be added the research on emotional responses of animals to frustration (for example, Marx, 1956). Similar and perhaps more revealing phenomena can be observed in young infants where, usually after and rarely before the sixth month of life, both the appearance of a stranger and the disappearance of the mother can give rise to signs of extreme distress. The fear shown by chimpanzees when confronted with the severed heads of other chimpanzees (Hebb, 1946) is another case which falls into this category of distress consequent on extreme perceptual discrepancy. It is at least difficult to fit these cases to a theory of anxiety which depends primitively on pain or any other archetypical trauma.

If it can be agreed that pain is not a necessary condition for the development of anxiety, another question comes to the fore. To what degree or in what fashion is pain a sufficient antecedent condition for the development of anxiety? The skeptical answer that appears to be warranted by the evidence is that the relation between pain and anxiety is rarely simple or obvious, and further that attention to the distinction between pain as a sensory event and the distress reaction which usually but does not always accompany pain may clarify the complexity somewhat. The presentation of this line of discourse is made easier by the recent appearance of a stimulating review by Barber (1959) of problems associated with pain. We will, therefore, only summarize what seem to be legitimate supports for the two-or-more-factor theory of pain and then move on to a more extended treatment of the nature of distress.

There is some, though admittedly very little, evidence that the appearance of discomfort with painful stimulation requires early experience of as-yet-unknown character. Puppies raised by Melzack and Scott (1957) in a restricted environment showed indifference to stimulation painful to normal dogs and great difficulty in learning to avoid objects associated with pain. These observations are of crucial importance to speculations about anxiety and warrant replication and extension. In human infants, there is a striking temporal difference between the first "defensive" response to painful stimulation (withdrawal or startle) and the second "distressful" response (crying, increased motility, and so on). Peiper (1956) reports that the first response has a latency of 0.2 second while the second response has a latency as high as 5–7 seconds.

A similar separability of what might be called cognitive pain and distress occurs in some cases of prefrontal surgical interference to deal with intractable pain. Barber (1959), in reviewing the evidence, concludes:

When prefrontal leucotomy alleviates intractable pain it does not necessarily elevate the pain threshold or alter "the sensation of pain." . . . [Further,] with few, if any, exceptions, investigators report that the "sensation" or "perception" of pain is practically unaltered by any of these procedures (p. 438).

Finally, Barber suggests that noxious painful stimulation has wide cortical effects and argues against a neurology of pain based exclusively on specific pain pathways or pain areas. The discomfort-pain association seems to depend on extensive cortical organization —in the words of the present argument, on experience of pain and discomfort.

The death of pain as original in all anxiety does not rule out alternative formulations of the traumatic or archetypical variety. Solomon and Brush (1956), for example, have taken students of aversive behavior to task for neglecting the investigation of noxious stimuli other than electric shock. When they ask, "Are all aversive anticipatory states alike?" they point to one alternative suggested by the elimination of pain as the sole antecedent of anxiety.

Another alternative, which will be explored here, is to examine a postulation of anxiety which is independent not only of pain, but of any archetypical traumatic event.

Nature of Fundamental Distress

It is our contention that a nontraumatic theory of the sources of anxiety can be defended and, further, that anxiety may be reduced or terminated by devices other than escape from and avoidance of threat. These alternative formulations are proposed as supplements to, rather than as substitutes for, the archetypical theories of anxiety.

The schematic model suggested here for the occurrence of anxiety—in distinction from the classical model of the organism fleeing the associations of pain—is the cyclical distress of the human newborn. There may be antecedent events which could account for the crying and increased activity we recognize as distressful in the young infant—for example, food privation, shifts in temperature, and so on—but *it is not necessary to specify or even to assume such a specific antecedent event.* It is a defensible proposition that the strong bent of the archetypical formulations to study those conditions of distress for which a specific evoker could be discerned seriously limits the range of proper investigation. The distress of the human newborn, as obviously "anxious" as a rat in a shuttle box, can be taken as an example of human anxiety and as a starting point for changes in speculations about human emotion, regardless of the absence of known or well-guessed "unconditioned" archetypical evokers. More than that, this modification suggests that there are cases in which the old and respected saw about anxiety as the conditioned form of the stimulus-specific fear reaction may be misleading; that is, there may be interesting cases in which a stimulus-specific fear (as indicated by flight or avoidance) may be better understood as a conditioned form of primitive anxiety or *fundamental distress*.[4]

To see anxiety as fundamental distress raises the ghosts of an old dispute in psychology—that between James and Cannon on the nature of emotion. Let us take a further theoretical step and suggest that the crucial event in fundamental distress is the perception or afferent effect of variable and intense autonomic, visceral activity. This is a rough restatement of James' position that emotions are the results of the perception of visceral events or are those perceptions themselves (James, 1890). Most of Cannon's counterarguments to such a position are not relevant to the postulation of such an effect during early infancy, since his position depends to a large extent on the identification of external threatening stimuli —a feat beyond the powers of the newborn (Cannon, 1927). But Cannon's major argument that emotional reactions take place with a latency far shorter than the latency of autonomic reactions deserves particular attention here. The delayed emotional response of the infant cited earlier, as well as the variable, badly organized reactions of infants, suggests just such a delayed emotional mechanism as Cannon ascribes to James. If we assume further (cf. Mandler & Kremen, 1958) that these visceral reactions are eventually represented centrally (in other words, that

"central" anxiety short-circuits visceral events), then ascription of a developmental shift from a Jamesian to a Cannonic mechanism becomes plausible.[5] A closely related point was recently made by Schneirla (1959):

although the James-Lange type of theory provides a useful basis for studying the early ontogeny of mammals, . . . a Cannon-type theory of higher-center control is *indispensable* for later stages of perceptual and motivational development. If ontogeny progresses well, specialized patterns of [approach] and [withdrawal] . . ., or their combinations, perceptually controlled, often short-circuit or modify the early viscerally dominated versions (p. 26).

One final comment on the nature of distress is warranted. It is not assumed that the distress reaction is usually terminated suddenly by the occurrence of an escape or of an avoidance response. Rather, we assume that, except for a few laboratory situations, the distress reaction is reverberatory in character. Particular events or responses do not terminate the anxiety immediately; moreover, the distress reaction will serve as a signal for further distress. Depending on partially understood environmental and organismic conditions, these reverberations will augment the initial anxiety (see Mednick, 1958) or gradually damp out and disappear.

In short, fundamental distress is held to be a state of discomfort, unease, or anxiety which bears no clear or neces-

4 Auersperg (1958) has presented a treatment of "fundamental anxiety" (*Fundamentalangst*) which bears on the present discussion.

5 The argument that visceral discomfort may become centrally represented does not necessarily imply that the visceral response will not thereafter occur; the postulation of central representation is required to explain the quick and efficient reaction of the adult to threatening events. However, given the possibility of rapid removal from the situation of threat, the "postthreat" visceral response may in fact not occur. Recent research by Solomon and Wynne (1954) supports a similar interpretation.

sary relation to a specific antecedent event (archetypical evoker). The model or "ideal case" of fundamental distress is held to be the recurrent distress of the human newborn. Examination of the notion of anxiety in the light of these propositions is compatible with a resolution of the conflict between James' and Cannon's views on the nature of emotion. What remains for consideration is an examination of the occasions of reduction or termination of anxiety and the relation of such occasions to fundamental distress.

Inhibition of Anxiety

The second departure from conventional views of anxiety has to do with techniques for the reduction or termination of anxiety. It is proposed that, in addition to the classical mechanisms of escape and avoidance of danger, anxiety is brought under control (that is, diminished or removed) by the operation of *specific inhibitors*. Before moving on to a discussion of the inhibitory mechanism, however, we must emphasize a point that is implicit in the foregoing treatment. The undifferentiated discomfort of the infant which we have taken as an example of fundamental distress may accompany particular conditions of need or drive; that is, the newborn may be hungry *and* distressed, thirsty *and* distressed, cold *and* distressed, and so on. With the removal of the privation or drive, the distress may disappear, but this reduction by the repair of a deficit—which is formally equivalent with escape from danger—is not of primary interest in the present discussion. Rather, our concern is with those responses of the organism and events in the environment which inhibit distress, *regardless of their rela-

tion to a specifiable need, drive, or privation.*

Anecdotal evidence of the operation of congenital inhibitors of anxiety in infants abounds, but there has been relatively little systematic exploration of these inhibitors in the newly born, human or animal. However, two recent empirical studies will serve to illustrate the character of the inhibitory mechanism; one of them is based on a response of the infant, the other on a particular pattern in the environment. Research by Kessen and his associates has shown that infant distress, as indicated by crying and hyperactivity, is dramatically reduced by the occurrence of empty—that is, nonnutritive—sucking as early as the fourth day of life. The performance of the congenital sucking response on a rubber nipple stuffed with cloth brings the newborn to a condition of motor and vocal quiescence. Thus, sucking appears to fit the pattern of the congenital inhibitor of distress, or, more broadly, of anxiety. Systematic observation of the effects of sucking on motility in the period immediately after birth will be necessary to demonstrate that the inhibition is not "secondary" to the experience of food. There can be cited the incidental observation that the hungry infant during the first days of life, with little or no experience of feeding, will quiet when given breast or bottle, even though it is unlikely that his hunger has been reduced during the first several sucking responses.

The second instance of distress-inhibition derives from Harlow's (1958) research with infant monkeys. These animals when distressed, whether by a frightful artificial Monster Rhesus or in the routine cyclicity of discomfort, seek out a situation—the experimental "mother"—which inhibits the distress. Harlow has made some provocative assumptions about the characteristics of the model which serve to reduce the infant monkey's distress and he has established an empirical procedure for testing them. What seems beyond doubt are the facts that a complex environmental event serves to terminate a condition of the animal that meets our usual criteria for the presence of anxiety and that this event bears no obvious relation to physiological privation or deficit.

There are undoubtedly several congenital or early developed inhibitors of distress which have not received adequate empirical examination; the quieting effects of rocking and the response of the 2-month-old infant to the adult face come to mind. A strong presumptive case can be made for the operation of a class of such distress terminators which do not depend for their effects on escape from or avoidance of an archetypical or traumatic evoker of distress.[6]

There is a further aspect of the problem of distress-inhibition which will illustrate the relation of fundamental distress and its inhibitors to anxiety of the archetypical variety. If distress is under control by the operation of an inhibitor, what is the effect of withdrawing the inhibitor? What, in other words, are the consequences of disinhibition of distress? For some occurrences

of some inhibitors—for example, rocking the hungry and distressful infant—it seems that disinhibition "releases" or "reinstates" the distress. For others—for example, sucking on the hands until asleep—the withdrawal of the inhibitor does not result in the recurrence of distress.

The following proposals can be made to deal with this kind of disjunction. Archetypical evokers (for example, pain, hunger) are accompanied by or lead to distress. This distress can usually be reduced in two quite distinct ways: by action of a specific inhibitor which reduces distress but does not necessarily affect the primitive evoker; or by changes acting directly on the level of the primitive evokers. The best example of how these mechanisms work together in nonlaboratory settings is nutritive sucking. The infant's *sucking* inhibits the fundamental distress accompanying hunger; at a slower rate, the *ingestion of food* "shuts off" the source of distress. It is maintained here that these two mechanisms for the reduction of distress or anxiety are profitably kept separate in psychological theory.[7]

The separation of distress reduction by specific inhibition and distress reduction by changes in archetypical evokers can be defended on other grounds as well. As noted earlier, much infantile (and later) distress is of a periodic variety without obvious relation to specific environmental evokers. Specific inhibitors may serve to tide the organism over the peaks of these distress cycles, whatever their source, until some other occurrence (for example, the on-

---

[6] One group of inhibitors of distress appears to be characterized by rhythmic periodicity: regular sounds, rocking, the nodding head of the adult, and so on. Investigation of the relation of this class of events to visceral rhythms would lead to increased precision in speculations about fundamental distress. It is interesting to speculate in this connection about the relation between distress-inhibition on one side and sympathetic-parasympathetic incompatibility on the other.

[7] These postulations are formally equivalent to the theory Deutsch (1960) has proposed to account for behavioral phenomena associated with hunger and thirst.

set of sleep) results in a more stable reduction of the level of organismic disturbance.

It is reasonable to assume that the inhibitory mechanism under discussion is not limited to the operation of primitive inhibitors early in development. Rather, events associated with inhibitors may, under appropriate circumstances, acquire learned or secondary inhibitory properties. Under this proposal, it can be maintained that the immediate "satisfying" effects of food may be ascribable to its association with the inhibition of distress by eating, rather than the other way round. F. D. Sheffield (unpublished) has proposed a mechanism for reinforcement which is closely akin to this argument.

With the foregoing reservations in view, we would argue finally that among the earliest differentiations the child makes are those that have to do with the handling of distress. Whether in regard to what we have called fundamental distress or in regard to distress set off by specific environmental events, much of early infant behavior can be related to the management of discomfort or unease. Furthermore, it is probably in these connections that the infant first learns about the consequences of interruption of organized response sequences or expectations. Just as it has been assumed that secondary inhibitors of distress can be developed, so it is assumed that learned signals of disinhibition—that is, the reinstatement of distress at the withdrawal of an inhibitor—can be developed over the course of infancy. Thus, the phenomenon of separation anxiety seen in the young child can be understood as the interruption of well-established inhibitory sequences. The failure of the mother to appear, that is, the omission of an important inhibitor, leads to the rearousal of distress.[8]

In short, anxiety is not only the trace of a trauma which must be fled, but is as well a condition of distress which can be met by the action of specific inhibitors. The model of fundamental distress and its inhibition which is proposed here may serve to provide a testable alternative to the current metaphysics of anxiety (May, Angel, & Ellenberger, 1958).

Summary: Contemporary theories of anxiety, while showing divergency in the statement of specific antecedents for and indicators of anxiety, have shared a dual emphasis. They have called on an archetypical evoker of anxiety (or trauma) to explain the first occurrences of anxiety and on the association of neutral events with the archetypical evoker in order to account for learned, symptomatic, or secondary anxiety. The second communality has been an emphasis on flight (escape or avoidance) from trauma or its signals as the basic mechanism for the control of anxiety.

We have presented evidence to suggest that the "flight from trauma" view of anxiety is incomplete. Specifically, the conception of pain as the sole source of later anxiety has been shown to be untenable.

Two supplements to the traumatic theory of anxiety were proposed. The burden of one was to point out the occurrence of anxiety or distress in the absence of any clearly discernible antecedent trauma. The periodic distress of the human newborn was taken as an example of this phenome-

---

[8] It is tempting to speculate that tendencies in the older organism to be active (Bühler's *Funktionslust*, 1930, or White's "competence motivation," 1959) may be related to the repeated arousal of distress as a consequence of the withdrawal or omission of a well-entrenched inhibitor of anxiety. In other words, the interruption of well-established behavior sequences may lead to anxiety and their continuation may ward it off. Such a position would suggest that in psychotherapy it may be as profitable for the patient to be able to complete interrupted behavior sequences as it is for him to avoid traumatic events.

non. The second modification suggested that anxiety may be controlled not only by flight from trauma and its signals but may be reduced by the action of specific inhibitors. These inhibitors may be responses of the organism (for example, the sucking

response of the newborn) or external environmental events (for example, Harlow's experimental "mother").

The implications of these supplementary proposals for a theory of anxiety were explored.

Psychological Review, 1955, vol. 62, pp. 378–390.

Relationships Between Shame and Guilt in the Socializing Process

David P. Ausubel

Guilt is one of the most important psychological mechanisms through which an individual becomes socialized in the ways of his culture. It is also an important instrument for cultural survival since it constitutes a most efficient watchdog within each individual, serving to keep his behavior compatible with the moral values of the society in which he lives. Without the aid rendered by guilt feelings, child rearing would be a difficult matter indeed. If children felt no sense of accountability or moral obligation to curb their hedonistic and irresponsible impulses, to conform to accepted social norms, or to acquire self-control, the socializing process would be slow, arduous, and incomplete. Sheer physical force, threat of pain, deprivation, and punishment, or withholding of love and approval would be the only available methods—combined with constant surveillance—to exact conformity to cultural standards of acceptable behavior. And since it is plainly evident that the maintenance of perpetual vigilance is impractical, that fear alone is never an effective deterrent against antisocial behavior, and

that the interests of personal expediency are not always in agreement with prescribed ethical norms, a social order unbuttressed by a sense of moral obligation in its members would enjoy precious little stability.

Within recent years, a number of social anthropologists (Benedict, 1946; Leighton & Kluckhohn, 1947; Mead, 1949; 1950) have advanced the notion that guilt is not universally present or prominent as a sanction in mediating and sustaining the culture. Instead they have identified guilt as a unique property of the characterology of individuals who as children experience the kinds of relationships with parents allowing for "superego" formation, that is, typically of persons growing up in cultures adhering to the Judaic-Christian tradition. Thus, among the Samoans, Iatmul, and Balinese, Margaret Mead believes that the culture is primarily transmitted through such external sanctions as expediency in conforming to the rules (1949, p. 514), shared, undifferentiated fear (1950, p. 369), and anticipation of physical reprisals (1950, p. 370), respectively. Ruth Benedict minimizes the importance of guilt and emphasizes the role of shame in regulating the social behavior of the Japanese (1946, p. 222). Leighton and Kluckhohn make the same point in reference to the Navaho: "Sensitivity to shame . . . largely takes the place that remorse and self-punishment have in preventing anti-social conduct in white society" (1947, p. 106). And even in characterizing the moral development of adolescents in our own society who undergo peer-group rather than parent-regulated socialization, Margaret Mead comments that "shame, the agony of being found wanting and exposed to the disapproval of others, becomes a more prominent sanction behind conduct than guilt, the fear of not measuring up to the high standard which was represented by the parents" (1949, p. 520).

In this paper we shall be concerned with a critical examination of the criteria that these anthropologists have used in differentiating between shame and guilt. We shall attempt to show that although the two kinds of sanctions are distinguishable from one another, they are nevertheless neither dichotomous nor mutually exclusive, and that the development of guilt feelings is not dependent upon highly specific aspects of a unique kind of parent-child relationship. Before turning to this task, however, it might be profitable to undertake a logical analysis of the developmental conditions under which the capacity for acquiring guilt behavior arises, as well as some of the basic relationships between shame and guilt. Because of the paucity of experimental or naturalistic evidence in this area of theoretical inquiry, it should be self-evident that the following paradigm is offered as a system of interrelated hypotheses rather than as an exposition of empirically established facts.

The Developmental Origins of Guilt

Guilt may be conceptualized as a special kind of negative self-evaluation which occurs when an individual acknowledges that his behavior is at variance with a given moral value to which he feels obligated to conform. It is a self-reaction to an injured conscience, if by conscience is meant an abstraction referring to a feeling of obligation to abide by all internalized moral values. The injury consists of a self-perceived violation of this obligation. Hence, in accordance with this formulation, one might hypothesize that before guilt feelings can become operative, the following developmental conditions must apply: (a) the individual must accept certain standards of right and wrong or good and bad as his own, (b) he must accept the obligation of regulating his behavior to conform to whatever standards he has thus adopted, and must feel accountable for lapses therefrom, and (c) he must possess sufficient self-critical ability to recognize when a discrepancy between behavior and internalized values occurs.

It goes without saying that none of these conditions can ever be satisfied at birth; under minimally favorable circumstances, however, all human beings should be potentially capable of acquiring the capacity for guilt behavior. Culture may make a difference in the form which this behavior takes and in the specific kinds of stimuli which instigate it; but the capacity itself should be so basically human and so fundamental to the sanctions by which social norms are maintained and transmitted to the young in any culture that differences among individuals within a culture would probably be as great as or greater than differences among cultures.

It is theoretically possible, of course, that in certain extreme cases a culture may be so anarchic and unstructured in terms of the obligations it engenders in its members that the potentiality for guilt experience is never realized, as, for example, among the Dobu (Benedict, 1934, p. 131). Ordinarily, however, we might expect that guilt feelings would be found universally; and, hence, the burden of proof regarding their alleged absence in a given culture more properly rests with the investigator making the allegation.

Despite the probable existence of many important culturally conditioned differences in children's acquisition of guilt behavior, there are presumptive grounds for believing that considerable communality prevails in the general pattern of sequential development. Such communality would be a product of various uniformities regarding (a) basic conditions of the parent-child relationship, (b) minimal cultural needs for socialization of the child, and (c) certain gross trends in cognitive and social growth that prevail from one culture to the next.

The cultural basis of conscience development in the individual may be found in the potent need of both parents and society to inculcate a sense of responsibility in the child. Not only the physical survival of its members, but also the perpetuation of its selective way of life is contingent upon the culture's degree of success in this undertaking. Thus, the attenuation of infantile irresponsibility might be consid-

ered part of the necessary process of ego devaluation and maturation that presumably characterizes personality development in all cultures. Socialization demands the learning of self-control and self-discipline, the subordination of personal desires to the needs and wishes of others, the acquisition of skills and self-sufficiency, the curbing of hedonistic and aggressive impulses, and the assimilation of culturally sanctioned patterns of behavior. It seems highly unlikely that any of these propensities could become thoroughly stable before conscience is firmly established.

We might postulate that the first step in the child's development of conscience involves his assimilation of parental values and standards.[1] Having no other frame of reference for judgments of good and bad, the prestige suggestion of parents easily holds sway. But acceptance of these values does not obligate him—in the absence of a still undeveloped sense of moral responsibility—to regulate his own behavior accordingly. Lapses on the part of *other* persons are perceived as "bad," but such judgments have no relevance for similar behavior of his *own* when gratification of his *own* impulses is at stake. At this stage of development his behavior can only be directed into acceptable channels by punishment or by anticipation of punishment in the form of pain, deprivation, ridicule, threatened separation from the parent, etc. Conformity to ethical standards, therefore, is "devoid of moral implications because it is only indicative of submis-

[1] In cultures characterized by an extended family group, or where persons other than parents take major responsibility for child rearing, both value assimilation and the subsequent development of moral obligation have from the very beginning a wider social base.

sion to authority rather than acceptance of it" (Ausubel, 1952, p. 122).

Behavior can first be regarded as manifesting moral properties when a sense of obligation is acquired. The central hypothesis of the present formulation is that this development typically takes place in children who are accepted and intrinsically valued by parents, and who thereby acquire a derived or vicarious status in consequence of this acceptance. By the fiat of parental acceptance they are provided with intrinsic feelings of security and adequacy despite their manifest dependency and incompetence to fend for themselves. They accordingly become disposed to accept parental values implicitly and unconditionally out of loyalty to the individuals[1] to whom they owe their status and self-esteem. Among other standards assimilated in this uncritical and subservient fashion "is the feeling of moral responsibility or accountability to conform to standards of behavior which have been given ethical implications. . . . Unlike other values which are ends in themselves, moral responsibility has [the] regulatory function of compelling adherence to internalized norms of behavior" (Ausubel, 1952, p. 135).

It is reasonable to suppose, however, that the inhibition of unacceptable behavior by feelings of personal loyalty and accountability, by the child's recognition of his parents' moral authority, and by his desire to avoid the self-punishing consequences of guilt develops relatively slowly. The old external sanctions of pain, punishment, threat, and ridicule continue to be applied, reinforced now by the more meaningful threat of withdrawal of love and approval. Delaying the consolidation of guilt behavior is the slow growth of both the self-critical faculty (making perception of discrepancies between precept and conduct difficult) and of the ability to generalize principles of right and wrong beyond specific situations.

During preadolescence and adolescence, as the child begins to lose his volitional dependence upon parents and becomes more concerned both with a primary status based upon his own competencies and with equal membership in the social order, the basis of conscience and guilt behavior apparently undergoes significant change. As Piaget has shown, greater experience in interpersonal relationships and in playing differentiated roles in complex social activities makes him more inclined to interpret rules of conduct as functional contrivances designed to facilitate social organization and interaction rather than as sacred and axiomatic givens (1932b, p. 106). Concomitantly, he develops a notion of moral law based upon principles of equity and embodying a system of reciprocal as opposed to unilateral moral obligations (1932, p. 387). The absolutism of his moral standards also tends to be weakened by his greater need for self-enhancement as an individual in his own right —a need that no longer favors unconditional adherence to an uncompromisable set of parental standards, and places a greater premium on the value of expediency. Finally, once the individual acquires this functional concept of moral law, conceives of himself as an independent entity striving for primary status in a social community, and recognizes the reciprocal nature of obligation, he completes the process of transferring "his feeling of moral accountability from parents to the moral authority of society" (Ausubel, 1952, p. 482).

In heterogeneous cultures, values tend to acquire a wider social base during adolescence. The individual is exposed to a variety of ethical standards and can, within limits, choose between alternative moral systems. And where the peer group plays the major role in adolescent socialization, parents are replaced by peers as the chief interpreters and enforcers of the moral code and, to some extent, as the source of moral authority. But neither set of conditions is essential for the maturational changes in the nature of moral organization that take place during and subsequent to preadolescence (Mead, 1949, p. 519; Nichols, 1930, p. 96). In certain homogeneous cultures also, the source of moral values and authority is referred almost from the beginning to persons outside the immediate family circle (Leighton & Kluckholn, 1947, p. 51).

Atypical Development of Guilt Behavior

The above description of the original and subsequent development of guilt behavior is hypothesized as the more typical course of moral growth in most children. It presupposes that the latter can achieve derived feelings of status through the medium of a dependent parent-child relationship, and can consequently internalize both values and a sense of moral obligation on the implicit basis of personal loyalty. In all cultures, however, a variable number of parents are psychologically incapable of extending acceptance and intrinsic valuation to their offspring. Thus deprived of the self-esteem derived from the fiat of unconditional parental acceptance, such children are from the very beginning obliged to seek primary status and feelings of adequacy

on the basis of their own competencies and performance ability. Accordingly, the basis on which they internalize values and moral obligations might be expected to be correspondingly different.

It would serve no useful purpose here to speculate further on the possible atypical courses that conscience development could take in rejected and extrinsically valued children (Ausubel, 1952). However, there is less reason to believe that rejecting and extrinsically valuing attitudes characterize *all* parents in a few rare cultures than that they may be found among *some* parents in almost all cultures. Hence, we would hypothesize that the probability of finding some conscienceless individuals in every culture is greater than that of finding conscienceless cultures.

Classification of Shame and Guilt

Generally, shame may be defined as an unpleasant emotional reaction by an individual to an actual or presumed negative judgment of himself by others resulting in self-depreciation vis-à-vis the group. This definition of shame is inclusive of instances in which the persons passing judgment are valued either positively or negatively by the individual being judged (Mead, 1950, p. 367), and of both moral and nonmoral causes for the instigation of such negative judgments. Typical examples of nonmoral shame are embarrassment in committing a breach of propriety or in having one's bodily intimacy exposed to public scrutiny (Nuttin, 1950, p. 350), and "loss of face" resulting from exposure of ignorance or incompetency. Moral shame, on the other hand, is a reaction to the negative moral judgments of others. It is a prominent sanction in many cultures both before and subsequent to the development of conscience.

Moral shame can, in turn, be divided into two categories—internalized and noninternalized. The latter variety occurs when an individual reacts with self-depreciation to the moral condemnation of others, but does not accept the moral value to which he has failed to conform, e.g., a young child may be shamed by being caught in a lie even if he does not accept the judgment that lying is wrong. Essential for this type of shame is the presence of witnesses to or eventual discovery of the misdeed in question. When the value is internalized, e.g., when the child *really* believes that lying is opprobrious, actual discovery is unnecessary; shame can result merely from presumed or fantasied reproach. Under the influence of such unwitnessed shame, the Ojibway may commit suicide (Mead, 1950, p. 367). According to Margaret Mead, internalized shame only occurs when the parent is the interpreter and enforcer of the sanction (Mead, 1950, p. 366). Observation of closely-knit adolescent peer groups, however, seem to indicate that genuine shame may occur when adolescents perceive or fantasy the moral disapproval of their fellows for offenses against norms established and enforced by the group itself.

The shame associated with guilt may be considered a special case of moral shame. In addition to an internalized moral value, a personal obligation to abide by that value is at stake, e.g., the child not only believes that lying is wrong and feels shame by experiencing or imagining the censure of others, but also feels shame in fantasying the reproach of others for violating a moral obligation. In either case an actual audience is unnecessary, but a presumed or fantasied judgment by others is. However, it is important to emphasize at this point that shame is only one component of guilt, the component involving external judgment and sanction. Guilt also involves other *self-reactions* that are independent of the judgment of others, namely, self-reproach, self-disgust, self-contempt, remorse, lowered self-esteem, anxiety, and various characteristic and subjectively identifiable visceral and vasomotor responses. And conversely, the shame of guilt is only one of many kinds of shame. Thus, the presence of guilt-related shame does not preclude the simultaneous operation of other forms of moral or nonmoral shame unassociated with guilt; nor does the excitation of any of these kinds of shame (associated or unassociated with guilt) preclude the operation of the various self-judgments characterizing guilt feelings.

Shame relies on external sanctions alone. Guilt relies on both internal and external sanctions. The latter sanctions consist of the presumed judgments of others regarding one's lapses with respect to moral obligations and the resulting self-depreciation vis-à-vis the group, as well as the customary social reprisals associated with the misdemeanors arousing guilt. In addition, feelings of guilt have external reference in that they acknowledge accountability for a moral offense against the group.

In the following section we shall critically appraise (a) the views of Margaret Mead and of Leighton and Kluckhohn, who hold that the development of guilt behavior requires a parent-child relationship in which an omniscient parent is the referent for and the source of moral authority, in addition to personally administering and interpreting moral sanctions (Mead, 1950, pp. 366, 367); and (b) Ruth Benedict's position that guilt is shameless, involves no external sanctions, and is concerned with inner convictions of sin (1946, pp. 222–223).

Ethnocentric Distinctions Between Shame and Guilt

SUPEREGO MODELS OF GUILT

The first ethnocentric conception of guilt referred to above equates the capacity for experiencing guilt feelings with neo-Freudian notions of superego formation. According to this conception, guilt feelings cannot arise unless the conditions essential for superego formation are not only present in childhood but are also maintained in subsequent years. Hence, guilt-like behavior in our own or other cultures that does not conform to these conditions is categorized as shame. The two basic conditions that are laid down for the development of guilt are: (a) the child must accept the parent or parent surrogate as omniscient or as qualitatively superior to himself in a moral sense, and (b) he must accept the parent as the source of moral authority, i.e., as the "referent" in whose name moral behavior is enjoined.

In reference to the former condition Margaret Mead states:

The adults in the society must think of the child as qualitatively different from themselves, in that the child has not yet attained their moral stature, but is subject to innate impulses which, if permitted unchecked expression, would eventuate in adult character different from and morally inferior to that of the parent (1949, p. 514).

Leighton and Kluckhohn similarly characterize guilt feelings as representing an individual's acknowledgment that he is "unworthy . . . for not living up to the high standards represented by [his] parents" (1947, p. 106). In explaining why "Navaho sensitivity to shame takes the place of guilt in our society," they go on to say:

"Conscience" is related to the belief in an omnipotent God who knows all. . . . In white society the child doesn't see the parent in many life situations. [But] in the circumstances of Navaho life a pose of omnipotence or omniscience on the part of parents would be speedily and almost daily exposed (1947, p. 106).

Only rarely does one hear the utterances on the part of Navaho parents which are so usual among white parents: "Do it because I say it is right," "do it because I say so," "do it because I am your father and children must obey their parents" (1947, p. 53).

In the first place, one may legitimately question the assumption that children do not acquire moral obligations unless a highly authoritarian, paternalistic, and hierarchical parent-child relationship exists, unless the parent sets himself up and is perceived as a qualitatively superior paragon of virtue. As long as the conditions for acquiring derived status are fulfilled, it seems reasonable to suppose that moral obligations are incurred provided that parents or parent surrogates make such expectations unambiguously clear. It undoubtedly increases the prestige suggestion with which the standards and expectations of parents are endowed if the latter individuals are perceived as omniscient; but there is neither convincing logical nor empirical justification for designating this criterion as a *sine qua non* for the acquisition of guilt behavior.

A second difficulty confronting the proposition that qualitative hierarchical distinctions must prevail between preceptor and learner in order for guilt feelings to develop is the suggestive evidence of Piaget, referred to above, showing that as children approach adolescence in our culture they become increasingly concerned with moral obligations based on principles of reciprocity (1932, pp. 106, 387). Cooperative and functional relationships with peers engender notions of obligation reflecting mutual respect between equals which gradually displace unilateral feelings of obligation based on implicit acceptance of authority (1932, p. 106).

The second condition imposed by adherents of the superego model of guilt behavior, i.e., that parents or parent surrogates must serve as the source of moral authority, runs into similar difficulties posed by developmental shifts in the organization of conscience. It presupposes, in the words of Margaret Mead, that

. . . teachers, the clergy, judicial officials, etc., partake of the character of the judging parent who metes out reward to the individual child (or, later, adult) who makes a satisfactory approximation to the desired behavior, and punishment to him who does not (1949, p. 514).

Such a requirement arbitrarily eliminates the possibility of guilt behavior developing in cultures like the Navaho where the authority for moral sanctions is from the earliest days of socialization referred to the group as a whole (Leighton & Kluckhohn, 1947, p. 51). The same criterion rules out the occurrence of guilt behavior among (a) adolescents in our own culture who accept the peer group as their major source of moral authority (see earlier quotation from Margaret Mead), (b) rejected and extrinsically valued children who never accept the moral authority of parents, but who may accept rational principles of equity and the moral authority of the group, and (c) adults in most cultures, who, in accordance with the developmental changes described above, transfer their allegiances from the moral authority of parents to the moral authority of society. The latter process does not necessarily require the intermediate adolescent step of repudiating adult authority and substituting peer standards. Sufficient for this outcome is a transformation of the basis upon which the authority of elders is accepted, i.e., a change from implicit acceptance of axiomatic truth by a dependent and ideationally subservient individual to a more rational acceptance of functionally necessary norms growing out of interpersonal relations by an independent member of adult society (Nichols, 1930, pp. 95–96).

To deny that guilt feelings can arise in the above four situations requires summary dismissal of the evidence of everyday experience with the behavioral content of others. It is admittedly difficult to evaluate the subjective emotional experience of other persons, particularly if they happen to be members of different cultures. Logical inference must always supplement the perceptions of even the most experienced observer. Nevertheless a decision regarding the meaning of behavior can never be reached on the basis of a priori criteria alone, especially when these lack irrefutable logical or face validity. An emotion is adjudged to be guilt or shame on the basis of its behavioral characteristics, its situational excitants, and its subjective properties, and not because it fails to meet certain arbitrary ethnocentric criteria that apply to a single culture or phase of development. In the next section we shall examine some ethnological materials presented by Leighton and Kluckhohn and by Ruth Benedict as illustrative of shame and show how such behavior can be more defensibly interpreted as guilt.

A conception of conscience or guilt behavior that makes no provision for developmental changes in the underlying personality structure upon which such behavior depends cannot be successfully integrated into any self-consistent theory of personality development. A theoretical framework must be found that is broad enough to encompass the guilt behavior of a child of eight and likewise of an adult of eighteen or eighty. We cannot conclude that eighteen-year-old guilt must be shame because it does not conform to an eight-year-old model of guilt.

Personality development is admittedly characterized by continuity as well as by change. A tendency to accept values and obligations uncritically, on the basis of personal allegiances, still continues in adult life. Similarly, early attitudes of unconditional loyalty to moral obligations tend to persist long beyond the span of childhood. Nevertheless although these continuing trends add much to the stability of conscience, they are largely supplanted by different moral orientations and enjoy only substrate existence in a generally changed gestalt. A precipitate of the experiences of the eight-year-old is represented in the behavior of the eighteen-year-old, but this precipitate has a phenomenologically different meaning and significance than its original form a decade earlier.

Pointing up the logical as well as the empirical untenability of a criterion of guilt that requires a qualitatively superior parent or parent surrogate as the source of moral authority is the discrepancy on this score between the two chief examples of allegedly "shaming cultures," i.e., certain North American Indian tribes and the Japanese. Leighton and Kluckhohn characterize the Navaho as a "shaming culture" in part because sanctions are applied laterally rather than from above, and are referred to group rather than to parental authority (1947, pp. 105–106). On the other hand, Ruth Benedict, using other criteria, regards the Japanese as a shaming culture despite the fact that the Japanese family is the ethnological example par excellence of unconditionally accepted, paternalistic (if not arbitrarily imposed) authority based upon hierarchical position (1946, pp. 55–57, 264). Obviously, then, this criterion for distinguishing between shame and guilt has little claim to universality.

GUILT AS A SHAMELESS, WHOLLY INTERNALIZED CONVICTION OF SIN

The second major ethnocentric (and psychoanalytically oriented) conception of guilt assumes that guilt and shame are mutually incompatible and that genuine guilt must be devoid of shame and all external sanctions. Thus, in cultures where shame plays a more prominent role in behavioral control than in our own culture, ethnologists sharing this conception of guilt have insisted that guilt feelings must *ipso facto* be either nonexistent or of negligible significance. Among the Japanese, according to Gorer, "mockery is the most important and most effective sanction for obtaining conformity in social life" (1942, p. 20). Ruth Benedict espouses the same opinion in stating that "shame has the same place of authority in Japanese ethics that 'a clear conscience,' 'being right with God,' and avoidance of sin have in Western ethics" (1946, p. 224). Leighton and Kluckhohn claim that Navahos do not internalize the "standards of their parents and elders," and that shame ("I would feel very uncomfortable if anyone saw me deviating from accepted norms") is the major deterrent to antisocial behavior (1947, p. 106). Margaret Mead goes even further by ruling out the occurrence of both guilt and shame in the sanction systems of the Samoans (1949, pp. 514–515), Balinese (1950, p. 369), and Iatmul (1950, pp. 369–370), and insisting that only such external sanctions as fear, expediency, and threat of physical reprisals are operative.

This dichotomization of shame and guilt, of internal and external sanctions, in addition to lacking logical self-consistency, simply does not conform to available naturalistic evidence. Both moral and nonmoral shame may be extremely important sanctions in a given culture, but they preclude the occurrence of neither the public (shame) nor the private (self-judgment) aspects of guilt. A culture so unstable and so anarchic that its members fail to respond to internal sanctions (i.e., feelings of moral obligation) is indeed an ethnological rarity. The inhabitants of Dobu (Benedict, 1934) may fit this description, but the case made out for the Samoans, Iatmul, and Balinese (Mead, 1949; 1950) is far from convincing; and descriptions of Japanese (Benedict, 1946; La Barre, 1948) and Navaho (Leighton & Kluckhohn, 1947) behavior tend to disprove the very contentions they are meant to illustrate. Conversely, a culture in which external sanctions are *not* applied at any stage

of moral development is also rare enough to qualify as an ethnological oddity.

The evidence seems clear enough that although Japanese and Navaho individuals are more responsive to shame than we are, much of this shame is really the shame of guilt, i.e., the shame accompanying awareness of violated moral obligations. The predominant pattern of parent-child relationships in both cultures is one of acceptance and intrinsic valuation of the child, leading to the first or implicit stage of moral responsibility based upon personal loyalty (Benedict, 1946, Ch. 12; 7, Ch. 1). Navaho children acquire a sense of responsibility between five and eight years of age, learning assiduousness in executing their chores. They learn "that they cannot always indulge themselves and that they have duties toward others" (Leighton & Kluckholn, 1947, p. 58). Navaho parents are strikingly devoted and attentive to the needs of their children (Leighton & Kluckholn, 1947, pp. 13–33), and children, in turn, even as adults, are very devoted to their parents and siblings (Leighton & Kluckholn, 1947, pp. 94–100). The Navaho adult is capable of very responsible conduct in relation to his social group despite the fact that responsibility is "divided and shared" (Leighton & Kluckholn, 1947, p. 107). If such behavior is not indicative of internalized moral obligation, what other credible explanation is there? Surely shame alone could not account for all of it.

Among the Japanese an even stronger case can be made for the importance of conscience and guilt behavior. Few other cultures lay greater stress upon the sanctity of moral obligations. "The strong according to Japanese verdict are those who disregard personal happiness and fulfill their obligations. . . . A man is weak if he pays attention to his personal desires when they conflict with the code of obligations" (Benedict, 1946, pp. 207–208). Obligations to others must be fulfilled even if one dislikes the latter personally (Benedict, 1946, p. 124). The Japanese sense of accountability is especially stringent. "Each man must accept responsibility for the outcome of his acts. He must acknowledge and accept all natural consequences of his weakness, his lack of persistence, his ineffectualness" (Benedict, 1946, p. 296).

What is even more impressive is the fact that in contrast to prevailing attitudes in our own culture, the self-discipline, the self-restraint, and any of the personal disadvantages incurred in honoring obligations are not regarded as self-sacrifice. The fulfillment of obligations is taken for granted on the grounds of reciprocity, and calls for no applause, reward, self-pity, or self-righteousness (Benedict, 1946, pp. 230–233). The notions of mutual dependence and indebtedness to one's society and one's past lie at the very heart of the Japanese concept of obligation. "One repays one's debts to one's forbears by passing on to one's children the care one oneself received" (Benedict, 1946, p. 122).

Despite this overwhelming evidence of conscience and guilt behavior, Ruth Benedict is misled by the dichotomized conception of shame and guilt, and insists upon referring to such behavior as shame on the grounds that guilt is supposedly shameless. But, as already pointed out above, what she calls "shame" is actually the shame component of guilt. La Barre paints essentially the same picture of Japanese character structure as she does and reaches

a diametrically opposite conclusion. He asserts that the Japanese superego is exceedingly strong (1948, p. 329). Nevertheless, even while minimizing the role of guilt among the Japanese, Ruth Benedict is grudgingly obliged to admit the existence of moral self-judgments unrelated to external sanctions.

They [the Japanese] are terribly concerned about what other people will think of their behavior, and they are also overcome by guilt when other people know nothing of their misstep. . . . Japanese sometimes react as strongly as any Puritan to a private accumulation of guilt (1946, pp. 2–3, 222).

We cannot escape the conclusion, therefore, that both guilt and shame, and internal and external sanctions, can and do exist side by side and mutually reinforce each other. The assertion that "true shame cultures rely on external sanctions for good behavior, not, as true guilt cultures do, on an internalized conviction of sin" (Benedict, 1946, p. 323) is unsupported by available evidence. The presence of the stock, the pillory, and the ducking stool in the public market place offers eloquent refutation to the statement that "the early Puritans who settled in the United States tried to base their whole morality on guilt" (Benedict, 1946, p. 223). Reinforcing most of the moral sanctions that we customarily assign to the domain of conscience is a parallel set of statutes and group pressures enforced by appropriate public reprisals. Even in cultures where moral obligations are highly internalized, we usually find a policeman on the corner giving a friendly nudge to sluggish consciences or a timely warning to impish consciences pondering a brief vacation from duty.

The regulation of conduct by moral self-judgment is also the *final* step in a long developmental process. In controlling the behavior of children in our own culture, parents may differ from Samoan, Balinese, and Iatmul parents in their propensity for premature sermonizing about right and wrong, filial duty, virtue, etc. But during the first few years of life such preachments are but empty verbalisms to our children, who actually respond as do children in all cultures to the accompanying external sanctions of reward and punishment. Guilt feelings also have external reference by virtue of their shame component which involves a self-deprecatory reaction to the presumed or actual moral censure of others for a transgression of moral obligation. Finally, the external reference of guilt is apparent in the fact that it is reduced by punishment and confession. It always implies an offense against the group which, therefore, can only be pardoned by group action.[2]

Another source for ethnocentric misinterpretation of Japanese guilt behavior lies in their lack of preoccupation with sin. The idea of sin, however, is in no way indigenous to a conscience founded on moral obligation; it merely tends to be associated with a specific variety of guilt behavior that is influenced by certain religious traditions and notions about the original nature of man. Nevertheless, by equating guilt with "an internalized conviction of sin" (Benedict, 1946, p. 223), and conscience with "the avoidance of sin" (Benedict, 1946, p. 224), Ruth Benedict finds further "justification" for regarding the Japanese as relatively guiltless.

Japanese neglect of the problem of

sin, however, stems from two other sources that can hardly be interpreted as detracting from the genuineness of their expressions of guilt. In the first place, since they do not regard indulgence in physical pleasure as inherently evil—providing that it is properly subordinated to moral obligation—they do not share our notion of "original sin" or our conception of human nature as constantly in need of redemption from inherently sinful desires (Benedict, 1946, pp. 191–192). Secondly, since the fulfillment of obligation is taken for granted and is not regarded as self-sacrifice or as a victory of virtue over innately evil propensities, Japanese good conscience is not burdened with the self-righteousness that comes from conquering sin; and, similarly, guilt is not "internalized conviction of sin," but simply awareness of the breakdown of moral obligation.

Because the Japanese lay great stress on certain "external" (shame) aspects of self-respect, such as acting with circumspection and paying scrupulous attention to the details of propriety, Western observers are prone to deduce that this precludes their association of the term *self*-respect with a criterion such as "consciously conforming to a worthy standard of conduct" (Benedict, 1946, p. 219). However, in the light of the foregoing description of Japanese concepts of moral obligation, we are only justified in concluding that *in addition* to sharing the meaning which is commonly placed on "self-respect" in our culture, the Japanese value other character traits (i.e., self-restraint, circumspection, respect for social niceties and for the feelings of others) sufficiently to dignify them by the same term that we usually reserve for moral uprightness.

Lastly, it is important to explain why

[2] In private confessionals, the priest serves as the moral representative of the group.

confession and atonement are such relatively inconspicuous aspects of Japanese guilt behavior.[3] The absence of these characteristics that so frequently accompany the expression of guilt in our culture does not prove, as Ruth Benedict suggests, that genuine guilt is lacking, since otherwise it would be relieved by confession (1946, p. 223). The Japanese does not, as alleged, avoid confession because his guilt is really only shame and, hence, would be aggravated rather than eased by being made public. The more credible explanation is that although confession would be guilt reducing it would also be too traumatic in view of the tremendous Japanese sensitivity to shame. Under such circumstances, overwhelming feelings of guilt can be relieved less painfully by suicide.

Summary: The capacity for experiencing guilt behavior (i.e., a constellation of negative self-reactions to the perceived violation of moral obligation) is conceived as so basically human and so fundamental to the sanctions by which social norms are maintained and transmitted to the young that under minimally favorable social conditions it should develop in all cultures. The only psychological conditions hypothesized as essential for the development of guilt behavior are (*a*) the acceptance of moral values, (*b*) the internalization of a sense of moral obligation to abide by these values, and (*c*) sufficient self-critical ability to perceive discrepancies between internalized values and actual behavior. The development of conscience typically embodies various sequential changes paralleling shifts in the individual's biosocial status. Ordinarily, greater differences in moral behavior may be anticipated among individuals within a culture than among different cultures.

Shame is a self-deprecatory reaction to the actual or presumed judgments of *others*. It may have moral or nonmoral reference. Guilt feelings always involve a special type of moral shame in addition to other negative *self*-judgments. In addition to the shame of guilt, conscience (guilt behavior) is customarily buttressed by such external sanctions as statutory law, public opinion, and ridicule. Thus, the sanctions of guilt are both external and internal in nature.

Various criteria have been advanced by different ethnologists for distinguishing between shame and guilt. It has been alleged (*a*) that guilt behavior can only arise when a hierarchically superior parent or parent surrogate serves as the source of moral authority, (*b*) that genuine guilt feelings can only exist when shame and other external sanctions are not operative, and (*c*) that, subjectively, guilt must be characterized by conviction of sin and need for atonement. Examination of Navaho and Japanese ethnological materials presented in support of these criteria shows that the latter lack both logical and empirical validity. Highly suggestive evidence of the operation of strong moral obligations and of guilt behavior was found in these supposedly prime examples of "shaming cultures."

The problem of shame and guilt is illustrative of a major methodological hazard in the cross-cultural investigation of personality traits, namely, of the ethnocentric tendency to define a given trait in terms of its *specific* attributes in one's own culture. This leads to a perversion of cultural relativism. Instead of demonstrating how a basic human capacity (e.g., guilt behavior) occurs under different conditions and assumes different forms in different cultures, this approach inevitably "discovers" that this very capacity is absent in other cultures because it does not conform to a specific set of ethnocentric criteria. The generalization is then made that the capacity is non-universal, culture-bound, and, hence, not basic. Cross-cultural investigations of personality must, therefore, start with definitions of traits that are both psychologically meaningful and general enough to encompass specific cultural variants.

---

[3] The practice of atonement is not entirely unknown in Japan. "Boys in later elementary school are sometimes confined to the house for kinshin, 'repentance,' and must occupy themselves with . . . the writing of diaries." Similarly, when ostracized by his schoolmates for offenses, the culprit "has to apologize and make promises before he is readmitted" (Benedict, 1946, pp. 273–274).

It is also important to avoid the error of circularity—setting up *a priori conditions* for the emergence of a trait, finding these conditions absent in a given culture, and concluding "empirically" therefrom that the *trait itself* is absent. This error can be avoided in part by paying attention to the subjective and expressive content of behavior and not merely to the postulated determinants of the trait in question.

The Report of Being Watched as a Measure of Guilty Behavior[1]

Martha E. Bernal

One of the problems facing the psychological investigator interested in guilt is that "guilt" is a label applied by the culture to a private emotional experience that has a large degree of interpersonal variance, and therefore cannot be experimentally manipulated. Rather than attempt to solve the many ramifications of this problem, the investigator examined some classes of behavior called "guilty," which are manifestations of historical variables, but not necessarily of the experience of guilt.

Two main classes of behavior can be observed when a person engages in guilty behavior. One class is physiological, and includes autonomic and skeletomuscular changes; the other class consists of defensive operations, more commonly called defense mechanisms. These two elements of behavior, correlated in time with the commission of

some socially unacceptable act or with the symbols representing the act, constitute what is called guilty behavior. When the clinician concludes that his patient is suffering from feelings of guilt, certain clues have led him to this conclusion. Evidences of perspiration, flushing, irregularity of speech, and fidgeting as the patient touches upon his life's experiences relating to forbidden behaviors arouse the clinician's suspicions. A further clue may take the form of the patient's efforts to "defend against" his guilt by denying it, projecting it onto others, rationalizing it, etc. These specific behaviors, occurring in a particular context, signal the occurrence of this patient's private experience to the therapist.

The purpose of this paper is to attempt to reproduce some classes of behavior called guilty and to demonstrate their sensitivity to subtle environmental cues. Physiological changes in autonomic and skeletal effector systems are not difficult to measure. Defensive maneuvers, however, by virtue of their definition are highly susceptible to modification and subtlety, since the individual uses them as a means of protection and adaptation after he evaluates the environment and determines

[1] This article is based on a doctoral dissertation submitted to Indiana University. The author wishes to express her appreciation to Arnold M. Binder for his generous assistance and to Leon H. Levy who devised the basic method for the research. Further thanks are due to Ralph Wetzel for his cogent criticisms leading to the present revision of an earlier paper and to Mary L. Martin and Alice Jwaidah who conducted Experiment 3. This research was partially supported by Indiana ONR Contract Nonr 908-15.

how to defend himself in different situations. This defensive process includes the making of subtle discriminations as part of a built-up chain of behaviors leading to the defense itself. For example, a young man drops food on his lap while dining in a restaurant with his date. He instantly looks up to see if she saw him; if she did, he may make some comment such as "slippery food." If she did not see him drop the food he may go on eating. However, assume that for some reason the lady has been unduly observant of her escort's manners and has "threatened" him. In this case, his behavior may be different; he drops the food, looks up, but instead of rationalizing, says nothing, perhaps because by doing so he can deprive her of the opportunity for criticism. In each of these examples, the chain of behaviors includes a fine discrimination between environmental stimuli which set the occasion for the behavior that follows. The search for the cue of being seen is part of this chain, and the discrimination made determines what defense follows.

The procedure for the three studies to be reported includes some of the basic elements of the two examples given above. Four subjects at a time were seated in each of four rooms equipped with one-way mirrors and provided with a telegraph key which they were to press every time they felt the experimenter was watching them through the mirrors. To obtain the pressing behavior, the experiment was represented as an extrasensory perception (ESP) study; subjects made "ESP guesses" about when they believed they were being watched. Each telegraph key was wired to an electric clock which recorded the amount of time the key was pressed; thus a Time Report, or

TR, was obtained for each subject. Two sets of questions were presented: guilt questions inquiring about a number of behaviors believed to be socially unacceptable for a population of female undergraduates, and neutral questions inquiring about benign behaviors. After subjects answered each of the questions with a "yes" or "no," they made TRs. Subjects were instructed in two different ways: in one case they were told they might be watched at any time, and in the second case they were told they would be watched during every TR period. The symbols for unacceptable behavior were presented and subjects admitted or denied having engaged in the behaviors, evaluated the available cues, and either pressed or did not press the key. The key-pressing and the failure to press communicated to the experimenter whether or not subjects believed they were being watched. In addition to the TR, selected autonomic changes were measured.

In pilot work, larger TRs were elicited following presentation of guilt questions than following neutral questions. These interesting results led to the design of two experiments in which the hypotheses were that guilt questions would elicit TRs and autonomic changes of greater magnitude than neutral questions. In the first of these two experiments, subjects were permitted to make TRs following any of the questions, and some subjects made very few or none at all in response to either type of question. These findings were interpreted as a problem of poor instructions, and the instructions for the second experiment were altered slightly to try to force subjects to make TRs following most of the questions. A third experiment was conducted in which the hypothesis of differences between magnitude of TRs to guilt and neutral questions was proposed, but no prediction was made as to the direction of the differences.

Method

EXPERIMENTS 1 AND 2

Subjects

The subjects were 20 female Indiana University undergraduates per experiment who were paid for their services. Selection of subjects was based on age (17 to 21 years), single marital status, fluent knowledge of English, and completion of a maximum of one semester of psychology. Some of these criteria were established in order to restrict the population with regard to level of general sophistication. They were randomly assigned to Guilt and Neutral groups and retained their group identification for the two phases of the research.

Apparatus

The electrocardiograph, pneumograph, and GSR recording apparatus have been described elsewhere (Ellson, Davis, Saltzman, and Burke, 1952). The transducer for the pneumograph was a mercury-filled rubber tube which changed resistance when stretched. These changes were amplified and recorded on a Stoelting servographic recorder.

GSR electrodes were attached to the left upper arm and palm. EKG electrodes were placed on the right upper arm and left leg. The rubber tube was placed around the upper thorax, just under the arms.

Autonomic and TR responses could not be obtained concurrently because of the extensive instrumentation required to record from four subjects at once. In order to minimize the effects of repeating the same questions on two different occasions, phrases expressing the content of the questions were used during the physiological recordings. The stimulus questions, a Guilt set and a Neutral set, are shown below in Table 1, with the phrases underlined; whenever necessary, the phrases are written in parentheses. Each set of phrases was recorded on five different tapes, each tape having a different random sequence of the phrases. During the tape recording, care was taken to use approximately the same voice inflection and volume throughout. Physiological measurements were taken

TABLE 1

LIST OF STIMULUS QUESTIONS

Guilt Questions	Neutral Questions
Are you failing any of your *courses*? (Fail courses)	*Do you *have* a *job*?
Do you *betray* your *friends*?	Are you a *native Hoosier*?
Do you *hate* one or both of your *parents*?	*Do you *enjoy* listening to *music*?
*Do you *tell lies*?	Are you a *fulltime student*?
Do you *indulge* in *petting* when on dates?	*Do you *participate* in *sports*?
Do you *break regulations* whenever possible?	Have you traveled overseas? (Travel overseas)
Are you a *cheating student*?	Do you *own* any *pets*?
*Do you *masturbate often*?	*Do you often *watch television*?
*Do you demand more of your parents than they can provide you? (Demanding daughter)	*Do you *drive* a *car*?
*Do you *deceive* your *parents* about what you do?	Do you *have* any *brothers*?
* Have you had any *homosexual experiences*?	Did you *eat breakfast* this morning?
*Do you *disappoint people* who count on you?	*Do you *read novels*?

* These questions were used in Experiment 3.

during playback of the phrases, and the complete questions were presented in written form on 5 x 8 inch index cards during the TR phase.

Physiological recordings were made while one subject at a time was seated in a sound-attenuated room equipped with a loudspeaker. The physiological recording instruments and tape recorder were in a separate room. The experimental setting for the TR phase consisted of four adjoining rooms, each having a one-way observation mirror along one wall. Subjects were seated at tables situated next to the one-way screen so that full view of only one subject at a time was possible from the enclosed corridor on the observation side of the screen.

Four army signal corps keys and four electric clocks were used to obtain TRs. A key was placed on the table at which the subject was seated. Each key was wired to its respective clock, thereby permitting the subject to start and stop the clock by pushing down and releasing the key. A buzzer signalled the start and finish of each TR period. A card on the subject's table noted the signals and their meaning.

Measurements

The autonomic response variables and their measures are shown in Table 2. Exploratory analyses of pilot data assisted in

selecting measures that best represented stimulus effects. To order the stimulus phrases according to magnitude of autonomic response, a "large" response was defined on the basis of absolute magnitude of change alone, regardless of the direction of change. For instance, whether breathing rate increased or decreased, only the magnitude of the change was measured. TR data were in seconds of time.

Procedure

Autonomic data were always acquired first, then TR data were collected at a later date. For the autonomic recordings, subjects were orally instructed to sit quietly while the experimenter said some phrases over the loudspeaker and responses were obtained. Subjects were told that the purpose of the recordings was to try to find out what kinds of experiences they had had in connection with the phrases. These instructions were designed to structure the situation so that subjects would believe that an effort was being made to expose them in a manner similar to the one they would encounter when answering the questions under observation by the experimenter.

For the TR phase, four subjects, from both Guilt and Neutral groups, were taken into the observation corridor and the operation of the one-way mirrors was explained. The general strategy was to try to convince

TABLE 2

AUTONOMIC RESPONSE VARIABLES, MEASUREMENTS, AND QUANTIFICATIONS

Variable	Measurement	Quantification
GSR size	Maximum decrease in resistance in 1st 15 secs. after stimulus.	Decrease as percent of base level at point immediately preceding stimulus onset.
Breathing-cycle time	Difference between mean time for 10 cycles before stimulus and for 10 cycles after stimulus.	Difference score in secs. per cycle.
Breathing amplitude	Difference between mean amplitude of inhalation for 10 cycles before stimulus and for 10 cycles after stimulus.	$\dfrac{\text{Difference score}}{\text{Pre-stimulus reading}} \times 100.$
Heart rate	Difference between mean beats per sec. for 5 cycles before stimulus and for 5 cycles after stimulus.	Difference score $\times$ 60 = beats per minute.

the subjects that ESP is a real phenomenon and that they would be taking part in one of a series of ESP studies. Subjects were given a definition of ESP as an individual's ability to guess what another person is thinking or doing when he is unable to see or communicate with the other person. Their task in the experiment was to try to guess when the experimenter was watching them through the one-way mirror without being able to see the experimenter. It was explained that they might be watched a short while or a long while; each would be observed one at a time. The ESP guess was made by pressing a telegraph key and holding it down for the period of time during which the subject believed she was being watched. In Experiment 2, it was specifically stressed that each subject would be observed during every ESP guess or TR period, whereas this was not made clear in the Experiment 1 instructions.[2] Presses could be repeated as many times as the subject believed the experimenter had resumed observation of her. Subjects read one question at a time, answered it, then put the card down and reported their guesses. One minute was allowed for reading and answering the question and two minutes for the TR. The experimenter recorded the total TR made by each subject at the end of each report period, so that at the end of the experiment there were 12 sets of TR scores per subject, each score corresponding to the amount of time a subject reported being watched following each question.

EXPERIMENT 3

Thirty female undergraduates participated in this study in partial fulfillment of introductory psychology course requirements. The TR procedure was different in

[2] In the dissertation research, Spearman rank order correlations were computed between autonomic changes and TRs to the Guilt stimuli. It was necessary to obtain data that would permit the assignment of ranks to all 12 Guilt stimuli in order to run these correlations. When Experiment 1 subjects failed to respond to so many of the questions, it was decided to try to force them to make TRs to each question. This decision led to the instructional change in Experiment 2.

three important respects: (1) only TR measurements were made; (2) each subject responded to both sets of questions, with the order of presentation of the two sets counterbalanced in a crossover design; and (3) abbreviated lists of Guilt and Neutral questions were used, each containing six questions of each type (marked by an asterisk in Table 1). The six Guilt questions which most consistently elicited the largest autonomic changes in Experiments 1 and 2 were selected in order to increase the threat value of the Guilt set. As in Experiment 2, subjects were instructed that each would be observed following presentation of every question.

Results

EXPERIMENTS 1 AND 2

The raw data for each of the autonomic variables and TR were set up in a matrix with rows representing subjects and columns representing stimuli. The data were totaled in the columns and the means of the columns computed. The one-tailed Mann-Whitney U Test with $n_1 = 12$, $n_2 = 12$ (Siegel, 1956) was used to evaluate autonomic responsiveness and TR differences between Guilt and Neutral groups.

The magnitude of breathing-cycle time and heart rate changes for the Guilt group were greater than for the Neutral group ($p < .05$ and $p < .001$ for Experiments 1 and 2, respectively). In addition, the GSR differences in Experiment 2 were highly significant, with the larger changes exhibited by the Guilt group ($p < .001$). Table 3 displays the values of U for these comparisons between Guilt and Neutral groups for all variables.

Guilt group TRs were significantly larger than Neutral group TRs in Experiment 1 ($U = 20$, $p < .001$), but in Experiment 2 the direction of the

TABLE 3

VALUES OF MANN-WHITNEY U FOR COMPARISONS BETWEEN
GUILT AND NEUTRAL RESPONSES

Experiment	Breathing-cycle time	Breathing amplitude	Heart rate	GSR	TR
1	39*	63	41*	——	20**
2	9**	68	17**	0**	39*

Note.—In Experiment 1, U values for respiration variables based on 9 Guilt and 10 Neutral Group subjects, and 8 Guilt and 6 Neutral Group subjects for TR variable. Experiment 1 GSR data lost due to recording difficulties. All other U values based on 10 subjects per group. One-tailed significance tests used throughout.

* $p < .05$.
** $p < .001$.

significant differences were reversed such that Neutral group TRs were larger than Guilt group TRs ($U = 39$, $p < .05$).

Analyses for the effects of position of either Guilt or Neutral stimuli in order of presentation on magnitude of autonomic and TR responses failed to show any systematic trends.

EXPERIMENT 3

Neutral questions elicited sigificantly larger TRs than Guilt questions when each subject was presented with both sets ($F = 5.47$, $p < .05$). Table 4 shows the analysis of variance of TR data for 30 subjects. It should be noted that the

TABLE 4

ANALYSIS OF VARIANCE COMPARING
TIME REPORTS TO GUILT
AND NEUTRAL QUESTIONS,
EXPERIMENT 3

Source	df	MS	F
Replications	29	3680.07	2.41
Order	1	1717.35	1.12
Treatments	1	8378.01	5.47*
Error	28	1529.18	

* $p < .05$.

order in which subjects answered the two sets of questions produced no systematic effect on TRs.

Discussion

The magnitude of autonomic changes following presentation of symbols representing socially unacceptable behavior was greater than following presentation of symbols representing more acceptable behaviors. These findings are important only in terms of the interpretation given them: members of the general class of physiological behaviors may be elicited by some of the stimuli that also elicit defensive behaviors.

The significance of the reported studies lies in the demonstration of the susceptibility of the report of being watched to subtle environmental cues. In the first experiment, subjects answering the Guilt questions reported being watched as the end response in a chain of behaviors instigated by symbols representing forbidden behaviors. The results of Experiment 2 suggested that subjects were responding to cues other than the type of question presented, namely, to the instruction that they would be observed during every one of the TR periods. One effect of these instructions was that Experiment 2 subjects had a greater incidence of TRs than Experiment 1 subjects, as was expected. However, if the instructional change had affected both groups uniformly, the direction of the differences in response to the two types of questions should have been the same as in Experiment 1, if any differences were found. The conclusion drawn was that there was probably an interactive effect between the instructions and the experimental condition, leading to an inhibition of the report of being watched under the Guilt condition. Experiment 3 represented an effort to clarify the issue of these contradictory results by increasing the threat effect of the experimental situation and using a more powerful design and statistical test. The hypothesis of differences between Guilt and Neutral group TRs was confirmed, with the larger TRs in favor of the Neutral

group. The conclusion drawn was that alteration of the social reinforcement contingencies led to defensive behavior consisting of a failure to make the pressing response which would communicate to the experimenter that subjects believed they were being watched under the Guilt condition.

One implication of this research is that it may be more profitable to explore the functional relationships between historical and environmental variables and classes of behaviors called guilty than to attempt to describe, define, or measure the experience of guilt. For the clinician involved in the treatment or manipulation of behavioral disorders related to guilt, knowledge about the parameters of reinforcement necessary to produce the disorders and data on the empirical relationships between specific stimulus conditions and guilty behaviors would be of greater value than theoretical formulas involving conflicting and condemning forces existing somewhere inside the patient.

Journal of Abnormal and Social Psychology, 1963, vol. 67, pp. 469–479

Thematic Hostility and Guilt Responses as Related to Self-Reported Hostility, Guilt, and Conflict[1]

George Saltz and Seymour Epstein

In a study of the sex drive Leiman and Epstein (1961) tested a modification of Miller's (1948, 1951) displacement model applied to projective tech-

[1] This study is part of a project on the measurement of drive and conflict which is being supported by Grant M-1293 from the National Institute of Mental Health, United States Public Health Service.

niques (see Epstein, 1962, for the most recent description of the model). They investigated thematic sexual responses as a function of drive, guilt, and stimulus relevance, i.e., the degree to which the stimulus elicits responses related to the drive in question. Thematic sexual responses were found to be directly related to drive, as measured by rate of outlet, and inversely to self-reported guilt. In accordance with the model, pictures of low relevance best differentiated the groups according to drive and pictures of high relevance according to guilt. When deprivation was used as an alternate index of drive, a significant interaction was found between guilt and drive. When guilt was low, thematic sexual responses were directly related to drive; when guilt was high the relationship was inverse. It was concluded that the level of awareness at which drive is measured and degree of guilt are critical factors in determining the relationship between projective responses and drive.

The major purpose of the present study is to investigate thematic hostility responses in a manner parallel to the Leiman and Epstein study on sexual responses. In addition, an independent self-report scale of conflict is used to test the assumption that simultaneous scores of high drive and high guilt on a self-report inventory are associated with high scores on self-reported conflict, and to provide a more direct criterion of conflict with which to evaluate the projective responses.

On the basis of the conflict model referred to above and the findings of thematic sexual responses by Leiman and Epstein (1961), the following hypotheses were formulated:

Hypothesis 1. There is a direct relationship between thematic hostility and feelings of hostility. This is based on the assumption that people project their drive states.

Hypothesis 2. There is a direct relationship between thematic guilt responses and feelings of guilt. This is based on the assumption that people project their feelings of guilt.

Hypothesis 3. There is an inverse relationship between thematic hostility responses and guilt over hostility. This is based on the assumption that guilt leads to an inhibition of guilt producing responses.

Hypothesis 4. Hostile responses to pictures of low relevance are primarily determined by drive, and hostile responses to pictures of high relevance by guilt. This follows from the assumption that the gradient of avoidance is steeper than the gradient of approach and is consistent with the findings of Leiman and Epstein (1961).

Hypothesis 5. There is an interaction between hostility and guilt on thematic responses such that the relationship between thematic hostility responses and feelings of hostility is stronger when guilt over hostility is low than when guilt over hostility is high. This is based on the assumption that inhibition is facilitated by strong cues, whether stimulus produced or drive produced, and is consistent with the findings of Leiman and Epstein (1961).

Hypothesis 6. With increasing conflict over hostility, there is an increasing tendency to overrespond to stimuli of low relevance and to underrespond to stimuli of high relevance. This is based on the assumption that conflict can be represented by the interaction of gradients of approach and avoidance, with the latter steeper than the former. Although the hypothesis was not supported by Leiman and Epstein (1961), it was of secondary importance in the design of their study, and their criterion of conflict was questionable.

Method

A specially constructed TAT-like test containing cues at two levels of hostility

Fig. 1. Pictures of low and high relevance for hostility. Presented second, third, and fifth in the series.

was administered, and followed by a questionnaire on hostility, guilt, and conflict over hostility. The questionnaire was administered last so that it would not influence the projective responses.

Thematic Apperception Test (TAT)

The test of thematic apperception consisted of six pictures. Two pictures of low relevance presented no direct cues of hostility but were appropriate for hostile and nonhostile responses, while a picture of high relevance portrayed a hostile act and allowed for response variation in terms of intensity, displacement, and denial. The latter picture was identical with TAT picture 18GF (Murray, 1943), except that men were substituted for women. Three other pictures served as buffers to separate the low from the high relevant pictures, and to insulate the questionnaire from the projective test. The three critical pictures are presented in Figure 1. The low relevant pictures were presented first in order to keep response generalization to a minimum. The procedure for administering the thematic test is indicated by the following instructions on the test booklet:

This is a test of your creative imagination. A number of pictures will be projected on the screen. You will have up to twenty seconds to look at the picture and then 5 minutes to make up a story about it. Notice that there is one page for each story.

To insure a complete story, include the following:

1) What led up to the scene?
2) What is happening, and what are the people feeling and thinking?
3) What will the outcome be?

Do not merely describe the pictures, but try to make up interesting and vivid stories about them. Make up a new story for each one rather than continue a story from a previous picture. Please do not tell humorous stories. Tell the story in the third person rather than as your own experience.

Two scores were obtained, Need Hostility (n Hostility) and TAT Guilt.

n Hostility. A basic weight was assigned to each story, as follows:

0—There is no indication that the hero is angry, nor does anyone other than the hero experience injury, either physically or psychologically.

1—The hero is slightly angry, or someone other than the hero is mildly injured physically or psychologically.

3—The hero is moderately angry, or someone other than the hero is moderately injured physically or psychologically.

5—The hero is very angry, or someone other than the hero is severely injured physically or psychologically.

The basic weights were modified up to one point by taking into account intensity

of hostility, vividness of description, emphasis, and importance of hostility to the plot. Before assigning values, judgments were empirically anchored by scanning the pool of stories and selecting one to represent each weight. The stories, devoid of identifying information, were all scored by the first author. Interscorer reliability as established for 39 randomly selected records scored by the second author was .97. It should be noted that the scale does not take account whether injury has its source in the behavior of the hero or of another figure. However, the responses were independently scored on the following scale of displacement, which does take into account the part played by the hero:

I—The hero is a person with whom identification is very likely (e.g., "young man," "college student") who feels angry or injures someone directly and purposely, without being under an abnormal influence (e.g., alcohol, drugs, hypnosis).

II—The hero is a person with whom identification is questionable (e.g., "a man who has been released from prison") who feels angry, purposely injures someone, or who has injured someone in the past, while not in an abnormal state.

III—The hero is a person with whom identification is very unlikely (e.g., "mental defective," "psychotic," "person from a distant planet"), or in an abnormal state and not responsible for his behavior, or injures others while trying to help them (e.g., "surgeon").

IV—The hero neither wished for, is an agent in, nor is pleased by whatever misfortune or injury occurs to others. He is neither accidentally nor purposely involved.

In all analyses two scores were investigated, one in which n Hostility was weighted for displacement and one in which it was not. Weighting for displacement was based on the assumption that displaced responses are weaker manifestations of hostility than direct responses. Accordingly, n Hostility scores in Displacement Level I were multiplied by 4, Level II by 3, Level III by 2, and Level IV by 1. It was found that the scores weighted for displacement added nothing to the unweighted scores, and only the analyses for unweighted scores are presented. The failure of weighting by displacement to make a difference is largely due to the pictures of low relevance eliciting almost no displacement.

TAT Guilt. A scale for scoring TAT Guilt was developed in an identical manner to the one for n Hostility, except that injury directed toward the hero rather than toward others was scored. An interscorer reliability coefficient of .77 was obtained for 39 records selected at random.

Questionnaire Hostility, Guilt, and Conflict

Ninety items, including all those in the Edwards (1959) scale on hostility, some from the MMPI, and some specially constructed ones were presented to six clinical psychologists to sort into four piles representing hostile feelings, guilt over hostility, conflict over hostility, or none of these. The judges were requested to consider the categories as independent and to avoid inferring conflict from the presence or absence of guilt or hostility alone, but to require evidence of simultaneous approach and avoidance tendencies toward hostile expression, or of disturbance about hostility. Items on which at least five of the six judges agreed were tentatively assigned to scales. An item analysis was then done by dividing the pooled group into thirds according to total score on each scale, and noting whether frequency of endorsement of an item increased as a function of total score. The 8 items in each scale which had the sharpest slopes were retained. The completed scale consisted of 54 items, including 20 buffer items, and 10 Lie (*L*) scale items from the MMPI. The purpose of the *L* scale was to discard unduly defensive subjects, to compare the experimental groups on defensiveness, and to provide descriptive information for comparison with future studies. Subjects were required to mark each item as 1, Definitely False; 2, Mostly False; 3, Mostly True; or 4, Definitely True. Scores consisted of the sum of the weights, after making reversals for oppositely worded items. For hostility, guilt, and conflict, the possible range of scores

was from 1 to 32, and for the *L* scale 1 to 40. Following are the items in each scale, with the number preceding the item indicating its position in the questionnaire. An "r" in parentheses following an item indicates that the scoring is reversed for that item.

Hostility scale:
7. I have daydreams that I make a fool of someone who knows more than I do.
11. I have daydreams about hurting someone I don't like.
29. I never get so mad as to feel like beating or smashing things. (r)
30. When someone annoys me, my first impulse is to tell him (her) off.
37. I am not easily angered. (r)
41. I picture myself taking revenge on someone I dislike.
45. I think of ways to get even with certain people.
53. I do not have unusually strong hostile feelings and impulses. (r)

It should be noted that all the hostility items refer to feelings and daydreams rather than overt behavior. This was done with the consideration that hostile behavior is a composite function of hostile impulses and inhibitory tendencies, and that consequently it is impossible to construct independent scales of hostile behavior and guilt. While inhibition influences feelings, it can be assumed to exert less of an effect on feelings than on behavior. For the present scale of hostility, a high score is equivalent to the statement, "I am a person with strong hostile feelings."

Guilt scale:
3. I feel that might makes right. (r)
9. I think it is wrong to seek revenge since two wrongs don't make a right.
15. It is foolish to be nice to those who are inconsiderate. (r)
22. I feel there are situations where one is justified in hurting another person's feelings. (r)
24. I believe that aggressive feelings should be expressed. (r)
26. I can never condone physical violence.
43. I feel that people are too much

concerned with satisfying their own desires at the expense of others.

47. We are never really justified in being hostile toward others.

Inspection of the items indicates that the scale measures negative attitudes toward expression of hostility. In this respect, the Guilt scale is not parallel to the Hostility scale, which refers to personal feelings. The decision to build a scale of negative attitude toward hostility followed from the wish to keep the Guilt scale independent of the hostility and conflict scales.

Conflict scale:

13. I wish I could find a way to handle my angry feelings more satisfactorily.

16. I try not to let things upset me because I have such a terrible temper.

20. When I express my anger, I am usually sorry afterwards.

27. I wonder why I act so nice to people I can't stand.

32. I feel sorry after telling someone off, even though he may have deserved it.

35. I fail to defend myself when I should, and I get overly aggressive when I shouldn't.

39. I find it hard to refuse favors, even to people I dislike.

49. Some of the destructive thoughts I have really frighten me.

It is evident that the items in the Conflict scale indicate disturbance over hostile feelings and behavior. A high score is summarized by the statement, "I am unhappy and disturbed about my hostile feelings and the manner in which I handle them."

Subjects

Subjects consisted of 181 male undergraduate volunteers from an introductory course in psychology at the University of Massachusetts. Two subjects who obtained scores on defensiveness that fell out of the distribution were eliminated. From the remaining pool of subjects, groups differing in hostility and guilt were selected according to three different experimental designs. In the first design, hostility and guilt were kept independent by dividing subjects above and below the median on self-reported hostility and self-reported guilt and then selecting 20 subjects in each cell so that the two levels of hostility had the same means and standard deviations on guilt, and the two levels of guilt had the same means and standard deviations on hostility. Within these limits, subjects were chosen to be as extreme on hostility and guilt as possible. Evidence that the variables were not originally independent was revealed by the initial fourfold table, where 34 subjects were found to be below the median on both scales, 63 below on hostility and above on guilt, 48 above on hostility and below on guilt, and 36 above the median on both scales. A chi square of 8.88, $df = 1$, indicates a significant inverse relationship between hostility and guilt at the .01 level. It is not surprising that the two variables are related, as considering oneself hostile while disapproving of hostility is obviously not conducive to a stable state of equilibrium. In Table 1, which presents descriptive data for the groups finally selected, it can be seen that they do not differ in defensiveness.

Selecting subjects on a double criterion of self-reporting hostility and guilt while keeping the two independent necessitated the elimination of many extreme subjects. While such selection provides an effective test of the interaction of hostility and guilt, it is of limited value in testing the main effects of the two variables because of sampling restriction. In the second design

TABLE 1

DESCRIPTIVE DATA FOR THE EXPERIMENTAL GROUPS
WITH HOSTILITY AND GUILT TREATED EQUALLY

Group	Hostility		Guilt		Defensiveness	
	M	Range	M	Range	M	Range
Low hostility-Low guilt	15.8	12–19	14.0	9–16	33.1	24–40
Low hostility-High guilt	14.2	9–19	21.8	18–26	31.8	24–37
High hostility-Low guilt	23.2	20–30	14.4	10–16	33.2	26–40
High hostility-High guilt	23.0	20–32	21.0	17–26	31.1	29–40

TABLE 2

Descriptive Data for the Experimental Groups with Hostility as the Major Variable

Group	Hostility		Guilt		Defensiveness	
	M	Range	M	Range	M	Range
Low hostility-Low guilt	10.7	9–12	19.4	18–20	32.0	26–36
Low hostility-High guilt	10.8	9–12	23.0	21–26	29.6	23–35
High hostility-Low guilt	25.2	23–20	12.5	10–16	33.2	30–40
High hostility-High guilt	26.1	23–32	19.2	16–25	33.6	30–39

TABLE 3

Descriptive Data for the Experimental Groups with Guilt as the Major Variable

Group	Hostility		Guilt		Defensiveness	
	M	Range	M	Range	M	Range
Low guilt-Low hostility	16.1	12–18	12.4	9–14	35.4	29–40
Low guilt-High hostility	23.5	19–30	12.6	10–14	32.6	26–40
High guilt-Low hostility	11.7	10–13	24.6	24–26	29.1	23–35
High guilt-High hostility	19.2	15–32	25.1	24–26	30.9	24–37

the 20 highest and lowest subjects on self-reported hostility were selected from the pool of 179 subjects without regard to self-reported guilt. A division within groups was then made by separating the 10 highest and lowest subjects on self-reported guilt. This design is particularly useful in examining the main effect of hostility and is also of some value in evaluating guilt and the interaction of hostility and guilt, as guilt can reasonably be considered contingent upon hostility. The reverse, of course, is not true. In the third design, extremes were selected on self-reported guilt, and subjects were subdivided on self-reported hostility. This design is useful in examining the

main effect of guilt, and the subdivision on hostility serves merely to refine the error variance. The descriptive data for the second and third designs are presented in Tables 2 and 3, where it can be seen that defensiveness, as revealed by *low* scores on the *L* scale, tends to be associated with low scores on hostility and high scores on guilt. However, the differences between groups on defensiveness are not significant.

In order to investigate self-reported conflict, three groups of 20 subjects each were selected from the pool of 179 subjects to represent the extremes and midpoint of the distribution. Table 4 presents the descriptive data for the three groups. It is apparent that they do not differ in defensiveness.

TABLE 4

Descriptive Data for the Three Conflict Groups

Group	Conflict		Defensiveness	
	M	Range	M	Range
Low conflict	12.7	10.14	31.7	26–38
Medium conflict	18.2	16–19	31.4	25–40
High conflict	24.1	21–27	33.3	27–39

Results

THEMATIC HOSTILITY AS A FUNCTION OF SELF-REPORTED HOSTILITY AND GUILT

It was originally planned to represent the two levels of stimulus relevance within a single analysis, where the combined ambiguous pictures would represent the level of low relevance and the single hostile picture the level of high relevance. However, there were too many zero responses at the level of low relevance to justify treatment within an analysis of variance. Accordingly, the data in each of the three designs were inspected to determine whether the levels of relevance were functionally similar. Where such was the case, a composite score was entered into the analysis of variance. Where the levels were functionally dissimilar, the pictures of high relevance were analyzed by analysis of variance, and the combined pictures of low relevance by chi square. By following a procedure described by Sutcliffe (1957), it was possible to obtain the interaction of hostility and guilt by chi square.

In testing the hypothesis that there is a direct relationship between n Hostility and self-reported hostility, the most appropriate analysis is the one comparing extremes on self-reported hostility. Inspection reveals that the two levels of relevance are functionally dissimilar. On the pictures of low relevance there is a direct relationship between n Hostility and self-reported hostility, with 6 out of 20 subjects of low self-reported hostility and 15 out of 20 subjects of high self-reported hostility producing at least one hostile response. Chi square is 8.12, which, with $df = 1$, is significant at the .01 level. On the picture of high relevance, the groups have almost identical thematic hostility scores, with means in order of increasing self-reported hostility of 3.55 and 3.80. If the pictures of low and high relevance are combined the results are no longer significant. Neither of the other designs produces significant confirming results but this can be attributed to the sampling restriction in these

designs. It may be concluded that self-reported hostility is directly related to thematic hostility as measured by pictures of low relevance.

When the low relevant pictures are analyzed individually, Picture 3 differentiates the groups reliably, and Picture 2 does not. On Picture 3, 4 out of 20 subjects of low self-reported hostility and 12 out of 20 subjects of high self-reported hostility produce a hostile response. Chi square is 6.66, which, with $df = 1$, is significant at the .01 level. On Picture 2, 5 out of 20 subjects of low self-reported hostility, and 10 out of 20 subjects of high self-reported hostility produce a hostile response, yielding a chi square of 2.67, which is not significant $(p = .10)$. In order to determine why some pictures are more effective than others, and to provide data for comparison with pictures in other studies, the response characteristics of each picture were determined. In Table 5 it can be seen that the two pictures of low relevance are similar in the frequency with which they elicit hostile responses, but Picture 3 elicits stronger responses and has a larger standard deviation, so that it is psychometrically a better measure of individual differences.

TABLE 5

RESPONSE CHARACTERISTICS
OF THE INDIVIDUAL PICTURES

Thematic hostility	Picture		
	2	3	5
Percentage of responses	36%	40%	84%
Mean response	0.43	1.12	3.03
Range	0–4	0–6	0–6
SD	1.19	1.45	1.95
Mean considering only responses greater than zero	1.90	2.78	3.62

In testing the hypothesis of an interaction between hostility and guilt, the most important analysis is the one in which self-rated hostility and guilt are represented orthogonally. Inspection of the data failed to reveal a functional difference between levels of stimulus relevance, so that an analysis of variance was carried out on a composite score. In Table 6 it can be seen that the interaction is significant at the .05 level.[3] Figure 2 reveals a direct relationship between n Hostility and self-reported hostility when guilt is low and an inverse relationship when guilt is high. Apparently the inverse relationship produced by subjects of high guilt canceled out the direct relationship produced by subjects of low guilt, accounting for the absence of a significant main effect for hostility. The same direction of interaction was found in the analysis of the extreme groups on hostility with guilt as a subordinate variable, but did not reach significance.

To test the hypothesis that there is an inverse relationship between self-reported guilt and n Hostility, the most important analysis is the one comparing extremes on self-reported guilt. Inspection reveals that the pictures of low and high relevance are functionally

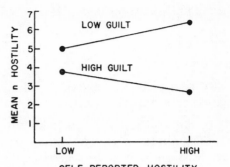

Fig. 2. Thematic hostility as a function of self-reported hostility and guilt.

similar. Analysis of variance of a composite score indicates that there is a significant relationship between n Hostility and self-reported guilt at the .05 level ($F = 2.89$, $df = 1/36$, one-tailed test). The relationship is inverse, confirming hypothesis, with a mean n Hostility score for the low guilt group of 3.90, and a mean for the high guilt group of 2.31. A similar inverse relationship at the .001 level is found in the analysis in which self-reported hostility and guilt are orthogonal.

As to the hypothesis that drive is best measured by responses to stimuli of low relevance and guilt by responses to stimuli of high relevance, support for the first part of the hypothesis has already been indicated. All three experimental designs have bearing on testing the second part of the hypothesis, but only the one comparing extreme groups on hostility is confirming. In this analysis it is found that n Hostility is significantly inversely related to self-reported guilt on the picture of high relevance at the .05 level ($F = 4.14$, $df = 1/36$), and is unrelated to self-reported guilt on the pictures of low relevance. If we take the three analyses together, and consider the low level of significance in the one confirming analysis, the findings on thematic responses as a function of

TABLE 6

ANALYSIS OF VARIANCE OF N HOSTILITY
AS A FUNCTION OF SELF-REPORTED
HOSTILITY AND GUILT

Source	df	MS	F
Hostility (A)	1	0.00	0.00
Guilt (B)	1	122.00	13.55**
A × B	1	30.00	3.33*
Subjects within groups	76	9.00	

* $p \leq .05$, one-tailed test.
** $p \leq .001$.

[3] Results in accordance with hypothesis were evaluated by one-tailed tests of significance.

stimulus relevance and self-reported guilt are equivocal and in need of further verification.

TAT GUILT AS A FUNCTION OF SELF-REPORTED GUILT

In order to test the hypothesis that TAT guilt is directly related to self-reported guilt, it is first necessary to equate the groups on n Hostility, as the greater the expression of hostility the greater the opportunity for a score on guilt. The results are consistent for all three designs, and only the findings on the orthogonal arrangement of self-reported guilt and hostility are reported. For purposes of the analysis, eight subjects in each of the four cells were so selected that their means and variances on n Hostility were almost identical. Analysis of variance indicates that TAT guilt and self-reported guilt are significantly related at the .05 level $(F = 4.81, df = 1/28)$. The relationship is direct, with the groups of low and high self-reported guilt obtaining mean TAT guilt scores, respectively, of 2.68 and 4.75.

SELF-REPORTED CONFLICT AS A FUNCTION OF SELF-REPORTED HOSTILITY AND GUILT

It was anticipated that subjects high on both self-reported hostility and guilt would be high on self-reported conflict over hostility. To test this assumption, self-reported conflict was treated as a dependent variable and entered into the same experimental designs as the ones used to evaluate n Hostility. The results are consistent for all three analyses, and only the findings on the orthogonal arrangement of self-reported hostility and guilt are presented. Self-reported conflict is significantly related to self-reported hostility at the .001 level $(F = 15.34, df = 1/76)$, but it is not significantly related to self-reported guilt nor to the interaction of self-reported hostility and guilt. The relationship is a direct one, with the group high on self-reported hostility obtaining a mean conflict score of 21.4 as compared to a mean of 18.3 for the group low on self-reported hostility. The mean conflict scores for all four groups are as follows: High hostility-High guilt, 21.8; High hostility-Low guilt, 21.4; Low hostility-High guilt, 19.4; Low hostility-Low guilt, 17.0. The group with high self-reported hostility and low self-reported guilt obtains almost the identical mean as the group high on both. Thus self-reported guilt adds nothing to self-reported hostility in selecting subjects high on self-reported conflict.

THEMATIC HOSTILITY AS A FUNCTION OF SELF-REPORTED CONFLICT

No support was found for the hypothesis that conflict over hostility is indicated by a simultaneous overproduction of hostile responses to cues of low relevance and a failure to produce appropriately hostile responses to cues of high relevance. The data were also examined for a relationship between self-reported conflict and avoidance tendencies as revealed by displacement of hostile responses. A nonsignificant tendency was found for displaced responses to be associated with low scores on self-reported conflict. However, when the criterion for avoidance was complete absence of a hostile response to the picture of high relevance, the findings were in the opposite direction. Of a total of eight subjects who behaved in this fashion, five were in the high conflict group, and one in the low conflict group. Thus only when the most extreme avoidance reactions are considered is self-reported conflict directly related to avoidance. This finding, of course, requires verification with a larger sample.

As a second approach to testing the hypothesis that simultaneously overresponding to cues of low relevance and underresponding to cues of high relevance is indicative of conflict, subjects were divided on the basis of their thematic responses, and self-reported conflict was treated as the dependent variable. This procedure corresponds to the clinical use of the TAT, where prediction is from the projective test to other forms of behavior. There are eight subjects who produce a hostile response to a picture of low relevance and either fail to produce a hostile response to the picture of high relevance or produce a highly displaced response, at Level III or IV. Three additional groups of eight subjects were selected to form a 2 × 2 table for presence and absence of hostility in the stimulus, and direct versus displaced or no hostility in the response. An analysis of variance failed to reveal any source of significance, and what tendency there was, was for direct hostile responses to be positively associated with self-reported conflict, no matter to which stimulus the hostile responses had been made. A comparison of the four groups on individual items in the self-reported conflict scale revealed a significant relationship between producing a hostile response to pictures of low relevance and endorsing Items 16 and 49, the two most extreme items as determined by frequency of endorsement in the entire pool of subjects. One of the items

attests to a terrible temper and the other to frightening and destructive thoughts. In that both refer to hostile impulses, the findings are consistent with the direct relationship reported between self-rated hostility and hostile responses to stimuli of low relevance. However, it is possible that extremeness alone is the critical factor, and in view of the total number of items investigated, not much significance can be attributed to the two items other than that they provide a lead for further work.

Discussion

The findings in the present study in some respects coincide with the findings in the Leiman and Epstein (1961) study on the sex drive, after which it was patterned, and in some respects do not. Both studies demonstrated an inverse relationship between thematic drive related responses and self-reported guilt, both found an interaction between drive and guilt such that drive related responses were directly related to drive when guilt was low and inversely when guilt was high, and both demonstrated that pictures of low relevance provided a better measure of drive than pictures of high relevance. Both studies were also in agreement in failing to verify the hypothesis that conflict is indicated by simultaneously overresponding to cues of low relevance and underresponding to cues of high relevance. Agreement was less complete in regard to the hypothesis that pictures of high relevance provide the best measures of guilt. While the hypothesis was confirmed in the study on the sex drive, the results in the present study were equivocal. The studies also differ in regard to the relationship between drive and drive related responses across pictures. While the Leiman and Epstein study reported a direct and significant relationship, such was not the case in the present study. There are at least three possible reasons for the discrepancy. One is that the pictures were not equivalent in features other than drive relevance. A second possibility is that the drives are not functionally similar. As will be seen later, there is good reason to believe such is the case. Third, the two drives were inferred from different kinds of evidence, sex from reported rate of orgasm, and hostility from reported feelings. It is obvious that the latter is more dependent upon self-awareness than the former.

A finding in both studies that is of particular importance theoretically and practically is the nature of the interaction of drive and guilt. When guilt was low there was a direct relationship between drive and drive related responses, but when guilt was high, the relationship was inverse. Of practical significance, this finding indicates that the clinician must recognize that an increase in drive can be revealed by either an increase or decrease in drive related responses, depending upon guilt. Of theoretical significance, the interaction provides evidence that guilt reactions can be directly conditioned to cues produced by the drive itself, so that drive cannot be varied independently of guilt. Thus an increase in drive can produce a yet greater increase in guilt, with a net effect in the direction of increased avoidance. Such an effect is consistent with the assumption that the gradient of inhibition as a function of drive relevant cues *from any source* is steeper than the gradient of expression. All in all, it is apparent that a more complex model is required than Mill-

er's (1951) model which represents approach and avoidance gradients as varying independently from each other. The same point has recently been made by Champion (1961), Feshbach (1961), Leiman and Epstein (1961), and Miller (1961). The interaction between drive and guilt has been demonstrated in a variety of contexts. Lesser (1957) reported a direct relationship between thematic hostility and behavioral aggression in boys whose mothers encouraged aggression, and for whom there was presumably little guilt over hostility, and an inverse relationship in boys whose mothers discouraged aggression, and who presumably experienced considerable guilt over expression of hostility. Clark (1952) reported an inverse relationship between experimental arousal of sexual drive and thematic sexual responses under classroom conditions, and a direct relationship following a beer party, which was assumed to reduce inhibition. Strizver (1961), using subjects of a lower social class, who might be expected to be less inhibited over sex (Kinsey, Pomeroy, & Martin, 1948) than Clark's subjects, found a direct relationship under the conditions in which Clark found an inverse relationship.

How do the findings in the present study compare with other investigations of the relationship of thematic and self-reported hostility? The results are not entirely consistent. Lindzey and Tejessey (1956) report highly significant positive correlations between several measures of thematic hostility and self-reported hostility, while Child, Frank, and Storm (1956) find no relationship. Davids, Henry, McArthur, and McNamara (1955) find a significant relationship for *direction* but not *amount* of thematic hostility. They report a direct relationship between self-rated hostility and a score of "anger out" in thematic hostility, and an inverse relationship for a score of "anger in." In the present study, in which the scoring system corresponds to "anger out," no relationship was found across pictures, but a positive relationship was found on the pictures of low relevance. Herein lies an explanation of the discrepancies among different studies. Namely, studies which use different pictures obtain different results, as stimulus characteristics are critical, and not enough is known about them to make appropriate allowances for the differences. The common practice of pooling across pictures is certainly unwarranted unless the individual pictures have been shown to be functionally similar. While the results in the present study and the Leiman and Epstein (1961) study are consistent with the conclusion that pictures of low relevance provide better measures of drive than pictures of high relevance, the data are far from conclusive. It is possible that uncontrolled features of the stimulus were confounded with drive relevance, and were responsible for the results. This can only be determined by doing a sufficient variety of pictures. A particularly important investigation would be one in which the stimulus dimension is kept as simple as possible, with the stimuli varying in no respect other than the degree of anger of the hero depicted.

It was previously stated that hostility and sex, although both socially restricted drives, do not function in a completely parallel manner. This is most clearly revealed by the relationship of self-reported conflict to self-reported drive and guilt. Leiman (1961) found that self-reported conflict over sex was directly related to both drive and self-reported guilt. Those subjects who were high on drive as well as guilt were highest on conflict over sex. On the other hand, in the present study, self-reported guilt was not related to self-reported conflict over hostility, while self-reported drive was. The discrepancy can be attributed to the social implications of the two drives. The college male who has negative attitudes toward sex is treated as a social outcast, while the one with negative attitudes toward hostile expression is generally socially rewarded. Moreover, to a greater extent than for sex, intrapersonal conflict between expressive and inhibitory tendencies for hostility reduces interpersonal conflict, i.e., guilt, or control from within, reduces fear of retaliation from without.

The results failed to support the hypothesis that conflict is revealed by simultaneous projection to cues of low relevance and inhibition to cues of high relevance. Apart from the possibility that the model is incorrect, there are at least two alternative considerations. One is that a self-report measure, to the extent that it involves insight, is self-defeating as a criterion of conflict, as insight reduces projection and denial. A second consideration is that the model may hold only for conflict in terms of expression and inhibition of words and thoughts, i.e., suppression and repression, and such conflict does not correspond to conflict as exhibited in approach-avoidance behavior, nor does it necessarily involve personal disturbance. Thus it is possible to acknowledge or express avoidance tendencies and to inhibit the recognition or expression of approach tendencies. In a study in which subjects were selected on the basis of expression and inhibition of hostile responses on a thematic apperception test (Nelson & Epstein, 1962), where self-ratings were not involved, the results supported hypotheses derived from the conflict model.

Summary: Thematic hostility and guilt responses were investigated as a function of hostile cues and self-reported drive, guilt, and conflict over hostility. From a pool of 181 college males, extreme groups of 20 each were selected on each of the self-report measures. It was found that (a) self-reported hostility across levels of guilt was directly related to TAT hostility on pictures of low relevance for hostility only; (b) TAT hostility across pictures was directly related to self-reported hostility when guilt was low and inversely when guilt was high; (c) TAT hostility was inversely, and TAT guilt directly, related to self-reported guilt; and (d) there was no evidence that conflict produces a simultaneous increase in drive related responses to cues of low relevance and decrease in drive related responses to cues of high relevance.

Chapter 9

FANTASY, DREAMS, AND UNCONSCIOUS PROCESSES

This last chapter includes several related concepts and processes. They are each very important for the study of motivation, even though they are frequently omitted from texts on this subject. Even more than in the previous chapter, these concepts seem to have little application to non-human behavior, and any interest in having such concepts generalize from animal to human data or vice versa must be considered irrelevant here. Because so much of the study of motivation has been dictated by concepts and theoretical positions derived from animal research, how-ever, topics such as fantasy, dreams, or unconscious processes have been inadequately treated by every formal theory of motivation except the Freudian psychoanalytic theory. Consequently, it has been only very recently that experimental investigations of these processes has been undertaken, derived either from psychoanalytic theory or from other points of view.

This state of affairs is still somewhat surprising because of the obvious-ness of fantasy processes in the everyday life of every person. It is quite amazing that fantasy has been ignored for so long, even though it is a difficult aspect of behavior to handle and manipulate. It is just this point, though, that McClelland addresses in the paper presented here, and for this reason his paper is placed first. He enters a strong plea to psycholo-gists to reconsider the content of responses rather than just their structure or, at worst, their mere numerosity. He argues that whole vistas of access to motivational data are available if one only listens to what the subjects are saying. Specifically, he is most strongly suggesting the use of projective-like instruments, such as the Thematic Apperception Test, because of their standardization, ease of administration, and richness of data regard-ing fantasy processes.

Freud's paper is a very brief example of both the unconscious motiva-tion underlying an act of forgetting, and, on a microscopic level, the essence of the processes of free association in action. Clark's paper is a nearly classic study, such as that sought by McClelland, on the use of a fantasy measure both to study motivation (sexual and aggressive in this instance) and, even more impressively, to study the effects of these motives on the fantasizing of the subjects. His results offer very strong support that fantasy is no mere epiphenomenon of motivational states, but also functions to control and mediate those states. Blum's study, now over ten years old, still points out a different facet of how psychoanalytic concepts can be rigorously tested in the laboratory without losing the meaning or context of the theory. His study is particularly interesting because he suggests that perceptual vigilance and perceptual defense, far from being quite different processes, are both reactions to potential danger to the individual. They differ only in the perceived remoteness of the danger; when it is quite removed, vigilance reactions should occur, enabling the person to keep track of the danger. If, however, it is very close and threatens to overwhelm the person when he has no means to handle it, then perceptual defense reactions designed to block the danger from view will be utilized. Blum's experiment represents a demonstration of how perceived remoteness controls these two defensive processes.

The next two papers, on dreaming, by Hall and by Dement, reflect very different methodologies and very different interests; Both, however, show that access to the scientific study of dreaming is not only possible but very fruitful. Dement's work, particularly, opens up many new approaches to the study of the functioning of dreams, especially because he can determine when a dream is in progress without interrupting the dream or the dreamer.

The final three papers are chosen to illustrate three different aspects of the motivational properties of unconscious processes. Projection is one of the principal defense mechanisms utilized to handle anxiety. The paper by Bramal proposes a new interpretation of defensive projection, one based on Festinger's dissonance theory, and presents some evidence to support this conceptualization. This paper was selected in part because it offers the possibility of new experimental approaches to the study of this defense mechanism.

On a quite different topic, Hilgard has provided an excellent discussion and review of a fundamental distinction in psychoanalytic theory between primary and secondary processes in thinking, a distinction that is central in analyses of thought processes, especially as influenced by motivational patterns of behavior.

In the last paper, Leventhal and his coworkers present a study of how motivational processes interact with decisions and feelings in a nonlaboratory situation. An extensive experimental literature has appeared on the effects of motivational states, especially fear and anxiety, on decision-making and on the rationalizations for decisions after they are made. The experiment included here reports how anxiety over acquiring tetanus can affect both an individual's attitudes and his behavior with respect to preventative action.

Psychological Review, 1955, vol. 62, pp. 297–302

The Psychology of Mental Content Reconsidered[1]

David C. McClelland

Psychologists used to be interested in what went on in people's heads. In fact, for thousands of years this was practically all they were interested in. Psychologists from Aristotle to John Stuart Mill were concerned primarily with ideas and associations between ideas, but with the rise of modern scientific psychology we lost interest in ideas, by and large. The history of this development is well known, but let us review it for a moment. The psychology of mental content collapsed in the United States under the impact of two heavy blows. First, introspectionism seemed to run into a dead end. Titchener had argued manfully for a scientific study of the contents of mind, a kind of mental chemistry in which the basic elements would all be discovered and sorted out, but his laboratories simply failed to produce enough data to back up his theoretical position. It was not so much that his position was untenable. It was just that the data collected by the introspectionists did not seem to lead anywhere—to fruitful hypotheses, for example, which would serve to make theoretical sense out of the flux of mental events.

The second blow was even more devastating. It was, of course, the behavioristic revolution. Particularly in

the United States, psychologists began to argue that conscious content could never form the basis of a science, whereas behavior could. J. B. Watson led the revolt in the name of scientific objectivity. After all, could you see or touch or feel or record with a machine a thought or a feeling? Now, a muscular contraction—an eye blink, a foot withdrawal, a right turn in a maze—that was something else again. That could be seen and touched and felt and often recorded entirely automatically by an impersonal, mechanical gadget. Here was the stuff of which a real science could be made!

Looking back with the perspective of 30 years we can begin to see why this movement was so appealing. In the first place, it did provide the kind of objectivity, methodologically speaking, that psychology had never had before and it could, therefore, lend real support to psychology's claim that it was a science. Secondly, it fit in with the traditional American pragmatic bias in favor of action rather than thought or feeling which were generally considered to be old-fashioned European concepts. After all, in the United States it is what a man does that counts, not what he says or thinks or feels. This tendency in American psychology is still so prevalent that to many of us prediction of behavior means *only* predicting gross

[1] This paper was delivered at the Fourteenth International Congress of Psychology in Montreal, June 9, 1954.

motor behavior rather than predicting thoughts, conflicts, doubts, imaginings, feelings, etc. as reflected in verbal behavior. Thirdly, behaviorism tended to focus attention on problems which were of vital topical interest to a new country in which many of its citizens were attempting to adjust to new ways of life. In fact, adjustment or *learning* became the key concept. And this was natural in a country in which so many immigrants or their children had to give up traditional European ways of behaving for new American habit patterns. It was at this point that psychology became almost exclusively interested in "process variables," in how people went about doing things rather than in what they did. This was the time when Woodworth was stressing that we should rewrite psychology in terms of "ing" words—e.g., perceiving, emoting, thinking, learning, etc. No one was interested in *what* people thought, *what* they perceived, *what* they learned, etc. Instead we were to be concerned only with the laws which governed the *process* of perceiving, learning, etc.

Even personality and social psychology, which by definition are content oriented and which, therefore, should have resisted this trend, fell under the spell of this widespread movement. In personality psychology we were primarily interested in self-descriptive inventories in which the subject answered a lot of questions about his aches, pains, and anxieties. But, mind you, we did not look at his answers. We added them up to get a neuroticism score or dominance score or what not. We were not interested even here in *what* he said about himself, in *what* his ideas were. We were only interested in the extent to which his answer contributed to a total score which meant something else.

To be sure, an individual clinician sometimes went so far as to look at the actual answers a person had given on a personality inventory, but then, he was not a scientist! In social psychology, too, we managed to get along without much concern with content, although here, too, it was a little difficult. The problem was solved with the help of the attitude concept. An attitude is essentially what I have been calling a process variable. We are interested in *how* attitudes get set up, in how we can measure them, in their consistency, in their rigidity, their generality or specificity, etc.—all process variables. But we are not interested in *what* they are, particularly. Any old attitude will do for our purpose, just as in studying learning, any old task will do for our purpose—a maze, a bar to press, a list of nonsense syllables, or what not. So social psychologists chose as the attitudes to be investigated whatever happened to be of current interest at the moment —e.g., internationalism, feminism, pacifism, race prejudice, and so on. Few if any people thought it was even worth asking which attitudes were the "important" ones to use in describing a person or his culture. Many people probably would have wondered whether such questions really fell within the province of psychology at all.

It is against the background of this widespread social movement in psychology that we can see the beginnings of the projective testing movement as the source of a change in attitude which is finally beginning to be felt today, possibly in large part because of the success of projective tests. But certainly projective testing did not start as a conscious revolt against this interest in process. Quite the contrary. The Rorschach test, as one of the oldest of these new instruments, probably gained as wide acceptance as it did in the United States largely because it became primarily process-oriented. It became concerned with *how* people perceive and only secondarily with *what* they perceive. Quantitative indices could be computed according to how many responses were determined primarily by form, by color, by movement, and the like. Nevertheless, the good clinicians often found that the particular content of the association given by the patient was of value to them in understanding the person. And this has always been the case with a good clinician. He *has* to be interested in *what* his patient thinks as well as in how he thinks it. Even though his formal psychological training gives him very little assistance at this level, he knows that in order to handle this particular person he has to be interested in the patient's ideas. This, it seems to me, has been the great and continuing contribution of the clinic and the projective test in a time when psychological theorists have talked themselves out of being interested in content altogether. I am reminded here of a comment made to me once by one of my more cynical colleagues who claimed that no new ideas of importance ever appeared in the universities. Usually they appear outside first, and then are only gradually claimed by the universities. Certainly if we think for a minute of men like Descartes, Darwin, Freud, or Einstein, there would seem to be something in what he said. And this development seems to be a case in point. The projective testing movement grew up largely *outside* the conservative academic tradition and finally, because of its clinical success, has managed to dent the calm assurance with which many

theoretical psychologists have discarded all problems of mental content.

But to continue with my story: The real change came with the development by Murray and his associates of the Thematic Apperception Test about 20 years ago. Now for the first time we had an instrument in which the primary concern was not form but content. The person interpreting a TAT record must ask such questions as: *What* motives activate this person? *What* conflicts plague him? *What* modes of defense does he adopt? *What* characteristics does the world have for him? No longer are we concerned primarily, as in the Rorschach, with *how* he approaches his task, although some have attempted to analyze the TAT in these terms. To help us in our analyses of such content, we have drawn heavily on psychoanalysis, the one system of content psychology which, isolated in the clinic, survived the mass attack of behaviorism in the laboratory. Murray in his original system of analysis for the TAT attempted to provide us with a much broader vocabulary for the analysis of content, but, by and large, in our analyses we draw upon relatively few general psychoanalytical concepts such as sex, aggression, parent-child relationships, and the like. This, to my way of thinking, is an impoverished set of concepts for dealing with mental content, but it is nonetheless the one real and vital one in the United States today.

What evidence is there that this tendency to concern oneself with mental content is of growing influence? In the first place, we must not underestimate the conservative resistance to the belief that such a psychology is possible. Even Freud's generalizations about the importance of certain basic conflicts such as those involved in the Oedipus complex are under constant attack. To some extent the attacks are motivated by the conviction that generalizations about content are really impossible. The argument runs that there are no general concepts which can serve to describe the human situation at *any* place or time in history. What about cultural relativism? After all, individuals differ widely in what they think and so do cultures. Some have an Oedipus complex and some do not. How can we generalize about anything except the process by which individuals arrive at their ideas? The ideas themselves are completely relative. One can perhaps be literary about them, but not scientific. This is the argument and there is no answer to it, except to prove that it can be done fruitfully. Many of us are convinced already, for example, that despite individual and cultural variations, it is a major scientific achievement to have focused attention on the framework of the mother-son relationship as of primary importance in the development of the individual, and to have worked out some of the taxonomy of this and the allied relationship with the father.

Meanwhile, there have been some new developments which would encourage us to believe that perhaps a psychology of content is possible. Take the research report on *The Authoritarian Personality* (Adorno, Frenkel-Brunswik, Levison, & Sanford, 1950), for example. I would contend that the essential issues raised by this research are issues in the psychology of content. It represents to some extent a fusion of psychoanalytic structural concepts with certain concepts drawn from political ideology. Whether we like the fusion or not does not really matter too much. From the methodological point of view it repre-

sents an exciting step forward since its authors have drawn on political ideology as well as psychoanalysis to help explain the structure of personality. When our science has matured to the point where we can draw not only on political ideology, but on economic, religious, esthetic ideologies, and the like, then we will be on the way toward developing a really full-blown psychology of mental content.

Our own research on *The Achievement Motive* (McClelland, Atkinson, Clark, & Lowell, 1953) has contributed as much to these conclusions as anything else. We started with the relatively simple task of identifying those types of imagery in a TAT-type record which indicated the presence of a motive to achieve or succeed. After we were able to identify reliably this item of mental content, we were able to select individuals whose thought processes contained a lot of such items and other individuals whose thought processes contained few such items. We were then faced with the question of how these people differed. Do they behave differently? Yes, they do. The ones with a lot of achievement imagery tend to learn faster, to perform better, to set different levels of aspiration, to have a better memory for incompleted tasks, to perceive the world in different terms, etc. Perhaps even more interesting was the question of how they got that way. How is it that some people tend to think more often in achievement terms? We were led back to the mother-son relationship and found that independence training seems to be associated with achievement motivation. That is, those mothers who encouraged their sons to develop independently to learn their way around by themselves, seemed to have sons with higher achievement motives. But we pushed the question one step further back. How is it that some mothers favor independence training more than others? This raised the question of values, and values raised the question of religious ideology. Then we found that attitudes toward independence training were not randomly distributed through various population subgroups. Instead, Protestant and Jewish parents were much more likely to favor early independence training than were Catholic parents and this, in turn, seemed to fit into the belief systems and emphases of these three religions (McClelland, Rindlisbacher, & DeCharms, 1955). And if this is so, we can begin to trace some of the details of the connection between Protestantism and the rise of capitalism as originally outlined by Max Weber (1930) and R. H. Tawney (1926).

So our recent research has led us into the relationships between religious values, independence training, achievement motivation, and economic development. We think we are beginning to discover some connections among these phenomena which can be traced out with a fair degree of scientific confidence. But whether we succeed or not, the point I am trying to make is that by concentrating on one item of mental content, namely achievement imagery, we have opened up a whole new set of problems in social science that can be investigated by psychology.

Now let us pause a minute and try to reconsider what has happened. The "new look" in the study of mental content really involves neither introspection nor projective testing in their pure forms. Instead I prefer to call it "thought sampling," and to use the analogy of the "blood count" from the medical laboratory to explain what I have in mind. Just as we need a sample of blood to make a white cell count, we want a sample of thoughts or ideas to make our imagery counts. In general, we get these samples by asking the subject to write stories to certain cues, usually verbal or visual. Having gotten our thought sample, we have to learn to recognize certain types of imagery, just as the medical technician has to learn to recognize a white blood cell when he sees one. This involves a great deal of preliminary work so that we can define the characteristics of the imagery carefully and then train individuals to recognize what they are looking for. It does require training, but probably no more training than a medical technician needs to be able to distinguish one type of blood cell from another. That is, it does not involve high-level judgment, but is essentially a "pointing" operation which is a little, but not much, more difficult to make than pointing to an animal's right turn in a maze. Watson need not have feared for the objectivity of this kind of analysis. The record is permanent. The same person can look at it again and again, or several people can analyze it. It is quite possible to get a reliable and objective result.

If we put the "new look" in mental content in these general terms, it is immediately clear that we have a number of problems to solve. For example, there is the sampling problem. Under what conditions should we get our thought samples? What cues should we use? Should we get long samples or short samples? What about the subject's set? How does it influence content? Here it becomes obvious that traditional projective testing elicits only a very small segment of the possible types of mental content. To the extent that we stay within the limited framework of the traditional TAT cards, for example, we are bound to have a biased sample of what goes on in a man's mind.

An even more important problem has to do with the decision as to what categories for content analysis we use. This is the heart of the problem, since we will get theoretically meaningful results, or generalizations that hold for a wide variety of situations, only if we choose the right categories to begin with. How does one discover the right categories? The literature of social science is strewn with content analyses of everything from open-ended interviews to "soap operas"—analyses which are purely *ad hoc*—for the immediate practical purpose in hand. I am certainly not arguing for more of this industrious busy work. The categories must be meaningful; they must be related to theory; they must be trans-situational— i.e., applicable to more situations than the one to which they are first applied. It takes inspiration or luck or hard work or something to discover such a category, just as it did in biology to discover what was the most useful of many possible ways to classify blood cells. The only concrete suggestion I have as to how to proceed, which comes from our own experience, is to choose those categories which show significant shifts as a result of experimental operations. Whether this is an unnecessarily restrictive rule, I do not know. At any rate it certainly eliminates many possible categories, and it seems to be roughly the one which the chemists have used in setting up the classification of elements.

This brings us back to Titchener. Looking back with the perspective of history, we can now see that Titchener's structural psychology failed for two reasons. In the first place, the content categories he chose did not turn out to be fruitful. They were not related to experimental operations on the one hand or to other types of behavior on the other. For these or other reasons, they simply did not lead to theoretical development. Therefore they were the wrong categories. In the second place, and this is of major methodological importance, his students categorized their own data. The essence of introspection is that the same person serves both as a source of data and as a categorizer of them. This has an obvious weakness, a weakness which has been perpetuated in self-descriptive personality inventories. It is simply that the subject may have a very imperfect or incorrect idea of what categories his thoughts belong in. This may be because his categories are different from the ones we as scientists want to use or because he may really misperceive himself. The great contribution that both Freud and the projective testing movement made was that neither asked the subject to pass judgment on his thoughts as they appeared to him. Both simply asked for a sample of those thoughts and then left the categorization process to an outside observer. This was an important methodological advance, the significance of which I think we are only just beginning to appreciate.

If psychologists are to re-enter the field of mental content and start classifying it according to categories of genuine theoretical fruitfulness, I fear they will have to return to disciplines they have long neglected. In the twenties, in the heyday of behaviorism, we were proud that we knew nothing of religion, of art, of history, of economics, or politics (except in a personal, often naive way). We didn't need to know about these things if we were only interested in process variables. We could make our own choice of a task situation—for example, the rat in a maze—and what we found out there about how the rat learned the maze would apply equally well to *all* (including human) learning situations. We could afford to be ignorant of many things that man has thought about. But if the psychology of content develops as I think it will, we shall have to go back to getting a broad, general education. Certainly nothing in my training *as a psychologist* prepared me to handle problems in religious belief systems or economic development. Yet these are typical of the problems which I think will begin to arise increasingly often in the new

psychology of content, and we simply cannot afford to be naive and pretend that research scholars in these fields have nothing to tell us.

If my analysis is correct, we are on the brink of an important new development in psychology. Because of methodological improvements, we are about to take up again some of the problems in mental content that formerly were considered to be an essential part of psychology. And it is my conviction that the projective testing movement is to be thanked for keeping an interest in content alive in an era when most theoretical psychologists were otherwise occupied, and for providing us with the methodological advance that enabled us to escape from the blind alley into which introspection had led us.

The Psychopathology of Everyday Life. London: Ernest Benn, Limited, 1904, Chapter 1, pp. 3–18

Unconscious Motivation in Everyday Life*

Sigmund Freud

Forgetting of Foreign Words

The ordinary vocabulary of our own language seems to be protected against forgetting within the limits of normal function, but it is quite different with words from a foreign language. The tendency to forget such words extends to all parts of speech. In fact, depending on our own general state and the degree of fatigue, the first manifestation of functional disturbance evinces itself in the irregularity of our control over

foreign vocabulary. In a series of cases, this forgetting follows the same mechanism as the one revealed in the example *Signorelli*. As a demonstration of this, I shall report a single analysis, characterized, however, by valuable features concerning the forgetting of a word, not a noun, from a Latin quotation. Before proceeding, allow me to give a full and clear account of this little episode.

Last summer, while journeying on my vacation, I renewed the acquaintance of a young man of academic edu-

* Excerpted and reprinted by permission of the publisher.

cation, who, as I soon noticed, was conversant with some of my works. In our conversation we drifted—I no longer remember how—to the social position of the race to which we both belonged. He, being ambitious, bemoaned the fact that his generation, as he expressed it, was destined to become stunted, that it was prevented from developing its talents and from gratifying its desires. He concluded his passionately felt speech with the familiar verse from Virgil: *Exoriare . . .* in which the unhappy *Dido* leaves her vengeance upon *Aeneas* to posterity. Instead of "concluded," I should have said, "wished to conclude," for he could not bring the quotation to an end, and attempted to conceal the open gap in his memory by transposing the words: "*Exoriar(e) ex nostris ossibus ultor!*" He finally became piqued and said: "Please don't make such a mocking face, as if you were gloating over my embarrassment, but help me. There is something missing in this verse. How does it read in its complete form?"

"With pleasure," I answered, and cited it correctly:

"*Exoriar(e) aliquis nostris ex ossibus ultor!*"

"It was too stupid to forget such a word," he said. "By the way, I understand you claim that forgetting is not without its reasons; I should be very curious to find out how I came to forget this indefinite pronoun '*aliquis*'"

I gladly accepted the challenge, as I hoped to get an addition to my collection, and said, "We can easily do this, but I must ask you to tell me frankly and without any criticism everything that occurs to your mind after you focus your attention, without any particular intention, on the forgotten word."

"Very well, the ridiculous idea comes

to me to divide the word in the following way: *a* and *liquis.*"

"What does that mean?"

"I don't know."

"What else does that recall to you?"

"The thought goes on to *reliques—liquidation—liquidity—fluid.*"

"Does that mean anything to you now?"

"No, not by a long shot."

"Just go ahead."

"I now think," he said, laughing sarcastically, "of Simon of Trent, whose relics I saw two years ago in a church in Trent. I think of the old accusation which has been brought against the Jews again, and of the work of *Kleinpaul,* who sees in these supposed sacrifices reincarnations or revivals, so to speak, of the Saviour."

"This stream of thoughts has some connection with the theme which we discussed before the Latin word escaped you."

"You are right. I now think of an article in an Italian journal which I have recently read. I believe it was entitled: 'What St. Augustine said Concerning Women.' What can you do with this?"

I waited.

"Now I think of something which surely has no connection with the theme."

"Oh, please abstain from all criticism, and—"

"Oh, I know! I recall a handsome old gentleman whom I met on my journey last week. He was really an *original* type. He looked like a big bird of prey. His name, if you care to know, is Benedict."

"Well, at least you give a grouping of saints and church fathers: *St. Simon, St. Augustine* and *St. Benedict.* I believe that there was a Church father named *Origines*. Three of these, more-over, are Christian names, like *Paul* in the name of *Kleinpaul*."

"Now I think of *St. Januarius* and his blood miracle—I find that the thoughts are running mechanically."

"Just stop a moment; both St. Janu-arius and St. Augustine have something to do with the calendar. Will you re-call to me the blood miracle?"

"Don't you know about it? The blood of St. Januarius is preserved in a phial in a church in Naples, and on a certain holiday, a miracle takes place causing it to liquefy. The people think a great deal of this miracle, and become very excited if the liquefying process is re-tarded, as happened once during the French occupation. The General in command—or Garibaldi, if I am not mistaken—then took the priest aside, and with a very significant gesture pointed out to him the soldiers arrayed without, and expressed his hope that the miracle would soon take place. And it actually took place. . . ."

"Well, what else comes to your mind? Why do you hesitate?"

"Something really occurred to me . . . but it is too intimate a matter to im-part . . . besides, I see no connection and no necessity for telling it."

"I will take care of the connection. Of course I cannot compel you to re-veal what is disagreeable to you, but then you should not have demanded that I tell you why you forgot the word '*aliquis*'."

"Really? Do you think so? Well, I suddenly thought of a woman from whom I could easily get a message that would be very annoying to us both."

"That she missed her courses?"

"How could you guess such a thing?"

"That was not very difficult. You pre-pared me for it long enough. Just think

of the *saints of the calendar, the lique-fying of the blood on a certain day, the excitement if the event does not take place, and the distinct threat that the miracle must take place*. . . . Indeed, you have elaborated the miracle of St. Januarius into a clever allusion to the courses of the woman."

"It was surely without my knowledge. And do you really believe that my in-ability to reproduce the word '*aliquis*' was due to this anxious expectation?"

"That appears to me absolutely cer-tain. Don't you recall dividing it into *a-liquis* and the associations: *reliques, liquidation, fluid?* Shall I also add to this connection the fact that St. Simon, to whom you got by way of *reliques*, was sacrificed as a child?"

"Please stop. I hope you do not take these thoughts—if I really entertained them—seriously. I will, however, con-fess to you that the lady is Italian, and that I visited Naples in her company. But may not all this be coincidental?"

"I must leave to your own judgment whether you can explain all these con-nections through the assumption of co-incidence. I will tell you, however, that every similar case that you analyze will lead you to just such remarkable 'coin-cidences'!"

I have more than one reason for valu-ing this little analysis, for which I am indebted to my travelling companion. First, because in this case, I was able to make use of a source which is otherwise inaccessible to me. Most of the exam-ples of psychic disturbances of daily life that I have here compiled, I was obliged to take from observation of my-self. I endeavored to evade the far richer material furnished me by my neurotic patients because I had to pre-clude the objection that the phenomena in question were only the result and manifestation of the neurosis. It was therefore of special value for my purpose to have a stranger free from a neurosis offer himself as a subject for such examination. This analysis is also important in other respects, inasmuch as it elucidates a case of word-forgetting *without* substituted recollection, and thus confirms the principle formulated above, namely, that the appearance or nonappearance of incorrect substitutive recollections does not constitute an essential distinction.

But the principal value of the example *aliquis* lies in another of its distinctions from the case *Signorelli*. In the latter example, the reproduction of the name becomes disturbed through the after-effects of a stream of thought which began shortly before and was interrupted, but whose content had no distinct relation to the new theme which contained the name Signorelli. Between the repression and the theme of the forgotten name, there existed only the relation of temporal contiguity, which reached the other in order that the two should be able to form a connection through an outer association. On the other hand, in the example *aliquis,* one can note no trace of such an independent repressed theme which could occupy conscious thought immediately before and then re-echo as a disturbance. The disturbance of the reproduction proceeded here from the inner part of the theme touched upon, and was brought about by the fact that unconsciously a contradiction arose against the wish-idea represented in the quotation.

The origin must be construed in the following manner: The speaker deplored the fact that the present generation of his people was being deprived of its rights, and like Dido, he presaged that a new generation would take upon itself vengeance against the oppressors. He therefore expressed the wish for posterity. In this moment, he was interrupted by the contradictory thought: "Do you really wish so much for posterity? That is not true. Just think in what a predicament you would be if you should now receive the information that you must expel posterity from the quarter you have in mind! No, you want no posterity—as much as you need it for your vengeance." This contradiction asserts itself, just as in the example *Signorelli,* by forming an outer association between one of his ideation elements and an element of the repressed wish, but here it is brought about in a most strained manner through what seems an artificial detour of associations. Another important agreement with the example *Signorelli* results from the fact that the contradiction originates from repressed sources and emanates from thoughts which would cause a deviation of attention.

So much for the diversity and the inner relationship of both paradigms of the forgetting of names. We have learned to know a second mechanism of forgetting, namely, the disturbance of thought through an inner contradiction emanating from the repression. In the course of this discussion, we shall repeatedly meet with this process, which seems to me to be the more easily understood.

Erroneously Carried-Out Actions

It is quite obvious that grasping the wrong thing may also serve a whole series of other obscure purposes. Here is a first example: It is very seldom that I break anything. I am not particularly dexterous, but by virtue of the anatomic integrity of my nervous and muscular apparatus, there are apparently no grounds in me for such awkward movements with undesirable results. I can recall no object in my home which I have ever broken. Owing to the narrowness of my study, it has often been necessary for me to work in the most uncomfortable position among my numerous antique clay and stone objects, of which I have a small collection. So much is this true that onlookers have expressed fear lest I topple down something and shatter it. But it never happened. Then, why did I brush to the floor the cover of my simple inkwell so that it broke into pieces?

My inkstand is made of a flat piece of marble which is hollowed out for the reception of the glass inkwell; the inkwell has a marble cover with a knob of the same stone. A circle of bronze statuettes with small terra-cotta figures is set behind this inkstand. I seated myself at the desk to write; I made a remarkably awkward outward movement with the hand holding the penholder, and so swept the cover of the inkstand, which already lay on the desk, to the floor.

It is not difficult to find the explanation. Some hours before, my sister had been in the room to look at some of my new acquisitions. She found them very pretty, and then remarked: "Now the desk really looks very well only the inkstand doesn't match. You must get a prettier one." I accompanied my sister out and did not return for several hours. But then, as it seems, I performed the execution of the condemned inkstand.

Did I perhaps conclude from my sister's words that she intended to present me with a prettier inkstand on the next festive occasion, and did I shatter the unsightly old one in order to force her to carry out her signified intention? If that be so, then my swinging motion was only apparently awkward; in reality, it was most skillful and designed, as it seemingly understood how to avoid all the valuable objects located near it.

I actually believe that we must accept this explanation for a whole series of seemingly accidental awkward movements. It is true that on the surface, these seem to show something violent and irregular, similar to spastic-ataxic movements, but on examination, they seem to be dominated by some intention, and they accomplish their aim with a certainty that cannot be generally credited to conscious arbitrary motions. In both characteristics, the force as well as the sure aim, they show besides a resemblance to the motor manifestations of the hysterical neurosis, and in part also to the motor accomplishments of somnambulism, which here as well as there, point to the same unfamiliar modification of the functions of innervation.

In latter years, since I have been collecting such observations, it has happened several times that I have shattered and broken objects of some value, but the examination of these cases convinced me that it was never the result of accident or of my unintentional awkwardness. Thus, one morning while in my bath-robe and straw slippers, I followed a sudden impulse as I passed a room, and hurled a slipper from my foot against the wall so that it brought down a beautiful little marble Venus from its bracket. As it fell to pieces, I recited quite unmoved the following verse from Busch:

Ach! Die Venus ist perdü—[1]
Klickeradoms!—von Medici!

[1] Alas! The Venus of Medici is lost!

This crazy action and my calmness at the sight of the damage are explained in the then existing situation. We had a very sick person in the family, of whose recovery I had personally despaired. That morning, I had been informed that there was a great improvement; I know that I had said to myself, "After all she will live." My attack of destructive madness served therefore as the expression of a grateful feeling toward fate, and afforded me the opportunity of performing an "act of sacrifice," just as if I had vowed, "If she gets well, I will give this or that as a sacrifice." That I chose the Venus of Medici as this sacrifice was only gallant homage to the convalescent. But even today, it is still incomprehensible to me that I decided so quickly, aimed so accurately, and struck no other object in close proximity.

Another breaking, in which I utilized a penholder falling from my hand, also signified a sacrifice, but this time, it was a pious offering to avert some evil. I had once allowed myself to reproach a true and worthy friend for no other reason than certain manifestations which I interpreted from his unconscious activity. He took it amiss and wrote me a letter in which he bade me not to treat my friends by psychoanalysis. I had to admit that he was right and appeased him with my answer. While writing this letter, I had before me my latest acquisition—a small, handsome, glazed Egyptian figure. I broke it in the manner mentioned, and then immediately knew that I had caused this mischief to avert a greater one. Luckily, both the friendship and the figure could be so cemented that the break would not be noticed.

A third case of breaking had a less serious connection; it was only a disguised "execution," to use an expression from Th. Vischer's *Auch Einer,* of an object that no longer suited my taste. For quite a while, I had carried a cane with a silver handle; through no fault of mine, the thin silver plate was once damaged and poorly repaired. Soon after the cane was returned, I mirthfully used the handle to angle for the leg of one of my children. In that way, it naturally broke and I got rid of it.

The indifference with which we accept the resulting damage in all these cases may certainly be taken as evidence for the existence of an unconscious purpose in their execution.

As can sometimes be demonstrated by analysis, the dropping of objects or the overturning and breaking of the same, are very frequently utilized as the expression of unconscious streams of thought, but more often, they serve to represent the superstitious or odd significances connected therewith in popular sayings. The meanings attached to the spilling of salt, the overturning of a wineglass, the sticking of a knife dropped to the floor, and so on, are well known. I shall discuss later the right to investigate such superstitious interpretations; here I shall simply observe that the individual awkward acts do not by any means always have the same meaning, but, depending on the circumstances, they serve to represent now this or that purpose.

Recently, we passed through a period in my house, during which an unusual number of glass and china dishes were broken. I myself largely contributed to the damage. This little endemic was readily explained by the fact that it preceded the public betrothal of my eldest daughter. At such festivities, it is customary to break some dishes and utter at the same time some felicitating expression. This custom may signify a sacrifice or express any other symbolic sense.

When servants destroy fragile objects by letting them fall, we certainly do not think in the first place of a psychic motive for it; still, some obscure motives are not improbable even here. Nothing lies farther from the uneducated than the appreciation of art and works of art. Our servants are dominated by a foolish hostility against these productions, especially when the objects, whose worth they do not realize, become a source of a great deal of work for them. On the other hand, persons of the same education and origin employed in scientific institutions often distinguish themselves by great dexterity and reliability in the handling of delicate objects, as soon as they begin to identify themselves with their masters and consider themselves an essential part of the staff.

I shall here add the report of a young mechanical engineer, which gives some insight into the mechanism of damaging things.

"Some time ago, I worked with many others in the laboratory of the High School on a series of complicated experiments on the subject of elasticity. It was a work that we undertook of our own volition, but it turned out that it took up more of our time than we expected. One day, while going to the laboratory with F., he complained of losing so much time, especially on this day, when he had so many other things to do at home. I could only agree with him, and he added half jokingly, alluding to an incident of the previous week: 'Let us hope that the machine will refuse to work, so that we can interrupt the experiment and go home earlier.'

"In arranging the work, it happened that F. was assigned to the regulation of the pressure valve; that is, it was his duty to carefully open the valve and let the fluid under pressure flow from the accumulator into the cylinder of the hydraulic press. The leader of the experiment stood at the manometer and called a loud 'Stop!' when the maximum pressure was reached. At this command, F. grasped the valve and turned it with all his force—to the left (all valves, without any exception, are closed to the right). This caused a sudden full pressure in the accumulator of the press, and as there was no outlet, the connecting pipe burst. This was quite a trifling accident to the machine, but enough to force us to stop our work for the day and go home.

"It is characteristic, moreover, that some time later on discussing this occurrence, my friend F. could not recall the remark that I positively remember he had made."

Similarly, to fall, to make a misstep, or to slip need not always be interpreted as an entirely accidental miscarriage of a motor action. The linguistic double meaning of these expressions points to diverse hidden phantasies, which may present themselves through the giving up of bodily equilibrium. I recall a number of lighter nervous ailments in women and girls which made their appearance after falling without injury, and which were conceived as traumatic hysteria as a result of the shock of the fall. At that time, I already entertained the impression that these conditions had a different connection, that the fall was already a preparation of the neurosis, and an expression of the same unconscious phantasies of sexual content which may be taken as the moving forces behind the symptoms. Was not this very thing meant in the proverb which says, *"When a maiden falls, she falls on her back"*?

We can also add to these mistakes the case of one who gives a beggar a gold piece in place of a copper or a silver coin. The solution of such mishandling is simple: it is an act of sacrifice designed to mollify fate, to avert evil, and so on. If we hear a tender mother or an aunt express concern regarding the health of a child, immediately before taking a walk during which she displays her charity, contrary to her usual habit, we can hardly doubt the sense of this apparently undesirable accident. In this manner, our faulty acts make possible the practice of all those pious and superstitious customs which must shun the light of consciousness, because of the strivings against them of our unbelieving reason.

That accidental actions are really intentional will find no greater credence in any other sphere than in sexual activity, where the border between the intention and accident hardly seems discernible. That an apparently clumsy movement may be utilized in a most refined way for sexual purposes, I can verify by a nice example, from my own experience. In a friend's house, I met a young girl visitor who excited in me a feeling of fondness which I had long believed extinct, thus putting me in a jovial, loquacious and complaisant mood. At that time, I endeavored to find out how this came about, as a year before this same girl made no impression on me.

As the girl's uncle, a very old man,

entered the room, we both jumped to our feet to bring him a chair which stood in the corner. She was more agile than I and also nearer the object, so that she was the first to take possession of the chair. She carried it with its back to her, holding both hands on the edge of the seat. As I got there later and did not give up the claim to carrying the chair, I suddenly stood directly back of her, and with both my arms was embracing her from behind, and for a moment, my hands touched her lap. I naturally solved the situation as quickly as it came about. Nor did it occur to anybody how dexterously I had taken advantage of this awkward movement.

Occasionally, I have had to admit to myself that the annoying, awkward stepping aside on the street, whereby for some seconds one steps here and there, yet always in the same direction as the other person, until finally both stop facing each other, that this "barring one's way" repeats an ill-mannered, provoking conduct of earlier times and conceals erotic purposes under the mask of awkwardness. From my psychoanalysis of neurotics, I know that the so-called naïveté of young people and children is frequently only such a mask employed in order that the subject may say or do the indecent without restraint.

The effects which result from mistakes of normal persons are, as a rule, of a most harmless nature. Just for this reason, it would be particularly interesting to find out whether mistakes of considerable importance, which could be followed by serious results, as, for example, those of physicians or druggists, fall within the range of our point of view.

As I am seldom in a position to deal

with active medical matters, I can only report one mistake from my own experience. I treated a very old woman, whom I visited twice daily for several years. My medical activities were limited to two acts, which I performed during my morning visits: I dropped a few drops of an eye lotion into her eyes and gave her a hypodermic injection of morphine. I prepared regularly two bottles—a blue one, containing the eye lotion, and a white one, containing the morphine solution. While performing these duties, my thoughts were mostly occupied with something else, for they had been repeated so often that the attention acted as if free. One morning, I noticed that the automaton worked wrong; I had put the dropper into the white instead of into the blue bottle, and had dropped into the eyes the morphine instead of the lotion. I was greatly frightened, but then calmed myself through the reflection that a few drops of a *two per cent* solution of morphine would not likely do any harm even if left in the conjunctival sac. The cause of the fright manifestly belonged elsewhere.

In attempting to analyze the slight mistake, I first thought of the phrase, "to seize the old woman by mistake," which pointed out the short way to the solution. I had been impressed by a dream which a young man had told me the previous evening, the contents of which could be explained only on the basis of sexual intercourse with his own mother. The strangeness of the fact that the Oedipus legend takes no offense at the age of Queen Jocasta seemed to me to agree with the assumption that in being in love with one's mother, we never deal with the present personality, but with her youthful

memory picture carried over from our childhood. Such incongruities always show themselves where one phantasy fluctuating between two periods is made conscious, and is then bound to one definite period.

Deep in thoughts of this kind, I came to my parent of over ninety; I must have been well on the way to grasp the universal character of the Oedipus fable as the correlation of the fate which the oracle pronounces, for I made a blunder in reference to or on the old woman. Here, again, the mistake was harmless; of the two possible errors, taking the morphine solution for the eye, or the eye lotion for the injection, I chose the one by far the least harmful. The question still remains open whether in mistakes in handling things which may cause serious harm, we can assume an unconscious intention as in the cases here discussed.

Determinism and Chance

As the general result of the preceding separate discussions, we must put down the following principle: *Certain inadequacies of our psychic functions —whose common character will soon be more definitely determined—and certain performances which are apparently unintentional prove to be well motivated when subjected to psychoanalytic investigation, and are determined through the consciousness of unknown motives.*

In order to belong to the class of phenomena which can thus be explained, a faulty psychic action must satisfy the following conditions:

(a) It must not exceed a certain measure, which is firmly established through our estimation, and is designated by the expression "within normal limits."

(b) It must evince the character of the momentary and temporary disturbance. The same action must have been previously performed more correctly or we must always rely on ourselves to perform it more correctly if we are corrected by others, we must immediately recognize the truth of the correction and the incorrectness of our psychic action.

(c) If we at all perceive a faulty action, we must not perceive in ourselves any motivation of the same, but must attempt to explain it through "inattention" or attribute it to an "accident."

Thus, there remain in this group the cases of forgetting, the errors, the lapses in speaking, reading, writing, the erroneously carried-out actions and the so-called chance actions. The explanations of these very definite psychic processes are connected with a series of observations which may in part arouse further interest.

By assuming that a part of our psychic function is unexplainable through purposive ideas, we ignore the realms of determinism in our mental life. Here, as in still other spheres, determinism reaches farther than we suppose. In the year 1900, I read an essay published in the *Zeit* written by the literary historian R. M. Meyer, in which he maintains and illustrates by examples, that it is impossible to compose nonsense intentionally and arbitrarily. For some time, I have been aware that it is impossible to think of a number, or even of a name, of one's own free will. If one investigates this seeming voluntary formation, let us say, of a number of many digits uttered in unrestrained mirth, it always proves

to be so strictly determined that the determination seems impossible. I will now briefly discuss an example of an "arbitrarily chosen" first name, and then exhaustively analyze an analogous example of a "thoughtlessly uttered" number.

While preparing the history of one of my patients for publication, I considered what first name I should give her in the article. There seemed to be a wide choice; of course, certain names were at once excluded by me, in the first place the real name, then the names of members of my family to which I would have objected, also some female names having an especially peculiar pronunciation. But, excluding these, there should have been no need of being puzzled about such a name. It would be thought, and I myself supposed, that a whole multitude of feminine names would be placed at my disposal. Instead of this, only one sprang up, no other besides it; it was the name Dora.

I inquired as to its determination: "Who else is called Dora?" I wished to reject the next idea as incredulous; it occurred to me that the nurse of my sister's children was named Dora. But I possess so much self-control, or practice, in analysis, if you like, that I held firmly to the idea and proceeded. Then a slight incident of the previous evening soon flashed through my mind which brought the looked-for determinant. On my sister's dining room table, I noticed a letter bearing the address, "Miss Rosa W." Astonished, I asked whose name this was, and was informed that the right name of the supposed Dora was really Rosa, and that on accepting the position, she had to lay aside her name because Rosa would also refer to my sister. I said pityingly; "Poor people! They cannot even retain their own names!" I now recall that on hearing this, I became quiet for a moment and began to think of all sorts of serious matters which merged into obscurity, but which I could now easily bring into my consciousness. Thus, when I sought a name for a person *who could not retain her own name,* no other except "Dora" occurred to me. The exclusiveness here is based, moreover, on firmer internal associations, for in the history of my patient, it was a stranger in the house, the governess, who exerted a decisive influence on the course of the treatment.

This slight incident found its unexpected continuation many years later. While discussing in a lecture the long since published history of the girl called Dora, it occurred to me that one of my two women pupils had the very name Dora, which I was obliged to utter so often in the different associations of the case. I turned to the young student whom I knew personally with the apology that I had really not thought that she bore the same name, and that I was ready to substitute it in my lecture by another name.

I was now confronted with the task of rapidly choosing another name and reflected that I must not now choose the first name of the other woman student, and so set a poor example to the class, who were already quite conversant with psychoanalysis. I was therefore well pleased when the name "Erna" occurred to me as the substitute for Dora, and Erna I used in the discourse. After the lecture, I asked myself whence the name "Erna" could possibly have originated and had to laugh as I observed that the feared possibility in the choice of the substitutive name had come to pass, in

part at least. The other lady's family name was Lucerna of which Erna was a part.

In a letter to a friend, I informed him that I had finished reading the proof sheets of *The Interpretation of Dreams,* and that I did not intend to make any further changes in it, "even if it contained 2,467 mistakes." I immediately attempted to explain to myself the number and added this little analysis as a postscript to the letter. It will be best to quote it now as I wrote it when I caught myself in this transaction:

"I will add hastily another contribution to the *Psychopathology of Everyday Life.* You will find in the letter the number 2,467 as a jocose and arbitrary estimation of the number of errors that may be found in the dream-book. I meant to write: no matter how large the number might be, and this one presented itself. But there is nothing arbitrary or undetermined in the psychic life. You will therefore rightly suppose that the unconscious hastened to determine the number which was liberated by consciousness. Just previous to this, I had read in the paper that General E. M. had been retired as Inspector-General of Ordnance. You must know that I am interested in this man. While I was serving as military medical student, he, then a colonel, once came into the hospital and said to the physician: 'You must make me well in eight days, as I have some work to do for which the Emperor is waiting.'

"At that time, I decided to follow this man's career, and just think, today (1899) he is at the end of it—Inspector-General of Ordnance and already retired. I wished to figure out in what time he had covered this road, and assumed that I had seen him in the hospital in 1882. That would make 17 years. I related this to my wife, and she remarked, 'Then you, too, should be retired.' And I protested, 'The Lord forbid!' After this conversation, I seated myself at the table to write to you. The previous train of thought continued, and for good reason. The figuring was incorrect; I had a definite recollection of the circumstances in my mind. I had celebrated my coming of age, my *24th* birthday, in the military prison (for being absent without permission). Therefore, I must have seen him in 1880, which makes it 19 years ago. You then have the number 24 in 2467! Now take the number that represents my age, 43, and add 24 years to it and you get 67! That is, to the question whether I wished to retire, I had expressed the wish to work 24 years more. Obviously, I am annoyed that in the interval during which I followed Colonel M., I have not accomplished much myself, and still there is a sort of triumph in the fact that he is already finished, while I still have all before me. Thus we may justly say that not even the unintentionally thrown-out number 2467 lacks its determination from the unconscious."

Free Will and Superstition

This understanding of the determination of apparently arbitrarily selected names, numbers, and words may perhaps contribute to the solution of another problem. As is known, many persons argue against the assumption of an absolute psychic determinism by referring to an intense feeling of conviction that there is a free will. This feeling of conviction exists, but is not incompatible with the belief in determinism. Like all normal feelings, it

must be justified by something. But, so far as I can observe, it does not manifest itself in weighty and important decisions; on these occasions, one has much more the feeling of the psychic compulsion and gladly falls back upon it. (Compare Luther's "Here I stand, I cannot do anything else.")

On the other hand, it is in trivial and indifferent decisions that one feels sure that he could just as easily have acted differently, that he acted of his own free will, and without any motives. From our analyses we therefore need not contest the right of the feeling of conviction that there is a free will. If we distinguish conscious from unconscious motivation, we are then informed by the feeling of conviction that the conscious motivation does not extend over all our motor resolutions. *Minima non curat praetor.* What is thus left free from the one side receives its motive from the other side, from the unconscious, and the determinism in the psychic realm is thus carried out uninterruptedly.

Although conscious thought must be altogether ignorant of the motivation of the faulty actions described above, yet it would be desirable to discover a psychologic proof of its existence; indeed, reasons obtained through a deeper knowledge of the unconscious make it probable that such proofs are to be discovered somewhere. As a matter of fact, phenomena can be demonstrated in two spheres which seem to correspond to an unconscious and hence, to a displaced knowledge of these motives.

(*a*) It is a striking and generally recognized feature in the behavior of paranoiacs, that they attach the greatest significance to trivial details in the behavior of others. Details which are usually overlooked by others they interpret and utilize as the basis of far-reaching conclusions. For example, the last paranoiac seen by me concluded that there was a general understanding among people of his environment, because at his departure from the railway station, they made a certain motion with one hand. Another noticed how people walked on the street, how they brandished their walking-sticks, and the like.

The category of the accidental, requiring no motivation, which the normal person lets pass as a part of his own psychic functions and faulty actions, is thus rejected by the paranoiac in his application to the psychic manifestations of others. All that he observes in others is full of meaning; all is explainable. But how does he come to look at it in this manner? Probably here, as in so many other cases, he projects into the mental life of others what exists in his own unconscious activity. Many things obtrude themselves on consciousness in paranoia, which in normal and neurotic persons can only be demonstrated through psychoanalysis as existing in their unconscious. In a certain sense, the paranoiac behavior is justified; he perceives something that escapes the normal person; he sees clearer than one of normal intellectual capacity, but his knowledge becomes worthless when he imputes to others the state of affairs he thus recognizes. I hope that I shall not be expected to justify every paranoiac interpretation. But the point which we grant to paranoia in this conception of chance actions will facilitate for us the psychologic understanding of the conviction which the paranoiac attaches to all these interpretations. *There is certainly some truth to it;* even our errors of judgment, which are not designated as morbid, acquire their feeling of conviction in the same way. This feeling is justified for a certain part of the erroneous train of thought or for the source of its origin, and we shall later extend to it the remaining relationships.

(*b*) The phenomena of superstition furnish another indication of the unconscious motivation in chance and faulty actions. I will make myself clear through the discussion of a simple experience which gave me the starting-point to these reflections.

Having returned from my vacation, my thoughts immediately turned to the patients with whom I was to occupy myself in the beginning of my year's work. My first visit was to a very old woman (see above) for whom I had twice daily performed the same professional services for many years. Owing to this monotony, unconscious thoughts have often found expression on the way to the patient and during my occupation with her. She was over ninety years old; it was therefore pertinent to ask oneself at the beginning of each year how much longer she was likely to live.

On the day of which I speak, I was in a hurry and took a carriage to her house. Every coachman at the cabstand near my house knew the old woman's address, as each of them had often driven me there. This day, it happened that the driver did not stop in front of her house, but before one of the same number in a nearby and really similar-looking parallel street. I noticed the mistake and reproached the coachman, who apologized for it.

Is it of any significance when I am taken to a house where the old woman is not to be found? Certainly not to me; but were I *superstitious,* I should see an omen in this incident, a hint of fate that this would be the last year for the old woman. A great many omens which have been preserved by history have been founded on no better symbolism. Of course, I explain the incident as an accident without further meaning.

The case would have been entirely different had I come on foot and, "absorbed in thought" or "through distraction," I had gone to the house in the parallel street instead of the correct one. I would not explain that as an accident, but as an action with unconscious intent requiring interpretation. My explanation of this "lapse in walking" would probably be that I expected that the time would soon come when I should no longer meet the old woman.

I therefore differ from a superstitious person in the following manner:

I do not believe that an occurrence in which my mental life takes no part can teach me anything hidden concerning the future shaping of reality; but I do believe that an unintentional manifestation of my own mental activity surely contains something concealed which belongs only to my mental life— that is, I believe in outer (real) chance, but not in inner (psychic) accidents. With the superstitious person, the case is reversed: he knows nothing of the motive of his chance and faulty actions; he believes in the existence of psychic contingencies; he is therefore inclined to attribute meaning to external chance, which manifests itself in actual occurrence, and to see in the accident a means of expression for something hidden outside of him. There are two differences between me and the superstitious person: first, he projects the motive to the outside, while I look for it in myself; second, he explains the accident by an event which I trace to a thought. What he considers hidden corresponds to the unconscious with me, and the compulsion not to let chance pass as chance, but to explain it as common to both of us.

Thus, I admit that this conscious ignorance and unconscious knowledge of the motivation of psychic accidentalness is one of the psychic roots of superstition. *Because* the superstitious person knows nothing of the motivation of his own accidental actions, and because the fact of this motivation strives for a place in his recognition, he is compelled to dispose of them by displacing them into the outer world. If such a connection exists, it can hardly be limited to this single case. As a matter of fact, I believe that a large portion of the mythological conception of the world which reaches far into the most modern religions, *is nothing but psychology projected to the outer world.* The dim perception (the endo-psychic perception, as it were) of psychic factors and relations[2] of the unconscious was taken as a model in the construction of a *transcendental reality,* which is destined to be changed again by science into *psychology of the unconscious.*

[2] Which naturally has nothing of the character of perception.

D. C. McClelland (Ed.), *Studies in Motivation.* New York: Appleton-Century-Crofts, Inc., 1955, Chapter 5, pp. 44–57

The Effects of Sexual Motivation on Phantasy*

Russell A. Clark

The purpose of the present research has been to investigate the measurement of sexual motivation by content analysis of "creative" stories written by subjects to pictures from the Thematic Apperception Test (TAT). The original impetus for this study came from some findings by McClelland *et al.* All of the TAT scoring categories employed by McClelland and his associates (McClelland, Atkinson, Clark, & Lowell, 1953) for measuring the need for achievement (*n* Achievement) varied as a direct function of increase in motivation. That is to say, with an increase in experimentally induced achievement motivation there was a corresponding increase in the frequency of appearance of the various achievement-related categories. This seems to indicate that for *n* Achievement there is no such thing as repression, suppression, or any sort of inhibition operating. Such a finding seems fairly plausible in view of the fact that in the American culture individuals are widely encouraged to work hard, get good grades in school, advance themselves in the business world, and so forth. There are few taboos attached to the attainment of achievement goals. However, these findings involved mean differences in frequencies based on groups of subjects. A further study by McClelland *et al.* (1953) involving case histories and psychiatric interviews indicated that there were a few individuals who were highly motivated to achieve but so anxious about achievement that they inhibited the expression of manifest achievement imagery in their TAT stories. This tentative finding ran contrary to the common assumption that projective measures circumvent the usual defenses of the individual.

For investigating the degree to which inhibition occurs in the TAT, it seemed desirable to select some motive which was apt to differ from *n* Achievement with regard to amount of anxiety that was apt to be involved. The sex motive, in our society at least, seems to have the necessary qualifications. There are all sorts of parental, social, and religious prohibitions against sexual activity. Because of this basis difference, and because it seemed possible to manipulate sex motivation experimentally, this motive was chosen as suitable for investigation.

Procedure

Two separate experiments will be described here. Each involved two groups of male college *S*s, one of which (aroused)

* Reprinted by permission of Appleton-Century-Crofts. Prepared especially for *Studies in Motivation,* but based in part on Clark, R. A., The projective measurement of experimentally induced sexual motivation. *Journal of experimental Psychology,* 1952, 44: 391–399.

took a group TAT after having been exposed to some type of sexually arousing stimulus. The other group (control) consisted of comparable Ss who took the group TAT without prior sexual stimulation. The difference between the two experiments is that the first was conducted in a classroom setting. That is to say, both the aroused and control groups were tested in lecture halls at regularly scheduled class meetings. This condition will hereafter be referred to as the nonalcohol or normal condition. The second experiment, however, was conducted in two different fraternity houses at night under a beer-party atmosphere. This condition will be referred to as the alcohol condition.

The TAT pictures employed were from the Murray 1943 series with one exception. They were presented in the following order: 7BM, 12BG, 14, 20, 10, 6F, Picture of a man working late at night in an office, and 6BM. However, under the normal (classroom) condition there was sufficient time to show only the first five of these TAT slides. In the alcohol condition all eight were given. The instructions which were employed for the administration of the group TAT are the standard instructions used by McClelland et al. (1953; McClelland, Clark, Roby, & Atkinson, 1949).

Nonalcohol Condition

The aroused group was first exposed to a series of photographic slides of attractive nude females and immediately thereafter given the TAT. The control group took the TAT immediately after having been exposed to a series of slides of landscape scenes, architecture, fashionably decorated rooms, and so forth.

The Ss were in two sections of an elementary psychology class. They were tested before there had been any formal discussion of projective techniques. Two Es (graduate students) met the control class; one to conduct an "investigation on factors affecting aesthetic judgment," which was the rationale for the control slides, and the other to conduct "a standardization of a test of creative imagination." The Ss were asked to rate each slide with respect to degree of attractiveness stating what it was about the picture that makes it attractive

or unattractive. They used mimeographed line rating scales with spaces for comments. All slides were presented briefly in order to enable Ss to get an over-all impression, and then on the second presentation the slides were shown for a longer period thus enabling Ss to make the ratings and pertinent comments. The TAT was given by the second E immediately thereafter. Every effort was made to convince Ss that the rating of the slides and the TAT were separate experiments.

The aroused group was tested on the next day by the author and one of the previous Es. After again doing a variety of things to give Ss the impression that the presentation of the slides and the TAT were two different experiments, the author gave the rationale for the presentation of the nude slides, which was an attempt to make the presentation of the nude slides seem very plausible to the Ss. This rationale gave as a reference the work of Sheldon (14) on the correlation between body type and certain physical and mental disorders, explained why the pictures of nude females were drawn from art photography (because of social pressure against standardized body-typing photographs), and requested Ss to use a mimeographed line rating scale with space for comments in evaluating the eight pictures to be shown. The E indicated that comments such as "breasts just the right size and shape" and "legs long and shapely" were adequate. In order to further set Ss for sexual stimulation by the slides, E then said:

I think that you will find that most of these pictures are of at least fairly attractive girls. We have purposely included mostly those body types that we feel should be fairly appealing. So when you use the rating scale, don't be concerned if many of the ratings fall towards the attractive end of the scale, but try to make fine discriminations among the more attractive girls. Now remember your job is to judge the sexual attractiveness of these girls. I don't think you will find this an especially unpleasant task.

The nudes were projected life-size on a large screen. After the Ss had finished their ratings and pertinent comments about these slides, *E* collected the papers, packed up the slides, and left. The other *E* then came forward and administered the TAT with the same remarks and instructions that were given the control group.

Alcohol Condition

In this condition the aroused group took the TAT in a fraternity beer-party setting after having been exposed to nude slides as compared with a control group also in a beer-party setting but without exposure to any kind of slides.[1]

Two presumably comparable fraternity groups were used as the aroused and control groups. The TAT was rationalized on the ground that it was desirable to determine the effects of informal environment and alcohol on the test of "creative imagination." The test was given approximately one and one-quarter hours after the start of the beer parties, and Ss were permitted to continue drinking during the test. The nude pictures were exposed on slides to the aroused group through clandestine arrangements with a "stooge" in the fraternity in a manner designed to dissociate these pictures from the later TAT. The TAT was given shortly after the last of eight nude pictures was shown.

Scoring

The scoring was done by the author and one other person. The author rescored the stories several times. The other scorer practiced on 150 stories under the author's tutelage before beginning the reliability check. In the case of the few discrepancies the final scoring was decided upon after a joint conference of the two scorers.

The first analysis of the TAT protocols was to reveal manifest sex imagery. Sexual relationships were categorized as (*a*) primary—explicit or implicit evidence for

[1] Neutral slides were omitted from this control group because a few stories in the nonalcohol condition seemed to be determined by a set for evaluation of the aesthetic qualities of the TAT slides which presumably was established by having rated the aesthetic qualities of the "control" slides. Also under beer party conditions it is difficult to get a rationale for looking at neutral slides. This was not true for the nude slides which were introduced as the private property of a member of the fraternity.

sexual intercourse, (*b*) secondary—evidence for the occurrence of such secondary sex activity as kissing, dancing, or fondling, (*c*) tertiary—characters in the stories perceived as sweethearts, on a date, courting, in love, and so on, but not engaged in either primary or secondary sexual activity. Sexual activity was scored only once for each story, and that which was biologically most sexual received priority.

The per cent agreement between the two scorers was 91 per cent for sexual imagery. This percentage was obtained by considering agreements to be those categories which both scorers had marked as being present. Those categories which one scorer had marked as being present but the other scorer had marked as absent were counted as disagreements. Those categories which both scorers had indicated as being absent were not considered in the above calculations. Thus, agreements of the present-present variety are considered but not agreements of the absent-absent variety.

Results and Discussion

Manifest Sex Imagery

Table 1 summarizes the results from these two experiments. This table clearly shows that under classroom (nonalcohol) conditions the sexually-aroused group expressed significantly less manifest sex than did the control group. This finding, of course, suggested that the aroused group was inhibiting expression of sexuality because of anxiety or guilt. Therefore the second experiment was conducted with the expectation that the consumption of alcohol would reduce this inhibition and permit the aroused group to exhibit an increased expression of sexuality. It is, of course, a very common assumption that alcohol reduces guilt, fear, or anxiety, and in fact, recent work by Conger (1951) with white rats seems to demonstrate that this is the case. Table 1 shows that this expectation is confirmed. Under the influence

TABLE 1

MEAN FREQUENCY OF MANIFEST SEXUAL IMAGERY EXPRESSED
BY BOTH THE CONTROL AND SEXUALLY AROUSED GROUPS
UNDER ALCOHOL AND NONALCOHOL CONDITIONS*

	Nonalcohol		Alcohol	
	Control	*Aroused*	*Control*	*Aroused*
Number of cases	38	40	27	35
Mean frequency of sex imagery	1.68	1.10	2.07	2.40
Differences	*Control vs. Aroused*		*Control vs. Aroused*	
Mean diff.	−.58		.33	
t	2.42		1.90	
p	<.01		.07	
	Nonalcohol vs. Alcohol			
Mean diff.	.88			
t	4.89			
p	<.01			

* The means in this table are based on the first five picture which all groups had in common. The *t* tests within the nonalcohol group and between the nonalcohol and alcohol groups were made using the error estimate obtained from all four groups to compute a more reliable estimate of the standard error of the mean difference (139 degrees of freedom). However, for the comparisons within the alcohol group eight pictures were available for use. Thus the *t* tests involved in these comparisons are based on the data for all eight pictures (not presented here) with the error estimate coming from these groups alone which would have of course only 60 degrees of freedom. All *p* values are based on two-tailed tests of significance.

of alcohol the aroused group expresses more rather than less manifest sexual imagery than the control group, and both alcohol groups taken together express significantly more sex than does the nonalcohol group.

In conclusion these results seem to indicate that under normal (nonalcohol) conditions the sexual arousal causes sufficient anxiety to lead to the inhibition of manifest sexual imagery whereas, under the influence of alcohol this anxiety or guilt is sufficiently reduced to permit increased expression of manifest sexuality reflecting directly the heightened state of arousal.

Sexual symbolism

With these foregoing results in hand a Freudian hypothesis immediately came to mind. When the manifest expression of sexuality is being inhibited, as seems to be the case for the aroused group under nonalcohol conditions, perhaps a disguised form of expression such as symbolism will be exhibited. Freud's discussion of this situation with respect to dreams is too well known to require any elaboration here. Therefore, it was decided to score for the presence of sexual symbolism. This presented certain difficulties. The major difficulty was encountered when we tried to score merely for the presence of all separate objects that are considered to be potential symbols. The reason for our difficulty was that the TAT pictures which were employed clearly depicted objects that are considered classical sexual symbols. For example, 12BG clearly shows a boat resting in a pond under a tree in a general wooded setting. The boat, tree, and rolling landscape are sexual symbols mentioned by Freud and others. Picture 14 shows the silhouette of a boy in a window. A window or portal is, of course, another sexual symbol. Other such examples could be cited. Thus, we were getting large numbers of symbols that were merely mentions of objects that were clearly depicted in the pictures. This did not seem to be a sensible procedure. Our final decision was not to score for the presence of symbolism if there was only the mere mention of a given classical symbol that was clearly depicted in the TAT picture. In fact, we did *not* score the mere mentioning of a classical symbol even if it wasn't clearly depicted in the picture. In order to be scored for symbolism a story had to meet the following criterion: The classical symbol or symbols mentioned had to be utilized or involved in some action which in and of itself could be interpreted as being symbolic. That is, isolated objects which fulfilled the requirements for sexual symbols were scored only if they appeared in a symbolic context that could be interpreted as signifying intercourse, masturbation, tumescence-detumescence cycles, and so on. For example, if in response to picture 14 a person wrote that this was a boy looking out of his dormitory *window,* this was *not* scored as symbolic, but if there were a thief *climbing up* to go through the *window* in order to steal the *jewels* in the *house,* this *was* scored as symbolic. In this latter statement the window which is a classical symbol and clearly represented in the picture is also a part of a classically symbolic action sequence, e.g., climbing, breaking into house, stealing jewels. In essence what we scored for was not the mere presence of isolated objects that could or could not be

symbols, but for themas that could be interpreted in a symbolic fashion. These themas, of course, involved objects which are considered to be the symbols for the male or female genitals, breasts, and so forth. For a discussion of classical symbolism see Gutheil (1939) or Hall (1953).

In scoring, the stories were given weights of two, one, or zero. A weight of two indicated that symbolism was strongly present in the story, a weight of one indicated that some symbolism was present, and zero indicated that no symbolism could be detected. An individual's total score was the sum of the weights given his five separate stories. The scoring was done independently by two scorers after they had familiarized themselves with the literature on sexual symbolism. The product-moment correlation between the initial two sets of total scores for both the alcohol and nonalcohol conditions was $+.82$. The scoring used for the present analysis represents a joint scoring in which differences in the two sets of scores were reconciled.

A t test of the difference between the two groups of the nonalcohol condition (cf. also Table 2) demonstrated that the aroused group $(N = 39)$ exhibited a significantly higher symbolic sex score than did the control group $(N = 38)$ $(t = 2.19, p < .05)$. It will be recalled, of course, that this aroused group showed significantly *less* manifest sexual content than its control group. This finding, then, is in line with Freud's general hypothesis that anxiety can cause manifest sex content to be inhibited, but that sexual motivation can find expression in symbolic form. Also if Freud's hypothesis is correct, one would expect the groups in the alcohol condition to express little symbolism because of the fact that once anxiety was reduced by the consumption of alcohol and the permissive party atmosphere all the sexual expression would be manifest in nature. This, in fact, turns out to be the case. In this condition both the controls and the aroused group express very little symbolism and in almost identical amounts. The average symbolism score for the combined groups in this condition was .45. This value is lower than that obtained for either the control or aroused groups of the nonalcohol condition. ($t = 1.79$, $p < .08$; $t = 3.87$, $p < .01$ respectively). These findings, of course, are in complete accord with the classical Freudian contention. That is, if anxiety is present the libido finds expression in a disguised or symbolic fashion. When anxiety is absent, sexual expression is channeled directly in manifest form.

A recent paper by Hall (1953), however, takes exception to this Freudian contention. In general Hall maintains that sexual symbolism in dreams is not a disguised expression of sex, the purpose of the disguise being to smuggle the content past the censor, but rather a means of representing as clearly as possible the particular conception of sexuality that the dreamer has in mind. One of several cogent reasons that Hall has for offering his alternative theory is that in his collection of dreams he often found both manifest and symbolic expression of sexual activity in the same dream or same sequence of dreams. The question that Hall raises concerns the efficacy of disguising the sexual content if at the next moment it is revealed in manifest form.

Hall's theory was of particular interest because the same phenomenon was noted in this study in the TAT stories.

That is, an individual would give both strong manifest and symbolic sex in the same story or series of stories. To throw additional light on this somewhat paradoxical question we decided to examine the intra-group relationship between symbolic and manifest expression of sex. If Freud's contention is correct, one would again expect a negative relationship between the two as was the case with the inter-group comparisons. If Hall's formulation is correct, one might possibly expect even a positive relationship. It was feasible to do this only for the two groups of the nonalcohol condition. The frequency of appearance of symbolism was so very low under conditions of alcohol that any kind of intra-group trend analysis was meaningless. The obtained relationship for the nonalcohol condition can be seen in Table 2 which presents the results of an analysis of variance in which both the aroused and control groups were divided into thirds as equally as possible based on the *manifest* sex score. This manifest sex score was derived by giving a weight of two to a primary sex story, a weight of one to a secondary or tertiary sex story, and a weight of zero to a story containing no manifest sex. The breakdown into thirds of the distribution was made separately for the control and aroused groups. That is, the "highs" in the aroused group represent those with the highest manifest sex content in their own group, but they have significantly lower manifest sex score than the "highs" in the control group. Lastly, the entries in the cells represent averages based on the total symbolic sex score previously described.

It can be seen from Table 2 that the relationship between manifest and symbolic sex is neither positively or nega-

TABLE 2

MEAN SCORES ON SEXUAL SYMBOLISM AS A FUNCTION OF EXPERIMENTAL CONDITION
AND MANIFEST SEX SCORE (NONALCOHOL CONDITION)*

	Experimental condition	High manifest sex score	Moderate manifest sex score	Low manifest sex score
Mean	Aroused	M 1.87	.64	1.70
sex	Group	N 15	14	10
symbolism	Control	M .89	.56	1.00
score	Group	N 9	16	13

	Source	Sums of squares	d.f.	Variance estimate
	1. Total	38.20	76	
	2. Experimental treatment	2.15	1	2.15
	3. Manifest sex score	3.18	2	1.59
Error	4. Interaction (2 × 3)	0.51	2	.26
	5. Within cells	32.36	71	.46

$$F = \frac{\text{Experimental treatment}}{\text{Error}} = 4.78 \ p < .05$$

$$F = \frac{\text{Manifest sex score}}{\text{Error}} = 3.53 \ p < .05$$

* In the statistical treatment of the data in this table the means are based on the raw data. However, the actual t tests or F tests were based on transformed data using the square root technique. This was done because the variance estimates were not homogeneous and seemed proportional to the means. Also in the analysis of variance adjustment was made for disproportionate sub-class frequencies according to the method offered by Johnson (1949).

tively linear but rather curvilinear, with those individuals who write either strong manifest sex stories or very weak manifest sex stories exhibiting the greatest amount of symbolism. This relationship can be seen more readily from the plot in Figure 1. That this trend is probably not a random one is evidenced by the F test involving the variation due to the different levels of manifest sex score. Also the fact that the interaction between the experimental treatment and manifest sex score is insignificant indicates that there is no evidence that the trends in the two groups are dissimilar.

This curvilinear relationship is rather a curious finding. The large amount of symbolism in the high manifest group is, of course, the major deviant finding and in need of explanation. This fol-

lows, because according to a Freudian formulation the writing of strong sex stories would seem to preclude the possibility of the presence of much anxiety. There are a number of ways

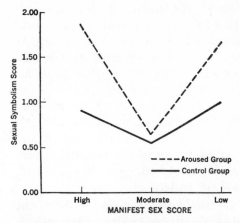

Fig. 1. Sexual Symbolism score as a function of manifest sex score for the aroused and control groups of the nonalcohol condition.

in which to account for this. One way is to assume that if sexual motivation becomes sufficiently high, there is the tendency for symbolism to be expressed without regard to the presence of anxiety. With this added assumption this interpretation would be in line with Hall's general formulation and could also account for the increased amount of symbolism in the aroused group.

One other possibility is, of course, that both Hall and Freud are correct. It may well be that symbolism is used as an alternative means of expressing sex even in the absence of anxiety but becomes more preferred to the extent that anxiety is involved. However, an examination of the data from the alcohol condition should help clarify this issue. The aroused group from this experiment represents a sexually aroused group presumably with much of the anxiety reduced by the alcohol and permissive party atmosphere. This group gave a large number of manifest sex stories. If Freud's formulation is correct, you would *not* expect much symbolism in this group because of the presumably low anxiety level. If the formulation which is more in line with Hall's theorizing is correct, you would expect a large amount of symbolism. As indicated previously from the comparisons involving the combined groups from the alcohol condition this is not the case. The average symbolism score for the aroused group alone was .41, which is lower than the aroused and control groups of the nonalcohol condition ($t = 3.88$, $p < .01$; $t = 1.83$, $p < .07$ respectively).

It would thus seem that to the extent that anxiety is lacking, symbolism is lacking, and that Freud's formulation is supported. However, there still re-mains the apparently paradoxical fact that in the intra-group breakdown for the nonalcohol condition those with high manifest scores also have high symbolism scores. This seems paradoxical because, as mentioned before, the writing of sex stories, especially of a primary nature, would seem to preclude the possibility of the presence of anxiety. However, there is one possibility that should not be ignored, and this involves the response-produced guilt that stems from writing stories of a sexual nature. The individuals who write strong sex stories must normally have a fairly low anxiety level which permits them to do this, but writing sexual stories, especially if primary in nature, may cue off enough guilt to channel the expression into symbolic form. This certainly did seem to be what was happening in some cases in which a primary manifest sex story was followed immediately by one containing symbolism.

The solution to this very paradox has been handled by Miller (1944) in slightly different terms in his treatment of approach-avoidance conflicts. Miller points out, "Similar paradoxical effects may be deduced when the attractiveness of the goal is held constant and its repulsiveness varied within the limits allowing the two gradients to cross. As the strength of avoidance at the goal is weakened, the subject will be expected to move forward. But as he moves forward, the strength of approach increases so that stronger avoidance must be aroused before his advance is stopped. The fact that the subject moves nearer to the dangerous goal more than compensates for its reduction in unattractiveness."

In this instance going closer to the goal would involve writing stories of a more primary nature. Therefore, it would be individuals with the initial low gradients of avoidance who would write the most sexual stories and thus be apt to experience the most response-produced guilt.

Therefore, what may possibly be happening is something like this. The individuals in the *low* manifest group (both aroused and controls) through past training are highly anxious about expressing sex. For the aroused subjects this anxiety is, of course, reinforced by the stimulation to which they were exposed. These individuals, therefore, would tend to express most of their sexuality in symbolic terms. The individuals in the *high* manifest group through past training have acquired less anxiety over sexuality and therefore approach close enough to the goal to write stories of a primary nature which in turn cues off quite a bit of guilt resulting in symbolic expression of sexuality. Now what about the individuals in the moderate manifest category? They could be individuals with a moderate amount of anxiety who write stories with mild sexuality in them, but this isn't enough to cue off much guilt, so they have only a moderate amount of symbolism in their stories.

There still remains at least one apparent inconsistency: Why is it that in the intra-group comparisons the individuals with the highest manifest sex scores give high symbolism; whereas, in the inter-group comparisons just the reverse holds true? Why shouldn't the control group of the nonalcohol condition give as much or more symbolism than the aroused group in view of the fact that they gave significantly more manifest sex? That is to say, isn't it possible that the increased response-produced guilt of the control-group is

enough to offset the stimulus-produced anxiety of the aroused group? One possible answer to this is that in the aroused group nearly *everyone* should have experienced a certain high level of anxiety as a function of examining the slides of attractive nude females; whereas, in the control group perhaps an equivalent level of guilt was reached by only those individuals who wrote stories of a primary manifest nature.

Although much of the foregoing has been *ad hoc* conjecture, a few tentative conclusions seem justifiable: (*a*) It does seem that classical symbolism serves as a disguised expression of sexuality. (*b*) Symbolism as a mode of expression seems to be preferred only to the extent that anxiety over sex is present. (*c*) The amount of symbolism in a story is not necessarily a direct measure of the "normal" level of anxiety. For example, if an individual's normal level is quite low, he may approach so close to the goal that this engenders a high level of response-produced guilt which may in turn produce symbolic expression of sexuality. (*d*) The above is a possible explanation of the seemingly paradoxical fact that both strong manifest and symbolic expressions of sexuality appear in the same phantasy sequences.

The relation between sexual and aggressive imagery

Throughout the psychological literature there appear scattered conjectures and evidence that sexuality and aggression are somehow intimately linked. Freud (1938) writes, "That cruelty and the sexual instinct are most intimately connected is beyond doubt taught by the history of civilization, but in the explanation of this connection no one has gone beyond the accentuation of the aggressive factors of the libido." Dollard, Doob, Miller, Mowrer & Sears (1939) report a study by Sollenberger in which there was shown to be a very marked relationship between aggressive behavior and male hormone content of adolescent boys. Ford and Beach (1951) cite numerous examples of aggressive behavior occurring during copulation up and down the phylogenetic scale. In a recent study by Lindner (1953) it was found that sexual offenders showed more aggression on a projective test than did a control group of non-sexual offenders.

A similar finding exists with the present data. The stories for both groups were scored for the presence of overt aggression. There were five general categories that constituted the scoring system for aggression: (a) all occurrences of death except by suicide,[2] (b) physical violence—beatings, auto accidents, combat, rape, and so forth, (c) personal tragedies and misfortunes—homes burning to the ground, loved ones ill, loss of life savings, and so on, (d) crimes—theft, breaking and entering, embezzlement, and so on, (e) quarrels—disagreements in which anger, hatred, resentment, or tension are involved. Also in this analysis punishment or imprisonment for crimes committed was *not* considered as aggression. The crimes were scored, of course, but not any attendant punishment. Finally, only aggressive acts directed against persons were considered in this present analysis. The scoring was done independently by two separate scorers. A product-moment reliability coefficient was calculated using as the score for

[2] For the purposes of the present and a later analysis, it was considered expedient to omit suicides because their theoretical significance is quite complex. A check was made, however, and it was found that their inclusion would not have altered the nature of the findings.

each individual the total frequency of appearance of aggressive incidents in his five stories. This correlation was .91.

Under nonalcohol conditions only 4 of the 39 Ss in the sexually aroused group gave at least three aggressive responses compared with 22 of the 38 Ss in the control group. This difference is highly significant (Chi-square, corrected for continuity, $= 17.57, P < .01$). It will be recalled that the sexually aroused group in the nonalcohol condition also expressed significantly less manifest sex. Consequently the *decrease in both manifest sex and aggression imagery resulting from sexual arousal* would appear to argue for a close linkage between sex and aggression. However, it is not at all clear what the exact nature of this linkage is. If there had been *more* aggression in the aroused group instead of less, this would have been consonant with the frustration-aggression hypothesis expounded by such writers as Dollard *et al.* (1939), on the assumption that arousal had increased sexual drives which could not be satisfied under the circumstances. A possibility is that there were greater aggressive tendencies in the aroused group, but these suffered the same fate for the same reason as the sexual tendencies discussed in the previous sections. That is to say, it might easily be that the expression of any frustration-produced aggression would be inhibited by the presence of anxiety over expressing aggression. It might be that some measure of a disguised or substitute form of aggression would show a higher frequency in the aroused group as was the case with expression of sexuality. Although it is a little difficult to conceive of "symbolic" aggression, there is a somewhat different approach that is pertinent. McClelland (1951) in his discussion of aggression cites evidence that if there is a strong anxiety present, aggressive tendencies appearing in phantasy will be projected into impersonal, vague, or unspecified agents. That is, a person is killed not at the hands of another person but by an animal, through sickness, accident, and so forth. Following this lead all instances of aggression appearing in the stories were scored as to whether the agent of the aggression was personal in source or whether the agent was impersonal or unspecified. Accidents were scored as impersonal because intent to harm is absent, and because the emphasis is definitely on the vehicle as the instrument of harm. Deaths in a war, although to an extent depersonalized, were scored as "personal" because war usually involves inter-personal conflict with intent to harm. Again the scoring was done independently by two individuals and product moment reliability coefficients were calculated. An individual's score consisted of the total number of personal or impersonal instances of aggression appearing in his record. Separate reliabilities were calculated for the two types of aggression. For aggres-

sion which was personal in source the correlation was .93, for impersonal aggression it was .88.

The results of this analysis showed that only 12 of the 35 Ss in the control group who showed any aggression attributed at least half of it to impersonal sources compared with 20 of the 30 Ss who showed any aggression in the sexually aroused group (Chi-square = 6.70, $P < .01$). Therefore, although the aroused group expresses significantly less aggression than the control group, an appreciably greater percentage of this aggression is impersonal in source. Thus a reasonable conclusion would seem to be that the aroused group was not only anxious about expressing manifest sex, but also anxious about expressing manifest aggression; and when it did express manifest aggression, there was a tendency to project it into impersonal or unspecified sources.

In short, in college males anxiety resulting from sexual arousal seems to result in a decrease and disguise not only of manifest sexual imagery but of thoughts of direct personal aggression as well.

Journal of Personality, 1963, vol. 31, pp. 336–345

Strangers in Dreams: An Empirical Confirmation of the Oedipus Complex[1]

Calvin Hall

The empirical foundations upon which Freud based his theory of personality consisted chiefly of the quali-

[1] This investigation was supported by a USPHS research grant, No. M-6475 (A) from the National Institute of Mental Health, USPHS.

tative analysis of verbal behavior of patients undergoing psychoanalysis. Although confirmation of hypotheses generated by Freudian theory still comes largely from observations of patient behavior, other empirical approaches are employed. Among these are observations of infant and child behavior, cross-cultural studies, responses to projective and objective tests, and controlled laboratory experiments.

One of the principal activities of the Institute of Dream Research is the testing of hypotheses derived from Freudian theory using dreams collected from a large number of persons differing in sex, age, ethnic groups, and other respects. The use of dreams for this purpose is particularly appropriate since from the very beginning of psychoanalysis, dreams and free associations to them have been an important source of data. Freud was convinced that dreaming makes manifest unconscious and otherwise inaccessible roots of personality.

Critics of psychoanalytic methodology have objected to the qualitative, subjective, and anecdotal character of the evidence secured from dreams and free associations of patients. Psychoanalysts have been criticized for generalizing findings obtained from a patient population to people in general.

With the Institute's large collection of dreams it is possible to obviate these criticisms. Objective, quantitative, and repeatable tests of Freudian theory can be made without violating the basic assumptions of the theory.

The investigation to be reported here is a test of the validity of the Oedipus complex. Testable hypotheses were formulated in terms of the contents of reported dreams and associations to these contents.

In the classical exposition of the development of the Oedipus complex, very young children of either sex are described as having a positive cathexis for the mother and a negative one for the father. The father is perceived by the child as an intruder, an unwelcome stranger, and a threat. He is resented and feared. In the course of development, the girl's feelings toward her mother and father diverge from those of the boy's. Recognizing that she lacks a penis and blaming her mother for this deficiency, she turns from the mother to the father. In spite of this turning, the earlier fantasies of the "good" mother and the "bad" father are not obliterated. In comparison with the boy whose nuclear Oedipus complex remains fairly constant, the girl is more ambivalent toward both parents. She neither fears nor resents the father as much as the boy does, nor does she love and covet the mother as much as he does.

The primary assumption upon which this investigation rests is that the earliest conception of the father as a resented and feared stranger is represented in dreams by male characters who are not known to the dreamer. The male stranger of the dream, it is asserted, symbolizes the father.

An equally important assumption is that the sleeping person dreams about people who are connected, directly or indirectly, with conflicts, frustrations, insecurities, anxieties, and other emotions which have their inception in early childhood.

The following testable hypotheses were formulated:

1. More strangers in dreams are males than females.

2. There is a higher proportion of male strangers in male dreams than in female dreams.

3. There is a higher proportion of aggressive encounters by the dreamer with male strangers than with any of the following classes of dream charac-

ters: (a) female strangers, (b) familiar males, and (c) familiar females.

4. The proportion of aggressive encounters with male strangers is greater for male dreamers than for female dreamers.

5. When Ss are asked to free associate to male strangers who appear in their dreams, they will give more father and male authority figure associations than any other class of association.

Method

The data for this investigation were obtained from the content analysis of six groups of male dreams and female dreams. A description of the six groups appears in Table 1. Groups 1 through 5 consist of single dreams and Group 6 consists of dream series. The number of dreams in the series ranges from 15 to 21.

With the exception of some of the dreams reported by young children which were taken down by adults, the dreams were reported by the dreamers themselves on standard report forms. These forms include questions about the dream and about the dreamer.

The dreams were analyzed for characters and aggressions using standard manuals prepared by the Institute of Dream Research (1962a, 1962b).

Although the groups vary in age from two to eighty, none of the hypotheses tested in this investigation is concerned with the age variable.

Results

Hypothesis 1 states that more strangers in dreams are male than female. This hypothesis was tested in two ways:

(1) An analysis of the characters appearing in the dreams (not counting the dreamer) was made. Four categories of characters were identified: known males, known females, male strangers, and female strangers. The hypothesis states that the proportion of male strangers will exceed the proportion of female strangers. The results are presented in Table 2. The standard formula for testing the significance of difference between proportions was used for Groups 1–5. The statistical treatment of Group 6 consisted of determining the proportions for each individual series, computing the mean and standard deviation for each distribution of proportions, and applying the standard formula for testing the significance of difference between means. If there were reason to believe that the two variables being compared were correlated, the formula for correlated means was employed. In Table 2 the differences between the proportions are all in the predicted direction except for the male dreamers of Group 2 who show a reversal and the female dreamers of

TABLE 1

A DESCRIPTION OF THE GROUPS USED IN THIS STUDY

	Males		Females	
Group	No. Dreamers	No. Dreams	No. Dreamers	No. Dreams
1 (Ages 2–12)	105	105	119	119
2 (Ages 13–18)	138	138	138	138
3 (Ages 18–27)	200	200	200	200
4 (Ages 20–24)	200	200	200	200
5 (Ages 30–80)	281	281	281	281
6 (Ages 18–26)	27	492	28	525

TABLE 2

COMPARISON OF PROPORTIONS OF MALE STRANGERS AND FEMALE STRANGERS
FOR THE SIX GROUPS OF DREAMS

	Male dreamers			Female dreamers		
	Male strangers	Female strangers		Male strangers	Female strangers	
Groups	Male characters	Female characters	p	Male characters	Female characters	p
1	.47	.16	.01	.35	.20	n.s.
2	.24	.35		.32	.14	.01
3	.42	.32	n.s.	.29	.29	
4	.54	.34	.01	.37	.24	.01
5	.51	.25	.001	.36	.27	.01
6	.55	.39	.01	.40	.30	.01

Group 3 where the proportions are equal. Among the other ten comparisons, eight are significant at the .01 or .001 level. The hypothesis appears to be confirmed.

(2) The second method of testing the hypothesis consisted of computing the proportion, male strangers/male + female strangers, and testing the significance of the difference of each proportion from the chance proportion of .50. The results are presented in Table 3. All of the proportions except the one for male dreamers in Group 2, exceed .50. Nine of the twelve proportions are significant at the .01 or .001 level, and the hypothesis appears to be confirmed.

Hypothesis 2 asserts that there is a higher proportion of male strangers in male dreams than in female dreams. This hypothesis could not be tested by the first method used in testing Hypothesis 1 because there are more strangers of both sexes in male dreams than in female dreams. Consequently, we compared the proportion, male strangers/male + female strangers, between male and female dreamers. The results are presented in Table 4.

With the exception of Group 2, all of the differences are in the predicted direction, but only two of the five differences meet a satisfactory level of significance. By combining the two similar age groups, 3 and 4, the difference is significant at the .05 level. Taking into consideration the relatively small numbers of male strangers in the first

TABLE 3

PROPORTION OF MALE STRANGERS IN EACH OF THE SEX GROUPS

	Male dreams		Female dreams	
	Male strangers		Female strangers	
Groups	Male+female strangers	p	Male+female strangers	p
1	.81	.001	.64	n.s.
2	.43		.69	.01
3	.63	.01	.52	n.s.
4	.71	.001	.67	.001
5	.80	.001	.59	.001
6	.69	.001	.59	.001

TABLE 4

COMPARISON OF THE PROPORTION OF MALE STRANGERS
BETWEEN MALE AND FEMALE DREAMERS

| Groups | Male Dreamers | Female Dreamers | |
| | Male Strangers | Female Strangers | p |
	Male+Female Strangers	Male+Female Strangers	
1	.81	.64	n.s.
2	.43	.69	
3	.63	.52	n.s.
4	.71	.67	n.s.
5	.80	.59	.001
6	.69	.59	.05
Combining 3 and 4	.69	.61	.05

five groups, and the fact that in Group 6 which has the largest number of dreams there is a significant difference, it appears to us that the hypothesis is confirmed.

Hypothesis 3 states that there is a higher proportion of aggressive encounters by the dreamer with male strangers than with any of the following classes of dream characters: (*a*) female strangers, (*b*) familiar males, and (*c*)

familiar females. The hypothesis states that the proportions in the first column of Table 5 will exceed those in each of the other three columns. This is the case in all of the 36 comparisons except for three. Fifteen of the comparisons are significant at the .05, .01, or .001 levels. In view of the small number of aggressions in some of the groups, these results appear to us to confirm the hypothesis.

TABLE 5

ANALYSIS OF AGGRESSIONS WITH DREAM CHARACTER

| Groups | Aggressions with Male Strangers | | Aggressions with Female Strangers | | Aggressions with Familiar Males | | Aggressions with Familiar Females | |
	No. Male Strangers		No. Female Strangers		No. Familiar Males		No. Familiar Females	
Male Dreamers								
1	.27		.67		.20	n.s.	.16	n.s.
2	.33		.10	.05	.15	n.s.	.18	n.s.
3	.29		.13	.05	.23	n.s.	.23	n.s.
4	.33		.18	.05	.25	n.s.	.15	.01
5	.21		.03	.01	.08	.01	.05	.01
6	.29		.05	.001	.15	.05	.12	.01
Female Dreamers								
1	.40		.27	n.s.	.24	n.s.	.16	.05
2	.31		.23	n.s.	.10	.01	.16	.05
3	.21		.19	n.s.	.15	n.s.	.10	.05
4	.28		.16	n.s.	.21	n.s.	.10	.001
5	.04		.01	n.s.	.03	n.s.	.03	n.s.
6	.15		.10	n.s.	.17		.15	

TABLE 6

COMPARISON OF THE PROPORTION OF AGGRESSIVE ENCOUNTERS
WITH MALE STRANGERS BY MALE AND FEMALE DREAMERS

| Group | Aggression with Male Strangers / Aggression with Male Strangers+Female Strangers | | |
	Male Dreamers	Female Dreamers	p
1	.64	.73	
2	.71	.75	
3	.79	.55	.05
4	.82	.78	n.s.
5	.96	.82	n.s.
6	.81	.36	.001

It will be observed that there are more significant differences for male dreamers than for female dreamers. This is to be expected on the basis of the next hypothesis.

Hypothesis 4 the proportion of aggressive encounters with male strangers is greater for male dreamers than for female dreamers. The proportion, aggression with male strangers/aggression with male strangers + aggression with female strangers, was computed for male and female dreamers in each of the six groups. The results appear in Table 6. For Groups 1 and 2, the difference is in the reverse direction from that predicted. For the other four groups, the differences are in the predicted direction but only two of them are significant. However, Group 6 which contains the greatest number of dreams and consequently the greatest number of aggressions yields a highly significant difference between male and female dreamers. We conclude, therefore, that the hypothesis is confirmed.

Hypothesis 5 asserts that when subjects are asked to free associate to male strangers who appear in their dreams, they will give more father and male authority figure associations than any other class of association. Free associ-

ations were obtained for 10 dreams from each of 12 male college students and 12 female college students. These free associations were collected by Dr. Walter Reis (1959) under conditions simulating a psychoanalytic session. Associations were given to all parts of each dream, not just to unknown males.

Thirty-one male strangers were identified in the 120 male dreams. These were all individual strangers, and not groups. One dreamer had no male stranger in his ten dreams. Thirty-three individual male strangers were identified in the 120 female dreams. Three dreamers had no male stranger in their dreams. All of the associations were listed. In some cases, more than one association was given. The associations were classified into the categories shown in Table 7.

For male dreamers, the hypothesis states that the sum of categories 1–4 will be greater than either category 5 or 6. The sum of the frequencies for the four categories is 20, which is greater than the frequency for 5 or 6. The difference between the summed frequencies for 1–4 and the larger of the other two categories, which is 13, fails to reach a p of .05, however. For female dreamers, the hypothesis states that the

TABLE 7

ASSOCIATIONS BY CATEGORIES

Male dreamers	No.	Female dreamers	No.
Father	9	Father	12
Stepfather	1	Grandfather	3
Another person's father	3	Uncle	1
Male authority figure or male with power or strength	7	Male authority figure or male with power or strength	2
Dreamer or some aspect of dreamer	13	Priest	1
Miscellaneous	4	Brother	2
		Male cousin	1
		Boy friend	7
		Mother	3
		Male sexuality	2
		Dreamer	1
		Miscellaneous	3
Total	37	Total	38

sum of categories 1–5 will be greater than the largest of the remaining categories. The sum of 1–5 is 19, and the largest frequency for the remaining categories is 7 for boy friend. The difference between these two frequencies is significant at less than the .01 level.

In view of the small number of cases, we are not willing to conclude that the hypothesis is confirmed. We believe, however, that the addition of more cases will establish its validity.

Discussion

When a theory tells us what we will find if we look in a certain place—and we look there and we do find what has been predicted—then the theory has done its work well. In the present instance, Oedipal theory told us correctly what we would find if we analyzed a population of dreams for certain variables. Had we not found what the theory said, or had the finding been ambiguous and equivocal, then we would have discussed why the theory or the empirical operations failed us, and what steps should be taken to revise the theory or improve the methodology.

But what is there to discuss when the findings fulfill the investigator's expectations?

The question is often asked, could not the results obtained have been predicted by another theory? Perhaps. The question is, however, an irrelevant one. An investigator usually has a commitment to, or at least a preference for, a particular theoretical system. Ours is to classical Freudian theory. As long as this theory maintains (a) its heuristic value, (b) its capacity for making sense out of a wide variety of phenomena, and (c) its ability to generate correct predictions, there is no necessity to consider empirical findings from the point of view of other theories.

A discussion of results often involves comparing them with results obtained in comparable investigations. Although empirical tests of hypotheses derived from Oedipal theory have been made (see, e.g., Friedman, 1952), none of them is comparable with this investigation of dreams. Nor is this the place to present a systematic, evaluative review of studies which purport to bear upon Oedipal theory.

What remains to be discussed then are the implications of some findings which appeared, so to speak, "out of the blue." Looking at Table 7, we see that male dreamers give 13 associations which have a self-reference, i.e. "I am the stranger" or "Some aspect of me—my conscience, sadism, or sexuality—is a stranger to me." One is reminded of A. E. Housman's oft-quoted lines, "I, a stranger and afraid/In a world I never made."

In only one instance does a female dreamer give a self-reference association. The sex difference very likely has no great significance because it is probably easier for male dreamers than for female dreamers to identify with male strangers.

Why do young men frequently conceive of themselves as the stranger in their dreams? Our guess is that when the young boy discovers his parents share certain activities from which he is excluded, the feeling appears that he and not the father is the stranger in the house. Chief among these activities from which he is excluded is the sexual one. But we still think, following Freudian theory, that the father-as-stranger fantasy precedes developmentally the self-as-stranger fantasy, and because of its prior entry it remains more potent throughout life for both males and females.

In line with this discussion it is appropriate to look, however briefly, at what is considered by many to be the finest example of the novel form in recent literature. We refer, of course, to Camus' *The Stranger*. Meursault, the hero, is Housman's stranger, although unafraid, living in a world he never made, i.e., an indifferent universe.

Camus does not tell us how he got that way; he only shows what happens to him. He is guillotined for killing a man. Had Meursault been brought to the couch rather than to the guillotine, it is our prediction that the impact of primal scene experiences would have been uncovered. The impact consists, we believe, on the one hand, in reinforcing the young boy's hatred of the father-stranger and, on the other hand, in originating the bleak view, "I am the stranger." For not only has the father excluded him—that is to be expected—but his mother has, too. The fantasy of being the excluded one, the outsider, would explain Meursault's indifference to his mother as well as the killing of a relative stranger. But this is literary exigesis and not scientific analysis.

Taking another look at Table 7 we see that the number of categories under female dreamers is larger than those under male dreamers. We suspect that women make more displacements from the father to other classes of males, e.g., brother, cousin, boy friend, than men do. Observe also that in spite of the fact that the stranger is a male, in three instances, women dreamers give the association "mother." The mother, according to Oedipal theory, is more likely to be seen as a stranger by her daughter than by her son.

Summary: Five hypotheses, all of them derived from Oedipal theory and all having to do with male strangers in the dreams of males and females, were tested. Four of them were confirmed, and the fifth was marginally confirmed. It is concluded that the male stranger in dreams often represents the young child's fantasy of the father as a hostile stranger.

Science, June 10, 1960, vol. 131, pp. 1705–1708

The Effect of Dream Deprivation*[1]

William Dement

About a year ago, a research program was initiated at the Mount Sinai Hospital which aimed at assessing the basic function and significance of dreaming. The experiments have been arduous and time-consuming and are still in progress. However, the results of the first series have been quite uniform, and because of the length of the program, it has been decided to issue this preliminary report.

In recent years, a body of evidence has accumulated which demonstrates that dreaming occurs in association with periods of rapid, binocularly synchronous eye movements (Aserinsky & Kleitman, 1955; Dement & Wolpert, 1958a; Goodenough, Shapiro, Holden & Steinschriber, 1959; Wolpert & Trasman, 1958; Dement, 1955; Dement & Kleitman, 1957b; Dement & Wolpert, 1958b). Furthermore, the amount and directional patterning of these eye movements and the associated dream *content* are related in such a way as to strongly suggest that the eye movements represent scanning movements made by the dreamer as he watches the events of the dream (Dement & Kleitman, 1957b; Dement & Wolpert, 1958b). In a study of undisturbed sleep (Dement & Kleitman,

1957a), the eye-movement periods were observed to occur regularly throughout the night in association with the lightest phases of a cyclic variation in depth of sleep, as measured by the electroencephalograph. The length of individual cycles averaged about 90 minutes, and the mean duration of single periods of eye movement was about 20 minutes. Thus, a typical night's sleep includes four or five periods of dreaming, which account for about 20 percent of the total sleep time.

One of the most striking facts apparent in all the works cited above was that a very much greater amount of dreaming occurs normally than had heretofore been realized—greater both from the standpoint of frequency and duration in a single night of sleep and in the invariability of its occurrence from night to night. In other words, dreaming appears to be an intrinsic part of normal sleep and, as such, although the dreams are not usually recalled, occurs every night in every sleeping person.

A consideration of this aspect of dreaming leads more or less inevitably to the formulation of certain rather fundamental questions. Since there appear to be no exceptions to the nightly occurrence of a substantial amount of dreaming in every sleeping person, it might be asked whether or not this amount of dreaming is in some way a

* Reprinted from *Science* by permission. Copyright © 1960 by the AAAS.
1 The research reported in this paper was aided by a grant from the Foundation's Fund for Research in Psychiatry.

necessary and vital part of our existence. Would it be possible for human beings to continue functioning normally if their dream life were completely or partially suppressed? Should dreaming be considered necessary in a psychological sense or a physiological sense or both?

The obvious attack on these problems was to study subjects who had somehow been deprived of the opportunity to dream. After a few unsuccessful preliminary trials with depressant drugs, it was decided to use the somewhat drastic method of awakening sleeping subjects immediately after the onset of dreaming and to continue this procedure throughout the night, so that each dream period would be artificially terminated right at its beginning.

Subjects and Method

The data in this article are from the first eight subjects in the research program, all males, ranging in age from 23 to 32. Eye movements and accompanying low voltage, nonspindling electroencephalographic patterns (Dement & Kleitman, 1957a) were used as the objective criteria of dreaming. The technique by which these variables are recorded, and their precise relationship to dreaming, have been extensively discussed elsewhere (Dement, 1955; Dement & Kleitman, 1957a). Briefly, the subjects came to the laboratory at about their usual bedtime. Small silver-disk electrodes were carefully attached near their eyes and on their scalps; then the subjects went to sleep in a quiet, dark room in the laboratory. Lead wires ran from the electrodes to apparatus in an adjacent room upon which the electrical potentials of eye movements and brain waves were recorded continuously throughout the night.

Eye movements and brain waves of each subject were recorded throughout a series of undisturbed nights of sleep, to evaluate his base-line total nightly dream time and over-all sleep pattern. After this, recordings were made throughout a number of nights in which the subject was awakened by the experimenter every time the eye-movement and electroencephalographic recordings indicated that he had begun to dream. These "dream-deprivation" nights were always consecutive. Furthermore, the subjects were requested not to sleep at any other time. Obviously, if subjects were allowed to nap, or to sleep at home on any night in the dream-deprivation period, an unknown amount of dreaming would take place, offsetting the effects of the deprivation. On the first night immediately after the period of dream deprivation, and for several consecutive nights thereafter, the subject was allowed to sleep without disturbance. These nights were designated "recovery nights." The subject then had a varying number of nights off, after which he returned for another series of interrupted nights which exactly duplicated the dream-deprivation series in number of nights and number of awakenings per night. The only difference was that the subject was awakened in the intervals between eye-movement (dream) periods. Whenever a dream period began, the subject was allowed to sleep on without interruption, and was awakened only after the dream had ended spontaneously. Next, the subject had a number of recovery nights of undisturbed sleep equal to the number of recovery nights in his original dream-deprivation series.

Altogether, as many as 20 to 30 all-night recordings were made for each subject, most of them on consecutive nights. Since, for the most part, tests could be made on only one subject at a time, and since a minute-by-minute all-night vigil was required of the experimenter to catch each dream episode immediately at its onset, it can be understood why the experiments have been called arduous and time-consuming.

Table 1 summarizes most of the pertinent data. As can be seen, the total number of base-line nights for the eight subjects was 40. The mean sleep time for the 40 nights was 7 hours and 2 minutes, the mean total nightly dream time was 82 minutes, and the mean percentage of dream time (total dream time to total sleep time × 100) was 19.4. Since total sleep time was not held absolutely constant, percentage figures were routinely calculated as a check on the possibility that differences in total nightly dream time were due to differences in total sleep time. Actually, this is not a plausible explanation for any but quite small differences in dream time, because the range of values for total sleep time for each subject turned out to be very narrow throughout the entire study. When averaged in terms of individuals rather than nights, the means were: total sleep time, 6 hours 50 minutes; total dream time, 80 minutes; percentage of dream time, 19.5; this indicates that the figures were not skewed by the disparate number of base-line nights per subject. The remarkable uniformity of the findings for individual nights is demonstrated by the fact that the standard deviation of the total nightly dream time was only plus or minus 7 minutes.

Progressive Increase in Dream "Attempts"

The number of consecutive nights of dream deprivation arbitrarily selected as a condition of the study was five. However, one subject left the study in a flurry of obviously contrived excuses after only three nights, and two subjects insisted on stopping after four nights but consented to continue with the recovery nights and the remainder of the schedule. One subject was pushed to seven nights. During each awakening the subjects were required to sit up in bed and remain fully awake for several minutes. On the first nights of dream deprivation, the return to sleep generally initiated a new sleep cycle, and the next dream period was postponed for the expected amount of time. However, on subsequent nights the number of forced awakenings required to suppress dreaming steadily mounted. Or, to put it another way, there was a progressive increase in the number of attempts to dream. The number of awakenings required on the first and last nights of deprivation are listed in Table 1. All the subjects showed this progressive increase, although there was considerable variation in the starting number and the amount of the increase. An important point is that each awakening was preceded by a minute or two of dreaming. This represented the time required for the experimenter to judge the emerging record and make the decision to awaken the subject after he first noticed the beginning of eye movements. In some cases the time was a little longer, as when an eye-movement period started while the experimenter was looking away from the recording apparatus. It is apparent from this that the method employed did not constitute absolute dream deprivation but, rather, about a 65- to 75-percent deprivation, as it turned out.

Nightly Dream Time Elevated after Deprivation

The data on the first night of the dream deprivation recovery period are summarized for each subject in Table 1. As was mentioned, one subject had quit the study. The mean total dream time on the first recovery night was 112 minutes, or 26.6 percent of the total mean sleep time. If the results for two subjects who did not show marked increases on the first recovery night are excluded, the mean dream time is 127 minutes or 29 percent, which represents a 50-percent increase over the group base-line mean. For all seven subjects together, on the first recovery night the increase in percentage of dream time over the base-line mean (Table 1, col. 3, mean percentage figures; col. 10, first recovery night percentages) was significant at the $p < .05$ level in a one-tail Wilcoxin matched-pairs signed-ranks test (Siegel, 1956).

It is important to mention, however, that one (S.M. in Table 1) of the two subjects alluded to above as exceptions was not really an exception because, although he had only 1 hour 1 minute of dreaming on his first recovery night, he showed a marked increase on *four* subsequent nights. His failure to show a rise on the first recovery night was in all likelihood due to the fact that he had imbibed several cocktails at a party before coming to the laboratory so that the expected increase in dream time was offset by the depressing effect of the alcohol. The other one of the two subjects (N.W. in Table 1) failed to show a significant increase in dream time on any of five consecutive recovery nights and therefore must be considered the single exception to the over-all results. Even so, it is hard to reconcile his lack of increase in dream time on recovery nights with the fact that during the actual period of dream deprivation he showed the largest build-up in number of awakenings required to suppress dreaming (11 to 30) of any subject in this group. One may only suggest that, although he was strongly affected by the dream loss, he could not increase his dream time on recovery nights because of an unusually stable basic sleep cycle that resisted modification.

The number of consecutive recovery nights for each subject in this series of tests was too small in some cases, mainly because it was naively supposed at the beginning of the study that an increase in dream time, if it occurred, would last only one or two nights. One subject had only one recovery night, another two, and another three. The dream time was markedly elevated above the base-line on all these nights. For how many additional nights each of these three subjects would have maintained an elevation in dream time can only be surmised in the absence of objective data. All of the remaining four subjects had five consecutive recovery nights. One was the single subject who showed no increase, two were nearing the base-line dream time by the fifth night, and one still showed marked elevation in dream time. From this admittedly incomplete sample it appears that about five nights of increased dreaming usually follow four or five nights of dream suppression achieved by the method of this study.

TABLE 1

SUMMARY OF EXPERIMENTAL RESULTS. TST, TOTAL SLEEP TIME; TDT, TOTAL DREAM TIME

Mean and range, base-line nights			Dream depri-vation nights (No.)	Awakenings (No.)		Dream-deprivation recovery nights				First control recovery night		
						First night						
TST	TDT	Percent		First night	Last night	No.	TST	TDT	Percent	TST	TDT	Percent
Subject W. T. (4 base-line nights)												
6^h36^m 6^h24^m–6^h48^m	1^h17^m 1^h10^m–1^h21^m	19.5 17.0–21.3	5	8	14	1	6^h43^m	2^h17^m	34.0	6^h50^m	1^h04^m	15.6
Subject H. S. (5 base-line nights)												
7^h27^m 7^h07^m–7^h58^m	1^h24^m 1^h07^m–1^h38^m	18.8 15.4–21.8	7	7	24	2	8^h02^m	2^h45^m	34.2	8^h00^m	1^h49^m	22.7
Subject N. W. (7 base-line nights)												
6^h39^m 5^h50^m–7^h10^m	1^h18^m 1^h11^m–1^h27^m	19.5 17.4–22.4	5	11	30	5	6^h46^m	1^h12^m	17.8	7^h10^m	1^h28^m	20.2
Subject B. M. (6 base-line nights)												
6^h59^m 6^h28^m–7^h38^m	1^h18^m 0^h58^m–1^h35^m	18.6 14.8–22.2	5	7	23	5	7^h25^m	1^h58^m	26.3	7^h48^m	1^h28^m	18.8
Subject R. G. (10 base-line nights)												
7^h26^m 7^h00^m–7^h57^m	1^h26^m 1^h13^m–1^h46^m	19.3 16.9–22.7	5	10	20	5	7^h14^m	2^h08^m	29.5	7^h18^m	1^h55^m	26.3
Subject W. D. (4 base-line nights)												
6^h29^m 5^h38^m–7^h22^m	1^h21^m 1^h08^m–1^h32^m	20.8 17.8–23.4	4	13	20	3	8^h53^m	2^h35^m	29.0			
Subject S. M. (2 base-line nights)												
6^h41^m 6^h18^m–7^h04^m	1^h12^m 1^h01^m–1^h23^m	17.9 16.2–19.3	4	22	30	6	5^h08^m 6^h32^m**	1^h01^m 1^h50^m**	19.8 28.1*	6^h40^m	1^h07^m	16.8
Subject W. G. (2 base-line nights)												
6^h16^m 6^h08^m–6^h24^m	1^h22^m 1^h17^m–1^h27^m	20.8 20.7–20.9	3	9	13							

* Second recovery night (see text).

Effect Not Due to Awakening

Six of the subjects underwent the series of control awakenings—that is, awakenings during non-dream periods. This series exactly duplicated the dream-deprivation series for each subject in number of nights, total number of awakenings, and total number of awakenings per successive night. The dream time on these nights was slightly below base-line levels as a rule. The purpose of this series was, of course, to see if the findings following dream deprivation were solely an effect of the multiple awakenings. Data for the first recovery nights after nights of control awakenings are included in Table 1. There was no significant increase for the group. The mean dream time was 88 minutes, and the mean percentage was 20.1. Subsequent recovery nights in this series also failed to show the marked rise in dream time that was observed after nights of dream deprivation. A moderate increase found on four out of a total of 24 recovery nights for the individuals in the control-awakening group was felt to be a response to the slight reduction in dream time on control-awakening nights.

Behavioral Changes

Psychological disturbances such as anxiety, irritability, and difficulty in concentrating developed during the period of dream deprivation, but these were not catastrophic. One subject, as was mentioned above, quit the study in an apparent panic, and two subjects insisted on stopping one night short of the goal of five nights of dream deprivation, presumably because the stress was too great. At least one subject exhibited serious anxiety and agitation. Five subjects developed a marked increase in appetite during the period of dream deprivation; this observation was supported by daily weight measurements which showed a gain in weight of 3 to 5 pounds in three of the subjects. The psychological changes disappeared as soon as the subjects were allowed to dream. The most important fact was that *none* of the observed changes were seen during the period of control awakenings.

The results have been tentatively interpreted as indicating that a certain amount of dreaming each night is a necessity. It is as though a pressure to dream builds up with the accruing dream deficit during successive dream-deprivation nights—a pressure which is first evident in the increasing frequency of attempts to dream and then, during the recovery period, in the marked increase in total dream time and percentage of dream time. The fact that this increase may be maintained over four or more successive recovery nights suggests that there is a more or less quantitative compensation for the deficit. It is possible that if the dream suppression were carried on long enough, a serious disruption of the personality would result.

Journal of Abnormal and Social Psychology, 1954, vol. 49, pp. 94–98

An Experimental Reunion of Psychoanalytic Theory With Perceptual Vigilance and Defense[1]

Gerald S. Blum

Psychoanalytic theory has long since grown accustomed to adolescent rebelliousness. Like the parent who conceives and cares for his offspring only to find one day that all past efforts are now met with ingratitude and desertion, psychoanalysis has spawned many concepts in psychology which somehow stray from home and eventually lose their parental identity. Some current emphases in the field of perception do not deviate from this familiar pattern.

The notions of perceptual vigilance and defense, for example, have their direct counterparts in psychoanalytic theory. Though the link between the two still receives some acknowledgment (we seem to be in the "early straying" stage now), the portents are ominous. The critics are once again assailing the untestability of the original psychoanalytic formulations—a certain cue for a quick fadeout. For example, Postman and Brown, in a recent comment on the mechanism of repression, say: "It seems to us that theoretical arguments relating perception to such general personality factors hold out little promise for the precise specification and experimental manipulation of the conditions under which variations in perceptual behavior occur" (Postman & Brown, 1952, p. 219).

Having advocated the testability of psychoanalytic hypotheses on other fronts (Blum, 1949; Blum & Miller, 1952), the present writer undertook the following experimental investigation in the area of perception.

Hypotheses

Psychoanalytic theory encourages the derivation of two hypotheses concerning the perception of psychosexual stimuli. First, sexual and aggressive impulses, denied conscious expression by the ego, still continue to strive actively to break through into consciousness. In other words, repressed psychosexual impulses, of which the individual is not consciously aware, are always pushing and seeking for an outlet in conscious behavior. If this theoretical formulation is correct, then *everyone* should, at the unconscious level, be sensitive and responsive to cues relevant to these potentially threatening impulses—a process which is now familiarly labeled "subception" (Lazarus & McCleary, 1951), "selective vigilance" (Bruner & Postman, 1947), "selective sensitization" (Lazarus, Eriksen & Fonda, 1951), etc.

[1] Based on a paper presented in a symposium on "Measuring Human Motivation" at the annual meeting of the American Psychological Association, Washington, D.C., 1952.

This study was made possible by a Rackham Faculty Research Fellowship at the University of Michigan for the summer of 1952.

This process, however, is expected to operate only at a level below conscious awareness, for when the impulses do begin to approach the surface, we have a second process, ego defense. Now, that which the organism basically desires must be warded off because of its threatening quality. At this point, rather than being vigilant for psychosexual cues, the individual seeks devious ways not to perceive them—a mechanism currently labeled "perceptual defense."

In sum, we are led by psychoanalytic theory to postulate two opposing tendencies—vigilance and defense—and to predict the exact operation of each by controlling the level of awareness.

Method

Investigation of the perception of psychosexual stimuli, upon which psychoanalytic theory focuses, required an initial choice of techniques. To tap perception we used a tachistoscope; to provide psychosexual stimuli we chose the Blacky Pictures (Blum, 1950). More specifically, the experimental design grew out of an earlier study by Clapp (1951), who presented pairs of Blacky Pictures tachistoscopically and asked groups of subjects to judge their relative clarity. In accordance with his predictions, the more traumatic picture in the pair tended to be judged as clearer at very fast speeds (vigilance) and the neutral picture as clearer at the slow speeds (defense). Clapp's group procedures, however, entailed certain complications, such as setting up fully satisfactory control groups and manipulating the set of the subjects experimentally. The generally positive results within the limitations of Clapp's research, however, pointed strongly to the feasibility of continuing to explore perceptual approaches to psychosexual motivation by means of the Blacky Pictures.

Subjects. Subjects (Ss) in the present study were seven men and seven women, ranging in age from 19 to 37, with a mean of 24. Their ranks included secretaries and

undergraduate and graduate students in a variety of fields. The sole criteria for selection were no prior knowledge of the Blacky Pictures and a willingness to participate. Approximately 30 other individuals of similar pedigree had been employed earlier in pretesting the experimental conditions.

Apparatus

The tachistoscope, constructed for use by one S at a time, was designed by R. Gerbrands, of Arlington, Massachusetts. The speeds of perception in the first and second parts of the experiment (described below), were .03 sec., assumed to represent a low level of awareness, and .20 sec., assumed to represent a relatively higher level of awareness, respectively. Illumination of the adapting field was 1.87 foot-lamberts, of the test field 1.15 foot-lamberts.

Procedure

The individual S was brought into the laboratory room, and after having been familiarized with the tachistoscope, was given these instructions:

"Now I'm going to flash some pictures very quickly, at a fraction of a second. There will be four pictures shown simultaneously at each flash—one at the Left, Right, Top, and Bottom. What I want you to do is simply to say which one of the four *stands out the most.* Obviously with these very fast speeds you won't be able to get any real idea even of what the pictures are, so you may feel quite uncertain of your judgments. But in every case make a guess. All I am interested in, for this part of the experiment, is your immediate impression. You will see different patterns or combinations of pictures during the series of flashes. Remember to say just Left, Right, Top, or Bottom, according to which picture appears to you to stand out the most. When I say Ready, focus on the dark spot in the center of the screen. That will give you the best chance to see all four pictures at once. I will flash the pictures right after the ready signal."

Then a pattern of Blacky Pictures was flashed at .03 sec. and S immediately indicated the position of the one which seemed to him to stand out most. Each pattern consisted of the following four

Blacky Pictures: Oral Sadism (II) and Masturbation Guilt (V), which were the two key experimental stimuli; and Oral Eroticism (I) and Identification Process (VII), which were slightly altered to serve as effective distractors. These four pictures were actually mounted on each of six cards, so that the position of every picture was systematically rotated.[2] The six cards were flashed sequentially for a total of 54 trials at the same speed, with short breaks after each series of 18 trials. After the first exposure S invariably expressed amazement that any one could see anything at all at speeds like that, but with minor reassurance settled down to the routine task of saying Left, Right, Top, or Bottom.

At the conclusion of the 54 trials the experimenter (E) asked S to guess what he had been looking at, since he had never seen or heard of the Blacky Pictures before. The almost universal reply was "elephants." In the beginning, a suspicion existed that this response might have been contaminated by the fact that the early Ss were run during the Republican convention, but there were still lots of elephant reports and only one or two donkeys two weeks later. The parsimonious interpretation seems to be that at .03 sec. the various projections (limbs, tails, etc.) in the pictures make Blacky resemble an elephant.

The purpose of these first 54 trials was to establish a base line of S's choices made solely from the physical properties of the pictures. Next came the sensitization experience, in which S was injected with an appropriate "type and dosage of psychosexual serum." This was accomplished by showing him the two experimental pictures placed adjacently (positions systematically varied) and saying:

"Now I'm going to show you two of the pictures from among the several which you just saw at fast speeds. They belong to a

[2] Photographic reproductions of these four stimulus patterns and tables of the raw data from this experiment have been deposited with the ADI. Order Document 4031 from the ADI Auxiliary Publications Project, Photoduplication Service, Library of Congress, Washington 25, D.C., remitting in advance $1.25 for 35-mm. microfilm or $1.25 for photostats readable without optical aid. Make checks payable to Chief, Photoduplication Service, Library of Congress.

psychological test which consists of a series of cartoons portraying the adventures of a dog named Blacky. I'll tell you what is happening in each picture when I show them to you." (Pictures then presented in full view.)

For the male Ss the Masturbation picture (V) was structured as the traumatic one by stating, "Over here, Blacky can't keep from licking his sexual parts even though he's been scolded for it," and the other stimulus picture (II) neutralized by the comment, "Over here, Blacky loves the free feeling of romping outdoors and retrieving things like this belt or collar." Also, Blacky's angry expression was deleted from the latter and the name "Mama" taken off the collar. For the females, it was just the reverse. Oral Sadism (II) was maximized by the comment, "Over here, Blacky is bitterly angry at her mother and feels like chewing Mama instead of her collar," (the fierce look and "Mama" were restored), and the other picture (V) was neutralized by, "Blacky is busily chasing flies after running around the fields on a hot summer afternoon." Then S was told: "Now, without saying anything out loud, look at the pictures and try to recall when you might have felt the way Blacky does in these scenes. Just think to yourself about similar experiences of your own, and I will not ask you afterward about your thoughts." The S was then ignored for 30 seconds of silent meditation.

The purpose of the sensitization process was, of course, to affect S's behavior in the subsequent parts of the experiment. The male and female Ss were given different sets to control the influence of any physical factors operating in the picture choice and also to demonstrate that any positive results obtained would apply to more than one psychosexual dimension. All the males were given the Masturbation set and all the females the Oral Sadism set for two reasons. In the original Blacky monograph (1) females were suggested to be more oral sadistic than males, and in the pretesting it was found to be more difficult to disguise Oral Sadism for the women and Masturbation Guilt for the men.

The third phase of the experiment consisted of an exact replication of the first—another 54 trials at .03 sec. with the same instructions. The only difference between the phases was that S had now seen two of the pictures and had, presumably, also thought privately about his own experiences in those areas. The theoretical prediction was that he should now be sensitized to the traumatic picture and consequently choose it as standing out the most, at this brief exposure of .03 sec., relatively more often than he had originally. This then was a test of the first hypothesis, dealing with the striving of repressed impulses for expression, since S still had no opportunity for conscious recognition of the stimuli.

The second hypothesis, dealing with perceptual defense against psychosexual stimuli presented at close to the conscious level of awareness, was tested as follows. After the vigilance series was completed, S was told:

"This time we're going to do something slightly different. The picture where Blacky is (holding the collar) (angry at Mama) (masturbating) (chasing flies) will be present in each one of the combinations. It will appear either at the left, the right, the top, or the bottom. And it will move around among all the positions—it won't be in the same position all the time. Also, it will appear in only one of the four positions at each flash. Your job will be to locate the correct position. Focus on the dark spot at the ready signal."

The S was asked to look alternately for one picture for six trials and then the other for six trials, up to 36 trials on each one. The designation of each picture conformed, of course, to its earlier structure in the sensitization experience.

The ego was brought into play in two ways: first, the time of exposure was increased from .03 to .20 sec.—a speed at which preliminary studies had shown that S very frequently recognized one or more of the pictures; and secondly, his task was now a conscious, ego-involving one of trying to locate a certain picture. The prediction in this case was the opposite of what it had been before: the traumatic picture, which now assumes an ego-threatening quality, should be correctly located *less* frequently than the neutral one. Because of S's emotional disturbance connected with the traumatic picture, he should be more

anxious and blocked in his attempts to find it, even though earlier he had unconsciously been more responsive to it in the vigilance series.

Results and Discussion

Vigilance series

The sensitization experience, in which S was exposed to relatively traumatic and neutral psychosexual stimuli, was intended to activate experimentally an underlying area of conflict already existing in his personality structure. In other words, the male is theoretically expected to be predisposed, in some degree to masturbation guilt and the female to conflict over oral sadism. The experimental sensitization served to link this "natural" predisposition with a specific picture stimulus, to which responses could then be predicted. In terms of the vigilance hypothesis, S should shift from pre- to post-sensitization in the direction of being more responsive to the traumatic picture during the later of the first two series of exposures.

This prediction was tested by noting for each S the relative proportions of choices of Pictures II and V before and after sensitization. An S who chose the traumatic picture relatively more often than the neutral one in the postsensitization condition than he had done earlier was behaving as predicted. By this sign test (set up in advance as the appropriate method of statistical analysis), the results show that 11 of the 14 Ss shifted in the predicted direction ($p < .05$).[3] Breaking down the data by

[3] Level of significance computed according to the procedure outlined in Dixon, W. J., & Mood, A. M. The statistical sign test. *J. Amer. stat. Ass.*, 1946, 41, 557–566. This nonparametric test is based on the binomial distribution and does not involve any assumption of continuity of data.

sexes, we find that six of the seven males shifted toward the traumatic picture (Masturbation Guilt) and five of the seven females shifted toward the traumatic one (Oral Sadism). Further examination of the extent of the shift in each individual reveals statistical significance beyond the .10 level of confidence in 6 of the 11 positive cases. Thus the vigilance hypothesis is supported by the results.

Defense series

The ego-defense hypothesis maintains that S should, at the close-to-conscious level, block more in response to the traumatic stimulus and therefore perform less effectively in locating it. The test here involves a comparison within each S of the number of correct locations of the two pictures during the 36 trials on each. Twelve of the 14 Ss performed as predicted ($p < .006$), i.e., made fewer correct locations of the traumatic than of the neutral picture. The breakdown by sexes shows that all seven females did more poorly looking for the traumatic stimulus (Oral Sadism), and five of the seven males were poorer on the traumatic one (Masturbation Guilt). Statistical significance of individual shifts exceeded the .10 level in five of the 12 cases. It should be noted that these positive results occurred despite the previously greater responsiveness to the traumatic picture in the vigilance trials.

The above findings contain implications which go beyond their specific support of hypotheses dealing with vigilance and defense. At the most general level we now have additional experimental evidence pointing to the testability of psychoanalytic hypotheses. Even such a seemingly elusive concept as the unconscious striving of repressed

impulses has, in this experiment, lent itself to operational definition within a perceptual framework. Also, by harnessing the predictive power of this potent theory of personality, despite its limitations, we can study behavior in a more appropriate setting. Previous experiments in this area (Lazarus & McCleary, 1951; McGinnies, 1949) have contented themselves with nonsense syllables, PGR equipment, and the like. The very same phenomenon of subception, now analyzed from the standpoint of strong, underlying impulses assumed to be operating commonly in personality structures, becomes demonstrable at the psychological as well as the physiological level of behavior. A psychosexual context, combining well-developed theory with translation into the form of Blacky Pictures, thus seems to provide the exploration of human personality with an easy entry into the experimental laboratory.[4]

The next research steps suggested by the data concern the problem of individual differences in perceptual response. The few exceptions in the present study, plus the differential degree of vigilance and defense effects noted in

[4] The importance of an appropriate setting is emphasized by the results of a supplementary study undertaken in conjunction with the present research. The reader will recall that the "natural" sets in the experiment proper were deemed to be Masturbation Guilt as the more traumatic for the male S and Oral Sadism for the female S. In order to test this assumption, the entire experiment was repeated on another group of Ss, with the traumatic and neutral sets reversed, i.e., Oral Sadism structured as the traumatic picture for the men and Masturbation Guilt for the women. The resulting vigilance and defense effects were somewhat slighter in the case of the men than they had been in the experiment proper (five out of seven in the predicted direction for both vigilance and defense), and disappeared completely in the case of the women (one out of seven on vigilance, two out of seven on defense in the predicted direction).

those Ss who did conform to the general pattern of behavior, point to the desirability of such an approach. Prior assessment of S's personality dynamics, particularly with reference to his characteristic use of defense mechanisms, seems most plausible in this regard. Theoretically, the accuracy of prediction should be augmented by knowledge of type and degree of psychosexual conflict and its accompanying defensive reactions. The feasibility of considering perceptual defense in the light of ego-defense mechanisms has already been shown by Eriksen (1951) and Lazarus, Eriksen & Fonda (1951). Further application to the process of selective vigilance follows directly from psychoanalytic theory. For example, the person who projects his unacceptable impulses is said to be extraordinarily sensitive to the existence of similar impulses in other individuals. Whether he will oblige in his tachistoscopic performance remains to be seen.

Summary: This experiment was designed to test, within the framework of perceptual behavior, two psychoanalytic hypotheses: (a) the unconscious striving for expression of underlying psychosexual impulses (vigilance); and (b) the warding off of these threatening impulses as they begin to approach conscious awareness (defense). In the vigilance series, patterns of Blacky Pictures were flashed tachistoscopically at .03 sec., and Ss (seven men and seven women) were asked to indicate the position of the one picture "standing out the most." In the defense series, the ego was brought more into play by slowing the speed to .20 sec. and instructing Ss to try to locate the correct positions of selected pictures.

The results were:

1. The vigilance hypothesis was supported in 11 of the 14 individual cases ($p < .05$). After a brief sensitization experience, most Ss responded relatively more often to a traumatic psychosexual stimulus (Masturbation Guilt for men, Oral Sadism for women) than they had done in pre-sensitization trials, despite the absence of any conscious recognition of the pictures throughout.

2. The defense hypothesis was supported in 12 of the 14 cases ($p < .006$). At the close-to-conscious level, most Ss experienced more difficulty in trying to locate a traumatic psychosexual stimulus picture than a relatively neutral one, in contrast to a previously greater sensitivity to the traumatic picture during the vigilance series.

The experimental findings were interpreted as further evidence for the testability of psychoanalytic formulations. In addition, the use of psychosexual content was considered to facilitate a more appropriate setting in the laboratory study of human personality.

Psychological Bulletin, 1962, vol. 59, pp. 477–488

Impulsive Versus Realistic Thinking:

AN EXAMINATION OF THE DISTINCTION BETWEEN PRIMARY AND SECONDARY PROCESSES IN THOUGHT[1]

Ernest R. Hilgard

Because we so commonly characterize Freudian psychoanalysis as a dynamic psychology, or a developmental psychology, or a psychology that emphasizes conflict or the relief of symptoms, we tend to translate the conceptions of psychoanalysis into an active mode. This tendency sometimes causes us to overlook the fact that psychoanalysis is very largely a *cognitive psychology* concerned primarily with mental representations, with hallucinations and dreams, with memories, their distortions and repression, with attention and inattention. Of course one might say that all psychology was mentalistic when Freud was writing, and that he was really talking about overt behavior and not about symbolic behavior. This I believe to be incorrect: Freud was very much concerned about symbols; his mental representations, condensations, displacements, and the rest are essentially cognitive. It is appropriate for us to consider Freud's views in this symposium, for his psychology was at once a cognitive psychology and a psychology of motivation.

The basic cleavage in thought, according to Freud, is between two processes, the earlier and more primitive *primary process,* and the later more orderly, rational, and reality-oriented *secondary process.* I wish to examine this distinction to see of what service it might be within general psychology.

The distinction between the illogical and impulsive in thought, on the one hand, and the logical and rational, on the other, is of course a very old one, and is not original with Freud. Every elementary logic course points out the circumstances that lead to fallacious thinking, and these include the *argumentum ad hominem,* and other kinds of argument that permit prejudice to blind judgment. The notion that "the wish is father to the thought" did not begin with Freud. Contemporary writers, too, such as Piaget and Werner, arrive at distinctions between earlier and later modes of thought. Hence some such distinction as that which Freud makes between primary and secondary process is plausible enough.

[1] Paper prepared for the Symposium on Motivation in Thinking, Western Psychological Association, Seattle, Washington, June 15, 1961; the paper has been somewhat revised since it was delivered. It constitutes a report from the Laboratory of Human Development, established under a grant from the Ford Foundation. The research program on hypnosis to which reference is made has been carried on with the additional support of the Robert C. Wheeler Foundation and the National Institute of Mental Health (Grant M-3859).

The question for us to face is not whether this distinction is plausible, but whether there are novel features in Freud's conception that are important, whether the concepts are clear, and whether there are suggestions for empirical work deriving from them.

Two Processes According to Freud

The distinction between primary and secondary processes is so pervasive in psychoanalysis that it often receives scant mention by psychoanalytic writers who fully accept it. This may be in part because the terms belong to the metapsychology, and the clinical literature of psychoanalysis is commonly not expressed in these terms. The more theoretical discussions of psychoanalytic theory invariably find a central place for these processes. Freud's biographer says: "It was this distinction on which rests Freud's chief claim to fame: even his discovery of the unconscious is subordinate to it" (Jones, 1955, p. 313), and the translator of his *Interpretation of Dreams* says in a footnote: "The distinction between primary and secondary systems, and the hypothesis that psychical functioning operates differently in them, are among the most fundamental of Freud's concepts" (Freud, 1953, p. 601). It is of some interest, therefore, to review the attention that Freud gave these terms, and then to try to assess their meaning for a general psychology of cognition.

Freud introduced the terms in his *Project for a Scientific Psychology*, prepared in 1895, but not published until after his death along with his letters to Fliess. The first mention was in a letter to Fliess dated October 20, 1895, with reference clearly to the *Project* upon which he was then working. The rele-

vant section in the *Project* is entitled "Primary Processes: Sleep and Dreams" (Freud, 1954, pp. 397–404). Here most of the later ideas are anticipated, although at this stage they are couched as a speculative neuronal theory—a theory that at least one competent reviewer finds to be in many ways an anticipation of contemporary developments in neurophysiology (Pribram, 1962).

The next full-scale discussion is in the *Interpretation of Dreams*, with the relevant section entitled "The Primary and Secondary Processes: Repression" (Freud, 1953, pp. 588–611). Freud returned briefly to the problem from time to time thereafter, the most important single paper being "Formulations on the Two Principles of Mental Functioning" (Freud, 1958). Later papers helped to coordinate the two processes with later developments in the theory, such as the new "death instinct" (Freud, 1955) and the new id, ego, superego structures (Freud, 1961).

The most painstaking effort to understand what Freud meant and to cast what he said into the form of conceptual models was made by Rapaport in a series of papers (Rapaport, 1950b, 1951a, 1951b, 1957, 1959, 1960a; Rapaport & Gill, 1959), all of which bear in one way or another on the problems of motivation in thinking. The main conclusion to which Rapaport came is that there are two kinds of organization of memory which become reflected in the two kinds of thinking: drive-organization[2] and conceptual-organization, the

[2] It is not possible in a brief paper to deal with all the puzzling problems that are raised in trying to be at once appreciative and critical of psychoanalysis. In accepting the *drive* concept from psychoanalysis, and coordinating it with what most psychologists mean by drive, we overlook a rigidity within writers on classi-

former representing, of course, primary process, the latter secondary process.

In carrying through the conceptual distinction between pimary and secondary process, Rapaport deduced from Freud primary models of action, cognition, and affect (indicating their characteristics when primary process is in control) and secondary models of each of these, when the delays of secondary process are introduced (Rapaport, 1959, pp. 71–78). The primary model of *action* is that familiar in the drive-reduction theory of motivation: aroused drive-tension, presence of the incentive and response to it (in psychoanalysis, sucking the mother's breast), followed by drive reduction. The primary model of *cognition* is aroused drive tension in the absence of the incentive, leading to hallucination of the incentive. Finally, the primary model of *affect* substitutes affect discharge for hallucination. Thus the hungry infant may scream instead of hallucinating the breast. All primary models indicate prompt response to the drive that reaches threshold intensity; all secondary models introduce delays. The secondary model of action introduces a derivative drive (similar again to learning theories that study the drive value of familiar paths and the secondary reinforcement value of sub-goals). The role of inhibition (in the absence of the goal-object) is also stressed; again something familiar in the learning-theorist discussion of frustration-induced drives (Amsel & Roussel, 1952; Marx, 1956). The secondary model of

---

cal psychoanalysis who recognize only two drives (sex and aggression), despite the primitive nature of pain, hunger, thirst, temperature, contact, curiosity, manipulation, and the other candidates for inclusion as drives. Freud did not settle the matter once and for all in 1920 when he proposed the death instinct, which for his followers made aggression a second drive along with sex.

cognition substitutes for the hallucination of the object a search for it, i.e., ordered thinking. The secondary model of affect substitutes for massive affect discharge a lesser anticipatory discharge that serves instead as a signal; behavior may be released which defends against the more massive affect discharge. There are complexities within each of these models that this brief summary cannot deal with.

Some of the characteristics of the two processes which we need to examine in relation to a general theory of thinking are the following:

1. Primary process is earlier in time and more primitive than secondary process. This does not mean that it is ever outgrown, however, for primary process functioning is characteristic of the normal adult as well as the infant, e.g., in dreams.

2. When the primary process holds sway, wishing ends in hallucinating; the infant is said to hallucinate the satisfaction of its internal needs when they cannot be gratified at once. Massive affective discharge is an alternative.

3. Primary process is coordinated with the pleasure principle, secondary process with the reality principle.

4. The pleasure principle "reigns unrestrictedly in the id" and the ego endeavors to substitute the reality principle.

5. The formal characteristics of primary and secondary processes differ, the characteristics of primary process being inferred largely from dreams. Thus the disregard for space and time and for ordinary logic is typical of primary process; the processes that Freud called the dreamwork are primary ones, especially condensation, displacement, and symbolization.

6. Primary process involves "mobile

cathexis" and the manipulation of large quantities of energy; secondary process involves "bound cathexis" and operates with small amounts of energy. The interaction between primary and secondary processes is conflictual, involving repression, defense, and the like.

7. Primary process is compelling, peremptory; secondary thought activity (practical thought, rational thought) we can "take or leave" (Rapaport, 1959, p. 76).

8. Primary process thinking in conscious subjects may be found "either out of strength or out of weakness" (Holt & Havel, 1960, p. 267). That is, primary process thinking may emerge out of ego weakness (as in a psychotic state) or because a person regresses to primary process thinking for fun or in order to open himself to creative ideas. This has come to be called "regression in the service of the ego" (Kris, 1952; Schafer, 1958).

Here then is a rich store of ideas. For these ideas to become a part of general psychology we need, first, to understand the theory in its own terms, second, to criticize it, and eventually, to reconstruct it. The ultimate contribution of Freud does not rest on a decision whether he was right or wrong; eventually we want to know more than he knew, but if he helped to stimulate the search, that will tribute enough to him.

√ Freudian Conceptions Examined

Let us pass quickly over some of the general ideas that in one form or another everyone finds acceptable. Some kind of *genetic-developmental* theory of thinking is acceptable, and a number of these have of course been proposed, such as those of Piaget (1955) and

Werner (1948). The details are a matter of some uncertainty, but there is probably some kind of continuous development rather than a saltatory or discontinuous transition from one stage to the next. The Freudian theory can be conceived in this continuous way, for primary process is never completely displaced by secondary process (Burstein, 1959). Freudian conceptions have been compared with those of Piaget by Wolff (1960).[3] Also some kind of contrast between prelogical, concrete, impulse-driven thinking and more abstract, dispassionate, realistic thinking (both forms found in the adult), is acceptable. It is important here, however, to know just what we are talking about, and Freud rests his case on the dream as the prototype of primary process; this can be objected to either on the grounds that dream thinking is not a good representative of illogical and fallacious thinking (even though it manifests these characteristics), or that Freud gave a one-sided picture of what dream thinking was like. French, who believes that dreams are attempts at problem solving and are more orderly than Freud thought, has reanalyzed Freud's Dora case in these terms (French, 1954, pp. 10–18).

The most controversial features of the Freudian scheme, either because

[3] While the tenor of Wolff's monograph is that the coordination of Piaget and Freud should be rather easy, he has given some penetrating analyses of their differences, particularly in the first stage of development, where the primary-secondary process distinction is most cogent. Here he points out that according to Piaget the organism's fundamental tendency is to assimilate the environment to itself, while Freud's theory is that it tries to rid itself of all stimulation (Wolff, 1960, p. 60). The development of ego-psychology within psychoanalysis now makes it easier for the classical analyst to accept early interaction with the environment, while not giving up any of his long-held views about intrapsychic processes.

they are unclear, unproven, or disputed, seem to me to be: (*a*) the theory of the interplay between the pleasure principle and the reality principle, especially in the negative definition of pleasure as tension-reduction, and the separation between affect and cognition, as implied in the notion that affect discharge is an alternative to hallucination as a means of primary tension reduction; (*b*) the conjecture that the infant hallucinates the absent incentive; and (*c*) the energetics involved in the contrast between primary and secondary processes. Each of these deserves some comment.

The tension-reduction theory of motivation has come in for a number of attacks, and attention has gradually shifted from the negatives of tension relief to the positive role of incentives (e.g., Hilgard, 1956, pp. 427–433; White, 1959). Freud's pleasure principle, while somewhat more complex than the typical motivational theory of the experimental students of learning, subjects Freud to the same kind of criticism, for example, for his neglect of joy and hope among the affects (e.g., Schachtel, 1959, pp. 19–21). This issue is being fought out within general psychology, and it would not take too much doctoring to fit the Freudian theory to whatever the outcome is.

A most original feature of Freud's theory is that the infant hallucinates the absent object. This is of course conjecture, based upon the predominantly visual nature of dreams, but the conjecture occurs repeatedly in Freud's writings. It should be noted that this cannot be mental activity at its earliest, for the hallucination is a *memory*, and some theory of prior perception and recovery is implied. The pleasure principle may be conceived to operate be-

fore modes of thought have developed at all. At one point Freud used the illustration of the bird inside the egg, with the nutrients there to be had immediately; the wish for nutrients cannot be distinguished from the availability of nutrients (Freud, 1958). Through some further steps, made necessary in human development because the object of gratification is not always there, *attention* and *memory* develop, and, out of them, *thought*. This is the course of development in the direction of the reality principle, but one thought-activity is split off: that is fantasy making. This is then the primary process that persists in thinking after secondary process thinking has also developed. The fact that the fantasy does not actually bring relief means that secondary process thinking must develop almost simultaneously; we are probably dealing with a ratio of the two processes from the start, more primary process gradually giving way to more secondary process.

How plausible is the conjecture that the infant hallucinates in response to its needs? Evidence would be hard to get, although working backwards by analogy from EEGs and eye movements in hallucinating adults we might be able to get some evidence; to my knowledge this does not exist. The truth is probably a metaphorical one, emphasizing the tendency of thought to move to the concrete, the specific, the pictorial, and attributing to the infant what is found in adult dreams and in the hallucinations of deprived adults (the mirage on the desert) and psychotics. The tendency for more primitive thought to take concrete forms is not without support in experimental studies, for example, the concrete-abstract distinction of Goldstein and Scheerer (1941), and the greater ease of attaining concrete over abstract concepts in general, for example, Heidbreder, Bensley, and Ivy (1948), and Grant (1951). Freud apparently was not completely satisfied with his treatment of hallucinations; at one point he suggested that the *negative* hallucination (i.e., denying the presence of stimulation) might be a better point of departure than the positive hallucination from which to start an explanation (Freud, 1957).

The energy concepts within Freudian psychology are difficult ones at best and pose a number of problems (Colby, 1955; Hilgard, 1962b). The term *cathexis* in Freudian theory is used for some kind of energy charge, but the analogy with physical energy is not a close one; the meaning is much more that of *interest,* or *attention,* or of Lewin's *valence.* In any case a highly cathected idea comes to awareness (i.e., can be attended to) in competition with less cathected ones and can be driven out of awareness by countercathexes. The notion of *mobile cathexis,* used in discussing primary process, is that, as Holt and Havel (1960) put it, "an idea and its cathexis are easily parted"—the search pattern or drive that can cause one idea to be cathected may as well cathect another one. Hence one idea easily substitutes for another in a dream. An idea and its cathexis are more closely bound when secondary process operates: when one idea is searched for in memory, or somehow comes across the threshold because of the state of its cathexis in relation to competing ideas, it comes in stable, reliable form. Poetry tends to deal in more mobile cathexes than science does ("to take up arms against a sea of troubles" versus "sea water contains sodium chloride"). Dealing with the distinction between pri-

mary and secondary process in terms of cathexes is metaphorical, but it communicates something that is comprehensible; still one is never sure but what he is missing something.[4] In addition to mobile and bound energy there is neutralized energy (Freud, 1961; Kris, 1950), referred to as delibidinized, deaggressivized, or sublimated. These forms are all said to have their roots in the innate drives (sex and aggression) but have been transformed from primary process so as to be at the service of secondary process; there may also be forms of neutralized energy that do not come from drives (Hartmann, 1950). Once neutralized energy is accepted the dichotomy between primary and secondary processes becomes less sharp (Rapaport, 1959, p. 92).

Another problem of energy in primary and secondary processes has to do with *amounts,* large amounts being involved in primary process, small amounts in secondary process. This is a little confusing because in physical outcome primary process tends to go on while the person is immobilized in sleep and incapable of putting out much energy; secondary process permits the physical outcome of energetic control over the environment. It is necessary to be repeatedly reminded that we

4 Obscure ideas sometimes seem less obscure to those who use them simply because they become familiar. Cathexis is, in fact, a very obscure idea; as in the case of other obscure ideas it becomes a difficult problem to determine when such an idea is merely obscure and when it is also profound. Attempts to clarify the concept have thus far not been very helpful (e.g., Rapaport, 1959, pp. 125–129). There is no doubt that the notion of cathexis attempts to deal with deep psychological problems, e.g., how the registration of a past experience stored in the nervous system becomes available to consciousness, how symbolization occurs. The question is how well it *solves* these problems.

are talking about amounts of psychic energy and not physical energy. Actually the matter has not been stated quite properly here: in primary process the quantity of energy dealt with is large because it is mobile and all discharged at once. This is what gives primary process manifestations their insistent quality; they, so to speak, "take over." The total quantity of energy dealt with in secondary processes may be the same, but its *regulation* is through small quantities of energy, just as a small thermostat may control a large heating plant. Hence secondary process is more finely tuned and can be turned on and off as primary process (usually) cannot be.

In order to take these ideas out of their metaphorical context and place them nearer to general psychology, we can look for some resemblances to familiar ideas:

1. Free association is more like primary process than controlled association because in controlled association we insist on bound cathexes, that is, on "appropriate" replies, as when we ask for a part-whole relationship, or a large-small relationship, and then give one member of a pair and ask for an associate. In free association, anything will do, so long as an answer is given. Under these circumstances (and this is where Freud comes in) unconscious factors are likely to provide the missing intermediaries between stimulus and response.

2. Some persistent ideas (as in obsessions) have about them a driven quality, as though we are helpless about them; they seem to happen from without, as though they happen *to* us rather than *by* us. Thus we do not feel ourselves to be the stage managers of our dreams. This is what is meant by the immediate and powerful discharge of primary processes.

3. We sometimes distinguish the affective consequences of punishment from the informative consequences. Too much affect may produce what Thorndike called irrelevant emotion; according to the Yerkes-Dodson law too much punishment interferes with learning. Thus the massive involvement of affect is inhibiting to realistic cognitive activity; if the affect comes in smaller doses, then the organism can profit by it in learning its way around. Here we have a clue to Freud's notion that secondary process experiments with small amounts of energy. The notion is also related to modern information theory, which distinguishes between the control mechanisms and the power operations that are controlled. Rapaport has noted this possible parallel (Rapaport, 1959, p. 91).

4. The opposition between primary and secondary processes is tempered somewhat in the notion of regression in the service of the ego earlier referred to; it is a regression from which one can escape, so that it does not have the full peremptory quality usually assigned to primary process. That is, we can go to a "kid party" and then change our clothes and become adult; we are not committed to hebephrenia by this act of temporary regression. The original discussion of regression in the service of the ego (Kris, 1952) is a very sketchy one; the best elaboration is by Schafer (1958). There is a curious quality about Schafer's account, however. He gives six conditions facilitating regression in the service of the ego; these are all conditions of good mental health or ego strength, and as he reviews them himself he sees that they are not quite appropriate to gifted artists, comics, and

scientists (who are supposed to use regression in the service of the ego unusually well). He resolves this problem by indicating that such regressions may serve different individual purposes. The trouble is probably not with his account but with the concept itself. Probably more is involved than that a regression permits primary process thoughts to appear. One might think of several possibilities, such as (a) a capacity for regressive experiences, for example, richness of imagination; (b) a tolerance for regressive experiences, for example, lack of anxiety when thought and imagination are given free range; and (c) skill in the utilization of regressive experiences, for example, ability to convert fantasy into acceptable artistic or other creative products, including humor.[5] These, or other aspects, may mean that the experience called regression in the service of the ego has several dimensions. Schachtel (1959, pp. 244–248) objects to the notion that the experiences are regressive at all; a certain openness to new ideas need not be regressive, but is better interpreted, he believes, as progressive.

When all the trappings of the theory of primary and secondary processes are removed there remains much in the major distinction that is plausible and familiar: enough to invite an examination of the more obscure conceptions.

Some Questions Subject to Answer

Let us now grant that as reference-concepts the primary and secondary processes are useful, and see how we can go on from there, outside the spe-

cial framework of the Freudian metapsychology. The basic classification, following David Rapaport, is between *drive organized* and *concept organized* memories as they enter into our thought processes. If primary process rules out thinking, the vehicles of thought, the ideas to which we can attend, are brought to awareness by the impulses or drives that are stirred up; thus our memories are drive organized. If my reactions to my boss are dictated by an unperceived relation between him and my father, then my thoughts of the boss are drive organized. If secondary process rules my thinking, then I may use what I have learned from interacting with my father, but I know my boss is not my father, and I react to him in accordance with the demands of the actual social situation. In this case, my thought is concept organized, according to the lines of command within the organization in which I work, the assignment I am working on, and so on. We have long been taught to distinguish between *reasoning* and *rationalization;* the former representing thought under the conceptual mode, the latter thought that is impulse driven.

If we grant the distinction between primary and secondary process, or drive organized and concept organized thought, then we have to decide how we are to use this distinction in talking about the wide range of things people do when they think. There are two chief ways of using a twofold scheme of this kind, one as a *dimension,* the other as a *mixture.*

The dimensional scheme takes off from the notion of growth, and assumes that primary process is primitive and early, secondary process more mature and later. One can then draw a line with primary process at one end and

[5] Some of these distinctions have been made by As, O'Hara, and Munger (1962) in attempting to discover regression-like experiences related to hypnotic susceptibility.

secondary process at the other, and place any act of thought along this line. The thoughts that are represented in the middle are *fusions,* if you wish, with some aspects of primary process and some aspects of secondary. I suppose one could go to a modern art exhibit and place the pictures along such a continuum, with the totally nonrepresentative pictures at one end, corresponding to impulse, with photographic representations of reality at the other; those in between would be the kinds of distorted or stylized pictures that combine impulse with reality. This scale would be a kind of analog of a scale from primary to secondary process. The dimensional position is the one favored by Rapaport (1951a, 1951b), Hartmann (1950), Kris (1952), Holt and Havel (1960.

The *mixture* scheme suggests that primary process and secondary process remain to some extent distinct, but one intrudes upon the other; their conflicts are compromised in various ways, but there is characteristically enough vacillation between them to keep their identities intact. As one grows older a larger part of his thought tends to be of the secondary process kind, but he reverts to primary process thinking in dreams and fantasy.

These two ways of schematizing the relationship between primary and secondary process can only be distinguished if the conceptual models are clear, for it is often hard to tell the difference between a fusion (implied in the dimensional scheme) and a mixture (implied when the two processes fight it out, but each continues its own existence).

These notions are too abstract to deal with unless we have some examples before us. Let us consider some examples of thinking.

1. A schizophrenic patient says to a physician: "I am 75 years old." The physician says to him: "You feel that you have suffered three times as much as most 25-year-olds." If the interpretation is correct, the patient has distorted reality, assigned himself a false age, as an expression of affect. But in so doing he has multiplied 25×3 correctly. The primary process interpretation is that the ideas that he manipulates come from his store of memories by way of impulse. He does not remember the age based on his birth certificate; he remembers the phenomenal time through which he has suffered. The fact that he can manipulate these ideas correctly does not deny their primary process origin.

2. A hypnotized subject is told that he is about to hear a very funny joke. The hypnotist tells him: "The whale is the largest living mammal." He laughs as though his sides would split. Aroused from the hypnotic state he is asked why this was so funny. One subject says: "It really wasn't funny. I just had a sort of laughing fit." Another says: "You should have seen the funny whale I pictured with a long snout and tiny legs. It sure was funny!" In the first of these, impulse and cognition were not fused, in the second they were.

3. A hypnotized subject is shown a small metal box with one real light on the left, but told that there are two lights, one on the left and one on the right. He sees both lights. Asked if they are both real, he says, "Yes." Told that one of them is *not* real, but to find which is which, he says: "The one on the right is not real; it casts no reflection in the metal surface, as the one on the left does." If the hallucination sig-

nifies primary process, the successful problem solving is secondary process. Here both go on simultaneously, but they remain distinct; the hallucination is not destroyed by the knowledge that it is not real.

4. A subject who volunteers to be hypnotized for the first time by a technique in which gradual eye-closure is suggested, raises his arms before his chest, moans, and sobs. Roused from hypnosis, he can give no account of any ideas associated with the display of affect. In a later interview outside hypnosis childhood memories were reviewed, and he demonstrated how he cowered in a chair when he was beaten by his mother. He re-enacted in the interview the positioning of his hands, his tightly closed eyes, his moaning and sobbing. His behavior in the hypnotic situation can be interpreted as the re-activation of a memory (nonverbal re-activation in this case) on the basis of some similarities between the hypnotic induction and the earlier submission to authority. This memory was drive organized rather than concept organized; it did not, however, involve hallucinations.

5. A subject who has just undergone a hypnotic session without very much success, when leaving the experiment suddenly experiences a spontaneous regression: she finds that her body is shrinking and she is becoming a small-sized girl again. Somewhat frightened by this distorted body-image, she looks about her to see that the world of objects has not changed, and she becomes her own size again. She is able to switch the experience on and off. For a while her regressed body-image coexisted with a real world; it is an important principle that in a regressed state not everything is regressed.

I have here given five illustrations to show what kinds of problems are to be faced in trying to assess primary and secondary process thinking, particularly in formulating them clearly enough to decide whether one should talk about fusions, or mixtures, or both.

Perhaps these illustrations themselves suggest experimental problems. I should like to suggest that more careful study of fantasy productions, eidetic images, and hallucinations will make important contributions, provided these studies are guided by theory. Hypnotic experimentation, from which most of my illustrations were drawn, provides a convenient way of getting into these areas, but other methods are available. Robert Holt and his associates, for example, have been studying primary process manifestations in Rorschach responses (Goldberger, 1958; Goldberger & Holt, 1958; Holt, 1956; Holt & Havel, 1960). Presumably there should be more secondary process in the TAT, and this might be a good place to examine the problem of fusion versus mixture.

Let me say a word about eidetic images. These have been very little studied in recent years, yet they can be detected when they are looked for. We find a good deal of evidence of their presence among our more hypnotizable subjects. The subject who was told stories by an Irish grandmother who believed in (and had actually seen) Leprechauns, has little trouble in seeing Leprechauns herself, as eidetic images. These are now memory images from childhood, but they bring a kind of gratification that is close to the original meaning of primary process, even though the gratification is derivative from the grandmother. The subjects in our sample who have these images tend *also* to be highly verbal and communicative, by contrast with the nonhypnotizable subjects who lack both fantasy and easy verbal expression. One might suppose words to be representative of secondary process, but they are heavily loaded with primary process too. Thus poetry, a verbal art, uses many of the same devices as the dream. There are many problems here.

A symposium is a good place to throw out problems for discussion, even though answers are hard to come by. Let me summarize some of the issues:

1. Is it possible to sharpen the characterization of primary and secondary process thinking so that the delineation will be clearer than it now is? For example, when is hallucination an essential part of primary process thinking?

2. In dealing with any illustration of thinking that we wish to classify in primary-secondary process terms, do we do better to describe *aspects* of the thinking as primary and secondary functioning, so as to place the illustration on a continuum, or do we describe the mixture and vacillation between the two processes? Or do we need a more complex model that encompasses *both* fusions and mixtures?

3. What kinds of experiments can we set up to help us sharpen these distinctions and bring them into line with our other ways of conceptualizing thinking and problem solving? For example, Charles Fisher's (1960) perceptual experiments suggest the possibility that less clearly perceived (perhaps subliminal) material tends to be recovered in memory through drive organized memories, while more clearly perceived material tends to evoke concept organized memories. Here is certainly the kind of hypothesis that can be put to test, once our criteria of the two types of organization are clearly formulated.

Summary

1. Freudian psychology is in many respects a cognitive psychology, concerned as it is with hallucinations, dreams, memories, symbols, and distortions of the thought process. It is at once a cognitive psychology and a psychology of motivation.

2. The distinction between primary and secondary processes is a very central one within psychoanalytic theory. The nature of these processes as described by Freud, and interpreted by Rapaport, is best summarized by asserting that there are drive organized and conceptually organized memories that enter into the two kinds of thinking.

3. Some of the problems of the Freudian theory are examined, and the plausibility of the theory is considered in the light of other approaches to the same phenomena. The theory is plausible, but much of its theoretical basis is obscure.

4. Some illustrations are given of the kinds of thought situations that raise questions about the two processes, whether a particular example should be viewed as a fusion of the processes or as a mixture of them. The answer is not clear, and a complete model might have to include both fusions and mixtures, if the distinction between the two processes is to be retained. There are empirical approaches to the problems possible by way of projective tests, hypnosis, and the experimental study of perception and dreams.

Journal of Abnormal and Social Psychology, 1962, vol. 64, pp. 121–129

A Dissonance Theory Approach to Defensive Projection[1]

Dana Bramel

Ego defensive processes, as discussed in psychoanalytic theory, often seem to bear some resemblance to the cognitive changes dealt with in Festinger's (1957) dissonance theory. This observation has led to a comparison of the two theories and to consideration of the possibility that certain of the Freudian defense mechanisms might occur in response to dissonance. Especially interesting from the point of view of social psychology is the concept of projection, since it clearly has implications for interpersonal relations.

Consider those situations, described in psychoanalytic theory, in which the individual's perception of some aspect of himself is contrary to his internalized standards of right and wrong (the superego). According to the theory the perception of this information arouses fear of punishment, perhaps especially a fear of painful guilt feelings (Fenichel, 1945). In order to avoid further anxiety and guilt feelings, the ego is said to initiate defensive measures.

In order to determine the relevance of dissonance theory to this phenomenon, one must ask whether dissonant relations would be expected to exist among the cognitions involved. Imagine, for example, a person who considers homosexuality a bad and disgusting thing; on some occasion he is suddenly exposed to information strongly implying that he has homosexual tendencies. According to classical psychoanalytic theory, the crucial relation is the conflict between the information or impulse and the demands of the superego. Is the new cognition—that one has homosexual tendencies—necessarily dissonant with one's belief that such tendencies are bad and that one should not have them? The answer is no. People who conceive of themselves as possessing a mixture of good and bad traits, or a preponderance of bad traits, would not generally expect that new information would be favorable to themselves or consistent with superego standards. It follows that a discrepancy between the new information and superego standards, although threatening in the psychoanalytic sense, would not necessarily be dissonant.

This is not to say, however, that dissonance would be completely absent from the cognition of the person who

[1] This article is based upon a doctoral dissertation submitted to Stanford University. The author wishes to express his indebtedness to Leon Festinger for valuable assistance throughout the research. Advice and criticism from Robert R. Sears, Nathan Maccoby, Quinn McNemar, and Stanley Schachter are gratefully acknowledged. Special thanks are also due Alvin I. Haimson for assistance in conducting the experiment.

recognizes that he is not perfect. For example, when he discovers he has homosexual tendencies, this knowledge may be dissonant with his specific belief that he is really quite masculine, even though it is not dissonant with his conviction that homosexuality is a bad thing.

The point can be clarified by a hypothetical example. Imagine two people, A and B. Both consider homosexuality a very bad thing, and both believe they are quite lacking in such motivation. A believes he is an extremely fine person in general; B sees himself as possessing almost no favorable characteristics. Both are then confronted with information that they have strong homosexual tendencies. For both this information is contrary to superego standards and dissonant with their belief that they are not homosexual. However, for A the information is also strongly dissonant with his belief that he is a nearly perfect person. For B, on the other hand, the information is quite consonant with his belief that he is a failure. The new information produces more dissonance for the person with high self-esteem, even though the conflict with the superego is substantially the same for the two people. This emphasis upon the actual self-concept in the dissonance theory approach reveals a difference in focus of the two theories.

Can dissonance involving the self-concept be reduced by projecting the offending trait onto other people? Perhaps the most effective mode of dissonance reduction would be to deny the implications of the information. Let us assume, however, that the information is so unambiguous that successful denial is not possible for the person. He is compelled to ascribe the undesirable trait to himself. Under these circum-

stances, attributing the trait to other persons might reduce dissonance in several ways. By attributing it to respected people, the projector may enable himself to re-evaluate the trait. If respected persons possess it, then perhaps it is not so bad a thing after all. Then possession of the trait would not be contradictory to a favorable level of self-esteem. Another possibility is that the person may attribute the trait to members of his reference or comparison group (Festinger, 1954). In this way he could convince himself that he does not deviate from the persons with whom he ordinarily compares himself. If he is only average in his possession of the trait, then subjectively his favorable level of self-esteem is not so strongly negated.

These possibilities suggest that indeed projection may be used as a means of reducing dissonance. There are several studies in the literature (for example, Backman & Secord, 1959 unpublished; Murstein, 1956; Wright, 1942) which are specifically relevant and show positive results, but all leave certain important issues unresolved. Consequently, the experiment reported here was conducted to test whether projection occurs in response to dissonance and to throw some light on the particular ways in which this attribution may reduce dissonance.

The hypotheses to be tested were these:

1. If a person is exposed to information strongly implying that he possesses an undesirable characteristic, he is more likely to attribute the trait to others if the information is dissonant with his level of self-esteem; the greater the dissonance, the more likely it is that projection will occur.

2. If a person is compelled to ascribe

an undesirable and dissonant characteristic to himself, he will be motivated to attribute the characteristic to favorably evaluated persons and/or to persons with whom he ordinarily compares himself.

Method

Overview

Subjects in the Favorable condition received falsified personality test results aimed at temporarily increasing their general level of self-esteem; subjects in the Unfavorable condition received parallel information intended to lower their general self-esteem. Subsequently, all subjects were privately exposed to further falsified information of an undesirable nature about themselves. It was hypothesized that this information, being more dissonant with the self-concept of subjects in the Favorable condition, would lead to more projection in that condition. Attribution was measured by asking each subject to rate another subject with whom he was paired.

First session

Each subject who signed up for the experiment appeared individually for the first session. He was told that the first part of the experiment was designed to discover what kinds of people had insight into themselves. He was asked to take a number of personality tests, which, he was told, would be carefully and confidentially analyzed by three members of the clinical psychology staff. He was informed that, after the tests were scored, he would learn the results in an interview, during which time his self-insight was to be measured. Among the tests included were the Taylor Manifest Anxiety scale, the *F, K,* and *L* scales from the MMPI, and an adjective checklist self-concept measure.

At the end of the hour, the subject was told that the second session would also include a measure of his ability to judge the personality of another person on the basis of a first impression.

Second session

On the basis of the self-concept measure subjects were paired for the second session by matching their level of self-esteem and their concept of their own masculinity.

At the beginning of the second session the two unacquainted subjects scheduled for the hour were introduced to each other. In order to aid subjects in forming an impression of each other, the experimenter asked each in turn (in the presence of the other) a set of questions about himself and his attitudes toward certain current events. At the conclusion of this meeting the subjects were separated and interviewed privately regarding the results of their personality tests.

Unknown to the subject, the "results" which he received had been prepared with no reference whatsoever to his actual test performance. There were only two test reports used in the experiment, one very favorable, and the other very unfavorable. The reports covered the personality "dimensions" of creativity, hostility, egocentricity, and over-all maturity. Each section of the report gave a rather detailed discussion of the test results bearing upon the particular dimension. The tone was objective and the general favorability was very consistent throughout the report. The two reports were very similar in form, but the specific contents were directly opposite in implication.

After having been assigned randomly to his experimental condition, the subject was read the report in private by the experimenter, and its discrepancies from the subject's present self-concept were explicitly pointed out by the experimenter. The report was finished in approximately 20 minutes. In each pair of subjects, one was assigned to the Favorable condition, one to the Unfavorable condition. Two interviewers were used for this part of the experiment, alternating between the two conditions.

Following the test report, the two subjects were brought together in another room, where they expected to make some personality judgments about each other. Each was then given a questionnaire consisting of 11 polar adjective seven-point scales, to be used to rate the other person. An over-all favorability score could be computed across the scales. Examples were masculine-feminine, friendly-hostile, competent-incompetent, and mature-immature. A self-concept measure followed, consisting of 16 polar adjective scales similar to those included in the prior rating of the other person. These were selected partially to tap dimensions covered in the personality reports, and to serve as a check on the manipulation of self-esteem. As in the previous set, they included the item, masculine-feminine, and could be summated to provide a general favorability score. Emphasis was placed upon the anonymity of the questionnaires and upon the earnest request that the subject respond "as *you* see yourself, from your own point of view at the present time."

Introducing the undesirable cognition

It was expected that informing a male undergraduate that he has homosexual tendencies would be sufficiently dissonant under certain conditions to provoke defensive behavior. Care was taken to ensure that the degree of threat was not extreme and that no damaging effects would remain at the end of the experiment. These precautions will be discussed in more detail below.

At this point in the experiment, while making ratings of partner and self, the two subjects were seated along one side of a long table, separated by about 4 feet, both facing a projection screen 6 feet in front of them. On the table in front of each subject was a small plywood box containing a galvanometer dial facing him. Issuing from the box were two wires with electrodes on the ends. Each box, with its dial, was completely shielded from the other persons in the room. Thus, each subject perceived his apparatus immediately in front of him and could not see the other subject's apparatus.

Next, the experimenter read a set of instructions to set the stage for the undesirable cognitions about homosexuality. These instructions were largely of a deceptive nature. It was explained that this part of the experiment would be concerned with the perception of sexual arousal. An elaborate explanation of the physiology of sexual arousal and the sensitive techniques for its measurement followed. Care was taken

to distinguish the galvanometer response to sexual arousal from that commonly associated with anxiety reactions, by pointing out the unmistakable signs of the former. Considerable emphasis was placed on the unconscious nature of sexual arousal and the impossibility of exerting conscious control over its expression in the "psychogalvanic skin response." It was further explained that the experimenter was investigating the perception of homosexual rather than heterosexual arousal. The task set for the subject was to observe his own sexual arousal response on his galvanometer for each of a series of photographs of men which would be projected onto the screen. He was to record this figure on a page of a small anonymous booklet. After he had recorded his own arousal level for the particular picture on the screen, he was to make an estimate of the needle indication of the other subject's apparatus for the same photograph. All subjects were explicitly told that movements of the dial would indicate homosexual arousal to the photographs. As a precaution against excessive threat, they were told that persons with very strong homosexual tendencies would consistently "go off the scale." Further, the anonymity and privacy of the situation were carefully spelled out, with the intention of convincing the subject that no one but he would know what his own responses had been.

Unknown to the subject, the supposed "psychogalvanic skin response apparatus" was not actually responding to changes in his own level of sexual arousal to the pictures. Rather, the galvanometers in each of the two boxes were controlled remotely by the experimenter. Concealed wires led from the galvanometers, in a direct current series circuit, to a calibrated variable resister. Thus, the experimenter exerted complete control over the movements of the needles, which were identical for the two subjects. Each photograph had been assigned an "appropriate" needle reading in advance, so that those depicting handsome men in states of undress received more current than did those depicting unattractive and fully clothed men. Both subjects were, thus, led to believe that they were sexually aroused by certain pictures and not by others, according to a consistent pattern.

Both subjects were confronted with exactly the same stimulus input at this point of the experiment.[2]

It was expected that the instructions would be so impressive to the subject that denial of the fact that homosexual arousal was being indicated would be very difficult. By closing off certain alternative avenues of dissonance reduction, such as the cognition that the apparatus was untrustworthy, it was intended that the situation would be conducive to the appearance of defensive projection. According to the hypothesis, subjects in the Favorable condition should experience considerable dissonance when observing their needle jump in response to photographs of attractive males. For subjects in the Unfavorable condition there would be many cognitions consonant with the new information concerning homosexuality, and not so many dissonant cognitions. For most subjects there would, no doubt, be some dissonance due to their prior belief that they are not homosexual, but the two conditions would not differ in this respect. Since the test reports contained no material concerning sexuality, subjects in the two conditions were not expected to differ in their concepts of their own masculinity or in their superego standards.

Fifteen photographs of men were used. Many of the men were almost entirely nude and had physiques somewhat more delicate and posed than those typically found in physical culture magazines. These photographs were chosen on the assumption that subjects might perceive them as being the type toward which homosexuals would be attracted.

Measuring attribution

It seemed that the most meaningful measure for testing the hypotheses would be a score representing the difference between the subject's own recorded score and his estimate of his partner's galvanic skin response. This should most accurately reflect the subject's comparison between himself and his partner. Therefore, a total score was computed for each subject, taking the algebraic sum of the differences between

[2] A similar experimental technique was independently devised by Harold Gerard (cf. Gerard, 1959; Gerard & Rabbie, 1960).

own and attributed scores across the 15 photographs. This summary score (P score) would be positive if the subject attributed (on the average) higher needle indications to his partner than to himself (i.e., attributed greater homosexual arousal). It would be zero if on the average there was no difference between own and attributed scores. It would be negative if the subject attributed lower needle indications to the other subject than to himself.

Following the threatening material, the subject responded to anonymous questions about his own and his partner's degree of possession of homosexual tendencies, and about his attitude toward the "psychogalvanic skin response" as a measure of such tendencies.

A considerable amount of time at the end of the experiment was allocated to explaining the true nature of the study and demonstrating in detail that the personality reports and the apparatus were incapable of giving a correct evaluation of a person. The expression of relief which often followed the unveiling of the deceptions indicated that the manipulations had been effective. The necessity for the deceptions used in the experimental analysis of such delicate processes was carefully explained, and all questions were answered. Not until the subjects seemed quite restored and satisfied was the session ended. All available evidence indicates that the subjects considered the experiment interesting and worthy of their participation.

Subjects

All subjects in the experiment were undergraduate men registered in the introductory psychology course. Not all of those who took part in the first session were selected to finish the experiment. Those who scored very high on the Taylor Manifest Anxiety scale and at the same time very low on the defensiveness scale of the MMPI were excluded from the second session, since there was the possibility that the manipulations might be too threatening for them. Of the 98 subjects who participated in both sessions of the experiment, 14 were excluded from the analysis—8 for suspicion regarding the procedure, 3 for excessive age (over 30), and 3 for failure to obey the instructions. Of those excluded, 7 were in the Favorable and 7 in the Unfavorable condition.

Results

Adequacy of experimental operations

The major independent variable was the level of self-esteem, or the number of favorable self-referent cognitions. A checklist measure of self-esteem administered before the manipulations revealed no initial difference between the groups. The effectiveness of the personality reports was determined by comparing the Favorable and Unfavorable groups on self-esteem as measured by adjective scales shortly after the manipulation. Mean favorability scores could range from a low of 1 to a high of 7. The results are shown in Table 1. The mean for the Favorable group was significantly higher than for the Unfavorable group ($t = 8.35$, $p < .001$).[3] We may infer, therefore, that the desired difference in self-esteem was successfully created by the fraudulent test reports.

Another important problem of experimental control had to do with the favorability of the subjects' ratings of each other prior to introduction of the cognitions concerning homosexuality. A score was calculated for each subject, taking the mean of his ratings of his partner (scored for favorability) across 10 polar adjective scales, excluding the item, masculine-feminine (considered separately below). The first half vs. second half reliability of the score was .57. Possible scores could range from 1 (very unfavorable) to 7 (very favorable). As shown in Table 1, there was no signifi-

[3] All reported significance levels are based upon two-tailed tests.

TABLE 1

MEANS AND STANDARD DEVIATIONS OF VARIABLES MEASURED PRIOR TO INTRODUCTION OF THE UNDESIRABLE COGNITION

Variable	Favorable (n = 42)	Unfavorable (n = 42)
Before self-esteem manipulation Initial self-esteem (checklist)		
M	14.5	15.1
SD	3.6	3.3
After self-esteem manipulation Self-esteem (seven-point scales)		
M	5.52	4.20
SD	.54	.86
Favorability of rating of partner		
M	4.79	4.90
SD	.69	.68
Rating of masculinity of partner		
M	5.39	5.30
SD	1.11	1.32
Rating of own masculinity		
M	5.87	5.56
SD	1.00	1.02

cant difference between the two conditions in favorability of rating of partner.

On the masculine-feminine scale, 1 indicated "very feminine" and 7 indicated "very masculine." Mean scores of the two groups did not differ on this scale, as shown in Table 1. Further, the groups did not differ significantly in their rating of their own "masculinity-femininity."

On the basis of these comparisons, it seems justifiable to conclude that the Favorable and Unfavorable groups did not differ regarding these possible artifactual effects of the self-esteem manipulations.

Self-esteem and projection

Before comparing the two experimental conditions on the attribution of homosexual arousal, let us check the reliability of the measure, the P score. For the first 23 subjects used in the experiment, the series of 15 photographs was repeated, yielding a set of 30 judgment situations for each subject. The discrepancies between his own recorded dial readings and his estimates of his partner's dial were summed separately for the first 15 and the second 15 exposures of the photographs. The correlation between these two sums (P scores) was .95. For subsequent analyses, only the P score for the first 15 photographs was used.

Subjects in the two conditions did not differ, on the average, in their own recorded scores. That is, they were equal in the accuracy with which they recorded scores. Therefore, the P scores, which were partially derived from the subjects' own recorded dial readings, could not differ between the two groups simply as a function of differences in own recorded scores.

For evidence concerning the relation between dissonance and projection, let us look first at the gross differences

TABLE 2

Means and Standard Deviations of Attribution Measured after Manipulation of Self-Esteem

Attribution	Favorable (n = 42)	Unfavorable (n = 42)
Raw P score		
M	−2.95	−11.45
SD	25.52	27.96
P score adjusted for prethreat judgment of masculinity of partner		
M	+4.65	−4.76
SD	24.28	23.99

between the experimental conditions. As shown in Table 2, the mean P score for the Favorable condition was −2.95; the mean for the Unfavorable condition was −11.45. Thus, subjects in the high dissonance condition tended to say that their partner's arousal level was about the same as their own, while those in the low dissonance condition tended to say their partner's arousal was somewhat less than their own. Attributing one's own characteristic to others was therefore more frequent in the high dissonance, or Favorable, group. The difference between the means yielded a t (for correlated means, due to matching) of 1.52, which is at the .13 level of significance. In order to arrive at a more firm conclusion regarding the outcome of this comparison, let us look at another source of variance which can be taken out of the gross variance in the P scores.

It had been anticipated that part of the variance in P scores would be due to the impression of masculinity created by the partner prior to the introduction of the undesirable cognition. If the subject rated his partner as very masculine on the masculine-feminine scale, then he would be likely to make somewhat lower (less homosexual) needle estimates for his partner than if he had rated him as very feminine. Correlations were therefore calculated between perceived masculinity of the partner (prethreat) and attribution of homosexual arousal to the photographs (P score). Within the Favorable group the resulting product-moment correlation was −.32 ($p < .05$); in the Unfavorable group the correlation was −.52 ($p < .01$). It will be remembered that the two groups did not differ in their mean (prethreat) rating of the masculinity of the partner (as measured by the masculine-feminine scale); in addition, the distributions of these ratings were very similar in the two groups. Therefore, it was decided that the rather similar within-groups correlations would justify combining the groups, calculating the correlation between the two variables in the total sample, and computing adjusted P scores as deviations from the regression line. By means of this procedure the variance associated with how masculine the partner appeared (*prior* to the threat) could be partialed out. Within the total sample ($N = 84$) the correlation between "masculinity" (prethreat) and P score was $-.42$. Each subject's P score deviation from the regression line was calculated, and the resulting scores were then interpreted as reflecting differences in attribution due to factors other than the initial perceived masculinity of the partner. The adjusted means for the groups are shown in

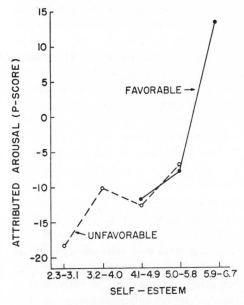

Fig. 1. Mean attribution of homosexuality as a function of level of self-esteem.

Table 2. A t test for correlated means yielded a t of 2.04 ($df = 40$), significant beyond the .05 level. On the basis of these results one may conclude that the groups differed in attribution in the direction predicted by the hypothesis relating dissonance and projection.

In all subsequent comparisons, the original, unadjusted P scores were used. The use of the simpler score should make interpretations clearer and more direct, especially in the case of within-conditions analyses.

It is of interest to look at the relation between self-esteem and attribution of arousal within the two experimental conditions. The product-moment correlation within the Favorable group was $+.29$ ($p < .07$); within the Unfavorable group the correlation was $+.10$ ($p < .55$). The relations are presented graphically in Figure 1, showing the mean raw P scores within each condition as a function of increasing self-esteem. The lack of correlation in the Unfavorable condition suggests that projection as a means of reducing dissonance occurred only when the amount of dissonance was quite high. From the point of view of the theory, this is not surprising. For the person with low self-esteem the undersirable information is actually consonant with his general self-evaluation (although dissonant with his specific cognitions about his adequate masculinity). Only for the person who believes he is consistently good will the undesirable information be strongly dissonant with his general self-esteem.

In Figure 1 it can be seen that the two groups show considerable continuity where they overlap in level of measured self-esteem. This fact is important because it implies that the self-esteem manipulations did not have strong opposed artifactual effects upon the amount of attribution of homosexual arousal. If the personality test report interviews had had effects on attribution in ways other than through the self-esteem variable, then differences between conditions might have appeared when considering subjects in the two groups with equivalent levels of self-esteem. Judging from Figure 1, persons in the two groups who had equivalent measured self-esteem levels apparently reacted similarly to the undesirable cognition.

Projection and attitude toward available social objects

There is a well-known judgmental tendency which leads a person to perceive others as possessing traits consistent with his general evaluation of those others (a halo effect). On the basis of the halo effect alone, one would expect a tendency to attribute homosexuality (an unfavorable trait) to persons who are evaluated in general relatively negatively. However, the presence of dissonance resulting from self-ascription of homosexuality should introduce a contrary tendency. To the extent that projection, of the type defined in this report, occurs, it should be aimed primarily at persons who are relatively favorably evaluated. Since in this experiment projection was expected to occur to a greater extent in the Favorable group, it follows that the empirical pattern of attribution in that condition should be some compromise between the projection pattern and the halo pattern, since one may expect both forces to be operating. In the Unfavorable condition, on the other hand, one would expect to find a pattern more closely resembling the pure

halo pattern, due to the absence of large amounts of dissonance.

In Figure 2 the results are shown separately for the two conditions. Mean P scores are shown as a function of increasingly favorable evaluation of the partner, as measured independently and prior to the introduction of the cognitions regarding homosexuality. It can be seen that the results are consistent with the hypothesis. For relatively negative and moderate levels of evaluation of the partner, subjects in the Favorable and Unfavorable conditions attributed homosexual arousal consistent with a halo effect. The less favorably they rated the other subject, the more homosexuality they attributed to him. However, when the partner had been evaluated very favorably, subjects in the two experimental conditions reacted in quite different ways. The Unfavorable group continued to follow the halo pattern, attributing very low homosexuality to the partner. The Favorable group, in contrast, exhibited no decrease in attribution when confronted with favorably evaluated objects. In fact, there was a slight but insignificant increase. The difference between the mean P scores of the Favorable $(n = 9)$ and Unfavorable $(n = 12)$ groups at the high respect point (5.4 to 6.4 in Figure 2) was significant beyond the .05 level by the t test. Since the subject's respect for his partner was not experimentally manipulated, it is possible that via self-selection other variables may be contributing to the observed difference. It should be pointed out, for example, that the measured self-esteem level of subjects in the Favorable group (with respected partner) was slightly higher than that of other subjects in the Favorable group, so that some of the

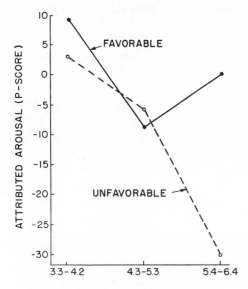

ATTITUDE TOWARD PARTNER
Fig. 2. Mean attribution of homosexuality as a function of favorability of attitude toward partner.

tendency of these particular subjects to project may be traceable to their higher self-esteem rather than to their attitude toward their partner. Unfortunately, the number of cases is too small to allow an internal analysis to throw light on this question. All things considered, one can be fairly confident that the difference between the conditions does reflect a tendency for projection to be directed toward favorably evaluated persons under these circumstances.

Discussion

The results provided good support for the central hypothesis, that projection can be a response to dissonance involving the self-concept. Subjects in the Favorable condition, for whom the undesirable information about homosexuality was more dissonant with the self-concept, attributed more arousal to

other persons. It is very unlikely that this difference was due to differences between conditions in severity of super-ego standards concerning homosexuality. In designing the experimental manipulations, care was taken to avoid any implications about the good or bad aspects of homosexuality. Since subjects were assigned randomly to conditions, it appears safe to assume that the groups did not differ on the average in their moral evaluation of homosexuality as such. The experiment was therefore capable of demonstrating the role of dissonance in projection while controlling the super-ego variable.

The finding that projection resulting from dissonance was aimed primarily at respected persons supported the second hypothesis. A number of defensive projection processes have been summoned in order to explain phenomena of prejudice toward out-groups (for example, Ackerman & Jahoda, 1950; Adorno, Frenkel-Brunswik, Levinson, & Sanford, 1950). It is important to note that in most cases projection is said to be aimed at persons and groups who are disliked and considered incomparable and inferior to the projector. This is, of course, quite different from the kind of projection revealed in the present experiment.

Let us consider possible alternative explanations for the results shown in Figure 2. Perhaps the dissonance introduced by the undersirable information in the Favorable condition led directly to a re-evaluation of homosexuality. That is, perhaps these subjects were able to change their attitude toward the trait without the intermediate step of associating it with favorably evaluated persons. This re-evaluation prior to attribution might then affect the pattern of attribution in such a way as to give the appearance, deceptively, of projection. Once the undesirability of the trait was reduced, there would be less tendency to attribute it differentially to disliked persons (halo effect). The effect of such a process would be to attenuate the halo pattern in the Favorable condition, and might be revealed in part as a greater tendency to attribute homosexuality to respected persons, as compared with subjects in the Unfavorable condition. Is this hypothesis capable of explaining the results of the experiment without resort to the hypothesis of defensive projection?

The data show that subjects in the Favorable condition did tend to follow the halo pattern when the partner was evaluated unfavorably or moderate in favorability. In Figure 2, the difference between the unfavorable ($n = 9$) and moderate ($n = 24$) points within the Favorable group was significant beyond the .10 level by the t test, and was at least as striking as the pattern for the Unfavorable group. If in fact the high dissonance in the Favorable condition had led directly to re-evaluation of homosexuality (without projection), then the halo effect would have been attenuated in this condition at all points in Figure 2. There is no apparent reason for supposing that re-evaluation of the trait (without defensive projection) would have occurred among Favorable subjects confronted with respected partners more so than among other subjects in the Favorable group.

Consider another alternative explanation of the results. Perhaps the personality test report led subjects in the Favorable condition to conclude that they were generally better than other

people, while those in the Unfavorable condition concluded they were worse than other people. Both groups of subjects then were given information that they possessed some degree of homosexual arousal. If subjects in the Favorable condition believed they were generally superior people, they might then have deduced that their partner was likely to be less worthy than themselves. This could result in rating the partner as possessing a greater amount of homosexual motivation. Persons in the Unfavorable condition would, by similar reasoning, conclude that their partner possessed a smaller amount of homosexual arousal. Such nondefensive processes could account for the over-all difference in attribution between the two experimental conditions.

The data, as presented in Figure 2, cast doubt upon this alternative explanation. If the over-all difference between conditions were due to nondefensive deductions from the personality test reports, one would expect to find differences between the Favorable and Unfavorable conditions at all points along the attitude-toward-partner dimension. It is apparent, on the contrary, that the difference between conditions occurred only when the partner had been rated favorably.

It is interesting to speculate about the conditions under which dissonance with the self-concept will lead to projection onto favorably evaluated persons. In this experiment the dissonance producing information was probably quite striking and unambiguous to the subjects. With great care the experimenter had explained that movement of the needle in response to looking at the photographs was a clear and indisputable sign of homosexual arousal. The situation was such that outright denial of the meaning of the needle movements would have been quite difficult for persons in reasonable touch with reality. It is very likely that these subjects were forced to accept the information as implying some degree of homosexual arousal in themselves. Under these circumstances of self-ascription, a good way to reduce the dissonance remaining was to try to get desirable people "into the same boat."

However, if the subjects had been able to deny the direct implications of the galvanic skin response, then a different pattern of attribution might have been observed. If the information were sufficiently ambiguous, so that partial denial occurred, then it would no longer be so comforting to attribute the undesirable trait to persons with whom the subject ordinarily classes himself. That is, when one is attempting to avoid self-ascription, it probably does not help to ascribe the trait to others who are seen as generally similar to one's self. Whether, when denial is possible, projection tends to be directed toward undesirable persons or outgroups, is an interesting question for further experimental exploration.

Summary: A laboratory experiment was conducted to investigate some of the conditions affecting the occurrence of defensive projection. It was hypothesized that such projection is a positive function of the amount of cognitive dissonance resulting from the introduction of a self-referent cognition of negative valence. Further, it was hypothesized that certain types of defensive projection are likely to be selectively aimed at persons who are favorably evaluated by the threatened individual. Two groups of normal subjects were prepared in such a way that different amounts of dissonance would result from their exposure to the same undesirable information about themselves. All subjects received fraudulent information to the effect that they possessed homosexual tendencies. During the presentation of the disturbing material, each subject made estimates of the degree of homosexual arousal of another subject with whom he was paired, and whom he had met only rather briefly just prior to this part of the experiment.

The results supported the hypotheses. On the average, subjects in the high dissonance condition attributed to their partner about the same degree of arousal as they themselves appeared to be having. Those in the low dissonance condition in general attributed to their partner a level of arousal less than their own. The evidence suggested that the high dissonance group projected only when confronted with a partner whom they had previously evaluated quite favorably on adjective rating scales.

The relation between the psychoanalytic and dissonance theory approaches to defensive processes was discussed. It was proposed that study of the selection of objects should throw light upon the possible existence of distinct varieties of defensive projection.

Journal of Personality and Social Psychology, 1965, vol. 1

The Effects of Fear and Specificity of Recommendation upon Attitudes and Behavior[*][1]

Howard Leventhal, Robert Singer, and Susan Jones

Information alone seldom provides sufficient impetus to change attitudes or actions toward a given object (Cohen, 1957; Klapper, 1960; Rosenberg, 1956). The information must not only instruct the audience but must create motivating forces that induce attitude and behavioral change. Janis and Feshbach (1953, 1954) were among the first to explore the effects of information that arouses fear or avoidant motivation on the changing of attitudes. Their results indicated that high fear-arousal produced less attitude change, presumably because high fear produced responses of defensive avoidance. Support for the finding of less attitude change with high than with low fear communications has also been presented by Goldstein (1959) and by Janis and Terwilliger (1962). In other recent studies, however, evidence has accumulated that suggests the need to reevaluate the relationship between fear-arousal and persuasion.

First, Berkowitz and Cottingham (1960) have demonstrated that, at relatively low levels, increments in fear may produce increased attitude change especially for subjects (Ss) for whom

* Adapted with permission.
1 This study was conducted under U.S.P.H.S. grant CH 00077-02. We would like to thank Drs. John S. Hathaway and James S. Davie of the Department of University Health for the cooperation and help they gave to this study.

the communication was less relevant. Leventhal and Niles (1963), and Niles (1964) have also found that fear-arousal increases persuasion. They obtained a positive correlation between reported fear and intentions to act (Leventhal and Niles, 1964) and increases in intentions with increasingly powerful communications (Niles, 1964). These effects were found by using stimuli considerably more vivid and frightening than those used in any of the earlier investigations. Thus, these experiments suggest that fear functions as a drive that promotes the acceptance of recommended actions, and, regardless of the absolute level of fear-arousal used in any study, the communication which arouses more fear will be more persuasive.

There are a number of incidental factors that may account for the different results in these studies; e.g., (1) Janis and Feshbach's topic was dental health, while Leventhal and Niles (1964) and Niles (1964) studied lung cancer. (2) Janis and Feshbach (1953) used high school students, Leventhal and Niles (1964) used people attending the New York City health exposition, and Niles (1964) used college students. While these factors might be responsible for the different outcomes, one variable that seems of particular importance is the availability of the recommended action. In their study, Janis and Fesh-bach (1935) suggested that fear-arousal could lead to increased persuasion if the action was immediately available. In the Leventhal and Niles study (1964), action was immediately available to all groups of Ss; i.e., they could get an X-ray, and, while stopping smoking may require concerted effort over a long period of time, it can be initiated immediately. In the Niles (1964) experiment, the arousal of fear increased desire to take action principally for Ss who did *not* see themselves as vulnerable to disease. Ss who felt vulnerable to disease showed relatively small increases in willingness to take preventive action when made fearful. Their greater resistance to persuasion seemed to be related to their tendency to judge the recommendations to prevent lung cancer as ineffective. In addition, Ss high in vulnerability scored low on a scale of self esteem that relates to seeing oneself as able to cope with the environment (Leventhal and Perloe, 1962; Dabbs, 1962). The findings suggest that when environmental conditions *or* the S's dispositional characteristics make action seem highly possible and effective, fear will promote action and attitude change.

The present study was designed to provide additional data on this question. Fear-arousing and non–fear-arousing communications were used to recommend a clear action (taking a tetanus shot) that is, for all intents and purposes, 100 percent effective. Thus, in line with our earlier findings (Leventhal and Niles, 1963; Niles, 1964), it was predicted that a greater degree of attitude change and a greater degree of action would be produced by the high fear conditions. Secondly, an attempt was made to manipulate experimentally the perceived availability of the recommended action by giving some Ss a *specific plan* to guide their action. It was hypothesized that adherence to the recommended act would be greater among Ss possessing a specific plan. Finally, an interaction was expected between fear and specificity: highly motivated Ss, that is, those exposed to the fear-arousing materials, were expected to show the greatest attitude and behavioral compliance when a clear plan for action was given to them.

Another question that was raised with regard to these divergent findings was the kind of emotion evoked by the stimulus. Careful attention has been given to discriminating levels of fear-arousal, and to the possibility that fear-arousing communications arouse aggression as well as anxiety (Janis and Feshbach, 1953; Robbins, 1962). Other studies in the current program (Leventhal, Jacobs, and Niles, 1963) suggest that "fear" may be experienced along with many other emotions. Therefore, several items were used to assess emotional arousal with the hope that these would provide added information on the nature of the fear associated with persuasion.

Method

Design and Subjects

The experimental design incorporated two levels of fear and two levels of information on the availability of the recommended action. Additional control groups were run to clarify questions unanswered by the factorial design. These are described in the results section. Booklets were used to present the fear-arousing stimuli and to deliver the recommendation for inoculation. The Ss completed a questionnaire after they had read the booklet.

All Ss were seniors at Yale College and were selected by taking every other name from the class list. Initial contacts were by mail, and specific appointments for the experimental session were made by phone. No inducements were offered for participating in the study and Ss knew only that they were to evaluate a public health pamphlet. All contacts with Ss were made using the name of the John Slade Ely Center and the University Department of Health.

Subjects were run individually and in a building 2½ blocks away from the University Health Service. Conducting the study in the University Health Building would have made it far too simple for Ss to get shots. When a student entered the experiment, he was given a pamphlet and told: "Would you please read this pamphlet carefully. When you are finished, please bring it back to me and I will give you a questionnaire to fill out about it." After reading the pamphlet and filling out the questionnaire the students departed. There was minimal conversation with the experimenters.

Experimental Manipulations

The booklets were composed of two sections: (1) a "fear section," dealing with the causes of tetanus and including a case history of a tetanus patient, and (2) a "recommendation section," dealing with the importance of shots in preventing the disease. There were two forms of each section: high fear and low fear, specific recommendation and nonspecific recommendation. Thus there were four pamphlets in all.

Fear Manipulation. The same facts about the disease were present on both fear levels. Three devices were used to manipulate fear: (1) coupling frightening or non-frightening facts with basic information on tetanus; (2) using emotion-provoking or non–emotion-provoking adjectives to describe the causes of tetanus, the tetanus case, and the treatment of tetanus; and (3) including different kinds of photographs to illustrate the pamphlet. For example, in the high fear booklet the incidence was described as being as high as that for polio, and the bacteria were described as "under your finger nails, in your mouth" etc., and as literally surrounding the reader. The low

treatment simply stated these facts in a nondramatic way. The aim of the high fear booklet was to create a strong feeling of personal vulnerability.

A case history, constructed from reports in medical journals, was presented to make vivid the severity of the disease. In the high fear condition, the wording was constructed to create a clear image of the patient's symptoms (convulsions; his back arched upwards, head whipped back, mouth slammed shut, etc.). Photographs were also included which showed a child in a tetanic convulsion and bedridden patients with gastric and tracheal tubes, and urinary catheters in place. Three of the photographs were in color. One illustrated a gaping tracheotomy wound, the others depicted patients with urinary catheters, tracheotomy drainage, and nasal tubes. The treatments illustrated are actually used in the therapy of severe cases of tetanus. They proved to be quite startling to these naïve subjects.

In the low fear condition, colored photographs were omitted, as were the pictures of the hospital patients and equipment. Two photographic copies of drawings of the facial expressions found in tetanus were included. The case history was described in unemotional terms and, where the patient died in the high fear booklet, he survived in the low fear case. Otherwise, the booklets were factually identical and were approximately of equal length (12 mimeographed pages).

The plan for action. After the presentation of the case history, all pamphlets contained identical paragraphs on the importance of controlling tetanus by inoculation. This point was illustrated by statistics that clearly demonstrated that shots are the only powerful and fully adequate protection against the disease. In addition, it was stated that the University was making shots available free of charge to all interested students.

For the high availability treatment, additional material was included urging the students to take a shot and providing a detailed set of suggestions as to how he could do this within the context of his daily activities. The points made can be paraphrased as follows:

1. The University Health Service expressed the hope that all students would

take the necessary action to protect themselves.

2. The location of the University Health Service was described and the times that shots were available were listed.

3. Precisely where to go and what to do to get a shot was indicated.

4. A map was presented of the campus with the University Health Building clearly circled.

5. A request was made that each student review his weekly schedule to locate a time when he would pass by the University Health so that he could stop in to be inoculated.

The specific recommendation, then, was essentially a detailed plan to make the S rehearse the various steps needed to take the suggested action. Thus, the low availability groups were told of the effectiveness of the shots and that they were available. The high availability groups had this information plus additional material helping them to plan and to review the specific steps needed to take the shots. It should be made clear, however, that since the Ss were seniors, they *all* knew the location of student health, and it is extremely likely that they had all visited the building at some time in the past. The plan, therefore, would simply make salient that which was *already* known rather than providing new information.

Response Measure

Two types of responses were observed for all subjects participating in this experiment. Immediately after the communication all subjects completed a questionnaire on which they reported their attitudes, feelings, and reactions to the experimental setting. In addition, a record was obtained of all Ss taking a tetanus inoculation.

Questionnaire measures. The questionnaire included items on:

1. Prior inoculation against tetanus.

2. Intentions to be inoculated.

3. Attitude regarding the importance of inoculation.

4. Judgments of the likelihood of contracting tetanus and its severity *if* contracted.

5. Emotions experienced while reading the communications.

6. Reactions to, and interest in the communications.

The items used will be reported in the result section.

Behavioral measures. The records of all participants were checked by student health authorities and a count was made of the subjects in each fear and availability category who were inoculated. The dates for inoculation were also obtained. Those students who were inoculated at the close of the semester, more than one month *after* the study termination, were not included in the inoculation count. (It is common practice for students taking trips abroad to receive inoculations at the end of the semester.)

The questionnaire also included a variety of items on many diseases besides tetanus. The items were included principally to suggest to S that the investigation was on *health,* rather than an attempt to coerce him into taking an inoculation. Thus, items asked about prior shots for polio, typhoid, and flu, and feelings of susceptibility to and the severity of six other diseases. These questions can also serve as a check on whether the attitude change effects are specific to the topic of the communication.

Results

Fear Arousal

As can be seen from Table 1, the fear manipulation was highly successful. Ss reported feeling greater fright, tension, nervousness, anxiety, discomfort, anger, and nausea in the high than in the low fear treatment.[2] All differences were significant at less than the .005 level. Incidental observations indicated that the high fear booklets were indeed distressing. All Ss were extremely intent and focused on the materials; some appeared pale, others

[2] The self reports of emotion were obtained by asking "While you were reading the pamphlet did you find that you had any of the following feelings?" A series of adjectives with 21-point scales followed this statement.

TABLE 1

REPORTED EMOTIONS BY TREATMENT AND PRIOR INOCULATION OF *S*

		Treatment				Significance data		
		High fear		Low fear				
Emotions[a]		No shot	Shot	No shot	Shot	F (Hi-Lo)	df	p
Fear[b]	X	9.25	8.47	4.51	3.21	43.19	1/139	.005
	N	(30)	(44)	(29)	(44)			
Baseline Recommendations only	X	2.61						
Tension	X	9.28	9.07	4.43	3.58	35.28	1/139	.005
	N	(30)	(44)	(29)	(44)			
Baseline Recommendations only	X	1.35						
Nervousness	X	7.85	7.79	3.93	2.70	36.40	1/139	.005
	N	(30)	(44)	(29)	(44)			
Baseline Recommendations only	X	1.53						
Anxiety	X	9.51	9.06	5.43	3.26	32.30	1/139	.005
	N	(30)	(44)	(29)	(44)			
Baseline Recommendations only	X	2.97						
Discomfort	X	11.43	10.40	4.47	3.36	63.84	1/139	.005
	N	(30)	(46)	(29)	(44)			
Baseline Recommendations only	X	3.87						
Anger	X	4.56	3.40	2.19	1.59	15.54	1/140	.005
	N	(30)	(45)	(29)	(44)			
Baseline Recommendations only	X	5.94						
Naseau[c]	X	7.34	5.22	2.61	2.19	27.81	1/140	.005
	N	(30)	(45)	(29)	(44)			
Baseline Recommendations only	X	3.87						

[a] Twenty-one points on scale. Higher numbers on all scales indicate higher reported affect.

[b] The means are *averages* of the means for specific non-specific for each fear level. This was done for ease in presentation. The analyses were conducted on the complete table using Walker and Lev (1953) technique for unequal *ns*. There were *no* significant interactions.

[c] Nausea was also effected by specificity. This will be reported in a later table.

shaken and many made other sounds and gestures indicating distress. These treatment effects were significant whether or not *Ss* had been inoculated against the disease. (Means are also presented for two control groups. One was not exposed to any communication and simply filled out the "Health Prac-tices Questionnaire." The other received only the specific recommendation material prior to completing the questionnaire.)[3]

[3] The control *Ss* completed essentially the same questionnaire as the experimental *Ss*. All references to the preceding communication were, however, omitted. The relatively high mean for anger reflects the initiation some con-

TABLE 2

IMPORTANCE OF TETANUS SHOTS AND INTENTIONS TO BE INOCULATED

A. Importance of Shots (13 point scale)

		No Prior Shots			Prior Shots	
		Hi Fear	Lo Fear		Hi Fear	Lo Fear
Specific	X	11.92	10.00		11.61	11.82
	N	(13)	(16)		(23)	(22)
Nonspecific	X	11.29	10.54		11.93	10.32
	N	(17)	(13)		(22)	(22)
Recommendations only		Baseline Control		8.82		
Control	8.76			(11)		
	(29)					

B. Intention To Get Shots (13 point scale)

		No Prior Shots			Prior Shots	
		Hi Fear	Lo Fear		Hi Fear	Lo Fear
Specific	X	11.23	10.00		8.43	5.90
	N	(13)	(15)		(23)	(22)
Nonspecific	X	11.29	9.69		7.52	7.55
	N	(17)	(13)		(21)	(20)
Recommendations only		Baseline Control		6.75		
Control	7.00			(10)		
	(29)					

	No Prior Shots	
	Hi Fear	Lo Fear
Strong Intention (13)	18	9
Moderate Intention (1–12)	12	20

$X^2 = 6.22$; df 1; $p < .02$.

Attitudes. On a 13-point scale, a general question (How important do you think it is to get a tetanus shot?) was used to assess the degree of importance that Ss attached to the tetanus shots. On the same scale, another question was used to assess his intentions to avail himself of inoculation (Do you intend to get a tetanus shot?). As can be seen in Table 2, Ss in the high fear conditions felt that the shots were more

trol Ss felt (and expounded upon) at having to answer the emotion items. Some control Ss found these questions annoying as they did not seem to have a clear referent.

important than did Ss in the low fear conditions (F = 8.45; df 1/140; p < .01)

For the intention question, there were two important trends. First Ss who had a shot within the last two years scored lower than those who had not had a shot (F = 16.8; df 1/136; p < .005). In addition, there was a trend for Ss in the high fear treatment, regardless of inoculation status to express stronger intentions to get shots than did Ss in the low fear condition (F = 3.55; df 1/136; p < .08). Since the distributions were skewed downwards and the means in the high fear cells were over 11, using a 13-point scale, it appeared that a ceiling effect was operating to minimize the differences. A test of the effect of fear on intentions was therefore performed by treating all scores of 13 as very strong intentions and scores of 12 and below as weak intentions. Using only those Ss who *had not* had a shot within the last two years (relevant Ss), a significantly greater number of Ss expressed a strong intention to be inoculated in the high fear treatment than in the low ($X^2 = 6.22$; df 1; $p < .02$).

Action. During the four to six week period between the experimental sessions and the end of classes, nine of the 59 eligible Ss went for shots. Of the nine, four were in the high fear specific, four in the low specific, one in the low fear nonspecific and none in the high fear nonspecific. A comparison between the 27.6 percent of specific takers and the 3.3 percent of nonspecific takers is significant ($CR = 2.65$; $p < .01$). Ss in the specific condition were more likely to get shots.[4] Thus, attitudes and actions appear to be affected by different factors. While a low fear nonspecific communication has little influence on either attitudes or actions, fear-arousing messages affect attitudes regardless of specificity of plan, and recommendations using specific plans affect actions regardless of the level of fear.[5]

Recommendations only control. Because the specificity factor did not interact with arousal as predicted, it was unclear whether the arousal of fear was a necessary condition for action. The main effect suggests that specific information may be a sufficient condition for the occurrence of action. To test this possibility, a control group was run of Ss exposed only to specific information. This group was run the following year and a time difference is involved which was absent in the other comparisons.

The procedures for contacting and dealing with Ss were identical to those used in the four experimental groups. Of the 30 eligible Ss in the group, not one availed himself of the opportunity to obtain an inoculation. Thus, specific information alone does not seem to be sufficient to influence actions or attitudes (see Table 2).

Action baseline. The date of tetanus inoculation for a sample of 60 students was also obtained to record the baserate of inoculation seeking during the experimental period. None of the students (eligibles or ineligibles) were inoculated during that period. Therefore, while the rate of shot taking was not high in the specific experimental treatments (27.6 percent), it is obviously greater than the base-rate.[6]

---

[4] Seven additional eligible Ss took shots following the close of classes. These were distributed as follows: four specific (two high and two low) and three nonspecific (two high and one low). Adding in these cases gives 41 percent specific, 13 percent nonspecific taking shots ($CR = 2.44$; $p < .02$). Among the ineligible Ss, two in the high fear, nonspecific condition took shots. It appears that most of these Ss were receiving shots as part of a series in preparation for travel.

[5] One could agree that the specificity effect was obtained because Ss in the nonspecific

condition *missed* the statement that shots could be obtained at University Health. However, when Ss were asked where they would get shots, 70 percent of those in the nonspecific treatment and 72 percent of those in the specific mentioned University Health.

[6] Only one of the Ss included in the experimental groups had had a shot just prior to participating. He had received it as treatment for an injury. Thus, there is little reason to believe that students spontaneously take shots during the year to protect themselves against tetanus.

Mediating Factors

Variables associated with attitude change. In addition to the fear measures, several other measures of reported feelings varied in the same manner as did attitudes toward tetanus inoculations. Ss in the high fear condition felt that tetanus was more serious than did subjects in the low fear treatments ("How serious do you think it would be if you contracted tetanus?"; F = 22.94; df 1/139; p < .005). In addition, Ss in the high fear conditions reported more concern about getting tetanus ("When you think about the possibility of getting tetanus, how concerned or worried do you feel about it?"; Table 3, F = 3.92; df 1/140; p < .05), more worry about the way they had treated cuts ("While you were reading the pamphlet, did you feel worried about the way you have treated abrasions, cuts, or bruises?"; F = 3.75; df 1/136; p < .10), and reported more irritation directed at the photographs than did subjects in the low fear condition ("Did the illustrations irritate you or make you angry?"; F = 6.94; df 1/136; p < .01). High fear Ss were also more certain than low fear Ss that the pictures used enhanced the pamphlet ("Did the illustrations in the pamphlet enhance the message of the pamphlet?"; F = 11.618; df 1/134; p < .001). These effects were significant regardless of the Ss' prior vaccination histories. As with the prior measures of emotional arousal, being vaccinated is no protection against the distressing emotions that appear to be elicited by the

TABLE 3

OTHER DIFFERENCES BETWEEN HIGH AND LOW FEAR
CORRELATED WITH ATTITUDE CHANGE

	High Fear		Low Fear				
	No prior shot	Prior shot	No prior shot	Prior shot	F (Hi-Lo)	df	p
1. Seriousness[a] of tetanus	10.88[b]	10.68	8.16	8.02	22.94	1/139	.005
Control (N = 11)	7.02						
Recommendations only (N = 30) 8.9							
2. Concern over contracting tetanus	10.48	10.59	9.13	7.67	3.92	1/140	.05
Control (N = 11)	5.58						
Recommendations only 7.53							
3. Worry over cuts and bruises	7.20	7.39	6.43	4.72	3.75	1/136	n.s.
Control (N = 11)	1.26						
Recommendations only 4.17							
4. Anger at illustrations	3.71	3.94	2.37	2.62	6.95	1/136	.01
5. Pictures Enhance pamphlet	7.06	7.13	5.69	5.55	11.62	1/134	.005

[a] Item 1 used a 13 point scale, item 2 and 3 used 21 point scales, and 4 and 5 used 9 point scales.

[b] Means reported are the average of the means for specific and non-specific cells.

pamphlet *per se*. It is also interesting to note that the arousal of aggression (anger and irritation) occurs in the same conditions as opinion change. The annoyance and irritation prompted by the communication and the illustrations, therefore, either does not minimize their effectiveness or was not of sufficient strength to arouse resistance to persuasion.

Variables associated with action. In examining data relating to action, we shall compare the means only for those Ss *eligible* for vaccination. Ss receiving specific recommendations tended to report stronger feelings of susceptibility to tetanus. Though the difference is at the .10 level, ("The chances are——in 100 that I will contract tetanus"; Table 4, F = 3.14; df 1/136; p < .10), the scores are highly skewed and do not approach significance using an appropriate test.

Ss receiving the specific recommendation reported feeling less nauseated than those getting the general recommendation (F = 6.14; df 1/140; p < .01). Thus, while nausea was increased by the high fear booklets, it was depressed by the specific recommendation and for the low fear

specific was below the control mean. In addition, the specific Ss reported more interest in the communication ("Did you find the pamphlet interesting?"; F = 4.26; df 1/137; p < .105). It seems, therefore, that the correlates of action are a greater interest in the outer environment and a lessening of what may be potentially inhibiting visceral reactions, though fear itself is high.

Takers versus nontakers. The analyses to the point appear to indicate that fear-arousal is sufficient to influence attitudes, while both arousal stimuli and specific recommendations are needed for action. Since an increase in the level of fear does not increase the rate of action taking, it may appear that actions and attitudes are no longer related to one another. To obtain further evidence on this question, a *post hoc* comparison was made of takers and nontakers on the questionnaire measures. In making the comparisons, a constant equal to the difference between the high and low fear means, was added to all scores in the low fear condition. This eliminated the main effects of arousal and allowed a comparison of shot takers and non-

TABLE 4

DIFFERENCES BETWEEN SPECIFIC AND NONSPECIFIC TREATMENTS
(NO PRIOR SHOT SUBJECTS ONLY)

		Specific		Nonspecific		Quest. Control	Rec. only Control
		High Fear	Low Fear	High Fear	Low Fear		
Susceptibility	X	7.089	13.569*	4.736	4.615	5.58	11.61*
(100 point scale)	N	(13)	(16)	(17)	(13)	(11)	(28)
Nausea	X	5.61	1.75	9.06	3.46	3.87	1.59
(21 point scale)	N	(13)	(16)	(17)	(13)		
Interested in							
Pamphlet	X	8.15	7.73	7.17	7.3	—	—
(9 point scale)	N	(13)	(15)	(17)	(13)		

* A few Ss had extremely high scores for these questions which caused an unduly inflated mean.

TABLE 5

COMPARISON OF SHOT TAKERS WITH NON-TAKERS

A. Emotion		Takers	Non-Takers	t	p[a]
Anxiety	X	11.90	9.07	1.548	.10
	N	(9)	(50)		
Fright	X	11.39	8.88	1.470	.10
	N	(9)	(50)		
B. Attitude					
Importance	X	11.96	10.49	1.885	.05
	N	(9)	(50)		
Illustrations Enhance	X	8.89	6.36	1.585	.10
		(9)	(48)		
Susceptibility[b]	X	19.16	10.32	1.275	.15
		(8)	(21)		

[a] One-tailed values
[b] Specific treatment Ss only

takers ignoring the effect of the fear treatment. The only values that approached significance were for anxiety, fright, importance of shots and feelings that the illustrations enhanced the pamphlet. Thus, shot takers, who are mainly in the specific recommendation condition, not only differ from non-takers in the *general* recommendation condition in the ways discussed before, but they *also* show higher scores on the above measures. Attitude and arousal are related, therefore, to action.

Discussion

The data lend mixed support to the hypotheses. As in the earlier experiments (Leventhal and Niles, 1963; Niles, 1964), fear-arousing communications increased attitudinal acceptance of the recommendations, in this case, favoring tetanus inoculations. Supporting evidence for the facilitating effect of fear on attitude change can also be found in Weiss, Rawson, and Passamanick (1963) where high scores on dispositional anxiety facilitated opinion change. These results are, however, contradictory to the data reported in two studies of acceptance of recommendations for dental hygiene (Janis and Feshbach, 1953; Goldstein, 1959) where increases in fear level appeared to be associated with resistance to the recommendations.[7] As suggested earlier (Leventhal and Niles, 1963; and Niles, 1964), the discrepancy between the experiments may relate to differences in the perceived effectiveness of the recommended actions. Thus, tetanus inoculations are far more effective as a preventive measure for tetanus than tooth brushing is for dental disease. No matter how one cares for his teeth, he is still likely to have some caries. On the other hand, the incidence of tetanus is practically 0 for protected people, and for lung cancer, the incidence is extremely low for nonsmokers. There-

[7] The Janis and Terwilliger (1962) experiment also tends to support the thesis that high fear increases resistance to persuasion. The experiment, however, was not specifically designed to test this hypothesis and the results on this particular issue were borderline; the trend for high fear (6–2/11) vs. low fear (11–0/16) on acceptance of a nonsmoking recommendation being only suggestive (CR = 1.35; p < .18 two tailed).

fore, when fear is aroused it may be critical to present an extremely effective (or effective-appearing) recommendation to minimize the possibility that Ss will leave the communication setting still in need of reassurance and thus open to counterpersuasion.

It has also been suggested (Weiss, *et al.*, 1963) that fear will have opposite effects upon attitude change depending upon the *S*'s initial position. When Ss hold competing opinions, the increased drive level could be predicted to strengthen the incorrect responses more than the correct ones (e.g., Farber and Spence, 1953). In the present experiment, it is clear from the control group data that Ss are initially favorable toward shots. It is possible, however, that Ss in the dental hygiene study (Janis and Feshbach, 1953, 1954) were negative toward some of the recommended practices and that fear strengthened the "incorrect" responses. This argument, however, loses some strength, as smokers in the lung cancer studies also showed more acceptance of recommendations with high levels of fear (Leventhal and Niles, 1963; Niles, 1964). Still, the actions recommended in the current setting are preventive, simple to take, and relatively painless.

Of greater interest, however, is that specific plans for action influence behavior while level of fear does not. But specific information alone is insufficient, as action is influenced only when specific information is combined with one of the fear-arousing communications. The group exposed only to specific information is generally quite similar to an unexposed control for reported emotions and very similar to the unexposed control attitudes concerning the importance of shots. Therefore, while emotional arousal is neces-

sary for attitudinal and behavioral change, it seems to be sufficient for the former and only necessary for the latter. Does this mean that behavior and attitudes are entirely independent of one another? In our first study on lung cancer (Leventhal and Niles, 1963), a very high correspondence was found between the intention to get X-rays and actually having one taken. In addition, X-ray takers reported more fear than nontakers. In the present study, the comparisons of takers and nontakers revealed a similar effect, that is, the takers regarded shots as more important (though intentions were *not* stronger) than the nontakers, and the takers had higher scores on some of the fear indices. Neither of these experiments show significant differences between fear treatments for the action measures. If one reexamines the setting for the lung cancer study, it soon becomes apparent that Ss in all conditions were given a highly specific plan for taking X-rays; that is, while delivering the recommendation for X-rays, "the experimenter pointed directly at the X-ray unit which was down the corridor from the 'theatre.' The unit was clearly visible to all Ss . . ." (Leventhal and Niles, 1963). Therefore, the effects on action are extremely similar in both studies and both studies produced a relationship between attitude and actions, though the relationship is weaker in the present experiment.

Although there is a positive relationship between attitudes and behavior, the present data show that the independent variables have different effects upon attitudes and actions. Specific information for taking action does not in itself produce favorable attitudes but does establish a link between attitude and action. What is the nature of this link that permits the attitude to be translated into action? In certain situations, for example, those in which the action is immediately possible, specificity may entail the elimination of barriers to action (Leventhal and Niles, 1963). In situations such as the present, however, in which the actions were carried out several days subsequent to the communication, other aspects of the manipulations, for example, rehearsing the action, making a decision to act, as well as simple information on how to make the response, could be responsible for the link. An examination of questionnaire affects associated with the specificity manipulation tentatively suggests that specificity altered S's emotional state. Thus, Ss receiving the specific plan for action were somewhat more interested in the materials and reported significantly less nausea, which can be interpreted to mean that the specific information eliminated various inward turning inhibitory features of the fear state. Several authors have distinguished between inhibitory or depressive fear states and excitatory fear states (Bull, 1962; Kollar, 1961; Shands, 1955) and have associated striving and protective activity with the latter. While it is clear, however, that those affective states can be distinguished in communication studies (Leventhal, Jacobs and Niles), the study of their relationship to persuasion and action has just begun. The present data do suggest, however, that providing a clear possibility or plan for action can re-duce the inhibitory properties of certain fear states.

Regardless of the exact process by which specific information links the evaluative and action components, it is still puzzling why more action did not occur in that condition in which the attitude change was greatest. There is a very simple hypothesis that can be suggested to account for this. If the effects of fear dissipate rapidly with time, then it may be that the failure to find more action in the high fear treatments reflects the fact that "attitudes" were measured *at* the time of exposure, while action took place after the fear-induced attitude effects had been dissipated. If this is the case, no relationship between attitude change and behavior could possibly be expected.

Summary: The study dealt with the effects of (1) level of fear and (2) specific plans for action versus general recommendations on attitudes toward tetanus inoculations and actually getting tetanus shots. The arousal of fear resulted in more favorable attitudes toward inoculation and the expression of stronger intentions to get shots. Actually getting shots occurred, however, significantly more often for subjects receiving a specific plan for action. Although action was unaffected by fear level, some level of arousal was necessary for action to occur. A specific plan was not sufficient for action to appear. Although the two dependent measures were affected by different independent variables, those people getting shots were also more favorable toward doing so. The results are compared with other studies on fear-arousal and actions, and speculations were presented on the role of specific action plans in the translation of attitudes into actions.

REFERENCES[1]

Ackerman, N. W., and Marie Jahoda. *Anti-Semitism and emotional disorder.* New York: Harper & Row, 1950.

Adametz, J. H. Rate of recovery in cats with rostral reticular lesions. *J. Neurosurg.,* 1959, *16:* 85–98.

Adams, J. K., and P. A. Adams. Realism of confidence judgments. *Psychol. Rev.,* 1961, *68:* 33–45.

Ader, R., and M. L. Belfer. Prenatal maternal anxiety and off-spring emotionality in the rat. *Psychol. Rep.,* 1962, *10:* 711–718.

*Ader, R., and P. M. Conklin. Handling of pregnant rats: effects on emotionality of their off-spring. *Science,* 1963, *142:* 411–412.

Adler, N., and J. A. Hogan. Classical conditioning and punishment of an instinctive response in Betta splendens. *Anim. Behav.,* 1963, *11:* 351–354.

Adrian, E. D. Impulses in sympathetic fibres and in slow afferent fibres. *J. Physiol.* (London), 930, *70:* Proc. Physiol. Soc. XX–XXI.

Adorno, T. W., Else Frenkel-Brunswik, D. J. Levinson, and R. N. Sanford. *The authoritarian personality.* New York: Harper & Row, 1950.

Aiken, E. G. The effort variable in the acquisition, extinction, and spontaneous recovery of an instrumental response. *J. exp. Psychol.,* 1957, *53:* 47–51.

Alexander, F. A contribution to a theory of play. *Psa. Quart.,* 1958, *27:* 175–193.

Allee, W. C., and N. Collias. The influence of estradiol on the social organization of flocks of hens. *Endocrinology,* 1940, *27:* 87–94.

Allee, W. C., N. E. Collias, and C. Z. Lutherman. Modification of the social order in flocks of hens by the injection of testosterone propionate. *Physiol. Zool.,* 1939, *12:* 412–440.

Allee, W. C., and D. Foreman. Effects of an androgen on dominance and subordinance in six common breeds of Gallus gallus. *Physiol. Zool.,* 1955, *28:* 89–115.

Allport, F. H. *Social psychology.* Boston: Houghton Mifflin, 1924.

Alpert, R. The perceptual determinants of affect. Unpublished master's thesis, Wesleyan Univer., 1953.

Alpert, R. Anxiety in academic achievement situations: Its measurement and relation to aptitude. Unpublished doctoral dissertation, Stanford Univer., 1957.

*Alpert, R., and R. N. Haber. Anxiety in academic achievement situations. *J. abnorm. soc. Psychol.,* 1960, *61:* 207–215.

Amsel, A. The role of frustrative non-reward in non-continuous reward situations. *Psychol. Bull.,* 1958, *55:* 102–119.

[1] Asterisked references are to articles included in this volume.

Amsel, A. Frustrative nonreward in partial reinforcement and discrimination learning; some recent history and a theoretical extension. *Psychol. Rev.*, 1962, *69:* 306–328.

Amsel, A., and J. Roussel. Motivational properties of frustration: I. Effect on a running response of the addition of frustration to the motivational complex. *J. exp. Psychol.*, 1952, *43:* 363–368.

Andersson, B. The effect of injections of hypertonic NaCl solutions into different parts of the hypothalamus of goats. *Acta. physiol. Scand.*, 1953, *28:* 188–201.

Andreas, B. G. Motor conflict behavior as a function of motivation and amount of training. *J. exp. Psychol.*, 1958, *55:* 173–178.

Andrew, R. J. Normal and irrelevant toilet behavior in Emberiza spp. *Brit. J. anim. Behav.*, 1956, *4:* 85–91.(a)

Andrew, R. J. Some remarks on behaviour in conflict situations, with special reference to Emberiza spp. *Brit. J. anim. Behav.*, 1956, *4:* 41–45.(b)

Angier, R. P. The aesthetics of unequal division. *Psychol. Rev.* (Monogr. Suppl.), 1903, *4:* 541–561.

Appel, J. B. Punishment and shock intensity. *Science,* 1963, *141:* 528–529.

Appleton, L. E. *A comparative study of the play of adult savages and civilized children.* Chicago: Univer. of Chicago Press, 1910.

Applezweig, M. H. Response potential as a function of effort. *J. comp. physiol. Psychol.*, 1951, *44:* 225–235.

*Argyle, M., and P. Robinson. Two origins of achievement motivation. *Brit. J. soc. clin. Psychol.*, 1962, *1:* 107–120.

Armstrong, E. A. *Bird display and behavior.* London: Cambridge Univer. Press, 1947.

Armstrong, E. A. The nature and function of displacement activities. *Symp. soc. exp. Biol.*, 1950, *4:* 361–386.

Armus, H. Effect of percentage of reinforcement and distribution of acquisition trials on extinction of conditioned fear. *Psychol. Rep.*, 1960, *6:* 387–390.

Arnold, Magda B. Physiological differentiation of emotional states. *Psychol. Rev.*, 1945, *52:* 35–48.

Aronson, E The effect of effort on the attractiveness of rewarded and unrewarded stimuli. *J. abnorm. soc. Psychol.*, 1961, *63:* 375–380.

Aronson, E., and J. M. Carlsmith. Performance expectancy as a determinant of actual performance. *J. abnorm. soc. Psychol.*, 1962, *65:* 178–183.

Aronson, E., and J. M. Carlsmith. Effect of the severity of threat on the devaluation of forbidden behavior. *J. abnorm. soc. Psychol.*, 1963, *66:* 584–588.

Aronson, E., and J. Mills. The effect of severity of initiation on liking for a group. *J. abnorm. soc. Psychol.*, 1959, *59:* 177–181.

Aronson, L. R. Hormones and reproductive behavior: Some phylogenetic considerations. In A. Gorbman (Ed.), *Comparative Endocrinology.* New York: Wiley, 1959. Pp. 98–120.

Arsenian, J. M. Young children in an insecure situation. *J. abnorm. soc. Psychol.*, 1943, *38:* 225–249.

Ås, A., J. W. O'Hara, and P. M. Munger. The measurement of subjective experiences presumably related to hypnotic susceptibility. *Scand. J. Psychol.,* 1962, *3:* 47–64.

Aserinsky, E., and N. Kleitman. A motility cycle in sleeping infants as manifested by ocular and gross bodily activity. *J. Appl. Physiol.,* 1955, *8:* 1.

Atkinson, J. W. Explorations using imaginative thought to assess the strength of human motives. In M. R. Jones (Ed.), *The Nebraska symposium on motivation: 1954.* Lincoln, Neb., Univer. of Nebraska Press.

Atkinson, J. W. Motivational determinants of risk-taking behavior. *Psychol. Rev.,* 1957, *64:* 359–372.

Atkinson, J. W. (Ed.), *Motives in fantasy, action, and society.* Princeton, N. J.: Van Nostrand, 1958.

Atkinson, J. W., R. W. Heyns, and J. Veroff. The effect of experimental arousal of the affiliation motive on thematic apperception. *J. abnorm. soc. Psychol.,* 1954, *49:* 405–410.

Atkinson, J. W., and G. H. Litwin. Achievement motive and test anxiety as motives to approach success and avoid failure. *J. abnorm. soc. Psychol.,* 1960, *60:* 52–63.

Attneave, F. D. Some informational aspects of visual perception. *Psychol. Rev.,* 1954, *61:* 183–193.

Auersperg, A. P. Vom Werden der Angst. *Nervenarzt,* 1958, *29:* 193–201.

Ausubel, D. P. *Ego development and the personality disorders.* New York: Grune & Stratton, 1952.

*Ausubel, D. P. Relationship between shame and guilt in the socializing process. *Psychol. Rev.,* 1955, *62:* 378–390.

Azrin, N. H. Some effects of two intermittent schedules of immediate and non-immediate punishment. *J. Psychol.,* 1956, *42:* 8–21.

Azrin, N. H. Punishment and recovery during fixed-ratio performance. *J. exp. anal. Behav.,* 1959, *2:* 301–305.

Azrin, N. H., and W. C. Holz. Punishment during fixed-interval reinforcement. *J. exp. Anal Behav.,* 1961, *4:* 343–347.

Azrin, N. H., W. C. Holz, and D. Hake. Intermittent reinforcement by removal of a conditioned aversive stimulus. *Science,* 1962, *136:* 781–782.

Baerends, G. P. The ethological analysis of incubation behavior. *Ibis,* 1959, *101:* 357–368.

Baerends, G. P., and J. M. Baerands-van Roon. An introduction to the ethology of cichlid fishes. *Behaviour,* suppl. 1, 1950, *1:* 1–243.

Baggerman, B., G. P. Baerends, H. S. Helkers, and J. M. Mook. Observations on the behavior of the black tern, Chlidonias n. niger (L.), in the breeding area. *Ardea,* 1956, *44:* 1–71.

Bailey, C. J., and N. E. Miller. The effect of sodium amytal on an approach-avoidance conflict in cats. *J. comp. physiol. Psychol.,* 1952, *45:* 205–208.

Baldwin, J. M., *Mental development in the child and in the race.* New York: Macmillan, 1895.

Balint, M. Individual differences of behavior in early infancy, and an objective method for recording them: II. Results and conclusions. *J. genet. Psychol.*, 1948, *73:* 81–117.

Bandura, A., and Aletha C. Huston. Identification as a process of incidental learning. *J. abnorm. soc. Psychol.*, 1961, *63:* 311–318.

Bandura, A., D. Ross, and S. A. Ross. Transmission of aggression through imitation of aggressive models. *J. abnorm. soc. Psychol.*, 1961, *63:* 575–583.

Bandura, A., and R. H. Walters. *Adolescent aggression.* New York: Ronald, 1959.

Barber, T. X. Toward a theory of pain: Relief of chronic pain by prefrontal leucotomy, opiates, placebos, and hypnosis. *Psychol. Bull.*, 1959, *56:* 430–460.

Barnett, S. A. Displacement behavior and psychosomatic disorder. *Lancet,* 1955, *2:* 1203–1208.

Baron, A., K. H. Brookshire, and R. A. Littman. Effects of infantile and adult shock-trauma upon learning in the adult white rat. *J. comp. physiol. Psychol.*, 1957, *50:* 530–534.

Barry, H. III, A. R. Wagner, and N. E. Miller. Effects of alcohol and amobarbital on performance inhibited by experimental extinction. *J. comp. physiol. Psychol.*, 1962, *55:* 464–468.

Bartlett, R. G., Jr., V. C. Bohr, R. H. Helmendach, G. L. Foster, and M. A. Miller. Evidence of an emotional factor in hypothermia produced by restraint. *Amer. J. Physiol.*, 1954, *179:* 343–346.

Bartlett, R. G., Jr., R. H. Helmendach, and V. C. Bohr. Effect of emotional stress, anesthesia, and death on body temperature of mice exposed to cold. *Proc. Soc. Exp. Biol.*, N.Y., 1953, *83:* 4–5.

Bartlett, R. G., Jr., R. H. Helmendach, and W. T. Inman. Effect of restraint on temperature regulation in the cat. *Proc. Soc. Exp. Biol.*, N.Y., 1954, *85:* 81–83.

Bastock, M., and A. Manning. The courtship of Drosophila melanogaster. *Behaviour,* 1955, *8:* 85–111.

Bastock, M., D. Morris, and M. Moynihan. Some comments on conflict and thwarting in animals. *Behavior,* 1953, *6:* 66–84.

Bates, R. W., O. Riddle, and E. L. Lahr. The mechanism of the anti-gonad action of prolactin. *Amer. J. Physiol.*, 1937, *119:* 610–614.

Beach, F. A. The neural basis of innate behavior. I. Effects of cortical lesions upon the maternal behavior pattern in the rat. *J. comp. Psychol.*, 1937, *24:* 393–436.

Beach, F. A. The neural basis of innate behavior. III. Comparison of learning ability and instinctive behavior in the rat. *J. comp. Psychol.*, 1939, *28:* 225–262.

Beach, F. A. Comparison of copulatory behavior in male rats raised in isolation, cohabitation, and segregation. *J. genet. Psychol.* 1942, *60:* 121–136.

Beach, F. A. Concepts of play in animals. *Amer. Naturalist,* 1945, *79:* 523–541.

Beach, F. A. A review of physiological and psychological studies of sexual behavior in mammals. *Physiol. Rev.*, 1947, *27:* 240–307.

*Beach, F. A. The descent of instinct. *Psychol. Rev.*, 1955, *62:* 401–410.

Beach, F. A. Characteristics of masculine "sex drive." In M. R. Jones (Ed.), *Nebraska symposium on motivation: 1956.* Lincoln, Nebr.: Univer. of Nebraska Press.

Beach, F. A. Normal sexual behavior in male rats isolated at fourteen days of age. *J. comp. physiol. Psychol.* 1958, *51:* 37–38.

Beach, F. A. Experimental investigations of species-specific behavior. *Amer. Psychol.* 1960, *15:* 1–18.

Beach, F. A., M. W. Conovitz, F. Steinberg, and A. C. Goldstein. Experimental inhibition and restoration of mating behavior in male rats. *J. genet. Psychol.,* 1956, *89:* 165–181.

Beach, F. A., and J. Jaynes. Effects of early experience upon the behavior of animals. *Psychol. Bull.,* 1954, *51:* 239–263.

Becker, G. M. Decision Making: Objective measures of subjective probability and utility. *Psychol. Rev.,* 1962, *69:* 136–148.

Beebe-Center, J. G. *The Psychology of Pleasantness and Unpleasantness.* New York: Van Nostrand, 1932.

Beling, I. Über des Zeitgeclächtuis der Bienen, *Z. Vergleich. Physiol.,* 1929, *9:* 259–338.

Bender, L. There is no substitute for family life. *Child Study,* 1946, *23:* 74.

Bender, L. Psychopathic behavior disorders in children. In R. M. Lindner & R. V. Seliger (Eds.), *Handbook of correctional psychology.* New York: Philosophical Library, 1947, pp. 360–378.

Bender, L., and P. Schilder. Unconditioned and conditioned reactions to pain in schizophrenia. *Amer. J. Psychiat.,* 1930, *10:* 365–384.

Benedict, Ruth. *Patterns of culture.* Boston: Houghton Mifflin, 1934.

Benedict, Ruth, *The chrysanthemum and the sword.* Boston: Houghton Mifflin, 1946.

Bennett, M. A. The social hierarchy in ring doves: The effect of treatment with testosterone propionate. *Ecology,* 1940, *21:* 148–165.

Bergmann, G. Theoretical psychology. *Ann. Rev. Psychol.,* 1953, *4:* 435–458.

Berkeley, A. W. Level of aspiration in relation to adrenal cortical activity and the concept of stress. *J. comp. physiol. Psychol.,* 1952, *45:* 443–449.

Berkowitz, L., and D. R. Cottingham. The interest value and relevance of fear-arousing communications. *J. abnorm. soc. Psychol.,* 1960, *60:* 37–43.

Berkun, M. M. Factors in the recovery from approach-avoidance conflict. *J. exp. Psychol.,* 1957, *54:* 65–73.

Berkun, M. M., Marion L. Kessen, and N. E. Miller. Hunger-reducing effects of food by mouth measured by consummatory response. *J. comp. physiol. Psychol.,* 1952, *45:* 550–554.

Berlyne, D. E. Novelty and curiosity as determinants of exploratory behavior. *Brit. J. Psychol.,* 1950, *41:* 68–80.

Berlyne, D. E. The arousal and satiation of perceptual curiosity in the rat. *J. comp. physiol. Psychol.,* 1955, *48:* 238–246.

Berlyne, D. E. Conflict and information-theory variables as determinants of human perceptual curiosity. *J. exp. Psychol.,* 1957, *53:* 399–404.

Berlyne, D. E. The influence of complexity and novelty in visual figures on orienting responses. *J. exp. Psychol.,* 1958, *55:* 289–296.

Berlyne, D. E. *Conflict, arousal and curiosity.* New York: McGraw-Hill, 1960.

Berlyne, D. E. Conflict and the orientation reaction. *J. exp. Psychol.*, 1961, *62:* 476–483.

Berlyne, D. E. Motivational problems raised by exploratory and epistemic behavior. In S. Koch (Ed.), *Psychology—a study of a science*. New York: McGraw-Hill, 1963, vol. 5, pp. 284–364. (a)

Berlyne, D. E. Complexity and incongruity variables as determinants of exploratory choice and evaluative ratings. *Canad. J. Psychol.*, 1963. *17:* 274–290.(b)

Berlyne, D. E. *Structure and direction in thinking*. New York: Wiley, 1964.

Berlyne, D. E., M. A. Craw, P. H. Salapatek, and J. L. Lewis. Novelty, complexity, incongruity, extrinsic motivation and the GSR. *J. exp. Psychol.*, 1963, *66:* 560–567.

Berlyne, D. E., and G. H. Lawrence. Effects of complexity and incongruity variables on exploratory behavior and verbally expressed preference. *J. genet. Psychol.*, 1964.

Berlyne, D. E., and J. L. Lewis. Effects of heightened arousal on human exploratory behavior. *Canad. J. Psychol.*, 1963, *17:* 398–410.

*Berlyne, D. E., and P. McDonnell. Effects of stimulus complexity and incongruity on duration of EEG desynchronization. *EEG clin. Neurophysiol.*, 1965, *18:* 156–161.

*Bernal, M. E. The report of being watched as a measure of guilty behavior. Published for the first time in this volume.

Bersch, P. J., J. M. Notterman, and W. N. Schoenfeld. *School of Aviation: USAF Rep. no. 56–79,* 1956.

Bexton, W. H., W. Heron, and T. H. Scott. Effects of decreased variation in the sensory environment. *Canad. J. Psychol.*, 1954, *8:* 70–76.

Bilodeau, I. McD. Conflict behavior as a function of the strengths of competing response tendencies. Unpublished doctoral dissertation, State Univer. of Iowa, 1950.

Bindra, D. *Motivation: A systematic reinterpretation*. New York: Ronald, 1959.

Bindra, D. Components of general activity and the analysis of behavior. *Psychol., Rev.*, 1961, *68:* 205–215.

Blauvelt, H. Dynamics of the mother-newborn relationship in goats. In B. Schaffner (Ed.), *Group Processes*, Tr. First Conference, Josiah Macy, Jr. Foundation, New York: 1955, pp. 221–258.

Block, J., and P. Petersen. Some personality correlates of confidence, caution, and speed in a decision situation. *J. abnorm. soc. Psychol.*, 1955, *51:* 34–41.

Blough, D. S. Technique for studying the effects of drugs on discrimination in the pigeon. *Ann. N.Y. Acad. Sci.*, 1956, *65:* 334–344.

Blum, G. S. A study of the psychoanalytic theory of psychosexual development. *Genet. Psychol. Monogr.*, 1949, *13:* 3–99.

Blum, G. S. *The Blacky Pictures: A technique for the exploration of personality dynamics*. New York: Psychological Corp., 1950.

*Blum, G. S. An experimental reunion of psychoanalytic theory with perceptual vigilance and defense. *J. abnorm. soc. Psychol.*, 1954, *49:* 94–98.

Blum, G. S., and H. F. Hunt. The validity of the Blacky Pictures. *Psychol. Bull.*, 1952, *49:* 238–250.

Blum, G. S., and D. R. Miller. Exploring the psychoanalytic theory of the "oral character." *J. Pers.*, 1952, *20:* 287–304.

Bol, Angela. A consummatory situation. The effect of eggs on the sexual behavior of a male three-spined stickleback (Gasterosteus aculeatus). *Experientia,* 1959, *15:* 115–117.

Bolles, R. C. The usefulness of the drive concept. In M. R. Jones (Ed.), *Nebraska symposium on motivation: 1958.* Lincoln, Nebr.: Univer. of Nebraska Press.

Bolles, R. C. Grooming behavior in the rat. *J. comp. physiol. Psychol.,* 1960, *53:* 306–310.

Boston Psychopathic Hospital. Experimental psychoses. *Sci. Amer.,* 1955, *192:*(6): 34–39.

Bovard, E. W. The effects of early handling on viability of the albino rat. *Psychol. Rev.,* 1958, *65:* 257–271.

Bovard, E. W. The effects of social stimuli on the response to stress. *Psychol. Rev.,* 1959, *5:* 267–275.

Bower, G. H., and N. E. Miller. Effect of amount of reward on strength of approach in an approach-avoidance conflict. *J. comp. physiol. Psychol.,* 1960, *53:* 59–62.

Bowlby, J. *Forty-four juvenile thieves, their characters and homelife.* London: 1946. (Reprint of *Internat. J. Psychoanal.* 1944, *25:* 19.)

*Bowlby, J. *Maternal care and mental health.* Geneva: World Health Organization, 1952.

Bowlby, J. The nature of the child's tie to his mother. *Internat. J. Psychoanal.,* 1958, part 5, *39:* 350–373.

Brady, J. V. Assessment of drug effects on behavior. *Science,* 1956, *123:* 1033–1034.

*Brady, J. V. Ulcers in "executive monkeys." *Sci. Amer.,* 1958, *199:* 95–103.

Brady, J. V., R. W. Porter, D. G. Conrad, and J. W. Mason. Avoidance behavior and the development of gastroduodenal ulcers. *J. exp. anal. Behav.,* 1958, *1:* 69–72.

*Bramel, D. A dissonance theory approach to defensive projection. *J. abnorm. soc. Psychol.,* 1962, *64:* 121–129.

Brattgård, S. O. The importance of adequate stimulation for the chemical composition of retinal ganglion cells during early post-natal development. *Acta. Radiol.,* Stockholm, suppl. 96, 1952.

Bridges, K. M. B. Emotional development in early infancy. *Child Develpm.* 1932, *3:* 324–341.

Brink, F. Excitation and conduction in the neuron. In S. S. Stevens (Ed.), *Handbook of experimental psychology.* New York: Wiley, 1951, pp. 50–93.

Britt, S. H., and S. Q. Janus. Toward a social psychology of human play. *J. soc. Psychol.,* 1941, *13:* 351–384.

Broadhurst, P. L. Emotionality and the Yerkes-Dodson Law. *J. exp. Psychol.,* 1957, *54:* 345–352.

Brogden, W. J. Acquisition and extinction of conditioned avoidance response in dogs. *J. comp. physiol. Psychol.,* 1949, *42:* 296–302.

Bronfenbrenner, U. Socialization and the social class through time and space. In

E. E. Maccoby, T. M. Newcomb, and E. L. Hartley (Eds.), *Readings in social psychology*. New York: Holt, 1958, pp. 400–425.

Bronfenbrenner, U. Freudian theories of identification and their derivatives. *Child Develpm.*, 1960, *31:* 15–40.

Bronshtein, A. D., T. G. Antonova, A. G. Kamenetskaya, N. N. Luppova, and V. A. Sytova. (On the development of the functions of analyzers in infants and some animals at the early stage of ontogenesis.) In *Problemy evolyutsii fiziologicheskikh funktsii* (Problems of evolution of physiological functions). (Office of Technical Services Report No. 60–61066, 1960, pp. 106–116. Translation obtainable from the United States Department of Commerce, Office of Technical Services.) Moscow-Leningrad: Akademiya Nauk SSSR, 1958.

Brookshire, K. H. An experimental analysis of the effects of infantile shock-trauma. *Diss. Abstr.*, 1958, *19:* 180.

Brookshire, K. H., R. A. Littman, and C. N. Stewart. Residua of shock-trauma in the white rat: a three-factor theory. *Psychol. Monogr.*, 1961, *75*(no. 10): whole no. 514.

Brown, J. S. A note on a temporal gradient of reinforcement. *J. exp. Psychol.*, 1939, *25:* 211–227.

Brown, J. S. Factors determining conflict reactions in difficult discriminations. *J. exp. Psychol.*, 1942, *31:* 272–292.

Brown, J. S. Gradients of approach and avoidance responses and their relation to level of motivation. *J. comp. physiol. Psychol.*, 1948, *41:* 450–465.

Brown, J. S. Problems presented by the concept of acquired drives. In M. R. Jones *Current theory and research in motivation: A symposium*. Lincoln, Nebr.: Univer. of Nebraska Press, 1953, pp. 1–21.

*Brown, J. S. Pleasure-seeking behavior and the drive-reduction hypothesis. *Psychol. Rev.*, 1955, *62:* 169–179.

Brown, J. S. *The Motivation of Behavior*. New York: McGraw-Hill, 1961.

Brown, J. S., and I. E. Farber. Emotions conceptualized as intervening variables—with suggestions toward a theory of frustration. *Psychol. Bull.*, 1951, *48:* 465–495.

*Brown, J. S., and A. Jacobs. The role of fear in the motivation and acquisition of responses. *J. exp. Psychol.*, 1949, *39:* 747–759.

*Brown, J. S., H. I. Kalish, and I. E. Farber. Conditioned fear as revealed by magnitude of startle response to an auditory stimulus. *J. exp. Psychol.*, 1951, *41:* 317–328.

*Brown, J. S., R. C. Martin, and M. W. Morrow. Self-punitive behavior in the rat: facilitative effects of punishment on resistance to extinction. *J. comp. physiol. Psychol.*, 1964, *57:* 127–133.

Brown, R. T., and A. R. Wagner. Resistance to punishment and extinction following training with shock or nonreinforcement. *J. exp. Psychol.*, 1964, *68:* 503–507.

Browne, L. B., and D. R. Evans. *J. Physiol. Psychol.*, 1960, *4:* 27.

Bruner, J. S., and L. Postman. Tension and tension-release as organizing factors in perception. *J. Pers.*, 1947, *15:* 300–308.

Bugelski, B. R. *The psychology of learning*. New York: Holt, 1956.

Buhler, K. *Die geistige Entwicklung des Kindes.* Jena: Fischer, 1918.

Buhler, K. Displeasure and pleasure in relation to activity. In M. L. Reymert (Ed.), *Feelings and emotions: the Wittenberg symposium.* Worcester, Mass.: Clark Univer. Press, 1928, chap. 14.

Buhler, K. *The mental development of the child.* New York: Harcourt, 1930.

Bull, N. *The Body and Its Mind.* New York: Las Americas Publishing Co., 1962.

Bullock, T. H. Problems in the comparative study of brain waves. *Yale J. Biol. Med.,* 1945, *17:* 657–679.

Bullock, T. H. Integration and rhythmicity in neural systems. *Amer. Zool.,* 1962, *2:* 97.

Bullock, T. H. Evolution of neurophysiological mechanisms. In A. Roe and G. G. Simpson (Eds.), *Behavior and Evolution.* New Haven: Yale Univer. Press, 1958.

Burlingham, D., and A. Freud. *Infants without families.* London: Internat. Univer. Press, 1943.

Burns, B. D. The mechanism of after-bursts in cerebral cortex. *J. Physiol.,* 1955, *127:* 168–188.

Burstein, A. G. Primary process in children as a function of age. *J. abnorm. soc. Psychol.,* 1959, *59:* 284–286.

Butler, R. A. Discrimination learning by rhesus monkeys to visual-exploration motivation. *J. comp. physiol. Psychol.,* 1953, *46:* 95–98.

Butler, R. A. Incentive conditions which influence visual exploration. *J. exp. Psychol.,* 1954, *48:* 19–23.

Buytendijk, F. J. J. *Wesen und Sinn des Spieles.* Berlin: K. Wolff, 1933.

*Byrne, D. Anxiety and the experimental arousal of affiliation. *J. abnorm. soc. Psychol.,* 1961, *63:* 660–662.

Campbell, B. A., and F. D. Sheffield. Relation of random activity to food deprivation. *J. comp. physiol. Psychol.,* 1953, *46:* 320–322.

Cannon, W. B. The James-Lange theory of emotions: a critical examination and an alternative theory. *Amer. J. Psychol.,* 1927, *39:* 106–124.

Cannon, W. B. *Bodily changes in pain, hunger, fear and rage* (2nd ed.) New York and London: D. Appleton, 1929.

Carey-Trefzer, C. J. The results of a clinical study of war-damaged children who attended the Child Guidance Clinic, the hospital for sick children, Great Ormond Street, London. *J. ment. Sci.,* 1949, *95:* 535.

Carlsmith, J. M. The effect of punishment on avoidance responses: The use of different stimuli for training and punishment. Paper read at Eastern Psychological Association, Philadelphia, April 1961.

*Carlsmith, J. M., and E. Aronson. Some hedonic consequences of the confirmation and disconfirmation of expectancies. *J. abnorm. soc. Psychol.,* 1963, *66:* 151–156.

Carmichael, L. The development of behavior in vertebrates experimentally removed from the influence of external stimulation. *Psychol. Rev.,* 1927, *34:* 34–47.

Carmichael, L. A re-evaluation of the concepts of maturation and learning as applied to the early development of behavior. *Psychol. Rev.,* 1936, *43:* 450–470.

Carmichael, L. The growth of sensory control of behavior before birth. *Psychol. Rev.*, 1947, *54:* 316–324.

Carpenter, C. R. A field study of the behavior and social relations of howling monkeys. *Comp. Psychol. Monograph no. 10,* 1934, 1.

Carper, J. W., and F. A. Polliard. Comparison of the intake of glucose and saccharin solutions under conditions of caloric need. *Amer. J. Psychol.*, 1953, *66:* 479–482.

Carr, H. A. The survival value of play. *Investigations of the department of psychology and education.* Boulder: Univer. of Colorado Press, 1902.

Cartwright, D. Relation of decision-time to the categories of response. *Amer. J. Psychol.*, 1941, *54:* 174–193.

Castaneda, A., B. R. McCandless, and D. S. Palermo. The children's form of the Manifest Anxiety Scale. *Child Develpm.*, 1956, *27:* 317–326.

Castaneda, A., and L. Worrell. Differential relation of latency and response vigor to stimulus similarity in brightness discrimination. *J. exp. Psychol.*, 1961, *61:* 309–314.

Champion, R. A. The acquisition and extinction of the fear response. *Austral. J. Psychol.*, 1961, *13:* 23–38.(a)

*Champion, R. A. Motivational effects in approach-avoidance conflict. *Psychol. Rev.*, 1961, *68:* 354–358.(b)

*Champion, R. A. The latency of the conditioned fear response. *Amer. J. Psychol.*, 1964, *77:* 75–83.

Champion, R. A., and J. E. Jones. Forward, backward, and pseudo-conditioning of the GSR. *J. exp. Psychol.*, 1961, *62:* 58–61.

Child, I. Children's preference for goals easy or difficult to obtain. *Psychol. Monogr.*, 1946, *60* (4, whole no. 280).

Child, I. L. Personality. *Ann. Rev. Psychol.*, 1954, *5:* 149–170.

Child, I. L., T. Storm, and J. Veroff. Achievement themes in folk tales related to socialization practice. In J. W. Atkinson (Ed.), *Motives in fantasy, action and society.* Princeton: Van Nostrand, 1958, chap. 34.

Child, I. L., Kitty F. Frank, and T. Storm. Self-ratings and TAT: Their relations to each other and to childhood background. *J. Pers.*, 1956, *25:* 96–114.

Chow, K. L., and W. Randall. Learning and EEG studies of cats with lesions in the reticular formation. Paper read at First Annual Meeting Psychonomic Society, Chicago, September 2–3, 1960.

Christie, R. Experimental naïveté and experiential naïveté, *Psychol. Bull.*, 1951, *48:* 327–339.

Christie, R. The effect of some early experience in the latent learning of adult rats. *J. exp. Psychol.*, 1952, *43:* 281–288.

Church, R. M. The varied effects of punishment on behavior. *Psychol. Rev.*, 1963, *70:* 369–402.

Ciurlo, L. Sulla funzione olfattoria nel neonato. *Valsalva*, 1934, *10:* 22–34.

Claparède, E. *Psychology of the child.* New York: Longmans, 1911.

Claparède, E. Sur la nature et la fonction du jeu. *Arch. de Psychol.*, 1934, *24:* 350–369.

Clapp, C. D. Two levels of unconscious awareness. Unpublished doctoral dissertation, Univer. of Michigan, 1951.

Clare, M. H., and G. H. Bishop. Properties of dendrites; apical dendrites of the cat cortex. *EEG clin. Neurophysiol.*, 1955, *7:* 85–98.

Clark, A. R., and S. Epstein. Food-related responses to ambiguous stimuli as a function of time without food and experimental set. *Amer. Psychol.* 1957, *12:* 394. (Abstract)

Clark, G., and H. G. Birch. Hormonal modifications of social behavior. I. The effect of sex-hormone administration on the social status of a male-castrate chimpanzee. *Psychosom. Med.*, 1945, *7:* 321–329.

Clark, G., and H. G. Birch. Hormonal modifications of social behavior. III. The effects of stilbestrol therapy on social dominance in the female-castrate chimpanzee. *Bull. Canad. Psychol.*, 1946, A. *6:* 1–3.

Clark, R. A. The projective measurement of experimentally induced levels of sexual motivation. *J. exp. Psychol.*, 1952, *44:* 391–399.

*Clark, R. A. The effects of sexual motivation on phantasy. In D. C. McClelland (Ed.), *Studies in motivation.* New York: Appleton, 1955, pp. 44–57.

Clark, R. A., R. Teevan, and H. N. Ricciuti. Hope of success and fear of failure as aspects of need for achievement. *J. abnorm. soc. Psychol.*, 1956, *53:* 182–186.

Clark, U. K., and P. Langley. *Nature*, 1962, *194:* 160.

Cleghorn, R. A. Discussion of F. L. Engel, General concepts of adrenocortical function in relation to the response to stress. *Psychosom. Med.*, 1953, *15:* 571–573.

Cofer, C. N. Motivation. *Ann. Rev. Psychol.*, 1959, *10:* 173–202.

Cohen, A. R. Need for cognition and order of communication as determinants of opinion change. In C. Hovland (Ed.), *Order of Presentation.* Published for the Institute of Human Relations, New Haven: Yale Univer. Press, 1957, pp. 79–97.

Colby, K. M. *Energy and structure in psychoanalysis.* New York: Ronald, 1955.

College Entrance Examination Board. *A description of the College Board Scholastic Aptitude Test.* Princeton: Educ. Testing Serv., 1956.

Collias, N. E. The analysis of socialization in sheep and goats. *Ecology*, 1956, *37:* 228–239.

Collier, G., and L. Myers. The loci of reinforcement. *J. exp. Psychol.*, 1961, *61:* 57–66.

Conger, J. J. The effects of alcohol on conflict behavior in the albino rat. *Quart. J. Stud. Alcohol*, 1951, *12:* 1–29.

Conger, J. J., W. L. Sawrey, and E. S. Turrell. An experimental investigation of the role of social experience in the production of gastric ulcers in hooded rats. *Amer. Psychol.*, 1957, *12:* 410. (Abstract)

Coons, E. E., and N. E. Miller. Conflict versus consolidation of memory traces to explain "retrograde amnesia" produced by ECS. *J. comp. physiol. Psychol.*, 1960, *53:* 524–531.

Corner, G. W. *Ourselves unborn.* New Haven: Yale Univer. Press, 1944.

Corwin, G. H. The involuntary response to pleasantness. *Amer. J. Psychol.*, 1921, *32:* 563–570.

Courts, F. A. Relations between muscular tension and performance. *Psychol. Bull.*, 1942, *39:* 347–367.

Cowen, Judith E. Test anxiety in high school students and its relationship to performance on group tests. Unpublished doctoral dissertation, School of Education, Harvard Univer., 1957.

Craig, W. The voices of pigeons regarded as a means of social control. *Amer. J. Sociol.*, 1908, *14:* 86–100.

Craig, W. The expression of emotion in the pigeons. I. The blond ring dove. *J. comp. Neurol.*, 1909, *19:* 29–80.

Crandall, V. J., A. Preston, and A. Rabson. Maternal reactions and the development of independence and achievement behavior in young children. *Child Develpm.*, 1960, *31:* 243–251.

Crane, Jocelyn. Basic patterns of display in fiddler crabs (Ocypodidae, genus Uca). *Zoologica* (N.Y.), 1957, *42:* 69–83.

Crespi, L. P. Quantitative variation of incentive and performance in the white rat. *Amer. J. Psychol.*, 1942, *55:* 467–517.

Crespi, L. P. Amount of reinforcement and level of performance. *Psychol. Rev.*, 1944, *51:* 341–357.

Cross, B. A. Nursing behaviour and the milk ejection reflex in rabbits. *J. Endocrinol.*, 1952, *8:* xiii–xiv.

Crum, J., W. L. Brown, and M. E. Bitterman. The effect of partial and delayed reinforcement on resistance to extinction. *Amer. J. Psychol.*, 1951, *64:* 228–237.

Cruze, W. W. Maturation and learning in chicks. *J. comp. Psychol.*, 1935, *19:* 371–409.

Curti, M. W. *Child psychology*. New York: Longmans, 1930.

Dabbs, J. Self-esteem, coping and influence. Unpub. doctoral dissertation, Yale Univer., 1962.

Dallenbach, K. M. Pain: History and present status. *Amer. J. Psychol.*, 1939, *52:* 331–347.

Dana, R. H. Manifest anxiety, intelligence, and psychopathology, *J. consult. Psychol.*, 1957, *21:* 38–40.

Darling, F. F. *Wild Country*. London: Cambridge Univer. Press, 1938.

Darrow, C. W. The galvanic skin reflex (sweating) and blood-pressure as preparatory and facilitative functions. *Psychol. Bull.*, 1936, *33:* 73–94.

Darrow, C. W. Psychological and psychophysiological significance of the electroencephalogram. *Psychol. Rev.*, 1947, *54:* 157–168.

Davey, K. G. The release by feeding of a pharmacologically active factor from the corpus cardiacum of Periplaneta. *J. insect Physiol.*, 1962, *8:* 205–208.(a)

Davey, K. G. The nervous pathway involved in the release by feeding of a pharmacologically active factor from the corpus cardiacum of Periplaneta Americana. *J. insect. Physiol.*, 1962, *8:* 579–583.(b)

Davey, K. G. The release by enforced activity of the cardiac accelerator from the corpus cardiacum of Periplaneta Americana. *J. insect Physiol.*, 1963, *9:* 375–381.

Davids, A. Relations among several objective measures of anxiety under different conditions of motivation. *J. consult. Psychol.*, 1955, *19:* 275–279.(a)

Davids, A. Some personality and intellectual correlates of intolerance of ambiguity. *J. abnorm. soc. Psychol.*, 1955, *51:* 415–420.(b)

Davids, A., and C. W. Eriksen. The relation of manifest anxiety to association productivity and intellectual attainment. *J. consult. Psychol.*, 1955, *19:* 219–222.

Davids, A., A. F. Henry, C. C. McArthur, and L. F. McNamara. Projection, self-evaluation, and clinical evaluation of aggression. *J. consult. Psychol.*, 1955, *19:* 437–440.

Davis, H. V., R. R. Sears, H. C. Miller, and A. J. Brodbeck. Effects of cup, bottle, and breast feeding on oral activities of newborn infants. *Pediatrics*, 1948, *2:* 549–558.

*Davis, J. D., and J. D. Keehn. Magnitude of reinforcement and consummatory behavior. *Science*, 1959, *130:* 269–270.

Davis, R. C. Modification of the galvanic reflex by daily repetition of a stimulus. *J. exp. Psychol.*, 1934, *17:* 504–535.

Davis, R. C., A. Lundervold, and J. D. Miller. The pattern of somatic response during a repetitive motor task and its modification by visual stimuli. *J. comp. physiol. Psychol.*, 1957, *50:* 53–60.

Davitz, J. R., and D. J. Mason. Socially facilitated reduction of a fear response in rats. *J. comp. physiol. Psychol.*, 1955, *48:* 149–151.

Dearborn, G. V. N. The emotion of joy. *Psychol. Rev.* (Monogr. suppl.), 1899, *2*(5).

Deese, J. *The psychology of learning.* New York: McGraw-Hill, 1958.

*Deevey, E. S. The hare and the haruspex. *Yale Rev.*, 1959, *49:* 161–179.

Dell, P. C. Humoral effects on the brain stem reticular formations. In H. H. Jasper, L. D. Proctor, R. S. Knighton, W. C. Noshay, & R. T. Costello (Eds.). *Reticular formation of the brain.* Toronto: Little, Brown, 1958, pp. 365–379.

Dell, P. C. Some basic mechanisms of the translation of bodily needs into behavior. In *Neurological basis of behavior.* London: Churchill, 1958.

DeLong, Erika, H. N. Uhley, and M. Friedman. Change in blood clotting time of rats exposed to a particular form of stress. *Amer. J. Physiol.*, 1959, *196:* 429–430.

DelVecchio, A., E. Genovese, and L. Martini. Hypothalamus and somatotrophic hormone release. *Proc. soc. exp. Biol.*, N.Y., 1958, *98:* 641–644.

Dember, W. N. Response by the rat to environmental change. *J. comp. physiol. Psychol.*, 1956, *49:* 93–95.

Dember, W. N., R. W. Earl, and N. Paradise. Response by rats to differential stimulus complexity. *J. comp. physiol. Psychol.*, 1957, *50:* 514–518.

Dement, W. Dream recall and eye movements during sleep in schizophrenics and normals. *J. nerv. ment. Dis.*, 1955, *122:* 263.

*Dement, W. The effect of dream deprivation. *Science*, 1960, *131:* 1705–1708.

Dement, W., and N. Kleitman. Cyclic variations in EEG during sleep and their relation to eye movements, body motility, and dreaming. *EEG clin. Neurophysiol.*, 1957, *9:* 673.(a)

Dement, W., and N. Kleitman. The relation of eye movements during sleep to dream activity: An objective method for the study of dreaming. *J. exp. Psychol.*, 1957, *53:* 339.(b)

Dement, W., and E. Wolpert. Relationships in the manifest context of dreams occuring in the same night. *J. nerv. ment. Dis.*, 1958, *126:* 568.(a)

Dement, W., and E. Wolpert. The relation of eye movements, body motility, and external stimuli to dream content. *J. exp. Psychol.*, 1958, *55:* 543.(b)

De Molina, A. F., and R. W. Hunsperger. Central representation of affective reactions in forebrain and brain stem: Electrical stimulation of amygdala, stria terminalis, and adjacent structures. *J. Physiol.*, 1959, *145:* 251–265.

Denenberg, V. H. Interactive effects of infantile and adult shock levels upon learning. *Psychol. Rep.*, 1959, *5:* 357–364.

Denenberg, V. H. The effects of early experience. In C. S. E. Hafez (Ed.), *The behavior of domestic animals.* London: Bailliere, Tindall and Cox, 1962, pp. 109–138.(a)

Denenberg, V. H. An attempt to isolate critical periods of development in the rat. *J. comp. physiol. Psychol.*, 1962, *55:* 813–815.(b)

*Denenberg, V. H., and R. W. Bell. Critical periods for the effects of infantile experience on adult learning. *Science*, 1960, *131:* 227–228.

Denenberg, V. H., and G. G. Karas. Interactive effects of age and duration of infantile experience on adult learning. *Psychol. Rep.*, 1960, *7:* 313–322.

Denenberg, V. H., and G. G. Karas. Interactive effects of infantile and adult experiences upon weight gain and mortality in the rat. *J. comp. physiol. Psychol.*, 1961, *54:* 685–689.

Denenberg, V. H., J. R. C. Morton, N. S. Kline, and L. J. Grota. Effects of duration of infantile stimulation upon emotionality. *Canad. J. Psychol.*, 1962, *16:* 72–76.

*Denenberg, V. H., and A. E. Whimbey. Behavior of adult rats is modified by experiences their mothers had as infants. *Science,* 1963, *142:* 1192–1193.

Dennis, W. Infant development under conditions of restricted practice and of minimum social stimulation: A preliminary report. *J. genet. Psychol.*, 1938, *53:* 149–158.

Dennis, W. Infant development under conditions of restricted practice. *Genet. psychol. Monogr.*, 1941, *23:* 143–189.

Dennis, W. Causes of retardation among institutional children: Iran. *J. genet. Psychol.*, 1960, *96:* 47–59.

Dennis, W., and Marsena G. Dennis. The effect of cradling practice upon the onset of walking in Hopi children. *J. genet. Psychol.*, 1940, *56:* 77–86.

Dennis, W., and Marsena G. Dennis. Infant development under conditions of restricted practice and minimum social stimulation. *Genet. psychol. Monogr.*, 1941, *23:* 149–155. Also as: Development under controlled environmental conditions. In W. Dennis (Ed.), *Readings in child psychology.* New York: Prentice-Hall, 1951, Part III, Chap. 1.

Dethier, V. G. The relation between olfactory response and receptor population in the blowfly. *Biol. Bull.*, 1952, *102:* 111–117.

Dethier, V. G. The physiology and histology of the contact chemoreceptors of the blowfly. *Quart. Rev. Biol.*, 1955, *30:* 348–371.

*Dethier, V. G. Microscopic brains. *Science,* 1964, *143:* 1138–1145.

Dethier, V. G., and D. Bodenstein. Hunger in the blowfly. *Z. Tierpsychol.*, 1958, *15:* 129–140.

Dethier, V. G., D. R. Evans, and M. V. Rhoades. Some factors controlling the ingestion of carbohydrates by the blowfly. *Biol. Bull.*, 1956, *111*(2): 204–222.

Dethier, V. G., and M. V. Rhoades. *J. exp. Zool.*, 1954, *126:* 177.

Deutsch, J. A. *The structural basis of behavior.* Chicago: Univer. of Chicago Press, 1960.

Deutsch, M., and H. B. Gerard. A study of normative and informational social influences upon individual judgment. *J. abnorm. soc. Psychol.*, 1955, *51:* 629–636.

Deutsch, M., and L. Solomon. Reactions to evaluations made by others as influenced by self-evaluations. *Sociometry,* 1959, *22:* 93–112.

Dewey, J. *The school and society.* Chicago: Univer. of Chicago Press (Phoenix Books, P3), 1960 (Originally published in 1900).

Dieterlen, F. Das Verhalten des syrischen Goldhamsters (*Mesocricetus auratus* Waterhouse); Untersuchungen zur Frage seiner Entwicklung und seiner angeborenen Anteile durch geruchsisolierte Aufzuchten. *Ztschr. f. Tier-psychol.*, 1959, *16:* 47–103.

Dinsmoor, J. A. A discrimination based on punishment. *Quart. J. exp. Psychol.*, 1952, *4:* 27–45.

Dinsmoor, J. A. Punishment: I. The avoidance hypothesis. *Psychol. Rev.*, 1954, *61:* 34–46.

Dinsmoor, J. A. Punishment: II. An interpretation of empirical findings. *Psychol. Rev.*, 1955, *62:* 96–105.

Dinsmoor, J. A. Variable-interval escape from stimuli accompanied by shocks. *J. exp. anal. Behav.*, 1962, *5:* 41–47.

Dollard, J., L. W. Doob, N. E. Miller, O. H. Mowrer, and R. R. Sears. *Frustration and aggression.* New Haven: Yale Univer. Press, 1939.

Dollard, J., and N. E. Miller. *Personality and psychotherapy.* New York: McGraw-Hill, 1950.

Doob, L. W., and R. R. Sears. Factors determining substitute behavior and the overt expression of aggression. *J. abnorm. soc. Psychol.*, 1939, *34:* 293–313.

Doty, R. W., E. C. Beck, and K. A. Koci. Effects of brain-stem lesions on conditioned responses in cats. *Exp. Neurol.* 1959, *1:* 360–385.

Doty, R. W., and C. Giurgea. Conditioned reflexes established by coupling electrical excitation of two cortical areas. In J. Delafresnaye (Ed.), *Brain mechanisms and learning.* London: Blackwell, 1961.

Doyle, G., and E. P. Yule. Grooming activities and freezing behavior in relation to emotionality in albino rats. *Animal Behav.*, 1959, *7:* 18.

Drescher, W. Regenerationsversuche Am Gehirru Von *Periplaneta Americana* Unter Berücksichtigung von verhaetensänderung und Neurosekretion. *Z. Morphol. Oekal. Tierre,* 1960, *48:* 576–649.

Drew, G. C. The function of punishment in learning. *J. genet. Psychol.*, 1938, *52:* 257–267.

Dubos, R. J. The effect of bacterial endotoxins on the water intake and body weight of mice. *J. exp. Med.*, 1961, *113:* 921–934.

Duffy, E. The measurement of muscular tension as a technique for the study of emotional tendencies. *Amer. J. Psychol.*, 1932, *44:* 146–162.

Duffy, E. Emotion: an example of the need for reorientation in psychology. *Psychol. Rev.,* 1934, *41:* 184–198.

Duffy, E. The conceptual categories of psychology: a suggestion for revision. *Psychol. Rev.,* 1941, *48:* 177–203. (a)

Duffy, E. An explanation of "emotional" phenomena without the use of the concept "emotion." *J. genet. Psychol.,* 1941, *25:* 283–293.(b)

Duffy, E. A systematic framework for the description of personality. *J. abnorm. soc. Psychol.,* 1949, *44:* 175–190.

Duffy, E. The concept of energy mobilization. *Psychol. Rev.,* 1951, *58:* 30–40.

Duffy, E. The psychological significance of the concept of "arousal" or "activation." *Psychol. Rev.,* 1957, *64:* 265–275.

Duffy, E. *Activation and behavior.* New York: Wiley, 1962.

*Duffy, E. The nature and development of the concept of activation. APA, 1963. Published for the first time in this volume.

Duffy, E., and O. L. Lacey. Adaptation in energy mobilization: changes in general level of palmar skin conductance. *J. exp. Psychol.,* 1946, *36:* 437–452.

Dufort, R. H., and G. A. Kimble. Changes in response strength with changes in the amount of reinforcement. *J. exp. Psychol.,* 1956, *51:* 185–191.

Duncan, D. Multiple range and multiple F tests. *Biometrics,* 1955, *11:* 1–45.

Dunlap, K. Are there any instincts? *J. abnorm. Psychol.,* 1919–1920, *14:* 35–50.

Dusser de Barenne, J. G. The labyrinthine and postural mechanisms. In C. Murchison (Ed.), *A handbook of general experimental psychology.* Worcester, Mass.: Clark Univer. Press, 1934, pp. 204–246.

Easterbrook, J. A. The effect of emotion on cue utilization and the organization of behavior. *Psychol. Rev.,* 1959, *66:* 183–201.

Eccles, J. C. *The neurophysiological basis of mind.* London: Oxford Univer. Press, 1953.

Edney, E. B. *Bull. Entomol. Res.,* 1937, *28:* 243.

Edwards, A. L. *The social desirability variable in personality assessment and research.* New York: Dryden, 1957.

Edwards, A. L. *Manual for Edwards' Personal Preference Schedule* (rev. ed.). New York: Psychological Corporation, 1959.

Edwards, A. L. *Experimental design in psychological research* (rev. ed.). New York: Holt, 1960.

Edwards, W. The theory of decision making. *Psychol. Bull.,* 1954, *51:* 380–417.

Edwards, W. Subjective probabilities inferred from decisions. *Psychol. Rev.,* 1962, *69:* 109–135.

Egger, M. D., and N. E. Miller. Will rats work to escape from conflict? *Amer. Psychol.,* 1960, *15:* 474. (Abstract)

Egger, M. D., and N. E. Miller. Secondary reinforcement in rats as a function of information value and reliability of the stimulus. *J. exp. Psychol.,* 1962, *64:* 97–104.

Eglash, A. Fixation and inhibition. *J. abnorm. soc. Psychol.,* 1954, *49:* 241–245.

*Elder, T., C. O. Noblin, and B. A. Maher. The extinction of fear as a function of distance versus dissimilarity from the original conflict situation. *J. abnorm. soc. Psychol.*, 1961, *63:* 530–533.

Ellis, P. E. *Anti-Locust Res. Bull.*, 1951, *7:* 1.

Ellis, P. E., and G. Hoyle. A physiological interpretation of the marching of hoppers of the African migratory locust (Locusta migratoria migratorioides R. & F.). *J. exp. Biol.*, 1954, *31:* 271–279.

Ellson, D. G., R. C. Davis, I. J. Saltzman, and C. J. Burke. A report of research on detection of deception (Contract N6onr-18011 with Office of Naval Research). Distributed by Dept. of Psychol., Indiana Univer., Bloomington, Ind., 1952.

Emerson, A. E. Ecology, evolution and society. *Amer. Nat.*, 1943, *77:* 97–118.

Epstein, S. Food-related responses to ambiguous stimuli as a function of hunger and ego strength. *J. consult. Psychol.*, 1961, *25:* 463–469.

Epstein, S. The measurement of drive and conflict in humans: Theory and experiment. In M. R. Jones (Ed.), *Nebraska symposium on motivation: 1962.* Lincoln, Nebr.: Univer. of Nebraska Press, 1962, pp. 127–206.

*Epstein, S., and H. Levitt. The influence of hunger on the learning and recall of food related words. *J. abnorm. soc. Psychol.*, 1962, *64:* 130–135.

Epstein, S., and R. Smith. Thematic apperception as a measure of the hunger drive. *J. proj. Tech.*, 1956, *20:* 373–384.

Epstein, S., and R. Smith. Thematic apperception, Rorschach content, and ratings of sexual attractiveness of women as measures of the sex drive. *J. consult. Psychol.*, 1957, *21:* 473–478.

Erikson, E. H. Configuration in play—clinical notes. *Psa. Quart.*, 1937, *6:* 138–214.

Erikson, E. H. Studies in the interpretation of play: I. Clinical observations of play disruption in young children. *Genet. Psychol. Monogr.*, 1940, *22:* 557–671.

Erikson, E. H. *Childhood and society.* New York: Norton, 1950.

Erikson, E. H. Sex differences in the play configurations of preadolescents. *Amer. J. Orthopsychiat.*, 1951, *21:* 667–692.

Erikson, E. H. The problem of ego identity. *J. Amer. Psychoanal. Assoc.*, 1956, *4:* 56–121.

Erikson, E. H. Growth and crises of the healthy personality. *Psychol. Issues*, 1959, *1:* 50–100.

Eron, L. D., T. J. Banta, L. O. Walder, and J. H. Laulicht. Comparison of data obtained from mothers and fathers on child-rearing practices and their relation to child aggression. *Child Developm.*, 1961, *32:* 457–472.

Esman, A. A case of self-castration. *J. nerv. ment. Dis.*, 1954, *120:* 79–82.

Estes, W. K. Discriminative conditioning: I. A discriminative property of conditioned anticipation. *J. exp. Psychol.*, 1943, *34:* 150–155.

Estes, W. K. An experimental study of punishment. *Psychol. Monogr.*, 1944, *57* (3, whole no. 263).

Estes, W. K. Discriminative conditioning: II. Effects of Pavlovian conditioned stimulus on a subsequently established operant response. *J. exp. Psychol.*, 1948, *38:* 173–177.

Estes, W. K. Comments on Dr. Bolles' paper. In M. R. Jones (Ed.), *Nebraska symposium on motivation: 1958.* Lincoln, Nebr.: Univer. of Nebraska Press, 1958, pp. 33–34. (a)

Estes, W. K. Stimulus-response theory of drive. In M. R. Jones (Ed.), *Nebraska symposium on motivation: 1958.* Lincoln, Nebr.: Univer. of Nebraska Press, 1958, pp. 35–69. (b)

Estes, W. K. Learning theory. *Ann. Rev. Psychol.,* 1962, *13:* 107–144.

Estes, W. K., and B. F. Skinner. Some quantitative properties of anxiety. *J. exp. Psychol.,* 1941, *29:* 390–400.

Evans, D. R., and L. B. Browne. *Amer. Midland Naturalist,* 1960, *64:* 282.

Evans, D. R., and V. G. Dethier. *J. insect Physiol,* 1957, *1:* 3.

Eysenck, H. J. *The dynamics of anxiety and hysteria.* London: Routledge & Kegan Paul, 1957.

Fabricius, E. Zur ethologie junger antiden. *Acta. Zool. Fennica,* 1951, *68:* 1.

Fairlee, C. W., Jr. The effect of shock at the moment of choice on the formation of a visual discrimination habit. *J. exp. Psychol.,* 1937, *21:* 662–669.

Fanconi, G., and F. Ferrazzini. Kongenitale Analgie: Kongenitale generalisierte Schmerzindifferenz. *Helv. paediat. Acta,* 1957, *12:* 79–115.

Farber, I. E. Response fixation under anxiety and non-anxiety conditions. *J. exp. Psychol.,* 1948, *38:* 111–131.

Farber, I. E. Anxiety as a drive state. In M. R. Jones (Ed.), *Nebraska symposium on motivation: 1954.* Lincoln, Nebr.: Univer. of Nebraska Press, 1954, pp. 1–46.

Farber, I. E. The role of motivation in verbal learning and performance. *Psychol. Bull.,* 1955, *52:* 311–327.

Farber, I. E., and K. W. Spence. Complex learning and conditioning as a function of anxiety. *J. exp. Psychol.,* 1953, *45:* 120–125.

Farber, I. E., and K. W. Spence. Effects of anxiety, stress, and task variables on reaction time. *J. Pers.,* 1956, *25:* 1–18.

Faust, R. Untersuchungen zum haherenproblem. *Zool. Jahrb. Abt. Allgem. Zool. Physiol. Tiere,* 1952, *63:* 325–366.

Feather, N. T. Subjective probability and decision under uncertainty. *Psychol. Rev.,* 1959, *66:* 150–164.(a)

Feather, N. T. Success probability and choice behavior. *J. exp. Psychol.,* 1959, *58:* 257–266.(b)

Feather, N. T. The relationship of persistence at a task to expectation of success and achievement related motives. *J. abnorm. soc. Psychol.,* 1961, *63:* 552–561.

Feather, N. T. The study of persistence. *Psychol. Bull.,* 1962, *59:* 94–115.

*Feather, N. T. Mowrer's revised two factor motive and the move-expectancy-value model. *Psychol. Rev.,* 1963, *60:* 500–515.(a)

Feather, N. T. The relationship of expectation of success to reported probability, task structure, and achievement related motivation. *J. abnorm. soc. Psychol.,* 1963, *66:* 231–238.(b)

Feather, N. T. Persistence at a difficult task with alternative task of intermediate difficulty. *J. abnormal soc. Psychol.,* 1963, *66:* 604–609.(c)

Fehrer, E. Effects of amount of reinforcement and of pre- and postreinforcement delays on learning and extinction. *J. exp. Psychol.,* 1956, *52:* 167–176.

Feirstein, A., and N. E. Miller. Learning to resist pain and fear: effects of electric shock before versus after reaching goal. *J. comp. physiol. Psychol.*, 1963, *56:* 797–800.

Feldman, S. M. Differential effect of shock as a function of intensity and cue factors in maze learning. Unpublished doctoral dissertation, McGill Univer., 1958.

Feldman, S. M. Differential effects of shock in human maze learning. *J. exp. Psychol.*, 1961, *62:* 171–178.

Feinichel, O. *Problems of psychoanalytic technique* (Trans. by D. Brunswick). New York: *Psychoanal. Quart.*, 1941.

Fenichel, O. *The psychoanalytic theory of neurosis.* New York: Norton, 1945.

Féré, C. *Sensation et mouvement: études éxperimentales de psychomécanique* (2nd ed. rev.). Paris: Ancienne Librarie Germer Baillière et Cie, 1900.

Ferster, C. B., and B. F. Skinner. *Schedules of reinforcement.* New York: Appleton, 1957.

Feshbach, S. The influence of drive arousal and conflict upon fantasy behavior. In J. Kagan & G. S. Lesser (Eds.), *Contemporary issues in thematic apperception methods.* Springfield, Ill.: Charles C Thomas, 1961, pp. 119–140.

Festinger, L. Development of differential appetite in the rat. *J. exp. Psychol.*, 1943, *32:* 226–234.

Festinger, L. *A Theory of cognitive dissonance.* New York: Harper & Row, 1957.

*Festinger, L. The psychological effects of insufficient rewards. *Amer. Psychol.*, 1961, *16:* 1–11.

Fiedler, F. E. The concept of an ideal therapeutic relationship. *J. consult. Psychol.*, 1950, *14:* 239–245.

Field, J., H. W. Magoun, and V. E. Hall. *Handbook of physiology. Sect. 1. Neurophysiology.* Washington, D. C.: Amer. Physiol. Soc., 1960. (3 vols.)

Finan, J. L. Quantitative studies of motivation. I. Strength of conditioning in rats under varying degrees of hunger. *J. comp. Psychol.*, 1940, *29:* 119–134.

Finch, G. Hunger as a determinant of conditional and unconditional salivary response magnitude. *Amer. J. Physiol.*, 1938, *123:* 379–382.

Finger, F. W. Quantitative studies of "conflict": I. Variations in latency and strength of the rat's response in a discrimination-jumping situation. *J. comp. Psychol.*, 1941, *31:* 97–127.

Fisher, A. E. The effects of differential early treatment on the social and exploratory behavior of puppies. Unpublished doctoral dissertation, Pennsylvania State Univer., 1955.

Fisher, C. Subliminal and supraliminal influences on dreams. *Amer. J. Psychiat.*, 1960, *116:* 1009–1017.

Fisher, Dorothy C. *A Montessori mother.* New York: Holt, 1912.

Fiske, D. W., and S. R. Maddi. *Functions of varied experience.* Homewood, Ill.: Dorsey, 1961.

Fitzgerald, O. Love deprivation and the hysterical personality. *J. ment. Sci.*, 1948, *94:* 701.

Flugel, J. C. *Man, morals and society.* New York: Internat. Univer. Press, 1945.

Fodor, N. Varieties of castration. *Amer. Imago.*, 1947, *2:* 32–48.

Fogel, M. L. The conditioning of fear·to internal stimuli. *Psychol. Rec.*, 1961, *11:* 169–176.

Foley, J. P., Jr. The effect of practice on the delayed reaction in the rhesus monkey. *J. genet. Psychol.*, 1934, *45:* 39–105.

Ford, C. S., and F. A. Beach. *Patterns of sexual behavior.* New York: Harper & Row, 1951.

Forgays, D. G., and Janet W. Forgays. The nature of the effect of free environmental experience in the rat. *J. comp. physiol. Psychol.*, 1952, *45:* 322–328.

Forgus, R. H. The effect of early perceptual learning on the behavioral organization of adult rats. *J. comp. physiol. Psychol.*, 1954, *47:* 331–336.

Fortier, C. Dual control of adrenocorticotrophic release. *Endocrinology*, 1951, *49:* 782–788.

Fourment, A., and M. A. Cramer. Réponses électrocorticales visuelles du lapin soumis durant son développement à une surstimulation lumineuse. *Rev. Neurol.*, 1961, *105:* 196–197.

Fourment, A., and J. Scherrer. Electrocortical responses of the rabbit reared in darkness. *J. physiol.* (Paris), 1961, *53:* 340.

Fox, S. S. Self-maintained sensory input and sensory deprivation in monkeys: A behavioral and neuropharmacological study. *J. comp. physiol. Psychol.*, 1962, *55:* 438–444.

Freeburne, C. M., and M. Schneider. Shock for right and wrong responses during learning and extinction in human subjects. *J. exp. Psychol.*, 1955, *49:* 181–186.

Freeburne, C. M., and J. E. Taylor. Discrimination learning with shock for right and wrong responses in the same subjects. *J. comp. physiol. Psychol.*, 1952, *45:* 264–268.

Freeman, G. L. The postural substrate. *Psychol. Rev.*, 1938, *45:* 324–334.

Freeman, G. L. The relationship between performance level and bodily activity level. *J. exp. Psychol.*, 1940, *26:* 602–608.

Freeman, G. L. *The energetics of human behavior.* Ithaca, N.Y.: Cornell University Press, 1948.

Freeman, M. J. The development of a test for the measurement of anxiety: A study of its reliability and validity. *Psychol. Monogr.*, 1953, *67* (3, whole no. 353).

French, Elizabeth G. Development of a measure of complex motivation. In J. W. Atkinson (Ed.), *Motives in fantasy, action, and society.* Princeton: Van Nostrand, 1958, pp. 242–248.

French, Elizabeth G., and Irene Chadwick. Some characteristics of affiliation motivation. *J. abnorm. soc. Psychol.*, 1956, *52:* 296–300.

French, J. D., Verzeano and H. W. Magoun, 1953.

French, T. M. *The integration of behavior*, vol. 2. *The integrative process in dreams.* Chicago: Univer. of Chicago Press, 1954.

Freud, Anna. *The ego and the mechanisms of defense.* London: Hogarth Press, 1936. Also publ. in New York by Internal. Univer. Press, 1946.

Freud, Anna, and Dorothy Burlingham. *Infants without families.* New York: Internat. Univer. Press, 1944.

*Freud, S. Unconscious motivation in everyday life. In S. Freud, *The psycho-pathology of everyday life*. London: Ernest Benn, 1904, pp. 3–18.

Freud, S. *The problem of anxiety*. New York: Norton, 1936 (Originally published in 1926).

Freud, S. *The basic writings of Sigmund Freud*. New York: Random House, 1938.(a)

Freud, S. The interpretation of dreams. In S. Freud, *The basic writings of Sigmund Freud*. New York: Modern Library, 1938 (Originally published in 1900), pp. 179–549.(b)

Freud, S. Three contributions to the theory of sex (Trans. by A. A. Brill). In S. Freud, *The basic writings of Sigmund Freud*. New York: Modern Library, 1938, pp. 553–629.(c)

Freud, S. Wit and its relation to the unconscious. In S. Freud, *The basic writings of Sigmund Freud* (Trans. by A. A. Brill). New York: Modern Library, 1938 (Originally published in 1905), pp. 631–803.(d)

Freud, S. Group psychology and the analysis of the ego. London: Hogarth, 1948 (Originally published in 1921).

Freud, S. The relation of the poet to day-dreaming. In S. Freud, *Collected papers*. London: Hogarth, 1948 (Originally published in 1908), vol. IV, pp. 184–191.(b)

Freud, S. The unconscious. In S. Freud, *Collected papers*. London: Hogarth, 1948 (Originally published in 1915), vol. IV, pp. 98–136.(c)

Freud, S. Analysis of a phobia in a five-year-old boy. In S. Freud, *Collected papers*. London: Hogarth, 1949, vol. III, pp. 149–295.(a)

Freud, S. *New introductory lectures on psychoanalysis*. London: Hogarth, 1949 (Originally published in 1933).(b)

Freud, S. Instincts and their vicissitudes. In S. Freud, *Collected papers*. London: Hogarth, 1950, vol. IV, pp. 60–83.

Freud, S. The interpretation of dreams. In J. Strachey (Ed.), *The standard edition of the complete psychological works of Sigmund Freud*. London: Hogarth, 1953 (originally published in 1900), vols. IV and V.(a)

Freud, S. *The origins of psychoanalysis: Letters to Wilhelm Fliess, drafts and notes, 1887–1902*. New York: Basic Books, 1953.(b)

Freud, S. Beyond the pleasure principle. In J. Strachey (Ed.), *The standard edition of the complete psychological works of Sigmund Freud*. London: Hogarth, 1955 (Originally published in 1920), vol. XVIII.

Freud, S. A metapsychological supplement to the theory of dreams. In J. Strachey (Ed.), *The standard edition of the complete psychological works of Sigmund Freud*. London: Hogarth, 1957 (Originally published in 1917), vol. XIV, pp. 219–235.

Freud, S. Formulations on the two principles of mental functioning. In J. Strachey (Ed.), *The standard edition of the complete psychological works of Sigmund Freud*. London: Hogarth, 1958 (Originally published in 1911), vol. X, pp. 213–226.

Freud, S. Creative writers and daydreaming. In J. Strachey (Ed.), *The standard edition of the complete psychological works of Sigmund Freud*. London: Hogarth, 1959 (originally published in 1908), vol. IX, pp. 141–154.(a)

Freud S. Inhibitions, symptoms and anxiety. In J. Strachey (Ed.), *The standard edition of the complete psychological works of Sigmund Freud*. London: Hogarth, 1959 (originally published in 1926), vol. XX, pp. 177–178.(b)

Freud, S. The ego and the id. In J. Strachey (Ed.), *The standard edition of the complete psychological works of Sigmund Freud*. London: Hogarth, 1961 (Originally published in 1923), vol. XIX, pp. 3–66.

Friedman, G. A. A cross-cultural study of the relationship between independence training and of achievement as revealed by mythology. Unpublished honor's thesis. Harvard Univer., 1950.

Friedman, S. M. An empirical study of the castration and Oedipus complexes. *Genet. Psychol. Monogr.*, 1952, *2*: 61–130.

Froebel, F. *The education of man* (Trans. by W. T. Harris). New York: Appleton, 1887.

Fuller, J. L., and J. P. Scott. Heredity and learning ability in infrahuman animals. *Eugenics Quart.*, 1954, *1*: 28–43.

*Fuster, J. M. Effects of stimulation of the brain stem on tachistoscopic perception. *Science*, 1958, *127*: 150.

Fuster, J. M. Excitation and inhibition of neuronal firing in visual cortex by reticular stimulation. *Science*, 1961, *133*: 2011–2012.

Galanter, E. The direct measurement of utility and subjective probability. *Amer. J. Psychol.*, 962, *75*: 208–220.

Gantt, W. H. *Experimental basis for neurotic behavior*. New York: Harper & Row, 1944.

Gantt, W. H. Psychosexuality in animals. In P. H. Hoch & J. Zubin (Eds.), *Psychosexual development in health and disease*. New York: Grune & Stratton, 1948, pp. 33–51.

Garmezy, N. Approach and avoidance behavior of schizophrenic and normal subjects as a function of reward and punishment. *Amer. Psychol.*, 1952, *7*: 334. (Abstract)(a)

Garmezy, N. Stimulus differentiation by schizophrenic and normal subjects under conditions of reward and punishment. *J. Pers.*, 1952, *20*: 253–276.(b)

Garner, W. R. *Uncertainty and conflict as psychological concepts*. New York: Wiley, 1962.

Garth, T. R., M. R. Moses, and C. N. Anthony. The color preferences of East Indians. *Amer. J. Psychol.*, 1938, *51*: 709–713.

Gauron, E. G., and W. C. Becker. The effects of early sensory deprivation on adult rat behavior under competition stress: An attempt at replication of a study by Alexander Wolf. *J. comp. physiol. Psychol.*, 1959, *52*: 689–693.

Geldard, F. A. *The human senses*. New York: Wiley, 1953.

Gellhorn, E., H. Nakao, and E. Redgate. The influence of lesions in the anterior and posterior hypothalamus on tonic and phasic autonomic reactions. *J. Physiol.*, 1956, *131*: 402–423.

Gerard, H. B. A specific study: Conflict and conformity. *Amer. Psychol.*, 1959, *14*: 413. (Abstract)

Gerard, H. B., and J. M. Rabbie. Fear, affiliation, and social comparison. *Amer. Psychol.,* 1960, *15:* 409. (Abstract)

Gerard, H. B., and J. M. Rabbie. Fear and social comparison. *J. abnorm. soc. Psychol.,* 1961, *62:* 586–592.

Ghent, Lila. The relation of experience to the development of hunger. *Canad. J. Psychol.,* 1951, *5:* 77–81.

Gilbert, T. F. Fundamental dimensional properties of the operant. *Psychol. Rev.,* 1958, *65:* 272–282.

Gilmore, J. B. The role of anxiety and cognitive factors in children's play behavior. Unpublished doctoral dissertation, Yale Univer., 1964.

*Gilmore, J. B. Motivational antecedents and effects of play. 1965. Published for the first time in this volume.

Ginsburg, B. E., and R. B. Hovda. On the physiology of gene controlled audiogenic seizures in mice. *Anat. Rec.,* 1947, *99:* 65–66.

Gloor, P. Electrophysiological studies on the connections of the amygdaloid nucleus in the cat. Part I: The neuronal organization of the amygdaloid projection system. *EEG clin. Neurophysiol.,* 1955, *7:* 223–242.(a)

Gloor, P. Electrophysiological studies on the connections of the amygdaloid nucleus in the cat. Part II. The electrophysiological properties of the amygdaloid projection system. *EEG clin. Neurophysiol.,* 1955, *7:* 243–264.(b)

Goldberger, L. Individual differences in the effects of perceptual isolation as related to Rorschach manifestations of the primary process. Unpublished doctoral dissertation, New York Univer., 1958.

Goldberger, L., and R. R. Holt, Experimental interference with reality contact (perceptual isolation): Method and group results. *J. nerv. ment. Dis.,* 1958, *127:* 99–112.

Goldfarb, W. The effects of early institutional care on adolescent personality. *J. exp. Educ.,* 1943, *12:* 106–129.

Goldfarb, W. Psychological privation in infancy and subsequent adjustment. *Amer. J. Orthopsychiat.,* 1945, *15:* 247.

Goldfarb, W. Variations in adolescent adjustment of institutionally-reared children. *Amer. J. Orthopsychiat.,* 1947, *17:* 449.

Goldfarb, W. Rorschach test differences between family-reared, institution-reared and schizophrenic children. *Amer. J. Orthopsychiat.,* 1949, *19:* 624–633.

Goldfarb, W. Emotional and intellectual consequences of psychologic deprivation in infancy: A re-evaluation. In P. Hoch & J. Zubin (Eds.), *Psychopathology of childhood.* New York: Grune & Stratton, 1955, pp. 105–119.

Goldstein, K., and M. Scheerer. Abstract and concrete behavior: An experimental study with special tests. *Psychol. Monogr.,* 1941, *53* (2, whole no. 239).

Goldstein, M. J. The relationship between coping and avoiding behavior and response to fear-arousing propaganda. *J. abnorm. soc. Psychol.,* 1959, *58:* 247–252.

Goldstein, M. S., E. R. Ramey, I. Fritz, and R. Levine. Reversal of effects of stress in adrenalectomized animals by autonomic blocking agents. *Amer. J. Physiol.,* 1952, *171:* 92–99.

Goodenough, D., A. Shapiro, M. Holden, and L. Steinschriber. A comparison of "dreamers" and "non-dreamers": Eye movements, electroencephalograms, and the recall of dreams. *J. abnorm. soc. Psychol.*, 1959, *59:* 295.

Goodrich, K. P. Running speed and drinking rate as functions of sucrose concentration and amount of consummatory activity. *J. comp. physiol. Psychol.*, 1960, *53:* 245–250.

Goodson, F. E., and A. Brownstein. Secondary reinforcing and motivating properties of stimuli contiguous with shock onset and termination. *J. comp. physiol. Psychol.*, 1955, *48:* 381–386.

Gordon, H. R. S. Displacement activities in fiddler crabs. *Nature,* 1955, *176:* 356.

Gorer, G. *Japanese character structure.* New York: Institute for Intercultural Studies, 1942.

Gough, H. *Manual of the California Personality Inventory.* Palo Alto: Consulting Psychologists Press, 1957.

Goy, R. W., and W. C. Young. Somatic basis of sexual behavior patterns in guinea pigs. *Psychosom. Med.*, 1957, *19:* 144–151.

Grabowski, U. Pragung eines Jungschafs auf den Menschen. *Z. Tierpsychol.*, 1941, *4:* 326–329.

Graham, B. F. Neuroendocrine components in the physiological response to stress. *Ann. N.Y. Acad. Sci.*, 1953, *56:* 184–194.

Grant, D. A. Perceptual vs. analytical responses to the number concept of a Weigl-type card sorting test. *J. exp. Psychol.*, 1951, *41:* 23–29.

Gray, P. H. Theory and evidence of imprinting in human infants. *J. Psychol.*, 1958, *46:* 155–166.

Gregory, R. L. The brain as an engineering problem. In W. H. Thorpe & O. L. Zangwill (Eds.), *Current problems in animal behavior.* London: Cambridge Univer. Press, 1961.

Grindley, G. C. Experiments on the influence of the amount of reward on learning in young chickens. *Brit. J. Psychol.*, 1929, *20:* 173–180.

Groos, K. *The play of animals.* New York: Appleton, 1898.

Groos, K. *The play of men.* New York: Appleton, 1908.(a)

Groos, K. Das Spiel als Katharsis. *Zeitschrift fur Pad. Psychol. u. Ex. Pad.*, 1908, December 7.(b)

Grossman, S. P. Behavioral effects of direct adrenergic and cholinergic stimulation of the hypothalamic mechanisms regulating food and water intake. Unpublished doctoral dissertation, Yale Univer., 1961.

Grota, L. J. Thesis, Purdue Univer., 1963.

Grundfest, H. Electrical inexcitability of synapses and some consequences in the central nervous system. *Physiol. Rev.*, 1957, *37:* 337–361.

Grunt, J. A., and W. C. Young. Differential reactivity of individuals and the response of the male guinea pig to testosterone propionate. *Endocrinology*, 1952, *51:* 237–248.

Grunt, J. A., and W. C. Young. Consistency of sexual behavior patterns in individual male guinea pigs following castration and androgen therapy. *J. comp. physiol. Psychol.*, 1953, *46:* 138–144.

Guhl, A. M., and L. I. Ortman. Visual patterns in the recognition of individuals among chickens. *Condor.*, 1953, *55:* 287–298.

Guillemin, R., G. W. Clayton, J. D. Smith, and H. S. Lipscomb. Measurement of free corticosteroids in rat plasma: Physiological validation of a method. *Endocrinology*, 1958, *63:* 349–358.

Gutheil, E. A. *The language of the dream.* New York: Macmillan, 1939.

Guthrie, E. R. *The psychology of learning.* New York: Harper & Row, 1935.

Guthrie, E. R. *The psychology of learning* (rev. ed.). New York: Harper & Row, 1952.

Guttman, N. Operant conditioning, extinction, and periodic reinforcement in relation to concentration of sucrose used as reinforcing agent. *J. exp. Psychol.*, 1953, *46:* 213–224.

Guttman, N. Equal-reinforcement values for sucrose and glucose solutions compared with equal-sweetness values. *J. comp. physiol. Psychol.*, 1954, *47:* 358–361.

Guttman, N. Laws of behavior and facts of perception. In S. Koch (Ed.), *Psychology: A study of a science.* New York: McGraw-Hill, 1963, pp. 114–178.

Guttman, N., and H. I. Kalish. Discriminability and stimulus generalization. *J. exp. Psychol.*, 1956, *51:* 79.

Gwinn, G. T. The effects of punishment on acts motivated by fear. *J. exp. Psychol.*, 1949, *39:* 260–269.

Gwinn, G. T. Resistance to extinction of learned fear-drives and avoidance behavior. Unpublished paper, 1950.

*Haber, R. N. Discrepancy from adaptation as a source of affect. *J. exp. Psychol.*, 1958, *56:* 370–375.

Haggard, E. A. On the application of analysis of variance to GSR data: I. The selection of an appropriate measure. *J. exp. Psychol.*, 1949, *39:* 378–392.

Hall, C. S. The inheritance of emotionality. *Sigma Xi Quart.*, 1938, *26:* 17–27.

Hall, C. S. Genetic differences in fatal audiogenic seizures between two inbred strains of house mice. *J. Hered.*, 1947, *38:* 2–6.

Hall, C. S. The genetics of behavior. In S. S. Stevens (Ed.), *Handbook of experimental psychology.* New York: Wiley, 1951.

Hall, C. S. A cognitive theory of dream symbols. *J. genet. Psychol.*, 1953, *48:* 169–186.

*Hall, C. S. Strangers in dreams: an empirical confirmation of the Oedipus complex. *J. Pers.*, 1963, *31:* 336–345.

Hall, G. S. *Youth.* New York: Appleton, 1906.

Hanström, B. *Vergleichende anatomie des nervensystems der Wirbellosen Tiere.* Berlin: Springer, 1928.

Hardy, J. D., H. G. Wolff, and Helen Goodell. Studies on pain. A new method for measuring pain threshold: Observations on spatial summation of pain. *J. clin. Invest.*, 1940, *19:* 649–658.

Harker, J. E. Factors controlling the diurnal rhythm of activity of periplaneta Americana L. *J. exp. Biol.*, 1956, *33:* 224–234.

Harlow, H. F. Mice, monkeys, men and motives. *Psychol. Rev.*, 1953, *60:* 23–32.(a)

Harlow, H. F. Motivation as a factor in the acquisition of new responses. In M. R. Jones (Ed.), *Current theory and research in motivation.* Lincoln, Nebr.: Univer. of Nebraska Press, 1953, pp. 24–49.(b)

Harlow, H. F. The nature of love. *Amer. Psychol.,* 1958, *13:* 673–685.

Harlow, H. F. In J. N. Spuhler (Ed.), *The evolution of man's capacity for culture.* Detroit, Mich.: Wayne Univer. Press, 1959.

Harlow, H. F., N. C. Blazek, and G. E. McClearn. Manipulatory motivation in the infant rhesus monkey. *J. comp. physiol. Psychol.,* 1956, *49:* 444–448.

Harlow, H. F., Margaret K. Harlow, and D. R. Meyer. Learning motivated by a manipulation drive. *J. exp. Psychol.,* 1950, *40:* 228–234.

Harlow, H. F., and G. E. McClearn. Object discrimination learned by monkeys on the basis of manipulation motives. *J. comp. physiol. Psychol.,* 1954, *47:* 73–76.

Harlow, H. F., and R. R. Zimmerman. The development of affectional responses in infant monkeys. *Proc. Amer. Phil. Soc.,* 1958, *102:* 501–509.

*Harlow, H. F., and R. R. Zimmerman. Affectional responses in the infant monkeys. *Science,* 1959, *130:* 421–431.

Harriman, A. E. An experimental investigation into the development of the dietary preference for salt in adrenalectomized rats and into the validity of the processes postulated to account for the manifestation of this preference. Unpublished doctoral dissertation, Cornell Univer., 1952.

Harris, G. W. Hypothalamic control of the anterior lobe of the hypophysis. In W. S. Fields, R. Guillemin, and C. A. Carton (Eds.), *Hypothalamic-hypophysial interrelationships.* Springfield, Ill.: Charles C Thomas, 1956, pp. 31–42.

Hartmann, H. Comments on the psychoanalytic theory of the ego. In *The psychoanalytic study of the child.* New York: Internat. Univer. Press, 1950, vol. II, pp. 74–96.

Hartmann, H., E. Kris, and R. M. Loewenstein. Comments on the formation of psychic structure. In *The psychoanalytic study of the child.* New York: Internat. Univer. Press, vol. II, pp. 11–38.

Haskell, P. T., and J. E. Moorhouse. *Nature,* 1963, *197:* 56.

Haslinger, F. Über den Geschmacksinn Von Calliphora Erythrocephala Meigen und Über Die Verwertung von Zuckern Und Zuckeralkoholen Durch Diesse Fliege. *Z. Vergleich Physiol.,* 1935, *22:* 614–640.

Hassenstein, B. Ommatidienraster und Afferent Bewegungsintegration. *Z. Vergleich Physiol.,* 1951, *33:* 301–326.

Hassenstein, B. Über Die Wahrnehmung Der Bewegung Von Figuren Und Unregelmässigen Helligkeitsmustern. *Z. Vergleich Physiol.,* 1958, *40:* 556–592.

Hassenstein, B. *Z. Naturforsch,* 1959, *146:* 659.

Hassenstein, B., and W. Reichardt. Wie Sehen Insekten Bewegungen? *Umschau,* 1959, *59:* 302–306.

Hassett, C. C., V. G. Dethier, and J. Gans. A comparison of nutritive values and taste thresholds of carbohydrates for the blowfly. *Biol. Bull.,* 1950, *99:* 446–453.

*Hearst, E. Simultaneous generalization gradients for appetitive and aversive behavior. *Science,* 1960, *132:* 1769–1770.

*Hearst, E. Escape from a stimulus associated with both reward and punishment. *J. comp. physiol. Psychol.*, 1963, *56:* 1027–1031.

Hearst, E., and M. Sidman. Some behavioral effects of a concurrently positive and negative stimulus. *J. exp. anal. Behav.*, 1961, *4:* 251–256.

Heathers, G. L. The avoidance of repetition of a maze reaction in the rat as a function of the time interval between trials. *J. Psychol.*, 1940, *10:* 359–380.

Hebb, D. O. Elementary school methods. *Teach Mag.* (Montreal), 1930, *12:* 23–26.

Hebb, D. O. On the nature of fear. *Psychol. Rev.*, 1946, *53:* 259–276.

Hebb, D. O. The effects of early experience on problem-solving at maturity. *Amer. Psychol.*, 1947, *2:* 306–307.

Hebb, D. O. *Organization of behavior*. New York: Wiley, 1949.

Hebb, D. O. Heredity and environment in mamalian behavior. *Brit. J. anim. Behav.*, 1953, *1:* 43–47.(a)

Hebb, D. O. On human thought. *Canad. J. Psychol.*, 1953, 7: 99–110.(b)

*Hebb, D. O. Drives and the CNS (conceptual nervous system). *Psychol. Rev.*, 1955, *62:* 243–254.

Hebb, D. O. *A textbook of psychology*. Philadelphia: Saunders, 1958.

Hebb, D. O. The American revolution. *Amer. Psychol.*, 1960, *15:* 735–745.

Hebb, D. O., and Helen Mahut. Motivation et recherche du changement perceptif chez le rat et chez l'homme. *J. Psychol. norm. path.*, 1955, *48:* 209–220.

Hebb, D. O., and A. H. Riesen. The genesis of irrational fears. *Bull. Canad. Psychol. Ass.*, 1943, *3:* 49–50.

Hebb, D. O., and W. R. Thompson. The social significance of animal studies. In G. Lindzey (Ed.), *Handbook of social psychology*. Cambridge, Mass.: Addison-Wesley, 1954, pp. 532–561.

Hebb, D. O., and K. Williams. A method of rating animal intelligence. *J. genet. Psychol.*, 1946, *34:* 59–65.

Hediger, H. *Wild animals in captivity* (Rev. ed.). London: Butterworth, 1950.

Heidbreder, E., M. Bensley, and M. Ivy. The attainment of concepts: IV. Regularities and levels. *J. Psychol.*, 1948, *25:* 299–329.

Heinroth, M., and O. Heinroth. *Die Vogel Mitteleuropas*. Berlin: Lichterfelde, 1924–1933.

Heinroth, O. Beitrage zur Biologie, namentlich Ethologie und Physiologie der Anatiden. *Verhandl. 5th Internat. Ornithol. Kong.*, 1910, pp. 589–702.

Helson, H. Adaptation-level as frame of reference for prediction of psychophysical data. *Amer. J. Psychol.*, 1947, *60:* 1–29.

Helson, H. Adaptation-level as a basis for a quantitative theory of frames of reference. *Psychol. Rev.*, 1948, *55:* 297–313.

Helson, H. Adaptation-level theory. In S. Koch (Ed.), *Psychology: A study of science*. New York: McGraw-Hill, 1959, pp. 565–621.

Hendrick, I. The discussion of the "instinct to master." *Psychoanal. Quart.*, 1943, *12:* 561–565.

Hendry, D. P., and R. Rasche. Analysis of a new nonnutritive positive reinforcer based on thirst. *J. comp. physiol. Psychol.*, 1961, *54:* 477–483.

Heron, W. T. The inheritance of maze learning ability in rats. *J. comp. Psychol.*, 1935, *19:* 77–89.

Hersher, L., A. U. Moore, and J. B. Richmond. Effect of postpartum separation of mother and kid on maternal care in the domestic goat. *Science*, 1958, *128:* 1342–1343.

Herter, K. Die Beziehungen zwischen Vorzugstemperatur und Hautbeschaffenheit bei Mausen. *Zool. Anz. Suppl.*, 1938, *11:* 48–55.

Hess, E. H. Effects of meprobamate on imprinting in waterfowl. *Ann. N.Y. Acad. Sci.*, 1957, *67:* 724.

Hess, E. H. "Imprinting" in animals. *Sci. Amer.*, 1958, *198:* 81–90.

*Hess, E. H. Imprinting. *Science*, 1959, *130:* 133–141.(a)

Hess, E. H. The relationship between printing and motivation. In M. R. Jones (Ed.), *Nebraska symposium on motivation: 1959*. Lincoln, Nebr.: Univer. of Nebraska Press, 1959, pp. 44–78.(b)

Hess, E. H. Two conditions limiting critical age for imprinting. *J. comp. physiol. Psychol.*, 1959, *52:* 515–518.(c)

Hess, E. H., and H. H. Schaefer. Innate behavior patterns as indicators of the "critical period." *Z. Tierpsychol.*, 1959, *16:* 155.

Hess, W. R. *Diencephalon. Autonomic and extrapyramidal functions*. New York: Grune & Stratton, 1954.

Heyns, R. W., J. Veroff, and J. W. Atkinson. A scoring manual for the affiliation motive. In J. W. Atkinson (Ed.), *Motives in fantasy, action, and society*. Princeton, N.J.: Van Nostrand, 1958, pp. 205–218.

Hilgard, E. R. *Theories of learning*. New York: Appleton, 1948.

Hilgard, E. R. *Theories of learning* (rev. ed.). New York: Appleton, 1956.

*Hilgard, E. R. Impulsive versus realistic thinking: an examination of the distinction between primary and secondary processes in thought. *Psychol. Bull.*, 1962, *59:* 477–488.(a)

Hilgard, E. R. The scientific status of psychoanalysis. In *Proceedings of the 1960 International Congress in Logic, Methodology, and Philosophy of Science*. Stanford, Calif.: Stanford Univer. Press, 1962, pp. 375–390.(b)

Hilgard, E. R., L. V. Jones, and S. J. Kaplan. Conditioned discrimination as related to anxiety. *J. exp. Psychol.*, 1951, *52:* 94–99.

Hilgard, E. R., and D. G. Marquis. *Conditioning and learning*. New York: Appleton, 1940.

*Hillix, W. A. Sensory deprivation in rats. Letter to the editors of Science. *Science*, 1963, *142:* 1021–1022.

Hinde, R. A. The behavior of the great tit (parus major) and some other related species. *Behaviour*, 1952, suppl. No. 2.

Hinde, R. A. The conflict between drives in the courtship and copulation of the chaffinch. *Behaviour*, 1953, *5:* 1–31.

Hinde, R. A. Changes in responsiveness to a constant stimulus. *Brit. J. anim. Behav.*, 1954, *2:* 41–55.

Hinde, R. A. The nest building behavior of domesticated canaries. *Proc. Zool. Soc. Lond.*, 1958, *131:* 1–48.

Hinde, R. A. Unitary drives. *Brit. J. anim. Behav.*, 1959, *1:* 130–141.

Hinde, R. A. Energy models of motivation. *Symp. Soc. Exp. Biol.*, 1960, *14:* 199–213.

Hinde, R. A., W. H. Thorpe, and M. A. Vince. The following responses of young coots and moorhens. *Behaviour*, 1956, *9:* 214–242.

Hingston, R. W. G. *Problems of instinct and intelligence.* London: Arnold, 1928.

Hockman, C. H. Prenatal maternal stress on the rat: its effects on emotional behavior in the offspring. *J. comp. physiol. Psychol.*, 1961, *54:* 679–684.

Hodgson, E. S., and S. Geldiay. Experimentally induced release of neurosecretory materials from roach corpora cardiaca. *Biol. Bull.*, 1959, *117:* 275–283.

Hodgson, R. E. An eight generation experiment in inbreeding swine. *J. Hered.*, 1935, *26:* 209–217.

Hollenberg, Eleanor, and Margaret Sperry. Some antecedents of aggression and effects of frustration in doll play. *Personality*, 1951, *1:* 32–43.

Holt, F. B. Animal drive and the learning process. New York: Holt, 1931.

Holt, R. R. Gauging primary and secondary processes in Rorschach responses. *J. proj. Tech.*, 1956, *20:* 14–25.

Holt, R. R., and Joan Havel. A method for assessing primary and secondary process in the Rorschach. In Maria A. Rickers-Ovsiankina (Ed.), *Rorschach psychology.* New York: Wiley, 1960, pp. 263–315.

Holz, W. C., and N. H. Azrin. Discriminative properties of punishment. *J. exp. anal. Behav.*, 1961, *4:* 225–232.

Holz, W. C., and N. H. Azrin. Interactions between the discriminative and aversive properties of punishment. *J. exp. anal. Behav.*, 1962, *5:* 229–234.

Holz, W. C., N. H. Azrin, and R. E. Ulrich. Punishment of temporally spaced responding. *J. exp. anal. Behav.*, 1963, *6:* 115–122.

Horenstein, B. R. Performance of conditioned responses as a function of strength of hunger drive. *J. comp. physiol. Psychol.*, 1951, *44:* 210–224.

Hoyle, G. Changes in the blood potassium concentration of the African migratory locust (Locusta migratoria migratorioides R. & F.) during food deprivation, and the effect on neuromuscular activity. *J. exp. Biol.*, 1954, *31:* 260–270.

Hoyle, G. The effects of some common cations on neuromuscular transmission in insects. *J. Physiol.* (London), 1955, *127:* 90–103.

Hovland, C. I., and R. R. Sears. Experiments on motor conflict. I. Types of conflict and their modes of resolution. *J. exp. Psychol.*, 1938, *23:* 477–503.

Huber, E. Evolution of facial musculature and cutaneous field of trigeminus. *Quart. Rev. Biol.*, 1930, *5:* (133): 389–437.

Huber, F. *Naturwissenshaften*, 1955, *42:* 566.

Huber, F. *Verhandl. Zool. Ges. Munster. Zool. Anz. Suppl.*, 1959, *23:* 248.

Huber, F. Untersuchungen Über Die Funktion Des Zentralnervensystems Und Insbesondere Des Gehirnes Bei Der Fortbewegung Und Der Lauterzeugung Der Grillen. *Z. Vergleich Physiol.*, 1960, *44:* 60–132.

Huber, F. *Evolution*, 1962, *4:* 429.(a)

Huber, F. *Fortschr. Zool.*, 1962, *15:* 165.(b)

Huber, F. The role of the CNS in Orthoptera during co-ordination and control of stimulation. In R. G. Busnel (Ed.), *L'Acoustique animal.* Amsterdam: Elsevier, 1962, pp. 440–489.(c)

Hull, C. L. Goal attraction and directing ideas conceived as habit phenomena. *Psychol. Rev.*, 1931, *38:* 487–506.

Hull, C. L. The goal-gradient hypothesis applied to some field-force problems in the behavior of young children. *Psychol. Rev.*, 1938, *45:* 271–299.

Hull, C. L. *Principles of behavior.* New York: Appleton, 1943.

Hull, C. L. *Essentials of behavior.* New Haven: Yale Univer. Press, 1951.

Hull, C. L. *A behavior system.* New Haven: Yale Univer. Press, 1952.

Humphreys, L. G. The effect of random alternation of reinforcement on the acquisition and extinction of conditioned eyelid reactions. *J. exp. Psychol.*, 1939, *25:* 141–158.

Hunt, H. F. Effects of drugs on emotional responses and abnormal behavior in animals. In *Conference on drugs and psychiatry.* Washington, D.C.: National Research Council, 1956.

Hunt, H. F., and J. V. Brady. Some quantitative and qualitative differences between "anxiety" and "punishment" conditioning. *Amer. Psychol.*, 1951, *6:* 276–277. (Abstract)

Hunt, H. F., and J. V. Brady. Some effects of punishment and intercurrent "anxiety" on a simple operant. *J. comp. physiol. Psychol.*, 1955, *48:* 305–310.

Hunt, J. McV. The effects of infant feeding frustration upon adult hoarding in the albino rat. *J. abnorm. soc. Psychol.*, 1941, *36:* 338–360.

Hunt, J. McV. (Ed.), *Personality and the behavior disorders.* New York: Ronald, 1944.

Hunt, J. McV. *Intelligence and experience.* New York: Ronald, 1961.

Hunt, J. McV. Motivation inherent in information processing and action. In O. J. Harvey (Ed.), *Motivation and social organization: the cognitive factors.* New York: Ronald, 1963.(a)

Hunt, J. McV. Piaget's observations as a source of hypotheses concerning motivation. *Merrill-Palmer Quart.*, 1963, *9:* 263–275.(b)

Hunt, J. McV. The psychological basis for using pre-school enrichment as an antidote for cultural deprivation. *Merrill-Palmer Quart.*, 1964, *10:* 209–248.

*Hunt, J. McV. The epigenesis of motivation and early cognitive learning. Published for the first time in this volume.

Hunt, J. McV., and H. Schlosberg. Behavior of rats in continuous conflict. *J. comp. physiol. Psychol.*, 1950, *43:* 351–357.

Hunter, T. A., and J. S. Brown. A decade-type electronic interval-timer. *Amer. J. Psychol.*, 1949, *62:* 570–575.

Hunter, W. S. Conditioning and extinction in the rat. *Brit. J. Psychol.*, 1935, *26:* 135–148.

Hunter, W. S. Muscle potentials and conditioning in the rat. *J. exp. Psychol.*, 1937, *21:* 611–624.

Hurlock, E. B. Experimental investigations of childhood play. *Psychol. Bull.*, 1934, *31:* 47–66.

Hurst, C. C. *Experiments in genetics.* Cambridge: Cambridge Univer. Press, 1925.

Hydén, H. Biochemical changes in glial cells and nerve cells at varying activity. In F. Brücke (Ed.), *Proc. 4th Internat. Congr. Biochem., III, Biochemistry of the central nervous system.* London: Pergamon, 1959, pp. 64–89.

Hymovitch, B. The effects of experimental variations on problem solving in the rat. *J. comp. physiol. Psychol.*, 1952, *45:* 313–321.

Imada, H. The effects of punishment on avoidance behavior. *Jap. psychol. Res.,* 1959, *1:* 27–38.

Institute of Dream Research. *A manual for classifying characters in dreams.* Technical Manual no. 1, 1962.(a)

Institute of Dream Research, *A manual for classifying aggressions, misfortune, friendly acts, and good fortunes in dreams.* Technical Manual no. 2, 1962.(b)

James, H. Flickers: An unconditioned stimulus for imprinting. *Canad. J. Psychol.,* 1959, *13:* 59–67.

James, W. *Principles of psychology.* New York: Holt, 1890.

Janis, I. L. *Physiological stress.* New York: Wiley, 1958.

Janis, I. L., and S. Feshbach. Effects of fear-arousing communication. *J. abnorm. soc. Psychol.,* 1953, *48:* 78–92.

Janis, I. L., and S. Feshbach. Personality differences associated with responsiveness to fear-arousing communications. *J. Pers.,* 1954, *23:* 154–166.

Janis, I. L., and R. Terwilliger. An experimental study of psychological resistances to fear-arousing communications. *J. abnorm. soc. Psychol.,* 1962, *65:* 403–410.

Jasper, H. H. Electroencephalography. In W. Penfield & T. C. Erickson (Eds.), *Epilepsy and cerebral localization.* Springfield, Ill.: Charles C Thomas, 1941, pp. 380–454.

Jasper, H. H. Diffuse projection systems: The integrative action of the thalamic reticular system. *EEG clin. Neurophysiol.,* 1949, *1:* 405.

Jaynes, J. Imprinting: The interaction of learned and innate behavior: I. Development and generalization. *J. comp. physiol. Psychol.,* 1956, *49:* 201.

Jaynes, J. Imprinting: The interaction of learned and innate behavior: II. The critical period. *J. comp. physiol. Psychol.,* 1957, *50:* 6–10.

Jaynes, J. Imprinting: The interaction of learned and innate behavior: III. Practical effects on performance, retention and fear. *J. comp. physiol. Psychol.,* 1958, *51:* 234–237.(a)

Jaynes, J. Imprinting: The interaction of learned and innate behavior: IV. Generalization and emergent discrimination. *J. comp. physiol. Psychol.,* 1958, *51:* 238–242.(b)

Jenkins, R. L. Guilt feelings—their function and dysfunction. In M. L. Reyment (Ed.), *Feelings and emotions.* New York: McGraw-Hill, 1950.

Jenkins, W. O., G. R. Pascal, and R. W. Walker. Deprivation and generalization. *J. exp. Psychol.,* 1958, *56:* 274.

Jenkins, W. O., and F. D. Sheffield. Rehearsal and guessing habits as sources of the "spread of effect." *J. exp. Psychol.,* 1946, *36:* 316–330.

Jenkins, W. O., and J. C. Stanley. Partial reinforcement: A review and critique. *Psychol. Bull.,* 1950, *47:* 193–234.

Jersild, A. T. *Child psychology* (rev. ed.). New York: Prentice-Hall, 1942.

Jersild, A. T., and F. B. Holmes. Children's fears. *Child Developm. Monogr. no. 20,* 1935, pp. ix & 358.

Johannsen, W. *Uber Erblichkeit in populationen und in reinen Linien.* Jena: Gustav Fisher, 1903.

Johnson, P. C., and J. W. Bean. Effect of sympathetic blocking agents on the toxic action of O_2 at high pressure. *Amer. J. Physiol.,* 1957, *188:* 593–598.

Johnson, P. O. *Statistical methods in research.* New York: Prentice-Hall, 1949.

Jones, E. *The life and work of Sigmund Freud.* New York: Basic Books, 1955, vol. II.

Jones, M. R. (Ed.) *Nebraska symposium on motivation: 1959.* Lincoln, Nebr.: Univer. of Nebraska Press, 1959.

Kagan, J., and H. A. Moss. Stability and validity of achievement fantasy. *J. abnorm. soc. Psychol.,* 1959, *58:* 357–364.

Kamin, L. J. The measurement of anxiety: A methodological note. *Canad. J. Psychol.,* 1957, *11:* 71–74.

Kamin, L. J. The delay-of-punishment gradient. *J. comp. physiol. Psychol.,* 1959, *52:* 434–437.

Kamin, L. J. Apparent adaptation effects in the acquisition of a conditioned emotional response. *Canad. J. Psychol.,* 1961, *15:* 176–188.

Kaplan, M. The effects of noxious stimulus intensity and duration during intermittent reinforcement of escape behavior. *J. comp. physiol. Psychol.,* 1952, *45:* 538–549.

Karsh, E. B. Effects of number of rewarded trials and intensity of punishment on running speed. *J. comp. physiol. Psychol.,* 1962, *55:* 44–51.

Karsh, E. B. Changes in intensity of punishment: Effect on runway behavior of rats. *Science,* 1963, *140:* 1084–1085.

Kasatkin, N. I. Early conditioned reflexes in the child. *Zh. vyssh. nervn. Deiatel.,* 1952, *2:* 572–581.

Kaufman, E. L., and N. E. Miller. Effect of number of reinforcements on strength of approach in an approach-avoidance conflict. *J. comp. physiol. Psychol.,* 1949, *42:* 63–74.

Keeler, C. E., and H. D. King. Multiple effects of coat color genes in the Norway rat, with special reference to temperament and domestication. *J. comp. Psychol.,* 1942, *34:* 241–250.

Keister, M. E. The behavior of young children in failure: An experimental attempt to discover and to modify undesirable responses of preschool children to failure. *Univer. of Iowa Stud. Child Welf.,* 1938, *14:* 27–82.

Kelleher, R. T., and L. R. Gollub. A review of positive conditioned reinforcement. *J. exp. anal. Behav.,* 1962, *5:* 543–597.

Keller, F. S., and W. N. Schoenfeld. *Principles of psychology.* New York: Appleton, 1950.

Kellogg, W. N. Electric shock as a motivating stimulus in conditioning experiments. *J. genet. Psychol.,* 1941, *25:* 85–96.

Kelly, G. A. *A psychology of personal constructs.* New York: Norton, 1955.

Kendler, H. H. Reflections and confessions of a reinforcement theorist. *Psychol. Rev.,* 1951, *58:* 368–374.

Kendler, H. H. Learning. *Ann. Rev. Psychol.,* 1959, *10:* 43–88.

Kennedy, D. The initiation of impulses in receptors. *Amer. Zool.,* 1962, *2:* 27.

Kennedy, J. S. Is modern ethology objective? *Brit. J. anim. Behav.,* 1954, *2:* 12–19.

Kessen, W., L. S. Hendry, and A. M. Leutzendorff. Measurement of movement in the human newborn: A new technique. *Child Develpm.*, 1961, *32:* 95–105.

*Kessen, W., G. A. Kimble, and B. M. Hillman. Effects of deprivation and scheduling on water intake in the white rat. *Science*, 1960, *131:* 1735–1736.

*Kessen, W., and A. M. Leutzendorff. The effect of nonnutritive sucking on movement in the human newborn. *J. comp. physiol. Psychol.*, 1963, *56:* 69–72.

*Kessen, W., and G. Mandler. Anxiety, pain, and the inhibition of distress. *Psychol. Rev.*, 1961, *68:* 396–404.

Kessen, W., E. J. Williams, and J. P. Williams. Selection and test of response measures in the study of the human newborn. *Child Develpm.*, 1961, *32:* 7–24.

Kimble, G. A. Shock intensity and avoidance learning. *J. comp. physiol. Psychol.*, 1955, *48:* 281–284.

Kinsey, A. C., W. B. Pomeroy, and C. E. Martin. *Sexual behavior in the human male.* Philadelphia: Saunders, 1948.

Klapper, J. T. *The effects of mass communications.* New York: Free Press, 1960.

Klein, M. A contribution to the psychogenesis of manic-depressive states. In *Contributions to psychoanalysis, 1921–1945.* London: Hogarth, 1948, p. 282.(a)

Klein, M. Personification in the play of children. In *Contributions to psychoanalysis.* London: Hogarth, 1948 (Originally published in 1929), pp. 215–226.(b)

Kobler, F. Description of an acute castration fear based on superstition. *Psychoanal. Rev.*, 1948, *35:* 285–289.

Koch, S., and W. J. Daniel. The effect of satiation on the behavior mediated by a habit of maximum strength. *J. exp. Psychol.*, 1945, *35:* 167–187.

Köhler, W. *The mentality of apes.* New York: Harcourt, 1925.

Kohn, M. Satiation of hunger from food injected directly into the stomach versus food ingested by mouth. *J. comp. physiol. Psychol.*, 1951, *44:* 412–422.

Kohn, M. L. Social class and the exercise of parental authority. *Amer. Sociol. Rev.*, 1959, *24:* 352–366.

Kollar, E. J. Psychological stress: A re-evaluation. *J. nerv. Ment. Dis.*, 1961, *132:* 382–396.

Konorski, J., and G. Szwejkowska. Chronic extinction and restoration of conditioned reflexes: IV. The dependence of the course of extinction and restoration of conditioned reflexes on the "history" of the conditioned stimulus (The principle of the primacy of first training). *Acta biol. Exp.*, 1952, *16:* 95–113.

Korman, M. Ego strength and conflict discrimination: An experimental construct validation of the ego strength scale. *J. consult. Psychol.*, 1960, *24:* 294–298.

Kortlandt, A. Wechselwirkung zwischen instinkten. *Arch. Neerl. Zool.*, 1940, *4:* 442–520.

Kovach, J. K., and E. H. Hess. Imprinting: Effects of painful stimulation upon the following response. *J. comp. physiol. Psychol.*, 1963, *56:* 461–464.

*Kraeling, Doris. Amount of reward as a variable in training. *J. comp. physiol. Psychol.*, 1961, *54:* 560–565.

Kramer, C. Y. Extension of multiple range tests to group means with unequal numbers of replications. *Biometrics*, 1956, *12:* 307–310.

Kratin, G. [Analysis of "indifferent" stimuli from the encephalogram in man]. *Fiziol. Zh. SSSR*, 1959, *45* (1): 16–23.

Kreindler, A., L. Unger, and D. Volanskii. Effects of a circumscribed lesion of reticular formation in brain stem on higher nervous activity of dogs. *Sechenov. Physiol. J. USSR*, 1959, *45:* 247–256.

Kris, E. On preconscious mental processes. *Psychoanal. Quart.*, 1950, *19:* 540–560.

Kris, E. *Psychoanalytic explorations in art.* New York: Internat. Univer. Press, 1952.

Kuethe, J. L., and C. W. Eriksen. Personality, anxiety, and muscle tension as determinants of response stereotypy. *J. abnorm. soc. Psychol.*, 1957, *54:* 400–404.

Kuo, Z. Y. A psychology without heredity. *Psychol. Rev.*, 1924, *31:* 427–451.

Kuo, Z. Y. Ontogeny of embryonic behavior in Aves. III. The structure and environmental factors in embryonic behavior. *J. comp. Psychol.*, 1932, *13:* 245–272.

Kurtz, K. H., and J. Pearl. The effects of prior fear experiences on acquired-drive learning. *J. comp. physiol. Psychol.*, 1960, *53:* 201–206.

Kurtz, K. H., and G. C. Walters. The effects of prior fear experiences on an approach-avoidance conflict. *J. comp. physiol. Psychol.*, 1962, *55:* 1075–1078.

LaBarre, W. Some observations on character structure in the Orient: The Japanese. *Psychiatry*, 1948, *8:* 319–342.

Lacey, J. I., and B. C. Lacey. Verification and extension of the principle of autonomic response—stereotypy. *Amer. J. Psychol.*, 1958, *71:* 50–73.(a)

Lacey, J. I., and B. C. Lacey. The relationship of resting autonomic activity to motor impulsivity. *Res. Publ. Ass. Res. Nerv. Ment. Dis.*, 1958, *36:* 144–209.(b)

Landis, C., and W. A. Hunt. The dimensional analysis of a new series of facial expressions. *J. Psychol.*, 1936, *2:* 215–219.

Landis, C., and W. A. Hunt. *The startle pattern.* New York: Holt, 1939.

Lange, K. Erganzungstheorie. Berlin: 1901.

Lashley, K. S. Experimental analysis of instinctive behavior. *Psychol. Rev.*, 1938, *45:* 445–471.

Lavenda, N., R. G. Bartlett, Jr., and V. E. Kennedy. Leucocyte changes in rodents exposed to cold with and without restraint. *Amer. J. Physiol.*, 1956, *184:* 624–626.

Lazarus, M. *Uber die Reize des Spiels.* Berlin: F. Dummler, 1883.

Lazarus, R. S., C. W. Eriksen, and C. P. Fonda. Personality dynamics and auditory perceptual recognition. *J. Pers.*, 1951, *19:* 471–482.

Lazarus, R. S., and R. A. McCleary. Autonomic discrimination without awareness: A study of subception. *Psychol. Rev.*, 1951, *58:* 113–122.

Lazarus, R. S., H. Yousem, and A. Arenberg. Hunger and perception. *J. Pers.*, 1953, *21:* 312–328.

Lee, W. A. Approach and avoidance to a cue paired with the beginning and end of pain. Unpublished manuscript, Wesleyan Univer., 1951.

*Lefkowitz, M. M., L. O. Walder, and L. D. Eron. Punishment, identification and aggression. *Merrill-Palmer Quart.*, 1963, *9:* 159–174.

Lehrman, D. S. A critique of Konrad Lorenz's theory of instinctive behavior. *Quart. Rev. Biol.*, 1953, *28:* 337–363.

Lehrman, D. S. The physiological basis of parental feeding behavior in the ring dove (*Streptopelia risoria*). *Behaviour*, 1955, *7:* 241–286.

Lehrman, D. S. Comparative physiology (behavior). *Ann. Rev. Physiol.*, 1956, *18:* 527–542.(a)

Lehrman, D. S. On the organization of maternal behavior and the problem of instinct. In P.-P. Grassé (Ed.), *L'Instinct dans le comportement des animaux et de l'homme.* Paris: Masson & Cie, 1956, pp. 475–520.(b)

Lehrman, D. S. Effect of female sex hormones on incubation behavior in the ring dove (*Streptopelia risoria*). *J. comp. physiol. Psychol.*, 1958, *51: 142–145.*(a)

Lehrman, D. S. Induction of broodiness by participation in courtship and nest-building in the ring dove (*Streptopelia risoria*). *J. comp. physiol. Psychol.*, 1958, *51:* 32–36.(b)

Lehrman, D. S. On the origin of the reproductive behavior cycle in doves. *Tr. New York Acad. Sci.*, 1959, *21:* 682–688.

Lehrman, D. S. Hormonal regulation of parental behavior in birds and infra-human mammals. In W. C. Young (Ed.), *Sex and internal secretions.* Baltimore: Williams & Wilkins, 1961, pp. 1268–1382.

*Lehrman, D. S. Interaction of hormonal and experiential influence on development of behavior. In E. L. Bliss (Ed.), *Roots of behavior.* New York: Harper & Row, 1962, pp. 142–156.

Leighton, Dorothea, and C. Kluckhohn. *Children of the people: The Navajo individual and his development.* Cambridge, Mass.: Harvard Univer. Press, 1947.

Leiman, A. H. Relationship of TAT sexual responses to sexual drive, sexual guilt and sexual conflict. Unpublished doctoral dissertation, Univer. of Mass., 1961.

Leiman, A. H., and S. Epstein. Thematic sexual responses as related to sexual drive and guilt. *J. abnorm. soc. Psychol.*, 1961, *63:* 169–175.

Lesser, G. S. The relationship between overt and fantasy aggression as a function of maternal response to aggression. *J. abnorm. soc. Psychol.*, 1957, *55:* 218–221.

Leventhal, H., R. Jacobs, and P. Niles. Negative emotions and persuasion. Unpublished manuscript.

Leventhal, H., and P. Niles. A field experiment on fear-arousal with data on the validity of questionnaire measures. Unpublished manuscript, 1963.

Leventhal, H., and S. Perloe. A relationship between self-esteem and persuasibility. *J. abnorm. soc. Psychol.*, 1962, *64:* 385.

*Leventhal, H., R. Singer, and S. Jones. The effects of fear and specificity of recommendation upon attitudes and behavior. *J. pers. soc. psychol.*, 1965, 1.

Levin, H., and D. G. Forgays. Sensory change as immediate and delayed reinforcement for maze learning. *J. comp. physiol. Psychol.*, 1960, *53:* 194–196.

Levin, H., and E. Wardwell. The research uses of doll play. *Psychol. Bull.*, 1962, *59:* 27–56.

Levine, R., I. Chein, and G. Murphy. The relation of the intensity of a need to the amount of perceptual distortion. *J. Psychol.*, 1942, *13:* 283–293.

Levine, S. A further study of infantile handling and adult avoidance learning. *J. Pers.*, 1956, *27:* 70–80.

Levine, S. Infantile experience and consummatory behavior in adulthood. *J. comp. physiol. Psychol.*, 1957, *50:* 609–612.

Levine, S. Effects of early deprivation and delayed weaning on avoidance learning in the albino rat. *Arch. neurol. Psychiat.*, 1958, *79:* 211–213.

Levine, S. The effects of differential infantile stimulation on emotionality at weaning. *Canad. J. Psychol.*, 1959, *13:* 243–247.

Levine, S. Plasma-free cortico-steroid response to electric shock in rats stimulated in infancy. *Science*, 1962, *135:* 795–796.(a)

Levine, S. The effects of infantile experience on adult behavior. In A. J. Bachrach (Ed.), *Experimental foundations of clinical psychology.* New York: Basic Books, 1962, pp. 139–169.(b)

Levine, S., M. Alpert, and G. W. Lewis. Infantile experience and the maturation of the pituitary-adrenal axis. *Science*, 1957, *127:* 1347.

Levine, S. J. Stimulation in infancy. *Sci. Amer.*, 1960, *202:* 80–86.

Levine, S. J. Psychophysiological effects of infantile stimulation. In E. L. Bliss (Ed.), *Roots of behavior.* New York: Hoeber, 1962.

Levine, S. J., J. A. Chevalier, and S. O. Korchin. The effects of early shock and handling in infancy on later avoidance learning. *J. Pers.* 1956, *24:* 475–493.

Levy, D. M. Primary affect hunger. *Amer. J. Psychiat.*, 1937, *94:* 643.

Lewin, K. Environmental forces. In C. Murchison (Ed.), *A handbook of child psychology.* Worcester, Mass.: Clark Univer. Press, 1933, pp. 590–625.

Lewin, K. *A dynamic theory of personality.* New York: McGraw-Hill, 1935.

Lewin, K. *Principles of topological psychology.* New York: McGraw-Hill, 1936.

Lewin, K., T. Dembo, L. Festinger, and P. S. Sears. Level of aspiration. In J. McV. Hunt (Ed.), *Personality and the behavior disorders.* New York: Ronald, 1944, pp. 333–378.

Lewis, D. J. Acquisition, extinction, and spontaneous recovery as a function of percentage of reinforcement and intertrial intervals. *J. exp. Psychol.*, 1956, *51:* 45–53.

*Lewis, M. Some nondecremental effects of effort. *J. comp. physiol. Psychol.*, 1964, *57:* 367–372.

Lewis, M. The effect of effort on value: An exploratory study of children. *Child Develpm.*, 1964.

Lewis, O. *The children of Sanchez.* New York: Random House, 1961.

Li, Choh-Luh, and H. Jasper. Microelectrode studies of the cerebral cortex in the cat. *J. Physiol.*, 1953, *121:* 117–140.

Lichtenstein, P. E. Studies of anxiety: I. The production of a feeding inhibition in dogs. *J. comp. physiol. Psychol.*, 1950, *43:* 16–29.

Lichtenstein, P. E. On "The dilemma of fear as a motivating force." *Psychol. Rep.*, 1957, *3:* 213–216.

Liddell, H. S. Animal studies bearing on the problem of pain. *Psychosom. Med.*, 1944, *6:* 261–263.

Liddell, H. S. Some specific factors that modify tolerance for environmental stress. In H. G. Wolff, S. G. Wolf, Jr., & C. C. Hare (Eds.), *Life stress and bodily disease.* Baltimore: Williams & Wilkins, 1950, pp. 155–171.

Lilly, J. C. True primary emotional state of anxiety-terror-panic in contrast to a "sham" emotion or "pseudo-affective" state evoked by a stimulation of hypo-thalamus. *Fed. Proc.*, 1957, *16:* 81. (Abstract)

Lindner, H. Sexual responsiveness to perceptual tests in a group of sexual offenders. *J. Pers.*, 1953, *21:* 364–374.

Lindquist, E. R. *Design and analysis of experiments in psychology and education.* New York: Houghton Mifflin, 1953.

Lindsley, D. B. Emotion. In S. S. Stevens (Ed.), *Handbook of experimental psychology.* New York: Wiley, 1951, pp. 473–516.

Lindsley, D. B. Psychophysiology and motivation. In M. R. Jones (Ed.), *Nebraska symposium on motivation: 1957.* Lincoln, Nebr.: Univer. of Nebraska Press, 1957, pp. 44–105.

Lindsley, D. B. The reticular system and perceptual discrimination. In H. H. Jasper *et al.* (Eds.), *Reticular formation of the brain.* Boston: Little, Brown, 1958, p. 513.

Lindsley, D. F., R. H. Wendt, R. Fugett, D. B. Lindsley, and W. R. Adey. Diurnal activity cycles in monkeys under prolonged visual-pattern deprivation. *J. comp. physiol. Psychol.*, 1962, *55:* 633–640.

Lindzey, G. *Assessment of human motives.* New York: Holt, 1958.

Lindzey, G., D. T. Lykken, and H. D. Winston. Infantile trauma, genetic factors, and adult temperament. *J. abnorm. soc. Psychol.*, 1960, *61:* 7–14.

Lindzey, G., and C. Tejessey. Thematic Apperception Test: Indices of aggression in relation to measures of overt and covert behavior. *Amer. J. Orthopsychiat.*, 1956, *26:* 567–576.

Linton, R. *The cultural background of personality.* New York: Appleton, 1945.

Lipton, E. L., J. B. Richmond, H. L. Weinberger, and L. Hersher. An approach to the evaluation of neonate autonomic responses. *Psychosom. Med.*, 1958, *20:* 409.

Lloyd, D. P. C. A direct central inhibitory action of dromically conducted impulses. *J. Neurophysiol.*, 1941, *4:* 184–190.

Lockhard, R. B. Self-regulated exposure to light by dark- or light-treated rats. *Science*, 1962, *135:* 377–378.

Loewald, H. On the therapeutic action of psychoanalysis. Unpublished manuscript, 1956.

Logan, F. A. *Incentive.* New Haven: Yale Univer. Press, 1960.

Lorente de Nó, R. Transmission of impulses through cranial motor nuclei. *J. Neurophysiol.*, 1939, *2:* 402–464.

Lorenz, K. The companion in the bird's world. The fellow-member of the species as releasing factor of social behavior. *J. Ornithol.*, 1935, *83:* 137–213.

Lorenz, K. Vergleichende Bewegungstudien an Anatinen. *J. Ornithol.*, 1941, *89:* 19–29.

Lorenz, K. The comparative method in studying innate behavior patterns. *Symp. Soc. exp. Biol.*, 1950, *4:* 221–268.

Lorenz, K. The past twelve years in the comparative study of behavior. In G. H. Schiller (Ed.), *Instinctive behavior.* New York: Internat. Univer. Press, 1957, pp. 288–310.

Loucks, R. B. The experimental delimitation of neural structures essential for learning: The attempt to condition striped muscle responses with faradization of the sigmoid gyri. *J. Psychol.*, 1935, *1:* 5–44.

Lowrey, L. G. Personality distortion and early institutional care. *Amer. J. Orthopsychiat.,* 1940, *10:* 516.

Lustman, S. L. Rudiments of the ego. *Psychoanal. Stud. Child,* 1956, *11:* 89–98.

Maatsch, J. L., H. M. Adelman, and M. R. Denny. Effort and resistance to extinction of the bar-pressing response. *J. comp. physiol. Psychol.,* 1954, *47:* 47–51.

MacCorquodale, K., and P. E. Meehl. A distinction between hypothetical constructs and intervening variables. *Psychol. Rev.,* 1948, *55:* 95–107.

MacCorquodale, K., and P. E. Meehl. Cognitive learning in the absence of competition of incentives. *J. comp. physiol. Psychol.,* 1949, *42:* 383–390.

MacDonald, A. The effect of adaptation to the unconditioned stimulus upon the formation of conditioned avoidance responses. *J. exp. Psychol.,* 1946, *36:* 1–12.

Magoun, H. W. *The waking brain.* Springfield, Ill.: Charles C Thomas, 1958.

Magoun, H. W., and R. Rhines. *Spacticity: The stretch reflex and extrapyramidal systems.* Springfield, Ill.: Charles C Thomas, 1947.

Maher, B. A., S. T. Elder, and C. D. Noblin. A differential investigation of avoidance reduction versus hypermotility following frontal ablation. *J. comp. physiol. Psychol.,* 1962, *55:* 449–455.

Maier, N. R. F. *Frustration: The study of behavior without a goal.* New York: McGraw-Hill, 1949.

Makkink, G. F. Die Kopulation der Brandente (Tadorna tadorna [L.]). *Ardea,* 1931, *20:* 18–22.

Makkink, G. F. An attempt at an ethogram of the European avocet (Recurvirostra avosetta L.) with ethological and psychological remarks. *Ardea,* 1936, *31:* 1–60.

Malmo, R. B. Anxiety and behavioral arousal. *Psychol. Rev.,* 1957, *64:* 276–287.

Malmo, R. B. Measurement of drive: An unsolved problem in psychology. In M. R. Jones (Ed.), *Nebraska symposium on motivation: 1958.* Lincoln, Nebr.: Univer. of Nebr. Press, 1958, pp. 229–265.

*Malmo, R. B. Activation: A neuropsychological dimension. *Psychol. Rev.,* 1959, *66:* 367–386.

Malmo, R. B., and C. Shagass. Physiological study of symptom mechanisms in psychiatric patients under stress. *Psychosom. Med.,* 1949, *11:* 25–29.

Maltzman, N. F. The process need. *Psychol. Rev.,* 1952, *59:* 40–48.

Mandlebaum, D. G. *Soldier groups and Negro soldiers.* Berkeley: Univer. of Calif., 1952, pp. 45–48.

Mandler, G. Anxiety and performance: Empirical and theoretical aspects of anxiety scales. Unpublished manuscript, Lab. Soc. Relat., Harvard Univer., 1954.

Mandler, G., and W. Kessen. *The language of psychology.* New York: Wiley, 1959.

Mandler, G., and I. Kremen. Autonomic feedback: A correlational study. *J. Pers.,* 1958, *26:* 388–399. (*Erratum,* 1960, *28:* 545.)

Mandler, G., and S. B. Sarason. A study of anxiety and learning. *J. abnorm. soc. Psychol.,* 1952, *47:* 166–173.

Mandler, J. M. Irregular maintenance schedules and drives. *Science,* 1957, *126:* 505.

Marshall, S. L. A. *Men against fire*. New York: Morrow, 1947.

Marquis, Dorothy P. A study of frustration in newborn infants. *J. exp. Psychol.,* 1943, *32:* 123–138.

*Martin, B. Reward and punishment associated with the same goal response: A factor in the learning of motives. *Psychol. Bull.,* 1963, *60:* 441–451.

Martin, R. C. Resistance to extinction of an escape response as a function of number of reinforcements. Unpublished master's thesis, Univer. of Florida, 1962.

Martire, J. G. Relationships between the self concept and differences in the strength and generality of achievement motivation. *J. Pers.,* 1956, *24:* 364–375.

Marx, M. H. Some relations between frustration and drive. In M. R. Jones (Ed.), *Nebraska symposium on motivation: 1956*. Lincoln, Nebr.: Univer. of Nebraska Press, 1956.

Marx, M. H., and F. A. Knarr. Long-term development of reinforcing properties of a stimulus as a function of temporal relationship to food reinforcement. *J. comp. physiol. Psychol.,* 1963, *56:* 546–550.

Marx, M. H., and W. W. Murphy. Resistance to extinction as a function of the presentation of a motivating cue in the startbox. *J. comp. physiol. Psychol.,* 1961, *54:* 207–210.

Mason, J. W., C. Theresa Harwood, and N. R. Rosenthal. Influence of some environmental factors on plasma and urinary 17-hydroxycorticosteroid levels in the rhesus monkey. *Amer. J. Physiol.,* 1957, *190:* 429–433.

Masserman, J. M. *Behavior and neurosis*. Chicago: Univer. of Chicago Press, 1943.

Masserman, J. M. *Principles of dynamic psychiatry*. Philadelphia: Saunders, 1946.

Masserman, J. M., and C. Pechtel. Neurosis in monkeys: A preliminary report of experimental observations. *Ann. N.Y. Acad. Sci.,* 1953, *56:* 253–265.

May, M. A. Experimentally acquired drives. *J. exp. Psychol.,* 1948, *38:* 66–77.

May, R., E. Angel, and H. F. Ellenberger (Eds.). *Existence: A new dimension in psychiatry and psychology*. New York: Basic Books, 1958.

Maynard, D. M. *Nature*, 1956, *117:* 529.

Maynard, D. M. Organization of neuropil. *Amer. Zool.,* 1962, *2:* 79.

*McClelland, D. C. The importance of early learning in the formation of motives. In D. C. McClelland, *Personality*. New York: Holt, 1951, pp. 441–458.

McClelland, D. C. *Personality*. New York: Holt, 1951.

McClelland, D. C. The psychology of mental content reconsidered. *Psychol. Rev.,* 1955, *62:* 297–302.

McClelland, D. C. Methods of measuring human motivation. In J. W. Atkinson (Ed.), *Motives in fantasy, action, and society*. Princeton, N.J.: Van Nostrand, 1958, pp. 7–42.

McClelland, D. C., and J. W. Atkinson. The projective expression of needs: I. The effect of different intensities of the hunger drive on perception. *J. Psychol.,* 1948, *25:* 205–222.

*McClelland, D. C., J. W. Atkinson, R. A. Clark, and E. A. Lowell. *The achievement motive*. New York: Appleton, 1953.

McClelland, D. C., R. A. Clark, T. Roby, and J. W. Atkinson. The projective expression of needs: IV. The effect of the need for achievement on thematic apperception. *J. exp. Psychol.,* 1949, *39:* 242–255.

McClelland, D. C., and G. A. Friedman. A cross-cultural study of the relationship between child-training practices and achievement motivation appearing in folk tales. In G. E. Swanson, T. M. Newcomb, & E. L. Hartley (Eds.), *Readings in social psychology.* New York: Holt, 1952.

McClelland, D. C., and D. R. McGowan. The effect of non-specific food reinforcement on the strength of a secondary reward. Unpublished manuscript, 1950.

McClelland, D. C., and D. R. McGowan. The effect of variable food reinforcement on the strength of a secondary reward. *J. comp. physiol. Psychol.,* 1953, *46:* 80–86.

McClelland, D. C., A. Rindlisbacher, and R. DeCharms. Religious and other sources of attitudes toward independence training. In D. C. McClelland (Ed.), *Studies in motivation.* New York: Appleton, 1955, pp. 389–397.

McClelland, W. J. Differential handling and weight gain in the rat. *Canad. J. Psychol.,* 1956, *10:* 19–22.

McDougall, W. Pleasure, pain and conation. *Brit. J. Psychol.,* 1927, *17:* 171–180.

McGeoch, J. A. *The psychology of human learning.* New York: Longmans, 1942.

McGinnies, E. Emotionality and perceptual defense. *Psychol. Rev.,* 1949, *56:* 244–251.

McGraw, M. B. *Growth: A study of Johnny and Jimmy.* New York: Appleton, 1935.

McGraw, M. B. Later development of children specially trained in infancy. *Child Develpm.,* 1939, *10:* 1–19.

McKay, D. M. Quantal aspects of scientific information. *Phil. Mag.,* 1950, *41:* 289–311.

Mead, Margaret. Social change and cultural surrogates. In C. Kluckhohn & H. A. Murray (Eds.), *Personality in nature, society and culture.* New York: Knopf, 1949.

Mead, Margaret. Some anthropological considerations concerning guilt. In M. L. Reymert (Ed.), *Feelings and emotions.* New York: McGraw-Hill, 1950.

Mednick, Martha T. Mediated generalization and the incubation effect as a function of manifest anxiety. *J. abnorm. soc. Psychol.,* 1957, *55:* 315–321.

Mednick, S. A. Generalization as a function of manifest anxiety and adaptation to psychological experiments. *J. consult. Psychol.,* 1957, *21:* 491–494.

Mednick, S. A. A learning theory approach to research in schizophrenia. *Psychol. Bull.,* 1958, *55:* 316–327.

Mednick, S. A., and J. L. Freedman. Stimulus generalization. *Psychol. Bull.,* 1960, *57:* 169.

Meehl, P. E. On the circularity of the law of effect. *Psychol. Bull.,* 1950, *47:* 52–75.

Melzack, R. The effects of early experience on the emotional responses to pain. Unpublished doctoral dissertation, McGill Univer., 1954.

Melzack, R., and T. H. Scott. The effects of early experience on the response to pain. *J. comp. physiol. Psychol.,* 1957, *50:* 155–161.

Menut, G. *La dissociation familiale et les troubles du charactère chez l'enfant.* Paris, 1943.

Meryman, J. J. Magnitude of the startle response as a function of hunger and fear. Unpublished master's thesis, State Univer. of Iowa, 1952.

Meryman, J. J. The magnitude of the unconditioned GSR as a function of fear conditioned at a long CS-UCS interval. Unpublished doctoral dissertation, State Univer. of Iowa, 1953.

Meyer, D. R., and M. E. Noble. Summation of manifest anxiety and muscular tension. *J. exp. Psychol.*, 1958, *55:* 599–602.

Milburn, N. S., and K. D. Roeder. *Gen. Comp. Endocrinol.*, 1962, *2:* 70.

Milburn, N. S., E. A. Weiant, and K. D. Roeder. The release of efferent nerve activity in the roach, Periplaneta Americana, by extracts of the corpus cardiacum. *Biol. Bull.*, 1960, *118:* 111–119.

Miller, D. R. On the definition of problems and the interpretation of symptoms. *J. consult. Psychol.*, 1962, *26:* 302–305.

Miller, G. A., E. H. Galanter, and K. H. Pribram. *Plans and the structure of behavior.* New York: Holt, 1960.

Miller, G. A., and P. Viek. An analysis of the rat's response to unfamiliar aspects of the hoarding situation. *J. comp. physiol. Psychol.*, 1944, *37:* 221–231.

Miller, N. E. A reply to "sign-gestalt or conditioned reflex?" *Psychol. Rev.*, 1935, *42:* 280–292.

Miller, N. E. Experimental studies of conflict. In J. McV. Hunt (Ed.), *Personality and the behavior disorders.* New York: Ronald, 1944, pp. 431–465.

Miller, N. E. Studies of fear as an acquirable drive: I. Fear as motivation and fear reduction as reinforcement in the learning of new responses. *J. exp. Psychol.*, 1948, *38:* 89–101.(a)

Miller, N. E. Theory and experiment relating psychoanalytic displacement to stimulus-response generalization. *J. abnorm. soc. Psychol.*, 1948, *43:* 155–178.(b)

Miller, N. E. Comments on theoretical models. *J. Pers.*, 1951, *20:* 82–100.(a)

Miller, N. E. Learnable drives and rewards. In S. S. Stevens (Ed.), *Handbook of experimental psychology.* New York: Wiley, 1951, pp. 435–472.(b)

Miller, N. E. Some studies of drive and drive reduction. Paper read at Amer. Psychol. Ass., Cleveland, September, 1953.

Miller, N. E. Shortcomings of food consumption as a measure of hunger: Results from other behavioral techniques. *Ann. N.Y. Acad. Sci.*, 1955, *63:* 141–143.

Miller, N. E. Experiments on motivation: Studies combining psychological and pharmacological techniques. *Science,* 1957, *126:* 1271–1278.(a)

Miller, N. E. Graphic communication and the crisis in education. *Audiovis. commun. Rev.*, 1957, *5:* 3.(b)

Miller, N. E. Liberalization of basic S-R concepts: Extensions to conflict behavior, motivation and social learning. In S. Koch (Ed.), *Psychology: A study of a science.* New York: McGraw-Hill, 1959, vol. II, pp. 196–292.

Miller, N. E. Learning resistance to pain and fear: Effects of overlearning, exposure, and rewarded exposure in context. *J. exp. Psychol.*, 1960, *60:* 137–145.(a)

Miller, N. E. Some motivational effects of brain stimulation and drugs. *Fed. Proc.*, 1960, *19:* 846–854.(b)

*Miller, N. E. Analytical studies of drive and reward. *Amer. Psychol.*, 1961, *16:* 739–754.(a)

Miller, N. E. Integration of neurophysiological and behavioral research. *Ann. N.Y. Acad. Sci.*, 1961, *92:* 830–839.(b)

Miller, N. E. Learning and performance motivated by direct stimulation of the brain. In D. E. Sheer (Ed.), *Electrical stimulation of the brain: Subcortical integrative systems.* Austin, Texas: Univer. of Texas Press, 1961, pp. 387–396.(c)

*Miller, N. E. Some recent studies of conflict behavior and drugs. *Amer. Psychol.*, 1961, *16:* 12–24.(d)

Miller, N. E., C. J. Bailey, and J. A. F. Stevenson. Decreased "hunger" but increased food intake from hypothalamic lesions. *Science,* 1950, *112:* 256–259.

Miller, N. E., and H. Barry. Motivational effects of drugs: Methods which illustrate some general problems in psychopharmacology. *Psychopharmacologia,* 1961, *1:* 169–199.

Miller, N. E., and J. Dollard. *Social learning and imitation.* New Haven: Yale Univer. Press, 1941.

Miller, N. E., and M. L. Kessen. Reward effects of food via stomach fistula compared with those of food via mouth. *J. comp. physiol. Psychol.*, 1952, *45:* 550–564.

Miller, N. E., and D. Kraeling. Displacement: Greater generalization of approach than avoidance in generalized approach-voidnce conflict. *J. exp. Psychol.*, 1952, *43:* 217–221.

Miller, N. E., and E. J. Murray. Displacement and conflict-learnable drive as a basis for the steeper gradient of approach than of avoidance. *J. exp. Psychol.*, 1952, *43:* 227–231.

Miller, N. E., R. I. Sampliner, and P. Woodrow. Thirst-reducing effects of water by stomach fistula vs. water by mouth measured by both a consummatory and and instrumental response. *J. comp. physiol. Psychol.*, 1957, *50:* 1–5.

Miller, N. E., and S. S. Stevenson. Agitated behavior of rats during experimental extinction and a curve of spontaneous recovery. *J. comp. Psychol.*, 1936, *21:* 205–231.

Millican, R. C., and E. F. Stohlman. Relative effectiveness of certain drugs against shock produced in mice from tourniquet and burn trauma. *Amer. J. Physiol.*, 1956, *185:* 195–200.

Mitchell, E. D., and B. S. Mason. *The theory of play.* New York: A. S. Barnes, 1934.

Mittelmann, B. Motility in infants, children, and adults. *Psychoanal. Stud. Child.*, 1954, *9:* 142–177.

Mittelstaedt, H. Control systems of orientation in insects. *Ann. Rev. Entomol.*, 1962, *7:* 177–198.

Moltz, H., and L. A. Rosenblum. Imprinting and associative learning: the stability of the following response in Peking ducks (Anas platyrhynchos). *J. comp. physiol. Psychol.*, 1958, *51:* 580–583.(a)

Moltz, H., and L. A. Rosenblum. The relation between habituation and the stability of following responses. *J. comp. physiol. Psychol.*, 1958, *51:* 658–661.(b)

Moltz, H., L. A. Rosenblum, and N. Halikas. Imprinting and level of anxiety. *J. comp. physiol. Psychol.*, 1959, *52:* 240–244.

Montessori, Maria. *The Montessori method.* New York: Frederick A. Stokes, 1909.

Montgomery, K. C. A test of two explanations of spontaneous alternation. *J. comp. physiol. Psychol.*, 1952, *45:* 287–293.

Montgomery, K. C. Exploratory behavior as a function of "similarity" of stimulus situations. *J. comp. physiol. Psychol.*, 1953, *46:* 129–133.(a)

Montgomery, K. C. The effect of activity deprivation upon exploratory behavior. *J. comp. physiol. Psychol.*, 1953, *46:* 438–441.(b)

Montgomery, K. C. The relation between fear induced by novel stimulation and exploratory drive. *J. comp. physiol. Psychol.*, 1955, *48:* 254–260.

Morgan, C. T. The hoarding instinct. *Psychol. Rev.*, 1947, *54:* 335–341.

Morgan, C. T. Physiological theory of drive. In S. Koch (Ed.), *Psychology: A study of a science.* New York: McGraw-Hill, 1959, vol. I, pp. 644–671.

Morris, D. The reproductive behavior of the zebra finch (poephilia tuttata) with special reference to pseudofemale behaviour and displacement activities. *Behaviour*, 1954, *6:* 271–322.

Morris, D. The feather postures of birds and the problem of the origins of social signals. *Behaviour*, 1956, *9:* 75–114.

Morton, J. R. C., V. H. Denenburg, and M. X. Zarrow. Modification of Sexual development through stimulation in infancy. *Endocrinology*, 1963, *72:* 439–442.

Moruzzi, G., and H. W. Magoun. Brain stem reticular formation and activation of the EEG. *EEG clin. Neurophysiol.*, 1949, *1:* 455–473.

Mosteller, F., and R. R. Bush. Selected quantitative techniques. In G. Lindzey (Ed.), *Handbook of social psychology*, Cambridge, Mass.: Addison-Wesley, 1954, vol. I.

Mowrer, O. H. A stimulus-response analysis of anxiety and its role as a reinforcing agent. *Psychol. Rev.*, 1939, *46:* 553–565.

Mowrer, O. H. An experimental analogue of "regression" with incidental observations on "reaction-formation." *J. abnorm. soc. Psychol.*, 1940, *35:* 56–87.(a)

Mowrer, O. H. Anxiety-reduction and learning. *J. exp. Psychol.*, 1940, *27:* 497–516.(b)

Mowrer, O. H. Dynamic theory of personality. In J. McV. Hunt (Ed.), *Personality and the behavior disorders.* New York: Ronald, 1944, vol. I.

Mowrer, O. H. On the dual nature of learning—a reinterpretation of "conditioning" and "problem-solving." *Harvard educ. Rev.*, 1947, *17:* 102–148.

Mowrer, O. H. *Learning theory and personality dynamics.* New York: Ronald, 1950.

Mowrer, O. H. Two-factor learning theory: Summary and comment. *Psychol. Rev.* 1951, *58:* 350–354.

Mowrer, O. H. Motivation. *Ann. Rev. Psychol.*, 1952, *3:* 419–438.

Mowrer, O. H. *Learning theory and the symbolic processes.* New York: Wiley, 1960.(a)

Mowrer, O. H. *Learning theory and behavior.* New York: Wiley, 1960.(b)

Mowrer, O. H., and E. G. Aiken. Contiguity vs. drive-reduction in conditioned fear: Variations in conditioned and unconditioned stimuli. *Amer. J. Psychol.,* 1954, *67:* 26–38.

Mowrer, O. H., and R. R. Lamoreaux. Fear as an intervening variable in avoidance conditioning. *J. comp. physiol. Psychol.,* 1946, *39:* 29–50.

Mowrer, O. H., and L. N. Solomon. Contiguity vs. drive-reduction in conditioned fear: The proximity and abruptness of drive-reduction. *Amer. J. Psychol.,* 1954, *67:* 15–25.

Moyer, K. E. A study of some of the variables of which fixation is a function. *J. genet. Psychol.,* 1955, *86:* 3–31.

Moyer, K. E. The effects of shock on anxiety-motivated behavior in the rat. *J. genet. Psychol.,* 1957, *91:* 197–203.

Moynihan, M. Some displacement activities of the black-headed gull. *Behaviour,* 1953, *5:* 58–80.

Muenzinger, K. F. Motivation in learning. I. Electric shock for correct response in the visual discrimination habit. *J. comp. Psychol.,* 1934, *17:* 267–277.

Muenzinger, K. F., and L. F. Baxter. The effect of training to approach vs. training to escape from electric shock upon subsequent discrimination learning. *J. comp. physiol. Psychol.,* 1957, *50:* 252–257.

Muenzinger, K. F., A. H. Bernstone, and L. Richards. Motivation in learning: VIII. Equivalent amounts of electric shock for right and wrong responses in a visual discrimination habit. *J. comp. Psychol.,* 1938, *26:* 177–186.

Muenzinger, K. F., W. O. Brown, W. J. Crow, and R. F. Powloski. Motivation in learning: XI. An analysis of electric shock for correct responses into its avoidance and accelerating components. *J. exp. Psychol.,* 1952, *43:* 115–119.

Muenzinger, K. F., and R. F. Powloski. Motivation in learning: X. Comparison of electric shock for correct turns in a corrective and non-corrective situation. *J. exp. Psychol.,* 1951, *42:* 118–124.

Muenzinger, K. F., and Alda Wood. Motivation in learning: IV. The function of punishment as determined by its temporal relation to the act of choice in the visual discrimination habit. *J. comp. physiol. Psychol.,* 1935, *20:* 95–106.

Munn, N. *Psychological development.* New York: Houghton Mifflin, 1938.

Munsinger, H., and W. Kessen. Uncertainty, structure and preference. *Psychol. Monogr.,* 1964, *78:* 586.

Murray, E. J. Conflict and repression during sleep deprivation. *J. abnorm. soc. Psychol.,* 1959, *59:* 95–101.

Murray, E. J., and M. M. Berkun. Displacement as a function of conflict. *J. abnorm. soc. Psychol.,* 1955, *51:* 47–56.

Murray, E. J., and N. E. Miller. Displacement: Steeper gradient of generalization of avoidance than of approach with age of habit controlled. *J. exp. Psychol.,* 1952, *43:* 222–226.

Murray, H. A. *Explorations in personality.* New York: Oxford, 1938.

Murray, H. A. *Thematic Apperception Test manual.* Cambridge: Harvard Univer. Press, 1943.

Murstein, B. I. The projection of hostility on the Rorschach and as a result of ego-threat. *J. proj. Tech.,* 1956, *20:* 418–428.

Musselman, D. R. Free choice as a function of adaptation to stimulus complexity. Paper read at Western Psychol. Ass. Convention, 1962.

Musselman, D. R. Unpubl. ied doctoral dissertation. Claremont Grad. School, 1963.

Mussen, P. H., and J. J. Conger. *Child development and personality.* New York: Harper & Row, 1956.

Myers, A. K., and N. E. Miller. Failure to find a learned drive based on hunger: Evidence for learning motivated by "exploration." *J. comp. physiol. Psychol.,* 1954, *47:* 428–436.

Myers, J. L. Secondary reinforcement: A review of recent experimentation. *Psychol. Bull.,* 1958, *55:* 284–301.

Nagaty, M. O. Effect of food reward immediately preceding performance on an instrumental conditioned response on extinction of that response. *J. exp. Psychol.,* 1951, *42:* 333–340.

Neilson, Anne J. Time-intensity studies. In A. D. Little, Inc., *Flavor research and food acceptance.* New York: Reinhold, 1958, pp. 88–93.

Nelson, J. T., and S. Epstein. Relationships among three measures of conflict over hostility. *J. consult. Psychol.,* 1962, *26:* 345–350.

Newton, G., J. Paul, and E. W. Bovard. Effect of emotional stress on finger temperature. *Psychol. Rep.,* 1957, *3:* 341–343.

Nice, M. M. Some experiences in imprinting ducklings. *Condor,* 1953, *55:* 33–37.

Nichols, C. A. *Moral education among North American Indians.* New York: Teachers Coll., Columbia Univer., 1930.

Niles, P. Two personality measures associated with responsiveness to fear-arousing communications. Unpublished doctoral dissertation, Yale Univer., 1964.

Nissen, H. W. A study of exploratory behavior in the white rat by means of the obstruction method. *J. genet. Psychol.,* 1930, *37:* 361–376.

Nissen, H. W. Instinct as seen by a psychologist. *Psychol. Rev.,* 1953, *60:* 291–294.

Nolte, A. Field observations on the behavior of Macaca radiata in South India. *Z. Tierpsychol.,* 1955, *12:* 77–87.

Notterman, J. M., W. N. Schoenfeld, and P. J. Bersh. Conditioned heart rate response in human beings during experimental anxiety. *J. comp. physiol. Psychol.,* 1952, *45:* 1–8.

Novin, D. The relation between electrical conductivity of brain tissue and thirst in the rat. *J. comp. physiol. Psychol.,* 1962, *55:* 145–155.

Nuttin, J. Intimacy and shame in the dynamic structure of personality. In M. L. Reymert (Ed.), *Feelings and emotions.* New York: McGraw-Hill, 1950.

Oberholzer, R. J. H., and F. Huber. Methodik der elektrischen Reizung und Ausschaltung im oberschlundganglion (gehirn) nicht-narkotisier Grillen (Acheta domesticus L. und Gryllus campestris L.) *Helv. physiol. pharmachol.* Acta, 1957, *15:* 185.

Olds, J. The acquisition of motives. Unpublished doctoral dissertation, Harvard Univer., 1952.

Olds, J. Influence of practice on the strength of secondary approach drives. *J. exp. Psychol.*, 1953, *46:* 232–236.

Olds, J. Physiological mechanisms of reward. In M. R. Jones (Ed.), *Nebraska symposium on motivation*. Lincoln, Nebr.: Univer. of Nebraska Press, 1955.

Olds, J. *The growth and structure of motives*. New York: Free Press, 1916.

Olds, J. *Physiol. Rev.,* 1962, *43:* 554.

Olds, J. and P. Milner. Positive reinforcement produced by electrical stimulation of septal area and other regions of rat brain. *J. comp. physiol. Psychol.,* 1954, *47:* 419–427.

Olszewski, J. The cytoarchitecture of the human reticular formation. In E. D. Adrian, F. Bremer, and H. H. Jasper (Eds.), *Brain mechanisms and consciousness*. Oxford: Blackwell, 1954.

Orlansky, H. Infant care and personality. *Psychol. Bull.,* 1949, *46:* 1–48.

Osgood, C. E. *Method and theory in experimental psychology*. New York: Oxford, 1953.

Osgood, C. E., G. J. Suci, and P. H. Tannenbaum. *The measurement of meaning*. Univer. of Illinois Press, 1957.

Ozbas, S., and E. S. Hodgson. Action of insect neurosecretion upon central nervous system in vitro and upon behavior. *Proc. Natl. Acad. Sci.,* 1958, *44*(8): 825–830.

Parsons, C. M., and F. R. Goetzl. Effect of induced pain on pain threshold. *Proc. Soc. exp. Biol.,* New York, 1945, *60:* 327–329.

Patel, M. D. The physiology of the formation of the pigeon's milk. *Physiol. Zool.,* 1936, *9:* 129–152.

Patrick, G. T. W. *The psychology of relaxation*. New York: Houghton Mifflin, 1916.

Pavlov, I. P. *Conditioned reflexes* (Trans. by G. V. Anrep) London: Oxford, 1927.

Pearl, J. The effect of prior experience of electric shock on the punishment value of loud noises. Unpublished master's thesis, Univer. of Buffalo, 1961.

Peck, Ruth. The influence of anxiety factors upon the effectiveness of an experimental "counselling session." Unpublished doctoral dissertation, State Univer. of Iowa, 1951.

Peiper, A. *Die Eigenart der kindlichen Hirntätigkeit* (2nd ed.). Leipzig: Thieme, 1956.

Peller, L. E. Libidinal phases, ego development, and play. In *The psychoanalytic study of the child*. New York: Internat. Univer. Press, pp. 178–198.

Persky, H., D. A. Hamburg, H. Basowitz, R. R. Grinker, M. Sabshin, S. J. Korchin, M. Herz, F. A. Board, and Helen A. Heath. Relation of emotional responses and changes in plasma hydrocortisone level after stressful interview. *Arch. Neurol. & Psychiat.,* 1958, *79:* 434–447.

Peters, H. N. Experimental studies of the judgmental theory of feeling: I. Learning of positive and negative reactions as a determinant of affective judgments. *J. exp. Psychol.,* 1938, *23:* 1–25.

Peterson, N. Control of behavior by presentation of an imprinted stimulus. *Science,* 1960, *132:* 1395–1396.

Pfaffenberger, C. J., and J. P. Scott. The relationship between delayed socialization and trainability in guide dogs. *J. genet. Psychol.*, 1959, *95:* 145.

Pfaffman, C. Taste and smell. In S. S. Stevens, *Handbook of experimental psychology*. New York: Wiley, 1951, pp. 1143–1171.

Pfaffman, C. Behavioral responses to taste and odor stimuli. In A. D. Little, Inc., *Flavor research and food acceptance*. New York: Reinhold, 1958, pp. 29–44.

Pfaffman, C., and J. K. Bare. Gustatory nerve discharges in normal and adrenalectomized rats. *J. comp. physiol. Psychol.*, 1950, *43:* 320–324.

Piaget, J. *Judgment and reasoning in the child*. New York: Harcourt, 1928.

Piaget, J. *The child's conception of the world*. New York: Harcourt, 1929.

Piaget, J. *The child's conception of physical causality*. London: Routledge & Kegan Paul, 1930.

Piaget, J. *The language and thought of the child* (2nd ed.). London: Routledge & Kegan Paul, 1932.(a)

Piaget, J. *The moral judgment of the child*. New York: Free Press, 1932.(b)

Piaget, J. *Play, dreams, and imitation in childhood*. London: William Heinemann Ltd., 1951 (Originally published in 1945).

Piaget, J. *The origins of intelligence in children* (Trans. by Margaret Cook). New York: Internat. Univer. Press, 1952 (Originally published in 1936).

Piaget, J. *The construction of reality in the child* (Trans. by Margaret Cook). New York: Basic Books, 1954 (Originally published in 1937).

Piaget, J. *The growth of logical thinking in the child*. New York: Basic Books, 1955.

Pinneau, S. R. The infantile disorders of hospitalism and anaclitic depression. *Psychol. Bull.*, 1955, *52:* 429–459.

Pomeroy, D. S. Ameliorative effects of "counselling" upon maze performance following experimentally induced stress. *Amer. Psychol.*, 1950, *5:* 327.

Postman, L. The history and present status of the law of effect. *Psychol. Bull.*, 1947, *44:* 489–563.

Postman, L., and D. R. Brown. The perceptual consequences of success and failure. *J. abnorm. soc. Psychol.*, 1952, *47:* 213–221.

Postman, L., and R. S. Crutchfield. The interaction of need, set, and stimulus-structure in a cognitive task. *Amer. J. Psychol.*, 1952, *65:* 196–217.

Powdermaker, C., H. T. Levis, and G. Touraine. Psychopathology and treatment of delinquent girls. *Amer. J. Orthopsychiat.*, 1937, *7:* 58.

Pribram, K. H. A review of theory in physiological psychology. *Ann. Rev. Psychol.*, 1960, *11:* 1–40.

Pribram, K. H. The neuropsychology of Sigmund Freud. In A. J. Bachrach (Ed.), *Experimental foundations of clinical psychology*. New York: Basic Books, 1962, pp. 442–468.

Prince, A. I., Jr. Effect of punishment on visual discrimination learning. *J. exp. Psychol.*, 1956, *52:* 381–385.

Pringle, J. W. S. *Phil. Trans. Roy. Soc. London*, 1948, *B233:* 347.

Prosser, C. L., and W. S. Hunter. The extinction of startle responses and spinal reflexes in the white rat. *Amer. J. Physiol.*, 1936, *117:* 609–618.

Rabbie, J. M. Factors influencing the magnitude and direction of affiliative tendencies under stress. Unpublished doctoral dissertation, Yale Univer., 1961.

Rabbie, J. M. Differential preference for companionship under threat. *J. abnorm. soc. Psychol.*, 1963, *67:* 643–648.

Räber, H. An analysis of mating behavior in a domesticated turkey (Meleagris). *Behaviour,* 1948, *1:* 237–266.

Ramey, Estelle R., and M, S. Goldstein. The adrenal cortex and the sympathetic nervous system. *Physiol. Rev.*, 1957, *37:* 155–195.

Ramond, C. Anxiety and task as determiners of verbal performance. *J. exp. Psychol.*, 1953, *46:* 120–124.

Ramsay, A. O. Familial recognition in domestic birds. *Auk,* 1951, *68:* 1–16.

Ramsay, A. O., and E. H. Hess. A laboratory approach to the study of imprinting. *Wilson Bull.*, 1954, *66:* 196–206.

Rank, O. *The trauma of birth.* New York: Harcourt, 1929.

Rapaport, D. *Emotions and memory* (2nd ed.). New York: Internat. Univer. Press, 1950.(a)

Rapaport, D. On the psychoanalytic theory of thinking. *Internat. J. Psychoanal.*, 1950, *31:* 161–170.(b)

Rapaport, D. The autonomy of the ego. *Bull. Menninger Clin.*, 1951, *15:* 113–123.(a)

Rapaport, D. The conceptual model of psychoanalysis. *J. Pers.*, 1951, *20:* 56–81.(b)

Rapaport, D. (Ed.). *Organization and pathology of thought.* New York: Columbia Univer. Press, 1951.(c)

Rapaport, D. Cognitive structures. In *Contemporary approaches to cognition: A symposium held at the University of Colorado.* Cambridge: Harvard Univer. Press, 1957.

Rapaport, D. The structure of psychoanalytic theory. In S. Koch (Ed.), *Psychology: A study of science,* vol. 3. New York: McGraw-Hill, 1959, pp. 55–183.

Rapaport, D. Motivation of thinking. In M. R. Jones (Ed.), *Nebraska symposium on motivation: 1960.* Lincoln, Nebr.: Univer. of Nebraska Press, 1960.(a)

Rapaport, D. Psychoanalysis as a developmental psychology. In B. Kaplan and S. Wapner (Eds.), *Perspectives in psychological theory: Essays in honor of Heinz Werner.* New York: Internat. Univer. Press, 1960, pp. 209–225.(b)

Rapaport, D., and M. M. Gill. The points of view and assumptions of metapsychology. *Internat. J. Psychoanal.*, 1959, *40:* 153–162.

Razran, G. The observable unconscious and the inferable conscious in current Soviet psychophysiology: Interoceptive conditioning, semantic conditioning, and the orienting reflex. *Psychol. Rev.*, 1961, *68:* 81–147.

Reaney, M. J. *The psychology of the organized group game.* London: Cambridge Univer. Press, 1916.

Redgate, E. S., and E. Gellhorn. Relation of anterior hypothalamic excitability to cardiovascular reflexes. *Amer. J. Physiol.*, 1955, *183:* 654. (Abstract)

Reis, W. J. A comparison of the interpretation of dream series with and without free associations. In M. F. DeMartino (Ed.), *Dreams and personality dynamics.* Springfield, Ill.: Charles C Thomas, 1959, pp. 211–225.

Reynolds, Bradley. The relationship between the strength of a habit and the degree of drive present during acquisition. *J. exp. Psychol.*, 1949, *39:* 296–305.

Reynolds, G. Behavioral contrast. *J. exp. anal. Behav.*, 1961, *4:* 57–71.

Ribble, M. A. *The rights of infants.* New York: Columbia Univer. Press, 1943.

Riddle, O. Physiological responses to prolactin. *Symposia Quant. Biol.* (Cold Spring Harbor, N.Y.), 1937, *5:* 218–228.

Riddle, O., and F. H. Burns. A conditioned emetic reflex in the pigeon. *Proc. Soc. exp. Biol.*, N.Y. 1931, *28:* 979–981.

Riddle, O., and E. L. Lahr. On broodiness of ring doves following implants of certain steroid hormones. *Endocrinology*, 1944, *35:* 255–260.

Riesen, A. H. The development of visual perception in man and chimpanzee. *Science*, 1947, *106:* 107–108.

Riesen, A. H. Plasticity of behavior: Psychological aspects. In H. F. Harlow & C. N. Woolsey (Eds.), *Biological and biochemical bases of behavior.* Madison: Univer. of Wisconsin Press, 1958, pp. 425–450.

Riesen, A. H. Stimulation as a requirement for growth and function in behavioral development. In D. W. Fiske & S. R. Maddi (Eds.), *Functions of varied experience.* Homewood, Ill.: Dorsey Press, 1961, pp. 57–80.

Riess, B. F. The isolation of factors of learning and native behavior in field and laboratory studies. *Ann. N.Y. Acad. Sci.*, 1950, *51:* 1093–1102.

Riss, W., E. S. Valenstein, J. Sinks, and W. C. Young. Development of sexual behavior in male guinea pigs from genetically different stocks under controlled conditioned of androgen treatment and aging. *Endrocrinology*, 1955, *57:* 193–146.

Robbins, P. R. An application of the method of successive intervals to the study of fear-arousing information. *Psychol. Rep.*, 1962, *11:* 757–760.

Roberts, C. L., M. H. Marx, and G. Collier. Light onset and light offset as reinforcers for the albino rat. *J. comp. physiol. Psychol.*, 1958, *51:* 575–579.

Robinson, E. S. The compensatory function of make-believe play. *Psychol. Rev.*, 1920, *27:* 429–439.

Robinson, J., and H. Cantt. The orienting reflex (questioning reaction): cardiac, respiratory, salivary and motor components. *Johns Hopk. Hosp. Bull.*, 1947, *80:* 231–253.

Robinson, P. The measurement of achievement motivation. Unpublished doctoral dissertation, Oxford Univer., 1961.

Roeder, K. D. *Insect physiology.* New York: Wiley, 1953, pp. 463–487.

Roeder, K. D. Spontaneous activity and behavior. *Sci. Monthly*, 1955, *80:* 362–376.

Roeder, K. D. Neural mechanisms of animal behavior. *Amer. Zool.*, 1962, *2:* 105–115.

Roeder, K. D., L. Tozian, and E. A. Weiant. Endogenous nerve activity and behavior in the mantis and cockroach. *J. insect Physiol.*, 1960, *4:* 45–62.

Rolleston, J. D. *The history of acute exasthemata.* London: William Heineman, 1937.

Rosen, B. C., and R. D'Andrade. The psychosocial origins of achievement motivation. *Sociometry,* 1959, *22:* 185–218.

Rosenbaum, G. Stimulus generalization as a function of clinical anxiety. *J. abnorm. soc. Psychol.,* 1956, *53:* 281–285.

Rosenberg, M. J. Cognitive structure and attitudinal affect. *J. abnorm. soc. Psychol.,* 1956, *53:* 367–372.

Rosenblatt, J. S., and L. R. Aronson. The decline of sexual behavior in male cats after castration with special reference to the role of prior sexual experience. *Behaviour,* 1958, *12:* 285–338.(a)

Rosenblatt, J. S., and L. R. Aronson. The influence of experience on the behavioural effects of androgen in prepuberally castrated male cats. *Animal Behav.,* 1958, *6:* 171–182.(b)

Ross, C. A., and S. A. Herczeg. Protective effects of ganglionic blocking agents on traumatic shock in the rat. *Proc. Soc. Exp. Biol.,* N.Y., 1956, *91:* 196–199.

Ross, L. E. Conditioned fear as a function of CS–UCS and probe stimulus intervals. *J. exp. Psychol.,* 1960, *61:* 265–273.

Ross, S., V. H. Denenberg, P. B. Sawin, and P. Meyer. Changes in nestbuilding behaviour in multiparous rabbits. *Brit. J. Animal Behav.,* 1956, *4:* 69–74.

Ross, W. R. D. and J. F. Davis. Stable bandpass filters for electroencephalography. *IRE Canad. Convention Rec. 1958,* Paper no. 860: 202–206.

Rossi, G. F., and A. Zanchetti. The brainstem reticular formation: Anatomy and physiology. *Arch. Ital. Biol.,* 1957, *95:* 199–435.

Rothballer, A. B. Studies on the adrenaline-sensitive component of the reticular activating system. *EEG Clin. Neurophysiol.,* 1956, *8:* 603–621.

Rothenberg, S., and A. B. Brenner. The number 13 as a castration fantasy. *Psychoanal. Quart.,* 1955, *24:* 545–559.

Rotter, J. B. *Social learning and clinical psychology.* New York: Prentice-Hall, 1954.

Rowell, C. H. F. Displacement grooming in the chaffinch. *Anim. Behav.,* 1961, *9:* 38–63.

Rundquist, E. A. The inheritance of spontaneous activity in rats. *J. comp. Psychol.,* 1933, *16:* 415–438.

*Sackett, G. P. Sensory deprivation in rats, a reply to Hillix. Letter to the editors of *Science,* 1963, *142:* 1022.

*Sackett, G. P., P. Keith-Lee, and R. Treat. Food versus perceptual complexity as reward for rats previously subjected to sensory deprivation. *Science,* 1963, *141:* 518–520.

Safran, M., A. V. Schally, and B. G. Benfey. Stimulation of the release of corticotropin from the adenohypophysis by a neurohypophysial factor. *Endocrinology,* 1955, *57:* 439–444.

Salama, A. A., and J. McV. Hunt. "Fixation" in the rat as a function of infantile shocking, handling, and gentling. *J. genet. Psychol.,* 1964, *105:* 131–162.

Saltz, E., and T. I. Myers. A method for group presentation of paired-associate learning materials. Paper read at Midwestern Psychological Association convention, Chicago, 1955.

*Saltz, G. and S. Epstein. Thematic hostility and guilt responses as related to self-reported hostility, guilt, and conflict. *J. abnorm. soc. Psychol.*, 1963, *67:* 469–479.

Saltzman, I., and S. Koch. Effect of low intensities of hunger on behavior mediated by a habit of maximum strength. *J. exp. Psychol.*, 1948, *38:* 347–370.

Sanford, N. The dynamics of identification. *Psychol. Rev.*, 1955, *62:* 106–117.

Sanford, R. N. The effect of abstinence from food upon imaginal processes: A preliminary experiment. *J. Psychol.*, 1936, *2:* 129–136.

Sarason, S. B., and G. Mandler. Some correlates of text anxiety. *J. abnorm. soc. Psychol.*, 1952, *47:* 810–817.

Sarason, S. B., G. Mandler, and P. C. Craighill. The effect of differential instructions on anxiety and learning. *J. abnorm. soc. Psychol.*, 1952, *47:* 561–565.

Sarnoff, I. Psychoanalytic theory and social attitudes. *Publ. opin. Quart.*, 1960, *24:* 251–279.(a)

Sarnoff, I. Reaction formation and cynicism. *J. Pers.*, 1960, *28:* 129–143.(b)

*Sarnoff, I., and S. M. Corwin. Castration anxiety and fear of death. *J. Pers.*, 1959, *27:* 374–385.

*Sarnoff, I., and P. G. Zimbardo. Anxiety, fear, and social affiliation. *J. abnorm. soc. Psychol.*, 1961, *62:* 356–363.

Schachtel, E. G. *Metamorphosis.* New York: Basic Books, 1959.

Schachter, S. *The psychology of affiliation.* Stanford: Stanford Univer. Press, 1959.

Schachter, S., and J. Singer. Cognitive, social, and physiological determinants of emotional states. *Psychol. Rev.*, 1962, *69:* 379–399.

Schaefer, H. H., and E. H. Hess. Color preferences in imprinting objects. *Z. Tierpsychol.*, 1959, *16:* 161.

Schaefer, V. H., H. J. Link, J. U. Farrar, D. Wiens, and J. M. Dinsmore. Lethality in rats as a function of frequency in constant-displacement vibration. *USA Med. Res. Lab. Rep.*, 1959, no. 390.

Schaefer, V. H., R. G. Ulmer, and H. J. Link. Some behavioral and physiological studies in vibration. *USA Med. Res. Lab. Rep.*, 1959, no. 389.

Schafer, R. Regression in the service of the ego: The relevance of a psychoanalytic concept for personality assessment. In G. Lindzey (Ed.), *Assessment of human motives.* New York: Holt, 1958, pp. 119–148.

Schenkel, R. Ausdrucks-Studien an Wolfen. *Behaviour,* 1947, *1:* 81–130.

Schiller, F. *Essays, aesthetical and philosophical.* London: Bell & Sons, 1875.

Schlosberg, H. Conditioned responses in the white rat. *J. genet. Psychol.*, 1934, *45:* 303–335.

Schlosberg, H. The description of facial expressions in terms of two dimensions. *J. exp. Psychol.*, 1952, *44:* 229–237.

Schlosberg, H. Three dimensions of emotion. *Psychol. Rev.*, 1954, *61:* 81–88.

Schmidt, H. D. Das Verhalten von Haushunden in Konflict-situationen. *Z. Psychol.*, 1956, *159:* 162–245.

Schneider, G. Die Halteren Der Schneissfliege (Calliphora) Als Sinnesorgane Und Als Mechanische Flugstabilisatoren. *Z. Vergleich. Physiol.*, 1953, *35:* 416–458.

Schneirla, T. C. Basic problems in the nature of insect behavior. In K. D. Roeder (Ed.), *Insect physiology*. New York: Wiley, 1953.(a)

Schneirla, T. C. Modifiability in insect behavior. In K. D. Roeder (Ed.), *Insect physiology*. New York: Wiley, 1953.(b)

Schneirla, T. C. Interrelationships of the innate and the acquired in instinctive behavior. In P.-P.. Grasse (Ed.), *L'Instinct dans le comportement des animaux et de l'homme*. Paris: Masson & Cie, 1956. Pp. 387–452.

Schneirla, T. C. The concept of development in comparative psychology. In D. B. Harris (Ed.), *The concept of development*. Minneapolis, Minn.: Univer. of Minn. Press, 1957. Pp. 78–108.

Schnore, W. N., J. J. Antonitis, and P. J. Bersch. A preliminary study of training conditions necessary for secondary reinforcement. *J. exp. Psychol.*, 1950, *40:* 40–45.

Schoettle, H. E. T. *Thesis*. Univer. of Penn., 1963.

Schoonhoven, L. M. Spontaneous Electrical Activity in the brains of Diapausing insects. *Science*, 1963, *141:* 173–174.

Schulz, R. E., and A. D. Calvin. A failure to replicate the findings of a negative correlations between manifest anxiety and ACE scores. *J. consult. Psychol.*, 1955, *19:* 223–224.

Schwartz, B. J. Measurement of castration anxiety and anxiety over loss of love. *J. Pers.*, 1955, *24:* 204–219.

Schwartz, B. J. An empirical test of two Freudian hypotheses concerning castration anxiety. *J. Pers.*, 1956, *24:* 318–327.

Scodel, A., P. Ratoosh, and J. S. Minas. Some personality correlates of decision making under conditions of risk. *Behav. Sci.*, 1959, *4:* 19–28.

Scott, E. D., and E. L. Wike. The effect of partially delayed reinforcement and trial distribution on the extinction of an instrumental response. *Amer. J. Psychol.*, 1956, *69:* 264–268.

Scott, J. P. Genetic differences in the social behavior of inbred strains of mice. *J. Hered.*, 1942, *33:* 11–15.

Scott, W. A. The avoidance of threatening material in imaginative behavior. *J. abnorm. soc. Psychol.*, 1956, *52:* 338–346.

Sears, P. S. Levels of aspiration in academically successful and unsuccessful children. *J. abnorm. soc. Psychol.*, 1940, *35:* 498–536.

Sears, R. R. Relation of early socialization experiences to aggression in middle childhood. Unpublished paper, 1961.

Sears, R. R., and C. I. Hovland. Experiments on motor conflict. II. Determination of mode of resolution by comparative strengths of conflicting responses. *J. exp. Psychol.*, 1941, *28:* 280–286.

Sears, R. R., E. Maccoby, and H. Levin. *Patterns of child rearing*. New York: Harper & Row, 1957.

Sears, R. R., J. W. M. Whiting, V. Nowlis, and P. S. Sears. Some child-rearing antecedents of aggression and dependency in young children. *Genet. Psychol. Monogr.*, 1953, *47:* 135–234.

Segundo, J. P., R. Arana, and J. D. French. Behavioral arousal by stimulation of the brain in the monkey. *J. Neurosurg.*, 1955, *12:* 601–613.

Seitz, P. F. D. The maternal instinct in animal subjects: I. *Psychosom. Med.*, 1958, *20:* 215–226.

Selye, H. *Stress.* Montreal: Acta, 1950.

Selye, H. *The story of the adaptation syndrome.* Montreal: Acta, 1952.

Selye, H. *The stress of life.* New York: McGraw-Hill, 1956.

Selye, H., and C. Fortier. Adaptive reactions to stress. In H. G. Wolff, S. G. Wolf, Jr., & C. C. Hare (Eds.) *Life stress and bodily disease.* Baltimore: Williams & Wilkins, 1950, pp. 3–18.

Sevenster, P. The mechanism of a displacement activity. *Arch. Neerl. Zool*, 1960, *13:* 576–579.

Sevenster, P. A causal analysis of a displacement activity (fanning in *Gasteroteus Aculeatus* L.). *Behaviour,* 1961, suppl. no. 9.

Seward, J. P. Drive, incentive, and reinforcement. *Psychol. Rev.,* 1956, *63:* 195–203.

Seward, J. P. Secondary reinforcement as tertiary motivation: A revision of Hull's revision. *Psychol. Rev.,* 1950, *57:* 362–374.

Seward, J. P., and D. C. Raskin. The role of fear in aversive behavior. *J comp. physiol. Psychol.,* 1960, *53:* 328–335.

Seward, J. P., and G. H. Seward. The effects on repetition on reaction to electric shock: With special reference to menstrual cycle. *Arch. Psychol.,* 1934, *27:* 103.

Shafer, L. F. *The psychology of adjustment.* Boston: Houghton Mifflin, 1936.

Shands, H. C. An outline of the process of recovery from severe trauma. *A.M.A. Arch. Neurol. Psychiat.,* 1955, *73:* 403–409.

Sharpless, S. K. Role of the reticular formation in habituation. Unpublished doctoral dissertation, McGill Univer., 1954.

Sheffield, F. D. Hilgard's critique of Guthrie. *Psychol. Rev.,* 1949, *45:* 284–291.

*Sheffield, F. D. A drive-induction theory of reinforcement. Published for the first time in this volume.

*Sheffield, F. D. New evidence on the drive-induction theory of motivation. Published for the first time in this volume.

Sheffield, F. D., and B. A. Campbell. The role of experience in the "spontaneous" activity of hungry rats. *J. comp. physiol. Psychol.,* 1954, *47:* 97–100.

Sheffield, F. D., and T. B. Roby. Reward value of a non-nutritive sweet taste. *J. comp. physiol. Psychol.,* 1950, *43:* 471–481.

Sheffield, F. D., T. B. Roby, and B. A. Campbell. Drive reduction versus consummatory behavior as determinants of reinforcement. *J. comp. physiol. Psychol.,* 1954, *47:* 349–354.

Sheffield, F. D., J. J. Wulff, and R. Backer. Reward value of copulation without sex drive reduction. *J. comp. physiol. Psychol.,* 1951, *44:* 3–8.

Sheffield, V. F. Extinction as a function of partial reinforcement and distribution of practice. *J. exp. Psychol.,* 1949, *39:* 511–526.

Sheldon, W. H. *Varieties of delinquent youth: An introduction to constitutional psychiatry.* New York: Harper & Row, 1949.

Sheldon, W. H., S. S. Stevens, and W. B. Tucker. *The varieties of human physique.* New York: Harper & Row, 1940.

Sherrington, C. S. *The integrative action of the nervous system.* New Haven: Yale Univer. Press, 1906.

Shimazu, K., Okada, M., Ban, T., & Kurotsu, T. Influence of stimulation of the hypothalamic nuclei upon the neurosecretory system in the hypothalamus and the neurohypophysis of rabbit. *Med. J. Osaka Univer.,* 1954, *5:* 701–727.

Shipley, T. E., and J. Veroff. A projective measure of need for affiliation. *J. exp. Psychol.,* 1952, *43:* 349–356.

Sidman, M. Two temporal parameters of the maintenance of avoidance behavior by the white rat. *J. comp. physiol. Psychol.,* 1953, *46:* 253–261.(a)

Sidman, M. Avoidance conditioning with brief shock and no exteroceptive warning signal. *Science,* 1953, *118:* 157.(b)

Sidman, M. The relationship of emotionality to the consummatory response of eating. Paper presented at East. Psychol. Assn. Convention, 1960.

Siegel, P. S., and J. J. Brantley. *J. exp. Psychol.,* 1951, *42:* 304.

Siegel, S. *Nonparametric statistics for the behavioral sciences.* New York: McGraw-Hill, 1956.

Skinner, B. F. *The behavior of organisms.* New York: Appleton, 1938.

Skinner, B. F. *Walden Two.* New York: Macmillan, 1948.

Skinner, B. F. *Science and human behavior.* New York: Macmillan, 1953.

Skinner, B. F. *Cumulative record.* New York: Appleton, 1961.

Slutskaya, M. M. Converting defensive into food reflexes in oligophrenics and in normal children. *Zh. Nevropatol.,* 1928, *21:* 195–210 (Reviewed in Razran, G. H. S., Conditioned reflexes in children. *Arch. Psychol.,* 1933, *23:* no. 148).

Sokolov, E. N. *Vospriiate i uslovny refleks.* (Perception and the conditioned reflex.) Moscow: Moscow Univer. Press, 1958.

*Solomon, R. L. Punishment. *Amer. Psychol.,* 1964, *19:* 239–353.

Solomon, R. L., and Elinor S. Brush. Experimentally derived conceptions of anxiety and aversion. In M. R. Jones (Ed.), *Nebraska symposium on motivation: 1956.* Lincoln, Nebr.: Univer. of Nebraska Press, 1956.

Solomon, R. L., L. J. Kamin, and L. C. Wynne. Traumatic avoidance learning: The outcomes of several extinction procedures with dogs. *J. abnorm. soc. Psychol.,* 1953, *48:* 291–302.

Solomon, R. L., and L. C. Wynne. Avoidance conditioning in normal dogs and in dogs deprived of normal autonomic functioning. *Amer. Psychol.,* 1950, *5:* 264. (Abstract)

Solomon, R. L., and L. C. Wynne. Traumatic avoidance learning: The principles of anxiety conservation and partial irreversibility. *Psychol. Rev.,* 1954, *61:* 353–385.

Sontag, L. W. The genetics of differences in psychosomatic patterns in childhood. *Amer. J. Orthopsychiat.,* 1950, *20:* 479–489.

Soulairac, A. Analyze expérimentale des actions hormonales sur le comportement sexuel du rat male normal. *J. physiol. path. Gén.,* 1952, *44:* 327–330.

Spence, K. W. Theoretical interpretations of learning. In S. S. Stevens (Ed.), *Handbook of experimental psychology.* New York: Wiley, 1951.

Spence, K. W. *Behavior theory and conditioning.* New Haven: Yale Univer. Press, 1956.

Spence, K. W. A theory of emotionally based drive (D) and its relation to performance in simple learning situations. *Amer. Psychol.*, 1958, *13:* 131–141.

Spence, K. W. *Behavior theory and learning.* Englewood Cliffs, N.J.: Prentice-Hall, 1960.

Spence, K. W., I. E. Farber, and H. McFann. The relation of anxiety (drive) level to performance in competitional and non-competitional paired associates learning. *J. exp. Psychol.*, 1956, *52:* 296–305.

Spence, K. W., and R. Lippitt. Latent learning of a simple maze problem with relevant needs satiated. *Psychol. Bull.*, 1940, *37:* 429.

Spence, K. W., and W. N. Runquist. Temporal effects of conditioned fear on the eyelid reflex. *J. exp. Psychol.*, 1958, *55:* 613–616.

Spence, K. W., and Janet A. Taylor. Anxiety and strength of the UCS as determiners of the amount of eyelid conditioning. *J. exp. Psychol.*, 1951, *42:* 183–188.

Spencer, H. *The principles of psychology.* New York: Appleton, 1873.

Spitz, R. A. Hospitalism: An inquiry into the genesis of psychiatric conditions in early childhood. *Psychoanal. Stud. Child,* 1945, *1:* 53–74.

Spitz, R. A. Hospitalism: A follow-up report. *Psychoanal. Stud. Child,* 1946, *2:* 113–117.

Spitz, R. A., and K. M. Wolf. Anaclitic depression: An inquiry into the genesis of psychiatric conditions in early childhood. II. *Psychoanal. Stud. Child,* 1946, *2:* 313.(a)

Spitz, R. A., and K. M. Wolf. The smiling response: A contribution to the ontogenesis of social relations. *Genet. Psychol. Monogr.*, 1946, *34:* 57(b)

Spragg, S. D. S. Morphine addiction in chimpanzees. *Comp. Psychol. Monogr.*, 1940, *15:* (7).

Sprague, J. M., W. W. Chambers, and E. Stellar. Attentive, affective, and adaptive behavior in the cat. *Science,* 1961, *133:* 165–173.

Stanley, W. C., and O. Elliot. Differential human handling as reinforcing events and as treatments influencing later social behavior in Basenji puppies. *Psychol. Rep.*, 1962, *10:* 775–788.

Starcke, A. The castration complex. *Internat. J. Psychoanal.*, 1921, *2:* 179–201.

Steele, J. *Nature,* 1961, *193:* 680.

Stellar, E. The physiology of motivation. *Psychol. Rev.*, 1954, *61:* 5–22.

Stellar, E., and J. H. Hill. The rat's rate of drinking as a function of water deprivation. *J. comp. physiol. Psychol.*, 1952, *45:* 96–102.

Stennett, R. G. The relationship of alpha amplitude to the level of palmar conductance. *EEG Clin. Neurophysiol.*, 1957, *9:* 131–138.(a)

Stennett, R. G. The relationship of performance level to level of arousal. *J. exp. Psychol.*, 1957, *54:* 54–61.(b)

Stevens, S. S. *Handbook of experimental Psychology.* New York: Wiley, 1951.

Stone, L. J., and W. L. Jenkins. Recent research in curaneous sensitivity. I. Pain and temperature. *Psychol. Bull.*, 1940, *37:* 285–311.

Storms, L. H., C. Boroczi, and W. E. Broen. Punishment inhibits an instrumental response in hooded rats. *Science,* 1962, *135:* 1133–1134.

Storms, L. H., C. Boroczi, and W. E. Broen. Effects of punishment as a function of strain of rat and duration of shock. *J. comp. physiol. Psychol.*, 1963, *56:* 1022–1026.

Stott, D. H. *Delinquency and human nature.* Dunfermline, 1950.

Strizver, G. L. Thematic sexual and guilt responses as related to stimulus-relevance and experimentally induced drive and inhibition. Unpublished doctoral dissertation, Univer. of Mass., 1961.

Surwillo, W. W. A device for recording variations in pressure of grip during tracking. *Amer. J. Psychol.*, 1955, *68:* 669–670.

Surwillo, W. W. Psychological factors in muscle-action potentials: EMG gradients. *J. exp. Psychol.*, 1956, *52:* 263–272.

Sutcliffe, J. P. A general method of analysis of frequency data for multiple classification designs. *Psychol. Bull.*, 1957, *54:* 134–137.

Szwejkowska, G. The transformation of differentiated inhibitory stimuli into positive conditioned stimuli. *Acta. biol. exp.*, 1959, *19:* 151–159.

Tapp, J. T., and H. Markowitz. Infant handling: Effects on avoidance learning, brain weight, cholinesterase activity. *Science*, 1963, *140:* 486–487.

Tawney, R. H. *Religion and the rise of capitalism.* New York: Harcourt, 1926.

Taylor, Janet A. The relationship of anxiety to the conditioned eyelid response. *J. exp. Psychol.*, 1951, *41:* 81–92.

Taylor, Janet A. A personality scale of manifest anxiety. *J. abnorm. soc. Psychol.*, 1953, *49:* 285–290.

Taylor, Janet A. The Taylor Manifest Anxiety Scale and Intelligence. *J. abnorm. soc. Psychol.*, 1955, *51:* 347.

Taylor, Janet A. Physiological need, set, and visual duration threshold. *J. abnorm. soc. Psychol.*, 1956, *52:* 96–99.

Taylor, Janet A., and K. W. Spence. The relationship of anxiety level to performance in serial learning. *J. exp. Psychol.*, 1952, *44:* 61–64.

Teitelbaum, P. The use of operant methods in the assessment and control of motivational states. In *Operant behavior and psychology.* New York: Appleton.

Teitelbaum, P., and A. N. Epstein. The lateral hypothalamic syndrome. *Psychol. Rev.*, 1962, *69:* 74–90.

Thomas, D. R., and R. A. King. Stimulus generalization as a function of level of generalization. *J. exp. Psychol.*, 1959, *57:* 323.

Thompson, W. R. The inheritance of behaviour: behavioural differences in fifteen mouse strains. *Canad. J. Psychol.*, 1953, *7:* 145–155.

Thompson, W. R. Influence of prenatal anxiety on emotionality in young rats. *Science*, 1957, *125:* 698.

Thompson, W. R., and W. Heron. The effects of restraining early experience on the problem-solving capacity of dogs. *Canad. J. Psychol.*, 1954, *8:* 17–31.

*Thompson, W. R., and M. W. O'Kieffe. Imprinting: Its effects on the response to stress in chicks. *Science*, 1962, *135:* 918–919.

Thompson, W. R., and L. M. Solomon. Spontaneous pattern discrimination in the rat. *J. comp. physiol. Psychol.;* 1954, *47:* 104–107.

Thompson, W. R., and L. W. Sontag. Behavioral effects in the offspring of rats subjected to audiogruic seizure during the gestational period. *J. comp. physiol. Psychol.*, 1956, *49:* 454.

Thorndike, E. L. Animal intelligence: An experimental study of the associative processes in animals. *Psychol. Rev., Mongr. Suppl.*, 1898, *2:* (4, whole no. 8).

Thorndike, E. L. *Animal Intelligence.* New York: Macmillan, 1911.

Thorndike, E. L. *Human learning.* New York: Appleton, 1931.

Thorndike, E. L. A proof of the law of affect. *Science*, 1933, *77:* 173–175.

Thorpe, W. H. Some problems of animal learning. *Proc. Linn. soc. Lond.*, 1944, *156:* 70–83.

Tibout, N. H. C. From a speech given at the *International Congress on Mental Health,* London, 1948, *2:* 12, 46.

Tinbergen, N. Die Ubersprungbewegung. *Z. Tierpsychol.*, 1940, *4:* 1–40.

Tinbergen, N. *The study of instinct.* Oxford: Oxford, 1951.

Tinbergen, N. "Deriver" activities: Their causation, biological significance, origin and emancipation during evolution. *Quart. Rev. Biol.*, 1952, *27:* 1–32.

Tinbergen, N., and J. J. A. van Iersel. Displacement reactions in the three-spined stickleback. *Behaviour*, 1947, *1:* 56–63.

Tinklepaugh, O. L. An experiment study of representative factors in monkeys. *J. comp. Psychol.*, 1928, *8:* 197–236.

Tinklepaugh, O. L. Social behavior in animals. In F. A. Moss (Ed.), *Comparative psychology* (2nd ed.). New York: Prentice-Hall, 1942.

Titchener, E. B. *A text-book of psychology.* New York: Macmillan, 1926.

Titmuss, R. M. *Problems of social policy.* London: H. M. Stationery Office and Longmans, 1950.

Tolman, E. C. *Purposive behavior in animals and men.* New York: Appleton, 1932.

Tolman, E. C., C. S. Hall, and E. P. Bretnall. A dis-proof of the law of effect and a substitution of the laws of emphasis, motivation, and disruption. *J. exp. Psychol.*, 1932, *15:* 601–614.

*Trapold, M. A. The effect of incentive motivation on an unrelated reflex response. *J. comp. physiol. Psychol.*, 1962, *55:* 1034–1039.

Trotter, J. R. An aid to field observation. *Anim. Behav.*, 1959, *7:* 107.

Tryon, R. C. Genetics of learning ability in rats. *Univer. of Calif. Publ. Psychol.*, 1929, *4:* 71–89.

Tugendhat, B. The disturbed feeding of the three-spined stickleback: I. Electric Shock is administered in the food area. *Behaviour*, 1960, *16:* 159–187.(a)

*Tugendhat, B. Feeding in conflict situations and following thwarting. *Science,* 1960, *132:* 896–897.(b)

Tugendhat, B. The normal feeding behavior of the three-spined stickleback (Gasterosteus aculeatus L.). *Behaviour*, 1960, *15:* 284.(c)

Turner, L. H., and R. L. Solomon. Human traumatic avoidance learning: Theory and experiments on the operant-respondent distinction and failures to learn. *Psychol. Mongr.*, 1962, *76*(40, whole no. 559).

Tyhurst, J. S. Individual reactions to community disaster: the natural history of psychiatric phenomena. *Amer. J. Psychiat.*, 1951, *107:* 764–769.

Ullman, A. D. The experimental production and analysis of a "compulsive eating" symptom in rats. *J. comp. physiol. Psychol.*, 1951, *44:* 575–581.

Ullman, A. D. Three factors involved in producing "compulsive eating" in rats. *J. comp. physiol. Psychol.*, 1952, *45:* 490–496.

Upton, M. The auditory sensitivity of guinea pigs. *Amer. J. Psychol.*, 1929, *41:* 412–421.

Valenstein, E. S., and R. W. Goy. Further studies of the organization and display of sexual behavior in male guinea pigs. *J. comp. physiol. Psychol.*, 1957, *50:* 115–119.

Valenstein, E. S., W. Riss, and W. C. Young. Sex drive in genetically heterogeneous and highly inbred strains of male guinea pigs. *J. comp. physiol. Psychol.*, 1954, *47:* 162–165.

Valenstein, E. S., W. Riss, and W. C. Young. Experiential and genetic factors in the organization of sexual behavior in male guinea pigs. *J. comp. physiol. Psychol.*, 1955, *48:* 397–403.

Valenstein, E. S., and W. C. Young. An experimental factor influencing the effectiveness of testosterone propionate in eliciting sexual behavior in male guinea pigs. *Endocrinology*, 1955, *56:* 173–177.

Valentine, C. W. The innate bases of fear. *J. genet. Psychol.*, 1930, *37:* 394–419.

Van der Kloot, W. G. Neurosecretion in insects. *Ann. Rev. Entomol.*, 1960, *5:* 35–52.

Van der Kloot, W. G. Muscle and its neural control. *Amer. Zool.* 1962, 2: 55.

Van der Kloot, W. G., and C. M. Williams. Cocoon construction by the cecropia silkworm: I. The role of the external environment. *Behaviour,* 1953, *5:* 141–156.(a)

Van der Kloot, W. G., and C. M. Williams. Cocoon construction by the cecropia silkworm: II. The role of the internal environment. *Behaviour,* 1953, *5:* 157–174.(b)

van Iersel, J. J. A., and Angela Bol. Preening of two tern species: A study on displacement activities. *Behaviour,* 1958, *13:* 1–88.

Verzeano, M., J. D. French, and H. W. Magoun. An extralemniseal sensory system in the brain. *AMA Arch. Neurol. Psychiat.*, 1953, *69:* 505–518.

Voskresenskaya, A. K. *Dokl. Akad. Nauk. SSSR,* 1957, *112:* 964.

Voskresenskaya, A. K., and V. L. Svidersky. The role of the central and sympathetic nervous system in the function of the tymbal muscles of cicadas. *J. Insect Physiol.*, 1961, *6:* 26–35.

Vowles, D. M. *Anim. Behav.,* 1954, *2:* 116.

Vowles, D. M. *Anim. Behav.,* 1958, *6:* 115.

Vowles, D. M. Natural mechanisms in insect behavior. In W. H. Thorpe & O. L. Zangwill (Eds.), *Current problems in animal behavior.* London: Cambridge Univer. Press, 1961, pp. 5–29.

Waddell, D. Hoarding behavior in the Golden Hamster. *J. comp. physiol. Psychol.*, 1951, *44:* 383–388.

Waelder, R. The psychoanalytic theory of play. *Psychoanal. Quart.,* 1933, 2: 208–224.

Wagenen, O. Van. The monkey. In E. J. Farris (Ed.), *The care and breeding of laboratory animals.* New York: Wiley, 1950, pp. 1–43.

Wagner, A. R. Effects of amount and percentage of reinforcement and number of acquisition trials on conditioning and extinction. *J. exp. Psychol.,* 1961, *62:* 234–242.

Wagner, A. R. Conditioned frustration as a learned drive. *J. exp. Psychol.,* 1963, *66:* 142–148.(a)

Wagner, A. R. Sodium amytal and partially reinforced runway performance. *J. exp. Psychol.,* 1963, *65:* 474–477.(b)

*Wagner, A. R. Frustration and punishment. Prepared especially for this volume.

Waite, R. R., S. B. Sarason, F. F. Lighthall, and K. S. Davidson. A study of anxiety and learning in children. *J. abnorm. soc. Psychol.,* 1958, *57:* 267–270.

Walder, L. O., R. P. Ableson, L. D. Eron, T. J. Banta, and J. H. Laulicht. Development of a peer-rating measure of aggression. *Psychol. Rep. Monogr. Suppl., 4*(9): 1961.

Walker, H. M., and J. Lev. *Statistical inference.* New York: Holt, 1953.

Walker, K. C. Effect of a discriminative stimulus transferred to a previously unassociated response. *J. exp. Psychol.,* 1942, *31:* 312–321.

*Walters, G. C. Frequency and intensity of pre-shock experiences as determinants of fearfulness in an approach-avoidance conflict. *Canad. J. Psychol.,* 1963, *17:* 412–418.

Walters, G. C., and J. V. Rogers. Aversive stimulation of the rat: long-term effects on subsequent behavior. *Science,* 1963, *142:* 70–71.

Warden, C. J., and M. Aylesworth. The relative value of reward and punishment in the formulation of a visual discrimination habit in the white rat. *J. comp. physiol. Psychol.,* 1927, *7:* 117–127.

Waters, R. H. The law of effect as a principle of learning. *Psychol. Bull.,* 1934, *31:* 408–425.

Watson, J. B. *Psychology from the standpoint of a behaviorist.* Philadelphia: Lippincott, 1924.

Watson, J. B. *Behaviorism.* New York: Norton, 1925.

Weatherley, D. Anti-Semitism and the expression of fantasy aggression. *J. abnorm. soc. Psychol.,* 1961, *62:* 454–457.

*Weatherley, D. Maternal permissiveness toward aggression and subsequent TAT aggression. *J. abnorm. soc. Psychol.,* 1962, *65:* 1–5.

Weber, M. *The Protestant ethic* (Trans. by Talcott Parsons). New York: Scribner's, 1930.

Weiner, I. H., and E. Stellar. Salt preferences of the rat determined by a single stimulus method. *J. comp. physiol. Psychol.,* 1951, *44:* 394–401.

Weinstock, S. Resistance to extinction of a running response following partial reinforcement under widely spaced trials. *J. comp. physiol. Psychol.,* 1954, *47:* 318–322.

Weiss, R. F., H. E. Rawson, and B. Pasamanick. Argument strength, delay of argument, and anxiety in the "conditioning" and "selective learning" of attitudes. *J. abnorm. soc. Psychol.,* 1963, *67.*

Welker, W. I. Escape, exploratory, and food-seeking responses of rats in a novel situation. *J. comp. physiol. Psychol.*, 1959, *52:* 106.

Welker, W. I. An analysis of exploratory and play behavior in animals. In D. W. Fiske & S. R. Maddi (Eds.), *Functions of varied experiences.* Homewood, Ill.; Dorsey Press, 1961, pp. 175–226.

Welsh, G. S. An anxiety index and an internalization ratio for the MMPI. *J. consult. Psychol.*, 1952, *16:* 65–72.

Wendt, G. R. An interpretation of inhibition of conditioned reflexes as competition between reaction systems. *Psychol. Rev.*, 1936, *43:* 258–281.

*Wendt, R. H., D. F. Lindsley, W. R. Adey, and S. S. Fox. Self-maintained visual stimulation in monkeys after long-term visual deprivation. *Science,* 1963, *139:* 336–338.

Werner, H. *Comparative psychology of mental development* (rev. ed.). New York: Follett, 1948.

Wert, J. E., C. O. Neidt, and J. S. Ahmann. *Statistical methods in educational and psychological research.* New York: Appleton, 1954.

West, L. J., and I. E. Farber. The role of pain in emotional development. University of Oklahoma Medical School, 1960. (Mimeo)

Wever, E. G. The upper limit of hearing in the cat. *J. comp. Psychol.*, 1930, *10:* 221–233.

White, R. W. Motivation reconsidered: The concept of competence. *Psychol. Rev.*, 1959, *66:* 297–333.

Whiteis, U. E. A study of the effects of punishment on avoidance behavior. Unpublished doctoral dissertation, Harvard University, 1953.

Whiteis, U. E. Punishment's influence on fear and avoidance. *Harv. educ. Rev.*, 1956, *26:* 360–373.

Whiting, J. W. M. Effects of conflict on drive. Unpublished paper, 1950.

Whiting, J. W. M., and I. L. Child. *Child training and personality.* New Haven: Yale Univer. Press, 1953.

Whiting, J. W. M., and O. H. Mowrer. Habit progression and regression—a laboratory study of some factors relevant to human socialization. *J. comp. physiol. Psychol.*, 1943, *36:* 229–253.

Whiting, M. G. A cross-cultural nutrition survey of 118 societies representing the major cultural and geographic areas of the world. Unpublished D. Sc. thesis, Harvard School of Public Health, 1958.

Whitney, L. F. Heredity of trail barking propensity of dogs. *J. Hered.*, 1929, *20:* 561–562.

Wiersma, C. A. G. The organization of the arthropod central nervous system. *Am. Zool.*, 1962, *2:* 67–78.

Wigglesworth, V. B. *Quart. J. Microscop. Sci.*, 1934, *77:* 191.

Wike, E. L., and H. J. McNemara. The effects of percentage of partially delayed reinforcement on the acquisition and extinction of an instrumental response. *J. comp. physiol., Psychol.*, 1957, *50:* 348–351.

Williams, J. P., and W. Kessen. Effect of hand-mouth contacting on neonatal movement. *Child Developm.*, 1961, *32:* 243–248.

Willis, R. H. Stimulus pooling and social perception. *J. abnorm. soc. Psychol.*, 1960, *60:* 365–373.

Wilson, N. H. and W. P. Wilson. The duration of human electroencephalographic arousal responses elicited by photic stimulation. *EEG clin. Neurophysiol.*, 1959, *11:* 85–91.

Wilson, W., E. J. Weiss, and A. Amsel. Two tests of the Sheffield hypothesis concerning resistance to extinction, partial reinforcement, and distribution of practice. *J. exp. Psychol.*, 1955, *50:* 51–60.

Winnicott, D. W. Pediatrics and psychiatry. *Brit. J. Med. Psychol.*, 1948, *21:* 229–240.

Winterbottom, M. R. The relation of need for achievement to learning experiences in independence and mastery. In J. W. Atkinson (Ed.), *Motives in fantasy, action and society*. Princeton, N.J.: Van Nostrand, 1958, chap. 33.

Wischner, G. J. The effect of punishment on discrimination learning in a non-correction situation. *J. exp. Psychol.*, 1947, *37:* 271–284.

Wispe, L. G. Physiological need, verbal frequency, and word association. *J. abnorm. soc. Psychol.*, 1954, *49:* 229–234.

Wolf, A. The dynamics of the selective inhibition of specific functions in neurosis: a preliminary report. *Psychosom. Med.*, 1943, *5:* 27–38. Reprinted in S. S. Tomkins (Ed.), *Contemporary psychopathology*. Cambridge: Harvard Univer. Press, 1943, chap. 31.

Wolf, T. H. The effect of praise and competition on the persistent behavior of kindergarten children. *Inst. Child Welf. Monogr.*, no. 15. Univ. of Minnesota Press, 1938.

Wolff, H. G. *Stress and disease*. Springfield, Ill.: Charles C Thomas, 1953.

Wolff, H. G., and H. Goodell. The relation of attitude and suggestion to the perception of and reaction to pain. *Res. publ. Ass. nerv. ment. Dis.*, 1943, *23:* 434–448.

Wolff, P. H. Observations on newborn infants. *Psychosom. Med.*, 1959, *21:* 110–118.

Wolff, P. H. The developmental psychologies of Jean Piaget and psychoanalysis. *Psychol. Issues*, 1960, *2:* (1, monogr. no. 5).

Wolpert, E., and H. Trasman. Studies in psychophysiology of dreams. I. Experimental evocation of sequential dream episodes. *AMA Arch. neurol. Psychiat.*, 1958, *79:* 603.

Woodrow, H. The measurement of attention. *Psychol. Monogr.*, 1914, *17:* (76): 43–44.

Woodworth, R. S. *Psychology*. New York: Holt, 1921.

Woodworth, R. S. *Dynamic psychology*. New York: Columbia Univer. Press, 1918.

Woodworth, R. S. *Experimental psychology*. New York: Holt, 1938.

Woodworth, R. S., and D. G. Marquis. *Psychology* (5th ed.). New York: Holt, 1947.

Woodworth, R. S., and H. Schlosberg. *Experimental psychology* (rev. ed.). New York: Holt, 1954.

Worell, L. A theory of conflict: Implications for some motivational studies of performances. Unpublished manuscript, Oklahoma State Univer., 1961.

*Worell, L. Response to conflict as determined by prior exposure to conflict. *J. abnorm. soc. Psychol.*, 1962, *64:* 438–445.

Worell, L., and A. Castaneda. Individual differences in conflict resolution and the ease of learning. *Amer. Psychol.*, 1961, *16:* 400. (Abstract).(a)

Worell, L., and A. Castaneda. Response to conflict as a function of response-defined anxiety. *J. Pers.*, 1961, *29:* 10–29.(b)

Worell, L., and L. Hill. Ego strength and anxiety in discrimination conflict resolution. *J. consult. Psychol.*, 1962.

Wright, B. A. Altruism in children and the perceived conduct of others. *J. abnorm. soc. Psychol.*, 1942, *37:* 218–233.

Wright, H. F. The influence of barriers upon strength of motivation. *Contr. psychol. Theory*, 1937, *1:* (whole no. 3).

Wundt, W. *Grundriss der Psychologie.* Leipzig: Kroner, 1913.

Wycoff, L. B. Toward a quantitative theory of secondary reinforcement. *Psychol. Rev.*, 1959, *66:* 68–78.

Wynne, L. C., and R. L. Solomon. Traumatic avoidance learning: Acquisition and extinction in dogs deprived of normal peripheral autonomic function. *Genet. Psychol. Monogr.*, 1955, *52:* 241–284.

Yaryan, R. B., and L. Festinger. The effect of preparatory action on belief in the occurrence of possible future events. Unpublished paper.

Yates, A. J. The application of learning theory to the treatment of tics. *J. abnorm. soc. Psychol.*, 1958, *56:* 175–182.

Yates, A. J. *Frustration and conflict.* New York: Wiley, 1962.

Yerkes, R. M. The heredity of savageness and wildness in rats. *J. Anim. Behav.*, 1913, *3:* 286–296.

Yerkes, R. M., and M. I. Tomilin. Mother-infant relations in chimpanzee. *J. comp. Psychol.*, 1935, *20:* 321.

Yoshioka, J. G. Size preference of albino rats. *J. genet. Psychol.*, 1930, *37:* 427–430.

Young, P. T. Food-seeking drive, affective process, and learning. *Psychol. Rev.*, 1949, *56:* 98–121.

Young, P. T. The role of hedonic processes in motivation. In M. R. Jones (Ed.), *The Nebraska symposium on motivation: 1955.* Lincoln, Nebr.: Univer. of Nebraska Press, 1955.

Young, P. T., and E. H., Shuford, Jr. Intensity, duration, and repetition of hedonic processes as related to acquisition of motives. *J. comp. physiol. Psychol.*, 1954, *47:* 298–305.

Young, R. D. Effects of prenatal maternal injection of epinephrine on post-natal offspring behavior. *J. comp. physiol. Psychol.*, 1963, *56:* 929–932.

Young, W. C. Genetic and psychological determinants of sexual behavior patterns. In H. Hoagland (Ed.), *Hormones, brain function, and behavior.* New York: Academic Press, 1957, pp. 75–98.

Young, W. C. and J. A. Grunt. The pattern and measurement of sexual behavior in the male guinea pig. *J. comp. physiol. Psychol.*, 1951, *44:* 492–500.

Zeaman, D. Response latency as a function of the amount of reinforcement. *J. exp. Psychol.,* 1949, *39:* 466–483.

*Zeigler, H. P. Displacement activity and motivational theory. *Psychol. Bull.,* 1964, *61:* 362–376.

Zuckerman, M. The development of an Affect Adjective Check List for the measurement of anxiety. *J. consult. Psychol.* 1960, *24:* 457–462.

Zuckerman, S. *Functional affinities of man, monkeys and apes.* London: Harcourt, 1933.

INDEX